DISCRETE TIME SYSTEMS

Edited by **Mario A. Jordán**
and **Jorge L. Bustamante**

INTECHOPEN.COM

Discrete Time Systems
Edited by Mario A. Jordán and Jorge L. Bustamante

CBS, Edition **2016**

Published by InTech
Janeza Trdine 9, 51000 Rijeka, Croatia

Publishing Process Manager Ivana Lorkovic

Technical Editor Teodora Smiljanic

Cover Designer InTech Design Team

Image Copyright Emelyano, 2010. Used under license from Shutterstock.com

Additional hard copies can be obtained from orders@intechopen.com

Discrete Time Systems, Edited by Mario A. Jordán and Jorge L. Bustamante
p.cm.
ISBN 978-953-307-200-5

INTECH

open science | open minds

Contents

Preface

Discrete-Time Systems comprehend an important and broad research field. The consolidation of digital-based computational means in the present, pushes a technological tool into the field with a tremendous impact in areas like Control, Signal Processing, Communications, System Modelling and related Applications. This fact has enabled numerous contributions and developments which are either genuinely original as discrete-time systems or are mirrors from their counterparts of previously existing continuous-time systems.

This book attempts to give a scope of the present state-of-the-art in the area of Discrete-Time Systems from selected international research groups which were specially convoked to give expressions to their expertise in the field.

The works are presented in a uniform framework and with a formal mathematical context.

In order to facilitate the scope and global comprehension of the book, the chapters were grouped conveniently in sections according to their affinity in 5 significant areas.

The first group focuses the problem of Filtering that encloses above all designs of State Observers, Estimators, Predictors and Smoothers. It comprises Chapters 1 to 6.

The second group is dedicated to the design of Fixed Control Systems (Chapters 7 to 12). Herein it appears designs for Tracking Control, Fault-Tolerant Control, Robust Control, and designs using LMI- and mixed LQR/Hoo techniques.

The third group includes Adaptive Control Systems (Chapter 13 to 15) oriented to the specialities of Predictive, Decentralized and Perturbed Control Systems.

The fourth group collects works that address Stability Problems (Chapter 16 to 20). They involve for instance Uncertain Systems with Multiple and Time-Varying Delays and Switched Linear Systems.

Finally, the fifth group concerns miscellaneous applications (Chapter 21 to 27). They cover topics in Multitone Modulation and Equalisation, Image Processing, Fault Diagnosis, Event-Based Dynamics and Analysis of Deterministic/Stochastic and Multidimensional Dynamics.

We think that the contribution in the book, which does not have the intention to be all-embracing, enlarges the field of the Discrete-Time Systems with signification in the present state-of-the-art. Despite the vertiginous advance in the field, we think also that the topics described here allow us also to look through some main tendencies in the next years in the research area.

Mario A. Jordán and Jorge L. Bustamante
IADO-CCT-CONICET
Dep. of Electrical Eng. and Computers
National University of the South
Argentina

Part 1

Discrete-Time Filtering

1

Real-time Recursive State Estimation for Nonlinear Discrete Dynamic Systems with Gaussian or non-Gaussian Noise

Kerim Demirbaş
Department of Electrical and Electronics Engineering
Middle East Technical University
Inonu Bulvari, 06531 Ankara
Turkey

1. Introduction

Many systems in the real world are more accurately described by nonlinear models. Since the original work of Kalman (Kalman, 1960; Kalman & Busy, 1961), which introduces the Kalman filter for linear models, extensive research has been going on state estimation of nonlinear models; but there do not yet exist any optimum estimation approaches for all nonlinear models, except for certain classes of nonlinear models; on the other hand, different suboptimum nonlinear estimation approaches have been proposed in the literature (Daum, 2005). These suboptimum approaches produce estimates by using some sorts of approximations for nonlinear models. The performances and implementation complexities of these suboptimum approaches surely depend upon the types of approximations which are used for nonlinear models. Model approximation errors are an important parameter which affects the performances of suboptimum estimation approaches. The performance of a nonlinear suboptimum estimation approach is better than the other estimation approaches for specific models considered, that is, the performance of a suboptimum estimation approach is model-dependent.

The most commonly used recursive nonlinear estimation approaches are the extended Kalman filter (EKF) and particle filters. The EKF linearizes nonlinear models by Taylor series expansion (Sage & Melsa, 1971) and the unscented Kalman filter (UKF) approximates *a posteriori* densities by a set of weighted and deterministically chosen points (Julier, 2004). Particle filters approximates *a posterior* densities by a large set of weighted and randomly selected points (called particles) in the state space (Arulampalam et al., 2002; Doucet et al., 2001; Ristic et al., 2004). In the nonlinear estimation approaches proposed in (Demirbaş, 1982; 1984; Demirbaş & Leondes, 1985; 1986; Demirbaş, 1988; 1989; 1990; 2007; 2010): the disturbance noise and initial state are first approximated by a discrete noise and a discrete initial state whose distribution functions the best approximate the distribution functions of the disturbance noise and initial state, states are quantized, and then multiple hypothesis testing is used for state estimation; whereas Grid-based approaches approximate *a posteriori* densities by discrete densities, which are determined by predefined gates (cells) in the predefined state space; if the state space is not finite in extent, then the state space necessitates some truncation of the state space; and grid-based estimation approaches assume the availability of the state transition density $p(x(k)|x(k-1))$, which may not easily be calculated for state models with nonlinear disturbance noise (Arulampalam et al., 2002; Ristic et al., 2004). The Demirbaş estimation approaches are more general than grid-based approaches since 1) the state space need not to be truncated, 2) the state transition density is not needed, 3) state models can be any nonlinear functions of the disturbance noise.

This chapter presents an online recursive nonlinear state filtering and prediction scheme for nonlinear dynamic systems. This scheme is recently proposed in (Demirbaş, 2010) and is referred to as the DF throughout this chapter. The DF is very suitable for state estimation of nonlinear dynamic systems under either missing observations or constraints imposed on state estimates. There exist many nonlinear dynamic systems for which the DF outperforms the extended Kalman filter (EKF), sampling importance resampling (SIR) particle filter (which is sometimes called the bootstrap filter), and auxiliary sampling importance resampling (ASIR) particle filter. Section 2 states the estimation problem. Section 3 first discusses discrete noises which approximate the disturbance noise and initial state, and then presents approximate state and observation models. Section 4 discusses optimum state estimation of approximate dynamic models. Section 5 presents the DF. Section 6 yields simulation results of two examples for which the DF outperforms the EKF, SIR, and ASIR particle filters. Section 7 concludes the chapter.

2. Problem statement

This section defines state estimation problem for nonlinear discrete dynamic systems. These dynamic systems are described by

State Model

$$x(k+1) = f(k, x(k), w(k)) \tag{1}$$

Observation Model

$$z(k) = g(k, x(k), v(k)), \tag{2}$$

where k stands for the discrete time index; $f : \mathbb{R}x\mathbb{R}^m x\mathbb{R}^n \to \mathbb{R}^m$ is the state transition function; $\mathbb{R}^m$ is the m-dimensional Euclidean space; $w(k) \in \mathbb{R}^n$ is the disturbance noise vector at time k; $x(k) \in \mathbb{R}^m$ is the state vector at time k; $g : \mathbb{R}x\mathbb{R}^m x\mathbb{R}^p \to \mathbb{R}^r$ is the observation function; $v(k) \in \mathbb{R}^p$ is the observation noise vector at time k; $z(k) \in \mathbb{R}^r$ is the observation vector at time k; $x(0)$, $w(k)$, and $v(k)$ are all assumed to be independent with known distribution functions. Moreover, it is assumed that there exist some constraints imposed on state estimates. The DF recursively yields a predicted value $\hat{x}(k|k-1)$ of the state $x(k)$ given the observation sequence from time one to time $k-1$, that is, $Z^{k-1} \triangleq \{z(1),\ z(2), \ldots, z(k-1)\}$; and a filtered value $\hat{x}(k|k)$ of the state $x(k)$ given the observation sequence from time one to time k, that is, Z^k. Estimation is accomplished by first approximating the disturbance noise and initial state with discrete random noises, quantizing the state, that is, representing the state model with a time varying state machine, and an online suboptimum implementation of multiple hypothesis testing.

3. Approximation

This section first discusses an approximate discrete random vector which approximates a random vector, and then presents approximate models of nonlinear dynamic systems.

3.1 Approximate discrete random noise

In this subsection: an approximate discrete random vector with n possible values of a random vector is defined; approximate discrete random vectors are used to approximate the disturbance noise and initial state throughout the chapter; moreover, a set of equations which must be satisfied by an approximate discrete random variable with n possible values of an absolutely continuous random variable is given (Demirbaş, 1982; 1984; 2010); finally, the approximate discrete random variables of a Gaussian random variable are tabulated.

Let w be an m-dimensional random vector. **An approximate discrete random vector with n possible values** of w, denoted by w_d, is defined as an m-dimensional discrete random vector with n possible values whose distribution function the best approximates the distribution function of w over the distribution functions of all m-dimensional discrete random vectors with n possible values, that is

$$w_d = \min_{y \epsilon D}^{-1}\{\int_{\mathbb{R}^n}[F_y(a) - F_w(a)]^2 da\} \tag{3}$$

where D is the set of all m-dimensional discrete random vectors with n possible values, $F_y(a)$ is the distribution function of the discrete random vector y, $F_w(a)$ is the distribution function of the random vector w, and $\mathbb{R}^m$ is the m-dimensional Euclidean space. An approximate discrete random vector w_d is, in general, numerically, offline-calculated, stored and then used for estimation. The possible values of w_d are denoted by w_{d1}, w_{d2}, ..., and w_{dn} ; and the occurrence probability of the possible value w_{di} is denoted by $P_{w_{di}}$, that is

$$P_{w_{di}} \triangleq Prob\{w_d = w_{di}\}. \tag{4}$$

where $Prob\{w_d(0) = w_{di}\}$ is the occurrence probability of w_{di}.

Let us now consider the case that w is an absolutely continuous random variable. Then, w_d is an approximate discrete random variable with n possible values whose distribution function the best approximates the distribution function $F_w(a)$ of w over the distribution functions of all discrete random variables with n possible values, that is

$$w_d = \min_{y \epsilon D}^{-1}\{J(F_y(a))\}$$

in which the distribution error function (the objective function) $J(F_y(a))$ is defined by

$$J(F_y(a)) \triangleq \int_{\mathbb{R}}[F_y(a) - F_w(a)]^2 da$$

where D is the set of all discrete random variables with n possible values, $F_y(a)$ is the distribution function of the discrete random variable y, $F_w(a)$ is the distribution function of the absolutely continuous random variable w, and $\mathbb{R}$ is the real line. Let the distribution function $F_y(a)$ of a discrete random variable y be given by

$$F_y(a) \triangleq \begin{cases} 0 & \text{if } a < y_1 \\ F_{y_i} & \text{if } y_i \le a < y_{i+1},\ i = 1,\ 2,\ \ldots, n-1 \\ 1 & \text{if } a \ge y_n. \end{cases}$$

Then the distribution error function $J(F_y(a))$ can be written as

$$J(F_y(a)) = \int_{-\infty}^{y_1} F_w^2(a)da + \sum_{i=1}^{n-1}\int_{y_i}^{y_{i+1}}[F_{y_i} - F_w(a)]^2 da + \int_{y_n}^{\infty}[1 - F_w(a)]^2 da.$$

Let the distribution function $F_{w_d}(a)$ of an approximate discrete random variable w_d be

$$F_{w_d}(a) \triangleq \begin{cases} 0 & \text{if } a < w_{d1} \\ F_{w_{di}} & \text{if } w_{di} \le a < w_{di+1},\ i = 1,\ 2,\ \ldots, n-1 \\ 1 & \text{if } a \ge w_{dn}. \end{cases}$$

It can readily be shown that the distribution function $F_{w_d}(a)$ of the approximate discrete random variable w_d must satisfy the set of equations given by

$$\begin{aligned} F_{w_{d1}} &= 2F_w(w_{d1}); \\ F_{w_{di}} + F_{w_{di+1}} &= 2F_w(w_{di+1}),\quad i = 1,\ 2,\ \ldots,\ n-2; \\ 1 + F_{w_{dn-1}} &= 2F_w(w_{dn}); \\ F_{w_{di}}[w_{di+1} - w_{di}] &= \int_{w_{di}}^{w_{di+1}} F_w(a)da,\quad i = 1,\ 2,\ \ldots,\ n-1. \end{aligned} \tag{5}$$

The values w_{d1}, w_{d2}, ..., w_{dn}, $F_{w_{d1}}$, $F_{w_{d2}}$, ...,$F_{w_{dn}}$ satisfying the set of Eqs. (5) determine the distribution function of w_d. These values can be, in general, obtained by numerically solving Eqs. (5). Then the possible values of the approximate discrete random variable w_d become w_{d1}, w_{d2}, ..., and w_{dn} ; and the occurrence probabilities of these possible values are obtained by

$$P_{w_{di}} = \begin{cases} F_{w_{d1}} & \text{if } i = 1 \\ F_{w_{di}} - F_{w_{di-1}} & \text{if } i = 2,\ 3,\ \ldots, n-1 \\ 1 - F_{w_{dn}} & \text{if } i = n. \end{cases}$$

where $P_{w_{di}} = Prob\{w_d = w_{di}\}$, which is the occurrence probability of w_{di}.
Let y be a Gaussian random variable with zero mean and unit variance. An approximate discrete random variable y_d with n possible values was numerically calculated for different n's by using the set of Eqs. (5). The possible values y_{d1}, y_{d2}, ..., y_{dn} of y_d and the occurrence probabilities $P_{y_{d1}}$, $P_{y_{d2}}$, ..., $P_{y_{dn}}$ of these possible values are given in Table 1, where $P_{y_{di}} \triangleq Prob\{y_d = y_{di}\}$. As an example, the possible values of an approximate discrete random variable with 3 possible values of a Gaussian random variable with zero mean and unit variance are -1.005, 0.0, and 1.005; and the occurrence probabilities of these possible values are 0.315, 0.370, and 0.315, respectively. Let w be a Gaussian random variable with mean $E\{w\}$ and variance σ^2. This random variable can be expressed as $w = y\sigma + E\{w\}$. Hence, the possible values of an approximate discrete random variable of w are given by $w_{di} = y_{di}\sigma + E\{w\}$, *where* $i = 1, 2, 3, ..., n$; and the occurrence probability of the possible value w_{di} is the same as the occurrence probability of y_{di}, which is given in Table 1.

3.2 Approximate models

For state estimation, the state and observation models of Eqs. (1)and (2) are approximated by the time varying finite state model and approximate observation model which are given by

Finite State Model

$$x_q(k+1) = Q(f(k, x_q(k), w_d(k))) \tag{6}$$

Approximate Observation Model

$$z(k) = g(k, x_q(k), v(k)), \tag{7}$$

n	y_{d1}	y_{d2}	y_{d3}	y_{d4}	y_{d5}	y_{d6}	y_{d7}	y_{d8}	y_{d9}	y_{d10}
	$P_{y_{d1}}$	$P_{y_{d2}}$	$P_{y_{d3}}$	$P_{y_{d4}}$	$P_{y_{d5}}$	$P_{y_{d6}}$	$P_{y_{d7}}$	$P_{y_{d8}}$	$P_{y_{d9}}$	$P_{y_{d10}}$
1	0.000									
	1.000									
2	-0.675	0.675								
	0.500	0.500								
3	-1.005	0.0	1.005							
	0.315	0.370	0.315							
4	-1.218	-0.355	0.355	1.218						
	0.223	0.277	0.277	0.223						
5	-1.377	-0.592	0.0	0.592	1.377					
	0.169	0.216	0.230	0.216	0.169					
6	-1.499	-0.768	-0.242	0.242	0.768	1.499				
	0.134	0.175	0.191	0.191	0.175	0.134				
7	-1.603	-0.908	-0.424	0.0	0.424	0.908	1.603			
	0.110	0.145	0.162	0.166	0.162	0.145	0.110			
8	-1.690	-1.023	-0.569	-0.184	0.184	0.569	1.023	1.690		
	0.092	0.124	0.139	0.145	0.145	0.139	0.124	0.092		
9	-1.764	-1.120	-0.690	-0.332	0	0.332	0.690	1.120	1.764	
	0.079	0.106	0.121	0.129	0.130	0.129	0.121	0.106	0.079	
10	-1.818	-1.199	-0.789	-0.453	-0.148	0.148	0.453	0.789	1.199	1.818
	0.069	0.093	0.106	0.114	0.118	0.118	0.114	0.106	0.093	0.069

Table 1. Approximate Discrete Random Variables the best Approximating the Gaussian Random Variable with Zero Mean and Unit Variance

where $w_d(k)$ is an approximate discrete random vector with, say, n possible values of the disturbance noise vector $w(k)$; this approximate vector is pre(offline)-calculated, stored and then used for estimation to calculate quantization levels at time $k+1$; the possible values of $w_d(k)$ are denoted by $w_{d1}(k)$, $w_{d2}(k)$, ..., and $w_{dn}(k)$; $Q : \mathbb{R}^m \rightarrow \mathbb{R}^m$ is a quantizer which first divides the m-dimensional Euclidean space into nonoverlapping generalized rectangles (called gates) such that the union of all rectangles is the m-dimensional Euclidean space, and then assigns to each rectangle the center point of the rectangle, Fig. 1 (Demirbaş, 1982; 1984; 2010); $x_q(k)$, $k > 0$, is the quantized state vector at time k and its quantization levels, whose number is (say) m_k, are denoted by $x_{q1}(k)$, $x_{q2}(k)$, ..., and $x_{qm_k}(k)$. The quantization levels of $x_q(k+1)$ are calculated by substituting $x_q(k) = x_{qi}(k)$ $(i = 1, 2, \ldots, m_k)$ for $x_q(k)$ and $w_d(k) = w_{dj}(k)$ $(j = 1, 2, \ldots, n)$ for $w_d(k)$ in the finite state model of Eq. (6). As an example, let the quantization level $x_{qi}(k)$ in the gate G_i be mapped into the gate G_j by the lth-possible value $w_{dl}(k)$ of $w_d(k)$, then, $x(k+1)$ is quantized to $x_{qj}(k+1)$, Fig. 1. One should note that the approximate models of Eqs. (6) and (7) approach the models of Eqs. (1) and (2) as the gate sizes $(GS) \rightarrow 0$ and $n \rightarrow \infty$. An optimum state estimation of the models of Eqs. (6) and (7) is discussed in the next section.

4. Optimum state estimation

This section discuses an optimum estimation of the models of Eqs. (6) and (7) by using multiple hypothesis testing. On the average overall error probability sense, optimum estimation of states of the models of Eqs. (6) and (7) is done as follows: Finite state model

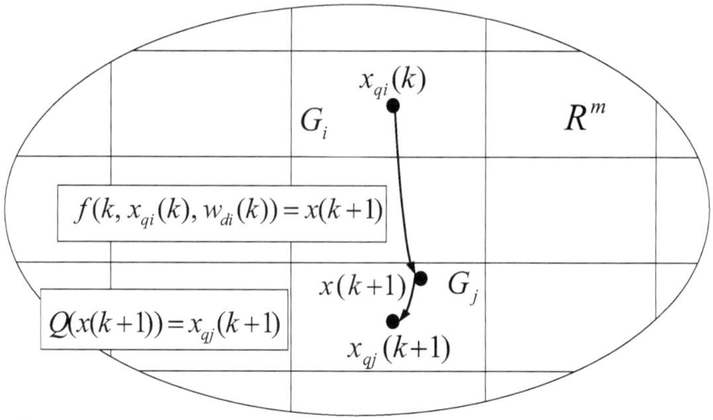

Fig. 1. Quantization of States

of Eq. (6) is represented by a trellis diagram from time 0 to time k (Demirbaş, 1982; 1984; Demirbaş & Leondes, 1985; Demirbaş, 2007). The nodes at time j of this trellis diagram represent the quantization levels of the state $x(j)$. The branches of the trellis diagram represent the transitions between quantization levels. There exist, in general, many paths through this trellis diagram. Let H^i denote the ith path (sometimes called the ith hypothesis) through the trellis diagram. Let $x_q^i(j)$ be the node (quantization level) through which the path H^i passes at time j. The estimation problem is to select a path (sometimes called the estimator path) through the trellis diagram such that the average overall error probability is minimized for decision (selection). The node at time k along this estimator path will be the desired estimate of the state $x(k)$. In Detection Theory (Van Trees, 2001; Weber, 1968): it is well-known that the optimum decision rule which minimizes the average overall error probability is given by

$$Select \;\; H^n \;\; as \; the \, estimator \; path \; if \; M(H^n) \geq M(H^l) \;\; for \; all \; l \neq n, \tag{8}$$

where $M(H^n)$ is called the metric of the path $M(H^n)$ and is defined by

$$M(H^n) \triangleq \ln\{p(H^n)Prob\{observation\ sequence \mid H^n\}\}, \tag{9}$$

where ln stands for the natural logarithm, $p(H^n)$ is the occurrence probability (or the *a priori probability*) of the path H^n, and $Prob\{observation\ sequence \mid H^n\}$ is the conditional probability of the observation sequence given that the actual values of the states are equal to the quantization levels along the path H^n. If the inequality in the optimum decision rule becomes an equality for an observation sequence, anyone of the paths satisfying the equality can be chosen as the estimator path, which is a path having the biggest metric.

It follows, from the assumption that samples of the observation noise are independent, that $Prob\{observation\ sequence \mid H^n\}$ can be expressed as

$$Prob\{observation\ sequence \mid H^n\} = \prod_{j=1}^{k} \lambda(z(j) \mid x_q^n(j)) \tag{10}$$

where

$$\lambda(z(j)|x_q^n)(j)) \triangleq \begin{cases} 1 & \text{if z(j) is neither available nor used for estimation} \\ p(z(j)|x_q^n(j)) & \text{if z(j) is available and used for estimation,} \end{cases} \tag{11}$$

in which, $p(z(j)|x_q^n(j))$ is the conditional density function of $z(j)$ given that the actual value of state is equal to $x_q^n(j)$, that is, $x(j) = x_q^n(j)$; and this density function is calculated by using the observation model of Eq. (2).

It also follows, from the assumption that all samples of the disturbance noise and the initial state are independent, that the *a priori probability* of H^n can be expressed as

$$p(H^n) = Prob\{x_q(0) = x_q^n(0)\} \prod_{j=1}^{k} T(x_q^n(j-1) \rightarrow x_q^n(j)), \tag{12}$$

where $Prob\{x_q(0) = x_q^n(0)\}$ is the occurrence probability of the initial node (or quantization level) $x_q^n(0)$, and $T(x_q^n(j-1) \rightarrow x_q^n(j))$ is the transition probability from the quantization level $x_q^n(j-1)$ to the quantization level $x_q^n(j))$, that is, $T(x_q^j(i-1) \rightarrow x_q^n(j)) \triangleq Prob\{x_q(j) = x_q^n(j)|x_q(j-1) = x_q^n(j-1)\}$, which is the probability that $x_q^n(j-1)$ is mapped to $x_q^n(j)$ by the finite state model of Eq. (6) with possible values of $w_d(j-1)$. Since the transition from $x_q^n(j-1)$ to $x_q^n(j)$ is determined by possible values of $w_d(j-1)$, this transition probability is the sum of occurrence probabilities of all possible values of $w_d(j-1)$ which map $x_q^n(j-1)$ to $x_q^n(j)$.

The estimation problem is to find the estimator path, which is the path having the biggest metric through the trellis diagram. This is accomplished by the Viterbi Algorithm (Demirbaş, 1982; 1984; 1989; Forney, 1973); which systematically searches all paths through the trellis diagram. The number of quantization levels of the finite state model, in general, increases exponentially with time k. As a result, the implementation complexity of this approach increases exponentially with time k (Demirbaş, 1982; 1984; Demirbaş & Leondes, 1985; Demirbaş, 2007). In order to overcome this obstacle, a block-by-block suboptimum estimation scheme was proposed in (Demirbaş, 1982; 1984; Demirbaş & Leondes, 1986; Demirbaş, 1988; 1989; 1990). In this estimation scheme: observation sequence was divided into blocks of constant length. Each block was initialized by the final state estimate from the last block. The initialization of each block with only a single quantization level (node), that is, the reduction of the trellis diagram to one node at the end of each block, results in state estimate divergence for long observation sequences, i.e., large time k, even though the implementation complexity of the proposed scheme does not increase with time (Kee & Irwin, 1994). The online and recursive state estimation scheme which is recently proposed in (Demirbaş, 2010) prevents state estimate divergence caused by one state initialization of each block for the block-by-block estimation. This recently proposed estimation scheme, referred to as the DF throughout this chapter, first prunes all paths going through the nodes which do not satisfy constraints imposed on estimates and then assigns a metric to each node (or quantization level) in the trellis diagram. Furthermore, at each time (step, or iteration), the number of considered state quantization levels (nodes) is limited by a selected positive integer MN, which stands for the maximum number of quantization levels considered through the trellis diagram; in other words , MN nodes having the biggest metrics are kept through the trellis diagram and all the paths going through the other nodes are pruned. Hence, the implementation complexity of the DF does not increase with time. The number MN is one of the parameters determining the implementation complexity and the performance of the DF.

5. Online state estimation

This section first yields some definitions, and then presents the DF.

5.1 Definitions

Admissible initial state quantization level : a possible value $x_{qi}(0) \triangleq x_{di}(0)$ of an approximate discrete random vector $x_q(0) \triangleq x_d(0)$ of the initial state vector $x(0)$ is said to be an admissible quantization level of the initial state vector (or an admissible initial state quantization level) if this possible value satisfies the constraints imposed on the state estimates. Obviously, if there do not exist any constraints imposed on the state estimates, then all possible values of the approximate discrete random vector $x_q(0)$ are admissible.

Metric of an admissible initial state quantization level: the natural logarithm of the occurrence probability of an admissible initial quantization level $x_{qi}(0)$ is referred to as the metric of this admissible initial quantization level. This metric is denoted by $M(x_{qi}(0))$, that is

$$M(x_{qi}(0)) \triangleq \ln\{Prob\{x_q(0) = x_{qi}(0)\}\}. \tag{13}$$

where $Prob\{x_q(0) = x_{qi}(0)\}$ is the occurrence probability of $x_{qi}(0)$.
Admissible state quantization level at time k: a quantization level $x_{qi}(k)$ of a state vector $x(k)$, where $k \geq 1$, is called an admissible quantization level of the state (or an admissible state quantization level) at time k if this quantization level satisfies the constraints imposed on the state estimates. Surely, if there do not exist any constraints imposed on the state estimates, then all the quantization levels of the state vector $x(k)$, which are calculated by Eq. (6), are admissible.

Maximum number of considered state quantization levels at each time: MN stands for the maximum number of admissible state quantization levels which are considered at each time (step or iteration) of the DF. MN is a preselected positive integer. A bigger value of MN yields better performance, but increases implementation complexity of the DF.
Metric of an admissible quantization level (or node) at time k, where $k \geq 1$: the metric of an admissible quantization level $x_{qj}(k)$, denoted by $M(x_{qj}(k))$, is defined by

$$\begin{aligned} M(x_{qj}(k)) \triangleq & \max_n\{M(x_{qn}(k-1)) + ln[T(x_{qn}(k-1) \rightarrow x_{qj}(k))]\} \\ & + ln[\lambda(z(k)|x_{qj}(k))], \end{aligned} \tag{14}$$

where the maximization is taken over all considered state quantization levels at time $k-1$ which are mapped to the quantization level $x_{qj}(k)$ by the possible values of $w_d(k-1)$; ln stands for the natural logarithm; $T(x_{qn}(k-1) \rightarrow x_{qj}(k))$ is the transition probability from $x_{qi}(k-1)$ to $x_{qj}(k)$ is given by

$$T(x_{qi}(k-1) \rightarrow x_{qj}(k)) = \sum_n Prob\{w_d(k-1) = w_{dn}(k-1)\}, \tag{15}$$

where $Prob\{w_d(k-1) = w_{dn}(k-1)\}$ is the occurrence probability of $w_{dn}(k-1)$ and the summation is taken over all possible values of $w_d(k-1)$ which maps $x_{qi}(k-1)$ to $x_{qj}(k)$; in other words, the summation is taken over all possible values of $w_d(k-1)$ such that

$$Q(f(k-1, x_{qi}(k-1), w_{dn}(k-1))) = x_{qj}(k); \tag{16}$$

and

$$\lambda(z(k)|x_{qj}(k)) \triangleq \begin{cases} 1 & \text{if z(j) is neither available nor used for estimation} \\ p(z(k)|x_{qj}(k)) & \text{if z(j) is available and used for estimation,} \end{cases} \tag{17}$$

in which, $p(z(k)|x_{qj}(k))$ is the conditional density function of $z(k)$ given that the actual value of state $x(k) = x_{qj}(k)$, and this density function is calculated by using the observation model of Eq. (2).

5.2 Estimation scheme (DF)

A flowchart of the DF is given in Fig. 3 for given $F_{w(k)}(a)$, $F_{x(0)}(a)$, MN, n, m , and GS; where $F_{w(k)}(a)$ and $F_{x(0)}(a)$ are the distribution functions of $w(k)$ and $x(0)$ respectively, n and m are the numbers of possible values of approximate random vectors of $w(k)$ and $x(0)$ respectively; GS is the gate size; and $z(k)$ is the observation at time k. The parameters MN, n, m , and GS determine the implementation complexity and performance of the DF. The number of possible values of the approximate disturbance noise $w_d(k)$ is assumed to be the same, n , for all iterations, i.e., for all k. The filtered value $\hat{x}(k|k)$ and predicted value $\hat{x}(k|k-1)$ of the state $x(k)$ are recursively determined by considering only MN admissible state quantization levels with the biggest metrics and discarding other quantization levels at each recursive step (each iteration or time) of the DF. Recursive steps of the DF is described below.
Initial Step (Step 0): an approximate discrete random vector $x_d(0)$ with m possible values of the initial state $x(0)$ is offline calculated by Eq. (3). The possible values of this approximate random vector are defined as the initial state quantization levels (nodes). These initial state quantization levels are denoted by $x_{q1}(0)$, $x_{q2}(0)$, ..., and $x_{qm}(0)$, where $x_{qi(0)} \triangleq x_{di(0)}$ $(i = 1\ 2\ ...m)$. Admissible initial state quantization levels, which satisfy the constraints imposed on state estimates, are determined and the other initial quantization levels are discarded. If the number of admissible initial quantization levels is zero, then the number, m, of possible values of the approximate initial random vector $x_d(0)$ is increased and *the initial step* of the DF is repeated from the beginning; otherwise, the metrics of admissible initial quantization levels are calculated by Eq. (13). The admissible initial state quantization levels (represented by $x_{q1}(0)$, $x_{q2}(0)$, ..., and $x_{qN_0}(0)$) and their metrics are considered in order to calculate state quantization levels and their metrics at time $k = 1$. These considered quantization levels are denoted by nodes (at time 0) on the first row (or column) of two rows (or columns) trellis diagram at the first step $k = 1$ of the DF, Fig. 2.
State estimate at time 0: if the mean value of $x(0)$ satisfies constraints imposed on state estimates such as the case that there do not exist any estimate constraints , then this mean value is taken as both $\hat{x}(0|0)$ and $\hat{x}(0|0-1)$; otherwise, the admissible initial state quantization level (node) with the biggest metric is taken as both the filtered value $\hat{x}(0|0)$ and predicted value $\hat{x}(0|0-1)$ of the state $x(0)$, given no observation.
Recursive Step (Step k): An approximate discrete disturbance noise vector $w_d(k-1)$ with n possible values of the disturbance noise $w(k-1)$ is offline obtained by Eq. (3). The quantization levels of the state vector at time k are calculated by using the finite state model of Eq. (6) with all the considered quantization levels (or nodes) $x_{q1}(k-1)$, $x_{q2}(k-1)$ ... $x_{qN_{k-1}}(k-1)$ at time $k-1$; and all possible values $w_{d1}(k-1)$, $w_{d2}(k-1)$, ..., $w_{dn}(k-1)$ of the approximate discrete disturbance noise vector $w_d(k-1)$. That is, substituting the

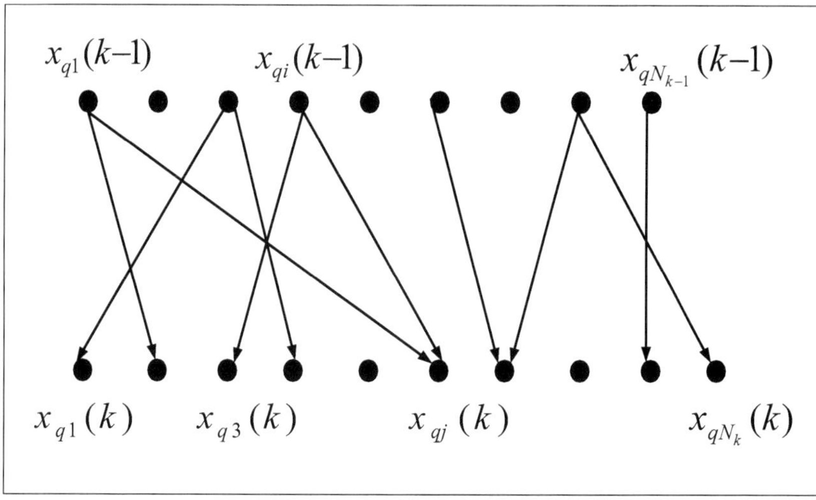

Fig. 2. Two Row Trellis Diagram of Admissible State Quantization Levels

considered state quantization levels $x_{qi}(k-1)$ ($i = 1, 2, \ldots, N_{k-1}$) for $x_q(k-1)$ and the possible values $w_d(k-1) = w_{dj}(k-1)$ ($j = 1, 2, \ldots, n$) for $w_d(k-1)$ in the finite state model of Eq. (6), the quantization levels of the state at time k are calculated (generated). The admissible quantization levels at time k, which satisfy constraints imposed on state estimates, are determined and non-admissible state quantization levels are discarded. If the number of admissible state quantization levels at time k is zero, then a larger n, MN or smaller GS is taken and *the recursive step at time k* of the DF is repeated from the beginning; otherwise, the metrics of all admissible state quantization levels at time k are calculated by using Eq. (14). If the number of admissible state quantization levels at time k is greater than MN, then only MN admissible state quantization levels with biggest metrics, otherwise, all admissible state quantization levels with their metrics are considered for the next step of the DF. The considered admissible quantization levels (denoted by $x_{q1}(k)$, $x_{q2}(k)$, ...,$x_{qN_k}(k)$) and their metrics are used to calculate the state quantization levels and their metrics at time $k+1$. The considered state quantization levels at time k are represented by the nodes on the second row (or column) of two rows (or columns) trellis diagram at *the recursive step k* and on the first row (or column) of two rows (or columns) trellis diagram at *the recursive step k* + 1, Fig. 2; where the subscript N_k, which is the number of considered nodes at the end of *Recursive step k*, is less than or equal to MN; and the transition from a node at time $k-1$, say $x_{qi}(k-1)$, to a node at time k , say $x_{qj}(k)$, is represented by a directed line which is called a branch. *Estimate at time k:* the admissible quantization level (node) with the biggest metric at time k is taken as the desired estimate of the state at time k, that is, the node with the biggest metric at time k is the desired predicted value of $x(k)$ if $z(k)$ is neither available nor used for estimation; otherwise, the node at time k with the biggest metric is the filtered value of $x(k)$. If there exist more than one nodes having the same biggest metric, anyone of these nodes can be taken as the desired estimate.

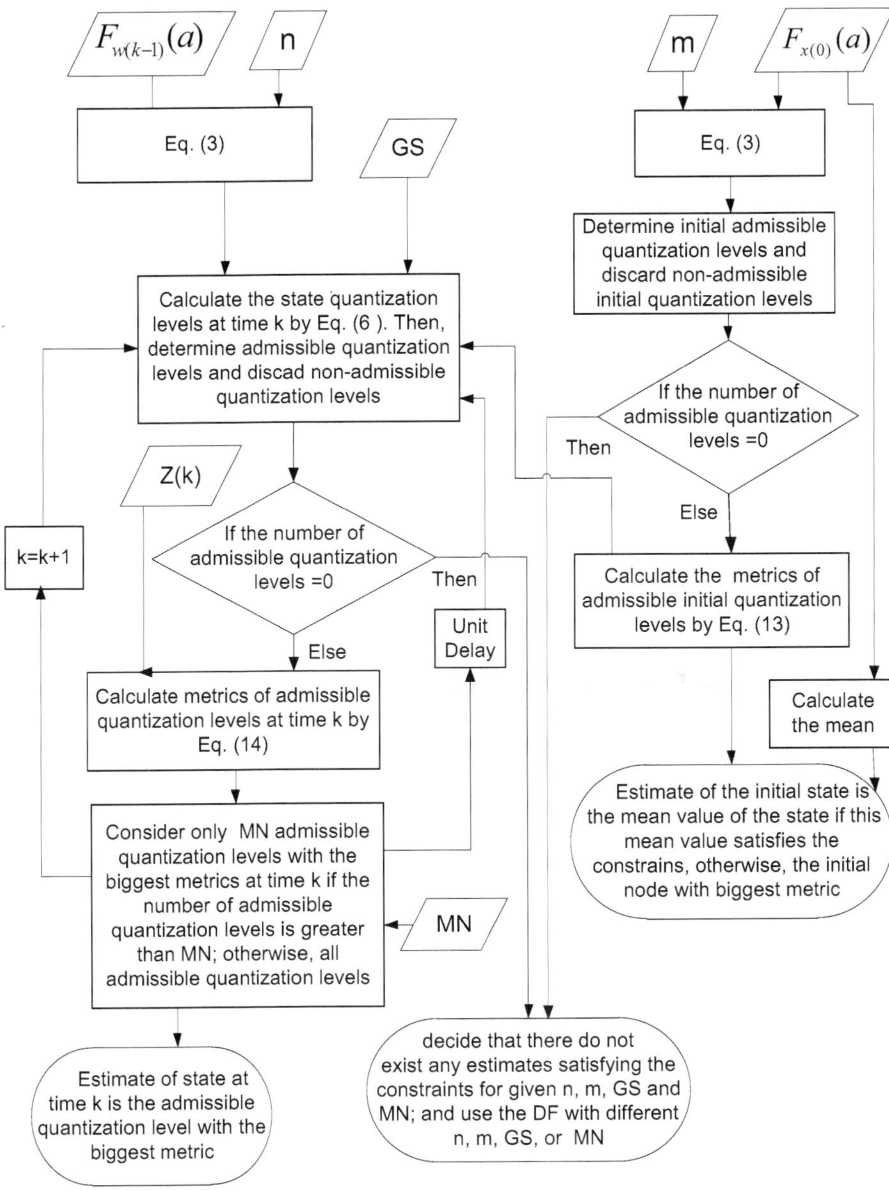

Fig. 3. Flowchart of the DF

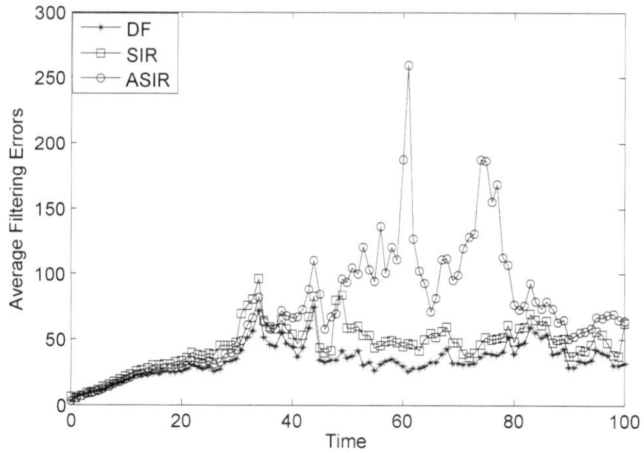

Fig. 4. Average Filtering Errors for Eqs. (18) and (19)

6. Simulations

In this section, Monte Carlo simulation results of two examples are given. More examples are presented in (Demirbaş, 2010). The first example is given by

State Model

$$x(k+1) = x(k)[1 + \frac{k}{k+1}\cos(0.8x(k) + 2w(k))] + w(k) \tag{18}$$

Observation Model

$$z(k) = \frac{6x(k)}{1 + x^2(k)} + v(k), \tag{19}$$

where the random variables $x(0)$, $w(k)$, and $v(k)$ are independent Gaussian random variables with means 6, 0, 0 and variances 13, 20, 15 respectively. It was assumed that there did not exist any constraints imposed on state estimates. The state model of Eq. (18) is an highly nonlinear function of the disturbance noise $w(k)$. The extended Kalman filter (EKF) and the grid-based approaches may not be used for the state estimation of this example, since the EKF assumes a linear disturbance noise in the state model and the grid based approaches assumes the availability of the state transition density $p(x(k)|x(k-1))$ which may not readily calculated (Arulampalam et al., 2002; Ristic et al., 2004). States of this example were estimated by using the DF, the sampling importance resampling (SIR) particle filter (which is sometimes called the bootstrap filter, and auxiliary sampling importance resampling (ASIR) particle filter (Arulampalam et al., 2002; Gordon et al., 1993). Average absolute filtering and prediction errors are sketched in Figs. 4 and 5 for 2000 runs each of which consists of 100 iterations. These estimation errors were obtained by using the SIR and ASIR particle filters with 1000 particles and the DF for which the random variables $x(0)$ and $w(k)$ were approximated by the approximate random variables with 3 possible values (which are given in Section 3); the gate size (GS) and MN were taken as 0.1 and 8 respectively. The average filtering and prediction errors per one estimation (one iteration) were 33.8445, 45.6377, 71.5145 and 34.0660, 45.4395,

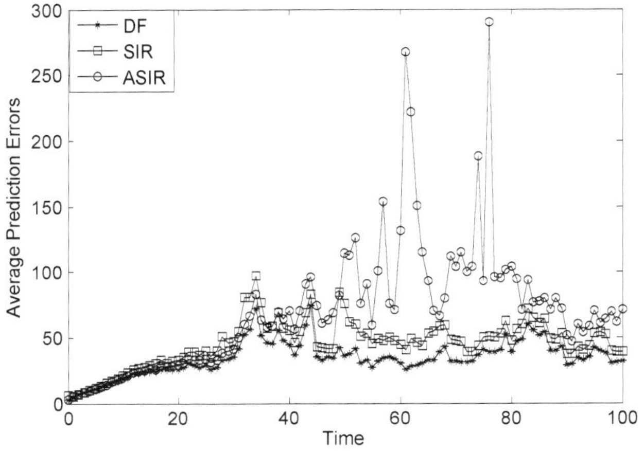

Fig. 5. Average Prediction Errors for Eqs. (18) and (19)

70.2305 respectively. A typical run with 100 iteration took 0.0818, 0.2753, 0.3936 seconds for the DF, SIR and ASIR particle filters, respectively. The DF clearly performs better than both the SIR and ASIR particle filter. Moreover, the DF is much faster than both the SIR and ASIR particle filters with 1000 particles.

The second example is described by

State Model

$$x(k+1) = x(k)[1 + \frac{k}{k+1}\cos(0.8x(k))] + w(k) \tag{20}$$

Observation Model

$$z(k) = \frac{6x(k)}{1+x^2(k)} + v(k), \tag{21}$$

where the random variables $x(0)$, $w(k)$,and $v(k)$ are independent Gaussian random variables with means 3, 0, 0 and variances 8, 9, 9 respectively. It was assumed that there did not exist any constraints imposed on state estimates. Average absolute filtering and prediction errors are sketched in Figs. 6 and 7 for 2000 runs each of which consists of 200 iterations. These estimation errors were obtained by using the SIR and ASIR particle filters with 1000 particles and the DF for which the random variables $x(0)$ and $w(k)$ were approximated by the approximate random variables with 3 possible values (which are given in Section 3); the gate size (GS) and MN were taken as 0.1 and 4 respectively. The average filtering and prediction errors per one estimation (one iteration) were 38.4913, 61.5432, 48.4791 and 38.5817, 61.4818, 48.5088 respectively. A typical run with 200 iteration took 0.0939, 0.5562, 0.8317 seconds for the DF, SIR and ASIR particle filters, respectively. The state model of the second example is a linear function of the disturbance noise. Hence, the extended Kalman filter (EKF) was also used for state estimation, but the EKF estimation errors quickly diverged, hence, the EKF state estimation errors are not sketched. The DF clearly performs better than the EKF, SIR and ASIR particle filters and also the DF is much faster than both the SIR and ASIR particle filters with 1000 particles for the second example.

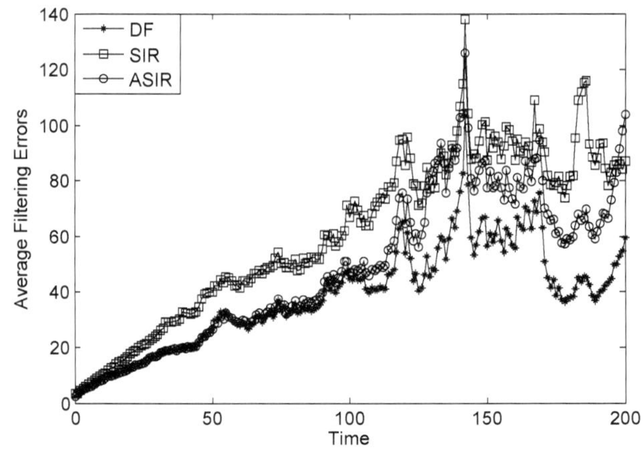

Fig. 6. Average Filtering Errors for Eqs. (20) and (21)

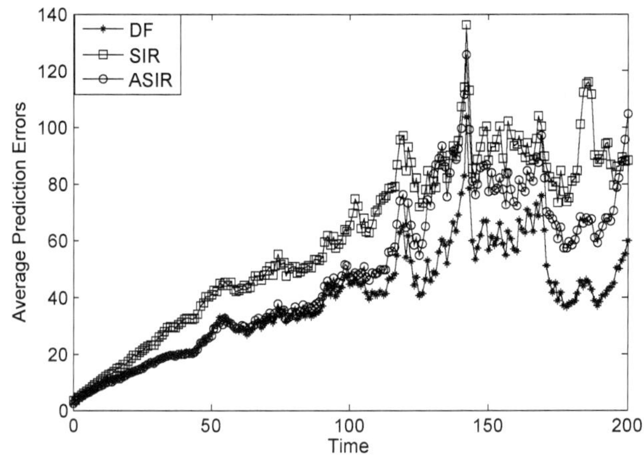

Fig. 7. Average Prediction Errors for Eqs. (20) and (21)

The performance of the DF is determined by the possible values (n and m) of the approximate discrete random disturbance noise and approximate discrete initial state, gate size (GS), maximum number (MN) of considered state quantization levels at each iteration. As GS goes to zero and the parameters n, m, and MN approach infinity, the approximate models of Eq. (6) and (7) approach the models of Eqs. (1) and (2), hence, the DF approaches an optimum estimation scheme, but the implementation complexity of the DF exponentially increases with time k. The parameters n, m, GS, MN which yield the best performance for given models are determined by Monte Carlo simulations for available hardware speed and storage. For given nonlinear models: the performances of the DF, EKF, particle filters, and others must be compared by Monte Carlo simulations with available hardware speed and storage. The estimation scheme yielding the best performance should be used. The EKF is surely much faster than both the DF and particle filters. The speed of the DF is based upon the parameters *n, m, GS, MN*; whereas the speeds of particle filters depend upon the number of particles used.

7. Conclutions

Presented is a real-time (online) recusive state filtering and prediction scheme for nonlinear discrete dynamic systems with Gaussian or non-Gaussian disturbance and observation noises. This scheme, referred to as the DF, is recently proposed in (Demirbaş, 2010). The DF is very suitable for state estimation of nonlinear dynamic systems under either missing observations or constraints imposed on state estimates. The DF is much more general than grid based estimation approaches. This is based upon discrete noise approximation, state quantization, and a suboptimum implementation of multiple hypothesis testing , whereas particle filters are based upon sequential Monte Carlo Methods. The models of the DF is as general as the models of particle filters, whereas the models of the extended Kalman filter (EKF) are linear functions of the disturbance and observation noises. The DF uses state models only to calculate transition probabilities from gates to gates. Hence, if these transition probabilities are known or can be estimated, state models are not needed for estimation with the DF, whereas state models are needed for both the EKF and particle filters. The performance and implementation complexity of the DF depend upon the gate size (*GS*), numbers n and m of possible values of approximate discrete disturbance noise and approximate discrete initial state, and maximum number (*MN*) of considered quantization levels at each iteration of the DF; whereas the performances and implementation complexities of particle filters depend upon numbers of particles used. The implementation complexity of the DF increases with a smaller value of *GS*, bigger values of n, m, and *MN*. These yield more accurate approximations of state and observation models; whereas the implementation complexities of particle filters increase with larger numbers of particles, which yield better approximations of conditional densities. Surely, the EKF is the simplest one to implement. The parameters (*GS, n,m, MN*) for which the DF yields the best performance for a real-time problem should be determined by Monte Carlo simulations. As $GS \to 0$, $n \to \infty$, $m \to \infty$,and $MN \to \infty$; the DF approaches the optimum one in the average overall error probability sense, but its implementation complexity exponentially increases with time. The performances of the DF, particle filters, EKF are all model-dependent. Hence, for a real-time problem with available hardware speed and storage; the DF, particle filters, and EKF (if applicable) should all be tested by Monte Carlo simulations, and the one which yields the best results should be used. The implementation complexity of the DF increases with the dimensions of multidimensional systems, as in the particle filters.

8. References

Arulampalam, M.S.; Maskell, S.; Gordon, N.; and Clapp, T. (2002), A tutorial on particle filters for online nonlinear/non-Gaussian bayesian tracking. *IEEE Transactions on Signal Processing*, Vol.50, pp. 174-188.

Daum, F.E. (2005). Nonlinear Filters: Beyond the Kalman Filter, *IEEE A&E Systems Magazine*, Vol. 20, No. 8, Part 2, pp. 57-69

Demirbaş K. (1982), New Smoothing Algorithms for Dynamic Systems with or without Interference, *The NATO AGARDograph Advances in the Techniques and Technology of Applications of Nonlinear Filters and Kalman Filters*, C.T. Leonde, (Ed.), AGARD, No. 256, pp. 19-1/66

Demirbaş, K. (1984). Information Theoretic Smoothing Algorithms for Dynamic Systems with or without Interference, *Advances in Control and Dynamic Systems,* C.T. Leonde, (Ed.), Volume XXI, pp. 175-295, Academic Press, New York

Demirbaş, K.; Leondes, C.T. (1985), Optimum decoding based smoothing algorithm for dynamic systems, *The International Journal of Systems Science,* Vol.16, No. 8, pp. 951-966

Demirbaş, K.; Leondes, C.T. (1986). A Suboptimum decoding based smoothing algorithm for dynamic Systems with or without interference, *The International Journal of Systems Science,* Vol.17, No.3, pp. 479-497.

Demirbaş, K. (1988). Maneuvering target tracking with hypothesis testing, *I.E.E.E. Transactions on Aerospace and Electronic Systems,* Vol.23, No.6, pp. 757-766.

Demirbaş, K. (1989). Manoeuvring-target Tracking with the Viterbi Algorithm in the Presence of Interference, *the IEE Proceedings-PartF, Communication, Radar and Signal Processing,* Vol. 136, No. 6, pp. 262-268

Demirbaş, K. (1990), Nonlinear State Smoothing and Filtering in Blocks for Dynamic Systems with Missing Observation, *The International Journal of Systems Science,* Vol. 21, No. 6, pp. 1135-1144

Demirbaş, K. (2007), A state prediction scheme for discrete time nonlinear dynamic systems, *the international journal of general systems,* Vol. 36, No. 5, pp. 501-511

Demirbaş, K. (2010). A new real-time suboptimum filtering and prediction scheme for general nonlinear discrete dynamic systems with Gaussian or non-Gaussian noise, to appear in *the international journal of Systems Science,* DOI: 10.1080/00207721003653682, first published in *www.informaworld.com* on 08 September 2010.

Doucet, A.; De Freitas, J.F.G.; and Gordon, N.J. (2001), An introduction to sequential Monte Carlo methods, *in Sequential Monte Carlo Methods in Practice,* A. Doucet, J.F.G de Freitas, and N.J.Gordon (Eds.), Springer-Verlag, New York

Forney, G.D. (1973). The Viterbi algorihm, *Proceedings of the IEEE,* Vol. 61, pp. 268-278

Gordon, N.; Salmond, D.; Smith, A.F.M. (1993). Novel approach to nonlinear and non-Gaussian Bayesian state estimation. *Proceedings of the Institute of Electrical Engineering F,* Vol.140, pp. 107-113

Kalman, R.E. (1960). A new approach to linear filtering and prediction problems, *Trans. ASME, Journal of Basic Engineering,* Vol. 82, pp. 35-45.

Kalman, R.E.; Busy R.S. (1960). New Results in Linear Filtering and Prediction Theory, *Trans. ASME, Journal of Basic Engineering,* Series D, Vol. 83, pp. 95-108

Kee, R.J.; Irwin, G.W. (1994). Investigation of trellis based filters for tracking, *IEE Proceedings Radar, Sonar and Navigation,* Vol. 141, No.1 pp. 9-18.

Julier S. J.; Uhlmann J. K. (2004). Unscented Filtering and Nonlinear Estimation *Proceedings of the IEEE,* **92**, pp. 401-422

Ristic B., Arulampalam S.; Gordon N. (2004). *Beyond the Kalman Filter: Particle Filters for Tracking Applications* , Artech House, London

Sage, A.P.; Melsa, J.L. (1971). *Estimation Theory with Applications to Communications and Control,* McGraw-Hill, New York

Van Trees, H. L. (2001). *Detection, Estimation and Modulation: Part I. Detection, Estimation, and Linesr Modulation Theory,* Jhon Wiley and Sons, Inc., New York, ISBN 0-471-09517-6

Weber, C. L. (1968), *Elements of Detection and Signal Design,* McGraw-Hill, New York

2

Observers Design for a Class of Lipschitz Discrete-Time Systems with Time-Delay

Ali Zemouche and Mohamed Boutayeb
Centre de Recherche en Automatique de Nancy, CRAN UMR 7039 CNRS, Nancy-Université, 54400 Cosnes et Romain France

1. Introduction

The observer design problem for nonlinear time-delay systems becomes more and more a subject of research in constant evolution Germani et al. (2002), Germani & Pepe (2004), Aggoune et al. (1999), Raff & Allgöwer (2006), Trinh et al. (2004), Xu et al. (2004), Zemouche et al. (2006), Zemouche et al. (2007). Indeed, time-delay is frequently encountered in various practical systems, such as chemical engineering systems, neural networks and population dynamic model. One of the recent application of time-delay is the synchronization and information recovery in chaotic communication systems Cherrier et al. (2005). In fact, the time-delay is added in a suitable way to the chaotic system in the goal to increase the complexity of the chaotic behavior and then to enhance the security of communication systems. On the other hand, contrary to nonlinear continuous-time systems, little attention has been paid toward discrete-time nonlinear systems with time-delay. We refer the readers to the few existing references Lu & Ho (2004a) and Lu & Ho (2004b), where the authors investigated the problem of robust H_∞ observer design for a class of Lipschitz time-delay systems with uncertain parameters in the discrete-time case. Their method show the stability of the state of the system and the estimation error simultaneously.
This chapter deals with observer design for a class of Lipschitz nonlinear discrete-time systems with time-delay. The main result lies in the use of a new structure of the proposed observer inspired from Fan & Arcak (2003). Using a *Lyapunov-Krasovskii* functional, a new nonrestrictive synthesis condition is obtained. This condition, expressed in term of LMI, contains more degree of freedom than those proposed by the approaches available in literature. Indeed, these last use a simple Luenberger observer which can be derived from the general form of the observer proposed in this paper by neglecting some observer gains.
An extension of the presented result to H_∞ performance analysis is given in the goal to take into account the noise which affects the considered system. A more general LMI is established. The last section is devoted to systems with differentiable nonlinearities. In this case, based on the use of the Differential Mean Value Theorem (DMVT), less restrictive synthesis conditions are proposed.

Notations : The following notations will be used throughout this chapter.

- $\|.\|$ is the usual Euclidean norm;

- $(\star)$ is used for the blocks induced by symmetry;
- A^T represents the transposed matrix of A;
- I_r represents the identity matrix of dimension r;
- for a square matrix S, $S > 0$ $(S < 0)$ means that this matrix is positive definite (negative definite);
- $z_t(k)$ represents the vector $x(k-t)$ for all z;
- The notation $\|x\|_{\ell_2^s} = \left(\sum_{k=0}^{\infty} \|x(k)\|^2\right)^{\frac{1}{2}}$ is the ℓ_2^s norm of the vector $x \in \mathbb{R}^s$. The set ℓ_2^s is defined by

$$\ell_2^s = \left\{x \in \mathbb{R}^s \ : \ \|x\|_{\ell_2^s} < +\infty\right\}.$$

2. Problem formulation and observer synthesis

In this section, we introduce the class of nonlinear systems to be studied, the proposed state observer and the observer synthesis conditions.

2.1 Problem formulation

Consider the class of systems described in a detailed forme by the following equations :

$$x(k+1) = Ax(k) + A_d x_d(k) + Bf\Big(Hx(k), H_d x_d(k)\Big) \tag{1a}$$

$$y(k) = Cx(k) \tag{1b}$$

$$x(k) = x^0(k), \ \text{for} \ k = -d, ..., 0 \tag{1c}$$

where the constant matrices A, A_d, B, C, H and H_d are of appropriate dimensions.
The function $f \ : \ \mathbb{R}^{s_1} \times \mathbb{R}^{s_2} \rightarrow \mathbb{R}^q$ satisfies the Lipschitz condition with Lipschitz constant γ_f, i.e :

$$\left\|f\Big(z_1, z_2\Big) - f\Big(\hat{z}_1, \hat{z}_2\Big)\right\| \leq \gamma_f \left\|\begin{bmatrix} z_1 - \hat{z}_1 \\ z_2 - \hat{z}_2 \end{bmatrix}\right\|, \ \forall \ z_1, z_2, \hat{z}_1, \hat{z}_2. \tag{2}$$

Now, consider the following new structure of the proposed observer defined by the equations (78) :

$$\begin{aligned} \hat{x}(k+1) &= A\hat{x}(k) + A_d\hat{x}_d(k) + Bf\Big(v(k), w(k)\Big) \\ &+ L\Big(y(k) - C\hat{x}(k)\Big) + L_d\Big(y_d(k) - C\hat{x}_d(k)\Big) \end{aligned} \tag{3a}$$

$$v(k) = H\hat{x}(k) + K^1\Big(y(k) - C\hat{x}(k)\Big) + K_d^1\Big(y_d(k) - C\hat{x}_d(k)\Big) \tag{3b}$$

$$w(k) = H_d\hat{x}_d(k) + K^2\Big(y(k) - C\hat{x}(k)\Big) + K_d^2\Big(y_d(k) - C\hat{x}_d(k)\Big). \tag{3c}$$

The dynamic of the estimation error is :

$$\varepsilon(k+1) = \Big(A - LC\Big)\varepsilon(k) + \Big(A_d - L_dC\Big)\varepsilon_d(k) + B\delta f_k \tag{4}$$

with

$$\delta f_k = f\Big(Hx(k), H_d x_d(k)\Big) - f\Big(v(k), w(k)\Big).$$

From (35), we obtain

$$\Big\|\delta f_k\Big\| \le \gamma_f \left\| \begin{bmatrix} (H - K^1C)\varepsilon(k) - K_d^1 C\varepsilon_d(k) \\ (H_d - K_d^2 C)\varepsilon_d(k) - K^2 C\varepsilon(k) \end{bmatrix} \right\|. \tag{5}$$

2.2 Observer synthesis conditions

This subsection is devoted to the observer synthesis method that provides a sufficient condition ensuring the asymptotic convergence of the estimation error towards zero. The synthesis conditions, expressed in term of LMI, are given in the following theorem.

Theorem 2.1. *The estimation error is asymptotically stable if there exist a scalar $\alpha > 0$ and matrices $P = P^T > 0$, $Q = Q^T > 0$, $R, R_d, \bar{K}^1, \bar{K}^2, \bar{K}_d^1$ and $\bar{K}_d^2$ of appropriate dimensions such that the following LMI is feasible :*

$$\begin{bmatrix} -P+Q & 0 & \mathbb{M}_{13} & \mathbb{M}_{14} & \mathbb{M}_{15}^T & \mathbb{M}_{16}^T \\ (\star) & -Q & \mathbb{M}_{23} & \mathbb{M}_{24} & \mathbb{M}_{25}^T & \mathbb{M}_{26}^T \\ (\star) & (\star) & \mathbb{M}_{33} & 0 & 0 & 0 \\ (\star) & (\star) & (\star) & -P & 0 & 0 \\ (\star) & (\star) & (\star) & (\star) & -\alpha\gamma_f^2 I_{s_1} & 0 \\ (\star) & (\star) & (\star) & (\star) & (\star) & -\alpha\gamma_f^2 I_{s_2} \end{bmatrix} < 0 \tag{6}$$

where

$$\mathbb{M}_{13} = A^T PB - C^T RB \tag{7a}$$
$$\mathbb{M}_{14} = A^T P - C^T R \tag{7b}$$
$$\mathbb{M}_{15} = \gamma_f^2\Big(\alpha H - \bar{K}^1 C\Big) \tag{7c}$$
$$\mathbb{M}_{16} = \gamma_f^2 \bar{K}^2 C \tag{7d}$$
$$\mathbb{M}_{23} = A_d^T PB - C^T R_d B \tag{7e}$$
$$\mathbb{M}_{24} = A_d^T P - C^T R_d \tag{7f}$$
$$\mathbb{M}_{25} = \gamma_f^2 \bar{K}_d^1 C \tag{7g}$$
$$\mathbb{M}_{26} = \gamma_f^2\Big(\alpha H_d - \bar{K}_d^2 C\Big) \tag{7h}$$
$$\mathbb{M}_{33} = B^T PB - \alpha I_q \tag{7i}$$

The gains L and L_d, K^1, K^2, K_d^1 and K_d^2 are given respectively by

$$L = P^{-1}R^T,\ L_d = P^{-1}R_d^T$$
$$K^1 = \frac{1}{\alpha}\bar{K}^1,\ K^2 = \frac{1}{\alpha}\bar{K}^2,$$
$$K_d^1 = \frac{1}{\alpha}\bar{K}_d^1,\ K_d^2 = \frac{1}{\alpha}\bar{K}_d^2.$$

Proof. Consider the following *Lyapunov-Krasovskii* functional :

$$V_k = \varepsilon^T(k)P\varepsilon(k) + \sum_{i=1}^{i=d}\Big(\varepsilon_i^T(k)Q\varepsilon_i(k)\Big). \tag{8}$$

Using the dynamics (4), we obtain

$$V_{k+1} - V_k = \zeta_k^T \mathbb{M}_1 \zeta_k$$

where

$$\mathbb{M}_1 = \begin{bmatrix} \tilde{A}^T P\tilde{A} - P + Q & \tilde{A}^T P\tilde{A}_d & \tilde{A}^T PB \\ (\star) & \tilde{A}_d^T P\tilde{A}_d - Q & \tilde{A}_d^T PB \\ (\star) & (\star) & B^T PB \end{bmatrix}, \tag{9a}$$

$$\zeta_k^T = \left[\varepsilon^T(k)\ \varepsilon_d^T(k)\ \delta f_k^T\right], \tag{9b}$$

$$\tilde{A} = A - LC, \tag{9c}$$

$$\tilde{A}_d = A_d - L_dC. \tag{9d}$$

Using the notations $\bar{K}^1 = \alpha K^1, \bar{K}^2 = \alpha K^2, \bar{K}_d^1 = \alpha K_d^1$ and $\bar{K}_d^2 = \alpha K_d^2$, the condition (5) can be rewritten as follows :

$$\zeta_k^T \mathbb{M}_2 \zeta_k \geq 0 \tag{10}$$

with

$$\mathbb{M}_2 = \begin{bmatrix} \frac{1}{\alpha\gamma_f^2}\mathbb{M}_3 & 0 \\ 0 & -\alpha I_q \end{bmatrix}, \tag{11a}$$

$$\mathbb{M}_3 = \begin{bmatrix} \mathbb{M}_{15}^T\mathbb{M}_{15} + \mathbb{M}_{16}^T\mathbb{M}_{16} & \mathbb{M}_{15}^T\mathbb{M}_{25} + \mathbb{M}_{16}^T\mathbb{M}_{26} \\ (\star) & \mathbb{M}_{26}^T\mathbb{M}_{26} + \mathbb{M}_{25}^T\mathbb{M}_{25} \end{bmatrix}, \tag{11b}$$

and $\mathbb{M}_{15}, \mathbb{M}_{16}, \mathbb{M}_{25}, \mathbb{M}_{26}$ are defined in (7).
Consequently

$$V_{k+1} - V_k \leq \zeta_k^T\Big(\mathbb{M}_1 + \mathbb{M}_2\Big)\zeta_k. \tag{12}$$

By using the *Schur lemma* (see the Appendix), we deduce that the inequality

$$\mathbb{M}_1 + \mathbb{M}_2 < 0$$

is equivalent to

$$\mathbb{M}_4 < 0$$

where

$$\mathbb{M}_4 = \begin{bmatrix} -P+Q & 0 & \tilde{A}^T PB & \tilde{A}^T P & \mathbb{M}_{15}^T & \mathbb{M}_{16}^T \\ (\star) & -Q & \tilde{A}_d^T PB & \tilde{A}_d^T P & \mathbb{M}_{25}^T & \mathbb{M}_{26}^T \\ (\star) & (\star) & \mathbb{M}_{33} & 0 & 0 & 0 \\ (\star) & (\star) & (\star) & -P & 0 & 0 \\ (\star) & (\star) & (\star) & (\star) & -\alpha\gamma_f^2 I_{s_1} & 0 \\ (\star) & (\star) & (\star) & (\star) & (\star) & -\alpha\gamma_f^2 I_{s_2} \end{bmatrix}. \qquad (13)$$

Using the notations $R = L^T P$ and $R_d = L_d^T P$, we deduce that the inequality $\mathbb{M}_4 < 0$ is identical to (6). This means that under the condition (6) of Theorem 2.1, the function V_k is strictly decreasing and therefore the estimation error is asymptotically stable. This ends the proof of Theorem 2.1. □

Remark 2.2. *The* Schur lemma *and its application in the proof of Theorem 2.1 are detailed in the Appendix of this paper.*

2.3 Illustrative example

In this section, we present a numerical example in order to valid the proposed results.

Consider an example of an instable system under the form (1) described by the following parameters :

$$A = \begin{bmatrix} 4 & 2 & 0 \\ 0 & 4 & 2 \\ 0 & 0 & 3 \end{bmatrix}, \quad A_d = \begin{bmatrix} 0 & 0.5 & 0.3 \\ 0.5 & 0 & 0.3 \\ 0.3 & 0.3 & 0 \end{bmatrix},$$

$$B = \begin{bmatrix} 0.01 & 0 \\ 0 & 0.01 \\ 0 & 0 \end{bmatrix}, \quad H = \begin{bmatrix} 1 & 0 & 1 \end{bmatrix},$$

$$H_d = \begin{bmatrix} 1 & 0 & 0 \end{bmatrix}, \quad C = \begin{bmatrix} 1 & 0 & 0 \end{bmatrix}$$

and

$$f(Hx, H_d x_d, y) = \gamma_f \begin{bmatrix} \sin(x^1(k) + x^3(k)) \\ \cos(x^2(k-1)) \end{bmatrix}$$

where

$$x = \begin{bmatrix} x^1 & x^2 & x^3 \end{bmatrix}^T$$

and $\gamma_f = 10$ is the Lipschitz constant of the function f.

Applying the proposed method (condition (6)), we obtain the following gains :

$$L = \begin{bmatrix} 0.0701 & 1.8682 & 2.9925 \end{bmatrix}^T,$$

$$L_d = \begin{bmatrix} 0.3035 & 0.2942 & 0.0308 \end{bmatrix}^T,$$

$$K^1 = 0.9961,\ K^2 = -2.8074 \times 10^{-5},$$

$$K_d^1 = -9.0820 \times 10^{-4},\ K_d^2 = -0.0075$$

and

$$\alpha = 10^{-7}.$$

3. Extension to H_∞ performance analysis

In this section, we propose an extension of the previous result to H_∞ robust observer design problem. In this case, we give an observer synthesis method which takes into account the noises affecting the system.
Consider the disturbed system described by the equations :

$$x(k+1) = Ax(k) + A_d x_d(k) + E_\omega \omega(k) + Bf\Big(Hx(k), H_d x_d(k)\Big) \tag{14a}$$

$$y(k) = Cx(k) + D_\omega \omega(k) \tag{14b}$$

$$x(k) = x^0(k),\ \text{for } k = -d, ..., 0 \tag{14c}$$

where $\omega(k) \in \ell_2^s$ is the vector of bounded disturbances. The matrices E_ω and D_ω are constants with appropriate dimensions.

The corresponding observer has the same structure as in (3). We recall it hereafter with some different notations.

$$\begin{aligned}\hat{x}(k+1) &= A\hat{x}(k) + A_d\hat{x}_d(k) + Bf\Big(v_1(k), v_2(k)\Big) \\ &\quad + L\Big(y(k) - C\hat{x}(k)\Big) + L_d\Big(y_d(k) - C\hat{x}_d(k)\Big)\end{aligned} \tag{15a}$$

$$v_1(k) = H\hat{x}(k) + K^1\Big(y(k) - C\hat{x}(k)\Big) + K_d^1\Big(y_d(k) - C\hat{x}_d(k)\Big) \tag{15b}$$

$$v_2(k) = H_d\hat{x}_d(k) + K^2\Big(y(k) - C\hat{x}(k)\Big) + K_d^2\Big(y_d(k) - C\hat{x}_d(k)\Big). \tag{15c}$$

Our aim is to design the matrices L, L_d, K^1, K^2, K_d^1 and K_d^2 such that (15) is an asymptotic observer for the system (14). The dynamics of the estimation error

$$\varepsilon(k) = x(k) - \hat{x}(k)$$

is given by the equation :

$$\begin{aligned}\varepsilon(k+1) &= \Big(A - LC\Big)\varepsilon(k) + \Big(A_d - L_dC\Big)\varepsilon_d(k) + B\delta f_k \\ &\quad + \Big(E_\omega - LD_\omega\Big)\omega(k) - L_dD_\omega\omega_d(k)\end{aligned} \tag{16}$$

with

$$\delta f_k = f\Big(Hx(k), H_d x_d(k)\Big) - f\Big(v_1(k), v_2(k))\Big)$$

satisfies (5).
The objective is to find the gains L, L_d, K^1, K^2, K_d^1 and K_d^2 such that the estimation error converges robustly asymptotically to zero, i.e :

$$\|\varepsilon\|_{\ell_2^s} \leq \lambda \|\omega\|_{\ell_2^s} \tag{17}$$

where $\lambda > 0$ is the disturbance attenuation level to be minimized under some conditions that we will determined later.
The inequality (17) is equivalent to

$$\|\varepsilon\|_{\ell_2^s} \leq \frac{\lambda}{\sqrt{2}}\Big(\|\omega\|_{\ell_2^s}^2 + \|\omega_d\|_{\ell_2^s}^2 - \sum_{k=-d}^{-1} \omega^2(k)\Big)^{\frac{1}{2}}. \tag{18}$$

Without loss of generality, we assume that

$$\omega(k) = 0 \ \text{ for } \ k = -d, ..., -1.$$

Then, (18) becomes

$$\|\varepsilon\|_{\ell_2^s} \leq \frac{\lambda}{\sqrt{2}}\Big(\|\omega\|_{\ell_2^s}^2 + \|\omega_d\|_{\ell_2^s}^2\Big)^{\frac{1}{2}}. \tag{19}$$

Remark 3.1. *In fact, if $\omega(k) \neq 0$ for $k = -d, ..., -1$, we must replace the inequality* (17) *by*

$$\|\varepsilon\|_{\ell_2^s} \leq \lambda\Big(\|\omega\|_{\ell_2^s}^2 + \frac{1}{2}\sum_{k=-d}^{-1} \omega^2(k)\Big)^{\frac{1}{2}} \tag{20}$$

in order to obtain (19).

Robust H_∞ observer design problem Li & Fu (1997) : Given the system (14) and the observer (15), then the problem of robust H_∞ observer design is to determine the matrices L, L_d, K^1, K^2, K_d^1 and K_d^2 so that

$$\lim_{k\to\infty} \varepsilon(k) = 0 \ \text{ for } \ \omega(k) = 0; \tag{21}$$

$$\|\varepsilon\|_{\ell_2^s} \leq \lambda \|\omega\|_{\ell_2^s} \ \forall \ \omega(k) \neq 0; \ \ \varepsilon(k) = 0, k = -d, ..., 0. \tag{22}$$

From the equivalence between (17) and (19), the problem of robust H_∞ observer design (see the Appendix) is reduced to find a *Lyapunov* function V_k such that

$$W_k = \Delta V + \varepsilon^T(k)\varepsilon(k) - \frac{\lambda^2}{2}\omega^T(k)\omega(k) - \frac{\lambda^2}{2}\omega_d^T(k)\omega_d(k) < 0 \tag{23}$$

where

$$\Delta V = V_{k+1} - V_k.$$

At this stage, we can state the following theorem, which provides a sufficient condition ensuring (23).

Theorem 3.2. *The robust H_∞ observer design problem corresponding to the system (14) and the observer (15) is solvable if there exist a scalar $\alpha > 0$ matrices $P = P^T > 0$, $Q = Q^T > 0$, $R, R_d, \bar{K}^1, \bar{K}^2, \bar{K}_d^1$ and $\bar{K}_d^2$ of appropriate dimensions so that the following convex optimization problem is feasible :*

$$\min(\gamma) \text{ subject to } \Gamma < 0 \tag{24}$$

where

$$\Gamma = \begin{bmatrix} \begin{bmatrix} -P+Q+I_n & 0 & \mathbb{M}_{13} & 0 & 0 \\ (\star) & -Q & \mathbb{M}_{23} & 0 & 0 \\ (\star) & (\star) & \mathbb{M}_{33} & \mathbb{M}_{34} & \mathbb{M}_{35} \\ (\star) & (\star) & (\star) & -\gamma I_s & 0 \\ (\star) & (\star) & (\star) & (\star) & -\gamma I_s \end{bmatrix} & \begin{bmatrix} \mathbb{M}_{14} & \mathbb{M}_{15}^T & \mathbb{M}_{16}^T \\ \mathbb{M}_{24}^T & \mathbb{M}_{25}^T & \mathbb{M}_{26}^T \\ 0 & 0 & 0 \\ E_\omega^T P - C^T R & 0 & 0 \\ -D_\omega R_d & 0 & 0 \end{bmatrix} \\ \begin{bmatrix} \mathbb{M}_{14} & \mathbb{M}_{15}^T & \mathbb{M}_{16}^T \\ \mathbb{M}_{24}^T & \mathbb{M}_{25}^T & \mathbb{M}_{26}^T \\ 0 & 0 & 0 \\ E_\omega^T P - C^T R & 0 & 0 \\ -D_\omega R_d & 0 & 0 \end{bmatrix}^T & \begin{bmatrix} -P & 0 & 0 \\ (\star) & -\alpha\gamma_f^2 I_{s_1} & 0 \\ (\star) & (\star) & -\alpha\gamma_f^2 I_{s_2} \end{bmatrix} \end{bmatrix} \tag{25}$$

with

$$\mathbb{M}_{34} = B^T P E_\omega - B^T R^T C, \tag{26a}$$

$$\mathbb{M}_{35} = -B^T R_d^T D_\omega, \tag{26b}$$

and $\mathbb{M}_{13}, \mathbb{M}_{14}, \mathbb{M}_{15}, \mathbb{M}_{16}, \mathbb{M}_{24}, \mathbb{M}_{25}, \mathbb{M}_{26}, \mathbb{M}_{33}$ are de□ned in (7).
The gains L and $L_d, K^1, K^2, K_d^1, K_d^2$ and the minimum disturbance attenuation level λ are given respectively by

$$L = P^{-1}R^T,\ L_d = P^{-1}R_d^T$$

$$K^1 = \frac{1}{\alpha}\bar{K}^1,\ K^2 = \frac{1}{\alpha}\bar{K}^2,$$

$$K_d^1 = \frac{1}{\alpha}\bar{K}_d^1,\ K_d^2 = \frac{1}{\alpha}\bar{K}_d^2,$$

$$\lambda = \sqrt{2\gamma}.$$

Proof. The proof of this theorem is an extension of that of Theorem 2.1.
Let us consider the same *Lyapunov-Krasovskii* functional defined in (8). We show that if the convex optimization problem (24) is solvable, we have $W_k < 0$. Using the dynamics (16), we obtain

$$W_k = \eta^T \mathbb{S}_1 \eta \tag{27}$$

where

$$\mathbb{S}_1 = \begin{bmatrix} \mathbb{M}_1 + \begin{bmatrix} I_n & 0 & 0 \\ 0 & 0 & 0 \\ 0 & 0 & 0 \end{bmatrix} & \begin{bmatrix} \tilde{A}^T P \tilde{E}_\omega & -\tilde{A}^T P \tilde{D}_\omega \\ \tilde{A}_d^T P \tilde{E}_\omega & -\tilde{A}_d^T P \tilde{D}_\omega \\ B^T P \tilde{E}_\omega & -B^T P \tilde{D}_\omega \end{bmatrix} \\ \begin{bmatrix} \tilde{A}^T P \tilde{E}_\omega & -\tilde{A}^T P \tilde{D}_\omega \\ \tilde{A}_d^T P \tilde{E}_\omega & -\tilde{A}_d^T P \tilde{D}_\omega \\ B^T P \tilde{E}_\omega & -B^T P \tilde{D}_\omega \end{bmatrix}^T & \begin{bmatrix} \tilde{E}_\omega^T P \tilde{E}_\omega - \gamma I_s & \tilde{E}_\omega^T P \tilde{D}_\omega \\ \tilde{D}_\omega^T P \tilde{E}_\omega & \tilde{D}_\omega^T P \tilde{D}_\omega - \gamma I_s \end{bmatrix} \end{bmatrix}, \tag{28}$$

where

$$\tilde{E_\omega} = E_\omega - LC \quad (29a)$$

$$\tilde{D_\omega} = L_d D_\omega \quad (29b)$$

$$\eta^T = \left[\varepsilon^T \ \varepsilon_d^T \ \delta f_k \ \omega^T \ \omega_d^T\right], \quad (29c)$$

$$\gamma = \frac{\lambda^2}{2}. \quad (29d)$$

The matrices $\mathbb{M}_1, \tilde{A}$ and $\tilde{A}_d$ are defined in (9).
As in the proof of Theorem 2.1, since δf_k satisfies (5), we deduce, after multiplying by a scalar $\alpha > 0$, that

$$\eta^T \mathbb{S}_2 \eta \geq 0 \quad (30)$$

where

$$\mathbb{S}_2 = \begin{bmatrix} \frac{1}{\alpha\gamma_f^2}\mathbb{M}_3 & 0 & 0 & 0 \\ 0 & -\alpha I_q & 0 & 0 \\ 0 & 0 & 0 & 0 \\ 0 & 0 & 0 & 0 \end{bmatrix} \quad (31)$$

and $\mathbb{M}_3$ is defined in (11b).
The inequality (31) implies that

$$W_k = \eta^T(\mathbb{S}_1 + \mathbb{S}_2)\eta. \quad (32)$$

Now, using the *Schur Lemma* and the notations $R = L^T P$ and $R_d = L_d^T P$, we deduce that the inequality $\mathbb{S}_1 + \mathbb{S}_2 < 0$ is equivalent to $\Gamma < 0$. The estimation error converges robustly asymptotically to zero with a *minimum* value of the disturbance attenuation level $\lambda = \sqrt{2\gamma}$ if the convex optimization problem (24) is solvable. This ends the proof of Theorem 3.2. □

Remark 3.3. *We can obtain a synthesis condition which contains more degree of freedom than the LMI (6) by using a more general design of the observer. This new design of the observer can take the following structure :*

$$\begin{aligned}\hat{x}(k+1) &= A\hat{x}(k) + A_d\hat{x}_d(k) + Bf\Big(v(k), w(k)\Big) \\ &+ L\Big(y(k) - C\hat{x}(k)\Big) + \sum_{i=1}^{d} L_i\Big(y_i(k) - C\hat{x}_i(k)\Big)\end{aligned} \quad (33a)$$

$$v(k) = H\hat{x}(k) + K^1\Big(y(k) - C\hat{x}(k)\Big) + \sum_{i=1}^{d} K_i^1\Big(y_i(k) - C\hat{x}_i(k)\Big) \quad (33b)$$

$$w(k) = H_d\hat{x}_d(k) + K^2\Big(y(k) - C\hat{x}(k)\Big) + \sum_{i=1}^{d} K_i^2\Big(y_i(k) - C\hat{x}_i(k)\Big). \quad (33c)$$

If such an observer is used, the adequate Lyapunov-Krasovskii *functional that we propose is under the following form :*

$$V_k = \varepsilon^T(k)P\varepsilon(k) + \sum_{j=1}^{j=d}\sum_{i=1}^{i=j}\left(\varepsilon_i^T(k)Q_j\varepsilon_i(k)\right). \tag{34}$$

4. Systems with differentiable nonlinearities

4.1 Reformulation of the problem

In this section, we need to assume that the function f is differentiable with respect to x. Rewrite also f under the detailed form :

$$f(Hx, H_d z) = \begin{bmatrix} f_1(H_1 x, H_1^d z) \\ \cdot \\ \cdot \\ \cdot \\ f_q(H_q x, H_q^d z) \end{bmatrix}. \tag{35}$$

where $H_i \in \mathbb{R}^{s_i \times n}$ and $H_i^d \in \mathbb{R}^{r_i \times n}$ for all $i \in \{1, ..., q\}$. Here, we use the following reformulation of the Lipschitz condition :

$$-\infty < a_{ij} \leq \frac{\partial f_i}{\partial \zeta_j^i}(\zeta^i, z^i) \leq b_{ij} < +\infty, \ \forall \, \zeta^i \in \mathbb{R}^{s_i}, \ \forall \, z^i \in \mathbb{R}^{r_i} \tag{36}$$

$$-\infty < a_{ij}^d \leq \frac{\partial f_i}{\partial \zeta_j^i}(x^i, \zeta^i) \leq b_{ij}^d < +\infty, \ \forall \, \zeta^i \in \mathbb{R}^{r_i}, \ \forall \, x^i \in \mathbb{R}^{s_i} \tag{37}$$

where $x^i = H_i x$ and $z^i = H_i^d z$.
The conditions (36)-(37) imply that the differentiable function f is γ_f-Lipschitz where

$$\gamma_f = \sqrt{\sum_{i=1}^{i=q} \max\left(\sum_{j=1}^{j=s_i} \max\left(|a_{ij}|^2, |b_{ij}|^2\right), \sum_{j=1}^{j=r_i} \max\left(|a_{ij}^d|^2, |b_{ij}^d|^2\right)\right)}$$

The reformulation of the Lipschitz condition for differentiable functions as in (36) and (37) plays an important role on the feasibility of the synthesis conditions and avoids high gain as shown in Zemouche et al. (2008). In addition, it is shown in Alessandri (2004) that the use of the classical Lipschitz property leads to restrictive synthesis conditions.

Remark 4.1. *For simplicity of the presentation, we assume, without loss of generality, that f satis□es* (36) *and* (37) *with $a_{ij} = 0$ and $a_{lm}^d = 0$ for all $i, l = 1, ..., q$, $j = 1, ..., s$ and $m = 1, ..., r$, where $s = \max_{1 \leq i \leq q}(s_i)$ and $r = \max_{1 \leq i \leq q}(r_i)$. Indeed, if there exist subsets $S_1, S_1^d \subset \{1, ..., q\}$, $S_2 \subset \{1, ..., s\}$ and $S_2^d \subset \{1, ..., r\}$ such that $a_{ij} \neq 0$ for all $(i, j) \in S_1 \times S_2$ and $a_{lm}^d \neq 0$ for all $(l, m) \in S_1^d \times S_2^d$, we can* *consider the nonlinear function*

$$\begin{aligned}\tilde{f}(x_k, x_{k-d}) = f(Hx_k, H_d x_{k-d}) - \Big(\sum_{(i,j)\in S_1\times S_2} a_{ij} H_{ij} H_i \Big) x_k \\ - \Big(\sum_{(l,m)\in S_1^d\times S_2^d} a_{lm}^d H_{lm}^d H_l^d \Big) x_{k-d}\end{aligned} \tag{38}$$

where

$$H_{ij} = e_q(i) e_{s_i}^T(j) \;\; and \;\; H_{lm}^d = e_q(l) e_{r_l}^T(m).$$

Therefore, $\tilde{f}$ *satis□es* (36) *and* (37) *with* $\tilde{a}_{ij} = 0$, $\tilde{a}_{ij}^d = 0$, $\tilde{b}_{ij} = b_{ij} - a_{ij}$ *and* $\tilde{b}_{ij}^d = b_{ij}^d - a_{ij}^d$, *and then we rewrite* (1a) *as*

$$x_{k+1} = \tilde{A} x_k + \tilde{A}_d x_{k-d} + B\tilde{f}(x_k, x_{k-d})$$

with

$$\tilde{A} = A + B \sum_{(i,j)\in S_1\times S_2} a_{ij} H_{ij} H_i, \;\; \tilde{A}_d = A_d + B \sum_{(i,j)\in S_1^d\times S_2^d} a_{ij}^d H_{ij}^d H_i^d$$

Inspired by Fan & Arcak (2003), we consider the following state observer :

$$\begin{aligned}\hat{x}_{k+1} = A\hat{x}_k + A_d \hat{x}_{k-d} + \sum_{i=1}^{i=q} B e_q(i) f_i(v_k^i, w_k^i) \\ + L\Big(y_k - C\hat{x}_k\Big) + L^d\Big(y_{k-d} - C\hat{x}_{k-d}\Big)\end{aligned} \tag{39a}$$

$$v_k^i = H_i \hat{x}_k + K_i\Big(y_k - C\hat{x}_k\Big) \tag{39b}$$

$$w_k^i = H_i^d \hat{x}_{k-d} + K_i^d\Big(y_{k-d} - C\hat{x}_{k-d}\Big) \tag{39c}$$

$$\hat{x}_k = \hat{x}_0, \; \forall\, k \in \{-d, ..., 0\} \tag{39d}$$

Therefore, the aim is to find the gains $L \in \mathbb{R}^{n\times p}$, $L^d \in \mathbb{R}^{n\times p}$, $K_i \in \mathbb{R}^{s_i\times p}$ and $K_i^d \in \mathbb{R}^{r_i\times p}$, for $i = 1, ..., q$, such that the estimation error

$$\varepsilon_k = x_k - \hat{x}_k \tag{40}$$

converges asymptotically towards zero.
The dynamics of the estimation error is given by :

$$\varepsilon_{k+1} = \Big(A - LC\Big)\varepsilon_k + \Big(A_d - L^d C\Big)\varepsilon_{k-d} + \sum_{i=1}^{i=q} B e_q(i)\delta f_i \tag{41}$$

where

$$\delta f_i = f_i(H_i x_k, H_i^d \hat{x}_k) - f_i(v_k^i, w_k^i).$$

Using the DMVT-based approach given firstly in Zemouche et al. (2008), there exist $z_i \in Co(H_i x, v^i), z_i^d \in Co(H_i^d x_{k-d}, w^i)$ for all $i = 1, ..., q$ such that :

$$\delta f_i = \sum_{j=1}^{j=s_i} h_{ij}(k) e_{s_i}^T(j)\chi_i + \sum_{j=1}^{j=r_i} h_{ij}^d(k) e_{r_i}^T(j)\chi_i^d \tag{42}$$

where

$$\chi_i = \Big(H_i - K_i C\Big)\varepsilon_k \tag{43}$$

$$\chi_i^d = \Big(H_i^d - K_i^d C\Big)\varepsilon_{k-d} \tag{44}$$

$$h_{ij}(k) = \frac{\partial f_i}{\partial v_j^i}\Big(z_i(k), H_i^d x_{k-d}\Big) \tag{45}$$

$$h_{ij}^d(k) = \frac{\partial f_i}{\partial v_j^i}\Big(v_k^i, z_i^d(k)\Big) \tag{46}$$

Hence, the estimation error dynamics (41) becomes :

$$\begin{aligned} \varepsilon_{k+1} = & \Big(A - LC\Big)\varepsilon_k + \Big(A_d - L^d C\Big)\varepsilon_{k-d} \\ & + \sum_{i=1}^{i=q}\sum_{j=1}^{j=s_i} h_{ij}(k) B H_{ij} \chi_i \\ & + \sum_{i=1}^{i=q}\sum_{j=1}^{j=r_i} h_{ij}^d(k) B H_{ij}^d \chi_i^d \end{aligned} \tag{47}$$

4.2 New synthesis method

The content of this section consists in a new observer synthesis method. A novel sufficient stability condition ensuring the asymptotic convergence of the estimation error towards zero is provided. This condition is expressed in term of LMI easily tractable.

Theorem 4.2. *The estimation error* (40) *converges asymptotically towards zero if there exist matrices* $P = P^T > 0$, $Q = Q^T > 0$, R, R^d, K_i *and* K_i^d, *for* $i = 1, ..., q$, *of adequate dimensions so that the following LMI is feasible :*

$$\begin{bmatrix} -P+Q & 0 & \mathbb{M} & 0 & A^T P - C^T R \\ (\star) & -Q & 0 & \mathbb{N} & A_d^T P - C^T R^d \\ (\star) & (\star) & -\mathrm{Y} & 0 & \Sigma^T P \\ (\star) & (\star) & (\star) & -\mathrm{Y}^d & (\Sigma^d)^T P \\ (\star) & (\star) & (\star) & (\star) & -P \end{bmatrix} < 0 \tag{48}$$

where

$$\mathbb{M} = \Big[\mathbb{M}_1(K_1) \cdots \mathbb{M}_q(K_q)\Big] \tag{49}$$

$$\mathbb{M}_i(K_i) = \Big[\underbrace{(H_i - K_i C)^T ... (H_i - K_i C)^T}_{s_i \text{ times}}\Big] \tag{50}$$

$$\mathbb{N} = \left[\mathbb{N}_1(K_1^d) \cdots \mathbb{N}_q(K_q^d)\right] \tag{51}$$

$$\mathbb{N}_i(K_i^d) = \left[\underbrace{(H_i^d - K_i^d C)^T ... (H_i^d - K_i^d C)^T}_{r_i \text{ times}}\right] \tag{52}$$

$$\Sigma = B\left[H_{11} \cdots H_{1s_1}\ H_{21} \cdots H_{qs_q}\right] \tag{53}$$

$$\Sigma^d = B\left[H_{11}^d \cdots H_{1r_1}^d\ H_{21} \cdots H_{qr_q}\right] \tag{54}$$

$$\Upsilon = diag\left(\beta_{11} I_{s_1}, ..., \beta_{1s_1} I_{s_1}, \beta_{21} I_{s_2}, ..., \beta_{qs_q} I_{s_q}\right) \tag{55}$$

$$\Upsilon^d = diag\left(\beta_{11}^d I_{r_1}, ..., \beta_{1r_1}^d I_{r_1}, \beta_{21}^d I_{r_2}, ..., \beta_{qr_q}^d I_{r_q}\right) \tag{56}$$

$$\beta_{ij} = \frac{2}{b_{ij}},\ \beta_{ij}^d = \frac{2}{b_{ij}^d} \tag{57}$$

Hence, the gains L, L^d are given, respectively, by $L = P^{-1}R^T$, $L^d = P^{-1}(R^d)^T$ and the matrices K_i, K_i^d are free solutions of the LMI (48).

Proof. For the proof, we use the following Lyapunov-Krasovskii functional candidate :

$$V_k = \varepsilon_k^T P \varepsilon_k + \sum_{i=1}^{i=d} \varepsilon_{k-i}^T Q \varepsilon_{k-i}$$

Considering the difference $\Delta V = V_{k+1} - V_k$ along the system (1), we have

$$\begin{aligned}
\Delta V = {} & \varepsilon_k^T \left[\left(A - LC\right)^T P \left(A - LC\right) - P + Q\right] \varepsilon_k + \varepsilon_{k-d}^T \left[\left(A_d - L^d C\right)^T P \left(A_d - L^d C\right) - Q\right] \varepsilon_{k-d} \\
& + 2\varepsilon_k^T \left(A - LC\right)^T P \left(A_d - L^d C\right) \varepsilon_{k-d} + 2\varepsilon_k^T \left(A - LC\right)^T P \left(\sum_{i=1}^{i=q} \sum_{j=1}^{j=s_i} BH_{ij}\zeta_{ij}\right) \\
& + 2\varepsilon_k^T \left(A - LC\right)^T P \left(\sum_{i=1}^{i=q} \sum_{j=1}^{j=r_i} BH_{ij}^d\zeta_{ij}^d\right) + 2\varepsilon_{k-d}^T \left(A_d - L^d C\right)^T P \left(\sum_{i=1}^{i=q} \sum_{j=1}^{j=s_i} BH_{ij}\zeta_{ij}\right) \\
& + 2\varepsilon_{k-d}^T \left(A_d - L^d C\right)^T P \left(\sum_{i=1}^{i=q} \sum_{j=1}^{j=r_i} BH_{ij}^d\zeta_{ij}^d\right) + \left(\sum_{i=1}^{i=q} \sum_{j=1}^{j=s_i} BH_{ij}\zeta_{ij}\right)^T P \left(\sum_{i=1}^{i=q} \sum_{j=1}^{j=s_i} BH_{ij}\zeta_{ij}\right) \\
& + \left(\sum_{i=1}^{i=q} \sum_{j=1}^{j=r_i} BH_{ij}^d\zeta_{ij}^d\right)^T P \left(\sum_{i=1}^{i=q} \sum_{j=1}^{j=r_i} BH_{ij}^d\zeta_{ij}^d\right)
\end{aligned} \tag{58}$$

where

$$\zeta_{ij} = h_{ij}(k)\chi_i,\ \zeta_{ij}^d = h_{ij}^d(k)\chi_i^d. \tag{59}$$

From (36) and (37), we have

$$\sum_{i=1}^{i=q}\sum_{j=1}^{j=s_i}\zeta_{ij}^T\left(\frac{1}{h_{ij}}-\frac{1}{b_{ij}}\right)\zeta_{ij}\geq 0 \tag{60}$$

$$\sum_{i=1}^{i=q}\sum_{j=1}^{j=r_i}(\zeta_{ij}^d)^T\left(\frac{1}{h_{ij}^d}-\frac{1}{b_{ij}^d}\right)\zeta_{ij}^d\geq 0 \tag{61}$$

Using (43) and (59), the inequalities (60) and (61) become, respectively,

$$\sum_{i=1}^{i=q}\sum_{j=1}^{j=s_i}\varepsilon^T\Big(H_i-K_iC\Big)^T\zeta_{ij}-\sum_{i=1}^{i=q}\sum_{j=1}^{j=s_i}\frac{1}{b_{ij}}\zeta_{ij}^T\zeta_{ij}\geq 0 \tag{62}$$

$$\sum_{i=1}^{i=q}\sum_{j=1}^{j=r_i}\varepsilon_{k-d}^T\Big(H_i^d-K_i^dC\Big)^T\zeta_{ij}^d-\sum_{i=1}^{i=q}\sum_{j=1}^{j=r_i}\frac{1}{b_{ij}^d}(\zeta_{ij}^d)^T\zeta_{ij}^d\geq 0 \tag{63}$$

Consequently,

$$\Delta V\leq\begin{bmatrix}\varepsilon_k\\ \varepsilon_{k-d}\\ \zeta_k\\ \zeta_k^d\end{bmatrix}^T\begin{bmatrix}\Gamma_{11} & \Gamma_{12} & \Gamma_{13} & \Gamma_{14}\\ (\star) & \Gamma_{22} & \Gamma_{23} & \Gamma_{24}\\ (\star) & (\star) & \Gamma_{33} & \Gamma_{34}\\ (\star) & (\star) & (\star) & \Gamma_{44}\end{bmatrix}\begin{bmatrix}\varepsilon_k\\ \varepsilon_{k-d}\\ \zeta_k\\ \zeta_k^d\end{bmatrix} \tag{64}$$

where

$$\Gamma_{11}=\Big(A-LC\Big)^TP\Big(A-LC\Big)-P+Q \tag{65}$$

$$\Gamma_{12}=\Big(A-LC\Big)^TP\Big(A_d-L^dC\Big) \tag{66}$$

$$\Gamma_{13}=\mathbb{M}^T(K_1,...,K_q)+\Big(A-LC\Big)^TP\Sigma \tag{67}$$

$$\Gamma_{14}=\Big(A-LC\Big)^TP\Sigma^d \tag{68}$$

$$\Gamma_{22}=\Big(A_d-L^dC\Big)^TP\Big(A_d-L^dC\Big)-Q \tag{69}$$

$$\Gamma_{23}=\Big(A_d-L^dC\Big)^TP\Sigma \tag{70}$$

$$\Gamma_{24}=\mathbb{N}^T(K_1^d,...,K_q^d)+\Big(A_d-L^dC\Big)^TP\Sigma^d \tag{71}$$

$$\Gamma_{33}=\Sigma^TP\Sigma-\Upsilon \tag{72}$$

$$\Gamma_{34}=\Sigma^TP\Sigma^d \tag{73}$$

$$\Gamma_{44}=(\Sigma^d)^TP\Sigma^d-\Upsilon^d \tag{74}$$

$$\zeta_k=[\zeta_{11}^T,...,\zeta_{1s_1}^T,\zeta_{21}^T,...,\zeta_{qs_q}^T]^T \tag{75}$$

$$\zeta_k^d=[(\zeta_{11}^d)^T,...,(\zeta_{1r_1}^d)^T,(\zeta_{21}^d)^T,...,(\zeta_{qr_q}^d)^T]^T \tag{76}$$

and $\mathbb{M}(K_1, ..., K_q)$, Σ, Υ are defined in (49), (53) and (55) respectively.
Using the Schur Lemma and the notation $R = L^T P$, the inequality (48) is equivalent to

$$\begin{bmatrix} \Gamma_{11} & \Gamma_{12} & \Gamma_{13} & \Gamma_{14} \\ (\star) & \Gamma_{22} & \Gamma_{23} & \Gamma_{24} \\ (\star) & (\star) & \Gamma_{33} & \Gamma_{34} \\ (\star) & (\star) & (\star) & \Gamma_{44} \end{bmatrix} < 0. \tag{77}$$

Consequently, we deduce that under the condition (48), the estimation error converges asymptotically towards zero. This ends the proof of Theorem 4.2. □

Remark 4.3. *Note that we can consider a more general observer with more degree of freedoms as follows :*

$$\hat{x}_{k+1} = A\hat{x}_k + A_d x_{k-d} + \sum_{i=1}^{i=q} Be_q(i) f_i(v_k^i, w_k^i) + \sum_{l=0}^{l=d} L_l \left(y_{k-l} - C\hat{x}_{k-l} \right) \tag{78a}$$

$$v_k^i = H_i \hat{x}_k + \sum_{l=0}^{l=d} K_{i,l} \left(y_{k-l} - C\hat{x}_{k-l} \right) \tag{78b}$$

$$w_k^i = H_i^d \hat{x}_{k-d} + \sum_{l=0}^{l=d} K_{i,l}^d \left(y_{k-d} - C\hat{x}_{k-d} \right) \tag{78c}$$

This leads to a more general LMI using the general Lyapunov-Krasovskii functional :

$$V_k = \varepsilon_k^T P \varepsilon_k + \sum_{j=1}^{j=d} \sum_{i=1}^{i=j} \varepsilon_{k-i}^T Q_j \varepsilon_{k-i}$$

4.3 Numerical example

Now, we present a numerical example to show the performances of the proposed method. We consider the modified chaotic system introduced in Cherrier et al. (2006), and described by :

$$\dot{x} = Gx + F(x(t), x(t-\tau)) \tag{79}$$

where

$$G = \begin{bmatrix} -\alpha & \alpha & 0 \\ 1 & -1 & 1 \\ 0 & -\beta & -\gamma \end{bmatrix}, \quad F(x(t), x(t-\tau)) = \begin{bmatrix} -\alpha\delta \tanh(x_1(t)) \\ 0 \\ \epsilon \sin(\sigma x_1(t-\tau)) \end{bmatrix}$$

Since the proposed method concerns discrete-time systems, then we consider the discrete-time version of (79) obtained from the Euler discretization with sampling period $T = 0.01$. Hence, we obtain a system under the form (1a) with the following parameters :

$$A = I_3 + TG, \quad A_d = 0_{\mathbb{R}^{3\times3}}, \quad B = \begin{bmatrix} -\alpha\delta T & 0 \\ 0 & 0 \\ 0 & \epsilon T \end{bmatrix}$$

and

$$f(x_k, x_{k-d}) = \begin{bmatrix} \tanh(x_1(k)) \\ \sin(\sigma x_1(k-d)) \end{bmatrix}$$

that we can write under the form (35) with

$$H_1 = \begin{bmatrix}1 & 0 & 0\end{bmatrix},\ H_1^d = \begin{bmatrix}0 & 0 & 0\end{bmatrix}$$

$$H_2 = \begin{bmatrix}0 & 0 & 0\end{bmatrix},\ H_2^d = \begin{bmatrix}\sigma & 0 & 0\end{bmatrix}$$

Assume that the first component of the state x is measured, *i.e.* : $C = \begin{bmatrix}1 & 0 & 0\end{bmatrix}$.
The system exhibits a chaotic behavior for the following numerical values :

$$\alpha = 9,\ \beta = 14,\ \gamma = 5,\ d = 2$$

$$\delta = 5,\ \epsilon = 1000,\ \sigma = 100$$

as can be shown in the figure 1.
The bounds of the partial derivatives of f are

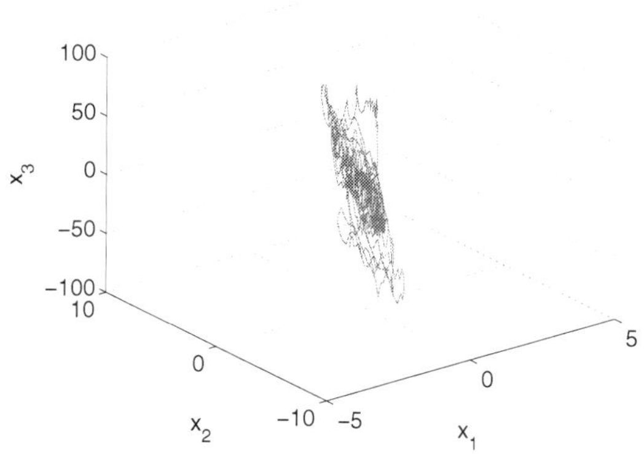

Fig. 1. Phase plot of the system

$$a_{11} = 1,\ b_{11} = 1,\ a_{21}^d = -1,\ b_{21}^d = 1$$

According to the remark 4.1, we must solve the LMI (48) with

$$\tilde{b}_{21}^d = b_{21}^d - a_{21}^d = 2,\ \tilde{A}_d = \begin{bmatrix}0 & 0 & 0\\ 0 & 0 & 0\\ 0 & 0 & -T\epsilon\sigma\end{bmatrix}$$

Hence, we obtain the following solutions :

$$L = \begin{bmatrix}1.3394\\ 4.9503\\ 40.8525\end{bmatrix},\ L^d = \begin{bmatrix}0\\ 0\\ -1000\end{bmatrix},\ K_1 = 0.9999,\ K_2 = -0.0425,\ K_1^d = -1.792 \times 10^{-13},\ K_2^d = 100$$

The simulation results are shown in figure 2.

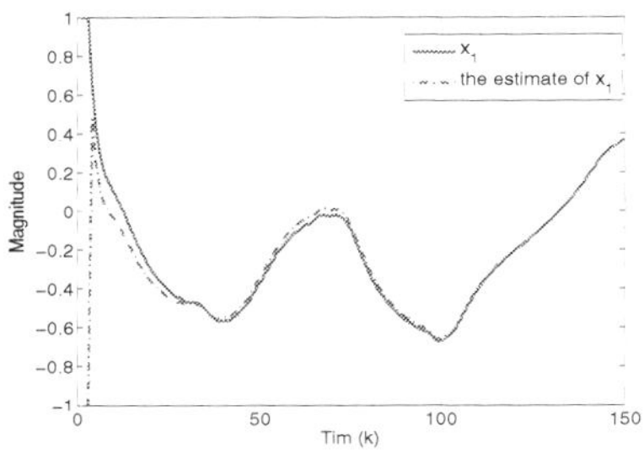

(a) The first component x_1 and its estimate $\hat{x}_1$

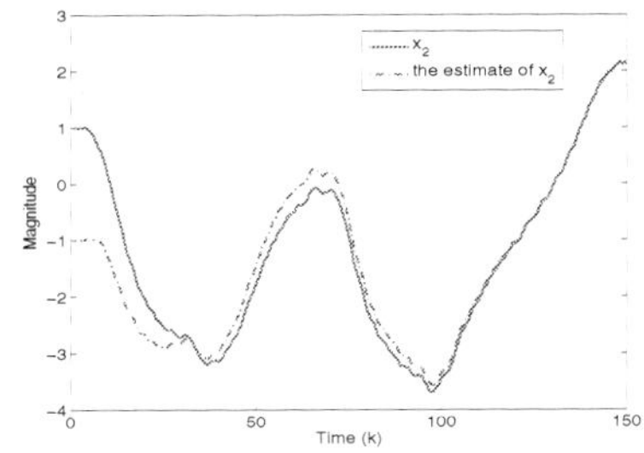

(b) The second component x_2 and its estimate $\hat{x}_2$

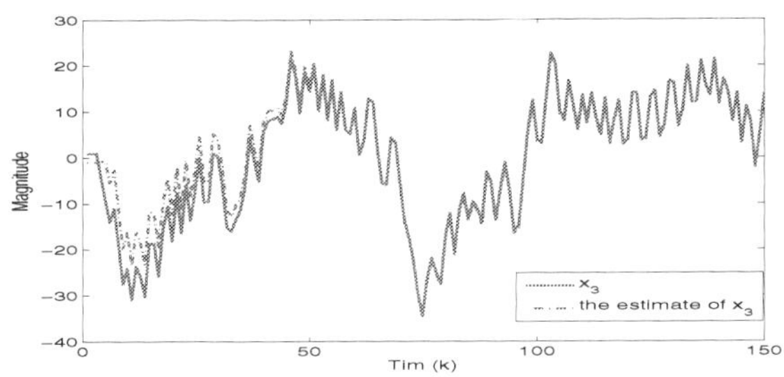

(c) The third component x_3 and its estimate $\hat{x}_3$

Fig. 2. Estimation error behavior

5. Conclusion

This chapter investigates the problem of observer design for a class of Lipschitz nonlinear time-delay systems in the discrete-time case. A new observer synthesis method is proposed, which leads to a less restrictive synthesis condition. Indeed, the obtained synthesis condition, expressed in term of LMI, contains more degree of freedom because of the general structure of the proposed observer. In order to take into account the noise (if it exists) which affects the considered system, a section is devoted to the study of H_∞ robustness. A dilated LMI condition is established particularly for systems with differentiable nonlinearities. Numerical examples are given in order to show the effectiveness of the proposed results.

A. Schur Lemma

In this section, we recall the *Schur lemma* and how it is used in the proof of Theorem 2.1.

Lemma A.1. *Boyd et al. (1994) Let Q_1, Q_2 and Q_3 be three matrices of appropriate dimensions such that $Q_1 = Q_1^T$ and $Q_3 = Q_3^T$. Then, the two following inequalities are equivalent :*

$$\begin{bmatrix} Q_1 & Q_2 \\ Q_2^T & Q_3 \end{bmatrix} < 0, \tag{80}$$

$$Q_3 < 0 \text{ and } Q_1 - Q_2 Q_3^{-1} Q_2^T < 0. \tag{81}$$

Now, we use the *Lemma A.1* to demonstrate the equivalence between $\mathbb{M}_1 + \mathbb{M}_2 < 0$ and $\mathbb{M}_4 < 0$.
We have

$$\begin{aligned} \mathbb{M}_1 + \mathbb{M}_2 = & \begin{bmatrix} -P+Q & 0 & \tilde{A}^T PB \\ (\star) & -Q & \tilde{A}_d^T PB \\ (\star) & (\star) & B^T PB - \alpha I_q \end{bmatrix} + \begin{bmatrix} \tilde{A}^T P \tilde{A} & \tilde{A}^T P \tilde{A}_d & 0 \\ (\star) & \tilde{A}_d^T P \tilde{A}_d & 0 \\ (\star) & (\star) & 0 \end{bmatrix} \\ & + \frac{1}{\alpha \gamma_f^2} \begin{bmatrix} \mathbb{M}_{15}^T \mathbb{M}_{15} + \mathbb{M}_{16}^T \mathbb{M}_{16} & \mathbb{M}_{15}^T \mathbb{M}_{25} + \mathbb{M}_{16}^T \mathbb{M}_{26} & 0 \\ (\star) & \mathbb{M}_{26}^T \mathbb{M}_{26} + \mathbb{M}_{25}^T \mathbb{M}_{25} & 0 \\ (\star) & (\star) & 0 \end{bmatrix}. \end{aligned} \tag{82}$$

By isolating the matrix

$$\Lambda = \begin{bmatrix} P & 0 & 0 \\ 0 & \alpha \gamma_f^2 I_{s_1} & 0 \\ 0 & 0 & \alpha \gamma_f^2 I_{s_2} \end{bmatrix}$$

we obtain

$$\mathbb{M}_1 + \mathbb{M}_2 = \begin{bmatrix} -P+Q & 0 & \tilde{A}^T PB \\ (\star) & -Q & \tilde{A}_d^T PB \\ (\star) & (\star) & B^T PB - \alpha I_q \end{bmatrix} - \begin{bmatrix} \tilde{A}^T & \mathbb{M}_{15}^T & \mathbb{M}_{16}^T \\ \tilde{A}_d^T & \mathbb{M}_{25}^T & \mathbb{M}_{26}^T \\ 0 & 0 & 0 \end{bmatrix} \mathrm{Y}(-\Lambda)^{-1}\mathrm{Y} \begin{bmatrix} \tilde{A} & \tilde{A}_d & 0 \\ \mathbb{M}_{15} & \mathbb{M}_{25} & 0 \\ \mathbb{M}_{16} & \mathbb{M}_{26} & 0 \end{bmatrix} \tag{83}$$

where

$$\mathrm{Y} = \begin{bmatrix} P & 0 & 0 \\ 0 & I_{s_1} & 0 \\ 0 & 0 & I_{s_2} \end{bmatrix}.$$

By setting

$$Q_1 = \begin{bmatrix} -P+Q & 0 & \tilde{A}^T PB \\ (\star) & -Q & \tilde{A}_d^T PB \\ (\star) & (\star) & B^T PB - \alpha I_q \end{bmatrix}, \; Q_2 = \begin{bmatrix} \tilde{A}^T & \mathbb{M}_{15}^T & \mathbb{M}_{16}^T \\ \tilde{A}_d^T & \mathbb{M}_{25}^T & \mathbb{M}_{26}^T \\ 0 & 0 & 0 \end{bmatrix} \mathrm{Y} \text{ and } Q_3 = -\Lambda$$

we have

$$\mathbb{M}_1 + \mathbb{M}_2 = Q_1 - Q_2 Q_3^{-1} Q_2^T. \tag{84}$$

Since $Q_3 < 0$, we deduce from the *Lemma A.1* that

$$\mathbb{M}_1 + \mathbb{M}_2 < 0$$

is equivalent to (80), which is equivalent to

$$\mathbb{M}_4 < 0$$

where $\mathbb{M}_4$ is defined in (13). This ends the proof of equivalence between $\mathbb{M}_1 + \mathbb{M}_2 < 0$ and $\mathbb{M}_4 < 0$. The *Lemma A.1* is used of the same manner in theorem 3.2.

B. Some Details on Robust H_∞ Observer Design Problem

Hereafter, we show why the problem of robust H_∞ observer design is reduced to find a *Lyapunov* function V_k so that $W_k < 0$, where W_k is defined in (23). In other words, we show that $W_k < 0$ implies that the inequalities (21) and (22) are satisfied.
If $\omega(k) = 0$, we have $W_k < 0$ implies that $\Delta V < 0$. Then, from the *Lyapunov* theory, we deduce that the estimation error converges asymptotically towards zero, and then we have (21).
Now, if $\omega(k) \neq 0$; $\varepsilon(k) = 0, k = -d, ..., 0$, we obtain $W_k < 0$ implies that

$$\sum_{k=0}^{N} \|\varepsilon(k)\|^2 < \frac{\lambda^2}{2} \sum_{k=0}^{N} \|\omega(k)\|^2 + \frac{\lambda^2}{2} \sum_{k=0}^{N} \|\omega_d(k)\|^2 - \sum_{k=0}^{N} (V_{k+1} - V_k) \tag{85}$$

Since without loss of generality, we have assumed that $\omega(k) = 0$ for $k = -d, ..., -1$ and $\varepsilon(k) = 0, k = -d, ..., 0$, we deduce that

$$\sum_{k=0}^{N} \|\varepsilon(k)\|^2 < \frac{\lambda^2}{2} \sum_{k=0}^{N} \|\omega(k)\|^2 + \frac{\lambda^2}{2} \sum_{k=0}^{N-d} \|\omega(k)\|^2 - V_N < \frac{\lambda^2}{2} \sum_{k=0}^{N} \|\omega(k)\|^2 + \frac{\lambda^2}{2} \sum_{k=0}^{N-d} \|\omega(k)\|^2. \tag{86}$$

When N tends toward infinity, we obtain

$$\sum_{k=0}^{\infty} \|\varepsilon(k)\|^2 \leq \frac{\lambda^2}{2} \sum_{k=0}^{\infty} \|\omega(k)\|^2 + \frac{\lambda^2}{2} \sum_{k=0}^{\infty-d} \|\omega(k)\|^2 \leq \frac{\lambda^2}{2} \sum_{k=0}^{N} \|\omega(k)\|^2 + \frac{\lambda^2}{2} \sum_{k=0}^{N-d} \|\omega(k)\|^2. \tag{87}$$

As

$$\sum_{k=0}^{\infty} \|\omega(k)\|^2 = \sum_{k=0}^{\infty-d} \|\omega(k)\|^2 = \|\omega\|^2_{\ell_2^s}$$

then the final relation (22) is inferred.

C. References

Aggoune, W., Boutayeb, M. & Darouach, M. (1999). Observers design for a class of nonlinear systems with time-varying delay, *CDC'1999, Phoenix, Arizona USA. December* .

Alessandri, A. (2004). Design of observers for Lipschitz nonlinear systems using LMI, *NOLCOS, IFAC Symposium on Nonlinear Control Systems, Stuttgart, Germany* .

Boyd, S., El Ghaoui, L., Feron, E. & Balakrishnan, V. (1994). Linear matrix inequalities in system and control theory, *SIAM Studies in Applied Mathematics*, Philadelphia, USA.

Cherrier, E., Boutayeb, M. & Ragot, J. (2005). Observers based synchronization and input recovery for a class of chaotic models, *Proceedings of the 44th IEEE Conference on Decision and Control and European Control Conference , Seville, Spain.*

Cherrier, E., Boutayeb, M. & Ragot, J. (2006). Observers-based synchronization and input recovery for a class of nonlinear chaotic models, *IEEE Trans. Circuits Syst. I* **53**(9): 1977–1988.

Fan, X. & Arcak, M. (2003). Observer design for systems with multivariable monotone nonlinearities, *Systems and Control Letters* **50**: 319–330.

Germani, A., Manes, C. & Pepe, P. (2002). A new approach to state observation of nonlinear systems with delayed output, *IEEE Trans. Autom. Control* **47**(1): 96–101.

Germani, A. & Pepe, P. (2004). An observer for a class of nonlinear systems with multiple discrete and distributed time delays, *16th MTNS, Leuven, Belgium* .

Li, H. & Fu, M. (1997). A linear matrix inequality approach to robust H_∞ filtering, *IEEE Trans. on Signal Processing* **45**(9): 2338–2350.

Lu, G. & Ho, D. W. C. (2004a). Robust H_∞ observer for a class of nonlinear discrete systems, *Proceedings of the 5th Asian Control Conference, ASCC2004*, Melbourne, Australia.

Lu, G. & Ho, D. W. C. (2004b). Robust H_∞ observer for a class of nonlinear discrete systems with time delay and parameter uncertainties, *IEE Control Theory Application* **151**(4).

Raff, T. & Allgöwer, F. (2006). An EKF-based observer for nonlinear time-delay systems, *2006 American Control Conference ACC'06*, Minneapolis, Minnesota, USA.

Trinh, H., Aldeen, M. & Nahavandi, S. (2004). An observer design procedure for a class of nonlinear time-delay systems, *Computers & Electrical Engineering* **30**: 61–71.

Xu, S., Lu, J., Zhou, S. & Yang, C. (2004). Design of observers for a class of discrete-time uncertain nonlinear systems with time delay, *Journal of the Franklin Institute* **341**: 295–308.

Zemouche, A., Boutayeb, M. & Bara, G. I. (2006). On observers design for nonlinear time-delay systems, *2006 American Control Conference ACC'06*, Minneapolis, Minnesota, USA.

Zemouche, A., Boutayeb, M. & Bara, G. I. (2007). Observer design for a class of nonlinear time-delay systems, *2007 American Control Conference ACC'07*, New York, USA.

Zemouche, A., Boutayeb, M. & Bara, G. I. (2008). Observers for a class of Lipschitz systems with extension to $\mathcal{H}_\infty$ performance analysis, *Systems & Control Letters* **57**(1): 18–27.

Distributed Fusion Prediction for Mixed Continuous-Discrete Linear Systems

Ha-ryong Song[1], Moon-gu Jeon[1] and Vladimir Shin[2]
[1]*School of Information and Communications, Gwangju Institute of Science and Technology*
Department of Information statistics, Gyeong sang National University
South Korea

1. Introduction

The integration of information from a combination of different types of observed instruments (sensors) are often used in the design of high-accuracy control systems. Typical applications that benefit from this use of multiple sensors include industrial tasks, military commands, mobile robot navigation, multi-target tracking, and aircraft navigation (see (hall, 1992, Bar-Shalom, 1990, Bar-Shalom & Li, 1995, Zhu, 2002, Ren & Key, 1989) and references therein). One problem that arises from the use of multiple sensors is that if all local sensors observe the same target, the question then becomes how to effectively combine the corresponding local estimates. Several distributed fusion architectures have been discussed in (Alouani, 2005, Bar-Shalom & Campo, 1986, Bar-Shalom, 2006, Li et al., 2003, Berg & Durrant-Whyte, 1994, Hamshemipour et al., 1998) and algorithms for distributed estimation fusion have been developed in (Bar-Shalom & Campo, 1986, Chang et al., 1997, Chang et al, 2002, Deng et al., 2005, Sun, 2004, Zhou et al., 2006, Zhu et al., 1999, Zhu et al., 2001, Roecker & McGillem, 1998, Shin et al, 2006). To this end, the Bar-Shalom and Campo fusion formula (Bar-Shalom & Campo, 1986) for two-sensor systems has been generalized for an arbitrary number of sensors in (Deng et al., 2005, Sun, 2004, Shin et al., 2007) The formula represents an optimal mean-square linear combination of the local estimates with matrix weights. The analogous formula for weighting an arbitrary number of local estimates using scalar weights has been proposed in (Shin et al., 2007, Sun & Deng, 2005, Lee & Shin 2007).
However, because of lack of prior information, in general, the distributed filtering using the fusion formula is globally suboptimal compared with optimal centralized filtering (Chang et al., 1997). Nevertheless, in this case it has advantages of lower computational requirements, efficient communication costs, parallel implementation, and fault-tolerance (Chang et al., 1997, Chang et al, 2002, Roecker & McGillem, 1998). Therefore, in spite of its limitations, the fusion formula has been widely used and is superior to the centralized filtering in real applications.
The aforementioned papers have not focused on prediction problem, but most of them have considered only distributed filtering in multisensory continuous and discrete dynamic models. Direct generalization of the distributed fusion filtering algorithms to the prediction problem is impossible. The distributed prediction requires special algorithms one of which for discrete-time systems was presented in (Song et al. 2009). In this paper, we generalize the results of (Song et al. 2009) on mixed continuous-discrete systems. The continuous-discrete

approach allows system to avoid discretization by propagating the estimate and error covariance between observations in continuous time using an integration routine such as Runge-Kutta. This approach yields the optimal or suboptimal estimate continuously at all times, including times between the data arrival instants. One advantage of the continuous-discrete filter over the alternative approach using system discretization is that in the former, it is not necessary for the sample times to be equally spaced. This means that the cases of irregular and intermittent measurements are easy to handle. In the absensce of data the optimal prediction is given by performing only the time update portion of the algorithm.
Thus, the primary aim of this paper is to propose two distributed fusion predictors using fusion formula with matrix weights, and analysis their statistical properties and relationship between them. Then, through a comparison with an optimal centralized predictor, performance of the novel predictors is evaluated.
This chapter is organized as follows. In Section 2, we present the statement of the continuous-discrete prediction problem in a multisensor environment and give its optimal solution. In Section 3, we propose two fusion predictors, derived by using the fusion formula and establish the equivalence between them. Unbiased property of the fusion predictors is also proved. The performance of the proposed predictors is studied on examples in Section 4. Finally, concluding remarks are presented in Section 5.

2. Statement of problem – centralized predictor

We consider a linear system described by the stochastic differential equation

$$\dot{x}_t = F_t x_t + G_t v_t, \quad t \geq 0, \tag{1}$$

where $x_t \in \Re^n$ is the state, $v_t \in \Re^q$ is a zero-mean Gaussian white noise with covariance $E\left(v_t v_s^T\right) = Q_t \delta(t\text{-}s)$, and $F_t \in \Re^{n\times n}$, $G_t \in \Re^{n\times q}$, and $Q_t \in \Re^{q\times q}$.
Suppose that overall discrete observations $Y_{t_k} \in \Re^m$ at time instants $t_1, t_2, \ldots$ are composed of N observation subvectors (local sensors) $y_{t_k}^{(1)}, \ldots, y_{t_k}^{(N)}$, i.e.,

$$Y_{t_k} = [y_{t_k}^{(1)^T} \cdots y_{t_k}^{(N)^T}]^T, \tag{2}$$

where $y_{t_k}^{(i)}$, i=1,…,N are determined by the equations

$$\begin{aligned} &y_{t_k}^{(1)} = H_{t_k}^{(1)} x_{t_k} + w_{t_k}^{(1)}, \quad y_{t_k}^{(1)} \in \Re^{m_1}, \\ &\quad\vdots \\ &y_{t_k}^{(N)} = H_{t_k}^{(N)} x_{t_k} + w_{t_k}^{(N)}, \quad y_{t_k}^{(N)} \in \Re^{m_N}, \\ &k=1,2,\ldots; \quad t_{k+1} > t_k \geq t_0 = 0; \quad m = m_1 + \cdots + m_N, \end{aligned} \tag{3}$$

where $y_{t_k}^{(i)} \in \Re^{m_i}$ is the local sensor observation, $H_{t_k}^{(i)} \in \Re^{n\times m_i}$, and $\left\{w_{t_k}^{(i)} \in \Re^{m_i},\ k=1,2,\ldots\right\}$ are zero-mean white Gaussian sequences, $w_{t_k}^{(i)} \sim \mathbb{N}\left(0, R_{t_k}^{(i)}\right)$, $i=1,\ldots,N$. The distribution of the initial state x_0 is Gaussian, $x_0 \sim \mathbb{N}(\bar{x}_0, P_0)$, and x_0, v_t, and $\left\{w_{t_k}^{(i)}\right\}$, $i=1,\ldots,N$ are assumed mutually uncorrelated.

A problem associated with such systems is to find the distributed weighted fusion predictor $\hat{x}_{t+\Delta}$, $\Delta \geq 0$ of the state $x_{t+\Delta}$ based on overall current sensor observations

$$Y_{t_1}^{t_k} = \left\{ Y_{t_1}, \ldots, Y_{t_k} \right\}, \quad t_1 < \ldots < t_k \leq t \leq t+\Delta, \ \Delta \geq 0. \tag{4}$$

2.1 The optimal centralized predictor

The optimal centralized predictor is constructed by analogy with the continuous-discrete Kalman filter (Lewis, 1986, Gelb, 1974). In this case the prediction estimate $\hat{x}_{t+\Delta}^{opt}$ and its error covariance $P_{t+\Delta}^{opt}$ are determined by the combining of *time update and observation update,*

$$\begin{cases} \dot{\hat{x}}_s^{opt} = F_s \hat{x}_s^{opt}, \quad t_k \leq s \leq t+\Delta, \quad \hat{x}_{s=t_k}^{opt} = \hat{x}_{t_k}^{opt}, \\ \dot{P}_s^{opt} = F_s P_s^{opt} + P_s^{opt} F_s^T + \tilde{Q}_s, \quad P_{s=t_k}^{opt} = P_{t_k}^{opt}, \end{cases} \tag{5}$$

where the initial conditions represent filtering estimate of the state $\hat{x}_{t_k}^{opt}$ and its error covariance $P_{t_k}^{opt}$ which are given by the continuous-discrete Kalman filter equations (Lewis, 1986, Gelb, 1974):

Time update between observations:

$$\begin{cases} \dot{\hat{x}}_\tau^{opt^-} = F_\tau \hat{x}_\tau^{opt^-}, \quad t_{k-1} \leq \tau \leq t_k, \quad \hat{x}_{\tau=t_{k-1}}^{opt^-} = \hat{x}_{t_{k-1}}^{opt}, \\ \dot{P}_\tau^{opt^-} = F_\tau P_\tau^{opt^-} + P_\tau^{opt^-} F_\tau^T + \tilde{Q}_\tau, \quad P_{\tau=t_{k-1}}^{opt^-} = P_{t_{k-1}}^{opt}, \end{cases} \tag{6a}$$

Observation update at time t_k:

$$\begin{cases} \hat{x}_{t_k}^{opt} = \hat{x}_{t_k}^{opt^-} + L_{t_k}^{opt} \left(Y_{t_k} - H_{t_k} \hat{x}_{t_k}^{opt^-} \right), \\ L_{t_k}^{opt} = P_{t_k}^{opt^-} H_{t_k}^T \left(H_{t_k} P_{t_k}^{opt^-} H_{t_k}^T + R_{t_k} \right)^{-1}, \\ P_{t_k}^{opt} = \left(I_n - L_{t_k}^{opt} H_{t_k} \right) P_{t_k}^{opt^-}. \end{cases} \tag{6b}$$

Here I_n is the $n \times n$ identity matrix, $\tilde{Q}_t = G_t Q_t G_t^T$, $Y_{t_k}^T = \left[y_{t_k}^{(1)^T} \ \ldots \ y_{t_k}^{(N)^T} \right]$, $H_{t_k}^T = \left[H_{t_k}^{(1)^T} \ \ldots \ H_{t_k}^{(N)^T} \right]$, $R_{t_k} = \mathrm{diag}\left[R_{t_k}^{(1)} \ \ldots \ R_{t_k}^{(N)} \right]$, and the matrices F_t, G_t, Q_t and $R_{t_k}^{(i)}$ are defined in (1)-(3). Note that in the absence of observation Y_{t_k}, the centralized predictor includes two *time update* equations (5) and (6a), and in case of presence at time $t = t_k$ the initial conditions $\hat{x}_{t_k}^{opt}$ and $P_{t_k}^{opt}$ for (5) computed by the *observation update* equations (6b).

Many advanced systems now make use of a large number of sensors in practical applications ranging from aerospace and defence, robotics automation systems, to the monitoring and control of process generation plants. Recent developments in integrated sensor network systems have further motivated the search for decentralized signal processing algorithms. An important practical problem in the above systems is to find a fusion estimate to combine the information from various local estimates to produce a global (fusion) estimate. Moreover, there are several limitations for the centralized estimators in practical implementation, such as computational cost and capacity of data transmission. Also numerical errors of the centralized estimator design are drastically increased with dimension of the state $x_t \in \Re^n$ and overall observations $Y_{t_k} \in \Re^m$. In these cases the centralized estimators may be impractical. In next Section, we propose two new fusion predictors for multisensor mixed continuous-discrete linear systems (1), (3).

3. Two distributed fusion predictors

The derivation of the fusion predictors is based on the assumption that the overall observation vector Y_{t_k} combines the local subvectors (individual sensors) $y_{t_k}^{(1)},\dots,y_{t_k}^{(N)}$, which can be processed separately. According to (1) and (3), we have N unconnected dynamic subsystems ($i=1,\dots,N$) with the common state x_t and local sensor $y_{t_k}^{(i)}$:

$$\begin{aligned} &\dot{x}_t = F_t x_t + G_t v_t, \quad t \ge t_0, \\ &y_{t_k}^{(i)} = H_{t_k}^{(i)} x_{t_k} + w_{t_k}^{(i)}, \\ &k=1,2,\dots; \quad t_{k+1} > t_k \ge t_0 = 0, \end{aligned} \tag{7}$$

where i is the index of subsystem. Then by the analogy with the centralized prediction equations (5), (6) the optimal local predictor $\hat{x}_{t+\Delta}^{(i)}$ based on the overall local observations $\left\{y_{t_1}^{(i)},\dots,y_{t_k}^{(i)}\right\}$, $t_k \le t \le t+\Delta$ satisfies the following *time update and observation update* equations:

$$\begin{cases} \dot{\hat{x}}_s^{(i)} = F_s \hat{x}_s^{(i)}, \quad t_k \le s \le t+\Delta, \quad \hat{x}_{s=t_k}^{(i)} = \hat{x}_{t_k}^{(i)}, \\ \dot{P}_s^{(ii)} = F_s P_s^{(ii)} + P_s^{(ii)} F_s^T + \tilde{Q}_s, \quad P_{s=t_k}^{(ii)} = P_{t_k}^{(ii)}, \end{cases} \tag{8}$$

where the initial conditions $\hat{x}_{t_k}^{(i)}$ and its error covariance $P_{t_k}^{(ii)}$ are given by the continuous-discrete Kalman filter equations

Time update between observations:

$$\begin{cases} \dot{\hat{x}}_\tau^{(i)-} = F_\tau \hat{x}_\tau^{(i)-}, \quad t_{k-1} \le \tau \le t_k, \quad \hat{x}_{\tau=t_{k-1}}^{(i)-} = \hat{x}_{t_{k-1}}^{(i)}, \\ \dot{P}_\tau^{(ii)-} = F_\tau P_\tau^{(ii)-} + P_\tau^{(ii)-} F_\tau^T + \tilde{Q}_\tau, \quad P_{\tau=t_{k-1}}^{(ii)-} = P_{t_{k-1}}^{(ii)}, \end{cases} \tag{9a}$$

Observation update at time t_k:

$$\begin{cases} \hat{x}_{t_k}^{(i)} = \hat{x}_{t_k}^{(i)-} + L_{t_k}^{(i)}\left(y_{t_k}^{(i)} - H_{t_k}^{(i)} \hat{x}_{t_k}^{(i)-}\right), \\ L_{t_k}^{(i)} = P_{t_k}^{(ii)-} H_{t_k}^{(i)^T}\left(H_{t_k}^{(i)} P_{t_k}^{(ii)-} H_{t_k}^{(i)^T} + R_{t_k}^{(i)}\right)^{-1}, \\ P_{t_k}^{(ii)} = \left(I_n - L_{t_k}^{(i)} H_{t_k}^{(i)}\right) P_{t_k}^{(ii)-}. \end{cases} \tag{9b}$$

Thus from (8) we have N local filtering $\hat{x}_t^{(i)} = \hat{x}_{s=t}^{(i)}$ and prediction $\hat{x}_{t+\Delta}^{(i)} = \hat{x}_{s=t+\Delta}^{(i)}$ estimates, and corresponding error covariances $P_t^{(ii)}$ and $P_{t+\Delta}^{(ii)}$ for $i=1,\dots,N$ and $t \ge t_k$. Using these values we propose two fusion prediction algorithms.

3.1 The fusion of local predictors (FLP Algorithm)

The fusion predictor $\hat{x}_{t+\Delta}^{FLP}$ of the state $x_{t+\Delta}$ based on the overall sensors (2), (3) is constructed from the local predictors $\hat{x}_{t+\Delta}^{(i)}$, $i=1,...,N$ by using the fusion formula (Zhou et al., 2006, Shin et al., 2006):

$$x_{t+\Delta}^{FLP}=\sum_{i=1}^{N}a_{t+\Delta}^{(i)}\hat{x}_{t+\Delta}^{(i)},\quad \sum_{i=1}^{N}a_{t+\Delta}^{(i)}=I_n, \tag{10}$$

where $a_{t+\Delta}^{(1)},\dots,a_{t+\Delta}^{(N)}$ are $n\times n$ time-varying matrix weights determined from the mean-square criterion,

$$J_{t+\Delta}^{FLP}=E\left[\left\|x_{t+\Delta}-\sum_{i=1}^{N}a_{t+\Delta}^{(i)}x_{t+\Delta}^{(i)}\right\|^2\right]. \tag{11}$$

The Theorems 1 and 2 completely define the fusion predictor $\hat{x}_{t+\Delta}^{FLP}$ and its overall error covariance $P_{t+\Delta}^{FLP}=\mathrm{cov}(\tilde{x}_{t+\Delta}^{FLP},\tilde{x}_{t+\Delta}^{FLP})$, $\tilde{x}_{t+\Delta}^{FLP}=x_{t+\Delta}-\hat{x}_{t+\Delta}^{FLP}$.

Theorem 1: *Let* $\hat{x}_{t+\Delta}^{(1)},\dots,\hat{x}_{t+\Delta}^{(N)}$ *are the local predictors of an unknown state* $x_{t+\Delta}$. *Then*

a. *The weights* $a_{t+\Delta}^{(1)},\dots,a_{t+\Delta}^{(N)}$ *satisfy the linear algebraic equations*

$$\sum_{i=1}^{N}a_{t+\Delta}^{(i)}\left[P_{t+\Delta}^{(ij)}-P_{t+\Delta}^{(iN)}\right]=0,\quad \sum_{i=1}^{N}a_{t+\Delta}^{(i)}=I_n,\ j=1,\dots,N-1; \tag{12}$$

b. *The local covariance* $P_{t+\Delta}^{(ii)}=\mathrm{cov}(\tilde{x}_{t+\Delta}^{(i)},\tilde{x}_{t+\Delta}^{(i)})$, $\tilde{x}_{t+\Delta}^{(i)}=x_{t+\Delta}-\hat{x}_{t+\Delta}^{(i)}$ *satisfies (8) and local cross-covariance* $P_{t+\Delta}^{(ij)}=\mathrm{cov}(\tilde{x}_{t+\Delta}^{(i)},\tilde{x}_{t+\Delta}^{(j)})$, $i\neq j$ *describes the time update and observation update equations:*

$$\begin{cases}\dot{P}_{\tau}^{(ij)^{-}}=F_{\tau}P_{\tau}^{(ij)^{-}}+P_{\tau}^{(ij)^{-}}F_{\tau}^{T}+\tilde{Q}_{\tau},\ P_{\tau=t_{k-1}}^{(ij)^{-}}=P_{t_{k-1}}^{(ij)},\ t_{k-1}\leq\tau\leq t_k,\\ P_{t_k}^{(ij)}=\left(I_n+L_{t_k}^{(i)}H_{t_k}^{(i)}\right)P_{t_k}^{(ij)^{-}}\left(I_n+L_{t_k}^{(j)}H_{t_k}^{(j)}\right)^{T},\ t=t_k,\\ \dot{P}_{s}^{(ij)}=F_{s}P_{s}^{(ij)}+P_{s}^{(ij)}F_{s}^{T}+\tilde{Q}_{s},\ P_{s=t_k}^{(ij)}=P_{t_k}^{(ij)},\ t_k\leq s\leq t+\Delta;\end{cases} \tag{13}$$

c. *The fusion error covariance* $\mathbf{P}_{t+\Delta}^{\mathbf{FLP}}$ *is given by*

$$P_{t+\Delta}^{FLP}=\sum_{i,j=1}^{N}a_{t+\Delta}^{(i)}P_{t+\Delta}^{(ij)}a_{t+\Delta}^{(j)^{T}}. \tag{14}$$

Theorem 2: *The local predictors* $\hat{x}_{t+\Delta}^{(1)},\dots,\hat{x}_{t+\Delta}^{(N)}$ *and fusion predictor* $\hat{x}_{t+\Delta}^{FLP}$ *are unbiased, i.e.,* $E\left(\hat{x}_{\tau}^{(i)}\right)=E(x_{\tau})$ *and* $E\left(\hat{x}_{t+\Delta}^{FLP}\right)=E(x_{t+\Delta})$ *for* $0\leq\tau\leq t+\Delta$.

The proofs of Theorems 1 and 2 are given in Appendix.

Thus the local predictors (8) and fusion equations (10)-(14) completely define the FLP algorithm. In particular case at $N=2$, formulas (10)-(12) reduce to the Bar-Shalom and Campo formulas (Bar-Shalom & Campo, 1986):

$$\hat{x}_{t+\Delta}^{FLP}=a_{t+\Delta}^{(1)}\hat{x}_{t+\Delta}^{(1)}+a_{t+\Delta}^{(2)}\hat{x}_{t+\Delta}^{(2)},$$
$$a_{t+\Delta}^{(1)}=\left[P_{t+\Delta}^{(22)}-P_{t+\Delta}^{(21)}\right]\left[P_{t+\Delta}^{(11)}+P_{t+\Delta}^{(22)}-P_{t+\Delta}^{(12)}-P_{t+\Delta}^{(21)}\right]^{-1}, \tag{15}$$
$$a_{t+\Delta}^{(2)}=\left[P_{t+\Delta}^{(11)}-P_{t+\Delta}^{(12)}\right]\left[P_{t+\Delta}^{(11)}+P_{t+\Delta}^{(22)}-P_{t+\Delta}^{(12)}-P_{t+\Delta}^{(21)}\right]^{-1}.$$

Further, in parallel with the FLP we offer the other algorithm for fusion prediction.

3.2 The prediction of fusion filter (PFF Algorithm)

This algorithm consists of two parts. The first part fuses the local filtering estimates $\hat{x}_{t_k}^{(1)},\dots,\hat{x}_{t_k}^{(N)}$. Using the fusion formula, we obtain the fusion filtering (FF) estimate

$$\hat{x}_{t_k}^{FF}=\sum_{i=1}^{N}b_{t_k}^{(i)}\hat{x}_{t_k}^{(i)},\quad \sum_{i=1}^{N}b_{t_k}^{(i)}=I_n, \tag{16}$$

where the weights $b_{t_k}^{(1)},\dots,b_{t_k}^{(N)}$ do not depend on lead Δ.

In the second part we predict the fusion filtering estimate $\hat{x}_{t_k}^{FF}$ using the *time update* prediction equations. Then the fusion predictor $\hat{x}_{t+\Delta}^{PFF}$ and its error covariance $P_{t+\Delta}^{PFF}=\mathrm{cov}(\tilde{x}_{t+\Delta}^{PFF},\tilde{x}_{t+\Delta}^{PFF})$, $\tilde{x}_{t+\Delta}^{PFF}=x_{t+\Delta}-\hat{x}_{t+\Delta}^{PFF}$ satisfy the following equations:

$$\begin{cases}\dot{\hat{x}}_s^{PFF}=F_s\hat{x}_s^{PFF},\quad t_k\le s\le t+\Delta,\quad \hat{x}_{s=t_k}^{PFF}=\hat{x}_{t_k}^{FF},\\ \dot{P}_s^{PFF}=F_sP_s^{PFF}+P_s^{PFF}F_s^T+\tilde{Q}_s,\quad P_{s=t_k}^{PFF}=P_{t_k}^{FF}.\end{cases} \tag{17}$$

Next Theorem completely defines the PFF algorithm.

Theorem 3: *Let* $\hat{x}_{t_k}^{(1)},\dots,\hat{x}_{t_k}^{(N)}$ *are the local filtering estimates of an unknown state* x_t. *Then*

a. *The weights* $b_{t_k}^{(1)},\dots,b_{t_k}^{(N)}$ *satisfy the linear algebraic equations*

$$\sum_{i=1}^{N}b_{t_k}^{(i)}\left[P_{t_k}^{(ij)}-P_{t_k}^{(iN)}\right]=0,\quad \sum_{i=1}^{N}b_{t_k}^{(i)}=I_n,\quad j=1,\dots,N-1; \tag{18}$$

b. *The local covariance* $P_{t_k}^{(ii)}$ *and cross-covariance* $P_{t_k}^{(ij)}$ *in (18) are determined by equations (9) and (13), respectively;*

c. *The initial conditions* $\hat{x}_{t_k}^{FF}$ *and* $P_{t_k}^{FF}$ *in (17) are determined by (16) and formula*

$$P_{t_k}^{FF}=\sum_{i,j=1}^{N}b_{t_k}^{(i)}P_{t_k}^{(ij)}b_{t_k}^{(j)^T}, \tag{19}$$

respectively;

d. *The fusion predictor* $\hat{x}_{t+\Delta}^{PFF}$ *in (17) is unbiased, i.e.,* $E(\hat{x}_{t+\Delta}^{PFF})=E(x_{t+\Delta})$.

The proof of Theorem 3 is given in Appendix.

3.3 The relationship between FLP and PFF

Here we establish the relationship between the prediction fusion estimates $\hat{x}_{t+\Delta}^{FLP}$ and $\hat{x}_{t+\Delta}^{PFF}$ determined by (10) and (16), respectively.

Theorem 4: *Let* $\hat{x}_{t+\Delta}^{FLP}$ *and* $\hat{x}_{t+\Delta}^{PFF}$ *be the fusion prediction estimates determined by (10) and (16), respectively, and the local error covariances* $P_s^{(ij)}$, $t_k \le s \le t+\Delta$, $i,j=1,\ldots,N$ *are nonsingular. Then*

$$\hat{x}_{t+\Delta}^{FLP}=\hat{x}_{t+\Delta}^{PFF} \quad \text{for} \quad \Delta > 0. \tag{20}$$

The proof of Theorem 4 is given in Appendix.

Remark 1 *(Uniqueness solution)*: When the local prediction covariances $P_{t+\Delta}^{(ij)}$, $i,j=1,\ldots,N$ are nonsingular, the quadratic optimization problem (11) has a unique solution, and the wights $a_{t+\Delta}^{(1)},\ldots,a_{t+\Delta}^{(N)}$ are defined by the expressions (11). The same result is true for the covariance $P_{t_k}^{(ij)}$ and the weights $b_{t_k}^{(1)},\ldots,b_{t_k}^{(N)}$ (Zhu et al., 1999, Zhu, 2002).

Remark 2 *(Computational complexity)*: According to Theorem 4, both the predictors FLP and PFF are equivalent; however, from a computational point of view they are different. To predict the state $x_{t+\Delta}$ using FLP we need to compute the matrix weights $a_{t+\Delta}^{(1)},\ldots,a_{t+\Delta}^{(N)}$ for each lead $\Delta > 0$. This contrasts with PFF, wherein the weights $b_{t_k}^{(1)},\ldots,b_{t_k}^{(N)}$ are computed only once, since they do not depend on the leads Δ. Therefore, FLP is deemed more complex than PFF, especially for large leads.

Remark 3 *(Real-time implementation)*: We may note that the local filter gains $L_t^{(i)}$, the error cross-covariances $P_t^{(ij)}$, $P_{t+\Delta}^{(ij)}$, and the weights $a_{t+\Delta}^{(i)}$, $b_{t_k}^{(i)}$ may be pre-computed, since they do not depend on the current observations $y_{t_k}^{(i)}$, $i=1,\ldots,N$, but only on the noises statistics Q_t and $R_t^{(i)}$, and system matrices F_t, G_t, $H_t^{(i)}$, which are part of the system model (1), (3). Thus, once the observation schedule has been settled, the real-time implementation of the fusion predictors FLP and PFF requires only the computation of the local estimates $\hat{x}_t^{(i)}$, $\hat{x}_{t+\Delta}^{(i)}$, $i=1,\ldots,N$ and final fusion predictors $\hat{x}_{t+\Delta}^{FLP}$ and $\hat{x}_{t+\Delta}^{PFF}$.

Remark 4 *(Parallel implementation)*: The local estimates $\hat{x}_t^{(i)}$, $\hat{x}_{t+\Delta}^{(i)}$, $i=1,\ldots,N$ are separated for different sensors. Therefore, they can be implemented in parallel for various types of observations $y_t^{(i)}$, $i=1,\ldots,N$.

4. Examples

4.1 The damper harmonic oscillator motion

System model of the harmonic oscillator is considered in (Lewis, 1986). We have

$$\dot{x}_t=\begin{bmatrix} 0 & 1 \\ -\omega_n^2 & -2\alpha \end{bmatrix} x_t+\begin{bmatrix} 0 \\ 1 \end{bmatrix} v_t, \quad 0 \le t \le t^*, \tag{21}$$

where $x_t=[x_{1,t}\ x_{2,t}]^T$, and $x_{1,t}$ is position, $x_{2,t}$ is velocity, and v_t is zero-mean white Gaussian noise with intensity q, $E(v_t v_s)=q\delta_{t-s}$, $x_0 \sim \mathbb{N}(\bar{x}_0, P_0)$. Assume that the observation system contains N sensors which are observing the position $x_{1,t}$. Then we have

$$\begin{aligned} y_{t_k}^{(1)}&=H_{t_k}^{(1)}x_{t_k}+w_{t_k}^{(1)}, \\ &\vdots \\ y_{t_k}^{(N)}&=H_{t_k}^{(N)}x_{t_k}+w_{t_k}^{(N)}, \quad 0=t_0<t_1<t_2<\ldots<t^*, \end{aligned} \tag{22}$$

where $H_{t_k}^{(j)}=[1 \quad 0]$, and $w_{t_k}^{(j)}$, $j=1,\ldots,N$ are uncorrelated zero-mean white Gaussian noises with constant variances $r^{(j)}$, respectively.

For model (21), (22), three predictors are applied: centralized predictor (CP) in (5), (6), FLP in (10) and PFF in (16), (17). The performance comparison of the fusion predictors for $N=2,3$ was expressed in the terms of computation load (CPU time T_{CPU}) and MSEs, $P_{i,t+\Delta}=E(x_{i,t+\Delta}-\hat{x}_{i,t+\Delta})^2$, where $\hat{x}_{i,t+\Delta}=\hat{x}^{CP}_{i,t+\Delta}, \hat{x}^{FLP}_{i,t+\Delta}$ or $\hat{x}^{PFF}_{i,t+\Delta}$, $i=1,2$. The model parameters, noise statistics, initial conditions, and lead are taken to

$$\begin{aligned}&\omega_n^2=3,\ \alpha=2.5,\ t^*=3,\ q=5,\ r^{(1)}=3.0, r^{(2)}=2.0,\ r^{(3)}=1.0,\\&\bar{x}_0=\begin{bmatrix}10.0 & 0.0\end{bmatrix}^T,\ P_0=\text{diag}\begin{bmatrix}0.5 & 0.5\end{bmatrix},\\&\Delta=0.1\sim0.5\ (\text{sec}),\ t_k-t_{k-1}=0.1.\end{aligned} \tag{23}$$

Figs. 1 and 2 illustrate the MSEs for position (x_1), $P^{CP}_{1,t+\Delta}$, $P^{FLP}_{1,t+\Delta}$, $P^{PFF}_{1,t+\Delta}$, and analogously for velocity (x_2), $P^{CP}_{2,t+\Delta}$, $P^{FLP}_{2,t+\Delta}$, $P^{PFF}_{2,t+\Delta}$ at $N=2,3$ and lead $\Delta=0.2$. The analysis of results in Figs. 1 and 2 show that the fusion predictors FLP and PFF have the same accuracy, i.e., $P^{FLP}_{i,t+\Delta}=P^{PFF}_{i,t+\Delta}$, and the MSEs of each predictor are reduced from $N=2$ to $N=3$. The usage of three sensors allows to increase the accuracy of fusion predictors compared with the optimal CP for two sensors, i.e., $P^{FLP}_{i,t+\Delta}(N=3)=P^{PFF}_{i,t+\Delta}(N=3)<P^{CP}_{i,t+\Delta}(N=2)$. Moreover the differences between optimal $P^{CP}_{i,t+\Delta}$ and fusion MSEs $P^{FLP}_{i,t+\Delta}$, $P^{PFF}_{i,t+\Delta}$ are small, especially for steady-state regime. The results of numerical experiments on an Intel® Core 2 Duo with 2.6GHz CPU and 3G RAM are reported. The CPU time for CP, FLP, and PFF are represented in Table 1. We find that although $P^{FLP}_{i,t+\Delta}$ and $P^{PFF}_{i,t+\Delta}$ are equal (see Theorem 4), the CPU time T^{PFF}_{CPU} for evaluation of the prediction $\hat{x}^{PFF}_{i,t+\Delta}$ is 4~5 times less than T^{FLP}_{CPU} for $\hat{x}^{FLP}_{i,t+\Delta}$ ($T^{PFF}_{CPU}<T^{FLP}_{CPU}$) and this difference tends to increase with increasing the dimension of the state n or the number of sensors N. This is due to the fact that the PFF's weights $b^{(i)}_{t_k}$ do not depend on the leads Δ in contrast to the FLP's weights $a^{(i)}_{t+\Delta}$. Also, since CPU time difference between CP and PFF is negligible, PFF algorithm prefer to implement in real application rather than CP, especially for distributed system or sensor network.

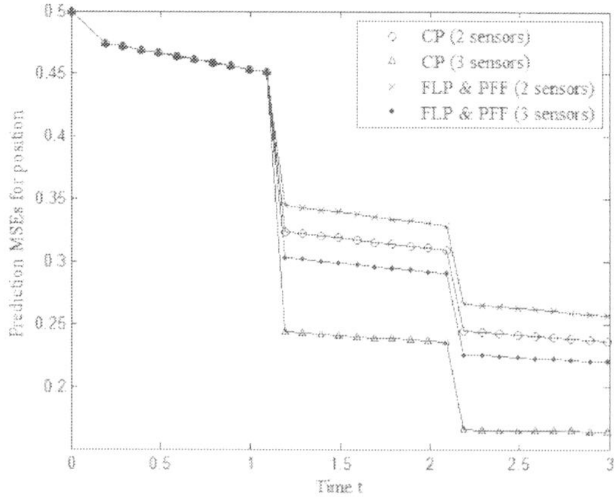

Fig. 1. Position MSE comparison of three predictors at $N=2,3$ and lead $\Delta=0.2$.

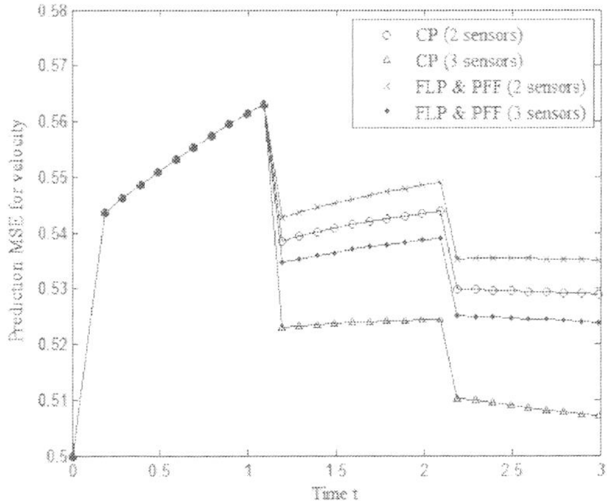

Fig. 2. Velocity MSE comparison of three predictors at N = 2,3 and lead Δ =0.2.

Number of sensors	Lead Δ (sec)	CPU time (sec)		
		T_{CPU}^{CP}	T_{CPU}^{FLP}	T_{CPU}^{PFF}
N = 2	0.1	0.172	0.826	0.185
	0.2	0.298	1.475	0.310
	0.3	0.384	1.863	0.405
	0.4	0.500	2.552	0.550
	0.5	0.656	3.137	0.691
N = 3	0.1	0.187	1.024	0.200
	0.2	0.305	1.743	0.340
	0.3	0.452	2.454	0.471
	0.4	0.602	3.306	0.621
	0.5	0.754	4.203	0.776

Table 1. Comparison of CPU time at $N = 2,3$ and $\Delta = 0.1 \sim 0.5$

4.2 The water tank mixing system

Consider the water tank system which accepts two types of different temperature of the water and throw off the mixed water simultaneously (Jannerup & Hendricks, 2006). This system is described by

$$\dot{x}_t = \begin{bmatrix} -0.0139 & 0 & 0 \\ 0 & -0.0277 & 0 \\ 0 & 0.1667 & -0.1667 \end{bmatrix} x_t + \begin{bmatrix} 1 \\ 1 \\ 1 \end{bmatrix} v_t, \quad t \geq 0, \tag{24}$$

where $x_t = [x_{1,t}\ x_{2,t}\ x_{3,t}]^T$ and $x_{1,t}$ is water level, $x_{2,t}$ is water temperature, $x_{3,t}$ is sensor temperature, and v_t is a white Gaussian noise with intensity q, $E(v_t v_s) = q\delta_{t-s}$, $x_0 \sim \mathbb{N}(\bar{x}_0, P_0)$. The measurement model contains two sensors (N = 2) which sense water level. Then we have

$$y_{t_k}^{(i)} = [1 \quad 0 \quad 0]x_{t_k} + w_{t_k}^{(i)}, \ 0=t_0<t_1<t_2<...<t^*, \ i=1,2, \quad (25)$$

where $w_{t_k}^{(1)}$ and $w_{t_k}^{(2)}$ are uncorrelated white Gaussian sequences with zero-mean and constant intensities $r^{(1)}$ and $r^{(2)}$, respectively.

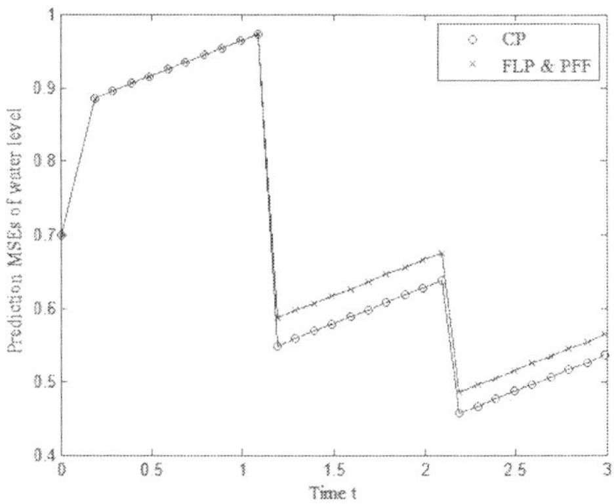

Fig. 3. CP, FLP and PFF MSEs for water level at lead Δ = 0.2s

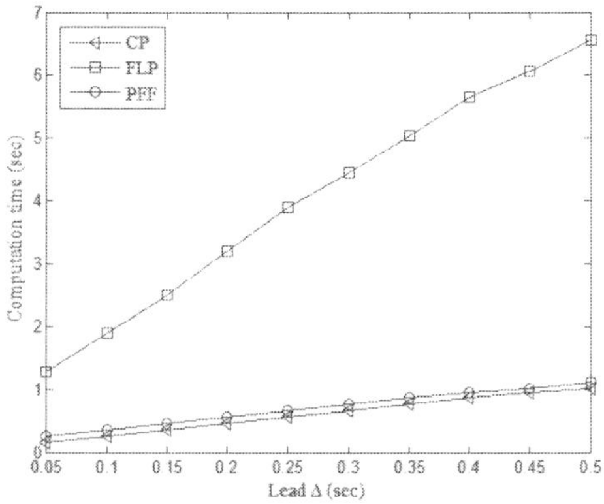

Fig. 4. Computational time of water tank mixing system using 3 predictors at leads Δ = 0.05, 0.1,…,0.5s.

The parameters are subjected to $q=1$, $r^{(1)}=2$, $r^{(2)}=1$, $t^*=3$, $\bar{x}_0=[1 \quad 1 \quad 0]^T$, $P_0 = diag[0.7 \quad 0.7 \quad 0.1]$, $t_k - t_{k-1} = 0.1$, $\Delta = 0.05 \sim 0.5$. Fig. 3 illustrates the MSEs of the water level $P_{1,t+\Delta}^{CP}$, $P_{1,t+\Delta}^{FLP}$ and $P_{1,t+\Delta}^{PFF}$ at lead Δ =0.2. As we can see in Fig. 3 the CP is better than the fusion predictors and the fusion MSEs for water level (x_1) of FLP and PFF are equal, i.e., $P_{1,t+\Delta}^{CP} < P_{1,t+\Delta}^{FLP} = P_{1,t+\Delta}^{PFF}$. The CPU times for CP, FLP and PFF are represented in Fig. 4, where it is shown that FLP requires considerably more CPU time than PFF, but CPU time of PFF is similar to CP.

Thus, from Examples 4.1 and 4.2 we can confirm that PFF is preferable to FLP in terms of computation efficiency.

5. Conclusions

In this chapter, two fusion predictors (FLP and PFF) for mixed continuous-discrete linear systems in a multisensor environment are proposed. Both of these predictors are derived by using the optimal local Kalman estimators (filters and predictors) and fusion formula. The fusion predictors represent the optimal linear combination of an arbitrary number of local Kalman estimators and each is fused by the MSE criterion. Equivalence between the two fusion predictors is established. However, the PFF algorithm is found to more significantly reduce the computational complexity, due to the fact that the PFF's weights $b_{t_k}^{(i)}$ do not depend on the leads $\Delta > 0$ in contrast to the FLP's weights $a_{t+\Delta}^{(i)}$.

Appendix

Proof of Theorem 1

(a), (c) Equation (12) and formula (14) immediately follow as a result of application of the general fusion formula [20] to the optimization problem (10), (11).

(b) In the absence of observations differential equation for the local prediction error $\tilde{x}_\tau^{(i)} = x_\tau - \hat{x}_\tau^{(i)}$ takes the form

$$\dot{\tilde{x}}_\tau^{(i)} = \dot{x}_\tau - \dot{\hat{x}}_\tau^{(i)} = F_\tau \tilde{x}_\tau^{(i)} + G_\tau v_\tau. \tag{A.1}$$

Then the prediction cross-covariance $P_\tau^{(ij)} = E\left(\tilde{x}_\tau^{(i)} \tilde{x}_\tau^{(j)T}\right)$ associated with the $\tilde{x}_\tau^{(i)}$ and $\tilde{x}_\tau^{(j)}$ satisfies the time update Lyapunov equation (see the first and third equations in (13)). At $t=t_k$ the local error $\tilde{x}_{t_k}^{(i)}$ can be written as

$$\tilde{x}_{t_k}^{(i)} = x_{t_k} - \hat{x}_{t_k}^{(i)} = x_{t_k} - \hat{x}_{t_k}^{(i)-} - L_{t_k}^{(i)}\left[y_{t_k}^{(i)} - H_{t_k}^{(i)} \hat{x}_{t_k}^{(i)-}\right] = \tilde{x}_{t_k}^{(i)-} - L_{t_k}^{(i)}\left[H_{t_k}^{(i)} x_{t_k} + w_{t_k}^{(i)} - H_{t_k}^{(i)} \hat{x}_{t_k}^{(i)-}\right] = \left(I_n - L_{t_k}^{(i)} H_{t_k}^{(i)}\right)\tilde{x}_{t_k}^{(i)-} - L_{t_k}^{(i)} w_{t_k}^{(i)}. \tag{A.2}$$

Given that random vectors $\tilde{x}_{t_k}^{(i)}$, $w_{t_k}^{(i)}$ and $w_{t_k}^{(j)}$ are mutually uncorrelated at $i \neq j$, we obtain observation update equation (13) for $P_{t_k}^{(ij)} = E\left(\tilde{x}_{t_k}^{(i)} \tilde{x}_{t_k}^{(j)T}\right)$.

This completes the proof of Theorem 1.

Proof of Theorem 2

It is well known that the local Kalman filtering estimates $\hat{x}_\tau^{(i)}$ are unbiased, i.e., $E(\hat{x}_\tau^{(i)}) = E(x_\tau)$ or $E\left(\tilde{x}_\tau^{(i)}\right) = E\left(x_\tau - \hat{x}_\tau^{(i)}\right) = 0$ at $0 \le \tau \le t_k$. With this result we can prove unbiased property at $t_k < \tau \le t+\Delta$. Using (8) we obtain

$$\dot{\tilde{x}}_\tau^{(i)} = \dot{x}_\tau - \dot{\hat{x}}_\tau^{(i)} = F_\tau \tilde{x}_\tau^{(i)} + G_\tau v_\tau, \quad \tilde{x}_{\tau=t_k}^{(i)} = \tilde{x}_{t_k}^{(i)}, \quad t_k \le \tau \le t+\Delta, \tag{A.3}$$

or

$$\frac{d}{d\tau} E\left(\tilde{x}_\tau^{(i)}\right) = F_\tau E\left(\tilde{x}_\tau^{(i)}\right), \quad E\left(\tilde{x}_{\tau=t_k}^{(i)}\right) = E\left(\tilde{x}_{t_k}^{(i)}\right) = 0, \quad t_k \le \tau \le t+\Delta. \tag{A.4}$$

Differential equation (A.4) is homogeneous with zero initial condition therefore it has zero solution $E\left(\tilde{x}_\tau^{(i)}\right) \equiv 0$ or $E\left(\hat{x}_\tau^{(i)}\right) = E\left(x_\tau\right)$, $t_k \le \tau \le t+\Delta$.

Since the local predictors $\hat{x}_{t+\Delta}^{(i)}$, $i = 1,\dots,N$ are unbiased, then we have

$$E\left(\hat{x}_{t+\Delta}^{FLP}\right) = \sum_{i=1}^{N} a_{t+\Delta}^{(i)} E\left(\hat{x}_{t+\Delta}^{(i)}\right) = \left[\sum_{i=1}^{N} a_{t+\Delta}^{(i)}\right] E\left(x_{t+\Delta}\right) = E\left(x_{t+\Delta}\right). \tag{A.5}$$

This completes the proof of Theorem 2.

Proof of Theorem 3

a., c. Equations (18) and (19) immediately follow from the general fusion formula for the filtering problem (Shin et al., 2006)

b. Derivation of observation update equation (13) is given in Theorem 1.

d. Unbiased property of the fusion estimate $\hat{x}_{t+\Delta}^{PFF}$ is proved by using the same method as in Theorem 2.

This completes the proof of Theorem 3.

Proof of Theorem 4

By integrating (8) and (17), we get

$$\hat{x}_{t+\Delta}^{(i)}=\Phi(t+\Delta,t_k)\hat{x}_{t_k}^{(i)},\ \ i=1,\dots,N,\ \ \hat{x}_{t+\Delta}^{PFF}=\Phi(t+\Delta,t_k)\hat{x}_{t_k}^{FF}, \tag{A.6}$$

where $\Phi(t,s)$ is the transition matrix of (8) or (17). From (10) and (16), we obtain

$$\begin{aligned}\hat{x}_{t+\Delta}^{FLP}&=\sum_{i=1}^{N}a_{t+\Delta}^{(i)}\hat{x}_{t+\Delta}^{(i)}=\sum_{i=1}^{N}a_{t+\Delta}^{(i)}\Phi(t+\Delta,t_k)\hat{x}_{t_k}^{(i)}=\sum_{i=1}^{N}A_{t,t_k,\Delta}^{(i)}\hat{x}_{t_k}^{(i)},\\ \hat{x}_{t+\Delta}^{PFF}&=\Phi(t+\Delta,t_k)\hat{x}_{t_k}^{FF}=\sum_{i=1}^{N}\Phi(t+\Delta,t_k)b_{t_k}^{(i)}\hat{x}_{t_k}^{(i)}=\sum_{i=1}^{N}B_{t,t_k,\Delta}^{(i)}\hat{x}_{t_k}^{(i)},\end{aligned} \tag{A.7}$$

where the new weights take the form:

$$A_{t,t_k,\Delta}^{(i)}=a_{t+\Delta}^{(i)}\Phi(t+\Delta,t_k),\ \ B_{t,t_k,\Delta}^{(i)}=\Phi(t+\Delta,t_k)b_{t_k}^{(i)}. \tag{A.8}$$

Next using (12) and (18) we will derive equations for the new weights (A.8). Multiplying the first (N-1) homogeneous equations (18) on the left hand side and right hand side by the nonsingular matrices $\Phi(t+\Delta,t_k)$ and $\Phi(t+\Delta,t_k)^T$, respectively, and multiplying the last non-homogeneous equation (18) by $\Phi(t+\Delta,t_k)$ we obtain

$$\begin{aligned}&\sum_{i=1}^{N}\Phi(t+\Delta,t_k)b_{t_k}^{(i)}\left[P_{t_k}^{(ij)}-P_{t_k}^{(iN)}\right]\Phi(t+\Delta,t_k)^T=0,\ \ j=1,\dots,N-1;\\ &\sum_{i=1}^{N}\Phi(t+\Delta,t_k)b_{t_k}^{(i)}=\Phi(t+\Delta,t_k).\end{aligned} \tag{A.9}$$

Using notation for the difference $\delta P_s^{(ijN)}=P_s^{(ij)}-P_s^{(iN)}$ we obtain equations for $B_{t,t_k,\Delta}^{(i)}$, $i=1,\dots,N$ such that

$$\sum_{i=1}^{N}B_{t,t_k,\Delta}^{(i)}\delta P_{t_k}^{(ijN)}\Phi(t+\Delta,t_k)^T=0,\ \ j=1,\dots,N-1;\ \ \sum_{i=1}^{N}B_{t,t_k,\Delta}^{(i)}=\Phi(t+\Delta,t_k). \tag{A.10}$$

Analogously after simple manipulations equation (12) takes the form

$$\begin{aligned}&\sum_{i=1}^{N}a_{t+\Delta}^{(i)}\Phi(t+\Delta,t_k)\Phi(t+\Delta,t_k)^{-1}\left[P_{t+\Delta}^{(ij)}-P_{t+\Delta}^{(iN)}\right]=\sum_{i=1}^{N}A_{t,t_k,\Delta}^{(i)}\Phi(t+\Delta,t_k)^{-1}\delta P_{t+\Delta}^{(ijN)}=0,\\ &\sum_{i=1}^{N}a_{t+\Delta}^{(i)}\Phi(t+\Delta,t_k)=\sum_{i=1}^{N}A_{t,t_k,\Delta}^{(i)}=\Phi(t+\Delta,t_k).\end{aligned} \tag{A.11}$$

or

$$\sum_{i=1}^{N} A_{t,t_k,\Delta}^{(i)} \Phi(t+\Delta,t_k)^{-1} \delta P_{t+\Delta}^{(ijN)}=0, \ j=1,...,N-1; \ \sum_{i=1}^{N} A_{t,t_k,\Delta}^{(i)}=\Phi(t+\Delta,t_k). \tag{A.12}$$

As we can see from (A.10) and (A.12) if the equality

$$\delta P_{t_k}^{(ijN)} \Phi(t+\Delta,t_k)^{T} = \Phi(t+\Delta,t_k)^{-1} \delta P_{t+\Delta}^{(ijN)} \tag{A.13}$$

will be hold then the new weights $A_{t,t_k,\Delta}^{(i)}$ and $B_{t,t_k,\Delta}^{(i)}$ satisfy the identical equations. To show that let consider differential equation for the difference $\delta P_s^{(ijN)}=P_s^{(ij)}-P_s^{(iN)}$. Using (13) we obtain the Lyapunov homogeneous matrix differential equation

$$\delta \dot{P}_s^{(ijN)}=\dot{P}_s^{(ij)}-\dot{P}_s^{(iN)}=F_s\left(P_s^{(ij)}-P_s^{(iN)}\right)+\left(P_s^{(ij)}-P_s^{(iN)}\right)F_s^T=F_s\delta P_s^{(ijN)}+\delta P_s^{(ijN)}F_s^T, \ t_k \le s \le t+\Delta, \tag{A.14}$$

which has the solution

$$\delta P_{t+\Delta}^{(ijN)}=\Phi(t+\Delta,t_k)\delta P_{t_k}^{(ijN)}\Phi(t+\Delta,t_k)^{T}. \tag{A.15}$$

By the nonsingular property of the transition matrix $\Phi(t+\Delta,t_k)$ the equality (A.13) holds, then $A_{t,t_k,\Delta}^{(i)} = B_{t,t_k,\Delta}^{(i)}$, and finally using (A.7) we get

$$\hat{x}_{t+\Delta}^{FLP}=\sum_{i=1}^{N} A_{t,t_k,\Delta}^{(i)} \hat{x}_{t_k}^{(i)} = \sum_{i=1}^{N} B_{t,t_k,\Delta}^{(i)} \hat{x}_{t_k}^{(i)} = \hat{x}_{t+\Delta}^{PFF}. \tag{A.16}$$

This completes the proof of Theorem 4.

6. References

Alouani, A. T. & Gray, J. E. (2005). Theory of distributed estimation using multiple asynchronous sensors, *IEEE Transations on Aerospace and Electronic Systems*, Vol. 41, No. 2, pp. 717-722.

Bar-Shalom, Y. & Campo, L. (1986). The effect of the common process noise on the two-sensor fused track covariance, *IEEE Transactions on Aerospace and Electronic Systems*, Vol. 22, No. 6, pp. 803–805.

Bar-Shalom, Y. (1990). *Multitarget-multisensor tracking: advanced applications*, Artech House, Norwood, MA.

Bar-Shalom, Y. & Li, X. R. (1995). *Multitarget-multisensor tracking: principles and techniques*, YBS Publishing.

Bar-Shalom, Y. (2006). On hierarchical tracking for the real world, *IEEE Transactions on Aerospace and Electronic Systems*, Vol. 42, No, 3, pp. 846–850.

Berg, T. M. & Durrant-Whyte, H. F. (1994). General decentralized Kalman filter, *Proceedings of American Control Conference*, pp. 2273-2274, Maryland.

Chang, K. C.; Saha, R. K. & Bar-Shalom, Y. (1997). On Optimal track-to-track fusion, *IEEE Transactions on Aerospace and Electronic Systems*, Vol. 33, No. 4, pp. 1271–1275.

Chang, K. C.; Tian, Z. & Saha, R. K. (2002). Performance evaluation of track fusion with information matrix filter, *IEEE Transactions on Aerospace and Electronic Systems*, Vol. 38, No. 2, pp. 455–466.

Deng, Z. L.; Gao, Y.; Mao, L. & Hao, G. (2005). New approach to information fusion steady-state Kalman filtering, *Automatica*, Vol. 41, No, 10, pp. 1695-1707.

Gelb, A. (1974). *Applied Optimal Estimation*, MIT Press, Cambridge, MA.

Hall, D. L. (1992). *Mathematical techniques in multisensor data Fusion*, Artech House, London.

Hashemipour, H. R.; Roy, S. & Laub, A. J. (1998). Decentralized structures for parallel Kalman filtering, *IEEE Transactions on Automatic Control*, Vol. 33, No. 1, pp. 88-94.

Jannerup, O. E. & Hendricks, E. (2006). *Linear Control System Design*, Technical University of Denmark.

Lee, S. H. & Shin, V. (2007). Fusion Filters Weighted by Scalars and Matrices for Linear Systems, *World Academy of Science, Engineering and Technology*, Vol. 34, pp. 88-93.

Lewis, F. L. (1986). *Optimal Estimation with an Introduction to Stochastic Control Theory*, John Wiley & Sons, New York.

Li, X. R.; Zhu, Y. M.; Wang, J. & Han, C. (2003). Optimal Linear Estimation Fusion - Part I: Unified Fusion Rules, *IEEE Transations on Information Theory*, Vol. 49, No. 9, pp. 2192-2208.

Ren, C. L. & Kay, M. G. (1989). Multisensor integration and fusion in intelligent systems, *IEEE Transactions on Systems, Man, and Cybernetics*, Vol. 19, No. 5, pp. 901-931.

Roecker, J. A. & McGillem, C. D. (1998). Comparison of two-sensor tracking methods based on state vector fusion and measurement fusion, *IEEE Transactions on Aerospace and Electronic Systems*, Vol. 24, No. 4, pp. 447–449.

Shin, V.; Lee, Y. & Choi, T. (2006). Generalized Millman's formula and its applications for estimation problems, *Signal Processing*, Vol. 86, No. 2, pp. 257–266.

Shin, V.; Shevlyakov, G. & Kim, K. S. (2007). A new fusion formula and its application to continuous-time linear systems with multisensor environment, *Computational Statistics & Data Analysis*, Vol. 52, No. 2, pp. 840-854.

Song, H. R.; Joen, M. G.; Choi, T. S. & Shin, V. (2009). Two Fusion Predictors for Discrete-Time Linear Systems with Different Types of Observations, *International Journal of Control, Automation, and Systems*, Vol. 7, No. 4, pp. 651-658.

Sun, S. L. (2004). Multi-sensor optimal information fusion Kalman filters with applications, *Aerospace Science and Technology*, Vol. 8, No. 1, pp. 57–62.

Sun, S. L. & Deng, Z. L. (2005). Multi-sensor information fusion Kalman filter weighted by scalars for systems with colored measurement noises, *Journal of Dynamic Systems, Measurement and Control*, Vol. 127, No. 4, pp. 663–667.

Zhou, J.; Zhu, Y.; You, Z. & Song, E. (2006). An efficient algorithm for optimal linear estimation fusion in distributed multisensor systems, IEEE Transactions on System, Man, Cybernetics, Vol. 36, No. 5, pp.1000–1009.

Zhu,Y. M. & Li, X. R. (1999). Best linear unbiased estimation fusion, *Proceeding of International Conference on Multisource-Multisensor Information Fusion*, Sunnyvale, CA, pp. 1054-1061.

Zhu,Y. M.; You, Z.; Zhao, J.; Zhang, K. & Li, X. R. (2001) The optimality for the distributed Kalman filtering fusion with feedback, *Automaica*, Vol. 37, No. 9, pp.1489–1493.

Zhu, Y. M. (2002) *Multisensor decision and estimation fusion*, Kluwer Academic, Boston.

4

New Smoothers for Discrete-time Linear Stochastic Systems with Unknown Disturbances

Akio Tanikawa
Osaka Institute of Technology
Japan

1. Introduction

We consider discrete-time linear stochastic systems with unknown inputs (or disturbances) and propose recursive algorithms for estimating states of these systems. If mathematical models derived by engineers are very accurate representations of real systems, we do not have to consider systems with unknown inputs. However, in practice, the models derived by engineers often contain modelling errors which greatly increase state estimation errors as if the models have unknown disturbances.

The most frequently discussed problem on state estimation is the optimal filtering problem which investigates the optimal estimate of state x_t at time t or x_{t+1} at time $t+1$ with minimum variance based on the observation $\mathbf{Y}_t$ of the outputs $\{y_0, y_1, \cdots, y_t\}$, i.e., $\mathbf{Y}_t = \sigma\{y_s, s = 0, 1, \cdots, t\}$ (the smallest σ-field generated by $\{y_0, y_1, \cdots, y_t\}$ (see e.g., Katayama (2000), Chapter 4)). It is well known that the standard Kalman filter is the optimal linear filter in the sense that it minimizes the mean-square error in an appropriate class of linear filters (see e.g., Kailath (1974), Kailath (1976), Kalman (1960), Kalman (1963) and Katayama (2000)). But we note that the Kalman filter can work well only if we have accurate mathematical modelling of the monitored systems.

In order to develop reliable filtering algorithms which are robust with respect to unknown disturbances and modelling errors, many research papers have been published based on the disturbance decoupling principle. Pioneering works were done by Darouach et al. (Darouach; Zasadzinski; Bassang & Nowakowski (1995) and Darouach; Zasadzinski & Keller (1992)), Chang and Hsu (Chang & Hsu (1993)) and Hou and Müller (Hou & Müller (1993)). They utilized some transformations to make the original systems with unknown inputs into some singular systems without unknown inputs. The most important preceding study related to this paper was done by Chen and Patton (Chen & Patton (1996)). They proposed the simple and useful optimal filtering algorithm, ODDO (Optimal Disturbance Decoupling Observer), and showed its excellent simulation results. See also the papers such as Caliskan; Mukai; Katz & Tanikawa (2003), Hou & Müller (1994), Hou & R. J. Patton (1998) and Sawada & Tanikawa (2002) and the book Chen & Patton (1999). Their algorithm recently has been modified by the author in Tanikawa (2006) (see Tanikawa & Sawada (2003) also).

We here consider smoothing problems which allow us time-lags for computing estimates of the states. Namely, we try to find the optimal estimate $\hat{x}_{t-L/t}$ of the state x_{t-L} based on the observation $\mathbf{Y}_t$ with $L > 0$. We often classify smoothing problems into the following three types. For the first problem, the fixed-point smoothing, we investigate the optimal estimate

$\hat{x}_{k/t}$ of the state x_k for a fixed k based on the observations $\{\mathbf{Y}_t, t = k+1, k+2, \cdots\}$. Algorithms for computing $\hat{x}_{k/t}, t = k+1, k+2, \cdots$, recursively are called fixed-point smoothers. For the second problem, the fixed-interval smoothing, we investigate the optimal estimate $\hat{x}_{t/N}$ of the state x_t at all times $t = 0, 1, \cdots, N$ based on the observation $\mathbf{Y}_N$ of all the outputs $\{y_0, y_1, \cdots, y_N\}$. Fixed-interval smoothers are algorithms for computing $\hat{x}_{t/N}, t = 0, 1, \cdots, N$ recursively. The third problem, the fixed-lag smoothing, is to investigate the optimal estimate $\hat{x}_{t-L/t}$ of the state x_{t-L} based on the observation $\mathbf{Y}_t$ for a given $L \geq 1$. Fixed-lag smoothers are algorithms for computing $\hat{x}_{t-L/t}, t = L+1, L+2, \cdots$, recursively. See the references such as Anderson & Moore (1979), Bryson & Ho (1969), Kailath (1975) and Meditch (1973) for early research works on smoothers. More recent papers have been published based on different approaches such as stochastic realization theory (e.g., Badawi; Lindquist & Pavon (1979) and Faurre; Clerget & Germain (1979)), the complementary models (e.g., Ackner & Kailath (1989a), Ackner & Kailath (1989b), Bello; Willsky & Levy (1989), Bello; Willsky; Levy & Castanon (1986) Desai; Weinert & Yasypchuk (1983) and Weinert & Desai (1981)) and others. Nice surveys can be found in Kailath; Sayed & Hassibi (2000) and Katayama (2000).

When stochastic systems contain unknown inputs explicitly, Tanikawa (Tanikawa (2006)) obtained a fixed-point smoother for the first problem. The second and the third problems were discussed in Tanikawa (2008). In this chapter, all three problems are discussed in a comrehensive and self-contained manner as much as possible. Namely, after some preliminary results in Section 2, we derive the fixed-point smoothing algorithm given in Tanikawa (2006) in Section 3 for the system with unknown inputs explicitly by applying the optimal filter with disturbance decoupling property obtained in Tanikawa & Sawada (2003). In Section 4, we construct the fixed-interval smoother given in Tanikawa (2008) from the fixed-point smoother obtained in Section 3. In Section 5, we construct the fixed-lag smoother given in Tanikawa (2008) from the optimal filter in Tanikawa & Sawada (2003).

Finally, the new feature and advantages of the obtained results are summarized here. To the best of our knowledge, no attempt has been made to investigate optimal fixed-interval and fixed-lag smoothers for systems with unknown inputs explicitly (see the stochastic system given by (1)-(2)) before Tanikawa (2006) and Tanikawa (2008). Our smoothing algorithms have similar recursive forms to the standard optimal filter (i.e., the Kalman filter) and smoothers. Moreover, our algorithms reduce to those known smoothers derived from the Kalman filter (see e.g., Katayama (2000)) when the unknown inputs disappear. Thus, our algorithms are consistent with the known smoothing algorithms for systems without unknown inputs.

2. Preliminaries

Consider the following discrete-time linear stochastic system for $t = 0, 1, 2, \cdots$:

$$x_{t+1} = A_t x_t + B_t u_t + E_t d_t + \zeta_t, \tag{1}$$

$$y_t = C_t x_t + \eta_t, \tag{2}$$

where

$x_t \in \mathbf{R}^n$	the state vector,
$y_t \in \mathbf{R}^m$	the output vector,

$u_t \in \mathbf{R}^r$ the known input vector,

$d_t \in \mathbf{R}^q$ the unknown input vector.

Suppose that ζ_t and η_t are independent zero mean white noise sequences with covariance matrices Q_t and R_t. Let A_t, B_t, C_t and E_t be known matrices with appropriate dimensions.
In Tanikawa & Sawada (2003), we considered the optimal estimate $\hat{x}_{t+1/t+1}$ of the state x_{t+1} which was proposed by Chen and Patton (Chen & Patton (1996) and Chen & Patton (1999)) with the following structure:

$$z_{t+1} = F_{t+1}\, z_t + T_{t+1}\, B_t\, u_t + K_{t+1}\, y_t, \tag{3}$$

$$\hat{x}_{t+1/t+1} = z_{t+1} + H_{t+1}\, y_{t+1}, \tag{4}$$

for $t = 0, 1, 2, \cdots$. Here, $\hat{x}_{0/0}$ is chosen to be z_0 for a fixed z_0. Denote the state estimation error and its covariance matrix respectively by e_t and P_t. Namely, we use the notations $e_t = x_t - \hat{x}_{t/t}$ and $P_t = \mathbf{E}\{e_t\, e_t{}^T\}$ for $t = 0, 1, 2, \cdots$. Here, $\mathbf{E}$ denotes expectation and T denotes transposition of a matrix. We assume in this paper that random variables $e_0, \{\eta_t\}, \{\zeta_t\}$ are independent. As in Chen & Patton (1996), Chen & Patton (1999) and Tanikawa & Sawada (2003), we consider state estimate (3)-(4) with the matrices $F_{t+1}, T_{t+1}, H_{t+1}$ and K_{t+1} of the forms:

$$K_{t+1} = K^1_{t+1} + K^2_{t+1}, \tag{5}$$

$$E_t = H_{t+1}\, C_{t+1}\, E_t, \tag{6}$$

$$T_{t+1} = I - H_{t+1}\, C_{t+1}, \tag{7}$$

$$F_{t+1} = A_t - H_{t+1}\, C_{t+1}\, A_t - K^1_{t+1}\, C_t, \tag{8}$$

$$K^2_{t+1} = F_{t+1}\, H_t. \tag{9}$$

The next lemma on equality (6) was obtained and used by Chen and Patton (Chen & Patton (1996) and Chen & Patton (1999)). Before stating it, we assume that E_k is a full column rank matrix. Notice that this assumption is not an essential restriction.

Lemma 2.1. *Equality (6) holds if and only if*

$$rank\,(C_{t+1}\, E_t) = rank\,(E_t)\,. \tag{10}$$

When this condition holds true, matrix H_{t+1} which satisfies (6) must have the form

$$H_{t+1} = E_t \left\{ (C_{t+1}\, E_t)^T\, (C_{t+1}\, E_t) \right\}^{-1} (C_{t+1}\, E_t)^T. \tag{11}$$

Hence, we have

$$C_{t+1}\, H_{t+1} = C_{t+1}\, E_t \left\{ (C_{t+1}\, E_t)^T\, (C_{t+1}\, E_t) \right\}^{-1} (C_{t+1}\, E_t)^T \tag{12}$$

which is a non-negative definite symmetric matrix. ∎

When the matrix K^1_{t+1} has the form

$$K^1_{t+1} = A^1_{t+1}\left(P_t\,C_t{}^T - H_t\,R_t\right)\left(C_t\,P_t\,C_t{}^T + R_t\right)^{-1}, \tag{13}$$

$$A^1_{t+1} = A_t - H_{t+1}\,C_{t+1}\,A_t, \tag{14}$$

we obtained the following result (Theorem 2.7 in Tanikawa & Sawada (2003)) on the optimal filtering algorithm.

Proposition 2.2. *If $C_t\,H_t$ and R_t are commutative, i.e.,*

$$C_t\,H_t\,R_t = R_t\,C_t\,H_t, \tag{15}$$

then the optimal gain matrix K^1_{t+1} which makes the variance of the state estimation error e_{t+1} minimum is determined by (13). Hence, we obtain the optimal filtering algorithm:

$$\hat{x}_{t+1/t+1} = A^1_{t+1}\left\{\hat{x}_{t/t} + G_t\left(y_t - C_t\,\hat{x}_{t/t}\right)\right\} + H_{t+1}\,y_{t+1} + T_{t+1}\,B_t\,u_t, \tag{16}$$

$$P_{t+1} = A^1_{t+1}\,M_t\,A^1_{t+1}{}^T + T_{t+1}\,Q_t\,T_{t+1}{}^T + H_{t+1}\,R_{t+1}\,H_{t+1}{}^T, \tag{17}$$

where

$$G_t = \left(P_t\,C_t{}^T - H_t\,R_t\right)\left(C_t\,P_t\,C_t{}^T + R_t\right)^{-1}, \tag{18}$$

and

$$M_t = P_t - G_t\left(C_t\,P_t - R_t\,H_t{}^T\right). \tag{19}$$

∎

Remark 2.3. If the matrix R_t has the form

$$R_t = r_t\,I$$

with some positive number r_t for each $t = 1, 2, \cdots$, then it is obvious to see that condition (15) holds. ∎

Finally, we have the following proposition which indicates that the standard Kalman filter is a special case of the optimal filter proposed in this section (see e.g., Theorem 5.2 (page 90) in Katayama (2000)).

Proposition 2.4. *Suppose that $E_t \equiv O$ holds for all t (i.e., the unknown input term is zero). Then, Lemma 2.1 cannot be applied directly. But, we can choose $H_t \equiv O$ for all t in this case, and the optimal filter given in Proposition 2.2 reduces to the standard Kalman filter.* ∎

3. The fixed-point smoothing

Let k be a fixed time. We study an iterative algorithm to compute the optimal estimate $\hat{x}_{k/t}$ of the state x_k based on the observation $\mathbf{Y}_t, t = k+1, k+2, \cdots$, with $\mathbf{Y}_t = \sigma\{y_s, s = 0, 1, \cdots, t\}$. We define state vectors $\theta_t, t = k, k+1, \cdots$, by

$$\theta_{t+1} = \theta_t, \ \ t = k, k+1, \cdots; \quad \theta_k = x_k. \tag{20}$$

It is easy to observe that the optimal estimate $\hat{\theta}_{t/t}$ of the state θ_t based on the observation $\mathbf{Y}_t$ is identical to the optimal smoother $\hat{x}_{k/t}$ in view of the equalities $\theta_t = x_k, t = k, k+1, \cdots$.
In order to derive the optimal fixed-point smoother, we consider the following augmented system for $t = k, k+1, \cdots$:

$$\begin{bmatrix} x_{t+1} \\ \theta_{t+1} \end{bmatrix} = \begin{bmatrix} A_t & O \\ O & I \end{bmatrix} \begin{bmatrix} x_t \\ \theta_t \end{bmatrix} + \begin{bmatrix} B_t \\ O \end{bmatrix} u_t + \begin{bmatrix} E_t \\ O \end{bmatrix} d_t + \begin{bmatrix} I \\ O \end{bmatrix} \zeta_t, \tag{21}$$

$$y_{t+1} = [C_{t+1} \; O] \begin{bmatrix} x_{t+1} \\ \theta_{t+1} \end{bmatrix} + \eta_{t+1}. \tag{22}$$

Denote these equations respectively by

$$\widetilde{x_{t+1}} = \widetilde{A_t}\, \widetilde{x_t} + \widetilde{B_t}\, u_t + \widetilde{E_t}\, d_t + \widetilde{J_t}\, \zeta_t, \tag{23}$$

$$y_{t+1} = \widetilde{C_{t+1}}\, \widetilde{x_{t+1}} + \eta_{t+1}, \tag{24}$$

where

$$\widetilde{x_t} = \begin{bmatrix} x_t \\ \theta_t \end{bmatrix}, \widetilde{A_t} = \begin{bmatrix} A_t & O \\ O & I \end{bmatrix}, \widetilde{B_t} = \begin{bmatrix} B_t \\ O \end{bmatrix}, \widetilde{E_t} = \begin{bmatrix} E_t \\ O \end{bmatrix}, \widetilde{J_t} = \begin{bmatrix} I \\ O \end{bmatrix}$$

and $\widetilde{C_{t+1}} = [C_{t+1} \; O]$.

Here, I and O are the identity matrix and the zero matrix respectively with appropriate dimensions. By making use of the notations

$$\widetilde{H_{t+1}} = \begin{bmatrix} H_{t+1} \\ O \end{bmatrix}, \; \widetilde{T_{t+1}} = \begin{bmatrix} I & O \\ O & I \end{bmatrix} - \widetilde{H_{t+1}}\, \widetilde{C_{t+1}},$$

we have the equalities:

$$\widetilde{C_{t+1}}\, \widetilde{E_t} = C_{t+1} E_t, \; \widetilde{T_{t+1}} = \begin{bmatrix} T_{t+1} & O \\ O & I \end{bmatrix}, \; \widetilde{A^1_{t+1}} = \widetilde{T_{t+1}}\, \widetilde{A_t} = \begin{bmatrix} A^1_{t+1} & O \\ O & I \end{bmatrix}.$$

We introduce the covariance matrix $\widetilde{P_t}$ of the state estimation error of the augmented system (23)-(24):

$$\widetilde{P_t} = \begin{bmatrix} P_t^{(1,1)} & P_t^{(1,2)} \\ P_t^{(2,1)} & P_t^{(2,2)} \end{bmatrix} = \mathbf{E} \left\{ \begin{bmatrix} x_t - \hat{x}_{t/t} \\ \theta_t - \hat{\theta}_{t/t} \end{bmatrix} \begin{bmatrix} x_t - \hat{x}_{t/t} \\ \theta_t - \hat{\theta}_{t/t} \end{bmatrix}^T \right\}. \tag{25}$$

Notice that $P_t^{(1,1)}$ is equal to P_t. Applying the optimal filter given in Proposition 2.2 to the augmented system (21)-(22), we obtain the following optimal fixed-point smoother.

Theorem 3.1. *If $C_t\, H_t$ and R_t are commutative, i.e.,*

$$C_t\, H_t\, R_t = R_t\, C_t\, H_t, \tag{26}$$

then we have the optimal fixed-point smoother for (21)-(22) as follows:

(i) the fixed-point smoother

$$\hat{x}_{k/t+1} = \hat{x}_{k/t} + D_t(k)\left[y_t - C_t\,\hat{x}_{t/t}\right], \tag{27}$$

(ii) the gain matrix

$$D_t(k) = P_t^{(2,1)}\,C_t^{\,T}\left(C_t\,P_t\,C_t^{\,T} + R_t\right)^{-1}, \tag{28}$$

(iii) the covariance matrix of the mean-square error

$$P_{t+1}^{(2,1)} = \left\{P_t^{(2,1)} - P_t^{(2,1)}\,C_t^{\,T}\left(C_t\,P_t\,C_t^{\,T} + R_t\right)^{-1}\left(C_t\,P_t\ - R_t\,H_t^{\,T}\right)\right\}A_{t+1}^{1\ \ T}, \tag{29}$$

$$P_{t+1}^{(2,2)} = P_t^{(2,2)} - P_t^{(2,1)}\,C_t^{\,T}\left(C_t\,P_t\,C_t^{\,T} + R_t\right)^{-1}C_t\,P_t^{(2,1)\,T}. \tag{30}$$

Here, we note that $P_k^{(2,1)} = P_k^{(2,2)} = P_k$. *We notice that* $\hat{x}_{t/t}$ *is the optimal filter of the original system (1)-(2) given in Tanikawa & Sawada (2003).*

Proof Applying the optimal filter given by (16)-(17) in Proposition (2.2) to the augmented system (23)-(24), we have

$$\widehat{\widetilde{x_{t+1/t+1}}} = \widetilde{A_{t+1}}^{1}\left\{\widehat{\widetilde{x_{t/t}}} + \widetilde{G_t}\left(y_t - C_t\,\widehat{\widetilde{x_{t/t}}}\right)\right\} + \widetilde{H_{t+1}}\,y_{t+1} + \widetilde{T_{t+1}}\,\widetilde{B_t}\,u_t. \tag{31}$$

This can be rewritten as

$$\begin{aligned}\begin{bmatrix}\hat{x}_{t+1/t+1}\\ \hat{\theta}_{t+1/t+1}\end{bmatrix} &= \begin{bmatrix}A_{t+1}^{1} & O\\ O & I\end{bmatrix}\left\{\begin{bmatrix}\hat{x}_{t/t}\\ \hat{\theta}_{t/t}\end{bmatrix} + \begin{bmatrix}P_t^{(1,1)}\,C_t^{\,T} - H_t R_t\\ P_t^{(2,1)}\,C_t^{\,T}\end{bmatrix}\right.\\ &\quad\left.\times\left(C_t\,P_t\,C_t^{\,T} + R_t\right)^{-1}\left(y_t - C_t\,\hat{x}_{t/t}\right)\right\} + \begin{bmatrix}H_{t+1}\,y_{t+1}\\ O\end{bmatrix} + \begin{bmatrix}T_{t+1}\,B_t\,u_t\\ O\end{bmatrix}.\end{aligned}$$

Thus, we have

$$\begin{aligned}\hat{x}_{t+1/t+1} &= A_{t+1}^{1}\left\{\hat{x}_{t/t} + \left(P_t^{(1,1)}\,C_t^{\,T} - H_t R_t\right)\left(C_t\,P_t\,C_t^{\,T} + R_t\right)^{-1}\left(y_t - C_t\,\hat{x}_{t/t}\right)\right\}\\ &\quad + H_{t+1}\,y_{t+1} + T_{t+1}\,B_t\,u_t\end{aligned} \tag{32}$$

and

$$\hat{\theta}_{t+1/t+1} = \hat{\theta}_{t/t} + P_t^{(2,1)}\,C_t^{\,T}\left(C_t\,P_t\,C_t^{\,T} + R_t\right)^{-1}\left(y_t - C_t\,\hat{x}_{t/t}\right). \tag{33}$$

Here, we used the equalities

$$\begin{aligned}\widetilde{C}_t\,\widetilde{P}_t\,\widetilde{C}_t^{\,T} + R_t &= [C_t\ \ O]\begin{bmatrix}P_t^{(1,1)} & P_t^{(1,2)}\\ P_t^{(2,1)} & P_t^{(2,2)}\end{bmatrix}\begin{bmatrix}C_t^{\,T}\\ O\end{bmatrix} + R_t\\ &= C_t\,P_t\,C_t^{\,T} + R_t\end{aligned} \tag{34}$$

and

$$
\begin{aligned}
\widetilde{G}_t &= \left(\widetilde{P}_t \begin{bmatrix} C_t{}^T \\ O \end{bmatrix} - \widetilde{H}_t R_t\right)\left(\widetilde{C}_t \widetilde{P}_t \widetilde{C}_t{}^T + R_t\right)^{-1} \\
&= \left(\begin{bmatrix} P_t^{(1,1)} & P_t^{(1,2)} \\ P_t^{(2,1)} & P_t^{(2,2)} \end{bmatrix}\begin{bmatrix} C_t{}^T \\ O \end{bmatrix} - \begin{bmatrix} H_t \\ O \end{bmatrix} R_t\right)\left(\widetilde{C}_t \widetilde{P}_t \widetilde{C}_t{}^T + R_t\right)^{-1} \\
&= \begin{bmatrix} P_t^{(1,1)} C_t{}^T - H_t R_t \\ P_t^{(2,1)} C_t{}^T \end{bmatrix}\left(C_t P_t C_t{}^T + R_t\right)^{-1}.
\end{aligned} \tag{35}
$$

Thus, equalities (27)-(28) can be obtained from (33) due to $\hat{\theta}_{t/t} = \hat{x}_{k/t}$.
By using the notation $\widetilde{M}_t$ for the augmented system (23)-(24)which corresponds to the matrix M_t in Proposition (2.2), we have

$$
\begin{aligned}
\widetilde{M}_t &= \begin{bmatrix} M_t^{(1,1)} & M_t^{(1,2)} \\ M_t^{(2,1)} & M_t^{(2,2)} \end{bmatrix} \\
&= \widetilde{P}_t - \widetilde{G}_t\left(\widetilde{C}_t \widetilde{P}_t - R_t\begin{bmatrix} H_t{}^T & O \end{bmatrix}\right) \\
&= \begin{bmatrix} P_t^{(1,1)} & P_t^{(1,2)} \\ P_t^{(2,1)} & P_t^{(2,2)} \end{bmatrix} - \begin{bmatrix} P_t^{(1,1)} C_t{}^T - H_t R_t \\ P_t^{(2,1)} C_t{}^T \end{bmatrix}\left(C_t P_t C_t{}^T + R_t\right)^{-1} \\
&\quad \times \left(\begin{bmatrix} C_t & O \end{bmatrix}\begin{bmatrix} P_t^{(1,1)} & P_t^{(1,2)} \\ P_t^{(2,1)} & P_t^{(2,2)} \end{bmatrix} - \begin{bmatrix} R_t H_t{}^T & O \end{bmatrix}\right).
\end{aligned}
$$

Thus, we have

$$
M_t^{(1,1)} = P_t^{(1,1)} - \left(P_t^{(1,1)} C_t{}^T - H_t R_t\right)\left(C_t P_t C_t{}^T + R_t\right)^{-1}\left(C_t P_t^{(1,1)} - R_t H_t{}^T\right), \tag{36}
$$

$$
M_t^{(1,2)} = P_t^{(1,2)} - \left(P_t^{(1,1)} C_t{}^T - H_t R_t\right)\left(C_t P_t C_t{}^T + R_t\right)^{-1} C_t P_t^{(1,2)}, \tag{37}
$$

$$
M_t^{(2,1)} = P_t^{(2,1)} - P_t^{(2,1)} C_t{}^T\left(C_t P_t C_t{}^T + R_t\right)^{-1}\left(C_t P_t^{(1,1)} - R_t H_t{}^T\right), \tag{38}
$$

and

$$
M_t^{(2,2)} = P_t^{(2,2)} - P_t^{(2,1)} C_t{}^T\left(C_t P_t C_t{}^T + R_t\right)^{-1} C_t P_t^{(1,2)}. \tag{39}
$$

It follows from (17) in Proposition 2.2 that

$$
\begin{aligned}
\widetilde{P_{t+1}} &= \widetilde{A_{t+1}^1}\,\widetilde{M}_t\,\widetilde{A_{t+1}^1}^T + \widetilde{T_{t+1}}\,\widetilde{J_{t+1}}\,Q_{t+1}\,\widetilde{J_{t+1}}^T\,\widetilde{T_{t+1}} + \widetilde{H_{t+1}}\,R_{t+1}\,\widetilde{H_{t+1}}^T \\
&= \begin{bmatrix} A_{t+1}^1 & O \\ O & I \end{bmatrix}\begin{bmatrix} M_t^{(1,1)} & M_t^{(1,2)} \\ M_t^{(2,1)} & M_t^{(2,2)} \end{bmatrix}\begin{bmatrix} A_{t+1}^1{}^T & O \\ O & I \end{bmatrix} \\
&\quad + \begin{bmatrix} T_{t+1} & O \\ O & I \end{bmatrix}\begin{bmatrix} I \\ O \end{bmatrix} Q_{t+1}\begin{bmatrix} I & O \end{bmatrix}\begin{bmatrix} T_{t+1}{}^T & O \\ O & I \end{bmatrix} \\
&\quad + \begin{bmatrix} H_{t+1} \\ O \end{bmatrix} R_{t+1}\begin{bmatrix} H_{t+1}{}^T & O \end{bmatrix}.
\end{aligned} \tag{40}
$$

Equalities (29)-(30) follow from (38)-(40). Finally, we have equalities $P_k^{(2,1)} = P_k^{(2,2)} = P_k^{(1,1)} = P_k$ by the definition of $\widetilde{P}_k$. ∎

We thus have derived the fixed-point smoothing algorithm for the state-space model which explicitly contains the unknown inputs. We can indicate that the algorithm has a rather simple form and also has consistency with both the Kalman filter and the standard optimal smoother derived from the Kalman filter as shown in the following remark.

Remark 3.2. Suppose that $E_t \equiv O$ holds for all t (i.e., the unknown input term is zero) and that $H_t \equiv O$ for all t(as in Proposition 2.4). In this case, it follows from Theorem 3.1 that

$$\hat{x}_{t+1/t+1} = A_t \left\{ \hat{x}_{t/t} + P_t C_t{}^T \left(C_t P_t C_t{}^T + R_t \right)^{-1} (y_t - C_t \hat{x}_{t/t}) \right\} + B_t u_t, \tag{41}$$

$$\hat{\theta}_{t+1/t+1} = \hat{\theta}_{t/t} + P_t^{(2,1)} C_t{}^T \left(C_t P_t C_t{}^T + R_t \right)^{-1} (y_t - C_t \hat{x}_{t/t}), \tag{42}$$

$$P_{t+1}^{(2,1)} = \left\{ P_t^{(2,1)} - P_t^{(2,1)} C_t{}^T \left(C_t P_t C_t{}^T + R_t \right)^{-1} C_t P_t \right\} A_t{}^T, \tag{43}$$

and

$$P_{t+1}^{(2,2)} = P_t^{(2,2)} - P_t^{(2,1)} C_t{}^T \left(C_t P_t C_t{}^T + R_t \right)^{-1} C_t P_t^{(2,1)^T}. \tag{44}$$

Here, we note that the state estimate $\hat{x}_{t+1/t+1}$ reduces to the state estimate $\hat{x}_{t+1/t}$ in Katayama (2000) when $H_t \equiv O$ holds. Moreover, Equalities (37)-(40) with the state estimates $\hat{x}_{t+1/t+1}$ and $\hat{x}_{t/t}$ replaced respectively by $\hat{x}_{t+1/t}$ and $\hat{x}_{t/t-1}$ are identical to those for the pair of the standard Kalman filter and the optimal fixed-point smoother in Katayama (2000). Thus, it has been shown that this algorithm reduces to the well known optimal smoother derived from the Kalman filter when the unknown inputs disappear. This indicates that our smoothing algorithm is a natural extension of the standard optimal smoother to linear systems possibly with unknown inputs. ∎

Let us introduce some notations:

$$\nu_t = y_t - C_t \hat{x}_{t/t}, \tag{45}$$

$$L_t = A_{t+1}^1 (I - G_t C_t), \tag{46}$$

$$\Psi(t,\tau) = \begin{cases} L_{t-1} L_{t-2} \cdots L_\tau \,, & t > \tau \\ I \,, & t = \tau \,, \end{cases} \tag{47}$$

where the matrix G_t was defined by (18), i.e.,

$$G_t = \left(P_t C_t{}^T - H_t R_t \right) \left(C_t P_t C_t{}^T + R_t \right)^{-1}. \tag{48}$$

We then have the following results due to (27).

Corollary 3.3. *We have the equalities:*

$$\hat{x}_{k/t+1} = \hat{x}_{k/k} + \sum_{i=k}^{t} D_i(k) \nu_i = \hat{x}_{k/k} + P_k \sum_{i=k}^{t} \Psi(i,k)^T C_i{}^T \left(C_i P_i C_i{}^T + R_i \right)^{-1} \nu_i \,. \tag{49}$$

∎

Proof It is straightforward to show the first equality from (27). For the second equality, it is sufficient to prove the equality

$$D_t(k) = P_k \Psi(t,k)^T C_t^T \left(C_t P_t C_t^T + R_t\right)^{-1} \tag{50}$$

for $t \geq k$. By virtue of (46), equality (29) can be rewritten as

$$P_t^{(2,1)} = P_{t-1}^{(2,1)} \left(I - C_{t-1}^T G_{t-1}^T\right) A_t^{1\,T} = P_{t-1}^{(2,1)} L_{t-1}^T. \tag{51}$$

By using this equality recursively, we have

$$\begin{aligned} P_t^{(2,1)} &= P_{t-2}^{(2,1)} L_{t-2}^T L_{t-1}^T = \cdots\cdots = P_k^{(2,1)} L_k^T L_{k+1}^T \cdots L_{t-1}^T \\ &= P_k \Psi(t,k)^T. \end{aligned} \tag{52}$$

Substituting this equality into (28), we obtain

$$D_t(k) = P_k \Psi(t,k)^T C_t^T \left(C_t P_t C_t^T + R_t\right)^{-1}, \tag{53}$$

i.e., (50). ∎

Finally, we study the reduction of the estimation error by the fixed-point smoothing over the optimal filtering. Due to (27), we have

$$P_t^{(2,2)} = \mathbf{E}\left[(x_k - \hat{x}_{k/t})(x_k - \hat{x}_{k/t})^T\right]. \tag{54}$$

Denote this matrix simply by $P_{k/t}$. It then follows from (30) that

$$P_{k/t+1} = P_{k/t} - P_t^{(2,1)} C_t^T \left(C_t P_t C_t^T + R_t\right)^{-1} C_t P_t^{(2,1)^T}. \tag{55}$$

Summing up these equalities for $t = k, k+1, \cdots, s$, we have

$$P_{k/k} - P_{k/s+1} = \sum_{i=k}^{s} P_i^{(2,1)} C_i^T \left(C_i P_i C_i^T + R_i\right)^{-1} C_i P_i^{(2,1)^T}. \tag{56}$$

Thus, the right hand side indicates the amount of the reduction of the estimation error by the fixed-point smoothing over the optimal filtering.

4. The fixed-interval smoothing

We consider the fixed-interval smoothing problem in this section. Namely, we investigate the optimal estimate $\hat{x}_{t/N}$ of the state x_t at all times $t = 0, 1, \cdots, N$ based on the observation $\mathbf{Y}_N$ of all the states $\{y_0, y_1, \cdots, y_N\}$. Applying equality (49), we easily obtain the following equality.

Lemma 4.1. *The equality*

$$\hat{x}_{t/N} = \hat{x}_{t/t+1} + P_t L_t^T P_{t+1}^{-1} (\hat{x}_{t+1/N} - \hat{x}_{t+1/t+1}) \tag{57}$$

holds for $t = 0, 1, \cdots, N-1$. ∎

Proof Using the notation

$$\tilde{v}_i = C_i^T \left(C_i P_i C_i^T + R_i \right)^{-1} v_i, \tag{58}$$

we have

$$\hat{x}_{k/t+1} = \hat{x}_{k/k} + P_k \sum_{i=k}^{t} \Psi(i,k)^T \tilde{v}_i \tag{59}$$

for $k \leq t$ due to (49). In view of (59) , we also have

$$\hat{x}_{k/t+1} = \hat{x}_{k/k} + P_k \tilde{v}_k + P_k \sum_{i=k+1}^{t} \Psi(i,k)^T \tilde{v}_i = \hat{x}_{k/k+1} + P_k \sum_{i=k+1}^{t} \Psi(i,k)^T \tilde{v}_i \tag{60}$$

for $k+1 \leq t$. Putting $t+1 = N$ and $k = t+1$ in equality (59), we have

$$\hat{x}_{t+1/N} = \hat{x}_{t+1/t+1} + P_{t+1} \sum_{i=t+1}^{N-1} \Psi(i,t+1)^T \tilde{v}_i. \tag{61}$$

Putting $t+1 = N$ and $k = t$ in equality (60), we have

$$\hat{x}_{t/N} = \hat{x}_{t/t+1} + P_t \sum_{i=t+1}^{N-1} \Psi(i,t)^T \tilde{v}_i = \hat{x}_{t/t+1} + P_t L_t^T \sum_{i=t+1}^{N-1} \Psi(i,t+1)^T \tilde{v}_i. \tag{62}$$

Substituting (61) into (62), we have

$$\hat{x}_{t/N} = \hat{x}_{t/t+1} + P_t L_t^T P_{t+1}^{-1} \left(\hat{x}_{t+1/N} - \hat{x}_{t+1/t+1} \right).$$

The above derivation is valid for $t = 0, 1, \cdots, N-2$. It is easy to observe that equality (57) also holds for $t = N-1$. ∎

It is a simple task to obtain the following Fraser-type algorithm from (57).

Theorem 4.2. *We obtain the fixed-interval smoother*

$$\hat{x}_{t/N} = \hat{x}_{t/t+1} + P_t L_t^T \lambda_{t+1}, \tag{63}$$

$$\lambda_t = L_t^T \lambda_{t+1} + C_t^T \left(C_t P_t C_t^T + R_t \right)^{-1} v_t. \tag{64}$$

for $t = N-1, N-2, \cdots, 1, 0$. *Here, we have* $\lambda_N = 0$. ∎

Proof For $t = 0, 1, \cdots, N$, we put

$$\lambda_t = P_t^{-1} \left(\hat{x}_{t/N} - \hat{x}_{t/t} \right). \tag{65}$$

We then have $\lambda_N = 0$. Substituting (65) into (57), we obtain equality (63). Then, by utilizing (63) and (65), we have

$$\lambda_t = P_t^{-1} \left(\hat{x}_{t/t+1} + P_t L_t^T \lambda_{t+1} - \hat{x}_{t/t} \right). \tag{66}$$

In view of the equality

$$\hat{x}_{t/t+1} - \hat{x}_{t/t} = P_t \tilde{v}_t \tag{67}$$

which follows from (27) in Tanikawa & Sawada (2003), we obtain

$$\begin{aligned}\lambda_t &= L_t{}^T \lambda_{t+1} + \tilde{\nu}_t \\ &= L_t{}^T \lambda_{t+1} + C_t{}^T \left(C_t P_t C_t{}^T + R_t\right)^{-1} \nu_t. \end{aligned} \tag{68}$$

Thus, we proved (64). ∎

Remark 4.3. When $E_t \equiv O$ holds for all t (i.e., the unknown input term is zero), we shall see that fixed-interval smoother (63)-(64) is identical to the fixed-interval smoother obtained from the standard Kalman filter (see e.g., Katayama (2000)). Thus, our algorithm is consistent with the known fixed-interval smoothing algorithm for systems without unknown inputs. This can be shown as follows. Assuming that $E_t = O$, we have $H_t = O$ for $t = 0, 1, \cdots, N$ (see Propositin 2.4). Note that in (59), i.e.,

$$\hat{x}_{k/t+1} = \hat{x}_{k/k} + P_k \sum_{i=k}^{t} \Psi(i,k)^T \tilde{\nu}_i$$

$\hat{x}_{k/t+1}$ and $\hat{x}_{k/k}$ respectively reduce to $\hat{x}_{k/t}$ and $\hat{x}_{k/k-1}$ which are respectively the optimal smoother and the optimal filter obtained from the standard Kalman filter. Then, the above equality is identical to (7.18) in Katayama (2000). Since the rest of the proof can be done in the same way as in Katayama (2000), we obtain the same smoother. ∎

5. The fixed-lag smoothing

We study the fixed-lag smoothing problem in this section. For a fixed $L > 0$, we investigate an iterative algorithm to compute the optimal state estimate $\hat{x}_{t-L/t}$ of the state x_{t-L} based on the observation $\mathbf{Y}_t$.

We consider the following augmented system:

$$\begin{bmatrix} x_{t+1} \\ x_t \\ \vdots \\ x_{t-L+1} \end{bmatrix} = \begin{bmatrix} A_t & O & \dots & O \\ I & O & \dots & O \\ & \ddots & & \\ O & & I & O \end{bmatrix} \begin{bmatrix} x_t \\ x_{t-1} \\ \vdots \\ x_{t-L} \end{bmatrix} + \begin{bmatrix} B_t \\ O \\ \vdots \\ O \end{bmatrix} u_t + \begin{bmatrix} E_t \\ O \\ \vdots \\ O \end{bmatrix} d_t + \begin{bmatrix} I \\ O \\ \vdots \\ O \end{bmatrix} \zeta_t, \tag{69}$$

$$y_{t+1} = [C_{t+1} \; O \; \dots \; O] \begin{bmatrix} x_{t+1} \\ x_t \\ \vdots \\ x_{t-L+1} \end{bmatrix} + \eta_{t+1}. \tag{70}$$

Denote these equations respectively by

$$\widetilde{x_{t+1}} = \widetilde{A_t}\, \widetilde{x_t} + \widetilde{B_t}\, u_t + \widetilde{E_t}\, d_t + \widetilde{J_t}\, \zeta_t, \tag{71}$$

$$y_{t+1} = \widetilde{C_{t+1}}\, \widetilde{x_{t+1}} + \eta_{t+1}, \tag{72}$$

where

$$\widetilde{x_t} = \begin{bmatrix} x_t \\ x_{t-1} \\ \vdots \\ x_{t-L} \end{bmatrix}, \ \widetilde{A_t} = \begin{bmatrix} A_t & O & \dots & O \\ I & O & \dots & O \\ & \ddots & & \\ O & & I & O \end{bmatrix}, \ \widetilde{B_t} = \begin{bmatrix} B_t \\ O \\ \vdots \\ O \end{bmatrix}, \ \widetilde{E_t} = \begin{bmatrix} E_t \\ O \\ \vdots \\ O \end{bmatrix},$$

$$\widetilde{J_t} = \begin{bmatrix} I \\ O \\ \vdots \\ O \end{bmatrix} \quad \text{and} \quad \widetilde{C_{t+1}} = [C_{t+1} \ O \ \dots \ O].$$

Here, I and O are the identity matrix and the zero matrix respectively with appropriate dimensions. By making use of the notations

$$\widetilde{H_{t+1}} = \begin{bmatrix} H_{t+1} \\ O \\ \vdots \\ O \end{bmatrix} \quad \text{and} \quad \widetilde{T_{t+1}} = I - \widetilde{H_{t+1}}\,\widetilde{C_{t+1}},$$

we have the equalities:

$$\widetilde{C_{t+1}}\,\widetilde{E_t} = [C_{t+1} \ O \ \dots \ O] \begin{bmatrix} E_t \\ O \\ \vdots \\ O \end{bmatrix} = C_{t+1}\,E_t,$$

$$\widetilde{T_{t+1}} = I - \begin{bmatrix} H_{t+1} \\ O \\ \vdots \\ O \end{bmatrix} [C_{t+1} \ O \ \dots \ O] = \begin{bmatrix} T_{t+1} & O & \dots & O \\ O & I & \dots & O \\ & & \ddots & \\ O & O & \dots & I \end{bmatrix},$$

$$\widetilde{A^1_{t+1}} = \widetilde{T_{t+1}}\,\widetilde{A_t} = \begin{bmatrix} T_{t+1} & O & \dots & O \\ O & I & \dots & O \\ & & \ddots & \\ O & O & \dots & I \end{bmatrix} \begin{bmatrix} A_t & O & \dots & O \\ I & O & \dots & O \\ & \ddots & & \\ O & & I & O \end{bmatrix} = \begin{bmatrix} A^1_{t+1} & O & \dots & O \\ I & O & \dots & O \\ & \ddots & & \\ O & & I & O \end{bmatrix}.$$

We introduce the covariance matrix $\widetilde{P_t}$ of the state estimation error of augmented system (71)-(72):

$$\widetilde{P_t} = \mathbf{E}\left\{ \begin{bmatrix} x_t - \hat{x}_{t/t} \\ x_{t-1} - \hat{x}_{t-1/t} \\ \vdots \\ x_{t-L} - \hat{x}_{t-L/t} \end{bmatrix} \begin{bmatrix} x_t - \hat{x}_{t/t} \\ x_{t-1} - \hat{x}_{t-1/t} \\ \vdots \\ x_{t-L} - \hat{x}_{t-L/t} \end{bmatrix}^T \right\}. \tag{73}$$

By using the notations

$$P_{t-i,t-j/t} = \mathbf{E}\left\{(x_{t-i} - \hat{x}_{t-i/t})\left(x_{t-j} - \hat{x}_{t-j/t}\right)^T\right\},$$
$$P_{t-i/t} = P_{t-i,t-i/t},$$

we can write

$$\widetilde{P}_t = \begin{bmatrix} P_{t/t} & P_{t,t-1/t} & \cdots & P_{t,t-L/t} \\ P_{t-1,t/t} & P_{t-1/t} & \cdots & P_{t-1,t-L/t} \\ \vdots & & \ddots & \vdots \\ P_{t-L,t/t} & P_{t-L,t-1/t} & \cdots & P_{t-L/t} \end{bmatrix}. \tag{74}$$

Here, it is easy to observe that $P_{t/t} = P_t$ holds. We also note that

$$\widetilde{C}_t \widetilde{P}_t \widetilde{C}_t^T + R_t = C_t P_{t/t} C_t^T + R_t. \tag{75}$$

From now on, we use the following notation for brevity:

$$\overline{C}_t := C_t P_t C_t^T + R_t. \tag{76}$$

Applying the optimal filter given in Proposition 2.2 to augmented system (71)-(72), we have

$$\widehat{\widetilde{x_{t+1/t+1}}} = \widetilde{A_{t+1}^1}\left\{\widehat{\widetilde{x_{t/t}}} + \widetilde{G_t}\left(y_t - \widetilde{C}_t \widehat{\widetilde{x_{t/t}}}\right)\right\} + \widetilde{H_{t+1}}\, y_{t+1} + \widetilde{T_{t+1}}\, \widetilde{B}_t\, u_t, \tag{77}$$

where

$$\widetilde{G}_t = \left(\widetilde{P}_t \widetilde{C}_t^T - \widetilde{H}_t R_t\right)\left(\widetilde{C}_t \widetilde{P}_t \widetilde{C}_t^T + R_t\right)^{-1} = \begin{bmatrix} P_{t/t} C_t^T - H_t R_t \\ P_{t-1,t/t} C_t^T \\ \vdots \\ P_{t-L,t/t} C_t^T \end{bmatrix} \overline{C}_t^{-1}. \tag{78}$$

Identifying the component matrices of (77)-(78), we have the following optimal fixed-lag smoother.

Theorem 5.1. *If $C_t\, H_t$ and R_t are commutative, i.e.,*

$$C_t H_t R_t = R_t C_t H_t, \tag{79}$$

then we have the optimal fixed-lag smoother for (1)-(2) as follows:
(i) the fixed-lag smoother

$$\hat{x}_{t-j/t+1} = \hat{x}_{t-j/t} + S_t(j)\,(y_t - C_t \hat{x}_{t/t}) \qquad (j = 0, 1, \cdots, L-1), \tag{80}$$

(ii) the optimal filter

$$\hat{x}_{t+1/t+1} = A_{t+1}^1\{\hat{x}_{t/t} + G_t(y_t - C_t \hat{x}_{t/t})\} + H_{t+1} y_{t+1} + T_{t+1} B_t u_t, \tag{81}$$

with G_t defined by (18) in Proposition 2.2,
(iii) the gain matrices

$$S_t(j) = \left(P_{t-j,t/t} C_t^T - \delta_{0,j} H_t R_t\right) \overline{C}_t^{-1} \qquad (j = 0, 1, \cdots, L-1), \tag{82}$$

where $\delta_{i,j}$ stands for the Kronecker's delta, i.e.,

$$\delta_{i,j} = \begin{cases} 1 & \text{for } i = j \\ 0 & \text{for } i \neq j \end{cases}, \tag{83}$$

(iv) the covariance matrix of the mean-square error

$$P_{t+1/t+1} = A^1_{t+1}\, M_t^{(0,0)}\, {A^1_{t+1}}^T + T_{t+1}\, Q_t\, {T_{t+1}}^T + H_{t+1}\, R_{t+1}\, {H_{t+1}}^T, \tag{84}$$

$$P_{t+1,t-j/t+1} = A^1_{t+1}\, M_t^{(0,j)} \qquad (j = 0, 1, \cdots, L-1), \tag{85}$$

$$P_{t-j,t+1/t+1} = \left(P_{t+1,t-j/t+1}\right)^T \qquad (j = 0, 1, \cdots, L-1), \tag{86}$$

$$P_{t-i,t-j/t+1} = M_t^{(i,j)} \qquad (i, j = 0, 1, \cdots, L-1), \tag{87}$$

and

$$M_t^{(i,j)} = P_{t-i,t-j/t} - \left(P_{t-i,t/t}\, {C_t}^T - \delta_{0,i}\, H_t\, R_t\right) {\overline{C}_t}^{-1} \left(C_t\, P_{t,t-j/t} - \delta_{0,j}\, R_t\, {H_t}^T\right) \qquad (i, j = 0, 1, \cdots, L). \tag{88}$$

∎

Remark 5.2. Since the equalities

$$P_{t/t} = P_t \quad (\text{ in Proposition 2.2 })$$

and

$$M_t^{(0,0)} = M_t \quad (\text{ in Proposition 2.2 })$$

hold, the part of the optimal filter in Theorem 5.1 is identical to that in Proposition 2.2. When $E_t \equiv O$ holds for all t (i.e., the unknown input term is zero), we shall see that fixed-lag smoother (80)-(88) is identical to the well known fixed-lag smoother (see e.g. Katayama (2000)) obtained from the standard Kalman filter. Thus, our algorithm is consistent with the known fixed-lag smoothing algorithm for systems without unknown inputs. This can be readily shown as in Remark 4.3. ∎

Proof of Theorem 5.1 Rewriting (77)-(78) with the component matrices explicitly, we have

$$\begin{bmatrix} \hat{x}_{t+1/t+1} \\ \hat{x}_{t/t+1} \\ \hat{x}_{t-1/t+1} \\ \vdots \\ \hat{x}_{t-L+1/t+1} \end{bmatrix} = \begin{bmatrix} A^1_{t+1}\left\{\hat{x}_{t/t} + \left(P_{t/t}{C_t}^T - H_t R_t\right) {\overline{C}_t}^{-1} (y_t - C_t \hat{x}_{t/t})\right\} \\ \hat{x}_{t/t} + \left(P_{t/t}\, {C_t}^T - H_t\, R_t\right) {\overline{C}_t}^{-1} (y_t - C_t\, \hat{x}_{t/t}) \\ \hat{x}_{t-1/t} + P_{t-1,t/t}\, {C_t}^T {\overline{C}_t}^{-1} (y_t - C_t\, \hat{x}_{t/t}) \\ \vdots \\ \hat{x}_{t-L+1/t} + P_{t-L+1,t/t}\, {C_t}^T {\overline{C}_t}^{-1} (y_t - C_t\, \hat{x}_{t/t}) \end{bmatrix} + \begin{bmatrix} H_{t+1}\, y_{t+1} + T_{t+1}\, B_t\, u_t \\ O \\ O \\ \vdots \\ O \end{bmatrix}. \tag{89}$$

The statements in (i)-(iii) easily follow from (89).
Let $\widetilde{M_t}$ be defined by

$$\widetilde{M_t} = \widetilde{P_t} - \widetilde{G_t}\left(\widetilde{C_t}\,\widetilde{P_t} - R_t\,\widetilde{H_t}^T\right)$$

$$= \widetilde{P_t} - \begin{bmatrix} P_{t/t}C_t^T - H_t R_t \\ P_{t-1,t/t}\, C_t^T \\ P_{t-2,t/t}\, C_t^T \\ \vdots \\ P_{t-L,t/t}\, C_t^T \end{bmatrix} \overline{C_t}^{-1} \begin{bmatrix} P_{t/t}C_t^T - H_t R_t \\ P_{t-1,t/t}\, C_t^T \\ P_{t-2,t/t}\, C_t^T \\ \vdots \\ P_{t-L,t/t}\, C_t^T \end{bmatrix}^T .$$

We also introduce component matrices of $\widetilde{M_t}$ as follows:

$$\widetilde{M_t} = \begin{bmatrix} M_t^{(0,0)} & M_t^{(0,1)} & M_t^{(0,2)} & \dots & M_t^{(0,L)} \\ M_t^{(1,0)} & M_t^{(1,1)} & M_t^{(1,2)} & \dots & M_t^{(1,L)} \\ M_t^{(2,0)} & M_t^{(2,1)} & M_t^{(2,2)} & \dots & M_t^{(2,L)} \\ \vdots & \vdots & \vdots & \ddots & \vdots \\ M_t^{(L,0)} & M_t^{(L,1)} & M_t^{(L,2)} & \dots & M_t^{(L,L)} \end{bmatrix} .$$

Concerning $\widetilde{P_{t+1}}$, we have

$$\widetilde{P_{t+1}} = \widetilde{A_{t+1}^1}\,\widetilde{M_t}\,\widetilde{A_{t+1}^1}^T + \widetilde{T_{t+1}}\,\widetilde{J_t}\,Q_t\,\widetilde{J_t}^T\,\widetilde{T_{t+1}}^T + \widetilde{H_{t+1}}\,R_{t+1}\,\widetilde{H_{t+1}}^T$$

$$= \begin{bmatrix} A_{t+1}^1 M_t^{(0,0)} {A_{t+1}^1}^T & A_{t+1}^1 M_t^{(0,0)} & A_{t+1}^1 M_t^{(0,1)} & \dots & A_{t+1}^1 M_t^{(0,L-1)} \\ M_t^{(0,0)} {A_{t+1}^1}^T & M_t^{(0,0)} & M_t^{(0,1)} & \dots & M_t^{(0,L-1)} \\ M_t^{(1,0)} {A_{t+1}^1}^T & M_t^{(1,0)} & M_t^{(1,1)} & \dots & M_t^{(1,L-1)} \\ \vdots & \vdots & \vdots & \ddots & \vdots \\ M_t^{(L-1,0)} {A_{t+1}^1}^T & M_t^{(L-1,0)} & M_t^{(L-1,1)} & \dots & M_t^{(L-1,L-1)} \end{bmatrix}$$

$$+ \begin{bmatrix} T_{t+1}Q_tT_{t+1}^T + H_{t+1}R_{t+1}H_{t+1}^T & O & O & \dots & O \\ O & O & O & \dots & O \\ O & O & O & \dots & O \\ \vdots & \vdots & \vdots & \ddots & \vdots \\ O & O & O & \dots & O \end{bmatrix} .$$

The final part (iv) can be obtained from the last three equalities. ∎

6. Conclusion

In this chapter, we considered discrete-time linear stochastic systems with unknown inputs (or disturbances) and studied three types of smoothing problems for these systems. We derived smoothing algorithms which are robust to unknown disturbances from the optimal filter for stochastic systems with unknown inputs obtained in our previous papers. These smoothing algorithms have similar recursive forms to the standard optimal filters and smoothers. Moreover, since our algorithms reduce to those known smoothers derived from the Kalman filter when unknown inputs disappear, these algorithms are consistent with the known smoothing algorithms for systems without unknown inputs.

This work was partially supported by the Japan Society for Promotion of Science (JSPS) under Grant-in-Aid for Scientific Research (C)-22540158.

7. References

Ackner, R. & Kailath, T. (1989a). Complementary models and smoothing, *IEEE Trans. Automatic Control*, Vol. 34, pp. 963–969

Ackner, R. & Kailath, T. (1989b). Discrete-time complementary models and smoothing, *Int. J. Control*, Vol. 49, pp. 1665–1682

Anderson, B. D. O. & Moore, J. B. (1979). *Optimal Filtering*, Prentice-Hall, Englewood Cliffs, NJ

Badawi, F. A.; Lindquist, A. & Pavon, M. (1979). A stochastic realization approach to the smoothing problem, *IEEE Trans. Automatic Control*, Vol. 24, pp. 878–888

Bello, M. G.; Willsky, A. S. & Levy, B. C. (1989). Construction and applications of discrete-time smoothing error models, *Int. J. Control*, Vol. 50, pp. 203–223

Bello, M. G.; Willsky, A. S.; Levy, B. C. & Castanon, D. A. (1986). Smoothing error dynamics and their use in the solution of smoothing and mapping problems, *IEEE Trans. Inform. Theory*, Vol. 32, pp. 483–495

Bryson, Jr., A. E. & Ho, Y. C. (1969). *Applied Optimal Control*, Blaisdell Publishing Company, Waltham, Massachusetts

Caliskan, F.; Mukai, H.; Katz, N. & Tanikawa, A. (2003). Game estimators for air combat games with unknown enemy inputs, *Proc. American Control Conference*, pp. 5381–5387, Denver, Colorado

Chang, S. & Hsu, P. (1993). State estimation using general structured observers for linear systems with unknown input, *Proc. 2nd European Control Conference: ECC'93*, pp. 1794–1799, Groningen, Holland

Chen, J. & Patton, R. J. (1996). Optimal filtering and robust fault diagnosis of stochastic systems with unknown disturbances, *IEE Proc. of Control Theory Applications*, Vol. 143, No. 1, pp. 31–36

Chen, J. & Patton, R. J. (1999). *Robust Model-based Fault Diagnosis for Dynamic Systems*, Kluwer Academic Publishers, Norwell, Massachusetts

Chen, J.; Patton, R. J. & Zhang, H. -Y. (1996). Design of unknown input observers and robust fault detection filters, *Int. J. Control*, Vol. 63, No. 1, pp. 85–105

Darouach, M.; Zasadzinski, M.; Bassang, O. A. & Nowakowski, S. (1995). Kalman filtering with unknown inputs via optimal state estimation of singular systems, *Int. J. Systems Science*, Vol. 26, pp. 2015–2028

Darouach, M.; Zasadzinski, M. & Keller, J. Y. (1992). State estimation for discrete systems with unknown inputs using state estimation of singular systems, *Proc. American Control Conference*, pp. 3014–3015

Desai, U. B.; Weinert, H. L. & Yasypchuk, G. (1983). Discrete-time complementary models and smoothing algorithms: The correlated case, *IEEE Trans. Automatic Control*, Vol. 28, pp. 536–539

Faurre, P.; Clerget, M. & Germain, F. (1979). *Operateurs Rationnels Positifs*, Dunod, Paris, France

Frank, P. M. (1990). Fault diagnosis in dynamic system using analytical and knowledge based redundancy: a survey and some new results, *Automatica*, Vol. 26, No. 3, pp. 459–474

Hou, M. & Müller, P. C. (1993). Unknown input decoupled Kalman filter for time-varying systems, *Proc. 2nd European Control Conference: ECC'93*, Groningen, Holland, pp. 2266–2270

Hou, M. & Müller, P. C. (1994). Disturbance decoupled observer design: a unified viewpoint, *IEEE Trans. Automatic Control*, Vol. 39, No. 6, pp. 1338–1341

Hou, M. & R. J. Patton, R. J. (1998). Optimal filtering for systems with unknown inputs, *IEEE Trans. Automatic Control*, Vol. 43, No. 3, pp. 445–449

Kailath, T. (1974). A view of three decades of linear filtering theory, *IEEE Trans. Inform. Theory*, Vol. 20, No. 2, pp. 146–181

Kailath, T. (1975). Supplement to a survey to data smoothing, *Automatica*, Vol. 11, No. 11, pp. 109–111

Kailath, T. (1976). *Lectures on Linear Least-Squares Estimation*, Springer

Kailath, T.; Sayed, A. H. & Hassibi, B. (2000). *Linear Estimation*, Prentice Hall

Kalman, R. E. (1960). A new approach to linear filtering and prediction problems, in *Trans. ASME, J. Basic Eng.*, Vol. 82D, No. 1, pp. 34–45

Kalman, R. E. (1963). New methods in Wiener filtering theory, *Proc. of First Symp. Eng. Appl. of Random Function Theory and Probability (J. L. Bogdanoff and F. Kozin, eds.)*, pp. 270-388, Wiley

Katayama, T. (2000). *Applied Kalman Filtering, New Edition*, in Japanese, Asakura-Shoten, Tokyo, Japan

Meditch, J. S. (1973). A survey of data smoothing for linear and nonlinear dynamic systems, *Automatica*, Vol. 9, No. 2, pp. 151–162

Patton, R. J.; Frank, P. M. & Clark, R. N. (1996). *Fault Diagnosis in Dynamic Systems: Theory and Application*, Prentice Hall

Sawada, Y. & Tanikawa, A. (2002). Optimal filtering and robust fault diagnosis of stochastic systems with unknown inputs and colored observation noises, *Proc. 5th IASTED Conf. Decision and Control*, pp. 149-154, Tsukuba, Japan

Tanikawa, A. (2006). On a smoother for discrete-time linear stochastic systems with unknown disturbances, *Int. J. Innovative Computing, Information and Control*, Vol. 2, No. 5, pp. 907–916

Tanikawa, A. (2008). On new smoothing algorithms for discrete-time linear stochastic systems with unknown disturbances, *Int. J. Innovative Computing, Information and Control*, Vol. 4, No. 1, pp. 15–24

Tanikawa, A. & Mukai, H. (2010). Minimum variance state estimators with disturbance decoupling property for optimal filtering problems with unknown inputs and fault detection (in preparation)

Tanikawa, A. & Sawada, Y. (2003). Minimum variance state estimators with disturbance decoupling property for optimal filtering problems with unknown inputs, *Proc. of the 35th ISCIE Int. Symp. on Stochastic Systems Theory and Its Appl.*, pp. 96-99, Ube, Japan

Weinert, H. L. & Desai, U. B. (1981). On complementary models and fixed-interval smoothing, *IEEE Trans. Automatic Control*, Vol. 26, pp. 863–867

5

On the Error Covariance Distribution for Kalman Filters with Packet Dropouts

Eduardo Rohr, Damián Marelli, and Minyue Fu
University of Newcastle
Australia

1. Introduction

The fast development of network (particularly wireless) technology has encouraged its use in control and signal processing applications. Under the control system's perspective, this new technology has imposed new challenges concerning how to deal with the effects of quantisation, delays and loss of packets, leading to the development of a new networked control theory Schenato et al. (2007). The study of state estimators, when measurements are subject to random delays and losses, finds applications in both control and signal processing. Most estimators are based on the well-known Kalman filter Anderson & Moore (1979). In order to cope with network induced effects, the standard Kalman filter paradigm needs to undergo certain modifications.

In the case of missing measurements, the update equation of the Kalman filter depends on whether a measurement arrives or not. When a measurement is available, the filter performs the standard update equation. On the other hand, if the measurement is missing, it must produce open loop estimation, which as pointed out in Sinopoli et al. (2004), can be interpreted as the standard update equation when the measurement noise is infinite. If the measurement arrival event is modeled as a binary random variable, the estimator's error covariance (EC) becomes a random matrix. Studying the statistical properties of the EC is important to assess the estimator's performance. Additionally, a clear understanding of how the system's parameters and network delivery rates affect the EC, permits a better system design, where the trade-off between conflicting interests must be evaluated.

Studies on how to compute the expected error covariance (EEC) can be dated back at least to Faridani (1986), where upper and lower bounds for the EEC were obtained using a constant gain on the estimator. In Sinopoli et al. (2004), the same upper bound was derived as the limiting value of a recursive equation that computes a weighted average of the next possible error covariances. A similar result which allows partial observation losses was presented in Liu & Goldsmith (2004). In Dana et al. (2007); Schenato (2008), it is shown that a system in which the sensor transmits state estimates instead of raw measurements will provide a better error covariance. However, this scheme requires the use of more complex sensors. Most of the available research work is concerned with the expected value of the EC, neglecting higher order statistics. The problem of finding the complete distribution function of the EC has been recently addressed in Shi et al. (2010).

This chapter investigates the behavior of the Kalman filter for discrete-time linear systems whose output is intermittently sampled. To this end we model the measurement arrival event as an independent identically distributed (i.i.d.) binary random variable. We introduce a method to obtain lower and upper bounds for the cumulative distribution function (CDF) of the EC. These bounds can be made arbitrarily tight, at the expense of increased computational complexity. We then use these bounds to derive upper and lower bounds for the EEC.

2. Problem description

In this section we give an overview of the Kalman filtering problem in the presence of randomly missing measurements. Consider the discrete-time linear system:

$$\begin{cases} x_{t+1} &= Ax_t + w_t \\ y_t &= Cx_t + v_t \end{cases} \tag{1}$$

where the state vector $x_t \in \mathbb{R}^n$ has initial condition $x_0 \sim N(0, P_0)$, $y \in \mathbb{R}^p$ is the measurement, $w \sim N(0, Q)$ is the process noise and $v \sim N(0, R)$ is the measurement noise. The goal of the Kalman filter is to obtain an estimate $\hat{x}_t$ of the state x_t, as well as providing an expression for the covariance matrix P_t of the error $\tilde{x}_t = x_t - \hat{x}_t$.

We assume that the measurements y_t are sent to the Kalman estimator through a network subject to random packet losses. The scheme proposed in Schenato (2008) can be used to deal with delayed measurements. Hence, without loss of generality, we assume that there is no delay in the transmission. Let γ_t be a binary random variable describing the arrival of a measurement at time t. We define that $\gamma_t = 1$ when y_t was received at the estimator and $\gamma_t = 0$ otherwise. We also assume that γ_t is independent of γ_s whenever $t \neq s$. The probability to receive a measurement is given by

$$\lambda = \mathcal{P}(\gamma_t = 1). \tag{2}$$

Let $\hat{x}_{t|s}$ denote the estimate of x_t considering the available measurements up to time s. Let $\tilde{x}_{t|s} = x_t - \hat{x}_{t|s}$ denote the estimation error and $\Sigma_{t|s} = E\{(\tilde{x}_{t|s} - E\{\tilde{x}_{t|s}\})(\tilde{x}_{t|s} - E\{\tilde{x}_{t|s}\})'\}$ denote its covariance matrix. If a measurement is received at time t (i.e., if $\gamma_t = 1$), the estimate and its EC are recursively computed as follows:

$$\hat{x}_{t|t} = \hat{x}_{t|t-1} + K_t(y_t - Cx_t) \tag{3}$$

$$\Sigma_{t|t} = (I - K_t C)\Sigma_{t|t-1} \tag{4}$$

$$\hat{x}_{t+1|t} = A\hat{x}_{t|t} \tag{5}$$

$$\Sigma_{t+1|t} = A\Sigma_{t|t}A' + Q, \tag{6}$$

with the Kalman gain K_t given by

$$K_t = \Sigma_{t|t-1}C'(C\Sigma_{t|t-1}C' + Q)^{-1}. \tag{7}$$

On the other hand, if a measurement is not received at time t (i.e., if $\gamma_t = 0$), then (3) and (4) are replaced by

$$\hat{x}_{t|t} = \hat{x}_{t|t-1} \tag{8}$$

$$\Sigma_{t|t} = \Sigma_{t|t-1}. \tag{9}$$

We will study the statistical properties of the EC $\Sigma_{t|t-1}$. To simplify the notation, we define $P_t = \Sigma_{t|t-1}$. Then, the update equation of P_t can be written as follows:

$$P_{t+1} = \begin{cases} \Phi_1(P_t), & \gamma_t = 1 \\ \Phi_0(P_t), & \gamma_t = 0 \end{cases} \tag{10}$$

with

$$\Phi_1(P_t) = AP_tA' + Q - AP_tC'(CP_tC' + R)^{-1}CP_tA' \tag{11}$$
$$\Phi_0(P_t) = AP_tA' + Q. \tag{12}$$

We point out that when all the measurements are available, and the Kalman filter reaches its steady state, the EC is given by the solution of the following algebraic Riccati equation

$$\underline{P} = A\underline{P}A' + Q - A\underline{P}C'(C\underline{P}C' + R)^{-1}C\underline{P}A'. \tag{13}$$

Throughout this chapter we use the following notation. For given $T \in \mathbb{N}$ and $0 \le m \le 2^T - 1$, the symbol S_m^T denotes the binary sequence of length T formed by the binary representation of m. We also use $S_m^T(i), i = 1, \cdots, T$ to denote the i-th entry of the sequence, i.e.,

$$S_m^T = \{S_m^T(1), S_m^T(2), \ldots, S_m^T(T)\} \tag{14}$$

and

$$m = \sum_{k=1}^{T} 2^{k-1} S_m^T(k). \tag{15}$$

(Notice that S_0^T denotes a sequence of length T formed exclusively by zeroes.) We use $|S_m^T|$ to denote the number of ones in the sequence S_m^T, i.e.,

$$|S_m^T| = \sum_{k=1}^{T} S_m^T(k). \tag{16}$$

For a given sequence S_m^T, and a matrix $P \in \mathbb{R}^{n \times n}$, we define the map

$$\phi(P, S_m^T) = \Phi_{S_m^T(T)} \circ \Phi_{S_m^T(T-1)} \circ \ldots \Phi_{S_m^T(1)}(P) \tag{17}$$

where $\circ$ denotes the composition of functions (i.e. $f \circ g(x) = f(g(x))$). Notice that if m is chosen so that

$$S_m^T = \{\gamma_{t-1}, \gamma_{t-2}, \ldots, \gamma_{t-T}\}, \tag{18}$$

then the map $\phi(\cdot, S_m^T)$ updates P_{t-T} according to the measurement arrivals in the last T sampling times, i.e.,

$$P_t = \phi(P_{t-T}, S_m^T) = \Phi_{\gamma_{t-1}} \circ \Phi_{\gamma_{t-1}} \circ \ldots \Phi_{\gamma_{t-T}}(P_{t-T}). \tag{19}$$

3. Bounds for the cumulative distribution function

In this section we present a method to compute lower and upper bounds for the limit CDF $F(x)$ of the trace of the EC, which is defined by

$$F(x) = \lim_{T\to\infty} F^T(x) \tag{20}$$

$$F^T(x) = \mathcal{P}\left(\mathrm{Tr}\{P_T\} < x\right) \tag{21}$$

$$= \sum_{m=0}^{2^T-1} \mathcal{P}\left(S_m^T\right) H\left(x - \mathrm{Tr}\{\phi(P_0, S_m^T)\}\right), \tag{22}$$

where $H(\cdot)$ is the Heaviside step function, and the probability to observe the sequence S_m^T is given by

$$\mathcal{P}\left(S_m^T\right) = \lambda^{|S_m^T|}(1-\lambda)^{T-|S_m^T|}. \tag{23}$$

The basic idea is to start with either the lowest or the highest possible value of EC, and then evaluate the CDF resulting from each starting value after a given time horizon T. Doing so, for each T, we obtain a lower bound $\underline{F}^T(x)$ and an upper bound $\overline{F}^T(x)$ for $F(x)$, i.e.,

$$\underline{F}^T(x) \leq F(x) \leq \overline{F}^T(x), \text{ for all } T \in \mathbb{R}. \tag{24}$$

As we show in Section 3.3, both bounds monotonically approach $F(x)$ as T increases.
To derive these results we make use of the following lemma stating properties of the maps $\Phi_0(\cdot)$ and $\Phi_1(\cdot)$ defined in (11)-(12).

Lemma 3.1. *Let $X, Y \in \mathbb{R}^{n\times n}$ be two positive semi-definite matrices. Then,*

$$\Phi_1(X) < \Phi_0(X). \tag{25}$$

If $Y \geq X$,

$$\Phi_0(Y) \geq \Phi_0(X) \tag{26}$$

$$\Phi_1(Y) \geq \Phi_1(X). \tag{27}$$

Proof: The proof of (25) is direct from (11)-(12). Equation (26) follows straightforwardly since $\Phi_0(X)$ is affine in X. Using the matrix inversion lemma, we have that

$$\Phi_1(X) = A(X^{-1} + C'R^{-1}C)^{-1}A' + Q \tag{28}$$

which shows that $\Phi_1(X)$ is monotonically increasing with respect to X. ∎

3.1 Upper bounds for the CDF

The smallest possible value of the EC is obtained when all the measurements are available and the Kalman filter reaches its steady state. In this case, the EC $\underline{P}$ is given by (13). Now, fix T, and suppose that m is such that $S_m^T = \{\gamma_{T-1}, \gamma_{T-2}, \ldots, \gamma_0\}$ describes the measurement arrival sequence. Then, assuming that[1] $P_0 \geq \underline{P}$, from (26)-(27), it follows that $P_T \geq \phi(\underline{P}, S_m^T)$. Hence, from (22), an upper bound of $F(x)$ is given by

$$\overline{F}^T(x) = \sum_{m=0}^{2^T-1} \mathcal{P}\left(S_m^T\right) H\left(x - \mathrm{Tr}\{\phi(\underline{P}, S_m^T)\}\right). \tag{29}$$

3.2 Lower bounds for the CDF

A lower bound for the CDF can be obtained using an argument similar to the one we used above to derive an upper bound. To do this we need to replace in (22) $\mathrm{Tr}\{\phi(P_0, S_m^T)\}$ by an upper bound of $\mathrm{Tr}\{P_T\}$ given the arrival sequence S_m^T. To do this we use the following lemma.

Lemma 3.2. *Let m be such that $S_m^T = \{\gamma_{T-1}, \gamma_{T-2}, \cdots, \gamma_0\}$ and $0 \leq t_1, t_2, \cdots, t_I \leq T-1$ denote the indexes where $\gamma_{t_i} = 1$, $i = 1, \cdots, I$. Define*

$$O = \begin{bmatrix} CA^{t_1} \\ CA^{t_2} \\ \vdots \\ CA^{t_I} \end{bmatrix}, \Sigma_Q = \begin{bmatrix} \sum_{j=0}^{t_1-1} CA^jQA'^{T-t_1+j} \\ \sum_{j=0}^{t_2-1} CA^jQA'^{T-t_2+j} \\ \vdots \\ \sum_{j=0}^{t_I-1} CA^jQA'^{T-t_I+j} \end{bmatrix}', \tag{30}$$

and the matrix $\Sigma_V \in \mathbb{R}^{pI \times pI}$, whose (i,j)-th submatrix $[\Sigma_V]_{i,j} \in \mathbb{R}^{p \times p}$ is given by

$$[\Sigma_V]_{i,j} = \sum_{k=0}^{\min\{t_i,t_j\}-1} CA^{t_i-1-k}QA'^{t_j-1-k}C' + R\delta(i,j) \tag{31}$$

where

$$\delta(i,j) = \begin{cases} 1, & i = j \\ 0, & i \neq j. \end{cases} \tag{32}$$

If O has full column rank, then

$$P_T \leq \overline{P}(S_m^T), \tag{33}$$

where the S_m^T-dependant matrix $\overline{P}(S_m^T)$ is given by

$$\overline{P}(S_m^T) = A^T\left(O'\Sigma_V^{-1}O\right)^{-1}A'^T + \sum_{j=0}^{T-1} A^jQA'^j - A^T(\Sigma_V^{-\frac{1}{2}}O)^\dagger\Sigma_V^{-\frac{1}{2}}\Sigma_Q' + \tag{34}$$
$$-\Sigma_Q\Sigma_V^{-\frac{1}{2}}(\Sigma_V^{-\frac{1}{2}}O)'^\dagger A'^T - \Sigma_Q\left(\Sigma_V^{-1} - \Sigma_V^{-1}O(O'\Sigma_V^{-1}O)^{-1}O'\Sigma_V^{-1}\right)\Sigma_Q',$$

with $(\Sigma_V^{-\frac{1}{2}}O)^\dagger$ denoting the Moore-Penrose pseudo-inverse of $\Sigma_V^{-\frac{1}{2}}O$ Ben-Israel & Greville (2003).

[1] If this assumption does not hold, one can substitute $\underline{P}$ by P_0 without loss of generality.

Proof: Let Y_T be the vector formed by the available measurements

$$Y_T = \left[y'_{t_1}\ y'_{t_2}\ \cdots\ y'_{t_I}\right]' \tag{35}$$
$$= Ox_0 + V_T, \tag{36}$$

where

$$V_T = \begin{bmatrix} \sum_{j=0}^{t_1-1} CA^{t_1-1-j}w_j + v_{t_1} \\ \sum_{j=0}^{t_2-1} CA^{t_2-1-j}w_j + v_{t_2} \\ \vdots \\ \sum_{j=0}^{t_I-1} CA^{t_I-1-j}w_j + v_{t_I} \end{bmatrix}. \tag{37}$$

From the model (1), it follows that

$$\begin{bmatrix} x_T \\ Y_T \end{bmatrix} \sim N\left(\begin{bmatrix} 0 \\ 0 \end{bmatrix}, \begin{bmatrix} \Sigma_x & \Sigma_{xY} \\ \Sigma'_{xY} & \Sigma_Y \end{bmatrix}\right) \tag{38}$$

where

$$\Sigma_x = A^T P_0 A'^T + \sum_{j=0}^{T-1} A^j Q A'^j \tag{39}$$

$$\Sigma_{xY} = A^T P_0 O' + \Sigma_Q \tag{40}$$

$$\Sigma_Y = OP_0O' + \Sigma_V. \tag{41}$$

Since the Kalman estimate $\hat{x}_T$ at time T is given by,

$$\hat{x}_T = E\left\{x_T | Y_T\right\}, \tag{42}$$

it follows from (Anderson & Moore, 1979, pp. 39) that the estimation error covariance is given by

$$P_T = \Sigma_x - \Sigma_{xY}\Sigma_Y^{-1}\Sigma'_{xY}. \tag{43}$$

Substituting (39)-(41) in (43), we have

$$P_T = A^T P_0 A'^T + \sum_{j=0}^{T-1} A^j Q A'^j + \tag{44}$$
$$- \left(A^T P_0 O' + \Sigma_Q\right) \left(OP_0O' + \Sigma_V\right)^{-1} \left(A^T P_0 O' + \Sigma_Q\right)'$$
$$= A^T \left(P_0 - P_0 O' \left(OP_0O' + \Sigma_V\right)^{-1} O' P_0\right) A^T + \sum_{j=0}^{T-1} A^j Q A'^j + \tag{45}$$
$$- A^T P_0 O' \left(OP_0O' + \Sigma_V\right)^{-1} \Sigma'_Q - \Sigma_Q \left(OP_0O' + \Sigma_V\right)^{-1} O' P_0 A^T +$$
$$- \Sigma_Q \left(OP_0O' + \Sigma_V\right)^{-1} \Sigma'_Q.$$

Now, from (19),

$$P_T = \phi(P_0, S_m^T). \tag{46}$$

Notice that for any P_0 we can always find a k such that $kI_n \geq P_0$, where I_n is the identity matrix of order n. From the monotonicity of $\phi(\cdot, S_m^T)$ (Lemma 3.1), it follows that

$$P_T \leq \lim_{k\to\infty} \phi(kI_n, S_m^T). \tag{47}$$

We then have that

$$P_T \leq P_{T,1} + P_{T,2} + P_{T,3} + P'_{T,3} + P_{T,4}, \tag{48}$$

with

$$\begin{aligned} P_{T,1} &= \lim_{k\to\infty} A^T \left(kI_n - k^2 O \left(kOO' + \Sigma_V\right)^{-1} O'\right) A'^T \qquad (49)\\ P_{T,2} &= \sum_{j=0}^{T-1} A^j Q A'^j \\ P_{T,3} &= -\lim_{k\to\infty} kA^T O \left(kOO' + \Sigma_V\right)^{-1} \Sigma'_Q \\ P_{T,4} &= -\lim_{k\to\infty} \Sigma_Q \left(kOO' + \Sigma_V\right)^{-1} \Sigma'_Q. \end{aligned}$$

Using the matrix inversion lemma, we have that

$$\begin{aligned} P_{T,1} &= A^T \lim_{k\to\infty} \left(k^{-1}I_n + O'\Sigma_V^{-1}O\right)^{-1} A'^T \qquad (50)\\ &= A^T \left(O'\Sigma_V^{-1}O\right)^{-1} A'^T. \qquad (51) \end{aligned}$$

It is straightforward to see that $P_{T,3}$ can be written as

$$\begin{aligned} P_{T,3} &= -\lim_{k\to\infty} A^T O' \left(OO' + \Sigma_V k^{-1}\right)^{-1} \Sigma'_Q \qquad (52)\\ &= -A^T \lim_{k\to\infty} O'\Sigma_V^{-\frac{1}{2}} \left(\Sigma_V^{-\frac{1}{2}} OO' \Sigma_V^{-\frac{1}{2}} + k^{-1}I_n\right)^{-1} \Sigma_V^{-\frac{1}{2}} \Sigma'_Q. \qquad (53) \end{aligned}$$

From (Ben-Israel & Greville, 2003, pp. 115), it follows that $\lim_{k\to\infty} X' \left(XX' + k^{-1}I_n\right) = X^{\dagger}$, for any matrix X. By making $X = \Sigma_V^{-\frac{1}{2}} O$, we have that

$$P_{T,3} = -A^T \left(\Sigma_V^{-\frac{1}{2}} O\right)^{\dagger} \Sigma_V^{-\frac{1}{2}} \Sigma'_Q. \tag{54}$$

Using the matrix inversion lemma, we have

$$\begin{aligned} P_{T,4} &= -\lim_{k\to\infty} \Sigma_Q \left(\Sigma_V^{-1} - \Sigma_V^{-1} O \left(O'\Sigma_V^{-1} O + k^{-1} I_n\right)^{-1} O'\Sigma_V^{-1}\right) \Sigma'_Q \qquad (55)\\ &= \Sigma_Q \left(\Sigma_V^{-1} - \Sigma_V^{-1} O \left(O'\Sigma_V^{-1} O\right)^{-1} O'\Sigma_V^{-1}\right) \Sigma'_Q \end{aligned}$$

and the result follows by substituting (51), (54) and (55) in (48). ∎

In order to keep the notation consistent with that of Section 3.1, with some abuse of notation we introduce the following definition:

$$\phi(\infty, S_m^T) \triangleq \begin{cases} \overline{P}(S_m^T), & \text{if } O \text{ has full column rank} \\ \infty I_n, & \text{otherwise} \end{cases} \tag{56}$$

where ∞I_n is an $n \times n$ diagonal matrix with ∞ on every entry of the main diagonal. Then, we obtain a lower bound for $F(x)$ as follows

$$\underline{F}^T(x) = \sum_{m=0}^{2^T-1} \mathcal{P}\left(S_m^T\right) H\left(x - \mathrm{Tr}\{\phi(\infty, S_m^T)\}\right). \tag{57}$$

3.3 Monotonic approximation of the bounds to $F(x)$

In this section we show that the bounds $\underline{F}^T(x)$ and $\overline{F}^T(x)$ in (24) approach monotonically $F(x)$, as T tends to infinity. This is stated in the following theorem.

Theorem 3.1. *We have that*

$$\underline{F}^{T+1}(x) \geq \underline{F}^T(x) \tag{58}$$

$$\overline{F}^{T+1}(x) \leq \overline{F}^T(x). \tag{59}$$

Moreover, the bounds $\underline{F}^T(x)$ and $\overline{F}^T(x)$ approach monotonically the true CDF $F(x)$ as T tends to ∞.

Proof: Let S_m^T be a sequence of length T. From (17) and Lemma 3.1 and for any $P_0 > 0$, we have

$$\phi(P_0, \{S_m^T, 0\}) = \phi(\Phi_0(P_0), S_m^T) \leq \phi(\infty, S_m^T). \tag{60}$$

From the monotonicity of $\phi(\cdot, S_m^T)$ and $\Phi_0(\cdot)$, stated in Lemma 3.1 we have

$$\phi(P_0, \{S_m^T, 0\}) = \phi(\Phi_0(P_0), S_m^T) \geq \phi(P_0, S_m^T) \tag{61}$$

which implies that

$$\phi(\infty, \{S_m^T, 0\}) \geq \phi(\infty, S_m^T). \tag{62}$$

From (60) and (62), we have

$$\phi(\infty, \{S_m^T, 0\}) = \phi(\infty, S_m^T). \tag{63}$$

Also, if the matrix O (defined in Lemma 3.2) resulting from the sequence S_m^T has full column rank, then so has the same matrix resulting from the sequence $\{S_m^T, 1\}$. This implies that

$$\phi(\infty, \{S_m^T, 1\}) \leq \phi(\infty, S_m^T). \tag{64}$$

Now, from Lemma 3.1, $\Phi_0(\underline{P}) \geq \underline{P}$, and therefore,

$$\phi(\underline{P}, \{S_m^T, 0\}) = \phi(\Phi_0(\underline{P}), S_m^T) \tag{65}$$

$$\geq \phi(\underline{P}, S_m^T). \tag{66}$$

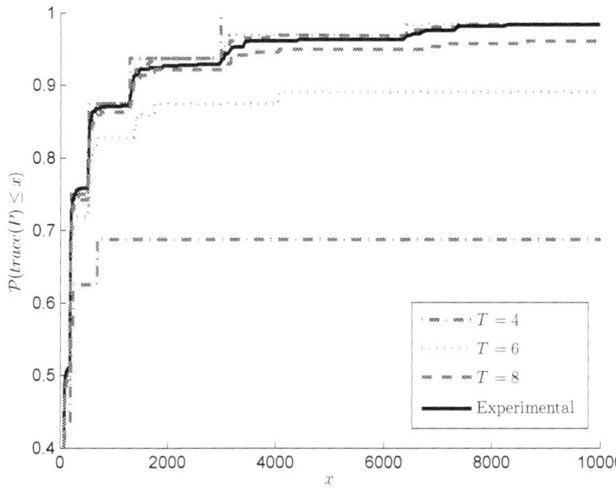

Fig. 1. Upper and lower bounds for the Error Covariance.

Also, since $\Phi_1(\underline{P}) = \underline{P}$, we have that

$$\phi(\underline{P}, \{S_m^T, 1\}) = \phi(\phi_1(\underline{P}), S_m^T) \tag{67}$$
$$= \phi(\underline{P}, S_m^T). \tag{68}$$

Hence, for any binary variable γ, we have that

$$\phi(\infty, \{S_m^T, \gamma\}) \leq \phi(\infty, S_m^T) \tag{69}$$
$$\phi(\underline{P}, \{S_m^T, \gamma\}) \geq \phi(\underline{P}, S_m^T). \tag{70}$$

Now notice that the bounds (29) and (57) only differ in the position of the step functions $H(\cdot)$. Hence, the result follows from (69) and (70). ∎

3.4 Example

Consider the system below, which is taken from Sinopoli et al. (2004),

$$A = \begin{bmatrix} 1.25 & 0 \\ 1 & 1.1 \end{bmatrix} \quad C = \begin{bmatrix} 1 \\ 1 \end{bmatrix}' \qquad Q = \begin{bmatrix} 20 & 0 \\ 0 & 20 \end{bmatrix} \quad R = 2.5, \tag{71}$$

with $\lambda = 0.5$. In Figure 1 we show the upper bound $\overline{F}^T(x)$ and the lower bound $\underline{F}^T(x)$, for $T = 3$, $T = 5$ and $T = 8$. We also show an estimate of the true CDF $F(x)$ obtained from a Monte Carlo simulation using $10,000$ runs. Notice that, as T increases, the bounds become tighter, and for $T = 8$, it is hard to distinguish between the lower and the upper bounds.

4. Bounds for the expected error covariance

In this section we derive upper and lower bounds for the trace G of the asymptotic EEC, i.e.,

$$G = \lim_{t\to\infty} \text{Tr}\{E\{P_t\}\}. \quad (72)$$

Since P_t is positive-semidefinite, we have that,

$$\text{Tr}\{E\{P_t\}\} = \int_0^\infty (1 - F^t(x))dx. \quad (73)$$

Hence, [2]

$$G = \int_0^\infty (1 - \lim_{t\to\infty} F^t(x))dx \quad (75)$$

$$= \int_0^\infty (1 - F(x))dx \quad (76)$$

4.1 Lower bounds for the EEC

In view of (76), a lower bound for G, can be obtained from an upper bound of $F(x)$. One such bound is $\overline{F}^T(x)$, derived in Section 3.1. A limitation of $\overline{F}^T(x)$ is that $\overline{F}^T(x) = 1$, for all $x > \phi(\underline{P}, S_0^T)$, hence it is too conservative for large values of x. To go around this, we introduce an alternative upper bound for $F(x)$, denoted by $\overline{F}_\star(x)$.
Our strategy for doing so is to group the sequences S_m^T, $m = 0, 1, \cdots, 2^T - 1$, according to the number of consecutive lost measurements at its end. Then, from each group, we only consider the worst sequence, i.e., the one producing the smallest EEC trace.
Notice that the sequences S_m^T with $m < 2^{T-z}$, $0 \le z \le T$, are those having the last z elements equal to zero. Then, from (25) and (26), it follows that

$$\underset{0\le m<2^{T-z}}{\arg\min}\, \text{Tr}\{\phi(X, S_m^T)\} = 2^{T-z} - 1, \quad (77)$$

i.e., from all sequences with z zeroes at its end, the one that produces the smallest EEC trace has its first $T - z$ elements equal to one. Using this, an upper bound for $F(x)$ is given by

$$F(x) \le \overline{F}_\star(x) \triangleq 1 - (1 - \lambda)^{k(x)} \quad (78)$$

where

$$k(x) = \begin{cases} 0, & x \le \underline{P} \\ \min\left\{j : \text{Tr}\left(\phi(\underline{P}, S_0^j)\right) > x\right\}, & x > \underline{P}. \end{cases} \quad (79)$$

---

[2] Following the argument in Theorem 3.1, it can be verified that $(1 - F^t(x)) \le \overline{F}(x)$ with

$$\overline{F}(x) = \begin{cases} 1 & x \le \text{Tr}\{P_0\} \\ F(x) & x > \text{Tr}\{P_0\}. \end{cases} \quad (74)$$

Hence, using Lebesgue's dominated convergence theorem, the limit can be exchanged with the integral whenever $\int_0^\infty (1 - F(x))dx < \infty$, i.e., whenever the asymptotic EEC is finite.

We can now use both $\overline{F}^T(x)$ and $\overline{F}_\star(x)$ to obtain a lower bound $\underline{G}^T$ for G as follows

$$\underline{G}^T = \int_0^\infty 1 - \min\{\overline{F}^T(x), \overline{F}_\star(x)\}dx. \tag{80}$$

The next lemma states the regions in which each bound is less conservative.

Lemma 4.1. *The following properties hold true:*

$$\overline{F}^T(x) \leq \overline{F}_\star(x), \ \forall x \leq \operatorname{Tr}\left(\phi(\underline{P}, S_0^T)\right) \tag{81}$$

$$\overline{F}^T(x) > \overline{F}_\star(x), \ \forall x > \operatorname{Tr}\left(\phi(\underline{P}, S_0^T)\right). \tag{82}$$

Proof: Define

$$Z(i,j) \triangleq \operatorname{Tr}\left(\phi(\underline{P}, S_i^j)\right). \tag{83}$$

To prove (81), notice that $\overline{F}^T(x)$ can be written as

$$\overline{F}^T(x) = \sum_{\substack{j=0 \\ j:Z(j,T)\leq x}}^{2^T-1} \mathcal{P}(S_j^T). \tag{84}$$

Substituting $x = Z(0,K)$ we have for all $1 < K \leq T$

$$\overline{F}^T(Z(0,K)) = \sum_{\substack{j=0 \\ j:Z(j,T)\leq Z(0,K)}}^{2^T-1} \mathcal{P}(S_j^T) \tag{85}$$

$$= 1 - \sum_{\substack{j=0 \\ j:Z(j,T)> Z(0,K)}}^{2^T-1} \mathcal{P}(S_j^T) \tag{86}$$

Now, notice that the summation in (86) includes, but is not limited to, all the sequences finishing with K zeroes. Hence

$$\sum_{\substack{j=0 \\ j:Z(j,T)> Z(0,K)}}^{2^T-1} \mathcal{P}(S_j^T) \geq (1-\lambda)^K \tag{87}$$

and we have

$$\overline{F}^T(Z(0,K)) \leq 1 - (1-\lambda)^K \tag{88}$$

$$= \overline{F}_\star(Z(0,K)). \tag{89}$$

Proving (82) is trivial, since $\overline{F}^T(x) = 1, x > Z(0,T)$. ∎

We can now present a sequence of lower bounds $\underline{G}^T$, $T \in \mathbb{N}$, for the EEC G. We do so in the next theorem.

Theorem 4.1. *Let E_j, $0 < j \leq 2^T$ denote the set of numbers* $\text{Tr}\left(\phi(\underline{P}, S_m^T)\right)$, $0 \leq m < 2^T$, *arranged in ascending order, (i.e.,* $E_j = \text{Tr}\left(\phi(\underline{P}, S_{m_j}^T)\right)$, *for some m_j, and $E_1 \leq E_1 \leq \cdots < E_{2^T}$). For each $0 < j \leq 2^T$, let $\pi_j = \sum_{k=0}^{m_j} \mathcal{P}(S_k^T)$. Also define $E_0 = \pi_0 = 0$. Then, $\underline{G}^T$ defined in (80) is given by*

$$\underline{G}^T = \underline{G}_1^T + \underline{G}_2^T \tag{90}$$

where

$$\underline{G}_1^T = \sum_{j=0}^{2^T-1} (1-\pi_j)(E_{j+1} - E_j) \tag{91}$$

$$\underline{G}_2^T = \sum_{j=T}^{\infty} (1-\lambda)^j \text{Tr}\left\{A^j \left(A\underline{P}A' + Q - \underline{P}\right) A'^j\right\} \tag{92}$$

Moreover, if the following condition holds

$$\max |\text{eig}(A)|^2 (1-\lambda) < 1, \tag{93}$$

and A is diagonalizable, i.e., it can be written as

$$A = VDV^{-1}, \tag{94}$$

with D diagonal, then,

$$\underline{G}_2^T = \text{Tr}\{\Gamma\} - \sum_{j=0}^{T-1} (1-\lambda)^j \text{Tr}\left\{A^j \left(A\underline{P}A' + Q - \underline{P}\right) A'^j\right\} \tag{95}$$

where

$$\Gamma \triangleq \left(X^{1/2} V'^{-1} \otimes V\right) \Delta \left(X^{1/2} V'^{-1} \otimes V\right)' \tag{96}$$

$$X \triangleq A\underline{P}A' + Q - \underline{P}. \tag{97}$$

Also, the $n^2 \times n^2$ matrix Δ is such that its i,j-th entry $[\Delta]_{i,j}$ is given by

$$[\Delta]_{i,j} \triangleq \frac{1}{1 - (1-\lambda)[\overrightarrow{D}]_i [\overrightarrow{D}]_j}, \tag{98}$$

where $\overrightarrow{D}$ denotes a column vector formed by stacking the columns of D, i.e.,

$$\overrightarrow{D} \triangleq \left[[D]_{1,1} \cdots [D]_{n,1} \; [D]_{1,2} \cdots [D]_{n,n} \right]' \tag{99}$$

Proof: In view of lemma 4.1, (90) can be written as

$$\underline{G}^T = \int_0^{Z(0,T)} (1 - \overline{F}^T(x))dx + \int_{Z(0,T)}^{\infty} (1 - \overline{F}_\star(x))dx \tag{100}$$

Now, $\overline{F}^T(x)$ can be written as

$$\overline{F}^T(x) = \pi_{i(x)},\ i(x) = \max\{i:\ E_i < x\}. \tag{101}$$

In view of (101), it is easy to verify that

$$\int_0^{Z(0,T)} 1 - \overline{F}^T(x)dx = \sum_{j=1}^{2^T}(1-\pi_j)(E_j - E_{j-1}) = \underline{G}_1^T. \tag{102}$$

The second term of (90) can be written using the definition of $\overline{F}_\star(x)$ as

$$\int_{Z(0,T)}^{\infty} 1 - \tilde{F}(x)dx = \sum_{j=T}^{\infty}(1-\lambda)^j\left(Z(0,j+1) - Z(0,j)\right) \tag{103}$$

$$= \sum_{j=T}^{\infty}(1-\lambda)^j \mathrm{Tr}\left\{A^j\left(A\underline{P}A' + Q - \underline{P}\right)A'^j\right\} \tag{104}$$

$$= \underline{G}_2^T. \tag{105}$$

and (90) follows from (100), (102) and (105).
To show (95), we use Lemma 7.1 (in the Appendix), with $b = (1-\lambda)$ and $X = A\underline{P}A' + Q - \underline{P}$, to obtain

$$\sum_{j=0}^{\infty}(1-\lambda)^j \mathrm{Tr}\left\{A^j\left(A\underline{P}A' + Q - \underline{P}\right)A'^j\right\} = \mathrm{Tr}\{\Gamma\}. \tag{106}$$

The result then follows immediately. ■

4.2 Upper bounds for the EEC

Using an argument similar to the one in the previous section, we will use lower bounds of the CDF to derive a family of upper bounds $\overline{G}^{T,N}$, $T \le N \in \mathbb{N}$, of G. Notice that, in general, there exists $\delta > 0$ such that $1 - \underline{F}^T(x) > \delta$, for all x. Hence, using $\underline{F}^T(x)$ in (76) will result in $\overline{G}$ being infinite valued. To avoid this, we will present two alternative lower bounds for $F(x)$, which we denote by $\underline{F}_\star^{T,N}(x)$ and $\underline{F}_\diamond^N(x)$.
Recall that $A \in \mathbb{R}^{n\times n}$, and define

$$N_0 \triangleq \min\left\{k\ :\ \mathrm{rank}\left(\begin{bmatrix} C \\ CA \\ CA^2 \\ \vdots \\ CA^{k-1}\end{bmatrix}\right) = n\right\}. \tag{107}$$

The lower bounds $\underline{F}_\star^{T,N}(x)$ and $\underline{F}_\diamond^N(x)$ are stated in the following two lemmas.

Lemma 4.2. *Let $T \le N \in \mathbb{N}$, with $N_0 \le T$ and N satisfying*

$$|S_m^N| \ge N_0 \Rightarrow \mathrm{Tr}\{\phi(\infty, S_m^N)\} < \infty. \tag{108}$$

For each $T \leq n \leq N$, let

$$\overline{P}^*(n) \triangleq \max_{m:|S_m^n|=N_0} \phi(\infty, S_m^n) \tag{109}$$

$$\overline{p}^*(n) \triangleq \text{Tr}(\overline{P}^*(n)). \tag{110}$$

Then, for all $\overline{p}^*(T) \leq x \leq \overline{p}^*(N)$,

$$F(x) \geq \underline{F}_\star^{T,N}(x), \tag{111}$$

where, for each $T \leq n < N$ and all $\overline{p}^*(n) \leq x \leq \overline{p}^*(n+1)$,

$$\underline{F}_\star^{T,N}(x) = 1 - \sum_{l=0}^{N_0-1} \lambda^l (1-\lambda)^{n-l} \frac{n!}{l!(n-l)!}. \tag{112}$$

Remark 4.1. *Lemma 4.2 above requires the existence of an integer constant N satisfying* (108). *Notice that such constant always exists since* (108) *is trivially satisfied by* N_0.

Proof: We first show that, for all $T \leq n < N$,

$$\overline{p}^*(n) < \overline{p}^*(n+1). \tag{113}$$

To see this, suppose we add a zero at the end of the sequence used to generate $\overline{p}^*(n)$. Doing so we have

$$\overline{P}^*(n) < \Phi_0\left(\overline{P}^*(n)\right) \leq \overline{P}^*(n+1). \tag{114}$$

Now, for a given n, we can obtain a lower bound for $F^n(x)$ by considering in (57) that $\text{Tr}(\phi(\infty, S_m^n)) = \infty$, whenever $|S_m^n| < N_0$. Also, from (25) we have that if $|S_m^n| \geq N_0$, then $\text{Tr}(\phi(\infty, S_m^n)) < \overline{p}^*(n)$. Hence, a lower bound for $F(x)$ is given by $\mathcal{P}(|S_m^n| < N_0)$, for $x \geq \overline{p}^*(n)$.

Finally, the result follows by noting that the probability to observe sequences S_m^n with m such that $|S_m^n| < N_0$ is given by

$$\mathcal{P}(|S_m^n| < N_0) = 1 - \sum_{l=0}^{N_0-1} \lambda^l (1-\lambda)^{n-l} \frac{n!}{l!(n-l)!}, \tag{115}$$

since $\lambda^l (1-\lambda)^{n-l}$ is the probability to receive a given sequence S_m^n with $|S_m^n| = l$, and the number of sequences of length n with l ones is given by the binomial coefficient

$$\binom{n}{l} = \frac{n!}{l!(n-l)!}. \tag{116}$$

■

Lemma 4.3. *Let N, $\overline{P}^*(N)$ and $\overline{p}^*(N)$ be as defined in Lemma 4.2, and let $L = \sum_{n=0}^{N_0-1} \binom{N}{n}$. Then, for all $x \geq \overline{p}^*(N)$,*

$$F(x) \geq \underline{F}_\diamond^N(x), \tag{117}$$

where, for each $n \in \mathbb{N}$ *and all* $\phi(\overline{P}^*(N), S_0^{n-1}) \leq x < \phi(\overline{P}^*(N), S_0^n)$,

$$\underline{F}_\diamond^N(x) = 1 - u'M^n z \tag{118}$$

with the vectors $u, z \in \mathbb{R}^L$ *defined by*

$$u = \begin{bmatrix} 1 \, 1 \cdots 1 \end{bmatrix}' \tag{119}$$

$$z = \begin{bmatrix} 1 \, 0 \cdots 0 \end{bmatrix}'. \tag{120}$$

The i, j*-th entry of the matrix* $M \in \mathbb{R}^{L \times L}$ *is given by*

$$[M]_{i,j} = \begin{cases} \lambda, & Z_i^N = U_+(Z_j^N, 1) \\ 1 - \lambda, & Z_i^N = U_+(Z_j^N, 0) \\ 0, & \text{otherwise.} \end{cases} \tag{121}$$

where Z_m^N, $m = 0, \cdots, L-1$ *denotes the set of sequences of length* N *with less than* N_0 *ones, with* $Z_0^N = S_0^N$, *but otherwise arranged in any arbitrary order (i.e.,*

$$|Z_m^N| < N_0 \text{ for all } m = 0, \cdots, L-1. \tag{122}$$

and $Z_m^N = S_{n_m}^N$, *for some* $n_m \in \{0, \cdots, 2^N - 1\}$*). Also, for* $\gamma \in \{0, 1\}$, *the operation* $U_+(Z_m^T, \gamma)$ *is defined by*

$$U_+(Z_m^T, \gamma) = \{Z_m^T(2), Z_m^T(3), \cdots, Z_m^T(T), \gamma\}. \tag{123}$$

Proof: The proof follows an argument similar to the one used in the proof of Lemma 4.2. In this case, for each n, we obtain a lower bound for $\underline{F}^n(x)$ by considering in (57) that $\text{Tr}(\phi(\infty, S_m^n)) = \infty$, whenever S_m^n does not contain a subsequence of length N with at least N_0 ones. Also, if S_m^n contains such a subsequence, the resulting EC is smaller that or equal to

$$\phi(\infty, \{S_{m^*}^N, S_0^n\}) = \phi(\phi(\infty, S_{m^*}^N), S_0^n) \tag{124}$$

$$= \phi(\overline{P}^*(N), S_0^n), \tag{125}$$

where $S_{m^*}^N$ denotes the sequence required to obtain $\overline{P}^*(N)$.
To conclude the proof we need to compute the probability $p_{N,n}$ of receiving a sequence of length $N + n$ that does not contain a subsequence of length N with at least N_0 ones. This is done in Lemma 7.2 (in the Appendix), where it is shown that

$$p_{N,n} = u'M^n z. \tag{126}$$

■

Now, for a given T and N, we can obtain an upper bound $\overline{G}^{T,N}$ for G using the lower bounds $\underline{F}^T(x)$, $\underline{F}_\star^{T,N}(x)$ and $\underline{F}_\diamond^N(x)$, as follows

$$\overline{G}^{T,N} = \int_0^\infty 1 - \max\{\underline{F}^T(x), \underline{F}_\star^{T,N}(x), \underline{F}_\diamond^N(x)\} dx. \tag{127}$$

We do so in the next theorem.

Theorem 4.2. *Let T and N be two given positive integers with $N_0 \leq T \leq N$ and such that for all $0 \leq m < 2^N$, $|S_m^N| \geq N_0 \Rightarrow \phi(\infty, S_m^N) < \infty$. Let J be the number of sequences such that $O(S_m^T)$ has full column rank. Let $E_0 \triangleq 0$ and $E_j, 0 < j \leq J$ denote the set of numbers* $\mathrm{Tr}\left(\phi(\infty, S_m^T)\right), 0 < m \leq J$, *arranged in ascending order, (i.e., $E_j = \mathrm{Tr}\left(\phi(\infty, S_{m_j}^T)\right)$, for some m_j, and $E_0 \leq E_1 \leq \cdots \leq E_f$). For each $0 \leq j < J$, let $\pi_j = \sum_{k=0}^{m_j} \mathcal{P}(S_k^T)$, and let M, u and v be as defined as in Lemma 4.3. Then, an upper bound for the EEC is given by*

$$G \leq \overline{G}^{T,N}, \tag{128}$$

where

$$\overline{G}^{T,N} = \mathrm{Tr}(\overline{G}_1^T + \overline{G}_2^{T,N} + \overline{G}_3^N), \tag{129}$$

and

$$\overline{G}_1^T = \sum_{j=0}^{J}(1-\pi_j)(E_{j+1} - E_j) \tag{130}$$

$$\overline{G}_2^{T,N} = \sum_{j=T}^{N-1}\sum_{l=0}^{N_0-1} \lambda^l (1-\lambda)^{j-l} \frac{j!}{l!(j-l)!}\left(\overline{P}^*(j+1) - \overline{P}^*(j)\right) \tag{131}$$

$$\overline{G}_3^N = \sum_{j=0}^{\infty} u' M^{N+j} z\{A^j(A\overline{P}^*(N)A' + Q - \overline{P}^*(N))A'^j\}. \tag{132}$$

Moreover, if A is diagonalizable, i.e.

$$A = VDV^{-1}, \tag{133}$$

with D diagonal, and

$$\max|\mathrm{eig}(A)|^2 \rho < 1, \tag{134}$$

where

$$\rho = (\max|\mathrm{sv}M|), \tag{135}$$

then the EEC is finite and

$$\overline{G}_3^N \leq u' M^N z \mathrm{Tr}(\Gamma^\star), \tag{136}$$

where

$$\Gamma^\star \triangleq \left(X^{1/2} V'^{-1} \otimes V\right) \Delta \left(X^{1/2} V'^{-1} \otimes V\right)' \tag{137}$$

$$X \triangleq A\underline{P}A' + Q - \underline{P}. \tag{138}$$

Also, the i,j-th entry $[\Delta]_{i,j}$ of the $n^2 \times n^2$ matrix Δ is given by

$$[\Delta]_{i,j} \triangleq \frac{\sqrt{2^{N_0}-1}}{1-\rho[\overrightarrow{D}]_i[\overrightarrow{D}]_j}. \tag{139}$$

Proof: First, notice that $\underline{F}^T(x)$ is defined for all $x > 0$, whereas $\underline{F}_\star^T(x)$ is defined on the range $\overline{P}^\star(T) < x \leq \overline{P}^\star(N)$ and $\underline{F}_\diamond^T(x)$ on $\overline{P}^\star(N) < x$. Now, for all $x \geq \overline{p}^*(T)$, we have

$$\underline{F}^T(x) = \sum_{j:|S_j^T|\geq N_0} \mathcal{P}(S_j^T) = 1 - \sum_{l=0}^{N_0-1} \lambda^l (1-\lambda)^{T-l} \frac{T!}{l!(T-l)!}, \tag{140}$$

which equals the probability of receiving a sequence of length T with N_0 or more ones. Now, for each integer $1 < n < N - T$, and for $\overline{p}^*(T+n) \leq x < \overline{p}^*(T+n+1)$, $\underline{F}_\star^{T,N}(x)$ represents the probability of receiving a sequence of length $T+n$ with more than or exactly N_0 ones. Hence, $\underline{F}_\star^{T,N}(x)$ is greater than $\underline{F}^T(x)$ on the range $\overline{P}^\star(T) < x \leq \overline{P}^\star(N)$. Also, $\underline{F}_\diamond^N(x)$ measures the probability of receiving a sequence of length N with a subsequence of length T with N_0 or more ones. Hence, it is greater than $\underline{F}^T(x)$ on $\overline{P}^\star(N) < x$. Therefore, we have that

$$\max\{\underline{F}^T(x), \underline{F}_\star^{T,N}(x), \underline{F}_\diamond^N(x)\} = \begin{cases} \underline{F}^T(x), & x \leq \overline{p}^*(T) \\ \underline{F}_\star^{T,N}(x), & \overline{p}^*(T) < x \leq \overline{p}^*(N) \\ \underline{F}_\diamond^N(x), & \overline{p}^*(N) < x. \end{cases} \tag{141}$$

We will use each of these three bounds to compute each term in (129). To obtain (130), notice that $\underline{F}^T(x)$ can be written as

$$\underline{F}^T(x) = \pi_{i(x)}, \; i(x) = \max\{i : E_i < x\}. \tag{142}$$

In view of the above, we have that

$$\int_0^{\overline{p}^*(T)} (1 - \underline{F}^T(x))dx = \sum_{j=0}^{J} (1-\pi_j)(E_{j+1} - E_j) = \overline{G}_1^T. \tag{143}$$

Using the definition of $\underline{F}_\star^{T,N}(x)$ in (112) we obtain

$$\int_{\overline{p}^*(T)}^{\overline{p}^*(N)} (1 - \underline{F}_\star^{T,N}(x))dx = \sum_{j=T}^{N-1} \sum_{l=0}^{N_0-1} \lambda^l (1-\lambda)^{j-l} \frac{j!}{l!(j-l)!} \left(\overline{P}^*(j+1) - \overline{P}^*(j)\right) \tag{144}$$

$$= \overline{G}_2^{T,N}. \tag{145}$$

Similarly, the definition of $\underline{F}_\diamond^N(x)$ in (118) can be used to obtain

$$\int_{\overline{p}^*(N)}^{\infty} (1 - \underline{F}_\diamond^N(x))dx = \sum_{j=0}^{\infty} u' M^j z \mathrm{Tr}\{A^j (A\overline{P}^*(N)A' + Q - \overline{P}^*(N))A'^j\} = \overline{G}_3^{T,N}. \tag{146}$$

To conclude the proof, notice that

$$\begin{aligned} uM^j z &= < u, M^j z > & (147)\\ &\leq \|u\|_2 \|M^j z\|_2 & (148)\\ &\leq \|u\|_2 \|M^j\| \|z\|_2 & (149)\\ &\leq \|u\|_2 \|M\|^j \|z\|_2 & (150)\\ &= \|u\|_2 (\max \mathrm{sv} M)^j \|z\|_2 & (151)\\ &= \sqrt{2^{N_0} - 1} (\max \mathrm{sv} M)^j. & (152) \end{aligned}$$

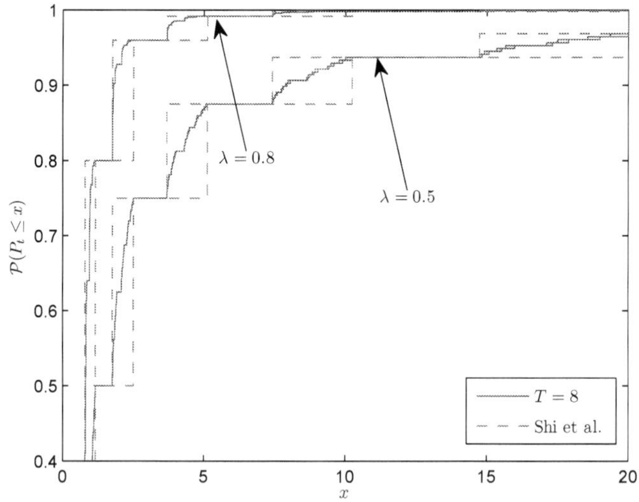

Fig. 2. Comparison of the bounds of the Cumulative Distribution Function.

where $\max \text{sv} M$ denotes the maximum singular value of M. Then, to obtain (136), we use the result in Lemma 7.1 (in the Appendix) with $b = \max \text{sv} M$ and $X = A\overline{P}^*(N)A' + Q - \overline{P}^*(N)$. ■

5. Examples

In this section we present a numerical comparison of our results with those available in the literature.

5.1 Bounds on the CDF

In Shi et al. (2010), the bounds of the CDF are given in terms of the probability to observe missing measurements in a row. Consider the scalar system below, taken from Shi et al. (2010).

$$A = 1.4, \ C = 1, \ Q = 0.2, \ R = 0.5 \tag{153}$$

We consider two different measurement arrival probabilities (i.e., $\lambda = 0.5$ and $\lambda = 0.8$) and compute the upper and lower bounds for the CDF. We do so using the expressions derived in Section 3, as well as those given in Shi et al. (2010). We see in Figure 2 how our proposed bounds are significantly tighter.

5.2 Bounds on the EEC

In this section we compare our proposed EEC bounds with those in Sinopoli et al. (2004) and Rohr et al. (2010).

Bound	Lower	Upper
From Sinopoli et al. (2004)	4.57	11.96
From Rohr et al. (2010)	-	10.53
Proposed	10.53	11.14

Table 1. Comparison of EEC bounds using a scalar system.

Bound	Lower	Upper
From Sinopoli et al. (2004)	2.15×10^4	2.53×10^5
From Rohr et al. (2010)	-	1.5×10^5
Proposed	9.54×10^4	3.73×10^5

Table 2. Comparison of EEC bounds using a system with a single unstable eigenvalue.

5.2.1 Scalar example

Consider the scalar system (153) with $\lambda = 0.5$. For the lower bound (90) we use $T = 14$, and for the upper bound (129) we use $T = N = 14$. Notice that in the scalar case $N_0 = 1$, that is, whenever a measurement is received, an upper bound for the EC is promptly available and using $N > T$ will not give any advantage. Also, for the upper bound in Rohr et al. (2010), we use a window length of 14 sampling times (notice that no lower bound for the EEC is proposed in Rohr et al. (2010)).
In Table 1 we compare the bounds resulting from the three works. We see that although the three upper bounds are roughly similar, our proposed lower bound is significantly tighter than that resulting from Sinopoli et al. (2004).

5.2.2 Example with single unstable eigenvalue

Consider the following system, taken from Sinopoli et al. (2004), where $\lambda = 0.5$ and

$$A = \begin{bmatrix} 1.25 & 1 & 0 \\ 0 & 0.9 & 7 \\ 0 & 0 & 0.6 \end{bmatrix} \quad C' = \begin{bmatrix} 1 \; 0 \; 2 \end{bmatrix} \qquad \qquad (154)$$
$$R = 2.5 \qquad Q = 20I.$$

Table 2 compares the same bounds described above, with $T = 10$ and $N = 40$. The same conclusion applies.

6. Conclusion

We considered a Kalman filter for a discrete-time linear system whose output is intermittently sampled according to an independent sequence of binary random variables. We derived lower and upper bounds for the CDF of the EC, as well as for the EEC. These bounds can be made arbitrarily tight, at the expense of increased computational complexity. We presented numerical examples demonstrating that the proposed bounds are tighter than those derived using other available methods.

7. Appendix

Lemma 7.1. *Let $0 \leq b \leq 1$ be a scalar, $X \in \mathbb{R}^{n\times n}$ be a positive-semidefinite matrix and $A \in \mathbb{R}^{n\times n}$ be diagonalizable, i.e., it can be written as*

$$A = VDV^{-1}, \tag{155}$$

with D diagonal. If

$$\max \text{eig}(A)^2 b < 1, \tag{156}$$

then,

$$\text{Tr}\left(\sum_{j=0}^{\infty} b^j A^j X A'^j\right) = \text{Tr}(\Gamma) \tag{157}$$

where

$$\Gamma \triangleq \left(X^{1/2}V'^{-1} \otimes V\right) \Delta \left(X^{1/2}V'^{-1} \otimes V\right)' \tag{158}$$

with $\otimes$ denoting the Kronecker product. The $n^2 \times n^2$ matrix Δ is such that its i,j-th entry $[\Delta]_{i,j}$ is given by

$$[\Delta]_{i,j} \triangleq \frac{1}{1 - b[\overrightarrow{D}]_i[\overrightarrow{D}]_j}, \tag{159}$$

where $\overrightarrow{D}$ denotes a column vector formed by stacking the columns of D, i.e.,

$$\overrightarrow{D} \triangleq \left[\, [D]_{1,1} \cdots [D]_{n,1}\ [D]_{1,2} \cdots [D]_{n,n} \right]'. \tag{160}$$

Proof: For any matrix

$$B = \begin{bmatrix} B_{1,1} & B_{1,2} & \dots & B_{1,n} \\ B_{2,1} & B_{2,2} & \dots & B_{2,n} \\ \vdots & \vdots & \ddots & \vdots \\ B_{n,1} & B_{n,2} & \dots & B_{n,n} \end{bmatrix} \tag{161}$$

with $B_{i,j} \in \mathbb{R}^{n\times n}$, we define the following linear transformation

$$\mathcal{D}_n(B) = \sum_{j=1}^{n} B_{j,j}. \tag{162}$$

Now, substituting (155) in (157), and using the vectorization operation $\overrightarrow{\cdot}$ defined above we have

$$\sum_{j=0}^{\infty} b^j A^j X A'^j = \sum_{j=0}^{\infty} b^j V D^j V^{-1} X^{1/2} \left(V D^j V^{-1} X^{1/2}\right)' \tag{163}$$

$$= \sum_{j=0}^{\infty} \mathcal{D}_n \left[b^j \overrightarrow{V D^j V^{-1} X^{1/2}} \left(\overrightarrow{V D^j V^{-1} X^{1/2}}\right)' \right] \tag{164}$$

$$= \mathcal{D}_n \left[\left(X^{1/2}V'^{-1} \otimes V\right) \sum_{j=0}^{\infty} b^j \overrightarrow{D^j}\, \overrightarrow{D^j}' \left(X^{1/2}V'^{-1} \otimes V\right)' \right], \tag{165}$$

where the last equality follows from the property

$$\overrightarrow{ABC} = (C' \otimes A)\overrightarrow{B}. \tag{166}$$

Let $\delta_{i,j}$ denote the i,j-th entry of $b\overrightarrow{D}\overrightarrow{D}'$, and $\mathrm{pow}(Y,j)$ denote the matrix obtained after elevating each entry of Y to the j-th power. Then, if every entry of $b\overrightarrow{D}\overrightarrow{D}'$ has magnitude smaller than one, we have that

$$\left[\sum_{j=0}^{\infty} b^j \overrightarrow{(D)^j}\,\overrightarrow{(D)^j}'\right]_{i,j} = \left[\sum_{j=0}^{\infty} \mathrm{pow}(b\overrightarrow{D}\overrightarrow{D}',j)\right]_{i,j} \tag{167}$$

$$= \frac{1}{1-\delta_{i,j}}. \tag{168}$$

where $[Y]_{i,j}$ denotes the i,j-th entry of Y. Notice that $\overrightarrow{D}\overrightarrow{D}'$ if formed by the products of the eigenvalues of A, so the series will converge if and only if

$$\max\ \mathrm{eig}(A)^2 b < 1. \tag{169}$$

Putting (168) into (165), we have that

$$\sum_{j=0}^{\infty} b^j A^j X A'^j = \mathcal{D}_n\left[\left(X^{1/2}V'^{-1}\otimes V\right)\Delta\left(X^{1/2}V'^{-1}\otimes V\right)'\right] \tag{170}$$

$$= \mathcal{D}_n(\Gamma) \tag{171}$$

and the result follows since $\mathrm{Tr}\{\mathcal{D}_n\{Y\}\} = \mathrm{Tr}\{Y\}$. ∎

Lemma 7.2. *Let u, z, N_0, L and M be as defined in Lemma 4.3. The probability $p_{N,n}$ of receiving a sequence of length $N+n$ that does not contain a subsequence of length N with at least N_0 ones is given by*

$$p_{N,n} = uM^{N+n}z. \tag{172}$$

Proof:
Let Z_m^N, $m = 0,\cdots,L-1$, and $U_+(Z_m^T,\gamma)$ be as defined in Lemma (4.3). Also, for each $N,t \in \mathbb{N}$, define the random sequence $V_t^N = \{\gamma_t,\gamma_{t-1},\cdots,\gamma_{t-N+1}\}$. Let W_t be the probability distribution of the sequences Z_m^N, i.e.

$$W_t = \begin{bmatrix} \mathcal{P}(V_t^N = Z_0^N) \\ \mathcal{P}(V_t^N = Z_1^N) \\ \cdots \\ \mathcal{P}(V_t^N = Z_{L-1}^N) \end{bmatrix}. \tag{173}$$

One can write a recursive equation for W_{t+1} as

$$W_{t+1} = MW_t. \tag{174}$$

Hence, for a given n, the distribution W_n of V_n^N is given by

$$W_n = M^n W_0. \tag{175}$$

To obtain the initial distribution W_0, we make $V_{-N}^N = Z_0^N$, which gives

$$W_{-N} = z. \tag{176}$$

Then, applying (175), we obtain

$$W_0 = M^N z. \tag{177}$$

Finally, to obtain the probability $p_{N,n}$, we add all the entries of the vector W_n by pre-multiplying W_n by u. Doing so, and substituting (177) in (175), we obtain

$$p_{N,n} = u M^{N+n} z. \tag{178}$$

■

8. References

Anderson, B. & Moore, J. (1979). *Optimal filtering*, Prentice-Hall Englewood Cliffs, NJ.

Ben-Israel, A. & Greville, T. N. E. (2003). *Generalized inverses*, CMS Books in Mathematics/Ouvrages de Mathématiques de la SMC, 15, second edn, Springer-Verlag, New York. Theory and applications.

Dana, A., Gupta, V., Hespanha, J., Hassibi, B. & Murray, R. (2007). Estimation over communication networks: Performance bounds and achievability results, *American Control Conference, 2007. ACC '07* pp. 3450 –3455.

Faridani, H. M. (1986). Performance of kalman filter with missing measurements, *Automatica* 22(1): 117–120.

Liu, X. & Goldsmith, A. (2004). Kalman filtering with partial observation losses, *IEEE Control and Decision* .

Rohr, E., Marelli, D. & Fu, M. (2010). Statistical properties of the error covariance in a kalman filter with random measurement losses, *Decision and Control, 2010. CDC 2010. 49th IEEE Conference on*.

Schenato, L. (2008). Optimal estimation in networked control systems subject to random delay and packet drop, *IEEE Transactions on Automatic Control* 53(5): 1311–1317.

Schenato, L., Sinopoli, B., Franceschetti, M., Poolla, K. & Sastry, S. (2007). Foundations of control and estimation over lossy networks, *Proc .IEEE* 95(1): 163.

Shi, L., Epstein, M. & Murray, R. (2010). Kalman filtering over a packet-dropping network: A probabilistic perspective, *Automatic Control, IEEE Transactions on* 55(3): 594 –604.

Sinopoli, B., Schenato, L., Franceschetti, M., Poolla, K., Jordan, M. & Sastry, S. (2004). Kalman filtering with intermittent observations, *IEEE Transactions on Automatic Control* 49(9): 1453–1464.

6

Kalman Filtering for Discrete Time Uncertain Systems

Rodrigo Souto, João Ishihara and Geovany Borges
University of Brasília
Brazil

1. Introduction

State estimation plays an important role in any application dealing with modeling of dynamic systems. In fact, many fields of knowledge use a mathematical representation of a behavior of interest, such as, but not limited to, engineering (mechanical, electrical, aerospace, civil and chemical), physics, economics, mathematics and biology Simon (2006).
A typical system dynamics can be represented as a transfer function or using the space-state approach. The state-space approach is based on the time-evolution of the "states" of the system, which are considered all the necessary information to represent its dynamic at the desired point of operation. That is why the knowledge about the states of a model is so important. However, in real applications there can be two reasons where the states of a system can not be measured: a) measuring a state implies in the need of a sensor. In order to measure all the states of a system it will be required a large amount of sensors, making the project more expensive and sometimes unfeasible. Usually the whole cost includes not only the price of the sensors, but also modifies the project itself to fix all of them (engineering hours, more material to buy, a heavier product). b) Some states are impossible to be physically measured because they are a mathematically useful representation of the system, such as, the attitude parameterization of an aircraft altitude.
Suppose we have access to all the states of a system. What can we do with them? As the states contain all the information necessary about the system, one can use them to:
a) Implement a state-feedback controller Simon (2006). Almost in the same time the state estimation theory was being developed, the optimal control was growing in popularity mainly because its theory can guarantees closed loop stability margins. However, the Linear-Quadratic-Gaussian (LQG) control problem (the most fundamental optimal control problem) requires the knowledge of the states of the model, which motivated the development of the state estimation for those states that could not be measured in the plant to be controlled.
b) Process monitoring. In this case, the knowledge of the state allows the monitoring of the system. This is very useful for navigation systems where it is necessary to know the position and the velocity of a vehicle, for instance, an aircraft or a submarine. In a radar system, this is its very purpose: keep tracking the position and velocity of all targets of interest in a given area. For an autonomous robot is very important to know its current position in relation to an inertial reference in order to keep it moving to its destiny. For a doctor is important to monitor the concentration of a given medicine in his patient.

c) Process optimization. Once it is possible to monitor the system, the natural consequence is to make it work better. An actual application is the next generation of smart planes. Based on the current position and velocity of a set of aircraft, it is possible to a computer to better schedule arrivals, departures and routes in order to minimize the flight time, which also considers the waiting time for a slot in an airport to land the aircraft. Reducing the flight time means less fuel consumed, reducing the operation costs for the company and the environmental cost for the planet. Another application is based on the knowledge of the position and velocities of cell phones in a network, allowing an improved handover process (the process of transferring an ongoing call or data session from one channel connected to the core network to another), implying in a better connection for the user and smart network resource utilization.
d) Fault detection and prognostics. This is another immediate consequence of process monitoring. For example, suppose we are monitoring the current of an electrical actuator. In the case this current drops below a certain threshold we can conclude that the actuator is not working properly anymore. We have just detected a failure and a warning message can be sent automatically. In military application, this is essentially important when a system can be damaged by exterior reasons. Based on the knowledge of a failure occurrence, it is possible to switch the controller in order to try to overcome the failures. For instance, some aircraft prototypes were still able to fly and land after losing 60% of its wing. Thinking about the actuator system, but in a prognostics approach, we can monitor its current and note that it is dropping along the time. Usually, this is not an abrupt process: it takes so time to the current drop below its acceptable threshold. Based on the decreasing rate of the current, one is able to estimate when the actuator will stop working, and then replace it before it fails. This information is very important when we think about the safety of a system, preventing accidents in cars, aircrafts and other critical systems.
e) Reduce noise effect. Even in cases where the states are measured directly, state estimation schemes can be useful to reduce noise effect Anderson & Moore (1979). For example, a telecommunication engineer wants to know the frequency and the amplitude of a sine wave received at his antenna. The environment and the hardware used may introduce some perturbations that disturb the sin wave, making the required measures imprecise. A state-state model of a sine wave and the estimation of its state can improve precision of the amplitude and frequency estimations.
When the states are not directly available, the above applications can still be performed by using estimates of the states. The most famous algorithm for state estimation is the Kalman filter Kalman (1960). It was initially developed in the 1960s and achieved a wide success to aerospace applications. Due its generic formulation, the same estimation theory could be applied to other practical fields, such as meteorology and economics, achieving the same success as in the aerospace industry. At our present time, the Kalman filter is the most popular algorithm to estimate the states of a system. Although its great success, there are some situations where the Kalman filter does not achieve good performance Ghaoui & Clafiore (2001). The advances of technology lead to smaller and more sensible components. The degradation of these component became more often and remarkable. Also, the number and complexity of these components kept growing in the systems, making more and more difficult to model them all. Even if possible, it became unfeasible to simulate the system with these amounts of details. For these reasons (lack of dynamics modeling and more remarkable parameters changes), it became hard to provide the accurate models assumed by the Kalman. Also, in a lot of applications, it is not easy to obtain the required statistic information about

noises and perturbations affecting the system. A new theory capable to deal with plant uncertainties was required, leading robust extensions of the Kalman filter. This new theory is referred as robust estimationGhaoui & Clafiore (2001).
This chapter presents a robust prediction algorithm used to perform the state estimation of discrete time systems. The first part of the chapter describes how to model an uncertain system. In the following, the chapter presents the new robust technique used when dealing with linear inaccurate models. A numerical example is given to illustrate the advantages of using a robust estimator when dealing with an uncertain system.

2. State Estimation

The Estimation Theory was developed to solve the following problem: given the values of a observed signal though time, [1] also known as measured signal, we require to estimate (smooth, correct or predict) the values of another signal that cannot be accessed directly or it is corrupted by noise or external perturbation.
The first step is to establish a relationship (or a model) between the measured and the estimated signal. Then we shall to define the criteria we will use to evaluate the model. In this sense, it is important to choose a criteria that is compatible with the model. The estimation is shown briefly at Figure 1.

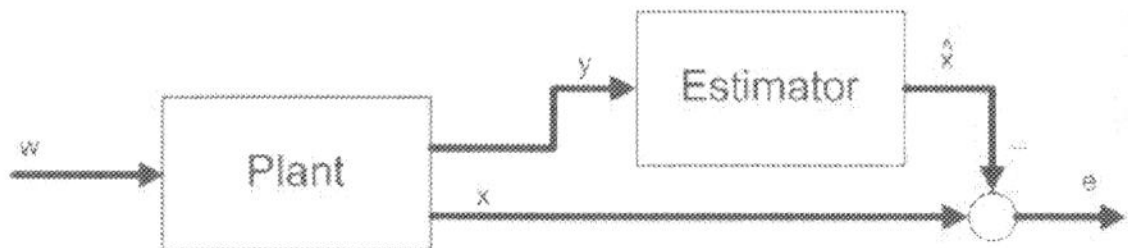

Fig. 1. Block diagram representing the estimation problem.

At Figure 1, we wish to estimate signal x. The signal y are the measured values from the plant. The signal w indicate an unknown input signal and it is usually represented by an stochastic behavior with known statistical properties. The estimation problem is about designing an algorithm that is able to provide $\hat{x}$, using the measures y, that are close of x for several realizations of y. This same problem can also be classically formulated as a minimization of the estimation error variance. At the figure, the error is represented by e and can be defined as $\hat{x}$ minus x. When we are dealing with a robust approach, our concern is to minimize an upper for the error variance as will be explained later on this chapter.
The following notation will be used along this chapter: $\mathbb{R}^n$ represents the n-dimensional Euclidean space, $\Re^{n\times m}$ is the set of real $n \times m$ matrices, $E\{\bullet\}$ denotes the expectation operator, $cov\{\bullet\}$ stands for the covariance, $Z^{\dagger}$ represents the pseudo-inverse of the matrix Z, $diag\{\bullet\}$ stands for a block-diagonal matrix.

3. Uncertain system modeling

The following discrete-time model is a representation of a linear uncertain plant:

$$x_{k+1} = A_{\Delta,k}x_k + \widetilde{w}_k, \quad (1)$$

$$y_k = C_{\Delta,k}x_k + \widetilde{v}_k, \quad (2)$$

[1] Signal here is used to define a data vector or a data set.

where $x_k \in \mathbb{R}^{n_x}$ is the state vector, $y_k \in \mathbb{R}^{n_y}$ stands for the output vector and $\widetilde{w}_k \in \mathbb{R}^{n_x}$ and $\widetilde{v}_k \in \mathbb{R}^{n_y}$ are the output and measurement noises respectively. The uncertainties are characterized as:

1. Additive uncertainties at the dynamic represented as $A_{\Delta,k} = A_k + \Delta A_k$, where A_k is the known, or expected, dynamic matrix and ΔA_k is the associated uncertainty.
2. Additive uncertainties at the output equation represented as $C_{\Delta,k} = C_k + \Delta C_k$, where C_k is the known output matrix and ΔC_k characterizes its uncertainty.
3. Uncertainties at the mean, covariance and cross-covariance of the noises $\widetilde{w}_k$ and $\widetilde{v}_k$. We assume that the initial conditions $\{x_0\}$ and the noises $\{\widetilde{w}_k, \widetilde{v}_k\}$ are uncorrelated with the statistical properties

$$E\left\{\begin{bmatrix} \widetilde{w}_k \\ \widetilde{v}_k \\ x_0 \end{bmatrix}\right\} = \begin{bmatrix} E\{\widetilde{w}_k\} \\ E\{\widetilde{v}_k\} \\ \overline{x}_0 \end{bmatrix}, \tag{3}$$

$$E\left\{\begin{bmatrix} \widetilde{w}_k - E\{\widetilde{w}_k\} \\ \widetilde{v}_k - E\{\widetilde{v}_k\} \\ x_0 - \overline{x}_0 \end{bmatrix}\begin{bmatrix} \widetilde{w}_j - E\left\{\widetilde{w}_j\right\} \\ \widetilde{v}_j - E\left\{\widetilde{v}_j\right\} \\ x_0 - \overline{x}_0 \end{bmatrix}^T\right\} = \begin{bmatrix} \widetilde{W}_k\delta_{kj} & \widetilde{S}_k\delta_{kj} & 0 \\ \widetilde{S}_k^T\delta_{kj} & \widetilde{V}_k\delta_{kj} & 0 \\ 0 & 0 & X_0 \end{bmatrix}, \tag{4}$$

where $\widetilde{W}_k$, $\widetilde{V}_k$ and X_0 denotes the noises and initial state covariance matrices, $\widetilde{S}_k$ is the cross covariance and δ_{kj} is the Kronecker delta function.
Although the exact values of the means and of the covariances are unknown, it is assumed that they are within a known set. The notation at (5) will be used to represent the covariances sets.

$$\widetilde{W}_k \in \mathcal{W}_k, \;\; \widetilde{V}_k \in \mathcal{V}_k, \;\; \widetilde{S}_k \in \mathcal{S}_k. \tag{5}$$

In the next sub section, it will be presented how to characterize a system with uncertain covariance as a system with known covariance, but with uncertain parameters.

3.1 The noises means and covariances spaces

In this sub section, we will analyze some features of the noises uncertainties. The approach shown above considered correlated $\widetilde{w}_k$ and $\widetilde{v}_k$ with unknown mean, covariance and cross covariance, but within a known set. As will be shown later on, these properties can be achieved when we define the following noises structures:

$$\widetilde{w}_k := B_{\Delta w,k}w_k + B_{\Delta v,k}v_k, \tag{6}$$
$$\widetilde{v}_k := D_{\Delta w,k}w_k + D_{\Delta v,k}v_k. \tag{7}$$

Also here we assume that the initial conditions $\{x_0\}$ and the noises $\{w_k\}, \{v_k\}$ are uncorrelated with the statistical properties

$$E\left\{\begin{bmatrix} w_k \\ v_k \\ x_0 \end{bmatrix}\right\} = \begin{bmatrix} \overline{w}_k \\ \overline{v}_k \\ \overline{x}_0 \end{bmatrix}, \tag{8}$$

$$E\left\{\begin{bmatrix} w_k - \overline{w}_k \\ v_k - \overline{v}_k \\ x_0 - \overline{x}_0 \end{bmatrix}\begin{bmatrix} w_j - \overline{w}_j \\ v_j - \overline{v}_j \\ x_0 - \overline{x}_0 \end{bmatrix}^T\right\} = \begin{bmatrix} W_k\delta_{kj} & S_k\delta_{kj} & 0 \\ S_k^T\delta_{kj} & V_k\delta_{kj} & 0 \\ 0 & 0 & X_0 \end{bmatrix}, \tag{9}$$

where W_k, V_k and X_0 denotes the noises and initial state covariance matrices and S_k stands for the cross covariance matrix of the noises.
Therefore using the properties (8) and (9) and the noises definitions (6) and (7), we can note that the noises $\widetilde{w}_k$ and $\widetilde{v}_k$ have uncertain mean given by

$$E\{\widetilde{w}_k\} = B_{\Delta w,k}\overline{w}_k + B_{\Delta v,k}\overline{v}_k, \tag{10}$$
$$E\{\widetilde{v}_k\} = D_{\Delta w,k}\overline{w}_k + D_{\Delta v,k}\overline{v}_k. \tag{11}$$

Their covariances are also uncertain and given by

$$E\left\{\begin{bmatrix} \widetilde{w}_k - E\{\widetilde{w}_k\} \\ \widetilde{v}_k - E\{\widetilde{v}_k\} \end{bmatrix}\begin{bmatrix} \widetilde{w}_j - E\left\{\widetilde{w}_j\right\} \\ \widetilde{v}_j - E\left\{\widetilde{v}_j\right\} \end{bmatrix}^T\right\} = \begin{bmatrix} \widetilde{W}_k\delta_{kj} & \widetilde{S}_k\delta_{kj} \\ \widetilde{S}_k^T\delta_{kj} & \widetilde{V}_k\delta_{kj} \end{bmatrix}. \tag{12}$$

Using the descriptions (6) and (7) for the noises, we obtain

$$\begin{bmatrix} \widetilde{W}_k\delta_{kj} & \widetilde{S}_k\delta_{kj} \\ \widetilde{S}_k^T\delta_{kj} & \widetilde{V}_k\delta_{kj} \end{bmatrix} = \begin{bmatrix} B_{\Delta w,k} & B_{\Delta v,k} \\ D_{\Delta w,k} & D_{\Delta v,k} \end{bmatrix}\begin{bmatrix} W_k\delta_{kj} & S_k\delta_{kj} \\ S_k^T\delta_{kj} & V_k\delta_{kj} \end{bmatrix}\begin{bmatrix} B_{\Delta w,k} & B_{\Delta v,k} \\ D_{\Delta w,k} & D_{\Delta v,k} \end{bmatrix}^T. \tag{13}$$

The notation at (13) is able to represent noises with the desired properties of uncertain covariance and cross covariance. However we can consider some simplifications and achieve the same properties. There are two possible ways to simplify equation (13):

1. Set

$$\begin{bmatrix} B_{\Delta w,k} & B_{\Delta v,k} \\ D_{\Delta w,k} & D_{\Delta v,k} \end{bmatrix} = \begin{bmatrix} B_{\Delta w,k} & 0 \\ 0 & D_{\Delta v,k} \end{bmatrix}. \tag{14}$$

In this case, the covariance matrices can be represented as

$$\begin{bmatrix} \widetilde{W}_k\delta_{kj} & \widetilde{S}_k\delta_{kj} \\ \widetilde{S}_k^T\delta_{kj} & \widetilde{V}_k\delta_{kj} \end{bmatrix} = \begin{bmatrix} B_{\Delta w,k}W_kB_{\Delta w,k}^T & B_{\Delta w,k}S_kD_{\Delta v,k}^T \\ D_{\Delta v,k}S_k^TB_{\Delta w,k}^T & D_{\Delta v,k}V_kD_{\Delta v,k}^T \end{bmatrix}\delta_{kj}. \tag{15}$$

2. The other approach is to consider

$$\begin{bmatrix} W_k\delta_{kj} & S_k\delta_{kj} \\ S_k^T\delta_{kj} & V_k\delta_{kj} \end{bmatrix} = \begin{bmatrix} W_k\delta_{kj} & 0 \\ 0 & V_k\delta_{kj} \end{bmatrix}. \tag{16}$$

In this case, the covariance matrices are given by

$$\begin{bmatrix} \widetilde{W}_k\delta_{kj} & \widetilde{S}_k\delta_{kj} \\ \widetilde{S}_k^T\delta_{kj} & \widetilde{V}_k\delta_{kj} \end{bmatrix} = \begin{bmatrix} B_{\Delta w,k}W_kB_{\Delta w,k}^T + B_{\Delta v,k}V_kB_{\Delta v,k}^T & B_{\Delta w,k}W_kD_{\Delta w,k}^T + B_{\Delta v,k}V_kD_{\Delta v,k}^T \\ D_{\Delta w,k}W_kB_{\Delta w,k}^T + D_{\Delta v,k}V_kB_{\Delta v,k}^T & D_{\Delta w,k}W_kD_{\Delta w,k}^T + D_{\Delta v,k}V_kD_{\Delta v,k}^T \end{bmatrix}\delta_{kj}. \tag{17}$$

So far we did not make any assumption about the structure of noises uncertainties at (6) and (7). As we did for the dynamic and the output matrices, it will be assumed additive uncertainties for the structure of the noises such as

$$B_{\Delta w,k} := B_{w,k} + \Delta B_{w,k}, \quad B_{\Delta v,k} := B_{v,k} + \Delta B_{v,k}, \tag{18}$$
$$D_{\Delta w,k} := D_{w,k} + \Delta D_{w,k}, \quad D_{\Delta v,k} := D_{v,k} + \Delta D_{v,k}, \tag{19}$$

where $B_{w,k}$, $B_{v,k}$, $D_{w,k}$ and $D_{v,k}$ denote the nominal matrices. Their uncertainties are represented by $\Delta B_{w,k}$, $\Delta B_{v,k}$, $\Delta D_{w,k}$ and $\Delta D_{v,k}$ respectively. Using the structures (18)-(19) for the uncertainties, then we are able to obtain the following representation

$$\widetilde{w}_k = \left(B_{w,k} + \Delta B_{w,k}\right) w_k + \left(B_{v,k} + \Delta B_{v,k}\right) v_k, \tag{20}$$

$$\widetilde{v}_k = \left(D_{w,k} + \Delta D_{w,k}\right) w_k + \left(D_{v,k} + \Delta D_{v,k}\right) v_k. \tag{21}$$

In this case, we can note that the mean of the noises depend on the uncertain parameters of the model. The same applies to the covariance matrix.

4. Linear robust estimation

4.1 Describing the model

Consider the following class of uncertain systems presented at (1)-(2):

$$x_{k+1} = \left(A_k + \Delta A_k\right) x_k + \widetilde{w}_k, \tag{22}$$

$$y_k = \left(C_k + \Delta C_k\right) x_k + \widetilde{v}_k, \tag{23}$$

where $x_k \in \mathbb{R}^{n_x}$ is the state vector, $y_k \in \mathbb{R}^{n_y}$ is the output vector and $\widetilde{w}_k \in \mathbb{R}^{n_x}$ and $\widetilde{v}_k \in \mathbb{R}^{n_y}$ are noise signals. It is assumed that the noise signals $\widetilde{w}_k$ and $\widetilde{v}_k$ are correlated and their time-variant mean, covariance and cross-covariance are uncertain but within known bounded sets. We assume that these known sets are described as presented previously at (20)-(21) with the same statistical properties as (8)-(9).

Using the noise modeling (20) and (21), the system (22)-(23) can be written as

$$x_{k+1} = \left(A_k + \Delta A_k\right) x_k + \left(B_{w,k} + \Delta B_{w,k}\right) w_k + \left(B_{v,k} + \Delta B_{v,k}\right) v_k, \tag{24}$$

$$y_k = \left(C_k + \Delta C_k\right) x_k + \left(D_{w,k} + \Delta D_{w,k}\right) w_k + \left(D_{v,k} + \Delta D_{v,k}\right) v_k. \tag{25}$$

The dimensions are shown at Table (1).

Matrix or vector	Set
x_k	$\mathbb{R}^{n_x}$
y_k	$\mathbb{R}^{n_y}$
w_k	$\mathbb{R}^{n_w}$
v_k	$\mathbb{R}^{n_v}$
A_k	$\mathbb{R}^{n_x \times n_x}$
$B_{w,k}$	$\mathbb{R}^{n_x \times n_w}$
$B_{v,k}$	$\mathbb{R}^{n_x \times n_v}$
C_k	$\mathbb{R}^{n_y \times n_x}$
$D_{w,k}$	$\mathbb{R}^{n_y \times n_w}$
$D_{v,k}$	$\mathbb{R}^{n_y \times n_v}$

Table 1. Matrices and vectors dimensions.

The model (24)-(25) with direct feedthrough is equivalent to one with only one noise vector at the state and output equations and that w_k and v_k could have cross-covariance Anderson & Moore (1979). However, we have preferred to use the redundant noise representation (20)-(21) with w_k and v_k uncorrelated in order to get a more accurate upper bound for the predictor covariance error. The nominal matrices A_k, $B_{w,k}$, $B_{v,k}$, C_k, $D_{w,k}$ and $D_{v,k}$ are known and the matrices ΔA_k, $\Delta B_{w,k}$, $\Delta B_{v,k}$, ΔC_k, $\Delta D_{w,k}$ and $\Delta D_{v,k}$ represent the associated uncertainties.

The only assumptions we made on the uncertainties is that they are additive and are within a known set. In order to proceed the analysis it is necessary more information about the uncertainties. Usually the uncertainties are assumed norm bounded or within a polytope. The second approach requires more complex analysis, although the norm bounded set is within the set represented by a polytope.
In this chapter, it will be considered norm bounded uncertainties. For the general case, each uncertainty of the system can be represented as

$$\begin{aligned} \Delta A_k &:= H_{A,k} F_{A,k} G_{A,k}, && (26)\\ \Delta B_{w,k} &:= H_{Bw,k} F_{Bw,k} G_{Bw,k}, && (27)\\ \Delta B_{v,k} &:= H_{Bv,k} F_{Bv,k} G_{Bv,k}, && (28)\\ \Delta C_k &:= H_{C,k} F_{C,k} G_{C,k}, && (29)\\ \Delta D_{w,k} &:= H_{Dw,k} F_{Dw,k} G_{Dw,k}, && (30)\\ \Delta D_{v,k} &:= H_{Dv,k} F_{Dv,k} G_{Dv,k}. && (31) \end{aligned}$$

where $H_{A,k}$, $H_{Bw,k}$, $H_{Bv,k}$, $H_{C,k}$, $H_{Dw,k}$, $H_{Dv,k}$, $G_{x,k}$, $G_{w,k}$ and $G_{v,k}$ are known. The matrices $F_{A,k}$, $F_{Bw,k}$, $F_{Bv,k}$, $F_{C,k}$, $F_{Dw,k}$ and $F_{Dv,k}$ are unknown, time varying and norm-bounded, *i.e.*,

$$F_{A,k}^T F_{A,k} \leq I, F_{Bw,k}^T F_{Bw,k} \leq I, F_{Bv,k}^T F_{Bv,k} \leq I, F_{C,k}^T F_{C,k} \leq I, F_{Dw,k}^T F_{Dw,k} \leq I, F_{Dv,k}^T F_{Dv,k} \leq I. \quad (32)$$

These uncertainties can also be represented at a matrix format as

$$\begin{aligned} &\begin{bmatrix} \Delta A_k & \Delta B_{w,k} & \Delta B_{v,k} \\ \Delta C_k & \Delta D_{w,k} & \Delta D_{v,k} \end{bmatrix} \\ &= \begin{bmatrix} H_{A,k}F_{A,k}G_{A,k} & H_{Bw,k}F_{Bw,k}G_{Bw,k} & H_{Bv,k}F_{Bv,k}G_{Bv,k} \\ H_{C,k}F_{C,k}G_{C,k} & H_{Dw,k}F_{Dw,k}G_{Dw,k} & H_{Dv,k}F_{Dv,k}G_{Dv,k} \end{bmatrix} \\ &= \begin{bmatrix} H_{A,k} & H_{Bw,k} & H_{Bv,k} & 0 & 0 & 0 \\ 0 & 0 & 0 & H_{C,k} & H_{Dw,k} & H_{Dv,k} \end{bmatrix} \\ &\times \, diag\left\{F_{A,k}, F_{Bw,k}, F_{Bv,k}, F_{C,k}, F_{Dw,k}, F_{Dv,k}\right\} \begin{bmatrix} G_{A,k} & 0 & 0 \\ 0 & G_{Bw,k} & 0 \\ 0 & 0 & G_{Bv,k} \\ G_{C,k} & 0 & 0 \\ 0 & G_{Dw,k} & 0 \\ 0 & 0 & G_{Dv,k} \end{bmatrix}. \quad (33) \end{aligned}$$

However, there is another way to represent distinct uncertainties for each matrix by the appropriate choice of the matrices H as follows

$$\begin{aligned} \begin{bmatrix} \Delta A_k \\ \Delta C_k \end{bmatrix} &:= \begin{bmatrix} H_{A,k} \\ H_{C,k} \end{bmatrix} F_{x,k} G_{x,k} && (34)\\ \begin{bmatrix} \Delta B_{w,k} \\ \Delta D_{w,k} \end{bmatrix} &:= \begin{bmatrix} H_{Bw,k} \\ H_{Dw,k} \end{bmatrix} F_{w,k} G_{w,k} && (35)\\ \begin{bmatrix} \Delta B_{v,k} \\ \Delta D_{v,k} \end{bmatrix} &:= \begin{bmatrix} H_{Bv,k} \\ H_{Dv,k} \end{bmatrix} F_{v,k} G_{v,k}, && (36) \end{aligned}$$

where the matrices $F_{x,k}$, $F_{w,k}$ and $F_{v,k}$ of dimensions $r_{x,k} \times s_{x,k}$, $r_{w,k} \times s_{w,k}$, $r_{v,k} \times s_{v,k}$ are unknown and norm-bounded, $\forall k \in [0, N]$, *i.e.*,

$$F_{x,k}^T F_{x,k} \leq I, \; F_{w,k}^T F_{w,k} \leq I, \; F_{v,k}^T F_{v,k} \leq I. \tag{37}$$

Rewriting the uncertainties into a matrix structure, we obtain

$$\begin{aligned} \begin{bmatrix} \Delta A_k & \Delta B_{w,k} & \Delta B_{v,k} \\ \Delta C_k & \Delta D_{w,k} & \Delta D_{v,k} \end{bmatrix} &= \begin{bmatrix} H_{A,k} F_{x,k} G_{x,k} & H_{Bw,k} F_{w,k} G_{w,k} & H_{Bv,k} F_{v,k} G_{v,k} \\ H_{C,k} F_{x,k} G_{x,k} & H_{Dw,k} F_{w,k} G_{w,k} & H_{Dv,k} F_{v,k} G_{v,k} \end{bmatrix} \\ &= \begin{bmatrix} H_{A,k} & H_{Bw,k} & H_{Bv,k} \\ H_{C,k} & H_{Dw,k} & H_{Dv,k} \end{bmatrix} \begin{bmatrix} F_{x,k} & 0 & 0 \\ 0 & F_{w,k} & 0 \\ 0 & 0 & F_{v,k} \end{bmatrix} \begin{bmatrix} G_{x,k} & 0 & 0 \\ 0 & G_{w,k} & 0 \\ 0 & 0 & G_{v,k} \end{bmatrix}. \end{aligned} \tag{38}$$

Our goal is to design a finite horizon robust predictor for state estimation of the uncertain system described by (24)-(37). We consider predictors with the following structure

$$\widehat{x}_{0|-1} = \overline{x}_0, \tag{39}$$

$$\widehat{x}_{k+1|k} = \Phi_k \widehat{x}_{k|k-1} + B_{w,k}\overline{w}_k + B_{v,k}\overline{v}_k + K_k \left(y_k - C_k \widehat{x}_{k|k-1} - D_{w,k}\overline{w}_k - D_{v,k}\overline{v}_k \right). \tag{40}$$

The predictor is intended to ensure an upper limit in the error estimation variance. In other words, we seek a sequence of non-negative definite matrices $\left\{ \overline{P}_{k+1|k} \right\}$ that, for all allowed uncertainties, satisfy for each k

$$cov\left\{ e_{k+1|k} \right\} \leq \overline{P}_{k+1|k}, \tag{41}$$

where $e_{k+1|k} = x_{k+1} - \widehat{x}_{k+1|k}$. The matrices Φ_k and K_k are time-varying and shall be determined in such way that the upper bound $\overline{P}_{k+1|k}$ is minimized.

4.2 A robust estimation solution

At this part, we shall choose an augmented state vector. There are normally found two options are found in the literature:

$$\tilde{x}_k := \begin{bmatrix} x_k \\ \widehat{x}_{k|k-1} \end{bmatrix}, \tilde{x}_k := \begin{bmatrix} x_k - \widehat{x}_{k|k-1} \\ \widehat{x}_{k|k-1} \end{bmatrix}. \tag{42}$$

One can note that there is a similarity transformation between both vectors. This transformation matrix and its inverse are given by

$$T = \begin{bmatrix} I & I \\ 0 & I \end{bmatrix}, T^{-1} = \begin{bmatrix} I & -I \\ 0 & I \end{bmatrix}. \tag{43}$$

Using the system definition (24)-(25) and the structure of the estimator in (40) then we define an augmented system as

$$\begin{aligned} \widetilde{x}_{k+1} &= \left(\widetilde{A}_k + \widetilde{H}_{x,k} F_{x,k} \widetilde{G}_{x,k} \right) \widetilde{x}_k + \left(\widetilde{B}_k + \widetilde{H}_{w,k} F_{w,k} G_{w,k} \right) w_k + \overline{\widetilde{B}}_k \overline{w}_k \\ &+ \left(\widetilde{D}_k + \widetilde{H}_{v,k} F_{v,k} G_{v,k} \right) v_k + \overline{\widetilde{D}}_k \overline{v}_k, \end{aligned} \tag{44}$$

where

$$\widetilde{D}_k = \begin{bmatrix} B_{v,k} \\ K_k D_{v,k} \end{bmatrix}, \widetilde{H}_{v,k} = \begin{bmatrix} H_{Bv,k} \\ K_k H_{Dv,k} \end{bmatrix}, \widetilde{G}_{x,k} = \begin{bmatrix} G_{x,k} \ 0 \end{bmatrix},$$
$$\widetilde{B}_k = \begin{bmatrix} B_{w,k} \\ K_k D_{w,k} \end{bmatrix}, \widetilde{H}_{w,k} = \begin{bmatrix} H_{Bw,k} \\ K_k H_{Dw,k} \end{bmatrix}, \widetilde{x}_k = \begin{bmatrix} x_k \\ \widehat{x}_{k|k-1} \end{bmatrix},$$
$$\widetilde{A}_k = \begin{bmatrix} A_k & 0 \\ K_k C_k & \Phi_k - K_k C_k \end{bmatrix}, \widetilde{H}_{x,k} = \begin{bmatrix} H_{A,k} \\ K_k H_{C,k} \end{bmatrix},$$
$$\widetilde{\widetilde{B}}_k = \begin{bmatrix} 0 \\ B_{w,k} - K_k D_{w,k} \end{bmatrix}, \widetilde{\widetilde{D}}_k = \begin{bmatrix} 0 \\ B_{v,k} - K_k D_{v,k} \end{bmatrix}. \tag{45}$$

Consider $\widetilde{P}_{k+1|k} = cov\{\widetilde{x}_{k+1}\}$. The next lemma give us an upper bound for the covariance matrix of the augmented system (44).

Lemma 1. An upper limit for the covariance matrix of the augmented system (44) is given by $P_{0|-1} = diag\{X_0, 0\}$ and

$$\begin{aligned} P_{k+1|k} &= \widetilde{A}_k P_{k|k-1} \widetilde{A}_k^T + \widetilde{B}_k W_{c,k} \widetilde{B}_k^T + \widetilde{D}_k V_{c,k} \widetilde{D}_k^T \\ &+ \widetilde{A}_k P_{k|k-1} \widetilde{G}_{x,k}^T \left(\alpha_{x,k}^{-1} I - \widetilde{G}_{x,k} P_{k|k-1} \widetilde{G}_{x,k}^T \right)^{-1} \widetilde{G}_{x,k} P_{k|k-1} \widetilde{A}_k^T \\ &+ \alpha_{x,k}^{-1} \widetilde{H}_{x,k} \widetilde{H}_{x,k}^T + \alpha_{w,k}^{-1} \widetilde{H}_{w,k} \widetilde{H}_{w,k}^T + \alpha_{v,k}^{-1} \widetilde{H}_{v,k} \widetilde{H}_{v,k}^T, \end{aligned} \tag{46}$$

where $\alpha_{x,k}^{-1}$, $\alpha_{w,k}^{-1}$ and $\alpha_{v,k}^{-1}$ satisfy

$$\alpha_{x,k}^{-1} I - \widetilde{G}_{x,k} P_{k|k-1} \widetilde{G}_{x,k}^T > 0, \tag{47}$$
$$\alpha_{w,k}^{-1} I - G_{w,k} W_k G_{w,k}^T > 0, \tag{48}$$
$$\alpha_{v,k}^{-1} I - G_{v,k} V_k G_{v,k}^T > 0. \tag{49}$$

Proof: Since $\widetilde{x}_k$, w_k and v_k are uncorrelated signals, and using (8), (9), (39) and (44), it is straightforward that $\widetilde{P}_{0|-1} = diag\{X_0, 0\}$ and

$$\begin{aligned} \widetilde{P}_{k+1|k} &= \left(\widetilde{A}_k + \widetilde{H}_{x,k} F_{x,k} \widetilde{G}_{x,k} \right) \widetilde{P}_{k|k-1} \left(\widetilde{A}_k + \widetilde{H}_{x,k} F_{x,k} \widetilde{G}_{x,k} \right)^T \\ &+ \left(\widetilde{B}_k + \widetilde{H}_{w,k} F_{w,k} G_{w,k} \right) W_k \left(\widetilde{B}_k + \widetilde{H}_{w,k} F_{w,k} G_{w,k} \right)^T \\ &+ \left(\widetilde{D}_k + \widetilde{H}_{v,k} F_{v,k} G_{v,k} \right) V_k \left(\widetilde{D}_k + \widetilde{H}_{v,k} F_{v,k} G_{v,k} \right)^T. \end{aligned}$$

Choose scaling parameters $\alpha_{x,k}^{-1}$, $\alpha_{w,k}^{-1}$ and $\alpha_{v,k}^{-1}$ satisfying (47)-(49). Using Lemma 2 of Wang et al. (1999) and Lemma 3.2 of Theodor & Shaked (1996), we have that the sequence $\left\{P_{k+1|k}\right\}$ given by (46) is such that $\widetilde{P}_{k+1|k} \leq P_{k+1|k}$ for all instants k. **QED**.

Replacing the augmented matrices (45) into (46), the upper bound $P_{k+1|k}$ can be partitioned as

$$P_{k+1|k} = \begin{bmatrix} P_{11,k+1|k} & P_{12,k+1|k} \\ P_{12,k+1|k}^T & P_{22,k+1|k} \end{bmatrix}, \tag{50}$$

where, using the definitions presented in Step 1 of Table 2, we obtain

$$P_{11,k+1|k} = A_k P_{11c,k} A_k^T + B_k U_{c,k} B_k^T + \Delta_{3,k}, \tag{51}$$

$$P_{12,k+1|k} = A_k P_{12c,k} \Phi_k^T + A_k S_{1,k} C_k^T K_k^T + \left(B_k U_{c,k} D_k^T + \Delta_{1,k} \right) K_k^T, \tag{52}$$

$$\begin{aligned} P_{22,k+1|k} &= \Phi_k P_{22c,k} \Phi_k^T + K_k C_k S_{2,k} \Phi_k^T + \Phi_k S_{2,k}^T C_k^T K_k^T \\ &+ K_k \left(C_k S_{3,k} C_k^T + D_k U_{c,k} D_k^T + \Delta_{2,k} \right) K_k^T \end{aligned} \tag{53}$$

with

$$U_{c,k} := \begin{bmatrix} W_{c,k} & 0 \\ 0 & V_{c,k} \end{bmatrix}, \tag{54}$$

$$\Delta_{1,k} := \alpha_{x,k}^{-1} H_{A,k} H_{C,k}^T + \alpha_{w,k}^{-1} H_{Bw,k} H_{Dw,k}^T + \alpha_{v,k}^{-1} H_{Bv,k} H_{Dv,k}^T, \tag{55}$$

$$\Delta_{2,k} := \alpha_{x,k}^{-1} H_{C,k} H_{C,k}^T + \alpha_{w,k}^{-1} H_{Dw,k} H_{Dw,k}^T + \alpha_{v,k}^{-1} H_{Dv,k} H_{Dv,k}^T, \tag{56}$$

$$\Delta_{3,k} := \alpha_{x,k}^{-1} H_{A,k} H_{A,k}^T + \alpha_{w,k}^{-1} H_{Bw,k} H_{Bw,k}^T + \alpha_{v,k}^{-1} H_{Bv,k} H_{Bv,k}^T, \tag{57}$$

$$M_k := G_{x,k}^T \left(\alpha_{x,k}^{-1} I - G_{x,k} P_{11,k|k-1} G_{x,k}^T \right)^{-1} G_{x,k}, \tag{58}$$

$$P_{11c,k} := P_{11,k|k-1} + P_{11,k|k-1} M_k P_{11,k|k-1}, \tag{59}$$

$$P_{12c,k} := P_{12,k|k-1} + P_{11,k|k-1} M_k P_{12,k|k-1}, \tag{60}$$

$$P_{22c,k} := P_{22,k|k-1} + P_{12,k|k-1}^T M_k P_{12,k|k-1}, \tag{61}$$

$$S_{1,k} := P_{11c,k} - P_{12c,k}, \tag{62}$$

$$S_{2,k} := P_{12c,k} - P_{22c,k}, \tag{63}$$

$$S_{3,k} := S_{1,k} - S_{2,k}^T. \tag{64}$$

Since $P_{k+1|k} \geq \widetilde{P}_{k+1|k} \geq 0, \forall k$, it is clear that if we define

$$\overline{P}_{k+1|k} = \begin{bmatrix} I & -I \end{bmatrix} P_{k+1|k} \begin{bmatrix} I & -I \end{bmatrix}^T, \tag{65}$$

then we have that $\overline{P}_{k+1|k}$ is an upper bound of the error variance on the state estimation. Using the definitions (50) and (65), the initial condition for $\overline{P}_{k+1|k}$ is $\overline{P}_{0|-1} = X_0$ and $\overline{P}_{k+1|k}$ can be written as

$$\begin{aligned} \overline{P}_{k+1|k} &= \left(A_k - K_k C_k \right) P_{11,c} \left(A_k - K_k C_k \right)^T - \left(A_k - K_k C_k \right) P_{12,c} \left(\Phi_k - K_k C_k \right)^T \\ &- \left(\Phi_k - K_k C_k \right) P_{12,c}^T \left(A_k - K_k C_k \right)^T + \left(\Phi_k - K_k C_k \right) P_{22,c1} \left(\Phi_k - K_k C_k \right)^T \\ &+ \left(B_{w,k} - K_k D_{w,k} \right) W_{c,k} \left(B_{w,k} - K_k D_{w,k} \right)^T \\ &+ \left(B_{v,k} - K_k D_{v,k} \right) V_{c,k} \left(B_{v,k} - K_k D_{v,k} \right)^T \\ &+ \alpha_{x,k}^{-1} \left(H_{A,k} - K_k H_{C,k} \right) \left(H_{A,k} -_k H_{C,k} \right)^T \\ &+ \alpha_{w,k}^{-1} \left(H_{Bw,k} - K_k H_{Dw,k} \right) \left(H_{Bw,k} - K_k H_{Dw,k} \right)^T \\ &+ \alpha_{v,k}^{-1} \left(H_{Bv,k} - K_k H_{Dv,k} \right) \left(H_{Bv,k} - K_k H_{Dv,k} \right)^T . \end{aligned} \tag{66}$$

Note that $\overline{P}_{k+1|k}$ given by (66) satisfies (41) for any Φ_k and K_k. In this sense, we can choose them to minimize the covariance of the estimation error given by $\overline{P}_{k+1|k}$. We calculate the first order partial derivatives of (66) with respect to Φ_k and K_k and making them equal to zero, *i.e.*,

$$\frac{\partial}{\partial \Phi_k}\overline{P}_{k+1|k} = 0 \tag{67}$$

$$\frac{\partial}{\partial K_k}\overline{P}_{k+1|k} = 0. \tag{68}$$

Then the optimal values $\Phi_k = \Phi_k^*$ and $K_k = K_k^*$ are given by

$$K_k^* = \left(A_k S_k C_k^T + \Psi_{1,k}\right)\left(C_k S_k C_k^T + \Psi_{2,k}\right)^{\dagger}, \tag{69}$$

$$\Phi_k^* = A_k + (A_k - K_k^* C_k)\left(P_{12c,k}P_{22c,k}^{\dagger} - I\right), \tag{70}$$

where

$$S_k := P_{11c,k} - P_{12c,k}P_{22c,k}^{\dagger}P_{12c,k}^T, \tag{71}$$

$$\Psi_{1,k} := B_{w,k}W_{c,k}D_{w,k}^T + B_{v,k}V_{c,k}D_{v,k}^T + \Delta_{1,k}, \tag{72}$$

$$\Psi_{2,k} := D_{w,k}W_{c,k}D_{w,k}^T + D_{v,k}V_{c,k}D_{v,k}^T + \Delta_{2,k}. \tag{73}$$

Actually Φ_k^* and K_k^* provide the global minimum of $\overline{P}_{k+1|k}$. This can be proved though the convexity of $\overline{P}_{k+1|k}$ at (66). We first have that $\widetilde{P}_{k+1|k} > 0$, $W_k > 0$ and $V_k > 0, \forall k$. Then we calculate the Hessian matrix to conclude that we have the global minimum:

$$He\left(\overline{P}_{k+1|k}\right) := \begin{bmatrix} \frac{\partial^2}{\partial^2 \Phi_k}\overline{P}_{k+1|k} & \frac{\partial^2}{\partial^2 [\Phi_k, K_k]}\overline{P}_{k+1|k} \\ \frac{\partial^2}{\partial^2 [K_k, \Phi_k]}\overline{P}_{k+1|k} & \frac{\partial^2}{\partial^2 K_k}\overline{P}_{k+1|k} \end{bmatrix} = \begin{bmatrix} 2P_{22,k|k-1} & 2C_k S_{2,k} \\ 2S_{2,k}^T C_k^T & C_k S_k C_k^T + \Psi_{3,k} \end{bmatrix} > 0.$$

At the previous equations we used the pseudo-inverse instead of the simple matrix inverse. Taking a look at the initial conditions $P_{12,0|-1} = P_{12,0|-1}^T = P_{22,0|-1} = 0$, one can note that $P_{22,0} = 0$ and, as consequence, the inverse does not exist for all instant k. However, it can be proved that the pseudo-inverse does exist.
Replacing (70) and (69) in (52) and (53), we obtain

$$\begin{aligned} P_{12,k+1|k} &= P_{12,k+1|k}^T = P_{22,k+1|k} = \\ &= A_k P_{12c,k}P_{22c,k}^{-1}P_{12c,k}^T A_k^T + \left(A_k S_k C_k^T + \Psi_{1,k}\right)\left(C_k S_k C_k^T + \Psi_{2,k}\right)^{\dagger}\left(A_k S_k C_k^T + \Psi_{1,k}\right)^T. \end{aligned} \tag{74}$$

Since (74) holds for any symmetric $P_{k+1|k}$, if we start with a matrix $P_{n+1|n}$ satisfying $P_{12,n+1|n} = P_{12,n+1|n}^T = P_{22,n+1|n}$ for some $n \geq 0$, then we can conclude that (74) is valid for any $k \geq n$.
The equality allows us some simplifications. The first one is

$$S_k = \overline{P}_{c,k|k-1} := \overline{P}_{k|k-1} + \overline{P}_{k|k-1}G_{x,k}^T\left(\alpha_{x,k}^{-1}I - G_{x,k}\overline{P}_{k|k-1}G_{x,k}^T\right)^{-1}G_{x,k}\overline{P}_{k|k-1}. \tag{75}$$

In fact, the covariance matrix of the estimation error presents a modified notation to deal with the uncertain system. At this point, we can conclude that $\alpha_{x,k}$ shall now satisfy

$$\alpha_{x,k}^{-1}I - G_{x,k}\overline{P}_{k|k-1}G_{x,k}^T > 0. \tag{76}$$

Using (74), we can simplify the expressions for Φ_k^*, K_k^* and $\overline{P}_{k+1|k}$. We can define Φ_k given in Step 4 of Table 2 as $\Phi_k = \Phi_k^*$. The simplified expression for the predictor gain is given by

$$K_k^* = \left(A_k \overline{P}_{c,k|k-1} C_k^T + \Upsilon_{1,k}\right)\left(C_k \overline{P}_{c,k|k-1} C_k^T + \Upsilon_{2,k}\right)^{\dagger},$$

which can be rewritten as presented in Step 4 of Table 2. The expression for the Riccati equation can be written as

$$\begin{aligned}\overline{P}_{k+1|k} = &\left(A_k - K_k^* C_k\right)\overline{P}_{c,k|k-1}\left(A_k - K_k^* C_k\right)^T \\ &+ \left(B_{w,k} - K_k^* D_{w,k}\right) W_{c,k} \left(B_{w,k} - K_k^* D_{w,k}\right)^T \\ &+ \left(B_{v,k} - K_k^* D_{v,k}\right) V_{c,k} \left(B_{v,k} - K_k^* D_{v,k}\right)^T \\ &+ \alpha_{x,k}^{-1}\left(H_{A,k} - K_k^* H_{C,k}\right)\left(H_{A,k} - K_k^* H_{C,k}\right)^T \\ &+ \alpha_{w,k}^{-1}\left(H_{Bw,k} - K_k^* H_{Dw,k}\right)\left(H_{Bw,k} - K_k^* H_{Dw,k}\right)^T \\ &+ \alpha_{v,k}^{-1}\left(H_{Bv,k} - K_k^* H_{Dv,k}\right)\left(H_{Bv,k} - K_k^* H_{Dv,k}\right)^T.\end{aligned}$$

Replacing the expression for K_k^* in $\overline{P}_{k+1|k}$, we obtain the Riccati equation given in Step 5 of Table 2.
Using an alternative representation, remember the predictor structure:

$$\widehat{x}_{k+1|k} = \Phi_k \widehat{x}_{k|k-1} + B_{w,k}\overline{w}_k + B_{v,k}\overline{v}_k + K_k\left(y_k - C_k \widehat{x}_{k|k-1} - D_{w,k}\overline{w}_k - D_{v,k}\overline{v}_k\right). \quad (77)$$

Replace Φ_k^* into (77) to obtain

$$\widehat{x}_{k+1|k} = A_{c,k}\widehat{x}_{k|k-1} + B_{w,k}\overline{w}_k + B_{v,k}\overline{v}_k + K_k\left(y_k - C_{c,k}\widehat{x}_{k|k-1} - D_{w,k}\overline{w}_k - D_{v,k}\overline{v}_k\right), \quad (78)$$

where

$$A_{c,k} := A_k + A_k \overline{P}_{k|k-1} G_{x,k}^T \left(\alpha_{x,k}^{-1} I - G_{x,k}\overline{P}_{k|k-1} G_{x,k}^T\right)^{-1} G_{x,k}, \quad (79)$$

$$C_{c,k} := C_k + C_k \overline{P}_{k|k-1} G_{x,k}^T \left(\alpha_{x,k}^{-1} I - G_{x,k}\overline{P}_{k|k-1} G_{x,k}^T\right)^{-1} G_{x,k}. \quad (80)$$

Once again, it is possible to obtain the classic estimator from the structure (79)-(80) for a system without uncertainties.

5. Numerical example

At this section we perform a simulation to illustrate to importance to consider the uncertainties at your predictor design.
One good way to quantify the performance of the estimator would be using its real variance to the error estimation. However, this is difficult to obtain from the response of the model. For this reason, we approximate the real variance of the estimation error using the ensemble-average (see Ishihara et al. (2006) and Sayed (2001)) given by:

$$var\left\{e_{i,k}\right\} \approx \frac{1}{N}\sum_{j=1}^{N}\left(e_{i,k}^{(j)} - E\left\{e_{i,k}^{(j)}\right\}\right)^2, \quad (81)$$

$$E\left\{e_{i,k}^{(j)}\right\} \approx \frac{1}{N}\sum_{j=1}^{N} e_{i,k}^{(j)}, \quad (82)$$

Step 0 (Initial conditions): $\widehat{x}_{0|-1} = \overline{x}_0$ and $\overline{P}_{0|-1} = X_0$.

Step 1: Obtain scalar parameters $\alpha_{x,k}$, $\alpha_{w,k}$ and $\alpha_{v,k}$ that satisfy (76), (48) and (49), respectively. Then define

$$\begin{aligned}
\Delta_{1,k} &:= \alpha_{x,k}^{-1} H_{A,k} H_{C,k}^T + \alpha_{w,k}^{-1} H_{Bw,k} H_{Dw,k}^T + \alpha_{v,k}^{-1} H_{Bv,k} H_{Dv,k}^T,\\
\Delta_{2,k} &:= \alpha_{x,k}^{-1} H_{C,k} H_{C,k}^T + \alpha_{w,k}^{-1} H_{Dw,k} H_{Dw,k}^T + \alpha_{v,k}^{-1} H_{Dv,k} H_{Dv,k}^T,\\
\Delta_{3,k} &:= \alpha_{x,k}^{-1} H_{A,k} H_{A,k}^T + \alpha_{w,k}^{-1} H_{Bw,k} H_{Bw,k}^T + \alpha_{v,k}^{-1} H_{Bv,k} H_{Bv,k}^T.
\end{aligned}$$

Step 2: Calculate the corrections due to the presence of uncertainties

$$\begin{aligned}
\overline{P}_{c,k|k-1} &:= \overline{P}_{k|k-1} + \overline{P}_{k|k-1} G_{x,k}^T \left(\alpha_{x,k}^{-1} I - G_{x,k} \overline{P}_{k|k-1} G_{x,k}^T\right)^{-1} G_{x,k} \overline{P}_{k|k-1},\\
W_{c,k} &:= W_k + W_k G_{w,k}^T \left(\alpha_{w,k}^{-1} I - G_{w,k} W_k G_{w,k}^T\right)^{-1} G_{w,k} W_k.\\
V_{c,k} &:= V_k + V_k G_{v,k}^T \left(\alpha_{v,k}^{-1} I - G_{v,k} V_k G_{v,k}^T\right)^{-1} G_{v,k} V_k,
\end{aligned}$$

Step 3: Define the augmented matrices

$$B_k := \begin{bmatrix} B_{w,k} & B_{v,k} \end{bmatrix}, D_k := \begin{bmatrix} D_{w,k} & D_{v,k} \end{bmatrix}, U_{c,k} := diag\left\{W_{c,k}, V_{c,k}\right\}.$$

Step 4: Calculate the parameters of the predictor as

$$\begin{aligned}
K_k &= \left(A_k \overline{P}_{c,k|k-1} C_k^T + B_k U_{c,k} D_k^T + \Delta_{1,k}\right)\left(C_k \overline{P}_{c,k|k-1} C_k^T + D_k U_{c,k} D_k^T + \Delta_{2,k}\right)^{\dagger},\\
\Phi_k &= A_k + (A_k - K_k C_k)\, \overline{P}_{k|k-1} G_{x,k}^T \left(\alpha_{x,k}^{-1} I - G_{x,k} \overline{P}_{k|k-1} G_{x,k}^T\right)^{-1} G_{x,k}.
\end{aligned}$$

Step 5: Update $\left\{\widehat{x}_{k+1|k}\right\}$ and $\left\{\overline{P}_{k+1|k}\right\}$ as

$$\begin{aligned}
\widehat{x}_{k+1|k} &= \Phi_k \widehat{x}_{k|k-1} + B_{w,k}\overline{w}_k + B_{v,k}\overline{v}_k + K_k\left(y_k - C_k \widehat{x}_{k|k-1} - D_{w,k}\overline{w}_k - D_{v,k}\overline{v}_k\right),\\
\overline{P}_{k+1|k} &= A_k \overline{P}_{c,k|k-1} A_k^T + B_k U_{c,k} B_k^T + \Delta_{3,k}\\
&\quad - \left(A_k \overline{P}_{c,k|k-1} C_k^T + \Delta_{1,k}\right)\left(C_k \overline{P}_{c,k|k-1} C_k^T + D_k U_{c,k} D_k^T + \Delta_{2,k}\right)^{\dagger}\left(A_k \overline{P}_{c,k|k-1} C_k^T + \Delta_{1,k}\right)^T
\end{aligned}$$

Table 2. The Enhanced Robust Predictor.

where $e_{i,k}^{(j)}$ is the i-th component of the estimation error vector $e_k^{(j)}$ of the realization j defined as

$$e_k^{(j)} := x_k^{(j)} - \widehat{x}_{k|k-1}^{(j)}. \tag{83}$$

Another way to quantify the performance of the estimation is though covariance ellipses. The use of covariance ellipses allows us to visualize the variance and the cross covariance of a system with two states.

Consider the benchmark model, used for instance in Fu et al. (2001) and Theodor & Shaked (1996), where we added uncertainties in order to affect every matrix of the system,

$$x_{k+1} = \begin{bmatrix} 0 & -0.5 \\ 1+\delta_{x,k} & 1+0.3\delta_{x,k} \end{bmatrix} x_k + \begin{bmatrix} -6 \\ 1+0.1\delta_{w,k} \end{bmatrix} w_k,$$
$$y_k = \begin{bmatrix} -100+5\delta_{x,k} & 10+1.5\delta_{x,k} \end{bmatrix} x_k + 100\delta_{v,k} v_k,$$

where $\delta_{n,k}$ varies uniformly at each step on the unit interval for $n = x, w, v$. We also use $\overline{w}_k = 0.1$, $\overline{v}_k = 0.9$, $W_k = 0.1$ and $V_k = 2$ with initial conditions $\overline{x}_0 = [2\ 1]^T$ and $X_0 = 0.1I$. The matrices associated to the uncertainties are given by

$$\begin{aligned} &H_{A,k} = \begin{bmatrix} 0 \\ 10 \end{bmatrix}, \; H_{Bw,k} = \begin{bmatrix} 0 \\ 10 \end{bmatrix}, \; H_{Bv,k} = \begin{bmatrix} 0 \\ 0 \end{bmatrix}, \\ &H_{C,k} = 50, \; H_{Dw,k} = 0, \; H_{Dv,k} = 100, \\ &G_{x,k} = \begin{bmatrix} 0.1 & 0.03 \end{bmatrix}, \; G_{w,k} = 0.01, \; G_{v,k} = 1. \end{aligned} \tag{84}$$

The scalar parameters are calculated at each step as

$$\alpha_{x,k}^{-1} = \sigma_{max}\left\{G_{x,k}\overline{P}_{k|k-1}G_{x,k}^T\right\} + \epsilon_x, \tag{85}$$

$$\alpha_{w,k}^{-1} = \sigma_{max}\left\{G_{w,k}W_k G_{w,k}^T\right\} + \epsilon_w, \tag{86}$$

$$\alpha_{v,k}^{-1} = \sigma_{max}\left\{G_{v,k}V_k G_{v,k}^T\right\} + \epsilon_v, \tag{87}$$

where $\sigma_{max}\{\bullet\}$ indicates the maximum singular value of a matrix. Numerical simulations show that, in general, smaller values of ϵ_x, ϵ_w and ϵ_v result in better bounds. However, this can lead to bad inverses calculation. In this example, we have chosen $\epsilon_x = \epsilon_w = \epsilon_v = 0.1$. The mean value of the covariance matrices obtained over 500 experiments at $k = 1500$ for the robust predictor and the classic predictor are

$$\overline{P}_{robust} = \begin{bmatrix} 14.4 & -22.7 \\ -22.7 & 76.4 \end{bmatrix}, \overline{P}_{classic} = \begin{bmatrix} 3.6 & -0.6 \\ -0.6 & 0.1 \end{bmatrix}.$$

Fig. 2 shows the time evolution of the mean value (over 500 experiments) of both states and of their estimated values using the classic and the robust predictors.. It can be verified that the estimates of the classic predictor keep oscillating while the robust predictor reaches an approximate stationary value. The dynamics of the actual model also presents approximate stationary values for both state. It means that the robust predictor were able to better estimate the dynamics of the model.

The covariance ellipses obtained from both predictors and the actually obtained states at $k = 1500$ are shown at Fig. 3. Although the size of the ellipse is smaller for the classic Kalman predictor, some states of the actual model are outside this bound. Fig. 4 presents the time evolution of the error variances for both states of the system. The error variances were approximated using the ensemble-average, defined in Sayed (2001).

The proposed filter reaches their approximate stationary states after a few steps while the Kalman filter did not. Fig. 4 also shows that the actual error variance of the proposed filter is always below its upper bound. Although the error variance of the Kalman filter is lower than the upper bound of the robust estimator, the actual error variance of the Kalman filter is above its error variance prediction, i.e., the Kalman filter does not guarantee the containment of the true signal y_k. This is a known result and it is presented in Ghaoui & Clafiore (2001).

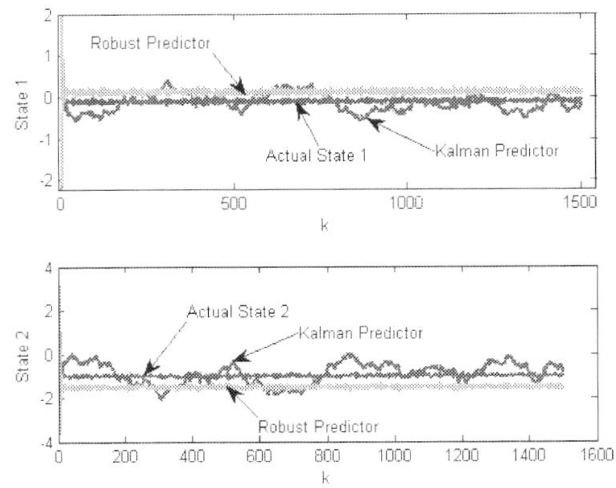

Fig. 2. Evolution of state 2 and its robust estimates.

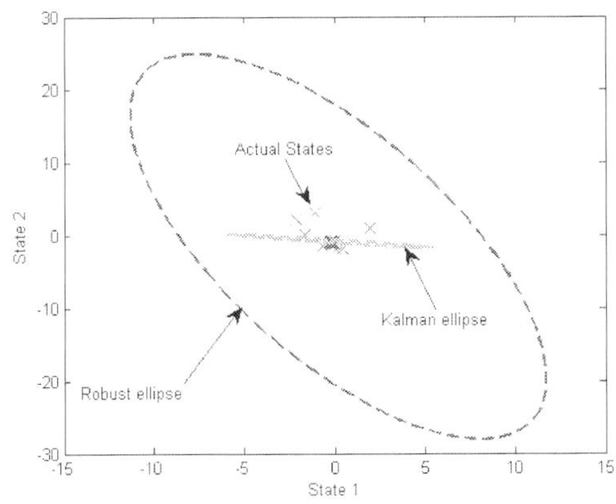

Fig. 3. Mean covariance ellipses after 1500 experiments.

A comparison with using the robust predictor presented here and another predictor found in the literature is shown at ?????. The results presented therein show that the enhanced predictor presented here provides a less conservative design, with lower upper bound and lower experimental value of the error variance.

6. Conclusions

This chapter presented how to design robust predictor for linear systems with norm-bounded and time-varying uncertainties in their matrices. The design is based on a guaranteed cost

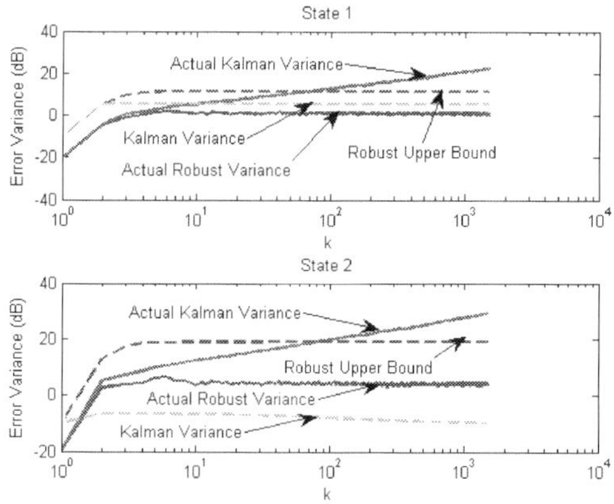

Fig. 4. Error variances for uncorrelated noise simulation.

approach using the Riccati equation. The obtained estimator is is capable of dealing with systems that present correlated dynamical and measurement noises with unknown mean and variance. In most of real life applications this is a common situation. It is also remarkable that the separated structure for the noises allows the estimator to have a less conservative upper bound for the covariance of the estimation error.

Further studies may include the use of approach of this chapter to design estimators for infinite time horizon discrete systems. Future studies may also investigate the feasibility to design a estimator for a more general description of systems: the descriptor systems.

7. References

Anderson, B. D. O. & Moore, J. B. (1979). *Optimal Filtering*, Prentice-Hall.

Fu, M., de Souza, C. E. & Luo, Z.-Q. (2001). Finite-horizon robust Kalman filter design, *IEEE Transactions on Signal Processing* 49(9): 2103–2112.

Ghaoui, L. E. & Clafiore, G. (2001). Robust filtering for discrete-time systems with bounded noise and parametric uncertainty, *IEEE Transactions on Automatic Control* 46(7): 1084–1089.

Ishihara, J. Y., Terra, M. H. & Campos, J. C. T. (2006). Robust Kalman filter for descriptor systems, *IEEE Transactions on Automatic Control* 51(8): 1354–1358.

Kalman, R. E. (1960). A New Approach to Linear Filtering and Prediction Problems, Transactions of the ASME 82 (1): 35-45.

Sayed, A. H. (2001). A framework for state space estimation with uncertain models, *IEEE Transactions on Automatic Control* 46(7): 998–1013.

Simon, D. (2006). Optimal State Estimation (2006). John Wiley and Sons.

Theodor, Y. & Shaked, U. (1996). Robust discrete-time minimum variance filtering, *IEEE Transactions on Signal Processing* 44(2): 181–189.

Wang, Z., Zhu, J. & Unbehauen, H. (1999). Robust filter design with time-varying parameter uncertainty and error variance constraints, *International Journal of Control* 72(1): 30–38.

Part 2

Discrete-Time Fixed Control

7

Stochastic Optimal Tracking with Preview for Linear Discrete Time Markovian Jump Systems

Gou Nakura

56-2-402, Gokasyo-Hirano, Uji, Kyoto, 611-0011, Japan

1. Introduction

It is well known that, for the design of tracking control systems, preview information of reference signals is very useful for improving performance of the systems, and recently much work has been done for preview control systems [Cohen & Shaked (1997); Gershon et al. (2004a); Gershon et al. (2004b); Nakura (2008a); Nakura (2008b); Nakura (2008c); Nakura (2008d); Nakura (2008e); Nakura (2009); Nakura (2010); Sawada (2008); Shaked & Souza (1995); Takaba (2000)]. Especially, in order to design tracking control systems for a class of systems with rapid or abrupt changes, it is effective in improving the tracking performance to construct tracking control systems considering future information of reference signals. Shaked et al. have constructed the H∞ tracking control theory with preview for continuous- and discrete-time linear time-varying systems by a game theoretic approach [Cohen & Shaked (1997); Shaked & Souza (1995)]. Recently the author has extended their theory to linear impulsive systems [Nakura (2008b); Nakura (2008c)]. It is also very important to consider the effects of stochastic noise or uncertainties for tracking control systems. By Gershon et al., the theory of stochastic H∞ tracking with preview has been presented for linear continuous- and discrete-time systems [Gershon et al. (2004a); Gershon et al. (2004b)]. The H∞ tracking theory by the game theoretic approach can be restricted to the optimal or stochastic optimal tracking theory and also extended to the stochastic H∞ tracking control theory. While some command generators of reference signals are needed in the papers [Sawada (2008); Takaba (2000)], a priori knowledge of any dynamic models for reference signals is not assumed on the game theoretic approach. Also notice that all these works have been studied for the systems with no mode transitions, i.e., the single mode systems. Tracking problems with preview for systems with some mode transitions are also very important issues to research.

Markovian jump systems [Boukas (2006); Costa & Tuesta (2003); Costa et al. (2005); Dragan & Morozan (2004); Fragoso (1989); Fragoso (1995); Lee & Khargonekar (2008); Mariton (1990); Souza & Fragoso (1993); Sworder (1969); Sworder (1972)] have abrupt random mode changes in their dynamics. The mode changes follow Markov processes. Such systems may be found in the area of mechanical systems, power systems, manufacturing systems, communications, aerospace systems, financial engineering and so on. Such systems are classified into continuous-time [Boukas (2006); Dragan & Morozan (2004); Mariton (1990);

Souza & Fragoso (1993); Sworder (1969); Sworder (1972)] and discrete-time [Costa & Tuesta (2003); Costa et al. (2005); Lee & Khargonekar (2008); Fragoso (1989); Fragoso et al. (1995)] systems. The optimal, stochastic optimal and H∞ control theory has been presented for each of these systems respectively [Costa & Tuesta (2003); Fragoso (1989); Fragoso et al. (1995); Souza & Fragoso (1993); Sworder (1969); Sworder (1972)]. The stochastic LQ and H∞ control theory for Markovian jump systems are of high practice. For example, these theories are applied to the solar energy system, the underactuated manipulator system and so on [Costa et al. (2005)]. Although preview compensation for hybrid systems including the Markovian jump systems is very effective for improving the system performance, the preview tracking theory for the Markovian jump systems had not been yet constructed. Recently the author has presented the stochastic LQ and H∞ preview tracking theories by state feedback for linear continuous-time Markovian jump systems [Nakura (2008d) Nakura (2008e); Nakura (2009)], which are the first theories of the preview tracking control for the Markovian jump systems. For the discrete-time Markovian jump systems, he has presented the stochastic LQ preview tracking theory only by state feedback [Nakura (2010)]. The stochastic LQ preview tracking problem for them by output feedback has not been yet fully investigated.

In this paper we study the stochastic optimal tracking problems with preview by state feedback and output feedback for linear discrete-time Markovian jump systems on the finite time interval and derive the forms of the preview compensator dynamics. In this paper it is assumed that the modes are fully observable in the whole time interval. We consider three different tracking problems according to the structures of preview information and give the control strategies for them respectively. The output feedback dynamic controller is given by using solutions of two types of coupled Riccati difference equations. Feedback controller gains are designed by using one type of coupled Riccati difference equations with terminal conditions, which give the necessary and sufficient conditions for the solvability of the stochastic optimal tracking problem with preview by state feedback, and filter gains are designed by using another type of coupled Riccati difference equations with initial conditions. Correspondingly compensators introducing future information are coupled with each other. This is our very important point in this paper. Finally we consider numerical examples and verify the effectiveness of the preview tracking theory presented in this paper.

The organization of this paper is as follows: In section 2 we describe the systems and problem formulation. In section 3 we present the solution of the stochastic optimal preview tracking problems over the finite time interval by state feedback. In section 4 we consider the output feedback problems. In section 5 we consider numerical examples and verify the effectiveness of the stochastic optimal preview tracking design theory. In the appendices we present the proof of the proposition, which gives the necessary and sufficient conditions of the solvability for the stochastic optimal preview tracking problems by state feedback, and the orthogonal property of the variable of the error system and that of the output feedback controller, which plays the important role to solve the output feedback problems.

Notations: Throughout this paper the superscript ' stands for the matrix transposition, $|\cdot|$ denotes the Euclidean vector norm and $|v|_R^2$ also denotes the weighted norm $v'Rv$. O denotes the matrix with all zero components.

2. Problem formulation

Let (Ω, F, P) be a probability space and, on this space, consider the following linear discrete-time time-varying system with reference signal and Markovian mode transitions.

$$
\begin{aligned}
x(k+1) &= A_{d,m(k)}(k)x(k) + G_{d,m(k)}(k)\omega_d(k) + B_{2d,m(k)}(k)u_d(k) + B_{3d,m(k)}(k)r_d(k) \\
z_d(k) &= C_{1d,m(k)}(k)x(k) + D_{12d,m(k)}(k)u_d(k) + D_{13d,m(k)}(k)r_d(k) \\
y(k) &= C_{2d,m(k)}(k)x(k) + H_{d,m(k)}(k)\omega_d(k) \\
& \qquad x(0) = x_0,\ m(0) = i_0
\end{aligned} \tag{1}
$$

where $x \in R^n$ is the state, $\omega_d \in R^{pd}$ is the exogenous random noise, $u_d \in R^m$ is the control input, $z_d \in R^{kd}$ is the controlled output, $r_d(\cdot) \in R^{rd}$ is known or measurable reference signal and $y \in R^k$ is the measured output. x_0 is an unknown initial state and i_0 is a given initial mode.

Let M be an integer and $\{m(k)\}$ is a Markov process taking values on the finite set $\varphi=\{1,2,\cdots,M\}$ with the following transition probabilities:

$$
P\{m(k+1)=j \mid m(k)=i\} := p_{d,ij}(k)
$$

where $p_{d,ij}(k) \geq 0$ is also the transition rate at the jump instant from the mode i to j, $i \neq j$, and $\sum_{j=1}^{M} p_{d,ij}(k) = 1$. Let $P_d(k) = [\, p_{d,ij}(k)]$ be the transition probability matrix. We assume that all these matrices are of compatible dimensions. Throughout this paper the dependence of the matrices on k will be omitted for the sake of notational simplicity.

For this system (1), we assume the following conditions:

A1: $D_{12d,m(k)}(k)$ is of full column rank.

A2: $D_{12d,m(k)}'(k)C_{1d,m(k)}(k)=O$, $D_{12d,m(k)}'(k)D_{13d,m(k)}(k)=O$

A3: $E\{x(0)\}=\mu_0$, $E\{\omega_d(k)\}=0$,
$E\{\omega_d(k)\omega_d'(k)1_{\{m(k)=i\}}\}=X_i$,
$E\{x(0)x'(0)\, 1_{\{m(0)=i_0\}}\}=Q_{i_0}(0)$,
$E\{\omega_d(0)x'(0)1_{\{m(0)=i_0\}}\}=O$,
$E\{\omega_d(k)x'(k)1_{\{m(k)=i\}}\}=O$,
$E\{\omega_d(k)u_d'(k)1_{\{m(k)=i\}}\}=O$,
$E\{\omega_d(k)r_d'(k)1_{\{m(k)=i\}}\}=O$

where E is the expectation with respect to m(k), and the indicator function $1_{\{m(k)=i\}}:=1$ if $m(k)=i$, and $1_{\{m(k)=i\}}:=0$ if $m(k)\neq i$.

The stochastic optimal tracking problems we address in this section for the system (1) are to design control laws $u_d(\cdot) \in l_2[0,N-1]$ over the finite horizon $[0,N]$, using the information available on the known part of the reference signal $r_d(\cdot)$ and minimizing the sum of the energy of $z_d(k)$, for the given initial mode i_0 and the given distribution of x_0. Considering the stochastic mode transitions and the average of the performance indices over the statistical information of the unknown part of r_d, we define the following performance index.

$$
\begin{aligned}
J_{dN}(x_0, u_d, r_d) := E\Bigg\{ & \sum_{k=0}^{N} E_{\overline{R}_k}\{|C_{1d,m(k)}(k)x(k) + D_{13d,m(k)}(k)r_d(k)|^2\} \\
& + \sum_{k=0}^{N-1} E_{\overline{R}_k}\{|D_{12d,m(k)}(k)u_d(k)|^2\} \Bigg\}
\end{aligned} \tag{2}
$$

$E_{\overline{R}_k}$ means the expectation over $\overline{R}_{k+h}$, h is the preview length of $r_d(k)$, and $\overline{R}_k$ denotes the future information on r_d at the current time k, i.e., $\overline{R}_k := \{r_d(l);\ k<l\leq N\}$. This introduction of

$E_{\overline{R_k}}$ means that the unknown part of the reference signal follows a stochastic process, whose distribution is allowed to be unknown.
Now we formulate the following optimal fixed-preview tracking problems for the system (1) and the performance index (2). In these problems, it is assumed that, at the current time k, $r_d(l)$ is known for $l \leq \min(N, k+h)$, where h is the preview length.
The Stochastic Optimal Fixed-Preview Tracking Problem by State Feedback:
Consider the system (1) and the performance index (2), and assume the conditions A1, A2 and A3. Then, find u_d^* minimizing the performance index (2) where the control strategy $u_d^*(k)$, $0 \leq k \leq N-1$, is based on the information $R_{k+h}:=\{r_d(l); 0 \leq l \leq k+h\}$ with $0 \leq h \leq N$ and the state information $X_k:=\{x(l); 0 \leq l \leq k\}$.
The Stochastic Optimal Fixed-Preview Tracking Problem by Output Feedback:
Consider the system (1) and the performance index (2), and assume the conditions A1, A2 and A3. Then, find u_d^* minimizing the performance index (2) where the control strategy $u_d^*(k)$, $0 \leq k \leq N-1$, is based on the information $R_{k+h}:=\{r_d(l); 0 \leq l \leq k+h\}$ with $0 \leq h \leq N$ and the observed information $Y_k:=\{y(l); 0 \leq l \leq k\}$.
Notice that, on these problems, at the current time k to decide the control strategies, R_{k+h} can include any noncausal information in the meaning of that it is allowed that the future information of the reference signals $\{r_d(l); k \leq l \leq k+h\}$ is inputted to the feedback controllers.

3. Design of tracking controllers by state feedback

In this section we consider the state feedback problems.
Now we consider the coupled Riccati difference equations [Costa et al. (2005); Fragoso (1989)]

$$X_i(k)=A_{d,i}'(k)E_i(X(k+1),k)A_{d,i}(k)+C_{1d,i}'C_{1d,i}-F_{2,i}'T_{2,i}F_{2,i}(k),\ k=0, 1, \cdots \tag{3}$$

where $E_i(X(k+1),k)=\sum_{j=1}^{M} p_{d,ij}(k)\, X_{j+1}(k+1)$, $X(k)=(X_1(k), \cdots, X_M(k))$,

$$\begin{aligned}
T_{2,i}(k) &= D_{12d,i}'D_{12d,i} + B_{2d,i}'E_i(X(k+1),k)B_{2d,i},\\
R_{2,i}(k) &= B_{2d,i}'E_i(X(k+1),k)A_{d,i},\\
F_{2,i}(k) &= -T_{2,i}^{-1}R_{2,i}(k)
\end{aligned}$$

and the following scalar coupled difference equations.

$$\alpha_i(k)=E_i(\alpha(k+1),k)+\mathrm{tr}\{G_{d,i}X_iG_{d,i}'E_i(X(k+1),k)\} \tag{4}$$

where $E_i(\alpha(k+1),k)=\sum_{j=1}^{M} p_{d,ij}(k),\ \alpha_j(k+1)$ and $\alpha(k)=(\alpha_1(k), \ldots, \alpha_M(k))$.

Remark 3.1 Note that these coupled Riccati difference equations (3) are the same as those for the standard stochastic linear quadratic (LQ) optimization problem of linear discrete-time Markovian jump systems without considering any exogeneous reference signals nor any preview information [Costa et al. (2005); Fragoso (1989)]. Also notice that the form of the equation (4) is different from [Costa et al. (2005); Fragoso (1989)] in the points that the solution $\alpha(\cdot)$ does not depend on any modes in [Costa et al. (2005)] and the noise matrix G_d does not depend on any modes in [Fragoso (1989)].

We obtain the following necessary and sufficient conditions for the solvability of the stochastic optimal fixed-preview tracking problem by state feedback and an optimal control strategy for it.

Theorem 3.1 Consider the system (1) and the performance index (2). Suppose A1, A2 and A3. Then the Stochastic Optimal Fixed-Preview Tracking Problem by State Feedback for (1) and (2) is solvable if and only if there exist matrices $X_i(k) \geq O$ and scalar functions $\alpha_i(k)$, i=1, ⋯,M, satisfying the conditions $X_i(N)=C_{1d,i}'(N)C_{1d,i}(N)$ and $\alpha_i(N)=0$ such that the coupled Riccati equations (3) and the coupled scalar equations (4) hold over [0,N]. Moreover an optimal control strategy for the tracking problem (1) and (2) is given by

$$u_d^*(k)=F_{2,i}(k)x(k)+D_{u,i}(k)r_d(k)+D_{\theta u,i}(k)E_i(\theta_c(k+1),k) \text{ for } i=1,\cdots,M$$

where $D_{u,i}(k)=-T_{2,i}^{-1}(k)B_{2d,i}'E_i(X(k+1),k)B_{3d,i}$ and $D_{\theta u,i}(k)=-T_{2,i}^{-1}(k)B_{2d,i}'$. $\theta_i(k)$, i=1, ⋯,M, $k \in [0,N]$ satisfies

$$\begin{aligned} &\theta_i(k)=\bar{A}_{d,i}'(k)E_i(\theta(k+1),k)+\bar{B}_{d,i}(k)r_d(k),\\ &\theta_i(N)=C_{1d,i}'D_{13d,i}r_d(N) \end{aligned} \tag{5}$$

where $E_i(\theta(k+1),k)=\sum_{j=1}^{M} p_{d,ij}(k)\,\theta_j(k+1)$ and $\theta(k)=(\theta_1(k),\cdots,\theta_M(k))$,

$$\begin{aligned} &\bar{A}_{d,i}'(k)=A_{d,i}-D_{\theta u,i}'T_{2,i}F_{2,i}(k),\\ &\bar{B}_{d,i}(k)=A_{d,i}'\,E_i(X(k+1),k)B_{3d,i}-F_{2,i}'T_{2,i}D_{u,i}(k)+C_{1d,i}'D_{13d,i} \end{aligned}$$

and $\theta_{c,i}(k)$ is the 'causal' part of $\theta_i(\cdot)$ at time k. This $\theta_{c,i}$ is the expected value of θ_i over $\bar{R}_k$ and given by

$$\begin{aligned} &\theta_{c,i}(l)=\bar{A}_{d,i}'(l)E_i(\theta_c(l+1),l)+\bar{B}_{d,i}(l)r_d(l),\ k+1\leq l\leq k+h,\\ &\theta_{c,i}(k+h+1)=0 \text{ if } k+h\leq N-1\\ &\theta_{c,i}(k+h+1)=C_{1d,i}'D_{13d,i}r_d(N),\ k+h=N \end{aligned} \tag{6}$$

where $E_i(\theta_c(k+1),k)=\sum_{j=1}^{M} p_{d,ij}(k)\,\theta_{c,j}(k+1)$ and $\theta_c(k)=(\theta_{c,1}(k),\cdots,\theta_{c,M}(k))$.

Moreover, the optimal value of the performance index is

$$\begin{aligned} J_{dN}(x0,u_d^*,r_d)&=tr\{Q_{i_0}X_{i_0}\}+\alpha_{i_0}(0)+E\{E_{\bar{R}_0}\{2\theta_{i_0}'x_0\}\}\\ &+E\{\sum_{k=0}^{N-1} E_{\bar{R}_k}\{|T_{2,m(k)}^{1/2}D_{\theta u,m(k)}(k)E_{m(k)}(\theta_c^-(k+1),k)|^2\}\}+\bar{J}_d(r_d) \end{aligned} \tag{7}$$

where $\theta_{c,m(k)}^-(k)=\theta_{m(k)}(k)-\theta_{c,m(k)}(k)$, $k \in [0,N]$,
$E_i(\theta_c^-(k+1),k)=\sum_{j=1}^{M} p_{d,ij}(k)\,\theta_{c,j}^-(k+1)$, $\theta_c^-(k)=(\theta_{c,1}^-(k),\cdots,\theta_{c,M}^-(k))$ and

$$\begin{aligned} \bar{J}_d(r_d)=E\Big\{E_{\bar{R}_N}\{|D_{13d,m(N)}(N)r_d(N)|^2\}\Big\}+E\Big\{\sum_{k=0}^{N-1} &E_{\bar{R}_k}\{-|T_{2,m(k)}^{1/2}D_{\theta u,m(k)}(k)E_{m(k)}(\theta(k+1),k)|^2\\ &-2E_{m(k)}(\theta'(k+1),k)D_{\theta u,m(k)}'T_{2,m(k)}D_{u,m(k)}(k)r_d(k)\\ &+2E_{m(k)}(\theta'(k+1),k)B_{3d,m(k)}(k)r_d(k)+J_{d,k,m(k)}(r_d)\}\Big\}, \end{aligned}$$

$$J_{d,k,m(k)}(r_d) = r_d'(k)\left[-D_{u,m(k)}'T_{2,m(k)}D_{u,m(k)}(k) + B_{3d,m(k)}'E_{m(k)}(X(k+1),k)B_{3d,m(k)}\right.$$
$$\left.+D_{13d,m(k)}'D_{13d,m(k)}\right]r_d(k).$$

(Proof) See the appendix 1.

Remark 3.2 Note that each dynamics (6) of $\theta_{c,i}$, which composes the compensator introducing the preview information, is coupled with the others. It corresponds to the characteristic that the Riccati difference equations (3) are coupled with each other, which give the necessary and sufficient conditions for the solvability of the stochastic optimal tracking problem by state feedback.

Next we consider the following two extreme cases according to the information structures (preview lengths) of r_d:

i. Stochastic Optimal Tracking of Causal $\{r_d(\cdot)\}$:

In this case, $\{r_d(k)\}$ is measured on-line, i.e., at time k, $r_d(l)$ is known only for $l\leq k$.

ii. Stochastic Optimal Tracking of Noncausal $\{r_d(\cdot)\}$:

In this case, the signal $\{r_d(k)\}$ is assumed to be known a priori for the whole time interval $k\in[0,N]$.

Utilizing the optimal control strategy for the stochastic optimal tracking problem in Theorem 3.1, we present the solutions to these two extreme cases.

Corollary 3.1 Consider the system (1) and the performance index (2). Suppose A1, A2 and A3. Then each of the stochastic optimal tracking problems for (1) and (2) is solvable by state feedback if and only if there exist matrices $X_i(k)\geq O$ and scalar functions $\alpha_i(k)$, i=1, ···,M, satisfying the conditions $X_i(N)=C_{1d,i}'(N)C_{1d,i}(N)$ and $\alpha_i(N)=0$ such that the coupled Riccati difference equations (3) and the coupled scalar equations (4) hold over [0,N]. Moreover, the following results hold using the three types of gains

$$K_{d,x,i}(k)=F_{2,i}(k),\ K_{rd,i}(k)=D_{u,i}(k) \text{ and } K_{d,\theta,i}(k)=D_{\theta u,i}(k) \text{ for } i=1,\cdots,M.$$

i. The control law for the Stochastic Optimal Tracking of Causal $\{r_d(\cdot)\}$ is

$$u_{d,s1}(k)=K_{d,x,i}(k)x(k)+K_{rd,i}(k)r_d(k) \text{ for } i=1,\cdots,M$$

and the value of the performance index is

$$J_{dN}(x_0,u_{d,s1},r_d)=\mathrm{tr}\{Q_{i_0}X_{i_0}\}+\alpha_{i_0}(0)+E\{E_{\overline{R_0}}\{2\theta_{i_0}'x_0\}\}$$
$$+E\{\sum_{k=0}^{N-1} E_{\overline{R_k}}\{|T_{2,m(k)}^{1/2}D_{\theta u,m(k)}(k)E_{m(k)}(\theta(k+1),k)|^2\}\}+\bar{J}_d(r_d).$$

ii. The control law for the Stochastic Optimal Tracking of Noncausal $\{r_d(\cdot)\}$ is

$$u_{d,s2}(k)=K_{d,x,i}(k)x(k)+K_{rd,i}(k)r_d(k)+K_{d,\theta,i}(k)E_i(\theta(k+1),k) \text{ for } i=1,\cdots,M$$

with $\theta_i(\cdot)$ given by (5) and the value of the performance index is

$$J_{dN}(x_0,u_{d,s2},r_d)=\mathrm{tr}\{Q_{i_0}X_{i_0}\}+\alpha_{i_0}(0)+2\theta_{i_0}'\mu_0+\bar{J}_d(r_d).$$

(Proof)

i. In this causal case, the control law is not affected by the effects of any preview information and so $\theta_c(k)=0$ for all $k\in[0,N]$ since the each dynamics of $\theta_{c,i}$ becomes autonomous. As a result we obtain θ (k)= θ_c^- (k) for all k $\in$ [0,N]. Therefore we obtain the value of the performance index $J_{dN}(x_0, u_{d,s1}, r_d)$.

ii. In this noncausal case, h=N-k and (5) and (6) becomes identical. As a result we obtain θ (k)= θ_c (k) for all k $\in$ [0,N]. Therefore we obtain θ_c^- (k)=0 for all k $\in$ [0,N] and the value of the performance index $J_{dN}(x_0, u_{d,s2}, r_d)$. Notice that, in this case, we can obtain the deterministic value of θ_{i_0} (0) using the information of $\{r_d(\cdot)\}$ until the final time N and so the term E{ $E_{\overline{R_0}}$ {2 θ_{i_0} 'x0}} in the right hand side of (7) reduces to 2 θ_{i_0} ' μ_0. (Q.E.D.)

4. Output feedback case

In this section, we consider the output feedback problems.
We first assume the following conditions:

$$\text{A4: } G_{d,m(k)}(k)H_{d,m(k)}'(k)=O,\ H_{d,m(k)}(k)H_{d,m(k)}'(k)>O$$

By the transformation

$$\bar{u}_{d,c}(k):=u_d(k)-D_{u,i}(k)r_d(k)-D_{\theta u,i}(k)E_i(\theta_c(k+1),k)$$

and the coupled difference equations (3) and (4), we can rewrite the performance index as follows:

$$\begin{aligned} J_{dN}(x_0,\bar{u}_{d,c},r_d) &= \mathrm{tr}\{Q_{i_0}X_{i_0}\} + \alpha_{i_0}(0) \\ &+E\left\{E_{\overline{R_0}}\{2'\theta_{i_0}x_0\}\right\} \\ &+E\left\{\sum_{k=0}^{N-1} E_{\overline{R_k}}\{|\bar{u}_{d,c}(k)-F_{2,m(k)}(k)x(k)\text{-}D_{\theta u,m(k)}(k)E_{m(k)}(\theta_c^-(k+1),k)|^2_{T_{2,m(k)}}\}\right\} \\ &+\bar{J}_d(r_d) \end{aligned}$$

and the dynamics can be written as follows:

$$x(k+1)=A_{d,m(k)}(k)x(k)+G_{d,m(k)}(k)\omega_d(k)+B_{2d,m(k)}(k)\bar{u}_{d,c}(k)+\bar{r}_{d,c}(k)$$

where

$$\bar{r}_{d,c}(k)=B_{2d,m(k)}\{D_{u,m(k)}(k)r_d(k)+D_{\theta u,m(k)}(k)E_{m(k)}(\theta_c(k+1),k)\}+B_{3d,m(k)}(k)r_d(k).$$

For this plant dynamics, consider the controller

$$\begin{aligned} \hat{x}_e(k+1) &= A_{d,m(k)}(k)\hat{x}_e(k)+B_{2d,m(k)}(k)\bar{u}_{d,c*}(k) \\ &+B_{3d,m(k)}(k)\bar{r}_{d,c}(k)-M_{m(k)}(k)[y(k)-C_{2d,m(k)}\hat{x}_e(k)] \\ \hat{x}_e(0) &= E\left\{E_{\overline{R_0}}\{x_0\}\right\}=\mu_0,\quad \bar{u}_{d,c*}(k)=F_{2,m(k)}(k)\hat{x}_e(k) \end{aligned} \tag{8}$$

where $M_{m(k)}$ are the controller gains to decide later, using the solutions of another coupled Riccati equations introduced below.
Define the error variable

$$e(k):=x(k)\text{-}\hat{x}_e(k)$$

and the error dynamics is as follows:

$$e(k+1)=A_{d,m(k)}(k)e(k)+G_{d,m(k)}(k)\omega_d(k)+M_{m(k)}(k)[y(k)-C_{2d,m(k)}\hat{x}_e(k)]$$
$$=[A_{d,m(k)}+M_{m(k)}C_{2d,m(k)}](k)e(k)+[G_{d,m(k)}+M_{m(k)}H_{d,m(k)}](k)\omega_d(k)$$

Note that this error dynamics does not depend on the exogenous inputs u_d nor r_d. Our objective is to design the controller gain $M_{m(k)}$ which minimizes

$$J_{dN}(x_0, \bar{u}_{d,c^*}, r_d)=tr\{Q_{i_0} X_{i_0}\}+\alpha_{i_0}(0)+E\{E_{\overline{R_0}}\{2\theta_{i_0}'x_0\}\}$$
$$+E\{\sum_{k=0}^{N-1} E_{\overline{R_k}}\{|F_{2,m(k)}(k)e(k)$$
$$-D_{\theta u,m(k)}(k)E_{m(k)}(\theta_c^-(k+1),k)|^2_{T_{2,m(k)}}\}\}+\bar{J}_d(r_d)$$

Notice that $e(k)$ and $E_{m(k)}(\theta_c^-(k+1),k)$ are mutually independent.
We decide the gain matrices $M_i(k)$, $i=1, \cdots, M$ by designing the LMMSE filter such that $\sum_{k=0}^{N-1} E\{E_{\overline{R_k}}\{|e(k)|^2\}\}$ is minimized. Now we consider the following coupled Riccati difference equations and the initial conditions.

$$Y_j(k+1)=\sum_{i\in J(k)} p_{d,ij}\Big[A_{d,i}'Y_i(k)A_{d,i}-A_{d,i}Y_i(k)C_{2d,i}'(H_{d,i}H_{d,i}'\pi_i(k)$$
$$+C_{2d,i}Y_i(k)C_{2d,i}')^{-1}C_{2d,i}Y_i(k)A_{d,i}'+\pi_i(k)G_{d,i}G_{d,i}'\Big], \tag{9}$$
$$Y_i(0)=\pi_i(0)(Q_{i_0}-\mu_0\mu_0')$$

where
$\pi_i(k):=P\{m(k)=i\}$, $\sum_{j=1}^{M} p_{d,ij}(k)\,\pi_i=\pi_j$, $\sum_{i=1}^{M}\pi_i(k)=1$, $J(k):=\{i\in N;\ \pi_i(k)>0\}$.
These equations are also called the filtering coupled Riccati difference equations [Costa & Tuesta (2003)].
Now since

$$E\{E_{\overline{R_0}}\{e(0)\}\}=E\{E_{\overline{R_0}}\{x_0\}-E\{E_{\overline{R_0}}\{x_0\}\}\}=E\{E_{\overline{R_0}}x_0\}\}-\mu_0=0$$

and $\bar{r}_{d,c}(0)$ is deterministic if $r_d(l)$ is known at all $l\in[0,k+h]$,

$$E\{E_{\overline{R_0}}\{e(0)\bar{r}_{d,c}'(0)1_{\{m(0)=i\}}\}\}=\pi_i(0)E\{E_{\overline{R_0}}\{e(0)\}\}\bar{r}_{d,c}'(0)=O$$

and so we obtain, for each $k\in[0,N]$,

$$E\{E_{\overline{R_k}}\{e(k)\bar{r}_{d,c}'(k)1_{\{m(k)=i\}}\}\}=\pi_i(k)E\{E_{\overline{R_k}}\{e(k)\}\}\bar{r}_{d,c}'(k)=O.$$

Namely there exist no couplings between $e(\cdot)$ and $\bar{r}_{d,c}(\cdot)$. The development of $e(\cdot)$ on time k is independent of the development of $\bar{r}_{d,c}(\cdot)$ on time k. Then we can show the following orthogonal property as [Theorem 5.3 in (Costa et al. (2005)) or Theorem 2 in (Costa & Tuesta (2003))] by induction on k (See the appendix 2).

$$E\{E_{\overline{R_k}}\{e(k)\hat{x}_e'(k)1_{\{m(k)=i\}}\}\}=O. \tag{10}$$

Moreover define

$$\overline{Y_i}(k):=E\{E_{\overline{R_k}}e(k)e'(k)1_{\{m(k)=i\}}\}$$

and then we can show

$$Y_i(k)=\overline{Y_i}(k).$$

From all these results (orthogonal properties), as the case of $r_d(\cdot)\equiv0$, using the solutions of the coupled difference Riccati equations, it can be shown that the gains $M_{m(k)}$ minimizing J_{dN} are decided as follows (cf. [Costa & Tuesta (2003); Costa et al. (2005)]):

$$M_i(k)=\begin{cases}-A_{d,i}Y_i(k)C_{2d,i}'\left(H_{d,i}H_{d,i}'\pi_i(k)+C_{2d,i}Y_i(k)C_{2d,i}'\right)^{-1}\text{ for } i\in J(k)\\ \\ 0 \text{ for } i\in J(k)\end{cases} \tag{11}$$

Finally the following theorem, which gives the solution of the output feedback problem, holds.

Theorem 4.1 Consider the system (1) and the performance index (2). Suppose A1, A2, A3 and A4. Then an optimal control strategy which, gives the solution of the Stochastic Optimal Fixed-Preview Tracking Problem by Output Feedback for (1) and (2) is given by the dynamic controller (8) with the gains (11) using the solutions of the two types of the coupled Riccati difference equations (3) with $X_i(N)=C_{1d,i}'(N)C_{1d,i}(N)$ and (9) with $Y_i(0)=\pi_i(0)(Q_{i_0}-\mu_0\mu_0')$.

Remark 4.1 Notice that

$$E\{E_{\overline{R_k}}\{|z_d(k)|^2\}\}=\sum_{i=1}^{M}tr\{C_{1d,i}C_{1d,i}'E\{E_{\overline{R_k}}\{x(k)x'(k)1_{\{m(k)=i\}}\}\}\}$$
$$+E\{E_{\overline{R_k}}\{|D_{12d,m(k)}(k)u_d(k)|^2+2x'(k)C_{1d,i}'D_{13d,i}r_d(k)\}\}.$$

Then, with regard to the performance index, the following result holds.

$$E\{E_{\overline{R_k}}\{|z_d(k)|^2\}\}=E\{E_{\overline{R_k}}\{|\hat{z}_e(k)|^2\}\}+\sum_{i=1}^{M}tr\{C_{1d,i}Y_i(k)C_{1d,i}'\}$$
$$+E\{\sum_{i=1}^{M}E_{\overline{R_k}}\{2e'(k)C_{1d,i}'D_{13d,i}r_d(k)1_{\{m(k)=i\}}\}\}$$

where

$$\hat{z}_e(k)=C_{1d,m(k)}\hat{x}_e(k)+D_{12d,m(k)}(k)u_d(k)+D_{13d,m(k)}(k)r_d(k)$$

and we have used the property

$$E\{E_{\overline{R_k}}\{x(k)x'(k)1_{\{m(k)=i\}}\}\}=E\{E_{\overline{R_k}}\{e(k)e'(k)1_{\{m(k)=i\}}\}\}+E\{E_{\overline{R_k}}\{\hat{x}_e(k)\hat{x}_e'(k)1_{\{m(k)=i\}}\}\}$$
$$=Y_i(k)+E\{E_{\overline{R_k}}\{\hat{x}_e(k)\hat{x}_e'(k)1_{\{m(k)=i\}}\}\}$$

by the orthogonal property (10).

Note that the second and third terms in the right hand side do not depend on the input u_d. Then we obtain

$$\begin{aligned} J_{dN}(x_0, u_d, r_d) = E\{\sum_{k=0}^{N} [E_{\overline{R}_k}\{|\hat{z}_e(k)|^2\} + \sum_{i=1}^{M} tr\{C_{1d,i} Y_i(k) C_{1d,i}'\} \\ + \sum_{i=1}^{M} E_{\overline{R}_k}\{2e'(k) C_{1d,i}' D_{13d,i} r_d(k) 1_{\{m(k)=i\}}\}] \\ + |C_{1d,m(N)} x(N) + D_{13d,m(N)} r_d(N)|^2\} \end{aligned} \tag{12}$$

Therefore minimizing (12) is equivalent to minimizing $E\{\sum_{k=0}^{N} E_{\overline{R}_k}\{|\hat{z}_e(k)|^2\}$ subject to the dynamics

$$\hat{x}_e(k+1) = A_{d,m(k)}(k)\hat{x}_e(k) + B_{2d,m(k)}(k)\overline{u}_{d,c^*}(k) + \overline{r}_{d,c}(k) - M_{m(k)}(k)v(k),\ \hat{x}_e(0) = E_{\overline{R}_0}\{x_0\} = \mu_0$$

where

$$v(k) = y(k) - C_{2d,m(k)}\hat{x}_e(k)$$

and $\overline{u}_{d,c^*}(k)$ is the state feedback controller with the form $K_{d,x,i}(k)\hat{x}_e(k) + K_{rd,i}(k) r_d(k) + K_{d,\theta,i}(k) E_i(\theta(k+1),k)$ for some gains $K_{d,x,i}$, $K_{rd,i}$ and $K_{d,\theta,i}$. Note that the term $M_{m(k)}(k)v(k)$ plays the same role as the "noise" term $G_{d,m(k)}(k)\omega_d(k)$ of the plant dynamics in the state feedback case.

Remark 4.2 As the case of $r_d(\cdot)\equiv 0$, the separation principle holds in the case of $r_d(\cdot)\not\equiv 0$. Namely we can design the state feedback gains $F_{2,m(k)}(k)$ and the filter gains $M_{m(k)}$ separately.

Utilizing the optimal control strategy for the stochastic optimal tracking problem in Theorem 4.1, we present the solutions to the two extreme cases.

Corollary 4.1 Consider the system (1) and the performance index (2). Suppose A1, A2, A3 and A4. Then optimal control strategies by output feedback for the two extreme cases are as follows using the solutions of the two types of the coupled Riccati difference equations (3) with $X_i(N) = C_{1d,i}'(N) C_{1d,i}(N)$ and (9) with $Y_i(0) = \pi_i(0)(Q_{i_0} - \mu_0\mu_0')$:

i. The control law by output feedback for the Stochastic Optimal Tracking of Causal $\{r_d(\cdot)\}$ is

$$\hat{x}_e(k+1) = A_{d,m(k)}(k)\hat{x}_e(k) + B_{2d,m(k)}(k)\overline{u}_{d,1^*}(k) + \overline{r}_{d,1}(k) - M_{m(k)}(k)v(k)$$
$$\hat{x}_e(0) = \mu_0$$
$$\overline{u}_{d,1}(k) := u_d(k) - D_{u,i}(k) r_d(k)$$
$$\overline{u}_{d,1^*}(k) = F_{2,m(k)}(k)\hat{x}_e(k)$$
$$\overline{r}_{d,1}(k) = B_{2d,m(k)} D_{u,m(k)}(k) r_d(k) + B_{3d,m(k)}(k) r_d(k)$$

and the value of the performance index is

$$\begin{aligned} J_{dN}(x_0, \overline{u}_{d,1^*}, r_d) = tr\{Q_{i_0} X_{i_0}\} + \alpha_{i_0}(0) + E\{E_{\overline{R}_0}\{2\theta_{i_0}' x_0\}\} \\ + E\{\sum_{k=0}^{N-1} E_{\overline{R}_k}\{|F_{2,m(k)}(k)e(k) \\ - D_{\theta u,m(k)}(k) E_{m(k)}(\theta(k+1),k)|^2_{T_{2,m(k)}}\}\} + \overline{J}_d(r_d). \end{aligned}$$

ii. The control law by output feedback for the Stochastic Optimal Tracking of Noncausal $\{r_d(\cdot)\}$ is

$$\hat{x}_e(k+1)=A_{d,m(k)}(k)\hat{x}_e(k)+B_{2d,m(k)}(k)\bar{u}_{d,2*}(k)+\bar{r}_{d,2}(k)-M_{m(k)}(k)v(k)$$
$$\hat{x}_e(0)=\mu_0$$
$$\bar{u}_{d,2}(k):=u_d(k)-D_{u,i}(k)r_d(k)-D_{\theta u,i}(k)E_i(\theta(k+1),k)$$
$$\bar{u}_{d,2*}(k)=F_{2,m(k)}(k)\hat{x}_e(k)$$
$$\bar{r}_{d,2}(k)=B_{2d,m(k)}\{D_{u,m(k)}(k)r_d(k)+D_{\theta u,m(k)}(k)E_{m(k)}(\theta(k+1),k)\}+B_{3d,m(k)}(k)r_d(k)$$

and the value of the performance index is

$$J_{dN}(x_0,\bar{u}_{d,2*},r_d)=\mathrm{tr}\{Q_{i_0}X_{i_0}\}+\alpha_{i_0}(0)+2\theta_{i_0}'\mu_0+E\{\sum_{k=0}^{N-1}E_{\overline{R_k}}\{|F_{2,m(k)}(k)e(k)|^2_{T_{2,m(k)}}\}\}+\bar{J}_d(r_d).$$

(Proof) As the state feedback cases, $\theta_c(k)=0$, i.e., $\theta(k)=\theta_c^-(k)$ for all $k\in[0,N]$ in the case i), and $\theta(k)=\theta_c(k)$, i.e., $\theta_c^-(k)=0$ for all $k\in[0,N]$ in the case ii).

5. Numerical examples

In this section, we study numerical examples to demonstrate the effectiveness of the presented stochastic LQ preview tracking design theory.
We consider the following two mode systems and assume that the system parameters are as follows. (cf. [Cohen & Shaked (1997); Shaked & Souza (1995)].):

$$\begin{aligned}
&x(k+1)=A_{d,m(k)}(k)x(k)+G_d(k)\omega_d(k)+B_{2d}(k)u_d(k)+B_{3d,m(k)}(k)r_d(k)\\
&x(0)=x_0,\ m(0)=i_0,m(k)=1,2\\
&z_d(k)=C_{1d,m(k)}(k)x(k)+D_{12d,m(k)}(k)u_d(k)+D_{13d,m(k)}(k)r_d(k)\\
&y(k)=C_{2d,m(k)}(k)x(k)+H_{d,m(k)}(k)\omega_d(k)
\end{aligned}\qquad(13)$$

where

Mode 1: Mode 2:

$$A_{d,1}=\begin{bmatrix}0&1\\-0.8&1.6\end{bmatrix},\ A_{d,2}=\begin{bmatrix}0&1\\1.6&1.6\end{bmatrix},\ G_d=\begin{bmatrix}0\\0.1\end{bmatrix},\ B_{2d}=\begin{bmatrix}0\\1\end{bmatrix},$$

$$B_{3d,1}=\begin{bmatrix}1.5\\0\end{bmatrix},\ B_{3d,2}=\begin{bmatrix}1.8\\0\end{bmatrix},$$

$$C_{1d,1}=\begin{bmatrix}-0.5&0.2\\0&0\end{bmatrix},\ C_{1d,2}=\begin{bmatrix}-0.5&0.1\\0&0\end{bmatrix},\ D_{12d}=\begin{bmatrix}0\\0.1\end{bmatrix},\ D_{13d}=\begin{bmatrix}-1.0\\0\end{bmatrix}$$

Let

$$P_d=\begin{bmatrix}0.3&0.7\\0.6&0.4\end{bmatrix}$$

be a stationary transition matrix of $\{m(k)\}$. We set $x_0=col(0,0)$ and $i_0=1$.

Then we introduce the following objective function.

$$J_{dN}(x_0, u_d, r_d) := E\{\sum_{k=0}^{N} E_{\overline{R}_k}\{| C_{1d,m(k)}(k)x(k)+D_{13d,m(k)}(k)r_d(k)|^2\}\}$$
$$+0.01E\{\sum_{k=0}^{N-1} E_{\overline{R}_k}\{| u_d(k)|^2\}\}$$

By the term $B_{3d,i}(k)r_d(k)$, i=1,2, the tracking performance can be expected to be improved as [Cohen & Shaked (1997); Shaked & Souza (1995)] and so on. The paths of m(k) are generated randomly, and the performances are compared under the same condition, that is, the same set of the paths so that the performances can be easily compared.
We consider the whole system (13) with mode transition rate P_d over the time interval $k \in [0,100]$. For this system (13) with the rate matrix P_d, we apply the results of the optimal tracking design theory by output feedback for $r_d(k)=0.5\sin(\pi k/20)$ and $r_d(k)=0.5\sin(\pi k/100)$ with various step lengths of preview, and show the simulation results for sample paths.

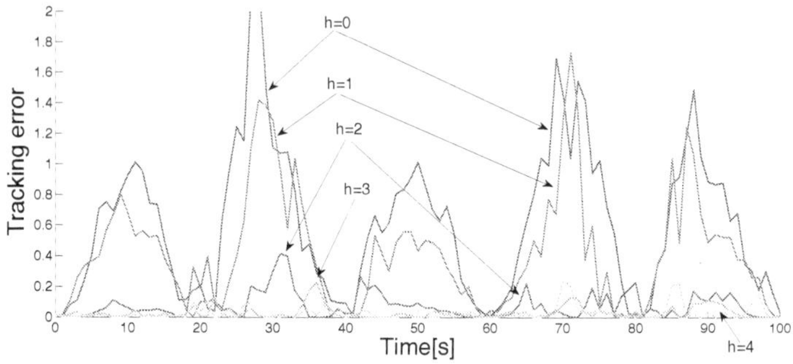

Fig. 1(a). $r_d(k)=0.5\sin(\pi k/20)$

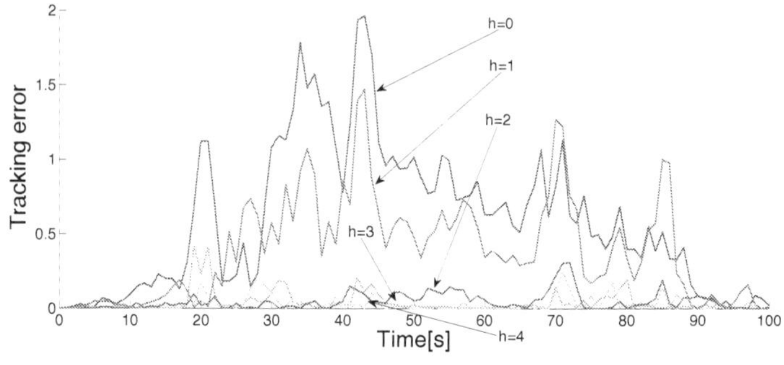

Fig. 1(b). $r_d(k)=0.5\sin(\pi k/100)$

Fig. 1. The whole system consisting of mode 1 and mode 2: The errors of tracking for various preview lengths

It is shown in Fig. 1(a) for $r_d(k)= 0.5\sin(\pi k/20)$ and Fig. 1(b) $r_d(k)=0.5\sin(\pi k/100)$ that increasing the preview steps from h=0 to h=1,2,3,4 improves the tracking performance. In fact, the square values $|C_{1d,i}(k)x(k) + D_{13d}(k)r_d(k)|^2$ of the tracking errors are shown in Fig. 1(a) and (b) and it is clear the tracking error decreases as increasing the preview steps by these figures.

6. Conclusion

In this paper we have studied the stochastic linear quadratic (LQ) optimal tracking control theory considering the preview information by state feedback and output feedback for the linear discrete-time Markovian jump systems affected by the white noises, which are a class of stochastic switching systems, and verified the effectiveness of the design theory by numerical examples. In order to solve the output feedback problems, we have introduced the LMMSE filters adapted to the effects of preview feedforward compensation. In order to design the output feedback controllers, we need the solutions of two types of coupled Riccati difference equations, i.e., the ones to decide the state feedback gains and the ones to decide the filter gains. These solutions of two types of coupled Riccati difference equations can be obtained independently i.e., the separation principle holds. Correspondingly the compensators introducing the preview information of the reference signal are coupled with each other. This is the very important research result in this paper.

We have considered both of the cases of full and partial observation. However, in these cases, we have considered the situations that the switching modes are observable over whole time interval. The construction of the design theory for the case that the switching modes are unknown is a very important further research issue.

Appendix 1. Proof of Proposition 3.1

(Proof of Proposition 3.1)

Sufficiency:

Let $X_i(k)>O$ and α_i, i=1, …, M, be solutions to (3) and (4) over [0,N] such that $X_i(N)=C_{1d,i}'(N)C_{1d,i}(N)$ and $\alpha_i(N)=0$.

Define

$$\phi_{k,m(k)} := E_{\overline{R_{k-1}}}\{E\{x'(k+1)X_{m(k+1)}(k+1)x(k+1)+\alpha_{m(k+1)}(k+1)\,|\,x(k),m(k)\}\}$$
$$- E_{\overline{R_k}}\{x'(k)X_{m(k)}x(k)+\alpha_{m(k)}(k)\}$$

We first consider the case of $r_d(\cdot)\equiv 0$. Then the following equalities hold by the assumptions A3.

$$\begin{aligned}
&E\{x'(k+1)X_{m(k+1)}(k+1)x(k+1)+\alpha_{m(k+1)}(k+1)\,|\,x(k),m(k)\}\\
&= E\{(A_{d,m(k)}(k)x(k)+G_{d,m(k)}(k)\omega_d(k)+B_{2d,m(k)}(k)u_d(k))'\\
&\quad\times X_{m(k+1)}(k+1)(A_{d,m(k)}(k)x(k)+G_{d,m(k)}(k)\omega_d(k)+B_{2d,m(k)}(k)u_d(k))\\
&\quad+\alpha_{m(k+1)}(k+1)\,|\,x(k),m(k)\}
\end{aligned}$$

$$=(A_{d,m(k)}(k)x(k)+B_{2d,m(k)}(k)u_d(k))'$$
$$\times\ E_{m(k)}(X(k+1),k)\ (A_{d,m(k)}(k)\ x(k)+B_{2d,m(k)}(k)u_d(k))$$
$$+\sum_{j=1}^{M} \mathrm{tr}\{G_{d,i}(k)X_i(k)G_{d,i}{}'(k)E_i(X(k+1),k)\}+E\{\alpha_{m(k+1)}(k+1)\,|\,x(k),m(k)\}$$

It can be shown that the following equality holds, using the system (1) and the coupled Riccati equations (3) and the coupled scalar equations (4). ([Costa et al. (2005); Fragoso (1989)])

$$\phi_{k,m(k)}=E_{\overline{R_k}}\{-|z_d(k)|^2+|T_{2,m(k)}^{1/2}(k)[u_d(k)-F_{2,m(k)}(k)\,x(k)]|^2\}$$

Moreover, in the genaral case that $r_d(\cdot)$ is arbitrary, we have the following equality.

$$\phi_{k,m(k)}=E_{\overline{R_k}}\{-|z_d(k)|^2+|T_{2,m(k)}^{1/2}(k)[u_d(k)-F_{2,m(k)}(k)x(k)]-D_{u,m(k)}(k)r_d(k)|^2$$
$$+\,2x'(k)\,\overline{B}_{d,m(k)}(k)r_d(k)+J_{d,k,m(k)}(r_d)\}$$

Notice that, in the right hand side of this equality, $J_{d,k,m(k)}(r_d)$, which means the tracking error without considering the effect of the preview information, is added.
Now introducing the vector $\theta_{m(k)}$, which can include some preview information of the tracking signals,

$$E_{\overline{R_{k+1}}}\{E\{\theta_{m(k+1)}{}'(k+1)x(k+1)\,|\,x(k),m(k)\}\}-E_{\overline{R_k}}\{\theta_{m(k)}{}'(k)x(k)\}$$
$$=E_{\overline{R_k}}\{E_{m(k)}(\theta'(k+1),k)(A_{d,m(k)}(k)x(k)+G_{d,m(k)}(k)\omega_d(k)$$
$$+B_{2d,m(k)}(k)u_d(k)+B_{3d,m(k)}(k)r_d(k))\}-E_{\overline{R_{k-1}}}\{\theta_{m(k)}{}'(k)x(k)\}$$

Then we obtain

$$\phi_{k,m(k)}+2\{E_{\overline{R_{k+1}}}\{E\{\theta_{m(k+1)}{}'(k+1)x(k+1)\,|\,x(k),m(k)\}\}-E_{\overline{R_k}}\{\theta_{m(k)}{}'(k)x(k)\}\}$$
$$=E_{\overline{R_k}}\{-|z_d(k)|^2+|T_{2,m(k)}^{1/2}(k)[u_d(k)-F_{2,m(k)}(k)x(k)-D_{u,m(k)}(k)r_d(k)]|^2$$
$$+\,2x'(k)\,\overline{B}_{d,m(k)}(k)r_d(k)+J_{d,k,m(k)}(r_d)\}$$
$$+2E_{\overline{R_k}}\{\{E_{m(k)}(\theta'(k+1),k)(A_{d,m(k)}(k)x(k)+G_{d,m(k)}(k)\omega_d(k) \tag{14}$$
$$+B_{2d,m(k)}(k)u_d(k)+B_{3d,m(k)}(k)r_d(k))\}-E_{\overline{R_{k-1}}}\{\theta_{m(k)}{}'(k)x(k)\}\}$$
$$=E_{\overline{R_k}}\{-|z_d(k)|^2+|T_{2,m(k)}^{1/2}(k)[u_d(k)-F_{2,m(k)}(k)x(k)-D_{u,m(k)}(k)r_d(k)$$
$$-D_{\theta u,m(k)}(k)E_{m(k)}(\theta(k+1),k)]|^2+\overline{J}_{d,k,m(k)}(r_d)\}$$

where

$$\theta_i(k)=\overline{A}_{d,i}{}'(k)E_i(\theta(k+1),k)+\overline{B}_{d,i}(k)r_d(k)$$

to get rid of the mixed terms of r_d and x, or $\theta_{m(k)}$ and x. $\bar{J}_{d,k,m(k)}(r_d)$ means the tracking error including the preview information vector θ and can be expressed by

$$\begin{aligned}\bar{J}_{d,k,m(k)}(r_d) =& -|\, T_{2,m(k)}^{1/2} D_{\theta u,m(k)}(k)E_{m(k)}(\theta(k+1),k)]\,|^2 \\ & -E_{m(k)}(\theta'(k+1),k)D_{\theta u,m(k)}{}' T_{2,m(k)}D_{u,m(k)}(k)r_d(k) \\ & +2\, E_{m(k)}(\theta'(k+1),k)B_{3d,m(k)}r_d(k)+J_{d,k,m(k)}(r_d)\end{aligned}$$

Taking the sum of the quantities (14) from k=0 to k=N-1 and adding $E\{|\,C_{1d,m(N)}(N)x(N)+D_{13d,m(N)}(N)r_d(N)\,|^2\}$ and taking the expectation E{ },

$$\begin{aligned}&\sum_{k=0}^{N-1} E\{E_{\overline{R_k}}\{|\, z_d(k)|^2\}\}+E\{|\,C_{1d,m(N)}(N)x(N)+ D_{13d,m(N)}(N)r_d(N)\,|^2\} \\ &\quad +\sum_{k=0}^{N-1} E\{\phi_{k,m(k)}+2\{E_{\overline{R_{k+1}}}\{E\{\theta_{m(k+1)}{}'(k+1)x(k+1)\,|\,x(k),m(k)\}\} \\ &\qquad - E_{\overline{R_k}}\{\theta_{m(k)}{}'(k)x(k)\}\}\,|\,x(k),m(k)\} \\ &= \sum_{k=0}^{N-1} E\{E_{\overline{R_k}}\{|\,\hat{u}_d(k)- D_{\theta u,m(k)}(k)\, E_{m(k)}(\theta(k+1),k)\,|^2_{T_{2,m(k)}(k)}\} \\ &\quad +E\{|\,C_{1d,m(N)}(N)x(N)+D_{13d,m(N)}(N)r_d(N)\,|^2\} \\ &\quad +\sum_{k=0}^{N-1} E\{E_{\overline{R_k}}\{\bar{J}_{d,k,m(k)}(r_d)\}\}\end{aligned}$$

where

$$\hat{u}_d(k)= u_d(k)-F_{2,m(k)}(k)\, x(k)-D_{u,m(k)}(k)r_d(k).$$

Since the left hand side reduces to

$$\begin{aligned}&\sum_{k=0}^{N-1} E\{E_{\overline{R_k}}\{|\,z_d(k)|^2\}\}+E\{|\,C_{1d,m(N)}(N)x(N)+D_{13d,m(N)}(N)r_d(N)\,|^2\} \\ &\quad + E\{2\,\theta_{m(N)}{}'(N)x(N)+x'(N)X_{m(N)}(N)x(N)+ \alpha_{m(N)}(N)\} \\ &\quad +E\{E_{\overline{R_0}}\{-2\,\theta_{i_0}{}'(0)x(0)-x'(0)\, X_{i_0}(0)x(0)- \alpha_{i_0}(0)\}\}\end{aligned}$$

noticing that the equality

$$\begin{aligned}&E_{\overline{R_N}}\{E\{x'(N)X_{m(N)}(N)x(N)+ \alpha_{m(N)}(N)+2\,\theta_{m(N)}{}'(N)x(N)\,|\,x(l),m(l)\}\} \\ &\quad - E_{\overline{R_l}}\{x'(l)X_{m(l)}x(l)+ \alpha_{m(l)}(l)+2\,\theta_{m(l)}{}'(l)x(l)\} \\ &= \sum_{k=l}^{N-1} E\{E_{\overline{R_{k+1}}}\{E\{x'(k+1)X_{m(k+1)}(k+1)x(k+1)+ \alpha_{m(k+1)}(k+1) \\ &\qquad +2\,\theta_{m(k+1)}{}'(k+1)x(k+1)\,|\,x(k),m(k)\}\}\end{aligned}$$

$$- E_{\overline{R_k}} \{x'(k)X_{m(k)}x(k)+ \alpha_{m(k)}(k)+2\,\theta_{m(k)}{}'(k)x(k)\} \mid x(l),m(l)\}$$
$$= \sum_{k=l}^{N-1} E\{\phi_{k,m(k)}$$
$$+2\{ E_{\overline{R_{k-1}}} \{E\{\theta_{m(k+1)}{}'(k+1)x(k+1) \mid x(k),m(k)\}\}$$
$$-\{ E_{\overline{R_k}}\, \theta_{m(k)}{}'(k)x(k)\}\}\, x(l),m(l)\}$$

holds for l, $0 \le l \le N-1$, we obtain

$$J_{dN}(x_0, u_d, r_d)=tr\{Q_{i_0}\ X_{i_0}\}+ \alpha_{i_0}(0)+E\{E_{\overline{R_0}}\{2\,\theta_{i_0}{}'(0)x_0\}\}$$
$$+E\{\sum_{k=0}^{N-1} E_{\overline{R_k}}\{|\,\hat{u}_d(k)-D_{\theta u,m(k)}(k)E_{m(k)}(\theta(k+1),k)\,|^2_{T_{2,m(k)}(k)}\}\}+E\{\bar{J}_d(r_d)\}$$

where we have used the terminal conditions $X_i(N)=C_{1d,i}'(N)C_{1d,i}(N)$, $\theta_i(N)=C_{1d,i}'D_{13d,i}r_d(N)$ and $\underline{\alpha_i}(N)=0$. Note that $\bar{J}_d(r_d)$ is independent of u_d and x_0. Since the average of $\theta^{-}_{c,m(k)}(k)$ over $\overline{R_k}$ is zero, including the 'causal' part $\theta_{c,m(k)}(k)$ of $\theta(\cdot)$ at time k, we adopt

$$\hat{u}^*_d(k)= D_{\theta u,m(k)}(k)\, E_{m(k)}(\theta_c(k+1),k)$$

as the minimizing control strategy.
Then finally we obtain

$$J_{dN}(x_0, u_d, r_d)=tr\{Q_{i_0}\ X_{i_0}\}+ \alpha_{i_0}(0)+E\{E_{\overline{R_0}}\{2\,\theta_{i_0}{}'(0)x_0\}\}$$
$$+E\{\sum_{k=0}^{N-1} E_{\overline{R_k}}\{|\,\hat{u}_d(k)-D_{\theta u,m(k)}(k)E_{m(k)}(\theta(k+1),k)\,|^2_{T_{2,m(k)}(k)}\}\}+E\{\bar{J}_d(r_d)\}$$
$$\ge tr\{Q_{i_0}\ X_{i_0}\}+ \alpha_{i_0}(0)+E\{E_{\overline{R_0}}\{2\,\theta_{i_0}{}'(0)x_0\}\}$$
$$+ E\{\sum_{k=0}^{N-1} E_{\overline{R_k}}\{|\,D_{\theta u,m(k)}(k)E_{m(k)}(\theta^{-}_c(k+1),k)\,|^2_{T_{2,m(k)}(k)}\}\}+E\{\bar{J}_d(r_d)\}$$
$$= J_{dN}(x_0, \hat{u}^*_d, r_d)$$

which concludes the proof of sufficiency.
Necessity:
Because of arbitrariness of the reference signal $r_d(\cdot)$, by considering the case of $r_d(\cdot) \equiv 0$, one can easily deduce the necessity for the solvability of the stochastic LQ optimal tracking problem [Costa et al. (2005); Fragoso (1989)]. Also notice that, in the proof of sufficiency, on the process of the evaluation of the performance index, by getting rid of the mixed terms of

r_d and x, or $\theta_{m(k)}$ and x, we necessarily obtain the form of the preview compensator dynamics. (Q.E.D.)

Appendix 2. Proof of Orthogonal Property (10)

In this appendix we give the proof of the orthogonal property (10).
We prove it by induction on k.
For k=0, since $\hat{x}_e(0)$ is deterministic,

$$E\{E_{\overline{R_0}}\{e(0)\hat{x}_e'(0)1_{\{m(0)=i\}}\}\}=\pi_i(0)\,E\{E_{\overline{R_0}}\{e(0)\}\}\hat{x}_e'(0)=O.$$

We have already shown that, for each $k\in[0,N]$,

$$E\{E_{\overline{R_k}}\{e(k)\bar{r}_{d,c}'(k)1_{\{m(k)=i\}}\}\}=O$$

in section 4. Suppose

$$E\{E_{\overline{R_k}}\{e(k)\hat{x}_e'(k)1_{\{m(k)=i\}}\}\}=O.$$

Then, since $\omega_d(k)$ is zero mean, not correlated with $\hat{x}_e(k)$ and $\bar{r}_{d,c}(k)$ and independent of m(k), we have

$$\begin{aligned}
&E\left\{E_{\overline{R_{k-1}}}\{e(k+1)\hat{x}_e'(k+1)\,1_{\{m(k+1)=i\}}\}\right\}\\
&=\sum_{i\in J(k)}p_{d,ij}\Big[\left[A_{d,i}+M_iC_i\right](k)E\left\{E_{\overline{R_k}}\{e(k)\hat{x}_e'(k)1_{\{m(k)=i\}}\}\right\}\left[A_{d,i}+M_iC_{2d,i}\right]'(k)\\
&\quad+\left[G_{d,i}+M_iH_{d,i}\right](k)E\left\{E_{\overline{R_k}}\{\omega_d(k)\hat{x}_e'(k)1_{\{m(k)=i\}}\}\right\}\left[A_{d,i}+M_iC_{2d,i}\right]'(k)\\
&\quad+\left[A_{d,i}+M_iC_{2d,i}\right](k)E\left\{E_{\overline{R_k}}\{e(k)\bar{u}_{d,c^*}'(k)1_{\{m(k)=i\}}\}\right\}B_{2d,i}'(k)\\
&\quad+\left[G_{d,i}+M_iH_{d,i}\right](k)E\left\{E_{\overline{R_k}}\{\omega_d(k)\bar{u}_{d,c^*}'(k)1_{\{m(k)=i\}}\}\right\}B_{2d,i}'(k)\\
&\quad+\left[A_{d,i}+M_iC_{2d,i}\right](k)E\left\{E_{\overline{R_k}}\{e(k)\bar{r}_{d,c}'(k)1_{\{m(k)=i\}}\}\right\}B_{3d,i}'(k)\\
&\quad+\left[G_{d,i}+M_iH_{d,i}\right](k)E\left\{E_{\overline{R_k}}\{\omega_d(k)\bar{r}_{d,c}'(k)1_{\{m(k)=i\}}\}\right\}B_{3d,i}'(k)\\
&\quad-\left[A_{d,i}+M_iC_{2d,i}\right](k)E\left\{E_{\overline{R_k}}\{e(k)y'(k)1_{\{m(k)=i\}}\}\right\}M_i'(k)\\
&\quad-\left[G_{d,i}+M_iH_{d,i}\right](k)E\left\{E_{\overline{R_k}}\{\omega_d(k)y'(k)1_{\{m(k)=i\}}\}\right\}M_i'(k)\Big]\\
&=\sum_{i\in J(k)}p_{d,ij}\Big[-\left[A_{d,i}+M_iC_{2d,i}\right](k)E\left\{E_{\overline{R_k}}\{e(k)y'(k)1_{\{m(k)=i\}}\}\right\}M_i'(k)\\
&\quad-\left[G_{d,i}+M_iH_{d,i}\right](k)E\left\{E_{\overline{R_k}}\{\omega_d(k)y'(k)1_{\{m(k)=i\}}\}\right\}M_i'(k)\Big]
\end{aligned}$$

where $\bar{u}_{d,c^*}(k)=F_{2,i}(k)\hat{x}_e(k)$, i=1, ···,M. Notice that

$$y(k)= C_{2d,m(k)}(k)x(k)+H_{d,m(k)}(k)\omega_d(k)= C_{2d,m(k)}(k)(e(k)+\hat{x}_e(k))+H_{d,m(k)}(k)\omega_d(k).$$

Then, by induction on k, we obtain

$$\begin{aligned}E\{E_{\overline{R_k}}\{e(k)y'(k)1_{\{m(k)=i\}}\}\}&= E\{E_{\overline{R_k}}\{e(k)e'(k)1_{\{m(k)=i\}}\}\}C_{2d,i}'(k)+E\{E_{\overline{R_k}}\{e(k)\hat{x}_e'(k)1_{\{m(k)=i\}}\}\}C_{2d,i}'(k)\\&\quad+E\{E_{\overline{R_k}}\{e(k)\omega_d'(k)1_{\{m(k)=i\}}\}\}H_{d,i}'(k)\\&=Y_i(k)C_{2d,i}'(k)\end{aligned}$$

We also obtain

$$\begin{aligned}&E\{E_{\overline{R_k}}\{\omega_d(k)y'(k)1_{\{m(k)=i\}}\}\}\\&= E\{E_{\overline{R_k}}\{\omega_d(k)e'(k)1_{\{m(k)=i\}}\}\}C_{2d,i}'(k)+E\{E_{\overline{R_k}}\{\omega_d(k)\hat{x}_e'(k)1_{\{m(k)=i\}}\}\}C_{2d,i}'(k)\\&\quad+E\{E_{\overline{R_k}}\{\omega_d(k)\omega_d'(k)1_{\{m(k)=i\}}\}\}H_{d,i}'(k)\\&= E\{\omega_d(k)\omega_d'(k)\}P\{m(k)=i\}H_{d,i}'(k)= \pi_i(k)H_{d,i}'(k).\end{aligned}$$

Then considering the assumption A4 $G_{d,i}(k)H_{d,i}'(k) = O$, i=1, ···,M, and

$$M_i(k)(H_{d,i}H_{d,i}'\pi_i(k)+ C_{2d,i}Y_i(k)C_{2d,i}')= - A_{d,i}Y_i(k)C_{2d,i}'$$

by (11), we finally obtain

$$\begin{aligned}&E\{E_{\overline{R_{k+1}}}\{e(k+1)\hat{x}_e'(k+1)1_{\{m(k+1)=i\}}\}\}\\&=\sum_{i\in J(k)}p_{d,ij}[-[A_{d,i}+M_iC_{2d,i}](k)Y_i(k)C_{2d,i}'(k)-[G_{d,i}+M_iH_{d,i}](k)\pi_i(k)H_{d,i}'(k)]M_i'(k)\\&=\sum_{i\in J(k)}p_{d,ij}[-A_{d,i}Y_i(k)C_{2d,i}'(k)-M_i(k)(H_{d,i}H_{d,i}'\pi_i(k)+C_{2d,i}Y_i(k)C_{2d,i}')]M_i'(k)\\&=\sum_{i\in J(k)}p_{d,ij}[-A_{d,i}Y_i(k)C_{2d,i}'(k)+A_{d,i}Y_i(k)C_{2d,i}']M_i'(k)\\&=0\end{aligned}$$

which concludes the proof. (Q.E.D.)

7. References

E. K. Boukas. (2006). *Stochastic Switching Systems: Analysis and Design,* Birkhauser, 0-8176-3782-6, Boston,

A. Cohen. & U. Shaked. (1997). Linear Discrete-Time H∞-Optimal Tracking with Preview. *IEEE Trans. Automat. Contr.,* 42, 2, 270-276

O. L. V. Costa. & E. F. Tuesta. (2003). Finite Horizon Quadratic Optimal Control and a Separation Principle for Markovian Jump Linear Systems. *IEEE Trans. Automat. Contr.,* 48, 10, 1836-1842

O. L. V. Costa.; M. D. Fragoso. & R. P. Marques. (2005). *Discrete-Time Markov Jump Linear Systems*, Springer, 1-85233-761-3, London

V. Dragan. & T. Morozan. (2004). The linear quadratic optimization problems for a class of linear stochastic systems with multiplicative white noise and Markovian jumping. *IEEE Trans. Automat. Contr.*, 49, 5, 665-675

M. D. Fragoso. (1989). Discrete-Time Jump LQG Problem. *Int. J. Systems Science*, 20, 12, 2539-2545

M. D. Fragoso.; J. B. R. do Val . & D. L. Pinto Junior. (1995). Jump Linear H∞ Control: the discrete-time case. *Control-Theory and Advanced Technology*, 10, 4, 1459-1474

E. Gershon.; D. J. N. Limebeer.; U. Shaked. & I. Yaesh. (2004). Stochastic H∞ Tracking with Preview for State-Multiplicative Systems. *IEEE Trans. Automat. Contr.*, 49, 11, 2061-2068

E. Gershon.; U. Shaked. & I. Yaesh. (2004). H∞ tracking of linear continuous-time systems with stochastic uncertainties and preview. *Int. J. Robust and Nonlinear Control*, 14, 7, 607-626

E. Gershon.; U. Shaked. & I. Yaesh. (2005). *H∞ Control and Estimation of State-Multiplicative Linear Systems*, LNCIS 318, Springer, 1-85233-997-7, London

J.-W. Lee. & P. P. Khargonekar. (2008). Optimal output regulation for discrete-time switched and Markovian jump linear systems, *SIAM J. Control Optim.*, 47, 1, 40-72

M. Mariton. (1990). *Jump Linear Systems in Automatic Control*, Marcel Dekker, 0-8247-8200-3, New York

G. Nakura. (2008a). Noncausal Optimal Tracking for Linear Switched Systems. In: *Hybrid Systems: Computation and Control: 11th International Workshop, HSCC 2008, St. Louis, MO, USA, April, 2008, Proceedings*, LNCS 4981, M. Egerstedt. & B. Mishra. (eds.), pp.372-385, Springer, 3-540-78928-6, Berlin, Heidelberg.

G. Nakura. (2008b). H∞ Tracking with Preview for Linear Systems with Impulsive Effects - State Feedback and Full Information Cases-. *Proceedings of the 17th IFAC World Congress*, TuA08.4 (CD-ROM), Seoul, Korea

G. Nakura. (2008c). H∞ Tracking with Preview by Output Feedback for Linear Systems with Impulsive Effects. *Proceedings of the 17th IFAC World Congress*, TuA08.5 (CD-ROM), Seoul, Korea

G. Nakura. (2008d). Stochastic Optimal Tracking with Preview for Linear Continuous-Time Markovian Jump Systems. *Proceedings of SICE Annual Conference 2008*, 2A09-2 (CD-ROM), Chofu, Tokyo, Japan

G. Nakura. (2008e). H∞ Tracking with Preview for Linear Continuous-Time Markovian Jump Systems. *Proceedings of SICE 8th Annual Conference on Control Systems*, 073-2-1 (CD-ROM), Kyoto, Japan

G. Nakura. (2009). Stochastic Optimal Tracking with Preview for Linear Discrete-Time Markovian Jump Systems (Extended Abstract). In: *Hybrid Systems: Computation and Control: 12th Conference, HSCC 2009, San Francisco, CA, USA, April, 2009, Proceedings*, LNCS 5469, R. Majumdar. & P. Tabuada. (Eds.), pp. 455-459, Springer, 3-642-00601-9, Berlin, Heidelberg

G. Nakura. (2010). Stochastic Optimal Tracking with Preview by State Feedback for Linear Discrete-Time Markovian Jump Systems. *International Journal of Innovative Computing, Information and Control (IJICIC)*, 6, 1, 15-27

Y. Sawada. (2008). Risk-sensitive tracking control of stochastic systems with preview action. *International Journal of Innovative Computing, Information and Control (IJICIC)*, 4, 1, 189-198

U. Shaked. & C. E. de Souza. (1995). Continuous-Time Tracking Problems in an $H\infty$ Setting: A Game Theory Approach. *IEEE Trans. Automat. Contr.*, 40, 5, 841-852

C. E. de Souza. & M. D. Fragoso. (1993). $H\infty$ Control for Linear Systems with Markovian Jumping Parameters. *Control-Theory and Advanced Technology*, 9, 2, 457-466

D. D. Sworder. (1969). Feedback Control of a Class of Linear Systems with Jump Parameters. *IEEE Trans. Automat. Contr.*, AC-14, 1, 9-14

D. D. Sworder. (1972). Control of Jump Parameter Systems with Discontinuous State Trajectories. *IEEE Trans. Automat. Contr.*, AC-17, 5, 740-741

K. Takaba. (2000). Robust servomechanism with preview action for polytopic uncertain systems. *Int. J. Robust and Nonlinear Control*, 10, 2, 101-111

8

The Design of a Discrete Time Model Following Control System for Nonlinear Descriptor System

Shigenori Okubo[1] and Shujing Wu[2]
[1]*Yamagata University*
[2]*Shanghai University of Engineering Science*
[1]*Japan*
[2]*P. R. China*

1. Introduction

This paper studies the design of a model following control system (MFCS) for nonlinear descriptor system in discrete time. In previous studies, a method of nonlinear model following control system with disturbances was proposed by Okubo,S. and also a nonlinear model following control system with unstable zero of the linear part, a nonlinear model following control system with containing inputs in nonlinear parts, and a nonlinear model following control system using stable zero assignment. In this paper, the method of MFCS will be extended to descriptor system in discrete time, and the effectiveness of the method will be verified by numerical simulation.

2. Expressions of the problem

The controlled object is described below, which is a nonlinear descriptor system in discrete time.

$$Ex(k+1) = Ax(k) + Bu(k) + B_f f(v(k)) + d(k) \tag{1}$$

$$v(k) = C_f x(k) \tag{2}$$

$$y(k) = Cx(k) + d_0(k) \tag{3}$$

The reference model is given below, which is assumed controllable and observable.

$$x_m(k+1) = A_m x_m(k) + B_m r_m(k) \tag{4}$$

$$y_m(k) = C_m x_m(k) \tag{5}$$

, where

$$x(k) \in R^n, d(k) \in R^n, u(k) \in R^\ell, y(k) \in R^\ell, y_m(k) \in R^\ell, d_0(k) \in R^\ell, f(v(k)) \in R^{\ell_f},$$

$v(k) \in R^{\ell_f}, r_m(k) \in R^{\ell_m}, x_m(k) \in R^{n_m}$, $y(k)$ is the available states output vector, $v(k)$ is the measurement output vector, $u(k)$ is the control input vector, $x(k)$ is the internal state vector

whose elements are available, $d(k), d_0(k)$ are bounded disturbances, $y_m(k)$ is the model output.
The basic assumptions are as follows:

1. Assume that (C, A, B) is controllable and observable, i.e.

$$rank[zE - A, B] = n, rank\begin{bmatrix} zE - A \\ C \end{bmatrix} = n \cdot$$

2. In order to guarantee the existence and uniqueness of the solution and have exponential function mode but an impulse one for (1), the following conditions are assumed.

$$|zE - A| \not\equiv 0, \quad rankE = \deg|zE - A| = r \le n$$

3. Zeros of $C[zE - A]^{-1} B$ are stable.

In this system, the nonlinear function $f(v(k))$ is available and satisfies the following constraint.

$$\|f(v(k))\| \le \alpha + \beta\|v(k)\|^{\gamma},$$

where $\alpha \ge 0, \beta \ge 0, 0 \le \gamma < 1$, $\|\cdot\|$ is Euclidean norm, disturbances $d(k), d_0(k)$ are bounded and satisfy

$$D_d(z)d(k) = 0 \tag{6}$$

$$D_d(z)d_0(k) = 0 \,. \tag{7}$$

Here, $D_d(z)$ is a scalar characteristic polynomial of disturbances. Output error is given as

$$e(k) = y(k) - y_m(k) \,. \tag{8}$$

The aim of the control system design is to obtain a control law which makes the output error zero and keeps the internal states be bounded.

3. Design of a nonlinear model following control system

Let z be the shift operator, Eq.(1) can be rewritten as follows.

$$C[zE - A]^{-1} B = N(z) / D(z)$$

$$C[zE - A]^{-1} B_f = N_f(z) / D(z),$$

where $D(z) = |zE - A|$, $\partial_{r_i}(N(z)) = \sigma_i$ and $\partial_{r_i}(N_f(z)) = \sigma_{f_i}$.
Then the representations of input-output equation is given as

$$D(z)y(k) = N(z)u(k) + N_f(z)f(v(k)) + w(k) \,. \tag{9}$$

Here $w(k) = Cadj[zE - A]d(k) + D(z)d_0(k)$, (C_m, A_m, B_m) is controllable and observable. Hence,

$$C_m[zI - A_m]^{-1} B_m = N_m(z) / D_m(z) \,.$$

Then, we have

$$D_m(z)y_m(k) = N_m(z)r_m(k), \tag{10}$$

where $D_m(z) = |zI - A_m|$ and $\partial_{r_i}(N_m(z)) = \sigma_{m_i}$.
Since the disturbances satisfy Eq.(6) and Eq.(7), and $D_d(z)$ is a monic polynomial, one has

$$D_d(z)w(k) = 0. \tag{11}$$

The first step of design is that a monic and stable polynomial $T(z)$, which has the degree of $\rho(\rho \geq n_d + 2n - n_m - 1 - \sigma_i)$, is chosen. Then, $R(z)$ and $S(z)$ can be obtained from

$$T(z)D_m(z) = D_d(z)D(z)R(z) + S(z), \tag{12}$$

where the degree of each polynomial is: $\partial T(z) = \rho, \partial D_d(z) = n_d, \partial D_m(z) = n_m$, $\partial D(z) = n, \partial R(z) = \rho + n_m - n_d - n$ and $\partial S(z) \leq n_d + n - 1$.
From Eq.(8)~(12), the following form is obtained:

$$T(z)D_m(z)e(k) = D_d(z)R(z)N(z)u(k) + D_d(z)R(z)N_f(z)f(v(k)) + S(z)y(k) - T(z)N_m(z)r_m(z).$$

The output error $e(k)$ is represented as following.

$$e(k) = \frac{1}{T(z)D_m(z)}\{[D_d(z)R(z)N(z) - Q(z)N_r]u(k) + Q(z)N_r u(k) + D_d(z)R(z)N_f(z)f(v(k)) + S(z)y(k) - T(z)N_m(z)r_m(k)\} \tag{13}$$

Suppose $\Gamma_r(N(z)) = N_r$, where $\Gamma_r(\cdot)$ is the coefficient matrix of the element with maximum of row degree, as well as $|N_r| \neq 0$. The next control law $u(k)$ can be obtained by making the right-hand side of Eq.(13) be equal to zero. Thus,

$$u(k) = -N_r^{-1}Q^{-1}(z)\{D_d(z)R(z)N(z) - Q(z)N_r\}u(k) - N_r^{-1}Q^{-1}(z)D_d(z)R(z)N_f(z)f(v(k)) - N_r^{-1}Q^{-1}(z)S(z)y(k) + u_m(k) \tag{14}$$

$$u_m(k) = N_r^{-1}Q^{-1}(z)T(z)N_m(z)r_m(k). \tag{15}$$

Here, $Q(z) = diag\left[z^{\delta_i}\right], \delta_i = \rho + n_m - n + \sigma_i (i = 1, 2, \cdots, \ell)$, and $u(k)$ of Eq.(14) is obtained from $e(k) = 0$. The model following control system can be realized if the system internal states are bounded.

4. Proof of the bounded property of internal states

System inputs are both reference input signal $r_m(k)$ and disturbances $d(k), d_0(k)$, which are all assumed to be bounded. The bounded property can be easily proved if there is no nonlinear part $f(v(k))$. But if $f(v(k))$ exits, the bound has a relation with it.
The state space expression of $u(k)$ is

$$u(k) = -H_1\xi_1(k) - E_2y(k) - H_2\xi_2(k) - E_3f(v(k)) - H_3\xi_3(k) + u_m(k) \tag{16}$$

$$u_m(k) = E_4r_m(k) + H_4\xi_4(k). \tag{17}$$

The following must be satisfied:

$$\xi_1(k+1) = F_1\xi_1(k) + G_1u(k) \tag{18}$$

$$\xi_2(k+1) = F_2\xi_2(k) + G_2y(k) \tag{19}$$

$$\xi_3(k+1) = F_3\xi_3(k) + G_3f(v(k)) \tag{20}$$

$$\xi_4(k+1) = F_4\xi_4(k) + G_4r_m(k). \tag{21}$$

Here,
$|zI - F_i| = |Q(z)|, \quad (i = 1,2,3,4)$.
Note that there are connections between the polynomial matrices and the system matrices, as follows:

$$N_r^{-1}Q^{-1}(z)\{D_d(z)R(z)N(z) - Q(z)N_r\} = H_1(zI - F_1)^{-1}G_1 \tag{22}$$

$$N_r^{-1}Q^{-1}(z)S(z) = H_2(zI - F_2)^{-1}G_2 + E_2 \tag{23}$$

$$N_r^{-1}Q^{-1}(z)D_d(z)R(z)N_f(z) = H_3(zI - F_3)^{-1}G_3 + E_3 \tag{24}$$

$$N_r^{-1}Q^{-1}(z)T(z)N_m(z) = H_4(zI - F_4)^{-1}G_4 + E_4\,. \tag{25}$$

Firstly, remove $u(k)$ from Eq.(1)~(3) and Eq.(18)~(21). Then, the representation of the overall system can be obtained as follows.

$$\begin{bmatrix} E & 0 & 0 & 0 \\ 0 & I & 0 & 0 \\ 0 & 0 & I & 0 \\ 0 & 0 & 0 & I \end{bmatrix}\begin{bmatrix} x(k+1) \\ \xi_1(k+1) \\ \xi_2(k+1) \\ \xi_3(k+1) \end{bmatrix} =$$

$$\begin{bmatrix} A - BE_2C & -BH_1 & -BH_2 & -BH_3 \\ -G_1E_2C & F_1 - G_1H_1 & -G_1H_2 & -G_1H_3 \\ G_2C & 0 & F_2 & 0 \\ 0 & 0 & 0 & F_3 \end{bmatrix}\begin{bmatrix} x(k) \\ \xi_1(k) \\ \xi_2(k) \\ \xi_3(k) \end{bmatrix} + \tag{26}$$

$$+\begin{bmatrix} BH_4 \\ G_1H_4 \\ 0 \\ 0 \end{bmatrix}\xi_4(k) + \begin{bmatrix} B_f - BE_3 \\ -G_1E_3 \\ 0 \\ G_3 \end{bmatrix}f(v(k)) + \begin{bmatrix} BE_4 \\ G_1E_4 \\ 0 \\ 0 \end{bmatrix}r_m(k) + \begin{bmatrix} d(k) - BE_2d_0(k) \\ -G_1E_2d_0(k) \\ G_2d_0(k) \\ 0 \end{bmatrix}$$

$$\xi_4(k+1) = F_4\xi_4(k) + G_4r_m(k) \tag{27}$$

$$v(k)=\begin{bmatrix} C_f & 0 & 0 & 0 \end{bmatrix}\begin{bmatrix} x(k) \\ \xi_1(k) \\ \xi_2(k) \\ \xi_3(k) \end{bmatrix} \tag{28}$$

$$y(k)=\begin{bmatrix} C & 0 & 0 & 0 \end{bmatrix}\begin{bmatrix} x(k) \\ \xi_1(k) \\ \xi_2(k) \\ \xi_3(k) \end{bmatrix}+d_0(k). \tag{29}$$

In Eq.(27), the $\xi_4(k)$ is bounded because $|zI-F_4|=|Q(z)|$ is a stable polynomial and $r_m(k)$ is the bounded reference input. Let $z(k), A_s, \tilde{E}, d_s(k), B_s, C_v, C_s$ be as follows respectively:

$$z(k)=\begin{bmatrix} x^T(k) & \xi_1^T(k) & \xi_2^T(k) & \xi_3^T(k) \end{bmatrix}^T, \quad A_s=\begin{bmatrix} A-BE_2C & -BH_1 & -BH_2 & -BH_3 \\ -G_1E_2C & F_1-G_1H_1 & -G_1H_2 & -G_1H_3 \\ G_2C & 0 & F_2 & 0 \\ 0 & 0 & 0 & F_3 \end{bmatrix}$$

$$\tilde{E}=\begin{bmatrix} E & 0 & 0 & 0 \\ 0 & I & 0 & 0 \\ 0 & 0 & I & 0 \\ 0 & 0 & 0 & I \end{bmatrix}, \quad d_s(k)=\begin{bmatrix} Bu_m(k)+d(k)-BE_2d_0(k) \\ G_1u_m(k)-G_1E_2d_0(k) \\ G_2d_0(k) \\ 0 \end{bmatrix}, \quad B_s=\begin{bmatrix} B_f-BE_3 \\ -G_1E_3 \\ 0 \\ G_3 \end{bmatrix}$$

$$C_v=\begin{bmatrix} C_f & 0 & 0 & 0 \end{bmatrix}, \quad C_s=\begin{bmatrix} C & 0 & 0 & 0 \end{bmatrix}.$$

With the consideration that $\xi_4(k)$ is bounded, the necessary parts to an easy proof of the bounded property are arranged as

$$\tilde{E}z(k+1)=A_sz(k)+B_sf(v(k))+d_s(k) \tag{30}$$

$$v(k)=C_vz(k) \tag{31}$$

$$y(k)=C_sz(k)+d_0(k), \tag{32}$$

where the contents of $A_s, \tilde{E}, d_s(k), B_s, C_v, C_s$ are constant matrices, and $d_s(k)$ is bounded. Thus, the internal states are bounded if $z(k)$ can be proved to be bounded. So it needs to prove that $|z\tilde{E}-A_s|$ is a stable polynomial. The characteristic polynomial of A_S is calculated as the next equation.

From Eq.(26), $|z\tilde{E}-A_s|$ can be shown as

$$|z\tilde{E}-A_s|=\begin{vmatrix} zE-A+BE_2C & BH_1 & BH_2 & BH_3 \\ G_1E_2C & zI-F_1+G_1H_1 & G_1H_2 & G_1H_3 \\ -G_2C & 0 & zI-F_2 & 0 \\ 0 & 0 & 0 & zI-F_3 \end{vmatrix}. \tag{33}$$

Prepare the following formulas:

$$\begin{vmatrix} X & Y \\ W & Z \end{vmatrix} = |Z||X - YZ^{-1}W|, (|Z| \neq 0),$$

$$I - X(I + YX)^{-1}Y = (I + XY)^{-1}$$

$$|I + XY| = |I + YX|.$$

Using the above formulas, $|z\tilde{E} - A_s|$ is described as

$$\begin{aligned} &|z\tilde{E} - A_s| \\ &= |zI - F_3||zI - F_2||zI - F_1||I + H_1[zI - F_1]^{-1}G_1| \\ &\cdot\ |zE - A + B\{I - H_1[zI - F_1 + G_1H_1]^{-1}G_1\}\{E_2 + H_2[zI - F_2]^{-1}G_2\}C| \\ &= |Q(z)|^3|I + H_1[zI - F_1]^{-1}G_1||zE - A + B\{I + H_1[zI - F_1]^{-1}G_1\}^{-1}\{E_2 + H_2[zI - F_2]^{-1}G_2\}C| \\ &= |Q(z)|^3|J_1||zE - A||I + BJ_1^{-1}J_2[zE - A]^{-1}| \\ &= |Q(z)|^3|zE - A||J_1 + J_2[zE - A]^{-1}B|. \end{aligned} \tag{34}$$

Here

$$J_1 = I + H_1[zI - F_1]^{-1}G_1 \tag{35}$$

$$J_2 = \{E_2 + H_2[zI - F_2]^{-1}G_2\}C. \tag{36}$$

From Eq.(22),(23),(35) and Eq.(36), we have

$$J_1 = N_r^{-1}Q^{-1}(z)D_d(z)R(z)N(z) \tag{37}$$

$$J_2 = N_r^{-1}Q^{-1}(z)S(z)C. \tag{38}$$

Using $C[zE - A]^{-1}B = N(z)/D(z)$ and $D(z) = |zE - A|$, furthermore, $|z\tilde{E} - A_s|$ is shown as

$$|z\tilde{E} - A_s| = T^{\ell}(z)D_m^{\ell}(z)|Q(z)|^2\frac{|N(z)||N_r|^{-1}}{D^{\ell-1}(z)}$$

and $V(z)$ is the zeros polynomial of $C[zE - A]^{-1}B = N(z)/D(z) = U^{-1}(z)V(z)$ (left coprime decomposition), $|U(z)| = D(z)$, that is, $|N(z)| = D^{\ell-1}(z)|V(z)|$. So $|z\tilde{E} - A_s|$ can be rewritten as

$$|z\tilde{E} - A_s| = |N_r|^{-1}T^{\ell}(z)D_m^{\ell}(z)|Q(z)|^2|V(z)| \tag{39}$$

As $T(z), D_m(z), |Q(z)|, |V(z)|$ are all stable polynomials, A_s is a stable system matrix. Consider the following:

$$z(k) = Q\bar{z}(k) = Q\begin{bmatrix} \bar{z}_1(k) \\ \bar{z}_2(k) \end{bmatrix}. \tag{40}$$

Using Eq.(40), one obtains

$$P\tilde{E}Q\bar{z}(k+1) = PA_sQ\bar{z}(k) + PB_sf(v(k)) + Pd_s(k).$$

Namely,

$$\begin{bmatrix} I & 0 \\ 0 & 0 \end{bmatrix}\begin{bmatrix} \bar{z}\ (k+1) \\ \bar{z}_2(k+1) \end{bmatrix} = \begin{bmatrix} A_{s1} & 0 \\ 0 & I \end{bmatrix}\begin{bmatrix} \bar{z}_1(k) \\ \bar{z}_2(k) \end{bmatrix} + \begin{bmatrix} B_{s1} \\ B_{s2} \end{bmatrix} f(v(k)) + \begin{bmatrix} d_{s1}(k) \\ d_{s2}(k) \end{bmatrix} \tag{41}$$

One can rewritten Eq.(41) as

$$\bar{z}_1(k+1) = A_{s1}\bar{z}_1(k) + B_{s1}f(v(k)) + d_{s1}(k) \tag{42}$$

$$0 = \bar{z}_2(k) + B_{s2}f(v(k)) + d_{s2}(k) \tag{43}$$

, where $\bar{z}(k), Pd_s(k), PA_sQ, PB_s$ can be represented by

$$\bar{z}(k) = \begin{bmatrix} \bar{z}_1(k) \\ \bar{z}_2(k) \end{bmatrix},\ Pd_s(k) = \begin{bmatrix} d_{s1}(k) \\ d_{s2}(k) \end{bmatrix},\ PA_sQ = \begin{bmatrix} A_{s1} & 0 \\ 0 & I \end{bmatrix},\ PB_s = \begin{bmatrix} B_{s1} \\ B_{s2} \end{bmatrix}. \tag{44}$$

Let $C_vQ = \begin{bmatrix} C_{v1} & C_{v2} \end{bmatrix}$, then

$$v(k) = C_{v1}\bar{z}_1(k) + C_{v2}\bar{z}_2(k). \tag{45}$$

From Eq.(43) and Eq.(45), we have

$$v(k) + C_{v2}B_{s2}f(v(k)) = C_{v1}\bar{z}(k) - C_{v2}d_{s2}(k). \tag{46}$$

From Eq.(46), we have

$$\frac{\partial}{\partial v^T(k)}(v(k) + C_{v2}B_{s2}f(v(k)) = I + C_{v2}B_{s2}\frac{\partial f(v(k))}{\partial v^T(k)}.$$

Existing condition of $v(k)$ is

$$\left| I + C_{v2}B_{s2}\frac{\partial f(v(k))}{\partial v^T(k)} \right| \neq 0. \tag{47}$$

From Eq.(44), we have

$$|P|\left|z\tilde{E} - A_s\right||Q| = \alpha_{PQ}\left|z\tilde{E} - A_s\right| = \begin{vmatrix} zI - A_{s1} & 0 \\ 0 & -I \end{vmatrix} = \alpha_I\left|zI - A_{s1}\right|. \tag{48}$$

Here, α_{PQ} and α_I are fixed. So, from Eq.(39), A_{s1} is a stable system matrix. Consider a quadratic Lyapunov function candidate

$$V(k) = \bar{z}_1^T(k)P_s\bar{z}_1(k). \tag{49}$$

The difference of $V(k)$ along the trajectories of system Eq.(42) is given by

$$\begin{aligned}\Delta V(k) &= V(k+1) - V(k) \\ &= \bar{z}_1^T(k+1)P_s\bar{z}_1(k+1) - \bar{z}_1^T(k)P_s\bar{z}_1(k) \\ &= \left[A_{s1}\bar{z}_1(k) + B_{s1}f(v(k)) + d_{s1}(k)\right]^T P_s\left[A_{s1}\bar{z}_1(k) + B_{s1}f(v(k)) + d_{s1}(k)\right] - \bar{z}_1^T(k)P_s\bar{z}_1(k)\end{aligned} \tag{50}$$

$$A_{s1}^T P_s A_{s1} - P_s = -Q_s, \tag{51}$$

where Q_s and P_s are symmetric positive definite matrices defined by Eq.(51). If A_{s1} is a stable matrix, we can get a unique P_s from Eq.(51) when Q_s is given. As $d_{s1}(k)$ is bounded and $0 \le \gamma < 1$, $\Delta V(k)$ satisfies

$$\begin{aligned}\Delta V(k) \le -\bar{z}_1^T(k)Q_s\bar{z}_1(k) + X_1\|\bar{z}_1(k)\|\|f(v(k))\| \\ + X_2\|\bar{z}_1(k)\| + \mu_2\|f(v(k))\|^2 + X_3\|f(v(k))\| + X_4\end{aligned} \tag{52}$$

From Eq.(40), we have

$$\|\bar{z}_1(k)\| \le M\|z(k)\|. \tag{53}$$

Here, M is positive constant. From Eq.(52), Eq.(53), we have

$$\begin{aligned}\Delta V(k) &\le -\mu_1\|z(k)\|^2 + X_5\|\bar{z}_1(k)\|^{1+\gamma} + X_6 \\ &\le -\mu_c\|z(k)\|^2 + X \\ &\le -\mu_{c1}\|\bar{z}_1(k)\|^2 + X \\ &\le -\mu_m V(k) + X,\end{aligned} \tag{54}$$

where $0 < \mu_1 = \lambda_{\min}(Q_s), \mu_2 \ge 0$ and $0 < \mu_m < \mu_c < \min(\mu_1, 1)$. Also, μ_1, μ_2, $X_i (i = 1 \sim 6)$ and X are positive constants. As a result of Eq.(54), $V(k)$ is bounded:

$$V(k) \le V(0) + X / \mu_m. \tag{55}$$

Hence, $\bar{z}_1(k)$ is bounded. From Eq.(43), $\bar{z}_2(k)$ is also bounded. Therefore, $z(k)$ is bounded. The above result is summarized as Theorem1.

[Theorem1]

In the nonlinear system

$$\begin{aligned}Ex(k+1) &= Ax(k) + Bu(k) + B_f f(v(k)) + d(k) \\ v(k) &= C_f x(k) \\ y(k) &= Cx(k) + d_0(k),\end{aligned} \tag{56}$$

where $x(k) \in R^n, u(k) \in R^\ell, y(k) \in R^\ell, v(k) \in R^{\ell_f}, d(k) \in R^n, d_0(k) \in R^\ell, f(v(k)) \in R^{\ell_f}$, $d(k)$ and $d_0(k)$ are assumed to be bounded. All the internal states are bounded and the output error $e(k) = y(k) - y_m(k)$ asymptotically converges to zero in the design of the model following control system for a nonlinear descriptor system in discrete time, if the following conditions are held:

1. Both the controlled object and the reference model are controllable and observable.
2. $|N_r| \neq 0$.
3. Zeros of $C[zE - A]^{-1} B$ are stable.
4. $\|f(v(k))\| \leq \alpha + \beta \|v(k)\|^{\gamma}, (\alpha \geq 0, \beta \geq 0, 0 \leq \gamma < 1)$.
5. Existing condition of $v(k)$ is $\left| I + C_{v2} B_{s2} \frac{\partial f(v(k))}{\partial v^T(k)} \right| \neq 0$.
6. $|zE - A| \not\equiv 0$ and $rank E = \deg |zE - A| = r \leq n$.

5. Numerical simulation

An example is given as follows:

$$\begin{bmatrix} 1 & 0 & 1 \\ 0 & 1 & 1 \\ 1 & 0 & 1 \end{bmatrix} x(k+1) = \begin{bmatrix} 0 & 1 & 0 \\ 0 & 0 & 1 \\ 0.2 & -0.5 & 0.6 \end{bmatrix} x(k) + \begin{bmatrix} 0 & 0 \\ 1 & 0 \\ 0 & 1 \end{bmatrix} u(k) + \begin{bmatrix} 1 \\ 0 \\ 1 \end{bmatrix} f(v(k)) + \begin{bmatrix} 0 \\ 1 \\ 1 \end{bmatrix} d(k)$$

$$\begin{aligned} v(k) &= \begin{bmatrix} 1 & 1 & 1 \end{bmatrix} x(k), \\ y(k) &= \begin{bmatrix} 0 & 0.1 & 0 \\ 0.1 & 0 & 0.1 \end{bmatrix} x(k) + \begin{bmatrix} 1 \\ 1 \end{bmatrix} \\ f(v(k)) &= \frac{3v^3(k) + 4v(k) + 1}{1 + v^4(k)} . \end{aligned} \tag{57}$$

Reference model is given by

$$\begin{aligned} x_m(k+1) &= \begin{bmatrix} 0 & 1 \\ -0.12 & 0.7 \end{bmatrix} x_m(k) + \begin{bmatrix} 0 \\ 1 \end{bmatrix} r_m(k) \\ y_m(k) &= \begin{bmatrix} 1 & 0 \end{bmatrix} x_m(k) \\ r_m(k) &= \sin(k\pi / 16) . \end{aligned} \tag{58}$$

In this example, disturbances $d(k)$ and $d_0(k)$ are ramp and step disturbances respectively. Then $d(k)$ and $d_0(k)$ are given as

$$\begin{aligned} d(k) &= 0.05(k - 85), (85 \leq k \leq 100) \\ d_0(k) &= 1.2, (20 \leq k \leq 50) \end{aligned} \tag{59}$$

We show a result of simulation in Fig. 1. It can be concluded that the output signal follows the reference even if disturbances exit in the system.

6. Conclusion

In the responses (Fig. 1) of the discrete time model following control system for nonlinear descriptor system, the output signal follows the references even though disturbances exit in the system. The effectiveness of this method has thus been verified. The future topic is that the case of nonlinear system for $\gamma \geq 1$ will be proved and analysed.

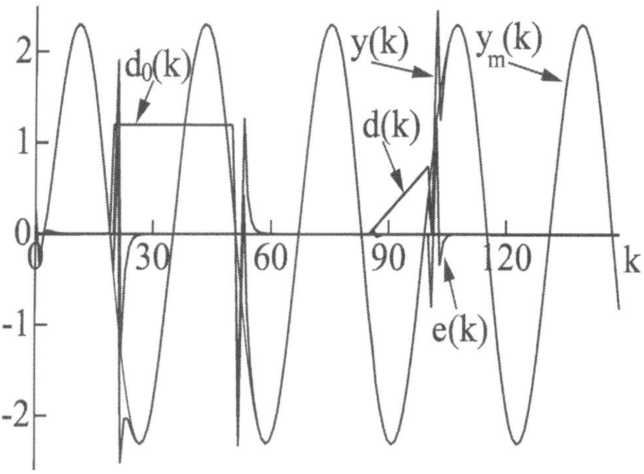

Fig. 1. Responses of the system for nonlinear descriptor system in discrete time

7. References

Wu,S.; Okubo,S.; Wang,D. (2008). Design of a Model Following Control System for Nonlinear Descriptor System in Discrete Time, *Kybernetika*, vol.44,no.4,pp.546-556.

Byrnes,C.I; Isidori,A. (1991). Asymptotic stabilization of minimum phase nonlinear system, *IEEE Transactions on Automatic Control*, vol.36,no.10,pp.1122-1137.

Casti,J.L. (1985). *Nonlinear Systems Theory*, Academic Press, London.

Furuta,K. (1989). *Digital Control (in Japanese)*, Corona Publishing Company, Tokyo.

Ishidori,A. (1995). *Nonlinear Control Systems*, Third edition, Springer-Verlag, New York.

Khalil,H.K. (1992). *Nonlinear Systems*, MacMillan Publishing Company, New York.

Mita,T. (1984). *Digital Control Theory (in Japanese)*, Shokodo Company, Tokyo.

Mori,Y. (2001). *Control Engineering (in Japanese)*, Corona Publishing Company, Tokyo.

Okubo,S. (1985). A design of nonlinear model following control system with disturbances (in Japanese), *Transactions on Instrument and Control Engineers*, vol.21,no.8,pp.792-799.

Okubo,S. (1986). A nonlinear model following control system with containing inputs in nonlinear parts (in Japanese), *Transactions on Instrument and Control Engineers*, vol.22,no.6,pp.714-716.

Okubo,S. (1988). Nonlinear model following control system with unstable zero points of the linear part (in Japanese), *Transactions on Instrument and Control Engineers*, vol.24,no.9,pp.920-926.

Okubo,S. (1992). Nonlinear model following control system using stable zero assignment (in Japanese), *Transactions on Instrument and Control Engineers*, vol.28, no.8, pp.939-946.

Takahashi,Y. (1985). *Digital Control (in Japanese)*, Iwanami Shoten,Tokyo.

Zhang,Y; Okubo,S. (1997). A design of discrete time nonlinear model following control system with disturbances (in Japanese), *Transactions on The Institute of Electrical Engineers of Japan*, vol.117-C,no.8,pp.1113-1118.

9

Output Feedback Control of Discrete-time LTI Systems: Scaling LMI Approaches

Jun Xu
National University of Singapore
Singapore

1. Introduction

Most physical systems have only limited states to be measured and fed back for system controls. Although sometimes, a reduced-order observer can be designed to meet the requirements of full-state feedback, it does introduce extra dynamics, which increases the complexity of the design. This naturally motivates the employment of output feedback, which only use measurable output in its feedback design. From implementation point of view, static feedback is more cost effective, more reliable and easier to implement than dynamic feedback (Khalil, 2002; Kučera & Souza, 1995; Syrmos et al., 1997). Moreover, many other problems are reducible to some variation of it. Simply stated, the static output feedback problem is to find a static output feedback so that the closed-loop system has some desirable characteristics, or determine the nonexistence of such a feedback (Syrmos et al., 1997). This problem, however, still marked as one important open question even for LTI systems in control engineering.
Although this problem is also known NP-hard (Syrmos et al., 1997), the curious fact to note here is that these early negative results have not prevented researchers from studying output feedback problems. In fact, there are a lot of existing works addressing this problem using different approaches, say, for example, Riccati equation approach, rank-constrained conditions, approach based on structural properties, bilinear matrix inequality (BMI) approaches and min-max optimization techniques (e.g., Bara & Boutayeb (2005; 2006); Benton (Jr.); Gadewadikar et al. (2006); Geromel, de Oliveira & Hsu (1998); Geromel et al. (1996); Ghaoui et al. (2001); Henrion et al. (2005); Kučera & Souza (1995); Syrmos et al. (1997) and the references therein). Nevertheless, the LMI approaches for this problem remain popular (Bara & Boutayeb, 2005; 2006; Cao & Sun, 1998; Geromel, de Oliveira & Hsu, 1998; Geromel et al., 1996; Prempain & Postlethwaite, 2001; Yu, 2004; Zečević & Šiljak, 2004) due to simplicity and efficiency.
Motivated by the recent work (Bara & Boutayeb, 2005; 2006; Geromel et al., 1996; Xu & Xie, 2005a;b; 2006), this paper proposes several scaling linear matrix inequality (LMI) approaches to static output feedback control of discrete-time linear time invariant (LTI) plants. Based on whether a similarity matrix transformation is applied, we divide these approaches into two parts. Some approaches with similarity transformation are concerned with the dimension and rank of system input and output. Several different methods with respect to the system state dimension, output dimension and input dimension are given based on whether the distribution matrix of input B or the distribution matrix of output C is full-rank. The other

approaches apply Finsler's Lemma to deal with the Lyapunov matrix and controller gain directly without similarity transformation. Compared with the BMI approach (e.g., Henrion et al. (2005)) or VK-like iterative approach (e.g.,Yu (2004)), the scaling LMI approaches are much more efficient and convergence properties are generally guaranteed. Meanwhile, they can significantly reduce the conservatism of non-scaling method, (e.g.,Bara & Boutayeb (2005; 2006)). Hence, we show that our approaches actually can be treated as alternative and complemental methods for existing works.

The remainder of this paper is organized as follows. In Section 2, we state the system and problem. In Section 3, several approaches based on similarity transformation are given. In Subection 3.1, we present the methods for the case that B is full column rank. Based on the relationship between the system state dimension and input dimension, we discuss it in three parts. In Subsection 3.2, we consider the case that C is full row rank in the similar way. In Subsection 3.3, we propose another formulations based on the connection between state feedback and output feedback. In Section 4, we present the methods based on Finsler's lemma. In Section 5, we compare our methods with some existing works and give a brief statistical analysis. In Section 6, we extend the latter result to H_∞ control. Finally, a conclusion is given in the last section. The notation in this paper is standard. $\mathcal{R}^n$ denotes the n dimensional real space. Matrix $A > 0$ ($A \geq 0$) means A is positive definite (semi-definite).

2. Problem formulation

Consider the following discrete-time linear time-invariant (LTI) system:

$$x(t+1) = A_o x(t) + B_o u(t) \tag{1}$$

$$y(t) = C_o x(t) \tag{2}$$

where $x \in \mathcal{R}^n, u \in \mathcal{R}^m$ and $y \in \mathcal{R}^l$. All the matrices mentioned in this paper are appropriately dimensioned. $m < n$ and $l < n$.

We want to stabilize the system (1)-(2) by static output feedback

$$u(t) = Ky(t) \tag{3}$$

The closed-loop system is

$$x(t+1) = \tilde{A}x(t) = (A_o + B_o K C_o)x(t) \tag{4}$$

The following lemma is well-known.

Lemma 1. *(Boyd et al., 1994) The closed-loop system (4) is (Schur) stable if and only if either one of the following conditions is satisfied:*

$$P > 0, \ \ \tilde{A}^T P \tilde{A} - P < 0 \tag{5}$$

$$Q > 0, \ \ \tilde{A} Q \tilde{A}^T - Q < 0 \tag{6}$$

3. Scaling LMIs with similarity transformation

This section is motivated by the recent LMI formulation of output feedback control (Bara & Boutayeb, 2005; 2006; Geromel, de Souze & Skelton, 1998) and dilated LMI formulation (de Oliveira et al., 1999; Xu et al., 2004).

3.1 B_o with full column-rank

We assume that B_o is of full column-rank, which means we can always find a non-singular matrix T_b such that $T_b B_o = \begin{bmatrix} I_m \\ 0 \end{bmatrix}$. In fact, using singular value decomposition (SVD), we can obtain such T_b. Hence the new state-space representation of this system is given by

$$A = T_b A_o T_b^{-1} = \begin{bmatrix} A_{11} & A_{12} \\ A_{21} & A_{22} \end{bmatrix}, B = T_b B_o, \; C = C_o T_b^{-1} \tag{7}$$

The closed-loop system (4) is stable if and only if

$$\tilde{A}_b = A + BKC \text{ is stable}$$

In this case, we divide it into 3 situations: $m = n - m$, $m < n - m$, and $m > n - m$. Let

$$P = \begin{bmatrix} P_{11} & P_{12} \\ P_{12}^T & P_{22} \end{bmatrix} \in \mathcal{R}^{n \times n}, P_{11} \in \mathcal{R}^{m \times m}, P_{12} \in \mathcal{R}^{m \times (n-m)} \tag{8}$$

For the third situation, let

$$P_{12} = [P_{12}^{(1)} \; P_{12}^{(2)}], \; P_{11} = \begin{bmatrix} P_{11}^{(1)} & P_{11}^{(2)} \\ P_{11}^{(2)T} & P_{11}^{(3)} \end{bmatrix} \tag{9}$$

where $P_{12}^{(1)} \in \mathcal{R}^{(n-m)\times(n-m)}$ and $P_{11}^{(1)} \in \mathcal{R}^{(n-m)\times(n-m)}$.

Theorem 1. *The discrete-time system (1)-(2) is stabilized by (3) if there exist $P > 0$ defined in (8) and R, such that*

$$\begin{cases} \Phi(\Theta_1) < 0, \; m = n - m \\ \Phi(\Theta_2) < 0, \; m < n - m \\ \Phi(\Theta_3) < 0, \; m > n - m \end{cases} \tag{10}$$

where $\varepsilon \in \mathcal{R}$,

$$\Phi(\Theta_1) = \begin{bmatrix} A^T \Theta_1 A - P & * \\ RC + [P_{11} \; P_{12}]A & -P_{11} \end{bmatrix} < 0 \tag{11}$$

$$\Theta_1 = \begin{bmatrix} 0 & 0 \\ 0 & P_{22} + \varepsilon^2 P_{11} - \varepsilon P_{12} - \varepsilon P_{12}^T \end{bmatrix}, \tag{12}$$

$$\Theta_2 = \begin{bmatrix} 0 & 0 \\ 0 & P_{22} - \varepsilon \begin{bmatrix} P_{12} \\ 0 \end{bmatrix} - \varepsilon [P_{12}^T \; 0] + \varepsilon^2 \begin{bmatrix} P_{11} & 0 \\ 0 & 0 \end{bmatrix} \end{bmatrix},$$

$$\Theta_3 = \begin{bmatrix} 0 & 0 \\ 0 & P_{22} - \varepsilon P_{12}^{(1)T} - \varepsilon P_{12}^{(1)} + \varepsilon^2 P_{11}^{(1)} \end{bmatrix}.$$

Furthermore, a static output feedback controller gain is given by

$$K = P_{11}^{-1} R \tag{13}$$

Proof: Noting that

$$(BKC)^T P (BKC) = C^T K^T P_{11} KC,$$

$$PBKC = \begin{bmatrix} P_{11} \\ P_{12}^T \end{bmatrix} KC$$

(5) is equivalent to

$$\begin{aligned} &([P_{11}\ P_{12}]A + P_{11}KC)^T P_{11}^{-1}([P_{11}\ P_{12}]A + P_{11}KC) \\ &-A^T \begin{bmatrix} P_{11} \\ P_{12}^T \end{bmatrix} P_{11}^{-1}[P_{11}\ P_{12}]A + A^T PA - P < 0 \end{aligned} \tag{14}$$

Considering that

$$P - \begin{bmatrix} P_{11} \\ P_{12}^T \end{bmatrix} P_{11}^{-1}[P_{11}\ P_{12}] = \begin{bmatrix} 0 & 0 \\ 0 & P_{22} - P_{12}^T P_{11}^{-1} P_{12} \end{bmatrix}$$

For the first situation $m = n - m$, consider the following inequality:

$$(P_{12} - \varepsilon P_{11})^T P_{11}^{-1}(P_{12} - \varepsilon P_{11}) \geq 0 \tag{15}$$

or equivalently

$$P_{12}^T P_{11}^{-1} P_{12} \geq \varepsilon P_{12}^T + \varepsilon P_{12} - \varepsilon^2 P_{11} \tag{16}$$

(14) is equivalent to

$$\begin{bmatrix} A^T \Theta_0 A - P & * \\ P_{11}KC + [P_{11}\ P_{12}]A & -P_{11} \end{bmatrix} < 0 \tag{17}$$

where

$$\Theta_0 = \begin{bmatrix} 0 & 0 \\ 0 & P_{22} - P_{12}^T P_{11}^{-1} P_{12} \end{bmatrix}$$

Using the fact (16), we have $\Theta_0 \leq \Theta_1$, and consequentially, $\Phi(\Theta_0) \leq \Phi(\Theta_1)$. Hence if (11) is satisfied, (5) is satisfied as well.

For the second situation, let the inequality

$$\left(\begin{bmatrix} P_{12} \\ 0 \end{bmatrix} - \varepsilon \begin{bmatrix} P_{11} & 0 \\ 0 & 0 \end{bmatrix} \right)^T \begin{bmatrix} P_{11} & 0 \\ 0 & I \end{bmatrix}^{-1} \left(\begin{bmatrix} P_{12} \\ 0 \end{bmatrix} - \varepsilon \begin{bmatrix} P_{11} & 0 \\ 0 & 0 \end{bmatrix} \right) \geq 0 \tag{18}$$

where $\begin{bmatrix} P_{12} \\ 0 \end{bmatrix} \in \mathcal{R}^{(n-m)\times(n-m)}$ and $\begin{bmatrix} P_{11} & 0 \\ 0 & I \end{bmatrix} \in \mathcal{R}^{(n-m)\times(n-m)}$. Note that (18) is equivalent to

$$P_{12}^T P_{11}^{-1} P_{12} \geq \varepsilon \begin{bmatrix} P_{12} \\ 0 \end{bmatrix}^T + \varepsilon \begin{bmatrix} P_{12} \\ 0 \end{bmatrix} - \varepsilon^2 \begin{bmatrix} P_{11} & 0 \\ 0 & 0 \end{bmatrix} \tag{19}$$

For the third situation, noting that

$$([\,P_{12}\ 0\,] - \varepsilon P_{11})^T P_{11}^{-1}([\,P_{12}\ 0\,] - \varepsilon P_{11}) \geq 0 \tag{20}$$

we have

$$\begin{bmatrix} P_{12}^T \\ 0 \end{bmatrix} P_{11}^{-1}\,[\,P_{12}\ 0\,] \geq \varepsilon \begin{bmatrix} P_{12}^T \\ 0 \end{bmatrix} + \varepsilon\,[\,P_{12}\ 0\,] - \varepsilon^2 P_{11} \tag{21}$$

(21) implies

$$P_{12}^T P_{11}^{-1} P_{12} \geq \varepsilon P_{12}^{(1)T} + \varepsilon P_{12}^{(1)} - \varepsilon^2 P_{11}^{(1)} \tag{22}$$

Hence we complete the proof.

Remark 1. *If $\varepsilon \equiv 0$ is set , then Theorem 1 recovers the result stated in (Bara & Boutayeb, 2006). We shall note that ε actually plays an important role in the scaling LMI formulation in Theorem 1. If $\varepsilon \equiv 0$, Theorem 1 implies $A_{22}^T P_{22} A_{22} - P_{22} < 0$ and $P_{22} > 0$, i.e., the system matrix A_{22} must be Schur stable, which obviously is an unnecessary condition and limits the application of this LMI formulation. However, with the aid of ε, we relax this constraint. A searching routine, such as fminsearch (simplex search method) in Matlab ©, can be applied to the following optimization problem (for a fixed ε, we have an LMI problem):*

$$\min_{\varepsilon,P,R} \lambda I, \ s.t. \ \Phi(\Theta) < \lambda I \tag{23}$$

The conservatism of Theorem 1 lies in these relaxations (15) or (16) on (5). To further relax the conservatism, we may choose a diagonal matrix $\triangle = diag\{\varepsilon_1, ..., \varepsilon_m\}, \varepsilon_i \geq 0$, instead of the single scalar ε. For example,

$$P_{12}^T P_{11}^{-1} P_{12} \geq P_{12}^T \triangle + \triangle P_{12} - \triangle P_{11} \triangle \tag{24}$$

Then we shall search the optimal value over multiple scalars for (23).

Remark 2. *In (Bara & Boutayeb, 2006), a different variable replacement is given:*

$$P_2 = P_{22} - P_{12}^T P_{11}^{-1} P_{12} \tag{25}$$

in (8). However, it is easily proved that these two transformations actually are equivalent. In fact, in (8), we have $P_{11} > 0$ and $P_2 > 0$ since $P > 0$. Based on (17), we have

$$\begin{bmatrix} A^T \begin{bmatrix} 0 & 0 \\ 0 & P_2 \end{bmatrix} A - \Lambda_0 & * \\ P_{11}KC + [P_{11} \ P_{12}]A & -P_{11} \end{bmatrix} < 0 \tag{26}$$

where

$$\Lambda_0 = \begin{bmatrix} P_{11} & P_{12} \\ P_{12}^T & P_2 + P_{12}^T P_{11}^{-1} P_{12} \end{bmatrix} = P \tag{27}$$

Hence, for the above three situations, we have an alternative condition, which is stated in the following lemma.

Theorem 2. *The discrete-time system (1)-(2) is stabilized by (3) if there exist $P_{11} > 0$, $P_2 > 0$, P_{12} and R with P defined in (27), such that*

$$\begin{cases} \Upsilon(\Lambda_1) < 0, & m = n - m \\ \Upsilon(\Lambda_2) < 0, & m < n - m \\ \Upsilon(\Lambda_3) < 0, & m > n - m \end{cases} \tag{28}$$

where $\varepsilon \in \mathcal{R}$,

$$\Upsilon(\Lambda_i) = \begin{bmatrix} A^T \begin{bmatrix} 0 & 0 \\ 0 & P_2 \end{bmatrix} A - \Lambda_i & * \\ RC + [P_{11} \ P_{12}]A & -P_{11} \end{bmatrix},$$

$$\Lambda_1 = \begin{bmatrix} P_{11} & P_{12} \\ P_{12}^T & P_2 - \varepsilon^2 P_{11} + \varepsilon P_{12} + \varepsilon P_{12}^T \end{bmatrix},$$

$$\Lambda_2 = \begin{bmatrix} P_{11} & P_{12} \\ P_{12}^T & P_2 + \varepsilon \begin{bmatrix} P_{12} \\ 0 \end{bmatrix} + \varepsilon [P_{12}^T \ 0] - \varepsilon^2 \begin{bmatrix} P_{11} & 0 \\ 0 & I \end{bmatrix} \end{bmatrix},$$

$$\Lambda_3 = \begin{bmatrix} P_{11} & P_{12} \\ P_{12}^T & P_2 + \varepsilon P_{12}^{(1)T} + \varepsilon P_{12}^{(1)} - \varepsilon^2 P_{11}^{(1)} \end{bmatrix}.$$

Furthermore, a static output controller gain is given by (13).

Proof: We only consider the first case. Replacing P_2 and R by P_{22} and K using (25) and (13), we can derive that (28) is a sufficient condition for (5) with the P defined in (8).

3.2 C_o with full row-rank

When C_o is full row rank, there exists a nonsingular matrix T_c such that $C_o T_o^{-1} = [I_l \ 0]$. Applying a similarity transformation to the system (1)-(2), the closed-loop system (4) is stable if and only if

$$\tilde{A}_c = A + BKC \text{ is stable}$$

where $A = T_c A_o T_c^{-1}$, $B = T_c B_o$ and $C = C_o T_c^{-1} = [I_l \ 0]$.
Similarly to Section 3.1, we can also divide this problem into three situations: $l = n - l$, $l < n - l$ and $l > n - l$. We use the condition (6) here and partition Q as $Q = \begin{bmatrix} Q_{11} & Q_{12} \\ Q_{12}^T & Q_{22} \end{bmatrix}$, where $Q_{11} \in \mathcal{R}^{l \times l}$.

Theorem 3. *The discrete-time system (1)-(2) is stabilized by (3) if there exist $Q > 0$ and R, such that*

$$\begin{cases} \Gamma(\bar{\Theta}_1) < 0, l = n - l \\ \Gamma(\bar{\Theta}_2) < 0, l < n - l \\ \Gamma(\bar{\Theta}_3) < 0, l > n - l \end{cases} \tag{29}$$

where $\varepsilon \in \mathcal{R}$,

$$\Gamma(\bar{\Theta}_i) = \begin{bmatrix} A\bar{\Theta}_i A^T - Q & * \\ (A[Q_{11} \ Q_{12}]^T + BR)^T & -Q_{11} \end{bmatrix},$$

$$\bar{\Theta}_1 = \begin{bmatrix} 0 & 0 \\ 0 & Q_{22} + \varepsilon^2 Q_{11} - \varepsilon Q_{12} - \varepsilon Q_{12}^T \end{bmatrix},$$

$$\bar{\Theta}_2 = \begin{bmatrix} 0 & 0 \\ 0 & Q_{22} + \varepsilon^2 \begin{bmatrix} Q_{11} & 0 \\ 0 & 0 \end{bmatrix} - \varepsilon \begin{bmatrix} Q_{12} \\ 0 \end{bmatrix} - \varepsilon [Q_{12}^T \ 0] \end{bmatrix},$$

$$\bar{\Theta}_3 = \begin{bmatrix} 0 & 0 \\ 0 & Q_{22} + \varepsilon^2 Q_{11}^{(1)} - \varepsilon Q_{12}^{(1)T} - \varepsilon Q_{12}^{(1)} \end{bmatrix},$$

$Q_{11}^{(1)}$ and $Q_{12}^{(1)}$ are properly dimensioned partitions of Q_{11} and Q_{12}. Furthermore, a static output feedback controller gain is given by

$$K = RQ_{11}^{-1} \tag{30}$$

Proof: We only prove the first case $l = n - l$, since the others are similar. Noting that $(BKC)Q(BKC)^T = BKQ_{11}K^TB$ and $BKCQ = BK[Q_{11}\ Q_{12}]$, (6) is equivalent to

$$
\begin{aligned}
&(A[Q_{11}\ Q_{12}]^T + BKQ_{11})Q_{11}^{-1}(A[Q_{11}\ Q_{12}]^T + BKQ_{11})^T \\
&-A\begin{bmatrix} Q_{11} \\ Q_{12}^T \end{bmatrix} Q_{11}^{-1}[Q_{11}\ Q_{12}]A^T + AQA^T - Q < 0
\end{aligned}
\tag{31}
$$

Using the fact that

$$
Q - \begin{bmatrix} Q_{11} \\ Q_{12}^T \end{bmatrix} Q_{11}^{-1}[Q_{11}\ Q_{12}] = \begin{bmatrix} 0 & 0 \\ 0 & Q_{12}^T Q_{11}^{-1} Q_{12} \end{bmatrix}
$$

we infer that stability of the close-loop system is equivalent to the existing of a $Q > 0$ such that

$$
\begin{bmatrix} A\bar{\Theta}_0 A^T - Q & * \\ (A[Q_{11}\ Q_{12}] + BKQ_{11})^T & -Q_{11} \end{bmatrix} < 0 \tag{32}
$$

where

$$
\bar{\Theta}_0 = \begin{bmatrix} 0 & 0 \\ 0 & Q_{22} - Q_{12}^T Q_{11}^{-1} Q_{12} \end{bmatrix}
$$

Since

$$
(Q_{12} - \varepsilon Q_{11})^T Q_{11}^{-1}(Q_{12} - \varepsilon Q_{11}) \geq 0 \tag{33}
$$

or equivalently,

$$
Q_{12}^T Q_{11}^{-1} Q_{12} \geq \varepsilon Q_{12}^T + \varepsilon Q_{12} - \varepsilon^2 Q_{11} \tag{34}
$$

It follows that (29) implies (32). Hence we complete the proof.

Remark 3. *How to compare the conditions in Theorem 3 and Theorem 1 remains a difficult problem. In the next section, we only give some experiential results based on numerical simulations, which give some suggestions on the dependence of the results with respect to m and l.*

3.3 Transformation-dependent LMIs

The result in this subsection builds a connection between the sets $\mathcal{L}$, $\mathcal{K}_c$, $\mathcal{K}_o$, $\tilde{\mathcal{K}_c}$ and $\tilde{\mathcal{K}_o}$, which are defined as follows. Without causing confusion, we omit the subscript $_o$ for A_o, B_o and C_o in this subsection.

$$
\mathcal{L} = \{K \in \mathcal{R}^{m\times l} : \bar{A}\ stable\} \tag{35}
$$

i.e., the set of all admissible output feedback matrix gains;

$$
\mathcal{K}_c = \{K_c \in \mathcal{R}^{m\times n} : A + BK_c\ \ stable\} \tag{36}
$$

i.e., the set of all admissible state feedback matrix gains;

$$
\mathcal{K}_o = \{K_o \in \mathcal{R}^{n\times l} : A + K_oC\ \ stable\} \tag{37}
$$

i.e., the set of all admissible observer matrix gains. Based on Lemma 1, we can easily formulate the LMI solution for sets $\mathcal{K}_c$ and $\mathcal{K}_o$. In fact, they are equivalent to following two sets respectively:

$$
\tilde{\mathcal{K}_c} = \{K_c = W_{c2}W_{c1}^{-1} \in \mathcal{R}^{m\times n} : (W_{c1}, W_{c2}) \in \mathcal{W}_c\} \tag{38}
$$

and

$$\mathcal{W}_c = \{W_{c1} \in \mathcal{R}^{n\times n}, W_{c2} \in \mathcal{R}^{m\times n} : W_{c1} > 0, \Psi_c < 0\} \tag{39}$$

where $\Psi_c = \begin{bmatrix} -W_{c1} & AW_{c1} + BW_{c2} \\ W_{c1}A^T + W_{c2}^T B^T & -W_{c1} \end{bmatrix}$.

$$\bar{\mathcal{K}}_o = \{K_o = W_{o1}^{-1} W_{o2} \in \mathcal{R}^{n\times l} : (W_{o1}, W_{o2}) \in \mathcal{W}_o\} \tag{40}$$

and

$$\mathcal{W}_o = \{W_{o1} \in \mathcal{R}^{n\times n}, W_{o2} \in \mathcal{R}^{n\times l} : W_{o1} > 0, \Psi_o < 0\} \tag{41}$$

where $\Psi_o = \begin{bmatrix} -W_{1o} & W_{o1}A + W_{o2}C \\ A^T W_{o1} + C^T W_{o2}^T & -W_{1o} \end{bmatrix}$.

Lemma 2. *$\mathcal{L} \neq \emptyset$ if and only if*

1. $\bar{\mathcal{K}}_c = \mathcal{K}_c \bigcap \{K_c : K_c Y_c = 0,\ Y_c = \mathcal{N}(C)\} \neq \emptyset$; *or*
2. $\bar{\mathcal{K}}_o = \mathcal{K}_o \bigcap \{K_c : Y_o K_o = 0,\ Y_o = \mathcal{N}(B')\} \neq \emptyset$.

In the affirmative case, any $K \in \mathcal{L}$ can be rewritten as

1. $K = K_c Q C^T (C Q C^T)^{-1}$; *or*
2. $K = (B^T P B)^{-1} B^T P K_o$.

where $Q > 0$ and $P > 0$ are arbitrarily chosen.

Proof: The first statement has been proved in Geromel et al. (1996). For complement, we give the proof of the second statement. The necessity is obvious since $K_o = BK$. Now we prove the sufficiency, i.e., given $K_o \in \bar{\mathcal{K}}_o$, there exists a K, such that the constraint $K_o = BK$ is solvable. Note that for $\forall P > 0$, $\Theta_o = \begin{bmatrix} B^T P \\ Y_o^T \end{bmatrix}$ is full rank, where $Y_o = \mathcal{N}(B^T)$. In fact, $rank(\Theta_o Y_o) = rank(\begin{bmatrix} B^T P Y_o \\ I_{n-m} \end{bmatrix}) \geq n - m$. Multiplying Θ_o at the both side of $K_o = BK$ we have

$$\begin{bmatrix} B^T P K_o \\ Y_o^T K_o \end{bmatrix} = \begin{bmatrix} B^T P B L \\ 0 \end{bmatrix}$$

Since $B^T P B$ is invertible, we have $K = (B^T P B)^{-1} B^T P K_0$. Hence, we can derive the result.

Lemma 3. *$\mathcal{L} \neq \emptyset$ if and only if there exists $E_c \in \mathcal{R}^{n\times(n-l)}$ or $E_o \in \mathcal{R}^{n\times(n-m)}$, such that one of the following conditions holds:*

1. $rank(T_c = \begin{bmatrix} C \\ E_c^T \end{bmatrix}) = n$ *and* $\mathcal{C}(E_c) \neq \emptyset$; *or*
2. $rank(T_o = \begin{bmatrix} B & E_o \end{bmatrix}) = n$ *and* $\mathcal{O}(E_o) \neq \emptyset$.

where

$$\mathcal{C}(E_c) = \mathcal{W}_c \bigcap \{(W_{c1}, W_{c2}) : C W_{c1} E_c = 0, W_{c2} E_c = 0\}$$

$$\mathcal{O}(E_o) = \mathcal{W}_o \bigcap \{(W_{o1}, W_{o2}) : B^T W_{o1} E_o = 0, E_o^T W_{o2} = 0\}$$

In the affirmative case, any $K \in \mathcal{L}$ can be rewritten as

1. $K = W_{c2} C^T (C W_{c1} C^T)^{-1}$; *or*
2. $K = (B^T W_{o1} B)^{-1} B^T W_{o2}$.

Proof: We only prove the statement 2, since the statement 1 is similar. For the necessity, if there exist $K \in \mathcal{L}$, then it shall satisfy Lemma 1. Now we let

$$W_{o1} = P, \; W_{o2} = PBK$$

Choose $E_o = P^{-1}Y_o$, $Y_o = \mathcal{N}(B^T)$. It is known that $\begin{bmatrix} B & E_o \end{bmatrix}$ is full rank. Then we have

$$B^T W_{o1} E = B^T Y_o = 0, E^T W_{o2} = Y_o^T BK = 0$$

For sufficiency, we assume there exists E_o such that the statement 2) is satisfied. Notice that $W_{o1} > 0$ and the item W_{o2} in Ψ_o can be rewritten as $W_{o1} W_{o1}^{-1} W_{o2}$.

$$W_{o1}^{-1} W_{o2} = T_o (T_o^T W_{o1} T_o)^{-1} T_o^T W_{o2} = B(B^T W_{o1} B)^{-1} B^T W_{o2} \tag{42}$$

since T_o is invertible and $B^T W_{o1} E = 0, E^T W_{o2} = 0$. Hence, $W_{o1}^{-1} W_{o2}$ can be factorized as BK, where $K = (B^T W_{o1} B)^{-1} B^T W_{o2}$. Now we can derive (5) from the fact $\Psi_o < 0$. Thus we complete the proof.

Remark 4. *For a given T_o, since $T_o^{-1} T_o = I_n$, $T_o^{-1} B = \begin{bmatrix} I_m \\ 0 \end{bmatrix}$ and $T_o^{-1} E = \begin{bmatrix} 0 \\ I_{n-m} \end{bmatrix}$. Similarly, For a given T_c, $C T_c^{-1} = \begin{bmatrix} I_l & 0 \end{bmatrix}$.*

Theorem 4. *$\mathcal{L} \neq \emptyset$ if and only if there exists T_c or T_o, such that one of the following conditions holds:*

1.

$$\tilde{\mathcal{W}}_c \neq \emptyset, \; \tilde{\mathcal{W}}_c = \{\hat{W}_{c1} \in \mathcal{R}^{n \times n}, \hat{W}_{c2} \in \mathcal{R}^{m \times n} : \hat{W}_{c1} > 0, \Phi_c < 0\} \tag{43}$$

where

$$\hat{A} = T_c A T_c^{-1}, \; \hat{B} = T_c B, \hat{W}_{c1} = \begin{bmatrix} W_{c11} & 0 \\ 0 & W_{c22} \end{bmatrix},$$

and

$$\hat{W}_{c2} = \begin{bmatrix} W_{c21} & 0 \end{bmatrix}, \quad W_{c11} \in \mathcal{R}^{l \times l}, \quad W_{c22} \in \mathcal{R}^{(n-l) \times (n-l)}, \quad W_{c21} \in \mathcal{R}^{m \times l},$$

$$\Phi_c = \begin{bmatrix} -\hat{W}_{c1} & \hat{A}\hat{W}_{c1} + \hat{B}\hat{W}_{c2} \\ \hat{W}_{c1}\hat{A}^T + \hat{W}_{c2}^T \hat{B}^T & -\hat{W}_{c1} \end{bmatrix};$$

2.

$$\tilde{\mathcal{W}}_o \neq \emptyset, \; \tilde{\mathcal{W}}_o = \{\check{W}_{o1} \in \mathcal{R}^{n \times n}, \check{W}_{o2} \in \mathcal{R}^{n \times r} : \check{W}_{o1} > 0, \Phi_o < 0\} \tag{44}$$

where

$$\check{A} = T_o^{-1} A T_o, \; \check{C} = C T_o, \quad \check{W}_{o1} = \begin{bmatrix} W_{o11} & 0 \\ 0 & W_{o22} \end{bmatrix},$$

and

$$\check{W}_{o2} = \begin{bmatrix} W_{o21} \\ 0 \end{bmatrix},$$

$$W_{o11} \in \mathcal{R}^{m \times m}, \quad W_{o22} \in \mathcal{R}^{(n-m) \times (n-m)}, \quad W_{o21} \in \mathcal{R}^{m \times r},$$

$$\Phi_o = \begin{bmatrix} -\check{W}_{o1} & \check{W}_{o1}\check{A} + \check{W}_{o2}\check{C} \\ \check{A}^T \check{W}_{o1} + \check{C}^T \check{W}_{o2}^T & -\check{W}_{o1} \end{bmatrix}.$$

In the affirmative case, any $K \in \mathcal{L}$ can be rewritten as

1. $K = W_{c21} W_{c11}^{-1}$; or

2. $K = W_{o11}^{-1} W_{o21}$.

Proof: We also only consider the statement 2) here. The sufficiency is obvious according to Lemma 3, hence, we only prove the necessity.
Note that

$$\begin{bmatrix} -\check{W}_{o1} & \check{W}_{o1}\check{A} + \check{W}_{o2}\check{C} \\ \check{A}^T\check{W}_{o1} + \check{C}^T\check{W}_{o2}^T & -\check{W}_{o1} \end{bmatrix}$$
$$= \mathcal{T}_o^T \begin{bmatrix} -W_{o1} & W_{o1}A + W_{o2}C \\ A^T W_{o1} + C^T W_{o2}^T & -W_{o1} \end{bmatrix} \mathcal{T}_o$$

where $\mathcal{T}_o = \begin{bmatrix} T_o & 0 \\ 0 & T_o \end{bmatrix}$. Hence, we can conclude that

$$\check{W}_{o1} = T_o^T W_{o1} T_o, \; \check{W}_{o2} = T_o^T W_{o2}$$

Since the system matrices also satisfy

$$B^T W_{o1} E = 0, E^T W_{o2} = 0$$

which implies

$$B^T T_o^{-T} \check{W}_{o1} T_o^{-1} E = 0, \; E^T T_o^{-T} \check{W}_{o2} = 0 \tag{45}$$

Let

$$\check{W}_{o1} = \begin{bmatrix} W_{o11} & W_{o12} \\ W_{o12}^T & W_{o22} \end{bmatrix}, \; \check{W}_{o2} = \begin{bmatrix} W_{o21} \\ W_{o23} \end{bmatrix}$$

With the conclusion from Remark 4, (45) implies

$$W_{o12} = 0, \; W_{o23} = 0$$

Hence we have the structural constraints on $\check{W}_{o1}$ and $\check{W}_{o2}$. Using the results of Lemma 3, we can easily get the controller L. Thus we complete the proof.

Remark 5. *The first statements of Lemma 3 and Theorem 4 are corollaries of the results in Geromel, de Souze & Skelton (1998); Geromel et al. (1996). Based on Theorem 4, we actually obtain a useful LMI algorithm for output feedback control design of general LTI systems with fixed E_c and/or E_o. For these LTI systems, we can first make a similarity transformation that makes $C = [I\ 0]$ (or $B^T = [I\ 0]$). Then we force the W_{c1} and W_{c2} (or W_{o1} and W_{o2}) to be constrained structure shown in Theorem 4. If the corresponding LMIs have solution, we may conclude that the output feedback gain exists; otherwise, we cannot make a conclusion, as the choice of E_c or E_o is simply a special case. Thus we can choose a scaled E_c or E_o, i.e., ϵE_c or ϵE_o to perform a one-dimensional search, which converts the LMI condition in Theorem 4 a scaling LMI. For example, Φ_c in (43) should be changed as* $\Phi_c = \begin{bmatrix} -\hat{W}_{1c} & A\hat{W}_{c1} + \varepsilon B\hat{W}_{c2} \\ \hat{W}_{c1}A^T + \varepsilon \hat{W}_{c2}^T B^T & -\hat{W}_{1c} \end{bmatrix}$.

All the approaches in this section require similarity transformation, which can be done by some techniques, such as the singular value decomposition (SVD). However, those transformations often bring numerical errors, which sometimes leads to some problems for the marginal solutions. Hence in the next section, using Finsler's lemma, we introduce some methods without the pretreatment on system matrices.

4. Scaling LMIs without similarity transformation

Finsler's Lemma has been applied in many LMI formulations, e.g., (Boyd et al., 1994; Xu et al., 2004). With the aid of Finsler's lemma, we can obtain scaling LMIs without similarity transformation.

Lemma 4. *(Boyd et al., 1994) The following expressions are equivalent:*

1. $x^T Ax > 0$ *for* $\forall x \neq 0$, *subject to* $Bx = 0$;
2. $B^{\perp T} AB^{\perp} > 0$, *where* $B^{\perp}$ *is the kernel of* B^T, *i.e.,* $B^{\perp} B^T = 0$;
3. $A + \sigma B^T B > 0$, *for some scale* $\sigma \in R$;
4. $A + XB + B^T X^T > 0$, *for some matrix X.*

In order to apply Finsler's lemma, several manipulation on the Lyapunov inequalities should be done first. Note that the condition (5) actually states $V(x(t)) = x^T(t)Px(t) > 0$ and $\Delta V(x) = V(x(t+1)) - V(x(t)) < 0$. The latter can be rewritten as

$$\xi^T \mathcal{P} \xi < 0,\ \xi = [x^T(t)\ x^T(t+1)]^T, \mathcal{P} = \begin{bmatrix} -P & 0 \\ 0 & P \end{bmatrix} \tag{46}$$

Define $\zeta = [x^T\ u^T]^T$. It is easy to verify:

$$\xi = M_p \zeta \tag{47}$$

$$[K\ -1]N_p \zeta = 0 \tag{48}$$

where

$$M_p = \begin{bmatrix} I & 0 \\ A & B \end{bmatrix}, N_p = \begin{bmatrix} C & 0 \\ 0 & I \end{bmatrix} \tag{49}$$

That is

$$(46)\ \text{s.t.}\ (47)\text{-}(48) \tag{50}$$

Now based on the statements 1) and 4) of Finsler's Lemma, we can conclude that (50) is equivalent to

$$M_p^T \mathcal{P} M_p + N_p^T \begin{bmatrix} K^T \\ -I \end{bmatrix} \mathcal{X}^T + \mathcal{X} \begin{bmatrix} K & -I \end{bmatrix} N_p < 0 \tag{51}$$

for some $\mathcal{X}$. Now we let

$$\mathcal{X}^T = [\varepsilon \tilde{Z}^T\ Z^T] \tag{52}$$

where ε is a given real scalar, $Z = [z_1^T, z_2^T, \cdots, z_m^T]^T \in \mathcal{R}^{m \times m}$ and $\tilde{Z} \in \mathcal{R}^{n \times m}$. Note that $\tilde{Z}$ is constructed from Z with n rows drawing from Z, i.e., $\tilde{Z} = [z_{\tilde{1}}^T, z_{\tilde{2}}^T, \cdots, z_{\tilde{n}}^T]^T$, where $z_{\tilde{i}}^T$, $1 \leq \tilde{i} \leq m$ is a vector from Z. Since $n \geq m$, there are some same vectors in $\tilde{Z}$. Now we define

$$W = ZK = [w_1^T, w_2^T, \cdots, w_m^T]^T \tag{53}$$

and

$$\tilde{W} = \tilde{Z}K = [w_{\tilde{1}}^T, w_{\tilde{2}}^T, \cdots, w_{\tilde{n}}^T]^T \tag{54}$$

where $w_{\tilde{i}}^T$, $1 \leq \tilde{i} \leq m$ is a vector from W. Then (51) can be transferred into following LMI:

$$M_p^T \mathcal{P} M_p + \begin{bmatrix} \varepsilon(C^T \tilde{W}^T + \tilde{W}C) & * \\ WC - \varepsilon \tilde{Z}^T & -(Z^T + Z) \end{bmatrix} < 0 \tag{55}$$

Since $Z^T + Z > B^T P B \geq 0$, Z is invertible, $K = Z^{-1}W$.

Theorem 5. *The discrete-time system (1)-(2) is stabilized by (3) if there exist $P > 0$ and Z, W, such that (55) is satisfied for some scalar ε. Furthermore, the controller is given by $K = Z^{-1}W$.*

The conservatism lies in the construction of $\tilde{Z}$, which has to be a special structure. $\tilde{Z}$ can be further relaxed using a transformation $\tilde{Z} = \varepsilon \hat{Z} Z$, where $\hat{Z} \in \mathcal{R}^{n\times m}$ is a given matrix. In Theorem 5, the condition (5) is applied. Based on the condition (6), we have the following Lemma.

Theorem 6. *The discrete-time system (1)-(2) is stabilized by (3) if there exist $Q > 0$ and Z, W, such that*

$$M_q \mathcal{Q} M_q^T + \begin{bmatrix} \varepsilon(\tilde{W}^T B^T + B\tilde{W}) & * \\ W^T B^T - \varepsilon \tilde{Z} & -(Z^T + Z) \end{bmatrix} < 0 \tag{56}$$

where

$$M_q = \begin{bmatrix} I & A \\ 0 & C \end{bmatrix}, \mathcal{Q} = \begin{bmatrix} -Q & 0 \\ 0 & Q \end{bmatrix} \tag{57}$$

is satisfied for some scalar ε. Furthermore, the controller is given by $K = Z^{-1}W$.

Proof: The condition (6) can be rewritten as

$$\begin{bmatrix} I \\ (BK)^T \end{bmatrix}^T M_q \mathcal{Q} M_q^T \begin{bmatrix} I \\ (BK)^T \end{bmatrix} < 0 \tag{58}$$

Since $\begin{bmatrix} I \\ (BK)^T \end{bmatrix}^T \begin{bmatrix} (BK) \\ -I \end{bmatrix} = 0$, (58) can be rewritten as

$$\begin{bmatrix} (BK) \\ -I \end{bmatrix}^{\perp} M_q \mathcal{Q} M_q^T \begin{bmatrix} (BK) \\ -I \end{bmatrix}^{\perp T} < 0 \tag{59}$$

Now applying Finsler's lemma, we have

$$M_q \mathcal{Q} M_q^T + \begin{bmatrix} (BK) \\ -I \end{bmatrix} \mathcal{X} + \mathcal{X}^T \begin{bmatrix} (BK) \\ -I \end{bmatrix}^T < 0 \tag{60}$$

for some $\mathcal{X} = [\varepsilon \tilde{Z}\ Z]$. Similar to (52), we construct $\tilde{Z}$ from Z with its columns. Hence we have (56), which is a sufficient condition for (6). Thus we complete the proof.

Remark 6. *The proof of Theorem 6 is based on the equivalence between 1 and 2 of Finsler's lemma. It also provides an alterative proof of Theorem 5 if we note that (5) is equivalent to*

$$\begin{bmatrix} I \\ KC \end{bmatrix}^T M_p^T \mathcal{P} M_p \begin{bmatrix} I \\ KC \end{bmatrix} < 0 \tag{61}$$

Remark 7. *Except for the case that $m = 1$ for Theorem 5 and $l = 1$ for Theorem 6, the construction of $\tilde{Z}$ is a problem to be considered. So far, we have no systematic method for this problem. However, based on our experience, the choose of different vectors and their sequence do affect the result.*

The following simple result is the consequence of the equivalence of 1 and 3 in Finsler's Lemma.

Theorem 7. *The discrete-time system (1)-(2) is stabilized by (3) if there exist $P > 0$ and K, such that*

$$\begin{bmatrix} -P - \varepsilon\bar{A} - \varepsilon\bar{A}^T + \varepsilon^2 I & \bar{A}^T \\ \bar{A} & P - I \end{bmatrix} < 0 \tag{62}$$

where $\varepsilon \in \mathcal{R}$.

Proof: It is obvious that inequality (42) holds subject to $[\bar{A} - I]\xi = 0$. Now we apply the equivalence between 1 and 3 of Finsler's lemma and obtain

$$\mathcal{P} - \sigma[\bar{A} - I]\begin{bmatrix} \bar{A} \\ -I \end{bmatrix} = \begin{bmatrix} -P - \sigma\bar{A}^T\bar{A} & \sigma\bar{A} \\ \sigma\bar{A} & P - \sigma I \end{bmatrix} < 0 \tag{63}$$

for some $\sigma > 0$. Note that $-\bar{A}^T\bar{A} < -\varepsilon\bar{A}^T - \varepsilon\bar{A} + \varepsilon^2 I$, (63) can be implied by

$$\begin{bmatrix} -P + \sigma(-\varepsilon\bar{A}^T - \varepsilon\bar{A} + \varepsilon^2 I) & \sigma\bar{A}^T \\ \sigma\bar{A} & P - \sigma I \end{bmatrix} < 0 \tag{64}$$

By redefining P as $\frac{1}{\sigma}P$, we can obtain the result.

Remark 8. *Inequality (51) is also equivalent to*

$$M_p^T \mathcal{P} M_p - \sigma N_p^T \begin{bmatrix} K^T \\ -I \end{bmatrix} \begin{bmatrix} K & -I \end{bmatrix} N_p < 0 \tag{65}$$

for some positive scalar σ. Hence, we have

$$M_p^T \tilde{\mathcal{P}} M_p - N_p^T \begin{bmatrix} K^T \\ -I \end{bmatrix} \begin{bmatrix} K & -I \end{bmatrix} N_p < 0 \tag{66}$$

where $\tilde{\mathcal{P}} = \begin{bmatrix} -\tilde{P} & 0 \\ 0 & \tilde{P} \end{bmatrix}$, $\tilde{P} = \sigma^{-1}P$. Using the fact that $(K - K_0)^T(K - K_0) \geq 0$, we may obtain an iterative solution from initial condition K_0, where K_0 may be gotten from Lemma 5.

5. Comparison and examples

We shall note that the comparisons of some existing methods (Bara & Boutayeb, 2005; Crusius & Trofino, 1999; Garcia et al., 2001) with the case of $\varepsilon = 0$ in Theorem 1 has been given in (Bara & Boutayeb, 2006), where it states that there are many numerical examples for which Theorem 1 with $\varepsilon = 0$ works successfully while the methods in (Bara & Boutayeb, 2005; Crusius & Trofino, 1999; Garcia et al., 2001) do not and vice-versa. It also stands for our conditions. Hence, in the section, we will only compare these methods introduced above. The LMI solvers used here are SeDuMi (v1.3) Sturm et al. (2006) and SDPT3 (v3.4) Toh et al. (2006) with YALMIP Löfberg (2004) as the interface.

In the first example, we will show the advantage of the scaling LMI with ε compared with the non-scaling ones. In the second example, we will show that different scaling LMI approaches have different performance for different situations. As a by-product, we will also illustrate the different solvability of the different solvers.

Example 1. *Consider the unstable system as follows.*

$$A_o = \begin{bmatrix} 0.82 & 0.0576 & 0.2212 & 0.8927 & 0.0678 \\ 0.0574 & 0.0634 & 0.6254 & 0.0926 & 0.9731 \\ 0.0901 & 0.7228 & 0.5133 & 0.2925 & 0.9228 \\ 0.6967 & 0.0337 & 0.5757 & 0.8219 & 0.9587 \\ 0.1471 & 0.6957 & 0.2872 & 0.994 & 0.5632 \end{bmatrix}$$

$$B_o = \begin{bmatrix} 0.9505 & 0.2924 \\ 0.3182 & 0.4025 \\ 0.2659 & 0.0341 \\ 0.0611 & 0.2875 \\ 0.3328 & 0.2196 \end{bmatrix}$$

$$C_o = \begin{bmatrix} 0.5659 & 0.255 & 0.5227 & 0.0038 & 0.3608 \\ 0.8701 & 0.5918 & 0.1291 & 0.3258 & 0.994 \end{bmatrix}$$

This example is borrowed from (Bara & Boutayeb, 2006), where output feedback controllers have been designed. For A_{22} from A, it has stable eigenvalue. In this paper, we compare the design problem with the maximum decay rate, i.e.,

$$\max \rho \quad s.t. \;\; \tilde{A}^T P \tilde{A} - P < -\rho P$$

Note that in this example, $m < n - m$. With $\varepsilon = 0$, i.e., using the method in (Bara & Boutayeb, 2006), we obtain the maximum $\rho = 0.16$, while Theorem 1 gives $\rho = 0.18$ with $\varepsilon = -0.09$. However, Theorem 5 only obtains a maximum $\rho = 0.03$ with a choice of $\hat{Z} = [I_2 \; I_2 \; 0]^T$. Note that the solvability heavily depends on the choice of ε. For example, when $\varepsilon = 0.09$ for Theorem 1, the LMI is not feasible.

Now we consider a case that A_{22} has an unstable eigenvalue. Consider the above example with slight changes on A_o

$$A_o = \begin{bmatrix} 0.9495 & 0.12048 & 0.14297 & 0.19192 & 0.019139 \\ 0.8656 & 0.28816 & 0.67152 & 0.01136 & 0.38651 \\ 0.5038 & 0.46371 & 0.9712 & 0.93839 & 0.42246 \\ 0.13009 & 0.76443 & 0.47657 & 0.54837 & 0.4089 \\ 0.34529 & 0.61187 & 0.15809 & 0.46639 & 0.53536 \end{bmatrix}$$

We can easily verify that A_{22} from A has one unstable eigenvalue 1.004. Hence, the method in (Bara & Boutayeb, 2006) cannot solve it. However, Theorem 1 generates a solution as $K = \begin{bmatrix} -0.233763 & -0.31506 \\ -3.61207 & 0.376493 \end{bmatrix}$. Meanwhile, Theorem 5 also can get a feasible solution for $\varepsilon = -0.1879$ and $K = \begin{bmatrix} 0.9373 & -0.4008 \\ 1.5244 & -0.7974 \end{bmatrix}$. Theorem 4 via a standard SVD without scaling can also obtain $K = \begin{bmatrix} -0.3914 & -0.3603 \\ -2.3604 & -1.1034 \end{bmatrix}$ using (43) or $K = \begin{bmatrix} 1.4813 & 0.5720 \\ -3.7203 & -1.8693 \end{bmatrix}$ using (44).

Example 2. *We randomly generate 5000 stabilizable and detectable systems of dimension* $n = 4(6, 6, 6, 7, 7)$, $m = 2(3, 1, 5, 4, 3)$ *and* $l = 2(3, 5, 1, 3, 4)$.

	T 1	T 3
SeDuMi	5000	4982
SDPT3	4975	5000

Table 1. Different solvability of different solvers

T 1$^{\alpha}$	T 3	4.2.2$^{\beta}$	6.3.3	6.1.5	6.5.1	7.4.3	7.3.4
Y	Y	4999	4999	4994	4996	4998	4998
Y	N	1	0	2	3	1	1
N	Y	0	1	4	1	1	1
N	N	0	0	0	0	0	0

Superscript$^{\gamma}$: Y (N) means that the problem can (not) be solved by the corresponding theorems. For example, the value 4 of third row and third column means that in the random 5000 examples, there are 4 cases that cannot be solved by Theorem 1 while can be solved by Theorem 3.

Table 2. Comparison of Theorem 1 and Theorem 3

Hence we can use Theorem 1 and Theorem 3 with $\varepsilon = 0$ to solve this problem. Note that different solvers may give different solvability. For example, given $n = 6$, $m = 3$ and $l = 3$, in a one-time simulation, the result is given in Table 1. Thus in order to partially eliminate the effect of the solvers, we choose the combined solvability result from two solvers in this section.

Table 2 shows the comparison of Theorem 1 and Theorem 3. Some phenomenons (the solvability of Theorem 1 and Theorem 3 depends on the l and m. When $m > l$, Theorem 1 tends to have a higher solvability than Theorem 3. And vise verse.) was observed from these results obtained using LMITOOLS provided by Matlab is not shown here.

6. Extension to H_∞ synthesis

The aforementioned results can contribute to other problems, such as robust control. In this section, we extend it to H_∞ output feedback control problem. Consider the following system:

$$x(t+1) = Ax(t) + B_2u(t) + B_1w \tag{67}$$

$$y(t) = Cx(t) + Dw \tag{68}$$

$$z(t) = Ex(t) + Fw \tag{69}$$

We only consider the case that B_2 is with full rank and assume that the system has been transferred into the form like (7). Using the controller as (3), the closed-loop system is

$$\begin{aligned} x(t+1) &= \hat{A}x(t) + \hat{B}w \\ &= (A + B_2KC)x(t) + (B_1 + B_2KD)w \end{aligned} \tag{70}$$

We attempt to design the controller, such that the L_2 gain $\sup \frac{\|z\|_2}{\|w\|_2} \leq \gamma$. It should be noted that all the aforementioned scaling LMI approaches can be applied here. However, we only choose one similar to Theorem 1.

Theorem 8. *The discrete-time system (67)-(69) is stabilized by (3) and satisfies H_∞, if there exist a matrix $P > 0$ defined in (8) and R, such that*

$$\begin{cases} \Re(\Theta_1) < 0, \ m = n - m \\ \Re(\Theta_2) < 0, \ m < n - m \\ \Re(\Theta_3) < 0, \ m > n - m \end{cases} \tag{71}$$

where $\varepsilon \in \mathcal{R}$, Θ_i is defined in Theorem 1,

$$\Re(\Theta_i) = \begin{bmatrix} -P_{11} & RC + [P_{11}\ P_{12}]A & RD + [P_{11}\ P_{12}]B_1 & 0 \\ * & A^T\Theta_i A - P & A^T\Theta_i B_1 & E^T \\ * & * & B_1^T\Theta_i B - \gamma I & F^T \\ * & * & * & -\gamma I \end{bmatrix} \tag{72}$$

Proof: Following the arguments in Theorem 1, we can see that (71) implies

$$\Re(\Theta_i) = \begin{bmatrix} \hat{A}^T P\hat{A} - P & \hat{A}^T P\hat{B} & E^T \\ * & \hat{B}^T P\hat{B} - \gamma I & F^T \\ * & * & -\gamma I \end{bmatrix} < 0 \tag{73}$$

Using bounded real lemma (Boyd et al., 1994), we can complete the proof.

7. Conclusion

In this paper, we have presented some sufficient conditions for static output feedback control of discrete-time LTI systems. Some approaches require a similarity transformation to convert B or C to a special form such that we can formulate the design problem into a scaling LMI problem with a conservative relaxation. Based on whether B or C is full rank, we consider several cases with respect to the system state dimension, output dimension and input dimension. These methods are better than these introduced in (Bara & Boutayeb, 2006) and might achieve statistical advantages over other existing results (Bara & Boutayeb, 2005; Crusius & Trofino, 1999; Garcia et al., 2001). The other approaches apply Finsler's lemma directly such that the Lyapunov matrix and the controller gain can be separated, and hence gain benefits for the design. All the presented approaches can be extended to some other problems. Note that we cannot conclude that the approaches presented in this paper is definitely superior to all the existing approaches, but introduce some alternative conditions which may achieve better performance than others in some circumstances.

8. References

Bara, G. I. & Boutayeb, M. (2005). static output feedback stabilization with h_∞ performance for linear discrete-time systems, *IEEE Trans. on Automatic Control* **50**(2): 250–254.

Bara, G. I. & Boutayeb, M. (2006). A new sufficient condition for the output feedback stabilization of linear discrete-time systems, *Technical report*, University Louis Pasteur, France.

Benton(Jr.), R. E. & Smith, D. (1998). Static output feedback stabilization with prescribed degree of stability, *IEEE Trans. on Automatic Control* **43**(10): 1493–1496.

Boyd, S., Ghaoui, L. E., Feron, E. & Balakrishnan, V. (1994). *Linear Matrix Inequalities in System and Control Theory*, Studies in applied mathematics, SIAM.

Cao, Y. & Sun, Y. (1998). Static output feedback simultaneous stabilization: ILMI approach, *International Journal of Control* **70**(5): 803–814.

Crusius, C. A. R. & Trofino, A. (1999). Sufficient LMI conditions for output feedback control problems, *IEEE Trans. on Automatic Control* **44**(5): 1053–1057.

de Oliveira, M. C., Bernussou, J. & Geromel, J. C. (1999). A new discrete-time robust stability condition, *Systems and Control Letters* **37**: 261–265.

Gadewadikar, J., Lewis, F., Xie, L., Kucera, V. & Abu-Khalaf, M. (2006). Parameterization of all stabilizing H_∞ static state-feedback gains: Application to output-feedback design, *Proc. Conference on Decision and Control*.

Garcia, G., Pradin, B. & Zeng, F. (2001). Stabilization of discrete time linear systems by static output feedback, *IEEE Trans. on Automatic Control* **46**(12): 1954–1958.

Geromel, J. C., de Oliveira, M. C. & Hsu, L. (1998). LMI characterization of structural and robust stability, *Linear Algebra and its Application* **285**: 69–80.

Geromel, J. C., de Souze, C. C. & Skelton, R. E. (1998). Static output feedback controllers: stability and convexity, *IEEE Trans. on Automatic Control* **43**(1).

Geromel, J. C., Peres, P. L. D. & Souza, S. R. (1996). Convex analysis of output feedback control problems: Robust stability and performance, *IEEE Trans. on Automatic Control* **41**(7): 997–1003.

Ghaoui, L. E., Oustry, F. & Aitrami, M. (2001). A cone complementarity linearization algorithm for static output feedback and related problems, *IEEE Trans. on Automatic Control* **42**(8): 870–878.

Henrion, D., Löfberg, J., Kočvara, M. & Stingl, M. (2005). Solving polynomial static output feedback problems with PENBMI, *Proc. Conference on Decision and Control*.

Khalil, H. K. (2002). *Nonlinear Systems*, 3rd edn, Pretince Hall, New Jersey, USA.

Kučera, V. & Souza, C. E. D. (1995). A necessary and sufficient condition for output feedback stabilizability, *Automatica* **31**(9): 1357–1359.

Löfberg, J. (2004). YALMIP : A toolbox for modeling and optimization in MATLAB, *the CACSD Conference*, Taipei, Taiwan.

Prempain, E. & Postlethwaite, I. (2001). Static output feedback stabilisation with H_∞ performance for a class of plants, *Systems and Control Letters* **43**: 159–166.

Sturm, J. F., Romanko, O. & Pólik, I. (2006). Sedumi: http: // sedumi.mcmaster.ca/, *User manual*, McMaster University.

Syrmos, V. L., Abdallab, C., Dprato, P. & Grigoriadis, K. (1997). Static output feedback - a survey, *Automatica* **33**(2): 125–137.

Toh, K. C., Tütüncü, R. H. & Todd, M. J. (2006). On the implementation and usage of SDPT3 - a MATLAB software package for semidefinite-quadratic-linear programming, version 4.0, *Manual*, National University of Singapore, Singapore.

Xu, J. & Xie, L. (2005a). H_∞ state feedback control of discrete-time piecewise affine systems, *IFAC World Congress*, Prague, Czech.

Xu, J. & Xie, L. (2005b). Non-synchronized H_∞ estimation of discrete-time piecewise linear systems, *IFAC World Congress*, Prague, Czech.

Xu, J. & Xie, L. (2006). Dilated LMI characterization and a new stability criterion for polytopic uncertain systems, *IEEE World Congress on Intelligent Control and Automation*, Dalian, China, pp. 243–247.

Xu, J., Xie, L. & Soh, Y. C. (2004). H_∞ and generalized H_2 estimation of continuous-time piecewise linear systems, *the 5th Asian Control Conference*, IEEE, Melbourne, Australia.

Yu, J. (2004). A new static output feedback approach to the suboptimal mixed $H_2 \backslash H_\infty$ problem, *Int. J. Robust Nonlinear Control* **14**: 1023–1034.

Zečević, A. I. & Šiljak, D. D. (2004). Design of robust static output feedback for large-scale systems, *IEEE Trans. on Automatic Control* **49**(11): 2040–2044.

10

Discrete Time Mixed LQR/H_∞ Control Problems

Xiaojie Xu
School of Electrical Engineering, Wuhan University
Wuhan, 430072,
P. R. China

1. Introduction

This chapter will consider two discrete time mixed LQR/ H_∞ control problems. One is the discrete time state feedback mixed LQR/ H_∞ control problem, another is the non-fragile discrete time state feedback mixed LQR/ H_∞ control problem. Motivation for mixed LQR/ H_∞ control problem is to combine the LQR and suboptimal H_∞ controller design theories, and achieve simultaneously the performance of the two problems. As is well known, the performance measure in optimal LQR control theory is the quadratic performance index, defined in the time-domain as

$$J := \sum_{k=0}^{\infty}(x^T(k)Qx(k) + u^T(k)Ru(k)) \tag{1}$$

while the performance measure in H_∞ control theory is H_∞ norm, defined in the frequency-domain for a stable transfer matrix $T_{zw}(z)$ as

$$\|T_{zw}(z)\|_\infty := \sup_{w\in[0,2\pi]} \sigma_{\max}[T_{zw}(e^{jw})]$$

where, $Q \geq 0$, $R > 0$, $\sigma_{\max}[\bullet]$ denotes the largest singular value.
The linear discrete time system corresponding to the discrete time state feedback mixed LQR/ H_∞ control problem is

$$x(k+1) = Ax(k) + B_1 w(k) + B_2 u(k) \tag{2.a}$$

$$z(k) = C_1 x(k) + D_{12} u(k) \tag{2.b}$$

with state feedback of the form

$$u(k) = Kx(k) \tag{3}$$

where, $x(k) \in R^n$ is the state, $u(k) \in R^m$ is the control input, $w(k) \in R^q$ is the disturbance input that belongs to $L_2[0,\infty)$, $z(k) \in R^p$ is the controlled output. A, B_1, B_2, C_1 and D_{12} are known matrices of appropriate dimensions. Let $x(0) = x_0$.
The closed loop transfer matrix from the disturbance input w to the controlled output z is

$$T_{zw}(z) = \left[\begin{array}{c|c} A_K & B_K \\ \hline C_K & 0 \end{array}\right] := C_K(zI - A_K)^{-1} B_K$$

where, $A_K := A + B_2K$, $B_K := B_1$, $C_K := C_1 + D_{12}K$.
Recall that the discrete time state feedback optimal LQR control problem is to find an admissible controller that minimizes the quadratic performance index (1) subject to the systems (2) (3) with $w = 0$, while the discrete time state feedback H_∞ control problem is to find an admissible controller such that $\|T_{zw}(z)\|_\infty < \gamma$ subject to the systems (2)(3) for a given number $\gamma > 0$. While we combine the two problems for the systems (2)(3) with $w \in L_2[0,\infty)$, the quadratic performance index (1) is a function of the control input $u(k)$ and disturbance input $w(k)$ in the case of $x(0)$ being given and γ being fixed. Thus, it is not possible to pose a mixed LQR/ H_∞ control problem that is to find an admissible controller that achieves the minimization of quadratic performance index (1) subject to $\|T_{zw}(z)\|_\infty < \gamma$ for the systems (2)(3) with $w \in L_2[0,\infty)$ because the quadratic performance index (1) is an uncertain function depending on the uncertain disturbance input $w(k)$. In order to eliminate this difficulty, the design criteria of state feedback mixed LQR/ H_∞ control problem should be replaced by the design criteria

$$\sup_{w \in L_{2+}} \inf_K \{J\} \text{ subject to } \|T_{zw}(z)\|_\infty < \gamma$$

because for all $w \in L_2[0,\infty)$, the following inequality always exists

$$\inf_K \{J\} \le \sup_{w \in L_{2+}} \inf_K \{J\}$$

The stochastic problem corresponding to this problem is the combined LQG/ H_∞ control problem that was first presented by Bernstein & Haddad (1989). This problem is to find an admissible fixed order dynamic compensator that minimizes the expected cost function of the form

$$J = \lim_{t \to \infty} \mathrm{E}(x^T Q x + u^T R u) \text{ subject to } \|T_{zw}\|_\infty < \gamma .$$

Here, the disturbance input w of this problem is restricted to be white noise. Since the problem of Bernstein & Haddad (1989) involves merely a special case of fixing weighting matrices Q and R, it is considered as a mixed H_2 / H_∞ problem in special case. Doyle et al. (1989b) considered a related output feedback mixed H_2 / H_∞ problem (also see Doyle et al., 1994). The two approaches have been shown in Yeh et al. (1992) to be duals of one another in some sense. Also, various approaches for solving the mixed H_2 / H_∞ problem are presented (Rotea & Khargonekar , 1991; Khargonekar & Rotea, 1991; Zhou et al., 1994; Limebeer et al. 1994; Sznaier ,1994; Rotstein & Sznaier, 1998 ; Sznaier et al. , 2000) . However, no approach has involved the mixed LQR/ H_∞ control problem until the discrete time state feedback controller for solving this problem was presented by Xu (1996). Since then, several approaches to the mixed LQR / H_∞ control problems have been presented in Xu (2007, 2008).
The first goal of this chapter is to, based on the results of Xu (1996,2007), present the simple approach to discrete time state feedback mixed LQR / H_∞ control problem by combining the Lyapunov method for proving the discrete time optimal LQR control pro-blem with an

extension of the discrete time bounded real lemma, the argument of compl-etion of squares of Furuta & Phoojaruenchanachi (1990) and standard inverse matrix man-ipulation of Souza & Xie (1992).
On the other hand, unlike the discrete time state feedback mixed LQR / H_∞ control problem, state feedback corresponding to the non-fragile discrete time state feedback mixed LQR/ H_∞ control problem is a function of controller uncertainty $\Delta F(k)$, and is given by

$$u(k) = \hat{F}_\infty x(k)\,,\ \hat{F}_\infty = F_\infty + \Delta F(k) \tag{4}$$

where, $\Delta F(k)$ is the controller uncertainty.
The closed-loop transfer matrix from disturbance input w to the controlled output z and quadratic performance index for the closed-loop system (2) (4) is respectively

$$\hat{T}_{zw}(z) = \left[\begin{array}{c|c} A_{\hat{F}_\infty} & B_{\hat{F}_\infty} \\ \hline C_{\hat{F}_\infty} & 0 \end{array}\right] := C_{\hat{F}_\infty}(zI - A_{\hat{F}_\infty})^{-1} B_{\hat{F}_\infty}$$

and

$$\hat{J} := \sum_{k=0}^{\infty} \{ \left\| Q^{1/2} x(k) \right\|^2 + \left\| R^{1/2} u(k) \right\|^2 - \gamma^2 \|w\|^2 \}$$

where, $A_{\hat{F}_\infty} := A + B_2 \hat{F}_\infty$, $B_{\hat{F}_\infty} := B_1$, $C_{\hat{F}_\infty} := C_1 + D_{12}\hat{F}_\infty$, $\gamma > 0$ is a given number.

Note that the feedback matrix $\hat{F}_\infty$ of the considered closed-loop system is a function of the controller uncertainty $\Delta F(k)$, this results in that the quadratic performance index (1) is not only a function of the controller F_∞ and disturbance input $w(k)$ but also a function of the controller uncertainty $\Delta F(k)$ in the case of $x(0)$ being given and γ being fixed. We can easily know that the existence of disturbance input $w(k)$ and controller uncertainty $\Delta F(k)$ makes it impossible to find $\sup_{w \in L_{2+}} \inf_K \{J\}$, while the existence of controller uncertainty $\Delta F(k)$ also makes it difficult to find $\sup_{w \in L_{2+}} \{J\}$. In order to eliminate these difficulties, the design criteria of non-fragile discrete time state feedback mixed LQR/ H_∞ control problem should be replaced by the design criteria

$$\sup_{w \in L_{2+}} \{\hat{J}\} \text{ subject to } \|T_{zw}(z)\|_\infty < \gamma\,.$$

Motivation for non-fragile problem came from Keel & Bhattacharyya (1997). Keel & Bhattacharyya (1997) showed by examples that optimum and robust controllers, designed by using the H_2, H_∞, l^1, and μ formulations, can produce extremely fragile controllers, in the sense that vanishingly small perturbations of the coefficients of the designed controller destabilize the closed-loop system; while the controller gain variations could not be avoided in most applications.This is because many factors, such as the limitations in available computer memory and word-length capabilities of digital processor and the A/D and D/A converters,result in the variation of the controller parameters in controller implementation. Also, the controller gain variations might come about because of external effects such as temperature changes.Thus, any controller must be insensitive to the above-mentioned contoller gain variation. The question arised from this is how to design a controller that is insensitive, or non-fragile to error/uncertainty in controller parameters for a given plant. This

problem is said to be a non-fragile control problem. Recently, the non-fragile controller approach has been used to a very large class of control problems (Famularo et al. 2000, Haddad et al. 2000, Yang et al 2000, Yang et al. 2001 and Xu 2007).
The second aim of this chapter is to, based on the results of Xu (2007), present a non-fragile controller approach to the discrete-time state feedback mixed LQR/ H_∞ control problem with controller uncertainty.
This chapter is organized as follows. In Section 2, we review several preliminary results, and present two extensions of the well known discrete time bounded real lamma. In Section 3, we define the discrete time state feedback mixed LQR/ H_∞ control problem. Based on this definition, we present the both Riccati equation approach and state space approach to the discrete time state feedback mixed LQR/ H_∞ control problem. In Section 4, we intro-duce the definition of non-fragile discrete time state feedback mixed LQR/ H_∞ control problem, give the design method of a non-fragile discrete time state feedback mixed LQR / H_∞ controller, and derive the necessary and sufficient conditions for the existence of this controller. In Section 5, we give two examples to illustrate the design procedures and their effectiveness, respectively. Section 6 gives some conclusions.
Throughout this chapter, A^T denotes the transpose of A, A^{-1} denotes the inverse of A, A^{-T} is the shorthand for $(A^{-1})^T$, $G^{\sim}(z)$ denotes the conjugate system of $G(z)$ and is the shorthand for $G^T(z^{-1})$, $L_2(-\infty,+\infty)$ denotes the time domain Lebesgue space, $L_2[0,+\infty)$ denotes the subspace of $L_2(-\infty,+\infty)$, $L_2(-\infty,0]$ denotes the subspace of $L_2(-\infty,+\infty)$, L_{2+} is the shorthand for $L_2[0,+\infty)$ and L_{2-} is the shorthand for $L_2(-\infty,0]$.

2. Preliminaries

This section reviews several preliminary results. First, we consider the discerete time Riccati equation and discrete time Riccati inequality, respectively

$$X = A^T X(I + RX)^{-1} A + Q \tag{5}$$

and

$$A^T X(I + RX)^{-1} A + Q - X < 0 \tag{6}$$

with $Q = Q^T \geq 0$ and $R = R^T > 0$.
We are particularly interested in solution s X of (5) and (6) such that $(I + RX)^{-1} A$ is stable. A symmetric matrix X is said to the stabilizing solution of discrete time Riccati equation (5) if it satisfies (5) and is such that $(I + RX)^{-1} A$ is stable. Moreover, for a sufficiently small constant $\delta > 0$, the discrete time Riccati inequality (6) can be rewritten as

$$X = A^T X(I + RX)^{-1} A + Q + \delta I \tag{7}$$

Based on the above relation, we can say that if a symmetric matrix X is a stabilizing solution to the discrete time Riccati equation (7), then it also is a stabilizing solution to the discrete time Riccati inequality (6). According to the concept of stabilizing solution of discrete time Riccati equation, we can define the stabilizing solution X to the discrete time Riccati inequality (6) as follow: if there exists a symmetric solution X to the discrete time Riccati inequality (6) such that $(I + RX)^{-1} A$ is stable, then it is said to be a stabilizing solution to the discrete time Riccati inequality (6).

If A is invertible, the stabilizing solution to the discerete time Riccati equation (5) can be obtained through the following simplectic matrix

$$S := \begin{bmatrix} A + RA^{-T}Q & -RA^{-T} \\ -A^{-T}Q & A^{-T} \end{bmatrix} \tag{8}$$

Assume that S has no eigenvalues on the unit circle, then it must have n eigenvalues in $|\lambda_i| < 1$ and n in $|\lambda_i| > 1$ ($i = 1,2,\cdots,n,n+1,\cdots,2n$). If n eigenvectors corresponding to n eigenvalues in $|\lambda_i| < 1$ of the simplectic matrix (8) is computed as

$$\begin{bmatrix} u_i \\ v_i \end{bmatrix}$$

then a stabilizing solution to the discerete time Riccati equation (5) is given by

$$X = \begin{bmatrix} v_1 & \cdots & v_n \end{bmatrix} \begin{bmatrix} u_1 & \cdots & u_n \end{bmatrix}^{-1}$$

Secondly, we will introduce the well known discrete time bounded real lemma (see Zhou et al. , 1996; Iglesias & Glover, 1991; Souza & Xie, 1992) .

Lemma 2.1 (Discrete Time Bounded Real Lemma)

Suppose that $\gamma > 0$, $M(z) = \left[\begin{array}{c|c} A & B \\ \hline C & D \end{array}\right] \in RH_\infty$, then the following two statements are equivalent:

i. $\|M(z)\|_\infty < \gamma$.

ii. There exists a stabilizing solution $X \ge 0$ ($X > 0$ if (C, A) is observable) to the discrete time Riccati equation

$$A^T XA - X + \gamma^{-2}(A^T XB + C^T D)U_1^{-1}(B^T XA + D^T C) + C^T C = 0$$

such that $U_1 = I - \gamma^{-2}(D^T D + B^T XB) > 0$.

In order to solve the two discrete time state feedback mixed LQR/ H_∞ control problems considered by this chapter, we introduce the following reference system

$$x(k+1) = Ax(k) + B_1 w(k) + B_2 u(k) \quad \hat{z}(k) = \begin{bmatrix} C_1 \\ \Omega^{\frac{1}{2}} \begin{bmatrix} I \\ 0 \end{bmatrix} \end{bmatrix} x(k) + \begin{bmatrix} D_{12} \\ \Omega^{\frac{1}{2}} \begin{bmatrix} 0 \\ I \end{bmatrix} \end{bmatrix} u(k) \tag{9}$$

where, $\Omega = \begin{bmatrix} Q & 0 \\ 0 & R \end{bmatrix}$ and $\hat{z}(k) = \begin{bmatrix} z(k) \\ z_0(k) \end{bmatrix}$.

The following lemma is an extension of the discrete time bounded real lemma.

Lemma 2.2 Given the system (2) under the influence of the state feedback (3), and suppose that $\gamma > 0$, $T_{zw}(z) \in RH_\infty$; then there exists an admissible controller K such that $\|T_{zw}(z)\|_\infty < \gamma$ if there exists a stabilizing solution $X_\infty \ge 0$ to the discrete time Riccati equation

$$A_K^T X_\infty A_K - X_\infty + \gamma^{-2} A_K^T X_\infty B_K U_1^{-1} B_K^T X_\infty A_K + C_K^T C_K + Q + K^T RK = 0 \tag{10}$$

such that $U_1 = I - \gamma^{-2} B_K^T X_\infty B_K > 0$.

Proof: Consider the reference system (9) under the influence of the state feedback (3), and define T_0 as

$$T_0(z) := \left[\begin{array}{c:c} A_K & B_K \\ \hdashline \Omega^{1/2}\begin{bmatrix} I \\ K \end{bmatrix} & 0 \end{array}\right]$$

then the closed-loop transfer matrix from disturbance input w to the controlled output $\hat{z}$ is $T_{\hat{z}w}(z) = \begin{bmatrix} T_{zw}(z) \\ T_0(z) \end{bmatrix}$. Note that $\gamma^2 I - T_{\hat{z}w}^{\sim} T_{\hat{z}w} > 0$ is equivalent to

$$\gamma^2 I - T_{zw}^{\sim} T_{zw} > T_0^{\sim} T_0 > 0 \text{ for all } w \in L_2[0,\infty) \ ,$$

and $T_{zw}(z) \in RH_\infty$ is equivalent to $T_{\hat{z}w}(z) \in RH_\infty$, so $\|T_{\hat{z}w}(z)\|_\infty < \gamma$ implies $\|T_{zw}(z)\|_\infty < \gamma$ Hence, it follows from Lemma 2.1. Q.E.D.

To prove the result of non-fragile discrete time state feedback mixed LQR/ H_∞ control problem, we define the inequality

$$A_{\hat{F}_\infty}^T X_\infty A_{\hat{F}_\infty} - X_\infty + \gamma^{-2} A_{\hat{F}_\infty}^T X_\infty B_{\hat{F}_\infty} U_1^{-1} B_{\hat{F}_\infty}^T X_\infty A_{\hat{F}_\infty} + C_{\hat{F}_\infty}^T C_{\hat{F}_\infty} + Q + \hat{F}_\infty^T R \hat{F}_\infty < 0 \qquad (11)$$

where, $U_1 = I - \gamma^{-2} B_{\hat{F}_\infty}^T X_\infty B_{\hat{F}_\infty} > 0$.

In terms of the inequality (11), we have the following lemma:

Lemma 2.3 Consider the system (2) under the influence of state feedback (4) with controler uncertainty, and suppose that $\gamma > 0$ is a given number, then there exists an admissible non-fragile controller F_∞ such that $\|T_{zw}\|_\infty < \gamma$ if for any admissible uncertainty $\Delta F(k)$, there exists a stabilizing solution $X_\infty \geq 0$ to the inequality (11) such that $U_1 = I - \gamma^{-2} B_{\hat{F}_\infty}^T X_\infty B_{\hat{F}_\infty} > 0$.

Proof: Suppose that for any admissible uncertainty $\Delta F(k)$, there exists a stabilizing solution $X_\infty \geq 0$ to the inequality (11) such that $U_1 = I - \gamma^{-2} B_{\hat{F}_\infty}^T X_\infty B_{\hat{F}_\infty} > 0$. This implies that the solution $X_\infty \geq 0$ is such that $A_{\hat{F}_\infty} + \gamma^{-2} B_{\hat{F}_\infty} U_1^{-1} B_{\hat{F}_\infty}^T X_\infty A_{\hat{F}_\infty}$ is stable.

Let $A_{F_\infty} = A + B_2 F_\infty$ and $C_{F_\infty} = C_1 + D_{12} F_\infty$; then we can rewrite (11) as

$$\begin{aligned} &A_{F_\infty}^T X_\infty A_{F_\infty} - X_\infty + \gamma^{-2} A_{F_\infty}^T X_\infty B_{\hat{F}_\infty} U_1^{-1} B_{\hat{F}_\infty}^T X_\infty A_{F_\infty} + C_{F_\infty}^T C_{F_\infty} + Q \\ &+ F_\infty^T R F_\infty - (A^T U_3 B_2 + F_\infty^T U_2) U_2^{-1} (B_2^T U_3 A + U_2 F_\infty) + \Delta N_F < 0 \end{aligned}$$

where, $U_2 = B_2^T U_3 B_2 + I + R$, $U_3 = \gamma^{-2} X_\infty B_{\hat{F}_\infty} U_1^{-1} B_{\hat{F}_\infty}^T X_\infty + X_\infty$,
$\Delta N_F = (A^T U_3 B_2 + F_\infty^T U_2 + \Delta F^T(k) U_2) U_2^{-1} (B_2^T U_3 A + U_2 F_\infty + U_2 \Delta F(k))$.

Since $\Delta F(k)$ is an admissible norm-bounded time- varying uncertainty, there exists a time-varying uncertain number $\delta(k) > 0$ satisfying

$$\begin{aligned} &A_{F_\infty}^T X_\infty A_{F_\infty} - X_\infty + \gamma^{-2} A_{F_\infty}^T X_\infty B_{\hat{F}_\infty} U_1^{-1} B_{\hat{F}_\infty}^T X_\infty A_{F_\infty} + C_{F_\infty}^T C_{F_\infty} + Q + F_\infty^T R F_\infty \\ &- (A^T U_3 B_2 + F_\infty^T U_2) U_2^{-1} (B_2^T U_3 A + U_2 F_\infty) + \Delta N_F + \delta(k) I = 0 \end{aligned} \qquad (12)$$

Note that $A_{\hat{F}_\infty} + \gamma^{-2} B_{\hat{F}_\infty} U_1^{-1} B_{\hat{F}_\infty}^T X_\infty A_{\hat{F}_\infty}$ is stable for any admissible uncertainty $\Delta F(k)$. This implies that $A_{F_\infty} + \gamma^{-2} B_{\hat{F}_\infty} U_1^{-1} B_{\hat{F}_\infty}^T X_\infty A_{F_\infty}$ is stable.
Hence, $(U_1^{-1} B_{\hat{F}_\infty}^T X_\infty A_{F_\infty}, A_{F_\infty})$ is detectable. Then it follows from standard results on Lyapunov equations (see Lemma 2.7 a), Iglesias & Glover 1991) and the equation (12) that A_{F_∞} is stable. Thus, $A_{\hat{F}_\infty} = A_{F_\infty} + B_2 \Delta F(k)$ is stable for any admissible uncertainty $\Delta F(k)$.
Define $V(x(k)) := x^T(k) X_\infty x(k)$, where, x is the solution to the plant equations for a given input w, then it can be easily established that

$$\begin{aligned}0 &= \sum_{k=0}^{\infty} \{-\Delta V(x(k)) + x^T(k+1) X_\infty x(k+1) - x^T(k) X_\infty x(k)\} \\ &= \sum_{k=0}^{\infty} \{-\Delta V(x(k)) - \|z\|^2 + \gamma^2 \|w\|^2 - \gamma^2 \left\| U_1^{1/2} (w - \gamma^{-2} U_1^{-1} B_{\hat{F}_\infty}^T X_\infty A_{\hat{F}_\infty} x) \right\|^2 \\ &\quad + x^T (A_{\hat{F}_\infty}^T X_\infty A_{\hat{F}_\infty} - X_\infty + \gamma^{-2} A_{\hat{F}_\infty}^T X_\infty B_{\hat{F}_\infty} U_1^{-1} B_{\hat{F}_\infty}^T X_\infty A_{\hat{F}_\infty} + C_{\hat{F}_\infty}^T C_{\hat{F}_\infty}) x\}\end{aligned}$$

Add the above zero equality to J to get

$$\begin{aligned}J &= \sum_{k=0}^{\infty} \{-\Delta V(x(k)) - \|z\|^2 + \gamma^2 \|w\|^2 - \gamma^2 \left\| U_1^{1/2} (w - \gamma^{-2} U_1^{-1} B_{\hat{F}_\infty}^T X_\infty A_{\hat{F}_\infty} x) \right\|^2 \\ &\quad + x^T (A_{\hat{F}_\infty}^T X_\infty A_{\hat{F}_\infty} - X_\infty + \gamma^{-2} A_{\hat{F}_\infty}^T X_\infty B_{\hat{F}_\infty} U_1^{-1} B_{\hat{F}_\infty}^T X_\infty A_{\hat{F}_\infty} + C_{\hat{F}_\infty}^T C_{\hat{F}_\infty} + Q + \hat{F}_\infty^T R \hat{F}_\infty) x\}\end{aligned}$$

Substituting (11) for the above formula,we get that for any $u(k)$ and $w(k)$ and $x(0) = 0$,

$$J < -\|z\|_2^2 + \gamma^2 \|w\|_2^2 - \gamma^2 \left\| U_1^{1/2} (w - \gamma^{-2} U_1^{-1} B_{\hat{F}_\infty}^T X_\infty A_{\hat{F}_\infty} x) \right\|_2^2$$

Note that $\|z_0\|_2^2 = \sum_{k=0}^{\infty} \hat{x}^T(k) \Omega \hat{x}(k)$, and define that $r := w - \gamma^{-2} U_1^{-1} B_{\hat{F}_\infty}^T X_\infty A_{\hat{F}_\infty} x$, we get

$$\|\hat{z}\|_2^2 - \gamma^2 \|w\|_2^2 < -\gamma^2 \left\| U_1^{1/2} r \right\|_2^2$$

Suppose that Γ is the operator with realization

$$\begin{aligned}x(k+1) &= (A + B_2 \hat{F}_\infty) x(k) + B_{\hat{F}_\infty} w(k) \\ r(k) &= -\gamma^{-2} U_1^{-1} B_{\hat{F}_\infty}^T X_\infty A_{\hat{F}_\infty} x(k) + w(k)\end{aligned}$$

which maps w to r.
Since Γ^{-1} exists (and is given by $x(k+1) = (A + B_2 \hat{F}_\infty + \gamma^{-2} B_{\hat{F}_\infty} U_1^{-1} B_{\hat{F}_\infty}^T X_\infty A_{\hat{F}_\infty}) x(k) + B_{\hat{F}_\infty} r(k)$, $w(k) = \gamma^{-2} U_1^{-1} B_{\hat{F}_\infty}^T X_\infty A_{\hat{F}_\infty} x(k) + r(k)$), we can write

$$\|\hat{z}\|_2^2 - \gamma^2 \|w\|_2^2 < -\gamma^2 \left\| U_1^{1/2} r \right\|_2^2 = -\gamma^2 \|\Gamma w\|_2^2 \le \kappa \|w\|_2^2$$

for some positive κ.This implies that there exists an admissible non-fragile controller such that $\|T_{\hat{z}w}\|_\infty < \gamma$. Note that $\gamma^2 I - T_{\hat{z}w}^{\sim} T_{\hat{z}w} > 0$ is equivalent to

$$\gamma^2 I - T_{zw}^{\sim} T_{zw} > T_0^{\sim} T_0 > 0 \text{ for all } w \in L_2[0,\infty)$$

so $\|T_{\hat{z}w}\|_\infty < \gamma$ implies $\|T_{zw}\|_\infty < \gamma$, and we conclude that there exists an admissible non-fragile controller such that $\|T_{zw}\|_\infty < \gamma$. Q. E. D.

3. State Feedback

In this section, we will consider the discrete time state feedback mixed LQR/ H_∞ control problem. This problem is defined as follows: Given the linear discrete-time systems (2)(3) with $w \in L_2[0,\infty)$ and $x(0) = x_0$ and the quadratic performance index (1), for a given number $\gamma > 0$, determine an admissible controller K that achieves

$$\sup_{w \in L_{2-}} \inf_{K} \{J\} \text{ subject to } \|T_{zw}(z)\|_\infty < \gamma .$$

If this controller K exists, it is said to be a discrete time state feedback mixed LQR/ H_∞ controller.

Here, we will discuss the simplified versions of the problem defined in the above. In order to do this, the following assumptions are imposed on the system

Assumption 1 (C_1, A) is detectable.

Assumption 2 (A, B_2) is stabilizable.

Assumption 3 $D_{12}^T \begin{bmatrix} C_1 & D_{12} \end{bmatrix} = \begin{bmatrix} 0 & I \end{bmatrix}$.

The solution to the problem defined in the above involves the discrete time Riccati equation

$$A^T X_\infty A - X_\infty - A^T X_\infty \hat{B}(\hat{B}^T X_\infty \hat{B} + \hat{R})^{-1} \hat{B}^T X_\infty A + C_1^T C_1 + Q = 0 \tag{13}$$

where, $\hat{B} = \begin{bmatrix} \gamma^{-1} B_1 & B_2 \end{bmatrix}$, $\hat{R} = \begin{bmatrix} -I & 0 \\ 0 & R + I \end{bmatrix}$. If A is invertible, the stabilizing solution to the discrete time Riccati equation (13) can be obtained through the following simplectic matrix

$$S_\infty := \begin{bmatrix} A + \hat{B}\hat{R}^{-1}\hat{B}^T A^{-T}(C_1^T C_1 + Q) & -\hat{B}\hat{R}^{-1}\hat{B}^T A^{-T} \\ -A^{-T}(C_1^T C_1 + Q) & A^{-T} \end{bmatrix}$$

In the following theorem, we provide the solution to discrete time state feedback mixed LQR/ H_∞ control problem.

Theorem 3.1 There exists a state feedback mixed LQR/ H_∞ controller if the discrete time Riccati equation (13) has a stabilizing solution $X_\infty \geq 0$ and $U_1 = I - \gamma^{-2} B_1^T X_\infty B_1 > 0$.

Moreover, this state feedback mixed LQR/ H_∞ controller is given by

$$K = -U_2^{-1} B_2^T U_3 A$$

where, $U_2 = R + I + B_2^T U_3 B_2$, and $U_3 = X_\infty + \gamma^{-2} X_\infty B_1 U_1^{-1} B_1^T X_\infty$.

In this case, the state feedback mixed LQR/ H_∞ controller will achieve

$$\sup_{w\in L_{2-}} \inf_K \{J\} = x_0^T (X_\infty + \gamma^{-2} X_w - X_z) x_0 \text{ subject to } \|T_{zw}\|_\infty < \gamma .$$

where, $\hat{A}_K = A_K + \gamma^{-2} B_K U_1^{-1} B_K^T X_\infty A_K$, $X_w = \sum_{k=0}^{\infty} \{(\hat{A}_K^k)^T A_K^T X_\infty B_K U_1^{-2} B_K^T X_\infty A_K \hat{A}_K^k\}$, and

$$X_z = \sum_{k=0}^{\infty} \{(\hat{A}_K^k)^T C_K^T C_K \hat{A}_K^k\} .$$

Before proving Theorem 3.1, we will give the following lemma.

Lemma 3.1 Suppose that the discrete time Riccati equation (13) has a stabilizing solution $X_\infty \geq 0$ and $U_1 = I - \gamma^{-2} B_1^T X_\infty B_1 > 0$, and let $A_K = A + B_2 K$ and $K = -U_2^{-1} B_2^T U_3 A$; then A_K is stable.

Proof: Suppose that the discrete time Riccati equation (13) has a stabilizing solution $X_\infty \geq 0$ and $U_1 = I - \gamma^{-2} B_1^T X_\infty B_1 > 0$. Observe that

$$\hat{B}^T X_\infty \hat{B} + \hat{R} = \begin{bmatrix} \gamma^{-1} B_1^T \\ B_2^T \end{bmatrix} X_\infty \begin{bmatrix} \gamma^{-1} B_1 & B_2 \end{bmatrix} + \begin{bmatrix} -I & 0 \\ 0 & R+I \end{bmatrix} = \begin{bmatrix} -U_1 & \gamma^{-1} B_1^T X_\infty B_2 \\ \gamma^{-1} B_2^T X_\infty B_1 & B_2^T X_\infty B_2 + R + I \end{bmatrix}$$

Also, note that $U_1 = I - \gamma^{-2} B_1^T X_\infty B_1 > 0$, $U_3 = X_\infty + \gamma^{-2} X_\infty B_1 U_1^{-1} B_1^T X_\infty$, and $U_2 = R + I + B_2^T U_3 B_2$; then it can be easily shown by using the similar standard matrix manipulations as in the proof of Theorem 3.1 in Souza & Xie (1992) that

$$(\hat{B}^T X_\infty \hat{B} + \hat{R})^{-1} = \begin{bmatrix} -U_1^{-1} + U_1^{-1} \hat{B}_1 U_2^{-1} \hat{B}_1^T U_1^{-1} & U_1^{-1} \hat{B}_1 U_2^{-1} \\ U_2^{-1} \hat{B}_1^T U_1^{-1} & U_2^{-1} \end{bmatrix}$$

where, $\hat{B}_1 = \gamma^{-1} B_1^T X_\infty B_2$.

Thus, we have

$$A^T X_\infty \hat{B} (\hat{B}^T X_\infty \hat{B} + \hat{R})^{-1} \hat{B}^T X_\infty A = -\gamma^{-2} A^T X_\infty B_1 U_1^{-1} B_1^T X_\infty A + A^T U_3 B_2 U_2^{-1} B_2^T U_3 A$$

Rearraging the discrete time Riccati equation (13), we get

$$\begin{aligned} X_\infty &= A^T X_\infty A + \gamma^{-2} A^T X_\infty B_1 U_1^{-1} B_1^T X_\infty A - A^T U_3 B_2 U_2^{-1} B_2^T U_3 A + C_1^T C_1 + Q \\ &= A^T X_\infty A + \gamma^{-2} A^T X_\infty B_1 U_1^{-1} B_1^T X_\infty A + C_1^T C_1 + Q - A^T U_3 B_2 U_2^{-1} B_2^T (X_\infty + \gamma^{-2} X_\infty B_1 U_1^{-1} B_1^T X_\infty) A \\ &\quad - A^T (X_\infty + \gamma^{-2} X_\infty B_1 U_1^{-1} B_1^T X_\infty) B_2 U_2^{-1} B_2^T U_3 A \\ &\quad + A^T U_3 B_2 U_2^{-1} [R + I + B_2^T (X_\infty + \gamma^{-2} X_\infty B_1 U_1^{-1} B_1^T X_\infty) B_2] U_2^{-1} B_2^T U_3 A \\ &= (A^T X_\infty A - A^T U_3 B_2 U_2^{-1} B_2^T X_\infty A - A^T X_\infty B_2 U_2^{-1} B_2^T U_3 A + A^T U_3 B_2 U_2^{-1} B_2^T X_\infty B_2 U_2^{-1} B_2^T U_3 A) \\ &\quad + (C_1^T C_1 + A^T U_3 B_2 U_2^{-1} U_2^{-1} B_2^T U_3 A) + A^T U_3 B_2 U_2^{-1} R U_2^{-1} B_2^T U_3 A + Q \\ &\quad + (\gamma^{-2} A^T X_\infty B_1 U_1^{-1} B_1^T X_\infty A - \gamma^{-2} A^T U_3 B_2 U_2^{-1} B_2^T X_\infty B_1 U_1^{-1} B_1^T X_\infty A \\ &\quad - \gamma^{-2} A^T X_\infty B_1 U_1^{-1} B_1^T X_\infty B_2 U_2^{-1} B_2^T U_3 A + \gamma^{-2} A^T U_3 B_2 U_2^{-1} B_2^T X_\infty B_1 U_1^{-1} B_1^T X_\infty B_2 U_2^{-1} B_2^T U_3 A) \\ &= (A - B_2 U_2^{-1} B_2^T U_3 A)^T X_\infty (A - B_2 U_2^{-1} B_2^T U_3 A) + (C_1 - D_{12} U_2^{-1} B_2^T U_3 A)^T (C_1 - D_{12} U_2^{-1} B_2^T U_3 A) \\ &\quad + K^T R K + Q + \gamma^{-2} (A - B_2 U_2^{-1} B_2^T U_3 A)^T X_\infty B_1 U_1^{-1} B_1^T X_\infty (A - B_2 U_2^{-1} B_2^T U_3 A) \end{aligned}$$

that is,

$$A_K^T X_\infty A_K - X_\infty + \gamma^{-2} A_K^T X_\infty B_K U_1^{-1} B_K^T X_\infty A_K + C_K^T C_K + Q + K^T R K = 0 \tag{14}$$

Since the discrete time Riccati equation (13) has a stabilizing solution $X_\infty \geq 0$, the discrete time Riccati equation (14) also has a stabilizing solution $X_\infty \geq 0$. This implies that $\hat{A}_K = A_K + \gamma^{-2} B_K U_1^{-1} B_K^T X_\infty A_K$ is stable. Hence $(U_1^{-1} B_K^T X_\infty A_K, A_K)$ is detectable. Based on this, it follows from standard results on Lyapunov equations (see Lemma 2.7 a), Iglesias & Glover 1991) that A_K is stable.Q. E. D.

Proof of Theorem 3.1: Suppose that the discrete time Riccati equation (13) has a stabilizing solution $X_\infty \geq 0$ and $U_1 = I - \gamma^{-2} B_1^T X_\infty B_1 > 0$. Then, it follows from Lemma 3.1 that A_K is stable. This implies that $T_{zw}(z) \in RH_\infty$. By using the same standard matrix manipulations as in the proof of Lemma 3.1, we can rewrite the discrete time Riccati equation (13) as follows:

$$A^T X_\infty A - X_\infty + \gamma^{-2} A^T X_\infty B_1 U_1^{-1} B_1^T X_\infty A - A^T U_3 B_2 U_2^{-1} B_2^T U_3 A + C_1^T C_1 + Q = 0$$

or equivalently,

$$A_K^T X_\infty A_K - X_\infty + \gamma^{-2} A_K^T X_\infty B_K U_1^{-1} B_K^T X_\infty A_K + C_K^T C_K + Q + K^T R K = 0$$

Thus, it follows from Lemma 2.2 that $\|T_{zw}(z)\|_\infty < \gamma$.

Define $V(x(k)) = x^T(k) X_\infty x(k)$, where X_∞ is the solution to the discrete time Riccati equation (13), then taking the difference $\Delta V(x(k))$ and completing the squares we get

$$\begin{aligned}
\Delta V(x(k)) &= x^T(k+1) X_\infty x(k+1) - x^T(k) X_\infty x(k) \\
&= x^T(k)(A_K^T X_\infty A_K - X_\infty) x(k) + x^T(k) A_K^T X_\infty B_K w(k) \\
&\quad + w^T(k) B_K^T X_\infty A_K x(k) + w^T(k) B_K^T X_\infty B_K w(k) \\
&= -\|z\|^2 + \gamma^2 \|w\|^2 - \gamma^2 \left\| U_1^{1/2} (w - \gamma^{-2} U_1^{-1} B_K^T X_\infty A_K x) \right\|^2 \\
&\quad + x^T (A_K^T X_\infty A_K - X_\infty + \gamma^{-2} A_K^T X_\infty B_K U_1^{-1} B_K^T X_\infty A_K + C_K^T C_K) x
\end{aligned}$$

Based on the above, the cost function J can be rewritten as:

$$\begin{aligned}
J = \sum_{k=0}^{\infty} \hat{x}^T(k) \Omega \hat{x}(k) = \sum_{k=0}^{\infty} \{ &-\Delta V(x(k)) - \|z\|^2 + \gamma^2 \|w\|^2 - \gamma^2 \left\| U_1^{1/2} (w - \gamma^{-2} U_1^{-1} B_K^T X_\infty A_K x) \right\|^2 \\
&+ x^T (A_K^T X_\infty A_K - X_\infty + \gamma^{-2} A_K^T X_\infty B_K U_1^{-1} B_K^T X_\infty A_K + C_K^T C_K + Q + K^T R K) x \}
\end{aligned} \tag{15}$$

On the other hand, it follows from the similar argumrnts as in the proof of Theorem 3.1 in Furuta & Phoojaruenchanachai (1990) that

$$\begin{aligned}
&A_K^T X_\infty A_K - X_\infty + \gamma^{-2} A_K^T X_\infty B_K U_1^{-1} B_K^T X_\infty A_K + C_K^T C_K + Q + K^T R K \\
&= A^T X_\infty A - X_\infty + \gamma^{-2} A^T X_\infty B_1 U_1^{-1} B_1^T X_\infty A - A^T U_3 B_2 U_2^{-1} B_2^T U_3 A + C_1^T C_1 + Q \\
&\quad + (K + U_2^{-1} B_2^T U_3 A)^T U_2 (K + U_2^{-1} B_2^T U_3 A)
\end{aligned}$$

At the same time note that

$$-\gamma^{-2}A^TX_\infty B_1U_1^{-1}B_1^TX_\infty A+A^TU_3B_2U_2^{-1}B_2^TU_3A$$
$$=A^TX_\infty\hat{B}\begin{bmatrix}-U_1^{-1}+U_1^{-1}\hat{B}_1U_2^{-1}\hat{B}_1^TU_1^{-1} & U_1^{-1}\hat{B}_1U_2^{-1}\\ U_2^{-1}\hat{B}_1^TU_1^{-1} & U_2^{-1}\end{bmatrix}\hat{B}^TX_\infty A$$
$$=A^TX_\infty\hat{B}(\hat{B}^TX_\infty\hat{B}+\hat{R})^{-1}\hat{B}^TX_\infty A$$

We have

$$A_K^TX_\infty A_K-X_\infty+\gamma^{-2}A_K^TX_\infty B_KU_1^{-1}B_K^TX_\infty A_K+C_K^TC_K+Q+K^TRK$$
$$=A^TX_\infty A-X_\infty-A^TX_\infty\hat{B}(\hat{B}^TX_\infty\hat{B}+\hat{R})^{-1}\hat{B}^TX_\infty A+C_1^TC_1+Q$$
$$+(K+U_2^{-1}B_2^TU_3A)^TU_2(K+U_2^{-1}B_2^TU_3A)$$

Also, noting that the discrete time Riccati equation (13) and substituting the above equality for (15), we get

$$J=\sum_{k=0}^{\infty}\hat{x}^T(k)\Omega\hat{x}(k)=\sum_{k=0}^{\infty}\{-\Delta V(x(k))-\|z\|^2+\gamma^2\|w\|^2-\gamma^2\left\|U_1^{1/2}(w-\gamma^{-2}U_1^{-1}B_K^TX_\infty A_Kx)\right\|^2$$
$$+\left\|U_2^{1/2}(K+U_2^{-1}B_2^TU_3A)x\right\|^2\} \tag{16}$$

Based on the above, it is clear that if $K=-U_2^{-1}B_2^TU_3A$, then we get

$$\inf_K\{J\}=x_0^TX_\infty x_0-\|z\|_2^2+\gamma^2\|w\|_2^2-\gamma^2\left\|U_1^{1/2}(w-\gamma^{-2}U_1^{-1}B_K^TX_\infty A_Kx)\right\|_2^2 \tag{17}$$

By letting $w(k)=\gamma^{-2}U_1^{-1}B_K^TX_\infty A_Kx(k)$ for all $k\geq 0$, we get that $x(k)=\hat{A}_K^kx_0$ with $\hat{A}_K$ which belongs to $L_2[0,+\infty)$ since $\hat{A}_K=A-\hat{B}(\hat{B}^TX_\infty\hat{B}+\hat{R})^{-1}\hat{B}^TX_\infty A$ is stable. Also, we have

$$\|w(k)\|_2^2=\gamma^{-4}x_0^TX_wx_0,\ \|z(k)\|_2^2=x_0^TX_zx_0$$

Then it follows from (17) that

$$\sup_{w\in L_{2-}}\inf_K\{J\}=x_0^T(X_\infty+\gamma^{-2}X_w-X_z)x_0$$

Thus we conclude that there exists an admissible state feedback controller such that

$$\sup_{w\in L_{2+}}\inf_K\{J\}=x_0^T(X_\infty+\gamma^{-2}X_w-X_z)x_0 \text{ subject to } \|T_{zw}\|_\infty<\gamma$$ Q.E.D.

4. Non-fragile controller

In this section, we will consider the non-fragile discrete-time state feedback mixed LQR/ H_∞ control problem with controller uncertainty. This problem is defined as follows: Consider the system (2) (4) satisfying Assumption 1-3 with $w\in L_2[0,\infty)$ and $x(0)=x_0$, for a given number $\gamma>0$ and any admissible controller uncertainty, determine an admissible non-fragile controller F_∞ such that

$$\sup_{w \in L_{2-}} \{\hat{J}\} \text{ subject to } \|T_{zw}(z)\|_\infty < \gamma .$$

where, the controller uncertainty $\Delta F(k)$ considered here is assumed to be of the following structure:

$$\Delta F(k) = H_K F(k) E_K$$

where, H_K and E_K are known matrices of appropriate dimensions. $F(k)$ is an uncertain matrix satisfying

$$F^T(k)F(k) \le I$$

with the elements of $F(k)$ being Lebesgue measurable.

If this controller exists, it is said to be a non-fragile discrete time state feedback mixed LQR/ H_∞ controller.

In order to solve the problem defined in the above, we first connect the its design criteria with the inequality (11).

Lemma 4.1 Suppose that $\gamma > 0$, then there exists an admissible non-fragile controller F_∞ that achieves

$$\sup_{w \in L_{2-}} \{\hat{J}\} = x_0^T X_\infty x_0 \text{ subject to } \|T_{zw}\|_\infty < \gamma$$

if for any admissible uncertainty $\Delta F(k)$, there exists a stabilizing solution $X_\infty \ge 0$ to the inequality (11) such that $U_1 = I - \gamma^{-2} B_{\hat{F}_\infty}^T X_\infty B_{\hat{F}_\infty} > 0$.

Proof: Suppose that for any admissible uncertainty $\Delta F(k)$, there exists a stabilizing solution $X_\infty \ge 0$ to the inequality (11) such that $U_1 = I - \gamma^{-2} B_{\hat{F}_\infty}^T X_\infty B_{\hat{F}_\infty} > 0$. This implies that the solution $X_\infty \ge 0$ is such that $A_{\hat{F}_\infty} + \gamma^{-2} B_{\hat{F}_\infty} U_1^{-1} B_{\hat{F}_\infty}^T X_\infty A_{\hat{F}_\infty}$ is stable. Then it follows from Lemma 2.3 that $\|T_{zw}\|_\infty < \gamma$. Using the same argument as in the proof of Lemma 2.3, we get that $A_{\hat{F}_\infty}$ is stable and J can be rewritten as follows:

$$\begin{aligned} J = \sum_{k=0}^{\infty} \{ & -\Delta V(x(k)) - \|z\|^2 + \gamma^2 \|w\|^2 - \gamma^2 \left\| U_1^{1/2} (w - \gamma^{-2} U_1^{-1} B_{\hat{F}_\infty}^T X_\infty A_{\hat{F}_\infty} x) \right\|^2 \\ & + x^T (A_{\hat{F}_\infty}^T X_\infty A_{\hat{F}_\infty} - X_\infty + \gamma^{-2} A_{\hat{F}_\infty}^T X_\infty B_{\hat{F}_\infty} U_1^{-1} B_{\hat{F}_\infty}^T X_\infty A_{\hat{F}_\infty} + C_{\hat{F}_\infty}^T C_{\hat{F}_\infty} + Q + \hat{F}_\infty^T R \hat{F}_\infty) x \} \end{aligned} \tag{18}$$

Substituting (11) for (18) to get

$$J < x_0^T X_\infty x_0 - \|z\|_2^2 + \gamma^2 \|w\|_2^2 - \gamma^2 \left\| U_1^{1/2} (w - \gamma^{-2} U_1^{-1} B_{\hat{F}_\infty}^T X_\infty A_{\hat{F}_\infty} x) \right\|_2^2 \tag{19a}$$

or

$$\hat{J} < x_0^T X_\infty x_0 - \|z\|_2^2 - \gamma^2 \left\| U_1^{1/2} (w - \gamma^{-2} U_1^{-1} B_{\hat{F}_\infty}^T X_\infty A_{\hat{F}_\infty} x) \right\|_2^2 \tag{19b}$$

By letting $w = \gamma^{-2} U_1^{-1} B_{\hat{F}_\infty}^T X_\infty A_{\hat{F}_\infty} x$ for all $k \ge 0$, we get that $x(k) = \hat{A}_{\hat{F}_\infty}^k x_0$ with $\hat{A}_{\hat{F}_\infty} = A_{\hat{F}_\infty} + \gamma^{-2} B_{\hat{F}_\infty} U_1^{-1} B_{\hat{F}_\infty}^T X_\infty A_{\hat{F}_\infty}$ which belongs to $L_2[0, +\infty)$ since $\hat{A}_{\hat{F}_\infty}$ is stable. It follows from (19b) that $\sup\{\hat{J}\}_{w\in L_{2-}} = x_0^T X_\infty x_0$. Thus, we conclude that there exists an admissible non-fragile controller such that $\sup\{\hat{J}\}_{w\in L_{2-}} = x_0^T X_\infty x_0$ subject to $\|T_{zw}\|_\infty < \gamma$. Q. E. D.

Remark 4.1 In the proof of Lemma 4.1, we let $w = \gamma^{-2}U_1^{-1}B_{\hat{F}_\infty}^T X_\infty A_{\hat{F}_\infty} x$ for all $k \geq 0$ to get that $x(k) = \hat{A}_{\hat{F}_\infty}^k x_0$ with $\hat{A}_{\hat{F}_\infty} = A_{\hat{F}_\infty} + \gamma^{-2}B_{\hat{F}_\infty}U_1^{-1}B_{\hat{F}_\infty}^T X_\infty A_{\hat{F}_\infty}$ which belongs to $L_2[0,+\infty)$ since $\hat{A}_{\hat{F}_\infty}$ is stable. Also, we have

$$\|w\|_2^2 = \gamma^{-4}x_0^T X_w x_0, \; \|z\|_2^2 = x_0^T X_z x_0 .$$

Then it follows from (19a) that

$$J < x_0^T(X_\infty + \gamma^{-2}X_w - X_z)x_0 \tag{20}$$

where, $X_w = \sum_{k=0}^{\infty}\{(\hat{A}_{\hat{F}_\infty}^k)^T A_{\hat{F}_\infty}^T X_\infty B_1 U_1^{-2} B_1^T X_\infty A_{\hat{F}_\infty} \hat{A}_{\hat{F}_\infty}^k\}$, and $X_z = \sum_{k=0}^{\infty}\{(\hat{A}_{\hat{F}_\infty}^k)^T C_{\hat{F}_\infty}^T C_{\hat{F}_\infty} \hat{A}_{\hat{F}_\infty}^k\}$.

Note that $\hat{A}_{\hat{F}_\infty}$ depends on the controller uncertainty $\Delta F(k)$, thus it is difficult to find an upper bound of either of X_w and X_z. This implies that the existence of controller uncertainty $\Delta F(k)$ makes it difficult to find $\sup_{w\in L_{2-}}\{J\}$ by using (20). Thus, it is clear that the existence of the controller uncertainty makes the performance of the designed system become bad.

In order to give necessary and sufficient conditions for the existence of an admissible non-fragile controller for solving the non-fragile discrete-time state feedback mixed LQR/ H_∞ control problem, we define the following parameter-dependent discrete time Riccati equation:

$$A^T X_\infty A - X_\infty - A^T X_\infty \hat{B}(\hat{B}^T X_\infty \hat{B} + \hat{R})^{-1}\hat{B}^T X_\infty A + \rho^2 E_K^T E_K + C_1^T C_1 + Q_\delta = 0 \tag{21}$$

where, $\hat{B} = \begin{bmatrix}\gamma^{-1}B_1 & B_2\end{bmatrix}$, $\hat{R} = \begin{bmatrix}-I & 0 \\ 0 & I+R\end{bmatrix}$, $Q_\delta = Q + \delta I$ with $\delta > 0$ being a sufficiently small constant, ρ is a given number satisfying $\rho^2 I - H_K^T U_2 H_K > 0$, $U_1 = I - \gamma^{-2}B_1^T X_\infty B_1 > 0$, $U_2 = B_2^T U_3 B_2 + I + R$ and $U_3 = X_\infty + \gamma^{-2}X_\infty B_1 U_1^{-1} B_1^T X_\infty$. If A is invertible, the parameter-dependent discrete time Riccati equation (21) can be solved by using the following symplectic matrix

$$\hat{S}_\infty := \begin{bmatrix} A + \hat{B}\hat{R}^{-1}\hat{B}^T A^{-T}(\rho^2 E_K^T E_K + C_1^T C_1 + Q_\delta) & -\hat{B}\hat{R}^{-1}\hat{B}^T A^{-T} \\ -A^{-T}(\rho^2 E_K^T E_K + C_1^T C_1 + Q_\delta) & A^{-T} \end{bmatrix}$$

The following theorem gives the solution to non-fragile discrete time state feedback mixed LQR/ H_∞ control problem.

Theorem 4.1 There exists a non-fragile discrete time state feedback mixed LQR/ H_∞ controller iff for a given number ρ and a sufficiently small constant $\delta > 0$, there exists a stabilizing solution $X_\infty \geq 0$ to the parameter-dependent discrete time Riccati equation (21) such that $U_1 = I - \gamma^{-2}B_1^T X_\infty B_1 > 0$ and $\rho^2 I - H_K^T U_2 H_K > 0$.

Moreover, this non-fragile discrete time state feedback mixed LQR/ H_∞ controller is

$$F_\infty = -U_2^{-1} B_2^T U_3 A$$

and achieves $\sup\{\hat{J}\}_{w \in L_{2+}} = x_0^T X_\infty x_0$ subject to $\|T_{zw}\|_\infty < \gamma$.
Proof: *Sufficiency*: Suppose that for a given number ρ and a sufficiently small constant $\delta > 0$, there exists a stabilizing solution $X_\infty \geq 0$ to the parameter-dependent Riccati equation (21) such that $U_1 = I - \gamma^{-2} B_1^T X_\infty B_1 > 0$ and $\rho^2 I - H_K^T U_2 H_K > 0$. This implies that the solution $X_\infty \geq 0$ is such that $A - \hat{B}(\hat{B}^T X_\infty \hat{B} + \hat{R})^{-1} \hat{B}^T X_\infty A$ is stable. Define respectively the state matrix and controlled output matrix of closed-loop system

$$A_{\hat{F}_\infty} = A + B_2(-U_2^{-1} B_2^T U_3 A + H_K F(k) E_K)$$
$$C_{\hat{F}_\infty} = C_1 + D_{12}(-U_2^{-1} B_2^T U_3 A + H_K F(k) E_K)$$

and let $A_{F_\infty} = A - B_2 U_2^{-1} B_2^T U_3 A$ and $\overline{F}_\infty = -U_2^{-1} B_2^T U_3 A + H_K F(k) E_K$, then it follows from the square completion that

$$\begin{aligned} &A_{\hat{F}_\infty}^T X_\infty A_{\hat{F}_\infty} - X_\infty + \gamma^{-2} A_{\hat{F}_\infty}^T X_\infty B_{\hat{F}_\infty} U_1^{-1} B_{\hat{F}_\infty}^T X_\infty A_{\hat{F}_\infty} + C_{\hat{F}_\infty}^T C_{\hat{F}_\infty} + Q + \overline{F}_\infty^T R \overline{F}_\infty \\ &= A^T X_\infty A - X_\infty + \gamma^{-2} A^T X_\infty B_1 U_1^{-1} B_1^T X_\infty A + C_1^T C_1 + Q + \overline{F}_\infty^T B_2^T U_3 A + A^T U_3 B_2 \overline{F}_\infty + \overline{F}_\infty^T U_2 \overline{F}_\infty \\ &= A^T X_\infty A - X_\infty + \gamma^{-2} A^T X_\infty B_1 U_1^{-1} B_1^T X_\infty A + C_1^T C_1 + Q - A^T U_3 B_2 U_2^{-1} B_2^T U_3 A + \Delta \overline{N} \end{aligned} \tag{22}$$

where, $\Delta \overline{N} = E_K^T F^T(k) H_K^T U_2 H_K F(k) E_K$.
Noting that $\rho^2 I - H_K^T U_2 H_K > 0$, we have

$$\Delta \overline{N} = -E_K^T F^T(k)(\rho^2 I - H_K^T U_2 H_K) F(k) E_K + \rho^2 E_K^T F^T(k) F(k) E_K \;\leq\; \rho^2 E_K^T E_K \tag{23}$$

Considering (22) and (23) to get

$$\begin{aligned} &A_{\hat{F}_\infty}^T X_\infty A_{\hat{F}_\infty} - X_\infty + \gamma^{-2} A_{\hat{F}_\infty}^T X_\infty B_{\hat{F}_\infty} U_1^{-1} B_{\hat{F}_\infty}^T X_\infty A_{\hat{F}_\infty} + C_{\hat{F}_\infty}^T C_{\hat{F}_\infty} + Q + \overline{F}_\infty^T R \overline{F}_\infty \\ &\leq A^T X_\infty A - X_\infty + \gamma^{-2} A^T X_\infty B_1 U_1^{-1} B_1^T X_\infty A + C_1^T C_1 + Q + \rho^2 E_K^T E_K - A^T U_3 B_2 U_2^{-1} B_2^T U_3 A \end{aligned} \tag{24}$$

Also, it can be easily shown by using the similar standard matrix manipulations as in the proof of Theorem 3.1 in Souza & Xie (1992) that

$$A^T X_\infty \hat{B}(\hat{B}^T X_\infty \hat{B} + \hat{R})^{-1} \hat{B}^T X_\infty A = -\gamma^{-2} A^T X_\infty B_1 U_1^{-1} B_1^T X_\infty A + A^T U_3 B_2 U_2^{-1} B_2^T U_3 A$$

This implies that (21) can be rewritten as

$$A^T X_\infty A - X_\infty + \gamma^{-2} A^T X_\infty B_1 U_1^{-1} B_1^T X_\infty A + C_1^T C_1 + Q_\delta - A^T U_3 B_2 U_2^{-1} B_2^T U_3 A + \rho^2 E_K^T E_K = 0 \tag{25}$$

Thus, it follows from (24) and (25) that there exists a non-negative-definite solution to the inequality

$$A_{\hat{F}_\infty}^T X_\infty A_{\hat{F}_\infty} - X_\infty + \gamma^{-2} A_{\hat{F}_\infty}^T X_\infty B_{\hat{F}_\infty} U_1^{-1} B_{\hat{F}_\infty}^T X_\infty A_{\hat{F}_\infty} + C_{\hat{F}_\infty}^T C_{\hat{F}_\infty} + Q + \overline{F}_\infty^T R \overline{F}_\infty < 0$$

Note that $A-\hat{B}(\hat{B}^T X_\infty \hat{B}+\hat{R})^{-1}\hat{B}^T X_\infty A = A_{F_\infty} + \gamma^{-2}B_1 U_1^{-1} B_1^T X_\infty A_{F_\infty}$ is stable and $\Delta F(k)$ is an admissible uncertainty, we get that $A_{\hat{F}_\infty} + \gamma^{-2} B_{\hat{F}_\infty} U_1^{-1} B_{\hat{F}_\infty}^T X_\infty A_{\hat{F}_\infty}$ is stable. By Lemma 4.1, there exists a non- fragile discrete time state feedback mixed LQR/ H_∞ controller.

Necessity: Suppose that there exists a non-fragile discrete time state feedback mixed LQR/ H_∞ controller. By Lemma 4.1, there exists a stabilizing solution $X_\infty \geq 0$ to the inequality (11) such that $U_1 = I - \gamma^{-2} B_{\hat{F}_\infty}^T X_\infty B_{\hat{F}_\infty} > 0$, i.e., there exists a symmetric non-negative-definite solution X_∞ to the inequality (11) such that $A_{\hat{F}_\infty} + \gamma^{-2} B_{\hat{F}_\infty} U_1^{-1} B_{\hat{F}_\infty}^T X_\infty A_{\hat{F}_\infty}$ is stable and $U_1 = I - \gamma^{-2} B_{\hat{F}_\infty}^T X_\infty B_{\hat{F}_\infty} > 0$ for any admissible uncertainty $\Delta F(k)$.

Rewriting (11) to get

$$\begin{aligned} &A_{F_\infty}^T X_\infty A_{F_\infty} - X_\infty + \gamma^{-2} A_{F_\infty}^T X_\infty B_1 U_1^{-1} B_1^T X_\infty A_{F_\infty} + C_{F_\infty}^T C_{F_\infty} + Q + F_\infty^T R F_\infty + \Delta\hat{N} < 0 \\ &\Delta\hat{N} = (A^T U_3 B_2 + F_\infty^T U_2)\Delta F(k) + \Delta F^T(k)(B_2^T U_3 A + U_2 F_\infty) + \Delta F^T(k) U_2 \Delta F(k) \end{aligned} \tag{26}$$

Note that $\rho^2 I - H_K^T U_2 H_K > 0$ and

$$\begin{aligned} \Delta\hat{N} &= \rho^2 E_K^T F^T(k) F(k) E_K + (A^T U_3 B_2 + F_\infty^T U_2) H_K (\rho^2 I - H_K^T U_2 H_K)^{-1} H_K^T \\ &\quad \times (B_2^T U_3 A + U_2 F_\infty) - ((A^T U_3 B_2 + F_\infty^T U_2) H_K (\rho^2 I - H_K^T U_2 H_K)^{-1} - E_K^T F^T(k)) \\ &\quad \times (\rho^2 I - H_K^T U_2 H_K)((\rho^2 I - H_K^T U_2 H_K)^{-1} H_K^T (B_2^T U_3 A + U_2 F_\infty) - F(k) E_K) \\ &\leq \rho^2 E_K^T E_K + (A^T U_3 B_2 + F_\infty^T U_2) H_K (\rho^2 I - H_K^T U_2 H_K)^{-1} H_K^T (B_2^T U_3 A + U_2 F_\infty) \end{aligned} \tag{27}$$

It follows from (26) and (27) that

$$\begin{aligned} &A_{F_\infty}^T X_\infty A_{F_\infty} - X_\infty + \gamma^{-2} A_{F_\infty}^T X_\infty B_1 U_1^{-1} B_1^T X_\infty A_{F_\infty} + C_{F_\infty}^T C_{F_\infty} + Q + F_\infty^T R F_\infty + \rho^2 E_K^T E_K \\ &+(A^T U_3 B_2 + F_\infty^T U_2) H_K (\rho^2 I - H_K^T U_2 H_K)^{-1} H_K^T (B_2^T U_3 A + U_2 F_\infty) < 0 \end{aligned} \tag{28}$$

Using the argument of completion of squares as in the proof of Theorem 3.1 in Furuta & Phoojaruenchanachai (1990), we get from (28) that $F_\infty = -U_2^{-1} B_2^T U_3 A$, where X_∞ is a symmetric non- negative-definite solution to the inequality

$$A^T X_\infty A - X_\infty + \gamma^{-2} A^T X_\infty B_1 U_1^{-1} B_1^T X_\infty A + C_1^T C_1 + Q - A^T U_3 B_2 U_2^{-1} B_2^T U_3 A + \rho^2 E_K^T E_K < 0$$

or equivalently, X_∞ is a symmetric non-negative-definite solution to the parameter-dependent discrete time Riccati equation

$$A^T X_\infty A - X_\infty + \gamma^{-2} A^T X_\infty B_1 U_1^{-1} B_1^T X_\infty A + C_1^T C_1 + Q_\delta - A^T U_3 B_2 U_2^{-1} B_2^T U_3 A + \rho^2 E_K^T E_K = 0 \tag{29}$$

Also, we can rewrite that Riccati equation (29) can be rewritten as

$$A^T X_\infty A - X_\infty - A^T X_\infty \hat{B}(\hat{B}^T X_\infty \hat{B} + \hat{R})^{-1} \hat{B}^T X_\infty A + \rho^2 E_K^T E_K + C_1^T C_1 + Q_\delta = 0 \tag{30}$$

by using the similar standard matrix manipulations as in the proof of Theorem 3.1 in Souza & Xie (1992). Note that $A-\hat{B}(\hat{B}^T X_\infty \hat{B}+\hat{R})^{-1}\hat{B}^T X_\infty A = A_{F_\infty}+\gamma^{-2}B_1 U_1^{-1}B_1^T X_\infty A_{F_\infty}$ and $\Delta F(k)$ is an admissible uncertainty, the assumption that $A_{\hat{F}_\infty}+\gamma^{-2}B_{\hat{F}_\infty}U_1^{-1}B_{\hat{F}_\infty}^T X_\infty A_{\hat{F}_\infty}$ is stable implies that $A-\hat{B}(\hat{B}^T X_\infty \hat{B}+\hat{R})^{-1}\hat{B}^T X_\infty A$ is stable Thus, we conclude that for a given number ρ and a sufficiently small number $\delta > 0$, the parameter-dependent discrete time Riccati equation (30) has a stabilizing solution X_∞ and $U_1 = I-\gamma^{-2}B_1^T X_\infty B_1 > 0$ and $\rho^2 I - H_K^T U_2 H_K > 0$. Q. E. D.

5. Numerical examples

In this section, we present two examples to illustrate the design method given by Section 3 and 4, respectively.

Example 1 Consider the following discrete-time system in Peres and Geromel (1993)

$$x(k+1) = Ax(k) + B_1 w(k) + B_2 u(k)$$
$$z(k) = C_1 x(k) + D_{12} u(k)$$

where,

$$A = \begin{bmatrix} 0.2113 & 0.0087 & 0.4524 \\ 0.0824 & 0.8096 & 0.8075 \\ 0.7599 & 0.8474 & 0.4832 \end{bmatrix},\ B_2 = \begin{bmatrix} 0.6135 & 0.6538 \\ 0.2749 & 0.4899 \\ 0.8807 & 0.7741 \end{bmatrix},$$

$$C_1 = \begin{bmatrix} 1 & 0 & 0 \\ 0 & 1 & 0 \\ 0 & 0 & 1 \\ 0 & 0 & 0 \\ 0 & 0 & 0 \end{bmatrix},\ D_{12} = \begin{bmatrix} 0 & 0 \\ 0 & 0 \\ 0 & 0 \\ 1 & 0 \\ 0 & 1 \end{bmatrix} \text{ and } B_1 = I.$$

In this example, we will design the above system under the influence of state feedback of the form (3) by using the discrete-times state feedback mixed LQR/ H_∞ control method displayed in Theorem 3.1. All results will be computed by using MATLAB. The above system is stabilizable and observable, and satisfies Assumption 3, and the eigenvalues of matrix A are $p_1 = 1.6133$, $p_2 = 0.3827$, $p_3 = -0.4919$;thus it is open-loop unstable.

Let $\gamma = 2.89$, $R = \begin{bmatrix} 1 & 0 \\ 0 & 1 \end{bmatrix}$, $Q = \begin{bmatrix} 1 & 0 & 0 \\ 0 & 1 & 0 \\ 0 & 0 & 1 \end{bmatrix}$, we solve the discrete-time Riccati equation (13) to get

$$X_\infty = \begin{bmatrix} 2.9683 & 1.1296 & 0.1359 \\ 1.1296 & 6.0983 & 2.4073 \\ 0.1359 & 2.4073 & 4.4882 \end{bmatrix} > 0,$$

$$U_1 = I - \gamma^{-2} B_1^T X_\infty B_1 = \begin{bmatrix} 0.6446 & -0.1352 & -0.0163 \\ -0.1352 & 0.2698 & -0.2882 \\ -0.0163 & -0.2882 & 0.4626 \end{bmatrix} > 0 .$$

Thus the discrete-time state feedback mixed LQR/ H_∞ controller is

$$K = \begin{bmatrix} -0.3640 & -0.5138 & -0.3715 \\ -0.2363 & -0.7176 & -0.7217 \end{bmatrix} .$$

Example 2 Consider the following discrete-time system in Peres and Geromel (1993)

$$\begin{aligned} x(k+1) &= Ax(k) + B_1 w(k) + B_2 u(k) \\ z(k) &= C_1 x(k) + D_{12} u(k) \end{aligned}$$

under the influences of state feedback with controller unceratinty of the form (4), where, A, B_1, B_2, C_1 and D_{12} are the same as ones in Example 1; the controller uncertainty $\Delta F(k)$ satisfies

$$\Delta F(k) = E_K F(k) E_K , \; F^T(k) F(k) \le I$$

where, $E_K = \begin{bmatrix} 1 & 0 & 0 \\ 0 & 1 & 0 \\ 0 & 1 & 1 \end{bmatrix}$, $H_K = \begin{bmatrix} 0.0100 & 0 & 0 \\ 0 & 0.0100 & 0 \end{bmatrix}$.

In this example, we illustrate the proposed method by Theorem 4.1 by using MATLAB. As stated in example 1, the system is stabilizable and observable, and satisfies Assumption 3, and is open-loop unstable.

Let $\gamma = 8.27$, $R = \begin{bmatrix} 1 & 0 \\ 0 & 1 \end{bmatrix}$, $Q = \begin{bmatrix} 1 & 0 & 0 \\ 0 & 1 & 0 \\ 0 & 0 & 1 \end{bmatrix}$, $\rho = 3.7800$, and $\delta = 0.0010$, then we solve the parameter-dependent discrete-time Riccati equation (21) to get

$$X_\infty = \begin{bmatrix} 18.5238 & 3.8295 & 0.1664 \\ 3.8295 & 51.3212 & 23.3226 \\ 0.1664 & 23.3226 & 22.7354 \end{bmatrix} > 0 ,$$

$$U_1 = I - \gamma^2 B_1^T X_\infty B_1 = \begin{bmatrix} 0.7292 & -0.0560 & -0.0024 \\ -0.0560 & 0.2496 & -0.3410 \\ -0.0024 & -0.3410 & 0.6676 \end{bmatrix} > 0 , \; U_2 = \begin{bmatrix} 609.6441 & 723.0571 \\ 723.0571 & 863.5683 \end{bmatrix} ,$$

$$\rho^2 I - H_K^T U_2 H_K = \begin{bmatrix} 14.2274 & -0.0723 & 0 \\ -0.0723 & 14.2020 & 0 \\ 0 & 0 & 14.2884 \end{bmatrix} > 0 .$$

Based on this, the non-fragile discrete-time state feedback mixed LQR/ H_∞ controller is

$$F_\infty = \begin{bmatrix} -0.4453 & -0.1789 & -0.0682 \\ -0.1613 & -1.1458 & -1.0756 \end{bmatrix}$$

6. Conclusion

In this chapter, we first study the discrete time state feedback mixed LQR/ H_∞ control problem. In order to solve this problem, we present an extension of the discrete time bounded real lemma. In terms of the stabilizing solution to a discrete time Riccati equation, we derive the simple approach to discrete time state feedback mixed LQR/ H_∞ control problem by combining the Lyapunov method for proving the discrete time optimal LQR control problem with the above extension of the discrete time bounded real lemma, the argument of completion of squares of Furuta & Phoojaruenchanachi (1990) and standard inverse matrix manipulation of Souza & Xie (1992).A related problem is the standard H_∞ control problem (Doyle et al., 1989a; Iglesias & Glover, 1991; Furuta & Phoojaruenchanachai, 1990; Souza & Xie, 1992; Zhou et al. 1996), another related problem is the H_∞ optimal control problem arisen from Basar & Bernhard (1991). The relations among the two related problem and mixed LQR/ H_∞ control problem can be clearly explained by based on the discrete time reference system (9)(3). The standard H_∞ control problem is to find an admissible controller K such that the H_∞-norm of closed-loop transfer matrix from disturbance input w to the controlled output z is less than a given number $\gamma > 0$ while the H_∞ optimal control roblem arisen from Basar & Bernhard (1991) is to find an admissible controller such that the H_∞-norm of closed-loop transfer matrix from disturbance input w to the controlled output z_0 is less than a given number $\gamma > 0$ for the discre time reference system (9)(3). Since the latter is equivalent to the problem that is to find an admissible controller K such that $\sup_{w \in L_{2+}} \inf_K \{\hat{J}\}$, we may recognize that the mixed LQR/ H_∞ control problem is a combination of the standard H_∞ control problem and H_∞ optimal control problem arisen from Basar & Bernhard (1991). The second problem considered by this chapter is the non-fragile discrete-time state feedback mixed LQR/ H_∞ control problem with controller uncertainty. This problem is to extend the results of discrete-time state feedback mixed LQR/ H_∞ control problem to the system (2)(4) with controller uncertainty. In terms of the stabilizing solution to a parameter-dependent discrete time Riccati equation, we give a design method of non-fragile discrete-time state feedback mixed LQR/ H_∞ controller, and derive necessary and sufficient conditions for the existence of this non-fragile controller.

7. References

T. Basar, and Bernhard P. (1991). H_∞-optimal control and related minmax design problems: a dynamic game approach. Boston, MA: Birkhauser.

D. S. Bernstein, and Haddad W. M. (1989). LQG control with an H_∞ performance bound: A Riccati equation approach, *IEEE Trans. Aut. Control.* 34(3), pp. 293- 305.

J. C. Doyle, Glover K., Khargonekar P. P. and Francis B. A. (1989a) . State-space solutions to standard H_2 and H_∞ control problems. *IEEE Trans. Aut. Control,* 34(8), pp. 831-847.

J. C. Doyle, Zhou K., and Bodenheimer B. (1989b). Optimal control with mixed H_2 and H_∞ performance objective. *Proceedings of 1989 American Control Conference*, Pittsburh, PA, pp. 2065- 2070, 1989.

J. C. Doyle, Zhou K., Glover K. and Bodenheimer B. (1994). Mixed H_2 and H_∞ performance objectives II: optimal control, *IEEE Trans. Aut. Control*, 39(8), pp.1575- 1587.

D. Famularo, Dorato P., Abdallah C. T., Haddad W. M. and Jadbabaie A. (2000). Robust non-fragile LQ controllers: the static state case, *INT. J. Control*, 73 (2),pp.159-165.

K. Furata, and Phoojaruenchanachai S. (1990). An algebraic approach to discrete-time H_∞ control problems. *Proceedings of 1990 American Control Conference*, San Diego, pp. 3067-3072, 1990.

W. M. Haddad, and Corrado J. R. (2000). Robust resilient dynamic controllers for systems with parametric uncertainty and controller gain variations, *INT. J. Control*, 73(15), pp. 1405- 1423.

P. A. Iglesias, and Glover K. (1991). State-space approach to discrete-time H_∞ control, *INT. J. Control*, 54(5), pp. 1031- 1073.

L. H. Keel, and Bhattacharyya S. P. (1997). Robust, fragile, or optimal ? *IEEE Trans. Aut. Control*, 42(8), pp. 1098-1105

L. H. Keel, and Bhattacharyya S. P. (1998). Authors' Reply. *IEEE Trans. Aut. Control*, 43(9), pp. 1268-1268.

P. P. Khargonekar, and Rotea M. A.(1991). Mixed H_2 / H_∞ control: A convex optimization approach, *IEEE Trans. Aut. Control*, 36(7), pp. 824-837.

V. Kucera (1972). A Contribution to matrix quadratic equations. *IEEE Trans. Aut. Control*, 17(3), pp. 344-347.

D. J. N. Limebeer, Anderson B. D. O., Khargonekar P. P. and Green M. (1992). A game theoretic approach to H_∞ control for time-varying systems. SIAM J. Control and Optimization, 30(2), pp.262-283.

D. J. N. Limebeer, Anderson B. D. O., and Hendel B. (1994). A Nash game approach to mixed H_2 / H_∞ control. *IEEE Trans. Aut. Control*, 39(1), pp. 69-82.

K. Ogata (1987). Discrete-time control systems. *Prentice Hall*, 1987.

T. Pappas, Laub A. J., Sandell N. R., Jr. (1980). On the numerical solution of the discrete - time algebraic Riccati equation. *IEEE Trans. Aut. Control*, 25(4), pp. 631-641.

P. L. D. Peres and Geromel J. C. (1993). H_2 control for discrete-time systems optimality and robustness. Automatica, Vol. 29, No. 1, pp. 225-228.

J. E. Potter (1966). Matrix quadratic solution. *J. SIAM App. Math.*, 14, pp. 496-501.

P. M. Makila (1998). Comments "Robust, Fragile, or Optimal ?". *IEEE Trans. Aut. Control.*, 43(9), pp. 1265-1267.

M. A. Rotea, and Khargonekar P. P. (1991). H_2-optimal control with an H_∞-constraint: the state-feedback case. Automatica, 27(2), pp. 307-316.

H. Rotstein, and Sznaier M. (1998). An exact solution to general four-block discrete-time mixed H_2 / H_∞ problems via convex optimization, *IEEE Trans. Aut. Control*, 43(10), pp. 1475-1480.

C. E. de Souza and Xie L. (1992). On the discrete-time bounded real lemma with application in the characterization of static state feedback H_∞ controllers, *Systems & Control Letters*, 18, pp. 61-71.

M. Sznaier (1994). An exact solution to general SISO mixed H_2 / H_∞ problems via convex optimization, *IEEE Trans. Aut. Control,* 39(12), pp. 2511-2517.

M. Sznaier, Rotstein H. , Bu J. and Sideris A. (2000). An exact solution to continuous-time mixed H_2 / H_∞ control problems, *IEEE Trans Aut. Control,* 45(11), pp.2095-2101.

X. Xu (1996). A study on robust control for discrete-time systems with uncertainty, *A Master Thesis of 1995,* Kobe university, Kobe, Japan, January,1996.

X. Xu (2007). Non-fragile mixed LQR/ H_∞ control problem for linear discrete-time systems with controller uncertainty. *Proceedings of the 26th Chinese Control Conference.* Zhangjiajie, Hunan, China, pp. 635-639, July 26-31, 2007.

X. Xu (2008). Characterization of all static state feedback mixed LQR/ H_∞ controllers for linear continuous-time systems. *Proceedings of the 27th Chinese Control Conference.* Kunming, Yunnan, China, pp. 678-682, July 16-18, 2008.

G. H. Yang, Wang J. L. and Lin C. (2000). H_∞ control for linear systems with additive controller gain variations, *INT. J. Control,* 73(16), pp. 1500-1506.

G. H. Yang, Wang J. L. (2001). Non-fragile H_∞ control for linear systems with multiplicative controller gain variations, *Automatica,* 37, pp. 727-737.

H. Yeh, Banda S. S. and Chang B. (1992). Necessary and sufficient conditions for mixed H_2 and H_∞ optimal control, *IEEE Trans. Aut. Control,* 37 (3), PP. 355-358.

K. Zhou, Glover K., Bodenheimer B. and Doyle J. C. (1994). Mixed H_2 and H_∞ performance objectives I: robust performance analysis, *IEEE Trans. Aut. Control,* 39 (8), PP. 1564-1574.

K. Zhou, Doyle J. C. and Glover K. (1996). Robust and optimal control, *Prentice-Hall, INC.,* 1996

11

Robust Control Design of Uncertain Discrete-Time Systems with Delays

Jun Yoneyama, Yuzu Uchida and Shusaku Nishikawa
Aoyama Gakuin University
Japan

1. Introduction

When we consider control problems of physical systems, we often see time-delay in the process of control algorithms and the transmission of information. Time-delay often appear in many practical systems and mathematical formulations such as electrical system, mechanical system, biological system, and transportation system. Hence, a system with time-delay is a natural representation for them, and its analysis and synthesis are of theoretical and practical importance. In the past decades, research on continuous-time delay systems has been active. Difficulty that arises in continuous time-delay system is that it is infinite dimensional and a corresponding controller can be a memory feedback. This class of controllers may minimize a certain performance index, but it is difficult to implement it to practical systems due to a memory feedback. To overcome such a difficulty, a memoryless controller is used for time-delay systems. In the last decade, sufficient stability conditions have been given via linear matrix inequalities (LMIs), and stabilization methods by memoryless controllers have been investigated by many researchers. Since Li and de Souza considered robust stability and stabilization problems in (8), less conservative robust stability conditions for continuous time-delay systems have been obtained ((7), (11)). Recently, H_∞ disturbance attenuation conditions have also been given ((10), (15), (16)).
On the other hand, research on discrete-time delay systems has not attracted as much attention as that of continuous-time delay systems. In addition, most results have focused on state feedback stabilization of discrete-time systems with time-varying delays. Only a few results on observer design of discrete-time systems with time-varying delays have appeared in the literature(for example, (9)). The results in (3), (12), (14), (18) considered discrete-time systems with time-invariant delays. Gao and Chen (4), Hara and Yoneyama (5), (6) gave robust stability conditions. Fridman and Shaked (1) solved a guaranteed cost control problem. Fridman and Shaked (2), Yoneyama (17), Zhang and Han (19) considered the H_∞ disturbance attenuation. They have given sufficient conditions via LMIs for corresponding control problems. Nonetheless, their conditions still show the conservatism. Hara and Yoneyama (5) and Yoneyama (17) gave least conservative conditions but their conditions require many LMI slack variables, which in turn require a large amount of computations. Furthermore, to authors' best knowledge, few results on robust observer design problem for uncertain discrete-time systems with time-varying delays have given in the literature.
In this paper, we consider the stabilization for a nominal discrete-time system with time-varying delay and robust stabilization for uncertain system counterpart. The system under consideration has time-varying delays in state, control input and output measurement. First, we obtain a stability condition for a nominal time-delay system. To this end, we define

a Lyapunov function and use Leibniz-Newton formula and free weighting matrix method. These methods are known to reduce the conservatism in our stability condition, which are expressed as linear matrix inequality. Based on such a stability condition, a state feedback design method is proposed. Then, we extend our stabilization result to robust stabilization for uncertain discrete-time systems with time-varying delay. Next, we consider observer design and robust observer design. Similar to a stability condition, we obtain a condition such that the error system, which comes from the original system and its observer, is asymptotically stable. Using a stability condition of the error system, we proposed an observer design method. Furthermore, we give a robust observer design method for an uncertain time-delay system. Finally, we give some numerical examples to illustrate our results and to compare with existing results.

2. Time-delay systems

Consider the following discrete-time system with a time-varying delay and uncertainties in the state and control input.

$$\begin{aligned} x(k+1) &= (A+\Delta A)x(k) + (A_d + \Delta A_d)x(k-d_k) + (B+\Delta B)u(k) \\ &\quad + (B_d + \Delta B_d)u(k-d_k) \end{aligned} \tag{1}$$

where $x(k) \in \Re^n$ is the state and $u(k) \in \Re^m$ is the control. A, A_d, B and B_d are system matrices with appropriate dimensions. d_k is a time-varying delay and satisfies $0 \le d_m \le d_k \le d_M$ and $d_{k+1} \le d_k$ where d_m and d_M are known constants. Uncertain matrices are of the form

$$\left[\Delta A\ \Delta A_d\ \Delta B\ \Delta B_d\right] = HF(k)\left[E\ E_d\ E_1\ E_b\right] \tag{2}$$

where $F(k) \in \Re^{l \times j}$ is an unknown time-varying matrix satisfying $F^T(k)F(k) \le I$ and H, E, E_d, E_1 and E_b are constant matrices of appropriate dimensions.

Definition 2.1. *The system (1) is said to be robustly stable if it is asymptotically stable for all admissible uncertainties (2).*

When we discuss a nominal system, we consider the following system.

$$x(k+1) = Ax(k) + A_d x(k-d_k) + Bu(k) + B_d u(k-d_k). \tag{3}$$

Our problem is to find a control law which makes the system (1) or (3) robustly stable. Let us now consider the following memoryless feedback:

$$u(k) = Kx(k) \tag{4}$$

where K is a control gain to be determined. Applying the control (4) to the system (1), we have the closed-loop system

$$x(k+1) = ((A+\Delta A) + (B+\Delta B)K)x(k) + ((A_d+\Delta A_d) + (B_d+\Delta B_d)K)x(k-d_k). \tag{5}$$

For the nominal case, we have

$$x(k+1) = (A+BK)x(k) + (A_d + B_d K)x(k-d_k). \tag{6}$$

In the following section, we consider the robust stability of the closed-loop system (5) and the stability of the closed-loop system (6).
The following lemma is useful to prove our results.

Lemma 2.2. *((13)) Given matrices $Q = Q^T$, H, E and $R = R^T > 0$ with appropriate dimensions.*

$$Q + HF(k)E + E^T F^T(k)H^T < 0$$

for all $F(k)$ satisfying $F^T(k)F(k) \leq R$ if and only if there exists a scalar $\varepsilon > 0$ such that

$$Q + \frac{1}{\varepsilon}HH^T + \varepsilon E^T RE < 0.$$

3. Stability analysis

This section analyzes the stability and robust stability of discrete-time delay systems. Section 3.1 gives a stability condition for nominal systems and Section 3.2 extends the stability result to a case of robust stability.

3.1 Stability for nominal systems

Stability conditions for discrete-time delay system (6) are given in the following theorem.

Theorem 3.1. *Given integers d_m and d_M, and control gain K. Then, the time-delay system (6) is asymptotically stable if there exist matrices $P_1 > 0$, $P_2 > 0$, $Q_1 > 0$, $Q_2 > 0$, $S > 0$, $M > 0$,*

$$L = \begin{bmatrix} L_1 \\ L_2 \\ L_3 \\ L_4 \\ L_5 \end{bmatrix}, \; N = \begin{bmatrix} N_1 \\ N_2 \\ N_3 \\ N_4 \\ N_5 \end{bmatrix}, \; T = \begin{bmatrix} T_1 \\ T_2 \\ T_3 \\ T_4 \\ T_5 \end{bmatrix}$$

satisfying

$$\Phi = \begin{bmatrix} \Phi_1 + \Xi_L + \Xi_L^T + \Xi_N + \Xi_N^T + \Xi_T + \Xi_T^T & \sqrt{d_M}Z \\ \sqrt{d_M}Z^T & -S \end{bmatrix} < 0 \tag{7}$$

where

$$\begin{aligned}
\Phi_1 &= \begin{bmatrix} P_1 & 0 & 0 & 0 & 0 \\ 0 & \Phi_{22} & 0 & 0 & 0 \\ 0 & 0 & -Q_1 - M & 0 & 0 \\ 0 & 0 & 0 & \Phi_{44} & -P_2 \\ 0 & 0 & 0 & -P_2 & P_2 - Q_2 \end{bmatrix}, \\
\Phi_{22} &= -P_1 + Q_1 + (d_M - d_m + 1)M, \\
\Phi_{44} &= P_2 + Q_2 + d_M S, \\
Z &= \begin{bmatrix} 0 \\ 0 \\ 0 \\ -P_2 \\ P_2 \end{bmatrix} + N, \\
\Xi_L &= \begin{bmatrix} L & -L & 0 & -L & 0 \end{bmatrix}, \\
\Xi_N &= \begin{bmatrix} 0 & N & -N & 0 & 0 \end{bmatrix}, \\
\Xi_T &= \begin{bmatrix} T & -T(A + BK) & -T(A_d + B_d K) & 0 & 0 \end{bmatrix}.
\end{aligned}$$

Proof: First, we note from Leibniz-Newton formula that

$$2\xi^T(k)L[x(k+1) - x(k) - e(k)] = 0, \tag{8}$$

$$2\xi^T(k)N[x(k) - x(k-d_k) - \sum_{i=k-d_k}^{k-1} e(i)] = 0 \tag{9}$$

where $e(k) = x(k+1) - x(k)$ and

$$\xi^T(k) = [x^T(k+1)\ x^T(k)\ x^T(k-d_k)\ e^T(k)\ e^T(k-d_k)].$$

It is also true that

$$2\xi^T(k)T[x(k+1) - (A+BK)x(k) - (A_d + B_dK)x(k-d_k)] = 0. \tag{10}$$

Now, we consider a Lyapunov function

$$V(k) = V_1(k) + V_2(k) + V_3(k) + V_4(k)$$

where

$$\begin{aligned}
V_1(k) &= x^T(k)P_1x(k) + \sum_{i=k-d_k}^{k-1} e^T(i)P_2 \sum_{i=k-d_k}^{k-1} e(i),\\
V_2(k) &= \sum_{i=k-d_k}^{k-1} x^T(i)Q_1x(i) + \sum_{i=k-d_k}^{k-1} e^T(i)Q_2e(i),\\
V_3(k) &= \sum_{i=-d_k}^{-1} \sum_{j=k+i}^{k-1} e^T(j)Se(j),\\
V_4(k) &= \sum_{j=-d_M}^{-d_m} \sum_{i=k+j}^{k-1} x^T(i)Mx(i),
\end{aligned}$$

and P_1, P_2, Q_1, Q_2, S and M are positive definite matrices to be determined. Then, we calculate the difference $\Delta V = V(k+1) - V(k)$ and add the left-hand-side of equations (8)-(10). Since $\Delta V_i(k),\ i = 1, \cdots, 4$ are calculated as follows;

$$\begin{aligned}
\Delta V_1(k) = & x^T(k+1)P_1x(k+1) + \sum_{i=k+1-d_{k+1}}^{k} e^T(i)P_2 \sum_{i=k+1-d_{k+1}}^{k} e(i)\\
& -x^T(k)P_1x(k) - \sum_{i=k-d_k}^{k-1} e^T(i)P_2 \sum_{i=k-d_k}^{k-1} e(i)\\
\leq & x^T(k+1)P_1x(k+1) - x^T(k)P_1x(k) + e^T(k)P_2e(k)\\
& -2e^T(k)P_2e(k-d_k) + 2e^T(k)P_2 \sum_{i=k-d_k}^{k-1} e(i)\\
& +e^T(k-d_k)P_2e(k-d_k) - 2e^T(k-d_k)P_2 \sum_{i=k-d_k}^{k-1} e(i),
\end{aligned}$$

$$
\begin{aligned}
\Delta V_2(k) &= \sum_{i=k+1-d_{k+1}}^{k} x^T(i)Q_1x(i) + \sum_{i=k+1-d_{k+1}}^{k} e^T(i)Q_2e(i) \\
&\quad - \sum_{i=k-d_k}^{k-1} x^T(i)Q_1x(i) - \sum_{i=k-d_k}^{k-1} e^T(i)Q_2e(i) \\
&\leq x^T(k)Q_1x(k) + e^T(k)Q_2e(k) - x^T(k-d_k)Q_1x(k-d_k) \\
&\quad - e^T(k-d_k)Q_2e(k-d_k), \\
\Delta V_3(k) &= d_{k+1}e^T(k)Se(k) - \sum_{i=k-d_{k+1}}^{k-1} e^T(i)Se(i) \cdots - \sum_{i=k-d_k}^{k-1} e^T(i)Se(i) \\
&\leq d_M e^T(k)Se(k) - \sum_{i=k-d_k}^{k-1} e^T(i)Se(i), \\
\Delta V_4(k) &= (d_M - d_m + 1)x^T(k)Mx(k) - \sum_{i=k-d_M+1}^{k-d_m} x^T(i)Mx(i) \\
&\leq (d_M - d_m + 1)x^T(k)Mx(k) - x^T(k-d_k)Mx(k-d_k),
\end{aligned}
$$

we have

$$
\begin{aligned}
\Delta V(k) &= \Delta V_1(k) + \Delta V_2(k) + \Delta V_3(k) + \Delta V_4(k) \\
&\leq \xi^T(k)[\Phi_1 + \Xi_L + \Xi_L^T + \Xi_N + \Xi_N^T + \Xi_T + \Xi_T^T]\xi(k) + \sum_{i=k-d_k}^{k-1} \xi^T(k)ZS^{-1}Z^T\xi(k) \\
&\quad - \sum_{i=k-d_k}^{k-1} (\xi^T(k)Z + e^T(i)S)S^{-1}(Z^T\xi(k) + Se(i)) \\
&\leq \xi^T(k)[\Phi_1 + \Xi_L + \Xi_L^T + \Xi_N + \Xi_N^T + \Xi_T + \Xi_T^T + d_M ZS^{-1}Z^T]\xi(k)
\end{aligned}
$$

If (7) is satisfied, by Schur complement formula, we have $\Phi_1 + \Xi_L + \Xi_L^T + \Xi_N + \Xi_N^T + \Xi_T + \Xi_T^T + d_M ZS^{-1}Z^T < 0$. It follows that $\Delta V(k) < 0$ and hence the proof is completed.

Remark 3.2. *We employ* $\sum_{i=k-d_k}^{k-1} (\star)$ *in our Lyapunov function instead of* $\sum_{i=k-d_M}^{k-1} (\star)$. *This gives a less conservative stability condition.*

3.2 Robust stability for uncertain systems

By extending Theorem 3.1, we obtain a condition for robust stability of uncertain system (5).

Theorem 3.3. *Given integers* d_m *and* d_M, *and control gain* K. *Then, the time-delay system (5) is robustly stable if there exist matrices* $P_1 > 0$, $P_2 > 0$, $Q_1 > 0$, $Q_2 > 0$, $S > 0$, $M > 0$,

$$
L = \begin{bmatrix} L_1 \\ L_2 \\ L_3 \\ L_4 \\ L_5 \end{bmatrix}, \; N = \begin{bmatrix} N_1 \\ N_2 \\ N_3 \\ N_4 \\ N_5 \end{bmatrix}, \; T = \begin{bmatrix} T_1 \\ T_2 \\ T_3 \\ T_4 \\ T_5 \end{bmatrix}
$$

and a scalar $\lambda > 0$ *satisfying*

$$\Pi = \begin{bmatrix} \Phi + \lambda \bar{E}^T \bar{E} & \bar{H}^T \\ \bar{H} & -\lambda I \end{bmatrix} < 0, \tag{11}$$

where Φ *is given in Theorem 3.1, and*

$$\bar{H} = \begin{bmatrix} -H^T T_1^T & -H^T T_2^T & -H^T T_3^T & -H^T T_4^T & -H^T T_5^T & 0 \end{bmatrix},$$

and

$$\bar{E} = \begin{bmatrix} 0 & E + E_1 K & E_d + E_b K & 0 & 0 & 0 \end{bmatrix}.$$

Proof: Replacing A, A_d, B and B_d in (7) with $A + HF(k)E$, $A_d + HF(k)E_d$, $B + HF(k)E_1$ and $B + HF(k)E_b$, respectively, we obtain a robust stability condition for the system (5).

$$\Phi + \bar{H}^T F(k) \bar{E} + \bar{E}^T F^T(k) \bar{H} < 0 \tag{12}$$

By Lemma 2.2, a necessary and sufficient condition that guarantees (12) is that there exists a scalar $\lambda > 0$ such that

$$\Phi + \lambda \bar{E}^T \bar{E} + \frac{1}{\lambda} \bar{H}^T \bar{H} < 0 \tag{13}$$

Applying Schur complement formula, we can show that (13) is equivalent to (11).

4. State feedback sabilization

This section proposes a state feedback stabilization method for the uncertain discrete-time delay system (1). First, stabilization of nominal system is considered in Section 4.1. Then, robust stabilization is proposed in Section 4.2

4.1 Stabilization

First, we consider stabilization for the nominal system (3). Our problem is to find a control gain K such that the closed-loop system (6) is asymptotically stable. Unfortunately, Theorem 3.1 does not give LMI conditions to find K. Hence, we must look for another method.

Theorem 4.1. *Given integers* d_m *and* d_M*, and scalars* ρ_i*,* $i = 1, \cdots, 5$*. Then, the controller (4) asymptotically stabilizes the time-delay system (3) if there exist matrices* $\bar{P}_1 > 0$*,* $\bar{P}_2 > 0$*,* $\bar{Q}_1 > 0$*,* $\bar{Q}_2 > 0$*,* $\bar{S} > 0$*,* $\bar{M} > 0$*,* G*,* Y

$$\bar{L} = \begin{bmatrix} \bar{L}_1 \\ \bar{L}_2 \\ \bar{L}_3 \\ \bar{L}_4 \\ \bar{L}_5 \end{bmatrix}, \quad \bar{N} = \begin{bmatrix} \bar{N}_1 \\ \bar{N}_2 \\ \bar{N}_3 \\ \bar{N}_4 \\ \bar{N}_5 \end{bmatrix},$$

satisfying

$$\Psi = \begin{bmatrix} \Psi_1 + \Theta_L + \Theta_L^T + \Theta_N + \Theta_N^T + \Theta_T + \Theta_T^T & \sqrt{d_M} \bar{Z} \\ \sqrt{d_M} \bar{Z}^T & -\bar{S} \end{bmatrix} < 0 \tag{14}$$

where

$$\Psi_1 = \begin{bmatrix} \bar{P}_1 & 0 & 0 & 0 & 0 \\ 0 & \Psi_{22} & 0 & 0 & 0 \\ 0 & 0 & -\bar{Q}_1 - \bar{M} & 0 & 0 \\ 0 & 0 & 0 & \Psi_{44} & -\bar{P}_2 \\ 0 & 0 & 0 & -\bar{P}_2 & \bar{P}_2 - \bar{Q}_2 \end{bmatrix},$$

$$\Psi_{22} = -\bar{P}_1 + \bar{Q}_1 + (d_M - d_m + 1)\bar{M},$$

$$\Psi_{44} = \bar{P}_2 + \bar{Q}_2 + d_M \bar{S},$$

$$\bar{Z} = \begin{bmatrix} 0 \\ 0 \\ 0 \\ -\bar{P}_2 \\ \bar{P}_2 \end{bmatrix} + \bar{N},$$

$$\Theta_L = \left[\bar{L}\ -\bar{L}\ 0\ -\bar{L}\ 0\right],$$

$$\Theta_N = \left[0\ \bar{N}\ -\bar{N}\ 0\ 0\right],$$

$$\Theta_T = \begin{bmatrix} \rho_1 Y^T & -\rho_1(AY^T + BG) & -\rho_1(A_d Y^T + B_d G) & 0 & 0 \\ \rho_2 Y^T & -\rho_2(AY^T + BG) & -\rho_2(A_d Y^T + B_d G) & 0 & 0 \\ \rho_3 Y^T & -\rho_3(AY^T + BG) & -\rho_3(A_d Y^T + B_d G) & 0 & 0 \\ \rho_4 Y^T & -\rho_4(AY^T + BG) & -\rho_4(A_d Y^T + B_d G) & 0 & 0 \\ \rho_5 Y^T & -\rho_5(AY^T + BG) & -\rho_5(A_d Y^T + B_d G) & 0 & 0 \end{bmatrix}.$$

In this case, a controller gain in the controller (4) is given by

$$K = GY^{-T} \tag{15}$$

Proof: Let $T_i = \rho_i Y^{-1}$, $i = 1, \cdots, 5$ where each ρ_i is given. We substitute them into (7). Then, we calculate $\Psi = \Sigma\Phi\Sigma^T$ with $\Sigma = \text{diag}[Y\ Y\ Y\ Y\ Y]$. Defining $\bar{P}_i = YP_iY^T$, $\bar{Q}_i = YQ_iY^T$, $i = 1, 2$, $\bar{S} = YSY^T$, $\bar{M} = YMY^T$, $\bar{L} = YLY^T$, $\bar{N} = YNY^T$, we obtain $\Theta < 0$ in (14) where we let $G = KY^T$. If the condition (14) hold, state feedback control gain matrix K is obviously given by (15).

Remark 4.2. *Should Y be singular, Let $\bar{L}_1 = 0$. In this case, it follows from $(1,1)$-block of Ψ that $\bar{P}_1 + \rho_1(Y + Y^T) < 0$. Then, if (14) holds, Y must be nonsingular.*

4.2 Robust stabilization

In a similar way to robust stability, we extend a stabilization result in the previous section to robust stabilization for uncertain discrete-time delay system (1).

Theorem 4.3. *Given integers d_m and d_M, and scalars ρ_i, $i = 1, \cdots, 5$. Then, the controller (4) robustly stabilizes the time-delay system (1) if there exist matrices $\bar{P}_1 > 0$, $\bar{P}_2 > 0$, $\bar{Q}_1 > 0$, $\bar{Q}_2 > 0$, $\bar{S} > 0$, $\bar{M} > 0$, G, Y*

$$\bar{L} = \begin{bmatrix} \bar{L}_1 \\ \bar{L}_2 \\ \bar{L}_3 \\ \bar{L}_4 \\ \bar{L}_5 \end{bmatrix}, \quad \bar{N} = \begin{bmatrix} \bar{N}_1 \\ \bar{N}_2 \\ \bar{N}_3 \\ \bar{N}_4 \\ \bar{N}_5 \end{bmatrix},$$

and a scalar $\lambda > 0$ *satisfying*

$$\Lambda = \begin{bmatrix} \Psi + \lambda \hat{H}^T \hat{H} & \hat{E}^T \\ \hat{E} & -\lambda I \end{bmatrix} < 0, \tag{16}$$

where

$$\hat{H} = \begin{bmatrix} -\rho_1 H^T & -\rho_2 H^T & -\rho_3 H^T & -\rho_4 H^T & -\rho_5 H^T & 0 \end{bmatrix},$$

and

$$\hat{E} = \begin{bmatrix} 0 & EY^T + E_1 G & E_d Y^T + E_b G & 0 & 0 & 0 \end{bmatrix}.$$

In this case, a controller gain in the controller (4) is given by (15).

Proof: Replacing A, A_d, B and B_d in (14) with $A + HF(k)E$, $A_d + HF(k)E_d$, $B + HF(k)E_1$ and $B + HF(k)E_b$, respectively, we obtain robust stability conditions for the system (1):

$$\Psi + \bar{H}^T F(k) \bar{E} + \bar{E}^T F^T(k) \bar{H} < 0 \tag{17}$$

By Lemma 2.2, a necessary and sufficient condition that guarantees (17) is that there exists a scalar $\lambda > 0$ such that

$$\Psi + \lambda \bar{H}^T \bar{H} + \frac{1}{\lambda} \bar{E}^T \bar{E} < 0 \tag{18}$$

Applying Schur complement formula, we can show that (18) is equivalent to (16).

5. State estimation

All the information on the state variables of the system is not always available in a physical situation. In this case, we need to estimate the values of the state variables from all the available information on the output and input. In the following, we make analysis of the existence of observers. Section 5.1 analyzes the observer of a nominal system, and Section 5.2 considers the robust observer analysis of an uncertain system.

5.1 Observer analysis

Using the results in the previous sections, we consider an observer design for the system (1), which estimates the state variables of the system using measurement outputs.

$$x(k+1) = (A + \Delta A)x(k) + (A_d + \Delta A_d)x(k - d_k), \tag{19}$$

$$y(k) = (C + \Delta C)x(k) + (C_d + \Delta C_d)x(k - d_k) \tag{20}$$

where uncertain matrices are of the form:

$$\begin{bmatrix} \Delta A & \Delta A_d \\ \Delta C & \Delta C_d \end{bmatrix} = \begin{bmatrix} H \\ H_2 \end{bmatrix} F(k) \begin{bmatrix} E & E_d \end{bmatrix}$$

where $F(k) \in \Re^{l \times j}$ is an unknown time-varying matrix satisfying $F^T(k)F(k) \leq I$ and H, H_2, E and E_d are constant matrices of appropriate dimensions.
We consider the following system to estimate the state variables:

$$\hat{x}(k+1) = A\hat{x}(k) + \bar{K}(y(k) - C\hat{x}(k)) \tag{21}$$

where $\hat{x}$ is the estimated state and $\bar{K}$ is an observer gain to be determined. It follows from (19), (20) and (21) that

$$x_c(k+1) = (\tilde{A} + \tilde{H}F(k)\tilde{E})x_c(k) + (\tilde{A}_d + \tilde{H}F(k)\tilde{E}_d)x_c(k-d_k). \quad (22)$$

where $x_c^T = [x^T \ e^T]^T$, $e(k) = x(k) - \hat{x}(k)$ and

$$\tilde{A} = \begin{bmatrix} A & 0 \\ 0 & A - \bar{K}C \end{bmatrix}, \ \tilde{A}_d = \begin{bmatrix} A_d & 0 \\ A_d - \bar{K}C_d & 0 \end{bmatrix},$$

$$\tilde{H} = \begin{bmatrix} H \\ H - \bar{K}H_2 \end{bmatrix}, \ \tilde{E} = \begin{bmatrix} E \ 0 \end{bmatrix}, \ \tilde{E}_d = \begin{bmatrix} E_d \ 0 \end{bmatrix}.$$

We shall find conditions for (22) to be robustly stable. In this case, the system (21) becomes an observer for the system (19) and (20).

For nominal case, we have

$$x_c(k+1) = \tilde{A}x_c(k) + \tilde{A}_d x_c(k-d_k). \quad (23)$$

We first consider the asymptotic stability of the system (23). The following theorem gives conditions for the system (23) to be asymptotically stable.

Theorem 5.1. *Given integers d_m and d_M, and observer gain $\bar{K}$. Then, the system (23) is asymptotically stable if there exist matrices $0 < \tilde{P}_1 \in \Re^{2n\times 2n}$, $< \tilde{P}_2 \in \Re^{2n\times 2n}$, $0 < \tilde{Q}_1 \in \Re^{2n\times 2n}$, $0 < \tilde{Q}_2 \in \Re^{2n\times 2n}$, $0 < \tilde{S} \in \Re^{2n\times 2n}$, $0 < \tilde{M} \in \Re^{2n\times 2n}$,*

$$\tilde{L} = \begin{bmatrix} \tilde{L}_1 \\ \tilde{L}_2 \\ \tilde{L}_3 \\ \tilde{L}_4 \\ \tilde{L}_5 \end{bmatrix} \in \Re^{10n\times 2n}, \ \tilde{N} = \begin{bmatrix} \tilde{N}_1 \\ \tilde{N}_2 \\ \tilde{N}_3 \\ \tilde{N}_4 \\ \tilde{N}_5 \end{bmatrix} \in \Re^{10n\times 2n}, \ \tilde{T} = \begin{bmatrix} \tilde{T}_1 \\ \tilde{T}_2 \\ \tilde{T}_3 \\ \tilde{T}_4 \\ \tilde{T}_5 \end{bmatrix} \in \Re^{10n\times 2n}$$

satisfying

$$\tilde{\Phi} = \begin{bmatrix} \tilde{\Phi}_1 + \tilde{\Xi}_L + \tilde{\Xi}_L^T + \tilde{\Xi}_N + \tilde{\Xi}_N^T + \tilde{\Xi}_T + \tilde{\Xi}_T^T & \sqrt{d_M}\tilde{Z} \\ \sqrt{d_M}\tilde{Z}^T & -\tilde{S} \end{bmatrix} < 0 \quad (24)$$

where

$$\tilde{\Phi}_1 = \begin{bmatrix} \tilde{P}_1 & 0 & 0 & 0 & 0 \\ 0 & \tilde{\Phi}_{22} & 0 & 0 & 0 \\ 0 & 0 & -\tilde{Q}_1 - \tilde{M} & 0 & 0 \\ 0 & 0 & 0 & \tilde{\Phi}_{44} & -\tilde{P}_2 \\ 0 & 0 & 0 & -\tilde{P}_2 & \tilde{P}_2 - \tilde{Q}_2 \end{bmatrix},$$

$$\tilde{\Phi}_{22} = -\tilde{P}_1 + \tilde{Q}_1 + (d_M - d_m + 1)\tilde{M},$$

$$\tilde{\Phi}_{44} = \tilde{P}_2 + \tilde{Q}_2 + d_M\tilde{S},$$

$$\tilde{Z} = \begin{bmatrix} 0 \\ 0 \\ 0 \\ -\tilde{P}_2 \\ \tilde{P}_2 \end{bmatrix} + \tilde{N},$$

$$\tilde{\Xi}_L = \begin{bmatrix} \tilde{L} & -\tilde{L} & 0 & -\tilde{L} & 0 \end{bmatrix},$$

$$\tilde{\Xi}_N = \begin{bmatrix} 0 & \tilde{N} & -\tilde{N} & 0 & 0 \end{bmatrix},$$

$$\tilde{\Xi}_T = \begin{bmatrix} \tilde{T} & -\tilde{T}\tilde{A} & -\tilde{T}\tilde{A}_d & 0 & 0 \end{bmatrix}.$$

Proof: We follow similar lines of proof of Theorem 3.1 for the stability of the system (23). Then, the result is straightforward.

5.2 Robust observer analysis

Now, we extend the result for the uncertain system (23).

Theorem 5.2. *Given integers d_m and d_M, and observer gain $\bar{K}$. Then, the system (22) is robustly stable if there exist matrices $0 < \tilde{P}_1 \in \Re^{2n\times 2n}$, $< \tilde{P}_2 \in \Re^{2n\times 2n}$, $0 < \tilde{Q}_1 \in \Re^{2n\times 2n}$, $0 < \tilde{Q}_2 \in \Re^{2n\times 2n}$, $0 < \tilde{S} \in \Re^{2n\times 2n}$, $0 < \tilde{M} \in \Re^{2n\times 2n}$,*

$$\tilde{L} = \begin{bmatrix} \tilde{L}_1 \\ \tilde{L}_2 \\ \tilde{L}_3 \\ \tilde{L}_4 \\ \tilde{L}_5 \end{bmatrix} \in \Re^{10n\times 2n},\ \tilde{N} = \begin{bmatrix} \tilde{N}_1 \\ \tilde{N}_2 \\ \tilde{N}_3 \\ \tilde{N}_4 \\ \tilde{N}_5 \end{bmatrix} \in \Re^{10n\times 2n},\ \tilde{T} = \begin{bmatrix} \tilde{T}_1 \\ \tilde{T}_2 \\ \tilde{T}_3 \\ \tilde{T}_4 \\ \tilde{T}_5 \end{bmatrix} \in \Re^{10n\times 2n}$$

and a scalar $\lambda > 0$ satisfying

$$\tilde{\Pi} = \begin{bmatrix} \tilde{\Phi} + \lambda \hat{E}^T \hat{E} & \hat{H}^T \\ \hat{H} & -\lambda I \end{bmatrix} < 0$$

where $\tilde{\Phi}$ is given in Theorem 5.1, and

$$\begin{aligned} \hat{H} &= \begin{bmatrix} -\tilde{H}^T \tilde{T}_1^T & -\tilde{H}^T \tilde{T}_2^T & -\tilde{H}^T \tilde{T}_3^T & -\tilde{H}^T \tilde{T}_4^T & -\tilde{H}^T \tilde{T}_5^T & 0 \end{bmatrix}, \\ \hat{E} &= \begin{bmatrix} 0 & \tilde{E} & \tilde{E}_d & 0 & 0 & 0 \end{bmatrix}. \end{aligned}$$

Proof: Replacing $\tilde{A}$ and $\tilde{A}_d$ in (24) with $\tilde{A} + \tilde{H}F(k)\tilde{E}$ and $\tilde{A}_d + \tilde{H}F(k)\tilde{E}_d$, respectively, and following similar lines of proof of Theorem 3.3, we have the desired result.

6. Observer design

This section gives observer design methods for discrete-time delay systems. Section 6.1 provides an observer design method for a nominal delay system, and Section 6.2 proposes for an uncertain delay system.

6.1 Nominal observer

Similar to Theorem 3.1, Theorem 5.1 does not give a design method of finding an observer gain $\bar{K}$. Hence, we obtain another theorem below.

Theorem 6.1. *Given integers d_m and d_M, and scalars ρ_i and $\hat{\rho}_i$, $i = 1, \cdots, 5$. Then, (21) becomes an observer for the system (19) and (20) with $\Delta A = \Delta A_d = 0$, $\Delta C = \Delta C_d = 0$ if there exist matrices $0 < \tilde{P}_1 \in \Re^{2n\times 2n}$, $0 < \tilde{P}_2 \in \Re^{2n\times 2n}$, $0 < \tilde{Q}_1 \in \Re^{2n\times 2n}$, $0 < \tilde{Q}_2 \in \Re^{2n\times 2n}$, $0 < \tilde{S} \in \Re^{2n\times 2n}$, $0 < \tilde{M} \in \Re^{2n\times 2n}$, $\tilde{G} \in \Re^{n\times n}$, $Y \in \Re^{n\times n}$*

$$\tilde{L} = \begin{bmatrix} \tilde{L}_1 \\ \tilde{L}_2 \\ \tilde{L}_3 \\ \tilde{L}_4 \\ \tilde{L}_5 \end{bmatrix} \in \Re^{10n\times 2n},\ \tilde{N} = \begin{bmatrix} \tilde{N}_1 \\ \tilde{N}_2 \\ \tilde{N}_3 \\ \tilde{N}_4 \\ \tilde{N}_5 \end{bmatrix} \in \Re^{10n\times 2n},\ T = \begin{bmatrix} T_1 \\ T_2 \\ T_3 \\ T_4 \\ T_5 \end{bmatrix} \in \Re^{5n\times n},\ \hat{T} = \begin{bmatrix} \hat{T}_1 \\ \hat{T}_2 \\ \hat{T}_3 \\ \hat{T}_4 \\ \hat{T}_5 \end{bmatrix} \in \Re^{5n\times n}$$

satisfying

$$\tilde{\Psi} = \begin{bmatrix} \tilde{\Psi}_1 + \tilde{\Theta}_L + \tilde{\Theta}_L^T + \tilde{\Theta}_N + \tilde{\Theta}_N^T + \tilde{\Theta}_T + \tilde{\Theta}_T^T & \sqrt{d_M}\tilde{Z} \\ \sqrt{d_M}\tilde{Z}^T & -\tilde{S} \end{bmatrix} < 0 \tag{25}$$

where

$$\tilde{\Psi}_1 = \begin{bmatrix} \tilde{P}_1 & 0 & 0 & 0 & 0 \\ 0 & \tilde{\Psi}_{22} & 0 & 0 & 0 \\ 0 & 0 & -\tilde{Q}_1 - \tilde{M} & 0 & 0 \\ 0 & 0 & 0 & \tilde{\Psi}_{44} & -\tilde{P}_2 \\ 0 & 0 & 0 & -\tilde{P}_2 & \tilde{P}_2 - \tilde{Q}_2 \end{bmatrix},$$

$$\tilde{\Psi}_{22} = -\tilde{P}_1 + \tilde{Q}_1 + (d_M - d_m + 1)\tilde{M},$$

$$\tilde{\Psi}_{44} = \tilde{P}_2 + \tilde{Q}_2 + d_M\tilde{S},$$

$$\tilde{Z} = \begin{bmatrix} 0 \\ 0 \\ 0 \\ -\tilde{P}_2 \\ \tilde{P}_2 \end{bmatrix} + \tilde{N},$$

$$\tilde{\Theta}_L = \begin{bmatrix} \tilde{L} & -\tilde{L} & 0 & -\tilde{L} & 0 \end{bmatrix},$$

$$\tilde{\Theta}_N = \begin{bmatrix} 0 & \tilde{N} & -\tilde{N} & 0 & 0 \end{bmatrix},$$

$$\tilde{\Theta}_T = \begin{bmatrix} T_1 & \rho_1 Y & -T_1 A & -\rho_1(YA - \tilde{G}C) & -T_1 A_d - \rho_1(YA_d - \tilde{G}C_d) & 0 & 0 & 0 & 0 & 0 \\ \hat{T}_1 & \hat{\rho}_1 Y & -\hat{T}_1 A & -\hat{\rho}_1(YA - \tilde{G}C) & -\hat{T}_1 A_d - \hat{\rho}_1(YA_d - \tilde{G}C_d) & 0 & 0 & 0 & 0 & 0 \\ T_2 & \rho_2 Y & -T_2 A & -\rho_2(YA - \tilde{G}C) & -T_2 A_d - \rho_2(YA_d - \tilde{G}C_d) & 0 & 0 & 0 & 0 & 0 \\ \hat{T}_2 & \hat{\rho}_2 Y & -\hat{T}_2 A & -\hat{\rho}_2(YA - \tilde{G}C) & -\hat{T}_2 A_d - \hat{\rho}_2(YA_d - \tilde{G}C_d) & 0 & 0 & 0 & 0 & 0 \\ T_3 & \rho_3 Y & -T_3 A & -\rho_3(YA - \tilde{G}C) & -T_3 A_d - \rho_3(YA_d - \tilde{G}C_d) & 0 & 0 & 0 & 0 & 0 \\ \hat{T}_3 & \hat{\rho}_3 Y & -\hat{T}_3 A & -\hat{\rho}_3(YA - \tilde{G}C) & -\hat{T}_3 A_d - \hat{\rho}_3(YA_d - \tilde{G}C_d) & 0 & 0 & 0 & 0 & 0 \\ T_4 & \rho_4 Y & -T_4 A & -\rho_4(YA - \tilde{G}C) & -T_4 A_d - \rho_4(YA_d - \tilde{G}C_d) & 0 & 0 & 0 & 0 & 0 \\ \hat{T}_4 & \hat{\rho}_4 Y & -\hat{T}_4 A & -\hat{\rho}_4(YA - \tilde{G}C) & -\hat{T}_4 A_d - \hat{\rho}_4(YA_d - \tilde{G}C_d) & 0 & 0 & 0 & 0 & 0 \\ T_5 & \rho_5 Y & -T_5 A & -\rho_5(YA - \tilde{G}C) & -T_5 A_d - \rho_5(YA_d - \tilde{G}C_d) & 0 & 0 & 0 & 0 & 0 \\ \hat{T}_5 & \hat{\rho}_5 Y & -\hat{T}_5 A & -\hat{\rho}_5(YA - \tilde{G}C) & -\hat{T}_5 A_d - \hat{\rho}_5(YA_d - \tilde{G}C_d) & 0 & 0 & 0 & 0 & 0 \end{bmatrix}.$$

In this case, an observer gain in the observer (21) is given by

$$\bar{K} = Y^{-1}\tilde{G}. \tag{26}$$

Proof: Proof is similar to that of Theorem 4.1. Let

$$T_i = \begin{bmatrix} T_i & \rho_i Y \\ \hat{T}_i & \hat{\rho}_i Y \end{bmatrix}, \; i = 1, \cdots, 5$$

where ρ_i and $\hat{\rho}_i$, $i = 1, \cdots, 5$ are given. We substitute them into (24). Defining $\tilde{G} = Y\bar{K}$, we obtain $\tilde{\Psi} < 0$ in (25). If the condition (25) hold, observer gain matrix $\bar{K}$ is obviously given by (26).

6.2 Robust observer

Extending Theorem 4.1, we have the following theorem, which proposes a robust observer design for an uncertain delay system.

Theorem 6.2. *Given integers d_m and d_M, and scalars ρ_i, $\hat{\rho}_i$, $i = 1, \cdots, 5$. Then, (21) becomes an observer for the system (19) and (20) if there exist matrices $0 < \tilde{P}_1 \in \Re^{2n\times 2n}$, $0 < \tilde{P}_2 \in \Re^{2n\times 2n}$, $0 < \tilde{Q}_1 \in \Re^{2n\times 2n}$, $0 < \tilde{Q}_2 \in \Re^{2n\times 2n}$, $0 < \tilde{S} \in \Re^{2n\times 2n}$, $0 < \tilde{M} \in \Re^{2n\times 2n}$, $G \in \Re^{n\times n}$, $Y \in \Re^{n\times n}$*

$$\tilde{L} = \begin{bmatrix} \tilde{L}_1 \\ \tilde{L}_2 \\ \tilde{L}_3 \\ \tilde{L}_4 \\ \tilde{L}_5 \end{bmatrix} \in \Re^{10n\times 2n},\ \tilde{N} = \begin{bmatrix} \tilde{N}_1 \\ \tilde{N}_2 \\ \tilde{N}_3 \\ \tilde{N}_4 \\ \tilde{N}_5 \end{bmatrix} \in \Re^{10n\times 2n},\ T = \begin{bmatrix} T_1 \\ T_2 \\ T_3 \\ T_4 \\ T_5 \end{bmatrix} \in \Re^{5n\times n},\ \hat{T} = \begin{bmatrix} \hat{T}_1 \\ \hat{T}_2 \\ \hat{T}_3 \\ \hat{T}_4 \\ \hat{T}_5 \end{bmatrix} \in \Re^{5n\times n},$$

and a scalar $\lambda > 0$ satisfying

$$\tilde{\Lambda} = \begin{bmatrix} \tilde{\Psi} + \lambda \tilde{E}^T \tilde{E} & \tilde{H}^T \\ \tilde{H} & -\lambda I \end{bmatrix} < 0 \tag{27}$$

where $\tilde{\Psi}$ is given in Theorem 6.1, and

$$\begin{aligned} \tilde{H} = -\ & [H^T T_1^T + \rho_1 (YH - \tilde{G}H_2)^T\ H^T \hat{T}_1^T + \hat{\rho}_1 (YH - \tilde{G}H_2)^T\ H^T T_2^T + \rho_2 (YH - \tilde{G}H_2)^T \\ & H^T \hat{T}_2^T + \hat{\rho}_2 (YH - \tilde{G}H_2)^T\ H^T T_3^T + \rho_3 (YH - \tilde{G}H_2)^T\ H^T \hat{T}_3^T + \hat{\rho}_3 (YH - \tilde{G}H_2)^T \\ & H^T T_4^T + \rho_4 (YH - \tilde{G}H_2)^T\ H^T \hat{T}_4^T + \hat{\rho}_4 (YH - \tilde{G}H_2)^T\ H^T T_5^T + \rho_5 (YH - \tilde{G}H_2)^T \\ & H^T \hat{T}_5^T + \hat{\rho}_5 (YH - \tilde{G}H_2)^T\ 0\ 0], \\ \tilde{E} =\ & [0\ 0\ E\ 0\ E_d\ 0\ 0\ 0\ 0\ 0\ 0\ 0]. \end{aligned}$$

In this case, an observer gain in the observer (21) is given by (26).

Proof: Replacing A and A_d in (27) with $A + HF(k)E$ and $A_d + HF(k)E_d$, respectively, and following similar lines of proof of Theorem 4.3, we have the desired result.

7. Examples

In this section, the following examples are provided to illustrate the proposed results. First example shows stabilization and robust stabilization. Second one gives observer design and robust observer design.

Example 7.1. *Consider the following discrete-time delay system:*

$$\begin{aligned} x(k+1) =\ & \begin{bmatrix} 1.1 + \alpha & 0 \\ 0 & 0.97 \end{bmatrix} x(k) + \begin{bmatrix} -0.1 & 0 \\ -0.1 & -0.1 \end{bmatrix} x(k - d_k) \\ & + \begin{bmatrix} 0.1 \\ 0.5 \end{bmatrix} u(k) + \begin{bmatrix} 0.2 \\ 0.3 \end{bmatrix} u(k - d_k) \end{aligned}$$

where α satisfies $|\alpha| \leq \bar{\alpha}$ for $\bar{\alpha}$ is an upper bound of $\alpha(k)$. First, we consider the stabilization for a nominal time-delay system with $\alpha(k) = 0$ by Theorem 4.1. Table 1 shows control gains for different time-invariant delay d_k, while Table 2 gives control gains for different time-varying delay d_k.
Next, we consider the robust stabilization for the uncertain time-delay system with $\alpha(k) \neq 0$. In this case, system matrices can be represented in the form of (1) with matrices given by

$$A = \begin{bmatrix} 1.1 & 0 \\ 0 & 0.97 \end{bmatrix},\ A_d = \begin{bmatrix} -0.1 & 0 \\ -0.1 & -0.1 \end{bmatrix},\ E = \begin{bmatrix} 1 & 0 \end{bmatrix},\ E_d = E_1 = \begin{bmatrix} 0 & 0 \end{bmatrix},$$

$$B = \begin{bmatrix} 0.1 \\ 0.5 \end{bmatrix},\ B_d = \begin{bmatrix} 0.2 \\ 0.3 \end{bmatrix},\ H = \begin{bmatrix} \bar{\alpha} \\ 0 \end{bmatrix},\ F(k) = \frac{\alpha(k)}{\bar{\alpha}}.$$

d_k	ρ's	K
1	$[0.1\ 0.1\ \ -0.1\ 0.5\ 0.1]$	$[-1.1316\ \ -0.1360]$
2	$[0.1\ 0.1\ \ -0.1\ 0.5\ 0.1]$	$[-0.9690\ \ -0.0976]$
3	$[0.1\ 0.1\ \ -0.1\ 0.5\ 0.1]$	$[-0.7908\ \ -0.0545]$
4	$[0.09\ 0.05\ \ -0.1\ 0.55\ 0.1]$	$[-0.5815\ \ -0.0306]$

Table 1. The stabilization for time-invariant delay d_k

d_k	ρ's	K
$0 \le d_k \le 1$	$[0.1\ 0.1\ \ -0.1\ 0.5\ 0.1]$	$[-1.1209\ \ -0.1174]$
$0 \le d_k \le 2$	$[0.1\ 0.1\ \ -0.1\ 0.5\ 0.1]$	$[-0.9429\ \ -0.0839]$
$0 \le d_k \le 3$	$[0.1\ 0.1\ \ -0.1\ 0.5\ 0.1]$	$[-0.7950\ \ -0.0469]$
$0 \le d_k \le 4$	$[0.09\ 0.05\ \ -0.1\ 0.55\ 0.1]$	$[-0.5586\ \ -0.0253]$

Table 2. The stabilization for time-varying delay d_k

d_k	$\bar{\alpha}$	ρ's	K
3	0.05	$[0.1\ 0.1\ \ -0.1\ 0.5\ 0.1]$	$[-0.8622\ \ -0.0059]$
3	0.10	$[0.1\ 0.1\ \ -0.1\ 0.5\ 0.1]$	$[-0.6243\ \ -0.0000]$
2	0.15	$[0.12\ 0.12\ \ -0.1\ 0.5\ 0.05]$	$[-1.2515\ \ -0.0115]$

Table 3. The robust stabilization for time-invariant delay d_k

d_k	$\bar{\alpha}$	ρ's	K
$0 \le d_k \le 3$	0.05	$[0.1\ 0.1\ \ -0.1\ 0.5\ 0.1]$	$[-0.8394\ \ -0.0047]$
$0 \le d_k \le 3$	0.10	$[0.12\ 0.1\ \ -0.1\ 0.5\ 0.1]$	$[-1.2539\ \ -0.0108]$
$0 \le d_k \le 2$	0.15	$[0.12\ 0.12\ \ -0.1\ 0.5\ 0.05]$	$[-1.1740\ \ -0.0015]$

Table 4. The robust stabilization for time-varying delay d_k

For time-invariant delay d_k, Theorem 4.3 gives control gains for different $\bar{\alpha}$ in Table 3. Table 4 provides the result for time-varying delay d_k.

Example 7.2. *Consider the following discrete-time delay system:*

$$\begin{aligned} x(k+1) &= \begin{bmatrix} 0.85+0.1\alpha & 0 \\ 0 & 0.97 \end{bmatrix} x(k) + \begin{bmatrix} -0.1 & 0 \\ -0.1 & -0.1 \end{bmatrix} x(k-d_k), \\ y(k) &= \begin{bmatrix} 0.5 \ 0.2 \end{bmatrix} x(k) + \begin{bmatrix} 0.1 \ 0.1 \end{bmatrix} x(k-d_k) \end{aligned}$$

where α satisfies $|\alpha| \le \bar{\alpha}$ for $\bar{\alpha}$ is an upper bound of $\alpha(k)$. We first consider the observer design for a nominal time-delay system with $\alpha(k) = 0$ by Theorem 6.1. Table 5 shows observer gains for different time-invariant delay d_k, while Table 6 gives observer gains for different time-varying delay d_k. In the following observer design, all ρ's are set to be zero for simplicity.
Next, we consider the robust observer design for the uncertain time-delay system with $\alpha(k) \ne 0$. In this case, system matrices can be represented in the form of (1) with matrices given by

$$A = \begin{bmatrix} 0.85 & 0 \\ 0 & 0.97 \end{bmatrix}, A_d = \begin{bmatrix} -0.1 & 0 \\ -0.1 & -0.1 \end{bmatrix}, \ E = \begin{bmatrix} \bar{\alpha} \ 0 \end{bmatrix}, E_d = E_1 = \begin{bmatrix} 0 \ 0 \end{bmatrix},$$

$$C = \begin{bmatrix} 0.5 \ 0.2 \end{bmatrix}, \ C_d = \begin{bmatrix} 0.1 \ 0.1 \end{bmatrix}, \ H = \begin{bmatrix} 0.1 \\ 0 \end{bmatrix}, \ F(k) = \frac{\alpha(k)}{\bar{\alpha}}.$$

d_k	$\hat{\rho}$'s	$\bar{K}$
1	$[-22.6\ 2.5\ -2.1\ -1.9\ -1.9]$	$\begin{bmatrix}0.4835\\0.3622\end{bmatrix}$
2	$[-21.9\ 6.7\ -0.3\ -2.6\ -1.9]$	$\begin{bmatrix}0.5372\\0.3348\end{bmatrix}$
3	$[-23.4\ 8.6\ 0.2\ -1.9\ -1.9]$	$\begin{bmatrix}0.5174\\0.3910\end{bmatrix}$
4	$[-9.0\ 26.4\ 0.2\ -2.5\ -1.9]$	$\begin{bmatrix}-3.2281\\0.0459\end{bmatrix}$
5	$[-9.0\ 25.9\ 0.2\ -2.5\ -1.9]$	$\begin{bmatrix}-2.3508\\-0.7232\end{bmatrix}$

Table 5. The observer design for time-invariant delay d_k

d_k	$\hat{\rho}$'s	$\bar{K}$
$0 \le d_k \le 1$	$[-20.2\ 6.5\ -2.1\ -2.5\ -1.9]$	$\begin{bmatrix}0.6295\\0.3777\end{bmatrix}$
$0 \le d_k \le 2$	$[-21.9\ 6.7\ -0.3\ -2.6\ -1.9]$	$\begin{bmatrix}0.5817\\0.3475\end{bmatrix}$
$0 \le d_k \le 3$	$[-22.0\ 8.6\ 0.2\ -1.9\ -1.9]$	$\begin{bmatrix}0.5490\\0.3037\end{bmatrix}$
$0 \le d_k \le 4$	$[-22.0\ 8.6\ 0.2\ -2.5\ -1.9]$	$\begin{bmatrix}0.5157\\0.2921\end{bmatrix}$
$0 \le d_k \le 5$	$[-22.5\ 8.6\ 0.2\ -1.9\ -3.1]$	$\begin{bmatrix}0.5170\\0.2956\end{bmatrix}$

Table 6. The observer design for time-varying delay d_k

d_k	$\bar{\alpha}$	$\hat{\rho}$'s	$\bar{K}$
1	0.5	$[-22.6\ 2.5\ -2.1\ -1.9\ -1.9]$	$\begin{bmatrix}0.5047\\0.3813\end{bmatrix}$
2	0.4	$[-21.9\ 6.7\ -0.3\ -2.6\ -1.9]$	$\begin{bmatrix}0.5625\\0.3633\end{bmatrix}$
3	0.3	$[-23.4\ 8.6\ 0.2\ -1.9\ -1.9]$	$\begin{bmatrix}0.5264\\0.3641\end{bmatrix}$
4	0.3	$[-9.0\ 26.4\ 0.2\ -2.5\ -1.9]$	$\begin{bmatrix}-2.6343\\-1.6768\end{bmatrix}$
5	0.2	$[-9.0\ 25.9\ 0.2\ -2.5\ -1.9]$	$\begin{bmatrix}-2.5959\\-1.5602\end{bmatrix}$

Table 7. The observer design for time-invariant delay d_k

For time-invariant delay d_k, Theorem 6.2 gives observer gains for different $\bar{\alpha}$ in Table 7. Table 8 provides observer gains for time-varying delay d_k by the same theorem.

8. Conclusions

In this paper, we proposed stabilization and robust stabilization method for discrete-time systems with time-varying delay. Our conditions were obtained by introducing new Lyapunov function and using Leibniz-Newton formula and free weighting matrix method.

d_k	$\bar{\alpha}$	$\bar{\rho}$'s	$\bar{K}$
$0 \le d_k \le 1$	0.5	$[-20.2\ \ 6.5\ \ -2.1\ \ -2.5\ \ -1.9]$	$\begin{bmatrix}0.6345\\0.3520\end{bmatrix}$
$0 \le d_k \le 2$	0.4	$[-21.9\ \ 6.7\ \ -0.3\ \ -2.6\ \ -1.9]$	$\begin{bmatrix}0.5870\\0.3153\end{bmatrix}$
$0 \le d_k \le 3$	0.3	$[-22.0\ \ 8.6\ \ 0.2\ \ -1.9\ \ -1.9]$	$\begin{bmatrix}0.5675\\0.3003\end{bmatrix}$
$0 \le d_k \le 4$	0.3	$[-22.0\ \ 8.6\ \ 0.2\ \ -2.5\ \ -1.9]$	$\begin{bmatrix}0.5375\\0.3444\end{bmatrix}$
$0 \le d_k \le 5$	0.2	$[-22.5\ \ 8.6\ \ 0.2\ \ -1.9\ \ -3.1]$	$\begin{bmatrix}0.5077\\0.3425\end{bmatrix}$

Table 8. The observer design for time-varying delay d_k

Similarly, we also gave observer design and robust observer design methods. Numerical examples were given to illustrate our proposed design method.

9. References

[1] Fridman, E. & Shaked, U. (2005). Stability and guaranteed cost control of uncertain discrete delay systems, *International Journal of Control*, Vol.78, 235-246.

[2] Fridman, E. & Shaked, U. (2005). Delay-dependent H_∞ control of uncertain discrete delay systems, *European Journal of Control*, Vol.11, 29-37.

[3] Gao, H.; Lam, J.:Wang, C. & Wang, Y. (2004). delay-dependent output feedback stabilization of discrete-time systems with time-varying state delay, *IEE Proc. Control Theory Appl.*, Vol.151, 691-698.

[4] Gao, H. & Chen, T. (2007). New results on stability of discrete-time systems with time-varying state delay, *IEEE Transactions on Automatic Control*, Vol.52, 328-334.

[5] Hara, M. & Yoneyama, J. (2008), New robust stability condition for uncertain discrete-time systems with time-varying delay, in *SICE Annual Conference 2008*, 743-747, Tokyo, August 2008.

[6] Hara, M. & Yoneyama, J. (2009). An improved robust stability condition for uncertain discrete time-varying delay systems, *Journal of Cybernetics and Systems*, Vol.2, 23-27.

[7] He, Y.; Wang, Q.; Xie, L. & Lin, C. (2007). Further improvement of free-weighting matrices technique for systems with time-varying delay, *IEEE Transactions on Automatic Control*, Vol.52, 293-299.

[8] Li, X. & de Souza, C. E. (1997). Delay dependent robust stability and stabilization of uncertain linear delay systems: a linear matrix inequality approach, *IEEE Transactions on Automatic Control*, Vol.42, 1144-1148.

[9] Liu, Y.; Wang, Z. & Liu, X. (2008). Robust H_∞ filtering for discrete nonlinear stochastic systems with time-varying delay, *Journal of Mathematical Analysis and Applications*, Vol.341, 318-336.

[10] Ma, S.; Zhang, C. & Cheng, Z. (2008). Delay-dependent Robust H_∞ Control for Uncertain Discrete-Time Singular Systems with Time-Delays, *Journal of Computational and Applied Mathematics*, Vol.217, 194-211.

[11] Mahmoud, M.S. (2000). *Robust Control and Filtering for Time-Delay Systems*, New York: Marcel Dekker, Inc.

[12] Palhares, R.M.; Campos, C.D.; Ekel, P. Ya.; Leles, M.C.R. & D'Angelo, M.F.S.V. (2005). Delay-dependent robust H_∞ control of uncertain linear systems with lumped delays, *IEE Proc. Control Theory Appl.*, Vol.152, 27-33

[13] Xie, L. (1996). Output Feedback H_∞ Control of systems with parameter uncertainty, *International Journal of Control*, Vol.63, 741-750.

[14] Xu, S.; Lam, J. & Zou, Y. (2005). Improved conditions for delay-dependent robust stability and stabilization of uncertain discrete-time systems, *Asian Journal of Control*, Vol.7, 344-348.

[15] Xu, S.; Lam, J. & Zou, Y. (2006). New results on delay-dependent robust H_∞ control for systems with time-varying delays, *Automatica*, Vol.42, 343-348.

[16] Ye, D. & Yang, G. H. (2008). Adaptive robust H_∞ state feedback control for linear uncertain systems with time-varying delay, *International Journal of Adaptive Control and Signal Processing*, Vol.22, 845-858.

[17] Yoneyama, J. (2008). H_∞ disturbance attenuation for discrete-time systems with time varying delays, *SICE Transactions*, Vol.44, 285-287(in Japanese).

[18] Yoneyama, J. & Tsuchiya, T. (2008). New delay-dependent conditions on robust stability and stabilisation for discrete-time systems with time-delay, *International Journal of Systems Science*, Vol.39, 1033-1040.

[19] Zhang, X.-M. & Han, Q.-L. (2008). A new finite sum inequality approach to delay-dependent H_∞ control of discrete-time systems with time-varying delay, *International Journal of Robust and Nonlinear Control*, Vol.18, 630-647.

12

Quadratic D Stabilizable Satisfactory Fault-tolerant Control with Constraints of Consistent Indices for Satellite Attitude Control Systems

Han Xiaodong[1] and Zhang Dengfeng[2]
[1]*Institute of Telecommunication Satellite, CAST, Beijing 100094*
[2]*Nanjing University of Science and Technology, Nanjing 210094, P.R. China*

1. Introduction

In the last twenty some years, much attention has been paid to the problem of fault-tolerant control in satellite attitude control systems and many methods have been developed and proven to be capable of tolerating certain types of system faults (see e.g., [1~5] and the references therein). However, these solutions focused mainly on keeping stability of the faulty systems and in less consideration of other performance indices. Actually, the performance requirements of practical satellite control systems are usually multi-objective even in faulty cases and it is desirable for fault tolerant systems to keep the required performance indices in a satisfactory and admissible region rather than the optimization of single index [6~7].

As is well known, in many practical applications, it is desirable to construct systems to achieve better transient property, strong anti-disturbance ability and adequate level of cost function performance. To this end, optimal controllers have been designed by assigning pole in a desired region (see e.g., [8] and [9]), using H_∞ norm-bound constraint on disturbance attenuation [10, 11] and the guaranteed cost control (see [12] and [13]), respectively. Unfortunately, few results have been considered such performance indices simultaneously. Meanwhile, once some components of satellite attitude control systems go wrong, it is difficult to confirm desired multiple performances by the existing fault-tolerant control. Thus, it is necessary to investigate the problem of fault-tolerant control with multiple performance constraints.

Therefore, it is our motivation to investigate the quadratic D stabilizable satisfactory fault-tolerant control problem with consistent indices constraints for a class of satellite attitude control uncertain discrete-time systems subject to actuator failures. In view of possible actuator failure as well as uncertainties which do not satisfy matching conditions existing in both the state and control input matrices, we first derive the existence conditions of satisfactory fault-tolerant state-feedback control law. Then by LMI technique, a convex optimization problem is formulated to find the corresponding controller. The state-feedback controller is designed to guarantee the closed-loop system satisfying the pre-specified quadratic D stabilizability index, H_∞ norm-bound constraint on disturbance attenuation and having the quadratic cost performance simultaneously, for all admissible value-bounded uncertainties and possible actuator failures. Furthermore, the consistency of the performance indices mentioned earlier is discussed for fault-tolerant control. Finally, simulative example is provided to illustrate the validity of the proposed method and the necessity of such a satisfactory fault-tolerant control.

2. Problem formulation

The systems considered in this paper can be described as follows:

$$\begin{aligned} \mathbf{x}(k+1) &= (\mathbf{A}+\Delta\mathbf{A})\mathbf{x}(k)+(\mathbf{B}+\Delta\mathbf{B})\mathbf{u}^f(k)+\mathbf{D}\boldsymbol{\omega}(k) \\ \mathbf{z}(k) &= \mathbf{C}\mathbf{x}(k)+\mathbf{E}\mathbf{u}^f(k) \end{aligned} \tag{1}$$

where $\mathbf{x}(k)\in\Re^n$ is the state vector, $\mathbf{u}^f(k)\in\Re^p$ is the control input from the actuator that may be fault, $\mathbf{z}(k)\in\Re^k$ is the controlled output, $\boldsymbol{\omega}(k)\in\Re^q$ is the input disturbance and $||\boldsymbol{\omega}(k)||_2\le\beta$, $\mathbf{A}$, $\mathbf{B}$, $\mathbf{C}$ and $\mathbf{D}$ are known real constant matrices with appropriate dimensions, $\Delta\mathbf{A}$ and $\Delta\mathbf{B}$ are unknown matrices representing parameter uncertainties in the state matrix and input matrix, respectively.
In much literature, time-varying matrices of uncertain parameters are assumed to be of the form $[\Delta\mathbf{A} \quad \Delta\mathbf{B}]=\mathbf{H}\mathbf{F}(k)[\mathbf{E}_a \quad \mathbf{E}_b]$, where $\mathbf{H}$, $\mathbf{E}_a$ and $\mathbf{E}_b$ are known real constant matrices with appropriate dimensions, $\mathbf{F}(k)$ is an unknown real matrix satisfying $\mathbf{F}(k)\in\Omega:=\{\mathbf{F}(k)\in\Re^{i^*j}\,|\,\mathbf{F}^T(k)\mathbf{F}(k)\le\mathbf{I}\}$. However, the uncertainty is often value bounded which is more universal and need not satisfy the so-called matching conditions in practical engineering. Thus, $\Delta\mathbf{A}$ and $\Delta\mathbf{B}$ denote value bounded uncertainties in this paper, i.e., $||\Delta\mathbf{A}||\le a$, $||\Delta\mathbf{B}||\le b$.
Suppose the states are available for state-feedback.

$$\mathbf{u}(k)=\mathbf{K}\mathbf{x}(k) \tag{2}$$

where $\mathbf{K}\in\Re^{p^*n}$ is the feedback gain matrix. For the control input, the following failure model in [18] is adopted for this study:

$$\mathbf{u}^f(k)=\mathbf{M}\mathbf{u}(k) \tag{3}$$

$$\mathbf{M}=diag\left[m_1,m_2,\cdots,m_p\right] \tag{4}$$

where $\mathbf{M}$ denotes the actuator faults function matrix, $0\le m_{il}\le m_i\le m_{iu}$, $m_{il}<1$, $m_{iu}\ge1$, $i=1,2,\cdots,p$.
Remark 1: In the above fault matrix $\mathbf{M}$, if $m_i=1$, it corresponds to the normal case $\mathbf{u}^f(k)=\mathbf{u}(k)$. If $m_i=0$, outage of actuator control signal occurs. If $0<m_{il}<m_i<m_{iu}$, $m_{il}<1$, $m_{iu}\ge1$ and $m_i\ne1$, the corresponding actuator would be in partial failure case. Hence, let $\mathbf{u}^f(k)$ denote the control input vector both in normal and actuator failures cases for fault-tolerant control research in this paper.
The decomposition of fault function $\mathbf{M}$ is given below with a similar manner in [7], which will be used for our main results. Define

$$\mathbf{M}_0=diag[m_{01},m_{02},\cdots,m_{0p}],\ \mathbf{J}=diag[j_1,j_2,\cdots,j_p],\ |\mathbf{L}|=diag[|l_1|,|l_2|,\cdots,|l_p|],$$

where $m_{0i} = (m_{il} + m_{iu}) / 2$, $j_i = (m_{iu} - m_{il}) / (m_{iu} + m_{il})$, $l_i = (m_i - m_{0i}) / m_{0i}$. So, we then have

$$\mathbf{M} = \mathbf{M}_0(\mathbf{I} + \mathbf{L}) \qquad |\mathbf{L}| \le \mathbf{J} \le \mathbf{I} \tag{5}$$

The faulty closed-loop system is given by

$$\begin{aligned} \mathbf{x}(k+1) &= \bar{\mathbf{A}}_C \mathbf{x}(k) + \mathbf{D}\boldsymbol{\omega}(k) \\ \mathbf{z}(k) &= \mathbf{C}_C \mathbf{x}(k) \end{aligned} \tag{6}$$

where $\bar{\mathbf{A}}_C = \mathbf{A}_C + \Delta\mathbf{A}_C$, $\mathbf{A}_C = \mathbf{A} + \mathbf{BMK}$, $\Delta\mathbf{A}_C = \Delta\mathbf{A} + \Delta\mathbf{BMK}$, $\mathbf{C}_C = \mathbf{C} + \mathbf{EMK}$.
The cost function associated with system (1) considered possible actuator faults (3) is

$$J = \sum_{k=0}^{\infty} \mathbf{x}^T(k)\left(\mathbf{Q} + (\mathbf{MK})^T \mathbf{R}(\mathbf{MK})\right)x(k) \tag{7}$$

where $\mathbf{Q} = \mathbf{Q}^T > 0$, $\mathbf{R} = \mathbf{R}^T > 0$ are given weighting matrices.
Definition 1: For system (1), if there exists state-feedback controller, such that the faulty closed-loop system (6) will meet the following indices constraints simultaneously,

a. The closed-loop system is quadratic D stabilizable with constraint $\Phi(q,r)$, $\Phi(q,r)$ denotes the disc with centre $q + j0$ and the radius r, where r and q are known constants with $|q| + r < 1$.
b. The H_∞ norm of the closed-loop transfer function is strictly less than a given positive scalar γ,
c. The closed-loop value of the cost function (7) exists an upper bound satisfying $J \le J^*$,

then for all admissible uncertainties and possible faults, the given indices, quadratic D stabilizability index $\Phi(q,r)$, H_∞ norm bound $\gamma > 0$ and cost function performance $J^* > 0$ are said to be consistent, state-feedback controller $\mathbf{u}(k) = \mathbf{Kx}(k)$ is said to be satisfactory fault-tolerant controller.
Now, the satisfactory fault-tolerant control problem considered in this paper is stated in the following.
Problem: For the system (1) with actuator failure, given the quadratic D stabilizability index $\Phi(q,r)$, H_∞ norm bound $\gamma > 0$ and the cost function (7), determine a control law $\mathbf{u}(k) = \mathbf{Kx}(k)$ so that the closed-loop system satisfies criteria (a), (b) and (c) simultaneously.

3. Main results

Lemma 1: Consider the actuator fault model (3), for any matrix $\mathbf{R} = \mathbf{R}^T > 0$ and scalar $\varepsilon > 0$, if $\mathbf{R}^{-1} - \varepsilon\mathbf{I} > 0$ then

$$\mathbf{MRM} \le \mathbf{M}_0\left(\mathbf{R}^{-1} - \varepsilon\mathbf{I}\right)^{-1}\mathbf{M}_0 + \varepsilon^{-1}\mathbf{M}_0\mathbf{JJM}_0 \tag{8}$$

Lemma 2: Consider the system (1) subject to faults, given index $\Phi(q,r)$, if there exists gain matrix $\mathbf{K}$ and symmetric positive matrix $\mathbf{P}$ such that the following matrix inequality

$$\begin{bmatrix} -\mathbf{P}^{-1} & \bar{\mathbf{A}}_C - q\mathbf{I} \\ \left(\bar{\mathbf{A}}_C - q\mathbf{I}\right)^T & -r^2\mathbf{P} \end{bmatrix} < 0 \tag{9}$$

holds for all admissible uncertainties and possible faults, then the system (1) is quadratically D stabilizable.

Remark 2: It can be easily shown that in the case when $q=0$, $r=1$, the definition of quadratic D stabilizability is reduced to quadratic stabilizability where no closed-loop pole constraints is considered. Therefore, Lemma 2 shows that if the uncertain system (1) is quadratic D stabilizable, then for some state feedback controllers both quadratic stabilizability and pole assignment constraints of the faulty closed-loop system are enforced simultaneously.

Theorem 1: Consider the system (1), for the given index $\Phi(q,r)$, if there exists symmetric positive matrix $\mathbf{X}$, matrix $\mathbf{Y}$ and scalars $\varepsilon_i > 0 (i = 1 \sim 3)$ such that the following linear matrix inequality

$$\begin{bmatrix} \Sigma_{11} & AX+BY-qX & 0 & \varepsilon_3 BJ & 0 \\ * & -r^2 X & X & Y^T & Y^T \\ * & * & -\varepsilon_1 I & 0 & 0 \\ * & * & * & -\varepsilon_2 I + \varepsilon_3 J & 0 \\ * & * & * & * & -\varepsilon_3 J^{-1} \end{bmatrix} < 0 \tag{10}$$

holds, where $\Sigma_{11} = -X + \varepsilon_1 a I + \varepsilon_2 b I + \varepsilon_3 BJB^T$. Then for all admissible uncertainties and possible faults $\mathbf{M}$, the faulty closed-loop system (6) with satisfactory fault-tolerant controller $\mathbf{u}(k) = \mathbf{K}\mathbf{x}(k) = \mathbf{M}_0^{-1}\mathbf{Y}\ \mathbf{X}^{-1}\mathbf{x}(k)$ is quadratically D stabilizable.

Remark 3: Theorem 1 shows us LMI with $\mathbf{X}$ and $\mathbf{Y}$, which can be tested with convex optimization to decide whether it is solvable, and Matlab LMI Control Toolbox can be utilized to solve it. If LMI (13) holds, there must exist state-feedback controller assigning the closed-loop poles within $\Phi(q,r)$, namely, the constraint (a) is met. In this case the system (1) is said to be robust fault-tolerant state feedback assignable for actuator faults case.

Lemma 3: Consider the system (1) in fault case and the cost function (7) as well as square integrable disturbance $\boldsymbol{\omega}(k)$, if there exists gain matrix $\mathbf{K}$ and symmetric positive matrix $\mathbf{P}$ such that the following matrix inequality

$$\bar{\mathbf{A}}_C^T \mathbf{P} \bar{\mathbf{A}}_C - \mathbf{P} + \mathbf{C}_C{}^T \mathbf{C}_C + \mathbf{Q} + \mathbf{K}^T \mathbf{MRMK} + \bar{\mathbf{A}}_C^T \mathbf{PD}\left(\gamma^2 \mathbf{I} - \mathbf{D}^T \mathbf{PD}\right)^{-1} \mathbf{D}^T \mathbf{P} \bar{\mathbf{A}}_C < 0 \tag{11}$$

holds for all admissible uncertainties and possible faults $\mathbf{M}$, then the faulty closed-loop system is asymptotically stable with an H_∞ norm-bound γ, and the cost function (7) has an upper bound

$$J < \mathbf{x}_0^T \mathbf{P} \mathbf{x}_0 + \gamma^2 \beta^2 \tag{12}$$

Remark 4: In some literature on the guaranteed cost control with regional pole constraint such as [12], the upper bound of cost function J is that $J \le V(0)/r^2 = \mathbf{x}_0^T \mathbf{P} \mathbf{x}_0 / r^2$. For $0 < r < 1$, it is certainly larger than the one in (12) when $\boldsymbol{\omega}(t) = 0$. So the result here provides an improved performance bound.

Remark 5: Note this upper bound in (12) which depends on the initial condition $\mathbf{x}_0$. To remove the dependence on the initial state, suppose $\mathbf{x}_0$ is arbitrary but belongs to the set $W = \{\mathbf{x}_0 \in \Re^n : \mathbf{x}_0 = \mathbf{U}\mathbf{v}, \mathbf{v}^T\mathbf{v} \le 1\}$, where $\mathbf{U}$ is a given matrix. The cost bound in (12) then leads to

$$J < \mathbf{x}_0^T \mathbf{P} \mathbf{x}_0 + \gamma^2 \beta^2 \le \lambda_{\max}\left(\mathbf{U}^T \mathbf{P} \mathbf{U}\right) + \gamma^2 \beta^2$$

Theorem 2: Consider the system (1) and the cost function (7), for the given index $\Phi(q,r)$ and H$_\infty$ norm-bound index γ, if there exists symmetric positive matrix $\mathbf{X}$, matrix $\mathbf{Y}$ and scalars $\varepsilon_i > 0 (i = 4 \sim 9)$ such that the following linear matrix inequality

$$\begin{bmatrix} -X & 0 & (AX+BY)^T & \Sigma_{21} \\ * & -\gamma^2 I & D^T & 0 \\ * & * & -X + \varepsilon_4 aI + \varepsilon_5 bI + \varepsilon_6 BJB^T & 0 \\ * & * & * & \Sigma_{22} \end{bmatrix} < 0 \tag{13}$$

holds, where $\Sigma_{21} = [(CX+EY)^T, X, X, Y^T, Y^T, Y^T, Y^T, Y^T, Y^T J]$, $\Sigma_{22} = diag[-I + \varepsilon_7 EJE^T, -Q^{-1}, -\varepsilon_4 I,$ $-\varepsilon_5 I + \varepsilon_8 J, -\varepsilon_6 J^{-1}, -\varepsilon_7 J^{-1}, -\varepsilon_8 J^{-1}, \varepsilon_9 I - R^{-1}, -\varepsilon_9 I]$. Then for all admissible uncertainties and possible faults $\mathbf{M}$, the faulty closed-loop system (6) with satisfactory fault-tolerant controller $\mathbf{u}(k) = \mathbf{K}\mathbf{x}(k) = \mathbf{M}_0^{-1}\mathbf{Y}\mathbf{X}^{-1}\mathbf{x}(k)$ is asymptotically stable with an H$_\infty$ norm-bound γ, and the corresponding closed-loop cost function (7) is with $J \le \lambda_{\max}(\mathbf{U}^T \mathbf{X}^{-1} \mathbf{U}) + \gamma^2 \beta^2$.

According to Theorem 1 and 2, the consistency of the quadratic D stabilizability constraint, H$_\infty$ performance and cost function indices for fault-tolerant control is deduced as the following optimization problem.

Theorem 3: Given quadratic D stabilizability index $\Phi(q,r)$, suppose the system (1) is robust fault-tolerant state feedback assignable for actuator faults case, then LMIs (10), (13) have a feasible solution. Thus, the following minimization problem is meaningful.

$$\min(\gamma): \left(\mathbf{X}, \mathbf{Y}, \gamma, \varepsilon_i\right) \text{ S.t. LMIs (10), (13)} \tag{14}$$

Proof: Based on Theorem 1, if the system (1) is robust fault-tolerant state feedback assignable for actuator faults case, then inequality

$$\bar{\mathbf{A}}_C^T \mathbf{P} \bar{\mathbf{A}}_C - \mathbf{P} < 0$$

has a feasible solution $\mathbf{P}$, $\mathbf{K}$. And existing $\lambda > 0$, $\delta > 0$, the following inequality holds

$$\lambda\left[\bar{\mathbf{A}}_C^T \mathbf{P} \bar{\mathbf{A}}_C - \mathbf{P}\right] + \mathbf{C}_C{}^T \mathbf{C}_C + \mathbf{Q} + \mathbf{K}^T \mathbf{MRMK} + \delta \mathbf{I} < 0 \tag{15}$$

Then existing a scalar γ_0, when $\gamma > \gamma_0$, it can be obtained that

$$\bar{\mathbf{A}}_C^T \mathbf{P}_1 \mathbf{D}\left(\gamma^2 \mathbf{I} - \mathbf{D}^T \mathbf{P}_1 \mathbf{D}\right)^{-1} \mathbf{D}^T \mathbf{P}_1 \bar{\mathbf{A}}_C < \delta \mathbf{I}$$

where $\mathbf{P}_1 = \lambda \mathbf{P}$. Furthermore, it follows that

$$\bar{\mathbf{A}}_C^T \mathbf{P}_1 \bar{\mathbf{A}}_C - \mathbf{P}_1 + \mathbf{C}_C{}^T \mathbf{C}_C + \mathbf{Q} + \mathbf{K}^T \mathbf{MRMK} + \bar{\mathbf{A}}_C^T \mathbf{P}_1 \mathbf{D}\left(\gamma^2 \mathbf{I} - \mathbf{D}^T \mathbf{P}_1 \mathbf{D}\right)^{-1} \mathbf{D}^T \mathbf{P}_1 \bar{\mathbf{A}}_C < 0$$

Using Schur complement and Theorem 2, it is easy to show that the above inequality is equivalent to linear matrix inequality (13), namely, $\mathbf{P}_1$, $\mathbf{K}$, γ is a feasible solution of LMIs

(10), (13). So if the system (1) is robust fault-tolerant state feedback assignable for actuator faults case, the LMIs (10), (13) have a feasible solution and the minimization problem (14) is meaningful. The proof is completed.

Suppose the above minimization problem has a solution $\mathbf{X}_L$, $\mathbf{Y}_L$, ε_{iL}, γ_L, and then any index $\gamma > \gamma_L$, LMIs (10), (13) have a feasible solution. Thus, the following optimization problem is meaningful.

Theorem 4: Consider the system (1) and the cost function (7), for the given quadratic D stabilizability index $\Phi(q,r)$ and H∞ norm-bound index $\gamma > \gamma_L$, if there exists symmetric positive matrix $\mathbf{X}$, matrix $\mathbf{Y}$ and scalars $\varepsilon_i > 0 (i = 1 \sim 9)$ such that the following minimization

$$\min \ \lambda + \gamma^2 \beta^2 \tag{16}$$

$$\text{S.t. (i)} \ (10), (13)$$

$$\text{(ii)} \ \begin{bmatrix} -\lambda \mathbf{I} & \mathbf{U}^T \\ \mathbf{U} & -\mathbf{X} \end{bmatrix} < 0$$

has a solution $\mathbf{X}_{\min}, \mathbf{Y}_{\min}, \varepsilon_{i\min}, \lambda_{\min}$, then for all admissible uncertainties and possible faults $\mathbf{M}$, $\mathbf{u}(k) = \mathbf{Kx}(k) = \mathbf{M}_0^{-1}\mathbf{Y}_{\min}\mathbf{X}_{\min}^{-1}\mathbf{x}(k)$ is an optimal guaranteed cost satisfactory fault-tolerant controller, so that the faulty closed-loop system (6) is quadratically D stabilizable with an H∞ norm-bound γ, and the corresponding closed-loop cost function (7) satisfies $J \le \lambda_{\min} + \gamma^2 \beta^2$.

According to Theorem 1~4, the following satisfactory fault-tolerant controller design method is concluded for the actuator faults case.

Theorem 5: Given consistent quadratic D stabilizability index $\Phi(q,r)$, H∞ norm index $\gamma > \gamma_L$ and cost function index $J^* > \lambda_{\min} + \gamma^2\beta^2$, suppose that the system (1) is robust fault-tolerant state feedback assignable for actuator faults case. If LMIs (10), (13) have a feasible solution $\mathbf{X}, \mathbf{Y}$, then for all admissible uncertainties and possible faults $\mathbf{M}$, $\mathbf{u}(k) = \mathbf{Kx}(k) = \mathbf{M}_0^{-1}\mathbf{Y}\mathbf{X}^{-1}\mathbf{x}(k)$ is satisfactory fault-tolerant controller making the faulty closed-loop system (6) satisfying the constraints (a), (b) and (c) simultaneously.

In a similar manner to the Theorem 5, as for the system (1) with quadratic D stabilizability, H∞ norm and cost function requirements in normal case, i.e., $\mathbf{M} = \mathbf{I}$, we can get the satisfactory normal controller without fault tolerance.

4. Simulative example

Consider a satellite attitude control uncertain discrete-time system (1) with parameters as follows:

$$\mathbf{A} = \begin{bmatrix} -2 & 2 \\ 2 & 4 \end{bmatrix}, \ \mathbf{B} = \begin{bmatrix} 1 & 1 \\ 0 & 1 \end{bmatrix}, \ \mathbf{C} = \begin{bmatrix} 0.2 & 0.3 \end{bmatrix}, \ \mathbf{D} = \begin{bmatrix} 0.1 \\ 0.5 \end{bmatrix}, \ \mathbf{Q} = \begin{bmatrix} 1 & 0 \\ 0 & 1 \end{bmatrix}, \ \mathbf{R} = \begin{bmatrix} 1 & 0 \\ 0 & 1 \end{bmatrix}, \ a = 0.1, \ b = 0.2 .$$

Suppose the actuator failure parameters $\mathbf{M}_l = diag\{0.4, 0.6\}$, $\mathbf{M}_u = diag\{1.3, 1.1\}$. Given the quadratic D stabilizability index $\Phi(0.5, 0.5)$, we can obtain state-feedback satisfactory fault-tolerant controller (SFTC), such that the closed-loop systems will meet given indices constraints simultaneously based on Theorem 5.

$$\mathbf{K}_{\text{SFTC}} = \begin{bmatrix} 0.5935 & 3.0187 \\ -6.7827 & -5.6741 \end{bmatrix}$$

In order to compare, we can obtain the state-feedback satisfactory normal controller (SNC) without fault-tolerance.

$$\mathbf{K}_{\text{SNC}} = \begin{bmatrix} 0.4632 & 2.4951 \\ -5.4682 & -4.9128 \end{bmatrix}$$

Through simulative calculation, the pole-distribution of the closed-loop system by satisfactory fault-tolerant controller and normal controller are illustrated in Figure 1, 2 and 3 for normal case and the actuator faults case respectively. It can be concluded that the poles of closed-loop system driven by normal controller lie in the circular disk $\Phi(0.5,0.5)$ for normal case (see Fig. 1). However, in the actuator failure case, the closed-loop system with normal controller is unstable; some poles are out of the given circular disk (see Fig. 2). In the contrast, the performance by satisfactory fault-tolerant controller still satisfies the given pole index (see Fig. 3). Thus the poles of closed-loop systems lie in the given circular disk by the proposed method.

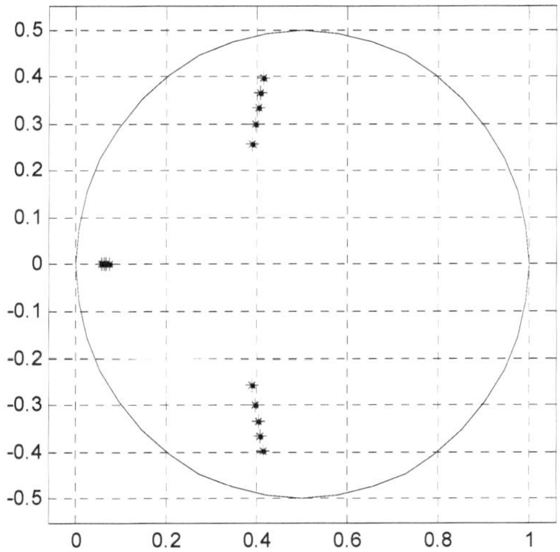

Fig. 1. Pole-distribution under satisfactory normal control without faults

5. Conclusion

Taking the guaranteed cost control in practical systems into account, the problem of satisfactory fault-tolerant controller design with quadratic D stabilizability and H_∞ norm-bound constraints is concerned by LMI approach for a class of satellite attitude systems subject to actuator failures. Attention has been paid to the design of state-feedback controller that guarantees, for all admissible value-bounded uncertainties existing in both the state and control input matrices as well as possible actuator failures, the closed-loop system to satisfy the pre-specified quadratic D stabilizability index, meanwhile the H_∞ index and cost function are restricted within the chosen upper bounds. So, the resulting closed-loop system can provide satisfactory stability, transient property, H_∞ performance and quadratic cost performance despite of possible actuator faults. The similar design method can be extended to sensor failures case.

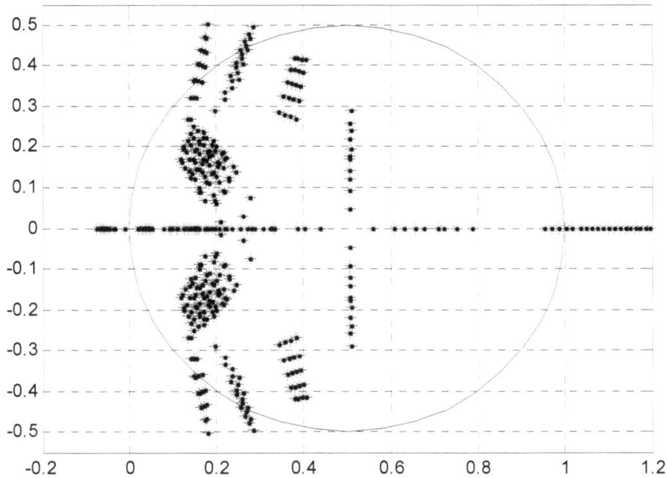

Fig. 2. Pole-distribution under satisfactory normal control with faults

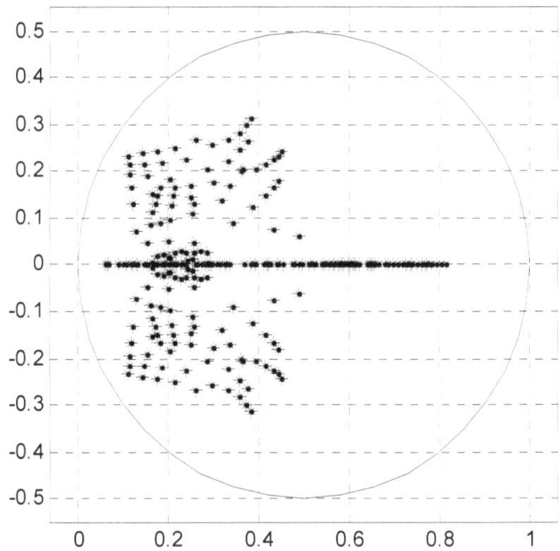

Fig. 3. Pole-distribution under satisfactory fault-tolerant control with faults

6. Acknowledgement

This work is supported by the National Natural Science Foundation of P. R. China under grants 60574082, 60804027 and the NUST Research Funding under Grant 2010ZYTS012.

7. Reference

H. Yang, B. Jiang, and M. Staroswiecki. Observer-based fault-tolerant control for a class of switched nonlinear systems, IET Control Theory Appl, Vol. 1, No. 5, pp. 1523-1532, 2007.

D. Ye, and G. Yang. Adaptive fault-tolerant tracking control against actuator faults with application to flight control, IEEE Trans. on Control Systems Technology, Vol. 14, No. 6, pp. 1088-1096, 2006.

J. Lunze, and T. Steffen. Control reconfiguration after actuator failures using disturbance decoupling methods, IEEE Trans. on Automatic Control, Vol. 51, No. 10, pp. 1590-1601, 2006.

Y. Wang, D. Zhou, and F. Gao. Iterative learning fault-tolerant control for batch processes, Industrial & Engineering Chemistry Research, Vol. 45, pp. 9050-9060, 2006.

M. Zhong, H. Ye, S. Ding, *et al.* Observer-based fast rate fault detection for a class of multirate sampled-data systems, IEEE Trans. on Automatic Control, Vol. 52, No. 3, pp. 520-525, 2007.

G. Zhang, Z. Wang, X. Han, *et al.* Research on satisfactory control theory and its application in fault-tolerant technology, Proceedings of the 5th World Congress on Intelligent Control and Automation, Hangzhou China, June 2004, Vol. 2, pp. 1521-1524.

D. Zhang, Z. Wang, and S. Hu. Robust satisfactory fault-tolerant control of uncertain linear discrete-time systems: an LMI approach, International Journal of Systems Science, Vol. 38, No. 2, pp. 151-165, 2007.

F. Wang, B. Yao, and S. Zhang. Reliable control of regional stabilizability for linear systems, Control Theory & Applications, Vol. 21, No. 5, pp. 835-839, 2004.

F. Yang, M. Gani, and D. Henrion. Fixed-order robust H_∞ controller design with regional pole assignment, IEEE Trans. on Automatic Control, Vol. 52, No. 10, pp. 1959-1963, 2007.

A. Zhang, and H. Fang. Reliable H_∞ control for nonlinear systems based on fuzzy control switching, Proceedings of the 2007 IEEE International Conference on Mechatronics and Automation, Harbin China, Aug. 2007, pp. 2587-2591.

F. Yang, Z. Wang, D. W.C.Ho, *et al.* Robust H_∞ control with missing measurements and time delays, IEEE Trans. on Automatic Control, Vol. 52, No. 9, pp. 1666-1672, 2007.

G. Garcia. Quadratic guaranteed cost and disc pole location control for discrete-time uncertain systems, IEE Proceedings: Control Theory and Applications, Vol. 144, No. 6, pp. 545-548, 1997.

X. Nian, and J. Feng. Guaranteed-cost control of a linear uncertain system with multiple time-varying delays: an LMI approach, IEE Proceedings: Control Theory and Applications, Vol. 150, No. 1, pp. 17-22, 2003.

J. Liu, J. Wang, and G. Yang. Reliable robust minimum variance filtering with sensor failures, Proceeding of the 2001 American Control Conference, Arlington USA, Vol. 2, pp. 1041-1046.

H. Wang, J. Lam, S. Xu, *et al*. Robust H_∞ reliable control for a class of uncertain neutral delay systems, International Journal of Systems Science, Vol. 33, pp. 611-622, 2002.
G. Yang, J. Wang, and Y. Soh. Reliable H_∞ controller design for linear systems, Automatica, Vol. 37, pp. 717-725, 2001.
Q. Ma, and C. Hu. An effective evolutionary approach to mixed H_2/H_∞ filtering with regional pole assignment, Proceedings of the 6th World Congress on Intelligent Control and Automation, Dalian China, June 2006, Vol. 2, pp. 1590-1593.
Y. Yang, G. Yang, and Y. Soh. Reliable control of discrete-time systems with actuator failures, IEE Proceedings: Control Theory and Applications, Vol. 147, No. 4, pp. 428-432, 2000.
L. Yu. An LMI approach to reliable guaranteed cost control of discrete-time systems with actuator failure, Applied Mathematics and Computation, Vol. 162, pp. 1325-1331, 2005.
L. Xie. Output feedback H_∞ control of systems with parameter uncertainty, International Journal of Control, Vol. 63, No. 4, pp. 741-750, 1996.

Part 3

Discrete-Time Adaptive Control

13

Discrete-Time Adaptive Predictive Control with Asymptotic Output Tracking

Chenguang Yang[1] and Hongbin Ma[2]
[1]*University of Plymouth*
[2]*Beijing Institute of Technology*
[1]*United Kingdom*
[2]*China*

1. Introduction

Nowadays nearly all the control algorithms are implemented digitally and consequently discrete-time systems have been receiving ever increasing attention. However, as to the development of nonlinear adaptive control methods, which are generally regarded as smart ways to deal with system uncertainties, most researches are conducted for continuous-time systems, such that it is very difficult or even impossible to directly apply many well developed methods in discrete-time systems, due to the fundamental difference between differential and difference equations for modeling continuous-time and discrete-time systems, respectively. Even some concepts for discrete-time systems have very different meaning from those for continuous-time systems, e.g., the "relative degrees" defined for continuous-time and discrete-time systems have totally different physical explanations Cabrera & Narendra (1999). Therefore, nonlinear adaptive control of discrete-time systems needs to be further investigated.

On the other hand, the early studies on adaptive control were mainly concerning on the parametric uncertainties, i.e., unknown system parameters, such that the designed control laws have limited robustness properties, where minute disturbances and the presence of nonparametric model uncertainties can lead to poor performance and even instability of the closed-loop systems Egardt (1979); Tao (2003). Subsequently, robustness in adaptive control has been the subject of much research attention for decades. However, due to the difficulties associated with discrete-time uncertain nonlinear system model, there are only limited researches on robust adaptive control to deal with nonparametric nonlinear model uncertainties in discrete-time systems. For example, in Zhang et al. (2001), parameter projection method was adopted to guarantee boundedness of parameter estimates in presence of small nonparametric uncertainties under certain wild conditions. For another example, the sliding mode method has been incorporated into discrete-time adaptive control Chen (2006). However, in contrast to continuous-time systems for which a sliding mode controller can be constructed to eliminate the effects of the general uncertain model nonlinearity, for discrete-time systems, the uncertain nonlinearity is normally required to be of small growth rate or globally bounded, but sliding mode control is yet not able to completely compensate for the effects of nonlinear uncertainties in discrete-time. As a matter of fact, unlike in continuous-time systems, it is much more difficulty in discrete-time systems to deal with

nonlinear uncertainties. When the size of the uncertain nonlinearity is larger than a certain level, even a simple first-order discrete-time system cannot be globally stabilized Xie & Guo (2000). In an early work on discrete-time adaptive systems, Lee (1996) it is also pointed out that when there is large parameter time-variation, it may be impossible to construct a global stable control even for a first order system. Moreover, for discrete-time systems, most existing robust approaches only guarantee the closed-loop stability in the presence of the nonparametric model uncertainties, but are not able to improve control performance by complete compensation for the effect of uncertainties.
Towards the goal of complete compensation for the effect of nonlinear model uncertainties in discrete-time adaptive control, the methods using output information in previous steps to compensate for uncertainty at current step have been investigated in Ma et al. (2007) for first order system, and in Ge et al. (2009) for high order strict-feedback systems. We will carry forward to study adaptive control with nonparametric uncertainty compensation for *NARMA system* (nonlinear auto-regressive moving average), which comprises a general nonlinear discrete-time model structure and is one of the most frequently employed form in discrete-time modeling process.

2. Problem formulation

In this chapter, *NARMA system* to be studied is described by the following equation

$$y(k+n) = \sum_{i=1}^{n} \theta_i^T \phi_i(\underline{y}(k+n-i)) + \sum_{j=1}^{m} g_j u(k-m+j) + \nu(z(k-\tau)) \tag{1}$$

where $y(k)$ and $u(k)$ are output and input, respectively. Here

$$\underline{y}(k) = [y(k), y(k-1), \ldots, y(k-n+1)]^T \tag{2}$$

$$\underline{u}(k) = [u(k-1), u(k-2), \ldots, u(k-m+1)]^T \tag{3}$$

and $z(k) = [\underline{y}^T(k), \underline{u}^T(k-1)]^T$. And for $i = 1, 2, \cdots, n$, $\phi_i(\cdot) : R^n \to R^{p_i}$ are known vector-valued functions, $\theta_i^T = [\theta_{i,1}, \ldots, \theta_{i,p_i}]$, and g_j are unknown parameters. And the last term $\nu(z(k-\tau))$ represents the nonlinear model uncertainties (which can be regarded as unmodeled dynamics uncertainties) with unknown time delay τ satisfying $0 \leq \tau_{\min} \leq \tau \leq \tau_{\max}$ for known constants $\tau_{\min}$ and $\tau_{\max}$. The control objective to make sure the boundedness of all the closed-loop signals while to make the output $y(k)$ *asymptotically* track a given bounded reference $y^*(k)$.
Time delay is an active topic of research because it is frequently encountered in engineering systems to be controlled Kolmanovskii & Myshkis (1992). Of great concern is the effect of time delay on stability and asymptotic performance. For continuous-time systems with time delays, some of the useful tools in robust stability analysis have been well developed based on the Lyapunov's second method, the Lyapunov-Krasovskii theorem and the Lyapunov-Razumikhin theorem. Following its success in stability analysis, the utility of Lyapunov-Krasovskii functionals were subsequently explored in adaptive control designs for continuous-time time delayed systems Ge et al. (2003; 2004); Ge & Tee (2007); Wu (2000); Xia et al. (2009); Zhang & Ge (2007). However, in the discrete-time case there dos not exist a counterpart of Lyapunov-Krasovskii functional. To resolve the difficulties associated with unknown time delayed states and the nonparametric nonlinear uncertainties, an augmented

states vector is introduced in this work such that the effect of time delays can be canceled at the same time when the effects of nonlinear uncertainties are compensated.
In the *NARMA system* described in (1), we can see that there is a "relative degree" n which can be regarded as response delay from input to output. Thus, the control input at the kth step, $u(k)$, will actually only determine the output at n-step ahead. The n-step ahead output $y(k+n)$ also depends on the following future outputs:

$$y(k+1), y(k+2), \ldots, y(k+n-2), y(k+n-1) \tag{4}$$

and ideally the controller should also incorporate the information of these states. However, dependence on these future states will make the controller non-causal!
If system (1) is linear, e.g., there is no nonlinear functions ϕ_i, we could find a so called Diophantine function by using which system (1) can be transformed into an n-step predictor where $y(k+n)$ only depends on outputs at or before the k-th step. Then, linear adaptive control can be designed under *certainty equivalence principal* to emulate a deadbeat controller, which forces the n-step ahead future output to acquire a desired reference value. However, transformation of the nonlinear system (1) into an n-step predictor form would make the known nonlinear functions and unknown parameters entangled together and thus not identifiable. Thus, we propose *future outputs prediction*, based on which adaptive control can be designed properly.
Throughout this chapter, the following notations are used.

- $\|\cdot\|$ denotes the Euclidean norm of vectors and induced norm of matrices.
- Z_t^+ represents the set of all integers which are not less than a given integer t.
- $\mathbf{0}_{[\mathbf{q}]}$ stands for q-dimension zero vector.
- $A := B$ means that A is defined as B.
- $(\hat{\cdot})$ and $(\tilde{\cdot})$ denote the estimates of unknown parameters and estimate errors, respectively.

3. Assumptions and preliminaries

Some reasonable assumptions are made in this section on the system (1) to be studied. In addition, some useful lemmas are introduced in this section to facilitate the later control design.

Assumption 3.1. *In system (1), the functional uncertainty $\nu(\cdot)$, satisfies Lipschitz condition, i.e., $\|\nu(\varepsilon_1) - \nu(\varepsilon_2)\| \le L_\nu \|\varepsilon_1 - \varepsilon_2\|$, $\forall \varepsilon_1, \varepsilon_2 \in R^n$, where $L_\nu < \lambda^*$ with λ^* being a small number defined in (58). The system functions $\phi_i(\cdot)$, $i = 1, 2, \ldots, n$, are also Lipschitz functions with Lipschitz coefficients L_j.*

Remark 3.1. *Any continuously derivable function is Lipschitz on a compact set, refer to Hirsch & Smale (1974) and any function with bounded derivative is globally Lipschitz. As our objective is to achieve global asymptotic stability, it is not stringent to assume that the nonlinearity is globally Lipschitz.*
In fact, Lipschitz condition is a common assumption for nonlinearity in the control community Arcak et al. (2001); Nešić & Laila (July, 2002); Nešić & Teel (2006); Sokolov (2003). In addition, it is usual in discrete-time control to assume that the uncertain nonlinearity is of small Lipschitz coefficient Chen et al. (2001); Myszkorowski (1994); Zhang et al. (2001); Zhu & Guo (2004). When the Lipschitz coefficient is large, discrete-time uncertain systems are not stabilizable as indicated in Ma (2008); Xie & Guo (2000); Zhang & Guo (2002). Actually, if the discrete-time

models are derived from continuous-time models, the growth rate of nonlinear uncertainty can always be made sufficient small by choosing sufficient small sampling time.

Assumption 3.2. *In system (1), the control gain coefficient g_m of current instant control input $u(k)$ is bounded away from zero, i.e., there is a known constant $\underline{g}_m > 0$ such that $|g_m| > \underline{g}_m$, and its sign is known a priori. Thus, without loss of generality, we assume $g_m > 0$.*

Remark 3.2. *It is called unknown control direction problem when the sign of the control gain is unknown. The unknown control direction problem of nonlinear discrete-time system has been well addressed in Ge et al. (2008); Yang et al. (2009) but it is out the scope of this chapter.*

Definition 3.1. *Chen & Narendra (2001) Let $x_1(k)$ and $x_2(k)$ be two discrete-time scalar or vector signals, $\forall k \in Z_t^+$, for any t.*

- *We denote $x_1(k) = O[x_2(k)]$, if there exist positive constants m_1, m_2 and k_0 such that $\|x_1(k)\| \leq m_1 \max_{k' \leq k} \|x_2(k')\| + m_2, \ \forall k > k_0$.*
- *We denote $x_1(k) = o[x_2(k)]$, if there exists a discrete-time function $\alpha(k)$ satisfying $\lim_{k\to\infty} \alpha(k) = 0$ and a constant k_0 such that $\|x_1(k)\| \leq \alpha(k) \max_{k' \leq k} \|x_2(k')\|$, $\forall k > k_0$.*
- *We denote $x_1(k) \sim x_2(k)$ if they satisfy $x_1(k) = O[x_2(k)]$ and $x_2(k) = O[x_1(k)]$.*

Assumption 3.3. *The input and output of system (1) satisfy*

$$u(k) = O[y(k+n)] \tag{5}$$

Assumption 3.3 implies that the system (1) is bounded-output-bounded-input (BOBI) system (or equivalently minimum phase for linear systems).
For convenience, in the followings we use $O[1]$ and $o[1]$ to denote bounded sequences and sequences converging to zero, respectively. In addition, if sequence $y(k)$ satisfies $y(k) = O[x(k)]$ or $y(k) = o[x(k)]$, then we may directly use $O[x(k)]$ or $o[x(k)]$ to denote sequence $y(k)$ for convenience.
According to Definition 3.1, we have the following proposition.

Proposition 3.1. *According to the definition on signal orders in Definition 3.1, we have following properties:*

(i) $O[x_1(k+\tau)] + O[x_1(k)] \sim O[x_1(k+\tau)], \forall \tau \geq 0$.

(ii) $x_1(k+\tau) + o[x_1(k)] \sim x_1(k+\tau), \forall \tau \geq 0$.

(iii) $o[x_1(k+\tau)] + o[x_1(k)] \sim o[x_1(k+\tau)], \forall \tau \geq 0$.

(iv) $o[x_1(k)] + o[x_2(k)] \sim o[|x_1(k)| + |x_2(k)|]$.

(v) $o[O[x_1(k)]] \sim o[x_1(k)] + O[1]$.

(vi) If $x_1(k) \sim x_2(k)$ *and* $\lim_{k\to\infty} \|x_2(k)\| = 0$, *then* $\lim_{k\to\infty} \|x_1(k)\| = 0$.

(vii) If $x_1(k) = o[x_1(k)] + o[1]$, *then* $\lim_{k\to\infty} \|x_1(k)\| = 0$.

(viii) Let $x_2(k) = x_1(k) + o[x_1(k)]$. *If* $x_2(k) = o[1]$, *then* $\lim_{k\to\infty} \|x_1(k)\| = 0$.

Proof. See Appendix A. ∎

Lemma 3.1. *Goodwin et al. (1980) (Key Technical Lemma) For some given real scalar sequences $s(k)$, $b_1(k)$, $b_2(k)$ and vector sequence $\sigma(k)$, if the following conditions hold:*

(i) $\lim_{k\to\infty} \frac{s^2(k)}{b_1(k)+b_2(k)\sigma^T(k)\sigma(k)} = 0$,
(ii) $b_1(k) = O[1]$ *and* $b_2(k) = O[1]$,
(iii) $\sigma(k) = O[s(k)]$.
Then, we have
a) $\lim_{k\to\infty} s(k) = 0$, *and b)* $\sigma(k)$ *is bounded.*

Lemma 3.2. *Define*

$$Z(k) = [z(k-\tau_{\max}), \ldots, z(k-\tau), \ldots, z(k-\tau_{\min})] \tag{6}$$

and

$$l_k = \arg\min_{l\leq k-n} \|Z(k) - Z(l)\| \tag{7}$$

such that

$$Z(l_k) = [z(l_k-\tau_{\max}), \ldots, z(l_k-\tau), \ldots, z(l_k-\tau_{\min})] \tag{8}$$

and

$$\Delta Z(k) = Z(k) - Z(l_k) \tag{9}$$

Then, if $\|Z(k)\|$ *is bounded we have* $\|\Delta Z(k)\| \to 0$ *as well as* $\|\nu(z(k-\tau)) - \nu(z(l_k-\tau))\| \to 0$.
Proof. Given the definition of l_k in (7), it has been proved in Ma (2006); Xie & Guo (2000) that the boundedness of sequence $Z(k)$ leads to $\|\Delta Z(k)\| \to 0$. As $0 \leq \|\nu(z(k-\tau)) - \nu(z(l_k-\tau))\| \leq \|\Delta Z(k)\|$, it is obvious that $\|\nu(z(k-\tau)) - \nu(z(l_k-\tau))\| \to 0$ as $k\to\infty$. ∎

According to the definition of $\Delta Z(k)$ in (9) and Assumption 3.1, we see that

$$|\nu(z(k-\tau)) - \nu(z(l_k-\tau))| \leq L_\nu \|\Delta Z(k))\| \tag{10}$$

The inequality above serves as a key to compensate for the nonparametric uncertainty, which will be demonstrated later.

4. Future output prediction

In this section, an approach to predict the future outputs in (4) is developed to facilitate control design in next section. To start with, let us define an auxiliary output as

$$y_a(k+n-1) = \sum_{i=1}^{n} \theta_i^T \phi_i(\underline{y}(k+n-i)) + \nu(z(k-\tau)) \tag{11}$$

such that (1) can be rewritten as

$$y(k+n) = y_a(k+n-1) + \sum_{j=1}^{m} g_j u(k-m+j) \tag{12}$$

It is easy to show that

$$\begin{aligned} y_a(k+n-1) &= y_a(k+n-1) - y_a(l_k+n-1) + y_a(l_k+n-1) \\ &= \sum_{i=1}^{n} \theta_i^T [\phi_i(\underline{y}(k+n-i)) - \phi_i(\underline{y}(l_k+n-i))] - \sum_{j=1}^{m} g_j u(l_k-m+j) \\ &\quad + y(l_k+n) + (\nu(z(k-\tau)) - \nu(z(l_k-\tau)) \end{aligned} \tag{13}$$

For convenience, we introduce the following notations

$$\Delta\phi_i(k+n-i) = \phi_i(\underline{y}(k+n-i)) - \phi_i(\underline{y}(l_k+n-i)) \tag{14}$$

$$\Delta u(k-m+j) = u(k-m+j) - u(l_k-m+j)$$

$$\Delta\nu(k-\tau) = \nu(z(k-\tau)) - \nu(z(l_k-\tau)) \tag{15}$$

for $i = 1, 2, \ldots, n$ and $j = 1, 2, \ldots, m$.

Combining (12) and (13), we obtain

$$y(k+n) = \sum_{i=1}^{n} \theta_i^T \Delta\phi_i(k+n-i) + \sum_{j=1}^{m} g_j \Delta u(k-m+j) + y(l_k+n) + \Delta\nu(k-\tau) \tag{16}$$

Step 1:

Denote $\hat{\theta}_i(k)$ and $\hat{g}_j(k)$ as the estimates of unknown parameters θ_i and g_j at the kth step, respectively. Then, according to (16), one-step ahead future output $y(k+1)$ can be predicted at the kth step as

$$\begin{aligned}\hat{y}(k+1|k) = &\sum_{i=1}^{n} \hat{\theta}_i^T(k-n+2)\Delta\phi_i(k-i+1) + \sum_{j=1}^{m} \hat{g}_j(k-n+2)\Delta u(k-m+j-n+1) \\ &+y(l_{k-n+1}+n)\end{aligned} \tag{17}$$

Now, based on $\hat{y}(k+1|k)$, we define

$$\Delta\hat{\phi}_1(k+1|k) = \phi_1(\underline{\hat{y}}(k+1|k)) - \phi_1(\underline{y}(l_{k-n+2}+n-1)) \tag{18}$$

which will be used in next step for prediction of two-step ahead output and where

$$\underline{\hat{y}}(k+1|k) = [\hat{y}(k+1|k), y(k), \ldots, y(k-n+2)]^T \tag{19}$$

Step 2: By using the estimates $\hat{\theta}_i$(k) and $\hat{g}_j(k)$ and according to (16), the two-step ahead future output $y(k+2)$ can be predicted at the kth step as

$$\begin{aligned}\hat{y}(k+2|k) = &\hat{\theta}_1^T(k-n+3)\Delta\hat{\phi}_1(k+1|k) + \sum_{i=2}^{n} \hat{\theta}_i^T(k-n+3)\Delta\phi_i(k-i+2) \\ &+ \sum_{j=1}^{m} \hat{g}_j(k-n+3)\Delta u(k-m+j-n+2) + y(l_{k-n+2}+n)\end{aligned} \tag{20}$$

Then, by using $\hat{y}(k+1|k)$ and $\hat{y}(k+2|k)$, we define

$$\Delta\hat{\phi}_1(k+2|k) = \phi_1(\underline{\hat{y}}(k+2|k)) - \phi_1(\underline{y}(l_{k-n+3}+n-1))$$

$$\Delta\hat{\phi}_2(k+1|k) = \phi_2(\underline{\hat{y}}(k+1|k)) - \phi_2(\underline{y}(l_{k-n+3}+n-2)) \tag{21}$$

which will be used for prediction in next step and where

$$\underline{\hat{y}}(k+2|k) = [\hat{y}(k+2|k), \hat{y}(k+1|k), y(k), \ldots, y(k-n+3)]^T \tag{22}$$

Continuing the procedure above, we have three-step ahead future output prediction and so on so forth until the $(n-1)$-step ahead future output prediction as follows:
Step $(n-1)$: The $(n-1)$-step ahead future output is predicted as

$$\begin{aligned}\hat{y}(k+n-1|k) &= \sum_{i=1}^{n-2} \hat{\theta}_i^T(k)\Delta\hat{\phi}_i(k+n-1-i|k) + \sum_{i=n-1}^{n} \hat{\theta}_i^T(k)\Delta\phi_i(k-(i-(n-1))) \\ &\quad + \sum_{j=1}^{m} \hat{g}_j(k)\Delta u(k-m+j-1) + y(l_{k-1}+n)\end{aligned} \tag{23}$$

where

$$\Delta\hat{\phi}_i(k+l|k) = \phi_i(\underline{\hat{y}}(k+l|k)) - \phi_i(\underline{y}(l_{k-n+i+l}+n-i)) \tag{24}$$

for $i = 1, 2, \ldots, n-2$ and $l = 1, 2, \ldots, n-i-1$.
The prediction law of future outputs is summarized as follows:

$$\begin{aligned}\hat{y}(k+l|k) &= \sum_{i=1}^{l-1} \hat{\theta}_i^T(k-n+l+1)\Delta\hat{\phi}_i(k+l-i|k) + \sum_{i=l}^{n} \hat{\theta}_i^T(k-n+l+1)\Delta\phi_i(k-(i-l)) \\ &\quad + \sum_{j=1}^{m} \hat{g}_j(k)\Delta u(k-m-n+l+j) + y(l_{k-n+l}+n)\end{aligned} \tag{25}$$

for $l = 1, 2, \ldots, n-1$.

Remark 4.1. *Note that $\hat{\theta}_i(k-n+l+1)$ and $\hat{g}_j(k-n+l+1)$ instead of $\hat{\theta}_i(k)$ and $g_j(k)$ are used in the prediction law of the l-step ahead future output. In this way, the parameter estimates appearing in the prediction of $\hat{y}(k+l|k)$ and $\hat{y}(k+l|k+1)$ are at the same time step, such that the analysis of prediction error will be much simplified.*

Remark 4.2. *Similar to the prediction procedure proposed in Yang et al. (2009), the future output prediction is defined in such a way that the j-step prediction is based on the previous step predictions. The prediction method Yang et al. (2009) is further developed here for the compensation of the effect of the nonlinear uncertainties $\nu(z(k-\tau))$. With the help of the introduction of previous instant l_k defined in (7), it can been seen that in the transformed system (16) that the output information at previous instants is used to compensate for the effect of nonparametric uncertainties $\nu(z(k-\tau))$ at the current instant according to (15).*

The parameter estimates in output prediction are obtained from the following update laws

$$\begin{aligned}\hat{\theta}_i(k+1) &= \hat{\theta}_i(k-n+2) - \frac{a_p(k)\gamma_p\Delta\phi_i(k-i+1)\tilde{y}(k+1|k)}{D_p(k)} \\ \hat{g}_j(k+1) &= \hat{g}_j(k-n+2) - \frac{a_p(k)\gamma_p\Delta u(k-m+j-n+1)\tilde{y}(k+1|k)}{D_p(k)} \\ i &= 1, 2, \ldots, n, \quad j = 1, 2, \ldots, m\end{aligned} \tag{26}$$

with

$$
\begin{aligned}
\tilde{y}(k+1|k) &= \hat{y}(k+1|k) - y(k+1) \\
D_p(k) &= 1 + \sum_{i=1}^{n} \|\Delta\phi_i(k-i+1)\|^2 + \sum_{j=1}^{m} \Delta u^2(k-m+j-n+1) \quad (27)\\
a_p(k) &= \begin{cases} 1 - \frac{\lambda\|\Delta Z(k-n+1)\|}{|\tilde{y}(k+1|k)|}, \\ \quad \text{if } |\tilde{y}(k+1|k)| > \lambda\|\Delta Z(k-n+1)\| \\ 0 \quad \text{otherwise} \end{cases} \quad (28)\\
\hat{\theta}_i(0) &= \mathbf{0}_{[q]}, \ \hat{g}_j(0) = 0 \quad (29)
\end{aligned}
$$

where $0 < \gamma_p < 2$ and λ can be chosen as a constant satisfying $L_v \le \lambda < \lambda^*$, with λ^* defined later in (58).

Remark 4.3. *The dead zone indicator $a_p(k)$ is employed in the future output prediction above, which is motivated by the work in Chen et al. (2001). In the parameter update law (38), the dead zone implies that in the region $|\tilde{y}(k+1|k)| \le \lambda\|\Delta Z(k-n+1)\|$, the values of parameter estimates at the $(k+1)$-th step are same as those at the $(k+n-2)$-th step. While the estimate values will be updated outside of this region. The threshold of the dead zone will converge to zero because $\lim_{k\to\infty} \|\Delta Z(k-n+1)\| = 0$, which will be guaranteed by the adaptive control law designed in the next section. The similar dead zone method will also be used in the parameter update laws of the adaptive controller in the next section.*

With the future outputs predicted above, we can establish the following lemma for the prediction errors.

Lemma 4.1. *Define $\tilde{y}(k+l|k) = \hat{y}(k+l|k) - y(k+l)$, then there exist constant c_l such that*

$$|\tilde{y}(k+l|k)| = o[O[y(k+l)]] + \lambda\Delta_s(k,l), \ \ l = 1,2,\ldots,n-1 \quad (30)$$

where

$$\Delta_s(k,l) = \max_{1\le k'\le l}\{\|\Delta Z(k-n+k')\|\} \quad (31)$$

Proof. See Appendix B. ■

5. Adaptive control design

By introducing the following notations

$$
\begin{aligned}
\bar{\theta} &= [\theta_1^T, \theta_2^T, \ldots, \theta_n^T]^T \\
\bar{\phi}(k+n-1) &= [\Delta\phi_1(\underline{y}(k+n-1)), \Delta\phi_2(\underline{y}(k+n-2)), \ldots, \Delta\phi_n(\underline{y}(k))]^T \\
\bar{g} &= [g_1, g_2, \ldots, g_m]^T \\
\bar{u}(k) &= [\Delta u_1(k-m+1), \Delta u_2(k-m+2), \ldots, \Delta u_m(k)]^T \quad (32)
\end{aligned}
$$

we could rewrite (16) in a compact form as follows:

$$y(k+n) = \bar{\theta}^T\bar{\phi}(k+n-1) + \bar{g}^T\bar{u}(k) + y(l_k+n) + \Delta\nu(k-\tau) \quad (33)$$

Define $\hat{\bar{\theta}}(k)$ and $\hat{\bar{g}}(k)$ as estimate of $\bar{\theta}$ and $\bar{g}$ at the kth step, respectively, and then, the controller will be designed such that

$$y^*(k+n) = \hat{\bar{\theta}}^T(k)\hat{\bar{\phi}}(k+n-1) + \hat{\bar{g}}(k)^T\bar{u}(k) + y(l_k+n) \tag{34}$$

Define the output tracking error as

$$e(k) = y(k) - y^*(k) \tag{35}$$

A proper parameter estimate law will be constructed using the following dead zone indicator which stops the update process when the tracking error is smaller than a specific value

$$a_c(k) = \begin{cases} 1 - \frac{\lambda\|\Delta Z(k-n)\|+|\beta(k-1)|}{|e(k)|}, \text{if } |e(k)| > \lambda\|\Delta Z(k-n)\| + |\beta(k-1)| \\ 0 \quad \text{otherwise} \end{cases} \tag{36}$$

where

$$\beta(k-1) = \hat{\bar{\theta}}^T(k-n)(\hat{\bar{\phi}}(k-1) - \bar{\phi}(k-1)) \tag{37}$$

and λ is same as that used in (28).
The parameter estimates in control law (34) are calculated by the following update laws:

$$\begin{aligned} \hat{\bar{\theta}}(k) &= \hat{\bar{\theta}}(k-n) + \frac{\gamma_c a_c(k)\bar{\phi}(k-1)}{D_c(k)}e(k) \\ \hat{\bar{g}}(k) &= \hat{\bar{g}}(k-n) + \frac{\gamma_c a_c(k)\bar{u}(k-n)}{D_c(k)}e(k) \end{aligned} \tag{38}$$

with

$$D_c(k) = 1 + \|\bar{\phi}(k-1)\|^2 + \|\bar{u}(k-n)\|^2 \tag{39}$$

and $0 < \gamma_c < 2$.

Remark 5.1. *To explicitly calculate the control input from (34), one can see that the estimate of g_m, $\hat{g}_m(k)$, which appears in the denominator, may lead to the so called "controller singularity" problem when the estimate $\hat{g}_m(k)$ falls into a small neighborhood of zero. To avoid the singularity problem, we may take advantage of the a priori information of the lower bound of g_m, i.e. $\underline{g}_m$, to revise the update law of $\hat{g}_m(k)$ in (38) as follows:*

$$\hat{\bar{g}}'(k) = \hat{\bar{g}}(k-n) + \frac{\gamma_c a_c(k)\bar{u}(k-n)}{D_c(k)}e(k)$$

$$\hat{\bar{g}}(k) = \begin{cases} \hat{\bar{g}}'(k), & \text{if } \hat{g}'_m(k) > \underline{g}_m \\ \hat{\bar{g}}_r(k) & \text{otherwise} \end{cases} \tag{40}$$

(41)

where

$$\begin{aligned} \hat{\bar{g}}'(k) &= [\hat{g}'_1(k), \hat{g}'_2(k), \ldots, \hat{g}'_m(k)] \\ \hat{\bar{g}}_r(k) &= [\hat{g}'_1(k), \hat{g}'_2(k), \ldots, \underline{g}_m]^T \end{aligned} \tag{42}$$

In (40), one can see that in case where the estimate of control gain $\hat{g}_m(k)$ falls below the known lower bound, the update laws force it to be at least as large as the lower bound such that the potential singularity problem will be solved.

6. Main results and closed-loop system analysis

The performance of the adaptive controller designed above is summarized in the following theorem:

Theorem 6.1. *Under adaptive control law (34) with parameter estimation law (38) and with employment of predicted future outputs obtained in Section 4, all the closed-loop signals are guaranteed to be bounded and, in addition, the asymptotic output tracking can be achieved:*

$$\lim_{k\to\infty} |y(k) - y^*(k)| = 0 \tag{43}$$

To prove the above theorem, we proceed from the expression of output tracking error. Substitute control law (34) into the transformed system (33) and consider the definition of output tracking error in (35), then we have

$$e(k) = -\tilde{\bar{\theta}}^T(k-n)\bar{\phi}(k-1) - \tilde{\bar{g}}^T(k-n)\bar{u}(k-n) - \beta(k-1) + \Delta\nu(k-n-\tau) \tag{44}$$

where $\tilde{\bar{\theta}}(k) = \hat{\bar{\theta}}(k) - \bar{\theta}$ and $\tilde{\bar{g}}(k) = \hat{\bar{g}}(k) - \bar{g}\,\Delta\nu(k-n-\tau)$ satisfies

$$\|\Delta\nu(k-n-\tau)\| \leq \lambda\|\Delta Z(k-n)\| \tag{45}$$

From the definition of dead zone indicator $a_c(k)$ in (36), we have

$$a_c(k)[|e(k)|(\lambda\|\Delta Z(k-n)\| + |\beta(k-1)|) - e^2(k)] = -a_c^2(k)e^2(k) \tag{46}$$

Let us choose a positive definite Lyapunov function candidate as

$$V_c(k) = \sum_{l=k-n+1}^{k} (\|\tilde{\bar{\theta}}(l)\|^2 + \|\tilde{\bar{g}}(l)\|^2) \tag{47}$$

and then by using (46) the first difference of the above Lyapunov function can be written as

$$\begin{aligned}
&\Delta V_c(k) = V_c(k) - V_c(k-1) \\
&\leq \tilde{\bar{\theta}}^T(k)\tilde{\bar{\theta}}(k) - \tilde{\bar{\theta}}^T(k-n)\tilde{\bar{\theta}}(k-n) + \tilde{\bar{g}}^2(k) - \tilde{\bar{g}}^2(k-n) \\
&= [\|\bar{\phi}(k-1)\|^2 + \|\bar{u}(k-n)\|^2]\frac{a_c^2(k)\gamma_c^2 e^2(k)}{D_c^2(k)} \\
&\quad + [\tilde{\bar{\theta}}^T(k-n)\bar{\phi}(k-1) + \tilde{\bar{g}}^T(k-n)\bar{u}(k-n)]e(k)\frac{2a_c(k)\gamma_c}{D_c(k)} \\
&\leq \frac{a_c^2(k)\gamma_c^2 e^2(k)}{D_c(k)} - \frac{2a_c(k)\gamma_c e^2(k)}{D_c(k)} \\
&\quad + \frac{2a_c(k)\gamma_c|e(k)|(\lambda\|\Delta Z(k-n)\| + |\beta(k-1)|)}{D_c(k)} \\
&\leq -\frac{\gamma_c(2-\gamma_c)a_c^2(k)e^2(k)}{D_c(k)}
\end{aligned} \tag{48}$$

Noting that $0 < \gamma_c < 2$, we have the boundedness of $V_c(k)$ and consequently the boundedness of $\hat{\bar{\theta}}(k)$ and $\hat{\bar{g}}(k)$. Taking summation on both hand sides of (48), we obtain

$$\sum_{k=0}^{\infty} \gamma_c(2-\gamma_c)\frac{a_c^2(k)e^2(k)}{D_c(k)} \leq V_c(0) - V_c(\infty)$$

which implies

$$\lim_{k\to\infty} \frac{a_c^2(k)e^2(k)}{D_c(k)} = 0 \tag{49}$$

Now, we will show that equation (49) results in $\lim_{k\to\infty} a_c(k)e(k) = 0$ using Lemma 3.1, the main stability analysis tool in adaptive discrete-time control. In fact, from the definition of dead zone $a_c(k)$ in (36), when $|e(k)| > \lambda\|\Delta Z(k-n)\| + |\beta(k-1)|$, we have

$$a_c(k)|e(k)| = |e(k)| - \lambda\|\Delta Z(k-n)\| - |\beta(k-1)| > 0$$

and when $|e(k)| \leq \lambda\|\Delta z(k-n)\| + |\beta(k-1)|$, we have

$$a_c(k)|e(k)| = 0 \geq |e(k)| - \lambda\|\Delta Z(k-n)\| - |\beta(k-1)|$$

Thus, we always have

$$|e(k)| - \lambda\|\Delta Z(k-n)\| - |\beta(k-1)| \leq a_c(k)|e(k)| \tag{50}$$

Considering the definition of $\beta(k-1)$ in (37) and the boundedness of $\hat{\hat{\theta}}(k)$, we obtain that $\beta(k-1) = o[O[y(k)]]$.
Since $y(k) \sim e(k)$, we have $\beta(k-1) = o[O[e(k)]]$. According to the Proposition 3.1, we have

$$\begin{aligned}
|y(k)| &\leq C_1 \max_{k'\leq k}\{|e(k')|\} + C_2 \\
&\leq C_1 \max_{k'\leq k}\{|e(k')| - \lambda\|\Delta Z(k'-n)\| - |\beta(k'-1)| \\
&\quad +\lambda\|\Delta Z(k'-n)\| + |\beta(k'-1)|\} + C_2 \\
&\leq C_1 \max_{k'\leq k}\{a_c(k')|e(k')|\} + \lambda C_1 \max_{k'\leq k}\{\|\Delta Z(k'-n)\|\} + C_1 \max_{k'\leq k}\{|\beta(k'-1)|\} \\
&\quad +C_2, \ \forall k \in Z^+_{-n}
\end{aligned} \tag{51}$$

According to Lemma 4.1 and Assumption 3.1, there exits a constant c_β such that

$$|\beta(k+n-1)| \leq o[O[y(k+n-1)]] + \lambda c_\beta \Delta_s(k, n-1) \tag{52}$$

Considering $\Delta Z(k)$ defined in (9) and $\Delta_s(k,m)$ defined in (31), Lemma (3.3), and noting the fact $l_k \leq k-n$, there exist constants $c_{z,1}, c_{z,2}, c_{s,1}$ and $c_{s,2}$ such that

$$\Delta Z(k-n) \leq c_{z,1} \max_{k'\leq k}\{|y(k')|\} + c_{z,2} \tag{53}$$

$$\begin{aligned}
\Delta_s(k, n-1) &= \max_{1\leq k'\leq n-1}\{\|Z(k-n+k') - Z(l_{k-n+k'})\|\} \\
&\leq c_{s,1} \max_{k'\leq k}\{|y(k'+n-1)|\} + c_{s,2}
\end{aligned} \tag{54}$$

According to the definition of $o[\cdot]$ in Definition 3.1, and (52), (54), it is clear that $\forall k \in Z^+_{-n}$

$$\begin{aligned}
|\beta(k+n-1)| &\leq o[O[y(k+n-1)]] + \lambda c_\beta \Delta_s(k, n-1) \\
&\leq (\alpha(k)c_{\beta,1} + \lambda c_\beta c_{s,1}) \max_{k'\leq k}\{|y(k'+n-1)|\} + \alpha(k)c_{\beta,2} + \lambda c_\beta c_{s,2}
\end{aligned} \tag{55}$$

where $\lim_{k\to\infty}\alpha(k) = 0$, and $c_{\beta,1}$ and $c_{\beta,2}$ are positive constants. Since $\lim_{k\to\infty}\alpha(k) = 0$, for any given arbitrary small positive constant ϵ_1, there exists a constants k_1 such that $\alpha(k) \leq \epsilon_1$, $\forall k > k_1$. Thus, it is clear that

$$|\beta(k+n-1)| \leq (\epsilon_1 c_{\beta,1} + \lambda c_\beta c_{s,1}) \max_{k'\leq k}\{|y(k'+n-1)|\} + \epsilon_1 c_{\beta,2} + \lambda c_\beta c_{s,2},\ \forall k > k_1 \quad (56)$$

From inequalities (51), (53), and (56), it is clear that there exist an arbitrary small positive constant ϵ_2 and constants C_3 and C_4 such that

$$\max_{k'\leq k}\{|y(k')|\} \leq C_1 \max_{k'\leq k}\{a_c(k')|e(k')|\} + (\lambda C_3 + \epsilon_2)\max_{k'\leq k}\{|y(k')|\} + C_4,\ k > k_1 \quad (57)$$

which implies the existence of a small positive constant

$$\lambda^* = \frac{1-\epsilon_2}{C_3} \quad (58)$$

such that

$$\max_{k'\leq k}\{|y(k')|\} \leq \frac{C_1}{1-\lambda C_3 - \epsilon_2}\max_{k'\leq k}\{a_c(k')|e(k')|\} + \frac{C_4}{1-\lambda C_3-\epsilon_2},\ k > k_1 \quad (59)$$

holds for all $\lambda < \lambda^*$, where $C_3 = (\bar{c}_c c_{z,1} + c_\beta c_{s,1})C_1$, $\epsilon_2 = \epsilon_1 c_{\beta,1} C_1$ and $C_4 = C_2 + \epsilon_1 c_{\beta,2} C_1 + \lambda \bar{c}_c c_{z,2} C_1 + \lambda c_\beta c_{s,2} C_1$. Note that inequality (59) implies $y(k) = O[a_c(k)e(k)]$. From $\bar{\phi}(y(k+n-1))$ defined in (32) and Assumption 3.1, it can be seen that $\bar{\phi}(y(k-1)) = O[y(k-1)]$. According to the definition of $D_c(k)$ in (39), $y(k) \sim e(k)$, $l_{k-n} \leq k-2n$, the boundedness of $y^*(k)$, and (53), we have

$$\begin{aligned} D_c^{\frac{1}{2}}(k) &\leq 1 + \|\bar{\phi}(k-1)\| + |\bar{u}(k-n)| \\ &= O[y(k)] = O[a_c(k)e(k)] \end{aligned}$$

Then, applying Lemma 3.1 to (49) yields

$$\lim_{k\to\infty} a_c(k)e(k) = 0 \quad (60)$$

From (59) and (60), we can see that the boundedness of $y(k)$ is guaranteed. It follows that tracking error $e(k)$ is bounded, and the boundedness of $u(k)$ and $z(k)$ in (75) can be obtained from (5) in Lemma 3.3, and thus all the signals in the closed-loop system are bounded. Due to the boundedness of $z(k)$, by Lemma 3.2, we have

$$\lim_{k\to\infty} \|\Delta Z(k)\| = 0 \quad (61)$$

which further leads to

$$\lim_{k\to\infty} \|\Delta_s(k, n-1)\| = 0 \quad (62)$$

Next, we will show that $\lim_{k\to\infty} a_c(k)e(k) = 0$ implies $\lim_{k\to\infty} e(k) = 0$. In fact, considering (52) and noting that $y(k) \sim e(k) \sim e(k)$, it follows that

$$|\beta(k-1)| \leq o[O[e(k)]] + \lambda c_\beta \Delta_s(k-n, n-1) \quad (63)$$

which yields

$$|e(k)| - |\beta(k-1)| + \lambda c_\beta \Delta_s(k-n, n-1) \geq |e(k)| - o[O[e(k)]] \\ \geq (1 - \alpha(k)m_1)|e(k)| - \alpha(k)m_2 \quad (64)$$

according to Definition 3.1, where m_1 and m_2 are positive constants, and $\lim_{k\to\infty} \alpha(k) = 0$. Since $\lim_{k\to\infty} \alpha(k) = 0$, there exists a constant k_2 such that $\alpha(k) \leq 1/m_1$, $\forall k > k_2$. Therefore, it can be seen from (64) that

$$|e(k)| - |\beta(k-1)| + \lambda c_\beta \Delta_s(k-n, n-1) + \alpha(k)m_2 \geq (1 - \alpha(k)m_1)|e(k)| \geq 0, \ \forall k > k_2 \quad (65)$$

From (50), it is clear that

$$|e(k)| - |\beta(k-1)| + \lambda c_\beta \Delta_s(k-n, n-1) + \alpha(k)m_2 \\ \leq a_c(k)|e(k)| + \lambda \|\Delta Z(k-n)\| + \lambda c_\beta \Delta_s(k-n, n-1) + \alpha(k)m_2 \quad (66)$$

which implies that $\lim_{k\to\infty} e(k) = 0$ according to (60)-(62), and (65), which further yields $\lim_{k\to\infty} e(k) = 0$ because of $e(k) \sim e(k)$. This completes the proof. ∎

Remark 6.1. *The underlying reason that the asymptotic tracking performance is achieved lies in that the uncertain nonlinear term $v(k-n-\tau)$ in the closed-loop tracking error dynamics (44) will converge to zero because $\lim_{k\to\infty} \|\Delta Z(k)\| = 0$ as shown in (61).*

7. Further discussion on output-feedback systems

In this section, we will make some discussions on the application of control design technique developed before to nonlinear system in lower triangular form. The research interest of lower triangular form systems lies in the fact that a large class of nonlinear systems can be transformed into strict-feedback form or output-feedback form, where the unknown parameters appear linearly in the system equations, via a global parameter-independent diffeomorphism. In a seminal work Kanellakopoulos et al. (1991), it is proved that a class of continuous nonlinear systems can be transformed to lower triangular parameter-strict-feedback form via parameter-independent diffeomorphisms. A similar result is obtained for a class of discrete-time systems Yeh & Kokotovic (1995), in which the geometric conditions for the systems transformable to the form are given and then the discrete-time backstepping design is proposed. More general strict-feedback system with unknown control gains was first studied for continuous-time systems Ye & Jiang (1998), in which it is indicated that a class of nonlinear triangular systems T_{1S} proposed in Seto et al. (1994) is transformable to this form. The discrete-time counterpart system was then studied in Ge et al. (2008), in which discrete Nussbaum gain was exploited to solve the unknown control direction problem. In addition to strict-feedback form systems, output-feedback systems as another kind of lower-triangular form systems have also received much research attention. The discrete-time output-feedback form systems have been studied in Zhao & Kanellakopoulos (2002), in which a set of parameter estimation algorithm using orthogonal projection is proposed and it guarantees the convergence of estimated parameters to their true values in finite steps. In Yang et al. (2009), adaptive control solving the unknown control direction problem has been developed for the discrete-time output-feedback form systems.

As mentioned in Section 1, NARMA model is one of the most popular representations of nonlinear discrete-time systemsLeontaritis & Billings (1985). In the following, we are going to show that the discrete-time output-feedback forms systems are transformable to the NARMA systems in the form of (1) so that the control design in this chapter is also applicable to the systems in the output-feedback form as below:

$$\begin{cases} x_i(k+1) = \theta_i^T \phi_i(x_1(k)) + g_i x_{i+1}(k) + v_i(x_1(k)),\ i = 1,2,\ldots,n-1 \\ x_n(k+1) = \theta_n^T \phi_n(x_1(k)) + g_n u(k) + v_n(x_1(k)) \\ y(k) = x_1(k) \end{cases} \tag{67}$$

where $x_i(k) \in R$, $i = 1,2,\ldots,n$ are the system states, $n \geq 1$ is system order; $u(k) \in R$, $y(k) \in R$ is the system input and output, respectively; θ_i are the vectors of unknown constant parameters; $g_i \in R$ are unknown control gains and $g_i \neq 0$; $\phi_i(\cdot)$, are known nonlinear vector functions; and $v_i(\cdot)$ are nonlinear uncertainties.
It is noted that the nonlinearities $\phi i(\cdot)$ as well as $v_{i(\cdot)}$ depend only on the output $y(k) = x_1(k)$, which is the only measured state. This justifies the name of "output-feedback" form.
According to Ge et al. (2009), for system (67) there exist prediction functions $F_{n-i}(\cdot)$ such that $y(k+n-i) = F_{n-i}(\underline{y}(k), \underline{u}(k-i))$, $i = 1,2,\ldots,n-1$, where

$$\underline{y}(k) = [y(k), y(k-1), \ldots, y(k-n+1)]^T \tag{68}$$

$$\underline{u}(k-i) = [u(k-i), u(k-i-1), \ldots, u(k-n+1)]^T \tag{69}$$

By moving the ith equation $(n-i)$ step ahead, we can rewrite system (67) as follows

$$\begin{cases} x_1(k+n) = \theta_1^T \phi_1(y(k+n-1)) + g_1 x_2(k+n-1) + v_1(y(k+n-1)) \\ x_2(k+n-1) = \theta_2^T \phi_2(y(k+n-2)) + g_2 x_3(k+n-2) + v_2(y(k+n-2)) \\ \vdots \\ x_n(k+1) = \theta_n^T \phi_n(y(k)) + g_n u(k) + v_n(y(k)) \end{cases} \tag{70}$$

Then, we submit the second equation to the first and obtain

$$\begin{aligned} x_1(k+n) &= \theta_1^T \phi_1(y(k+n-1)) + g_1 \theta_2^T \phi_2(y(k+n-2)) \\ &\quad + g_1 g_2 x_3(k+n-2) + v_1(y(k+n-1)) + g_1 v_2(F_{n-2}(\underline{y}(k), \underline{u}(k-2)) \end{aligned} \tag{71}$$

Continuing the iterative substitution, we could finally obtain

$$y(k+n) = \sum_{i=1}^{n} \theta_{fi}^T \phi_i(y(k+n-i)) + g u(k) + v(z(k)) \tag{72}$$

where

$$\theta_{f_1} = \theta_1,\ \theta_{f_i} = \theta_i \prod_{j=1}^{i-1} g_j,\ \ i = 2,3,\ldots,n$$

$$g_{f_1} = 1,\ \ g_{f_i} = \prod_{j=1}^{i-1} g_j,\ \ i = 2,3,\ldots,n,\ \ g = \prod_{j=1}^{n} g_j \tag{73}$$

and

$$v(z(k)) = \sum_{i=1}^{n} g_{f_i} v_i(z(k)),\ \ z(k) = [\underline{y}^T(k), \underline{u}^T(k-1)]^T \tag{74}$$

with

$$\begin{aligned} v_i(z(k)) &= v_i(y(k+n-i)) = v_i(F_{n-i}(\underline{y}(k), \underline{u}(k-i))), \; i = 1, 2, \ldots, n-1, \\ v_n(z(k)) &= v_n(y(k)) \end{aligned} \tag{75}$$

with $z(k)$ defined in the same manner as in (1). Now, it is obvious that the transformed output-feedback form system (72) is a special case of the general NARMA model (1).

8. Study on periodic varying parameters

In this section we shall study the case where the parameters θ_i and g_j, $i = 1, 2, \ldots, n$, $j = 1, 2, \ldots, m$ in (1) are periodically time-varying. The lth element of $\theta_i(k)$ is periodic with known period $N_{i,l}$ and the period of $g_i(k)$ is N_{gi}, i.e. $\theta_{i,l}(k) = \theta_{i,l}(k - N_{i,l})$ and $g_j(k) = g_j(k - N_{gj})$ for known positive constants $N_{i,l}$ and N_{gj}, $l = 1, 2, \ldots, p_i$.

To deal with periodic varying parameters, *periodic adaptive control* (PAC) has been developed in literature, which updates parameters every N steps, where N is a common period such that every period $N_{i,l}$ and N_{gj} can divide N with an integer quotient, respectively. However, the use of the common period will make the periodic adaptation inefficient. If possible, the periodic adaptation should be conducted according to individual periods. Therefore, we will employ the lifting approach proposed in Xu & Huang (2009).

Firstly, we define the augmented parametric vector and corresponding vector-valued nonlinearity function. As there are $N_{i,j}$ different values of the jth element of θ_i at different steps, denote an augmented vector combining them together by

$$\bar{\theta}_{i,l} = [\theta_{i,j,1}, \theta_{i,j,2}, \ldots, \theta_{i,j,N_{i,l}}]^T \tag{76}$$

with constant elements. We can construct an augmented vector including all p_i periodic parameters

$$\Theta_i = [\bar{\theta}_{i,1}^T, \bar{\theta}_{i,2}^T, \ldots, \bar{\theta}_{i,p_i}^T]^T = [\theta_{i,1,1}, \ldots, \theta_{i,1,N_{i,1}}, \ldots, \theta_{i,p_i,1}, \ldots, \theta_{i,p_i,N_{i,p_i}}]^T \tag{77}$$

with all elements being constant. Accordingly, we can define an augmented vector

$$\Phi_i(\underline{y}(k+n-1)) = [\bar{\phi}_{i,1}(\underline{y}(k+n-1)), \ldots, \bar{\phi}_{i,p_i}(\underline{y}(k+n-1))]^T \tag{78}$$

where $\bar{\phi}_{i,l}(\underline{y}(k+n-1)) = [0, \ldots, 0, \phi_i(\underline{y}(k+n-i)), 0, \ldots, 0]^T \in R^{N_{i,l}}$ and the element $\phi_i(k)$ appears in the qth position of $\bar{\phi}_{i,l}(\underline{y}(k+n-1))$ only when $k = sN_{i,l} + q$, for $i = 1, 2, \ldots, N_{i,l}$. It can be seen that n functions $\phi_i(k)$, rotate according to their own periodicity, $N_{i,l}$, respectively. As a result, for each time instance k, we have

$$\theta_i^T(k)\phi_i(\underline{y}(k+n-i)) = \Theta_i^T \Phi_i(\underline{y}(k+n-1)) \tag{79}$$

which converts periodic parameters into an augmented time invariant vector.

Analogously, we convert $g_i(k)$ into an augmented vector $\bar{g}_i = [g_{i,1}, g_{i,2}, \ldots, g_{i,N_{gj}}]$ and meanwhile define a vector

$$\varphi_j(k) = [0, \ldots, 0, 1, 0, \ldots, 0]^T \in R^{N_{gj}} \tag{80}$$

where the element 1 appears in the qth position of $\varphi_j(k)$ only when $k = sN_{gj} + q$. Hence for each time instance k, we have $g_j(k) = \bar{g}_j \varphi_j(k)$, i.e., $g_i(k)$ is converted into an augmented time-invariant vector.

Then, system (1) with periodic time-varying parameters $\theta_i(k)$ and $g_j(k)$ can be transformed into

$$y(k+n) = \sum_{i=1}^{n} \Theta_i^T \Phi_i(y(k+n-i)) + \sum_{j=1}^{m} \bar{g}_j \varphi_j(k) u(k-m+j) + \nu(z(k-\tau)) \tag{81}$$

such that the method developed in Sections 4 and 5 is applicable to (81) for control design.

9. Conclusion

In this chapter, we have studied *asymptotic tracking* adaptive control of a general class of *NARMA* systems with both parametric and nonparametric model uncertainties. The effects of nonlinear nonparametric uncertainty, as well as of the unknown time delay, have been compensated for by using information of previous inputs and outputs. As the *NARMA* model involves future outputs, which bring difficulties into the control design, a future output prediction method has been proposed in Section 4, which makes sure that the prediction error grows with smaller order than the outputs.

Combining the uncertainty compensation technique, the prediction method and adaptive control approach, a predictive adaptive control has been developed in Section 5 which guarantees stability and leads to *asymptotic tracking* performance. The techniques developed in this chapter provide a general control design framework for high order nonlinear discrete-time systems in *NARMA* form. In Sections 7 and 8, we have shown that the proposed control design method is also applicable to output-feedback systems and extendable to systems with periodic varying parameters.

10. Acknowledgments

This work is partially supported by National Nature Science Foundation (NSFC) under Grants 61004059 and 60904086. We would like to thank Ms. Lihua Rong for her careful proofreading.

11. Appendix A: Proof of Proposition 3.1

Only proofs of properties (ii) and (viii) are given below. Proofs of other properties are easy and are thus omitted here.

(ii) From Definition 3.1, we can see that $\|o[x(k)]\| \leq \alpha(k) \max_{k' \leq k+\tau} \|x(k')\|$, $\forall k > k_0, \tau \geq 0$, where $\lim_{k\to\infty} \alpha(k) = 0$. It implies that there exist constants k_1 and $\bar{\alpha}_1$ such that $\alpha(k) \leq \bar{\alpha}_1 < 1$, $\forall k > k_1$. Then, we have

$$\|x(k+\tau) + o[x(k)]\| \leq \|x(k+\tau)\| + \|o[x(k)]\| \leq (1+\bar{\alpha}_1) \max_{k' \leq k+\tau} \|x(k')\|, \forall k > k_1$$

which leads to $x(k+\tau) + o[x(k)] = O[x(k+\tau)]$. On the other hand, we have

$$\begin{aligned}
\max_{k_1 < k' \leq k+\tau} \|x(k')\| &\leq \|\max_{k_1 < k' \leq k+\tau} x(k') + o[x(k)]\| + \|o[x(k)]\| \\
&\leq \|\max_{k_1 < k' \leq k+\tau} x(k') + o[x(k)]\| + \bar{\alpha}_1 \max_{k_1 < k' \leq k+\tau} \{\|x(k')\}
\end{aligned}$$

and

$$\max_{k_1 < k' \leq k+\tau} \|x(k')\| \leq \frac{1}{1-\bar{\alpha}_1} \|\max_{k_1 < k' \leq k} x(k') + o[x(k')]\|, \forall k > k_1$$

which implies $x(k+\tau) = O[x(k) + o[x(k)]]$. Then, it is obvious that $x(k+\tau) + o[x(k)] \sim x(k)$.
(viii) First, let us suppose that $x_1(k)$ is unbounded and define $i_k = \arg\max_{i\leq k} \|x_1(i)\|$. Then, it is easy to see that $i_k \to \infty$ as $k \to \infty$. Due to $\lim_{k\to\infty} \alpha(k) = 0$, there exist a constant k_2 such that $\alpha(i_k) \leq \frac{1}{2}$ and $\|o[x_1(k)]\| \leq \frac{1}{2}\max_{k'\leq k} \|x_1(k')\|$, $\forall k > k_2$. Considering $x_2(k) = x_1(k) + o[x_1(k)]$, we have

$$\|x_2(i_k)\| = \|x_1(i_k) + o[x_1(i_k)]\| \geq \|x_1(i_k)\| - \|o[x_1(i_k)]\| \geq \frac{1}{2}\|x_1(i_k)\|, \forall k > k_2$$

which leads to $\|x_1(i_k)\| \leq 2\|x_2(i_k)\|$, $\forall k \geq k_2$. Then, the unboundedness of $x_1(k)$ conflicts with $\lim_{k\to\infty} \|x_2(k)\| = 0$. Therefore, $x_1(k)$ must be bounded. Noting that $\alpha(k) \to 0$, we have

$$0 \leq \|x_1(k)\| \leq \|x_1(k) + o[x_1(k)]\| + \|o[x_1(k)]\| \leq \|x_2(k)\| + \alpha(k)\max_{k'\leq k} \|x_1(k')\| \to 0$$

which implies $\lim_{k\to\infty} \|x_1(k)\| = 0$.

12. Appendix B: Proof of Lemma 4.1

It follows from (16) and (17) that

$$\begin{aligned}
&\tilde{y}(k+1|k) = \hat{y}(k+1|k) - y(k+1) \\
&= \sum_{i=1}^{n} \tilde{\theta}_i^T(k-n+2)\Delta\phi_i(k-i+1) + \sum_{i=1}^{m} \tilde{g}_j(k-n+2)\Delta u(k-m+j-n+1) \\
&-\Delta v(k-n+1-\tau)
\end{aligned} \quad (82)$$

which results in

$$\begin{aligned}
&-\{\sum_{i=1}^{n} \tilde{\theta}_i^T(k-n+2)\Delta\phi_i(k-i+1) + \sum_{j=1}^{m} \tilde{g}_j(k-n+2)\Delta u(k-m+j-n+1)\}\tilde{y}(k+1|k) \\
&= -\{\tilde{y}(k+1|k) + \Delta v(k-n+1-\tau)\}\tilde{y}(k+1|k) \\
&= -\tilde{y}^2(k+1|k) - \Delta v(k-n+1-\tau)\tilde{y}(k+1|k) \\
&\leq -\tilde{y}^2(k+1|k) + \lambda|\tilde{y}(k+1|k)|\|\Delta Z(k-n+1)\|
\end{aligned} \quad (83)$$

To prove the boundedness of all the estimated parameters, let us choose the following Lyapunov function candidate

$$V_p(k) = \sum_{l=k-n+2}^{k} \left(\sum_{i=1}^{n} \tilde{\theta}_i^2(l) + \sum_{j=1}^{m} \tilde{g}_j^2\right) \quad (84)$$

Using the parameter update law (26), the difference of $V_p(k)$ is

$$\begin{aligned}
&\Delta V_p(k) = V_p(k+1) - V_p(k) \\
&= \sum_{i=1}^{n}[\tilde{\theta}_i^2(k+1) - \tilde{\theta}_i^2(k-n+2)] + \sum_{j=1}^{m}[\tilde{g}_j^2(k+1) - \tilde{g}_j^2(k-n+2)] \\
&= \frac{a_p^2(k)\gamma_p^2\tilde{y}^2(k+1|k)[\sum_{i=1}^{n}\|\Delta\phi_i(k-i+1)\|^2 + \sum_{j=1}^{m}\Delta u^2(k-m+j-n+1)]}{D_p^2(k)} - \frac{2a_p(k)\gamma}{D_p(k)} \times \\
&\{\sum_{i=1}^{n} \tilde{\theta}_i^T(k-n+2)\Delta\phi_i(k-i+1) + \sum_{j=1}^{m} \tilde{g}_j(k-n+2)\Delta u(k-m+j-n+1)\}\tilde{y}(k+1|k)
\end{aligned}$$

According to the definition of $D_p(k)$ in (27) and inequality (83), the difference of $V_p(k)$ above can be written as

$$\begin{aligned}\Delta V_p(k) &\leq \frac{a_p^2(k)\gamma^2\tilde{y}^2(k+1|k)}{D_p(k)} - \frac{2a_p(k)\gamma\tilde{y}^2(k+1|k)}{D_p(k)} \\ &+ \frac{2a_p(k)\gamma_p\lambda|\tilde{y}(k+1|k)|\|\Delta Z(k-n+1)\|}{D_p(k)} \\ &= \frac{a_p^2(k)\gamma_p^2\tilde{y}^2(k+1|k)}{D_p(k)} - \frac{2a_p^2(k)\gamma\tilde{y}^2(k+1|k)}{D_p(k)} \\ &= -\frac{a_p^2(k)\gamma_p(2-\gamma_p)\tilde{y}^2(k+1|k)}{D_p(k)} \end{aligned} \tag{85}$$

where the following equation obtained from the definition of dead zone (28) is used:

$$\begin{aligned}-2a_p^2(k)\gamma\tilde{y}^2(k+1|k) &= -2a_p(k)\gamma\tilde{y}^2(k+1|k) \\ &+2a_p(k)\gamma_p\lambda|\tilde{y}(k+1|k)|\|\Delta Z(k-n+1)\|\end{aligned} \tag{86}$$

Noting that $0 < \gamma_p < 2$, we can see from (85) that the difference of Lyapunov function $V_p(k)$, is non-positive and thus, the boundedness of $V_p(k)$ is guaranteed. It further implies the boundedness of $\hat{\theta}_i(k)$ and $\hat{g}_j(k)$. Thus, there exist finite constants b_{θ_i} and b_{g_j} such that

$$\|\hat{\theta}_i(k)\| \leq b_{\theta_i}, \; \hat{g}_j(k) \leq b_{g_j}, \; \forall k \in Z^+_{-n} \tag{87}$$

Taking summation on both hand sides of (85), we obtain

$$\sum_{k=0}^{\infty} \frac{a_p^2(k)\gamma(2-\gamma)\tilde{y}^2(k+1|k)}{D_p(k)} \leq V_p(0) - V_p(\infty) \tag{88}$$

Note that the left hand side of inequality (88) is the summation of a non-decreasing sequence and thus the boundedness of $V_p(k)$ implies

$$\frac{a_p^2(k)\tilde{y}^2(k+1|k)}{D_p(k)} := \alpha(k) \to 0 \tag{89}$$

Noting that $l_{k-n+1} \leq k-2n+1$ by (7) and considering Assumption 3.1, (5) in Lemma 3.3, we see that $D_p(k)$ in (27) satisfies

$$D_p^{\frac{1}{2}}(k) = O[y(k+1)] \tag{90}$$

From (89) and (90), we have

$$a_p(k)|\tilde{y}(k+1|k)| = \alpha^{\frac{1}{2}}(k)D_p^{\frac{1}{2}}(k) = o[D_p^{\frac{1}{2}}(k)] = o[O[y(k+1)]] \tag{91}$$

From the definition of dead zone in (28), when $|\tilde{y}(k+1|k)| > \lambda\|\Delta Z(k-n+1)\|$, we have

$$a_p(k)|\tilde{y}(k+1|k)| = |\tilde{y}(k+1|k)| - \lambda\|\Delta Z(k-n+1)\| > 0$$

while when $|\tilde{y}(k+1|k)| \leq \lambda \hat{c}_p(k-n+2)\|\Delta Z(k-n+1)\|$, we have

$$a_p(k)|\tilde{y}(k+1|k)| = 0 \geq |\tilde{y}(k+1|k)| - \lambda\|\Delta Z(k-n+1)\|.$$

In summary, the definition of dead zone in (28) guarantees the following inequality

$$|\tilde{y}(k+1|k)| \leq a_p(k)|\tilde{y}(k+1|k)| + \lambda \hat{c}_p(k-n+2)\|\Delta Z(k-n+1)\| \tag{92}$$

which together with (91), boundedness of the parameter estimates, and the definition of $\Delta_s(k,m)$ in (31) yields

$$|\tilde{y}(k+1|k)| \leq o[O[y(k+1)]] + \lambda c_1 \Delta_s(k,1) \tag{93}$$

with $c_1 = 1$. Now, let us analyze the two-step prediction error:

$$\begin{aligned}\tilde{y}(k+2|k) &= \hat{y}(k+2|k) - y(k+2)\\ &= \tilde{y}(k+2|k+1) + \breve{y}(k+2|k)\end{aligned} \tag{94}$$

where

$$\begin{aligned}\tilde{y}(k+2|k+1) &= \hat{y}(k+2|k+1) - y(k+2)\\ \breve{y}(k+2|k) &= \hat{y}(k+2|k) - \hat{y}(k+2|k+1)\end{aligned} \tag{95}$$

From (93), it is easy to see that

$$|\tilde{y}(k+2|k+1)| \leq o[O[y(k+2)]] + \lambda c_1 \Delta_s(k,2) \tag{96}$$

From (17), and (20), it is clear that $\breve{y}(k+2|k)$ in (95) can be written as

$$\begin{aligned}\breve{y}(k+2|k) &= \hat{y}(k+2|k) - \hat{y}(k+2|k+1)\\ &= \hat{\theta}_1^T(k-n+3)[\Delta\hat{\phi}(k+1|k) - \Delta\phi(k+1)]\end{aligned} \tag{97}$$

Using (93) and the Lipschitz condition of $\Delta\phi_i(\cdot)$ (or equivalently $\phi_i(\cdot)$) with Lipschitz coefficient L_i, we have

$$\|\Delta\hat{\phi}(k+1|k) - \Delta\phi(k+1)\| \leq L_1|\tilde{y}(k+1|k)| \leq o[O[y(k+1)]] + \lambda c_1 L_1 \Delta_s(k,1) \tag{98}$$

which yields

$$|\breve{y}(k+2|k)| \leq o[O[y(k+1)]] + \lambda L_1 b_{\theta_1} \Delta_s(k,1) \tag{99}$$

From (94), (96) and (99), it is clear that there exists a constant c_2 such that

$$|\tilde{y}(k+2|k)| \leq o[O[y(k+2)]] + \lambda c_2 \Delta_s(k,2) \tag{100}$$

Continuing the analysis above, for l-step estimate error $\tilde{y}(k+l|k)$, we have

$$\begin{aligned}\tilde{y}(k+l|k) &= \hat{y}(k+l|k) - y(k+l)\\ &= \breve{y}(k+l|k) + \tilde{y}(k+l|k+1)\end{aligned} \tag{101}$$

where

$$\begin{aligned}\tilde{y}(k+l|k+1) &= \hat{y}(k+l|k+1) - y(k+l)\\ \breve{y}(k+l|k) &= \hat{y}(k+l|k) - \hat{y}(k+l|k+1)\end{aligned} \tag{102}$$

For $(l-1)$-step estimate error $\tilde{y}(k+l-1|k)$, it can be seen that there exist constants $\tilde{c}_{l-1}$ and $\check{c}_{l-1}$ such that

$$\begin{aligned} |\tilde{y}(k+l-1|k)| &\leq o[O[y(k+l-1)]] + \lambda\tilde{c}_{l-1}\Delta_s(k,l-1) \\ |\check{y}(k+l-1|k)| &\leq o[O[y(k+l-2)]] + \lambda\check{c}_{l-1}\Delta_s(k,l-2) \end{aligned} \quad (103)$$

From (25) and (102), it is clear that $\check{y}(k+l|k)$ can be expressed as

$$\check{y}(k+l|k) = \sum_{i=1}^{l-1} \hat{\theta}_i^T(k-n+l+1)[\Delta\hat{\phi}(k+l-i|k) - \Delta\hat{\phi}(k+l-i|k+1)] \quad (104)$$

From (102), we have

$$\hat{y}(k+l-i|k) - \hat{y}(k+l-i|k+1) = \check{y}(k+l-i|k) \quad (105)$$

According to the Lipschitz condition of $\phi(\cdot)$ and (105), the following equality holds:

$$\sum_{i=1}^{l-1} \|\Delta\hat{\phi}(k+l-i|k) - \Delta\phi(k+l-i)\| \leq \max\{L_j\}_{1\leq j\leq l-1} \sum_{i=1}^{l-1} |\check{y}(k+l-i|k)| \quad (106)$$

From (93),(101)-(106), it follows that there exist constants c_l such that

$$|\tilde{y}(k+l|k)| \leq o[O[y(k+l)]] + \lambda c_l \Delta_s(k,l)$$

which completes the proof.

13. References

Arcak, M., Teel, A. & Kokotovic, P. (2001). Robust nonlinear control of feedforward systems with unmodeled dynamics, *Automatica* **37**(2): 265–272.

Cabrera, J. B. D. & Narendra, K. S. (1999). Issues in the application of neural networks for tracking based on inverse control, *IEEE Transactions on Automatic Control* **44**(11): 2007–2027.

Chen, L. J. & Narendra, K. S. (2001). Nonlinear adaptive control using neural networks and multiple models, *Automatica* **37**(8): 1245–1255.

Chen, X. K. (2006). Adaptive sliding mode control for discrete-time multi-input multi-output systems, *Automatica* **42**(3): 427–435.

Chen, X. K., Fukuda, T. & Young, K. D. (2001). Adaptive quasi-sliding-mode tracking control for discrete uncertain input-output systems, *IEEE Transactions on Industrial Electronics* **48**(1): 216–224.

Egardt, B. (1979). *Stability of Adaptive Control*, Springer-Verlag, New York.

Ge, S. S., Hong, F. & Lee, T. H. (2003). Adaptive neural network control of nonlinear systems with unknown time delays, *IEEE Transactions on Automatic Control* **48**(11): 2004–2010.

Ge, S. S., Hong, F. & Lee, T. H. (2004). Adaptive neural control of nonlinear time-delay systems with unknow virtual control coefficients, *IEEE Transactions on Systems, Man, and Cybernetics, Part B* **34**(1): 499–516.

Ge, S. S. & Tee, K. P. (2007). Approximation-based control of nonlinear mimo time-delay systems, *Automatica* **43**(1): 31–43.

Ge, S. S., Yang, C., Dai, S.-L., Jiao, Z. X. & Lee, T. H. (2009). Robust adaptive control of a class of nonlinear strict-feedback discrete-time systems with exact output tracking, *Automatica* **45**(11): 2537–2545.

Ge, S. S., Yang, C. & Lee, T. H. (2008). Adaptive robust control of a class of nonlinear strict-feedback discrete-time systems with unknown control directions, *Systems & Control Letters* **57**(11): 888–895.

Goodwin, G. C., Ramadge, P. J. & Caines, P. E. (1980). Discrete-time multivariable adaptive control, *IEEE Transactions on Automatic Control* **25**(3): 449–456.

Hirsch, M. W. & Smale, S. (1974). *Differential Equations,Dynamical Systems, and Linear Algebra*, San Diego, CA:Acadamic Press, Inc.

Kanellakopoulos, I., Kokotovic, P. V. & Morse, A. S. (1991). Systematic design of adaptive controller for feedback linearizable systems, *IEEE Transactions on Automatic Control* **36**(11): 1241–1253.

Kolmanovskii, V. B. & Myshkis, A. (1992). *Applied theory of functional differential equations (Vol. 85)*, Kluwer Academic Publisher, Dordrecht.

Lee, T. H. (1996). Adaptive control of time-varying discrete-time systems: Stability and instability analysis for a first-order process, *Journal of Systems Engineering* **6**(1): 12–19.

Leontaritis, I. J. & Billings, S. A. (1985). Input-output parametric models for nonlinear systems, *International Journal of Control* **41**(2): 303–344.

Ma, H. B. (2006). *Capability and Limitation of Feedback Mechanism in Dealing with Uncertainties of Some Discrete-time Control Systems*, Phd thesis, Graduate School of Chinese Academy of Sciences, Beijing, China.

Ma, H. B. (2008). Further results on limitations to the capability of feedback, *International Journal of Control* **81**(1): 21–42.
URL: *http://dx.doi.org/10.1080/00207170701218333*

Ma, H. B., Lum, K. Y. & Ge, S. S. (2007). Adaptive control for a discrete-time first-order nonlinear system with both parametric and non-parametric uncertainties, *Proceedings of the 46th IEEE Conference on Decision and Control*, New Orleans, Louisiana USA, pp. 4839–4844.

Myszkorowski, P. (1994). Robust control of linear discrete-time systems, *Systems & Control Letters* **22**(4): 277–280.

Nešić, D. & Laila, D. S. (July, 2002). A note on input-to-state stabilization for nonlinear sampled-data systems, *IEEE Transactions on Automatic Control* **47**(7): 1153–1158.

Nešić, D. & Teel, A. R. (2006). Stabilization of sampled-data nonlinear systems via backstepping on their euler approximate model, *Automatica* **42**(10): 1801–1808.

Seto, D., Annaswamy, A. M. & Baillieul, J. (1994). Adaptive control of nonlinear systems with a triangular structure, *IEEE Transactions on Automatic Control* **39**: 1411–1428.

Sokolov, V. F. (2003). Adaptive suboptimal tracking for the first-order plant with Lipschitz uncertainty, *IEEE Transactions on Automatic Control* **48**(4): 607–612.

Tao, G. (2003). *Adaptive Control Design and Analysis*, John Wiley & Sons, Hoboken, NJ.

Wu, H. (2000). Adaptive stabilizing state feedback controllers of uncertaindynamical systems with multiple time delays, *IEEE Transactions on Automatic Control* **45**(9): 1697–1701.

Xia, Y., Fu, M. & Shi, P. (2009). *Analysis and Synthesis of Dynamical Systems with Time-Delays*, Vol. 387 of *Lecture Notes in Control and Information Sciences*, Springer, Berlin Heidelberg.

Xie, L. L. & Guo, L. (2000). How much uncertainty can be dealt with by feedback?, *IEEE Transactions on Automatic Control* **45**(12): 2203–2217.

Xu, J.-X. & Huang, D. (2009). Discrete-time adaptive control for a class of nonlinear systems with periodic parameters: A lifting approach, *Proceedings of 2009 Asian Control Conference*, Hong Kong, pp. 678–683.

Yang, C., Ge, S. S. & Lee, T. H. (2009). Output feedback adaptive control of a class of nonlinear discrete-time systems with unknown control directions, *Automatica* **45**(1): 270–276.

Ye, X. & Jiang, J. (1998). Adaptive nonlinear design without *a priori* knowledge of control directions, *IEEE Transactions on Automatic Control* **43**(11): 1617–1621.

Yeh, P. C. & Kokotovic, P. V. (1995). Adaptive control of a class of nonlinear discrete-time systems, *International Journal of Control* **62**(2): 303–324.

Zhang, T. & Ge, S. (2007). Adaptive neural control of MIMO nonlinear state time-varying delay systems with unknown dead-zones and gain signs, *Automatica* **43**(6): 1021–1033.

Zhang, Y., Wen, C. Y. & Soh, Y. C. (2001). Robust adaptive control of nonlinear discrete-time systems by backstepping without overparameterization, *Automatica* **37**(4): 551 – 558.

Zhang, Y. X. & Guo, L. (2002). A limit to the capability of feedback, *IEEE Transactions on Automatic Control* **47**(4): 687–692.

Zhao, J. & Kanellakopoulos, I. (2002). Active Identification for Discrete-Time Nonlinear Control-Part I: Output-Feedback Systems, *IEEE Transactions on Automatic Control* **47**(2): 210–224.

Zhu, Q. M. & Guo, L. Z. (2004). Stable adaptive neurocontrol for nonlinear discrete-time systems, *IEEE Transactions on Neural Networks* **15**(3): 653–662.

14

Decentralized Adaptive Control of Discrete-Time Multi-Agent Systems

Hongbin Ma[1], Chenguang Yang[2] and Mengyin Fu[3]
[1]Beijing Institute of Technology
[2]University of Plymouth
[3]Beijing Institute of Technology
[1,3]China
[2]United Kingdom

1. Introduction

In this chapter, we report some work on decentralized adaptive control of discrete-time multi-agent systems. Multi-agent systems, one important class of models of the so-called complex systems, have received great attention since 1980s in many areas such as physics, biology, bionics, engineering, artificial intelligence, and so on. With the development of technologies, more and more complex control systems demand new theories to deal with challenging problems which do not exist in traditional single-plant control systems.
The new challenges may be classified but not necessarily restricted in the following aspects:

- The increasing number of connected plants (or subsystems) adds more complexity to the control of whole system. Generally speaking, it is very difficult or even impossible to control the whole system in the same way as controlling one single plant.
- The couplings between plants interfere the evolution of states and outputs of each plant. That is to say, it is not possible to completely analyze each plant independently without considering other related plants.
- The connected plants need to exchange information among one another, which may bring extra communication constraints and costs. Generally speaking, the information exchange only occurs among coupled plants, and each plant may only have local connections with other plants.
- There may exist various uncertainties in the connected plants. The uncertainties may include unknown parameters, unknown couplings, unmodeled dynamics, and so on.

To resolve the above issues, multi-agent system control has been investigated by many researchers. Applications of multi-agent system control include scheduling of automated highway systems, formation control of satellite clusters, and distributed optimization of multiple mobile robotic systems, etc. Several examples can be found in Burns (2000); Swaroop & Hedrick (1999).
Various control strategies developed for multi-agent systems can be roughly assorted into two architectures: centralized and decentralized. In the decentralized control, local control for each agent is designed only using locally available information so it requires less

computational effort and is relatively more scalable with respect to the swarm size. In recent years, especially since the so-called Vicsek model was reported in Vicsek et al. (1995), decentralized control of multi-agent system has received much attention in the research community (e.g. Jadbabaie et al. (2003a); Moreau (2005)). In the (discrete-time) Vicsek model, there are n agents and all the agents move in the plane with the same speed but with different headings, which are updated by averaging the heading angles of neighor agents. By exploring matrix and graph properties, a theoretical explanation for the consensus behavior of the Vicsek model has been provided in Jadbabaie et al. (2003a). In Tanner & Christodoulakis (2005), a discrete-time multi-agent system model has been studied with fixed undirected topology and all the agents are assumed to transmit their state information in turn. In Xiao & Wang (2006), some sufficient conditions for the solvability of consensus problems for discrete-time multi-agent systems with switching topology and time-varying delays have been presented by using matrix theories. In Moreau (2005), a discrete-time network model of agents interacting via time-dependent communication links has been investigated. The result in Moreau (2005) has been extended to the case with time-varying delays by set-value Lyapunov theory in Angeli & Bliman (2006). Despite the fact that many researchers have focused on problems like consensus, synchronization, etc., we shall notice that the involved underlying dynamics in most existing models are essentially evolving with time in an invariant way determined by fixed parameters and system structure. This motivates us to consider decentralized adaptive control problems which essentially involve distributed agents with ability of adaptation and learning. Up to now, there are limited work on decentralized adaptive control for discrete-time multi-agent systems.

The theoretical work in this chapter has the following motivations:

1. The research on the capability and limitation of the feedback mechanism (e.g. Ma (2008a;b); Xie & Guo (2000)) in recent years focuses on investigating how to identify the maximum capability of feedback mechanism in dealing with *internal uncertainties of one single system.*
2. The decades of studies on traditional adaptive control (e.g. Aström & Wittenmark (1989); Chen & Guo (1991); Goodwin & Sin (1984); Ioannou & Sun (1996)) focus on investigating how to identify *the unknown parameters of a single plant*, especially a linear system or linear-in-parameter system.
3. The extensive studies on complex systems, especially the so-called *complex adaptive systems* theory Holland (1996), mainly focus on *agent-based modeling and simulations* rather than rigorous mathematical analysis.

Motivated by the above issues, to investigate how to deal with *coupling uncertainties* as well as internal uncertainties, we try to consider decentralized adaptive control of multi-agent systems, which exhibit complexity characteristics such as parametric internal uncertainties, parametric coupling uncertainties, unmodeled dynamics, random noise, and communication limits. To facilitate mathematical study on adaptive control problems of complex systems, the following simple yet nontrivial theoretical framework is adopted in our theoretical study:

1. The whole system consists of many dynamical agents, and evolution of each agent can be described by a state equation with optional output equation. Different agents may have different structures or parameters.
2. The evolution of each agent may be interacted by other agents, which means that the dynamic equations of agents are coupled in general. Such interactions among agents are usually restricted in local range, and the extent or intensity of reaction can be parameterized.

3. There exist information limits for all of the agents: (a) Each agent does *not* have access to internal structure or parameters of other agents while it may have complete or limited knowledge to its own internal structure and values of internal parameters. (b) Each agent does *not* know the intensity of influence from others. (c) However, each agent can observe the states of neighbor agents besides its own state.
4. Under the information limits above, each agent may utilize all of the information in hand to estimate the intensity of influence and to design local control so as to change the state of itself, consequently to influence neighbor agents. In other words, each agent is selfish and it aims to maximize its local benefits via minimizing the local tracking error.

Within the above framework, we are to explore the answers to the following basic problem: *Is it possible for all of the agents to achieve a global goal based on the local information and local control?* Here the global goal may refer to global stability, synchronization, consensus, or formation, etc. We shall start from a general model of discrete-time multi-agent system and discuss adaptive control design for several typical cases of this model. The ideas in this chapter can be also applied in more general or complex models, which may be considered in our future work and may involve more difficulties in the design and theoretical analysis of decentralized adaptive controller.

The remainder of this chapter is organized as follows: first, problem formulation will be given in Section 2 with the description of the general discrete-time multi-agent system model and several cases of local tracking goals; then, for these various local tracking tasks, decentralized adaptive control problem for a stochastic synchronization problem is discussed in Section 3 based on the recursive least-squares estimation algorithm; in Section 4, decentralized adaptive control for a special deterministic tracking problem, whereas the system has uncertain parameters, is given based on least-squares estimation algorithm; and Section 5 studies decentralized adaptive control for the special case of a hidden leader tracking problem, based on the normalized gradient estimation algorithm; finally, we give some concluding remarks in the last section.

2. Problem formulation

In this section, we will first describe the network of dynamic systems and then formulate the problems to be studied. We shall study a simple discrete-time dynamic network. In this model, there are N subsystems (plants), and each subsystem represents evolution of one agent. We denote the state of Agent i at time t by $x_i(t)$, and, for simplicity, we assume that linear influences among agents exist in this model. For convenience, we define the concepts of "neighbor" and "neighborhood" as follows: Agent j is a *neighbor* of Agent i if Agent j has influence on Agent i. Let $\mathcal{N}_i$ denote the set of all neighbors of Agent i and Agent i itself. Obviously *neighborhood* $\mathcal{N}_i$ of Agent i is a concept describing the communication limits between Agent i and others.

2.1 System model

The general model of each agent has the following state equation ($i = 1, 2, \ldots, N$) :

$$x_i(t+1) = f_i(z_i(t)) + u_i(t) + \gamma_i \bar{x}_i(t) + w_i(t+1) \tag{2.1}$$

with $z_i(t) = [\underline{x}_i(t), \underline{u}_i(t)]^T$, $\underline{x}_i(t) = [x_i(t), x_i(t-1), \ldots, x_i(t-n_i+1)]^T$ and $\underline{u}_i(t) = [u_i(t), u_i(t-1), \ldots, u_i(t-m_i+1)]^T$, where $f_i(\cdot)$ represents the internal structure of Agent i, $u_i(t)$ is the local control of Agent i, $w_i(t)$ is the unobservable random noise sequence, and

$\gamma_i \bar{x}_i(t)$ reflects the influence of the other agents towards Agent i. Hereinafter, $\bar{x}_i(t)$ is the weighted average of states of agents in the neighborhood of Agent i, i.e.,

$$\bar{x}_i(t) = \sum_{j \in \mathcal{N}_i} g_{ij} x_j(t) \tag{2.2}$$

where the nonnegative constants $\{g_{ij}\}$ satisfy $\sum_{j \in \mathcal{N}_i} g_{ij} = 1$ and γ_i denotes the *intensity of influence*, which is unknown to Agent i. From graph theory, the network can be represented by a directed graph with each node representing an agent and the neighborhood of Node i consists of all the nodes that are connected to Node i with an edge directing to Node i. This graph can be further represented by an adjacent matrix

$$G = (g_{ij}), g_{ij} = 0 \text{ if } j \notin \mathcal{N}_i. \tag{2.3}$$

***Remark* 2.1.** Although model (2.1) is simple enough, it can capture all essential features that we want, and the simple model can be viewed as a prototype or approximation of more complex models. Model (2.1) highlights the difficulties in dealing with coupling uncertainties as well as other uncertainties by feedback control.

2.2 Local tracking goals

Due to the limitation in the communication among the agents, generally speaking, agents can only try to achieve local goals. We assume that the *local tracking goal* for Agent i is to follow a reference signal x_i^{ref}, which can be a known sequence or a sequence relating to other agents as discussed below:

Case I (deterministic tracking). In this case, $x_i^{\text{ref}}(t)$ is a sequence of deterministic signals (bounded or even unbounded) which satisfies $|x_i^{\text{ref}}(t)| = O(t^\delta)$.

Case II (center-oriented tracking). In this case, $x_i^{\text{ref}}(t) = \bar{x}(t) \triangleq \frac{1}{N}\sum_{i=1}^N x_i(t)$ is the center state of all agents, i.e., average of states of all agents.

Case III (loose tracking). In this case, $x_i^{\text{ref}}(t) = \lambda \bar{x}_i(t)$, where constant $|\lambda| < 1$. This case means that the tracking signal $x_i^{\text{ref}}(t)$ is close to the (weighted) average of states of neighbor agents of Agent i, and factor λ describes how close it is.

Case IV (tight tracking). In this case, $x_i^{\text{ref}}(t) = \bar{x}_i(t)$. This case means that the tracking signal $x_i^{\text{ref}}(t)$ is exactly the (weighted) average of states of agents in the neighborhood of Agent i.

In the first two cases, all agents track a common signal sequence, and the only differences are as follows: In Case I the common sequence has nothing with every agent's state; however, in Case II the common sequence is the center state of all of the agents. The first two cases mean that a common "leader" of all of agents exists, who can communicate with and send commands to all agents; however, the agents can only communicate with one another under certain *information limits*. In Cases III and IV, no common "leader" exists and all agents attempt to track the average state $\bar{x}_i(t)$ of its neighbors, and the difference between them is just the factor of tracking tightness.

2.3 Decentralized adaptive control problem

In the framework above, Agent i does not know the intensity of influence γ_i; however, it can use the historical information

$$\{x_i(t), \bar{x}_i(t), u_i(t-1), x_i(t-1), \bar{x}_i(t-1), u_i(t-2), \ldots, x_i(1), \bar{x}_i(1), u_i(0)\} \tag{2.4}$$

to estimate γ_i and can further try to design its local control $u_i(t)$ to achieve its local goal. Such a problem is called a *decentralized adaptive control problem* since the agents must be smart enough so as to design a stabilizing adaptive control law, rather than to simply follow a common rule with fixed parameters such as the so-called *consensus protocol*, in a coupling network. Note that in the above problem formulation, besides the uncertain parameters γ_i, other uncertainties and constraints are also allowed to exist in the model, which may add the difficulty of decentralized adaptive control problem. In this chapter, we will discuss several concrete examples of designing decentralized adaptive control laws, in which coupling uncertainties, external noise disturbance, internal parametric uncertainties, and even functional structure uncertainties may exist and be dealt with by the decentralized adaptive controllers.

3. Decentralized synchronization with adaptive control

Synchronization is a simple global behavior of agents, and it means that all agents tend to behave in the same way as time goes by. For example, two fine-tuned coupled oscillators may gradually follow almost the same pace and pattern. As a kind of common and important phenomenon in nature, synchronization has been extensively investigated or discussed in the literature (e.g., Time et al. (2004); Wu & Chua (1995); Zhan et al. (2003)) due to its usefulness (e.g. secure communication with chaos synchronization) or harm (e.g. passing a bridge resonantly). Lots of existing work on synchronization are conducted on chaos (e.g.Gade & Hu (2000)), coupled maps (e.g.Jalan & Amritkar (2003)), scale-free or small-world networks (e.g.Barahona & Pecora (2002)), and complex dynamical networks (e.g.Li & Chen (2003)), etc. In recent years, several synchronization-related topics (*coordination*, *rendezvous*, *consensus*, *formation*, etc.) have also become active in the research community (e.g.Cao et al. (2008); Jadbabaie et al. (2003b); Olfati-Saber et al. (2007)). As for adaptive synchronization, it has received the attention of a few researchers in recent years (e.g.Yao et al. (2006); Zhou et al. (2006)), and the existing work mainly focused on deterministic continuous-time systems, especially chaotic systems, by constructing certain update laws to deal with parametric uncertainties and applying classical Lyapunov stability theory to analyze corresponding closed-loop systems.

In this section, we are to investigate a synchronization problem of a stochastic dynamic network. Due to the presence of random noise and unknown parametric coupling, unlike most existing work on synchronization, we need to introduce new concepts of synchronization and the decentralized learning (estimation) algorithm for studying the problem of decentralized adaptive synchronization.

3.1 System model

In this section, for simplicity, we assume that the internal function $f_i(\cdot)$ is known to each agent and the agents are in a common noisy environment, i.e. the random noise $\{w(t), \mathcal{F}_t\}$ are commonly present for all agents. Hence, the dynamics of Agent i ($i = 1, 2, \ldots, N$) has the following state equation:

$$x_i(t+1) = f_i(z_i(t)) + u_i(t) + \gamma_i \bar{x}_i(t) + w(t+1). \tag{3.1}$$

In this model, we emphasize that coupling uncertainty γ_i is the main source to prevent the agents from achieving synchronization with ease. And the random noise makes that traditional analysis techniques for investigating synchronization of deterministic systems cannot be applied here because it is impossible to determine a fixed common orbit for all agents to track asymptotically. These difficulties make the rather simple model here non-trivial for studying the synchronization property of the whole system, and we will find that proper estimation algorithms, which can be somewhat regarded as learning algorithms and make the agents smarter than those machinelike agents with fixed dynamics in previous studies, is critical for each agent to deal with these uncertainties.

3.2 Local controller design

As the intensity of influence γ_i is unknown, Agent i is supposed to estimate it on-line via commonly-used *recursive least-squares* (RLS) algorithm and design its local control based on the intensity estimate $\hat{\gamma}_i(t)$ via the certainty equivalence principle as follows:

$$u_i(t) = -f_i(z_i(t)) - \hat{\gamma}_i(t)\bar{x}_i(t) + x_i^{\text{ref}}(t) \tag{3.2}$$

where $\hat{\gamma}_i(t)$ is updated on-line by the following recursive LS algorithm

$$\begin{aligned} \hat{\gamma}_i(t+1) &= \hat{\gamma}_i(t) + \bar{\sigma}_i(t)\bar{p}_i(t)\bar{x}_i(t)[y_i(t+1) - \hat{\gamma}_i(t)\bar{x}_i(t)] \\ \bar{p}_i(t+1) &= \bar{p}_i(t) - \bar{\sigma}_i(t)[\bar{p}_i(t)\bar{x}_i(t)]^2 \end{aligned} \tag{3.3}$$

with $y_i(t) = x_i(t) - f_i(z_i(t-1)) - u_i(t-1)$ and

$$\bar{\sigma}_i(t) \stackrel{\Delta}{=} \left[1 + \bar{p}_i(t)\bar{x}_i^2(t)\right]^{-1}, \bar{p}_i(t) \stackrel{\Delta}{=} \left[\sum_{k=0}^{t-1} \bar{x}_i^2(k)\right]^{-1} \tag{3.4}$$

Let $e_{ij}(t) \stackrel{\Delta}{=} x_i(t) - x_j(t)$, and suppose that $x_i^{\text{ref}}(t) = x^*(t)$ for $i = 1, 2, \ldots, N$ in Case I. And suppose also matrix G is an irreducible primitive matrix in Case IV, which means that all of the agents should be connected and matrix G is cyclic (or periodic from the point of view of Markov chain).

Then we can establish almost surely convergence of the decentralized LS estimator and the global synchronization in Cases I—IV.

3.3 Assumptions

We need the following assumptions in our analysis:

Assumption 3.1. *The noise sequence $\{w(t), \mathcal{F}_t\}$ is a martingale difference sequence (with $\{\mathcal{F}_t\}$ being a sequence of nondecreasing σ-algebras) such that*

$$\sup_t E\left[|w(t+1)|^\beta | \mathcal{F}_t\right] < \infty \quad a.s. \tag{3.5}$$

for a constant $\beta > 2$.

Assumption 3.2. *Matrix $G = (g_{ij})$ is an irreducible primitive matrix.*

3.4 Main result

Theorem 3.1. *For system (3.1), suppose that Assumption 3.1 holds in Cases* I—IV *and Assumption 3.2 holds also in Case* IV. *Then the decentralized LS-based adaptive controller has the following closed-loop properties:*

(1) *All of the agents can asymptotically correctly estimate the intensity of influence from others, i.e.,*

$$\lim_{t\to\infty} \hat{\gamma}_i(t) = \gamma_i. \tag{3.6}$$

(2) *The system can achieve synchronization in sense of mean, i.e.,*

$$\lim_{T\to\infty}\frac{1}{T}\sum_{t=1}^{T}|e_{ij}(t)|=0,\quad \forall i\neq j. \tag{3.7}$$

(3) *The system can achieve synchronization in sense of mean squares, i.e.,*

$$\lim_{T\to\infty}\frac{1}{T}\sum_{t=1}^{T}|e_{ij}(t)|^2=0,\quad \forall i\neq j. \tag{3.8}$$

3.5 Lemmas

Lemma 3.1. *Suppose that Assumption 3.1 holds in Cases I, II, III, and IV. Then, in either case, for $i=1,2,\ldots,N$ and $m\geq 1$, $0\leq d<m$, we have*

$$\begin{aligned}\sum_{k=1}^{t}|\tilde{\gamma}_i(mk-d)\bar{x}_i(mk-d)|^2&=o(t)\ a.s.,\\ \sum_{k=1}^{t}|\tilde{\gamma}_i(mk-d)\bar{x}_i(mk-d)|&=o(t)\ a.s.\end{aligned} \tag{3.9}$$

Proof. See Ma (2009). ■

Lemma 3.2. *Consider the following iterative system:*

$$X_{t+1}=A_tX_t+W_t, \tag{3.10}$$

where $A_t\to A$ as $t\to\infty$ and $\{W_t\}$ satisfies

$$\sum_{k=1}^{t}\|W_k\|^2=o(t). \tag{3.11}$$

If the spectral radius $\rho(A)<1$, then

$$\sum_{k=1}^{t}\|X_k\|=o(t),\quad \sum_{k=1}^{t}\|X_k\|^2=o(t). \tag{3.12}$$

Proof. See Ma (2009). ■

Lemma 3.3. *The estimation $\hat{\gamma}_i(t)$ of γ_i converges to the true value γ_i almost surely with the convergence rate*

$$|\tilde{\gamma}_i(t)|=O\left(\sqrt{\frac{\log\bar{r}_i(t)}{\bar{r}_i(t)}}\right). \tag{3.13}$$

where $r_i(t)$ and $\bar{r}_i(t)$ are defined as follows

$$\begin{aligned}r_i(t)&\triangleq 1+\textstyle\sum_{k=0}^{t-1}x_i^2(k)\\ \bar{r}_i(t)&\triangleq 1+\textstyle\sum_{k=0}^{t-1}\bar{x}_i^2(k)\end{aligned} \tag{3.14}$$

Proof. This lemma is just the special one-dimensional case of (Guo, 1993, Theorem 6.3.1). ■

3.6 Proof of theorem 3.1

Putting (3.2) into (3.1), we have

$$\begin{aligned} x_i(t+1) &= -\hat{\gamma}_i(t)\bar{x}_i(t) + x_i^{\text{ref}}(t) + \gamma_i\bar{x}_i(t) + w(t+1) \\ &= x_i^{\text{ref}}(t) + \tilde{\gamma}_i(t)\bar{x}_i(t) + w(t+1). \end{aligned} \tag{3.15}$$

Denote

$$\begin{aligned} X(t) &= (x_1(t), x_2(t), \ldots, x_N(t))^T, \\ Z(t) &= (x_1^{\text{ref}}(t), x_2^{\text{ref}}(t), \ldots, x_N^{\text{ref}}(t))^T, \\ \bar{X}(t) &= (\bar{x}_1(t), \bar{x}_2(t), \ldots, \bar{x}_N(t))^T, \\ W(t+1) &= w(t+1)\mathbf{1} = (w(t+1), w(t+1), \ldots, w(t+1))^T, \\ \tilde{\Gamma}(t) &= \text{diag}(\tilde{\gamma}_1(t), \tilde{\gamma}_2(t), \ldots, \tilde{\gamma}_N(t)), \\ 1 &= [1, \ldots, 1]^T. \end{aligned} \tag{3.16}$$

Then we get

$$X(t+1) = Z(t) + \tilde{\Gamma}(t)\bar{X}(t) + W(t+1). \tag{3.17}$$

According to (2.2), we have

$$\bar{X}(t) = GX(t), \tag{3.18}$$

where the matrix $G = (g_{ij})$. Furthermore, we have

$$\bar{X}(t+1) = GX(t+1) = GZ(t) + G\tilde{\Gamma}(t)\bar{X}(t) + W(t+1). \tag{3.19}$$

By Lemma 3.3, we have $\tilde{\gamma}(t) \to 0$ as $t \to \infty$. Thus, $\tilde{\Gamma}(t) \to 0$.
By (3.15), we have

$$x_i(t+1) - x_i^{\text{ref}}(t) - w(t+1) = \tilde{\gamma}_i(t)\bar{x}_i(t). \tag{3.20}$$

Let $e_{ij}(t) \stackrel{\Delta}{=} x_i(t) - x_j(t)$, $\eta_i(t) = \tilde{\gamma}_i(t)\bar{x}_i(t)$. Then

$$e_{ij}(t+1) = [\eta_i(t) - \eta_j(t)] + [x_i^{\text{ref}}(t) - x_j^{\text{ref}}(t)]. \tag{3.21}$$

For convenience of later discussion, we introduce the following notations:

$$\begin{aligned} G^T &= (\zeta_1, \zeta_2, \ldots, \zeta_N), \\ E(t) &= (e_{1N}(t), e_{2N}(t), \ldots, e_{N-1,N}(t), 0)^T, \\ \eta(t) &= (\eta_1(t), \eta_2(t), \ldots, \eta_N(t))^T. \end{aligned} \tag{3.22}$$

Case I. In this case, $x_i^{\text{ref}}(t) = x^*(t)$, where $x^*(t)$ is a bounded deterministic signal. Hence,

$$e_{ij}(t+1) = \eta_i(t) - \eta_j(t). \tag{3.23}$$

Consequently, by Lemma 3.1, we obtain that $(i \neq j)$

$$\sum_{k=1}^{t} |e_{ij}(k+1)|^2 = O\left(\sum_{k=1}^{t} \eta_i^2(t)\right) + O\left(\sum_{k=1}^{t} \eta_j^2(t)\right) = o(t), \tag{3.24}$$

and similarly $\sum_{k=1}^{t} |e_{ij}(k+1)| = o(t)$ also holds.

Case II. In this case, $x_i^{\text{ref}}(t) = \bar{x}(t) = \frac{1}{N}\sum_{i=1}^{N} x_i(t)$. The proof is similar to Case I.

Case III. Here $x_i^{\text{ref}}(t) = \lambda\bar{x}_i(t) = \lambda\zeta_i^T X(t)$. Noting that $\zeta_i^T\mathbf{1} = 1$ for any i, we have

$$\zeta_i^T X(t) - \zeta_j^T X(t) = \zeta_i^T [X(t) - x_N(t)\mathbf{1}] - \zeta_j^T [X(t) - x_N(t)\mathbf{1}] = \zeta_i^T E(t) - \zeta_j^T E(t), \tag{3.25}$$

and, thus,

$$\begin{aligned} e_{ij}(t+1) &= [\eta_i(t) - \eta_j(t)] + \lambda[\bar{x}_i(t) - \bar{x}_j(t)] \\ &= [\eta_i(t) - \eta_j(t)] + \lambda[\zeta_i^T X(t) - \zeta_j^T X(t)] \\ &= [\eta_i(t) - \eta_j(t)] + \lambda[\zeta_i^T E(t) - \zeta_j^T E(t)]. \end{aligned} \tag{3.26}$$

Taking $j = N$ and $i = 1, 2, \ldots, N$, we can rewrite (3.26) into matrix form as

$$E(t+1) = [\eta(t) - \eta_N(t)\mathbf{1}] + \lambda[G - \mathbf{1}\zeta_N^T]E(t) = \lambda H E(t) + \xi(t), \tag{3.27}$$

where

$$H = G - G_N = G - \mathbf{1}\zeta_N^T, \;\; \xi(t) = \eta(t) - \eta_N(t). \tag{3.28}$$

By Lemma 3.1, we have

$$\sum_{k=1}^{t} \|\eta(k)\|^2 = o(t). \tag{3.29}$$

Therefore,

$$\sum_{k=1}^{t} \|\xi(k)\|^2 = o(t). \tag{3.30}$$

Now we prove that $\rho(H) \leq 1$. In fact, for any vector v such that $v^T v = 1$, we have

$$\begin{aligned} |v^T H v| &= |v^T G v - v^T G_N v| \\ &\leq \max\left(\lambda_{\max}(G)\|v\|^2 - \lambda_{\min}(G_N)\|v\|^2, \right. \\ &\quad \left. \lambda_{\max}(G_N)\|v\|^2 - \lambda_{\min}(G)\|v\|^2\right) \\ &\leq \max\left(\|v\|^2, \lambda_{\max}(G_N)\|v\|^2\right) \\ &= 1 \end{aligned} \tag{3.31}$$

which implies that $\rho(H) \leq 1$.
Finally, by (3.27), together with Lemma 3.2, we can immediately obtain

$$\sum_{k=1}^{t} \|E(k)\| = o(t), \quad \sum_{k=1}^{t} \|E(k)\|^2 = o(t). \tag{3.32}$$

Thus, for $i = 1, 2, \ldots, N-1$, as $t \to \infty$, we have proved

$$\frac{1}{t}\sum_{k=1}^{t} |e_{iN}(k)| \to 0, \quad \frac{1}{t}\sum_{k=1}^{t} [e_{iN}(k)]^2 \to 0. \tag{3.33}$$

Case IV. The proof is similar to that for Case III. We need only prove that the spectral radius $\rho(H)$ of H is less than 1, i.e., $\rho(H) < 1$; then we can apply Lemma 3.2 like in Case III.
Consider the following linear system:

$$z(t+1) = Gz(t). \tag{3.34}$$

Noting that G is a stochastic matrix, then, by Assumption 3.2 and knowledge of the Markov chain, we have

$$\lim_{t\to\infty} G^t = \mathbf{1}\pi^T, \tag{3.35}$$

where π is the unique stationary probability distribution of the finite-state Markov chain with transmission probability matrix G. Therefore,

$$z(t) = G^t z(0) \to \mathbf{1}\pi^T x_0^{\text{ref}} = (\pi^T x_0^{\text{ref}})\mathbf{1} \tag{3.36}$$

which means that all elements of $z(t)$ converge to a same constant $\pi^T x_0^{\text{ref}}$. Furthermore, let $z(t) = (x_1^{\text{ref}}(t), x_2^{\text{ref}}(t), \ldots, x_N^{\text{ref}}(t))^T$ and $\nu(t) = (\nu_1(t), \nu_2(t), \ldots, \nu_{N-1}(t), 0)^T$, where $\nu_i(t) = x_i^{\text{ref}}(t) - x_N^{\text{ref}}(t)$ for $i = 1, 2, \ldots, N$. Then we can see that

$$\nu(t+1) = (G - G_N)\nu(t) = H\nu(t) \tag{3.37}$$

and $\lim_{t\to\infty} \nu(t) = 0$ for any initial values $\nu_i(0) \in \mathcal{R}$, $i = 1, 2, \ldots, N-1$. Obviously $\nu(t) = H^t \nu(0)$, and each entry in the Nth row of H^t is zero since each entry in the Nth row of H is zero. Thus, denote

$$H^t \triangleq \begin{bmatrix} H_0(t) & * \\ 0 & 0 \end{bmatrix}, \tag{3.38}$$

where $H_0(t)$ is an $(N-1) \times (N-1)$ matrix. Then, for $i = 1, 2, \ldots, N-1$, taking $\nu(0) = \mathbf{e}_i$, respectively, by $\lim\limits_{t\to\infty} \nu(t) = 0$ we easily know that the ith column of $H_0(t)$ tends to zero vector as $t \to \infty$. Consequently, we have

$$\lim_{t\to\infty} H_0(t) = 0, \tag{3.39}$$

which implies that each eigenvalue of $H_0(t)$ tends to zero too. By (3.38), eigenvalues of H^t are identical with those of $H_0(t)$ except for zero, and, thus, we obtain that

$$\lim_{t\to\infty} \rho\left(H^t\right) = 0 \tag{3.40}$$

which implies that

$$\rho(H) < 1. \tag{3.41}$$

This completes the proof of Theorem 3.1. ■

4. Decentralized tracking with adaptive control

Decentralized tracking problem is critical to understand the fundamental relationship between (local) stability of individual agents and the global stability of the whole system, and tracking problem is the basis for investigating more general or complex problems such as formation control. In this section, besides the parametric coupling uncertainties and external random noise, parametric internal uncertainties are also present for each agent, which require each agent to do more estimation work so as to deal with all these uncertainties. If each agent needs to deal with both parametric and non-parametric uncertainties, the agents should adopt more complex and smart leaning algorithms, whose ideas may be partially borrowed from Ma & Lum (2008); Ma et al. (2007a); Yang et al. (2009) and the references therein.

4.1 System model

In this section, we study the case where the internal dynamics function $f_i(\cdot)$ is not completely known but can be expressed into a linear combination with unknown coefficients, such that (2.1) can be expressed as follows:

$$x_i(t+1) + \sum_{k=1}^{n_i} a_{ik} x_i(t-k+1) = \sum_{k=1}^{m_i} b_{ik} u_i(t-k+1) + \gamma_i \sum_{j\in\mathcal{N}_i} g_{ij} x_j(t) + w_i(t+1) \tag{4.1}$$

which can be rewritten into the well-known ARMAX model with additional coupling item $\sum_{j\in\mathcal{N}_i}\bar{g}_{ij}x_j(t)$ (letting $\bar{g}_{ij}\stackrel{\Delta}{=}\gamma_i g_{ij}$) as follows:

$$A_i(q^{-1})x_i(t+1) = B_i(q^{-1})u_i(t) + w_i(t+1) + \sum_{j\in\mathcal{N}_i}\bar{g}_{ij}x_j(t) \tag{4.2}$$

with $A_i(q^{-1}) = 1+\sum_{j=1}^{n_i}a_{ij}q^{-j}$, $B_i(q^{-1}) = b_{i1}+\sum_{j=2}^{m_i}b_{ij}q^{-j+1}$ and back shifter q^{-1}.

4.2 Local controller design

For Agent i, we can rewrite its dynamic model as the following regression model

$$x_i(t+1) = \boldsymbol{\theta}_i^T\boldsymbol{\phi}_i(t) + w_i(t+1) \tag{4.3}$$

where $\boldsymbol{\theta}_i$ holds all unknown parameters and $\phi_i(t)$ is the corresponding regressor vector. Then, by the following LS algorithm

$$\begin{array}{lcl} \hat{\boldsymbol{\theta}}_i(t+1) & = & \hat{\boldsymbol{\theta}}_i(t)+\sigma_i(t)P_i(t)\boldsymbol{\phi}_i(t)[x_i(t+1)-\boldsymbol{\phi}_i^T(t)\hat{\boldsymbol{\theta}}_i(t)] \\ P_i(t+1) & = & P_i(t)-\sigma_i(t)P_i(t)\boldsymbol{\phi}_i(t)\boldsymbol{\phi}_i^T(t)P_i(t) \\ \sigma_i(t) & = & [1+\boldsymbol{\phi}_i^T(t)P_i(t)\boldsymbol{\phi}_i(t)]^{-1} \end{array} \tag{4.4}$$

we can obtain the estimated values $\hat{\boldsymbol{\theta}}_i(t)$ of $\boldsymbol{\theta}_i$ at time t. For Agent i, to track a given local reference signal $x_i^{ref}(t)\doteq x_i^*(t)$, with the parameter estimate $\hat{\boldsymbol{\theta}}_i(t)$ given by the above LS algorithm, it can then design its adaptive control law $u_i(t)$ by the "certainty equivalence" principle, that is to say, it can choose $u_i(t)$ such that

$$\hat{\boldsymbol{\theta}}_i^T(t)\boldsymbol{\phi}_i(t) = x_i^*(t+1) \tag{4.5}$$

where $x_i^*(t)$ is the bounded desired reference signal of Agent i, i.e. Agent i is to track the deterministic given signal $x_i^*(t)$.
Consequently we obtain

$$\begin{array}{rcl} u_i(t) & = & \frac{1}{\hat{b}_{i1}(t)}\{x_i^*(t+1) \\ & & +[\hat{a}_{i1}(t)x_i(t)+\cdots+\hat{a}_{i,p_i}(t)x_i(t-p_i+1)] \\ & & -[\hat{b}_{i2}(t)u_i(t-1)+\cdots+\hat{b}_{i,q_i}(t)u_i(t-q_i+1)] \\ & & -\hat{\boldsymbol{g}}_i^T(t)\bar{\boldsymbol{X}}_i(t)\} \end{array} \tag{4.6}$$

where $\hat{\boldsymbol{g}}_i(t)$ is a vector holding the estimates $\hat{g}_{ij}(t)$ of g_{ij} ($j\in\mathcal{N}_i$) and $\bar{\boldsymbol{X}}_i(t)$ is a vector holding the states $x_{ij}(t)$ ($j\in\mathcal{N}_i$).
In particular, when the high-frequency gain b_{i1} is known *a priori*, let $\bar{\boldsymbol{\theta}}_i$ denote the parameter vector $\boldsymbol{\theta}_i$ without component b_{i1}, $\bar{\boldsymbol{\phi}}_i(t)$ denote the regression vector $\phi_i(t)$ without component $u_i(t)$, and similarly we introduce notations $\bar{a}_i(t), \bar{P}_i(t)$ corresponding to $a_i(t)$ and $P_i(t)$, respectively. Then, the estimate $\bar{\boldsymbol{\theta}}_i(t)$ at time t of $\bar{\boldsymbol{\theta}}_i$ can be updated by the following algorithm:

$$\begin{array}{lcl} \bar{\boldsymbol{\theta}}_i(t+1) & = & \bar{\boldsymbol{\theta}}_i(t)+\bar{\sigma}_i(t)\bar{P}_i(t)\bar{\boldsymbol{\phi}}_i(t) \\ & & \times[x_i(t+1)-b_{i1}u_i(t)-\bar{\boldsymbol{\phi}}_i^T(t)\bar{\boldsymbol{\theta}}_i(t)] \\ \bar{P}_i(t+1) & = & \bar{P}_i(t)-\bar{\sigma}_i(t)\bar{P}_i(t)\bar{\boldsymbol{\phi}}_i(t)\bar{\boldsymbol{\phi}}_i^T(t)\bar{P}_i(t) \\ \bar{\sigma}_i(t) & = & [1+\bar{\boldsymbol{\phi}}_i^T(t)\bar{P}_i(t)\bar{\boldsymbol{\phi}}_i(t)]^{-1} \end{array} \tag{4.7}$$

When the high-frequency gain b_{i1} is unknown *a priori*, to avoid the so-called singularity problem of $\hat{b}_{i1}(t)$ being or approaching zero, we need to use the following modified $\hat{b}_{i1}(t)$, denoted by $\hat{\hat{b}}_{i1}(t)$, instead of original $\hat{b}_{i1}(t)$:

$$\hat{\hat{b}}_{i1}(t) = \begin{cases} \hat{b}_{i1}(t) & \text{if } |\hat{b}_{i1}(t)| \geq \frac{1}{\sqrt{\log r_i(t)}} \\ \hat{b}_{i1}(t) + \frac{\operatorname{sgn}(\hat{b}_{i1}(t))}{\sqrt{\log r_i(t)}} & \text{if } |\hat{b}_{i1}(t)| < \frac{1}{\sqrt{\log r_i(t)}} \end{cases} \tag{4.8}$$

and consequently the local controller of Agent i is given by

$$\begin{aligned} u_i(t) = & \frac{1}{\hat{\hat{b}}_{i1}(t)}\{x_i^*(t+1) \\ & +[\hat{a}_{i1}(t)x_i(t) + \cdots + \hat{a}_{i,p_i}(t)x_i(t-p_i+1)] \\ & -[\hat{b}_{i2}(t)u_i(t-1) + \cdots + \hat{b}_{i,q_i}(t)u_i(t-q_i+1)] \\ & -\hat{\boldsymbol{g}}_i^T(t)\bar{\boldsymbol{X}}_i(t)\}. \end{aligned} \tag{4.9}$$

4.3 Assumptions

Assumption 4.1. (noise condition) $\{w_i(t), \mathcal{F}_t\}$ *is a martingale difference sequence, with* $\{\mathcal{F}_t\}$ *being a sequence of nondecreasing* σ*-algebras, such that*

$$\sup_{t\geq 0} E[|w_i(t+1)|^\beta|\mathcal{F}_t] < \infty, a.s.$$

for some $\beta > 2$ *and*

$$\lim_{t\to\infty} \frac{1}{t}\sum_{k=1}^{t} |w_i(k)|^2 = R_i > 0, a.s.$$

Assumption 4.2. (minimum phase condition) $B_i(z) \neq 0, \forall z \in \mathcal{C} : |z| \leq 1$.

Assumption 4.3. (reference signal) $\{x_i^*(t)\}$ *is a bounded deterministic signal.*

4.4 Main result

Theorem 4.1. *Suppose that Assumptions 4.1—4.3 hold for system (4.1). Then the closed-loop system is stable and optimal, that is to say, for* $i = 1, 2, \ldots, N$, *we have*

$$\limsup_{t\to\infty} \frac{1}{t}\sum_{k=1}^{t} [|x_i(k)|^2 + |u_i(k-1)|^2] < \infty, \quad a.s.$$

and

$$\lim_{t\to\infty} \frac{1}{t}\sum_{k=1}^{t} |x_i(k) - x_i^*(k)|^2 = R_i, \quad a.s.$$

Although each agent only aims to track a local reference signal by local adaptive controller based on recursive LS algorithm, the whole system achieves global stability. The optimality can also be understood intuitively because in the presence of noise, even when all the parameters are known, the limit of

$$J_i(t) \triangleq \lim_{t\to\infty} \frac{1}{t}\sum_{k=0}^{t-1} |x_i(k+1) - x_i^*(k+1)|^2$$

cannot be smaller than R_i.

4.5 Lemmas

Lemma 4.1. *Under Assumption 4.1, we have* $|w_i(t)| = O(d_i(t))$*, where* $\{d_i(t)\}$ *is an increasing sequence and can be taken as* t^δ *(*δ *can be any positive number).*

Proof. In fact, by using Markov inequality, we obtain that

$$\sum_{t=1}^{\infty} P(|w_i(t+1)|^2 \geq t^{2\delta}|\mathcal{F}_t) \leq \sum_{t=1}^{\infty} \frac{E[|w_i(t+1)|^\beta|\mathcal{F}_t]}{t^{\beta\delta}} < \infty$$

holds almost surely. By applying the Borel-Cantelli-Levy lemma, immediately we have $|w_i(t+1)| = O(t^\delta), a.s.$ ■

Lemma 4.2. *If* $\xi(t+1) = B(z)u(t), \forall t > 0$*, where polynomial (*$q \geq 1$*)*

$$B(z) = b_1 + b_2 z + \cdots + b_q z^{q-1}$$

satisfies

$$B(z) \neq 0, \forall z : |z| \leq 1, \tag{4.10}$$

then there exists a constant $\lambda \in (0,1)$ *such that*

$$|u(t)|^2 = O(\sum_{k=0}^{t+1} \lambda^{t+1-k}|\xi(k)|^2). \tag{4.11}$$

Proof. See Ma et al. (2007b). ■

Lemma 4.3. *Under Assumption 4.1, for* $i = 1, 2, \ldots, N$*, the LS algorithm has the following properties almost surely:*

(a)

$$\tilde{\boldsymbol{\theta}}_i^T(t+1)P_i^{-1}(t+1)\tilde{\boldsymbol{\theta}}_i(t+1) = O(\log r_i(t))$$

(b)

$$\sum_{k=1}^{t} \alpha_i(k) = O(\log r_i(t))$$

where

$$\begin{aligned} \delta_i(t) &\triangleq \mathrm{tr}(P_i(t) - P_i(t+1)) \\ \sigma_i(k) &\triangleq [1 + \phi_i^T(k)P_i(k)\phi_i(k)]^{-1} \\ \alpha_i(k) &\triangleq \sigma_i(k)|\tilde{\boldsymbol{\theta}}_i^T(k)\phi_t(k)|^2 \\ r_i(t) &\triangleq 1 + \sum_{k=1}^{t} \phi_i^T(k)\phi_i(k) \end{aligned} \tag{4.12}$$

Proof. This is a special case of (Guo, 1994, Lemma 2.5). ■

Lemma 4.4. *Under Assumption 4.1, for* $i = 1, 2, \ldots, N$*, we have*

$$\sum_{k=1}^{t} |x_i(k)|^2 \to \infty, \ \liminf_{t\to\infty} \frac{1}{t} \sum_{k=1}^{t} |x_i(k)|^2 \geq R_i > 0, \ a.s. \tag{4.13}$$

Proof. This lemma can be obtained by estimating lower bound of $\sum_{k=1}^{t} [x_i(k+1)]^2$ with the help of Assumption 4.1 and the martingale estimation theorem. Similar proof can be found in Chen & Guo (1991). ■

4.6 Proof of Theorem 4.1

To prove Theorem 4.1, we shall apply the main idea, utilized in Chen & Guo (1991) and Guo (1993), to estimate the bounds of signals by analyzing some linear inequalities. However, there are some difficulties in analyzing the closed-loop system of decentralized adaptive control law. Noting that each agent only uses local estimate algorithm and control law, but the agents are coupled, therefore for a fixed Agent i, we cannot estimate the bounds of state $x_i(t)$ and control $u_i(t)$ without knowing the corresponding bounds for its neighborhood agents. This is the main difficulty of this problem. To resolve this problem, we first analyze every agent, and then consider their relationship globally, finally the estimation of state bounds for each agent can be obtained through both the local and global analysis.

In the following analysis, $\delta_i(t)$, $\sigma_i(k)$, $\alpha_i(k)$ and $r_i(t)$ are defined as in Eq. (4.12).

Step 1: In this step, we analyze dynamics of each agent. We consider Agent i for $i = 1, 2, \ldots, N$. By putting the control law (4.9) into (4.3), noting that (4.5), we have

$$\begin{aligned} x_i(t+1) &= \boldsymbol{\theta}_i^T \phi_i(t) + w_i(t+1) \\ &= x_i^*(t+1) - \hat{\boldsymbol{\theta}}_i^T(t)\phi_i(t) + \boldsymbol{\theta}_i^T \phi_i(t) + w_i(t+1) \\ &= x_i^*(t+1) + \tilde{\boldsymbol{\theta}}_i^T(t)\phi_i(t) + w_i(t+1) \end{aligned}$$

By Lemma 4.1, we have $|w_i(t)|^2 = O(d_i(t))$. Noticing also

$$\begin{aligned} |\tilde{\boldsymbol{\theta}}_i(t)\phi_i(t)|^2 &= \alpha_i(t)[1 + \phi_i^T(t)P_i(t)\phi_i(t)] \\ &= \alpha_i(t)[1 + \phi_i^T(t)P_i(t+1)\phi_i(t)] \\ &\quad + \alpha_i(t)\phi_i^T(t)[P_i(t) - P_i(t+1)]\phi_i(t) \\ &\leq \alpha_i(t)[2 + \delta_i(t)\|\phi_i(t)\|^2] \end{aligned}$$

and the boundedness of $x_i^*(t+1)$, we can obtain that

$$|x_i(t+1)|^2 \leq 2\alpha_i(t)\delta_i(t)\|\phi_i(t)\|^2 + O(d_i(t)) + O(\log r_i(t)). \tag{4.14}$$

Now let us estimate $\|\phi_i(t)\|^2$. By Lemma 4.2, there exists $\lambda_i \in (0, 1)$ such that

$$|u_i(t)|^2 = O(\sum_{k=0}^{t+1} \lambda_i^{t+1-k}(|x_i(k)|^2 + \|\bar{\boldsymbol{X}}_i(k)\|^2 + |w_i(k+1)|^2)).$$

It holds for all $i = 1, 2, \ldots, N$, but we cannot estimate $|u_i(t)|^2$ directly because it involves $\{x_j(k), j \in \mathcal{N}_i\}$ in $\bar{\boldsymbol{X}}_i(k)$.

Let

$$\begin{aligned} \rho &= \max(\lambda_1, \cdots, \lambda_N) \in (0, 1) \\ \boldsymbol{X}(k) &= [x_1(k), \cdots, x_N(k)]^T \\ \bar{d}(k) &= \max(d_1(k), \cdots, d_N(k)). \end{aligned}$$

Obviously we have

$$|x_i(k)|^2 = O(\|\boldsymbol{X}(k)\|^2), \|\bar{\boldsymbol{X}}_i(k)\|^2 = O(\|\boldsymbol{X}(k)\|^2).$$

Now define

$$L_t \stackrel{\Delta}{=} \sum_{k=0}^{t} \rho^{t-k}\|\boldsymbol{X}(k)\|^2.$$

Then, for $i = 1, 2, \ldots, N$, we have

$$\begin{aligned}|u_i(t)|^2 &= O(L_{t+1}) + O(\sum_{k=0}^{t+1} \rho^{t+1-k}\bar{d}(k)) \\ &= O(L_{t+1}) + O(\bar{d}(t+1)).\end{aligned}$$

Since

$$\phi_i(t) = [x_i(t), \cdots, x_i(t-p_i+1), \quad u_i(t-1), \cdots, u_i(t-q_i+1), \bar{\boldsymbol{X}}_i^T(t)]^T$$

we can obtain that

$$\begin{aligned}\|\phi_i(t)\|^2 &= O(\|\boldsymbol{X}(t)\|^2) + O(L_t) + O(\bar{d}(t)) \\ &\quad + O(\log r_i(t) + d_i(t)) \\ &= O(L_t + \log \bar{r}(t) + \bar{d}(t))\end{aligned}$$

where

$$\bar{r}(t) \stackrel{\Delta}{=} \max(r_1(t), r_2(t), \cdots, r_N(t)).$$

Hence by (4.14), for Agent i, there exists $C_i > 0$ such that

$$\begin{aligned}|x_i(t+1)|^2 \le\ & C_i\alpha_i(t)\delta_i(t)L_t \\ & + O(\alpha_i(t)\delta_i(t)[\log \bar{r}(t) + \bar{d}(t)]) \\ & + O(d_i(t) + \log r_i(t)).\end{aligned}$$

Then noticing

$$\alpha_i(t)\delta_i(t) = O(\log r_i(t))$$

we obtain that

$$|x_i(t+1)|^2 \le C_i\alpha_i(t)\delta_i(t)L_t + O(\log r_i(t)[\log \bar{r}(t) + \bar{d}(t)]). \tag{4.15}$$

Step 2: Because (4.15) holds for $i = 1, 2, \ldots, N$, we have

$$\begin{aligned}\|\boldsymbol{X}(t+1)\|^2 &= \sum_{i=1}^{N} |x_i(t+1)|^2 \\ &\le [\sum_{i=1}^{N} C_i\alpha_i(t)\delta_i(t)]L_t \\ &\quad + O(N\bar{d}(t)\log \bar{r}(t)) + O(N\log^2 \bar{r}(t)).\end{aligned}$$

Thus by the definition of L_t, we have

$$\begin{aligned}L_{t+1} &= \rho L_t + \|\boldsymbol{X}(t+1)\|^2 \\ &\le [\rho + C\sum_{i=1}^{N} \alpha_i(t)\delta_i(t)]L_t \\ &\quad + O(N\bar{d}(t)\log \bar{r}(t)) + O(N\log^2 \bar{r}(t))\end{aligned}$$

where

$$C = \max(C_1, C_2, \cdots, C_N).$$

Let $\eta(t) = \sum_{i=1}^{N} \alpha_i(t)\delta_i(t)$, then

$$\begin{aligned}L_{t+1} &= O(N\bar{d}(t)\log r(t) + N\log^2 \bar{r}(t)) \\ &\quad + O(N\sum_{k=0}^{t-1} \prod_{l=k+1}^{t} [\rho + C\eta(l)] \\ &\qquad \times [\bar{d}(k)\log \bar{r}(k) + \log^2 \bar{r}(k)]).\end{aligned} \tag{4.16}$$

Since

$$\sum_{k=0}^{\infty} \delta_i(k) = \sum_{k=0}^{\infty} [\operatorname{tr} P_i(k) - \operatorname{tr} P_i(k+1)] \le \operatorname{tr} P_i(0) < \infty,$$

we have $\delta_i(k) \to 0$ as $k \to \infty$. By Lemma 4.3,

$$\sum_{k=0}^{\infty} \alpha_i(k) = O(\log r_i(k)) = O(\log \bar{r}(k)).$$

Then, for $i = 1, 2, \ldots, N$ and arbitrary $\epsilon > 0$, there exists $k_0 > 0$ such that

$$\rho^{-1} C \sum_{k=t_0}^{t} \alpha_i(k) \delta_i(k) \le \tfrac{1}{N} \epsilon \log \bar{r}(t)$$

for all $t \ge t_0 \ge k_0$. Therefore

$$\rho^{-1} C \sum_{k=t_0}^{t} \eta(k) \le \epsilon \log \bar{r}(t).$$

Then, by the inequality $1 + x \le e^x, \forall x \ge 0$ we have

$$\begin{aligned} \prod_{k=t_0}^{t} [1 + \rho^{-1} C \eta(k)] &\le \exp\{\rho^{-1} C \sum_{k=t_0}^{t} \eta(k)\} \\ &\le \exp\{\epsilon \log \bar{r}(t)\} = \bar{r}^{\epsilon}(t). \end{aligned}$$

Putting this into (4.16), we can obtain

$$L_{t+1} = O(\log r_i(t)[\log \bar{r}(t) + \bar{d}(t)]\bar{r}^{\epsilon}(t)).$$

Then, by the arbitrariness of ϵ, we have

$$L_{t+1} = O(\bar{d}(t)\bar{r}^{\epsilon}(t)), \forall \epsilon > 0.$$

Consequently, for $i = 1, 2, \ldots, N$, we obtain that

$$\begin{aligned} &\|\boldsymbol{X}(t+1)\|^2 \le L_{t+1} = O(\bar{d}(t)\bar{r}^{\epsilon}(t)) \\ &|u_i(t)|^2 = O(L_{t+1} + \bar{d}(t+1)) = O(\bar{d}(t)\bar{r}^{\epsilon}(t)) \\ &\|\phi_i(t)\|^2 = O(L_t + \log \bar{r}(t) + \bar{d}(t)) = O(\bar{d}(t)\bar{r}^{\epsilon}(t)). \end{aligned} \tag{4.17}$$

Step 3: By Lemma 4.4, we have

$$\liminf_{t \to \infty} \tfrac{r_i(t)}{t} \ge R_i > 0, \quad a.s.$$

Thus $t = O(r_i(t)) = O(\bar{r}(t))$, together with $\bar{d}(t) = O(t^{\delta}), \forall \delta \in (\frac{2}{\beta}, 1)$, then we conclude that $\bar{d}(t) = O(\bar{r}^{\epsilon}(t))$. Putting this into (4.17), and by the arbitrariness of ϵ, we obtain that

$$\|\phi_i(t)\|^2 = O(\bar{r}^{\delta}(t)), \forall \delta \in (\tfrac{2}{\beta}, 1).$$

Therefore

$$\begin{aligned}
&\sum_{k=0}^{t} |\tilde{\boldsymbol{\theta}}_i^T(k)\phi_i(k)|^2 \\
&\quad = \sum_{k=0}^{t} \alpha_i(k)[1+\phi_i^T(k)P_i(k)\phi_i(k)] \\
&\quad = O(\log r_i(t)) + O(\sum_{k=0}^{t} \alpha_i(k)\|\phi_i(k)\|^2) \\
&\quad = O(\log \bar{r}(t)) + O(\bar{r}^{\delta}(t)\sum_{k=0}^{t} \alpha_i(k)) \\
&\quad = O(\bar{r}^{\delta}(t)\log \bar{r}(t)), \forall \delta \in (\tfrac{2}{\beta}, 1).
\end{aligned}$$

Then, by the arbitrariness of δ, we have

$$\sum_{k=0}^{t} |\tilde{\boldsymbol{\theta}}_i^T(k)\phi_i(k)|^2 = O(\bar{r}^{\delta}(t)), \forall \delta \in (\tfrac{2}{\beta}, 1). \tag{4.18}$$

Since

$$x_i(t+1) = \tilde{\boldsymbol{\theta}}_i^T(t)\phi_i(t) + x_i^*(t+1) + w_i(t+1)$$

we have

$$\begin{aligned}
\sum_{k=0}^{t} |x_i(k+1)|^2 &= O(\bar{r}^{\delta}(t)) + O(t) + O(\log \bar{r}(t)) \\
&= O(\bar{r}^{\delta}(t)) + O(t) \\
\sum_{k=0}^{t} |u_i(k-1)|^2 &= O(\bar{r}^{\delta}(t)) + O(t)
\end{aligned}$$

From the above, we know that for $i = 1, 2, \ldots, N$,

$$\begin{aligned}
r_i(t) = 1 + \sum_{k=0}^{t} \|\phi_i(k)\|^2 &= O(\bar{r}^{\delta}(t)) + O(t) \\
&\forall \delta \in (\tfrac{2}{\beta}, 1).
\end{aligned}$$

Hence

$$\begin{aligned}
\bar{r}(t) &= \max\{r_i(t), 1 \le i \le N\} \\
&= O(\bar{r}^{\delta}(t)) + O(t), \forall \delta \in (\tfrac{2}{\beta}, 1).
\end{aligned}$$

Furthermore, we can obtain

$$\bar{r}(t) = O(t)$$

which means that the closed-loop system is stable.

Step 4: Now we give the proof of the optimality.

$$\begin{aligned}
&\sum_{k=0}^{t} |x_i(k+1) - x_i^*(k+1)|^2 \\
&\quad = \sum_{k=0}^{t} [w_i(k+1)]^2 + \sum_{k=0}^{t} [\psi_i(k)]^2 + 2\sum_{k=0}^{t} \psi_i(k)w_i(k+1)
\end{aligned} \tag{4.19}$$

where

$$\psi_i(k) \stackrel{\Delta}{=} \tilde{\boldsymbol{\theta}}_i^T(k)\phi_i(k).$$

By (4.18) and the martingale estimate theorem, we can obtain that the orders of last two items in (4.19) are both $O(\bar{r}^{\delta}(t))$, $\forall \delta \in (\frac{2}{\beta}, 1)$. Then we can obtain

$$\lim_{t\to\infty} \frac{1}{t} \sum_{k=0}^{t} |x_i(k+1) - x_i^*(k+1)|^2 = R_i, \quad a.s.$$

Furthermore

$$\begin{aligned}\sum_{k=0}^{t} |x_i(k) - x_i^*(k) - w_i(k)|^2 &= \sum_{k=0}^{t} \|\psi_i(k)\|^2 \\ &= O(\bar{r}^{\delta}(t)) = o(t), \quad a.s.\end{aligned}$$

This completes the proof of the optimality of the decentralized adaptive controller. ■

5. Hidden leader following with adaptive control

In this section, we consider a hidden leader following problem, in which the leader agent knows the target trajectory to follow but the leadership of itself is unknown to all the others, and the leader can only affect its neighbors who can sense its outputs. In fact, this sort of problems may be found in many real applications. For example, a capper in the casino lures the players to follow his action but at the same time he has to keep not recognized. For another example, the plainclothes policeman can handle the crowd guide work very well in a crowd of people although he may only affect people around him. The objective of hidden leader following problem for the multi-agent system is to make each agent eventually follow the hidden leader such that the whole system is in order. It is obvious that the hidden leader following problem is more complicated than the conventional leader following problem and investigations of this problem are of significance in both theory and practice.

5.1 System model

For simplicity, we do not consider random noise in this section. The dynamics of the multi-agent system under study is in the following manner:

$$A_i(q^{-1})x_i(t+1) = B_i(q^{-1})u_i(t) + \gamma_i \bar{x}_i(t) \tag{5.1}$$

with $A_i(q^{-1}) = 1 + \sum_{j=1}^{n_i} a_{ij} q^{-j}$, $B_i(q^{-1}) = b_{i1} + \sum_{j=2}^{m_i} b_{ij} q^{-j+1}$ and back shifter q^{-1}, where $u_i(t)$ and $x_i(t)$, $i = 1, 2, \ldots, N$, are input and output of Agent i, respectively. Here $\bar{x}_i(t)$ is the average of the outputs from the neighbors of Agent i:

$$\bar{x}_i(t) \triangleq \frac{1}{N_i} \sum_{j\in\mathcal{N}_i} x_j(t) \tag{5.2}$$

where

$$\mathcal{N}_i = \{s_{i,1}, s_{i,2}, \ldots, s_{i,N_i}\} \tag{5.3}$$

denotes the indices of Agent i's neighbors (excluding Agent i itself) and N_i is the number of Agent i's neighbors. In this model, we suppose that the parameters a_{ij} ($j = 1, 2, \ldots, m_j$), b_{ij} ($j = 1, 2, \ldots, n_j$) and γ_i are all *a priori* unknown to Agent i.

Remark 5.1. *From (5.1) we can find that there is no information to indicate which agent is the leader in the system representation.*

5.2 Local Controller design

Dynamics equation (5.1) for Agent i can be rewritten into the following regression form

$$x_i(t+1) = \boldsymbol{\theta}_i^T \phi_i(t)$$

where $\boldsymbol{\theta}_i$ holds all unknown parameters and $\phi_i(t)$ is the corresponding regressor vector. We assume that the bounded desired reference $x^*(k)$ is only available to the hidden leader and satisfies $x^*(k+1) - x^*(k) = o(1)$. Without loss of generality, we suppose that the first agent is the hidden leader, so the control $u_1(t)$ for the first agent can be directly designed by using the certainty equivalence principle to track $x_1^{\text{ref}}(k) \overset{\Delta}{=} x^*(k)$:

$$\hat{\boldsymbol{\theta}}_1^T(t)\phi_1(t) = x^*(t+1) \tag{5.4}$$

which leads to

$$\begin{aligned} u_1(t) = & \tfrac{1}{\hat{b}_{11}(t)}\{x^*(t+1) + [\hat{a}_{11}(t)x_1(t) + \cdots + \hat{a}_{1,n_1}(t)x_1(t-n_1+1)] \\ & -[\hat{b}_{12}(t)u_1(t-1) + \cdots + \hat{b}_{1,m_1}(t)u_1(t-m_1+1)] \\ & -\hat{\gamma}_1(t)\bar{x}_1(t)\}. \end{aligned} \tag{5.5}$$

As for the other agents, they are unaware of either the reference trajectory or the existence of the leader and the outputs of their neighbors are the only external information available for them, consequently, the jth ($j = 2, 3, \cdots, N$) agent should design its control $u_j(t)$ to track corresponding local center $x_j^{\text{ref}}(t) \overset{\Delta}{=} \bar{x}_j(t)$ such that

$$\hat{\boldsymbol{\theta}}_j^T(t)\phi_j(t) = \bar{x}_j(t) \tag{5.6}$$

from which we can obtain the following local adaptive controller for Agent j:

$$\begin{aligned} u_j(t) = & \tfrac{1}{\hat{b}_{j1}(t)}\{\bar{x}_j(t) + [\hat{a}_{j1}(t)x_j(t) + \cdots + \hat{a}_{j,n_1}(t)x_j(t-n_j+1)] \\ & -[\hat{b}_{j2}(t)u_j(t-1) + \cdots + \hat{b}_{j,m_j}(t)u_j(t-m_j+1)] \\ & -\hat{\gamma}_j(t)\bar{x}_j(t)\}. \end{aligned} \tag{5.7}$$

Define

$$\tilde{y}_1(t) = x_1(t) - x^*(t) \tag{5.8}$$

and

$$\tilde{y}_j(t) = x_j(t) - \bar{x}_j(t-1), \quad j = 2, 3, \cdots, N. \tag{5.9}$$

The update law for the estimated parameters in the adaptive control laws (5.5) and (5.7) is given below ($j = 1, 2, \ldots, N$):

$$\begin{aligned} \hat{\theta}_j(t) &= \hat{\theta}_j(t-1) + \tfrac{\mu_j \tilde{y}_j(t)\phi_j(t-1)}{D_j(t-1)} \\ D_j(k) &= 1 + \|\phi_j(k)\|^2 \end{aligned} \tag{5.10}$$

where $0 < \mu_j < 2$ is a tunable parameter for tuning the convergence rate. Note that the above update law may not guarantee that $\hat{b}_{j1}(t) \geq \underline{b}_{j1}$, hence when the original $\hat{b}_{j1}(t)$ given by (5.10), denoted by $\hat{b}'_{j1}(t)$ hereinafter, is smaller than $\underline{b}_{j1}$, we need to make minor modification to $\hat{b}_{j1}(t)$ as follows:

$$\hat{b}_{j1}(t) = \underline{b}_{j1} \quad \text{if } \hat{b}'_{j1}(t) < \underline{b}_{j1}. \tag{5.11}$$

In other words, $\hat{b}_{j1}(t) = \max(\hat{b}'_{j1}(t), \underline{b}_{j1})$ in all cases.

5.3 Assumptions

Assumption 5.1. *The desired reference $x^*(k)$ for the multi-agent system is a bounded sequence and satisfies $x^*(k+1) - x^*(k) = o(1)$.*

Assumption 5.2. *The graph of the multi-agent system under study is strongly connected such that its adjacent matrix G_A is irreducible.*

Assumption 5.3. *Without loss of generality, it is assumed that the first agent is a hidden leader who knows the desired reference $x^*(k)$ while other agents are unaware of either the desired reference or which agent is the leader.*

Assumption 5.4. *The sign of control gain b_{j1}, $1 \leq j \leq n$, is known and satisfies $|b_{j1}| \geq \underline{b}_{j1} > 0$. Without loss of generality, it is assumed that b_{j1} is positive.*

5.4 Main result

Under the proposed decentralized adaptive control, the control performance for the multi-agent system is summarized as the following theorem.

Theorem 5.1. *Considering the closed-loop multi-agent system consisting of open loop system in (5.1) under Assumptions 5.1-5.4, adaptive control inputs defined in (5.5) and (5.7), parameter estimates update law in (5.10), the system can achieve synchronization and every agent can asymptotically track the reference $x^*(t)$, i.e.,*

$$\lim_{t\to\infty} e_j(t) = 0,\ j = 1, 2, \ldots, N \tag{5.12}$$

where $e_j(k) = x_j(k) - x^*(k)$.

Corollary 5.1. *Under conditions of Theorem 5.1, the system can achieve synchronization in sense of mean and every agent can successfully track the reference $x^*(t)$ in sense of mean, i.e.,*

$$\lim_{t\to\infty} \frac{1}{t} \sum_{k=1}^{t} |e_j(k)| = 0,\ j = 1, 2, \ldots, N \tag{5.13}$$

5.5 Notations and lemmas

Define

$$X(k) = [x_1(k), x_2(k), \ldots, x_N(k)]^T \tag{5.14}$$
$$\tilde{Y}(k) = [\tilde{y}_1(k), \tilde{y}_2(k), \ldots, \tilde{y}_n(k)]^T \tag{5.15}$$
$$H = [1, 0, \ldots, 0]^T \in \mathcal{R}^N \tag{5.16}$$

From (5.2) and (5.14), we have

$$[0, \bar{x}_2(k), \ldots, \bar{x}_n(k)] = \Lambda G_A X(k) \tag{5.17}$$

where

$$\Lambda = \begin{bmatrix} 0 & 0 & \cdots & 0 \\ 0 & \frac{1}{N_2} & \cdots & 0 \\ \vdots & \vdots & \ddots & \vdots \\ 0 & 0 & \cdots & \frac{1}{N_N} \end{bmatrix}. \tag{5.18}$$

and G_A is an adjacent matrix of the multi-agent system (5.1), whose (i, j)th entry is 1 if $j \in \mathcal{N}_i$ or 0 if $j \notin \mathcal{N}_i$. Consequently, the closed-loop multi-agent system can be written in the following compact form by using equality

$$X(k+1) = \Lambda G_A X(k) + Hx^*(k+1) + \tilde{Y}(k+1) \tag{5.19}$$

Definition 5.1. *A sub-stochastic matrix is a square matrix each of whose rows consists of nonnegative real numbers, with at least one row summing strictly less than 1 and other rows summing to 1.*

Lemma 5.1. *According to Assumption 5.2, the product matrix ΛG_A is a substochastic matrix (refer to Definition 5.1) such that $\rho(\Lambda G_A) < 1$ (Dong et al. (2008)), where $\rho(A)$ stands for the spectral radius of a matrix A.*

Definition 5.2. *(Chen & Narendra, 2001) Let $x_1(k)$ and $x_2(k)$ be two discrete-time scalar or vector signals, $\forall k \in Z_t^+$, for any t.*

- *We denote $x_1(k) = O[x_2(k)]$, if there exist positive constants m_1, m_2 and k_0 such that $\|x_1(k)\| \leq m_1 \max_{k' \leq k} \|x_2(k')\| + m_2$, $\forall k > k_0$.*
- *We denote $x_1(k) = o[x_2(k)]$, if there exists a discrete-time function $\alpha(k)$ satisfying $\lim_{k\to\infty} \alpha(k) = 0$ and a constant k_0 such that $\|x_1(k)\| \leq \alpha(k) \max_{k' \leq k} \|x_2(k')\|$, $\forall k > k_0$.*
- *We denote $x_1(k) \sim x_2(k)$ if they satisfy $x_1(k) = O[x_2(k)]$ and $x_2(k) = O[x_1(k)]$.*

For convenience, in the followings we use $O[1]$ and $o[1]$ to denote bounded sequences and sequences converging to zero, respectively. In addition, if sequence $y(k)$ satisfies $y(k) = O[x(k)]$ or $y(k) = o[x(k)]$, then we may directly use $O[x(k)]$ or $o[x(k)]$ to denote sequence $y(k)$ for convenience.
According to Definition 5.2, we have the following lemma

Lemma 5.2. *According to the definition on signal orders in Definition 5.2, we have following properties:*

(i) $O[x_1(k+\tau)] + O[x_1(k)] \sim O[x_1(k+\tau)]$, $\forall \tau \geq 0$.

(ii) $x_1(k+\tau) + o[x_1(k)] \sim x_1(k+\tau)$, $\forall \tau \geq 0$.

(iii) $o[x_1(k+\tau)] + o[x_1(k)] \sim o[x_1(k+\tau)]$, $\forall \tau \geq 0$.

(iv) $o[x_1(k)] + o[x_2(k)] \sim o[|x_1(k)| + |x_2(k)|]$.

(v) $o[O[x_1(k)]] \sim o[x_1(k)] + O[1]$.

(vi) If $x_1(k) \sim x_2(k)$ and $\lim_{k\to\infty} \|x_2(k)\| = 0$, then $\lim_{k\to\infty} \|x_1(k)\| = 0$.

(vii) If $x_1(k) = o[x_1(k)] + o[1]$, then $\lim_{k\to\infty} \|x_1(k)\| = 0$.

(viii) Let $x_2(k) = x_1(k) + o[x_1(k)]$. If $x_2(k) = o[1]$, then $\lim_{k\to\infty} \|x_1(k)\| = 0$.

The following lemma is a special case of Lemma 4.4 in Ma (2009).

Lemma 5.3. *Consider the following iterative system*

$$X(k+1) = A(k)X(k) + W(k) \tag{5.20}$$

where $\|W(k)\| = O[1]$, and $A(k) \to A$ as $k \to \infty$. Assume that $\rho(A)$ is the spectral radius of A, i.e. $\rho(A) = \max\{|\lambda(A)|\}$ and $\rho(A) < 1$, then we can obtain

$$X(k+1) = O[1]. \tag{5.21}$$

5.6 Proof of Theorem 5.1

In the following, the proof of mathematic rigor is presented in two steps. In the first step, we prove that $\tilde{x}_j(k) \to 0$ for all $j = 1, 2, \ldots, N$, which leads to $x_1(k) - x^*(k) \to 0$ such that the hidden leader follows the reference trajectory. In the second step, we further prove that the output of each agent can track the output of the hidden leader such that the control objective is achieved.

Step 1: Denote $\tilde{\theta}_j(k) \triangleq \hat{\theta}_j(k) - \boldsymbol{\theta}_j(k)$, especially $\tilde{b}_{j1}(k) \triangleq \hat{b}_{j1}(k) - b_{j1}$. For convenience, let $\tilde{b}'_{j1} \triangleq \hat{b}'_{j1} - b_{j1}$, where $\hat{b}'_{j1}$ denotes the original estimate of b_{j1} without further modification. From the definitions of $\hat{b}'_{j1}$ and $\hat{b}_{j1}$, since $\hat{b}_{j1}(t) = \max(\hat{b}'_{j1}(t), \underline{b}_{j1})$ and $b_{j1} \geq \underline{b}_{j1}$, obviously we have

$$\tilde{b}_{j1}^2(k) \leq \tilde{b}_{j1}'^2(k). \tag{5.22}$$

Consider a Lyapunov candidate

$$V_j(k) = \|\tilde{\theta}_j(k)\|^2 \tag{5.23}$$

and we are to show that $V_j(k)$ is non-increasing for each $j = 1, 2, \ldots, N$, i.e. $V_j(k) \leq V_j(k-1)$. Noticing the fact given in (5.22), we can see that the minor modification given in (5.11) will not increase the value of $V_j(k)$ when $\hat{b}'_{j1}(k) < \underline{b}_{j1}$, therefore, in the sequel, we need only consider the original estimates without modification. Noting that

$$\|\hat{\theta}_j(k) - \hat{\theta}_j(k-1)\| = \|\tilde{\theta}_j(k) - \tilde{\theta}_j(k-1)\| \tag{5.24}$$

the difference of Lyapunov function $V_j(k)$ can be written as

$$\begin{aligned}
\Delta V_j(k) &= V_j(k) - V_j(k-1) \\
&= \|\tilde{\theta}_j(k)\|^2 - \|\tilde{\theta}_j(k-1)\|^2 \\
&= \|\hat{\theta}_j(k) - \hat{\theta}_j(k-1)\|^2 + 2\tilde{\theta}_j^T(k-1)[\hat{\theta}_j(k) - \hat{\theta}_j(k-1)].
\end{aligned} \tag{5.25}$$

Then, according to the update law (5.10), the error dynamics (5.8) and (5.9), we have

$$\begin{aligned}
&\|\hat{\theta}_j(k) - \hat{\theta}_j(k-1)\|^2 + 2\tilde{\theta}_j^T(k-1)[\hat{\theta}_j(k) - \hat{\theta}_j(k-1)] \\
&\leq \frac{\mu_j^2 \tilde{y}_j^2(k)}{D_j(k-1)} - \frac{2\mu_j \tilde{y}_j^2(k)}{D_j(k-1)} = -\frac{\mu_j(2-\mu_j)\tilde{y}_j^2(k)}{D_j(k-1)}.
\end{aligned}$$

Noting $0 < \mu_j < 2$, we see that $\Delta V_j(k)$ is guaranteed to be non-positive such that the boundedness of $V_j(k)$ is obvious, and immediately the boundedness of $\hat{\theta}_j(k)$ and $\hat{b}_{j1}(k)$ is guaranteed. Taking summation on both sides of the above equation, we obtain

$$\sum_{k=0}^{\infty} \mu_j(2-\mu_j)\frac{\tilde{y}_j^2(k)}{D_j(k-1)} \leq V_j(0) \tag{5.26}$$

which implies

$$\lim_{k\to\infty} \frac{\tilde{y}_j^2(k)}{D_j(k-1)} = 0, \text{ or } \tilde{y}_j(k) = \alpha_j(k) D_j^{\frac{1}{2}}(k-1) \tag{5.27}$$

with $\alpha_j(k) \in L^2[0,\infty)$.
Define

$$\bar{Y}_j(k) = [x_j(k), Y_j^T(k)]^T \tag{5.28}$$

where $Y_j(k)$ is a vector holding states, at time k, of the jth agent's neighbors. By (5.5) and (5.7), we have

$$\begin{aligned} u_j(k) &= O[\bar{Y}_j(k+1)] \\ \phi_j(k) &= O[\bar{Y}_j(k)] \end{aligned} \tag{5.29}$$

then it is obvious that

$$\begin{aligned} D_j^{\frac{1}{2}}(k-1) &\leq 1 + \|\phi_j(k-1)\| + |u_j(k-1)| \\ &= 1 + O[\bar{Y}_j(k)]. \end{aligned} \tag{5.30}$$

From (5.27) we obtain that

$$\tilde{y}_j(k) = o[1] + o[\bar{Y}_j(k)],\ j = 1, 2, \ldots, N \tag{5.31}$$

Using $o[X(k)] \sim o[x_1(k)] + o[x_2(k)] + \ldots + o[x_n(k)]$, we may rewrite the above equation as

$$\begin{aligned} \tilde{Y}(k) \sim\ & \mathrm{diag}(o[1], \ldots, o[1])(G_A + I)X(k) \\ & + [o[1], \ldots, o[1]]^T \end{aligned} \tag{5.32}$$

where I is the $n \times n$ identity matrix. Substituting the above equation into equation (5.19), we obtain

$$\begin{aligned} X(k+1) = & (\Lambda G_A + \mathrm{diag}(o[1], \ldots, o[1])(G_A + I))X(k) \\ & + [x^*(k+1) + o[1], o[1], \ldots, o[1]]^T. \end{aligned}$$

Since

$$(\Lambda G_A + \mathrm{diag}(o[1], \ldots, o[1])(G_A + I))Y(k) \to \Lambda G_A \tag{5.33}$$

as $k \to \infty$, noting $\rho(\Lambda G_A) < 1$, according to Lemma 5.1 and

$$[x^*(k+1) + o[1], o[1], \ldots, o[1]]^T = O[1] \tag{5.34}$$

from Lemma 5.3, we have

$$X(k+1) = O[1]. \tag{5.35}$$

Then, together with equation (5.32), we have $\tilde{Y}(k) = [o[1], \ldots, o[1]]^T$, which implies

$$\tilde{y}_j(k) \to 0 \text{ as } k \to \infty, j = 1, 2, \ldots, N \tag{5.36}$$

which leads to $x_1(k) - x^*(k) \to 0$.
Step 2: Next, we define a vector of the errors between each agent's output and the hidden leader's output as follows

$$E(k) = X(k) - [1,\ 1, \ldots,\ 1]^T x_1(k) = [e_{11}(k), e_{21}(k), \ldots, e_{n1}(k)]^T \tag{5.37}$$

where $e_{j1}(k)$ satisfies

$$\begin{aligned} e_{11}(k+1) &= x_1(k+1) - x_1(k+1) = 0, \\ e_{j1}(k+1) &= x_j(k+1) - x_1(k+1) = \bar{x}_j(k+1) - x_1(k+1) + \tilde{x}_j(k+1), \\ &\quad j = 2, 3, \ldots, N. \end{aligned} \tag{5.38}$$

Noting that except the first row, the summations of the other rows in the sub-stochastic matrix ΛG_A are 1, we have

$$[0, 1, \ldots, 1]^T = \Lambda G_A [0, 1, \ldots, 1]^T$$

such that equations in (5.38) can be written as

$$\begin{aligned} E(k+1) = \Lambda G X(k) - \Lambda G_A [0, 1, \ldots, 1]^T x_1(k+1) \\ + \operatorname{diag}(0, 1, \ldots, 1) \tilde{Y}(k). \end{aligned} \tag{5.39}$$

According to Assumption 5.1, we obtain

$$\begin{aligned} E(k+1) &= \Lambda G_A (X(k) - [0, 1, \ldots, 1]^T x_1(k)) \\ &\quad + [0, 1, \ldots, 1]^T (x_1(k) - x_1(k+1)) \\ &\quad + [o[1], \ldots, o[1]]^T \\ &= \Lambda G E(k) + [o[1], \ldots, o[1]]^T. \end{aligned} \tag{5.40}$$

Assume that ρ' is the spectral radius of ΛG_A, then there exists a matrix norm, which is denoted as $\|\cdot\|_p$, such that

$$\|E(k+1)\|_p \leq \rho' \|E(k)\|_p + o[1] \tag{5.41}$$

where $\rho' < 1$. Then, it is straightforward to show that

$$\|E(k+1)\|_p \to 0 \tag{5.42}$$

as $k \to \infty$. This completes the proof. ∎

6. Summary

The decentralized adaptive control problems have wide backgrounds and applications in practice. Such problems are very challenging because various uncertainties, including coupling uncertainties, parametric plant uncertainties, nonparametric modeling errors, random noise, communication limits, time delay, and so on, may exist in multi-agent systems. Especially, the decentralized adaptive control problems for the discrete-time multi-agent systems may involve more technical difficulties due to the nature of discrete-time systems and lack of mathematical tools for analyzing stability of discrete-time nonlinear systems.

In this chapter, within a unified framework of multi-agent decentralized adaptive control, for a typical general model with coupling uncertainties and other uncertainties, we have investigated several decentralized adaptive control problems, designed efficient local adaptive controllers according to local goals of agents, and mathematically established the global properties (synchronization, stability and optimality) of the whole system, which in turn reveal the fundamental relationship between local agents and the global system.

7. Acknowledgments

This work is partially supported by National Nature Science Foundation (NSFC) under Grants 61004059, 61004139 and 60904086. And this work is also supported by Program for New Century Excellent Talents in University, BIT Scientific Base Supporting Funding, and BIT Basic Research Funding. We would like to thank Ms. Lihua Rong for her careful proofreading.

8. References

Angeli, D. & Bliman, P. A. (2006). Stability of leaderless discrete-time multi-agent systems, *Mathematics of Control, Signals, and Systems* 18(4): 293–322.

Aström, K. & Wittenmark, B. (1989). *Adaptive Control*, Addison-Wesley Pupl. Comp.

Barahona, M. & Pecora, L. M. (2002). Synchronization in small-world systems, *Physical Review Letters* 89(5).

Burns, R. (2000). TechSat21: Formation design, control, and simulation, *Proceedings of IEEE Aerospace Conference* pp. 19–25.

Cao, M., Morse, A. S. & Anderson, B. D. O. (2008). Reaching a consensus in a dynamically changing environment: A graphical approach, *SIAM Journal of Control and Optimization.* 47: 575–600.

Chen, H. F. & Guo, L. (1991). *Identification and Stochastic Adaptive Control*, Birkhäuser, Boston, MA.

Chen, L. J. & Narendra, K. S. (2001). Nonlinear adaptive control using neural networks and multiple models, *Automatica* 37(8): 1245–1255.

Dong, G. H., He, H. G. & Hu, D. W. (2008). A strict inequality on spectral radius of nonnegative matrices and its probabilistic proof, *Proceedings of the 27th chinese Control conference* pp. 138–140.

Gade, P. M. & Hu, C.-K. (2000). Synchronous chaos in coupled map lattices with small-world interactions, *Physical Review E* 62(5).

Goodwin, G. & Sin, K. (1984). *Adaptive Filtering, Prediction and Control*, Prentice-Hall, Englewood Cliffs, NJ.

Guo, L. (1993). *Time-varing stochastic systems*, Ji Lin Science and Technology Press. (in Chinese).

Guo, L. (1994). Stability of recursive stochastic tracking algorithms, *SIAM Journal of Control and Optimization* 32(5): 1195.

Holland, J. H. (1996). *Hidden Order: How Adaptation Builds Complexity*, Addison-Wesley, New York.

Ioannou, P. A. & Sun, J. (1996). *Robust adaptive control*, Prentice Hall, Englewood, Cliffs, NJ.

Jadbabaie, A., Lin, J. & Morse, A. S. (2003a). Coordination of groups of mobile autonomous agents using nearest neighbor rules, *IEEE Transactions on Automatic Control* 48(6): 988–1001.

Jadbabaie, A., Lin, J. & Morse, A. S. (2003b). Coordination of groups of mobile autonomous agents using nearest neighbor rules, *IEEE Transactions on Automatic Control* 48: 998–1001.

Jalan, S. & Amritkar, R. E. (2003). Self-organized and driven phase synchronization in coupled maps, *Physical Review Letters* 90(1): 014101.

Li, X. & Chen, G. (2003). Synchronization and desynchronization of complex dynamical networks: An engineering viewpoint, *IEEE Transactions on Circuits and Systems - I* 50: 1381–1390.

Ma, H. B. (2008a). Further results on limitations to the capability of feedback, *International Journal of Control* 81(1): 21–42.
URL: *http://dx.doi.org/10.1080/00207170701218333*

Ma, H. B. (2008b). An "impossibility" theorem on a class of high-order discrete-time nonlinear control systems, *Systems & Control Letters* 57(6): 497–504.
URL: *http://dx.doi.org/10.1016/j.sysconle.2007.11.008*

Ma, H. B. (2009). Decentralized adaptive synchronization of a stochastic discrete-time multi-agent dynamic model, *SIAM Journal of Control and Optimization* 48(2): 859–880. Published February 25, 2009.
URL: *http://dx.doi.org/10.1137/070685610*

Ma, H. B. & Lum, K. Y. (2008). Adaptive estimation and control for systems with parametric and nonparametric uncertainties, *Adaptive Control*, I-Tech Education and Publishing, chapter 2, pp. 15–64.

Ma, H. B., Lum, K. Y. & Ge, S. S. (2007a). Adaptive control for a discrete-time first-order nonlinear system with both parametric and non-parametric uncertainties, *Proceedings of the 46th IEEE Conference on Decision and Control*, New Orleans, Louisiana USA, pp. 4839–4844.

Ma, H. B., Lum, K. Y. & Ge, S. S. (2007b). Decentralized Aström-Wittenmark self-tuning regulator of a multi-agent uncertain coupled ARMAX system, *Proceedings of the 2007 IEEE Multi-conference on Systems and Control*, p. 363.

Moreau, L. (2005). Stability of multiagent systems with time-dependent communication links, *IEEE Transactions on Automatic Control* 50(2): 169–182.

Olfati-Saber, R., Fax, J. A. & Murray, R. M. (2007). Consensus and cooperation in networked multi-agent systems, *Proceedings of IEEE* 95: 215–233.

Swaroop, D. & Hedrick, J. K. (1999). Constant spacing strategies for platooning in automated highway systems, *ASME Journal of Dynamic Systems, Measurement, and Control* 121: 462–476.

Tanner, H. G. & Christodoulakis, D. K. (2005). State synchronization in local-interaction networks is robust with respect to time delays, *Proceedings of the 44th IEEE Conference on Decision and Control, and the European Control Conference*, pp. 4945–4950.

Time, M., Wolf, F. & Geisl, T. (2004). Toplogical speed limits to network synchronization, *Phys. Rev. Lett.* 92(7): 074101.

Vicsek, T., Czirok, A., Jacob, E. B., Cohen, I. & Schochet, O. (1995). Novel type of phase transitions in a system of self-driven particles, *Physical Review Letter* 75: 1226–1229.

Wu, C. W. & Chua, L. O. (1995). Synchronization in an array of linearly coupled dynamical systems, *IEEE Transactions Circuits and Systems -I* 42(8): 430–447.

Xiao, F. & Wang, L. (2006). State consensus for multi-agent systems with switching topologies and time-varying delays, *International Journal of Control* 79(10): 1277–1284.

Xie, L. L. & Guo, L. (2000). How much uncertainty can be dealt with by feedback?, *IEEE Transactions on Automatic Control* 45(12): 2203–2217.

Yang, C., Dai, S.-L., Ge, S. S. & Lee, T. H. (2009). Adaptive asymptotic tracking control of a class of discrete-time nonlinear systems with parametric and nonparametric uncertainties, *Proceedings of 2009 American Control Conference*, Hyatt Regency Riverfront, St. Louis, MO, USA, pp. 580–585.

Yao, J., Hill, D. J., Guan, Z. H. & Wang, H. O. (2006). Synchronization of complex dynamical networks with switching topology via adaptive control, *Proceedings of 45th IEEE Conference on Decision and Control*, San Diego, CA, pp. 2819–2824.

Zhan, M., Wang, X., Gong, X., Wei, G. W. & Lai, C.-H. (2003). Complete synchronization and generalized synchronization of one-way coupled time-delay systems, *Physical Review E.* 68(036208).

Zhou, J., Lu, J. A. & Lü, J. (2006). Adaptive synchronization of an uncertain complex dynamical network, *IEEE Transactions on Automatic Control* 51: 652–656.

15

A General Approach to Discrete-Time Adaptive Control Systems with Perturbed Measures for Complex Dynamics - Case Study: Unmanned Underwater Vehicles

Mario Alberto Jordán and Jorge Luis Bustamante
Argentine Institute of Oceanography (IADO-CONICET) and Department of Electrical Engineering and Computers, National University of the South (DIEC-UNS), Florida 8000, B8000FWB Bahía Blanca
Argentina

1. Introduction

New design tools and systematic design procedures has been developed in the past decade to adaptive control for a set of general classes of nonlinear systems with uncertainties (Krstić et al., 1995; Fradkov et al., 1999). In the absence of modeling uncertainties, adaptive controllers can achieve in general global boundness, asymptotic tracking, passivity of the adaptation loop and systematic improvement of transient performance. Also, other sources of uncertainty like intrinsic disturbances acting on measures and exogenous perturbations are taking into account in many approaches in order for the controllers to be more robust.

The development of adaptive guidance systems for unmanned vehicles is recently starting to gain in interest in different application fields like autonomous vehicles in aerial, terrestrial as well as in subaquatic environments (Antonelli, 2007; Sun & Cheah, 2003; Kahveci et al., 2008; Bagnell et al., 2010). These complex dynamics involve a high degree of uncertainty (specially in the case of underwater vehicles), namely located in the inertia, added mass, Coriolis and centripetal forces, buoyancy and linear and nonlinear damping.

When applying digital technology, both in computing and communication, the implementation of controllers in digital form is unavoidable. This fact is strengthened by many applications where the sensorial components work inherently digitally at regular periods of time. However, usual applications in path tracking of unmanned vehicles are characterized by analog control approaches (Fossen, 1994; Inzartev, 2009).

The translation of existing analog-controller design approaches to the discrete-time domain is commonly done by a simple digitalization of the controlling action, and in the case of adaptive controllers, of the adaptive laws too (Cunha et al., 1995; Smallwood & Whitcomb, 2003). This way generally provides a good control system behavior. However the role played by the sampling time in the stability and performance must be cautiously investigated. Additionally, noisy measures and digitalization errors may not only affect the stability properties significantly but also increase the complexity of the analysis even for the simplest

approaches based on Euler or Tustin discretization methods (Jordán & Bustamante, 2009a; Jordán & Bustamante, 2009b; Jordán et al., 2010).
On the other side, controller designs being carried out directly in the discrete-time domain seem to be a more promising alternative than the translation approaches. This is sustained on the fact that model errors as well as perturbations are included in the design approach directly to ensure stability and performance specifications.
This work is concerned about a novel design of discrete-time adaptive controllers for path tracking of unmanned underwater vehicles subject to perturbations and measure disturbances. The presented approach is completely developed in the discrete time domain. Formal proofs are presented for stability and performance. Finally, a case study related to a complex guidance system in 6 degrees of freedom (DOF´s) is worked through to illustrate the features of the proposed approach.

2. Notation

Throughout the chapter, vectors are denoted in lower case and bold letters, scalars in lower case letters, matrices in capital letters. A function dependence on a variable is denoted with brackets as for instance $F[x]$. Also brackets are employed to enclose the elements of a vector. Elements of a set are described as enclosed in braces. Parentheses are only used to separate factors with terms of an expression. Subscripts are applied to reference elements in sequences, in matrices or sample-time points. In time sequences, one will distinguish between a prediction x_{n+1} at time t_n from a sample $x[t_n] = x_{t_n}$ at sample time t_n. Often we apply the notation for a derivative of a scalar function with respect to a quadratic matrix, meaning a new matrix with elements describing the derivative of the scalar function with respect to each element of the original matrix. For instance: let the functional Q be depending on the elements x_{ij} of the matrix X in the form $Q = (MX\mathbf{v}_1)^T\mathbf{v}_2$, then it has a derivative $\partial Q/\partial X = M^T\mathbf{v}_2\mathbf{v}_1^T$. Finally we will also make reference to $\partial Q/\partial \mathbf{x}_j$ meaning a gradient vector of the functional Q with respect to the vector $\mathbf{x}_j$, being this the column j of X.

3. Vehicle dynamics

3.1 Physical dynamics from ODEs

Many systems are described as the conjugation of two ODEs in generalized variables, namely one for the kinematics and the other one for the inertia (see Fig. 1). The block structure embraces a wide range of vehicle systems like mobile robots, unmanned aerial vehicles (UAV), spacecraft and satellite systems, autonomous underwater vehicles (AUV) and remotely operated vehicles (ROV), though with slight distinctive modifications in the structure among them.
Let $\boldsymbol{\eta}= [x, y, z, \varphi, \theta, \psi]^T$ be the generalized position vector referred on a earth-fixed coordinate system termed O', with displacements x, y, z, and rotation angles φ, θ, ψ about these directions, respectively. The motions associated to the elements of $\boldsymbol{\eta}$ are referred to as surge, sway, heave, roll, pitch and yaw, respectively.

Additionally let $\mathbf{v}= [u, v, w, p, q, r]^T$ be the generalized rate vector referred on a vehicle-fixed coordinate system termed O, oriented according to their main axes with translation rates u, v, w and angular rates p, q, r about these directions, respectively.

The vehicle dynamics is described as (see Jordán & Bustamante, 2009c; cf. Fossen, 1994)

$$\dot{\mathbf{v}}=M^{-1}\left(-C[\mathbf{v}]\mathbf{v}-D[|\mathbf{v}|]\mathbf{v}-\mathbf{g}[\boldsymbol{\eta}]+\boldsymbol{\tau}_c+\boldsymbol{\tau}\right) \quad (1)$$

$$\dot{\boldsymbol{\eta}}=J[\boldsymbol{\eta}](\mathbf{v}+\mathbf{v}_c). \quad (2)$$

Here M, C and D are the inertia, the Coriolis-centripetal and the drag matrices, respectively and J is the matrix expressing the transformation from the inertial frame to the vehicle-fixed frame. Moreover, $\mathbf{g}$ is the restoration force due to buoyancy and weight, $\boldsymbol{\tau}$ is the generalized propulsion force (also the future control action of a controller), $\boldsymbol{\tau}_c$ is a generalized perturbation force (for instance due to wind as in case of UAVs, fluid flow in AUVs, or cable tugs in ROVs) and $\mathbf{v}_c$ is a velocity perturbation (for instance the fluid current in ROVs/AUVs or wind rate in UAVs), all of them applied to O.
Also disturbances acting on the measures are indicated as $\delta\boldsymbol{\eta}$ and $\delta\mathbf{v}$, while noisy measures are referred to as $\boldsymbol{\eta}_\delta$ and $\mathbf{v}_\delta$, respectively.
Particularly, in fluid environment the mass is broken down into

$$M = M_b + M_a, \quad (3)$$

with M_b body mass matrix, M_a the additive mass matrix related to the dragged fluid mass in the surroundings of the moving vehicle.
For future developments in the controller design, it is convenient to factorize the system matrices into constant and variable arrays as (Jordán & Bustamante, 2009c)

$$C[\mathbf{v}] = \sum_{i=1}^{6} C_i . \times C_{v_i}[\mathbf{v}] \quad (4)$$

$$D[|\mathbf{v}|] = D_l + \sum_{i=1}^{6} D_{q_i} |v_i| \quad (5)$$

$$\mathbf{g}[\boldsymbol{\eta}] = B_1\, \mathbf{g}_1[\boldsymbol{\eta}]+B_2\mathbf{g}_2[\boldsymbol{\eta}], \quad (6)$$

with ".×" being an element-by-element array product. The matrices C_i, D_l, D_{q_i}, B_1 and B_2 are constant and supposed unknown, while $C_{v_i}, \mathbf{g}_1$ and $\mathbf{g}_2$ are state-dependent and computable arrays and v_i is an element of $\mathbf{v}$.
The generalized propulsion force $\boldsymbol{\tau}$ applied on O is broken down into force components provided by each thruster. These components termed f_i are arranged in the vector $\mathbf{f}$ which obeys the relation

$$\mathbf{f}=B^T\left(BB^T\right)^{-1}\boldsymbol{\tau}, \quad (7)$$

with B a commonly rectangular matrix that expresses the transformation of $\boldsymbol{\tau}$ into these thrust components.
On the other hand, $\mathbf{f}$ is related to a strong nonlinear characteristic which is proper of each thruster. Specially for underwater vehicles this is modelled by (cf. Fossen, 1994)

$$\mathbf{f}=K_1\left(|\mathbf{n}|.\mathbf{n}\right)-K_2\left(|\mathbf{n}|.\mathbf{v}_\mathrm{a}\right), \quad (8)$$

where K_1 and K_2 are constant matrices accounting for the influence of the thruster angular velocity $\mathbf{n}$ and the state $\mathbf{v}_\mathrm{a}$ related to every thruster force component in $\mathbf{f}$.

The thruster dynamics usually corresponds to a controlled system with input $\mathbf{n}_{ref}$ and output $\mathbf{n}$ given generally by a linear dynamics indicated generically as some linear vector funcion $\mathbf{k}$ in Laplace variable form

$$\mathbf{n}=\mathbf{k}[\mathbf{n}_{ref},\mathbf{v}], \tag{9}$$

where $\mathbf{n}_{ref}$ is the reference angular velocity referred to as the real input of the vehicle dynamics.

Usually in the literature it is assumed that the rapid thruster dynamics is parasitic in comparison with the dominant vehicle dynamics. In the same way we will neglect this parasitics and so the equality $\mathbf{n}=\mathbf{n}_{ref}$ will be employed throughout the chapter.

Moreover, we will concentrate henceforth on disturbed measures $\boldsymbol{\eta}_\delta$ and $\mathbf{v}_\delta$, and not on exogenous perturbations $\boldsymbol{\tau}_c$ and $\mathbf{v}_c$, so we have set $\boldsymbol{\tau}_c=\mathbf{v}_c=0$ throughout the paper. Similarly, $\mathbf{v}=\bar{\mathbf{v}}$ and $\boldsymbol{\eta}=\bar{\boldsymbol{\eta}}$ (see Fig. 1). For details of the influence of $\boldsymbol{\tau}_c$ and $\mathbf{v}_c$ on adaptive guidance systems see (Jordán and Bustamante, 2008; Jordán and Bustamante 2007), respectively.

3.2 Sampled-data behavior

For the continuous-time dynamics there exists an associated exact sampled-data dynamics described by the set of sequences $\{\boldsymbol{\eta}[t_i],\mathbf{v}[t_i]\}=\left\{\boldsymbol{\eta}_{t_i},\mathbf{v}_{t_i}\right\}$ for the states $\boldsymbol{\eta}[t]$ and $\mathbf{v}[t]$ at sample times t_i with a sampling rate h.

On the other side, we let the sampled measures for the kinematics and positioning state vectors be disturbed. So this is characterized in discrete time through the noisy measurements in the sequence set $\{\boldsymbol{\eta}_\delta[t_i],\mathbf{v}_\delta[t_i]\}=\left\{\boldsymbol{\eta}_{\delta_{t_i}},\mathbf{v}_{\delta_{t_i}}\right\}$ as illustrated in Fig. 1.

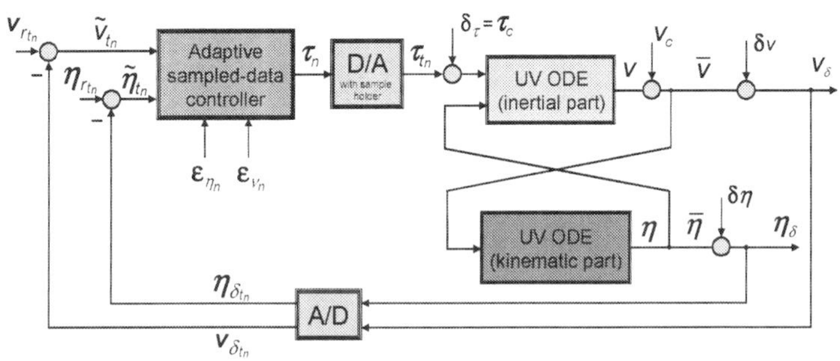

Fig. 1. Adaptive digital control system for underwater vehicles (UV) with noisy measures, model errors and exogenous perturbations

3.3 Sampled-data model

Usually, sampled-data behavior can be modelled by n-steps-ahead predictors (Jordán & Bustamante, 2009a). Accordingly, we attempt now to translate the continuous time dynamics of the system into a discrete-time model. The ODEs in (1)-(2) can be described in a compact form by

$$\dot{\mathbf{v}} = M^{-1}\mathbf{p}[\boldsymbol{\eta},\mathbf{v}]+M^{-1}\boldsymbol{\tau} \tag{10}$$

$$\dot{\boldsymbol{\eta}} = \mathbf{q}[\boldsymbol{\eta},\mathbf{v}], \tag{11}$$

with $\mathbf{p}$ and $\mathbf{q}$ being Lipschitz vector functions located at the right-hand memberships of (1) and (2), respectively. Here no exogenous perturbation was considered as agreed above.
Let us contemplate an approximation of first order of an Adams-Bashforth approximator (Jordán & Bustamante, 2009b). It is valid

$$\mathbf{v}_{n+1} = \mathbf{v}_{t_n} + hM^{-1}\left(\mathbf{p}_{\delta_{t_n}} + \boldsymbol{\tau}_n\right) \quad (12)$$
$$\boldsymbol{\eta}_{n+1} = \boldsymbol{\eta}_{t_n} + h\mathbf{q}_{t_n}, \quad (13)$$

where $\boldsymbol{\eta}_{n+1}$ and $\mathbf{v}_{n+1}$ are one-step-ahead predictions at the present time t_n. Moreover, $\boldsymbol{\tau}_n$ is the discrete-time control action at t_n, which is equal to the sample $\boldsymbol{\tau}[t_n]$ because of the employed zero-order sample holder.
More precisely it is valid with (1)-(2)

$$\mathbf{p}_{t_n} = -\sum_{i=1}^{6} C_i. \times C_{v_{i_{t_n}}} \mathbf{v}_{t_n} - D_l \mathbf{v}_{t_n} - \quad (14)$$
$$-\sum_{i=1}^{6} D_{q_i} \left|v_{i_{t_n}}\right| \mathbf{v}_{t_n} - B_1\, \mathbf{g}_{1_{t_n}} - B_2\, \mathbf{g}_{2_{t_n}}$$
$$\mathbf{q}_{t_n} = J_{t_n} \mathbf{v}_{t_n} \quad (15)$$

where $C_{v_{i_{t_n}}}$ means $C_{v_i}[\mathbf{v}_{t_n}]$, $\mathbf{g}_{1_{t_n}}$ and $\mathbf{g}_{2_{t_n}}$ mean $\mathbf{g}_1[\boldsymbol{\eta}_{t_n}]$ and $\mathbf{g}_2[\boldsymbol{\eta}_{t_n}]$ respectively, $J_{t_n}^{-1}$ means $J^{-1}[\boldsymbol{\eta}_{t_n}]$ and $v_{i_{t_n}}$ is an element of $\mathbf{v}_{t_n}$. Similar expressions can be obtained for the other sampled functions $\mathbf{p}_{t_i}$ and $\mathbf{q}_{t_i}$ in (18)-(19). Besides, the control action $\boldsymbol{\tau}$ is retained one sampling period h by a sample holder, so it is valid $\boldsymbol{\tau}_n = \boldsymbol{\tau}_{t_n}$.
The accuracy of one-step-ahead predictions is defined by the local model errors as

$$\boldsymbol{\varepsilon}_{v_{n+1}} = \mathbf{v}_{t_{n+1}} - \mathbf{v}_{n+1} \quad (16)$$
$$\boldsymbol{\varepsilon}_{\eta_{n+1}} = \boldsymbol{\eta}_{t_{n+1}} - \boldsymbol{\eta}_{n+1}, \quad (17)$$

with $\boldsymbol{\varepsilon}_{\eta_{n+1}}, \boldsymbol{\varepsilon}_{v_{n+1}} \in \mathcal{O}[h]$ and $\mathcal{O}$ being the order function that expresses the order of magnitude of the sampled-data model errors. It is noticing that local errors are by definition completely lacking of the influence from sampled-data disturbances.
Since $\mathbf{p}$ and $\mathbf{q}$ are Lipschitz continuous in the attraction domains in $\mathbf{v}$ and $\boldsymbol{\eta}$, then the samples, predictions and local errors all yield bounded. So it is valid the property $\mathbf{v}_{n+1} \to \mathbf{v}_{t_{n+1}}$ and $\boldsymbol{\eta}_{n+1} \to \boldsymbol{\eta}_{t_{n+1}}$ for $h \to 0$.
Next, the disturbed dynamics subject to sampled-data noisy measures is dealt with in the following.

3.4 1st-order predictor with disturbances

The one-step-ahead predictions with disturbances result from (18) and (19) as

$$\mathbf{v}_{n+1} = \mathbf{v}_{t_n} + \delta\mathbf{v}_{t_n} + hM^{-1}\left(\mathbf{p}_{\delta_{t_n}} + \boldsymbol{\tau}_n\right) \quad (18)$$
$$\boldsymbol{\eta}_{n+1} = \boldsymbol{\eta}_{t_n} + \delta\boldsymbol{\eta}_{t_n} + h\mathbf{q}_{\delta_{t_n}}, \quad (19)$$

where $\mathbf{v}_{t_n}+\delta\mathbf{v}_{t_n}=\mathbf{v}_{\delta_{t_n}}$ and $\boldsymbol{\eta}_{t_n}+\delta\boldsymbol{\eta}_{t_n}=\boldsymbol{\eta}_{\delta_{t_n}}$ are samples of the measure disturbances (see Fig. 1), and $\mathbf{p}_{\delta_{t_n}}$ and $\mathbf{q}_{\delta_{t_n}}$ are perturbed functions defined as $\mathbf{p}_{\delta_{t_n}}=\mathbf{p}\left[\mathbf{v}_{t_n}+\delta\mathbf{v}_{t_n},\boldsymbol{\eta}_{t_n}+\delta\boldsymbol{\eta}_{t_n}\right]$ and $\mathbf{q}_{\delta_{t_n}}=\mathbf{q}\left[\mathbf{v}_{t_n}+\delta\mathbf{v}_{t_n},\boldsymbol{\eta}_{t_n}+\delta\boldsymbol{\eta}_{t_n}\right]$.

3.5 Disturbed local error

Assuming bounded noise vectors $\delta\mathbf{v}_i$ and $\delta\boldsymbol{\eta}_i$, we can expand (18) and (19) in series of Taylor about the values of undisturbed measures $\mathbf{v}[t_n]$ and $\boldsymbol{\eta}[t_n]$. So it is accomplished

$$
\begin{aligned}
\bar{\boldsymbol{\varepsilon}}_{v_{n+1}} &= \boldsymbol{\varepsilon}_{v_{n+1}}+\Delta\delta\mathbf{v}_{t_{n+1}}-hM^{-1}\left(\frac{\partial\mathbf{p}_{\delta}^{T}}{\partial\mathbf{v}}\delta\mathbf{v}_{t_n}+\frac{\partial\mathbf{p}_{\delta}^{T}}{\partial\boldsymbol{\eta}}[t_n]\delta\boldsymbol{\eta}_{t_n}+\right.\\
&\left.+\frac{\partial\boldsymbol{\tau}_n^{T}}{\partial\mathbf{v}}\delta\mathbf{v}_{t_n}+\frac{\partial\boldsymbol{\tau}_n^{T}}{\partial\boldsymbol{\eta}}\delta\boldsymbol{\eta}_{t_n}+\mathbf{o}[\delta\mathbf{v}^2]+\mathbf{o}[\delta\boldsymbol{\eta}^2]\right) \qquad (20)\\
\bar{\boldsymbol{\varepsilon}}_{\eta_{n+1}} &= \boldsymbol{\varepsilon}_{\eta_{n+1}}+\Delta\delta\boldsymbol{\eta}_{t_{n+1}}-h\left(\frac{\partial\mathbf{q}_{\delta}^{T}}{\partial\mathbf{v}}[t_n]\delta\mathbf{v}_{t_n}+\right.\\
&\left.+\frac{\partial\mathbf{q}_{\delta}^{T}}{\partial\boldsymbol{\eta}}[t_n]\delta\boldsymbol{\eta}_{t_n}+\mathbf{o}[\delta\mathbf{v}^2]+\mathbf{o}[\delta\boldsymbol{\eta}^2]\right), \qquad (21)
\end{aligned}
$$

where $\boldsymbol{\varepsilon}_{v_{n+1}}$ and $\boldsymbol{\varepsilon}_{\eta_{n+1}}$ are the model local errors and $\Delta\delta\mathbf{v}_{t_{n+1}}=\delta\mathbf{v}_{t_{n+1}}-\delta\mathbf{v}_{t_n}$ and $\Delta\delta\boldsymbol{\eta}_{t_{n+1}}=\delta\boldsymbol{\eta}_{t_{n+1}}-\delta\boldsymbol{\eta}_{t_n}$. The functions $\mathbf{o}$ are truncating error vectors of the Taylor series expansions, all of them belonging to $\mathcal{O}[h^2]$. Moreover, $\frac{\partial\mathbf{p}_{\delta}^{T}}{\partial\mathbf{v}}$, $\frac{\partial\mathbf{p}_{\delta}^{T}}{\partial\boldsymbol{\eta}}$, $\frac{\partial\mathbf{q}_{\delta}^{T}}{\partial\mathbf{v}}$ and $\frac{\partial\mathbf{q}_{\delta}^{T}}{\partial\boldsymbol{\eta}}$ are Jacobian matrices of the system which act as variable gains that strengthen the sampled-data disturbances along the path.

It is worth noticing that the Jacobian matrices $\frac{\partial\boldsymbol{\tau}_n^{T}}{\partial\mathbf{v}}$ and $\frac{\partial\boldsymbol{\tau}_n^{T}}{\partial\boldsymbol{\eta}}$ in (20) will be obtained from the feedback law $\boldsymbol{\tau}_n[\bar{\boldsymbol{\eta}}_{t_n},\bar{\mathbf{v}}_{t_n}]$ of the adaptive control loop.

4. Sampled-data adaptive controller

The next step is devoted to the stability and performance study of a general class of adaptive control systems whose state feedback law is constructed from noisy measures and model errors.

A design of a general completely adaptive digital controller based on speed-gradient control laws is presented in (Jordán & Bustamante, 2011). To this end let us suppose the control goal lies on the path tracking of both geometric and kinematic reference as $\boldsymbol{\eta}_{r_{t_n}}$ and $\mathbf{v}_{r_{t_n}}$, respectively.

4.1 Control action

Accordingly to the digital model translation, we try out the following definitions for the exact path errors

$$
\begin{aligned}
\widetilde{\boldsymbol{\eta}}_{t_n} &= \boldsymbol{\eta}_{t_n}+\delta\boldsymbol{\eta}_{t_n}-\boldsymbol{\eta}_{r_{t_n}} \qquad (22)\\
\widetilde{\mathbf{v}}_{t_n} &= \mathbf{v}_{t_n}+\delta\mathbf{v}_{t_n}-J_{\delta_{t_n}}^{-1}\dot{\boldsymbol{\eta}}_{r_{t_n}}+J_{\delta_{t_n}}^{-1}K_p\widetilde{\boldsymbol{\eta}}_{t_n}. \qquad (23)
\end{aligned}
$$

where $K_p = K_p^T \geq 0$ is a design gain matrix affecting the geometric path error and $J_{\delta_{t_n}}^{-1}$ means $J^{-1}[\eta_{t_n}+\delta\eta_{t_n}]$. Clearly, if $\breve{\eta}_{t_n}\equiv\mathbf{0}$, then by (23) and (2), it yields $\mathbf{v}_{t_n}+\delta\mathbf{v}_{t_n}-\mathbf{v}_{r_{t_n}}\equiv\mathbf{0}$.
Then, replacing (18) and (19) in (22) for t_{n+1} one gets

$$\breve{\eta}_{t_{n+1}} = \left(I - hJ_{t_n}J_{\delta_{t_n}}^{-1}K_p\right)\breve{\eta}_{t_n}+\eta_{r_{t_n}}-\eta_{r_{t_{n+1}}}+\delta\eta_{t_{n+1}}-\delta\eta_{t_n} \tag{24}$$
$$+\varepsilon_{\eta_{n+1}}+h\left(J_{t_n}\breve{\mathbf{v}}_{t_n}+J_{t_n}\delta\mathbf{v}_{t_n}+J_{t_n}J_{\delta_{t_n}}^{-1}\dot{\eta}_{r_{t_n}}\right).$$

Similarly, with (18) and (19) in (23) for t_{n+1} one obtains

$$\breve{\mathbf{v}}_{t_{n+1}} = \breve{\mathbf{v}}_{t_n}+J_{\delta_{t_n}}^{-1}\dot{\eta}_{r_{t_n}}-J_{\delta_{t_{n+1}}}^{-1}\dot{\eta}_{r_{t_{n+1}}}-J_{\delta_{t_n}}^{-1}K_p\breve{\eta}_{t_n}+ \tag{25}$$
$$+J_{\delta_{t_{n+1}}}^{-1}K_p\breve{\eta}_{t_{n+1}}+\varepsilon_{v_{n+1}}+\delta\mathbf{v}_{t_{n+1}}-\delta\mathbf{v}_{t_n}+hM^{-1}\left(\mathbf{p}_{\delta_{t_n}}+\tau_n\right).$$

We now define a cost functional of the path error energy as

$$Q_{t_n} = \breve{\eta}_{t_n}^T\breve{\eta}_{t_n}+\breve{\mathbf{v}}_{t_n}^T\breve{\mathbf{v}}_{t_n}, \tag{26}$$

which is a positive definite and radially unbounded function in the error vector space. Then we state

$$\Delta Q_{t_n} = Q_{t_{n+1}} - Q_{t_n}= \tag{27}$$
$$= \left(\left(I - hJ_{t_n}J_{\delta_{t_n}}^{-1}K_p\right)\breve{\eta}_{t_n}+h\left(J_{t_n}\breve{\mathbf{v}}_{t_n}+J_{t_n}\delta\mathbf{v}_{t_n}+J_{t_n}J_{\delta_{t_n}}^{-1}\dot{\eta}_{r_{t_n}}\right)+\right.$$
$$\left.+\eta_{r_{t_n}}-\eta_{r_{t_{n+1}}}+\varepsilon_{\eta_{n+1}}+\delta\eta_{t_{n+1}}-\delta\eta_{t_n}\right)^2-\breve{\eta}_{t_n}^2+$$
$$+\left(\breve{\mathbf{v}}_{t_n}+J_{\delta_{t_n}}^{-1}\dot{\eta}_{r_{t_n}}-J_{\delta_{t_{n+1}}}^{-1}\dot{\eta}_{r_{t_{n+1}}}-J_{\delta_{t_n}}^{-1}K_p\breve{\eta}_{t_n}+J_{\delta_{t_{n+1}}}^{-1}K_p\breve{\eta}_{t_{n+1}}\right.$$
$$\left.+hM^{-1}\left(\mathbf{p}_{\delta_{t_n}}+\tau_n\right)+\delta\mathbf{v}_{t_{n+1}}-\delta\mathbf{v}_{t_n}+\varepsilon_{v_{n+1}}\right)^2-\breve{\mathbf{v}}_{t_n}^2.$$

The ideal path tracking demands that

$$\lim_{t_n\to\infty}\Delta Q_{t_n} = \lim_{t_n\to\infty}\left(Q_{t_{n+1}} - Q_{t_n}\right) = 0. \tag{28}$$

Bearing in mind the presence of disturbances and model uncertainties, the practical goal would be at least achieved that $\{\Delta Q_{t_n}\}$ remains bounded for $t_n \to \infty$.
In (Jordán & Bustamante, 2011) a flexible design of a completely adaptive digital controller was proposed. Therein all unknown system matrices (C_i, D_{q_i}, D_l, B_1 and B_2) that influence the stability of the control loop are adapted in the feedback control law with the unique exception of the inertia matrix M from which only a lower bound $\underline{M}$ is demanded. In that work a guideline to obtained an adequate value of that bound is indicated.
Here we will transcribe those results and continue afterwards the analysis to the aimed goal.
First we can conveniently split the control thrust τ_n into two terms as

$$\tau_n = \tau_{1_n} + \tau_{2_n}, \tag{29}$$

where the first one is

$$\tau_{1_n} = -K_v \breve{\mathbf{v}}_{t_n} - \frac{1}{h}\underline{M}\left(J^{-1}_{\delta_{t_n}} \dot{\boldsymbol{\eta}}_{r_{t_n}} + J^{-1}_{\delta_{t_n}} K_p \breve{\boldsymbol{\eta}}_{t_n} + \right. \\ \left. + J^{-1}_{\delta_{t_{n+1}}} \dot{\boldsymbol{\eta}}_{r_{t_{n+1}}} - J^{-1}_{\delta_{t_{n+1}}} K_p \breve{\boldsymbol{\eta}}_{t_{n+1}} \right) - \mathbf{r}_{\delta_{t_n}}, \tag{30}$$

with $K_v = K_v^T \geq 0$ being another design matrix like K_p, but affecting the kinematic errors instead. The vector $\mathbf{r}_{\delta_{t_n}}$ is

$$\mathbf{r}_{\delta_{t_n}} = \sum_{i=1}^{6} U_i . \times C_{v_{i_{t_n}}} \mathbf{v}_{\delta_{t_n}} + U_7 \mathbf{v}_{\delta_{t_n}} + \\ + \sum_{i=1}^{6} U_{7+i} |v_{i_{t_n}}| \mathbf{v}_{\delta_{t_n}} + U_{14} \mathbf{g}_{1_{\delta_{t_n}}} + U_{15}\, \mathbf{g}_{2_{\delta_{t_n}}}, \tag{31}$$

where the matrices U_i in $\mathbf{r}_{\delta_{t_n}}$ will account for every unknown system matrix in $\mathbf{p}_{\delta_{t_n}}$ in order to build up the partial control action τ_{1_n}. Moreover, the U_i´s represent the matrices of the adaptive sampled-data controller which will be designed later. Besides, it is noticing that $\mathbf{r}_{\delta_{t_n}}$ and $\mathbf{p}_{\delta_{t_n}}$ contain noisy measures.
The definition of the second component τ_{2_n} of τ_n is more cumbersome than the first component τ_{1_n}.
Basically we attempt to modify ΔQ_{t_n} farther to confer the quadratic form particular properties of sign definiteness. To this end let us first put (30) into (27). Thus

$$\Delta Q_{t_n} = Q_{t_{n+1}} - Q_{t_n} = \\ = \left(\left(I - h J_{t_n} J^{-1}_{\delta_{t_n}} K_p \right) \breve{\boldsymbol{\eta}}_{t_n} + h \left(J_{t_n} \breve{\mathbf{v}}_{t_n} + J_{t_n} \delta \mathbf{v}_{t_n} + J_{t_n} J^{-1}_{\delta_{t_n}} \dot{\boldsymbol{\eta}}_{r_{t_n}} \right) \right. \\ \left. + \boldsymbol{\eta}_{r_{t_n}} - \boldsymbol{\eta}_{r_{t_{n+1}}} + \boldsymbol{\varepsilon}_{\eta_{n+1}} + \delta \boldsymbol{\eta}_{t_{n+1}} - \delta \boldsymbol{\eta}_{t_n} \right)^2 - \breve{\boldsymbol{\eta}}^2_{t_n} + \\ + \left(\breve{\mathbf{v}}_{t_n} + J^{-1}_{\delta_{t_n}} \dot{\boldsymbol{\eta}}_{r_{t_n}} - J^{-1}_{\delta_{t_{n+1}}} \dot{\boldsymbol{\eta}}_{r_{t_{n+1}}} - J^{-1}_{\delta_{t_n}} K_p \breve{\boldsymbol{\eta}}_{t_n} + J^{-1}_{\delta_{t_{n+1}}} K_p \breve{\boldsymbol{\eta}}_{t_{n+1}} - \right. \\ - h M^{-1} K_v \breve{\mathbf{v}}_{t_n} - M^{-1} \underline{M} \left(J^{-1}_{\delta_{t_n}} \dot{\boldsymbol{\eta}}_{r_{t_n}} - J^{-1}_{\delta_{t_n}} K_p \breve{\boldsymbol{\eta}}_{t_n} - J^{-1}_{\delta_{t_{n+1}}} \dot{\boldsymbol{\eta}}_{r_{t_{n+1}}} + J^{-1}_{\delta_{t_{n+1}}} K_p \breve{\boldsymbol{\eta}}_{t_{n+1}} \right) \\ \left. + h M^{-1} \left(\mathbf{p}_{\delta_{t_n}} - \mathbf{r}_{\delta_{t_n}} \right) + h M^{-1} \tau_{2_n} + \delta \mathbf{v}_{t_{n+1}} - \delta \mathbf{v}_{t_n} + \boldsymbol{\varepsilon}_{v_{n+1}} \right)^2 - \breve{\mathbf{v}}^2_{t_n}, \tag{32}$$

where the old definition of $J^{-1}_{\delta_{t_n}} = J^{-1}[\boldsymbol{\eta}_{t_n} + \delta \boldsymbol{\eta}_{t_n}]$ can be rewritten as

$$J^{-1}_{\delta_{t_n}} = J^{-1}_{t_n} + \Delta J^{-1}_{t_n}. \tag{33}$$

Now defining an motion vector function (combination of acceleration and velocity) in the form

$$\mathbf{s}_{t_n} = J^{-1}_{\delta_{t_n}} \dot{\boldsymbol{\eta}}_{r_{t_n}} - J^{-1}_{\delta_{t_{n+1}}} \dot{\boldsymbol{\eta}}_{r_{t_{n+1}}} - J^{-1}_{\delta_{t_n}} K_p \breve{\boldsymbol{\eta}}_{t_n} + J^{-1}_{\delta_{t_{n+1}}} K_p \breve{\boldsymbol{\eta}}_{t_{n+1}}, \tag{34}$$

the (32) turns into

$$\begin{aligned}
\Delta Q_{t_n} &= Q_{t_{n+1}} - Q_{t_n} = \\
&= \Big((I - hK_p)\, \hat{\boldsymbol{\eta}}_{t_n} - hJ_{t_n}\Delta J^{-1}_{t_n} K_p \hat{\boldsymbol{\eta}}_{t_n} + h\left(J_{t_n}\check{\mathbf{v}}_{t_n} + \dot{\boldsymbol{\eta}}_{r_{t_n}} \right) + J_{t_n}\delta\mathbf{v}_{t_n} + J_{t_n}\Delta J^{-1}_{t_n}\dot{\boldsymbol{\eta}}_{r_{t_n}} \\
&+ \boldsymbol{\eta}_{r_{t_n}} - \boldsymbol{\eta}_{r_{t_{n+1}}} + \boldsymbol{\varepsilon}_{\eta_{n+1}} + \delta\boldsymbol{\eta}_{t_{n+1}} - \delta\boldsymbol{\eta}_{t_n} \Big)^2 - \hat{\boldsymbol{\eta}}^2_{t_n} + \\
&+ \Big(\left(I - hM^{-1}K_v \right) \hat{\mathbf{v}}_{t_n} + \left(I - M^{-1}\underline{M} \right) \mathbf{s}_{t_n} - \\
&+ h\left(\mathbf{p}_{\delta_{t_n}} - M^{-1}\mathbf{r}_{\delta_{t_n}} \right) + hM^{-1}\boldsymbol{\tau}_{2_n} + \delta\mathbf{v}_{t_{n+1}} - \delta\mathbf{v}_{t_n} + \boldsymbol{\varepsilon}_{v_{n+1}} \Big)^2 - \check{\mathbf{v}}^2_{t_n}.
\end{aligned} \tag{35}$$

From this expression one achieves

$$\begin{aligned}
\Delta Q_{t_n} &= a(M^{-1}\boldsymbol{\tau}_{2_n})^2 + \mathbf{b}^T M^{-1}\boldsymbol{\tau}_{2_n} + c + \\
&+ \hat{\boldsymbol{\eta}}^T_{t_n}\sqrt{a}K_p\left(\sqrt{a}K_p - 2I\right)\hat{\boldsymbol{\eta}}_{t_n} + \\
&+ \check{\mathbf{v}}^T_{t_n}\sqrt{a}K^*_v\left(\sqrt{a}K^*_v - 2I\right)\check{\mathbf{v}}_{t_n} + \\
&+ f_{\Delta Q_{1n}}\left[\boldsymbol{\varepsilon}_{\eta_{n+1}}, \boldsymbol{\varepsilon}_{v_{n+1}}, \delta\boldsymbol{\eta}_{t_{n+1}}, \delta\mathbf{v}_{t_{n+1}}\right],
\end{aligned} \tag{36}$$

where K^*_v is an auxiliary matrix equal to $K^*_v = M^{-1}K_v$. The polynomial coefficients a, $\mathbf{b}$ and c are

$$a = h^2 \tag{37}$$

$$\begin{aligned}
\mathbf{b} &= 2h(I - hK^*_v)\check{\mathbf{v}}_{t_n} + 2h\left(I - M^{-1}\underline{M} \right)\mathbf{s}_{t_n} + 2hM^{-1}(\mathbf{p}_{\delta_{t_n}} - \mathbf{r}_{\delta_{t_n}}) \\
&+ 2h\left(\delta\mathbf{v}_{t_{n+1}} - \delta\mathbf{v}_{t_n} + \boldsymbol{\varepsilon}_{v_{n+1}} \right)
\end{aligned} \tag{38}$$

$$\begin{aligned}
c &= h^2\left(J_{t_n}\check{\mathbf{v}}_{t_n} + \dot{\boldsymbol{\eta}}_{r_{t_n}} \right)^2 + \\
&+ 2h\left(J_{t_n}\check{\mathbf{v}}_{t_n} + \dot{\boldsymbol{\eta}}_{r_{t_n}} \right)^T\left(\boldsymbol{\eta}_{r_{t_n}} - \boldsymbol{\eta}_{r_{t_{n+1}}} \right) + \\
&+ \left(\boldsymbol{\eta}_{r_{t_n}} - \boldsymbol{\eta}_{r_{t_{n+1}}} \right)^T\left(\boldsymbol{\eta}_{r_{t_n}} - \boldsymbol{\eta}_{r_{t_{n+1}}} \right) + \\
&+ 2\left((I - hK_p)\,\hat{\boldsymbol{\eta}}_{t_n} \right)^T\left(h(J_{t_n}\check{\mathbf{v}}_{t_n} + \dot{\boldsymbol{\eta}}_{r_{t_n}}) + \boldsymbol{\eta}_{r_{t_n}} - \boldsymbol{\eta}_{r_{t_{n+1}}} \right) + \\
&+ \left(I - M^{-1}\underline{M} \right)^2 \mathbf{s}^2_{t_n} + h^2M^{-1}(\mathbf{p}_{\delta_{t_n}} - \mathbf{r}_{\delta_{t_n}})^2 + \left(\delta\mathbf{v}_{t_{n+1}} - \delta\mathbf{v}_{t_n} + \boldsymbol{\varepsilon}_{v_{n+1}} \right)^2 \\
&+ 2\left(\left(I - M^{-1}\underline{M} \right)\mathbf{s}_{t_n} + hM^{-1}(\mathbf{p}_{\delta_{t_n}} - \mathbf{r}_{\delta_{t_n}}) \right)^T\left(\delta\mathbf{v}_{t_{n+1}} - \delta\mathbf{v}_{t_n} + \boldsymbol{\varepsilon}_{v_{n+1}} \right)
\end{aligned} \tag{39}$$

and $f_{\Delta Q_{1n}}$ is a sign-undefined energy function of the model errors and measure disturbances defined as

$$f_{\Delta Q_{1n}}\left[\varepsilon_{\eta_{n+1}},\varepsilon_{v_{n+1}},\delta\eta_{t_{n+1}},\delta\mathbf{v}_{t_{n+1}}\right]= \tag{40}$$
$$\left(\varepsilon_{\eta_{n+1}}+\delta\eta_{t_{n+1}}-\delta\eta_{t_n}-hJ_{t_n}\Delta J_{t_n}^{-1}K_p\widetilde{\boldsymbol{\eta}}_{t_n}+J_{t_n}\delta\mathbf{v}_{t_n}+J_{t_n}\Delta J_{t_n}^{-1}\dot{\boldsymbol{\eta}}_{r_{t_n}}\right)^2$$
$$+2\left(\left(I-hK_p\right)\widetilde{\boldsymbol{\eta}}_{t_n}+h\left(J_{t_n}\widetilde{\mathbf{v}}_{t_n}+\dot{\boldsymbol{\eta}}_{r_{t_n}}\right)+\boldsymbol{\eta}_{r_{t_n}}-\boldsymbol{\eta}_{r_{t_{n+1}}}\right)^T\times$$
$$\left(\varepsilon_{\eta_{n+1}}+\delta\eta_{t_{n+1}}-\delta\eta_{t_n}-hJ_{t_n}\Delta J_{t_n}^{-1}K_p\widetilde{\boldsymbol{\eta}}_{t_n}+J_{t_n}\delta\mathbf{v}_{t_n}+J_{t_n}\Delta J_{t_n}^{-1}\dot{\boldsymbol{\eta}}_{r_{t_n}}\right).$$

Clearly, there are many variables involved like the system matrices, model errors and measure disturbances which are not known beforehand.
The idea now is to construct $\boldsymbol{\tau}_{2_n}$ so that the sum $a(M^{-1}\boldsymbol{\tau}_{2_n})^2+\mathbf{b}^TM^{-1}\boldsymbol{\tau}_{2_n}+c$ in (36) be null. As there are many variables in the sum which are unknown, we can construct an approximation of it with measurable variables. So, it results

$$\bar{a}\left(M^{-1}\boldsymbol{\tau}_{2_n}\right)^2+\overline{\mathbf{b}}_n^TM^{-1}\boldsymbol{\tau}_{2_n}+\bar{c}_n=0. \tag{41}$$

Now, the polynomial coefficients $\bar{a}$ $\overline{\mathbf{b}}_n$ and $\bar{c}_n$ are explained below. Here, there appear three error functions, namely $f_{\Delta Q_{1n}}$, and the new functions $f_{\Delta Q_{2n}}$ and $f_{U_{in}}$, all containing noisy and unknown variables which are described in the sequel.
The polynomial coefficients result

$$\bar{a}=a=h^2 \tag{42}$$
$$\overline{\mathbf{b}}_n=2h(I-hK_v^*)\widetilde{\mathbf{v}}_{t_n}+2h\underline{M}^{-1}(\overline{\mathbf{p}}_{\delta_{t_n}}-\mathbf{r}_{\delta_{t_n}}) \tag{43}$$

$$\bar{c}_n=h^2\left(\left(J_{t_n}\widetilde{\mathbf{v}}_{t_n}+\dot{\boldsymbol{\eta}}_{r_{t_n}}\right)^2+\left(\Delta J_{\delta t_n}\widetilde{\mathbf{v}}_{t_n}\right)^2+2\left(J_{t_n}\widetilde{\mathbf{v}}_{t_n}+\dot{\boldsymbol{\eta}}_{r_{t_n}}\right)^T\Delta J_{\delta t_n}\widetilde{\mathbf{v}}_{t_n}\right)+ \tag{44}$$
$$+2h\left(J_{t_n}\widetilde{\mathbf{v}}_{t_n}+\dot{\boldsymbol{\eta}}_{r_{t_n}}\right)^T\left(\boldsymbol{\eta}_{r_{t_n}}-\boldsymbol{\eta}_{r_{t_{n+1}}}\right)+2h\left(\Delta J_{\delta t_n}\widetilde{\mathbf{v}}_{t_n}\right)^T\left(\boldsymbol{\eta}_{r_{t_n}}-\boldsymbol{\eta}_{r_{t_{n+1}}}\right)+$$
$$+\left(\boldsymbol{\eta}_{r_{t_n}}-\boldsymbol{\eta}_{r_{t_{n+1}}}\right)^T\left(\boldsymbol{\eta}_{r_{t_n}}-\boldsymbol{\eta}_{r_{t_{n+1}}}\right)+$$
$$+2\left(\left(I-hK_p\right)\widetilde{\boldsymbol{\eta}}_{t_n}\right)^T\left(h\left(J_{t_n}\widetilde{\mathbf{v}}_{t_n}+\dot{\boldsymbol{\eta}}_{r_{t_n}}\right)+\boldsymbol{\eta}_{r_{t_n}}-\boldsymbol{\eta}_{r_{t_{n+1}}}\right)+2\left(\left(I-hK_p\right)\widetilde{\boldsymbol{\eta}}_{t_n}\right)^T\left(h\Delta J_{\delta t_n}\widetilde{\mathbf{v}}_{t_n}\right)+$$
$$+h^2\underline{M}^{-1}\left(\overline{\mathbf{p}}_{\delta_{t_n}}-\mathbf{r}_{\delta_{t_n}}\right)^2+2\left(h\underline{M}^{-1}(\overline{\mathbf{p}}_{\delta_{t_n}}-\mathbf{r}_{\delta_{t_n}})^T\right)(I-hK_v^*)\widetilde{\mathbf{v}}_{t_n},$$

with $\overline{\mathbf{p}}_{\delta_{t_n}}$ being an estimation of $\mathbf{p}_{\delta_{t_n}}$ in (14) given by

$$\overline{\mathbf{p}}_{\delta_{t_n}}=\underline{M}\frac{\mathbf{v}_{t_n}-\mathbf{v}_{t_{n-1}}}{h}-\boldsymbol{\tau}_n. \tag{45}$$

The second component $\boldsymbol{\tau}_{2_n}$ of $\boldsymbol{\tau}_n$ was contained in the condition (41) like a root pair that enables ΔQ_{t_n} be the expression (47). It is

$$\boldsymbol{\tau}_{n_2}=\underline{M}\left(\frac{-\overline{\mathbf{b}}}{2\bar{a}}\pm\frac{1}{2\bar{a}}\sqrt{\frac{\overline{\mathbf{b}}^T\overline{\mathbf{b}}-4\bar{a}\bar{c}}{6}}\mathbf{1}\right), \tag{46}$$

with $\mathbf{1}$ being a vector with ones.
With the choice of (41) and (46) in ΔQ_{t_n} one gets finally

$$\begin{aligned}\Delta Q_{t_n} = {} & \breve{\boldsymbol{\eta}}_{t_n}^T hK_p\left(hK_p-2I\right)\breve{\boldsymbol{\eta}}_{t_n}+ \\ & +\breve{\mathbf{v}}_{t_n}^T hK_v^*\left(hK_v^*-2I\right)\breve{\mathbf{v}}_{t_n}+f_{\Delta Q_{1_n}}\left[\boldsymbol{\varepsilon}_{\eta_{n+1}},\boldsymbol{\varepsilon}_{v_{n+1}},\delta\boldsymbol{\eta}_{t_{n+1}},\delta\mathbf{v}_{t_{n+1}}\right]+ \\ & +f_{\Delta Q_{2_n}}\left[\boldsymbol{\varepsilon}_{\eta_{n+1}},\boldsymbol{\varepsilon}_{v_{n+1}},\delta\boldsymbol{\eta}_{t_{n+1}},\delta\mathbf{v}_{t_{n+1}}\right]+f_{U_{i_n}}\left[\left(U_i^*-U_i\right),M^{-1}\underline{M}\right].\end{aligned} \tag{47}$$

The matrices U_i^* that appear in $f_{U_{i_n}}$ take particular constant values of the adaptive controller matrices U_i´s. They take the values equal to the system matrices in (1)-(2) (Jordán and Bustamante, 2008), namely

$$U_i^* = C_i, \text{ with } i=1,...,6 \tag{48}$$

$$U_7^* = D_l \tag{49}$$

$$U_i^* = D_{q_i}, \text{ with } i=8,...,13 \tag{50}$$

$$U_{14}^* = B_1 \tag{51}$$

$$U_{15}^* = B_2\ . \tag{52}$$

Moreover, the error functions $f_{\Delta Q_{2n}}$ and $f_{U_{i_n}}$ in (47) are respectively

$$\begin{aligned}f_{\Delta Q_{2n}}\left[\boldsymbol{\varepsilon}_{\eta_{n+1}},\boldsymbol{\varepsilon}_{v_{n+1}},\delta\boldsymbol{\eta}_{t_{n+1}},\delta\mathbf{v}_{t_{n+1}}\right] = {} & 2h\left(\delta\mathbf{v}_{t_{n+1}}-\delta\mathbf{v}_{t_n}+\boldsymbol{\varepsilon}_{v_{n+1}}\right)\times \\ \times M^{-1}\underline{M}\left(-\frac{\overline{\mathbf{b}}}{2\bar{a}}\pm\frac{1}{2\bar{a}}\sqrt{\frac{\overline{\mathbf{b}}^T\overline{\mathbf{b}}-4\bar{a}\bar{c}}{6}}\mathbf{1}\right) & -h^2\left(\Delta J_{\delta t_n}\breve{\mathbf{v}}_{t_n}\right)^2- \\ -2h^2\left(\Delta J_{\delta t_n}\breve{\mathbf{v}}_{t_n}\right)\left(\boldsymbol{\eta}_{r_{t_n}}-\boldsymbol{\eta}_{r_{t_{n+1}}}\right) & -2h^2\left(J_{t_n}\breve{\mathbf{v}}_{t_n}+\dot{\boldsymbol{\eta}}_{r_{t_n}}\right)^T\Delta J_{\delta t_n}\breve{\mathbf{v}}_{t_n}- \\ -2h\left(\left(I-hK_p\right)\breve{\boldsymbol{\eta}}_{t_n}\right)^T\Delta J_{\delta t_n}\breve{\mathbf{v}}_{t_n} & +\left(\delta\mathbf{v}_{t_{n+1}}-\delta\mathbf{v}_{t_n}+\boldsymbol{\varepsilon}_{v_{n+1}}\right)^2+ \\ +2\left(\left(I-M^{-1}\underline{M}\right)\mathbf{s}_{t_n}+hM^{-1}\left(\mathbf{p}_{\delta_{t_n}}-\mathbf{r}_{\delta_{t_n}}\right)\right)^T & \left(\delta\mathbf{v}_{t_{n+1}}-\delta\mathbf{v}_{t_n}+\boldsymbol{\varepsilon}_{v_{n+1}}\right),\end{aligned} \tag{53}$$

with $\Delta\mathbf{b}=\mathbf{b}-\overline{\mathbf{b}}$ from (38) and (43), and

$$f_{U_{i_n}}[(U_i^*-U_i), M^{-1}\underline{M}] = \tag{54}$$

$$\frac{\left(M^{-1}\underline{M}\,\overline{\mathbf{b}}\right)^T\left(M^{-1}\underline{M}\,\overline{\mathbf{b}}\right)}{4\bar{a}}+\frac{\mathbf{1}^T(M^{-1}\underline{M})^T(M^{-1}\underline{M})\mathbf{1}\left(\overline{\mathbf{b}}^T\,\overline{\mathbf{b}}\right)}{24\bar{a}}-\frac{\overline{\mathbf{b}}^T M^{-1}\underline{M}\,\overline{\mathbf{b}}}{2\bar{a}}\mp$$

$$\mp\overline{\mathbf{b}}^T\left(\left(M^{-1}\underline{M}\right)^T\left(M^{-1}\underline{M}\right)-M^{-1}\underline{M}\right)\frac{1}{2\bar{a}}\sqrt{\frac{\overline{\mathbf{b}}^T\,\overline{\mathbf{b}}-4\bar{a}\bar{c}}{6}}\mathbf{1}+$$

$$+2\left(h^2(M^{-1}-\underline{M}^{-1})K_v\check{\mathbf{v}}_{t_n}+h^2M^{-1}(\mathbf{p}_{\delta_{t_n}}-\mathbf{r}_{t_n})-h^2\underline{M}^{-1}(\bar{\mathbf{p}}_{t_n}-\mathbf{r}_{\delta_{t_n}})-\right.$$

$$\left.-h\left(I-M^{-1}\underline{M}\right)\mathbf{s}_{t_n}\right)^T M^{-1}\underline{M}\left(-\frac{\overline{\mathbf{b}}}{2\bar{a}}\pm\frac{1}{2\bar{a}}\sqrt{\frac{\overline{\mathbf{b}}^T\,\overline{\mathbf{b}}-4\bar{a}\bar{c}}{6}}\mathbf{1}\right)+h^2M^{-2}(\mathbf{p}_{\delta_{t_n}}-\mathbf{r}_{\delta_{t_n}})^2+$$

$$+\left(I-M^{-1}\underline{M}\right)^2\mathbf{s}_{t_n}^2+2h\left(M^{-1}(\mathbf{p}_{\delta_{t_n}}-\mathbf{r}_{\delta_{t_n}})\right)^T\left(I-M^{-1}\underline{M}\right)\mathbf{s}_{t_n}+$$

$$+2\left(h\left(M^{-1}(\mathbf{p}_{\delta_{t_n}}-\mathbf{r}_{\delta_{t_n}})\right)^T+\mathbf{s}_{t_n}^T\left(I-M^{-1}\underline{M}\right)^T\right)(I-hM^{-1}K_v)\check{\mathbf{v}}_{t_n}-$$

$$-h^2\underline{M}^{-2}\left(\overline{\mathbf{p}}_{\delta_{t_n}}-\mathbf{r}_{\delta_{t_n}}\right)^2-2\left(h\left(\underline{M}^{-1}\left(\overline{\mathbf{p}}_{\delta_{t_n}}-\mathbf{r}_{\delta_{t_n}}\right)\right)^T\right)(I-h\underline{M}^{-1}K_v)\check{\mathbf{v}}_{t_n}.$$

It is seeing from (40), (53) and (54), that the error functions go to lower bounds when $U_i=U_i^*$ (it is, when $\overline{\mathbf{p}}_{\delta_{t_n}}=\mathbf{r}_{\delta_{t_n}}$), $M^{-1}\underline{M}=I$ and $\delta\eta_{t_{n+1}}=\delta\mathbf{v}_{t_{n+1}}=\mathbf{0}$. These bounds will ultimately depend on the model errors $\varepsilon_{\eta_{n+1}}$ and $\varepsilon_{v_{n+1}}$ only.
It is noticing from (46) that the roots may be either real or complex. Clearly when the roots are real, (41) is accomplished. If eventually complex roots appear, one can chose only the real part of the resulting complex roots, namely $\overline{\boldsymbol{\tau}}_{2_n}=\underline{M}\frac{-\overline{\mathbf{b}}_n}{2\bar{a}}$. The implications of that choice will be analyzed later in the section dedicated to the stability study.
Finally, the control action to be applied to the vehicle system is $\boldsymbol{\tau}_n=\boldsymbol{\tau}_{1_n}+\boldsymbol{\tau}_{2_n}$ with the two components given in (30) and (46), respectively.

4.2 Adaptive laws

According to a speed-gradient law (Fradkov et al., 1999), the adaptation of the system behavior occurs by the permanent actualization of the controller matrices U_i.
Let the following adaptive law be valid for $i=1,...,15$

$$U_{i_{n+1}}\triangleq U_{i_n}-\Gamma_i\frac{\partial\Delta Q_{t_n}}{\partial U_i}, \tag{55}$$

with a gain matrix $\Gamma_i=\Gamma_i^T\geq 0$ and $\frac{\partial\Delta Q_{t_n}}{\partial U_{i_n}}$ being a gradient matrix for U_{i_n}.

First we can define an expression for the gradient matrix upon ΔQ_{t_n} in (47) but considering that M is known. This expression is referred to the ideal gradient matrix

$$\frac{\partial \Delta Q_{t_n}}{\partial U_i} = -2h^2 M^{-T}\left(M^{-1}\boldsymbol{\tau}_{2_n}\right)\left(\frac{\partial \mathbf{r}_{\delta_{t_n}}}{\partial U_i}\right)^T - \tag{56}$$
$$-2h^2 M^{-T} M^{-1}(\mathbf{p}_{\delta_{t_n}} - \mathbf{r}_{\delta_{t_n}})\left(\frac{\partial \mathbf{r}_{\delta_{t_n}}}{\partial U_i}\right)^T -$$
$$-2hM^{-T}(I - hK_v^*)\widehat{\mathbf{v}}_{t_n}\left(\frac{\partial \mathbf{r}_{\delta_{t_n}}}{\partial U_i}\right)^T.$$

Now, in order to be able to implement adaptive laws like (55) we have to replace the unknown M in (56) by its lower bound $\underline{M}$. In this way, we can generate implementable gradient matrices which will be denote by $\frac{\partial \overline{\Delta Q}_{t_n}}{\partial U_i}$ and is

$$\frac{\partial \overline{\Delta Q}_{t_n}}{\partial U_i} = -2h^2 \underline{M}^{-T}\left(\underline{M}^{-1}\boldsymbol{\tau}_{2_n}\right)\left(\frac{\partial \mathbf{r}_{\delta_{t_n}}}{\partial U_i}\right)^T - \tag{57}$$
$$-2h^2 \underline{M}^{-T} \underline{M}^{-1}(\overline{\mathbf{p}}_{\delta_{t_n}} - \mathbf{r}_{\delta_{t_n}})\left(\frac{\partial \mathbf{r}_{\delta_{t_n}}}{\partial U_i}\right)^T -$$
$$-2h\underline{M}^{-T}(I - hK_v^*)\widehat{\mathbf{v}}_{t_n}\left(\frac{\partial \mathbf{r}_{\delta_{t_n}}}{\partial U_i}\right)^T,$$

with the property

$$\frac{\partial \overline{\Delta Q}_{t_n}}{\partial U_i} = \frac{\partial \Delta Q_{t_n}}{\partial U_i} + \Delta_{U_{i_n}}, \tag{58}$$

where

$$\Delta_{U_{i_n}} = \delta_{M^{-2}} A_{i_n} + \delta_{M^{-1}} B_{i_n}, \tag{59}$$

and $\delta_{M^{-2}} = \left(\underline{M}^{-T}\underline{M}^{-1} - M^{-T}M^{-1}\right) \geq 0$ and $\delta_{M^{-1}} = \left(\underline{M}^{-1} - M^{-1}\right) \geq 0$. Here A_{i_n} and B_{i_n} are sampled state functions obtained from (56) after extracting of the common factors $\delta_{M^{-2}}$ and $\delta_{M^{-1}}$, respectively.

It is worth noticing that ΔQ_{t_n} and $\overline{\Delta Q}_{t_n}$, satisfy convexity properties in the space of elements of the U_i's.

Moreover, with (58) in mind we can conclude for any pair of values of U_i, say $U_i^{'}$ of $U_i^{''}$, it is valid

$$\Delta Q_{t_n}(U_i^{'}) - \Delta Q_{t_n}(U_i^{''}) \leq \frac{\partial \Delta Q_{t_n}(U_i^{''})}{\partial U_i}\left(U_i^{'} - U_i^{''}\right) \leq \tag{60}$$
$$\leq \frac{\partial \overline{\Delta Q}_{t_n}(U_i^{''})}{\partial U_i}\left(U_i^{'} - U_i^{''}\right). \tag{61}$$

This feature will be useful in the next analysis.

In summary, the practical laws which conform the digital adaptive controller are

$$U_{i_{n+1}} \triangleq U_{i_n} - \Gamma_i \frac{\partial \overline{\Delta Q}_{t_n}}{\partial U_i}. \tag{62}$$

Finally, it is seen from (57) that also here the noisy measures $\boldsymbol{\eta}_{\delta_{t_n}}$ and $\mathbf{v}_{\delta_{t_n}}$ will propagate into the adaptive laws $\frac{\partial \overline{\Delta Q}_{t_n}}{\partial U_i}$.

5. Stability analysis

In this section we prove stability, boundness of all control variables and convergence of the tracking errors in the case of path following for the case of 6 DOF´s involving references trajectories for position and kinematics.

5.1 Preliminaries

Let first the controller matrices U_i's to take the values U_i^*'s in (48)-(52). So, using these constant system matrices in (1),(4)-(6) and (14), a fixed controller can be designed.
For this particular controller we consider the resulting $\Delta Q_{t_n}^*$ from (47) accomplishing

$$\begin{aligned}\Delta Q_{t_n}^* &= \breve{\boldsymbol{\eta}}_{t_n}^T hK_p \left(hK_p - 2I\right) \breve{\boldsymbol{\eta}}_{t_n} + \\ &+ \breve{\mathbf{v}}_{t_n}^T hK_v^* \left(hK_v^* - 2I\right) \breve{\mathbf{v}}_{t_n} + \\ &+ f_{\Delta Q_n}^* [\boldsymbol{\varepsilon}_{\eta_{n+1}}, \boldsymbol{\varepsilon}_{v_{n+1}}, \delta\boldsymbol{\eta}_{t_n}, \delta\mathbf{v}_{t_n}, M^{-1}\underline{M}],\end{aligned} \tag{63}$$

where $f_{\Delta Q_n}^*$ is the sum of all errors obtained from (47) with (53) and (54). It fulfills with $\mathbf{p}_{\delta_{t_n}} = \mathbf{r}_{\delta_{t_n}}$

$$f_{\Delta Q_n}^* = f_{\Delta Q_{1n}} + f_{\Delta Q_{2n}}[\mathbf{p}_{\delta_{t_n}} = \mathbf{r}_{\delta_{t_n}}] + f_{U_{i_n}}[\mathbf{p}_{\delta_{t_n}} = \mathbf{r}_{\delta_{t_n}}]. \tag{64}$$

Later, a norm of $f_{\Delta Q_n}^*$ will be indicated.

Since $\left(\boldsymbol{\varepsilon}_{\eta_{n+1}} + \delta\boldsymbol{\eta}_{t_{n+1}} - \delta\boldsymbol{\eta}_{t_n}\right), \left(\delta\mathbf{v}_{t_{n+1}} - \delta\mathbf{v}_{t_n} + \boldsymbol{\varepsilon}_{v_{n+1}}\right) \in l_\infty$ and $M^{-1}\underline{M} \in l_\infty$, then one concludes $f_{\Delta Q_n}^* \in l_\infty$ as well.

So, it is noticing that $\Delta Q_{t_n}^* < 0$, at least in an attraction domain equal to

$$\mathcal{B} = \left\{ \breve{\boldsymbol{\eta}}_{t_n}, \breve{\mathbf{v}}_{t_n} \in \mathcal{R}^6 \cap \mathcal{B}_0^* \right\}, \tag{65}$$

with $\mathcal{B}_0^*$ a residual set around zero

$$\mathcal{B}_0^* = \left\{ \breve{\boldsymbol{\eta}}_{t_n}, \breve{\mathbf{v}}_{t_n} \in \mathcal{R}^6 / \Delta Q_{t_n}^* - f_{\Delta Q_n}^* \leq 0 \right\} \tag{66}$$

and with the design matrices satisfying the conditions

$$\frac{2}{h} I > K_p \geq 0 \tag{67}$$

$$\frac{2}{h} I > K_v^* \geq 0, \tag{68}$$

which is equivalent to

$$\frac{2}{h}M \geq \frac{2}{h}\underline{M} > K_v \geq 0. \tag{69}$$

The residual set $\mathcal{B}_0^*$ depends not only on $\varepsilon_{\eta_{n+1}}$ and $\varepsilon_{v_{n+1}}$ and the measure noises $\delta\boldsymbol{\eta}_{t_n}$ and $\delta\mathbf{v}_{t_n}$, but also on $M^{-1}\underline{M}$. In consequence, $\mathcal{B}_0^*$ becomes the null point at the limit when $h \to 0$, $\delta\boldsymbol{\eta}_{t_n}$, $\delta\mathbf{v}_{t_n} \to 0$ and $\underline{M} = M$.

5.2 Stability proof

The problem of stability of the adaptive control system is addressed in the sequel. Let a Lyapunov function be

$$V_{t_n} = Q_{t_n} + \frac{1}{2}\sum_{i=1}^{15}\sum_{j=1}^{6}\left(\widetilde{\mathbf{u}}_j^T\right)_{i_{n+1}}\Gamma_i^{-1}\left(\widetilde{\mathbf{u}}_j\right)_{i_{n+1}} - \frac{1}{2}\sum_{i=1}^{15}\sum_{j=1}^{6}\left(\widetilde{\mathbf{u}}_j^T\right)_{i_n}\Gamma_i^{-1}\left(\widetilde{\mathbf{u}}_j\right)_{i_n}, \tag{70}$$

with $\left(\widetilde{\mathbf{u}}_j\right)_{i_n} = \left(\mathbf{u}_j - \mathbf{u}_j^*\right)_{i_n}$, where $\mathbf{u}_j$ and $\mathbf{u}_j^*$ are vectors corresponding to the column j of the adaptive controller matrix U_i and its corresponding one U_i^* in the fixed controller, respectively. Then the differences $\Delta V_{t_n} = V_{t_{n+1}} - V_{t_n}$ can be bounded as follows

$$\begin{aligned}
\Delta V_{t_n} &= \Delta Q_{t_n} + \frac{1}{2}\sum_{i=1}^{15}\sum_{j=1}^{6}\left(\Delta\mathbf{u}_j^T\right)_{i_n}\Gamma_i^{-1}\left(\left(\widetilde{\mathbf{u}}_j\right)_{i_{n+1}} + \left(\widetilde{\mathbf{u}}_j\right)_{i_n}\right) \\
&= \Delta Q_{t_n} + \sum_{i=1}^{15}\sum_{j=1}^{6}\left(\Delta\mathbf{u}_j^T\right)_{i_n}\Gamma_i^{-1}\left(\widetilde{\mathbf{u}}_j\right)_{i_n} - \frac{1}{2}\sum_{i=1}^{15}\sum_{j=1}^{6}\left(\Delta\mathbf{u}_j^T\right)_{i_n}\Gamma_i^{-1}\left(\Delta\mathbf{u}_j\right)_{i_n} \\
&\leq \Delta Q_{t_n} - \sum_{i=1}^{15}\sum_{j=1}^{6}\left(\frac{\partial \Delta Q_{t_n}}{\partial \mathbf{u}_j}\right)^T\left(\widetilde{\mathbf{u}}_j\right)_{i_n} \\
&\leq \Delta Q_{t_n} - \sum_{i=1}^{15}\sum_{j=1}^{6}\left(\frac{\partial \overline{\Delta Q}_{t_n}}{\partial \mathbf{u}_j}\right)^T\left(\widetilde{\mathbf{u}}_j\right)_{i_n} \\
&\leq \Delta Q_{t_n}^* < 0 \text{ in } \mathcal{B} \cap \mathcal{B}_0^*,
\end{aligned} \tag{71}$$

with $\left(\Delta\mathbf{u}_j\right)_{i_n}$ a column vector of $\left(U_{i_{n+1}} - U_{i_n}\right)$.

The column vector $\left(\Delta\mathbf{u}_j\right)_{i_n}$ at the first inequality was replaced by the column vector $-\Gamma_i\left(\frac{\partial \Delta Q_{t_n}}{\partial \mathbf{u}_j}\right)$ and then by $-\Gamma_i\left(\frac{\partial \overline{\Delta Q}_{t_n}}{\partial \mathbf{u}_j}\right)$ in the right member according to (58) and (60)-(61). So in the second and third inequality, the convexity property of ΔQ_{t_n} in (60) was applied for any pair $\left(U' = U_{i_n}, U'' = U_i^*\right)$.

This analysis has proved convergence of the error paths when real square roots exist from $\sqrt{\overline{\mathbf{b}}_n^T\overline{\mathbf{b}}_n - 4\bar{a}\bar{c}_n}$ of (46).

If on the contrary $4\bar{a}\bar{c}_n > \overline{\mathbf{b}}_n^T \overline{\mathbf{b}}_n$ occurs at some time t_n, one chooses the real part of the complex roots in (46). So a suboptimal control action is employed instead, In this case, it is valid

$$\boldsymbol{\tau}_{2_n} = \frac{-1}{2\bar{a}} \underline{M}^{-1} \overline{\mathbf{b}}_n = \frac{-M^{-1}}{h} (I - hK_v^*) \widetilde{\mathbf{v}}_{t_n}. \quad (72)$$

So it yields a new functional $\Delta Q_{t_n}^{**}$ in

$$\Delta V_{t_n} \leq \Delta Q_{t_n}^{**} = \Delta Q_{t_n}^{*} + \bar{c}_n - \frac{1}{4h^2} \overline{\mathbf{b}}_n^T \overline{\mathbf{b}}_n < 0 \text{ in } \mathcal{B} \cap \mathcal{B}_0^{**}, \quad (73)$$

where $\Delta Q_{t_n}^*$ is (63) with a real root of (46) and $\mathcal{B}_0^{**}$ is a new residual set. It is worth noticing that the positive quantity $\left(\bar{c}_n - \frac{1}{4h^2} \overline{\mathbf{b}}_n^T \overline{\mathbf{b}}_n \right)$ can be reduced by choosing h small. Nevertheless, $\mathcal{B}_0^{**}$ results larger than $\mathcal{B}_0^*$ in (71), since its dimension depends not only on $\varepsilon_{\eta_{n+1}}$ and $\varepsilon_{v_{n+1}}$ but also on the magnitude of $\left(\bar{c}_n - \frac{1}{4h^2} \overline{\mathbf{b}}_n^T \overline{\mathbf{b}}_n \right)$.
This closes the stability and convergence proof.

5.3 Variable boundness

With respect to the boundness of the adaptive matrices U_i´s it is seen from (57) that the gradients are bounded. Also the third term is more dominant than the remainder ones for h small ($h << 1$), and so, the kinematic error $\widetilde{\mathbf{v}}_{t_n}$ influences the intensity and sign of $\partial \overline{\Delta Q}_{t_n} / \partial U_i$ more significantly than the others. From (62) one concludes than the increasing of $|U_i|$ may not be avoided long term, however some robust modification techniques like a projection zone can be employed to achieve boundness. This is not developed here. The author can consult for instance (Ioannou and Sun, 1995).

5.4 Incidence of model errors and noisy measures

It is seen in (66) that the residual set $\mathcal{B}_0^*$ is conformed by the perturbation error function $f_{\Delta Q_n}^*$. In this section some guidelines can be given for a proper selection of the design parameters in order to diminish the incidence of model errors and noisy measures. This concerns the design matrices K_p and K_v as well as operation parameters like the cruise vehicle velocity and the control action self.
To this end, let the sign-undefined term $f_{\Delta Q_n}^*$ be upper bounded by

$$\begin{aligned} \left| f_{\Delta Q_n}^* \right| \leq\; & |\mathbf{f}_1| \, |\varepsilon_{\eta_{n+1}} + \delta\boldsymbol{\eta}_{t_{n+1}} - \delta\boldsymbol{\eta}_{t_n}| + |\mathbf{f}_1| \, |J_{t_n}| \left| \Delta J_{t_n}^{-1} K_p \widetilde{\boldsymbol{\eta}}_{t_n} + \Delta J_{t_n}^{-1} \dot{\boldsymbol{\eta}}_{r_{t_n}} \right| + |\mathbf{f}_1| \, |J_{t_n}| \, |\delta\mathbf{v}_{t_n}| + \quad (74) \\ & + |\mathbf{f}_2| \left| \Delta J_{\delta t_n} \widetilde{\mathbf{v}}_{t_n} \right| + |\mathbf{f}_3| \, |\varepsilon_{v_{n+1}} + \delta\mathbf{v}_{t_{n+1}} - \delta\mathbf{v}_{t_n}| + \\ & 2h \left| M^{-1} \boldsymbol{\tau}_{2_n} \right| |\varepsilon_{v_{n+1}} + \delta\mathbf{v}_{t_{n+1}} - \delta\mathbf{v}_{t_n}| + h^2 \left| \Delta J_{\delta t_n} \widetilde{\mathbf{v}}_{t_n} \right|^2 \\ & + \left| \varepsilon_{\eta_{n+1}} + \delta\boldsymbol{\eta}_{t_{n+1}} - \delta\boldsymbol{\eta}_{t_n} - h J_{t_n} \Delta J_{t_n}^{-1} K_p \widetilde{\boldsymbol{\eta}}_{t_n} + J_{t_n} \delta\mathbf{v}_{t_n} + J_{t_n} \Delta J_{t_n}^{-1} \dot{\boldsymbol{\eta}}_{r_{t_n}} \right|^2 \\ & + |\varepsilon_{v_{n+1}} + \delta\mathbf{v}_{t_{n+1}} - \delta\mathbf{v}_{t_n}|^2 + \\ & + |f_4| \left| I - M^{-1} \underline{M} \right|, \end{aligned}$$

where $\mathbf{f}_1$,$\mathbf{f}_2$ and $\mathbf{f}_3$ are bounded vector functions

$$\mathbf{f}_1^T = 2\left(\left(I - hK_p\right)\widehat{\boldsymbol{\eta}}_{t_n} + h\left(J_{t_n}\widehat{\mathbf{v}}_{t_n} + \dot{\boldsymbol{\eta}}_{r_{t_n}}\right) + \boldsymbol{\eta}_{r_{t_n}} - \boldsymbol{\eta}_{r_{t_{n+1}}}\right)^T \tag{75}$$

$$\mathbf{f}_2^T = -2h\left(h\left(\boldsymbol{\eta}_{r_{t_n}} - \boldsymbol{\eta}_{r_{t_{n+1}}}\right) + h\left(J_{t_n}\widehat{\mathbf{v}}_{t_n} + \dot{\boldsymbol{\eta}}_{r_{t_n}}\right) + \left(I - hK_p\right)\widehat{\boldsymbol{\eta}}_{t_n}\right)^T \tag{76}$$

$$\mathbf{f}_3^T = \left(\left(I - M^{-1}\underline{M}\right)\mathbf{s}_{t_n}\right)^T, \tag{77}$$

and f_4 is also a bounded scalar function which can be identified from (54) with $\mathbf{p}_{\delta_{t_n}} = \mathbf{r}_{\delta_{t_n}}$ as

$$fu_i\left[\mathbf{p}_{\delta_{t_n}} = \mathbf{r}_{\delta_{t_n}}\right] = \tag{78}$$

$$\frac{\left(M^{-1}\underline{M}\,\overline{\mathbf{b}}\right)^T\left(M^{-1}\underline{M}\,\overline{\mathbf{b}}\right)}{4\bar{a}} + \frac{\mathbf{1}^T\left(M^{-1}\underline{M}\right)^T\left(M^{-1}\underline{M}\right)\mathbf{1}\left(\overline{\mathbf{b}}^T\,\overline{\mathbf{b}}\right)}{24\bar{a}} - \frac{\overline{\mathbf{b}}^T M^{-1}\underline{M}\,\overline{\mathbf{b}}}{2\bar{a}} \mp$$

$$\mp\overline{\mathbf{b}}^T\left(\left(M^{-1}\underline{M}\right)^T\left(M^{-1}\underline{M}\right) - M^{-1}\underline{M}\right)\frac{1}{2\bar{a}}\sqrt{\frac{\overline{\mathbf{b}}^T\,\overline{\mathbf{b}} - 4\bar{a}\bar{c}}{6}}\mathbf{1} +$$

$$+2\left(h^2\left(M^{-1} - \underline{M}^{-1}\right)K_v\widehat{\mathbf{v}}_{t_n} - h\left(I - M^{-1}\underline{M}\right)\mathbf{s}_{t_n}\right)^T M^{-1}\overline{\boldsymbol{\tau}}_{2_n} +$$

$$+\left(I - M^{-1}\underline{M}\right)^2\mathbf{s}_{t_n}^2 + 2\,\mathbf{s}_{t_n}^T\left(I - M^{-1}\underline{M}\right)^T\left(I - hM^{-1}K_v\right)\widehat{\mathbf{v}}_{t_n},$$

where the norm $\left|I - M^{-1}\underline{M}\right|$ is implicitly contained herein.

Clearly, if $h \to 0$, $\delta\boldsymbol{\eta}_{t_n}$, $\delta\mathbf{v}_{t_n} \to 0$ and $\underline{M} = M$, then $f^*_{\Delta Q_n}$ tends to zero conjointly.

At the first glance in (64) and (53), one notices that the inertia matrix M appears in $\mathbf{f}_3$. So, it is valid

$$\frac{|\mathbf{f}_3|}{|\mathbf{s}_{t_n}|} \leq \left(1 - \lambda_{\min}\left[M^{-1}\underline{M}\right]\right)|| \tag{79}$$

which does reveal that the influence of M on $\mathbf{f}_3$ is reduced whatever $\underline{M}$ be a good estimate of M, it is when $\lambda_{\min}\left[M^{-1}\underline{M}\right]$ be close to one. Besides, no dependence of the sampling time h on $\mathbf{f}_3$ is observed any longer in the tightest bound in (79).

Since the body inertia matrix M_b is plausible to be good estimated, we can choose $\underline{M} = M_b$. So it is valid

$$\frac{|\mathbf{f}_3|}{|\mathbf{s}_{t_n}|} \leq 1 - \left|\left(M_b + M_a\right)^{-1}\right|\left|M_b\right|. \tag{80}$$

Particularly, AUVs are designed with hydrodynamically slender profiles, they have commonly much more smaller values of M_a than in the case of ROVs. In this sense, it is expected that the uncertainty M_a affect more the steady-state performance in ROVs than in AUVs.

The same analysis can be carried out for $\mathbf{f}_1$ in (74). In particular, a choice of K_p in $\mathbf{f}_1$ that is as close as possible to the value I/h (see (67)), will reduce partially $|\mathbf{f}_1|$. Analogously, the same result for K_p could be obtained from $\mathbf{f}_2$.

On the other side, one sees that small differences of $\left(\eta_{r_{t_n}} - \eta_{r_{t_{n+1}}}\right)$ or equivalently small values of $\dot{\eta}_{r_{t_n}}$ have the influence of decreasing $|\mathbf{f}_1|$ as well. Since the quantity $\dot{\eta}_{r_{t_n}} - \frac{\eta_{r_{t_{n+1}}} - \eta_{r_{t_n}}}{h}$ assumes small values for h small, then large cruise velocities do not affect the performance if the sampling time is chosen relatively small.

Besides, the term $hJ_{t_n}\widetilde{\mathbf{v}}_{t_n}$ in $\mathbf{f}_1$ leads to the same conclusion about the effect of h. However, it is interesting to stress the fact that appears in vehicle rotations which may rise the norm of $J_{t_n}[\varphi, \theta, \psi]$ considerably when the pitch angle goes above about 30° (Jordán & Bustamante, 2011).

The scalar function f_4, whose bound is implicitly included in (78) gets small when particularly the vector $\overline{\mathbf{b}}$ is small (this means also $\overline{\tau}_{n_2}$ small), and the motion vector function $\mathbf{s}_{t_n}$ is also rather moderate.

Finally, there is the term $2h\overline{\tau}_{2_n}$ in (74) that also contributes to increase $f_{\Delta Q_{2n}}$ particularly when saturation values of the thrusters are achieved. Since $\overline{\tau}_{2_n}$ is fixed by the controller, the only countermeasure to be applied lays in the fact that the controller always choose the lower $\overline{\tau}_{2_n}$ of the two possible roots in (46). So, the perturbation energy $f_{\Delta Q_{2n}}$ is reduced as far as possible by the controller.

From (63) one can draw out that the choice $K_v = \frac{1}{h} M_b$ in the negative definite terms is much more appropriate to increase the negativeness of $\Delta Q^*_{t_n}$. Equally the choice of K_p in the same manner helps the trajectories to get the residual set more rapid.

Besides, the model errors and noisy measures $(\varepsilon_{v_{n+1}} + \delta\mathbf{v}_{t_{n+1}} - \delta\mathbf{v}_{t_{n+1}})$ and $\left(\varepsilon_{\eta_{n+1}} + \delta\eta_{t_{n+1}} - \delta\mathbf{v}_{t_{n+1}}\right)$ enter linearly and quadratically in the energy equation (74). As they are usually small, only the linear terms are magnified/attenuated by $\mathbf{f}_1$, $\mathbf{f}_2$, $\mathbf{f}_3$ and $\overline{\tau}_{2_n}$, while f_4 impacts nonlinearly in $\overline{\tau}_{n_2}$ and $\mathbf{s}_{t_n}$ as seen in (54).

5.5 Instability for large sampling time

Broadly speaking, the influence of the analyzed parameters will play a role in the instability when (on the chosen h is something large, even smaller than one, because the quadratic terms rise significantly to turn to be dominant in the error function $f^*_{\Delta Q_n}$.

The study of this phenomenon is rather complex but it generally involves the function $\Delta Q^*_{t_n}$ in (63) and $f^*_{\Delta Q_n}$ in (64).

For instante, when

$$f^*_{\Delta Q_n} > \widetilde{\eta}^T_{t_n} hK_p \left(hK_p - 2I\right) \widetilde{\eta}_{t_n} + \widetilde{\mathbf{v}}^T_{t_n} hK^*_v \left(hK^*_v - 2I\right) \widetilde{\mathbf{v}}_{t_n}, \tag{81}$$

the path trajectories may not be bounded into a residual set because the domain for the initial conditions in this situation is partially repulsive. So, depending on the particular initial conditions and for $h >> 0$ the adaptive control system may turn unstable.

In conclusion, when comparing two digital controllers, the sensitivity of the stability to h is fundamental to draw out robust properties and finally to range them.

6. Adaptive control algorithm

The adaptive control algorithm can be summarized as follows.

<u>*Preliminaries:*</u>

1) Estimate a lower bound $\underline{M}$, for instance $\underline{M} = M_b$ (Jordán & Bustamante, 2011),

2) Select a sampling time h as smaller as possible
3) Choose design gain matrices K_p and K_v according to (68)-(69), and simultaneously in order to reduce $f^*_{\Delta Q_n}$ and $\Delta Q^*_{t_n}$ (see related commentary in previous section),
4) Define the adaptive gain matrices Γ_i (usually $\Gamma_i = \alpha_i I$ with $\alpha_i > 0$),
5) Stipulate the desired sampled-data path references for the geometric and kinematic trajectories in 6 DOF´s: $\boldsymbol{\eta}_{r_{t_n}}$ and $\mathbf{v}_{r_{t_n}}$, respectively (see related commentary in previous section).
Continuously at each sample point:
6) Calculate the control thrust τ_n with components τ_{1_n} in (30) and τ_{2_n} (46) (or (72)), respectively,
7) Calculate the adaptive controller matrices (56) with the lower bound $\underline{M}$ instead of M.
Long-term tuning:
7) Redefine K_p, K_v and h in order to achieve optimal tracking performance.

7. Case study

7.1 Setup

With the end of illustrating the features of our control system approach, we simulate a path-tracking problem in 6 DOF´s for an underwater vehicle in a planar motion with some sporadic immersions to the floor.
A continuous-time model of a fully-maneuverable underwater vehicle is employed for the numerical simulations. Details of this dynamics are given in (Jordán & Bustamante, 2009c). The propulsion system is composed by 8 thrusters, distributed in 4 vertical and 4 horizontal. The simulated reference path η_r and the navigation path η are reproduced together by means of a visualization program (see a photogram in Fig. 2). The units for the path run away are in meters.
Basically the vehicle turns around a planar path. At a certain coordinate A it leaves the plane and submerses to the point A' for picking up a sample (of weight 10 (Kgf)) on the sea floor and returns back to A with a typical maneuver (backward movement and rotation). Then it continues on the planar trajectory till the coordinate B in where it submerses again to the point B' in order to place an equipment on the floor (of weight 20 (Kgf)) before to retreat and turn back to B and to complete finally the cycle. The vehicle weight is about 60 (kgf).
Additionally to the geometric path, the rate function $\mathbf{v}_r(t) = J^{-1}(\eta_r)\dot{\eta}_r(t)$ along it, is also specified, with short periods of rest at points A' and B' before beginning and after ending the maneuvers on the bottom.
At the start point of the mission (represented by O in Fig. 2), it is assumed for the adaptive control there is no information available about the vehicle dynamics matrices. Moreover, the maneuvers at stretches A-A' and B-B' imply considerable changes of moments acting on the vehicle in both a positive and negative quantities.
The reference velocity is programmed to be constant equal to 0.25(m/s) for the advance and as well as for the descent/ascent along the path. This rate will be referred to as the cruise velocity.
By the simulations, the adaptive control algorithm summarized in the previous section, is implemented. It is coupled with the ODE (1)-(2) for the vehicle dynamics, whose solution is numerically calculated in continuous time using Runge-Kutta approximators (the so-called *ODE45*). The computed control action is connected to a zero-order sample&hold previously to excite the vehicle.

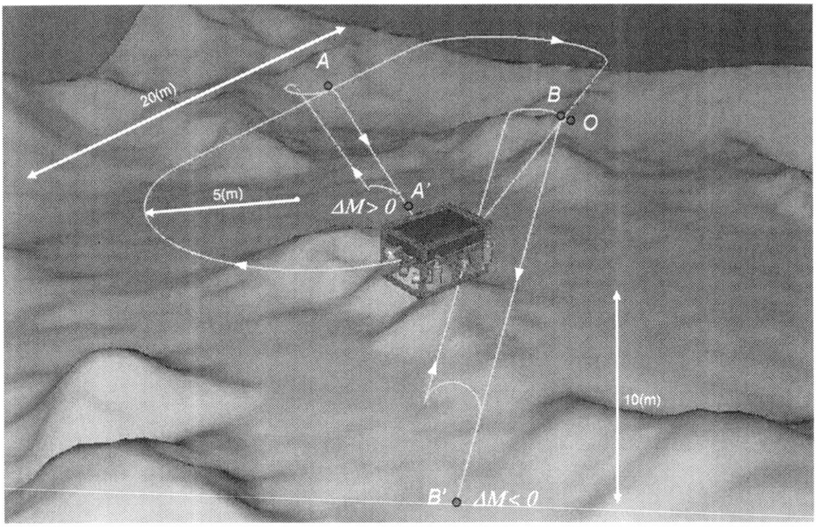

Fig. 2. Path tracking with grab sampling at coordinate A', and with placing of an equipment on the seafloor at coordinate B'

7.2 Design parameters

The most important *a-priori* information for the adaptive controller design is the ODE-structure in (1)-(2) but not its dynamics matrices, with the exception of the lower bound for the inertia matrix M. This takes the form

$$M = M_b + M_a \tag{82}$$

with the components: the body matrix M_b and the additive matrix M_a given by

$$M_b = M_{b_n} + \delta(t - t_{A'})\, M_{b\Delta^+} - \delta(t - t_{B'})\, M_{b\Delta^-} \tag{83}$$
$$M_a = M_{a_n} + \delta(t - t_{A'})\, M_{a\Delta^+} - \delta(t - t_{B'})\, M_{a\Delta^-}, \tag{84}$$

where M_{b_n} and M_{a_n} are nominal values of M_b and M_a at the start point O, and $M_{b\Delta^-}$, $M_{b\Delta^+}$,$M_{a\Delta+}$ and $M_{a\Delta-}$ are positive and negative variations at instants $t_{A'}$ and $t_{B'}$ on the points A' and B' of Fig. 2. Here $\delta(t - t_i)$ represents the Dirac function.
For our application M_{b_n} is determinable beforehand experimentally and it is set as the lower bound $\underline{M}$ for the control and adaptive laws. In the simulated scenario, $M_{b\Delta^-}$ is assumed known because it is about of an equipment deposited on the seafloor. In the case of $M_{b\Delta^+}$, $M_{a\Delta^+}$ and even $M_{a\Delta^-}$, we depart from unknown values.
The property of $M_a \geq 0$ is not affected by the sign of $M_{a\Delta^+}$ and $M_{a\Delta^-}$, which may be positive and negative as well. For that reason, a valid lower bound is chosen as $\underline{M} = M_{b_n} - M_{b\Delta^-}$.
Taking into account the simulation setup for the weight changes (the weight picked up from the seafloor at $t_{A'}$ and the second weight deposited on the seafloor at $t_{B'}$), the lower bound for $\underline{M}$ is

$$\underline{M} = \text{diag}(60, 60, 60, 5, 10, 10), \tag{85}$$

and the mass variations are

$$M_{b\Delta^+} = \text{diag}(10, 10, 10, 0.6250, 4.2250, 3.6) \quad (86)$$
$$M_{b\Delta^-} = \text{diag}(20, 20, 20, 1.25, 1.25, 0) \quad (87)$$
$$M_{a\Delta^+} = \text{diag}(6.3, 15.4, 0.115, 0.115, 0.261, 0.276) \quad (88)$$
$$M_{a\Delta^-} = \text{diag}(12.6, 30.8, 0.23, 0.23, 0.521, 0.551). \quad (89)$$

The design gain matrices for the controller are

$$\begin{aligned} K_p &= \text{diag}\,(5, 5, 5, 5, 5, 5) \\ K_v &= \text{diag}\,(300, 300, 300, 25, 50, 50) \end{aligned} \quad (90)$$

and the adaptive gain matrices about

$$\Gamma_i = I. \quad (91)$$

Finally we have proposed a sampling time $h = 0.2$(s).
All quantities are expressed in the SI Units.

7.3 Control performance

Here the acquired performance by the autonomously guided vehicle under the described simulated setup will be evaluated. First, in Fig. 3, the path error evolution corresponding to every mode with their respective rates is shown for the different transient phases, namely: the controller autotuning at the initial phase (to the left), the sampling phase on the sea bottom at A' (in the middle), and the release of an equipment on the floor at B' (to the right).
The largest path errors had occurred during the initial phase because the amount of information for the control adaptation was null. Here, the longest transient took about 5(s) which is considered outstanding in comparison to the commonly slow open loop behavior. Later, after the mass changes, the path errors behaved much more moderate and were insignificant in magnitude (only a few centimeters or a few hundredths of a radian according to translation/rotation). Among them, the errors in the surge, sway and pitch modes (x, z and θ) resulted more perturbed than the remainder ones because they were more excited from the main motion provided by the stipulated mission. In all evolutions the adaptations occurred quick and smoothly.
The same scenario of control performance can be observed in Fig. 4 from the side of the velocity path errors for every mode of motion. Qualitatively, all kinematic path errors were attenuated rapid and smoothly in the autotuning phase as well as during the mass-change periods. The magnitude of these errors is also related to the rapid changes of the reference $\mathbf{v}_{ref}$ in the programmed maneuvers.
In the Fig. 5, the time evolution of the actuator thrust for two arbitrarily selected thrusters (one horizontal and one vertical) is shown. Analogously as previous results, the forces are compared within the three periods of transients. One observes that the intervention of the controller after a sudden change of mass occurred immediately. Also the transients of these interventions up to the practical steady state were relatively short.
Fig. 6 illustrates the time evolution of some controller matrices U_i. To this end, we had chosen the induced norm of U_8 which is partially related to the adaptation of the linear damping.
One sees that the norm of U_8 evolved with significative changes. In contrast to analog adaptive controllers of the speed-gradient class, here the U_i's do not tend asymptotically to

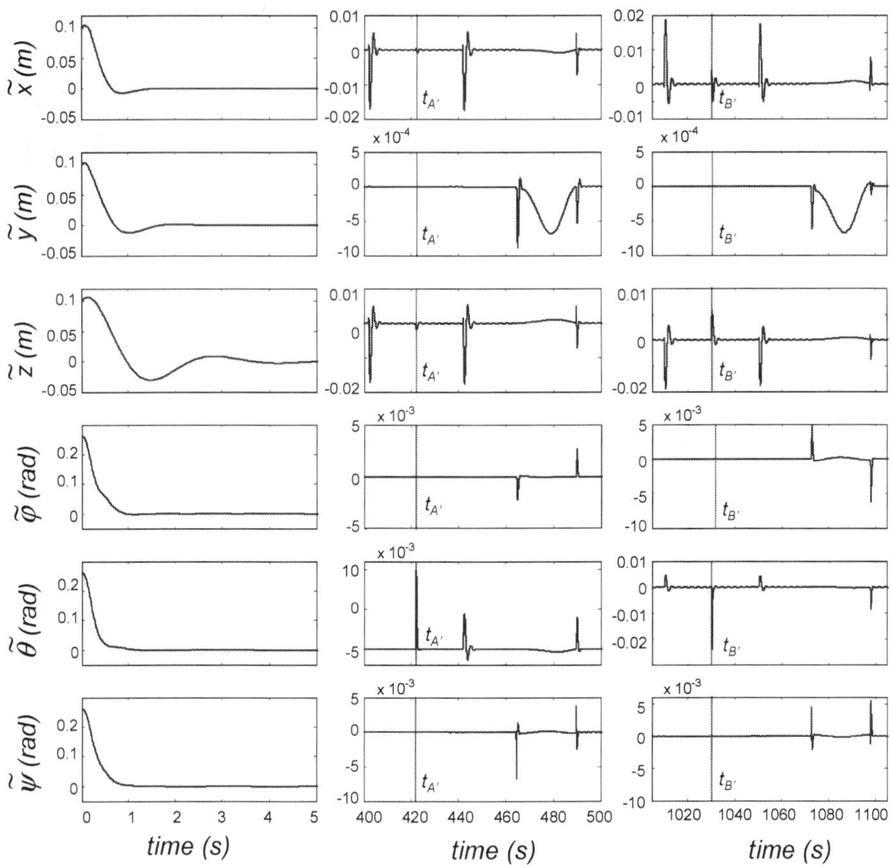

Fig. 3. Position path errors during transients in three different periods (from left to right column: autotuning, adaptation by weight pick up and adaptation by weight deposit)

constant matrices because of the difference between $\underline{M}^{-1}$ and M^{-1} in (58)-(59) (cf. Jordán & Bustamante, 2009c).

8. Conclusions

In this paper a novel design of adaptive control systems was presented. This is based on speed-gradient techniques which are widespread in the form of continuous-time designs in the literature. Here, we had focused their counterparts namely sampled-data adaptive controllers.

The work was framed into the path tracking control problem for the guidance of vehicles in many degrees of freedom. Particularly, the most complex dynamics of this class

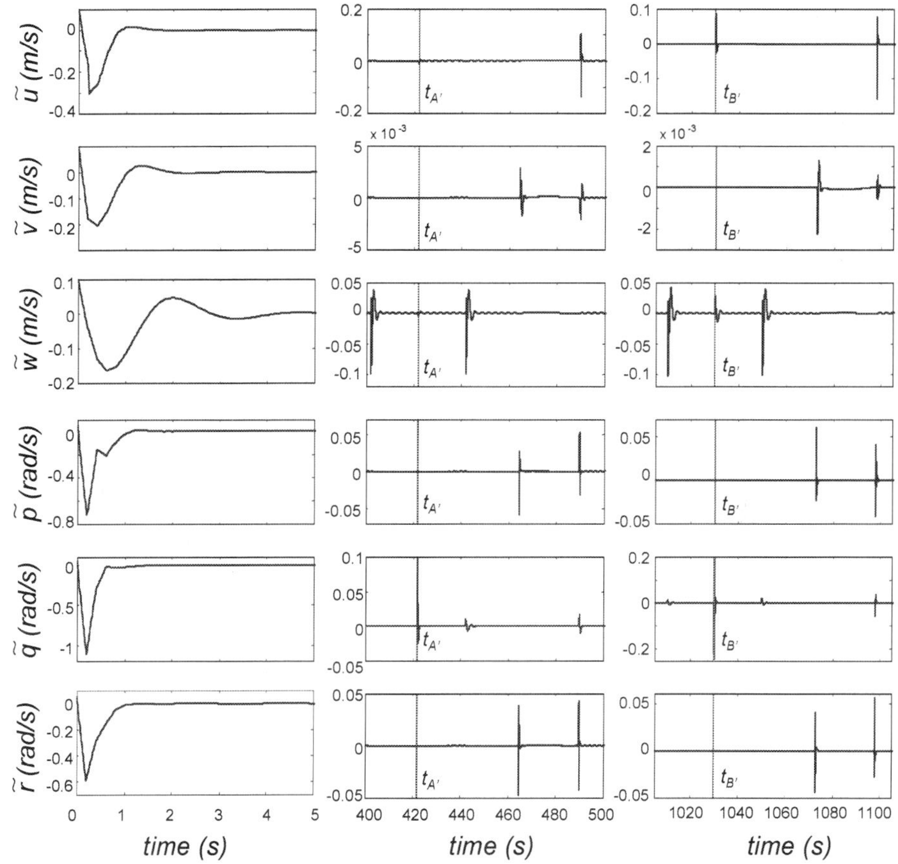

Fig. 4. Velocity path errors during transients in three different periods (from left to right column: autotuning, adaptation by weight pick up and adaptation by weight deposit)

corresponding to unmanned underwater vehicles was worked through in this work. Noisy measures as well as model uncertainties were considered by the design and analysis.
Formal proofs for stability of the digital adaptive control system and convergence of the path error trajectories were presented and an extensive analysis of the control performance was given.
It was shown that it is possible to stabilize the control loop adaptively in the six degrees of freedom without any a-priori knowledge of the vehicle system matrices with the exception of a lower bound for the inertia matrix.
Providing the noisy measures remain bounded, the adaptive controller can reduce asymptotically the path errors up to a residual set in the space state. The residual set contains the null equilibrium point and its magnitude depends on the upper bounds of the measure noises and on the sampling time. This signalizes the quality of the control performance.

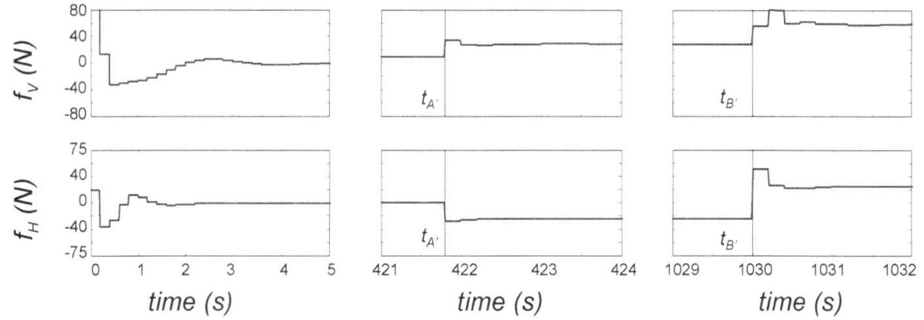

Fig. 5. Evolution of the thrust for one horizontal and one vertical thruster of the propulsion set

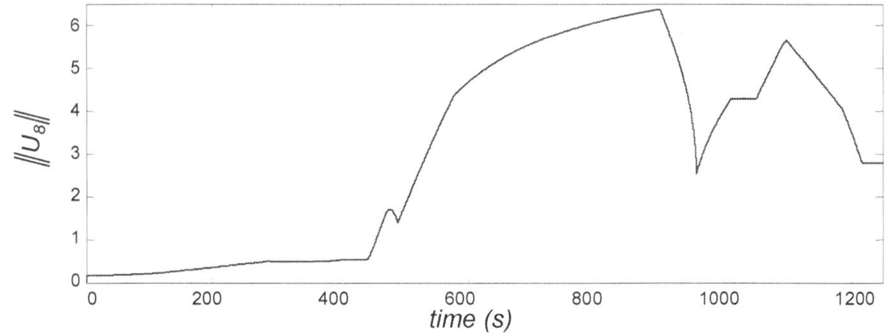

Fig. 6. Evolution of adaptive controller matrices

However, as generally occurs by digital controllers, it was observed that a large sampling time is an instabilizing factor.

It was also indicated the plausibility of obtaining a lower bound of the inertia matrix by simply calculating the inertia matrix of the body only.

We will emphasize that the design presented here was completely carried out in the discrete time domain. Other usual alternative design is the direct translation of a homologous but analog adaptive controller by digitalizing both the control and the adaptive laws. Recent results like in (Jordán & Bustamante, 2011) have shown that this alternative may lead to unstable behaviors if the sampling time is particularly not sufficiently small. This fact stands out the usefulness of our design here.

Finally, a case study was presented for an underwater vehicle in simulated sampling mission. The features of the implemented adaptive control system were highlighted by an all-round very good quality in the control performance.

9. References

[1] Antonelli, G. (2010). On the Use of Adaptive/Integral Actions for Six-Degrees-of-Freedom Control of Autonomous Underwater Vehicles, *IEEE Journal of Oceanic Engineering*. Vol. 32 (2), 300-312.

[2] Bagnell, J.A., Bradley, D., Silver, D., Sofman, B. &Stentz, A. (2010). Learning for Autonomous Navigation,
IEEE Robotics & Automation Magazine, Vol. 17(2), 74 – 84.

[3] Cunha, J.P.V.S, Costa R.R. & L. Hsu (1995). Design of a High Performance Variable Structure Position Control of ROV's, *IEEE J. of Oceanic Engineering*, Vol. 20(1), 42-55.

[4] Fossen, T.I. (1994) *Guidance and Control of Ocean Vehicles*, New York: John Wiley&Sons.

[5] Fradkov, A.L., Miroshnik, I.V. & Nikiforov, V.O. (1999). *Nonlinear and adaptive control of complex systems*, Dordrecht, The Netherlands: Kluwer Academic Publishers.

[6] Ioannou, P.A. and Sun, J. (1996). *Robust adaptive control*. PTR Prentice-Hall, Upper Saddle River, New Jersey.

[7] Inzartev , A.V. (2009)(Editor), *Underwater Vehicles*, Vienna, Austria: In-Tech.

[8] Jordán, M.A. and Bustamante, J.L. (2007) On The Presence Of Nonlinear Oscillations In The Teleoperation Of Underwater Vehicles Under The Influence Of Sea Wave And Current, *26th American Control Conference (2007 ACC)*. New York City, USA, July 11-13.

[9] Jordán, M.A. and Bustamante, J.L. (2008). Guidance Of Underwater Vehicles With Cable Tug Perturbations Under Fixed And Adaptive Control Modus, *IEEE Journal of Oceanic Engineering* , Vol. 33 (4), 579 – 598.

[10] Jordán, M.A. & Bustamante, J.L. (2009a). Adams-Bashforth Approximations for Digital Control of Complex Vehicle Dynamics, *4th Int. Scientific Conf. on Physics and Control (PHYSCON 2009)*, Catania, Italy, Sep. 1-4.

[11] Jordán, M.A. & Bustamante, J.L. (2009b). A General Approach to Sampled-Data Modeling and Digital Control of Vehicle Dynamics, *3rd IEEE Multi-conference on Systems and Control (MSC 2009)*. Saint Petersburg, Russia, July 8-10, 2009b.

[12] Jordán, M.A. and Bustamante, J.L. (2009c). *Adaptive Control for Guidance of Underwater Vehicles*, Underwater Vehicles, A.V. Inzartev (Editor), Vienna, Austria: In-Tech, Chapter 14, 251-278.

[13] Jordán, M.A. and Bustamante, J.L. (2011). An Approach to a Digital Adaptive Controller for guidance of Unmanned Vehicles - Comparison with Digitally-Translated Analog Counterparts, presented to 18th IFAC World Congress, Milan, Italia, August 29-September 2, 2011.

[14] Jordán, M.A., Bustamante, J.L. & Berger,C. (2010.) Adams-Bashforth Sampled-Data Models for Perturbed Underwater-Vehicle Dynamics, *IEEE/OES South America International Symposium*, Buenos Aires, Argentina, April 12-14.

[15] Kahveci, N.E., Ioannou, P.A. & Mirmirani, M.D. (2008). Adaptive LQ Control With Anti-Windup Augmentation to Optimize UAV Performance in Autonomous Soaring Applications, *IEEE Transactions On Control Systems Technology*, Vol. 16 (4).

[16] Krstić, M., Kanellakopoulus, I. & Kokotović, P.V. (1995). *Nonlinear and adaptive control design*. New York: John Wiley and Sons.

[17] Smallwood, D.A. & Whitcomb, L.L. (2003). Adaptive Identification of Dynamically Positioned Underwater Robotic Vehicles, *IEEE Trans. on Control Syst. Technology*, Vol. 11(4), 505-515.

[18] Sun, Y.C. & Cheah, C.C. (2003). Adaptive setpoint control for autonomous underwater vehicles, *IEEE Conf. Decision Control*, Maui, HI, Dec. 9-12.

Part 4

Stability Problems

16

Stability Criterion and Stabilization of Linear Discrete-time System with Multiple Time Varying Delay

Xie Wei
College of Automation Science and Technology, South China University of Technology Guangzhou, China

1. Introduction

The control of discrete systems with time-varying delays has been researched extensively in the last few decades. Especially in recent years there are increasing interests in discrete-time systems with delays due to the emerging fields of networked control and network congestion control (Altman & Basar 1999; Sichitiu et al., 2003; Boukas & Liu 2001). Stability problem for linear discrete-time systems with time-delays has been studied in (Kim & Park 1999; Song & Kim 1998; Mukaidani et al., 2005; Chang et al., 2004; Gao et al., 2004). These results are divided into delay-independent and delay-dependent conditions. The delay-independent conditions are more restrictive than delay-dependent conditions. In general, for discrete-time systems with delays, one might tend to consider augmenting the system and convert a delay problem into a delay-free problem (Song & Kim 1998; Mukaidani et al.,2005). The guaranteed cost control problem for a class of uncertain linear discrete-time systems with both state and input delays has been considered in (Chen et al., 2004). Recently, in (Boukas, 2006) new LMI-based delay-dependent sufficient conditions for stability have been developed for linear discrete-time systems with time varying delay in the state. In these papers above the time-varying delay of discrete systems is assumed to be unique in state variables.

On the other hand, in practice there always exist multiple time-varying delays in state variables, especially in network congestion control. Control problems of linear continuous-time systems with multiple time-varying delays have been studied in (Xu 1997). Quadratic stabilization for a class of multi-time-delay discrete systems with norm-bounded uncertainties has been studied in (Shi et al., 2009).

To the best of author's knowledge, stabilization problem of linear discrete systems has not been fully investigated for the case of multiple time-varying delays in state, and this will be the subject of this paper. This paper address stabilization problem of linear discrete-time systems with multiple time-varying delays by a memoryless state feedback. First, stability analysis conditions of these systems are given in the form of linear matrix inequalities (LMIs) by a Lyapunov function approach. It provides an efficient numerical method to analyze stability conditions. Second, based on the LMIs formulation, sufficient conditions of stabilization problem are derived by a memoryless state feedback. Meanwhile, robust stabilization problem is considered based on these formulations and they are numerically tractable.

2. Problem statement

Considering the dynamics of the discrete system with multiple time-varying time delays as

$$x_{k+1} = Ax_k + \sum_{i=1}^{N} A_{di}x_{k-d_{ki}} + Bu_k, x_k = \phi_k, \quad k \in \left[-\overline{d}_{\max}, \quad \ldots, \quad 0\right], \tag{1}$$

where $x_k \in \Re^n$ is the state at instant k, the matrices $A \in \Re^{n\times n}, A_{di} \in \Re^{n\times n}$ are constant matrices, ϕ_k represents the initial condition, and d_{ki} are positive integers representing multiple time-varying delays of the system that satisfy the following:

$$\underline{d}_i \le d_{ki} \le \overline{d}_i, \quad i = 1,\cdots,N, \tag{2}$$

where $\underline{d}_i$ and $\overline{d}_i$ are known to be positive and finite integers, and we let

$$\overline{d}_{\max} = \max(\overline{d}_i), i = 1,\ldots,N.$$

The aim of this paper is to establish sufficient conditions that guarantee the stability of the class of system (1). Based on stability conditions, the stabilization problem of this system (1) will be handled, too. The control law is given with a memoryless state-feedback as:

$$u_k = Kx_k, \; x_k = \phi_k, \quad k = 0,-1,\ldots,-\overline{d}_i,$$

where K is the control gain to be computed.

3. Stability analysis

In this section, LMIs-based conditions of delay-dependent stability analysis will be considered for discrete-time systems with multiple time-varying delays. The following result gives sufficient conditions to guarantee that the system (1) for $u_k = 0, k \ge 0$ is stable.
Theorem 1: For a given set of upper and lower bounds $\underline{d}_i, \overline{d}_i$ for corresponding time-varying delays d_{ki}, if there exist symmetric and positive-definite matrices $P_1 \in \Re^{n\times n}, Q_i \in \Re^{n\times n}$ and $R_i \in \Re^{n\times n}$, $i = 1,\ldots,N$ and general matrices P_2 and P_3 such that the following LMIs hold:

$$M = \begin{bmatrix} \sum_{i=1}^{N} Q_i + \sum_{i=1}^{N}(\overline{d}_i - \underline{d}_i)R_i + P_1 - A^T P_2 - P_2^T A & * & * & * & \cdots & * \\ P_2 - P_3^T A & P_1 + P_3 + P_3^T & * & * & \cdots & * \\ -A_{d1}^T P_2 & -A_{d1}^T P_3 & -Q_1 & * & \cdots & * \\ -A_{d2}^T P_2 & -A_{d2}^T P_3 & 0 & -Q_2 & * & \vdots \\ \vdots & \vdots & \vdots & 0 & \ddots & * \\ -A_{dN}^T P_2 & -A_{dN}^T P_3 & 0 & \cdots & 0 & -Q_N \end{bmatrix} < 0 \tag{3}$$

$$Q_i < R_i$$

Terms denoted by * are deduced by symmetry. Then the system (1) is stable.
Proof: Consider the following change of variables:

$$x_{k+1} = y_k, \quad 0 = -y_k + Ax_k + \sum_{i=1}^{N} A_{di} x_{k-d_{ki}} \tag{4}$$

Define $\tilde{x}_k = [x_k^T \quad y_k^T \quad x_{k-d1}^T \quad \cdots \quad x_{k-dN}^T]^T$, and consider the following Lyapunov-Krasovskii candidate functional:

$$V(\tilde{x}_k) = V_1(\tilde{x}_k) + V_2(\tilde{x}_k) + V_3(\tilde{x}_k) \tag{5}$$

with

$V_1(\tilde{x}_k) = \tilde{x}_k^T E^T P \tilde{x}_k,$

$V_2(\tilde{x}_k) = \sum_{i=1}^{N} \sum_{l=k-d_{ki}}^{k-1} x_l^T Q_i x_l$

and

$V_3(\tilde{x}_k) = \sum_{i=1}^{N} \sum_{l=-\bar{d}_i+2}^{-\underline{d}_i+1} \sum_{m=k+l-1}^{k-1} x_m^T R_i x_m,$

where $Q_i > 0$ and $R_i > 0$, and E and P are, respectively, singular and nonsingular matrices with the following forms:

$$E = \begin{bmatrix} I & 0 & 0 & \cdots & 0 \\ 0 & 0 & 0 & \cdots & 0 \\ 0 & 0 & 0 & 0 & 0 \\ \vdots & \vdots & 0 & \ddots & \vdots \\ 0 & 0 & 0 & \cdots & 0 \end{bmatrix}, \quad P = \begin{bmatrix} P_1 & 0 & 0 & \cdots & 0 \\ P_2 & P_3 & 0 & \cdots & 0 \\ 0 & 0 & I & 0 & 0 \\ \vdots & \vdots & 0 & \ddots & \vdots \\ 0 & 0 & 0 & \cdots & I \end{bmatrix}$$

where P_1 is a symmetric and positive-definite matrix.
The difference $\Delta V(\tilde{x}_k)$ is given by

$$\Delta V(\tilde{x}_k) = \Delta V_1(\tilde{x}_k) + \Delta V_2(\tilde{x}_k) + \Delta V_3(\tilde{x}_k) \tag{6}$$

Let us now compute $\Delta V_1(\tilde{x}_k)$:

$$\Delta V_1(\tilde{x}_k) = V_1(\tilde{x}_{k+1}) - V_1(\tilde{x}_k) = \tilde{x}_{k+1}^T E^T P \tilde{x}_{k+1} - \tilde{x}_k^T E^T P \tilde{x}_k$$

$$= y_k^T P_1 y_k - x_k^T P_1 x_k = y_k^T P_1 y_k - 2\begin{bmatrix} x_k^T & 0 & 0 & \cdots & 0 \end{bmatrix} P_1 \begin{bmatrix} \frac{1}{2} x_k \\ 0 \\ 0 \\ \vdots \\ 0 \end{bmatrix}$$

which has the following equivalent formulation using the fact that $0 = -y_k + Ax_k + \sum_{i=1}^{N} A_{di} x_{k-d_{ki}}$ as

$$\Delta V_1(\tilde{x}_k) = \tilde{x}_k^T \left[\begin{bmatrix} 0 & 0 & 0 & \cdots & 0 \\ 0 & P_1 & 0 & \cdots & 0 \\ 0 & 0 & 0 & 0 & 0 \\ \vdots & \vdots & 0 & \ddots & 0 \\ 0 & 0 & 0 & 0 & 0 \end{bmatrix} - P^T \begin{bmatrix} \frac{1}{2}I & 0 & 0 & \cdots & 0 \\ A & -I & A_{d1} & \cdots & A_{dN} \\ 0 & 0 & 0 & \cdots & 0 \\ \vdots & \vdots & \vdots & \ddots & \vdots \\ 0 & 0 & 0 & \cdots & 0 \end{bmatrix} - \begin{bmatrix} \frac{1}{2}I & A^T & 0 & \cdots & 0 \\ 0 & -I & 0 & \cdots & 0 \\ 0 & A_{d1}^T & 0 & \cdots & 0 \\ \vdots & \vdots & \vdots & \ddots & \vdots \\ 0 & A_{dN}^T & 0 & \cdots & 0 \end{bmatrix} P \right] \tilde{x}_k \qquad (7)$$

The difference $\Delta V_2(\tilde{x}_k)$ is given by

$$\Delta V_2(\tilde{x}_k) = V_2(\tilde{x}_{k+1}) - V_2(\tilde{x}_k) = \sum_{i=1}^{N} \sum_{l=k+1-d_{ki}}^{k} x_l^T Q_i x_l - \sum_{i=1}^{N} \sum_{l=k-d_{ki}}^{k-1} x_l^T Q_i x_l$$

Note that

$$\sum_{i=1}^{N} \sum_{l=k+1-d_{ki}}^{k} x_l^T Q_i x_l = \sum_{i=1}^{N} \sum_{l=k+1-d_{ki}}^{k-\underline{d}_i} x_l^T Q_i x_l + \sum_{i=1}^{N} \sum_{l=k+1-\underline{d}_i}^{k-1} x_l^T Q_i x_l + \sum_{i=1}^{N} x_k^T Q_i x_k$$

$$\sum_{i=1}^{N} \sum_{l=k-d_{ki}}^{k-1} x_l^T Q_i x_l = \sum_{i=1}^{N} \sum_{l=k+1-d_{ki}}^{k-1} x_l^T Q_i x_l + \sum_{i=1}^{N} x_{k-d_{ki}}^T Q_i x_{k-d_{ki}}$$

Using this, $\Delta V_2(\tilde{x}_k)$ can be rewritten as

$$\begin{aligned} \Delta V_2(\tilde{x}_k) &= \sum_{i=1}^{N} x_k^T Q_i x_k - \sum_{i=1}^{N} x_{k-d_{ki}}^T Q_i x_{k-d_{ki}} + \sum_{i=1}^{N} \sum_{l=k+1-d_{ki}}^{k-\underline{d}_i} x_l^T Q_i x_l \\ &+ \sum_{i=1}^{N} \sum_{l=k+1-\underline{d}_i}^{k-1} x_l^T Q_i x_l - \sum_{i=1}^{N} \sum_{l=k+1-d_{ki}}^{k-1} x_l^T Q_i x_l. \end{aligned} \qquad (8)$$

For $\Delta V_3(\tilde{x}_k)$, we have

$$\begin{aligned} \Delta V_3(\tilde{x}_k) &= \sum_{i=1}^{N} \sum_{l=-\bar{d}_i+2}^{-\underline{d}_i+1} \sum_{m=k+l}^{k} x_m^T R_i x_m - \sum_{i=1}^{N} \sum_{l=-\bar{d}_i+2}^{-\underline{d}_i+1} \sum_{m=k+l-1}^{k-1} x_m^T R_i x_m \\ &= \sum_{i=1}^{N} \sum_{l=-\bar{d}_i+2}^{-\underline{d}_i+1} [\sum_{m=k+l}^{k-1} x_m^T R_i x_m + x_k^T R_i x_k - \sum_{m=k+l}^{k-1} x_m^T R_i x_m - x_{k+l-1}^T R_i x_{k+l-1}] \\ &= \sum_{i=1}^{N} \sum_{l=-\bar{d}_i+2}^{-\underline{d}_i+1} [x_k^T R_i x_k - x_{k+l-1}^T R_i x_{k+l-1}] = \sum_{i=1}^{N} [(\bar{d}_i - \underline{d}_i) x_k^T R_i x_k - \sum_{l=k+1-\bar{d}_i}^{k-\underline{d}_i} x_l^T R_i x_l]. \end{aligned} \qquad (9)$$

Note that $\underline{d}_i \le d_{ki} \le \bar{d}_i$ for all i, we get

$$\sum_{i=1}^{N} \sum_{l=k+1-\underline{d}_i}^{k-1} x_l^T Q_i x_l \le \sum_{i=1}^{N} \sum_{l=k+1-d_{ki}}^{k-1} x_l^T Q_i x_l, \quad \sum_{i=1}^{N} \sum_{l=k+1-d_{ki}}^{k-\underline{d}_i} x_l^T Q_i x_l \le \sum_{i=1}^{N} \sum_{l=k+1-\bar{d}_i}^{k-\underline{d}_i} x_l^T Q_i x_l$$

$$\sum_{i=1}^{N} \sum_{l=k+1-\bar{d}_i}^{k-\underline{d}_i} x_l^T Q_i x_l \le \sum_{i=1}^{N} \sum_{l=k+1-\bar{d}_i}^{k-\underline{d}_i} x_l^T R_i x_l, \text{ since } Q_i < R_i .$$

Finally, by using (7), (8) and (9) together with these inequalities, we obtain

$$\Delta V(\tilde{x}_k) \le [x_k \quad y_k \quad x_{k-d1} \quad \cdots \quad x_{k-dN}]^T M \begin{bmatrix} x_k \\ y_k \\ x_{k-d1} \\ \vdots \\ x_{k-dN} \end{bmatrix} < 0,$$

where

$$M = \begin{bmatrix} \sum_{i=1}^{N} Q_i + \sum_{i=1}^{N} (\bar{d}_i - \underline{d}_i) R_i + P_1 - A^T P_2 - P_2^T A & * & * & * & \cdots & * \\ P_2 - P_3^T A & P_1 + P_3 + P_3^T & * & * & \cdots & * \\ -A_{d1}^T P_2 & -A_{d1}^T P_3 & -Q_1 & * & \cdots & * \\ -A_{d2}^T P_2 & -A_{d2}^T P_3 & 0 & -Q_2 & * & \vdots \\ \vdots & \vdots & \vdots & 0 & \ddots & * \\ -A_{dN}^T P_2 & -A_{dN}^T P_3 & 0 & \cdots & 0 & -Q_N \end{bmatrix} \quad (10)$$

This implies that the system is stable, and then the claim (3) can be established. □

Remark:

As to robust stability analysis of discrete time systems with poytopic-type uncertainties, robust stability analysis can be considered by the formulation above. When system state matrices in (1) are assumed as

$$[A(\lambda(k)) \quad A_{di}(\lambda(k))] = \sum_{j=1}^{L} \partial_j(k) \begin{bmatrix} A_j & A_{dij} \end{bmatrix}, \quad \partial_j(k) \ge 0, \sum_{j=1}^{L} \partial_j(k) = 1.$$

Robust state feedback synthesis can be formulated as:

For a given set of upper and lower bounds $\underline{d}_i, \bar{d}_i$ for corresponding time-varying delays d_{ki}, if there exist symmetric and positive-definite matrices $P_1 \in \Re^{n\times n}, Q_i \in \Re^{n\times n}$ and $R_i \in \Re^{n\times n}$, $i = 1, \ldots, N$ and general matrices P_2 and P_3 such that the following LMIs hold:

$$\begin{bmatrix} \sum_{i=1}^{N} Q_i + \sum_{i=1}^{N} (\bar{d}_i - \underline{d}_i) R_i + P_1 - A_j^T P_2 - P_2^T A_j & * & * & * & \cdots & * \\ P_2 - P_3^T A_j & P_1 + P_3 + P_3^T & * & * & \cdots & * \\ -A_{d1j}^T P_2 & -A_{d1j}^T P_3 & -Q_1 & & \ddots & \\ -A_{d2j}^T P_2 & -A_{d2j}^T P_3 & 0 & -Q_2 & * & \vdots \\ \vdots & \vdots & \vdots & 0 & \ddots & * \\ -A_{dNj}^T P_2 & -A_{dNj}^T P_3 & 0 & \cdots & 0 & -Q_N \end{bmatrix} < 0 \quad (11)$$

$$Q_i < R_i$$
$$j = 1, \ldots, L$$

Terms denoted by * are deduced by symmetry. Then the system with poytopic-type uncertainties is stable.

4. Stabilizability

The aim of this section is to design a memoryless state-feedback controller which stabilizes the system (1). When the memoryless state-feedback is substituted with plant dynamics (3), the dynamics of closed-loop system is obtained as

$$x_{k+1} = (A + BK)x_k + \sum_{i=1}^{N} A_{di} x_{k-d_{ki}}, \quad x_k = \phi_k, \quad k = 0,-1,\ldots,-\bar{d}_i \,. \tag{12}$$

Note that stability analysis condition (3) is not convenient for us to design a memoryless state-feedback. By Schur Complememt lemma, equivalent conditions of (3) are given easily to solve such a memoryless state-feedback which guarantees the closed-loop system (12) is stable. Due to

$$\begin{bmatrix} -Q_1 & 0 & \cdots & 0 \\ 0 & -Q_2 & 0 & \vdots \\ \vdots & 0 & \ddots & 0 \\ 0 & \cdots & 0 & -Q_N \end{bmatrix} < 0,$$

The equivalent formulation of (3) could be obtained as

$$\begin{bmatrix} \sum_{i=1}^{N} Q_i + \sum_{i=1}^{N} (\bar{d}_i - \underline{d}_i) R_i - P_1 - A^T P_2 - P_2^T A & * \\ P_2 - P_3^T A & P_1 + P_3 + P_3^T \end{bmatrix}$$

$$+ \begin{bmatrix} -P_2^T A_{d1} & -P_2^T A_{d2} & \cdots & -P_2^T A_{dN} \\ -P_3^T A_{d1} & -P_3^T A_{d2} & \cdots & -P_3^T A_{dN} \end{bmatrix} \begin{bmatrix} -Q_1 & 0 & \cdots & 0 \\ 0 & -Q_2 & 0 & \vdots \\ \vdots & 0 & \ddots & 0 \\ 0 & \cdots & 0 & -Q_N \end{bmatrix}^{-1} \begin{bmatrix} -A_{d1}^T P_2 & -A_{d1}^T P_3 \\ -A_{d2}^T P_2 & -A_{d1}^T P_3 \\ \vdots & \vdots \\ -A_{dN}^T P_2 & -A_{d1}^T P_3 \end{bmatrix} < 0$$

If we denote by X the inverse of P, we have

$$X = \begin{bmatrix} X_1 & 0 \\ X_2 & X_3 \end{bmatrix}, \quad X_1 = P_1^{-1},$$

$$0 = P_2 X_1 + P_3 X_2, \quad X_3 = P_3^{-1} .$$

$$X_1 = P_1^{-1}$$

Pre- and post multiplying the above LMI, respectively, by X^T and X and using these relations, we will get

$$\begin{bmatrix} \sum_{i=1}^{N} X_1^T Q_i X_1 + \sum_{i=1}^{N}(\bar{d}_i - \underline{d}_i) X_1^T R_i X_1 - X_1 & * \\ X_2 - AX_1 & X_3 + X_3^T \end{bmatrix} + \begin{bmatrix} X_2^T \\ X_3^T \end{bmatrix} P_1 \begin{bmatrix} X_2 & X_3 \end{bmatrix}$$

$$+ \begin{bmatrix} 0 & 0 & \cdots & 0 \\ A_{d1} & A_{d2} & \cdots & A_{dN} \end{bmatrix} \begin{bmatrix} -Q_1 & 0 & \cdots & 0 \\ 0 & -Q_2 & 0 & \vdots \\ \vdots & 0 & \ddots & 0 \\ 0 & \cdots & 0 & -Q_N \end{bmatrix}^{-1} \begin{bmatrix} 0 & -A_{d1}^T \\ 0 & -A_{d1}^T \\ \vdots & \vdots \\ 0_2 & -A_{d1}^T \end{bmatrix} < 0$$

Let $S_i = Q_i^{-1}$ and $T_i = R_i^{-1}$, we have

$$\begin{bmatrix}
-X_1 & * & \cdots & * & \cdots & * & & \cdots & * & & \cdots & & * \\
-AX_1 - BF + X_2 & X_3 + X_3^T & & \vdots & & & & & & & & & \\
X_2 & X_3 & -X_1 & * & \vdots & \vdots & \vdots & & & & & \vdots & \\
0 & -S_1 A_{d1}^T & 0 & -S_1 & & & & \ddots & * & & & & \\
0 & -S_2 A_{d2}^T & \vdots & 0 & -S_2 & * & & & & & & * & \vdots \\
\vdots & \vdots & 0 & \cdots & 0 & \ddots & * & & \vdots & & & & \\
0 & -S_N A_{dN}^T & & & & \ddots & -S_N & & & & & & \\
X_1 & 0 & \vdots & & & & 0 & -S_1 & * & \ddots & \ddots & & \vdots \\
\vdots & \vdots & & & \cdots & & & 0 & \ddots & & & & \\
X_1 & 0 & \vdots & & & & & & \ddots & -S_N & & & \\
\vdots & \vdots & & & \cdots & & & \cdots & & 0 & -\frac{T_1}{\bar{d}_1 - \underline{d_1}} & * & \\
\vdots & \vdots & & & & & & & & & \ddots & \ddots & * \\
X_1 & 0 & 0 & & 0 & & \cdots & 0 & & \cdots & 0 & 0 & -\frac{T_N}{\bar{d}_N - \underline{d_N}}
\end{bmatrix} < 0 \quad (13)$$

$$\begin{bmatrix}
-X_1 & * & \cdots & * & \cdots & * & & \cdots & * & & \cdots & & * \\
-AX_1 - BF + X_2 & X_3 + X_3^T & & \vdots & & & & & & & & & \\
X_2 & X_3 & -X_1 & * & \vdots & \vdots & \vdots & & & & & \vdots & \\
0 & -S_1 A_{d1}^T & 0 & -S_1 & & & & \ddots & * & & & & \\
0 & -S_2 A_{d2}^T & \vdots & 0 & -S_2 & * & & & & & & * & \vdots \\
\vdots & \vdots & 0 & \cdots & 0 & \ddots & * & & \vdots & & & & \\
0 & -S_N A_{dN}^T & & & & \ddots & -S_N & & & & & & \\
X_1 & 0 & \vdots & & & & 0 & -S_1 & * & \ddots & \ddots & & \vdots \\
\vdots & \vdots & & & \cdots & & & 0 & \ddots & & & & \\
X_1 & 0 & \vdots & & & & & & \ddots & -S_N & & & \\
\vdots & \vdots & & & \cdots & & & \cdots & & 0 & -\frac{T_1}{\bar{d}_1 - \underline{d_1}} & * & \\
\vdots & \vdots & & & & & & & & & \ddots & \ddots & * \\
X_1 & 0 & 0 & & 0 & & \cdots & 0 & & \cdots & 0 & 0 & -\frac{T_N}{\bar{d}_N - \underline{d_N}}
\end{bmatrix} < 0 \quad (14)$$

Theorem 2: For a given set of upper and lower bounds $\underline{d}_i, \overline{d}_i$ for corresponding time-varying delays d_{ki}, if there exist symmetric and positive-definite matrices $X_1 \in \Re^{n\times n}$, $S_i \in \Re^{n\times n}$ and $T_i \in \Re^{n\times n}$, $i = 1,\ldots,N$ and general matrices X_2 and X_3 such that LMIs below hold, the memoryless state-feedback gain is given by $K = FX_1^{-1}$.

Proof: Now we consider substituting system matrices of (12) into LMIs conditions (13), the LMIs-based conditions of the memoryless state-feedback problem can be obtained directly as (14). □

Remark:

When these time delays are constant, that is, $d = \overline{d}_i = \underline{d}_i$, $i = 1,\ldots,N$, theorem 2 is reduced to the following condition

$$\begin{bmatrix} -X_1 & * & \cdots & * & \cdots & * & * & \cdots & \cdots & * \\ -AX_1 + X_2 & X_3 + X_3^T & \vdots & \vdots & \cdots & & & \cdots & * & \vdots \\ X_2 & X_3 & X_1 & * & \cdots & \vdots & \vdots & * & \cdots & \vdots \\ 0 & -S_1 A_{d1}^T & 0 & -S_1 & & & & & \vdots & * \\ 0 & -S_2 A_{d2}^T & 0 & 0 & -S_2 & \ddots & * & & * & \vdots \\ \vdots & \vdots & \vdots & \vdots & 0 & \ddots & \vdots & & \vdots & \vdots \\ 0 & -S_N A_{dN}^T & 0 & 0 & \vdots & \vdots & -S_N & \vdots & \vdots & \vdots \\ X_1 & 0 & 0 & 0 & \cdots & \cdots & 0 & -S_1 & * & * \\ \vdots & \vdots & \vdots & \vdots & \vdots & \vdots & \vdots & 0 & \ddots & * \\ X_1 & 0 & 0 & 0 & 0 & \cdots & 0 & \cdots & 0 & -S_N \end{bmatrix} < 0 \qquad (15)$$

The condition above is delay-independent, which is more restrictive than delay-dependent conditions (14).

Remark:

When the time-varying delay of discrete systems is assumed to be unique in state variables, that is, $N = 1$, these results in theorem 2 could be reduced to those obtained in (Boukas, E. K., 2006).

Remark:

As to robust control problem of discrete time systems with poytopic-type uncertainties, robust state feedback synthesis can be considered by these new formulations. When system state matrices in (11) are assumed as

$$[A(\lambda(k)) \;\; A_{di}(\lambda(k)) \;\; B(\lambda(k))] = \sum_{j=1}^{L} \partial_j(k) \begin{bmatrix} A_j & A_{dij} & B_j \end{bmatrix},$$

$$\partial_j(k) \geq 0, \sum_{j=1}^{L} \partial_j(k) = 1,$$

Robust state feedback synthesis can be formulated as:

For a given set of upper and lower bounds $\underline{d}_i, \overline{d}_i$ for corresponding time varying delays d_{ki}, if there exist symmetric and positive definite matrices $X_1 \in \Re^{n\times n}$, $S_i \in \Re^{n\times n}$ and $T_i \in \Re^{n\times n}$, $i = 1,\ldots,N$ and general matrices X_2 and X_3 such that LMIs (16) hold, the memoryless state-feedback gain is given by $K = FX_1^{-1}$.

$$\begin{bmatrix}
-X_1 & * & \cdots & * & \cdots & * & & \cdots & * & & \cdots & & * \\
-A_jX_1-B_jF+X_2 & X_3+X_3^T & & \vdots & & & & & & & & & \\
X_2 & X_3 & -X_1 & * & \vdots & \vdots & \vdots & & & & & \vdots & \\
0 & -S_1A_{d1j}^T & 0 & -S_1 & & & & \ddots & * & & & & \\
0 & -S_2A_{d2j}^T & \vdots & 0 & -S_2 & * & & & & & & * & \vdots \\
\vdots & \vdots & 0 & \cdots & 0 & \ddots & * & & \vdots & & & & \\
0 & -S_NA_{dNj}^T & & & & \ddots & -S_N & & & & & & \\
X_1 & 0 & \vdots & & & & 0 & -S_1 & * & \ddots & \ddots & & \vdots \\
\vdots & \vdots & & & \cdots & & & 0 & \ddots & & & & \\
X_1 & 0 & \vdots & & & & & & \ddots & -S_N & & & \\
\vdots & \vdots & & & \cdots & & & \cdots & & 0 & -\frac{T_1}{\bar{d}_1-\underline{d}_1} & * & \\
\vdots & \vdots & & & & & & & & & \ddots & \ddots & * \\
X_1 & 0 & 0 & & 0 & & \cdots & 0 & & \cdots & 0 & 0 & -\frac{T_N}{\bar{d}_N-\underline{d}_N}
\end{bmatrix} < 0 \quad (16)$$

$$j = 1,\ldots,L.$$

5. Numerical example

To illustrate the usefulness of the previous theoretical results, let us give the following numerical examples.

Consider a discrete system with multiple time-varying delays $N = 2$ as

$$A = \begin{bmatrix} 0 & 1 \\ -2 & -3 \end{bmatrix},\ B = \begin{bmatrix} 0 \\ 1 \end{bmatrix},\ A_{d1} = \begin{bmatrix} 0.01 & 0.01 \\ 0 & 0.01 \end{bmatrix}$$

$$\text{and } A_{d2} = \begin{bmatrix} 0.02 & 0.25 \\ 0.10 & 0.01 \end{bmatrix}$$

with $1 \le d_1 \le 2$, $2 \le d_2 \le 3$. Now the stabilization of this system will be considered with a memoryless state feedback.

Using Matlab LMI toolbox (P. Gahinet, et al., 1995), solving (21) we can get

$$X_1 = \begin{bmatrix} 1.36e-3 & 4.26e-3 \\ 4.26e-3 & 1.62e-2 \end{bmatrix},\ X_2 = \begin{bmatrix} 7.31e-3 & 2.70e-2 \\ 1.95e-2 & 7.15e-2 \end{bmatrix}$$

$$\text{and } X_3 = \begin{bmatrix} -2.73e-4 & 1.89e-4 \\ -1.565e-3 & -3.42e-3 \end{bmatrix},$$

$$S_1 = \begin{bmatrix} 2.17e2 & 62.5 \\ 62.5 & 3.45e2 \end{bmatrix},\ S_2 = \begin{bmatrix} 1.64e2 & 47.8 \\ 47.8 & 8.56e2 \end{bmatrix},$$

$$T_1 = \begin{bmatrix} 4.04e2 & 1.22e2 \\ 1.22e2 & 6.32e2 \end{bmatrix},\ T_2 = \begin{bmatrix} 2.84e2 & 96.6 \\ 96.6 & 1.03e3 \end{bmatrix}.$$

Therefore, a memoryless state-feedback gain is given by $K = FX_1^{-1} = [2.0\ 3.0]$.
The closed-loop discrete-time system with multiple time-varying time delay is simulated in case of $d_1 = 1, d_2 = 2$, $d_1 = 1, d_2 = 3$, $d_1 = 2, d_2 = 2$, and $d_1 = 2, d_2 = 3$, respectively. And these results are illustrated in Figure 1, Figure 2, Figure 3 and Figure 4. These figures show that this system is stabilized by the state feedback.

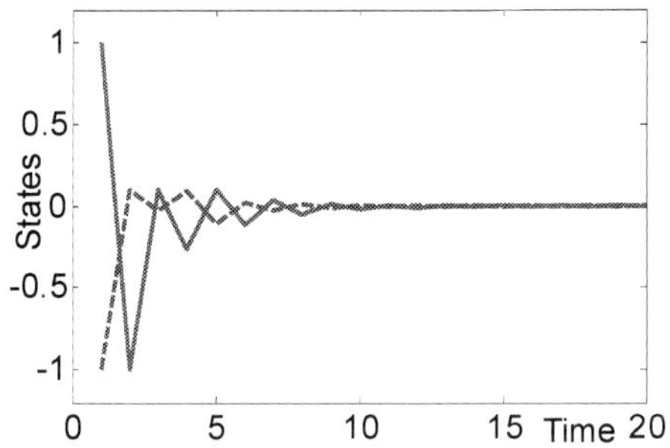

Fig. 1. The behavior of the states in case of $d_1 = 1, d_2 = 2$

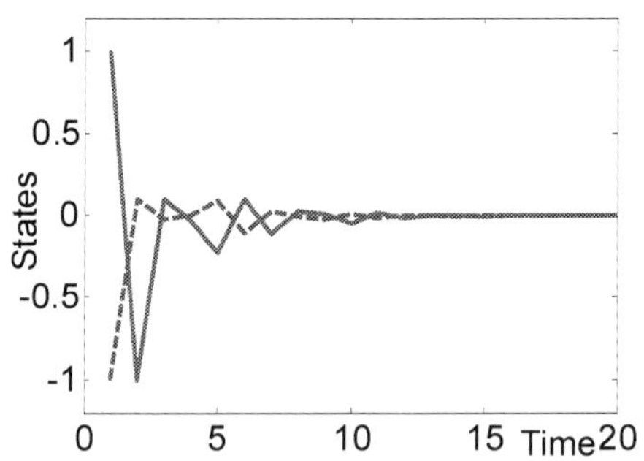

Fig. 2. The behavior of the states in case of $d_1 = 1, d_2 = 3$

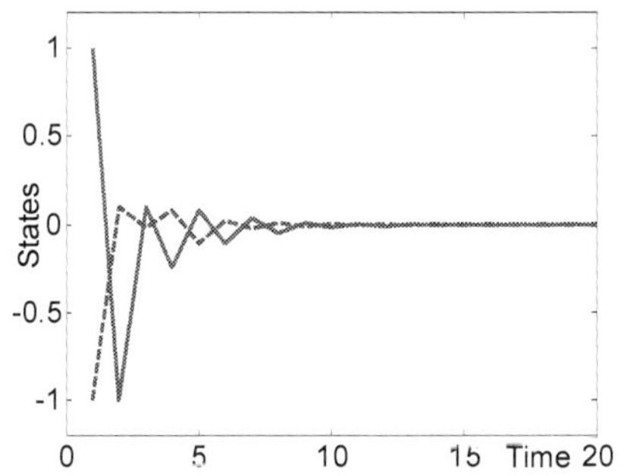

Fig. 3. The behavior of the states in case of $d_1 = 2, d_2 = 2$

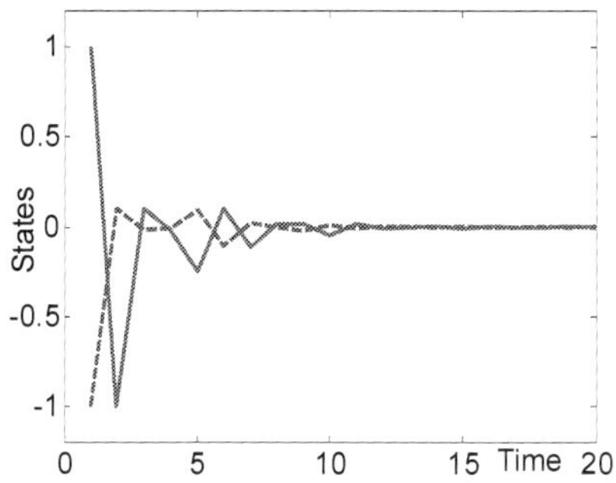

Fig. 4. The behavior of the states in case of $d_1 = 2, d_2 = 3$

6. Conclusion

Stability Criterion and Stabilization for linear discrete-time systems with multiple time-varying delays have been considered. Main results have been given in terms of linear matrix inequalities formulation. It provided us an efficient numerical method to stabilize these systems. Based on these results, it can be also extended to the memory state feedback problem of these systems in the future research.

7. Acknowledgements

This work is supported by the National Natural Science Foundation of China (Grant no. 6070422), the Fundamental Research Funds for the Central Universities, SCUT 2009ZZ0051, and NCET-08-0206.

8. References

Altman, E., Basar, T., & Srikant, R. (1999). Congestion control as a stochastic control problem with action delays. In *Proceedings of the 34th IEEE conference on decision and control*, pp. 1389–1394, New Orleans

Sichitiu, M. L., Bauer, P. H., & Premaratne, K. (2003). The effect of uncertain time-variant delays in ATM networks with explicit rate feedback: A control theoretic approach. *IEEE/ACM Transactions on Networking*, *11*(4) 628–637

Boukas, E. K and Liu, Z. K. (2001). Robust H infinity control of discrete-time Markovian jump linear systems with mode-dependent time-delays, *IEEE Transactions on Automatic Control* 46, no. 12, 1918-1924

Kim, J. H and Park, H. B, (1999). H infinity state feedback control for generalized continuous/discrete time-delay system, *Automatica* 35, no. 8, 1443-1451

Song, S. H and Kim, J. K, (1998). H infinity control of discrete-time linear systems with norm-bounded uncertainty and time delay in state, *Automatica* 34, no. 1, 137-139

Mukaidani, H., Sakaguchi, S., and Tsuji, T. (2005). LMI-based neurocontroller for guaranteed cost control of uncertain time-delay systems, *Proceedings of IEEE International Symposium on Circuits and Systems*, vol. 4, Kobe, pp. 3407-3050

Chang, Y. C., Su, S. F., and Chen, S. S. (2004). LMI approach to static output feedback simultaneous stabilization of discrete-time interval systems with time delay, *Proceedings of International Conference on Machine Learning and Cybernetics*, Vol. 7, Shanghai, pp. 4144-4149

Gao, H., Lam, J., Wang, C., and Wang, Y. (2004). Delay-dependent output-feedback stabilisation of discrete-time systems with time-varying state delay, *IEE Proceedings-Control Theory and Applications* 151, no. 6, 691-698

Guan, X, Lin, Z and Duan, G. (1999). Robust guaranteed cost control for discrete-time uncertain systems with delay, *IEE Proc. Control Theory*, 146, (6), pp. 598-602

Chen, W, Guan, Z and Lu, X. (2004). Delay-dependent guaranteed cost control for uncertain discrete-time systems with both state and input delays, *Journal of the Franklin Institute*, vol. 341, pp. 419-430

Chen, W, Guan, Z and Lu, X. (2004). Delay-dependent output feedback guaranteed cost control for uncertain time-delay systems, *Automatica*, vol. 40, pp. 1263-1268

Boukas, E. K., Discrete-time systems with time-varying time delay: Stability and Stabilizability, *Mathematical Problems in Engineering*, Vol. 2006, ID 42489, 1-10

Xie, W., Xie, L. H., Xu, B. G., stability analysis for linear discrete-time systems with multiple time-varying delays, 2007 IEEE International Conference on Control and Automation, pp. 3078-3080

Xie, W., Multi-objective H infinity/alpha-stability controller synthesis of LTI systems, IET Control Theory and Applications, Vol. 2, no. 1, pp.51-55, 2008

Xu, B. G. (1997) .Stability robustness bounds for linear systems with multiply time-varying delayed perturbations, International Journal of Systems Science, Vol.28, No.12, pp. 1311-1317

Shi, J. X., Ma, Y. C, Yang, B and Zhang, X. F. (2009). Quadratic stabilization for multi-time-delay uncertain discrete systems, Chinese Control and Decision Conference, pp. 4064-4068

Gahinet, P., Nemirovskii, A. , Laub, A. J. and Chilali, M. (1995). LMI Control Toolbox. Natick, MA: Mathworks

17

Uncertain Discrete-Time Systems with Delayed State: Robust Stabilization with Performance Specification via LMI Formulations

Valter J. S. Leite[1], Michelle F. F. Castro[2], André F. Caldeira[3], Márcio F. Miranda[4] and Eduardo N. Gonçalves[6]
[1,2,3]*CEFET–MG* / campus Divinópolis
[4]*UFMG* / *COLTEC* [5]*CEFET–MG* / campus *II*
Brazil

1. Introduction

This chapter is about techniques for robust stability analysis and robust stabilization of discrete-time systems with delay in the state vector. The relevance of this study is mainly due to the unavoidable presence of delays in dynamic systems. Even small time-delays can reduce the performance of systems and, in some cases, lead them to instability. Examples of such systems are robotics, networks, metal cutting, transmission lines, chemical and thermal processes among others as can be found in the books from Gu et al. (2003), Richard (2003), Niculescu (2001) and Kolmanovskii & Myshkis (1999).

Studies and techniques for dealing with such systems are not new. Since the beginning of control theory, researchers has been concerned with this issue, either in the input-output approach or in state-space approach. For the input-output approach, techniques such as Padé approximation and the Smith predictor are widely used, mainly for process control. The use of state space approach allows to treat both cases. For both approaches delays can be constant or time-varying. Besides, both the delay and the systems can be precisely known or affected by uncertainties.

In this chapter the class of uncertain discrete-time systems with state delay is studied. For these systems, the techniques for analysis and design could be delay dependent or delay independent, can lead with precisely known or uncertainty systems (in a polytopic or in a norm-bonded representation, for instance), and can consider constant or time-varying delays. For discrete-time systems with constant and known delay in the state it is always possible to study an augmented delay-free system Kapila & Haddad (1998), Leite & Miranda (2008a). However, this solution does not seem to be suitable to several cases such as time-varying delay or uncertain systems.

For these systems, most of the applied techniques for robust stability analysis an robust control design are based on Lyapunov-Krasovskii (L-K) approach, which can be used to obtain convex formulation problems in terms of linear matrix inequalities (LMIs).

In the literature it is possible to find approaches based on LMIs for stability analysis, most of them based on the quadratic stability (QS), i.e., with the matrices of the Lyapunov-Krasovskii function being constant and independent of the uncertain parameters.

In the context of QS, non-convex formulations of delay-independent type have been proposed, for example, in Shi et al. (2003) where the delay is considered time-invariant. In Fridman &

Shaked (2005a) and Fridman & Shaked (2005b), delay dependent conditions, convex to the analysis of stability and non-convex for the synthesis, are formulated using the approach of descriptor systems. These works consider systems with both polytopic uncertainties — see Fridman & Shaked (2005a) — and with norm-bounded uncertainties as done by Fridman & Shaked (2005b).

Some other different aspects of discrete-time systems with delayed state have been studied. Kandanvli & Kar (2009) present a proposal with LMI conditions for robust stability analysis of discrete time delayed systems with saturation. In the work of Xu & Yu (2009), bi-dimensional (2D) discrete-time systems with delayed state are investigated, and delay-independent conditions for norm-bounded uncertainties and constant delay are given by means of nonconvex formulations. In the paper from Ma et al. (2008), convex conditions have been proposed for discrete-time singular systems with time-invariant delay. Discrete-time switched systems with delayed state have been studied by Hetel et al. (2008) and Ibrir (2008). The former establishes the equivalence between the approach used here (Lyapunov-Krasovskii functions) and the one used, in general, for the stability of switched systems with time-varying delay. The latter gives nonconvex conditions for switched systems where each operation mode is subject to a norm-bounded uncertainty and constant delay.

The problem of robust filtering for discrete-time uncertain systems with delayed state is considered in some papers. Delayed state systems with norm-bounded uncertainties are studied by Yu & Gao (2001), Chen et al. (2004) and Xu et al. (2007) and with polytopic uncertainties by Du et al. (2007). The results of Gao et al. (2004) were improved by Liu et al. (2006), but the approach is based on QS and the design conditions are nonconvex depending directly on the Lyapunov-Krasovskii matrices.

The problem of output feedback has attracted attention for discrete-time systems with delay in the state and the works of Gao et al. (2004), He et al. (2008) and Liu et al. (2006) can be cited as examples of on going research. In special, He et al. (2008) present results for precisely known systems with time-varying delay including both static output feedback (SOF) and dynamic output feedback (DOF). However, the conditions are presented as an interactive method that relax some matrix inequalities.

The main objective of this chapter is to study the robust analysis and synthesis of discrete-time systems with state delay. This chapter is organized as follows. In Section 2 some notations and statements are presented, together the problems that are studied and solved in the next sections. In sections 3 and 4 solutions are presented for, respectively, robust stability analysis and robust design, based in a L-K function presented in section 2. In Section 5 some additional results are given by the application of the techniques developed in previous sections are presented, such as: extensions for switched systems, to treat actuator failure and to make design with pole location. In the last section it is presented the final comments.

2. Preliminaries and problem statement

In this chapter the uncertain discrete time system with time-varying delay in the state vector is given by

$$\Omega(\alpha) : \begin{cases} x_{k+1} &= A(\alpha)x_k + A_d(\alpha)x_{k-d_k} + B(\alpha)u_k + B_w(\alpha)w_k, \\ z_k &= C(\alpha)x_k + C_d(\alpha)x_{k-d_k} + D(\alpha)u_k + D_w(\alpha)w_k, \end{cases} \tag{1}$$

where k is the k-th sample-time, matrices $A(\alpha)$, $A_d(\alpha)$, $B(\alpha)$, B_w, $C(\alpha)$, $C_d(\alpha)$, $D(\alpha)$ and $D_w(\alpha)$ are time-invariant, uncertain and with adequate dimensions defined in function of the signals $x_k = x(k) \in \mathbb{R}^n$, the state vector at sample-time k, $u_k = u(k) \in \mathbb{R}^m$, representing the control vector with m control signals, $w_k = w(k) \in \mathbb{R}^\ell$, the exogenous input vector with ℓ input signals, and $z_k = z(k) \in \mathbb{R}^p$, the output vector with p weight output signals. These matrices can be described by a polytope $\mathcal{P}$ with known vertices

$$\mathcal{P} = \left\{ \Omega(\alpha) \in \mathbb{R}^{n+p \times 2n+m+\ell} : \Omega(\alpha) = \sum_{i=1}^{N} \alpha_i \Omega_i,\ \alpha \in \Upsilon \right\}, \tag{2}$$

where

$$\Upsilon = \left\{ \alpha : \sum_{i=1}^{N} \alpha_i = 1,\ \alpha_i \geq 0,\ \ i \in \mathcal{I}[1, N] \right\} \tag{3}$$

and

$$\Omega_i = \left[\begin{array}{cc|c|c} A_i & A_{di} & B_i & B_{wi} \\ \hline C_i & C_{di} & D_i & D_{wi} \end{array} \right],\ \ i \in \mathcal{I}[1, N]. \tag{4}$$

The delay, denoted by d_k, is supposed to be time-varying and given by:

$$d_k \in \mathcal{I}\left[\underline{d}, \bar{d}\right], (\underline{d}, \bar{d}) \in \mathbb{N}_*^2 \tag{5}$$

with $\underline{d}$, $\bar{d}$ representing the minimum and maximum values of d_k, respectively. Thus, any system $\Omega(\alpha) \in \mathcal{P}$ can be written as a convex combination of the N vertices Ω_i, $i \in \mathcal{I}[1, N]$, of $\mathcal{P}$.

The following control law is considered in this chapter:

$$u_k = K x_k + K_d x_{k-d_k} \tag{6}$$

with $[K|K_d] \in \mathbb{R}^{m \times 2n}$. By replacing (6) in (1)-(4), the resulting uncertain closed-loop system is given by

$$\tilde{\Omega}(\alpha) : \begin{cases} x_{k+1} &= \tilde{A}(\alpha) x_k + \tilde{A}_d(\alpha) x_{k-d_k} + B_w(\alpha) w_k \\ z_k &= \tilde{C}(\alpha) x_k + \tilde{C}_d(\alpha) x_{k-d_k} + D_w(\alpha) w_k \end{cases} \tag{7}$$

with $\tilde{\Omega}(\alpha) \in \tilde{\mathcal{P}}$,

$$\tilde{\mathcal{P}} = \left\{ \tilde{\Omega}(\alpha) \in \mathbb{R}^{n+p \times 2n+\ell} : \tilde{\Omega}(\alpha) = \sum_{i=1}^{N} \alpha_i \tilde{\Omega}_i,\ \ \alpha \in \Upsilon \right\} \tag{8}$$

where

$$\tilde{\Omega}_i = \left[\begin{array}{cc|c} \tilde{A}_i & \tilde{A}_{di} & B_{wi} \\ \hline \tilde{C}_i & \tilde{C}_{di} & D_{wi} \end{array} \right],\ \ i \in \mathcal{I}[1, N]. \tag{9}$$

and matrices $\tilde{A}_i$, $\tilde{A}_{di}$, $\tilde{C}_i$ e $\tilde{C}_{di}$ are defined by

$$\tilde{A}_i = A_i + B_i K, \quad \tilde{A}_{di} = A_{di} + B_i K_d, \tag{10}$$

$$\tilde{C}_i = C_i + D_i K, \quad \tilde{C}_{di} = C_{di} + D_i K_d \tag{11}$$

Note that, control law (6) requires that both x_k and x_{k-d_k} are available at each sample-time. Eventually, this can be achieved in physical systems by employing, for instance, a time-stamped in the measurements or in the estimated states Srinivasagupta et al. (2004). In case of d_k is not known, it is sufficient to assume $K_d = \mathbf{0}$.

2.1 Stability conditions

Since the stability of system $\tilde{\Omega}(\alpha)$ given in (7) plays a central rule in this work, it is addressed in the sequence. Note that, without loss of generality, it is possible to consider the stability of the system (7) with $w_k = \mathbf{0}$, $\forall\, k \in \mathbb{N}$.
Consider the sequence composed by $\bar{d}+1$ null vectors

$$\hat{\phi}_{\bar{d}} = \underbrace{\{\mathbf{0},\ldots,\mathbf{0}\}}_{(\bar{d}+1)\ \text{terms}}$$

In this chapter null initial conditions are always assumed, that is,

$$x_k = \phi_{0,k} = \hat{\phi}_{\bar{d}}, \;\; k \in \mathcal{I}[-\bar{d},0] \tag{12}$$

If $\phi_{t,k} = \hat{\phi}_{\bar{d}}$, then an equilibrium solution for system (7) with $w_k = \mathbf{0}$, $\forall\, k \in \mathbb{N}$, is achieved because $x_{k+1} = x_k = \mathbf{0}$, $\forall k > t$ and $\alpha \in \tilde{\Omega}$.

Definition 1 (Uniform asymptotic stability). *For a given $\alpha \in \Upsilon$, the trivial solution of (7) with $w_k = \mathbf{0}$, $\forall\, k \in \mathbb{N}$ is said uniformly asymptotically stable if for any $\kappa \in \mathbb{R}_+$ such that for all initial conditions $x_k \in \phi^{\bar{d}}_{0,k} \in \Phi^{\kappa}_{\bar{d}}$, $k \in \mathcal{I}[-\bar{d},0]$, it is verified*

$$\lim_{t\to\infty} \phi^{\bar{d}}_{t,j,k} = \mathbf{0}, \quad \forall j \in \mathcal{I}[1,\bar{d}+1]$$

This allows the following definition:

Definition 2 (Robust stability). *System (7) subject to (3), (5) and (8) is said robustly stable if its respective trivial solution is uniformly asymptotically stable $\forall\, \alpha \in \Upsilon$.*

The main objective in this work is to formulate convex optimization problems, expressed as LMIs, allowing an efficient numerical solution to a set of stability and performance problems.

2.2 Problems

Two sets of problems are investigated in this chapter. The first set concerns stability issues related to uncertain discrete time with time varying delay in the state vector as presented in the sequence.

Problem 1 (Robust stability analysis). *Determine if system (7) subject to (3), (5) and (8) is robustly stable.*

Problem 2 (Robust control design). *Determine a pair of static feedback gains, K and K_d, such that (1)-(5) controlled by (6) is robustly stable.*

The other set of problems is related to the performance of the class of systems considered in this chapter. In this proposal, the $\mathcal{H}_\infty$ index is used to quantify the performance of the system as stated in the following problems:

Problem 3 ($\mathcal{H}_\infty$ guaranteed cost). *Given the uncertain system $\tilde{\Omega}(\alpha) \in \tilde{\mathcal{P}}$, determine an estimation for $\gamma > 0$ such that for all $w_k \in \ell_2$ there exist $z_k \in \ell_2$ satisfying*

$$\|z_k\|_2 < \gamma \|w_k\|_2 \tag{13}$$

for all $\alpha \in \Upsilon$. In this case, γ is called an $\mathcal{H}_\infty$ guaranteed cost for (7).

Problem 4 (Robust $\mathcal{H}_\infty$ control design). *Given the uncertain system $\Omega(\alpha) \in \tilde{\mathcal{P}}$, (1), and a scalar $\gamma > 0$, determine robust state feedback gains K and K_d, such that the uncertain closed-loop system $\tilde{\Omega}(\alpha) \in \tilde{\mathcal{P}}$, (7), is robustly stable and, additionally, satisfies (13) for all w_k and z_k belonging to ℓ_2.*

It is worth to say that, in cases where time-delay depends on a physical parameter (such as velocity of a transport belt, the position of a steam valve, etc.) it may be possible to determine the delay value at each sample-time. As a special case, consider the regenerative chatter in metal cutting. In this process a cylindrical workpiece has an angular velocity while a machine tool (lathe) translates along the axis of this workpiece. For details, see (Gu et al., 2003, pp. 2). In this case the delay depends on the angular velocity and can be recovered at each sample-time k. However, the study of a physical application is not the objective in this chapter.
The following parameter dependent L-K function is used in this paper to investigate problems 1-4:

$$V(\alpha,k) = \sum_{v=1}^{3} V_v(\alpha,k) > 0 \tag{14}$$

with

$$V_1(\alpha,k) = x_k' P(\alpha) x_k, \tag{15}$$

$$V_2(\alpha,k) = \sum_{j=k-d_k}^{k-1} x_j' Q(\alpha) x_j, \tag{16}$$

$$V_3(\alpha,k) = \sum_{\ell=2-\bar{d}}^{1-\underline{d}} \sum_{j=k+\ell-1}^{k-1} x_j' Q(\alpha) x_j, \tag{17}$$

The dependency of matrices $P(\alpha)$ and $Q(\alpha)$ on the uncertain parameter α is a key issue on reducing the conservatism of the resulting conditions. Here, a linear relation on α is assumed. Thus, consider the following structure for these matrices:

$$P(\alpha) = \sum_{i=1}^{N} \alpha_i P_i; \quad Q(\alpha) = \sum_{i=1}^{N} \alpha_i Q_i \tag{18}$$

with $\alpha \in \Upsilon$. Note that, more general structures such as $P(\alpha)$ and $Q(\alpha)$ depending homogeneously on α — see Oliveira & Peres (2005) — may result in less conservative conditions, but at the expense of a higher numerical complexity of the resulting conditions.
To be a L-K function, the candidate (14) must be positive definite and satisfy

$$\Delta V(\alpha,k) = V(\alpha,k+1) - V(\alpha,k) < 0 \tag{19}$$

for all $\begin{bmatrix} x_k^T & x_{k-d_k}^T \end{bmatrix}^T \neq \mathbf{0}$ and $\alpha \in \Upsilon$.
The following result is used in this work to obtain less conservative results and to decouple the matrices of the system from the L-K matrices $P(\alpha)$ and $Q(\alpha)$.

Lemma 1 (Finsler's Lemma). *Let $\varphi \in \mathbb{R}^n$, $\mathcal{M}(\alpha) = \mathcal{M}(\alpha)^T \in \mathbb{R}^{n\times n}$ and $\mathcal{G}(\alpha) \in \mathbb{R}^{m\times n}$ such that* $\operatorname{rank}(\mathcal{G}(\alpha)) < n$. *Then, the following statements are equivalents:*

i) $\varphi^T \mathcal{M}(\alpha)\varphi < 0, \ \forall \varphi : \mathcal{G}(\alpha)\varphi = 0, \ \varphi \neq 0$

ii) $\mathcal{G}(\alpha)^{\perp T} \mathcal{M}(\alpha) \mathcal{G}(\alpha)^{\perp} < 0,$

iii) $\exists\, \mu(\alpha) \in \mathbb{R}_+ : \mathcal{M}(\alpha) - \mu(\alpha)\mathcal{G}(\alpha)^T\mathcal{G}(\alpha) < \mathbf{0}$

iv) $\exists\, \mathcal{X}(\alpha) \in \mathbb{R}^{n\times m} : \mathcal{M}(\alpha) + \mathcal{X}(\alpha)\mathcal{G}(\alpha) + \mathcal{G}(\alpha)^T\mathcal{X}(\alpha)^T < \mathbf{0}$

In the case of parameter independent matrices, the proof of this theorem can be found in de Oliveira & Skelton (2001). The proof for the case depending on α follows similar steps.

3. Robust stability analysis and $\mathcal{H}_\infty$ guaranteed cost

In this section it is presented the conditions for stability analysis and calculation of $\mathcal{H}_\infty$ guaranteed cost for system (7). The objective here is to present sufficient convex conditions for solving problems 1 and 3.

3.1 Robust stability analysis

Theorem 1. *If there exist symmetric matrices* $\mathbf{0} < P_i \in \mathbb{R}^{n\times n}$, $\mathbf{0} < Q_i \in \mathbb{R}^{n\times n}$, *a matrix* $\mathcal{X} \in \mathbb{R}^{3n\times n}$, $d_k \in \mathcal{I}[\underline{d}, \bar{d}]$ *with* $\bar{d}$ *and* $\underline{d}$ *belonging to* $\mathbb{N}_*$, *such that*

$$\Psi_i = \mathcal{Q}_i + \mathcal{X}\mathcal{B}_i + \mathcal{B}_i^T\mathcal{X}^T < \mathbf{0}; \quad i = 1,\ldots,N \tag{20}$$

with

$$\mathcal{Q}_i = \begin{bmatrix} P_i & \mathbf{0} & \mathbf{0} \\ \star & \beta Q_i - P_i & \mathbf{0} \\ \star & \star & -Q_i \end{bmatrix} \tag{21}$$

$$\beta = \bar{d} - \underline{d} + 1 \tag{22}$$

and

$$\mathcal{B}_i = \begin{bmatrix} \mathbf{I} & -A_i & -A_{di} \end{bmatrix} \tag{23}$$

is verified $\forall\ \alpha$ *admissible, then system (7) subject to (5) is robustly stable. Besides, (14)-(17) is a Lyapunov-Krasovskii function assuring the robust stability of the considered system.*

Proof. The positivity of the function (14) is assured with the hypothesis of $P_i = P_i^T > \mathbf{0}$, $Q_i = Q_i^T > \mathbf{0}$. For the equation (14) be a Lyapunov-Krasovskii function, besides its positivity, it is necessary to verify (19) $\forall\ \alpha \in \Omega$. From hereafter, the α dependency is omitted in the expressions $V_v(k), v = 1,\ldots,3$, To calculate (19), consider

$$\Delta V_1(k) = x_{k+1}^T P(\alpha) x_{k+1} - x_k^T P(\alpha) x_k \tag{24}$$

$$\Delta V_2(k) = x_k^T Q(\alpha) x_k - x_{k-d(k)}^T Q(\alpha) x_{k-d(k)} + \sum_{i=k+1-d(k+1)}^{k-1} x_i^T Q(\alpha) x_i - \sum_{i=k+1-d(k)}^{k-1} x_i^T Q(\alpha) x_i \tag{25}$$

and

$$\Delta V_3(k) = (\bar{d} - \underline{d}) x_k^T Q(\alpha) x_k - \sum_{i=k+1-\bar{d}}^{k-\underline{d}} x_i^T Q(\alpha) x_i \tag{26}$$

Observe that the third term in equation (25) can be rewritten as

$$\begin{aligned} \Xi_k \equiv \sum_{i=k+1-d(k+1)}^{k-1} x_i^T Q(\alpha) x_i &= \sum_{i=k+1-\underline{d}}^{k-1} x_i^T Q(\alpha) x_i + \sum_{i=k+1-d(k+1)}^{k-\underline{d}} x_i^T Q(\alpha) x_i \\ &\leq \sum_{i=k+1-d(k)}^{k-1} x_i^T Q(\alpha) x_i + \sum_{i=k+1-\bar{d}}^{k-\underline{d}} x_i^T Q(\alpha) x_i \end{aligned} \tag{27}$$

Using (27) in (25), one gets

$$\Delta V_2(k) \leq x_k^T Q(\alpha) x_k - x_{k-d(k)}^T Q(\alpha) x_{k-d(k)} + \sum_{i=k+1-\bar{d}}^{k-\underline{d}} x_i^T Q(\alpha) x_i \tag{28}$$

So, considering (24), (26) and (28) the following upper bound for (19) can be obtained

$$\Delta V(k) \leq x_{k+1}^T P(\alpha) x_{k+1} + x_k^T [\beta Q(\alpha) - P(\alpha)] x_k - x_{k-d(k)}^T Q(\alpha) x_{k-d(k)} < 0 \tag{29}$$

Taking into account (7) and using Lemma 1 with

$$\varphi = \xi_k = \begin{bmatrix} x_{k+1}^T \; x_k^T \; x_{k-d_k}^T \end{bmatrix}^T \tag{30}$$

$$\mathcal{M}(\alpha) = \begin{bmatrix} P(\alpha) & 0 & 0 \\ \star & \beta Q(\alpha) - P(\alpha) & 0 \\ \star & \star & -Q(\alpha) \end{bmatrix} \tag{31}$$

$$\mathcal{G}(\alpha) = \begin{bmatrix} \mathbf{I} & -A(\alpha) & -A_d(\alpha) \end{bmatrix} \tag{32}$$

then (29) is equivalent to

$$\Psi(\alpha) = \mathcal{M}(\alpha) + \mathcal{X}(\alpha)\mathcal{G}(\alpha) + \mathcal{G}(\alpha)^T \mathcal{X}(\alpha)^T < \mathbf{0}. \tag{33}$$

which is assured whenever (20) is verified by taking $\mathcal{X}(\alpha) = \mathcal{X}$,

$$\mathcal{M}(\alpha) = \sum_{i=1}^{N} \alpha_i \mathcal{Q}_i; \quad \mathcal{G}(\alpha) = \sum_{i=1}^{N} \alpha_i \mathcal{B}_i, \tag{34}$$

$\alpha \in \Upsilon$, $\mathcal{Q}_i$ and $\mathcal{B}_i$ given in (21) and (23), respectively, completing the proof. □

An important issue in Theorem 1 is that there is no product between the matrices of the system and the matrices of the Lyapunov-Krasovskii proposed function, (14). This can be exploited to reduce conservatism in both analysis and synthesis methods.

Example 1 (Stability Analysis). *In this example the stability analysis condition given in Theorem 1 is used to investigate system (7), with* $D_w = \mathbf{0}$, *where*

$$\tilde{A}_1 = \begin{bmatrix} 0.6 & 0 \\ 0.35 & 0.7 \end{bmatrix} \quad \text{and} \quad \tilde{A}_{d1} = \begin{bmatrix} 0.1 & 0 \\ 0.2 & 0.1 \end{bmatrix}. \tag{35}$$

This system has been investigated by Liu et al. (2006), Boukas (2006) and Leite & Miranda (2008a). The objective here is to establish the larger delay interval such that this system remains stable. The results are summarized in Table 1.

Although Theorem 1 and the condition from Liu et al. (2006) achieve the same upper bound for d_k, *the L-K function employed by Liu et al. (2006) has* 5 *parts while Theorem 1 uses a function with only* 3 *parts, as given by (14)-(17).*

Consider that (35) is affected by an uncertain parameter being described by a polytope (8) with $\tilde{A}_1$ *and* $\tilde{A}_{d1}$ *given by (35) and* $\tilde{A}_2 = 1.1\tilde{A}_1$ *and* $\tilde{A}_{d2} = 1.1\tilde{A}_{d1}$. *In this case the conditions of Boukas (2006) are no longer applicable and those from Liu et al. (2006) are not directly applied, because of type of the system uncertainty. Using Theorem 1 it is possible to assure the robust stability of this system for* $|d_{k+1} - d_k| \leq 3$.

Condition	$\underline{d}$	$\bar{d}$
Boukas (2006)[Theorem 3.1]	2	10
Liu et al. (2006)	2	13
Theorem 1	2	13

Table 1. Maximum delay intervals such that (7) with (35) is stable.

3.2 Estimation of $\mathcal{H}_\infty$ guaranteed cost

Theorem 2 presented in the sequel states a convex condition for checking if a given γ is an $\mathcal{H}_\infty$ guaranteed cost for system (7).

Theorem 2. *If there exist symmetric matrices $\mathbf{0} < P_i \in \mathbb{R}^{n\times n}$, $\mathbf{0} < Q_i \in \mathbb{R}^{n\times n}$, a matrix $\mathcal{X}_\mathcal{H} \in \mathbb{R}^{3n+p+\ell\times n+p}$, $d_k \in \mathcal{I}[\underline{d}, \bar{d}]$ with $\bar{d}$ and $\underline{d}$ belonging to $\mathbb{N}_*$, and a scalar $\mu = \gamma^2 \in \mathbb{R}_+$, such that*

$$\Psi_{\mathcal{H}i} = \mathcal{Q}_{\mathcal{H}i} + \mathcal{X}_\mathcal{H}\mathcal{B}_{\mathcal{H}i} + \mathcal{B}_{\mathcal{H}i}^T\mathcal{X}_\mathcal{H}^T < \mathbf{0}, \quad i = 1, \ldots, N, \tag{36}$$

with

$$\mathcal{Q}_{\mathcal{H}i} = \begin{bmatrix} \mathcal{Q}_i & \mathbf{0} \\ \star & \begin{bmatrix} \mathbf{I}_\ell & \mathbf{0} \\ \star & -\mu\mathbf{I}_p \end{bmatrix} \end{bmatrix} \tag{37}$$

where $\mathcal{Q}_i$ is given by (21) and

$$\mathcal{B}_{\mathcal{H}i} = \begin{bmatrix} \mathcal{B}_i & \mathbf{0} & B_{wi} \\ \begin{bmatrix} \mathbf{0} & \tilde{C}_i & \tilde{C}_{di} \end{bmatrix} & -\mathbf{I} & D_{wi} \end{bmatrix} \tag{38}$$

with $\mathcal{B}_i$ given by (23), then system (7) subject to (5) with null initial conditions, see (12), is robustly stable with an $\mathcal{H}_\infty$ guaranteed cost given by $\gamma = \sqrt{\mu}$. Besides, (14)-(17) is a L-K function assuring the robust stability of the considered system.

Proof. Following the proof given for Theorem 1, it is possible to conclude that the positivity of (14) is assured with the hypothesis of $P(\alpha) = P(\alpha)^T > \mathbf{0}$, $Q(\alpha) = Q(\alpha)^T > \mathbf{0}$ and, by (29) that

$$\Delta V(k) \leq x_{k+1}' P(\alpha) x_{k+1} + x_k'[\beta Q(\alpha) - P(\alpha)]x_k - x_{k-d(k)}' Q(\alpha) x_{k-d(k)} < 0 \tag{39}$$

Consider system (7) as robustly stable with null initial conditions given by (12), assume $\mu = \gamma^2$ and signals w_k and z_k belonging to ℓ_2. In this case, it is possible to verify that $V(\alpha, 0) = 0$ and $V(\alpha, \infty)$ approaches zero, whenever w_k goes to zero as k increases, or to a constant $\tilde{\phi} < \infty$, whenever w_k approaches $\phi < \infty$ as k increases. Also, consider the $\mathcal{H}_\infty$ performance index given by

$$J(\alpha, k) = \sum_{k=0}^{\infty} \left[z_k^T z_k - \mu w_k^T w_k \right] \tag{40}$$

Then, using (39), $J(\alpha, k)$ can be over bounded as

$$\begin{aligned} J(\alpha, k) &\leq \sum_{k=0}^{\infty} \left[z_k^T z_k - \mu w_k^T w_k + \Delta V(\alpha, k) \right] \\ &\leq \sum_{k=0}^{\infty} \left[z_k^T z_k - \mu w_k^T w_k + x_{k+1}' P(\alpha) x_{k+1} + x_k'[\beta Q(\alpha) - P(\alpha)]x_k - x_{k-d(k)}' Q(\alpha) x_{k-d(k)} \right] \end{aligned}$$

which can be rewritten as

$$J(\alpha,k) \leq \sum_{k=0}^{\infty} \zeta_k^T \mathcal{Q}_{\mathcal{H}}(\alpha)\zeta_k \tag{41}$$

with $\zeta_k = \begin{bmatrix} \xi_k^T & z_k^T & w_k^T \end{bmatrix}^T$, ξ_k defined in (30), and $\mathcal{Q}_{\mathcal{H}}(\alpha) = \sum_{i=1}^{N} \alpha_i \mathcal{Q}_{\mathcal{H}i}$, $\alpha \in \Upsilon$. Then, applying Lemma 1 to

$$\zeta_k^T \mathcal{Q}_{\mathcal{H}}(\alpha)\zeta_k < 0 \text{ subject to (7)}, \tag{42}$$

with $\mathcal{M}(\alpha) = \mathcal{Q}_{\mathcal{H}}(\alpha)$, $\varphi = \zeta_k$,

$$\mathcal{G}(\alpha) = \mathcal{B}_{\mathcal{H}}(\alpha) = \begin{bmatrix} \mathcal{B}(\alpha) & \mathbf{0} & B_w(\alpha) \\ \begin{bmatrix} \mathbf{0} & \tilde{C}(\alpha) & \tilde{C}_d(\alpha) \end{bmatrix} & -\mathbf{I} & D_w(\alpha) \end{bmatrix}, \tag{43}$$

and $\alpha \in \Upsilon$, (42) is equivalent to

$$\Psi_{\mathcal{H}}(\alpha) = \mathcal{Q}_{\mathcal{H}}(\alpha) + \mathcal{X}_{\mathcal{H}}(\alpha)\mathcal{B}_{\mathcal{H}}(\alpha) + \mathcal{B}_{\mathcal{H}}(\alpha)^T \mathcal{X}_{\mathcal{H}}(\alpha)^T < 0. \tag{44}$$

Once (36) is verified, (44) is assured with the special choice $\mathcal{X}_{\mathcal{H}}(\alpha) = \mathcal{X}_{\mathcal{H}} \in \mathbb{R}^{3n+p+\ell \times n+p}$ — i.e., eliminating the dependency on the uncertain parameter α — and noting that $\mathcal{G}(\alpha) = \sum_{i=1}^{N} \alpha_i \mathcal{B}_{\mathcal{H}i}$, convexity is achieved, and (36) can be used to recover (44) by $\Psi_{\mathcal{H}}(\alpha) = \sum_{i=1}^{N} \alpha_i \Psi_{\mathcal{H}i}$, $\alpha \in \Upsilon$. Thus, this assures the negativity of $J(\alpha,k)$ for all $w_k \in \ell_2$ implying that (7) is robustly stable with $\mathcal{H}_\infty$ guaranteed cost given by $\gamma = \sqrt{\mu}$. □

In case of time-varying uncertainties, i.e. $\alpha = \alpha_k = \alpha(k)$, the conditions formulated in both Theorem 1 and Theorem 2 can be adapted to match the quadratic stability approach. In this case, it is enough to use $P_i = P$, $Q_i = Q$, $i \in \mathcal{I}[1,N]$. This yields conditions similar to (20) and (36), respectively, with constant L-K matrices. See Subsection (5.1) for a more detailed discussion on this issue.

Note that, it is possible to use the conditions established by Theorem 2 to formulate the following optimization problem that allows to minimize the value of $\mu = \gamma^2$:

$$\mathcal{E}_{\mathcal{H}_\infty} : \begin{cases} \min\limits_{P_i > 0;\, Q_i > 0;\, \mathcal{X}} & \mu \\ \text{such that} & \text{(36) is feasible} \end{cases} \tag{45}$$

4. Robust $\mathcal{H}_\infty$ feedback design

The stability analysis conditions can be used to obtain convex synthesis counterpart formulations for designing robust state feedback gains K and K_d, such that control law (6) applied in (1) yields a robustly stable closed-loop system, and, therefore, provides a solution to problems 2 and 4. In this section, such conditions for synthesis are presented for both robust stabilization and robust $\mathcal{H}_\infty$ control design.

4.1 Robust stabilization

The following Theorem provides some LMI conditions depending on the difference $\bar{d} - \underline{d}$ to design robust state feedback gains K and K_d that assure the robust stability of the closed-loop system.

Theorem 3. *If there exist symmetric matrices* $\mathbf{0} < \tilde{P}_i \in \mathbb{R}^{n\times n}$, $\mathbf{0} < \tilde{Q}_i \in \mathbb{R}^{n\times n}$, $i = 1,\dots,N$, *matrices* $\mathcal{F} \in \mathbb{R}^{n\times n}$, $W \in \mathbb{R}^{m\times n}$ *and* $W_d \in \mathbb{R}^{m\times n}$, $d_k \in \mathcal{I}[\underline{d},\bar{d}]$ *with* $\bar{d}$ *and* $\underline{d}$ *belonging to* $\mathbb{N}_*$, *such that*

$$\tilde{\Psi}_i = \begin{bmatrix} \tilde{P}_i + \mathcal{F} + \mathcal{F}^T & -(A_i\mathcal{F} + B_iW) & -(A_{di}\mathcal{F} + B_iW_d) \\ \star & \beta\tilde{Q}_i - \tilde{P}_i & \mathbf{0} \\ \star & \star & -\tilde{Q}_i \end{bmatrix} < \mathbf{0}, \quad i = 1,\dots,N \tag{46}$$

are verified with β *given by (22), then system (1)-(3) is robustly stabilizable with (6), where the robust static feedback gains are given by*

$$K = W\mathcal{F}^{-1} \quad and \quad K_d = W_d\mathcal{F}^{-1} \tag{47}$$

yielding a convex solution to Problem 2.

Proof. Observe that, if (46) is feasible, then $\mathcal{F}$ is regular, once block $(1,1)$ of (46) assures $\tilde{P}_i + \mathcal{F} + \mathcal{F}^T < \mathbf{0}$, allowing to define

$$\mathcal{T} = \mathbf{I}_3 \otimes \mathcal{F}^{-T} \tag{48}$$

Then, by replacing W and W_d by $K\mathcal{F}$ and $K_d\mathcal{F}$, respectively obtained from (47), it is possible to recover $\Psi_i = \mathcal{T}\tilde{\Psi}_i\mathcal{T}^T < \mathbf{0}$ with $\mathcal{X} = \begin{bmatrix} \mathcal{F}^{-T} & \mathbf{0} & \mathbf{0} \end{bmatrix}^T$, $P_i = \mathcal{F}^{-T}\tilde{P}_i\mathcal{F}^{-1}$, $Q_i = \mathcal{F}^{-T}\tilde{Q}_i\mathcal{F}^{-1}$ and the closed-loop system matrices $\tilde{A}_i = (A + B_iK)$ and $\tilde{A}_{di} = (A_{di} + B_iK_d)$ replacing A_i and A_{di} in (20), which completes the proof. □

Note that, conditions in Theorem 3 encompass quadratic stability approach, since it is always possible to choose $P_i = P$ and $Q_i = Q$, $i = 1,\dots,N$. Also observe that, if d_k is not available at each sample-time, and therefore x_{k-d_k} cannot be used in the feedback, then it is enough to choose $W_d = \mathbf{0}$ leading to a control law given by $u_k = Kx_k$. Finally, note the convexity of the conditions stated in Theorem 3. This is a relevant issue, once most of the results available in the literature depend on a nonlinear algorithm to solve the stabilization problem.

Example 2 (Robust Stabilization). *Consider the discrete-time system studied in Leite & Miranda (2008a) with delayed state described by (1) with* $D_w = \mathbf{0}$ *and*

$$A = \begin{bmatrix} 0 & 1 \\ -2 & -3 \end{bmatrix}; \quad A_d = \begin{bmatrix} 0.01 & 0.1 \\ 0 & 0.1 \end{bmatrix}; \quad B = \begin{bmatrix} 0 \\ 1 \end{bmatrix} \tag{49}$$

Suppose that this system is affected by uncertain parameters $|\rho| \le 0.07$, $|\theta| \le 0.1$ *and* $|\eta| \le 0.1$, *such that*

$$A(\rho) = (1+\rho)A; \quad A_d(\theta) = (1+\theta)A_d; \quad B(\eta) = (1+\eta)B \tag{50}$$

These parameters yield a polytope with 8 vertices determined by the combination of the extreme values of ρ, θ *and* η. *Also, suppose that delay is not available on line and it is bounded as* $1 \le d_k \le 10$. *By applying the conditions presented in Theorem 3 with* $W_d = \mathbf{0}$ *— this is a necessary issue once the delay value is not known at each sample-time — it is possible to get the robust stabilizing gain*

$$K = \begin{bmatrix} 1.9670 & 2.7170 \end{bmatrix}. \tag{51}$$

The behavior of the states of the closed-loop response of this uncertain discrete-time system with time-varying delay is shown in Figure 4. It has been simulated the time response of this system at

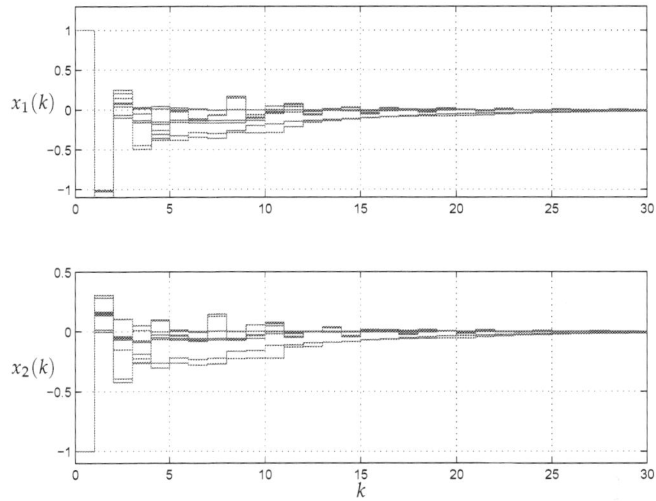

Fig. 1. The behavior of the states $x_1(k)$ (top) and $x_2(k)$ (bottom), with $d_k \in \mathcal{I}[1, 10]$ randomly genereated and the robust state feedback gain (51).

each vertex of the polytope that defines the uncertain closed-loop system. The initial conditions have been chosen as

$$\phi_{0,k} = \underbrace{\left\{ \begin{bmatrix} 1 \\ -1 \end{bmatrix}, \ldots, \begin{bmatrix} 1 \\ -1 \end{bmatrix} \right\}}_{11 \text{ terms}},$$

and the value of the delay, d_k, has been varied randomly. Please see Leite & Miranda (2008a) for details. In Figure 4, it is illustrated the stability of the uncertain close-loop system, assured by the robust state feedback gain (51).

4.2 Robust $\mathcal{H}_\infty$ feedback design

An stabilization condition assuring the $\mathcal{H}_\infty$ cost of the feedback system is stated in the sequel.

Theorem 4. *If there exist symmetric matrices $\mathbf{0} < \tilde{P}_i \in \mathbb{R}^{n\times n}$, $\mathbf{0} < \tilde{Q}_i \in \mathbb{R}^{n\times n}$, matrices $\mathcal{F} \in \mathbb{R}^{n\times n}$, $W \in \mathbb{R}^{m\times n}$, $W_d \in \mathbb{R}^{m\times n}$, a scalar variable $\theta \in]0,1]$ and for a given $\mu = \gamma^2 \in \mathbb{R}_+$ such that*

$$\begin{bmatrix} \tilde{P}_i - \mathcal{F} - \mathcal{F}^T & A_i\mathcal{F} + B_iW & A_{di}\mathcal{F} + B_iW_d & \mathbf{0} & B_{wi} \\ \star & \beta\tilde{Q}_i - \tilde{P}_i & \mathbf{0} & \mathcal{F}^TC_i^T + W^TD_i^T & \mathbf{0} \\ \star & \star & -\tilde{Q}_i & \mathcal{F}^TC_{di}^T + W_d^TD_i^T & \mathbf{0} \\ \star & \star & \star & -\theta I & D_{wi} \\ \star & \star & \star & \star & -\mu I \end{bmatrix} < \mathbf{0}, \quad i = 1, \ldots, N \quad (52)$$

are feasible with β given by (22), then system (1)-(3) is robustly stabilizable with (6) assuring a guaranteed $\mathcal{H}_\infty$ cost given by γ to the closed-loop system by robust state feedback gains K and K_d given by (47).

Proof. To demonstrate the sufficiency of (52), firstly note that, if it is verified, then the regularity of $\mathcal{F}$ is assured due to its block $(1,1)$ that verifies $\tilde{P}_i - \mathcal{F} - \mathcal{F}^T < \mathbf{0}$. Besides, there exist a real scalar $\kappa \in]0,2[$ such that for $\theta \in]0,1]$, $\kappa(\kappa-2) = -\theta$. Thus, replacing block $(4,4)$ of (52) by $\kappa(\kappa-2)\mathbf{I}_p$, the optimization variables W and W_d by $K\mathcal{F}$ and $K_d\mathcal{F}$, respectively, using the definitions given by (10)–(11) and pre- and post-multiplying the resulting LMI by $\mathcal{T}_{\mathcal{H}}$ (on the left) and by $\mathcal{T}_{\mathcal{H}}^T$ (on the right), with

$$\mathcal{T}_{\mathcal{H}} = \begin{bmatrix} \mathcal{T} & \mathbf{0} \\ \star & \begin{bmatrix} G & \mathbf{0} \\ \star & \mathbf{I}_\ell \end{bmatrix} \end{bmatrix}^{-1} \tag{53}$$

with $\mathcal{T}$ given by (48) and $G \in \mathbb{R}^{p\times p}$, it is possible to obtain $\tilde{\Psi}_{\mathcal{H}i} < \mathbf{0}$, with $\tilde{\Psi}_{\mathcal{H}i}$ given by

$$\tilde{\Psi}_{\mathcal{H}i} = \begin{bmatrix} \mathcal{F}^{-T}\tilde{P}_i\mathcal{F}^{-1} - \mathcal{F}^{-T} - \mathcal{F}^{-1} & \mathcal{F}^{-T}\underbrace{(A_i + B_iK)}_{\tilde{A}_i} & \mathcal{F}^{-T}\underbrace{(Ad_i + B_iK_d)}_{\tilde{A}_{di}} & \mathbf{0} & FBw \\ \star & \beta\mathcal{F}^{-T}\tilde{Q}_i\mathcal{F}^{-1} - \mathcal{F}^{-T}\tilde{P}_i\mathcal{F}^{-1} & \mathbf{0} & \underbrace{\left(C_i^T + K^TD_i^T\right)}_{\tilde{C}_i}G^T & \mathbf{0} \\ \star & \star & -\mathcal{F}^{-T}\tilde{Q}_i\mathcal{F}^{-1} & \underbrace{\left(Cd_i^T + K_d^TD_i^T\right)}_{\tilde{C}_{di}}G^T & \mathbf{0} \\ \star & \star & \star & G\left(\kappa^2 - 2\kappa\right)G^T & GDw \\ \star & \star & \star & \star & -\mu I_\ell \end{bmatrix} \tag{54}$$

Observe that, assuming $G = -\frac{1}{\kappa}\mathbf{I}_p$, block $(4,4)$ of (54) can be rewritten as

$$\begin{aligned} G\left(\kappa^2 - 2\kappa\right)G^T &= \left(-\frac{1}{\kappa}\mathbf{I}_p\right)\left(\kappa^2 - 2\kappa\right)\left(-\frac{1}{\kappa}\mathbf{I}_p\right) \\ &= \left(1 - \frac{2}{\kappa}\right)\mathbf{I}_p \\ &= \mathbf{I}_p - \frac{1}{\kappa}\mathbf{I}_p - \frac{1}{\kappa}\mathbf{I}_p \\ &= \mathbf{I}_p + G + G^T \end{aligned} \tag{55}$$

assuring the feasibility of $\Psi_{\mathcal{H}i} < \mathbf{0}$ given in (36) with $P_i = \mathcal{F}^{-T}\tilde{P}_i\mathcal{F}^{-1}$, $Q_i = \mathcal{F}^{-T}\tilde{Q}_i\mathcal{F}^{-1}$, $i \in \mathcal{I}[1,N]$, and

$$\mathcal{X}_H = \begin{bmatrix} \mathcal{F}^{-1} & \mathbf{0} \\ \mathbf{0} & \mathbf{0} \\ \mathbf{0} & \mathbf{0} \\ \mathbf{0} & G \\ \mathbf{0} & \mathbf{0} \end{bmatrix}$$

completing the proof. □

Theorem 4 provides a solution to Problem 4. This kind of solution can be efficiently achieved by means of, for example, interior point algorithms. Note that *all* matrices of the system can be affected by polytopic uncertainties which states a difference w.r.t. most of the proposals found in the literature. Another remark concerns the technique used to obtain the synthesis condition: differently from the usual approach for delay free systems, here it is not enough to replace matrices in the analysis conditions with their respective closed-loop versions and to make a linearizing change of variables. This makes clear that the $\mathcal{H}_\infty$ control of systems with delayed state is more complex than with delay free systems. Also, note that the design of state feedback gains K and K_d can be done minimizing the guaranteed $\mathcal{H}_\infty$ cost, $\gamma = \sqrt{\mu}$, of the uncertain closed-loop system. In this case, it is enough to solve the following convex optimization problem:

$$\mathcal{S}_{\mathcal{H}_\infty} : \begin{cases} \quad \min & \mu \\ \tilde{P}_i > \mathbf{0}; \tilde{Q}_i > \mathbf{0}; 0 < \theta \leq 1; & \\ \quad W;\ W_d;\ F & \\ \quad \text{such that} & \text{(52) is feasible} \end{cases} \tag{56}$$

Example 3 ($\mathcal{H}_\infty$ Design). *A physically motivated problem is considered in this example. It consists of a fifth order state space model of an industrial electric heater investigated in Chu (1995). This furnace is divided into five zones, each of them with a thermocouple and a electric heater as indicated in Figure 2. The state variables are the temperatures in each zone ($x_1, \ldots, x_5$), measured by thermocouples, and the control inputs are the electrical power signals ($u_1, \ldots, u_5$) applied to each electric heater. The*

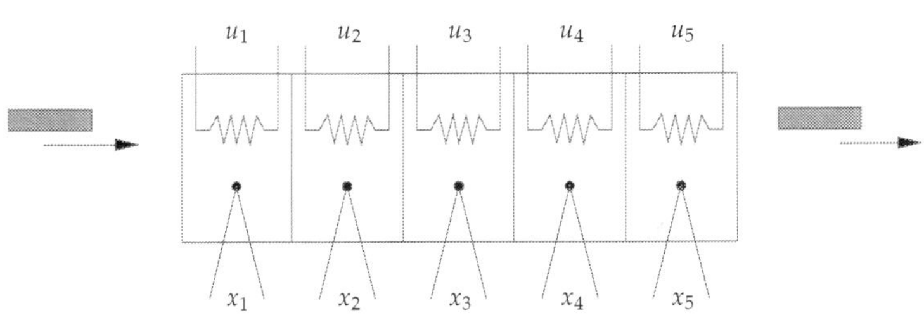

Fig. 2. Schematic diagram of the industrial electric heater.

temperature of each zone of the process must be regulated around its respective nominal operational conditions (see Chu (1995) for details). The dynamics of this system is slow and can be subject to several load disturbances. Also, a time-varying delay can be expected, since the velocity of the displacement of the mass across the furnace may vary. A discrete-time with delayed state model for this system has been obtained as given by (1) with $d_k = d = 15$, where

$$A = A_0 = \begin{bmatrix} 0.97421 & 0.15116 & 0.19667 & -0.05870 & 0.07144 \\ -0.01455 & 0.88914 & 0.26953 & 0.11866 & -0.22047 \\ 0.06376 & 0.12056 & 1.00049 & -0.03491 & -0.02766 \\ -0.05084 & 0.09254 & 0.28774 & 0.82569 & 0.02570 \\ 0.01723 & 0.01939 & 0.29285 & 0.03544 & 0.87111 \end{bmatrix} \tag{57}$$

$$A_d = A_{d0} = \begin{bmatrix} -0.01000 & -0.08837 & -0.06989 & 0.18874 & 0.20505 \\ 0.02363 & 0.03384 & 0.05282 & -0.09906 & -0.00191 \\ -0.04468 & -0.00798 & 0.05618 & 0.00157 & 0.03593 \\ -0.04082 & 0.01153 & -0.07116 & 0.16472 & 0.00083 \\ -0.02537 & 0.03878 & -0.04683 & 0.05665 & -0.03130 \end{bmatrix}, \quad (58)$$

$$B = B_0 = \begin{bmatrix} 0.53706 & -0.11185 & 0.09978 & 0.04652 & 0.25867 \\ -0.51718 & 0.73519 & 0.57518 & 0.40668 & -0.12472 \\ 0.29469 & 0.31528 & 1.16420 & -0.29922 & 0.23883 \\ -0.20191 & 0.19739 & 0.41686 & 0.66551 & 0.11366 \\ -0.11835 & 0.16287 & 0.20378 & 0.23261 & 0.36525 \end{bmatrix}, \quad (59)$$

and $C = D = \mathbf{I}_5$, $C_d = \mathbf{0}$, $D_w = \mathbf{0}$, $B_w = 0.1\mathbf{I}$ *with* A_0, A_{d0}, *and* B_0 *being the nominal matrices of this system. Note that, this nominal system has unstable modes. The design of a stabilizing state feedback gain for this system has been considered in Chu (1995) by using optimal control theory, designed by an augmented delay-free system with order equal to* 85 *and a time-invariant delay* $d = 15$*, by means of a Riccati equation.*

Here, robust $\mathcal{H}_\infty$ *state feedback gains are calculated to stabilize this system subject to uncertain parameters given by* $|\rho| \leq 0.4$, $|\eta| \leq 0.4$ *and* $|\sigma| \leq 0.08$ *that affect the matrices of the system as follows:*

$$A(\rho) = A(1+\rho), \quad A_d(\theta) = A_d(1+\theta), \quad B(\sigma) = B(1+\sigma) \quad (60)$$

This set of uncertainties defines a polytope with 8 vertices, obtained by combination of the upper and lower bounds of uncertain parameters. Also, it is supposed in this example that the system has a time-varying delay given by $10 \leq d_k \leq 20$.

In these conditions, an $\mathcal{H}_\infty$ *guaranteed cost* $\gamma = 6.37$ *can be obtained by applying Theorem 4 that yields the robust state feedback gains presented in the sequel.*

$$K = \begin{bmatrix} -2.2587 & -1.0130 & -0.0558 & 0.4113 & 0.9312 \\ -2.0369 & -2.1037 & 0.0822 & 1.5032 & 0.0380 \\ 0.9410 & 0.5645 & -0.7523 & -0.8688 & 0.3801 \\ -0.5796 & -0.2559 & 0.0454 & -1.0495 & 0.4072 \\ -0.0801 & 0.4106 & -0.4369 & 0.5415 & -2.4452 \end{bmatrix} \quad (61)$$

$$K_d = \begin{bmatrix} -0.0625 & 0.2592 & 0.0545 & -0.2603 & -0.5890 \\ -0.1865 & 0.1056 & -0.0508 & 0.1911 & -0.4114 \\ 0.1108 & -0.0460 & -0.0483 & -0.0612 & 0.1551 \\ 0.0309 & 0.0709 & 0.1404 & -0.3511 & -0.1736 \\ 0.0516 & -0.1016 & 0.1324 & -0.0870 & 0.1158 \end{bmatrix} \quad (62)$$

5. Extensions

In this section some extensions to the conditions presented in sections 3 and 4 are presented.

5.1 Quadratic stability approach

The quadratic stability approach is the source of many results of control theory presented in the literature. In such approach, the Lyapunov matrices are taken constant and independent of the uncertain parameter. As a consequence, their achieved results may be very conservative, specially when applied to uncertain time-invariant systems. See, for instance, the works of Leite & Peres (2003), de Oliveira et al. (2002) and Leite et al. (2004). Perhaps the main advantages of the quadratic stability approach are the simple formulation — with low numerical complexity — and the possibility to deal with time-varying systems. In this case, all equations given in Section 2 can be reformulated by using time-dependency on the uncertain parameter, i.e., by using $\alpha = \alpha_k$. In special, the uncertain open-loop system (1) can be described by

$$\Omega_v(\alpha_k) : \begin{cases} x_{k+1} &= A(\alpha_k)x_k + A_d(\alpha_k)x_{k-d_k} + B(\alpha_k)u_k + B_w(\alpha_k)w_k, \\ z_k &= C(\alpha_k)x_k + C_d(\alpha_k)x_{k-d_k} + D(\alpha_k)u_k + D_w(\alpha_k)w_k, \end{cases} \tag{63}$$

with $\alpha_k \in \Upsilon_v$

$$\Upsilon_v = \left\{ \alpha_k : \sum_{i=1}^{N} \alpha_{ki} = 1,\ \alpha_{ki} \geq 0,\ \ i \in \mathcal{I}[1, N] \right\} \tag{64}$$

which allows to define the polytope $\mathcal{P}$ given in (2) with α_k replacing α. Still considering control law (6), the resulting closed-loop system is given by

$$\tilde{\Omega}_v(\alpha_k) : \begin{cases} x_{k+1} &= \tilde{A}(\alpha_k)x_k + \tilde{A}_d(\alpha_k)x_{k-d_k} + B_w(\alpha_k)w_k, \\ z_k &= \tilde{C}(\alpha_k)x_k + \tilde{C}_d(\alpha_k)x_{k-d_k} + D_w(\alpha_k)w_k, \end{cases} \tag{65}$$

with $\tilde{\Omega}(\alpha_k) \in \tilde{\mathcal{P}}$ given in (8) with α_k replacing α.
The convex conditions presented can be simplified to match with quadratic stability formulation. This can be done in the analysis cases by imposing $P_i = P > \mathbf{0}$ and $Q_i = Q > \mathbf{0}$ in (20) and (36) and, in the synthesis cases, by imposing $\tilde{P}_i = \tilde{P} > \mathbf{0}$, $\tilde{Q}_i = \tilde{Q} > \mathbf{0}$, $i = 1, \ldots, N$. This procedure allows to establish the following Corollary.

Corollary 1 (Quadratic stability). *The following statements are equivalent and sufficient for the quadratic stability of system $\tilde{\Omega}_v(\alpha_k)$ given in (65):*

i) There exist symmetric matrices $\mathbf{0} < P \in \mathbb{R}^{n\times n}$, $\mathbf{0} < Q \in \mathbb{R}^{n\times n}$, matrices $F \in \mathbb{R}^{n\times n}$, $G \in \mathbb{R}^{n\times n}$ and $H \in \mathbb{R}^{n\times n} \in \mathbb{R}^{n\times n}$, $d_k \in \mathcal{I}[\underline{d}, \bar{d}]$ with $\bar{d}$ and $\underline{d}$ belonging to $\mathbb{N}_*$, such that

$$\Psi_{qi} = \begin{bmatrix} P + F^T + F & G^T - FA_i & H^T - FA_{di} \\ \star & \beta Q - P - A_i^T G^T - GA_i & -A_i^T H^T - G^T A_{di} \\ \star & \star & -(Q + HA_{di} + A_{di}^T H^T) \end{bmatrix} < \mathbf{0}, \tag{66}$$

is verified for $i = 1, \ldots, N$.

ii) There exist symmetric matrices $\mathbf{0} < P \in \mathbb{R}^{n\times n}$, $\mathbf{0} < Q \in \mathbb{R}^{n\times n}$, $d_k \in \mathcal{I}[\underline{d}, \bar{d}]$ with $\bar{d}$ and $\underline{d}$ belonging to $\mathbb{N}_*$, such that

$$\Phi_i = \begin{bmatrix} A_i^T P A_i + \beta Q - P & A_i^T P A_{di} \\ \star & A_{di}^T P A_{di} - Q \end{bmatrix} < \mathbf{0} \tag{67}$$

is verified for $i = 1, \ldots, N$.

Proof. Condition (66) can be obtained from (20) by imposing $P_i = P > \mathbf{0}$ and $Q_i = Q > \mathbf{0}$. This leads to a Lyapunov-Krasovskii function given by

$$V(x_k) = x_k' P x_k + \sum_{j=k-d(k)}^{k-1} x_j' Q x_j + \sum_{\ell=2-\bar{d}}^{1-\underline{d}} \sum_{j=k+\ell-1}^{k-1} x_j' Q x_j$$

which is sufficient for the quadratic stability of $\tilde{\Omega}_v(\alpha_k)$. This condition is not necessary for the quadratic stability because this function is also not necessary, even for the stability of the precisely known system. The equivalence between (66) and (67) can be stated as follows: *i)* $\Rightarrow$ *ii)* if (66) is verified, then (67) can be recovered by $\Phi_i = \mathcal{T}_{qi}^T \Psi_{qi} \mathcal{T}_{qi}$ with

$$\mathcal{T}_{qi} = \left[\frac{A_i \; A_{di}}{\mathbf{I}_{2n}} \right]$$

i) $\Leftarrow$ *ii)* On the other hand, if (67) is verified, then it is possible by its Schur's complement to obtain

$$\Phi_i < \mathbf{0} \Leftrightarrow \begin{bmatrix} -P & PA_i & PA_{di} \\ \star & \beta Q - P & \mathbf{0} \\ \star & \star & -Q \end{bmatrix} < \mathbf{0}, \quad i = 1, \ldots, N \tag{68}$$

which assures the feasibility of (66) with $F = -P$, $G = H = \mathbf{0}$, completing the proof. □

It is possible to obtain quadratic stability conditions corresponding to each of the formulations presented by theorems 2, 3, 4 following similar steps of those taken to obtain Corollary 1. However, due to the straight way to obtain such conditions, they are not shown here.
Nevertheless, quadratic stability based conditions may lead to results that are, in general, more conservative than those achieved by similar formulations that employ parameter dependent Lyapunov-Krasovskii functions.

5.2 Actuator failure

Partial or total actuator failures are important issues on real word systems and the formulations presented in this chapter can also be used to investigate the robust stability as well as to design robust state feedback control gains assuring stability and $\mathcal{H}_\infty$ guaranteed performance for the uncertain closed-loop system under such failures. The robustness against actuator failures plays an important role in industry, representing not only an improvement in the performance of the closed-loop system, but also a crucial security issue in many plants Leite et al. (2009). In this case, the problem of actuator failures is cast as a special type of uncertainty affecting the input matrix B, being modeled as $B\rho(t)$, with $\rho(t) \in \mathcal{I}[0,1]$. If $\rho(t) = 1$, then the actuator is perfectly working. On the other hand, when the value of $\rho(t)$ is reduced, it means that the actuator cannot delivery all energy required by the control law. The limit is when $\rho(t) = 0$, meaning that the actuator is off. Once the actuator failure implies on time-varying matrix $B(\alpha)$, i.e., $B(\alpha_k)$, it is necessary to employ quadratic stability approach, as described in subsection 5.1.

5.3 Switched systems with delayed state

Another class of time-varying systems is composed by the discrete-time switched systems with delay in the state vector. In this case the system can be described by

$$x_{k+1} = A(\alpha_k)x_k + A_d(\alpha_k)x_{k-d_k} + B(\alpha_k)u(\alpha_k) \tag{69}$$

with adequate initial conditions and the uncertain parameter $\alpha_k = \alpha(k)$ is

$$\alpha_i(k) = \begin{cases} 1, \text{for } i = \sigma_k \\ 0, \text{otherwise} \end{cases} \tag{70}$$

and σ_k is an arbitrary switching function defined as

$$\sigma_k : \mathbb{N} \to \mathcal{I}[1, N] \tag{71}$$

where N is the number of subsystems. The matrices $[A(\alpha_k)|A_d(\alpha_k)|B(\alpha_k)] \in \mathbb{R}^{n\times 2n+m}$ are switched matrices depending on the switching function (71) and can be written as the vertices of the polytope defined by the set of submodes of the system. Naturally, except the vertices, no element of this polytope is reached by the system. Therefore, function σ_k can select one of the subsystems $[A|A_d|B]_i$, $i = 1, \ldots, N$, at each instant k. Those definitions can be done with all other matrices presented in (69) or (65).
It is usual to take the following hypothesis when dealing with switched delay systems:

Hypothesis 1. *The switching function is not known* a priori, *but it is available at each sample-time, k.*

Hypothesis 2. *All matrices of system (69) (or* mutatis mutandis *(65)) are switched simultaneously by (71).*

Hypothesis 3. *Both state vectors, x_k and x_{k-d_k}, are available for feedback.*

These hypotheses can be considered on both stabilization and $\mathcal{H}_\infty$ control problems proposed in sections 3 and 4. An important difference w.r.t. the main stabilization problems investigated in this chapter is that, if σ_k is known, it is reasonable to use also a switched control law given by

$$u_k = K(\alpha_k)x_k + K_d(\alpha_k)x_{k-d_k} \tag{72}$$

where the gains $K(\alpha_k)$ and $K_d(\alpha_k)$ are considered to stabilize the respective subsystem i, $i = 1, \ldots, N$, and assure stable transitions $\sigma_k \to \sigma_{k+1}$. Thus, the switched closed-loop system may be stabilizable by a solution of this problem, being written as in (65) with

$$\tilde{A}(\alpha_k) \equiv A(\alpha_k) + B(\alpha_k)K(\alpha_k) \quad \tilde{A}_d(\alpha_k) \equiv A_d(\alpha_k) + B(\alpha_k)K_d(\alpha_k) \tag{73}$$

The stability of the closed-loop system can be tested with the theorem presented in the sequel.

Theorem 5. *If there exist symmetric matrices $0 < P_i \in \mathbb{R}^{n\times n}$, $0 < Q_i \in \mathbb{R}^{n\times n}$, matrices $F_i \in \mathbb{R}^{n\times n}$, $G_i \in \mathbb{R}^{n\times n}$ and $H_i \in \mathbb{R}^{n\times n}$, $i = 1, \ldots, N$, and a scalar $\beta = \bar{d} - \underline{d} + 1$, with $\underline{d}$ and $\bar{d}$ known, such that*

$$\begin{bmatrix} P_j + F_i^T + F_i & G_i^T - F_iA_i & H_i^T - F_iA_{di} \\ \star & \beta Q_i - P_i - A_i^TG_i^T - G_iA_i & -A_i^TH_i^T - G_iA_{di} \\ \star & \star & -(Q_\ell + H_iA_{di} + A_{di}^TH_i^T) \end{bmatrix} < 0, \tag{74}$$

for $(i, j, \ell) \in \mathcal{I}[1, N] \times \mathcal{I}[1, N] \times \mathcal{I}[1, N]$, then the switched time-varying delay system (69)-(73) with $u_k = 0$ is stable for arbitrary switching function σ_k.

As it can be noted, a relevant issue of (74) is that the extra matrices are also dependent on the switching function σ_k. This condition can be casted in a similar form of (20) as follows

$$\Psi_{\sigma i,j,\ell} = \mathcal{Q}_{i,j,\ell} + \mathcal{X}_i\mathcal{B}_i + \mathcal{B}_i^T\mathcal{X}_i^T < 0, \quad (i, j, \ell) \in \mathcal{I}[1, N] \times \mathcal{I}[1, N] \times \mathcal{I}[1, N] \tag{75}$$

where

$$\mathcal{Q}_{i,j,\ell} = \begin{bmatrix} P_j & 0 & 0 \\ \star & \beta Q_i - P_i & 0 \\ \star & \star & -Q_\ell \end{bmatrix}.$$

The synthesis case, i.e. to solve the problem of designing K_i and K_{di}, $i = 1, \ldots, N$, such that the (69)–(72) is robustly stable, is presented in the following theorem.

Theorem 6. *If there exist symmetric matrices* $\mathbf{0} < P_i \in \mathbb{R}^{n\times n}$, $\mathbf{0} < Q_i \in \mathbb{R}^{n\times n}$, *matrices* $F_i \in \mathbb{R}^{n\times n}$, $W_i \in \mathbb{R}^{n\times \ell}$ *and* $W_{di} \in \mathbb{R}^{n\times \ell}$, $i = 1, \ldots, N$, *and a scalar* $\beta = \bar{d} - \underline{d} + 1$, *with* $\underline{d}$ *and* $\bar{d}$ *known, such that*

$$\tilde{\Psi}_i = \begin{bmatrix} \tilde{P}_j + \mathcal{F}_i + \mathcal{F}_i^T & -(A_i\mathcal{F}_i + B_iW_i) & -(A_{di}\mathcal{F}_i + B_iW_{di}) \\ \star & \beta\tilde{Q}_i - \tilde{P}_i & \mathbf{0} \\ \star & \star & -\tilde{Q}_\ell \end{bmatrix} < \mathbf{0}, \tag{76}$$

for $(i, j, \ell) \in \mathcal{I}[1, N] \times \mathcal{I}[1, N] \times \mathcal{I}[1, N]$, *then the switched system with time-varying delay (69) is robustly stabilizable by the control law (72) with*

$$K_i = W_iF_i^{-1} \quad \textit{and} \quad K_{di} = W_{di}F_i^{-1} \tag{77}$$

The proof of theorems 5 and 6 can be found in Leite & Miranda (2008b) and are omitted here. An important issue of Theorem 6 is the use of one matrix $\mathcal{X}_i$ for each submode. This is possible because of the switched nature of the system that reaches only the vertices of the polytope.

Example 4. *Consider the switched discrete-time system with time varying delay described by (69) where where* $A(\sigma_k) = A_n + (-1)^{\sigma_k}\rho L'J$, $A_d(\sigma_k) = (0.225 + (-1)^{\sigma_k}0.025)A_n$ *and*

$$B(\sigma_k) = [0\ 1.5\ 0\ 1.5]' + (-1)^{\sigma_k}[0\ 0.5\ 0\ 0.5]'$$

with

$$A_n = \begin{bmatrix} 0.8 & -0.25 & 0 & 1 \\ 1 & 0 & 0 & 0 \\ 0 & 0 & 0.2 & 0.03 \\ 0 & 0 & 1 & 0 \end{bmatrix} \tag{78}$$

$L = [0,\ 0,\ 1,\ 0]'$, $J = [0.8,\ -0.5,\ 0,\ 1]$, $\sigma_k \in \{1,\ 2\}$, $\rho = 0.35$. *This system with 2 submodes has been investigated by Leite & Miranda (2008b). Note that, even for* $\underline{d} = \bar{d} = 1$, *conditions from Theorem 5 fail to identify this system as a stable one. Observe that, once the delay is time-varying, conditions presented in Montagner et al. (2005), Phat (2005) and Yu et al. (2007) cannot be applied. Supposing* $\underline{d} = 1$, *a search on* $\bar{d}$ *has been done to find its maximum value such that the considered system is stabilizable. Two alternatives are pursued: firstly, consider that only* x_k *is available for feedback, i.e.,* $K_d = \mathbf{0}$. *Conditions of Theorem 6 are feasible until* $\bar{d} = 15$, *for which value it is possible to determine the following gains:*

$$K_{Th\ 6,1} = \begin{bmatrix} 0.1215\ 0.0475\ -1.6326\ -0.4744 \end{bmatrix}$$

$$K_{Th\ 6,2} = \begin{bmatrix} -0.1494\ 0.1551\ -0.8168\ -0.5002 \end{bmatrix}$$

Secondly, consider that both x_k *and* x_{k-d_k} *are available for feedback. By using Theorem 6 it is possible to stabilize the switched system for* $1 \leq d_k \leq 335$. *In this case, with* $\bar{d} = 335$, *conditions of Theorem 6 lead to*

$$K_1 = \begin{bmatrix} -0.6129\ 0.3269\ -1.2873\ -1.1935 \end{bmatrix} \tag{79}$$

$$K_2 = \begin{bmatrix} -0.2199\ 0.1107\ -0.6450\ -0.4890 \end{bmatrix} \tag{80}$$

$$K_{d1} = \begin{bmatrix} -0.1291\ 0.0677\ -0.3228\ -0.2685 \end{bmatrix} \tag{81}$$

$$K_{d2} = \begin{bmatrix} -0.0518\ 0.0271\ -0.1291\ -0.1076 \end{bmatrix} \tag{82}$$

These gains are used in a numerical simulation where random signals for $\sigma_k \in \{1,\ 2\}$ *and for* $1 \leq d(k) \leq 335$ *have been generated as indicated in Figure 3. The initial condition used in this simulation*

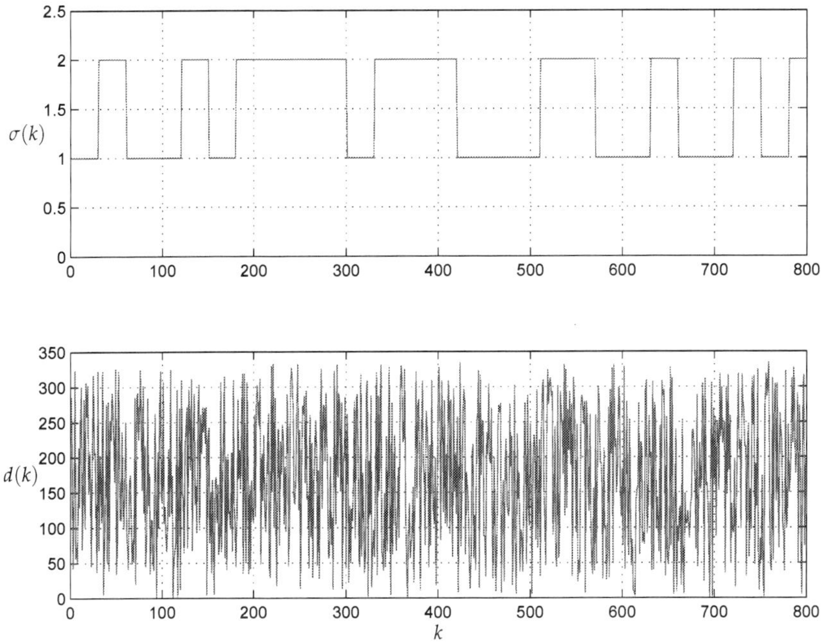

Fig. 3. The switched function, $\sigma(k)$ and the varying delay, d_k.

is

$$\phi_{0,k} = \underbrace{\left\{ \begin{bmatrix} 1 \\ -1 \\ 1 \\ -1 \end{bmatrix}, \ldots, \begin{bmatrix} 1 \\ -1 \\ 1 \\ -1 \end{bmatrix} \right\}}_{336 \text{ terms}}.$$

Thus, it is expected that the delayed state degenerate the overall system response, at least for the first $\bar{d} = 335$ samples, since it is like an impulsive state action arrives at each sample instant for $0 \leq k \leq 335$. Note that, this initial condition is harder than the ones usually found in the literature. The state behavior of the switched closed-loop system with time-varying delay is presented in Figure 4. Observe that the initial value of the state are not presented due to the scale choice. As can be noted by the response behavior presented in Figure 4, the states are almost at the equilibrium point after 400 samples. The control signal is presented in Figure 5. In the top part of this figure, it is shown the control signal part due to $K_{\sigma_k}x(k)$ and in the bottom the control signal due to $K_{d\sigma_k}x(k-d_k)$. The actual control signal is, thus, the addition of these two signals. If quadratic stability is used in the system of this example, the results are more conservative as can be seen in Leite & Miranda (2008b).

5.4 Decentralized control

It is interesting to note that the synthesis conditions proposed in this chapter, i.e. theorems 3, 4, 6 as well as the convex optimization problem $\mathcal{S}_{\mathcal{H}_\infty}$, can be easily used to design decentralized

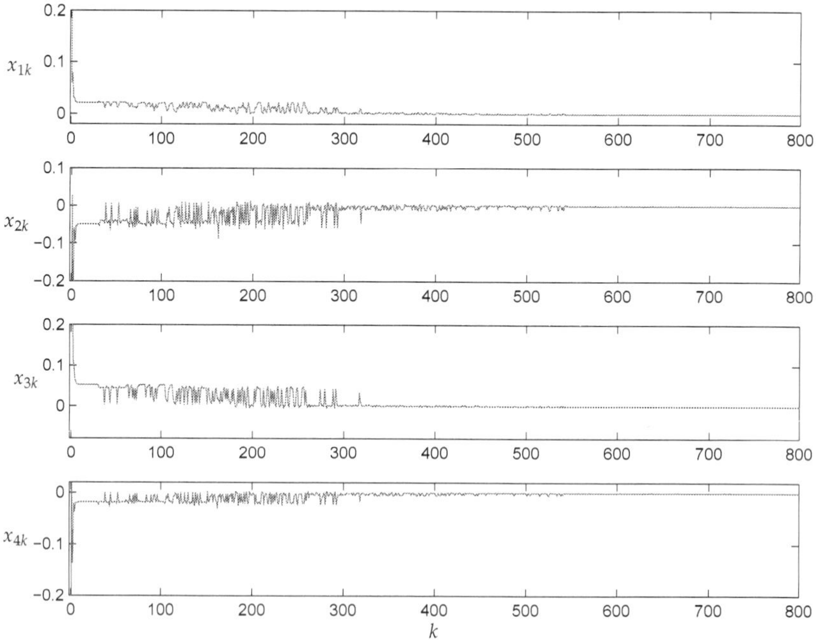

Fig. 4. The behaviors of the states x_{1k} to x_{4k}, with $1 \leq d(k) \leq 335$ (see Fig. 3).

control gains. This kind of control gain is usually employed when interconnected systems must be controlled by means of local information only. In this case, decentralized control gains $K = K_D$ and $K_d = K_{dD}$ can be obtained by imposing block-diagonal structure to matrices W, W_d and $\mathcal{F}$ as follows

$$W = W_D = \text{block-diag}\{W^1, \dots, W^{\varrho}\},$$
$$W_d = W_{dD} = \text{block-diag}\{W_d^1, \dots, W_d^{\varrho}\},$$
$$\mathcal{F} = \mathcal{F}_D = \text{block-diag}\{\mathcal{F}^1, \dots, \mathcal{F}^{\varrho}\}$$

where ϱ denote the number of defined subsystems. In this case, it is possible to get robust block-diagonal state feedback gains $K_D = W_D \mathcal{F}_D^{-1}$ and $K_{dD} = W_{dD} \mathcal{F}_D^{-1}$. It is worth to mention that the matrices of the Lyapunov-Krasovskii function, $\tilde{P}(\alpha)$ and $\tilde{Q}(\alpha)$, do not have any restrictions in their structures, which may leads to less conservative designs.

5.5 Static output feedback

When only a linear combination of the states is available for feedback and the output signal is given by $y_k = \tilde{C}x_k$, it may be necessary to use the static output feedback. See the survey made by Syrmos et al. (1997) on this subject. In case of $\tilde{C}$ with full row rank, it is always possible to find a regular matrix L such that $\tilde{C}L^{-1} = \begin{bmatrix} \mathbf{I}_p | \mathbf{0} \end{bmatrix}$. Using such matrix L in a similarity transformation applied to (1) it yields

$$\hat{x}_{k+1} = \hat{A}(\alpha)\hat{x}_k + \hat{A}_d(\alpha)\hat{x}_{k-d_k} + \hat{B}(\alpha)u_k, \tag{83}$$

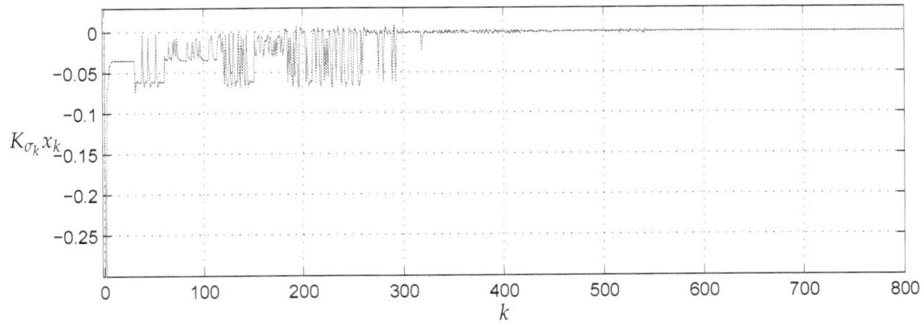

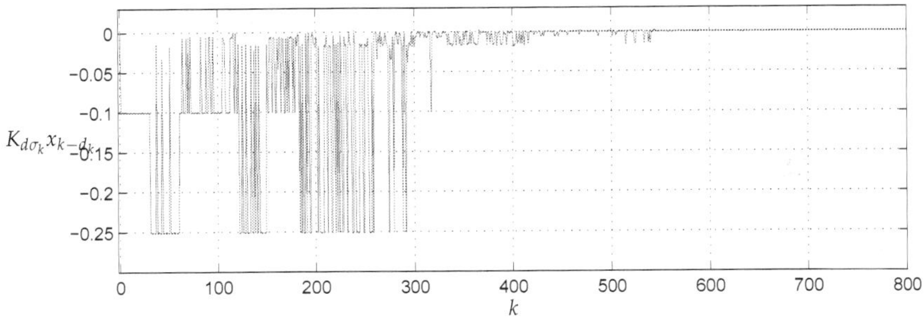

Fig. 5. Control signal $u_k = K_{\sigma_k}x_k + K_{d,\sigma_k}x_{k-d_k}$, with $K_{\sigma_k}x_k$ and $K_{d,\sigma_k}x_{k-d_k}$ shown in the top and bottom parts, respectively.

where $\hat{A}(\alpha) = L\tilde{A}(\alpha)L^{-1}$, $\hat{A}_d(\alpha) = L\tilde{A}_d(\alpha)L^{-1}$ and $\hat{B}(\alpha) = L\tilde{B}(\alpha)$, $\hat{x}_k = Lx_k$ and the output signal is given by $y_k = \begin{bmatrix} \mathbf{I}_p | \mathbf{0} \end{bmatrix} \hat{x}_k$. Thus, the objective here is to find robust static feedback gains $\mathcal{K} \in \mathbb{R}^{p\times\ell}$ and $\mathcal{K}_d \in \mathbb{R}^{p\times\ell}$ such that (83) is robustly stabilizable by the control law

$$u_k = \mathcal{K}y_k + \mathcal{K}_d y_{k-d_k} \tag{84}$$

These gains can be determined by using the conditions of theorems 3, 4, 6 with the following structures

$$\mathcal{F} = \left[\begin{array}{c|c} \mathcal{F}_o^{11} & \mathbf{0} \\ \hline \mathcal{F}_o^{21} & \mathcal{F}_o^{22} \end{array}\right], \quad W = \begin{bmatrix} W_{\mathcal{K}} | \mathbf{0} \end{bmatrix}, \quad W_d = \begin{bmatrix} W_{\mathcal{K}_d} | \mathbf{0} \end{bmatrix}$$

with $\mathcal{F}_o^{11} \in \mathbb{R}^{p\times p}$, $\mathcal{F}_o^{21} \in \mathbb{R}^{(n-p)\times p}$, $\mathcal{F}_o^{22} \in \mathbb{R}^{(n-p)\times(n-p)}$, $W_{\mathcal{K}} \in \mathbb{R}^{p\times n}$, $W_{\mathcal{K}_d} \in \mathbb{R}^{p\times n}$ which yields

$$K = \begin{bmatrix} \mathcal{K} | \mathbf{0} \end{bmatrix} \quad \text{and} \quad K_d = \begin{bmatrix} \mathcal{K}_d | \mathbf{0} \end{bmatrix}$$

Note that, similarly to the decentralized case, no constraint is taken over the Lyapunov-Krasovskii function matrices leading to less conservative conditions, in general.

5.6 Input delay

Another relevant issue in Control Theory is the study of stability and stabilization of input delay systems, which is quite frequent in many real systems Yu & Gao (2001), Chen et al.

(2004). In this case, consider the controlled system given by

$$x_{k+1} = A(\alpha)x_k + B(\alpha)u_{k-d_k} \tag{85}$$

with $A(\alpha)$ and $B(\alpha)$ belonging to polytope (2), $A_{di} = \mathbf{0}$ and $\alpha \in \Upsilon$. In Zhang et al. (2007) this system is detailed investigated and the problem is converted into an optimization problem in Krein space with an stochastic model associated. Here, the delayed input control signal is considered as

$$u_{k-d_k} = K_d x_{k-d_k} \tag{86}$$

The closed-loop-system is given by

$$x_{k+1} = \tilde{A}(\alpha)x_k + \tilde{A}_d(\alpha)x_{k-d_k} \tag{87}$$

with $\tilde{A}(\alpha) = A(\alpha)$, $\tilde{A}_d(\alpha) = B(\alpha)K_d$. Thus, with known K_d, closed-loop system (87) is equivalent to (7) with null exogenous signal w_k. This leads to simple analysis stability conditions obtained from Theorem 1 replacing $\tilde{A}_i$ by A_i and $\tilde{A}_{di}$ by B_iK_d, $i = 1, \ldots, N$. Besides, similar replacements can be used with conditions presented in theorems 2 and 5 and in Corollary 1. The possibility to address both controller fragility and input delay is a side result of this proposal. In the former it is required that no uncertainty affects the input matrix, i.e., $B(\alpha) = B$, $\forall \alpha \in \Upsilon$, while the latter can be used to investigate the bounds of stability of a closed-loop system with a delay due to, for example, digital processing or information propagation.
In case of the design of K_d it is possible to take similar steps with conditions of theorems 3, 4 and 6. In this case, it is sufficient to impose, $A_{di} = \mathbf{0}, i = 1, \ldots, N$ and $W = \mathbf{0}$ that yield $K = \mathbf{0}$. Finally, observe that static delayed output feedback control can be additionally addressed here by considering what is pointed out in Subsection 5.5.

5.7 Performance by delay-free model specification

Some well developed techniques related to model-following control (or internal model control) can be applied in the context of delayed state systems. The major advantage of such techniques for delayed systems concerns with the design with performance specification based on zero-pole location. See, for example, the works of Mao & Chu (2009) and Silva et al. (2009). Generally, the model-following control design is related to an input-output closed-loop model, specified from its poles, zeros and static gain, from which the controller is calculated. As the proposal presented in this chapter is based on state feedback control, it does not match entirely with the requirements for following-model, because doing state feedback only the poles can be redesigned, but not the zeros and the static gain. To develop a complete following model approach an usual way is to deal with output feedback, that yields a non-convex formulation. One way to match all the requirements of following model by using state feedback and maintaining the convexity of the formulation, is to use the technique presented by Coutinho et al. (2009) where the model to be matched is separated into two parts: One of them is used to coupe the static gain and zeros of the closed loop system with the prescribed model and the other part is matched by state feedback control. Consider the block diagram presented in Figure 6. In this figure, $\Omega(\alpha)$ is the system to controlled with signal u_k. This system is subject to input w_k which is required to be reject at the output y_k. Please, see equation (1). Ω_m stands for a specified delay-free model with realization given by $\left[\begin{array}{c|c} A_m & B_m \\ \hline C_m & D_m \end{array}\right]$. The model receives the same exogenous input of the system to be controlled, w_k, and has an output signal y_{mk} at the instant k.

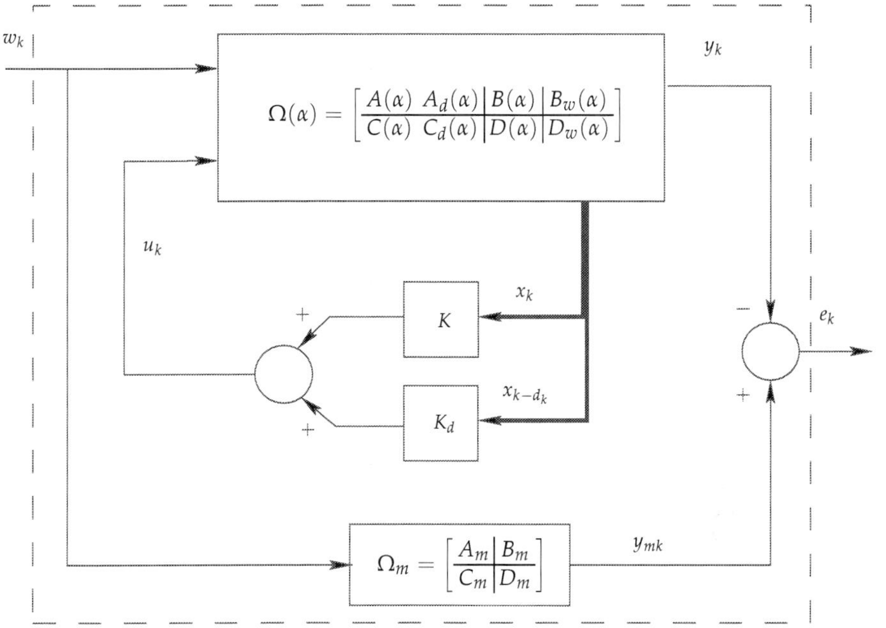

Fig. 6. Following model inspired problem.

The objective here is to design robust state feedback gains K and K_d to implement the control law (6) such that the $\mathcal{H}_\infty$ guaranteed cost between the input w_k and the output $e_k = y_k - y_{mk}$ is minimized. In other words, it is desired that the disturbance rejection of the uncertain system with time-varying delay in the state have a behavior as close as possible to the behavior of the specified delay-free model Ω_m. The dashed line in Figure 6 identifies the enlarged system required to have its $\mathcal{H}_\infty$ guaranteed cost minimized.
Taking the closed-loop system (7) and the specified model of perturbation rejection given by

$$x_{mk+1} = A_m x_{mk} + B_m w_k \tag{88}$$
$$y_{mk} = C_m x_{mk} + D_m w_k \tag{89}$$

where $x_{mk} \in \mathbb{R}^{n_m}$ is the model state vector at the k-th sample-time, $y_{mk} \in \mathbb{R}^p$ is the output of the model at the same sample-time and $w_k \in \mathbb{R}^\ell$ is the same perturbation affecting the controlled system, the difference $e_k = y_{mk} - z_k$ is obtained as

$$e_k = \begin{bmatrix} C_m & -(C(\alpha) + D(\alpha)K) & -(C_d(\alpha) + D(\alpha)K_d) \end{bmatrix} \begin{bmatrix} x_{mk} \\ x_k \\ x_{k-d_k} \end{bmatrix} + \begin{bmatrix} D_m - D_w(\alpha) \end{bmatrix} w_k \tag{90}$$

Thus, by using (1) with (88)-(89) and (90) it is possible to construct an augmented system composed by the state of the system and those from model yielding the following system

$$\hat{\Omega}(\alpha) : \begin{cases} \hat{x}_{k+1} = \hat{A}(\alpha)\hat{x}_k + \hat{A}_d(\alpha)\hat{x}_{k-d_k} + \hat{B}_w(\alpha)w_k \\ e_k = \hat{C}(\alpha)\hat{x}_k + \hat{C}_d(\alpha)\hat{x}_{k-d_k} + \hat{D}_w(\alpha)w_k \end{cases} \tag{91}$$

with $\hat{x}_k = \begin{bmatrix} x_{mk}^T & x_k^T \end{bmatrix}^T \in \mathbb{R}^{n_m+n}$, $\hat{\Omega}(\alpha) \in \hat{\mathcal{P}}$,

$$\hat{\mathcal{P}} = \left\{ \hat{\Omega}(\alpha) \in \mathbb{R}^{n+n_m+p\times 2(n+n_m)+\ell} : \hat{\Omega}(\alpha) = \sum_{i=1}^{N} \alpha_i \hat{\Omega}_i, \;\; \alpha \in \Upsilon \right\} \tag{92}$$

where

$$\begin{aligned}\hat{\Omega}_i &= \left[\begin{array}{c|c|c} \hat{A}_i & \hat{A}_{di} & \hat{B}_{wi} \\ \hline \hat{C}_i & \hat{C}_{di} & \hat{D}_{wi} \end{array}\right] \\ &= \left[\begin{array}{cc|cc|c} A_m & 0 & 0 & 0 & B_m \\ 0 & A_i + B_i K & 0 & A_{di} + B_i K_d & B_{wi} \\ \hline C_m & -(C_i + D_i K) & 0 & -(C_{di} + D_i K_d) & D_m - D_{wi} \end{array}\right], \;\; i \in \mathcal{I}[1, N].\end{aligned} \tag{93}$$

Therefore, matrices in (93) — $\hat{A}_i$, $\hat{A}_{di}$, $\hat{B}_{wi}$, $\hat{C}_i$, $\hat{C}_{di}$, $\hat{D}_{wi}$ — can be used to replace their respective in (38) and (23). As a consequence, LMI (36) becomes with $3(n + n_m) + 2(p + \ell)$ rows. Since the main interest in this section is to design K and K_d that minimize the $\mathcal{H}_\infty$ guaranteed cost between e_k and w_k, only the design condition is presented in the sequel. To achieve such condition, similar steps of those taken in the proof of Theorem 4 are taken. The main differences are related to *i)* the size and structure of the matrices and *ii)* the manipulations done to keep the convexity of the formulation.

Theorem 7. *If there exist symmetric matrices* $0 < \tilde{P}_i = \begin{bmatrix} \tilde{P}_{11i} & \tilde{P}_{12i} \\ \star & \tilde{P}_{22i} \end{bmatrix} \in \mathbb{R}^{n+n_m\times n+n_m}$, $0 < \tilde{Q}_i = \begin{bmatrix} \tilde{Q}_{11i} & \tilde{Q}_{12i} \\ \star & \tilde{Q}_{22i} \end{bmatrix} \in \mathbb{R}^{n+n_m\times n+n_m}$, *matrices* $\mathcal{F} = \begin{bmatrix} \mathcal{F}_{11} & \mathcal{F}_{12} \\ \mathcal{F}_{22}\Lambda & \mathcal{F}_{22} \end{bmatrix} \in \mathbb{R}^{n+n_m\times n+n_m}$, $\Lambda \in \mathbb{R}^{n\times n_m}$ *is a given matrix,* $W \in \mathbb{R}^{p\times n}$, $W_d \in \mathbb{R}^{p\times n}$, *a scalar variable* $\theta \in]0, 1]$ *and for a given* $\mu = \gamma^2$ *such that*

$$\Psi_i = \begin{bmatrix} \tilde{P}_{11i} - \mathcal{F}_{11} - \mathcal{F}_{11}^T & \tilde{P}_{12i} - \mathcal{F}_{12} - \Lambda^T \mathcal{F}_{22}^T & A_m \mathcal{F}_{11} & A_m \mathcal{F}_{12} & 0 & 0 & 0 & B_m \\ \star & \tilde{P}_{22i} - \mathcal{F}_{22} - \mathcal{F}_{22}^T & (A_i \mathcal{F}_{22} + B_i W)\Lambda & A_i \mathcal{F}_{22} + B_i W & (A_{di}\mathcal{F}_{22} + B_i W_d)\Lambda & A_{di}\mathcal{F}_{22} + B_i W_d & 0 & B_{wi} \\ \star & \star & \beta \tilde{Q}_{11i} - \tilde{P}_{11i} & \beta \tilde{Q}_{12i} - \tilde{P}_{12i} & 0 & 0 & \mathcal{F}_{11}^T C_m^T - \Lambda^T (W^T D_i^T + \mathcal{F}_{22}^T C_i^T) & 0 \\ \star & \star & \star & \beta \tilde{Q}_{22i} - \tilde{P}_{22i} & 0 & 0 & \mathcal{F}_{12}^T C_m^T - (W^T D_i^T + \mathcal{F}_{22}^T C_i^T) & 0 \\ \star & \star & \star & \star & -\tilde{Q}_{11i} & -\tilde{Q}_{12i} & -\Lambda^T (W_d^T D_i^T + \mathcal{F}_{22}^T C_{di}^T) & 0 \\ \star & \star & \star & \star & \star & -\tilde{Q}_{22i} & -(W_d^T D_i^T + \mathcal{F}_{22}^T C_{di}^T) & 0 \\ \star & \star & \star & \star & \star & \star & -\theta \mathbf{I}_p & D_m - D_{wi} \\ \star & \star & \star & \star & \star & \star & \star & -\mu \mathbf{I}_\ell \end{bmatrix} < 0$$

$$i = 1, \ldots, N \tag{94}$$

then system (1)–(5) is robustly stabilizable by (6) with

$$K = W\mathcal{F}_{22}^{-1} \quad \text{and} \quad K_d = W_d \mathcal{F}_{22}^{-1} \tag{95}$$

providing an $\mathcal{H}_\infty$ guaranteed cost $\gamma = \sqrt{\mu}$ between the output e_k, as defined by (93), and the input signal w_k.

Proof. The proof follows similar steps to those of the proof of the Theorem 4. Once (94) is verified, then the regularity of $\mathcal{F} = \begin{bmatrix} \mathcal{F}_{11} & \mathcal{F}_{12} \\ \mathcal{F}_{22}\Lambda & \mathcal{F}_{22} \end{bmatrix}$ is assured by the block

$$\tilde{P}_i - \mathcal{F} - \mathcal{F}^T = \begin{bmatrix} \tilde{P}_{11i} - \mathcal{F}_{11} - \mathcal{F}_{11}^T & \tilde{P}_{12i} - \mathcal{F}_{12} - \Lambda^T \mathcal{F}_{22}^T \\ \star & \tilde{P}_{22i} - \mathcal{F}_{22} - \mathcal{F}_{22}^T \end{bmatrix} < 0.$$

Thus it is possible to define the congruence transformation $\mathcal{T}_\mathcal{H}$ given by (53) with

$$\mathcal{T} = \mathbf{I}_3 \otimes \mathcal{F}^{-T} = \mathbf{I}_3 \otimes \begin{bmatrix} \mathcal{F}_{11} & \mathcal{F}_{12} \\ \mathcal{F}_{22}\Lambda & \mathcal{F}_{22} \end{bmatrix}^{-T}$$

to get $\hat{\Psi}_i = \mathcal{T}_\mathcal{H} \tilde{\Psi}_i \mathcal{T}_\mathcal{H}^T$. In block $(7,7)$ of $\hat{\Psi}_i$, it always exist a real scalar $\kappa \in]0,2[$ such that for $\theta \in]0,1]$, $\kappa(\kappa-2) = -\theta$. Thus, replacing this block by $\kappa(\kappa-2)\mathbf{I}_p$, the optimization variables W and W_d by $K\mathcal{F}_{22}$ and $K_d\mathcal{F}_{22}$, respectively, and using the definitions given by (91)–(93) it is possible to verify (36) by *i)* replacing matrices $\tilde{A}_i$, $\tilde{A}_{di}$, $\tilde{C}_i$, $\tilde{C}_{di}$, B_{wi} and D_{wi} by $\hat{A}_i$, $\hat{A}_{di}$, $\hat{C}_i$, $\hat{C}_{di}$, $\hat{B}_{wi}$ and $\hat{D}_{wi}$, respectively, given in (93); *ii)* choosing $G = \frac{1}{\kappa}\mathbf{I}_p$ that leads block $(7,7)$ to be rewritten as in (55); *iii)* assuming

$$P_i = \begin{bmatrix} \mathcal{F}_{11} & \mathcal{F}_{12} \\ \mathcal{F}_{22}\Lambda & \mathcal{F}_{22} \end{bmatrix}^{-T} \begin{bmatrix} \tilde{P}_{11i} & \tilde{P}_{12i} \\ \star & \tilde{P}_{22i} \end{bmatrix} \begin{bmatrix} \mathcal{F}_{11} & \mathcal{F}_{12} \\ \mathcal{F}_{22}\Lambda & \mathcal{F}_{22} \end{bmatrix}^{-1}$$

$$Q_i = \begin{bmatrix} \mathcal{F}_{11} & \mathcal{F}_{12} \\ \mathcal{F}_{22}\Lambda & \mathcal{F}_{22} \end{bmatrix}^{-T} \begin{bmatrix} \tilde{Q}_{11i} & \tilde{Q}_{12i} \\ \star & \tilde{Q}_{22i} \end{bmatrix} \begin{bmatrix} \mathcal{F}_{11} & \mathcal{F}_{12} \\ \mathcal{F}_{22}\Lambda & \mathcal{F}_{22} \end{bmatrix}^{-1}$$

and

$$\mathcal{X}_H = \begin{bmatrix} \begin{bmatrix} \mathcal{F}_{11} & \mathcal{F}_{12} \\ \mathcal{F}_{22}\Lambda & \mathcal{F}_{22} \end{bmatrix}^{-1} & \mathbf{0} \\ \mathbf{0} & \mathbf{0} \\ \mathbf{0} & \mathbf{0} \\ \mathbf{0} & \frac{1}{\kappa}\mathbf{I}_p \\ \mathbf{0} & \mathbf{0} \end{bmatrix}$$

which completes the proof. □

An important aspect of Theorem 7 is the choice of $\Lambda \in \mathbb{R}^{n \times n_m}$ in (94). This matrix plays an important role in this optimization problem, once it is used to adjust the dimensions of block $(2,1)$ of $\mathcal{F}$ that allows to use $\mathcal{F}_{22}$ to design both robust state feedback gains K and K_d. This kind choice made *a priori* also appears in some results found on the literature of filtering theory. Another possibility is to use an interactive algorithm to search for a better choice of Λ. This can be done by taking the following steps:

1. **Set** *max_iter*$\longleftarrow$ `maximum number of iterations;` $j \longleftarrow 0$; $\epsilon =$`precision;`
2. **Choose** an initial value of $\Lambda_j \longleftarrow \Lambda$ such that (94) is feasible.
   (a) **Set** $\mu_j \longleftarrow \mu$; $\Delta\mu \longleftarrow \mu_j$; $\mathcal{F}_{22,j} \longleftarrow \mathcal{F}_{22}$; $W_j \longleftarrow W$; $W_{d,j} \longleftarrow W_d$.
3. **While** $(\Delta\mu > \epsilon)$**AND**$(j <$ *max_iter*$)$

(a) **Set** $j \longleftarrow j+1$;

(b) **If** j is odd

i. **Solve** (94) with $\mathcal{F}_{22} \longleftarrow \mathcal{F}_{22,j}$; $W \longleftarrow W_j$; $W_d \longleftarrow W_{d,j}$.

ii. **Set** $\Lambda \longleftarrow \Lambda_j$;

Else

i. **Solve** (94) with $\Lambda \longleftarrow \Lambda_j$.

ii. **Set** $\mathcal{F}_{22,j} \longleftarrow \mathcal{F}_{22}$; $W_j \longleftarrow W$; $W_{d,j} \longleftarrow W_d$.

End_if

(c) **Set** $\mu_j \longleftarrow \mu$; $\Delta\mu \longleftarrow |(\mu_j - \mu_{j-1})|$;

End_while

4. **Calculate** K and K_d by means of (95);

5. **Set** $\mu_\star = \mu_j$

Once this is a non-convex algorithm — only steps *3.(b).i* are convex — different initial guesses for Λ may lead to different final values for the controllers K and K_d, as well as to the $\gamma = \sqrt{\mu_\star}$ To overcome the main drawback of this proposal, two approaches can be stated. The first follows the ideas of Coutinho et al. (2009) by designing an external loop to the closed-loop system proposed in Figure 6. In this sense, it is possible to design a transfer function that can adjust the gain and zeros of the controlled system. The second approach is based on the work of Rodrigues et al. (2009) where a dynamic output feedback controller is proposed. However, in this case the achieved conditions are non-convex and a relaxation algorithm is required. In the example presented in the sequel, Theorem 7 with

$$\Lambda = \begin{bmatrix} \mathbf{I}_{n_m} \\ \mathbf{0}_{n-n_m \times n_m} \end{bmatrix} \tag{96}$$

Example 5. *Consider the uncertain discrete-time system with time-varying delay $d_k \in \mathcal{I}[2,13]$ as given in (1) with uncertain matrices belonging to polytope (2)-(3) with 2 vertices given by*

$$A_1 = \begin{bmatrix} 0.6 & 0 \\ 0.35 & 0.7 \end{bmatrix}, \quad A_{d1} = \begin{bmatrix} 0.1 & 0 \\ 0.2 & 0.1 \end{bmatrix}, \quad A_2 = 1.1A_1, \quad A_{d2} = 1.1A_{d1} \tag{97}$$

$$B_{w1} = \begin{bmatrix} 0 \\ 1 \end{bmatrix}, \quad B_1 = \begin{bmatrix} 0 \\ 1 \end{bmatrix}, \quad B_{w2} = 1.1B_{w1}, \quad B_2 = 1.1B_1 \tag{98}$$

$$C_1 = \begin{bmatrix} 1 & 0 \end{bmatrix}, \quad C_{d1} = \begin{bmatrix} 0 & 0.05 \end{bmatrix}, \quad C_2 = 1.1C_1, \quad C_{d2} = 1.1C_{d1} \tag{99}$$

$$D_{w1} = 0.2, \quad D_1 = 0.1, \quad D_{w2} = 1.1D_{w1} \quad D_2 = 1.1D_1 \tag{100}$$

It is desired to design robust state feedback gains for control law (6) such that the output of this uncertain system approaches the behavior of delay-free model given by

$$\Omega_m = G(z) = \frac{0.1847z - 0.01617}{z+0.3} = \left[\begin{array}{c|c} -0.3 & 0.25 \\ \hline -0.2864 & 0.1847 \end{array}\right] \tag{101}$$

Thus, it is desired to minimize the $\mathcal{H}_\infty$ guaranteed cost between signals e_k and w_k identified in Figure 6. The static gain of model (101) was adjusted to match the gain of the controlled system. This procedure is similar to what has been proposed by Coutinho et al. (2009). The choice of the pole and the zero was arbitrary. Obviously, different models result in different value of $\mathcal{H}_\infty$ guaranteed cost.

By applying Theorem 7 to this problem, with Λ *given in (96), it has been found an* $\mathcal{H}_\infty$ *guaranteed cost* $\gamma = 0.2383$ *achieved with the robust state feedback gains:*

$$K = \begin{bmatrix} 1.8043 & -0.7138 \end{bmatrix} \quad \text{and} \quad K_d = \begin{bmatrix} -0.1546 & -0.0422 \end{bmatrix} \tag{102}$$

In case of unknown d_k*, Theorem 7 is unfeasible for the considered variation delay interval, i.e., imposing* $K_d = \mathbf{0}$*. On the other hand, if this interval is narrower, this system can be stabilized with an* $\mathcal{H}_\infty$ *guaranteed cost using only the current state. So, reducing the value of* $\bar{d}$ *from* $\bar{d} = 13$*, it has been found that Theorem 7 is feasible for* $d_k \in \mathcal{I}[2,10]$ *with*

$$K = \begin{bmatrix} -2.7162 & -0.6003 \end{bmatrix} \quad \text{and} \quad K_d = \mathbf{0} \tag{103}$$

and $\gamma = 0.3427$*. Just for a comparison, with this same delay interval, if K and* K_d *are designed, then the* $\mathcal{H}_\infty$ *guaranteed cost is reduced about 37.8% yielding an attenuation level given by* $\gamma = 0.2131$*. Thus, it is clear that, whenever the information about the delay is used it is possible to reduce the* $\mathcal{H}_\infty$ *guaranteed cost. Some numerical simulations have been done considering gains (102), and a disturbance input given by*

$$w_k = \begin{cases} 0, & \text{if } k = 0 \text{ or } k \geq 11 \\ 1, & \text{if } 1 \leq 10 \end{cases} \tag{104}$$

Two conditions were considered: i) $d_k = 13, \forall k \leq 0$ *and different values of* $\alpha_1 \in [0,1]$*; and* ii) $d_k = d = \in \mathcal{I}[2,13]$ *with* $\alpha_1 = 1$ *(i.e., only for the first vertex). The output responses of the controlled system have been performed with* $d_k = 13, \forall k \geq 0$*. This family of responses and that of the reference model are shown at the top of Figure 7 with solid lines. A red dashed line is used to indicate the desired model response. The absolute value of the error* ($|e_k| = |y_k - y_{mk}|$) *is shown in solid lines at the bottom of Figure 7 and the estimate* $\mathcal{H}_\infty$ *guaranteed cost provide by Theorem 7 in dashed red line. The respective control signals are shown in Figure 8.*
The other set of time simulations has been performed using only vertex number 1 ($\alpha_1 = 1$)*. In this numerical experiment, the perturbation (104) has been applied to system defined by vertex 1 and twelve numerical simulations were performed, one for each constant delay value* $d_k = d \in [2,13]$*. The results are shown in Figure 9: at the top, a red dashed line indicates the model response and at the bottom it is shown the absolute value of the error* ($|e_k| = |y_k - y_{mk}|$) *in solid lines and the estimate* $\mathcal{H}_\infty$ *guaranteed cost provide by Theorem 7 in dashed red line. This value is the same provide in Figure 7, once it is the same design. The respective control signals performed in simulations shown in Figure 9 are shown in Figure 10.*
At last, the frequency response considering the input w_k *and the output* e_k *is shown in Figure 11 with* a time-invariant delay. *For each value of delay in the interval* $[2,13]$ *and* $\alpha \in [0,1]$*, a frequency sweep has been performed on both open loop and closed-loop systems. The gains used in the closed-loop system are given in (102). It is interesting to note that, once it is desired that* y_k *approaches* y_{mk}*, i.e.,* e_k *approaches zero, the gain frequency response of the closed-loop should approaches zero. By Figure 11 the* $\mathcal{H}_\infty$ *guaranteed cost of the closed-loop system* with time invariant delay *is about* 0.1551*, but this value refers to the case of time-invariant delay only. The estimative provided by Theorem 7 is* 0.2383 *and considers a* time varying *delay.*

6. Final remarks

In this chapter, some sufficient convex conditions for robust stability and stabilization of discrete-time systems with delayed state were presented. The system considered is uncertain with polytopic representation and the conditions were obtained by using parameter dependent Lyapunov-Krasovskii functions. The Finsler's Lemma was used to obtain LMIs

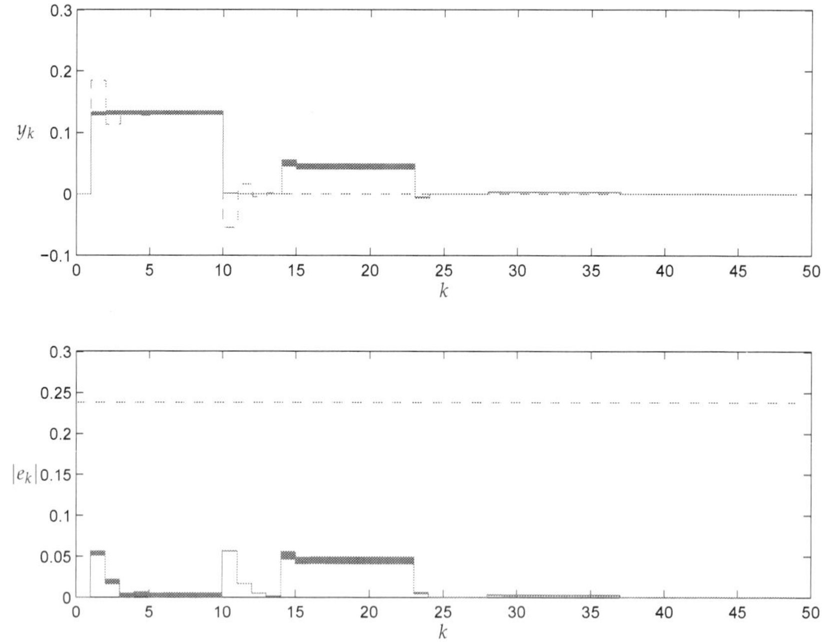

Fig. 7. Time behavior of y_k and $|e_k|$ in blue solid lines and model response (top) and estimated $\mathcal{H}_\infty$ guaranteed cost (bottom) in red dashed lines, for $d_k = 13$ and $\alpha \in [0, 1]$.

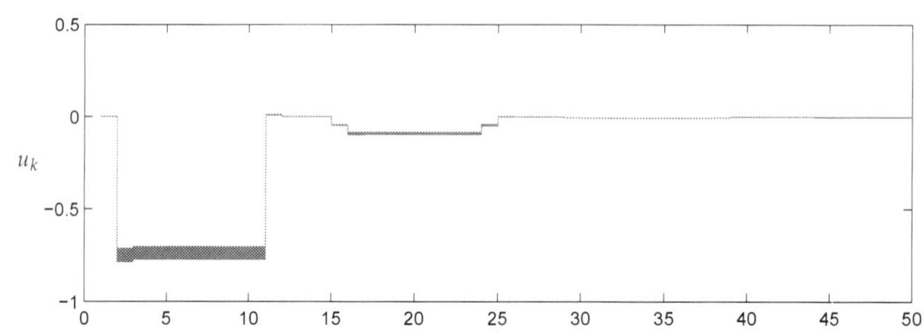

Fig. 8. Control signals used in time simulations presented in Figure 7.

condition where the Lyapunov-Krasovskii variables are decoupled from the matrices of the system. The fundamental problem of robust stability analysis and stabilization has been dealt. The $\mathcal{H}_\infty$ guaranteed cost has been used to improve the performance of the closed-loop system. It is worth to say that even all matrices of the system are affected by polytopic uncertainties, the proposed design conditions are convex, formulated in terms of LMIs.
It is shown how the results on robust stability analysis, synthesis and on $\mathcal{H}_\infty$ guaranteed cost estimation and design can be extended to match some special problems in control theory such

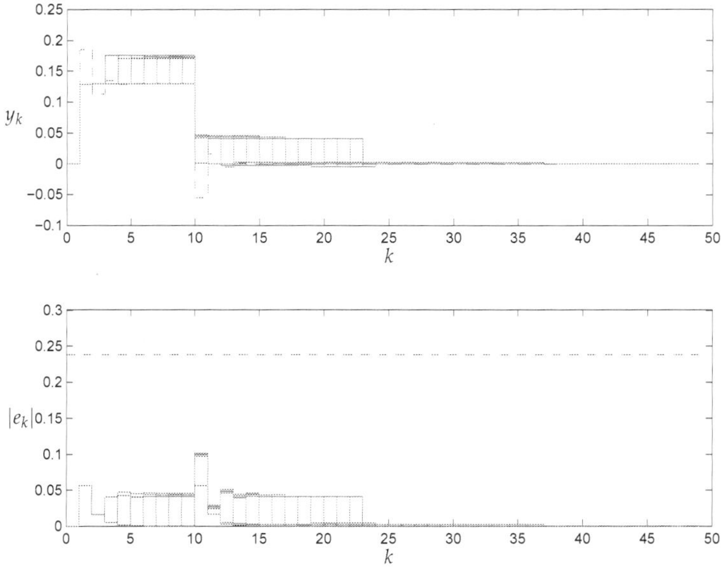

Fig. 9. Time behavior of y_k and $|e_k|$ in blue solid lines and model response (top) and estimated $\mathcal{H}_\infty$ guaranteed cost (bottom) in red dashed lines, for vertex 1 and delays from 2 to 13.

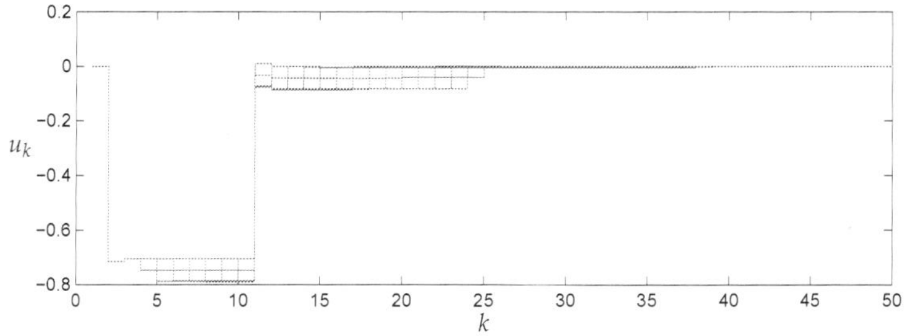

Fig. 10. Control signals used in time simulations presented in Figure 9.

as decentralized control, switched systems, actuator failure, output feedback and following model conditions.

It has been shown that the proposed convex conditions can be systematically obtained by *i)* defining a suitable positive definite parameter dependent Lyapunov-Krasovskii function; *ii)* calculating an over bound for $\Delta V(k) < \mathbf{0}$ and *iii)* applying Finsler's Lemma to get a set of LMIs, formulated in a enlarged space, where cross products between the matrices of the system and the matrices of the Lyapunov-Krasovskii function are avoided. In case of robust design conditions, they are obtained from the respective analysis conditions by congruence transformation and, in the $\mathcal{H}_\infty$ guaranteed cost design, by replacing some matrix blocs by their over bounds. Numerical examples are given to demonstrated some relevant aspects of the proposed conditions.

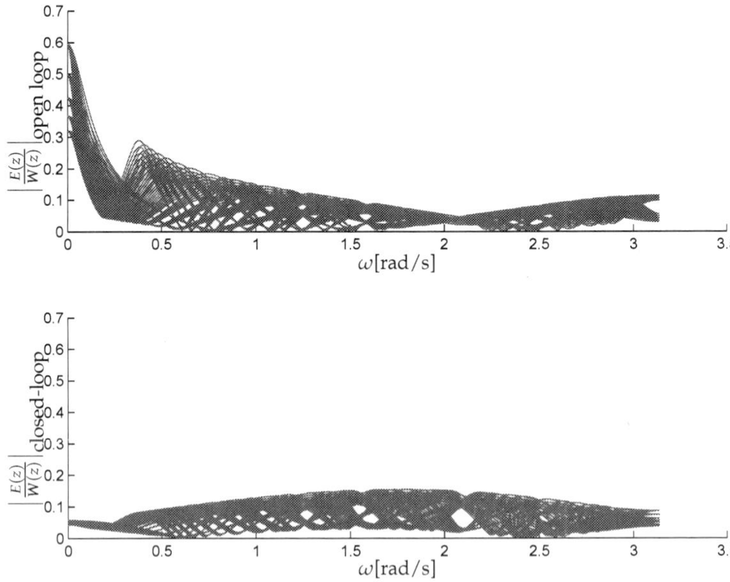

Fig. 11. Gain frequency response between signals e_k and w_k for the open loop (top) and closed-loop (bottom) cases for delays from 2 to 13 and a sweep on $\alpha \in [0,1]$.

The approach used in this proposal can be used to deal with more complete Lyapunov-Krasovskii functions, yielding less conservative conditions for both robust stability analysis and design, including closed-loop performance specifications as presented in this chapter.

7. References

Boukas, E.-K. (2006). Discrete-time systems with time-varying time delay: stability and stabilizability, *Mathematical Problems in Engineering* 2006: 1–10.

Chen, W. H., Guan, Z. H. & Lu, X. (2004). Delay-dependent guaranteed cost control for uncertain discrete-time systems with both state and input delays, *Journal of The Franklin Institute* 341(5): 419–430.

Chu, J. (1995). Application of a discrete optimal tracking controller to an industrial electric heater with pure delays, *Journal of Process Control* 5(1): 3–8.

Coutinho, D. F., Pereira, L. F. A. & Yoneyama, T. (2009). Robust $\mathcal{H}_2$ model matching from frequency domain specifications, *IET Control Theory and Applications* 3(8): 1119–1131.

de Oliveira, M. C. & Skelton, R. E. (2001). Stability tests for constrained linear systems, *in* S. O. Reza Moheimani (ed.), *Perspectives in Robust Control*, Vol. 268 of *Lecture Notes in Control and Information Science*, Springer-Verlag, New York, pp. 241–257.

de Oliveira, P. J., Oliveira, R. C. L. F., Leite, V. J. S., Montagner, V. F. & Peres, P. L. D. (2002). LMI based robust stability conditions for linear uncertain systems: a numerical comparison, *Proceedings of the 41st IEEE Conference on Decision and Control*, Las Vegas, pp. 644–649.

Du, D., Jiang, B., Shi, P. & Zhou, S. (2007). $\mathcal{H}_\infty$ filtering of discrete-time switched systems with state delays via switched Lyapunov function approach, *IEEE Transactions on Automatic Control* 52(8): 1520–1525.

Fridman, E. & Shaked, U. (2005a). Delay dependent $\mathcal{H}_\infty$ control of uncertain discrete delay system, *European Journal of Control* 11(1): 29–37.

Fridman, E. & Shaked, U. (2005b). Stability and guaranteed cost control of uncertain discrete delay system, *International Journal of Control* 78(4): 235–246.

Gao, H., Lam, J., Wang, C. & Wang, Y. (2004). Delay-dependent robust output feedback stabilisation of discrete-time systems with time-varying state delay, *IEE Proceedings — Control Theory and Applications* 151(6): 691–698.

Gu, K., Kharitonov, V. L. & Chen, J. (2003). *Stability of Time-delay Systems*, Control Engineering, Birkhäuser, Boston.

He, Y., Wu, M., Liu, G.-P. & She, J.-H. (2008). Output feedback stabilization for a discrete-time system with a time-varying delay, *IEEE Transactions on Automatic Control* 53(11): 2372–2377.

Hetel, L., Daafouz, J. & Iung, C. (2008). Equivalence between the Lyapunov-Krasovskii functionals approach for discrete delay systems and that of the stability conditions for switched systems, *Nonlinear Analysis: Hybrid Systems* 2: 697–705.

Ibrir, S. (2008). Stability and robust stabilization of discrete-time switched systems with time-delays: LMI approach, *Applied Mathematics and Computation* 206: 570–578.

Kandanvli, V. K. R. & Kar, H. (2009). Robust stability of discrete-time state-delayed systems with saturation nonlinearities: Linear matrix inequality approach, *Signal Processing* 89: 161–173.

Kapila, V. & Haddad, W. M. (1998). Memoryless $\mathcal{H}_\infty$ controllers for discrete-time systems with time delay, *Automatica* 34(9): 1141–1144.

Kolmanovskii, V. & Myshkis, A. (1999). *Introduction to the Theory and Applications of Functional Differential Equations*, Mathematics and Its Applications, Kluwer Academic Publishers.

Leite, V. J. S. & Miranda, M. F. (2008a). Robust stabilization of discrete-time systems with time-varying delay: an LMI approach, *Mathematical Problems in Engineering* pp. 1–15.

Leite, V. J. S. & Miranda, M. F. (2008b). Stabilization of switched discrete-time systems with time-varying delay, *Proceedings of the 17th IFAC World Congress*, Seul.

Leite, V. J. S., Montagner, V. F., de Oliveira, P. J., Oliveira, R. C. L. F., Ramos, D. C. W. & Peres, P. L. D. (2004). Estabilidade robusta de sistemas lineares através de desigualdades matriciais lineares, *SBA Controle & Automação* 15(1).

Leite, V. J. S. & Peres, P. L. D. (2003). An improved LMI condition for robust $\mathcal{D}$-stability of uncertain polytopic systems, *IEEE Transactions on Automatic Control* 48(3): 500–504.

Leite, V. S. J., Tarbouriech, S. & Peres, P. L. D. (2009). Robust $\mathcal{H}_\infty$ state feedback control of discrete-time systems with state delay: an LMI approach, *IMA Journal of Mathematical Control and Information* 26: 357–373.

Liu, X. G., Martin, R. R., Wu, M. & Tang, M. L. (2006). Delay-dependent robust stabilisation of discrete-time systems with time-varying delay, *IEE Proceedings — Control Theory and Applications* 153(6): 689–702.

Ma, S., Zhang, C. & Cheng, Z. (2008). Delay-dependent robust $\mathcal{H}_\infty$ control for uncertain discrete-time singular systems with time-delays, *Journal of Computational and Applied Mathematics* 217: 194–211.

Mao, W.-J. & Chu, J. (2009). $\mathcal{D}$-stability and $\mathcal{D}$-stabilization of linear discrete time-delay systems with polytopic uncertainties, *Automatica* 45(3): 842–846.

Montagner, V. F., Leite, V. J. S., Tarbouriech, S. & Peres, P. L. D. (2005). Stability and stabilizability of discrete-time switched linear systems with state delay, *Proceedings of the* 2005 *American Control Conference*, Portland, OR.

Niculescu, S.-I. (2001). *Delay Effects on Stability: A Robust Control Approach*, Vol. 269 of *Lecture Notes in Control and Information Sciences*, Springer-Verlag, London.

Oliveira, R. C. L. F. & Peres, P. L. D. (2005). Stability of polytopes of matrices via affine parameter-dependent Lyapunov functions: Asymptotically exact LMI conditions, *Linear Algebra and Its Applications* 405: 209–228.

Phat, V. N. (2005). Robust stability and stabilizability of uncertain linear hybrid systems with state delays, *IEEE Transactions on Circuits and Systems Part II: Analog and Digital Signal Processing* 52(2): 94–98.

Richard, J.-P. (2003). Time-delay systems: an overview of some recent advances and open problems, *Automatica* 39(10): 1667–1694.

Rodrigues, L. A., Gonçalves, E. N., Leite, V. J. S. & Palhares, R. M. (2009). Robust reference model control with LMI formulation, *Proceedings of the IASTED International Conference on Identification, Control and Applications*, Honolulu, HW, USA.

Shi, P., Boukas, E. K., Shi, Y. & Agarwal, R. K. (2003). Optimal guaranteed cost control of uncertain discrete time-delay systems, *Journal of Computational and Applied Mathematics* 157(2): 435–451.

Silva, L. F. P., Leite, V. J. S., Miranda, M. F. & Nepomuceno, E. G. (2009). Robust $\mathcal{D}$-stabilization with minimization of the $\mathcal{H}_\infty$ guaranteed cost for uncertain discrete-time systems with multiple delays in the state, *Proceedings of the 49th IEEE Conference on Decision and Control*, IEEE, Atlanta, GA, USA. CD ROM.

Srinivasagupta, D., Schättler, H. & Joseph, B. (2004). Time-stamped model predictive previous control: an algorithm for previous control of processes with random delays, *Computers & Chemical Engineering* 28(8): 1337–1346.

Syrmos, C. L., Abdallah, C. T., Dorato, P. & Grigoriadis, K. (1997). Static output feedback — a survey, *Automatica* 33(2): 125–137.

Xu, J. & Yu, L. (2009). Delay-dependent guaranteed cost control for uncertain 2-D discrete systems with state delay in the FM second model, *Journal of The Franklin Institute* 346(2): 159 - 174.
URL: *http://www.sciencedirect.com/science/article/B6V04-4TM9NGD1/2/85 cff1b946 d134a052d36dbe498df5bd*

Xu, S., Lam, J. & Mao, X. (2007). Delay-dependent $\mathcal{H}_\infty$ control and filtering for uncertain markovian jump systems with time-varying delays, *IEEE Transactions on Circuits and Systems Part I: Fundamamental Theory and Applications* 54(9): 2070–2077.

Yu, J., Xie, G. & Wang, L. (2007). Robust stabilization of discrete-time switched uncertain systems subject to actuator saturation, *Proceedings of the* 2007 *American Control Conference*, New York, NY, USA, pp. 2109–2112.

Yu, L. & Gao, F. (2001). Optimal guaranteed cost control of discrete-time uncertain systems with both state and input delays, *Journal of The Franklin Institute* 338(1): 101 - 110.
URL: *http://www.sciencedirect.com/science/article/B6V04-4286KHS -9/2/8197c 8472fdf444d1396b19619d4dcaf*

Zhang, H., Xie, L. & Duan, D. G. (2007). $\mathcal{H}_\infty$ control of discrete-time systems with multiple input delays, *IEEE Transactions on Automatic Control* 52(2): 271–283.

18

Stability Analysis of Grey Discrete Time Time-Delay Systems: A Sufficient Condition

Wen-Jye Shyr[1] and Chao-Hsing Hsu[2]
[1]*Department of Industrial Education and Technology, National Changhua University of Education*
[2]*Department of Computer and Communication Engineering Chienkuo Technology University Changhua 500, Taiwan, R.O.C.*

1. Introduction

Uncertainties in a control system may be the results modeling errors, measurement errors, parameter variations and a linearization approximation. Most physical dynamical systems and industrial process can be described as discrete time uncertain subsystems. Similarly, the unavoidable computation delay may cause a delay time, which can be considered as time-delay in the input part of the original systems. The stability of systems with parameter perturbations must be investigated. The problem of robust stability analysis of a nominally stable system subject to perturbations has attracted wide attention (Mori and Kokame, 1989). Stability analysis attempts to decide whether a system that is pushed slightly from a steady-state will return to that steady state. The robust stability of linear continuous time-delay system has been examined (Su and Hwang, 1992; Liu, 2001). The stability analysis of an interval system is very valuable for the robustness analysis of nominally stable system subject to model perturbations. Therefore, there has been considerable interest in the stability analysis of interval systems (Jiang, 1987; Chou and Chen, 1990; Chen, 1992).

Time-delay is often encountered in various engineering systems, such as the turboject engine, microwave oscillator, nuclear reactor, rolling mill, chemical process, manual control, and long transmission lines in pneumatic and hydraulic systems. It is frequently a source of the generation of oscillation and a source of instability in many control systems. Hence, stability testing for time-delay has received considerable attention (Mori, et al., 1982; Su, et al., 1988; Hmamed, 1991). The time-delay system has been investigated (Mahmoud, et al., 2007; Hassan and Boukas, 2007).

Grey system theory was initiated in the beginning of 1980s (Deng, 1982). Since then the research on theory development and applications is progressing. The state-of-the-art development of grey system theory and its application is addressed (Wevers, 2007). It aims to highlight and analysis the perspective both of grey system theory and of the grey system methods. Grey control problems for the discrete time are also discussed (Zhou and Deng, 1986; Liu and Shyr, 2005). A sufficient condition for the stability of grey discrete time systems with time-delay is proposed in this article. The proposed stability criteria are simple to be checked numerically and generalize the systems with uncertainties for the stability of grey discrete time systems with time-delay. Examples are given to compare the proposed method with reported (Zhou and Deng, 1989; Liu, 2001) in Section 4.

The structure of this paper is as follows. In the next section, a problem formulation of grey discrete time system is briefly reviewed. In Section 3, the robust stability for grey discrete time systems with time-delay is derived based on the results given in Section 2. Three examples are given to illustrate the application of result in Section 4. Finally, Section 5 offers some conclusions.

2. Problem formulation

Considering the stability problem of a grey discrete time system is described using the following equation

$$x(k+1) = A(\otimes)x(k) \tag{1}$$

where $x(k) \in R^n$ represents the state, and $A(\otimes)$ represents the state matrix of system (1). The stability of the system when the elements of $A(\otimes)$ are not known exactly is of major interest. The uncertainty can arise from perturbations in the system parameters because of changes in operating conditions, aging or maintenance-induced errors.

Let $\otimes_{ij}$ $(i, j = 1,2,...,n)$ of $A(\otimes)$ cannot be exactly known, but $\otimes_{ij}$ are confined within the intervals $e_{ij} \le \otimes_{ij} \le f_{ij}$. These e_{ij} and f_{ij} are known exactly, and $\tilde{\otimes}_{ij} \in \left[\underline{\otimes}, \overline{\otimes}\right]$. They are called white numbers, while $\otimes_{ij}$ are called grey numbers. $A(\otimes)$ has a grey matrix, and system (1) is a grey discrete time system.

For convenience of descriptions, the following Definition and Lemmas are introduced.

Definition 2.1

From system (1), the system has

$$A(\otimes) = [\otimes_{ij}]_{n\times n} = \begin{bmatrix} \otimes_{11} & \otimes_{12} & \cdots & \otimes_{1n} \\ \otimes_{21} & \otimes_{22} & \cdots & \otimes_{2n} \\ \vdots & \vdots & & \vdots \\ \otimes_{n1} & \otimes_{n2} & \cdots & \otimes_{nn} \end{bmatrix} \tag{2}$$

$$E = [e_{ij}]_{n\times n} = \begin{bmatrix} e_{11} & e_{12} & \cdots & e_{1n} \\ e_{21} & e_{22} & \cdots & e_{2n} \\ \vdots & \vdots & & \vdots \\ e_{n1} & e_{n2} & \cdots & e_{nn} \end{bmatrix} \tag{3}$$

$$F = [f_{ij}]_{n\times n} = \begin{bmatrix} f_{11} & f_{12} & \cdots & f_{1n} \\ f_{21} & f_{22} & \cdots & f_{2n} \\ \vdots & \vdots & & \vdots \\ f_{n1} & f_{n2} & \cdots & f_{nn} \end{bmatrix} \tag{4}$$

where E and F represent the minimal and maximal punctual matrices of $A(\otimes)$, respectively. Suppose that A represents the average white matrix of $A(\otimes)$ as

$$A = [a_{ij}]_{n\times n} = \left[\frac{e_{ij} + f_{ij}}{2}\right]_{n\times n} = \frac{E+F}{2} \tag{5}$$

and

$$A_G = [a_{gij}]_{n\times n} = [\tilde{\otimes}_{ij} - a_{ij}]_{n\times n} = A(\otimes) - A \tag{6}$$

$$M = [m_{ij}]_{n\times n} = [f_{ij} - a_{ij}]_{n\times n} = F - A \tag{7}$$

where A_G represents a bias matrix between $A(\otimes)$ and A; M represents the maximal bias matrix between F and A. Then we have

$$|A_G|_m \le |M|_m \tag{8}$$

where $|M|_m$ represents the modulus matrix of M; $r[M]$ represents the spectral radius of matrix M; I represents the identity matrix, and $\lambda(M)$ is the eigenvalue of matrix M. This assumption enables some conditions to be derived for the stability of the grey discrete system. Therefore, the following Lemmas are provided.

Lemma 2.1 (Chen, 1984)
The zero state of $x(k+1) = Ax(k)$ is asymptotically stable if and only if

$$|\det(zI - A)| > 0, \quad for \quad |z| \ge 1.$$

Lemma 2.2 (Ortega and Rheinboldt, 1970)
For any $n\times n$ matrices R, T and V, if $|R|_m \le V$, then

a. $r[R] \le r\left[|R|_m\right] \le r[V]$

b. $r[RT] \le r\left[|R|_m |T|_m\right] \le r\left[V|T|_m\right]$

c. $r[R+T] \le r\left[|R+T|_m\right] \le r\left[|R|_m + |T|_m\right] \le r\left[V + |T|_m\right]$.

Lemma 2.3 (Chou, 1991)
If $G(z)$ is a pulse transfer function matrix, then

$$|G(z)|_m \le \sum_{k=0}^{\infty} |G(K)|_m \equiv H(G(K)), \quad for \quad |z| \ge 1,$$

where $G(K)$ is the pulse-response sequence matrix of the multivariable system $G(z)$.

Lemma 2.4 (Chen, 1989)
For an $n\times n$ matrix R, if $r[R] < 1$, then $|\det(I \pm R)| > 0$.

Theorem **2.1**
The grey discrete time systems (1) is asymptotically stable, if $A(\otimes)$ is an asymptotically stable matrix, and if the following inequality is satisfied,

$$r\left[H(G(K))|M|_m\right] < 1 \tag{9}$$

where $H(G(K))$ and $|M|_m$ are defined in Lemma 2.3 and equation (8), and $G(K)$ is the pulse-response sequence matrix of the system

$$G(z) = (zI - A)^{-1}$$

Proof
By the identity

$$\det[RT] = \det[R]\det[T],$$

for any two $n \times n$ matrices R and T, we have

$$|\det[zI - A(\otimes)]| = |\det[zI - (A + A_G)]| = \left|\det[I - (zI - A)^{-1}(A_G)]\right| \left|\det[zI - A]\right| \quad (10)$$

Since A represents an asymptotically stable matrix, then applying Lemma 2.1 clearly shows that

$$|\det[zI - A] > 0|, \text{ for } |z| \geq 1 \quad (11)$$

If inequality (9) is satisfied, then Lemmas 2.2 and 2.3 give

$$\begin{aligned} r[(zI - A)^{-1}(A_G)] &= r[G(z)(A_G)] \leq r[|G(z)|_m |A_G|_m] \\ &\leq r[|G(z)|_m |M|_m] \\ &\leq r[H(G(K))|M|_m] \\ &< 1, \quad for\ |z| \geq 1 \end{aligned} \quad (12)$$

From equations (10)-(12) and Lemma 2.4, we have

$$\begin{aligned} |\det[zI - A(\otimes)]| &= |\det[zI - (A + A_G)]| \\ &= \left|\det[I - (zI - A)^{-1}(A_G)]\right| |\det[zI - A]| > 0, \quad for\ |z| \geq 1. \end{aligned}$$

Hence, the grey discrete time system (1) is asymptotically stable by Lemma 2.1.

3. Grey discrete time systems with time-delay

Considering the grey discrete time system with a time-delay as follows:

$$x(k+1) = A_I(\otimes)x(k) + B_I(\otimes)x(k-1) \quad (13)$$

where $A_I(\otimes)$ and $B_I(\otimes)$ denotes interval matrices with the properties as

$$A_I(\otimes) = [\otimes_{ij}^{a}]_{n\times n} \text{ and } B_I(\otimes) = [\otimes_{ij}^{b}]_{n\times n} \quad (14)$$

where $a_{ij}^1 \leq \otimes_{ij}^a \leq a_{ij}^2$ and $b_{ij}^1 \leq \otimes_{ij}^b \leq b_{ij}^2$.
Indicate

$$A_1 = [a_{ij}^1]_{n\times n},\ A_2 = [a_{ij}^2]_{n\times n},\ B_1 = [b_{ij}^1]_{n\times n},\ B_2 = [b_{ij}^2]_{n\times n}. \quad (15)$$

and let

$$A = [a_{ij}]_{n\times n} = \frac{[a_{ij}^1 + a_{ij}^2]_{n\times n}}{2} = \frac{(A_1 + A_2)}{2} \quad (16a)$$

and

$$B = [b_{ij}]_{n\times n} = \frac{[b_{ij}^1 + b_{ij}^2]_{n\times n}}{2} = \frac{(B_1 + B_2)}{2} \tag{16b}$$

where A and B are the average matrices between A_1 and A_2, B_1 and B_2, respectively. Moreover,

$$\Delta A_m = [a_{ij}^m]_{n\times n} = [\otimes_{ij}^a - a_{ij}]_{n\times n} = A_I(\otimes) - A \tag{17a}$$

and

$$\Delta B_m = [b_{ij}^m]_{n\times n} = [\otimes_{ij}^b - b_{ij}]_{n\times n} = B_I(\otimes) - B \tag{17b}$$

where ΔA_m and ΔB_m are the bias matrices between A_I and A, and B_I and B, respectively. Additionally,

$$M_1 = [m_{ij}^1]_{n\times n} = [a_{ij}^2 - a_{ij}]_{n\times n} = A_2 - A \tag{18a}$$

and

$$N_1 = [n_{ij}^1]_{n\times n} = [b_{ij}^2 - b_{ij}]_{n\times n} = B_2 - B \tag{18b}$$

where M_1 and N_1 are the maximal bias matrices between A_2 and A, and B_2 and B, respectively. Then we have

$$|\Delta A_m|_m \leq |M_1|_m \text{ and } |\Delta B_m|_m \leq |N_1|_m . \tag{19}$$

The following theorem ensures the stability of system (13) for all admissible matrices $A, \Delta A_m, B$ and ΔB_m with constrained (19).

Theorem 3.1

The grey discrete time with a time-delay system (13) is asymptotically stable, if nominal system $A_I(\otimes)$ is an asymptotically stable matrix, and if the following inequality is satisfied,

$$r\left[H(G_d(K))(|M_1|_m + |B|_m + |N_1|_m)\right] < 1 \tag{20}$$

where $H(G_d(K))$ are as defined in Lemma 2.3, and $G_d(K)$ represents the pulse-response sequence matrix of the system

$$G_d(z) = (zI - A)^{-1}$$

Proof

By the identity

$$\det[RT] = \det[R]\det[T],$$

for any two $n\times n$ matrices R and T, we have

$$\begin{aligned} &\left|\det[zI - (A_I(\otimes) + B_I(\otimes)z^{-1})]\right| = \left|\det[zI - (A + \Delta A_m + (B + \Delta B_m)z^{-1})]\right| \\ &= \left|\det[I - (zI - A)^{-1}(\Delta A_m + (B + \Delta B_m)z^{-1})]\right| \left|\det[zI - A]\right| \end{aligned} \tag{21}$$

Since A is an asymptotically stable matrix, then applying Lemma 2.1 clearly shows that

$$\left|\det[zI - A]\right| > 0, \text{ for } |z| \geq 1 \tag{22}$$

If inequality (20) is satisfied, then Lemmas 2.2 and 2.3 give

$$\begin{aligned} r\left[(zI-A)^{-1}\left(\Delta A_m + (B+\Delta B_m)z^{-1}\right)\right] &= r\left[G_d(z)\left(\Delta A_m + (B+\Delta B_m)z^{-1}\right)\right] \\ &\leq r\left[\left|G_d(z)\right|_m\left(\left|\Delta A_m + (B+\Delta B_m)z^{-1}\right|_m\right)\right] \\ &\leq r\left[\left|G_d(z)\right|_m\left(\left|\Delta A_m\right|_m + \left|(B+\Delta B_m)z^{-1}\right|_m\right)\right] \\ &\leq r\left[\left|G_d(z)\right|_m\left(\left|\Delta A_m\right|_m + \left|(B+\Delta B_m)\right|_m\left|z^{-1}\right|_m\right)\right] \\ &\leq r\left[\left|G_d(z)\right|_m\left(\left|\Delta A_m\right|_m + \left|(B+\Delta B_m)\right|_m\right)\right] \\ &\leq r\left[\left|G_d(z)\right|_m\left(\left|\Delta A_m\right|_m + \left|B\right|_m + \left|\Delta B_m\right|_m\right)\right] \\ &\leq r\left[H(G_d(K))\left(\left|M_1\right|_m + \left|B\right|_m + \left|N_1\right|_m\right)\right] \\ &< 1, \; for \; |z| \geq 1 \end{aligned} \tag{23}$$

Equations (21)-(23) and Lemma 2.4 give

$$\begin{aligned} \left|\det[zI - (A_I(\otimes) + B_I(\otimes)z^{-1})]\right| &= \left|\det[zI - (A + \Delta A_m + (B+\Delta B_m)z^{-1})]\right| \\ &= \left|\det[I - (zI-A)^{-1}(\Delta A_m + (B+\Delta B_m)z^{-1})]\right| \left|\det[zI - A]\right| > 0, \; for \; |z| \geq 1 \end{aligned}$$

Therefore, by Lemma 2.1, the grey discrete time with a time-delay system (13) is asymptotically stable.

4. Ilustrative examples

Example 4.1
Consider the stability of grey discrete time system (1) as follows:

$$x(k+1) = A(\otimes)x(k),$$

where

$$A(\otimes) = \begin{bmatrix} \otimes_{11}^a & \otimes_{12}^a \\ \otimes_{21}^a & \otimes_{22}^a \end{bmatrix}$$

with $-0.5 \leq \otimes_{11}^a \leq 0.5,\ 0.1 \leq \otimes_{12}^a \leq 0.8,\ -0.3 \leq \otimes_{21}^a \leq 0.2, -0.4 \leq \otimes_{22}^a \leq 0.5$.

From equations (2)-(5), the average matrices is

$$A = \begin{bmatrix} 0 & 0.15 \\ -0.05 & 0.05 \end{bmatrix},$$

and from equations (6)-(7), the maximal bias matrix M is

$$M=\begin{bmatrix} 0.5 & 0.35 \\ 0.25 & 0.45 \end{bmatrix}.$$

By Lemma 2.3, we obtain

$$H(G(K))=\begin{bmatrix} 1.0241 & 0.4826 \\ 0.0536 & 1.0725 \end{bmatrix}$$

Then, the equation (9) is

$$r\left[H(G(K))|M|_m\right]=0.9843<1.$$

Therefore, the system (1) is asymptotically stable in terms of Theorem 2.1.

Remark 1

Zhou and Deng (1989) have illustrated that the grey discrete time system (1) is asymptotically stable if the following inequality holds:

$$\rho(k)<1 \tag{24}$$

By applying the condition (24) as given by Zhou and Deng, the sufficient condition can be obtained as $\rho(k)=0.9899<1$ to guarantee that the system (1) is still stable.

The proposed sufficient condition (9) of Theorem 2.1 is less conservative than the condition (24) proposed by Zhou and Deng.

Example 4.2

Considering the grey discrete time with a time-delay system (Shyr and Hsu, 2008) is described by (13) as follows:

$$x(k+1)=A_{\mathbf{I}}(\otimes)x(k)+B_{\mathbf{I}}(\otimes)x(k-1)$$

where

$$A_I(\otimes)=\begin{bmatrix} \otimes_{11}^a & \otimes_{12}^a \\ \otimes_{21}^a & \otimes_{22}^a \end{bmatrix},\ B_I(\otimes)=\begin{bmatrix} \otimes_{11}^b & \otimes_{12}^b \\ \otimes_{21}^b & \otimes_{22}^b \end{bmatrix}, \tag{25}$$

with

$$-0.2\le\otimes_{11}^a\le 0.2,\ -0.2\le\otimes_{12}^a\le 0.1,\ -0.1\le\otimes_{21}^a\le 0.1, -0.1\le\otimes_{22}^a\le 0.2$$

and

$$0.1\le\otimes_{11}^b\le 0.2,\ 0.1\le\otimes_{12}^b\le 0.2, 0.1\le\otimes_{21}^b\le 0.15,\ 0.2\le\otimes_{22}^b\le 0.25.$$

Equation (15) and (25) give

$$A_1=\begin{bmatrix} -0.2 & -0.2 \\ -0.1 & -0.1 \end{bmatrix},\ A_2=\begin{bmatrix} 0.2 & 0.1 \\ 0.1 & 0.2 \end{bmatrix},\ B_1=\begin{bmatrix} 0.1 & 0.1 \\ 0.1 & 0.2 \end{bmatrix},\ B_2=\begin{bmatrix} 0.2 & 0.2 \\ 0.15 & 0.25 \end{bmatrix}$$

From equations (16), the average matrices are

$$A=\begin{bmatrix} 0 & -0.05 \\ 0 & 0.05 \end{bmatrix}, \quad B=\begin{bmatrix} 0.15 & 0.15 \\ 0.125 & 0.225 \end{bmatrix},$$

and from equations (18), the maximal bias matrices M_1 and N_1 are

$$M_1=\begin{bmatrix} 0.2 & 0.15 \\ 0.1 & 0.15 \end{bmatrix}, \quad N_1=\begin{bmatrix} 0.05 & 0.05 \\ 0.025 & 0.025 \end{bmatrix}.$$

By Lemma 2.3, we obtain

$$\mathrm{H}(\mathrm{G_d}(\mathrm{K}))=\begin{bmatrix} 0.0526 & 0.0526 \\ 0 & 1.0526 \end{bmatrix}.$$

From Theorem 3.1, the system (13) is stable, because

$$r\left[H(G_d(K))(|M_1|_m+|B|_m+|N_1|_m)\right]=0.4462<1.$$

Example 4.3

Considering the grey discrete time-delay systems (Zhou and Deng, 1989) is described by (13), where

$$A_I(\otimes)=\begin{bmatrix} \otimes_{11}^a & \otimes_{12}^a \\ \otimes_{21}^a & \otimes_{22}^a \end{bmatrix}, \; B_I(\otimes)=\begin{bmatrix} \otimes_{11}^b & \otimes_{12}^b \\ \otimes_{21}^b & \otimes_{22}^b \end{bmatrix},$$

with $-0.24 \le \otimes_{11}^a \le 0.24,\ 0.12 \le \otimes_{12}^a \le 0.24,\ -0.12 \le \otimes_{21}^a \le 0.12,\ 0.12 \le \otimes_{22}^a \le 0.24$ and $0.12 \le \otimes_{11}^b \le 0.24,\ 0.12 \le \otimes_{12}^b \le 0.24,\ 0.12 \le \otimes_{21}^b \le 0.18,\ 0.24 \le \otimes_{22}^b \le 0.30.$

Equation (15) and (25) give

$$A_1=\begin{bmatrix} -0.24 & 0.12 \\ -0.12 & 0.12 \end{bmatrix}, A_2=\begin{bmatrix} 0.24 & 0.24 \\ 0.12 & 0.24 \end{bmatrix}, B_1=\begin{bmatrix} 0.12 & 0.12 \\ 0.12 & 0.24 \end{bmatrix}, B_2=\begin{bmatrix} 0.24 & 0.24 \\ 0.18 & 0.30 \end{bmatrix}.$$

From (16)-(18), we obtain the matrices

$$A=\begin{bmatrix} 0 & 0.18 \\ 0 & 0.18 \end{bmatrix}, \; M_1=\begin{bmatrix} 0.24 & 0.06 \\ 0.12 & 0.06 \end{bmatrix}, \; B=\begin{bmatrix} 0.18 & 0.18 \\ 0.15 & 0.27 \end{bmatrix}, \; N_1=\begin{bmatrix} 0.06 & 0.06 \\ 0.03 & 0.03 \end{bmatrix}$$

By Lemma 2.3, we obtain

$$\mathrm{H}(\mathrm{G_d}(\mathrm{K}))=\begin{bmatrix} 0.5459 & 0.3790 \\ 0.3659 & 0.4390 \end{bmatrix}.$$

From Theorem 3.1, the system (13) is stable, because

$$r\left[H(G_d(K))(|M_1|_m+|B|_m+|N_1|_m)\right]=0.8686<1$$

According to Theorem 3.1, we know that system (13) is asymptotically stable.

Remark 2

If the following condition holds (Liu, 2001)

$$\min\left\{\max_i \sum_{j=1}^{n}\left(e_{ij}+f_{ij}\right),\ \max_i \sum_{j=1}^{n}\left(e_{ji}+f_{ji}\right)\right\}<1 \tag{26}$$

then system (13) is stable $i,j=1,2,\ldots,n$, where

$$E=[e_{ij}],\ e_{ii}=a_{ij}^2,\ e_{ij}=\max\{\left|\otimes_{ij}^{a}\right|,\left|a_{ij}^{2}\right|\} \qquad \text{for } i\neq j$$

and

$$F=[f_{ij}],\ f_{ii}=b_{ij}^2,\ f_{ij}=\max\{\left|\otimes_{ij}^{a}\right|,\left|b_{ij}^{2}\right|\} \qquad \text{for } i\neq j$$

The foregoing criterion is applied in our example and we obtain

$$\min\left\{\max_i \sum_{j=1}^{n}\left(e_{ij}+f_{ij}\right),\ \max_i \sum_{j=1}^{n}\left(e_{ji}+f_{ji}\right)\right\}=1.02>1$$

which cannot be satisfied in (26).

5. Conclusions

This paper proposes a sufficient condition for the stability analysis of grey discrete time systems with time-delay whose state matrices are interval matrices. A novel sufficient condition is obtained to ensure the stability of grey discrete time systems with time-delay. By mathematical analysis, the stability criterion of the proposed is less conservative than those of previous results. In Remark 1, by mathematical analysis, the presented criterion is less conservative than that proposed by Zhou and Deng (1989). In Remarks 2, by mathematical analysis, the presented criterion is to be less conservative than that proposed by Liu (2001). Therefore, the results of this paper indeed provide an additional choice for the stability examination of the grey discrete time time-delay systems. The proposed examples clearly demonstrate that the criteria presented in this paper for the stability of grey discrete time systems with time-delay are useful.

6. References

Chen, C. T. (1984). Linear system theory and design, New York: Pond Woods, Stony Brook.

Chen, J. (1992). Sufficient conditions on stability of interval matrices: connections and new results, IEEE Transactions on Automatic Control, Vol.37, No.4, pp.541-544.

Chen, K. H. (1989). Robust analysis and design of multi-loop control systems, Ph. D. Dissertation National Tsinghua University, Taiwan, R.O.C.

Chou, J. H. (1991). Pole-assignment robustness in a specified disk, Systems Control Letters, Vol.6, pp.41-44.

Chou, J. H. and Chen, B. S. (1990). New approach for the stability analysis of interval matrices, Control Theory and Advanced Technology, Vol.6, No.4, pp.725-730.

Deng, J. L. (1982). Control problem of grey systems, Systems & Control Letters, Vol.1, No.5, pp.288-294.

Hassan, M. F. and Boukas, K. (2007). Multilevel technique for large scale LQR with time-delays and systems constraints, International Journal of Innovative Computing Information and Control, Vol.3, No.2, pp.419-434.

Hmamed, A. (1991). Further results on the stability of uncertain time-delay systems, International Journal of Systems Science, Vol.22, pp.605-614.

Jiang, C. L. (1987). Sufficient condition for the asymptotic stability of interval matrices, International Journal of Control, Vol.46, No.5, pp.1803.

Liu, P. L. (2001). Stability of grey continuous and discrete time-delay systems, International Journal of Systems Science, Vol.32, No.7, pp.947-952.

Liu, P. L. and Shyr, W. J. (2005). Another sufficient condition for the stability of grey discrete-time systems, Journal of the Franklin Institute-Engineering and Applied Mathematics, Vol.342, No.1, pp.15-23.

Lu, M. and Wevers, K. (2007). Grey system theory and applications: A way forward, Journal of Grey System, Vol.10, No.1, pp.47-53.

Mahmoud, M. S., Shi, Y. and Nounou, H. N. (2007). Resilient observer-based control of uncertain time-delay systems, International Journal of Innovative Computing Information and Control, Vol.3, No.2, pp. 407-418.

Mori, T. and Kokame, H. (1989). Stability of $\dot{x}(t) = Ax(t) + Bx(t-\tau)$, IEEE Transactions on Automatic Control, Vol. 34, No.1, pp.460-462.

Mori, T., Fukuma, N. and Kuwahara, M. (1982). Delay-independent stability criteria for discrete-delay systems, IEEE Transactions on Automatic Control, Vol.27, No.4, pp.964-966.

Ortega, J. M. and Rheinboldt, W. C. (1970). Interactive soluation of non-linear equation in several variables, New York : Academic press.

Shyr W. J. and Hsu, C. H. (2008). A sufficient condition for stability analysis of grey discrete-time systems with time delay, International Journal of Innovative Computing Information and Control, Vol.4, No.9, pp.2139-2145.

Su, T. J. and Hwang, C. G. (1992). Robust stability of delay dependence for linear uncertain systems, IEEE Transactions on Automatic Control, Vol.37, No.10, pp.1656-1659.

Su, T. J., Kuo, T. S. and Sun, Y. Y. (1988). Robust stability for linear time-delay systems with linear parameter perturbations, International Journal of Systems Science, Vol.19, pp.2123-2129.

Zhou, C. S. and Deng, J. L. (1986). The stability of the grey linear system, International Journal of Control, Vol. 43, pp.313-320.

Zhou, C. S. and Deng, J. L. (1989). Stability analysis of grey discrete-time systems, IEEE Transactions on Automatic Control, Vol.34, No.2, pp.173-175.

19

Stability and $\mathcal{L}_2$ Gain Analysis of Switched Linear Discrete-Time Descriptor Systems

Guisheng Zhai

Department of Mathematical Sciences, Shibaura Institute of Technology, Saitama 337-8570 Japan

1. Introduction

This article is focused on analyzing stability and $\mathcal{L}_2$ gain properties for switched systems composed of a family of linear discrete-time descriptor subsystems. Concerning descriptor systems, they are also known as singular systems or implicit systems and have high abilities in representing dynamical systems [1, 2]. Since they can preserve physical parameters in the coefficient matrices, and describe the dynamic part, static part, and even improper part of the system in the same form, descriptor systems are much superior to systems represented by state space models. There have been many works on descriptor systems, which studied feedback stabilization [1, 2], Lyapunov stability theory [2, 3], the matrix inequality approach for stabilization, $\mathcal{H}_2$ and/or $\mathcal{H}_\infty$ control [4–6].

On the other hand, there has been increasing interest recently in stability analysis and design for switched systems; see the survey papers [7, 8], the recent books [9, 10] and the references cited therein. One motivation for studying switched systems is that many practical systems are inherently multi-modal in the sense that several dynamical subsystems are required to describe their behavior which may depend on various environmental factors. Another important motivation is that switching among a set of controllers for a specified system can be regarded as a switched system, and that switching has been used in adaptive control to assure stability in situations where stability can not be proved otherwise, or to improve transient response of adaptive control systems. Also, the methods of intelligent control design are based on the idea of switching among different controllers.

We observe from the above that switched descriptor systems belong to an important class of systems that are interesting in both theoretic and practical sense. However, to the authors' best knowledge, there has not been much works dealing with such systems. The difficulty falls into two aspects. First, descriptor systems are not easy to tackle and there are not rich results available up to now. Secondly, switching between several descriptor systems makes the problem more complicated and even not easy to make clear the well-posedness of the solutions in some cases.

Next, let us review the classification of problems in switched systems. It is commonly recognized [9] that there are three basic problems in stability analysis and design of switched systems: (i) find conditions for stability under arbitrary switching; (ii) identify the limited but useful class of stabilizing switching laws; and (iii) construct a stabilizing switching law.

Specifically, Problem (i) deals with the case that all subsystems are stable. This problem seems trivial, but it is important since we can find many examples where all subsystems are stable but improper switchings can make the whole system unstable [11]. Furthermore, if we know that a switched system is stable under arbitrary switching, then we can consider higher control specifications for the system. There have been several works for Problem (i) with state space systems. For example, Ref. [12] showed that when all subsystems are stable and commutative pairwise, the switched linear system is stable under arbitrary switching. Ref. [13] extended this result from the commutation condition to a Lie-algebraic condition. Ref. [14, 15] and [16] extended the consideration to the case of $\mathcal{L}_2$ gain analysis and the case where both continuous-time and discrete-time subsystems exist, respectively. In the previous papers [17, 18], we extended the existing result of [12] to switched linear descriptor systems. In that context, we showed that in the case where all descriptor subsystems are stable, if the descriptor matrix and all subsystem matrices are commutative pairwise, then the switched system is stable under impulse-free arbitrary switching. However, since the commutation condition is quite restrictive in real systems, alternative conditions are desired for stability of switched descriptor systems under impulse-free arbitrary switching.

In this article, we propose a unified approach for both stability and $\mathcal{L}_2$ gain analysis of switched linear descriptor systems in discrete-time domain. Since the existing results for stability of switched state space systems suggest that the common Lyapunov functions condition should be less conservative than the commutation condition, we establish our approach based on common quadratic Lyapunov functions incorporated with linear matrix inequalities (LMIs). We show that if there is a common quadratic Lyapunov function for stability of all descriptor subsystems, then the switched system is stable under impulse-free arbitrary switching. This is a reasonable extension of the results in [17, 18], in the sense that if all descriptor subsystems are stable, and furthermore the descriptor matrix and all subsystem matrices are commutative pairwise, then there exists a common quadratic Lyapunov function for all subsystems, and thus the switched system is stable under impulse-free arbitrary switching. Furthermore, we show that if there is a common quadratic Lyapunov function for stability and certain $\mathcal{L}_2$ gain of all descriptor subsystems, then the switched system is stable and has the same $\mathcal{L}_2$ gain under impulse-free arbitrary switching. Since the results are consistent with those for switched state space systems when the descriptor matrix shrinks to an identity matrix, the results are natural but important extensions of the existing results.

The rest of this article is organized as follows. Section 2 gives some preliminaries on discrete-time descriptor systems, and then Section 3 formulates the problem under consideration. Section 4 states and proves the stability condition for the switched linear discrete-time descriptor systems under impulse-free arbitrary switching. The condition requires in fact a common quadratic Lyapunov function for stability of all the subsystems, and includes the existing commutation condition [17, 18] as a special case. Section 5 extends the results to $\mathcal{L}_2$ gain analysis of the switched system under impulse-free arbitrary switching, and the condition to achieve the same stability and $\mathcal{L}_2$ gain properties requires a common quadratic Lyapunov function for all the subsystems. Finally, Section 6 concludes the article.

2. Preliminaries

Let us first give some preliminaries on linear discrete-time descriptor systems. Consider the descriptor system

$$\begin{cases} Ex(k+1) = Ax(k) + Bw(k) \\ z(k) = Cx(k), \end{cases} \tag{2.1}$$

where the nonnegative integer k denotes the discrete time, $x(k) \in \mathcal{R}^n$ is the descriptor variable, $w(k) \in \mathcal{R}^p$ is the disturbance input, $z(k) \in \mathcal{R}^q$ is the controlled output, $E \in \mathcal{R}^{n\times n}$, $A \in \mathcal{R}^{n\times n}$, $B \in \mathcal{R}^{n\times p}$ and $C \in \mathcal{R}^{q\times n}$ are constant matrices. The matrix E may be singular and we denote its rank by $r = \text{rank}\, E \leq n$.

Definition 1: Consider the linear descriptor system (2.1) with $w = 0$. The system has a unique solution for any initial condition and is called *regular*, if $|zE - A| \not\equiv 0$. The finite eigenvalues of the matrix pair (E, A), that is, the solutions of $|zE - A| = 0$, and the corresponding (generalized) eigenvectors define exponential modes of the system. If the finite eigenvalues lie in the open unit disc of z, the solution *decays exponentially*. The infinite eigenvalues of (E, A) with the eigenvectors satisfying the relations $Ex_1 = 0$ determine static modes. The infinite eigenvalues of (E, A) with generalized eigenvectors x_k satisfying the relations $Ex_1 = 0$ and $Ex_k = x_{k-1}$ $(k \geq 2)$ create *impulsive modes*. The system has no impulsive mode if and only if rank E = deg $|sE - A|$ (deg $|zE - A|$). The system is said to be *stable* if it is regular and has only decaying exponential modes and static modes (without impulsive modes). ∎

Lemma 1 (Weiertrass Form)[1, 2] If the descriptor system (2.1) is regular, then there exist two nonsingular matrices M and N such that

$$MEN = \begin{bmatrix} I_d & 0 \\ 0 & J \end{bmatrix}, \quad MAN = \begin{bmatrix} \Lambda & 0 \\ 0 & I_{n-d} \end{bmatrix} \tag{2.2}$$

where d = deg $|zE - A|$, J is composed of Jordan blocks for the finite eigenvalues. If the system (2.1) is regular and there is no impulsive mode, then (2.2) holds with $d = r$ and $J = 0$. If the system (2.1) is stable, then (2.2) holds with $d = r$, $J = 0$ and furthermore Λ is Schur stable. ∎

Let the singular value decomposition (SVD) of E be

$$E = U \begin{bmatrix} E_{11} & 0 \\ 0 & 0 \end{bmatrix} V^T, \quad E_{11} = \text{diag}\{\sigma_1, \cdots, \sigma_r\} \tag{2.3}$$

where σ_i's are the singular values, U and V are orthonormal matrices ($U^T U = V^T V = I$). With the definitions

$$\bar{x} = V^T x \triangleq \begin{bmatrix} \bar{x}_1 \\ \bar{x}_2 \end{bmatrix}, \quad U^T AV = \begin{bmatrix} A_{11} & A_{12} \\ A_{21} & A_{22} \end{bmatrix}, \tag{2.4}$$

the difference equation in (2.1) (with $w = 0$) takes the form of

$$\begin{aligned} E_{11}\bar{x}_1(k+1) &= A_{11}\bar{x}_1(k) + A_{12}\bar{x}_2(k) \\ 0 &= A_{21}\bar{x}_1(k) + A_{22}\bar{x}_2(k). \end{aligned} \tag{2.5}$$

It is easy to obtain from the above that the descriptor system is regular and has not impulsive modes if and only if A_{22} is nonsingular. Moreover, the system is stable if and only if A_{22} is nonsingular and furthermore $E_{11}^{-1}\left(A_{11} - A_{12}A_{22}^{-1}A_{21}\right)$ is Schur stable. This discussion will be used again in the next sections.

Definition 2: Given a positive scalar γ, if the linear descriptor system (2.1) is stable and satisfies

$$\sum_{j=0}^{k} z^T(j)z(j) \leq \phi(x(0)) + \gamma^2 \sum_{j=0}^{k} w^T(j)w(j) \tag{2.6}$$

for any integer $k > 0$ and any l_2-bounded disturbance input w, with some nonnegative definite function $\phi(\cdot)$, then the descriptor system is said to be stable and have $\mathcal{L}_2$ gain less than γ. ▮

The above definition is a general one for nonlinear systems, and will be used later for switched descriptor systems.

3. Problem formulation

In this article, we consider the switched system composed of $\mathcal{N}$ linear discrete-time descriptor subsystems described by

$$\begin{cases} Ex(k+1) = A_i x(k) + B_i w(k) \\ \quad\;\; z(k) = C_i x(k)\,, \end{cases} \tag{3.1}$$

where the vectors x, w, z and the descriptor matrix E are the same as in (2.1), the index i denotes the i-th subsystem and takes value in the discrete set $\mathcal{I} = \{1, 2, \cdots, \mathcal{N}\}$, and thus the matrices A_i, B_i, C_i together with E represent the dynamics of the i-th subsystem.

For the above switched system, we consider the stability and $\mathcal{L}_2$ gain properties under the assumption that all subsystems in (3.1) are stable and have $\mathcal{L}_2$ gain less than γ. As in the case of stability analysis for switched linear systems in state space representation, such an analysis problem is well posed (or practical) since a switched descriptor system can be unstable even if all the descriptor subsystems are stable and there is no variable (state) jump at the switching instants. Additionally, switchings between two subsystems can even result in impulse signals, even if the subsystems do not have impulsive modes themselves. This happens when the variable vector $x(k_r)$, where k_r is a switching instant, does not satisfy the algebraic equation required in the subsequent subsystem. In order to exclude this possibility, Ref. [19] proposed an additional condition involving consistency projectors. Here, as in most of the literature, we assume for simplicity that there is no impulse occurring with the variable (state) vector at every switching instant, and call such kind of switching *impulse-free*.

Definition 3: Given a switching sequence, the switched system (3.1) with $w = 0$ is said to be *stable* if starting from any initial value the system's trajectories converge to the origin exponentially, and the switched system is said to have $\mathcal{L}_2$ gain less than γ if the condition (2.6) is satisfied for any integer $k > 0$. ▮

In the end of this section, we state two analysis problems, which will be dealt with in Section 4 and 5, respectively.

Stability Analysis Problem: Assume that all the descriptor subsystems in (3.1) are stable. Establish the condition under which the switched system is stable under impulse-free arbitrary switching.

$\mathcal{L}_2$ Gain Analysis Problem: Assume that all the descriptor subsystems in (3.1) are stable and have $\mathcal{L}_2$ gain less than γ. Establish the condition under which the switched system is also stable and has $\mathcal{L}_2$ gain less than γ under impulse-free arbitrary switching.

Remark 1: There is a tacit assumption in the switched system (3.1) that the descriptor matrix E is the same in all the subsystems. Theoretically, this assumption is restrictive at present. However, as also discussed in [17, 18], the above problem settings and the results later can be applied to switching control problems for linear descriptor systems. This is the main motivation that we consider the same descriptor matrix E in the switched system. For example, if for a single descriptor system $Ex(k+1) = Ax(k) + Bu(k)$ where $u(k)$ is the control input, we have designed two stabilizing descriptor variable feedbacks $u = K_1x$, $u = K_2x$, and furthermore the switched system composed of the descriptor subsystems characterized by $(E, A + BK_1)$ and $(E, A + BK_2)$ are stable (and have $\mathcal{L}_2$ gain less than γ) under impulse-free arbitrary switching, then we can switch arbitrarily between the two controllers and thus can consider higher control specifications. This kind of requirement is very important when we want more flexibility for multiple control specifications in real applications. ∎

4. Stability analysis

In this section, we first state and prove the common quadratic Lyapunov function (CQLF) based stability condition for the switched descriptor system (3.1) (with $w = 0$), and then discuss the relation with the existing commutation condition.

4.1 CQLF based stability condition

Theorem 1: The switched system (3.1) (with $w = 0$) is stable under impulse-free arbitrary switching if there are nonsingular symmetric matrices $P_i \in \mathcal{R}^{n\times n}$ satisfying for $\forall i \in \mathcal{I}$ that

$$E^T P_i E \geq 0 \tag{4.1}$$

$$A_i^T P_i A_i - E^T P_i E < 0 \tag{4.2}$$

and furthermore

$$E^T P_i E = E^T P_j E\,,\ \forall i,j \in \mathcal{I},\ i \neq j\,. \tag{4.3}$$

Proof: The necessary condition for stability under arbitrary switching is that each subsystem should be stable. This is guaranteed by the two matrix inequalities (4.1) and (4.2) [20].
Since the rank of E is r, we first find nonsingular matrices M and N such that

$$MEN = \begin{bmatrix} I_r & 0 \\ 0 & 0 \end{bmatrix}. \tag{4.4}$$

Then, we obtain from (4.1) that

$$(N^T E^T M^T)(M^{-T} P_i M^{-1})(MEN) = \begin{bmatrix} P_{11}^i & 0 \\ 0 & 0 \end{bmatrix} \geq 0\,, \tag{4.5}$$

where

$$M^{-T} P_i M^{-1} \triangleq \begin{bmatrix} P_{11}^i & P_{12}^i \\ (P_{12}^i)^T & P_{22}^i \end{bmatrix}. \tag{4.6}$$

Since P_i (and thus $M^{-T} P_i M^{-1}$) is symmetric and nonsingular, we obtain $P_{11}^i > 0$.

Again, we obtain from (4.3) that

$$(N^T E^T M^T)(M^{-T} P_i M^{-1})(MEN) = (N^T E^T M^T)(M^{-T} P_j M^{-1})(MEN), \tag{4.7}$$

and thus

$$\begin{bmatrix} P_{11}^i & 0 \\ 0 & 0 \end{bmatrix} = \begin{bmatrix} P_{11}^j & 0 \\ 0 & 0 \end{bmatrix} \tag{4.8}$$

which leads to $P_{11}^i = P_{11}^j$, $\forall i, j \in \mathcal{I}$. From now on, we let $P_{11}^i = P_{11}$ for notation simplicity. Next, let

$$MA_i N = \begin{bmatrix} \bar{A}_{11}^i & \bar{A}_{12}^i \\ \bar{A}_{21}^i & \bar{A}_{22}^i \end{bmatrix} \tag{4.9}$$

and substitute it into the equivalent inequality of (4.2) as

$$(N^T A_i^T M^T)(M^{-T} P_i M^{-1})(MA_i N) - (N^T E^T M^T)(M^{-T} P_i M^{-1})(MEN) < 0 \tag{4.10}$$

to reach

$$\begin{bmatrix} \Lambda_{11} & \Lambda_{12} \\ \Lambda_{12}^T & \Lambda_{22} \end{bmatrix} < 0, \tag{4.11}$$

where

$$\begin{aligned} \Lambda_{11} &= (\bar{A}_{11}^i)^T P_{11} \bar{A}_{11}^i - P_{11} + (\bar{A}_{21}^i)^T (P_{12}^i)^T \bar{A}_{11}^i + (\bar{A}_{11}^i)^T P_{12}^i \bar{A}_{21}^i + (\bar{A}_{21}^i)^T P_{22}^i \bar{A}_{21}^i \\ \Lambda_{12} &= (\bar{A}_{11}^i)^T P_{11} \bar{A}_{12}^i + (\bar{A}_{11}^i)^T P_{12}^i \bar{A}_{22}^i + (\bar{A}_{21}^i)^T (P_{12}^i)^T \bar{A}_{12}^i + (\bar{A}_{21}^i)^T P_{22}^i \bar{A}_{22}^i \\ \Lambda_{22} &= (\bar{A}_{12}^i)^T P_{11} \bar{A}_{12}^i + (\bar{A}_{22}^i)^T (P_{12}^i)^T \bar{A}_{12}^i + (\bar{A}_{12}^i)^T P_{12}^i \bar{A}_{22}^i + (\bar{A}_{22}^i)^T P_{22}^i \bar{A}_{22}^i . \end{aligned} \tag{4.12}$$

At this point, we declare $\bar{A}_{22}^i$ is nonsingular from $\Lambda_{22} < 0$. Otherwise, there is a nonzero vector v such that $\bar{A}_{22}^i v = 0$. Then, $v^T \Lambda_{22} v < 0$. However, by simple calculation,

$$v^T \Lambda_{22} v = v^T (\bar{A}_{12}^i)^T P_{11} \bar{A}_{12}^i v \geq 0 \tag{4.13}$$

since P_{11} is positive definite. This results in a contradiction.

Multiplying the left side of (4.11) by the nonsingular matrix $\begin{bmatrix} I & -(\bar{A}_{21}^i)^T (\bar{A}_{22}^i)^{-T} \\ 0 & I \end{bmatrix}$ and the right side by its transpose, we obtain

$$\begin{bmatrix} (\tilde{A}_{11}^i)^T P_{11} \tilde{A}_{11}^i - P_{11} & * \\ (*)^T & \Lambda_{22} \end{bmatrix} < 0, \tag{4.14}$$

where $\tilde{A}_{11}^i = \bar{A}_{11}^i - \bar{A}_{12}^i (\bar{A}_{22}^i)^{-1} \bar{A}_{21}^i$.
With the same nonsingular transformation $\bar{x}(k) = N^{-1} x(k) = [\bar{x}_1^T(k) \;\; \bar{x}_2^T(k)]^T$, $\bar{x}_1(k) \in \mathcal{R}^r$, all the descriptor subsystems in (3.1) take the form of

$$\begin{aligned} \bar{x}_1(k+1) &= \bar{A}_{11}^i \bar{x}_1(k) + \bar{A}_{12}^i \bar{x}_2(k) \\ 0 &= \bar{A}_{21}^i \bar{x}_1(k) + \bar{A}_{22}^i \bar{x}_2(k), \end{aligned} \tag{4.15}$$

which is equivalent to

$$\bar{x}_1(k+1) = \tilde{A}_{11}^i \bar{x}_1(k) \tag{4.16}$$

with $\bar{x}_2(k) = -(\bar{A}_{22}^i)^{-1}\bar{A}_{21}^i\bar{x}_1(k)$. It is seen from (4.14) that

$$(\tilde{A}_{11}^i)^T P_{11} \tilde{A}_{11}^i - P_{11} < 0\,, \tag{4.17}$$

which means that all $\tilde{A}_{11}^i$'s are Schur stable, and a common positive definite matrix P_{11} exists for stability of all the subsystems in (4.16). Therefore, $\bar{x}_1(k)$ converges to zero exponentially under impulse-free arbitrary switching. The $\bar{x}_2(k)$ part is dominated by $\bar{x}_1(k)$ and thus also converges to zero exponentially. This completes the proof. ∎

Remark 2: When $E = I$ and all the subsystems are Schur stable, the condition of Theorem 1 actually requires a common positive definite matrix P satisfying $A_i^T P A_i - P < 0$ for $\forall i \in \mathcal{I}$, which is exactly the existing stability condition for switched linear systems composed of $x(k+1) = A_i x(k)$ under arbitrary switching [12]. Thus, Theorem 1 is an extension of the existing result for switched linear state space subsystems in discrete-time domain. ∎

Remark 3: It can be seen from the proof of Theorem 1 that $\bar{x}_1^T P_{11} \bar{x}_1$ is a common quadratic Lyapunov function for all the subsystems (4.16). Since the exponential convergence of $\bar{x}_1$ results in that of $\bar{x}_2$, we can regard $\bar{x}_1^T P_{11} \bar{x}_1$ as a common quadratic Lyapunov function for the whole switched system. In fact, this is rationalized by the following equation.

$$\begin{aligned} x^T E^T P_i E x &= (N^{-1}x)^T (MEN)^T (M^{-T} P_i M^{-1})(MEN)(N^{-1}x) \\ &= \begin{bmatrix} \bar{x}_1 \\ \bar{x}_2 \end{bmatrix}^T \begin{bmatrix} I_r & 0 \\ 0 & 0 \end{bmatrix} \begin{bmatrix} P_{11} & P_{12}^i \\ (P_{12}^i)^T & P_{22}^i \end{bmatrix} \begin{bmatrix} I_r & 0 \\ 0 & 0 \end{bmatrix} \begin{bmatrix} \bar{x}_1 \\ \bar{x}_2 \end{bmatrix} \\ &= \bar{x}_1^T P_{11} \bar{x}_1 \end{aligned} \tag{4.18}$$

Therefore, although $E^T P_i E$ is not positive definite and neither is $V(x) = x^T E^T P_i E x$, we can regard this $V(x)$ as a common quadratic Lyapunov function for all the descriptor subsystems in discrete-time domain. ∎

Remark 4: The LMI conditions (4.1)-(4.3) include a nonstrict matrix inequality, which may not be easy to solve using the existing LMI Control Toolbox in Matlab. As a matter of fact, the proof of Theorem 1 suggested an alternative method for solving it in the framework of strict LMIs: (a) decompose E as in (4.4) using nonsingular matrices M and N; (b) compute MA_iN for $\forall i \in \mathcal{I}$ as in (4.9); (c) solve the strict LMIs (4.11) for $\forall i \in \mathcal{I}$ simultaneously with respect to $P_{11} > 0$, P_{12}^i and P_{22}^i; (d) compute the original P_i with $P_i = M^T \begin{bmatrix} P_{11} & P_{12}^i \\ (P_{12}^i)^T & P_{22}^i \end{bmatrix} M$. ∎

Although we assumed in the above that the descriptor matrix is the same for all the subsystems (as mentioned in Remark 1), it can be seen from the proof of Theorem 1 that what we really need is the equation (4.4). Therefore, Theorem 1 can be extended to the case where the subsystem descriptor matrices are different as in the following corollary.

Corollary 1: Consider the switched system composed of $\mathcal{N}$ linear descriptor subsystems

$$E_i x(k+1) = A_i x(k)\,, \tag{4.19}$$

where E_i is the descriptor matrix of the ith subsystem and all the other notations are the same as before. Assume that all the descriptor matrices have the same rank r and there are common nonsingular matrices M and N such that

$$ME_iN = \begin{bmatrix} I_r & 0 \\ 0 & 0 \end{bmatrix}, \quad \forall i \in \mathcal{I}. \tag{4.20}$$

Then, the switched system (4.19) is stable under impulse-free arbitrary switching if there are symmetric nonsingular matrices $P_i \in \mathcal{R}^{n\times n}$ $(i = 1, \cdots, \mathcal{N})$ satisfying for $\forall i \in \mathcal{I}$

$$E_i^T P_i E_i \geq 0, \quad A_i^T P_i A_i - E_i^T P_i E_i < 0 \tag{4.21}$$

and furthermore

$$E_i^T P_i E_i = E_j^T P_j E_j, \quad \forall i, j \in \mathcal{I}, \ i \neq j. \tag{4.22}$$

∎

4.2 Relation with existing commutation condition

In this subsection, we consider the relation of Theorem 1 with the existing commutation condition proposed in [17].

Lemma 2:([17]) If all the descriptor subsystems are stable, and furthermore the matrices E, $A_1, \cdots, A_{\mathcal{N}}$ are commutative pairwise, then the switched system is stable under impulse-free arbitrary switching. ∎

The above lemma establishes another sufficient condition for stability of switched linear descriptor systems in the name of pairwise commutation. It is well known [12] that in the case of switched linear systems composed of the state space subsystems

$$x(k+1) = A_i x(k), \quad i \in \mathcal{I}, \tag{4.23}$$

where all subsystems are Schur stable and the subsystem matrices commute pairwise ($A_iA_j = A_jA_i$, $\forall i, j \in \mathcal{I}$), there exists a common positive definite matrix P satisfying

$$A_i^T P A_i - P < 0. \tag{4.24}$$

One then tends to expect that if the commutation condition of Lemma 2 holds, then a common quadratic Lyapunov function $V(x) = x^T E^T P_i E x$ should exist satisfying the condition of Theorem 1. This is exactly established in the following theorem.

Theorem 2: If all the descriptor subsystems in (3.1) are stable, and furthermore the matrices $E, A_1, \cdots, A_{\mathcal{N}}$ are commutative pairwise, then there are nonsingular symmetric matrices P_i's $(i = 1, \cdots, \mathcal{N})$ satisfying (4.1)-(4.3), and thus the switched system is stable under impulse-free arbitrary switching.

Proof: For notation simplicity, we only prove the case of $\mathcal{N} = 2$. Since (E, A_1) is stable, according to Lemma 1, there exist two nonsingular matrices M, N such that

$$MEN = \begin{bmatrix} I_r & 0 \\ 0 & 0 \end{bmatrix}, \quad MA_1N = \begin{bmatrix} \Lambda_1 & 0 \\ 0 & I_{n-r} \end{bmatrix} \tag{4.25}$$

where Λ_1 is a Schur stable matrix. Here, without causing confusion, we use the same notations M, N as before. Defining

$$N^{-1}M^{-1} = \begin{bmatrix} W_1 & W_2 \\ W_3 & W_4 \end{bmatrix} \tag{4.26}$$

and substituting it into the commutation condition $EA_1 = A_1E$ with

$$(MEN)(N^{-1}M^{-1})(MA_1N) = (MA_1N)(N^{-1}M^{-1})(MEN), \tag{4.27}$$

we obtain

$$\begin{bmatrix} W_1\Lambda_1 & W_2 \\ 0 & 0 \end{bmatrix} = \begin{bmatrix} \Lambda_1 W_1 & 0 \\ W_3 & 0 \end{bmatrix}. \tag{4.28}$$

Thus, $W_1\Lambda_1 = \Lambda_1 W_1$, $W_2 = 0$, $W_3 = 0$.
Now, we use the same nonsingular matrices M, N for the transformation of A_2 and write

$$MA_2N = \begin{bmatrix} \Lambda_2 & X_1 \\ X_2 & X \end{bmatrix}. \tag{4.29}$$

According to another commutation condition $EA_2 = A_2E$,

$$\begin{bmatrix} W_1\Lambda_2 & W_1X_1 \\ 0 & 0 \end{bmatrix} = \begin{bmatrix} \Lambda_2 W_1 & 0 \\ X_2W_1 & 0 \end{bmatrix} \tag{4.30}$$

holds, and thus $W_1\Lambda_2 = \Lambda_2 W_1$, $W_1X_1 = 0$, $X_2W_1 = 0$. Since NM is nonsingular and $W_2 = 0$, $W_3 = 0$, W_1 has to be nonsingular. We obtain then $X_1 = 0, X_2 = 0$. Furthermore, since (E, A_2) is stable, Λ_2 is Schur stable and X has to be nonsingular.
The third commutation condition $A_1A_2 = A_2A_1$ results in

$$\begin{bmatrix} \Lambda_1 W_1 \Lambda_2 & 0 \\ 0 & W_4X \end{bmatrix} = \begin{bmatrix} \Lambda_2 W_1 \Lambda_1 & 0 \\ 0 & XW_4 \end{bmatrix}. \tag{4.31}$$

We have $\Lambda_1 W_1 \Lambda_2 = \Lambda_2 W_1 \Lambda_1$. Combining with $W_1\Lambda_1 = \Lambda_1 W_1$, $W_1\Lambda_2 = \Lambda_2 W_1$, we obtain that

$$W_1\Lambda_1\Lambda_2 = \Lambda_1 W_1 \Lambda_2 = \Lambda_2 W_1 \Lambda_1 = W_1\Lambda_2\Lambda_1 \tag{4.32}$$

which implies Λ_1 and Λ_2 are commutative ($\Lambda_1\Lambda_2 = \Lambda_2\Lambda_1$) since W_1 is nonsingular.
To summarize the above discussion, we get to

$$MA_2N = \begin{bmatrix} \Lambda_2 & 0 \\ 0 & X \end{bmatrix}, \tag{4.33}$$

where Λ_2 is Schur stable, X is nonsingular, and $\Lambda_1\Lambda_2 = \Lambda_2\Lambda_1$. According to the existing result [12], there is a common positive definite matrix P_{11} satisfying $\Lambda_i^T P_{11}\Lambda_i - P_{11} < 0$, $i = 1, 2$. Then, with the definition

$$P_1 = P_2 = M^T \begin{bmatrix} P_{11} & 0 \\ 0 & -I \end{bmatrix} M, \tag{4.34}$$

it is easy to confirm that

$$(MEN)^T(M^{-T}P_iM^{-1})(MEN) = \begin{bmatrix} P_{11} & 0 \\ 0 & 0 \end{bmatrix} \geq 0 \tag{4.35}$$

and

$$\begin{aligned} &(MA_1N)^T(M^{-T}P_1M^{-1})(MA_1N) - (MEN)^T(M^{-T}P_1M^{-1})(MEN) \\ &\quad = \begin{bmatrix} \Lambda_1^T P_{11}\Lambda_1 - P_{11} & 0 \\ 0 & -I \end{bmatrix} < 0, \\ &(MA_2N)^T(M^{-T}P_2M^{-1})(MA_2N) - (MEN)^T(M^{-T}P_2M^{-1})(MEN) \\ &\quad = \begin{bmatrix} \Lambda_2^T P_{11}\Lambda_2 - P_{11} & 0 \\ 0 & -X^TX \end{bmatrix} < 0. \end{aligned} \tag{4.36}$$

Since P_{11} is common for $i = 1, 2$ and N is nonsingular, (4.35) and (4.36) imply that the matrices in (4.34) satisfy the conditions (4.1)-(4.3). ∎

It is observed from (4.34) that when the conditions of Theorem 2 hold, we can further choose $P_1 = P_2$, which certainly satisfies (4.3). Since the actual Lyapunov function for the stable descriptor system $Ex[k+1] = A_ix[k]$ takes the form of $V(x) = x^TE^TP_iEx$ (as mentioned in Remark 3), the commutation condition is more conservative than the LMI condition in Theorem 1. However, we state for integrity the above observation as a corollary of Theorem 2.

Corollary 2: If all the descriptor subsystems in (3.1) are stable, and furthermore the matrices E, A_1, $\cdots$, $A_{\mathcal{N}}$ are commutative pairwise, then there is a nonsingular symmetric matrix P satisfying

$$E^TPE \geq 0 \tag{4.37}$$

$$A_i^TPA_i - E^TPE < 0, \tag{4.38}$$

and thus the switched system is stable under impulse-free arbitrary switching. ∎

5. $\mathcal{L}_2$ gain analysis

In this section, we extend the discussion of stability to $\mathcal{L}_2$ gain analysis fro the switched linear descriptor system under consideration.

Theorem 3: The switched system (3.1) is stable and the $\mathcal{L}_2$ gain is less than γ under impulse-free arbitrary switching if there are nonsingular symmetric matrices $P_i \in \mathcal{R}^{n\times n}$ satisfying for $\forall i \in \mathcal{I}$ that

$$E^TP_iE \geq 0 \tag{5.1}$$

$$\begin{bmatrix} A_i^TP_iA_i - E^TP_iE + C_i^TC_i & A_i^TP_iB_i \\ B_i^TP_iA_i & B_i^TP_iB_i - \gamma^2 I \end{bmatrix} < 0 \tag{5.2}$$

together with (4.3).

Proof: Since (5.1) is the same as (4.1) and (5.2) includes (4.2), we conclude from Theorem 1 that the switched descriptor system is exponentially stable under impulse-free arbitrary switching. What remains is to prove the $\mathcal{L}_2$ gain property.

Consider the Lyapunov function candidate $V(x) = x^T E^T P_i E x$, which is always nonnegative due to (5.1) and always continuous due to (4.3). Then, on any discrete-time interval where the i-th subsystem is activated, the difference of $V(x)$ along the system's trajectories satisfies

$$\begin{aligned} V(x(k+1)) - V(x(k)) &= x^T(k+1)E^T P_i E x(k+1) - x^T(k)E^T P_i E x(k) \\ &= (Ex(k+1))^T P_i (Ex(k+1)) - x^T(k)E^T P_i^T E x(k) \\ &= (A_i x(k) + B_i w(k))^T P_i (A_i x(k) + B_i w(k)) - x^T(k) E^T P_i^T E x(k) \\ &= \begin{bmatrix} x(k) \\ w(k) \end{bmatrix}^T \begin{bmatrix} A_i^T P_i A_i - E^T P_i E & A_i^T P_i B_i \\ B_i^T P_i A_i & B_i^T P_i B_i \end{bmatrix} \begin{bmatrix} x(k) \\ w(k) \end{bmatrix} \\ &\le \begin{bmatrix} x(k) \\ w(k) \end{bmatrix}^T \begin{bmatrix} -C_i^T C_i & 0 \\ 0 & \gamma^2 I \end{bmatrix} \begin{bmatrix} x(k) \\ w(k) \end{bmatrix} \\ &= -z^T(k)z(k) + \gamma^2 w^T(k) w(k), \end{aligned} \tag{5.3}$$

where the condition (5.2) was used in the inequality.

Now, for an impulse-free arbitrary piecewise constant switching signal and any given $k > 0$, suppose $k_1 < k_2 < \cdots < k_r$ ($r \ge 1$) be the switching points of the switching signal on the discrete-time interval $[0, k)$. Then, according to (5.3), we obtain

$$\begin{aligned} V(x(k+1)) - V(x(k_r^+)) &\le \sum_{j=k_r}^{k} \{-z^T(j)z(j) + \gamma^2 w^T(j)w(j)\} \\ V(x(k_r^-)) - V(x(k_{r-1}^+)) &\le \sum_{j=k_{r-1}}^{k_r-1} \{-z^T(j)z(j) + \gamma^2 w^T(j)w(j)\} \\ &\cdots\cdots \\ V(x(k_2^-)) - V(x(k_1^+)) &\le \sum_{j=k_1}^{k_2-1} \{-z^T(j)z(j) + \gamma^2 w^T(j)w(j)\} \\ V(x(k_1^-)) - V(x(0)) &\le \sum_{j=0}^{k_1-1} \{-z^T(j)z(j) + \gamma^2 w^T(j)w(j)\}, \end{aligned} \tag{5.4}$$

where

$$V(x(k_j^+)) = \lim_{k \to k_j + 0} V(x(k)), \quad V(x(k_j^-)) = \lim_{k \to k_j - 0} V(x(k)). \tag{5.5}$$

However, due to the condition (4.3), we obtain $V(x(k_j^+)) = V(x(k_j^-))$ at all switching instants. Therefore, summing up all the inequalities of (5.4) results in

$$V(x(k+1)) - V(x(0)) \le \sum_{j=0}^{k} \left\{-z^T(j)z(j) + \gamma^2 w^T(j)w(j)\right\}. \tag{5.6}$$

Since $V(x(k+1)) \geq 0$, we obtain that

$$\sum_{j=0}^{k} z^T(j)z(j) \leq V(x(0)) + \gamma^2 \sum_{j=0}^{k} w^T(j)w(j), \tag{5.7}$$

which implies the $\mathcal{L}_2$ gain of the switched system is less than γ. ∎

Remark 5: When $E = I$, the conditions (5.1)-(5.2) and (4.3) require a common positive definite matrix P satisfying

$$\begin{bmatrix} A_i^T P_i A_i - P_i + C_i^T C_i & A_i^T P_i B_i \\ B_i^T P_i A_i & B_i^T P_i B_i - \gamma^2 I \end{bmatrix} < 0 \tag{5.8}$$

for all $\forall i \in \mathcal{I}$, which is the same as in [15]. Thus, Theorem 3 extended the $\mathcal{L}_2$ gain analysis result from switched time space systems to switched descriptor systems in discrete-time domain. In addition, it can be seen from the proof that $V(x) = x^T E^T P_i E x$ plays the important role of a common quadratic Lyapunov function for stability and $\mathcal{L}_2$ gain γ of all the descriptor subsystems. ∎

6. Concluding remarks

We have established a unified approach to stabilility and $\mathcal{L}_2$ gain analysis for switched linear discrete-time descriptor systems under impulse-free arbitrary switching. More precisely, we have shown that if there is a common quadratic Lyapunov function for stability of all subsystems, then the switched system is stable under impulse-free arbitrary switching. Furthermore, we have extended the results to $\mathcal{L}_2$ gain analysis of the switched descriptor systems, also in the name of common quadratic Lyapunov function approach. As also mentioned in the remarks, the common quadratic Lyapunov functions proposed are not positive definite with respect to all states, but they actually play the role of a Lyapunov function as in classical Lyapunov stability theory. The approach in this article is unified in the sense that it is valid for both continuous-time [21] and discrete-time systems, and it takes almost the same form in both stability and $\mathcal{L}_2$ gain analysis.

7. Acknowledgment

The authors would like to thank Prof. Xuping Xu with California Baptist University, USA, Mr. Ryuuen Kou, Prof. Joe Imae and Prof. Tomoaki Kobayashi with Osaka Prefecture University, Japan, for valuable discussions. This research has been supported in part by the Japan Ministry of Education, Sciences and Culture under Grant-in-Aid for Scientific Research (C) 21560471.

8. References

[1] D. Cobb, "Descriptor variable systems and optimal state regulation," *IEEE Transactions on Automatic Control*, vol. 28, no. 5, pp. 601–611, 1983.

[2] F. L. Lewis, "A survey of linear singular systems," *Circuits Systems Signal Process*, vol. 5, no. 1, pp. 3–36, 1986.

[3] K. Takaba, N. Morihira, and T. Katayama, "A generalized Lyapunov theorem for descriptor systems," *Systems & Control Letters*, vol. 24, no. 1, pp. 49–51, 1995.

[4] I. Masubuchi, Y. Kamitane, A. Ohara, and N. Suda, "$\mathcal{H}_\infty$ control for descriptor systems: A matrix inequalities approach," *Automatica*, vol. 33, no. 4, pp. 669–673, 1997.

[5] E. Uezato and M. Ikeda, "Strict LMI conditions for stability, robust stabilization, and $\mathcal{H}_\infty$ control of descriptor systems," in *Proceedings of the 38th IEEE Conference on Decision and Control*, Phoenix, USA, pp. 4092–4097, 1999.

[6] M. Ikeda, T. W. Lee, and E. Uezato, "A strict LMI condition for $\mathcal{H}_2$ control of descriptor systems," in *Proceedings of the 39th IEEE Conference on Decision and Control*, Sydney, Australia, pp. 601–604, 2000.

[7] D. Liberzon and A. S. Morse, "Basic problems in stability and design of switched systems," *IEEE Control Systems Magazine*, vol. 19, no. 5, pp. 59–70, 1999.

[8] R. DeCarlo, M. S. Branicky, S. Pettersson, and B. Lennartson, "Perspectives and results on the stability and stabilizability of hybrid systems," *Proceedings of the IEEE*, vol. 88, no. 7, pp. 1069–1082, 2000.

[9] D. Liberzon, *Switching in Systems and Control*, Birkhäuser, Boston, 2003.

[10] Z. Sun and S. S. Ge, *Switched Linear Systems: Control and Design*, Springer, London, 2005.

[11] M. S. Branicky, "Multiple Lyapunov functions and other analysis tools for switched and hybrid Systems," *IEEE Transactions on Automatic Control*, vol. 43, no. 4, pp. 475-482, 1998.

[12] K. S. Narendra and J. Balakrishnan, "A common Lyapunov function for stable LTI systems with commuting *A*-matrices," *IEEE Transactions on Automatic Control*, vol. 39, no. 12, pp. 2469–2471, 1994.

[13] D. Liberzon, J. P. Hespanha, and A. S. Morse, "Stability of switched systems: A Lie-algebraic condition," *Systems & Control Letters*, vol. 37, no. 3, pp. 117–122, 1999.

[14] G. Zhai, B. Hu, K. Yasuda, and A. N. Michel, "Disturbance attenuation properties of time-controlled switched systems," *Journal of The Franklin Institute*, vol. 338, no. 7, pp. 765–779, 2001.

[15] G. Zhai, B. Hu, K. Yasuda, and A. N. Michel, "Stability and $\mathcal{L}_2$ gain analysis of discrete-time switched systems," *Transactions of the Institute of Systems, Control and Information Engineers*, vol. 15, no. 3, pp. 117–125, 2002.

[16] G. Zhai, D. Liu, J. Imae, and T. Kobayashi, "Lie algebraic stability analysis for switched systems with continuous-time and discrete-time subsystems," *IEEE Transactions on Circuits and Systems II*, vol. 53, no. 2, pp. 152–156, 2006.

[17] G. Zhai, R. Kou, J. Imae, and T. Kobayashi, "Stability analysis and design for switched descriptor systems," *International Journal of Control, Automation, and Systems*, vol. 7, no. 3, pp. 349–355, 2009.

[18] G. Zhai, X. Xu, J. Imae, and T. Kobayashi, "Qualitative analysis of switched discrete-time descriptor systems," *International Journal of Control, Automation, and Systems*, vol. 7, no. 4, pp. 512–519, 2009.

[19] D. Liberzon and S. Trenn, "On stability of linear switched differential algebraic equations," in *Proceedings of the 48th IEEE Conference on Decision and Control*, Shanghai, China, pp. 2156–2161, 2009.

[20] S. Xu and C. Yang, "Stabilization of discrete-time singular systems: A matrix inequalities approach," *Automatica*, vol. 35, no. 9, pp. 1613–1617, 1999.

[21] G. Zhai and X. Xu, "A unified approach to analysis of switched linear descriptor systems under arbitrary switching," in *Proceedings of the 48th IEEE Conference on Decision and Control*, Shanghai, China, pp. 3897-3902, 2009.

20

Robust Stabilization for a Class of Uncertain Discrete-time Switched Linear Systems

Songlin Chen, Yu Yao and Xiaoguan Di
Harbin Institute of Technology
P. R. China

1. Introduction

Switched systems are a class of hybrid systems consisting of several subsystems (modes of operation) and a switching rule indicating the active subsystem at each instant of time. In recent years, considerable efforts have been devoted to the study of switched system. The motivation of study comes from theoretical interest as well as practical applications. Switched systems have numerous applications in control of mechanical systems, the automotive industry, aircraft and air traffic control, switching power converters, and many other fields. The basic problems in stability and design of switched systems were given by (Liberzon & Morse, 1999). For recent progress and perspectives in the field of switched systems, see the survey papers (DeCarlo et al., 2000; Sun & Ge, 2005).

The stability analysis and stabilization of switching systems have been studied by a number of researchers (Branicky, 1998; Zhai et al., 1998; Margaliot & Liberzon, 2006; Akar et al., 2006). Feedback stabilization strategies for switched systems may be broadly classified into two categories in (DeCarlo et al., 2000). One problem is to design appropriate feedback control laws to make the closed-loop systems stable for any switching signal given in an admissible set. If the switching signal is a design variable, then the problem of stabilization is to design both switching rules and feedback control laws to stabilize the switched systems. For the first problem, there exist many results. In (Daafouz et al., 2002), the switched Lyapunov function method and LMI based conditions were developed for stability analysis and feedback control design of switched linear systems under arbitrary switching signal. There are some extensions of (Daafouz et al., 2002) for different control problem (Xie et al., 2003; Ji et al., 2003). The pole assignment method was used to develop an observer-based controller to stabilizing the switched system with infinite switching times (Li et al., 2003).

It is should be noted that there are relatively little study on the second problem, especially for uncertain switched systems. Ji had considered the robust H_∞ control and quadratic stabilization of uncertain discrete-time switched linear systems via designing feedback control law and constructing switching rule based on common Lyapunov function approach (Ji et al., 2005). The similar results were given for the robust guaranteed cost control problem of uncertain discrete-time switched linear systems (Zhang & Duan, 2007). Based on multiple Lyapunov functions approach, the robust H_∞ control problem of uncertain continuous-time switched linear systems via designing switching rule and state feedback was studied (Ji et al., 2004). Compared with the switching rule based on common Lyapunov function approach (Ji et al., 2005; Zhang & Duan, 2007), the one based on multiple Lyapunov functions approach (Ji et al., 2004) is much simpler and more practical, but discrete-time case was not considered.

Motivated by the study in (Ji et al., 2005; Zhang & Duan, 2007; Ji et al., 2004), based on the multiple Lyapunov functions approach, the robust control for a class of discrete-time switched systems with norm-bounded time-varying uncertainties in both the state matrices and input matrices is investigated. It is shown that a state-depended switching rule and switched state feedback controller can be designed to stabilize the uncertain switched linear systems if a matrix inequality based condition is feasible and this condition can be dealt with as linear matrix inequalities (LMIs) if the associated scalar parameters are selected in advance. Furthermore, the parameterized representation of state feedback controller and constructing method of switching rule are presented. All the results can be considered as extensions of the existing results for both switched and non-switched systems.

2. Problem formulation

Firstly, we consider a class of uncertain discrete-time switched linear systems described by

$$\begin{cases} x(k+1) = \underbrace{(A_{\sigma(k)} + \Delta A_{\sigma(k)})}_{\overline{A}_{\sigma(k)}} x(k) + \underbrace{(B_{\sigma(k)} + \Delta B_{\sigma(k)})}_{\overline{B}_{\sigma(k)}} u(k) \\ y(k) = C_{\sigma(k)} x(k) \end{cases} \tag{1}$$

where $x(k) \in \mathbb{R}^n$ is the state, $u(k) \in \mathbb{R}^m$ is the control input, $y(k) \in \mathbb{R}^q$ is the measurement output and $\sigma(k) \in \Xi = \{1,2,\cdots N\}$ is a discrete switching signal to be designed. Moreover, $\sigma(k) = i$ means that the ith subsystem (A_i, B_i, C_i) is activated at time k (For notational simplicity, we may not explicitly mention the time-dependence of the switching signal below, that is, $\sigma(k)$ will be denoted as σ in some cases). Here A_i , B_i and C_i are constant matrices of compatible dimensions which describe the nominal subsystems. The uncertain matrices ΔA_i and ΔB_i are time-varying and are assumed to be of the forms as follows.

$$\Delta A_i = M_{ai} F_{ai}(k) N_{ai} \quad \Delta B_i = M_{bi} F_{bi}(k) N_{bi} \tag{2}$$

where M_{ai} , N_{ai} , M_{bi} , N_{bi} are given constant matrices of compatible dimensions which characterize the structures of the uncertainties, and the time-varying matrices $F_{ai}(k)$ and $F_{bi}(k)$ satisfy

$$F_{ai}^{\mathrm{T}}(k) F_{ai}(k) \le I, F_{bi}^{\mathrm{T}}(k) F_{bi}^{\mathrm{T}}(k) \le I \quad \forall i \in \Xi \tag{3}$$

where I is an identity matrix.

We assume that no subsystem can be stabilized individually (otherwise the switching problem will be trivial by always choosing the stabilized subsystem as the active subsystem). The problem being addressed can be formulated as follows:

For the uncertain switched linear systems (1), we aim to design the switched state feedback controller

$$u(k) = K_{\sigma} x(k) \tag{4}$$

and the state-depended switching rule $\sigma(x(k))$ to guarantee the corresponding closed-loop switched system

$$x(k+1) = [A_\sigma + \Delta A_\sigma + (B_\sigma + \Delta B_\sigma)K_\sigma]x(k) \tag{5}$$

is asymptotically stable for all admissible uncertainties under the constructed switching rule.

3. Main results

In order to derive the main result, we give the two main lemmas as follows.
Lemma 1: (Boyd, 1994) Given any constant ε and any matrices M, N with compatible dimensions, then the matrix inequality

$$MFN + N^T F^T M^T < \varepsilon MM^T + \varepsilon^{-1} N^T N$$

holds for the arbitrary norm-bounded time-varying uncertainty F satisfying $F^T F \le I$.
Lemma 2: (Boyd, 1994) (Schur complement lemma) Let S, P, Q be given matrices such that $Q = Q^T, P = P^T$, then

$$\begin{bmatrix} P & S^T \\ S & Q \end{bmatrix} < 0 \Leftrightarrow Q < 0, P - S^T Q^{-1} S < 0.$$

A sufficient condition for existence of such controller and switching rule is given by the following theorem.
Theorem 1: The closed-loop system (5) is asymptotically stable when $\Delta A_i = \Delta B_i = 0$ if there exist symmetric positive definite matrices $X_i \in \mathbb{R}^{n\times n}$, matrices $G_i \in \mathbb{R}^{n\times n}$, $Y_i \in \mathbb{R}^{m\times n}$, scalars $\varepsilon_i > 0$ $(i \in \Xi)$ and scalars $\lambda_{ij} < 0$ $(i, j \in \Xi, \lambda_{ii} = -1)$ such that

$$\begin{bmatrix} \sum_{j\in\Xi} \lambda_{ij}(G_i^T + G_i - X_i) & * & * & * & \cdots & * \\ A_i G_i + B_i Y_i & -X_i & * & * & \cdots & * \\ G_i & 0 & \lambda_{i1}^{-1} X_1 & * & \cdots & * \\ G_i & 0 & 0 & \lambda_{i2}^{-1} X_2 & \cdots & * \\ \vdots & \vdots & \vdots & \vdots & \ddots & * \\ G_i & 0 & 0 & 0 & 0 & \lambda_{iN}^{-1} X_N \end{bmatrix} < 0 \quad \forall i \in \Xi \tag{6}$$

is satisfied ($*$ denotes the corresponding transposed block matrix due to symmetry), then the state feedback gain matrices can be given by (4) with

$$K_i = Y_i G_i^{-1} \tag{7}$$

and the corresponding switching rule is given by

$$\sigma(x(k)) = \arg\min_{i\in\Xi}\{x^T(k) X_i^{-1} x(k)\} \tag{8}$$

Proof. Assume that there exist $G_i, X_i, Y_i, \varepsilon_i$ and λ_{ij} such that inequality (6) is satisfied.
By the symmetric positive definiteness of matrices X_i, we get

$$(G_i - X_i)^T X_i^{-1} (G_i - X_i) \ge 0$$

which is equal to

$$G_i^{\mathrm{T}} X_i^{-1} G_i \geq G_i^{\mathrm{T}} + G_i - X_i$$

It follows from (6) and $\lambda_{ij} < 0$ that

$$\begin{bmatrix} \sum_{j\in\Xi} \lambda_{ij} G_i^{\mathrm{T}} X_i^{-1} G_i & * & * \\ A_i G_i + B_i Y_i & -X_i & * \\ \Gamma_i & 0 & \Phi_i \end{bmatrix} < 0 \tag{9}$$

where $\Gamma_i = [G_i, G_i, \cdots G_i]^{\mathrm{T}}$, $\Phi_i = \mathrm{diag}\{1/\lambda_{i1}X_1, 1/\lambda_{i2}X_2, \cdots, 1/\lambda_{i(i-1)}X_{i-1}, 1/\lambda_{i(i+1)}X_{i+1}, \cdots, 1/\lambda_{iN}X_N\}$
Pre- and post- multiplying both sides of inequality (9) by $\mathrm{diag}\{G_i^{-1}, I, I\}^{\mathrm{T}}$ and $\mathrm{diag}\{G_i^{-1}, I, I\}$, we get

$$\begin{bmatrix} \sum_{j\in\Xi} \lambda_{ij} X_i^{-1} & * & * \\ A_i + B_i K_i & -X_i & * \\ \Pi_i & 0 & \Phi_i \end{bmatrix} < 0 \tag{10}$$

where $\Pi_i = [I, I, \cdots I]^{\mathrm{T}}$.
By virtue of the properties of the Schur complement lemma, inequality (10) is equal to

$$\begin{bmatrix} -X_i^{-1} + \sum_{j\in\Xi, j\neq i} \lambda_{ij}(X_i^{-1} - X_j^{-1}) & * \\ A_i + B_i K_i & -X_i \end{bmatrix} < 0 \tag{11}$$

Letting $P_i = X_i^{-1}$ and applying Schur complement lemma again yields

$$(A_i + B_i K_i)^{\mathrm{T}} P_i (A_i + B_i K_i) - P_i + \sum_{j\in\Xi, j\neq i} \lambda_{ij}(P_i - P_j) < 0 \tag{12}$$

Since $P_i = X_i^{-1} (\forall i \in \mathrm{E})$, the switching rule (8) can be rewritten as

$$\sigma(x(k)) = \arg\min_{i\in\Xi}\{x^{\mathrm{T}}(k) P_i x(k)\}. \tag{13}$$

By (13), $\sigma(k) = i$ implies that

$$x^T(k)(P_i - P_j)x(k) \leq 0, \qquad \forall j \in \Xi, j \neq i. \tag{14}$$

Multiply the above inequalities by negative scalars λ_{ij} for each $j \in \Xi, j \neq i$ and sum to get

$$x^{\mathrm{T}}(k)\left[\sum_{j\in\Xi, j\neq i} \lambda_{ij}(P_i - P_j)\right] x(k) \geq 0 \tag{15}$$

Associated with the switching rule (13), we take the multiple Lyapunov functions $V(x(k))$ as

$$V_{\sigma(k)}(x(k)) = x^T(k)P_{\sigma(k)}x(k) \tag{16}$$

then the difference of $V(x(k))$ along the solution of the closed-loop switched system (5) is

$$\Delta V = V(x(k+1)) - V(x(k)) = x^{\mathrm{T}}(k+1)P_{\sigma(k+1)}x(k+1) - x^{\mathrm{T}}(k)P_{\sigma(k)}x(k)$$

At non-switching instant, without loss of generality, letting $\sigma(k+1) = \sigma(k) = i (i \in \Xi)$, and applying switching rule (13) and inequality (15), we get

$$\Delta V = x^{\mathrm{T}}(k+1)P_i x(k+1) - x^{\mathrm{T}}(k)P_i x(k) = x^{\mathrm{T}}(k)\left[(A_i + B_i K_i)^{\mathrm{T}} P_i (A_i + B_i K_i) - P_i\right]x(k) \le 0 \tag{17}$$

It follows from (12) and (15) that $\Delta V < 0$ holds.
At switching instant, without loss of generality, let $\sigma(k+1) = j, \sigma(k) = i (i, j \in \Xi, i \ne j)$ to get

$$\Delta V = x^{\mathrm{T}}(k+1)P_j x(k+1) - x^{\mathrm{T}}(k)P_i x(k) \le x^{\mathrm{T}}(k+1)P_i x(k+1) - x^{\mathrm{T}}(k)P_i x(k) \le 0 \tag{18}$$

It follows from (17) and (18) that $\Delta V < 0$ holds. In virtue of multiple Lyapunov functions technique (Branicky, 1998), the closed-loop system (5) is asymptotically. This concludes the proof.
Remark 1: If the scalars λ_{ij} are selected in advance, the matrices inequalities (19) can be converted into LMIs with respect to other unknown matrices variables, which can be checked with efficient and reliable numerical algorithms available.
Theorem 2: The closed-loop system (5) is asymptotically stable for all admissible uncertainties if there exist symmetric positive definite matrices $X_i \in \mathbb{R}^{n\times n}$, matrices $G_i \in \mathbb{R}^{m\times n}$, $Y_i \in \mathbb{R}^{m\times n}$, scalars $\varepsilon_i > 0$ $(i \in \Xi)$ and scalars $\lambda_{ij} < 0$ $(i, j \in \Xi, \lambda_{ii} = -1)$ such that

$$\begin{bmatrix} \sum_{j\in\Xi} \lambda_{ij}(G_i^{\mathrm{T}} + G_i - X_i) & * & * & * & * & * & \cdots & * \\ A_i G_i + B_i Y_i & \Theta_i & * & * & * & * & \cdots & * \\ N_{ai} G_i & 0 & -\varepsilon_i I & * & * & * & \cdots & * \\ N_{bi} Y_i & 0 & 0 & -\varepsilon_i I & * & * & \cdots & * \\ G_i & 0 & 0 & 0 & \lambda_{i1}^{-1} X_1 & * & \cdots & * \\ G_i & 0 & 0 & 0 & 0 & \lambda_{i2}^{-1} X_2 & \cdots & * \\ \vdots & \vdots & \vdots & \vdots & \vdots & \vdots & \ddots & * \\ G_i & 0 & 0 & 0 & 0 & 0 & 0 & \lambda_{iN}^{-1} X_N \end{bmatrix} < 0 \quad \forall i \in \Xi \tag{19}$$

is satisfied, where

$$\Theta_i = -X_i + \varepsilon_i [M_{ai} M_{ai}^{\mathrm{T}} + M_{bi} M_{bi}^{\mathrm{T}}],$$

then the state feedback gain matrices can be given by (4) with

$$K_i = Y_i G_i^{-1} \tag{20}$$

and the corresponding switching rule is given by

$$\sigma(x(k)) = \arg\min_{i\in\Xi}\{x^{\mathrm{T}}(k)X_i^{-1}x(k)\} \tag{21}$$

Proof. By theorem 1, the closed-loop system (5) is asymptotically stable for all admissible uncertainties if that there exist G_i, X_i, Y_i and λ_{ij} such that

$$\begin{bmatrix} \sum_{j\in\Xi}\lambda_{ij}(G_i^{\mathrm{T}}+G_i-X_i) & * & * \\ \bar{A}_iG_i+\bar{B}_iY_i & \Theta_i & * \\ \Gamma_i & 0 & \Phi_i \end{bmatrix} < 0 \tag{22}$$

where $\Gamma_i = [G_i, G_i, \cdots G_i]^{\mathrm{T}}$,

$\Phi_i = \mathrm{diag}\{1/\lambda_{i1}X_1, 1/\lambda_{i2}X_2, \cdots, 1/\lambda_{i(i-1)}X_{i-1}, 1/\lambda_{i(i+1)}X_{i+1}, \cdots, 1/\lambda_{iN}X_N\}$,

which can be rewritten as

$$\tilde{A}_i + \tilde{M}_i\tilde{F}_i(k)\tilde{N}_i + \tilde{N}_i^{\mathrm{T}}\tilde{F}_i^{\mathrm{T}}(k)\tilde{M}_i^{\mathrm{T}} < 0$$

where

$$\tilde{A}_i = \begin{bmatrix} \sum_{j\in\Xi}\lambda_{ij}(G_i^{\mathrm{T}}+G_i-X_i) & * & * \\ A_iG_i+B_iY_i & \Theta_i & * \\ \Gamma_i & 0 & \Phi_i \end{bmatrix}, \quad \tilde{M}_i = \begin{bmatrix} 0 & 0 \\ M_{ai} & M_{bi} \\ 0 & 0 \end{bmatrix},$$

$$\tilde{F}_i(k) = \mathrm{diag}(F_{ai}(k), F_{bi}(k)), \quad \tilde{N}_i = \begin{bmatrix} N_{ai}G_i & 0 & 0 \\ N_{bi}K_i & 0 & 0 \end{bmatrix}$$

It follows from Lemma 1 and $\tilde{F}_i^{\mathrm{T}}(t)\tilde{F}_i^{\mathrm{T}}(t) \le I$ that

$$\tilde{A}_i + \tilde{M}_i\tilde{M}_i^{\mathrm{T}} + \tilde{N}_i^{\mathrm{T}}\tilde{N}_i < 0 \tag{23}$$

By virtue of the properties of the Schur complement lemma, inequality (19) can be rewritten as

$$\begin{bmatrix} \sum_{j\in\Xi}\lambda_{ij}(G_i^{\mathrm{T}}+G_i-X_i) & * & * & * & * \\ A_iG_i+B_iY_i & \Theta_i & * & * & * \\ \Gamma_i & 0 & \Phi_i & * & * \\ N_{ai}G_i & 0 & 0 & -\varepsilon_iI & * \\ N_{bi}Y_i & 0 & 0 & 0 & -\varepsilon_iI \end{bmatrix} < 0 \quad \forall i \in \Xi \tag{24}$$

It is obvious that inequality (24)is equal to inequality (19), which finished the proof.

Let the scalars $\lambda_{ij} = 0$ and $X_i = X_j = X$, it is easily to obtain the condition for robust stability of the closed-loop system (5) under arbitrary switching as follows.

Corollary 1: The closed-loop system (5) is asymptotically stable for all admissible uncertainties under arbitrary switching if there exist a symmetric positive definite matrix $X_i \in \mathbb{R}^{n\times n}$, matrices $G_i \in \mathbb{R}^{m\times n}$, $Y_i \in \mathbb{R}^{m\times n}$, scalars $\varepsilon_i > 0$ and such that

$$\begin{bmatrix} -G_i^{\mathrm{T}} - G_i + X_i & * & * & * \\ A_i G_i + B_i Y_i & \Theta_i & * & * \\ N_{ai} G_i & 0 & -\varepsilon_i I & * \\ N_{bi} Y_i & 0 & 0 & -\varepsilon_i I \end{bmatrix} < 0 \quad \forall i \in \Xi \tag{25}$$

is satisfied, where $\Theta_i = -X_i + \varepsilon_i [M_{ai} M_{ai}^{\mathrm{T}} + M_{bi} M_{bi}^{\mathrm{T}}]$, then the state feedback gain matrices can be given by (4) with

$$K_i = Y_i G_i^{-1} \tag{26}$$

4. Example

Consider the uncertain discrete-time switched linear system (1) with N =2. The system matrices are given by

$$A_1 = \begin{bmatrix} 1.5 & 1.5 \\ 0 & -1.2 \end{bmatrix}, B_1 = \begin{bmatrix} 1 \\ 0 \end{bmatrix}, M_{a1} = \begin{bmatrix} 0.5 \\ 0.2 \end{bmatrix}, \quad N_{a1} = \begin{bmatrix} 0.4 & 0.2 \end{bmatrix}, M_{b1} = \begin{bmatrix} 0.3 \\ 0.4 \end{bmatrix}, N_{b1} = \begin{bmatrix} 0.2 \end{bmatrix},$$

$$A_2 = \begin{bmatrix} 1.2 & 0 \\ 0.6 & 1.2 \end{bmatrix}, B_2 = \begin{bmatrix} 0 \\ 1 \end{bmatrix}, M_{a2} = \begin{bmatrix} 0.3 \\ 0.4 \end{bmatrix}, \quad N_{a2} = \begin{bmatrix} 0.3 & 0.2 \end{bmatrix}, M_{b2} = \begin{bmatrix} 0.3 \\ 0.3 \end{bmatrix}, N_{b2} = \begin{bmatrix} 0.1 \end{bmatrix}.$$

Obviously, the two subsystems are unstable, and it is easy to verify that neither subsystem can be individually stabilized via state feedback for all admissible uncertainties. Thus it is necessary to design both switching rule and feedback control laws to stabilize the uncertain switched system. Letting $\lambda_{12} = -10$ and $\lambda_{21} = -10$, the inequality (19) in Theorem 1 is converted into LMIs. Using the LMI control toolbox in MATLAB, we get

$$X_1 = \begin{bmatrix} 41.3398 & -8.7000 \\ -8.7000 & 86.6915 \end{bmatrix}, X_2 = \begin{bmatrix} 38.1986 & -8.6432 \\ -8.6432 & 93.8897 \end{bmatrix}$$

$$G_1 = \begin{bmatrix} 41.3415 & -8.6656 \\ -8.7540 & 86.4219 \end{bmatrix}, Y_1 = \begin{bmatrix} -51.2846 \\ -26.5670 \end{bmatrix}^T,$$

$$G_2 = \begin{bmatrix} 38.1665 & -8.6003 \\ -8.6186 & 93.6219 \end{bmatrix}, Y_2 = \begin{bmatrix} -44.3564 \\ 54.4478 \end{bmatrix}^T,$$

$$\varepsilon_1 = 56.6320, \varepsilon_1 = 24.3598$$

With $K_i = Y_i G_i^{-1}$, the switched state feedback controllers are

$$K_1 = \begin{bmatrix} -1.4841 & -1.1505 \end{bmatrix}, K_2 = \begin{bmatrix} -1.0527 & 0.4849 \end{bmatrix}.$$

It is obvious that neither of the designed controllers stabilizes the associated subsystem. Letting that the initial state is $x_0 = [-3,2]$ and the time-varying uncertain $F_{ia}(k) = F_{ib}(k) = f(k)$ $(i = 1,2)$ as shown in Figure 1 is random number between -1 and 1, the simulation results as shown in Figure 2, 3 and 4 are obtained, which show that the given uncertain switched system is stabilized under the switched state feedback controller together with the designed switching rule.

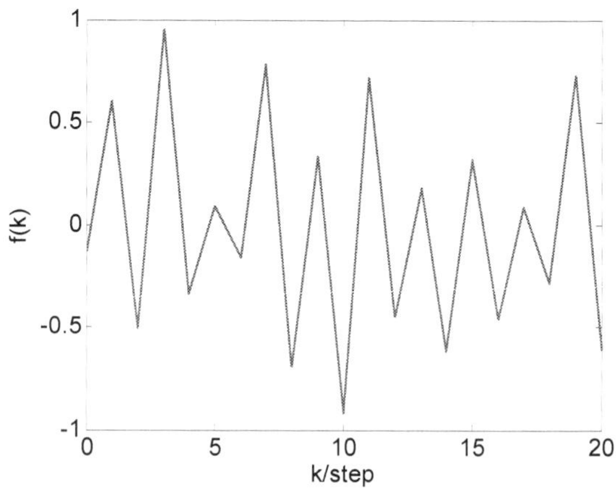

Fig. 1. The time-varying uncertainty f(k)

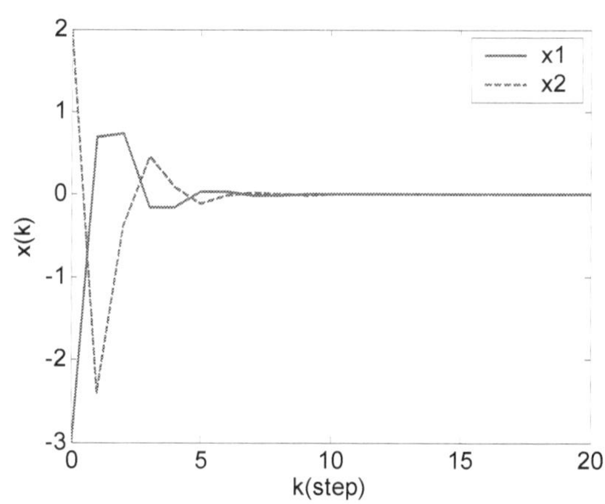

Fig. 2. The state response of the closed-loop system

5. Conclusion

This paper focused on the robust control of switched systems with norm-bounded time-varying uncertainties with the help of multiple Lyapunov functions approach and matrix inequality technique. By the introduction of additional matrices, a new condition expressed in terms of matrices inequalities for the existence of a state-based switching strategy and state feedback control law is derived. If some scalars parameters are selected in advance, the conditions can be dealt with as LMIs for which there exists efficient numerical software available. All the results can be easily extended to other control problems (H_2, H_∞ control, etc.).

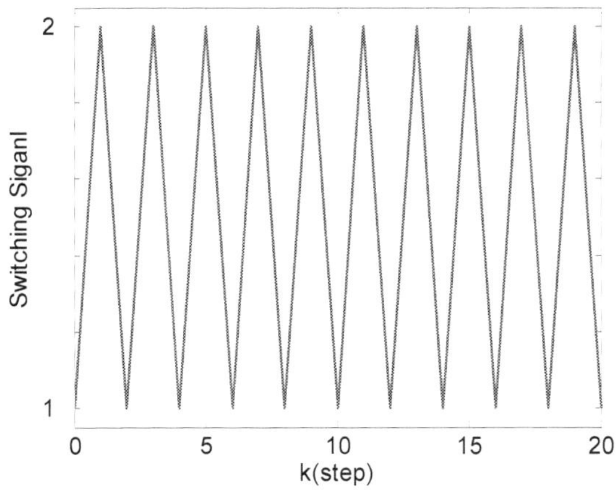

Fig. 3. The switching signal

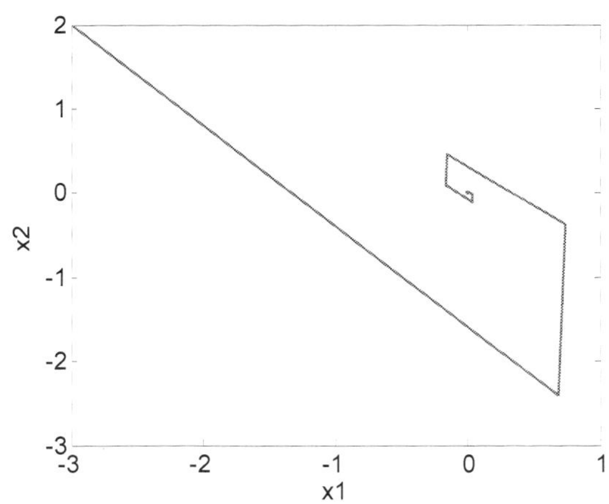

Fig. 4. The state trajectory of the closed-loop system

6. Acknowledgment

This paper is supported by the National Natural Science Foundation of China (60674043).

7. References

Liberzon, D. & Morse, A.S. (1999). Basic problems in stability and design of switched systems, *IEEE Control Syst. Mag.*, Vol 19, No. 5, Oct. 1999, pp. 59-70

DeCarlo, R. A.; Branicky, M. S.; Pettersson, S. & Lennartson, B. (2000). Perspectives and results on the stability and stabilizability of hybrid systems, *Proceedings of the IEEE*, Vol 88, No. 7, Jul. 2000, pp. 1069-1082.

Sun, Z. & Ge, S. S. (2005). Analysis and synthesis of switched linear control systems, *Automatica*, Vol 41, No 2, Feb. 2005, pp. 181-195.

Branicky, M. S. (1998). Multiple Lyapunov functions and other analysis tools for switched and hybrid systems, *IEEE Transactions on Automatic Control*, Vol 43, No.4, Apr. 1998, pp. 475-482.

G. S. Zhai, D. R. Liu, J. Imae, (1998). Lie algebraic stability analysis for switched systems with continuous-time and discrete-time subsystems, *IEEE Transactions on Circuits and Systems II-Express Briefs*, Vol 53, No. 2, Feb. 2006, pp. 152-156.

Margaliot, M. & Liberzon, D. (2006). Lie-algebraic stability conditions for nonlinear switched systems and differential inclusions, *Systems and Control Letters*, Vol 55, No. 1, Jan. 2006, pp. 8-16.

Akar, M.; Paul, A.; & Safonov, M. G. (2006). Conditions on the stability of a class of second-order switched systems, *IEEE Transactions on Automatic Control*, Vol 51, No. 2, Feb. 2006, pp. 338-340.

Daafouz, J.; Riedinger, P. & Iung, C. (2002). Stability analysis and control synthesis for switched systems: A switched Lyapunov function approach, *IEEE Transactions on Automatic Control*, Vol 47, No. 11, Nov. 2002, pp. 1883-1887.

Xie, D.; Wang, Hao, L. F. & Xie, G. (2003). Robust stability analysis and control synthesis for discrete-time uncertain switched systems, *Proceedings of the 42nd IEEE Conference on Decision and Control*, Maui, HI, Dec. 2003, pp. 4812-4817.

Ji, Z.; Wang, L. and Xie, G. (2003). Stabilizing discrete-time switched systems via observer-based static output feedback, *IEEE Int. Conf. SMC*, Washington, D.C, October 2003, pp. 2545-2550.

Li, Z. G.; Wen, C. Y. & Soh, Y. C. (2003). Observer based stabilization of switching linear systems, *Automatica*. Vol. 39 No. 3, Feb. 2003, pp:17-524.

Ji, Z. & Wang, L. (2005). Robust H∞ control and quadratic stabilization of uncertain discrete-time switched linear systems, *Proceedings of the American Control Conference*. Portland, OR, Jun. 2005, pp. 24-29.

Zhang, Y. & Duan, G. R. (2007). Guaranteed cost control with constructing switching law of uncertain discrete-time switched systems, *Journal of Systems Engineering and Electronics*, Vol 18, No. 4, Apr. 2007, pp. 846-851.

Ji, Z.; Wang, L. & Xie, G. (2004). Robust H∞ Control and Stabilization of Uncertain Switched Linear Systems: A Multiple Lyapunov Functions Approach, *The 16th Mathematical Theory of Networks and Systems Conference*. Leuven, Belgium, Jul. 2004, pp. 1~17.

Boyd, S.; Ghaoui, L.; Feron, E. & Balakrishnan, V. (1994). *Linear Matrix Inequalities in System and Control Theory*, SIAM, Philadelphia.

Part 5

Miscellaneous Applications

21

Half-overlap Subchannel Filtered MultiTone Modulation and Its Implementation

Pavel Silhavy and Ondrej Krajsa
Department of Telecommunications, Faculty of Electrical Engineering and Communication, Brno University of Technology, Czech Republic

1. Introduction

Multitone modulations are today frequently used modulation techniques that enable optimum utilization of the frequency band provided on non-ideal transmission carrier channel (Bingham, 2000). These modulations are used with especially in data transmission systems in access networks of telephone exchanges in ADSL (asymmetric Digital Subscriber Lines) and VDSL (Very high-speed Digital Subscriber Lines) transmission technologies, in systems enabling transmission over power lines - PLC (Power Line Communication), in systems for digital audio broadcasting (DAB) and digital video broadcasting (DVB) [10]. And, last but not least, they are also used in WLAN (Wireless Local Area Network) networks according to IEEE 802.11a, IEEE 802.11g, as well as in the new WiMAX technology according to IEEE 802.16. This modulation technique makes use of the fact that when the transmission band is divided into a sufficient number of parallel subchannels, it is possible to regard the transmission function on these subchannels as constant. The more subchannels are used, the more the transmission function approximates ideal characteristics (Bingham, 2000). It subsequently makes equalization in the receiver easier. However, increasing the number of subchannels also increases the delay and complication of the whole system. The dataflow carried by individual subchannels need not be the same and the number of bytes carried by one symbol in every subchannel is set such that it maintains a constant error rate with flat power spectral density across the frequency band used. The mechanism of allocating bits to the carriers is referred to as bit loading algorithm. The resulting bit-load to the carriers thus corresponds to an optimum distribution of carried information in the provided band at a minimum necessary transmitting power.
In all the above mentioned systems the known and well described modulation DMT (Discrete MultiTone) (Bingham, 2000) or OFDM (Orthogonal Frequency Division Multiplexing) is used. As can be seen, the above technologies use a wide spectrum of transmission media, from metallic twisted pair in systems ADSL and VDSL, through radio channel in WLAN and WiMAX to power lines in PLC systems.
Using multitone modulation, in this case DMT and OFDM modulations, with adaptive bit loading across the frequency band efficient data transmission is enabled on higher frequencies than for which the transmission medium was primarily designed (xDSL, PLC) and it is impossible therefore to warrant here its transfer characteristics. In terrestrial

transmission the relatively long symbol duration allows effective suppression of the influence of multi-path signal propagation (DAB, DVB, WiMAX, WLAN).

Unfortunately, DMT and OFDM modulation ability will fail to enable quite an effective utilization of transmission channels with specially formed spectral characteristic with sharp transients, which is a consequence of individual subchannel frequency characteristic in the form of sinc function. It is also the reason for the transmission rate loss on channels with the occurrence of narrow-band noise disturbance, both metallic and terrestrial. Moreover, multi-path signal propagation suppression on terrestrial channels is achieved only when the delay time is shorter than symbol duration. For these reasons the available transmission rate is considerably limited in these technologies.

Alternative modulation techniques are therefore ever more often sought that would remove the above described inadequacies. The first to be mentioned was the DWMT modulation (Discrete Wavelet MultiTone) (Sandberg & Tzanes, 1995). This technique using the FWT (Fast Wavelet Transform) transform instead of the FFT transform in DMT or OFDM enabled by changing the carrier shape and reducing the sinc function side lobes from - 13 dB to - 45 dB a reduction of the influence of some of the above limitations. The main disadvantage of DWMT was the necessity to modulate carriers with the help of one-dimensional Pulse-Amplitude Modulation (PAM) instead of two-dimensional QAM, as with the DMT or OFDM system, i.e. a complex number implementing the QAM modulator bank. Another drawback was the high computational complexity.

Another modulation method, which is today often mentioned, is the filter bank modulation, referred to as FMT (Filtered MultiTone or Filter bank MultiTone) (Cherubini et al.2000). FMT modulation represents a modulation technique using filter banks to divide the frequency spectrum. The system input is complex symbols, obtained with the help of QAM modulation, similar to classical DMT. The number of bits allocated to individual carriers is also determined during the transmission initialization according to the levels of interference and attenuation for the given channel, the same as with DMT. By upsampling the input signals their spectra will be periodized; subsequent filtering will select the part which will be transmitted on the given carrier. The filters in individual branches are frequency-shifted versions of the filter in the first branch, the so-called prototype filter – the lowpass filter (Cherubini et al.2000). Thanks to the separation of individual subchannel spectra, the interchannel interferences, ICI, are, contrary to the DMT, severely suppressed, down to a level comparable with the other noise. On the other hand, the intersymbol interferences, ISI, occur on every subchannel, event if the transmission channel is ideal (Benvenuto et al., 2002). Therefore, it is necessary to perform an equalization of not only the transmission channel but also the filters. This equalization may be realized completely in the frequency domain. FMT also facilitates the application of frequency division duplex, because there is no power emission from one channel into another.

2. DMT and OFDM modulations

A signal transmitted by DMT or OFDM modulator can be described as shown by equation:

$$x(t) = \Re\left\{ \frac{1}{\sqrt{2N}} \sum_{k=-\infty}^{\infty} \sum_{i=1}^{N-1} X_i^k h\left(t - kT_{sym}\right) e^{j\frac{2\pi i t}{T}} \right\} \tag{1}$$

where

$$h(t)\begin{cases}1 & \text{for } t\in\langle 0,T)\\ 0 & \text{otherwise}\end{cases},\ f_i=\frac{i}{T}=\frac{f_s\cdot i}{2N},\ T=\frac{2N}{f_s},\ T_{CP}=\frac{CP}{f_s}$$

and $T_{sym}=\dfrac{2N+CP}{f_s}$

In DMT modulation, N - 1 is the number of carriers and so $2N$ is the number of samples in one symbol, k is the ordinal number of symbol, i is the carrier index, and X_i^k is the QAM symbol of ith carrier of kth symbol. In OFDM modulation all $2N$ carriers are modulated independently, and so the output signal $x(t)$ is complex. The symbols are shaped by a rectangular window $h(n)$, therefore the spectrum of each carrier is a *sinc(f)* function. The individual carriers are centred at frequencies f_i and mutually overlapped. The transmission through the ideal channel enables a perfect demodulation of the DMT or OFDM signal on the grounds of the orthogonality between the individual carriers, which is provided by the FFT transformation.

However, the transmission through non-ideal channels, mentioned in the first section, leads to the loss of orthogonality and to the occurrence of Inter-Symbol (ISI) and Inter-Carrier Interferences (ICI). To suppress the effect of the non-ideal channel, time intervals of duration T_{CP} (so-called cyclic prefixes) are inserted between individual blocks in the transmitted data flow in the transmitter. The cyclic prefix (CP) is generated by copying a certain number of samples from the end of next symbol. In the receiver the impulse response of the channel is reduced by digital filtering, called Time domain EQualizer (TEQ), so as not to exceed the length of this cyclic prefix. The cyclic prefix is then removed. This method of transmission channel equalisation in the DMT modulation is described in [6].

The spectrum of the carriers is a *sinc(f)* function and so the out-of-transmitted-band emission is much higher. There is a problem with the duplex transmission realisation by Frequency dividing multiplex (FDM) and with the transmission medium shared by another transmission technology. Figure 1 shows an example of ADSL technology. In ADSL2+ the frequency band from 7th to 31st carrier is used by the upstream channel and from 32nd to 511th carriers by the downstream channel. The base band is used by the plain old telephone services (POTS).

In ADSL, the problem with out-of-transmitted-band emission is solved by digital filtering of the signal transmitted using digital IIR filters. The out-of-transmitted-band emission is reduced (see Fig. 1.), but this filtering participates significantly in giving rise to ICI and ISI interferences. The carriers on the transmission band border are degraded in particular. Unfortunately, additional filtering increases the channel equalization complexity, because channel with transmit and receive filters creates a band-pass filter instead of low-pass filter. The difficulty is greater in upstream direction especially for narrow band reason. Therefore, a higher order of TEQ filter is used and the signal is sampled with two-times higher frequency compared to the sampling theorem. Also, when narrow-band interference appears in the transmission band, it is not only the carriers corresponding to this band that are disturbed but also a whole series of neighbouring carriers.

The above disadvantages lead to a suboptimal utilization of the transmission band and to a reduced data rate. This is the main motivation for designing a new realisation of the MCM modulation scheme. Recently, a filter bank realisation of MCM has been the subject of discussion. This method is called Filtered MultiTone modulation (FMT).

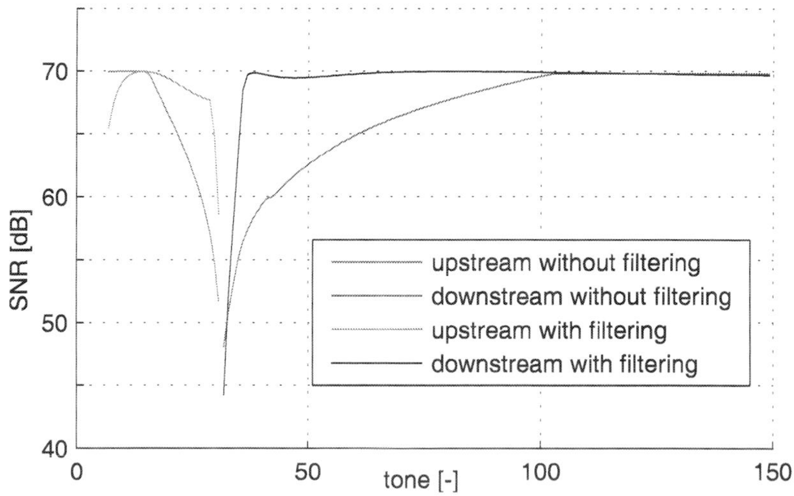

Fig. 1. SNR comparison of upstream and part of downstream frequency bands of ADSL2+ technology with and without additional digital filtering. PSD= -40 dBm/Hz, AWGN=-110 dBm/Hz and -40 dB hybrid suppression.

3. Filtered multitone modulation

This multicarrier modulation realization is sometimes called Filter bank Modulation Technique (Cherubini et al.2000). Figure 2 shows a FMT communication system realized by a critically sampled filter bank. The critically sampled filter bank, where the upsampling factor is equal to the size of filter bank 2N, can be realized efficiently with the help of the FFT algorithm, which will be described later. More concretely, the filter bank is non-critical, if the upsampling factor is higher than the size of filter bank (2N).

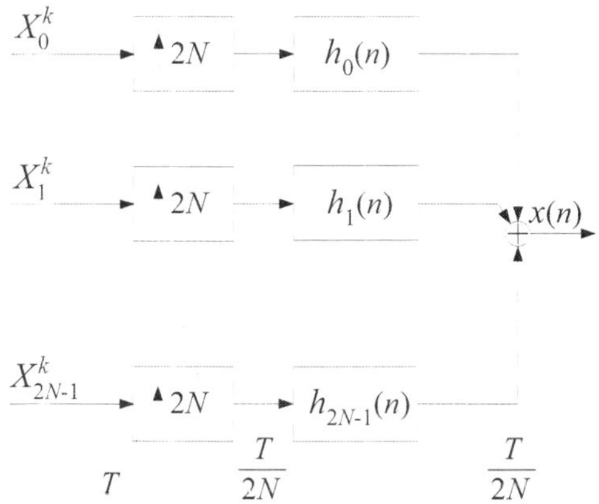

Fig. 2. Basic principle of Filtered MultiTone modulation.

The output signal $x(n)$ of the FMT transmitter given in Fig. 2 can be described using relation:

$$x(n)=\frac{1}{\sqrt{2N}}\sum_{k=-\infty}^{\infty}\sum_{i=0}^{2N-1}X_i^k h_i(n-2kN) \tag{2}$$

The polyphase FIR filters with the impulse response $h_i(n)$ are the frequency-shifted versions of low pass filter with impulse response $h(n)$, called prototype filter:

$$h_i(n)=\frac{1}{\sqrt{2N}}h(n)\;\mathrm{e}^{\mathrm{j}\frac{2\pi ni}{2N}} \tag{3}$$

In equation (3) $h(n)$ is the impulse response of the prototype FIR filter. The order of this filter is $2\gamma N$, where γ is the overlapping factor in the time domain.
For a perfect demodulation of received signal after transmission through the ideal channel the prototype filter must be designed such that for the polyphase filters the condition hold, which is expressed by the equation:

$$\sum_n h_i(n)h_{i'}^*(n-2Nk)=\delta_{i-i'}\delta_k \tag{4}$$

for $0 \le i, i' \le 2N-1$ and $k = \ldots, -1, 0, 1, \ldots$
In equation (4) δi is the Kronecker delta function. The equation defining the orthogonality between the polyphase filters is a more general form of the Nyquist criterion (Cherubini et al.2000). For example, condition (4) of perfect reconstruction is satisfied in the case of DMT modulation, given in equation (1), because the sinc spectrums of individual carriers have zero-values for the rest of corresponding carriers. The ideal frequency characteristic of the prototype filter to realize a non-overlapped FMT modulation system is given by the equation (5).

$$\left|H\left(\mathrm{e}^{\mathrm{j}\pi fT}\right)\right| = \begin{cases} 1 & \text{for } -\dfrac{1}{2T}\le f\le\dfrac{1}{2T} \\ 0 & \text{otherwise} \end{cases} \tag{5}$$

The prototype filter can be designed by the sampling the frequency characteristic (5) and applying the optimal window. Figure 3 shows the spectrum of an FMT modulation system for γ = 10. The prototype filter was designed with the help of the Blackmen window. Suitable windows enabling the design of orthogonal filter bank are e.g. the Blackman window, Blackmanharris window, Hamming window, Hann window, flattop window and Nuttall window. Further examples of the prototype filter design can be found in (Cherubini et al., 2000) and (Berenguer & Wassel, 2002).
The FMT realization of N - 1 carriers modulation system according to Fig. 4 needs $2N$ FIR filters with real coefficients of the order of $2\gamma N$. In (Berenguer & Wassel, 2002) a realization of FMT transmitter using the FFT algorithm is described. This realization is shown in Fig. 4.
In comparison with DMT modulation, each output of IFFT is filtered additionally by an FIR filter $h_i(m)$ of the order of γ. The coefficient of the $h_i(m)$ filter can be determined from the prototype filter $h(n)$ of the order of $2\gamma N$:

$$h_i(m)=h(2mN+i) \tag{6}$$

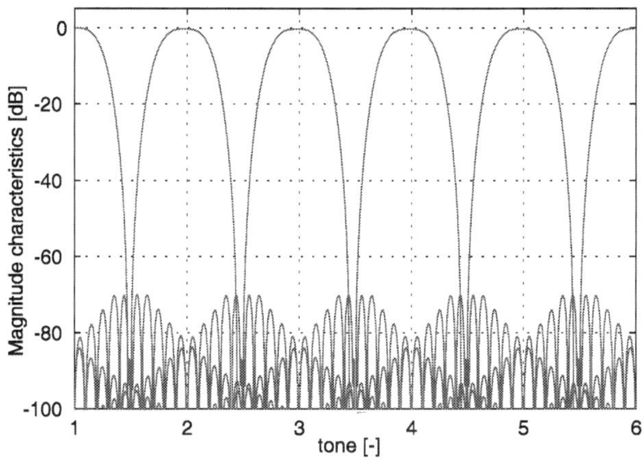

Fig. 3. FMT spectrum for $\gamma = 10$ and Blackman window.

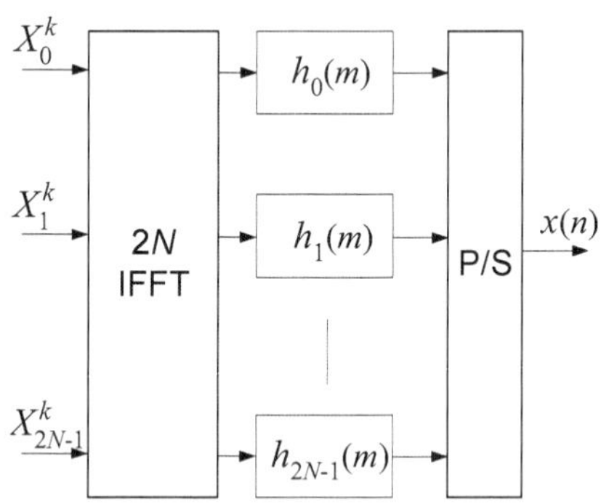

Fig. 4. The realization of FMT transmitter using FFT algorithm.

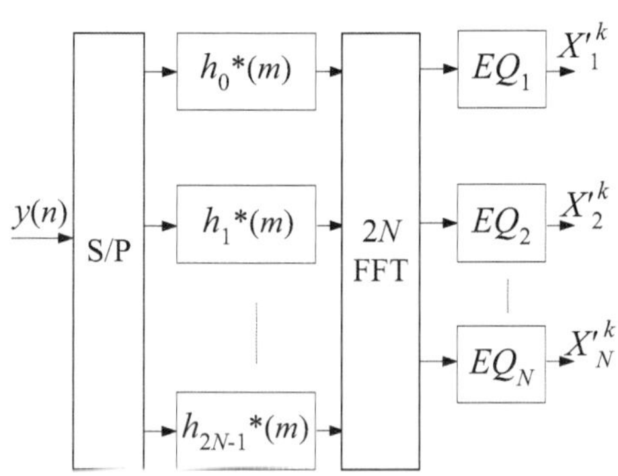

Fig. 5. The realization of FMT receiver using FFT algorithm.

The principle of FMT signal demodulation can be seen in fig 5. Since the individual carriers are completely separated, no ICI interference occurs. Equalization to minimize ISI interference can be performed in the frequency domain without the application of cyclic prefix (Benvenuto et al., 2002). Duplex transmission can be solved by both FDM and EC, without any further filtering, which is the case of DMT. If a part of the frequency band is shared (EC duplex method), the echo cancellation can be realized easily in the frequency domain.

4. Overlapped FMT modulation

The FMT modulation type mentioned in the previous section can be called non-overlapped FMT modulation. The individual carriers are completely separated and do not overlap each other. FMT realization of multicarrier modulation offers a lot of advantages, as mentioned in the preceding chapter. In particular, the frequency band provided is better utilized in the border parts of the spectrum designed for individual transmission directions, where in the case of DMT there are losses in the transmission rate. The out-of-transmission-band emission is eliminated almost completely. If we use the EC duplex method, the simpler suppression of echo signal enables sharing a higher frequency band. A disadvantage of FMT modulation is the increase in transmission delay, which increases with the filter order γ. The FMT transmission delay is minimally γ times higher than the transmission delay of a comparable DMT system and thus the filter order γ must be chosen as a compromise. The suboptimal utilization of provided frequency band in the area between individual carriers belongs to other disadvantages of non-overlapped FMT modulation. Individual carriers are completely separated, but a part of the frequency band between them is therefore not utilized optimally, as shown in Fig. 6. The requirement of closely shaped filters by reason of this unused part minimization just leads to the necessity of the high order of polyphase filters.

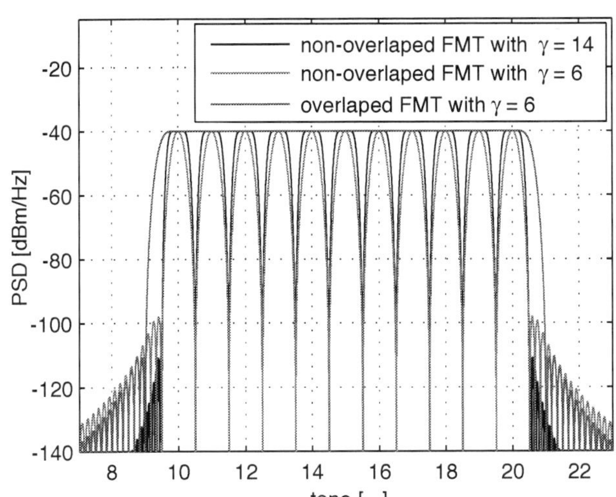

Fig. 6. Comparison of PSD of overlapped and non-overlapped FMT.

The above advantages and disadvantages of the modulations presented in the previous section became the motivation for designing the half subchannel overlapped FMT modulation. An example of this overlapped FMT modulation is shown in Fig. 7. As the Figure shows, individual carriers overlap one half of each other. The side-lobe attenuation is smaller than 100 dB. For example, the necessary signal-to-noise ratio (SNR) for 15 bits per symbol QAM is approximately 55 dB.

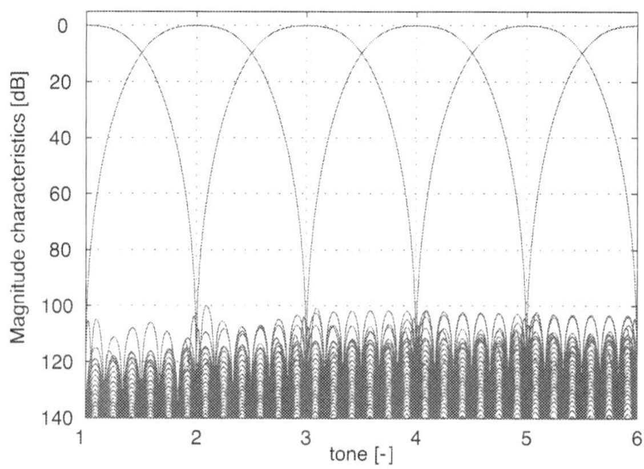

Fig. 7. Overlapped FMT spectrum for $\gamma = 6$ and Nuttall window.

The ratio between transmitted total power in overlapped and non-overlapped FMT modulations of equivalent peak power are shown in Table 1. Suboptimal utilization of the frequency band occurs for smaller filter orders. As has been mentioned, a higher order of filters increases the system delay. The whole system delay depends on the polyphase filter order, number of carriers and delay, which originates in equalizers.

γ[1] [-]	Pp/Pn [2] [dB]	window [3]
4	4.3	Hamming
6	5.4	Blackmen
8	3.5 / 6.0	Blackman /Nuttall
10	2.5 / 4.3	Blackman /Nuttall
12	1.7 / 3.1	Blackman /Nuttall
14	1.0 / 2.4	Blackman /Nuttall
16	1.0 / 1.8	Blackman /Nuttall

[1]Polyphase filter order;
[2]Ratio between power of overlapped and non-overlapped FMT modulation;
[3]Used window;

Table 1. Comparison of ratio between whole transmitted power of overlapped and non-overlapped FMT modulation for the same peak power.

The designed filter has to meet the orthogonal condition, introduced by equation (4). An efficient realization of overlapped FMT modulation is the same as that of non overlapped FMT modulation introduced in Fig. 4. The difference is in the design of the filter coefficients only. Polyphase filters can be of a considerably lower order than filters in non-overlapped FMT modulation, because they need not be so closely shaped in the transient part. The shape of individual filters must be designed so as to obtain a flat power spectral density (PSD) in the frequency band utilized, because it enables an optimal utilization of the frequency band provided. Figure 7 shows an example of such overlapped FMT modulation with γ = 6. The ideal frequency characteristic of overlapped FMT prototype filter can be defined with the help of two conditions:

$$\begin{aligned} &\left|H\left(e^{j\pi fT}\right)\right| = 0 \quad \text{for} \quad |f| \leq \frac{1}{2T} \\ &\left|H\left(e^{j\pi f T}\right)\right|^2 + \left|H\left(e^{j\pi(f T+1/2)}\right)\right|^2 = 1 \quad \text{for} \quad |f| > \frac{1}{2T} \end{aligned} \tag{7}$$

In the design of polyphase filters of very low order it is necessary to chose a compromise between both conditions, i.e. between the ripple in the band used and the stopband attenuation. Examples of some design results for polyphase filter orders of 2, 4 and 6 are shown in (Silhavy, 2008). The filter design method based on the prototype filter was described in the previous chapter.

5. Equalization in overlapped FMT modulation

In overlapped FMT modulation as well as in non-overlapped FMT modulation the inter-symbol interferences (ISI) occur even on an ideal channel, which is given by the FMT modulation system principle. Equalization for ISI interference elimination can be solved in the same manner as in non-overlapped FMT modulation with the help of DFE equalizers, in the frequency domain (see Fig. 5).

If the prototype filter was designed to satisfy orthogonal condition (4), ICI interferences do not occur even in overlapped FMT modulation. More exactly, the ICI interference level is comparable with non-overlapped FMT modulation. This is demonstrated by the simulation results shown in Figures 8 and 9.

In the Figures the 32-carrier system (Figure 8) and 256-carrier system (Figure 9) have been simulated, both with the order of polyphase filters γ equal to 8. The systems were simulated on an CSA-mid loop in the 1MHz frequency band. From a comparison of Figures 8a and 8b it can be seen that ICI interferences in overlapped and non-overlapped FMT modulations are comparable. In the case of a smaller order of polyphase filters γ the ICI interferences are lower even in overlapped FMT. Figure 9 shows the system with 256 carriers. It can be seen that the effect of channel and the ICI interferences are decreasing with growing number of subchannels. The level of ICI interferences is dependent on the order of polyphase filters γ, the type of window used and the number of carriers.

As has been mentioned, the channel equalization whose purpose is to minimize ISI interference can be performed in the frequency domain. Each of the EQn equalizers (see Figure 5.) can be realized as a Decision Feedback Equalizer (DFE). The Decision Feedback Equalizer is shown in Fig. 10. The equalizer works with complex values (Sayed, 2003).

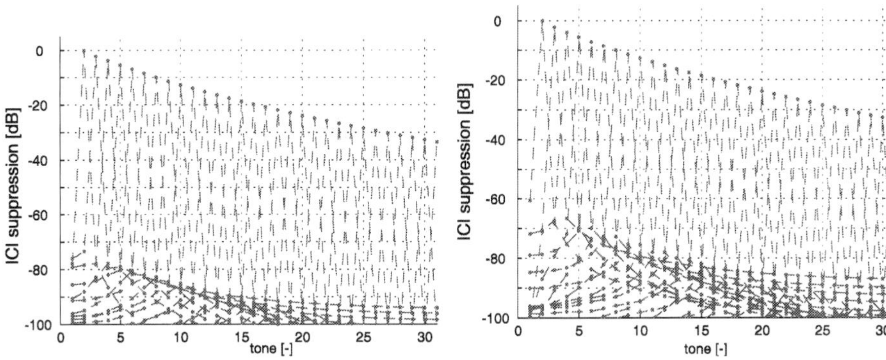

(a) (b)

Fig. 8. ICI suppression in overlapped FMT (a) and in non-overlapped FMT (b) modulation with N = 32, γ= 8 and Nuttal window.

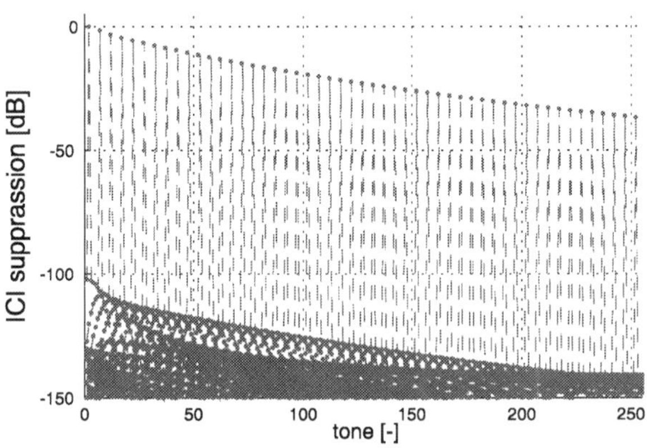

Fig. 9. ICI suppression in overlapped FMT modulation with N = 256, γ = 8 and Nuttal window.

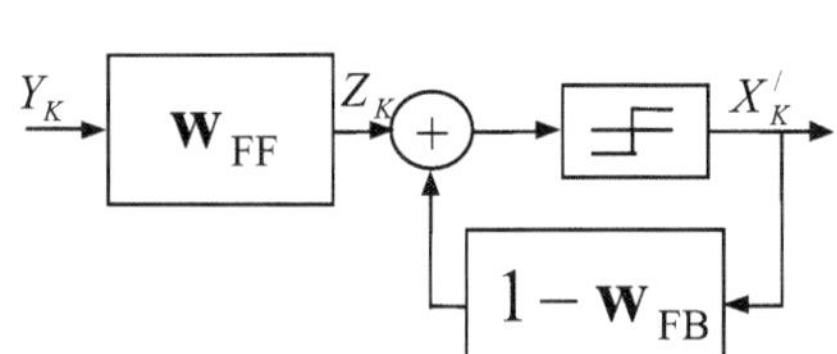

Fig. 10. Decision Feedback equalizer.

The Decision Feedback Equalizer contains two digital FIR (Finite impulse response) filters and a decision circuit. The feedforward filter (FF) with the coefficients $\mathbf{w}_{FF}$ and of the order of M is to shorten the channel impulse response to the feedback filter (FB) length R. The feedforward filter is designed to set the first coefficient of the shortened impulse response of channel to unity. With the help of the feedback filter (FB) with the coefficients 1- $\mathbf{w}_{FB}$ and order R we subtract the rest of the shortened channel impulse response. The whole DFE equalizer thus forms an infinite impulse response (IIR) filter. A linear equalizer, realized only by a feedforward filter, would not be sufficient to eliminate the ISI interference of the FMT system on the ideal channel.

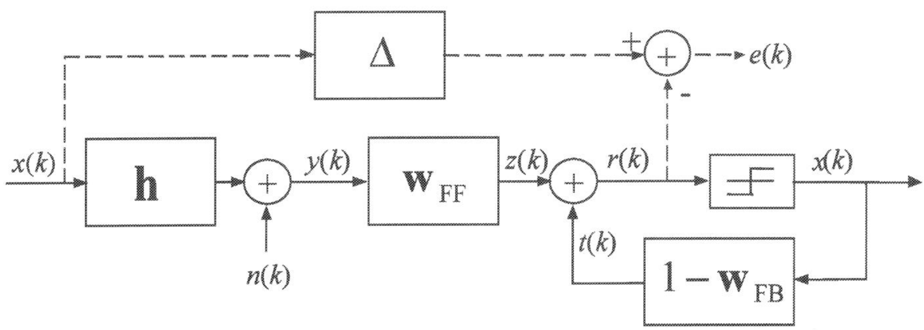

Fig. 11. Description of the sought MMSE minimization for the computation of FIR filters coefficients of equalizer

The sought minimization of mean square error (MMSE) is described in Fig. 11. The transmission channel with the impulse response $\mathbf{h}$ includes the whole of a complex channel of the FMT modulation from X_K to Y_K. The equalization result element $r(k)$ is compared with the delayed transmitted element $x(k)$. The delay Δ is also sought it optimizes the minimization and is equal to the delay inserted by the transmission channel and the feedforward filter. The minimization of the mean square error is described by equation (8).

$$\begin{aligned} e(k) &= x(k-\Delta) - r(k) = x(k-\Delta) - t(k) - z(k) = \\ &= x(k-\Delta) - \hat{x}(k-\Delta) + \sum_{n=0}^{R\text{-}1} \hat{x}(k-n-\Delta)\cdot w_{FB}(n) - \sum_{n=0}^{M-1} y(k-n)\cdot w_{FF}(n) \\ &\text{and } w_{FB}(0) = 1 \end{aligned} \tag{8}$$

On the assumption of correct estimate and thus the validity of $x(k-\Delta) = \hat{x}(k-\Delta)$ we can simplify equation (8):

$$e(k) = \sum_{n=0}^{R\text{-}1} x(k-n-\Delta)\cdot w_{FB}(n) - \sum_{n=0}^{M-1} y(k-n)\cdot w_{FF}(n) \qquad \text{and } w_{FB}(0) = 1 \tag{9}$$

The MMSE can be sought:

$$m_{\text{DFE-MMSE}} = E\{|e(k)|^2\} = \mathbf{w}_{FB}^{H}\mathbf{R}_{xx}\mathbf{w}_{FB} - \mathbf{w}_{FB}^{H}\mathbf{R}_{xy\Delta}\mathbf{w}_{FF} - \mathbf{w}_{FF}^{H}\mathbf{R}_{yx\Delta}\mathbf{w}_{FB} + \mathbf{w}_{FF}^{H}\mathbf{R}_{yy}\mathbf{w}_{FF} \tag{10}$$

The sought minimization $m_{\text{DFE-MMSE}}$ under unity constraint on the first element of shortened response (Silhavy, 2007), introduced by equation (11), is shown by equation (12):

$$m_{\text{DFE-MMSE}} = \mathbf{w}_{\text{FB}}^{\text{H}} \mathbf{R}_{\text{X}|\text{Y}} \mathbf{w}_{\text{FB}} + \lambda\left(1 - \mathbf{f}_0^{\ \text{T}} \mathbf{w}_{\text{FB}}\right) \tag{11}$$

$$m_{\text{DFE-MMSE}} = \frac{1}{\mathbf{f}_0^{\ \text{T}} \mathbf{R}_{\text{X}|\text{Y}}^{\ -1} \mathbf{f}_0} \tag{12}$$

where

$$\mathbf{R}_{\text{X}|\text{Y}} = \mathbf{R}_{\text{xx}} - \mathbf{R}_{\text{xy}\Delta} \mathbf{R}_{\text{yy}}^{\ -1} \mathbf{R}_{\text{yx}\Delta} \tag{13}$$

and $\mathbf{f}_0$ is the column zero vector of the same length as feedforward filter R with element one in the first position: $\mathbf{f}_0^{\text{T}} = [1 \quad \mathbf{0}_{\text{R-1}}]$

In this equation, $\mathbf{R}_{\mathbf{xx}}$ is the autocorrelation matrix of the input signal of M x M size, $\mathbf{R}_{\mathbf{xy}}\Delta$ and $\mathbf{R}_{\mathbf{yx}\Delta}$are the correlation matrices between the input and output signals of M x R and R x M sizes. These matrices are dependent on the parameter delay Δ, which defines the shift between the input and the output signals. For these matrices it holds that $\mathbf{R}_{\text{xy}\Delta} = \mathbf{R}_{\text{yx}\Delta}^{\text{H}}$. During the computation it is necessary to find the optimal delay Δ_{opt}, which can be determined based on computed minimization $m_{\text{DFE-MMSE}}$. The optimal delay, however, must be set the same for the whole equalizer bank. During the heuristic optimal delay search for each equalizer the most frequent delay needs to be determined and this delay must be used for coefficient computation of each equalizer of demodulator. In opposite case, the individual symbols would be mutually shifted, which would cause demodulation difficulties. $\mathbf{R}_{\text{yy}}$ is the autocorrelation matrix of the output signal of R x R size. This matrix includes the influence of the channel impulse response $\mathbf{h}$ and noise.

The vectors of coefficients of equalizer for a given delay Δ can be computed as shown by the following equations:

$$\mathbf{w}_{\text{FB}} = \frac{\mathbf{R}_{\text{X}|\text{Y}}^{\ -1} \mathbf{f}_0}{\mathbf{f}_0^{\ \text{T}} \mathbf{R}_{\text{X}|\text{Y}}^{\ -1} \mathbf{f}_0} \tag{14}$$

$$\mathbf{w}_{\text{FF}} = \mathbf{R}_{\text{yy}}^{\ -1} \mathbf{R}_{\text{yx}\Delta} \mathbf{w}_{\text{FB}} \tag{15}$$

Alternatively, we can based the computation of the coefficients of individual DFE equalizer filters on channel impulse response $\mathbf{h}$ only, without including the input signal and noise $\mathbf{n}$. This solution can be simply derived based on the previous solution after following derivation. The convolution matrix of a channel with impulse response $\mathbf{h}$ and length k is defined by the equation:

$$\mathbf{H} = \begin{bmatrix} h_0 & 0 & \cdots & 0 \\ h_1 & h_0 & \cdots & 0 \\ \vdots & \vdots & \ddots & \vdots \\ h_{k-1} & h_{k-2} & \cdots & h_{k-M} \\ 0 & h_{k-1} & \cdots & h_{k-M+1} \\ \vdots & \vdots & \ddots & \vdots \\ 0 & 0 & \cdots & h_{k-1} \end{bmatrix} \tag{16}$$

From this matrix we chose the shortened part in the terms of delay Δ with the help of vector **G**:

$$G = \text{diag}\big(\underbrace{0, \, \dots \, , 0,}_{\Delta} \overbrace{\underbrace{1, \, \dots \, , 1,}_{R} \, 0, \, \dots, 0}^{k+M-1 \text{ samples}}\big) \tag{17}$$

The sought matrix $\mathbf{R}_{X|Y}$, introduced by equation (13), of the Zero-forcing solution is shown by equation (18):

$$\mathbf{R}_{X|Y\_ZeroForce} = \mathbf{I} - \mathbf{GH}\left(\mathbf{H}^{H} \cdot \mathbf{H}\right)^{-1} \mathbf{H}^{H}\mathbf{G}^{H} \tag{18}$$

The approach presented enables determining the individual equalizer filter coefficients from the channel impulse response **h** only. The matrix **G** determines the maximized area and thus the delay Δ between the input and the output signals. In some cassis the matrix $\mathbf{R}_{X|Y\_ZeroForce}$ is not invertible. This problem can be fixed by increasing the components in the main diagonal, as shows by the equation:

$$\bar{\mathbf{A}} = \mathbf{A} + k_{opt} \cdot \max\{\text{diag}(\mathbf{A})\} \cdot \mathbf{I} \tag{19}$$

where max{daig(**A**)} is the maximal element of the main diagonal of matrix **A**, and k_{opt} is the optimization factor, which can be increased in several steps (e.g. 10^{-10}, 10^{-8}, 10^{-6}, ...).

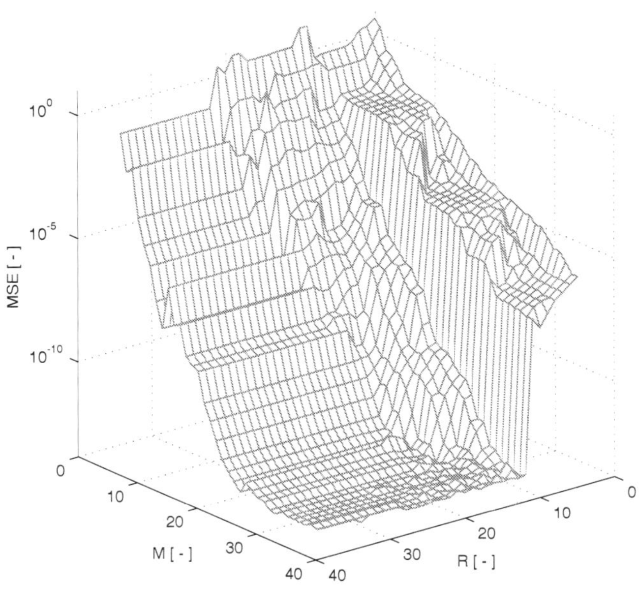

Fig. 12. Achieved MSE in dependence on both filter order for overlapped FMT system with γ =10, Nuttalwin window and ANSI 7 channel.

For the purpose of analyses we choose an FMT system with N = 32 carriers, a sampling frequency of 2 MHz, the Nuttalwin window type and the polyphase filter order γ =10, 12 and 14. Selected tested channels were the ideal channel and ANSI 7. The channels were modeled by an infinite impulse response (IIR) filter of the order of 60. In Figures 12, 13 and 14 for the purpose of comparing whole FMT systems the MSE is computed as summation of MSE of all N carriers. Figure 12 shows the dependence of achieved MSE on the order of both filters for overlapped FMT system with γ =12, Nuttalwin window and ANSI 7 channel. The optimal combination of orders can be different for different FMT systems and channel types. From Figures 13 a) and 13 b) it can be seen that the transmit and receive filters are of primary influence on the appearance of ISI interference. The necessary equalizer filter order is a little higher than the polyphase filter order.

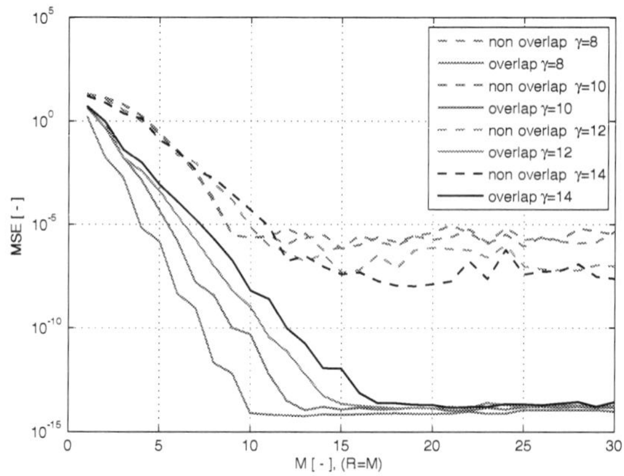

(a)

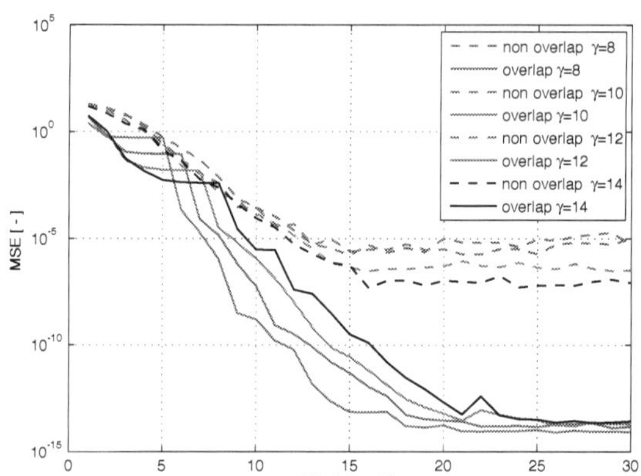

(b)

Fig. 13. Achieved MSE in dependence on filters order M=R for different FMT systems on ideal channel (a) and ANSI 7 channel (b).

6. Implementation of Filtered MultiTone in Matlab and on DSP

This chapter is devoted to describtion of the implementation of FMT and DMT modulations. Theoretical properties of the FMT modulations with all advantages and disadvantages have been described in previous chapters. Implementation of FMT modulation in Matlab-Simulink and on DSP is necessary for comparison of characteristics of this modulation with other ones in various communication systems.

Design of proper prototype filter is the first step in implementation of FMT. Prototype filter design methods are mentioned in chapter 3. Prototype filters for the implementation have been designed by the windowing method, using the Blackman, Modified Blackman and Nutall windows. The polyphase filters for non-overlap FMT modulation were of the order γ =14 (Blackman window) and in half-overlap FMT modulation filters of the order γ =6 (Modified Blackman window, subchannel crossing at -3dB) and γ =8 (Nuttall window, subchannel crossing at -6dB).

As mentioned above, almost twice higher order of polyphase filters in the non-overlap FMT had to be used because of the need for a spectral separation of individual subchannels, i.e. the need for a sharp transition from pass-band to stop-band. Two variants of half-overlapped FMT were used for comparison of spectral characteristics and power spectral density.

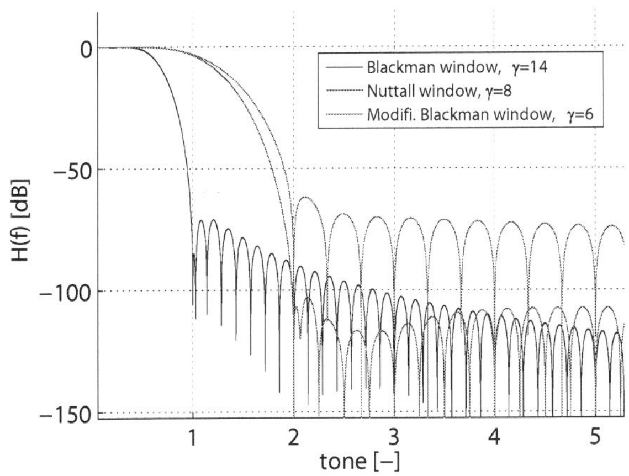

Fig. 14. Prototype filters used in implementation

Furthermore, we proposed a suitable model of FMT Modulation in Matlab-Simulink. As a source of pseudorandom binary sequence the Bernoulli random binary generator was chosen. Binary data are transmitted to the bank of QAM modulators, number of bits per channel is determined by signal to noise ratio on carrier, for example by the help of a bit-loading algorithm (Akujobi & Shen, 2008). After it the IFFT modulation is performed. In the model, we consider transmission over metallic lines and also comparison of the FMT with DMT modulation, so it is necessary to complement the modulation symbols to the number $2N$ according to (1) before IFFT. Filtering of IFFT output by the filter bank is the final step on the transmitter side. The filter bank was built-up from polyphase components of prototype filter mentioned above.

The procedure in the receiver is inverted. Firstly the received signal is filtered by receiver filter bank and after that, FFT is performed. In the next step the added symbols are removed i.e. the symbols *0* and *N...2N*. Through the characteristics of FMT modulation mentioned in chapter 5 is necessary to use equalization. DFE equalization with RLS adaptive algorithm is used in our model. Equalized symbols are then demodulated by a bank of QAM demodulators.

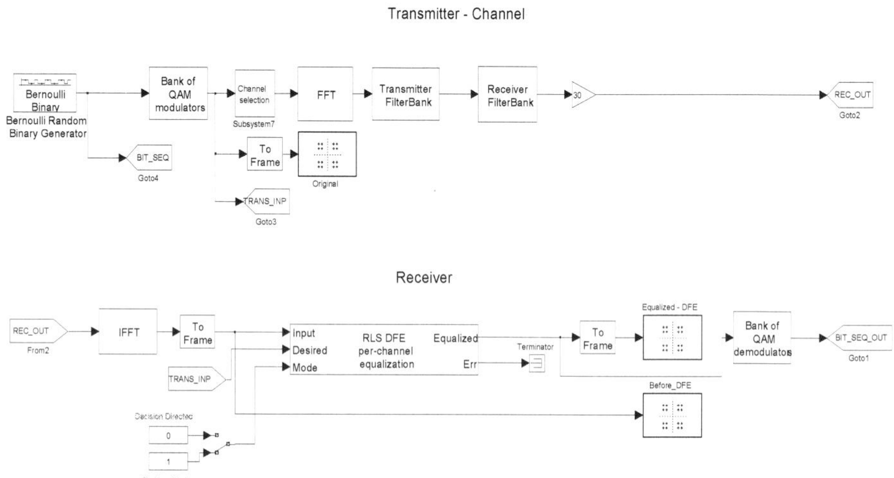

Fig. 15. FMT system in Matlab-Simulink

The resistance of narrowband noise on chosen carrier was tested on this model. This type of interference is very common in real conditions. Narrowband noise on 10th carrier was applied in our case.

The evaluation was done by measuring the signal to noise ratio, SNR. For the half-overlap FMT modulation the measurements were performed only for variants with subchannel crossing at level -3dB. The results of the measurements are presented in Fig.17. It is obvious that the DMT modulation has the worst properties, where the narrowband interference on 10th carrier degrades SNR on a large number of surrounding carriers. The opposite case is FMT modulation, in both variants the SNR is degraded only on the carrier with narrowband interference. For the half-overlap FMT modulation degradation on two nearby carriers was expected, but the measurement shows degradation only on 10th carrier.

The model described above can be adjusted and implemented on DSP. The chosen development kit uses the TI C6713 floating-point digital signal processor. The model is divided into part of transmitter and part of receiver. The signal processing procedure is identical to the model. After generation of pseudorandom binary sequence, QAM modulation is performed. The number of bits transmitted on the sub-carrier is chosen before the actual implementation. After it the IFFT modulation is performed and each output is filtered by the transmitter filter bank. The last step is to adjust the amplitude of the transmitted signal to the range of DAC converter. In this way modified model was then compiled and implemented on digital signal processor with the help of the Link for CCS toolbox.

This way of generating code is fully functional and they allow measuring the proposed algorithm directly in the digital signal processor but they definitely cannot be considered optimized. It is convenient to use libraries that are optimized for a given processor and replace the standard Simulink blocks by optimized ones. It is also possible to replace the original number formats by formats corresponding to the processor. Also the filterbank can be designed in two ways. The first way is independent filtering in each branch of filterbank (Sysel, Krajsa 2010).

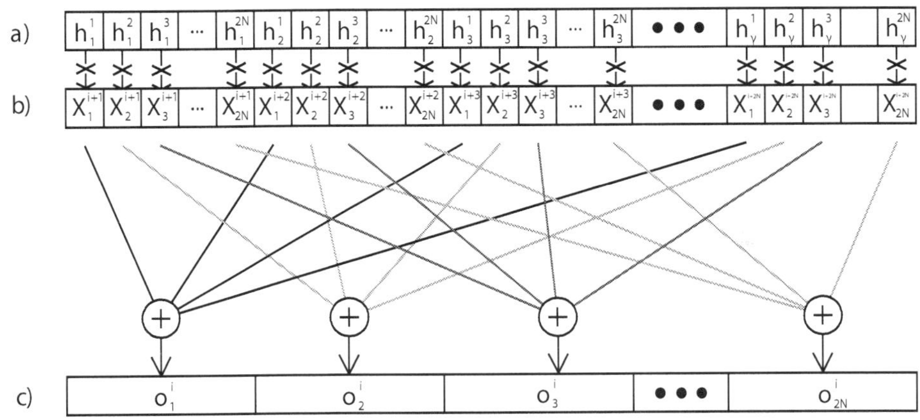

Fig. 16. Efficient filterbank implementation

The second one is described on Fig. 16, where h_n^m is n-th coefficient of m-th filter, X_m^i is i-th IFFT symbol in m-th branch and o_m^i is i-th output sample in m-th branch. We have three buffers, one (a) for prototype coefficients, one (b) for input symbols from IFFT, and the last one (c) for output frame. Buffer b is FIFO buffer, samples are written in frames of 2N samples. This way of filtering is more effective, because we need only one for cycle for computing one output frame.

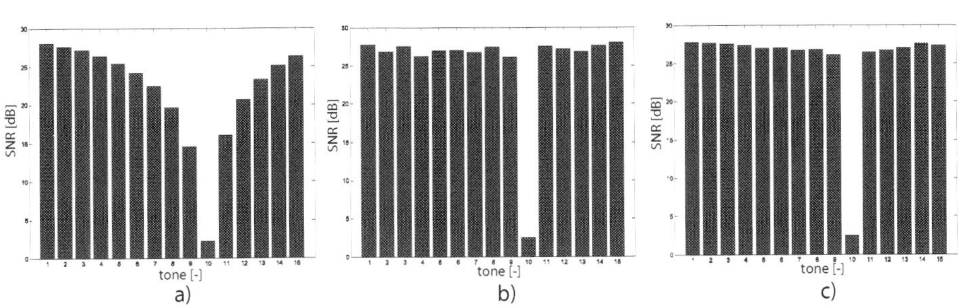

Fig. 17. SNR for a) DMT, b) Non-overlapped FMT, c) Half-overlapped FMT with narrowband noise

In the term of testing and comparing the implementation on DSP is interesting for the possibility of power spectral density measurement and for its characteristics inside and outside of the transmission band of partial subchannels on real line. In Fig. 19 is measured PSD for the considered modulations.

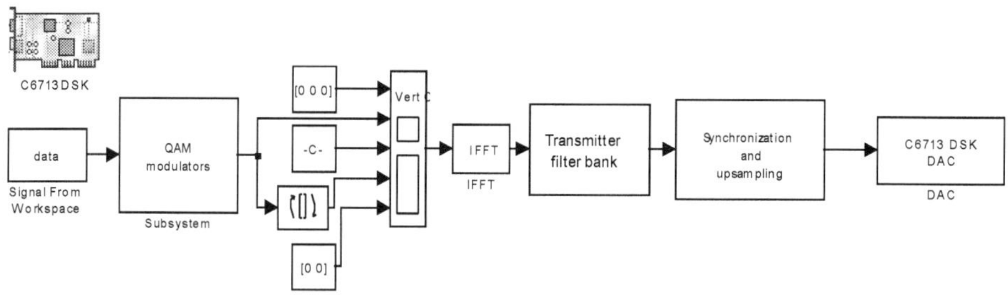

Fig. 18. FMT transmitter adjusted for implementation

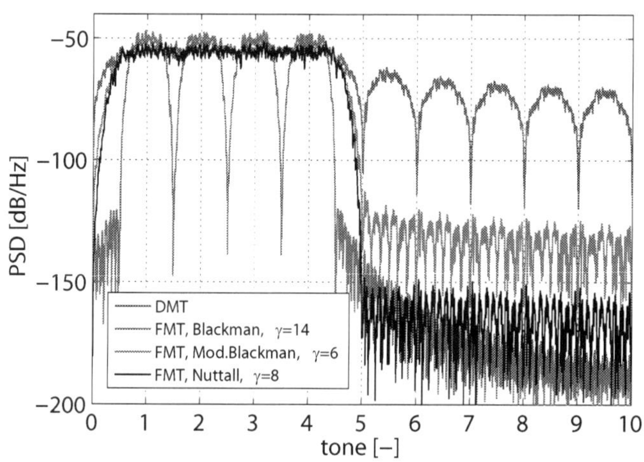

Fig. 19. Measured power spectral densit

It is clear that the implementation results confirm the theoretical assumptions about the properties of implemented modulations, mainly about their spectral properties. For the half-overlap FMT modulation the PSD measured was flat, as well as with DMT modulation, but the side lobes are suppressed by up to 50 dB. For the non-overlap FMT modulation perfectly separated subchannels and strongly repressed side lobes are again evident.

In the implementation the computational complexity of individual modulation was also compared. The most common form of DMT modulation needs to implement only the *2N*-point FFT, while with FMT each FFT output must be filtered. This represents an increase in the required computational power and in the memory used. A comparison of DMT and FMT for different systems is shown in the table. It compares the number of MAC instructions needed for processing one frame of length *2N*.

7. Conclusion

Based on a comparison of DMT and non-overlapped FMT multicarrier modulations we introduced in this contribution the half-overlap subchannel FMT modulation. This modulation scheme enables using optimally the available frequency band, such as DMT modulation, because the resultant power spectral density of the signal is flat. Also, the border frequency band is used optimally, the same as in non-overlapped FMT modulation. Compared to non-overlapped FMT modulation the subchannel width is double and the carriers cannot be too closely shaped. That enables using a smaller polyphase filter order and thus obtaining a smaller delay. In section 5 we demonstrated that if the prototype filter was designed to satisfy the orthogonal condition, even in overlapped FMT modulation the ICI interferences do not occur. Furthermore, a method for channel equalization with the help of DFE equalizer has been presented and the computation of individual filter coefficients has been derived.

8. Acknowledgments

This work was prepared within the solution of the MSM 021630513 research programme and the Grant Agency of Czech Republic project No. 102/09/1846.

9. References

Akujuobi C.M.; Shen J. (2008) Efficient Multi-User Parallel Greedy Bit-Loading Algorithm with Fairness Control For DMT Systems,In: Greedy Algorithms, Witold Bednorz, 103-130, In-tech, ISBN:978-953-7619-27-5

Cherubini G.; Eleftheriou E.; Olcer S., Cioffi M. (2000) Filter bank modulation techniques for VHDSL. *IEEE Communication Magazine*, (May 2000), pp. 98 - 104, ISSN: 0163-6804

Bingham, J, A. C.(2000) *ADSL, VDSL, and multicarrier modulation*, John Wiley & Sons, Inc., ISBN 0-471-29099-8, New York

Benvenuto N.; Tomasin S.; Tomba L.(2002) Equalization methods in DMT and FMT Systems for Broadband Wireless Communications. In *IEEE Transactions on Communications*, vol. 50, no. 9(September 2002), pp. 1413-1418, ISSN: 0090-6778

Berenguer, I.; Wassell J. I. (2002) FMT modulation: receiver filter bank definition for the derivation of an efficient implementation, IEEE 7th International OFDM workshop, Hamburg, (Germany, September 2002)

Sandberg S. D. & Tzannes M. A. (1995) Overlapped Discrete Multitone Modulation for High Speed Copper Wire Communications. *IEEE Journal on Selected Areas in Communications*, vol. 13, no.9, (December 1995), pp. 1571 - 1585, ISSN: 0733-8716

Sayed, A.H. (2003) *Fundamentals of Adaptive Filtering*, John Wiley & Sons, Inc, ISBN 0-471-46126-1, New York

Silhavy, P. (2007) Time domain equalization in modern communication systems based on discrete multitone modulation. *Proceedings of Sixth International Conference of Networking*.pp. , ISBN: 0-7695-2805-8 , Sante-Luce, Martinique, , April 2007, IARIA

Silhavy, P.(2008) Half-overlap subchannel Filtered MultiTone Modulation with the small delay. *Proceedings of the Seventh International Conference on Networking 2008*, pp. 474-478, ISBN: 978-0-7695-3106-9, Cancun, Mexico, April 2008, IARIA

Sysel, P.; Krajsa, O.(2010) Optimization of FIR filter implementation for FMT on VLIW DSP. *Proceedings of the 4th International Conference on Circuits, Systems and Signals (CSS'10).* ISBN: 978-960-474-208- 0, Corfu, 2010 WSEAS Press

Adaptive Step-size Order Statistic LMS-based Time-domain Equalisation in Discrete Multitone Systems

Suchada Sitjongsataporn and Peerapol Yuvapoositanon
Centre of Electronic Systems Design and Signal Processing (CESdSP)
Mahanakorn University of Technology
Thailand

1. Introduction

Discrete multitone (DMT) is a digital implementation of the multicarrier transmission technique for digital subscriber line (DSL) standard (Golden et al., 2006; Starr et al., 1999). An all-digital implementation of multicarrier modulation called *DMT modulation* has been standardised for asymmetric digital subscriber line (ADSL), ADSL2, ADSL2+ and very high bit rate DSL (VDSL) (ITU, 2001; 2002; 2003). ADSL modems rely on DMT modulation, which divides a broadband channel into many narrowband subchannels and modulated encoded signals onto the narrowband subchannels. The major impairments such as the intersymbol interference (ISI), the intercarrier interference (ICI), the channel distortion, echo, radio-frequency interference (RFI) and crosstalk from DSL systems are induced as a result of large bandwidth utilisation over the telephone line. However, the improvement can be achieved by the equalisation concepts. A time-domain equaliser (TEQ) has been suggested for equalisation in DMT-based systems (Bladel & Moenclaey, 1995; Baldemair & Frenger, 2001; Wang & Adali, 2000) and multicarrier systems (Lopez-Valcarce, 2004).
The so-called shortened impulse response (SIR) which is basically the convolutional result of TEQ and channel impulse response (CIR) is preferably shortened as most as possible. By employing a TEQ, the performance of a DMT system is less sensitive to the choice of length of cyclic prefix. It is inserted between DMT symbols to provide subchannel independency to eliminate intersymbol interference (ISI) and intercarrier interference (ICI). TEQs have been introduced in DMT systems to alleviate the effect of ISI and ICI in case that the length of SIR or shorter than the length of cyclic prefix (F-Boroujeny & Ding, 2001). The target impulse response (TIR) is a design parameter characterising the derivation of the TEQ. By employing a TEQ, the performance of a DMT system is less sensitive to the choice of length of the cyclic prefix. In addition to TEQ, a frequency-domain equaliser (FEQ) is provided for each tone separately to compensate for the amplitude and phase of distortion. An ultimate objective of most TEQ designs is to minimise the mean square error (MSE) between output of TEQ and TIR which implies that TEQ and TIR are optimised in the MSE sense (F-Boroujeny & Ding, 2001).
Existing TEQ algorithms are based upon mainly in the MMSE-based approach (Al-Dhahir & Cioffi, 1996; Lee et al., 1995; Yap & McCanny, 2002; Ysebaert et al., 2003). These include

the MMSE-TEQ design algorithm with the unit tap constraint (UTC) in (Lee et al., 1995) and the unit energy constraint (UEC) in (Ysebaert et al., 2003). Only a few adaptive algorithms for TEQ are proposed in the literature. In (Yap & McCanny, 2002), a combined structure using the order statistic normalised averaged least mean fourth (OS-NALMF) algorithm for TEQ and order statistic normalised averaged least mean square (OS-NALMS) for TIR is presented. The advantage of a class of order statistic least mean square algorithms has been presented in (Haweel & Clarkson, 1992) which are similar to the usual gradient-based least mean square (LMS) algorithm with robust order statistic filtering operations applied to the gradient estimate sequence.

The purpose of this chapter is therefore finding the adaptive low-complexity time-domain equalisation algorithm for DMT-based systems which more robust as compared to existing algorithms. The chapter is organised as follows. In Section 2 , we describe the overview of system and data model. In Section 3 , the MMSE-based time-domain equalisation is reviewed. In Section 4 , the derivation of normalised least mean square (NLMS) algorithm with the constrained optimisation for TEQ and TIR are introduced. We derive firstly the stochastic gradient-based TEQ and TIR design criteria based upon the well known low-complexity NLMS algorithm with the method of Lagrange multiplier. It is simple and robust for ISI and ICI. This leads into Section 5 , where the order statistic normalised averaged least mean square (OS-NALMS) TEQ and TIR are presented. Consequently, the adaptive step-size order statistic normalised averaged least mean square (AS-OSNALMS) algorithms for TEQ and TIR can be introduced as the solution of MSE sense. This allows to track changing channel conditions and be quite suitable and flexible for DMT-based systems. In Section 6 , the analysis of stability of proposed algorithm for TEQ and TIR is shown. In Section 7 and Section 8 , the simulation results and conclusion are presented.

2. System and data model

The basic structure of the DMT transceiver is illustrated in Fig. 1. The incoming bit stream is likewise reshaped to a complex-valued transmitted symbol for mapping in quadrature amplitude modulation (QAM). Then, the output of QAM bit stream is split into N parallel bit streams that are instantaneously fed to the modulating inverse fast Fourier transform (IFFT). After that, IFFT outputs are transformed into the serial symbols including the cyclic prefix (CP) between symbols in order to prevent intersymbol interference (ISI) (Henkel et al., 2002) and then fed to the channel. The transmission channel will be used throughout the chapter is based on parameters in (ITU, 2001). The transmitted signal sent over the channel with impulse response is generally corrupted by the additive white Gaussian noise (AWGN).

The received signal is also equalised by TEQ. The number of coefficients of TEQ is particularly used to make the shortened-channel impulse response (SIR) length, which is the desired length of the channel after equalisation. The frequency-domain equaliser (FEQ) is essentially a one-tap equaliser that is the fast Fourier transform (FFT) of the composite channel of the convolution between the coefficients of the channel ($\mathbf{h}$) and the tap-weight vector ($\mathbf{w}$) of TEQ. The parallel of received symbols are eventually converted into serial bits in the frequency-domain.

The data model is based on a finite impulse response (FIR) model of transmission channel and will be used for equaliser in DMT-based systems. The basic data model is assumed that the transmission channel, including the transmitter and receiver filter front end. This can be represented with an FIR model $\mathbf{h}$. The k-th received sample vector which is used for the detection of the k-th transmitted symbol vector $\mathbf{x}_{k,N}$, is given by

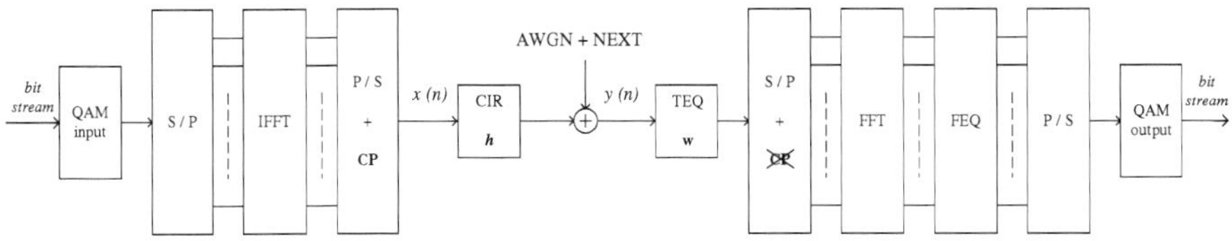

Fig. 1. Block diagram for time-domain equalisation.

$$\underbrace{\begin{bmatrix} y_{k,l+\Delta} \\ \vdots \\ y_{k,N-l+\Delta} \end{bmatrix}}_{\mathbf{y}_{k,l+\Delta:N-1+\Delta}} = \underbrace{\begin{bmatrix} \mathbf{0}_{(1)} & \overbrace{\begin{vmatrix} [\,\bar{\mathbf{h}}^T\,]\; 0 \cdots \\ \ddots\;\ddots \\ \cdots\; 0\; [\,\bar{\mathbf{h}}^T\,] \end{vmatrix}}^{\mathbf{H}_T} & \mathbf{0}_{(2)} \end{bmatrix}}_{\mathbf{H}} \cdot (\mathbf{I} \otimes \mathbf{P}_\nu \mathcal{F}_N^H) \cdot \underbrace{\begin{bmatrix} \mathbf{x}_{k-1,N} \\ \mathbf{x}_{k,N} \\ \mathbf{x}_{k+1,N} \end{bmatrix}}_{\mathbf{x}_{k-1:k+1,N}} + \underbrace{\begin{bmatrix} \eta_{k,l+\Delta} \\ \vdots \\ \eta_{k,N-l+\Delta} \end{bmatrix}}_{\eta_{k,l+\Delta:N-1+\Delta}}, \tag{1}$$

where

- The notation for the received sample vectors $\mathbf{y}_{k,l+\Delta:N-l+\Delta}$ and the received samples $y_{k,l+\Delta}$ are introduced by

$$\mathbf{y}_{k,l+\Delta:N-l+\Delta} = [\; y_{k,l+\Delta} \;\; \cdots \;\; y_{k,N-l+\Delta} \;]^T, \tag{2}$$

  where l determines the first considered sample of the k-th received DMT-symbol and depends on the number of equaliser taps L. The parameter Δ is a synchronisation delay.
- $\bar{\mathbf{h}}$ is the CIR vector $\mathbf{h}$ with coefficients in reverse order.
- $\mathbf{I}$ is an $n \times n$ identity matrix and $\otimes$ denotes the Kronecker product. The $(N+\nu) \times N$ matrix $\mathcal{P}_\nu$, which adds the cyclic prefix of length ν , is introduced by

$$\mathbf{x}_{k,-\nu:N-1} = \underbrace{\begin{bmatrix} \mathbf{0}_{\nu \times (N-\nu)} \,|\mathbf{I}_\nu \\ \hline \mathbf{I}_N \end{bmatrix}}_{\mathcal{P}_\nu} \mathbf{x}_{k,0:N-1}, \tag{3}$$

  where the sample vector $\mathbf{x}_{k,-\nu:-1}$ is called a cyclic prefix (CP).
- $\mathcal{F}_N^H = \mathcal{F}_N^*$ is the $N \times N$ IDFT matrix.
- The $N \times 1$ transmitted symbol vector $\mathbf{x}_{k,N}$ is introduced by

$$\mathbf{x}_{k,N} = [\; x_{k,0} \;\; \cdots \;\; x_{k,N-1} \;]^T = [\; x^*_{k,N-1} \;\; \cdots \;\; x^*_{k,\frac{N}{2}+1} \;]^T, \tag{4}$$

- The vector $\eta_{k,l+\Delta:N-1+\Delta}$ is a sample vector with additive channel noise, and its autocorrelation matrix is denoted as $\Sigma^2_\eta = E\{\eta_k \eta_k^T\}$.
- The matrices $\mathbf{0}_{(1)}$ and $\mathbf{0}_{(2)}$ in Eq.(1) are the zero matrices of size $(N-l) \times (N-L+2\nu+\Delta+l)$ and $(N-l) \times (N+\nu-\Delta)$, respectively.
- The transmitted symbol vector is denoted as $\mathbf{x}_{k-1:k+1,N}$, where $\mathbf{x}_{k-1,N}$ and $\mathbf{x}_{k+1,N}$ introduce ISI. The $\mathbf{x}_{k,N}$ is the symbol vector of interest.

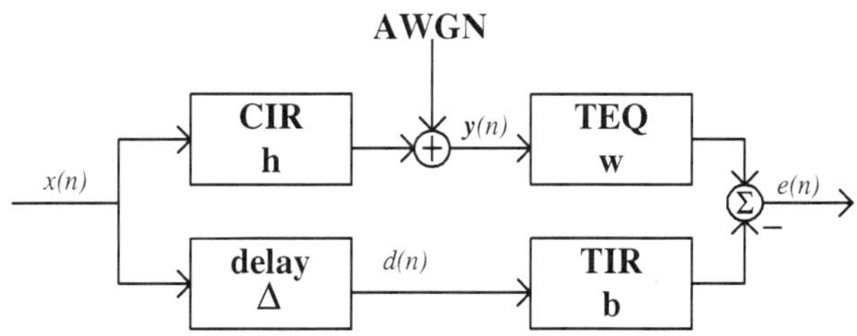

Fig. 2. Block diagram of MMSE-TEQ.

Some notation will be used throughout this chapter as follows: $E\{\cdot\}, (\cdot)^T, (\cdot)^H$ denote as the expectation, transpose and Hermitian operators, respectively. The vectors are in bold lowercase and matrices are in bold uppercase.

3. Minimum mean square error-based time-domain equalisation

The design of minimum mean square error time-domain equalisation (MMSE-TEQ) is based on the block diagram in Figure 2. The transmitted symbol $\mathbf{x}$ is sent over the channel with the impulse response $\mathbf{h}$ and corrupted by AWGN η. The convolution of the L-tap TEQ filter $\mathbf{w}$ and the CIR $\mathbf{h}$ of $N_h + 1$ samples are sufficiently shortened so that overall of impulse response has length $\nu + 1$ that should make TEQ as a channel shortener $\mathbf{c} = \mathbf{h} * \mathbf{w}$, called the shorten impulse response (SIR). Then the orthogonality between the tones are restored and ISI vanishes (Melsa et al., 1996).
The result of time-domain error e between the TEQ output and the TIR output is then minimised in the mean-square sense as

$$\min_{\mathbf{w},\mathbf{b}} E\{|e|^2\} = \min_{\mathbf{w},\mathbf{b}} E\{|\mathbf{y}^T\mathbf{w} - \mathbf{x}_\Delta^T\mathbf{b}|^2\} \tag{5}$$

$$= \min_{\mathbf{w},\mathbf{b}} \mathbf{w}^T\Sigma_{\mathbf{y}}^2\mathbf{w} + \mathbf{b}^T\Sigma_{\mathbf{x}}^2\mathbf{b} - 2\mathbf{b}^T\Sigma_{\mathbf{xy}}(\Delta)\mathbf{w}, \tag{6}$$

where $\Sigma_{\mathbf{y}}^2 = E\{\mathbf{y}\mathbf{y}^T\}$ and $\Sigma_{\mathbf{x}}^2 = E\{\mathbf{x}\mathbf{x}^T\}$ are autocorrelation matrices, and where $\Sigma_{\mathbf{xy}}(\Delta) = E\{\mathbf{x}_\Delta\mathbf{y}^T\}$ is a cross-correlation matrix.
To avoid the trivial all-zero solution $\mathbf{w} = \mathbf{0}, \mathbf{b} = \mathbf{0}$, a constraint on the TEQ or TIR is therefore imposed.
Some constraints that are added on the TEQ and TIR (Ysebaert et al., 2003) as follows.

1. The unit-norm constraint (UNC) on the TIR
   By solving Eq.(6) subject to
   $$\mathbf{b}^T\mathbf{b} = 1. \tag{7}$$
   The solution of $\mathbf{b}$ is the eigen-vector and $\mathbf{w}$ can be given as
   $$\mathbf{w} = (\Sigma_{\mathbf{y}}^2)^{-1}\Sigma_{\mathbf{xy}}^T\,\mathbf{b}. \tag{8}$$
2. The unit-tap constraint (UTC) on the TEQ
   A UTC on $\mathbf{w}$ can be calculated with the method of the linear equation
   $$\mathbf{e}_j^T\,\mathbf{w} = 1 \quad \text{or} \quad \mathbf{e}_j^T\,\mathbf{w} = -1, \tag{9}$$

where $\mathbf{e}_j$ is the canonical vector with element one in the j-th position. By determining the dominant generalised eigen-vector, the vector $\mathbf{w}$ can be obtained as the closed-form solution

$$\mathbf{w} = \frac{\mathbf{A}^{-1}\,\mathbf{e}_j}{\mathbf{e}_j^T\,\mathbf{A}^{-1}\,\mathbf{e}_j}, \tag{10}$$

where $\mathbf{A} = \Sigma_{\mathbf{y}}^2 - \Sigma_{\mathbf{xy}}^T\,(\Sigma_{\mathbf{x}}^2)^{-1}\,\Sigma_{\mathbf{xy}}$.

3. The unit-tap constraint (UTC) on the TIR
   Similarly, a UTC on $\mathbf{b}$ can be described as

$$\mathbf{e}_j^T\,\mathbf{b} = 1 \quad \text{or} \quad \mathbf{e}_j^T\,\mathbf{b} = -1\,, \tag{11}$$

   After computing the solution for $\mathbf{b}$ as

$$\mathbf{b} = \frac{\mathbf{A}^{-1}\,\mathbf{e}_j}{\mathbf{e}_j^T\,\mathbf{A}^{-1}\,\mathbf{e}_j}\,. \tag{12}$$

   The coefficients of TEQ $\mathbf{w}$ can be computed by Eq.(8).

4. The unit-energy constraint (UEC) on TEQ and TIR
   Three UECs can be considered as

$$\mathbf{w}^{\mathbf{T}}\Sigma_{\mathbf{y}}^2\mathbf{w} = 1 \;\text{ or }\; \mathbf{b}^{\mathbf{T}}\Sigma_{\mathbf{x}}^2\mathbf{b} = 1 \;\text{ or }\; \mathbf{w}^{\mathbf{T}}\Sigma_{\mathbf{y}}^2\mathbf{w} = 1 \;\&\; \mathbf{b}^{\mathbf{T}}\Sigma_{\mathbf{x}}^2\mathbf{b} = 1. \tag{13}$$

   It has been shown that each of all constraints results in Eq.(13), which can be incorporated into the one-tap FEQs in frequency domain (Ysebaert et al., 2003).

Most TEQ designs are based on the block-based computation to find TIR (Al-Dhahir & Cioffi, 1996; F-Boroujeny & Ding, 2001; Lee et al., 1995), it will make high computational complexity for implementation. However, this algorithm has much better performance and is used for the reference for on-line technique.

4. The proposed normalised least mean square algorithm for TEQ and TIR

We study the use of the LMS algorithm by means of the simplicity of implementation and robust performance. But the main limitation of the LMS algorithm is slow rate of convergence (Diniz, 2008; Haykin, 2002). Most importantly, the normalised least mean square (NLMS) algorithm exhibits a rate of convergence that is potentially faster than that of the standard LMS algorithm. Following (Haykin, 2002), we derive the normalised LMS algorithm for TEQ and TIR as follows.

Given the channel-filtered input vector $\mathbf{y}(n)$ and the delay input vector $\mathbf{d}(n)$, to determine the tap-weight vector of TEQ $\mathbf{w}(n+1)$ and the tap-weight vector of TIR $\mathbf{b}(n+1)$. So, the change $\delta\mathbf{w}(n+1)$ and $\delta\mathbf{b}(n+1)$ are defined as

$$\delta\mathbf{w}(n+1) = \mathbf{w}(n+1) - \mathbf{w}(n)\,, \tag{14}$$

$$\delta\mathbf{b}(n+1) = \mathbf{b}(n+1) - \mathbf{b}(n)\,, \tag{15}$$

and subject to the constraints

$$\mathbf{w}^H(n+1)\,\mathbf{y}(n) = g_1(n)\,, \tag{16}$$

$$\mathbf{b}^H(n+1)\,\mathbf{d}(n) = g_2(n)\,, \tag{17}$$

where $e(n)$ is the estimation error

$$e(n) = \mathbf{w}^H(n+1)\,\mathbf{y}(n) - \mathbf{b}^H(n+1)\,\mathbf{d}(n)\,. \tag{18}$$

The squared Euclidean norm of the change $\delta\mathbf{w}(n+1)$ and $\delta\mathbf{b}(n+1)$ may be expressed as

$$\|\,\delta\mathbf{w}(n+1)\|^{\,2} = \sum_{k=0}^{M-1} |\,\mathbf{w}_k(n+1) - \mathbf{w}_k(n)|^{\,2}\,, \tag{19}$$

$$\|\,\delta\mathbf{b}(n+1)\|^{\,2} = \sum_{k=0}^{M-1} |\,\mathbf{b}_k(n+1) - \mathbf{b}_k(n)|^{\,2}\,. \tag{20}$$

Given the tap-weight of TEQ $\mathbf{w}_k(n)$ and TIR $\mathbf{b}_k(n)$ for $k = 0, 1, \ldots, M-1$ in terms of their real and imaginary parts by

$$\mathbf{w}_k(n) = a_k(n) + j\,b_k(n)\,, \tag{21}$$

$$\mathbf{b}_k(n) = u_k(n) + j\,v_k(n)\,. \tag{22}$$

The tap-input vectors $\mathbf{y}(n)$ and $\mathbf{d}(n)$ are defined in term of real and imaginary parts as

$$\mathbf{y}(n) = y_1(n) + j\,y_2(n)\,, \tag{23}$$

$$\mathbf{d}(n) = d_1(n) + j\,d_2(n)\,. \tag{24}$$

Let the constraints $g_1(n)$ and $g_2(n)$ be expressed in terms of their real and imaginary parts as

$$g_1(n) = g_{1a}(n) + j\,g_{1b}(n)\,, \tag{25}$$

$$g_2(n) = g_{2a}(n) + j\,g_{2b}(n)\,. \tag{26}$$

To rewrite the complex constraint of Eq.(16) as the pair of real constraints

$$\begin{aligned}
g_1(n) &= \sum_{k=0}^{M-1} [\mathbf{w}_k(n+1)]^H\,\mathbf{y}(n) \\
&= \sum_{k=0}^{M-1} \left\{[a_k(n+1) + j\,b_k(n+1)]^*\,[y_1(n-k) + j\,y_2(n-k)]\right\} \\
&= \sum_{k=0}^{M-1} \{[a_k(n+1)y_1(n-k) + b_k(n+1)y_2(n-k)] \\
&\qquad + j\,[a_k(n+1)y_2(n-k) - b_k(n+1)y_1(n-k)]\} \\
&= g_{1a}(n) + j\,g_{1b}(n)\,.
\end{aligned} \tag{27}$$

Therefore,

$$g_{1a}(n) = \sum_{k=0}^{M-1} [a_k(n+1)y_1(n-k) + b_k(n+1)y_2(n-k)]\,, \tag{28}$$

$$g_{1b}(n) = \sum_{k=0}^{M-1} [a_k(n+1)y_2(n-k) - b_k(n+1)y_1(n-k)]\,. \tag{29}$$

To formulate the complex constraint of Eq.(17) as the pair of real constraints.

$$\begin{aligned} g_2(n) &= \sum_{k=0}^{M-1} [\mathbf{b}_k(n+1)]^H \mathbf{d}(n) \\ &= \sum_{k=0}^{M-1} \{[u_k(n+1) + j\,v_k(n+1)]^* [d_1(n-k) + j\,d_2(n-k)]\} \\ &= \sum_{k=0}^{M-1} \{[u_k(n+1)d_1(n-k) + v_k(n+1)d_2(n-k)] \\ &\qquad + j\,[u_k(n+1)d_2(n-k) - v_k(n+1)d_1(n-k)]\} \\ &= g_{2a}(n) + j\,g_{2b}(n)\,. \end{aligned} \tag{30}$$

Therefore,

$$g_{2a}(n) = \sum_{k=0}^{M-1} [u_k(n+1)d_1(n-k) + v_k(n+1)d_2(n-k)]\,, \tag{31}$$

$$g_{2b}(n) = \sum_{k=0}^{M-1} [u_k(n+1)d_2(n-k) - v_k(n+1)d_1(n-k)]\,. \tag{32}$$

4.1 The proposed normalised least mean square time-domain equalisation (NLMS-TEQ)

We define the real-valued cost function $J_1(n)$ for the constrained optimisation using *Lagrange multiplier.*[1] (Haykin, 2002)

$$\begin{aligned} J_1(n) &= \|\,\delta\mathbf{w}(n+1)\|^2 + \lambda_1 \{\,[a_k(n+1)y_1(n-k) + b_k(n+1)y_2(n-k)]\, - g_{1a}(n)\} \\ &\qquad + \lambda_2 \{\,[a_k(n+1)y_2(n-k) - b_k(n+1)y_1(n-k)]\, - g_{1b}(n)\} \\ &= \sum_{k=0}^{M-1} \{\,[a_k(n+1) - a_k(n)]^{\,2} + [b_k(n+1) - b_k(n)]^{\,2}\} \\ &\quad + \lambda_1 \{\sum_{k=0}^{M-1} [a_k(n+1)y_1(n-k) + b_k(n+1)y_2(n-k)] - g_{1a}(n)\} \\ &\quad + \lambda_2 \{\sum_{k=0}^{M-1} [a_k(n+1)y_2(n-k) - b_k(n+1)y_1(n-k)] - g_{1b}(n)\}\,, \end{aligned} \tag{33}$$

where λ_1 and λ_2 are *Lagrange multipliers*. We find the optimum values of $a_k(n+1)$ and $b_k(n+1)$ by differentiating the cost function $J_1(n)$ with respect to these parameters and set the both results equal to zero. Hence,

$$\frac{\partial J_1(n)}{\partial a_k(n+1)} = 0\,,$$

[1] The method of Lagrange multiplier is defined as a new real-valued Lagrange function $h(w)$

$$h(w) = f(w) + \lambda_1 Re\,[C(w)] + \lambda_2 Im\,[C(w)]$$

where $f(w)$ is the real function and $C(w)$ is the complex constraint function. The parameters λ_1 and λ_2 are the Lagrange multipliers, where $\lambda = \lambda_1 + j\,\lambda_2$

and

$$\frac{\partial J_1(n)}{\partial b_k(n+1)} = 0 \,.$$

The results are given by

$$2\,\left[a_k(n+1) - a_k(n)\right] + \lambda_1 y_1(n-k) + \lambda_2 y_2(n-k) = 0\,, \tag{34}$$

$$2\,\left[b_k(n+1) - b_k(n)\right] + \lambda_1 y_2(n-k) - \lambda_2 y_1(n-k) = 0\,. \tag{35}$$

From Eq.(21) and Eq.(23), we combine these two real results into a single complex one as

$$\frac{\partial J_1(n)}{\partial \mathbf{w}_k(n+1)} = \frac{\partial J_1(n)}{\partial a_k(n+1)} + j\,\frac{\partial J_1(n)}{\partial b_k(n+1)} = 0\,. \tag{36}$$

Therefore,

$$\begin{aligned} \frac{\partial J_1(n)}{\partial \mathbf{w}_k(n+1)} &= \{2\,\left[a_k(n+1) - a_k(n)\right] + \lambda_1 y_1(n-k) + \lambda_2 y_2(n-k)\} + \\ &\qquad j\,\{2\,\left[b_k(n+1) - b_k(n)\right] + \lambda_1 y_2(n-k) - \lambda_2 y_1(n-k)\} \\ &= 2\,\left[a_k(n+1) + j\,b_k(n+1)\right] - 2\,\left[a_k(n) + j\,b_k(n)\right] + \\ &\qquad \lambda_1\left[y_1(n-k) + j\,y_2(n-k)\right] - j\,\lambda_2\left[y_1(n-k) + j\,y_2(n-k)\right] \\ &= 2\,\left[a_k(n+1) + j\,b_k(n+1)\right] - 2\,\left[a_k(n) + j\,b_k(n)\right] + \\ &\qquad (\lambda_1 - j\,\lambda_2)\left[y_1(n-k) + j\,y_2(n-k)\right] \\ &= 0\,. \end{aligned} \tag{37}$$

Thus, we get

$$2\,\left[\mathbf{w}_k(n+1) - \mathbf{w}_k(n)\right] + \lambda_w^* \mathbf{y}(n-k) = 0,\ for\ k = 0, 1, \ldots, M-1 \tag{38}$$

where λ_w is a complex Lagrange multiplier for TEQ as

$$\lambda_w = \lambda_1 + j\,\lambda_2\,. \tag{39}$$

In order to find the unknown λ_w^*, we multiply both sides of Eq.(38) by $\mathbf{y}^*(n-k)$ and then sum over all integer values of k for 0 to $M-1$. Thus, we have

$$\begin{aligned} 2\,\left[\mathbf{w}_k(n+1) - \mathbf{w}_k(n)\right]\,\mathbf{y}^*(n-k) &= -\lambda_w^*\,\mathbf{y}(n-k)\,\mathbf{y}^*(n-k) \\ 2\sum_{k=0}^{M-1}\left[\,\mathbf{w}_k(n+1)\mathbf{y}^*(n-k) - \mathbf{w}_k(n)\mathbf{y}^*(n-k)\,\right] &= -\lambda_w^*\sum_{k=0}^{M-1}|\mathbf{y}(n-k)|^2 \\ 2\left[\mathbf{w}^T(n+1)\,\mathbf{y}^*(n) - \mathbf{w}^T(n)\,\mathbf{y}^*(n)\right] &= -\lambda_w^*\|\mathbf{y}(n)\|^2 \end{aligned}$$

Therefore, the complex conjugate Lagrange multiplier λ_w^* can be formulated as

$$\lambda_w^* = \frac{-2}{\|\mathbf{y}(n)\|^2}\left[\mathbf{w}^T(n+1)\,\mathbf{y}^*(n) - \mathbf{w}^T(n)\,\mathbf{y}^*(n)\right]\,, \tag{40}$$

where $\|\mathbf{y}(n)\|^2$ is the Euclidean norm of the tap-input vector $\mathbf{y}(n)$.
From the definition of the estimation error $e(n)$ in Eq.(18), the conjugate of $e(n)$ is written as

$$e^*(n) = \mathbf{w}^T(n+1)\,\mathbf{y}^*(n) - \mathbf{b}^T(n+1)\,\mathbf{d}^*(n)\,. \tag{41}$$

The mean-square error $|e(n)|^2$ is minimised by the derivative of $|e(n)|^2$ with respect to $\mathbf{w}(n+1)$ be equal to zero.

$$\frac{\partial |e(n)|^2}{\partial \mathbf{w}(n+1)} = \left[\mathbf{w}^H(n+1)\,\mathbf{y}(n) - \mathbf{b}^H(n+1)\,\mathbf{d}(n)\right]\mathbf{y}^*(n) = 0\,. \tag{42}$$

Hence, we have

$$\mathbf{w}^H(n+1)\,\mathbf{y}(n) = \mathbf{b}^H(n+1)\,\mathbf{d}(n)\,, \tag{43}$$

and the conjugate of Eq.(43) may expressed as

$$\mathbf{w}^T(n+1)\,\mathbf{y}^*(n) = \mathbf{b}^T(n+1)\,\mathbf{d}^*(n)\,. \tag{44}$$

To substitute Eq.(44) and Eq.(41) into Eq.(40) and then formulate λ_w^* as

$$\lambda_w^* = \frac{2}{\|\mathbf{y}(n)\|^2}\,e^*(n)\,. \tag{45}$$

We rewrite Eq.(38) using Eq.(14) by writing,

$$2\,\delta\mathbf{w}(n+1) = -\lambda_w^*\,\mathbf{y}(n) \tag{46}$$

The change $\delta\mathbf{w}(n+1)$ is redefined by substituting Eq.(45) in Eq.(46). We thus have

$$\delta\mathbf{w}(n+1) = \frac{-1}{\|\mathbf{y}(n)\|^2}\,\mathbf{y}(n)\,e^*(n)\,. \tag{47}$$

To introduce a step-size for TEQ denoted by μ_w and then we may express the change $\delta\mathbf{w}(n+1)$ as

$$\delta\mathbf{w}(n+1) = \frac{-\mu_w}{\|\mathbf{y}(n)\|^2}\,\mathbf{y}(n)\,e^*(n)\,. \tag{48}$$

We rewrite the tap-weight vector of TEQ $\mathbf{w}(n+1)$ as

$$\mathbf{w}(n+1) = \mathbf{w}(n) + \delta\mathbf{w}(n+1)\,. \tag{49}$$

Finally, we may obtain the tap-weight vector of TEQ $\mathbf{w}(n+1)$ in the well-known NLMS algorithm.

$$\mathbf{w}(n+1) = \mathbf{w}(n) - \frac{\mu_w}{\|\mathbf{y}(n)\|^2}\,\mathbf{y}(n)\,e^*(n)\,. \tag{50}$$

where $e^*(n)$ is described in Eq.(41).

4.2 The proposed normalised least mean square-target impulse response (NLMS-TIR)

We formulate the real-valued cost function $J_2(n)$ for the constrained optimisation problem using *Lagrange multiplier*.

$$\begin{aligned}
J_2(n) &= \|\,\delta\mathbf{b}(n+1)\|^2 + \lambda_3\,\{\,[u_k(n+1)d_1(n-k) + v_k(n+1)d_2(n-k)] \;-\; g_{2a}(n)\} \\
&\qquad\qquad\qquad\qquad + \lambda_4\,\{\,[u_k(n+1)d_2(n-k) - v_k(n+1)d_1(n-k)] \;-\; g_{2b}(n)\} \\
&= \sum_{k=0}^{M-1}\{\,[u_k(n+1) - u_k(n)]^{\,2} + [v_k(n+1) - v_k(n)]^{\,2}\} \\
&\quad + \lambda_3\,\{\sum_{k=0}^{M-1}\;[u_k(n+1)d_1(n-k) + v_k(n+1)d_2(n-k)] - g_{2a}(n)\} \\
&\quad + \lambda_4\,\{\sum_{k=0}^{M-1}\;[u_k(n+1)d_2(n-k) - v_k(n+1)d_1(n-k)] - g_{2b}(n)\}\,,
\end{aligned} \tag{51}$$

where λ_3 and λ_4 are *Lagrange multipliers*. We find the optimum values of $u_k(n+1)$ and $v_k(n+1)$ by differentiating the cost function $J_2(n)$ with respect to these parameters and then set the results equal to zero. Hence,

$$\frac{\partial J_2(n)}{\partial u_k(n+1)} = 0\,,$$

and

$$\frac{\partial J_2(n)}{\partial v_k(n+1)} = 0\,.$$

The results are

$$2\;[u_k(n+1) - u_k(n)] + \lambda_3 d_1(n-k) + \lambda_4 d_2(n-k) = 0\,, \tag{52}$$

$$2\;[v_k(n+1) - v_k(n)] + \lambda_3 d_2(n-k) - \lambda_4 d_1(n-k) = 0\,. \tag{53}$$

From Eq.(22) and Eq.(24), we combine these two real results into a single complex one as

$$\frac{\partial J_2(n)}{\partial \mathbf{b}_k(n+1)} = \frac{\partial J_2(n)}{\partial u_k(n+1)} + j\,\frac{\partial J_2(n)}{\partial v_k(n+1)} = 0\,. \tag{54}$$

Therefore,

$$\begin{aligned}
\frac{\partial J_2(n)}{\partial \mathbf{b}_k(n+1)} &= \{2\;[u_k(n+1) - u_k(n)] + \lambda_3 d_1(n-k) + \lambda_4 d_2(n-k)\} + \\
&\qquad\qquad j\,\{2\;[v_k(n+1) - v_k(n)] + \lambda_3 d_2(n-k) - \lambda_4 d_1(n-k)\} \\
&= \;2\;[u_k(n+1) + j\,v_k(n+1)] - 2\;[u_k(n) + j\,v_k(n)] + \\
&\qquad\qquad \lambda_3\,[d_1(n-k) + j\,d_2(n-k)] - j\,\lambda_4\,[d_1(n-k) + j\,d_2(n-k)] \\
&= \;2\;[u_k(n+1) + j\,v_k(n+1)] - 2\;[u_k(n) + j\,v_k(n)] + \\
&\qquad\qquad (\lambda_3 - j\,\lambda_4)\,[d_1(n-k) + j\,d_2(n-k)] \\
&= \;0\,.
\end{aligned} \tag{55}$$

Thus, we have

$$2\,[\mathbf{b}_k(n+1)-\mathbf{b}_k(n)]+\lambda_b^*\mathbf{d}(n-k)=0,\ for\,k=0,1,\ldots,M-1 \tag{56}$$

where λ_b is a complex Lagrange multiplier for TIR

$$\lambda_b=\lambda_3+j\,\lambda_4 \tag{57}$$

To multiply both side of Eq.(56) by $\mathbf{d}^*(n-k)$ to find the unknown λ_b^* and then sum over all possible integer values of k for 0 to $M-1$. Thus, we get

$$2\,[\mathbf{b}_k(n+1)-\mathbf{b}_k(n)]\,\mathbf{d}^*(n-k)=-\lambda_b^*\,\mathbf{d}(n-k)\,\mathbf{d}^*(n-k)$$
$$2\sum_{k=0}^{M-1}[\mathbf{b}_k(n+1)\mathbf{d}^*(n-k)-\mathbf{b}_k(n)\mathbf{d}^*(n-k)]=-\lambda_b^*\sum_{k=0}^{M-1}|\mathbf{d}(n-k)|^2$$
$$2\left[\mathbf{b}^T(n+1)\,\mathbf{d}^*(n)-\mathbf{b}^T(n)\,\mathbf{d}^*(n)\right]=-\lambda_b^*\|\mathbf{d}(n)\|^2$$

Therefore,

$$\lambda_b^*=\frac{-2}{\|\mathbf{d}(n)\|^2}\left[\mathbf{b}^T(n+1)\,\mathbf{d}^*(n)-\mathbf{b}^T(n)\,\mathbf{d}^*(n)\right]. \tag{58}$$

where $\|\mathbf{d}(n)\|^2$ is the Euclidean norm of the tap-input vector $\mathbf{d}(n)$.
To substitute Eq.(41) and Eq.(44) into Eq.(58) and then formulate λ_b^* as

$$\lambda_b^*=\frac{2}{\|\mathbf{d}(n)\|^2}\,e^*(n)\,. \tag{59}$$

We rewrite Eq.(56) using Eq.(15) by

$$2\,\delta\mathbf{b}(n+1)=\lambda_b^*\,\mathbf{d}(n) \tag{60}$$

To redefine the change $\delta\mathbf{b}(n+1)$ by substituting Eq.(59) in Eq.(60). We thus get,

$$\delta\mathbf{b}(n+1)=\frac{1}{|\mathbf{d}(n)|^2}\,\mathbf{d}(n)\,e^*(n)\,. \tag{61}$$

To introduce a step-size for TIR μ_b and then we redefine the change $\delta\mathbf{b}(n+1)$ simply as

$$\delta\mathbf{b}(n+1)=\frac{\mu_b}{\|\mathbf{d}(n)\|^2}\,\mathbf{d}(n)\,e^*(n)\,, \tag{62}$$

where μ_b is the step-size for the NLMS-TIR.
We rewrite the tap-weight vector of TIR $\mathbf{b}(n+1)$ as

$$\mathbf{b}(n+1)=\mathbf{b}(n)+\delta\mathbf{b}(n+1)\,. \tag{63}$$

Finally, we may formulate the tap-weight vector of TIR $\mathbf{b}(n+1)$ in the normalised LMS algorithm.

$$\mathbf{b}(n+1)=\mathbf{b}(n)+\frac{\mu_b}{\|\mathbf{d}(n)\|^2}\,\mathbf{d}(n)\,e^*(n)\,, \tag{64}$$

where $e^*(n)$ is given in Eq.(41).
To comply with the Euclidean norm constraint, the tap-weight vector of TIR $\mathbf{b}(n+1)$ is normalised as

$$\mathbf{b}(n+1)=\frac{\mathbf{b}(n+1)}{\|\mathbf{b}(n+1)\|}\,. \tag{65}$$

5. Adaptive step-size order statistic-normalised averaged least mean square-based time-domain equalisation

Based on least mean square (LMS) algorithm, a class of adaptive algorihtms employing order statistic filtering of the sampled gradient estimates has been presented in (Haweel & Clarkson, 1992), which can provide with the development of simple and robust adaptive filter across a wide range of input environments. This section is therefore concerned with the development of simple and robust adaptive time-domain equalisation by defining normalised least mean square (NLMS) algorithm.

Following (Haweel & Clarkson, 1992), we present the NLMS algorithm which replaces linear smoothing of gradient estimates by order statistic averaged LMS filter. A class of order statistic normalised averaged LMS algorithm with the adaptive step-size scheme for the proposed NLMS algorithm in Eq.(50) and Eq.(64) that are shown as (Sitjongsataporn & Yuvapoositanon, 2007).

$$\widehat{\mathbf{w}}(n+1) = \widehat{\mathbf{w}}(n) - \frac{\mu_w(n)}{\|\mathbf{y}(n)\|^2}\,\mathcal{M}_w\,\boldsymbol{a}_w\,, \tag{66}$$

$$\widehat{\mathbf{b}}(n+1) = \widehat{\mathbf{b}}(n) + \frac{\mu_b(n)}{\|\mathbf{d}(n)\|^2}\,\mathcal{M}_b\,\boldsymbol{a}_b\,, \tag{67}$$

with

$$\mathcal{M}_w = \tilde{T}\{\,\tilde{e}^*(n)\mathbf{y}(n),\ \tilde{e}^*(n-1)\mathbf{y}(n-1),\ldots,\ \tilde{e}^*(n-N_w+1)\mathbf{y}(n-N_w+1)\}\,, \tag{68}$$

$$\mathcal{M}_b = \tilde{T}\{\,\tilde{e}^*(n)\mathbf{d}(n),\ \tilde{e}^*(n-1)\mathbf{d}(n-1),\ldots,\ \tilde{e}^*(n-N_b+1)\mathbf{d}(n-N_b+1)\}\,, \tag{69}$$

$$\tilde{e}(n) = \widehat{\mathbf{w}}^H(n)\mathbf{y}(n) - \widehat{\mathbf{b}}^H(n)\mathbf{d}(n)\,, \tag{70}$$

and

$$\boldsymbol{a}_w = [a_w(1), a_w(2), \ldots, a_w(N_w)]\,, \qquad a_w(i) = 1/N_w\,; \qquad i = 1,2,\ldots,N_w. \tag{71}$$

$$\boldsymbol{a}_b = [a_b(1), a_b(2), \ldots, a_b(N_b)]\,, \qquad a_b(j) = 1/N_b\,; \qquad j = 1,2,\ldots,N_b. \tag{72}$$

where $\tilde{e}(n)$ is a priori estimation error and $\tilde{T}\{\cdot\}$ operation denotes as the algebraic ordering transformation. The parameters $\boldsymbol{a}_w$ and $\boldsymbol{a}_b$ are the average of the gradient estimates of weighting coefficients as described in (Chambers, 1993). The parameters $\mu_w(n)$ and $\mu_b(n)$ are the step-size of $\widehat{\mathbf{w}}(n)$ and $\widehat{\mathbf{b}}(n)$. The parameters N_w and N_b are the number of tap-weight vectors for TEQ and TIR, respectively.

Following (Benveniste et al., 1990), we demonstate the derivation of adaptive step-size algorithms of $\mu_w(n)$ and $\mu_b(n)$ based on the proposed NLMS algorithm in Eq.(50) and Eq.(64). The cost function $J_{min}(n)$ may be expressed as

$$J_{min}(n) = \min_{\mathbf{w},\mathbf{b}} E\{|e(n)|^2\}\,, \tag{73}$$

$$e(n) = \mathbf{w}^H(n+1)\,\mathbf{y}(n) - \mathbf{b}^H(n+1)\,\mathbf{d}(n)\,. \tag{74}$$

We then form the stochastic approximation equations for $\mu_w(n+1)$ and $\mu_b(n+1)$ as (Kushner & Yang, 1995)

$$\mu_w(n+1) = \mu_w(n) + \alpha_w\{-\nabla J_{min}(\mu_w)\}\,, \tag{75}$$

$$\mu_b(n+1) = \mu_b(n) + \alpha_b\{-\nabla J_{min}(\mu_b)\}\,, \tag{76}$$

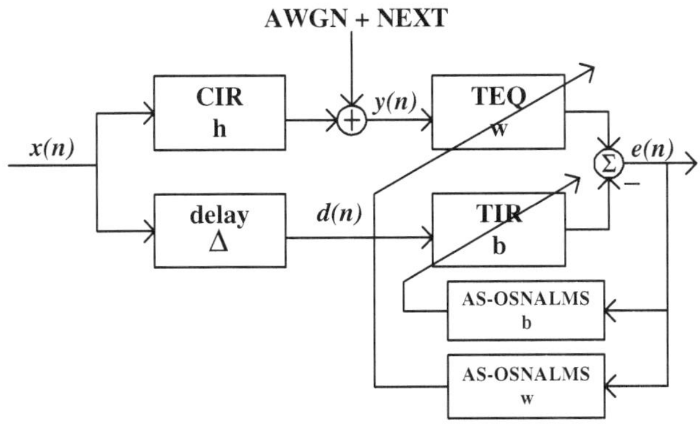

Fig. 3. Block diagram of adaptive step-size order statistic normalised averaged least mean square (AS-OSNALMS) TEQ and TIR.

where $\nabla J_{min}(\mu_w)$ and $\nabla J_{min}(\mu_b)$ denote as the value of the gradient vectors. The parameters α_w and α_b are the adaptation constant of μ_w and μ_b, respectively.
By differentiating the cost function in Eq.(73) with respect to μ_w and μ_b, we get

$$\frac{\partial J_{min}}{\partial \mu_w} = \nabla J_{min}(\mu_w) = e(n)\, \mathbf{y}^T(n)\Psi_w\,, \tag{77}$$

$$\frac{\partial J_{min}}{\partial \mu_b} = \nabla J_{min}(\mu_b) = -e(n)\, \mathbf{d}^T(n)\Psi_b\,, \tag{78}$$

where $\Psi_w = \frac{\partial \mathbf{w}(n)}{\partial \mu_w}$ and $\Psi_b = \frac{\partial \mathbf{b}(n)}{\partial \mu_b}$ are the derivative of $\mathbf{w}(n+1)$ in Eq.(50) with respect to $\mu_w(n)$ and of $\mathbf{b}(n+1)$ in Eq.(64) with respect to $\mu_b(n)$ (Moon & Stirling, 2000).
By substituting Eq.(77) and Eq.(78) in Eq.(75) and Eq.(76), we get the adaptive step-size $\mu_w(n)$ and $\mu_b(n)$ as

$$\mu_w(n+1) = \mu_w(n) - \alpha_w\{e(n)\, \mathbf{y}^T(n)\Psi_w\}\,, \tag{79}$$

$$\mu_b(n+1) = \mu_b(n) + \alpha_b\{e(n)\, \mathbf{d}^T(n)\Psi_b\}\,, \tag{80}$$

where

$$\Psi_w(n+1) = \left[\mathbf{I} - \frac{\mathbf{y}(n)}{\|\mathbf{y}(n)\|^2}\, \mu_w(n)\, \mathbf{y}^T(n)\right]\Psi_w(n) - \frac{\mathbf{y}(n)}{\|\mathbf{y}(n)\|^2}\, e^*(n)\,, \tag{81}$$

$$\Psi_b(n+1) = \left[\mathbf{I} - \frac{\mathbf{d}(n)}{\|\mathbf{d}(n)\|^2}\, \mu_b(n)\, \mathbf{d}^T(n)\right]\Psi_b(n) + \frac{\mathbf{d}(n)}{\|\mathbf{d}(n)\|^2}\, e^*(n)\,. \tag{82}$$

Then, we apply the order statistic scheme in Eq.(81) and Eq.(82) as

$$\widetilde{\Psi}_w(n+1) = \left[\mathbf{I} - \frac{\mathbf{y}(n)}{\|\mathbf{y}(n)\|^2}\, \mu_w(n)\, \mathbf{y}^T(n)\right]\widetilde{\Psi}_w(n) - \frac{\mathcal{M}_w\, \boldsymbol{a}_w}{\|\mathbf{y}(n)\|^2}\,, \tag{83}$$

$$\widetilde{\Psi}_b(n+1) = \left[\mathbf{I} - \frac{\mathbf{d}(n)}{\|\mathbf{d}(n)\|^2}\, \mu_b(n)\, \mathbf{d}^T(n)\right]\widetilde{\Psi}_b(n) + \frac{\mathcal{M}_b\, \boldsymbol{a}_b}{\|\mathbf{d}(n)\|^2}\,, \tag{84}$$

where $\mathcal{M}_w$, $\mathcal{M}_b$, $\boldsymbol{a}_w$, $\boldsymbol{a}_b$ and $\tilde{e}(n)$ are given in Eq.(68)-Eq.(72).

6. Stability analysis of the proposed AS-OSNALMS TEQ and TIR

In this section, the stability of the proposed AS-OSNALMS algorithm for TEQ and TIR are based upon the NLMS algorithm as given in (Haykin, 2002). This also provides for the optimal step-size parameters for TEQ and TIR.
According to the tap-weight estimate vector $\widehat{\mathbf{w}}(n)$ and $\widehat{\mathbf{b}}(n)$ computed in Eq.(66) and Eq.(67), the difference between the optimum tap-weight vector $\mathbf{w}^{opt}$ and $\widehat{\mathbf{w}}(n)$ is calculated by the weight-error vector of TEQ as

$$\Delta\,\mathbf{w}(n) = \mathbf{w}^{opt} - \widehat{\mathbf{w}}(n)\,, \tag{85}$$

and, in the similar fashion, the weight-error vector of TIR is given by

$$\Delta\,\mathbf{b}(n) = \mathbf{b}^{opt} - \widehat{\mathbf{b}}(n)\,, \tag{86}$$

By substituting Eq.(66) and Eq.(67) from $\mathbf{w}^{opt}$ and $\mathbf{b}^{opt}$, we have

$$\Delta\,\mathbf{w}(n+1) = \Delta\,\mathbf{w}(n) + \frac{\mu_w(n)}{\|\mathbf{y}(n)\|^2}\mathcal{M}_w\,\boldsymbol{a}_w\,, \tag{87}$$

where $\mathcal{M}_w$ and $\boldsymbol{a}_w$ are defined in Eq.(68) and Eq.(71).

$$\Delta\,\mathbf{b}(n+1) = \Delta\,\mathbf{b}(n) - \frac{\mu_b(n)}{\|\mathbf{d}(n)\|^2}\mathcal{M}_b\,\boldsymbol{a}_b\,, \tag{88}$$

where $\mathcal{M}_b$ and $\boldsymbol{a}_b$ are given in Eq.(69) and Eq.(72).
The stability analysis of the proposed AS-OSNALMS TEQ and TIR are based on the mean square deviation (MSD) as

$$\mathcal{D}_w(n) = E\{\|\Delta\mathbf{w}(n)\|^2\}\,, \tag{89}$$

$$\mathcal{D}_b(n) = E\{\|\Delta\mathbf{b}(n)\|^2\}\,, \tag{90}$$

where $\mathcal{D}_w(n)$ and $\mathcal{D}_b(n)$ denote as the MSD on TEQ and TIR.
By taking the squared Euclidean norms of both sides of Eq.(87) and Eq.(88), we get

$$\begin{aligned}\|\Delta\mathbf{w}(n+1)\|^2 &= \|\Delta\mathbf{w}(n)\|^2 + 2\,\frac{\mu_w(n)}{\|\mathbf{y}(n)\|^2}\,\Delta\mathbf{w}^H(n)\cdot(\mathcal{M}_w\,\boldsymbol{a}_w)\\ &\quad + \frac{\mu_w^2(n)}{\|\mathbf{y}(n)\|^2}\,\frac{(\mathcal{M}_w\,\boldsymbol{a}_w)^H\,(\mathcal{M}_w\,\boldsymbol{a}_w)}{\|\mathbf{y}(n)\|^2}\,,\end{aligned} \tag{91}$$

$$\begin{aligned}\|\Delta\mathbf{b}(n+1)\|^2 &= \|\Delta\mathbf{b}(n)\|^2 - 2\,\frac{\mu_b(n)}{\|\mathbf{d}(n)\|^2}\,\Delta\mathbf{b}^H(n)\cdot(\mathcal{M}_b\,\boldsymbol{a}_b)\\ &\quad + \frac{\mu_b^2(n)}{\|\mathbf{d}(n)\|^2}\,\frac{(\mathcal{M}_b\,\boldsymbol{a}_b)^H\,(\mathcal{M}_b\,\boldsymbol{a}_b)}{\|\mathbf{d}(n)\|^2}\,.\end{aligned} \tag{92}$$

Then taking expectations and rearranging terms with Eq.(89) and Eq.(90), the MSD of $\widehat{\mathbf{w}}(n)$ is defined by

$$\begin{aligned}\mathcal{D}_w(n+1) &= \mathcal{D}_w(n) + 2\,\mu_w(n)\,E\{\Re(\Delta\mathbf{w}^H(n)\,\boldsymbol{\xi}_w(n))\}\\ &\quad + \mu_w^2(n)\,E\{\Re(\boldsymbol{\xi}_w^H(n)\,\boldsymbol{\xi}_w(n))\}\,,\end{aligned} \tag{93}$$

where $\boldsymbol{\xi}_w(n)$ is given by

$$\boldsymbol{\xi}_w(n) = E\left\{ \frac{\mathcal{M}_w \, \boldsymbol{a}_w}{\|\mathbf{y}(n)\|^2} \right\}, \tag{94}$$

and $\Re(\cdot)$ denote as the real operator.
Thus, the MSD of $\widehat{\mathbf{b}}(n)$ can be computed as

$$\mathcal{D}_b(n+1) = \mathcal{D}_b(n) - 2\,\mu_b(n)\, E\left\{ \Re\left(\Delta\mathbf{b}^H(n)\, \boldsymbol{\xi}_b(n) \right) \right\} + \mu_b^2(n)\, E\left\{ \Re\left(\boldsymbol{\xi}_b^H(n)\, \boldsymbol{\xi}_b(n) \right) \right\}, \tag{95}$$

where $\boldsymbol{\xi}_b(n)$ is calculated by

$$\boldsymbol{\xi}_b(n) = E\left\{ \frac{\mathcal{M}_b \, \boldsymbol{a}_b}{\|\mathbf{d}(n)\|^2} \right\}. \tag{96}$$

Following these approximations

$$\lim_{n\to\infty} \mathcal{D}_w(n+1) = \lim_{n\to\infty} \mathcal{D}_w(n), \tag{97}$$

$$\lim_{n\to\infty} \mathcal{D}_b(n+1) = \lim_{n\to\infty} \mathcal{D}_b(n), \tag{98}$$

are taken into Eq.(93) and Eq.(95). The normalised step-size parameters $\mu_w(n)$ and $\mu_b(n)$ are bounded as

$$0 < \mu_w(n) < 2 \left| \Re\left(\frac{\Delta\mathbf{w}^H(n)\, \boldsymbol{\xi}_w(n)}{\boldsymbol{\xi}_w^H(n)\, \boldsymbol{\xi}_w(n)} \right) \right|, \tag{99}$$

$$0 < \mu_b(n) < 2\, \Re\left(\frac{\Delta\mathbf{b}^H(n)\, \boldsymbol{\xi}_b(n)}{\boldsymbol{\xi}_b^H(n)\, \boldsymbol{\xi}_b(n)} \right). \tag{100}$$

Therefore, the optimal step-size parameters μ_w^{opt} and μ_b^{opt} can be formulated by

$$\mu_w^{opt} = \left| \Re\left(\frac{\Delta\mathbf{w}^H(n)\, \boldsymbol{\xi}_w(n)}{\boldsymbol{\xi}_w^H(n)\, \boldsymbol{\xi}_w(n)} \right) \right|, \tag{101}$$

$$\mu_b^{opt} = \Re\left(\frac{\Delta\mathbf{b}^H(n)\, \boldsymbol{\xi}_b(n)}{\boldsymbol{\xi}_b^H(n)\, \boldsymbol{\xi}_b(n)} \right). \tag{102}$$

7. Simulation results

We implemented the ADSL transmission channel based on parameters as follows: the sampling rate $f_s = 2.208$ MHz, the size of FFT $N = 512$, and the input signal power of -40dBm/Hz. The standard ADSL system parameters were shown in Table 1. The ADSL downstream starting at active tones 38 up to tone 255 that comprises 512 coefficients of channel impulse response. The signal to noise ratio gap of 9.8dB, the coding gain of 4.2dB and the noise margin of 6dB were chosen for all active tones. The additive white Gaussian noise (AWGN) with a power of -140dBm/Hz and near-end cross talk (NEXT) from 24

Asymmetric Digital Subscriber Line (ADSL) Specifications			
Taps of $\widehat{\mathbf{w}}$ (N_w)	32	FFT size (N)	512
Taps of $\widehat{\mathbf{b}}$ (N_b)	32	Cyclic prefix (ν)	32
Sampling rate (f_s)	2.208 MHz	Signal to noise ratio gap	9.8 dB
Tone spacing	4.3125 KHz	Noise margin	6 dB
TX-DMT block (M)	400	Coding gain	4.2 dB
TX sequence	$M \times N$	Input power	-40dBm/Hz
Input impedance	100 Ω	AWGN power	-140dBm/Hz

Table 1. The standard ADSL system for simulation.

ADSL disturbers were included over the entire test channel. The optimal synchronisation delay (Δ) can be obtained from the proposed algorithm that was equal to 45. The ADSL downstream simulations with the carrier serving area (CSA) loop no. 1 was the representative of simulations with all 8 CSA loops as detailed in (Al-Dhahir & Cioffi, 1996). The CSA#1 loop is a 7700 ft, 26 gauge loop with 26 gauge bridged tap of length of 600 ft at 5900 ft.

The initial parameters of the proposed AS-OSNALMS algorithm were $\widehat{\mathbf{w}}(0) = \widehat{\mathbf{b}}(0) = \widetilde{\Psi}_w(0) = \widetilde{\Psi}_b(0) = [0.001\ \ 0\ \ \cdots\ \ 0]^T$ and of NLMS algorithm were $\mu_w = 0.15, \mu_b = 0.075$. The NLMS algorithm was calculated with the fixed step-size for TEQ and TIR with the method as described in Section 4. Fig. 4 depicts the original simulated channel, SIR and TIR of the proposed AS-OSNALMS algorithm which compared with SIR of MMSE-UEC. It is noted that the comparable lengths of SIR and TIR of proposed algorithm are shorter than the original channel. This explains the channel-shortening capability of the proposed algorithm. Fig. 5 illustrates the MSE curves of proposed AS-OSNALMS and NLMS algorithms. The MSE curve of proposed algorithm is shown to converge to the MMSE. Fig. 6 and Fig. 7 show the mean square deviation (MSD) on TEQ and TIR of proposed AS-OSNALMS and NLMS algorithms. The trajectories of $\mu_w(n)$ and $\mu_b(n)$ at the different of initial step-size μ_{w_0} and μ_{b_0} are presented with the fixed at the adaptation parameters α_w and α_b in Fig. 8 and Fig. 9 and with the different α_w and α_b in Fig. 10 and Fig. 11. Comparing the proposed AS-OSNALMS algorithm with the fixed at the adaptation parameters, it has been shown that the proposed algorithms have faster initial convergence rate with the different setting of initial step-size and adaptation parameters. Their are shown to converge to their own equilibria.

8. Conclusion

In this chapter, we present the proposed adaptive step-size order statistic LMS-based TEQ and TIR for DMT-based systems. We introduce how to derive the updated tap-weight vector $\widehat{\mathbf{w}}(n)$ and $\widehat{\mathbf{b}}(n)$ as the solution of constrained optimisation to obtain a well-known NLMS algorithm, which an averaged order statistic scheme is replaced linear smoothing of the gradient estimation. We demonstrate the derivation of adaptive step-size mechanism for the proposed order statistic normalised averaged least mean square algorithm. The proposed algorithms for TEQ and TIR can adapt automatically the step-size parameters. The adaptation of MSE, MSD of TEQ and MSD of TIR curves of the proposed algorithms are shown to converge to the MMSE in the simulated channel. According to the simulation results, the proposed algorithms provide a good approach and are appeared to be robust in AWGN and NEXT channel as compared to the existing algorithm.

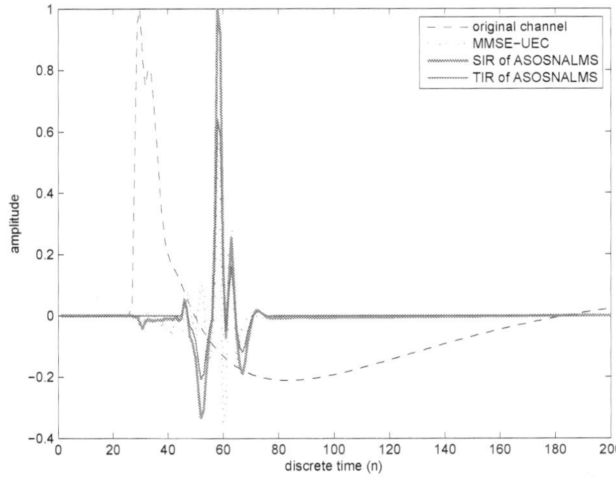

Fig. 4. Original channel, SIR of proposed ASOS-NALMS and TIR of AS-OSNALMS which compared with SIR of MMSE-UEC, when the samples of CSA loop are loop #1. Other parameters are $\mu_{w_0} = 0.415, \mu_{b_0} = 0.095, \alpha_w = 1.25 \times 10^{-6}$ and $\alpha_b = 1.5 \times 10^{-6}$.

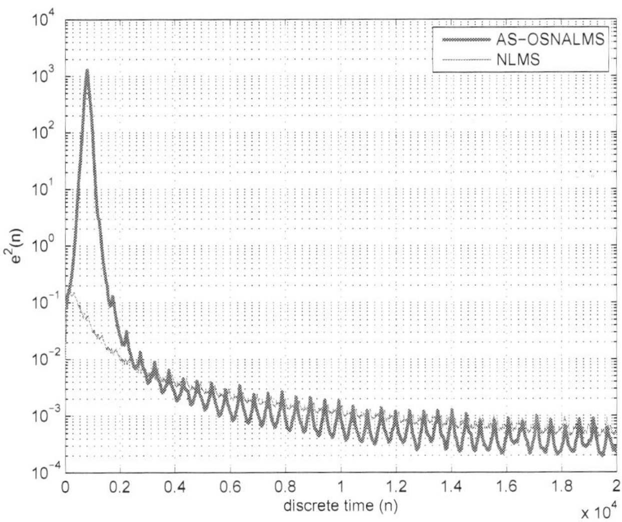

Fig. 5. Learning Curves of MSE of proposed AS-OSNALMS and NLMS algorithms for TEQ and TIR, when the samples of CSA loop are loop #1. Other parameters of AS-OSNALMS algorithm are $\mu_{w_0} = 0.415$, $\mu_{b_0} = 0.095$, $\alpha_w = 1.25 \times 10^{-6}$, $\alpha_b = 1.5 \times 10^{-6}$ and of NLMS alorithm are $\mu_w = 0.15$, $\mu_b = 0.075$.

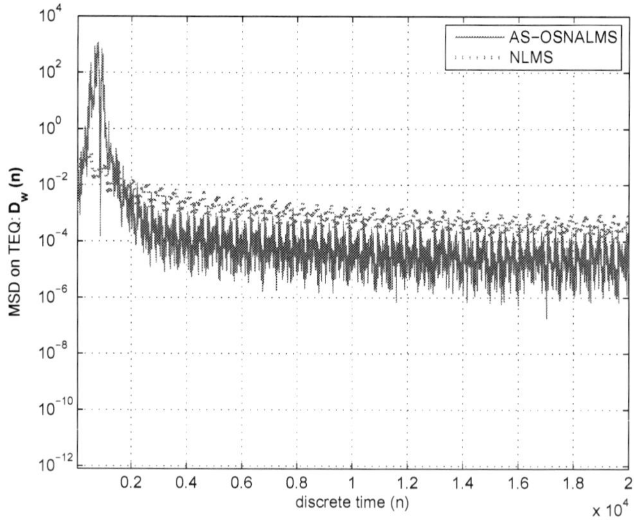

Fig. 6. Learning Curves of MSD $\mathcal{D}_w(n)$ of proposed AS-OSNALMS and NLMS algorithms for TEQ, when the samples of CSA loop are loop #1. Other parameters of AS-OSNALMS algorithm are $\mu_{w_0} = 0.415$, $\mu_{b_0} = 0.095$, $\alpha_w = 1.25 \times 10^{-6}$, $\alpha_b = 1.5 \times 10^{-6}$ and of NLMS algorithm are $\mu_w = 0.15$, $\mu_b = 0.075$.

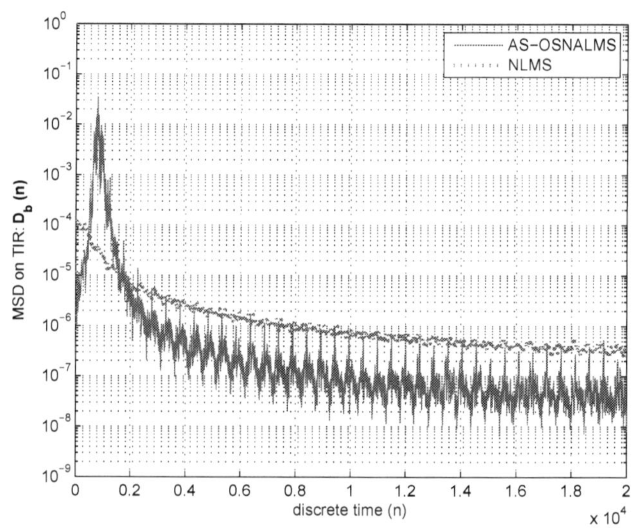

Fig. 7. Learning Curves of MSD $\mathcal{D}_b(n)$ of proposed AS-OSNALMS and NLMS algorithms for TIR, when the samples of CSA loop are loop #1. Other parameters of AS-OSNALMS algorithm are $\mu_{w_0} = 0.415$, $\mu_{b_0} = 0.095$, $\alpha_w = 1.25 \times 10^{-6}$, $\alpha_b = 1.5 \times 10^{-6}$ and of NLMS algorithm are $\mu_w = 0.15$, $\mu_b = 0.075$.

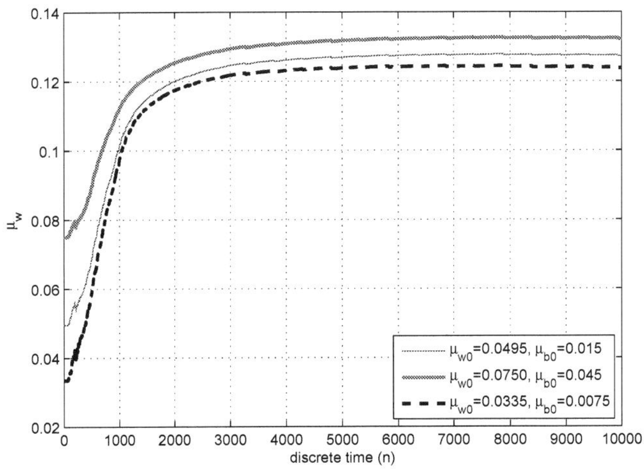

Fig. 8. Trajectories of μ_w of proposed AS-OSNALMS algorithm for TEQ using different setting of μ_{w_0} and μ_{b_0} for TEQ and TIR with fixed at $\alpha_w = 4.45 \times 10^{-4}$ and $\alpha_b = 1.75 \times 10^{-4}$, when the samples of CSA loop are loop #1.

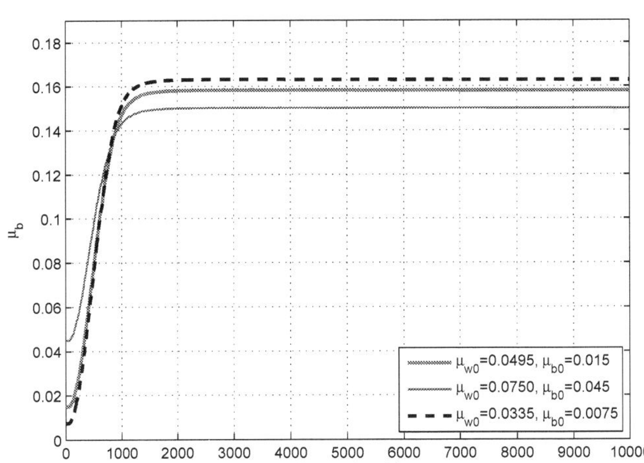

Fig. 9. Trajectories of μ_b of proposed AS-OSNALMS algorithm for TIR using different setting of μ_{w_0} and μ_{b_0} for TEQ and TIR with fixed at $\alpha_w = 4.45 \times 10^{-4}$ and $\alpha_b = 1.75 \times 10^{-4}$, when the samples of CSA loop are loop #1.

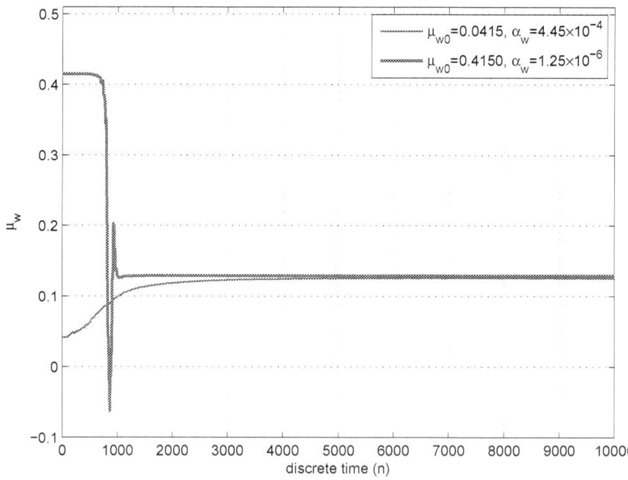

Fig. 10. Trajectories of μ_w of proposed AS-OSNALMS algorithm for TEQ using different setting of μ_{w_0} and μ_{b_0} for TEQ and TIR with different at $\alpha_w = 4.45 \times 10^{-4}$ and $\alpha_w = 1.25 \times 10^{-6}$, when the samples of CSA loop are loop #1.

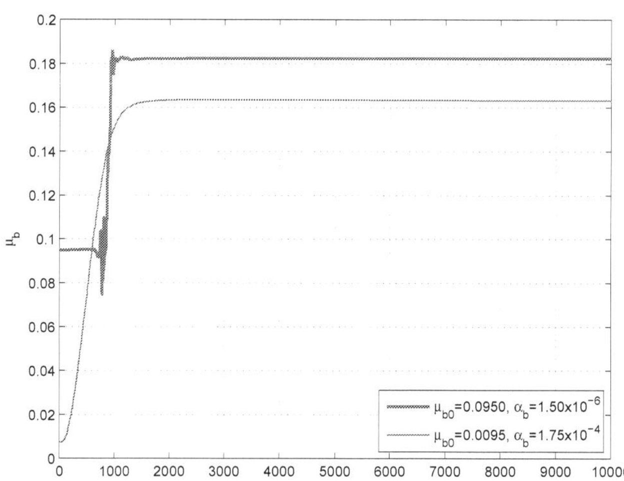

Fig. 11. Trajectories of μ_b of proposed AS-OSNALMS algorithm for TIR using different setting of μ_{w_0} and μ_{b_0} for TEQ and TIR with different at $\alpha_b = 1.75 \times 10^{-4}$ and $\alpha_b = 1.5 \times 10^{-6}$, when the samples of CSA loop are loop #1.

9. References

Al-Dhahir, N. & Cioffi, J.M. (1996). Optimum Finite-Length Equalization for Multicarrier Transceivers, *IEEE Trans. on Comm.*, vol. 44, no. 1, pp. 56-64, Jan. 1996.

Benveniste, A.; Métivier, M. & Priouret, P. (1990). *Adaptive Algorithms and Stochastic Approximations*, Springer-Verlag.

Bladel, M.V. & Moeneclaey, M. (1995). Time-Domain Equalization for Multicarrier Communication, *Proceedings of IEEE Global Comm. Conf. (GLOBECOM)*, pp.167-171, Nov. 1995.

Baldemair, R. & Frenger, P. (2001). A Time-domain Equalizer Minimizing Intersymbol and Intercarrier Interference in DMT Systems, *Proceedings of IEEE Global Comm. Conf. (GLOBECOM)*, vol.1, pp.381-385, Nov. 2001.

Chambers, J.A. (1993). Normalization of Order Statistics LMS Adaptive Filters Sequential Parameter Estimation, *Schlumberger Cambridge Research*, U.K., 1993.

Diniz, P.S.R. (2008) *Adaptive Filtering Algorithms and Practical Implementation*, Springer.

F-Boroujeny, B. & Ding, M. (2001). Design Methods for Time-Domain Equalizers in DMT Transceivers, *IEEE Trans. on Comm.*, vol. 49, no. 3, pp. 554-562, Mar. 2001.

Golden, P.; Dedieu H. & Jacobsen, K.S. (2006). *Fundamentals of DSL Technology*, Auerbach Publications, Taylor & Francis Group, New York.

Hayes, M.H. (1996). *Statistical Digital Signal Processing and Modeling*, John Wiley & Sons, 1996.

Haykin, S. (2002). *Adaptive Filter Theory*, Prentice Hall, Upper Saddle River, New Jersey.

Haweel, T.I. & Clarkson, P.M. (1992). A Class of Order Statistics LMS Algorithms, *IEEE Trans. on Signal Processing*, vol.40, no.1, pp.44-53, 1992.

Henkel, W., Tauböck, G., Ödling, P.; Börjesson, P.O. & Petersson, N. (2002). The Cyclic Prefix of OFDM/DMT-An Analysis, *Proceedings of IEEE Int.Zurich Seminar on Broadband Comm. Access-Transmission-Networking*, pp. 22.1-22.3, Feb. 2002.

International Telecommunications Union (ITU) (2001). Recommendation G.996.1, *Test Procedures for Asymmetric Digital Subscriber Line (ADSL) Transceivers*, February 2001.

International Telecommunications Union (ITU) (2002). Recommendation G.992.3, *Asymmetric Digital Subscriber Line (ADSL) Transceivers-2 (ADSL)*, July 2002.

International Telecommunications Union (ITU) (2003). Recommendation G.992.5, *Asymmetric Digital Subscriber Line (ADSL) Transceivers-Extened Bandwidth ADSL2 (ADSL2+)*, May 2003.

Kushner, H.J. & Yang, J. (1995). Analysis of Adaptive Step-Size SA Algorithms for Parameter Tracking, *IEEE Trans. on Automatic Control*, vol. 40, no. 8, pp. 1403-1410, Aug. 1995.

Lee, I., Chow, J.S. & Cioffi, J.M. (1995). Performance evaluation of a fast computation algorithm for the DMT in high-speed subscriber loop, *IEEE J. on Selected Areas in Comm.*, pp. 1564-1570, vol.13, Dec. 1995.

López-Valcarce, R. (2004). Minimum Delay Spread TEQ Design in Multicarrier Systems, *IEEE Signal Processing Letters*, vol. 11, no. 8, Aug. 2004.

Melsa, P.J.W., Younce, R.C. & Rohrs, C.E. (1996). Impulse Response Shortening for Discrete Multitone Transceivers, *IEEE Trans. on Communications*, vol. 44, no. 12, pp. 1662-1672, Dec. 1996.

Moon, T.K. & Stirling, W.C. (2000). *Mathmatical Methods and Algorithms for Signal Processing*, Prentice Hall, Upper Saddle River, New Jersey.

Nafie, M. & Gather, A. (1997). Time-Domain Equalizer Training for ADSL, *Proceedings of IEEE Int. Conf. on Communications (ICC)*, pp.1085-1089, June 1997.

Sitjongsataporn, S. & Yuvapoositanon, P. (2007). An Adaptive Step-size Order Statistic Time Domain Equaliser for Discrete Multitone Systems, *Proceedings of IEEE Int. Symp. on Circuits and Systems (ISCAS)*, pp. 1333-1336, New Orleans, LA., USA., May 2007.

Starr, T., Cioffi, J.M. & Silvermann, P.J. (1999) *Understanding Digital Subscriber Line Technology*, Prentice Hall, New Jersey.

Wang, B. & Adali, T. (2000). Time-Domain Equalizer Design for Discrete Multitone Systems, *Proceedings of IEEE Int. Conf. on Communications (ICC)*, pp.1080-1084, June 2000.

Yap, K.S. & McCanny, J.V. (2002). Improved time-domain equalizer initialization algorithm for ADSL modems, *Proceedings of Int. Symp. on DSP for communication systems (DSPCS)*, pp.253-258, Jan. 2002.

Ysebaert, G., Acker, K.Van, Moonen, M. & De Moor, B. (2003). Constraints in channel shortening equalizer design for DMT-based systems, *Signal Processing*, vol. 83, no. 3, pp. 641-648, Mar. 2003.

23

Discrete-Time Dynamic Image-Segmentation System

Ken'ichi Fujimoto, Mio Kobayashi and Tetsuya Yoshinaga
The University of Tokushima
Japan

1. Introduction

The modeling of oscillators and their dynamics has interested researchers in many fields such as those in physics, chemistry, engineering, and biology. The Hodgkin-Huxley (Hodgkin & Huxley, 1952) and Fitzhugh-Nagumo models (FitzHugh, 1961), which corresponds to the Bonhöffer van der Pol (BvP) equation, are well-known models of biological neurons. They have been described by differential equations, i.e., they are continuous-time relaxation oscillators. Discrete-time oscillators, e.g., one consisting of a recurrent neural network (Haschke & Steil, 2005) and another consisting of a spiking neuron model (Rulkov, 2002), have been proposed.

Synchronization observed in coupled oscillators has been established to be an important topic (Pikovsky et al., 2003; Waller & Kapral, 1984). Research on coupled oscillators has involved studies on pattern formation (Kapral, 1985; Oppo & Kapral, 1986), image segmentation (Shareef et al., 1999; Terman & Wang, 1995; Wang & Terman, 1995; 1997), and scene analysis (Wang, 2005). Of these, a locally excitatory globally inhibitory oscillator network (LEGION) (Wang & Terman, 1995), which is a continuous-time dynamical system, has been spotlighted as an ingenious image-segmentation system. A LEGION can segment an image and exhibit segmented images in a time series, i.e., it can spatially and temporally segment an image. We call such processing dynamic image segmentation. A LEGION consists of relaxation oscillators arranged in a two-dimensional (2D) grid and an inhibitor globally connected to all oscillators and it can segment images according to the synchronization of locally coupled oscillators. Image segmentation is the task of segmenting a given image so that homogeneous image blocks are disjoined; it is a fundamental technique in computer vision, e.g., object recognition for a computer-aided diagnosis system (Doi, 2007) in medical imaging. The problem with image segmentation is still serious, and various frameworks have been proposed (Pal & Pal, 1993; Suri et al., 2005) to solve this.

We proposed a discrete-time oscillator model consisting of a neuron (Fujimoto et al., 2008), which was modified from a chaotic neuron model (Aihara, 1990; Aihara et al., 1990), coupled with an inhibitor. Despite discrete-time dynamics as well as the recurrent neural network (Haschke & Steil, 2005), a neuron in our oscillator can generate a similar oscillatory response formed by a periodic point to an oscillation as observed in a continuous-time relaxation oscillator model, e.g., the BvP equation. This is a key attribute in our idea. Moreover, we proposed a neuronal network system consisting of our neurons (discrete-time oscillators) arranged in a 2D grid and an inhibitor globally coupled to all neurons. As well as a LEGION, our neuronal network system can work as a dynamic image-segmentation system according to the oscillatory responses of neurons. Our system provides much faster dynamic image segmentation than a LEGION on a digital computer because numerical integration is not required (Fujimoto et al., 2008). Another advantage of our system is that it simplifies the investigation of bifurcations of fixed points and periodic points due to the discrete-time dynamical system. A fixed point and a periodic point correspond to non-oscillatory and periodic oscillatory responses. Knowledge on the bifurcations of responses allows us to directly design appropriate system parameters to dynamically segment images. The assigned system parameters are made available by implementing our dynamic image-segmentation system into hardware such as field-programmable gate array devices (Fujimoto et al., 2011b). This article describes the derivation of a model reduced from our dynamic image-segmentation system that can simplify bifurcation analysis. We also explain our method of bifurcation analysis based on dynamical systems theory. Through analysis in reduced models with two or three neurons using our method of analysis, we find parameter regions where a fixed point or a periodic point exists. We also demonstrate that our dynamic image-segmentation system, whose system parameters were appropriately assigned according to the analyzed results, can work for images with two or three image regions. To demonstrate that segmentation is not limited to three in the system, we also present a successive algorithm for segmenting an image with an arbitrary number of image regions using our dynamic image-segmentation system.

2. Discrete-time dynamic image-segmentation system

2.1 Single neuronal system

Figure 1(a) illustrates the architecture of a system consisting of a neuron (Fujimoto et al., 2008) and an inhibitor. Here, let us call it a single neuronal system. Our neuron model modified from a chaotic neuron model (Aihara, 1990; Aihara et al., 1990) has two internal state variables, x and y; z corresponds to the internal state variable of an inhibitor, in which $x, y, z \in \mathbb{R}$ with $\mathbb{R}$ denoting the set of real numbers. Let the sum of internal state values in a neuron, i.e. $x + y$, be the activity level of a neuron. The dynamics of the single neuronal system is described by difference equations:

$$x(t+1) = k_f x(t) + d + W_x \cdot g(x(t) + y(t), \theta_c) - W_z \cdot g(z(t), \theta_z) \tag{1a}$$

$$y(t+1) = k_r y(t) - \alpha \cdot g(x(t) + y(t), \theta_c) + a \tag{1b}$$

$$z(t+1) = \phi \left\{ g\left(g(x(t) + y(t), \theta_f), \theta_d \right) - z(t) \right\}. \tag{1c}$$

The $t \in \mathbb{Z}$ denotes the discrete time where $\mathbb{Z}$ expresses the set of integers. $g(\cdot, \cdot)$ is the output function of a neuron or an inhibitor and is described as

$$g(u(t), \theta) = \frac{1}{1 + \exp(-(u(t) - \theta)/\varepsilon)}. \tag{2}$$

Note that $g(\cdot, \theta_d)$ where $g(x(t) + y(t), \theta_f)$ is nested in Eq. (1c) is neither output function, but a function to find the firing of a neuron that corresponds to a high level of activity. Therefore, an inhibitor plays roles in detecting a fired neuron and suppressing the activity level of a neuron at the next discrete time. The k_f, k_r, and ϕ are coefficients corresponding to the gradient of x, y, and z. The d denotes an external direct-current (DC) input. The W_x and α are self-feedback gains in a neuron, and W_z is the coupling coefficient from an inhibitor to a neuron. The a is a bias term in a neuron. The θ_c and θ_z are threshold parameters in output functions of a neuron and an inhibitor, respectively. Also, θ_f and θ_d are threshold parameters to define the firing of a neuron and to detect a fired neuron, respectively. The ε is a parameter that determines the gradient of the sigmoid function (2) at $u(t) = \theta$.

When we set all the parameters to certain values, our neuron can generate a similar oscillatory response formed by a periodic point to an oscillation as observed in a continuous-time relaxation oscillator model. For instance, the time evolution of a generated response, in which this is a waveform, is shown in Fig. 1(b) for initial values, $(x(0), y(0), z(0)) = (32.108, -31.626, 0.222)$, at $k_f = 0.5$, $d = 2$, $W_x = 15$, $\theta_c = 0$, $W_z = 15$, $\theta_z = 0.5$, $k_r = 0.89$, $\alpha = 4$, $a = 0.5$, $\phi = 0.8$, $\theta_f = 15$, $\theta_d = 0$, and $\varepsilon = 0.1$. To clarify the effect of the inhibitor, we have shown the activity level of the neuron and the internal state of the inhibitor on the vertical axis in this figure. The points marked with open circles "∘" indicate the values of $x + y$ and z at discrete time t. Although the response of a neuron or an inhibitor is formed by a series of points because of its discrete-time dynamics, we drew lines between temporally adjacent points as a visual aid. Therefore, our neuron coupled with an inhibitor is available as a discrete-time oscillator.

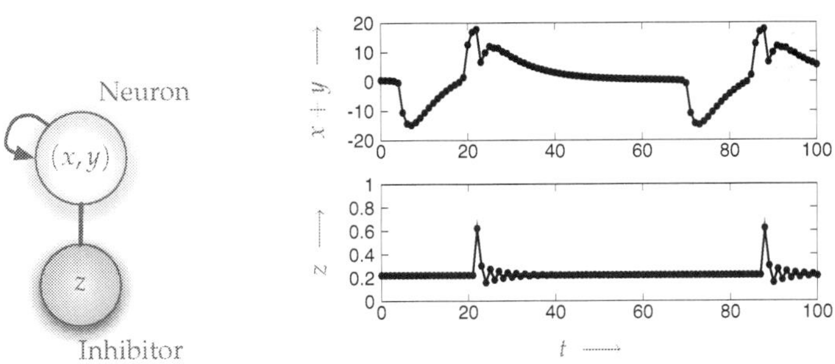

(a) Architecture (b) Oscillatory response

Fig. 1. Architecture of single neuronal system and generated oscillatory response

2.2 Neuronal network system

We have proposed a neuronal network system for dynamic image segmentation (Fujimoto et al., 2008). Figure 2(a) outlines the architecture of our system for a 2D image with P pixels. It is composed of our neurons that have as many pixels as in a given image and an inhibitor that is called a global inhibitor because it is connected with all neurons. All neurons are arranged in a 2D grid so that one corresponds to a pixel, and a neuron can have excitatory connections to its neighboring neurons. Here, we assumed that a neuron could connect to its four-neighboring ones. The formation of local connections between neighboring neurons is determined according to the value of DC input to each neuron. Note that, we can use our neuronal network system, in which neurons are arranged in a 3D grid so that one neuron corresponds to a voxel, which means a volumetric picture element, as a dynamic image-segmentation system for a 3D image.

The architecture for the ith neuron in a neuronal network system is illustrated in Fig. 2(b). The open and closed circles at the ends of the arrows correspond to excitatory and inhibitory

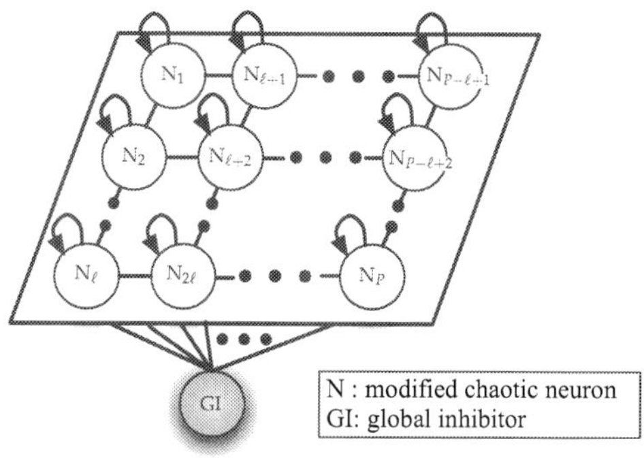

(a) Neuronal network system

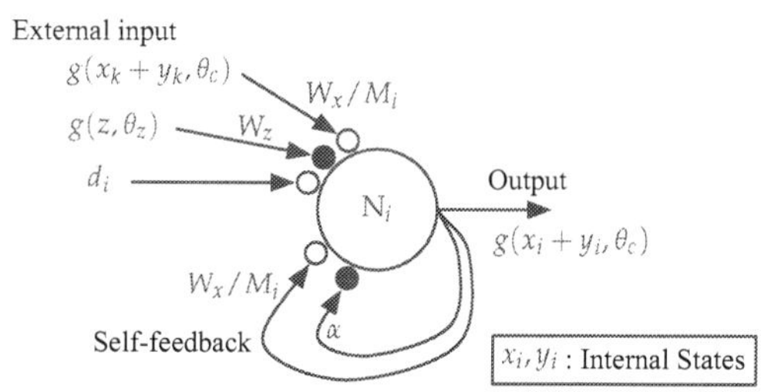

(b) The ith neuron

Fig. 2. Architecture of neuronal network system and a neuron

couplings. A neuron can receive external inputs from neighboring ones connected to it. An external input from another neuron can induce in-phase synchronization in the responses of connected neurons. Note that the number of external inputs in Fig. 2(b) indexed by $g(x_k + y_k, \theta_c)$ is the same as that of the other neurons connected to the ith neuron; moreover, when the DC-input value to the ith neuron is low, positive self-feedback vanishes and the neuron also has no connection to the others. W_x/M_i and W_z in external inputs represent coupling weights; the other W_x/M_i and α are feedback gains, where M_i denotes the number of connections to the ith neuron and neighboring neurons. What M_i means will be explained later.
The dynamics of our neuronal network system is described as

$$x_i(t+1) = k_f x_i(t) + d_i + \sum_{k \in L_i} \frac{W_x}{M_i} g(x_k(t) + y_k(t), \theta_c) - W_z \cdot g(z(t), \theta_z) \tag{3a}$$

$$y_i(t+1) = k_r y_i(t) - \alpha \cdot g(x_i(t) + y_i(t), \theta_c) + a \tag{3b}$$

$$(i = 1, 2, \ldots, P)$$

$$z(t+1) = \phi \left\{ g\left(\sum_{n=1}^{P} g(x_n(t) + y_n(t), \theta_f), \theta_d \right) - z(t) \right\}. \tag{3c}$$

The $g(\cdot,\cdot)$ was already defined in Eq. (2). The third term on the right hand side of Eq. (3a) denotes the ith neuron's self-feedback and external inputs from neighboring neurons, in which L_i represents an index set for neurons connected to the ith one. Therefore, the maximum number of elements in L_i is five in the architecture in Fig. 2(a). The M_i expresses the number of elements in L_i. Note that, when the ith neuron has no connection to neighboring neurons including itself, i.e., $M_i = 0$, we treat it as $W_x/M_i = 0$ because division by zero occurs.
As seen in Eq. (3c), the dynamics of a global inhibitor is improved from that in Eq. (1c) so that it can detect one or more firing neurons; moreover, it suppresses the activity levels of all neurons via negative couplings described at the fourth term in the right hand side of Eq. (3a). Therefore, when we set all the parameter values in Eq. (3) to those described in Sec. 2.1, only neurons with self-feedback can generate oscillatory responses.

2.3 Scheme of dynamic image segmentation

There is an image segmentation scheme using our neuronal network system in Fig. 3. For simplicity, let us now consider a simple gray-level image with 3×3 pixels. The image contains two image regions consisting of the same gray-level pixels: the first is composed of the first and fourth pixels, and the second is made up of only the ninth pixel.
Nine neurons are arranged in a 3×3 grid for the given image. The value of DC input, d_i, is associated with the gray level of the ith pixels. A neuron with a high DC-input value forms positive self-feedback and also connects to neighboring ones with similar DC-input values. Therefore, the red and blue neurons in this schematic have positive self-feedback connections and can generate oscillatory responses; the others corresponding to black pixels have no self-feedback and do not fire. Direct connection is formed between the red neurons because they correspond to pixels with the same gray levels, i.e., they have the same DC-input values. As seen from the red waveforms in Fig. 3, direct connection induces in-phase synchronization in the responses of coupled neurons. However, as seen from the red and blue waveforms, the responses of uncoupled neurons corresponding to pixels in different image regions are out of phase. This effect is produced by the global inhibitor that detects one or more firing neurons and suppresses the activity levels of all neurons with its own kindling. By assigning

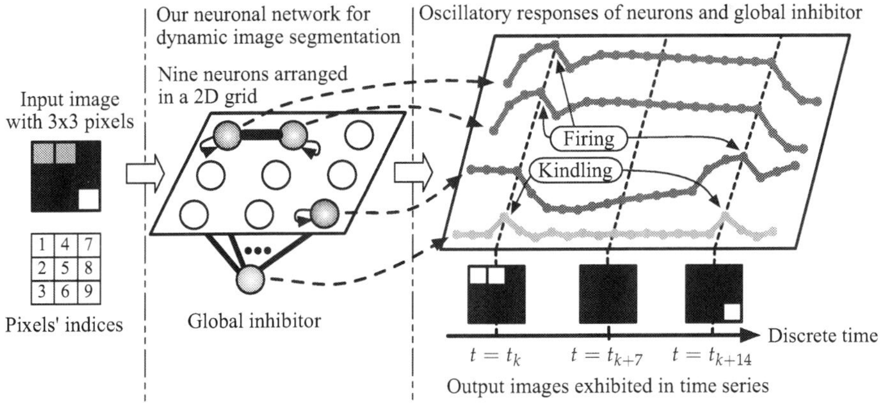

Fig. 3. Scheme of dynamic image segmentation using our system

the ith pixel value in the output image at time t to a high value corresponding to the white pixel only if $x_i(t) + y_i(t) \geq \theta_f$, segmented images are output and are exhibited in a time series. As a result, the given image is spatially and temporally segmented, i.e., dynamic image segmentation is achieved.

3. Analysis for parameter design

3.1 Reduced model

Our neuronal network model has complex dynamics and a variety of nonlinear phenomena such as synchronized neuron responses and bifurcations in these responses are therefore expected to occur in our system. From the viewpoint of dynamical systems theory, detailed analyses of the local and global bifurcations observed in our system would be interesting. However, we have only concentrated on analysis to design appropriate parameter values for dynamic image segmentation in this article, i.e., to find parameter regions where there are stable non-oscillatory or periodic oscillatory responses.

First, we need to derive a reduced model to simplify bifurcation analysis. Let us consider a dynamic image-segmentation system for a P-pixel image with Q image regions, where generally $Q \ll P$. A reduced model consists of a global inhibitor and Q neurons without direct coupling to the others as illustrated in Fig. 4. Here, we call it a Q-coupled system. A neuron in a Q-coupled system stands for neurons corresponding to all pixels in the same image region in our original neuronal system in Fig. 2(a). This reduced model is derived from three assumptions (Fujimoto et al., 2009b) in our dynamic image segmentation system for an image with Q image regions: 1) all pixel values in an identical image region are the same; viz., all neurons corresponding to pixels in an image region have the same DC-input values and are locally coupled with one another, 2) the responses of all neurons corresponding to pixels in an identical image region are synchronized in phase; this arises naturally from the first assumption, and 3) connections from the global inhibitor to the neurons are negligible because neurons corresponding to pixels with low gray-levels do not fire.

A non-oscillatory response and a periodic oscillatory response correspond to a fixed point and a periodic point. Therefore, knowing about their bifurcations in a Q-coupled system allows us to directly design appropriate parameter values to dynamically segment any sized image with Q image regions.

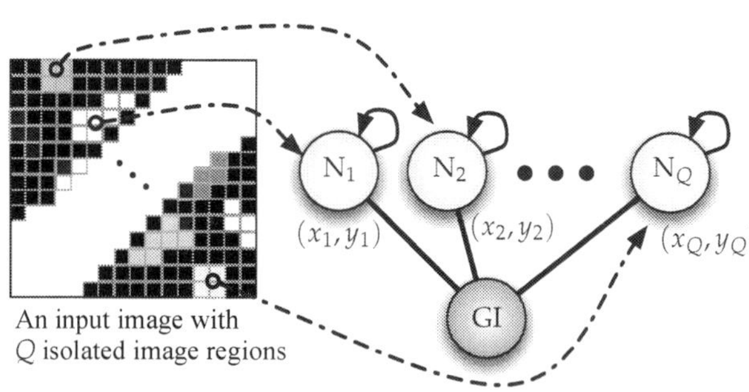

Fig. 4. Architecture of Q-coupled system and its correspondence to image with Q image regions

Now, let $\boldsymbol{x}(t) = (x_1(t), y_1(t), \ldots, x_Q(t), y_Q(t), z(t))^\top \in \mathbb{R}^V$, where $\top$ denotes the transpose of a vector. The dynamics of the Q-coupled system is described by a V-dimensional discrete-time dynamical system where $V = 2Q + 1$ as

$$\boldsymbol{x}(t+1) = \boldsymbol{f}(\boldsymbol{x}(t)), \tag{4}$$

or equivalently, an iterated map defined by

$$\boldsymbol{f} : \mathbb{R}^V \to \mathbb{R}^V; \boldsymbol{x} \mapsto \boldsymbol{f}(\boldsymbol{x}). \tag{5}$$

The nonlinear function, $\boldsymbol{f}$, describes the dynamics of the Q-coupled system given by

$$\boldsymbol{f}\begin{pmatrix} x_1 \\ y_1 \\ \vdots \\ x_Q \\ y_Q \\ z \end{pmatrix} = \begin{pmatrix} k_f x_1 + d_1 + W_x \cdot g(x_1 + y_1, \theta_c) - W_z \cdot g(z, \theta_z) \\ k_r y_1 - \alpha \cdot g(x_1 + y_1, \theta_c) + a \\ \vdots \\ k_f x_Q + d_Q + W_x \cdot g(x_Q + y_Q, \theta_c) - W_z \cdot g(z, \theta_z) \\ k_r y_Q - \alpha \cdot g(x_Q + y_Q, \theta_c) + a \\ \phi \left\{ g\left(\sum_{n=1}^{Q} g(x_n + y_n, \theta_f), \theta_d \right) - z \right\} \end{pmatrix} \tag{6}$$

where $g(\cdot, \cdot)$ was defined in Eq. (2).

3.2 Method of bifurcation analysis

A non-oscillatory response observed in the Q-coupled system corresponds to a fixed point of $\boldsymbol{f}$ in Eq. (5), and a periodic oscillatory response is formed by a periodic point of $\boldsymbol{f}$. Therefore, we can find their local bifurcations for the change in a system parameter value using a method of analysis based on qualitative bifurcation theory for discrete-time dynamical systems. The results from analyzing bifurcation in a reduced model enabled us to design suitable parameter values in our neuronal network system for dynamic image segmentation.

The following explains our method of analysis. Let us now consider a point, $\boldsymbol{x}^*$, satisfying

$$\boldsymbol{x}^* - \boldsymbol{f}(\boldsymbol{x}^*) = \boldsymbol{0}. \tag{7}$$

This is called a fixed point of $\boldsymbol{f}$ in Eq. (5) and corresponds to a non-oscillatory response observed in the Q-coupled system. The characteristic equation of $\boldsymbol{x}^*$ is defined as

$$\det(\mu \boldsymbol{E} - D\boldsymbol{f}(\boldsymbol{x}^*)) = 0, \tag{8}$$

where $\boldsymbol{E}$ and $D\boldsymbol{f}(\boldsymbol{x}^*)$ correspond to the $V \times V$ identity matrix and the Jacobian matrix of $\boldsymbol{f}$ at $\boldsymbol{x} = \boldsymbol{x}^*$. Moreover, the roots of Eq. (8), i.e., characteristic multipliers, are described as

$$\{\mu_1, \mu_2, \ldots, \mu_V\} = \{\mu_i \in \mathbb{C} \mid \det(\mu \boldsymbol{E} - D\boldsymbol{f}(\boldsymbol{x}^*)) = 0\}, \tag{9}$$

where $\mathbb{C}$ denotes the set of complex numbers. When the values of all $|\mu_i|$s are neither unity nor zero, we say that $\boldsymbol{x}^*$ is hyperbolic. Now, let us assume $\boldsymbol{x}^*$ is a hyperbolic fixed point. Let $\boldsymbol{U}$ be the intersection of $\mathbb{R}^V$ and the direct sum of the generalized eigenspaces of $D\boldsymbol{f}(\boldsymbol{x}^*)$ such that $|\mu_i| > 1, \forall i$; $\boldsymbol{U}$ is called the unstable subspace of $\mathbb{R}^V$. Moreover, let $\boldsymbol{H} = D\boldsymbol{f}(\boldsymbol{x}^*)|_{\boldsymbol{U}}$. The topological type of a hyperbolic fixed point is classified according to the value of $\dim \boldsymbol{U}$ and the sign of $\det \boldsymbol{H}$ (Kawakami, 1984).

A hyperbolic fixed point bifurcates when its stability is varied, or more correctly its topological type is changed, according to variations in a system parameter value; change in a topological type occurs when one or more characteristic multipliers are on the unit circle in the complex plane. There are generally three types of co-dimension-one bifurcations, i.e., tangent (saddle-node), period-doubling, and Neimark-Sacker bifurcations. D-type of branching (pitchfork bifurcation) can also appear as a degenerate case of tangent bifurcation in only a dynamical system that is symmetrical. Tangent bifurcation or D-type of branching appears if $\mu = +1$, period-doubling bifurcation occurs when $\mu = -1$, and Neimark-Sacker bifurcation is generated when $\mu = e^{j\varphi}$, where $j = \sqrt{-1}$ except for $\mu = \pm 1$.

A bifurcation point of $\boldsymbol{x}^*$ is computed by solving simultaneous equations consisting of Eqs. (7) and (8) as the values of $\boldsymbol{x}^*$ and a system parameter are unknown; we employed Newton's method for the numerical determination. The Jacobian matrix of the simultaneous equations used in Newton's method is derived from the first and second derivatives of $\boldsymbol{f}$. Note that, in Eq. (7), a fixed point, $\boldsymbol{x}^*$, becomes an m-periodic point by replacing $\boldsymbol{f}$ with $\boldsymbol{f}^m$, which denotes the m-times iteration of $\boldsymbol{f}$, where m is a natural number such that $m \geq 2$. We can define an m-periodic point and its bifurcations according to $\boldsymbol{f}^m$; moreover, we can numerically compute the bifurcation points of an m-periodic point as well as those of a fixed point.

As previously mentioned, we focused on bifurcation analysis to design suitable parameter values for our dynamic image segmentation system. Therefore, we will next illustrate parameter regions where there are stable fixed or stable periodic points in two-parameter bifurcation diagrams.

3.3 Results of analysis

We will now illustrate parameter regions where there are stable fixed or periodic points with our method of analyzing bifurcations. Knowing about the bifurcations allows us to directly set system-parameter values that yield successful results for dynamic image segmentation.

We treated a single neuronal system and two- and three-coupled systems and set the system parameter values in Eqs. (2) and (6) except for k_r, ϕ, and d_is to $\varepsilon = 0.1$, $k_f = 0.5$, $W_x = 15$, $\theta_c = 0$, $W_z = 15$, $\theta_z = 0.5$, $\alpha = 4$, $a = 0.5$, $\theta_f = 15$, and $\theta_d = 0$. In the bifurcation diagrams that follow, we used symbols G_ℓ^m, I_ℓ^m, NS_ℓ^m, and D_ℓ^m to denote tangent, period-doubling, and Neimark-Sacker bifurcations, and D-type of branching for an m-periodic point. The subscript series number ℓ was appended to distinguish bifurcation sets of the same type for an m-periodic point. Note that these symbols indicate bifurcations of a fixed point if $m = 1$.

3.3.1 Single neuronal system

This is the reduced model of a dynamic image segmentation system for an image with only one image region. Its architecture is outlined in Fig. 1(a). It may seem that the analysis of bifurcations observed in this reduced model is meaningless for dynamic image segmentation. However, the existence of a fixed point in this model leads to considerable knowledge to devise an algorithm for dynamic image segmentation as will be explained later.

We set $d = 2$ and used k_r and ϕ as unfixed parameters to analyze bifurcation. As shown in Fig. 1(b), an oscillatory response was observed in this model with $k_r = 0.89$ and $\phi = 0.8$. Moreover, we found a stable fixed point, $\boldsymbol{x}^* = (32.244, -23.333, 0.22222)$, at $k_r = 0.85$ and $\phi = 0.8$. We investigated a parameter region where there was a stable fixed point and also found the genesis of the oscillatory response (Fujimoto et al., 2009b).

Figure 5 shows a two-parameter bifurcation diagram on a fixed point in the (k_r, ϕ)-plane. We found three Neimark-Sacker bifurcation sets and located the shaded parameter region where there was a stable fixed point. When we gradually changed the value of k_r under $\phi = 0.8$ so that the parameter point passed through the bifurcation line indexed by NS_1^1 from the shaded region to the non-shaded region, the stable fixed point destabilized on the Neimark-Sacker bifurcation line. As a result, an oscillatory response was generated as seen in Fig. 6. In the numerical simulation, we set $k_r = 0.88975$ and $\phi = 0.8$ that correspond to the parameter point in the neighborhood at right of NS_1^1 in Fig. 5; the initial values were set to $\boldsymbol{x}(0) = (32.10, -31.58, 0.2222)$, which is in the vicinity of the destabilized fixed point. That is, this figure gives the time evolution in the transient state that starts from the destabilized fixed point to generate an oscillatory response. Although we observed an oscillatory response in the other non-shaded region surrounded by NS_2^1 and NS_3^1, it is not suited to dynamic image segmentation because of its small amplitude and short period.

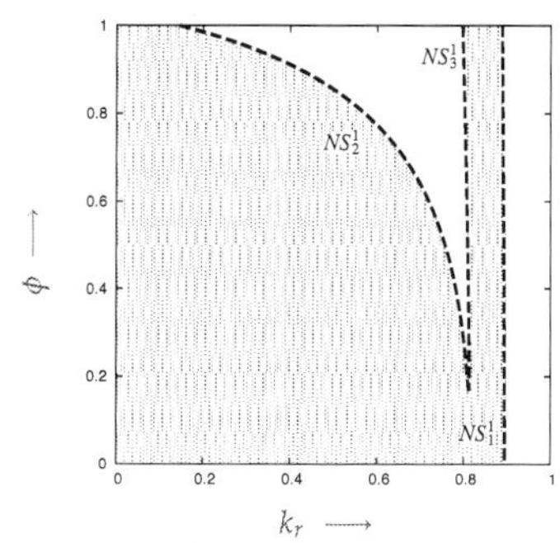

Fig. 5. Bifurcations of fixed point observed in single neuronal system

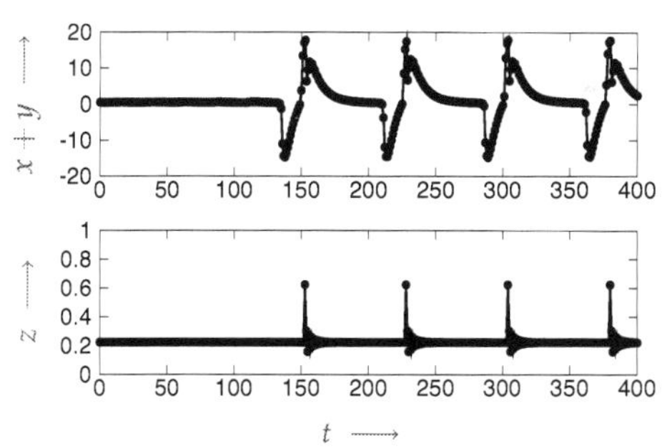

Fig. 6. Oscillatory response caused by Neimark-Sacker bifurcation of stable fixed point

3.3.2 Two-coupled system

This two-coupled system consists of a global inhibitor and two neurons without direct coupling to other neuron. This was derived as a reduced model of our scheme to dynamically segment an image with two image regions.

Here, the unfixed parameters were set to $d_1 = d_2 = 2$, which means that all pixel values in the two image regions are the same. Therefore, this system is symmetrical for the exchange of

(x_1, y_1) and (x_2, y_2) from Eq. (6) at $d_1 = d_2$. The k_r and ϕ were used as unfixed parameters in the analysis of bifurcation that is discussed below.

First, we investigated the bifurcations of a fixed point in a symmetrical two-coupled system (Fujimoto et al., 2009b) where we observed a stable fixed point, $\boldsymbol{x}^* = (32.244, 32.244, -23.333, -23.333, 0.222)$, at $k_r = 0.85$ and $\phi = 0.8$. The occurrence of a fixed point is adverse for dynamic image segmentation because only black images are output; this means dynamic image segmentation has failed. By analyzing bifurcation for the fixed point, we obtained the two-parameter bifurcation diagram in Fig. 5, i.e., this is the same as that for the results obtained for the fixed point in the single neuronal system.

We observed two types of oscillatory responses formed by periodic points at $k_r = 0.89$ and $\phi = 0.8$. Figure 7 shows in-phase and out-of-phase oscillatory responses in which the blue and red points correspond to the responses of the first and second neurons. To understand their phases better, we also drew phase portraits.

Figure 8(a) illustrates bifurcation sets of several in-phase periodic points, and the line marked NS_1^1 at the bottom left corresponds to the Neimark-Sacker bifurcation set of the fixed point. As seen in the figure, we found the tangent bifurcations of in-phase periodic points. There is a stable in-phase m-periodic point in the shaded parameter region surrounded by G_1^m and G_2^m for $m = 60, 61, \ldots, 70$. Therefore, in-phase periodic points could be observed in the shaded parameter regions in the right parameter regions of NS_1^1. Note that in-phase periodic points

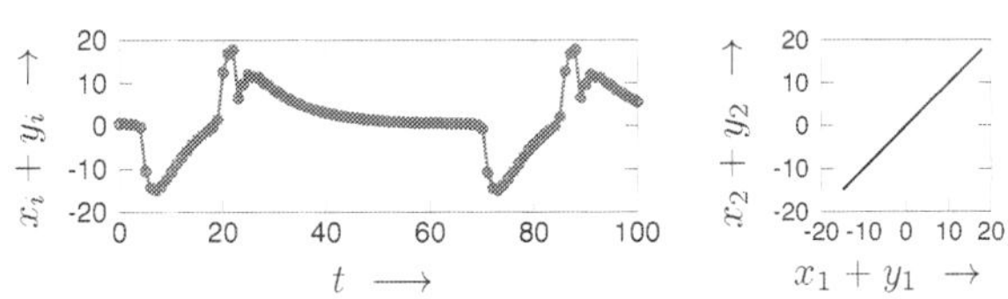

(a) In-phase oscillatory response

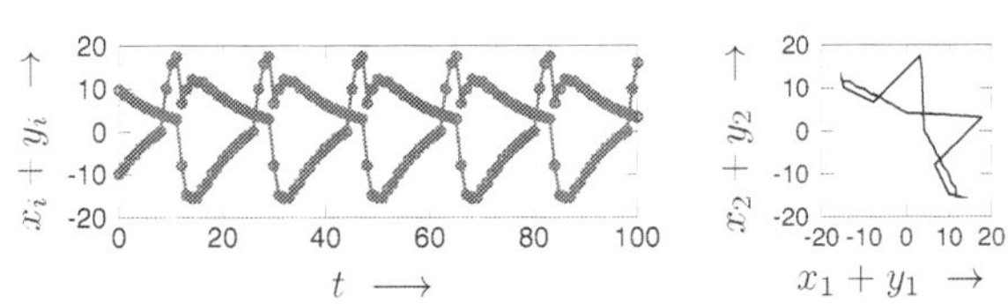

(b) Out-of-phase oscillatory response

Fig. 7. Different types of oscillatory responses observed in symmetric two-coupled system at $k_r = 0.89$ and $\phi = 0.8$

are inappropriate for dynamically segmenting an image with two image regions (Fujimoto et al., 2009b).

Next, we investigated the bifurcations of out-of-phase periodic points on the (k_r, ϕ)-plane. (Musashi et al., 2009). As shown in Fig. 8(b), their tangent bifurcations and D-type of branchings were found. For example, there are stable out-of-phase m-periodic points in the shaded parameter region surrounded by G_ℓ^m and D_1^m for $m = 30, 32, 34, 36$ for the observed periodic points. Note that the overlapping parameter region indicates that

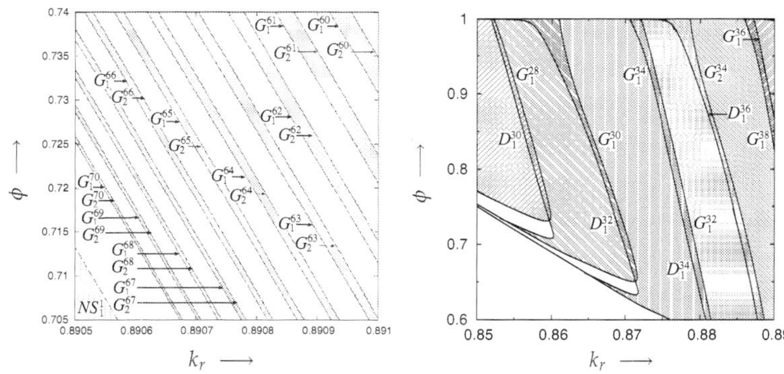

(a) In-phase periodic points (b) Out-of-phase periodic points

Fig. 8. Bifurcations of perodic points observed in symmetric two-coupled system

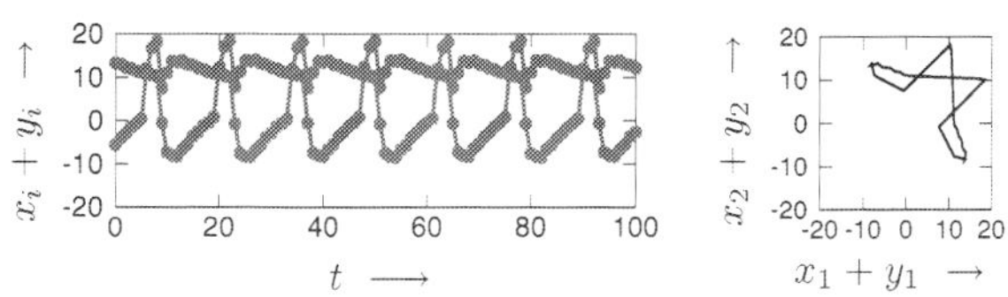

Fig. 9. Out-of-phase oscillatory response observed in asymmetric two-coupled system at $k_r = 0.85$ and $\phi = 0.8$

out-of-phase periodic points coexist. The whole parameter region where there are stable out-of-phase periodic points is much wider than that of stable in-phase periodic points. This is favorable for dynamic image segmentation, because an in-phase periodic point is unsuitable and an out-of-phase periodic point is suitable.

We set $d_1 \neq d_2$ in the two-coupled system, and therefore, the symmetry for the exchange of (x_1, y_1) and (x_2, y_2) in Eq. (6) is lost. This asymmetric two-coupled system corresponds to a situation where an input image contains two image regions of different colors. No symmetric periodic points occur in this system; however, we could observe the asymmetric out-of-phase periodic point shown in Fig. 9. Note that it is difficult to determine whether a periodic point is symmetric only from waveforms and phase portraits; however, this is not important because the feasibility of dynamic image segmentation is not dependent on whether there is symmetry or not but on the number of phases in a periodic point.

Figure 10(a) shows bifurcation sets of out-of-phase periodic points observed at $d_1 = 2$ and $d_2 = 1.9$. Different from the symmetric system, D-type of branching never appeared due to the asymmetric system; instead, period-doubling bifurcations were found. Comparing the extent of all the shaded parameter regions in Figs. 8(b) and 10(a), the asymmetric system is as wide as the symmetric system. Moreover, we set $d_1 = 2$ and $\phi = 0.8$ and investigated their bifurcations on the (k_r, d_2)-plane as seen in Fig. 10(b). This indicates that there were stable out-of-phase periodic points even if the value of $|d_1 - d_2|$ was large; in other words, the difference between the gray levels of the pixels in the two image regions is large. This is also favorable for a dynamic image segmentation system.

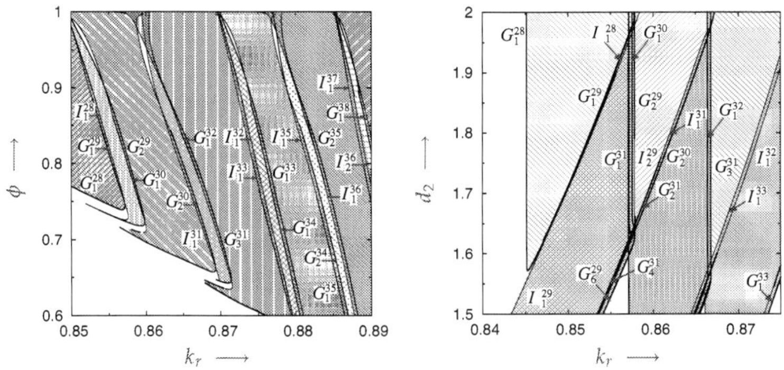

(a) Case of $d_1 = 2$ and $d_2 = 1.9$

(b) Case of $d_1 = 2$ and $\phi = 0.8$

Fig. 10. Bifurcations of out-of-phase perodic points observed in asymmetric two-coupled system

3.3.3 Three-coupled system

This model is composed of a global inhibitor and three neurons without direct coupling to the others and was derived as a reduced model of our dynamic segmentation of an image containing three image regions. As well as the aforementioned reduced models, we drew several two-parameter bifurcation diagrams to find the parameter regions such that a stable fixed point or a stable m-periodic point existed.

When we set $d_1 = d_2 = d_3 = 2$, the three-coupled system was symmetric for a circular exchange of (x_i, y_i) for (x_{i+1}, y_{i+1}), $i = 1,2,3$ where the value of $i+1$ returns to 1 if $i = 3$. In this symmetric system, we found a stable fixed point, $\boldsymbol{x}^* = (32.244, -29.167, 32.244, -29.167, 32.244, -29.167, 0.222)$, at $k_r = 0.88$ and $\phi = 0.8$. In the results we investigated, we found the bifurcation diagram on the fixed point on the (k_r, ϕ)-plane was the same as the one in Fig. 5. Moreover, as well as those in the symmetric two-coupled system, we could observe in-phase oscillatory responses in only the right hand side region of NS_1^1. The waveform of an in-phase oscillatory response and its phase portraits are shown in Fig. 11(a), where the blue, red, and green points correspond to the responses of the first, second, and third neurons. The results suggest that the Neimark-Sacker bifurcation set, NS_1^1, causes in-phase oscillatory responses to generate and these are similar to those of the symmetric two-coupled system (Fujimoto et al., 2009b; Musashi et al., 2009). Therefore, this implies that the global bifurcation structure of a fixed point and the generation of in-phase oscillatory responses are intrinsic properties of the symmetric Q-coupled system.

We also observed several oscillatory responses in certain parameter regions. Figures 11(b) and 11(c) show a two-phase and a three-phase periodic points. For the following reasons, we only focused on the bifurcations of three-phase periodic points that were appropriate for dynamically segmenting an image with three image regions.

Figure 13 shows bifurcation sets of three-phase periodic points observed in the symmetric system. Tangent, period-doubling, and Neimark-Sacker bifurcations were observed. The

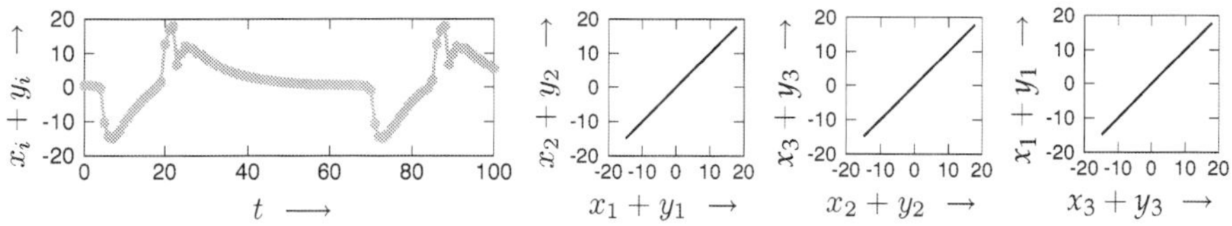

(a) In-phase oscillatory response

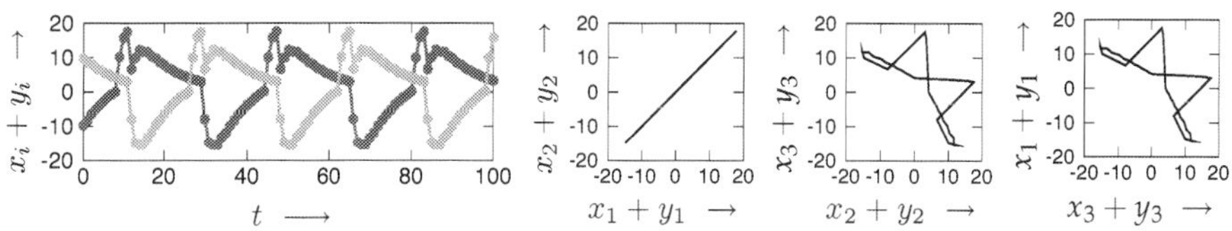

(b) Two-phase oscillatory response

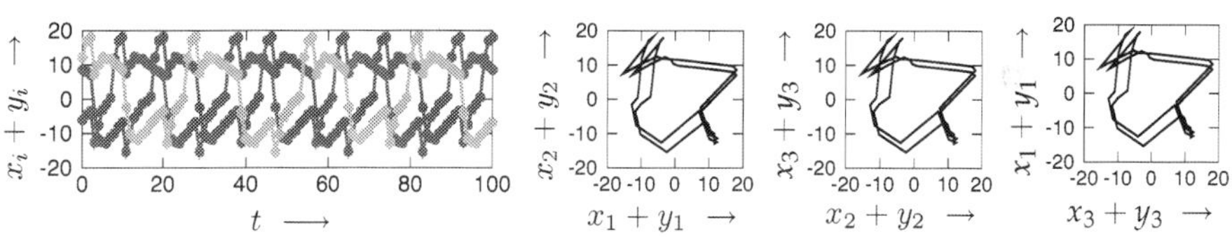

(c) Three-phase oscillatory response

Fig. 11. Different types of oscillatory responses observed in symmetric three-coupled system at $d_1 = d_2 = d_3 = 2$, $k_r = 0.89$, and $\phi = 0.8$

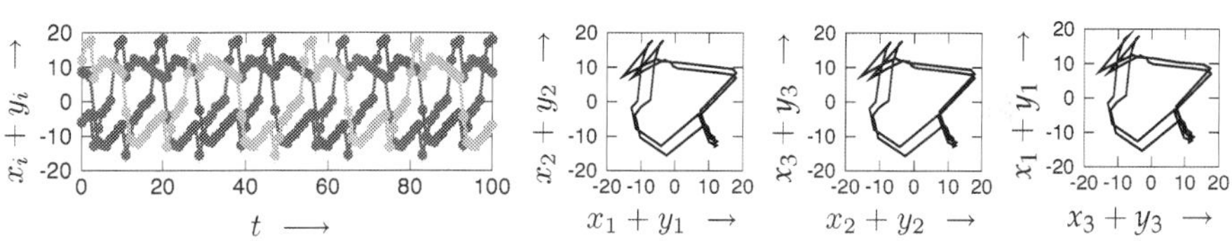

Fig. 12. Three-phase oscillatory response observed in asymmetric three-coupled system at $d_1 = 2$, $d_2 = 1.9$, $d_3 = 1.8$, $k_r = 0.89$, and $\phi = 0.8$

respective periodic points are symmetrical for the aforementioned circular exchange. However, as seen in Fig. 13, we could find no D-type of branching in these investigations. There is a stable three-phase periodic point in each shaded parameter region. Compared with the extent of the entire shaded parameter region in Fig. 8(b), that of the three-phase periodic points is small; however, it is sufficient to design the parameters of our dynamic image segmentation system.

Next, we set $d_1 \neq d_2 \neq d_3$, i.e., this model is asymmetric. Although this three-coupled system loses symmetry, there is a three-phase periodic point in certain parameters as shown in Fig. 12. We investigated the bifurcations of several three-phase periodic points observed in the asymmetric system and drew two bifurcation diagrams. Figure 14(a) shows the bifurcation sets of three-phase periodic points on the (k_r, ϕ)-plane. Of course, we found no D-type of

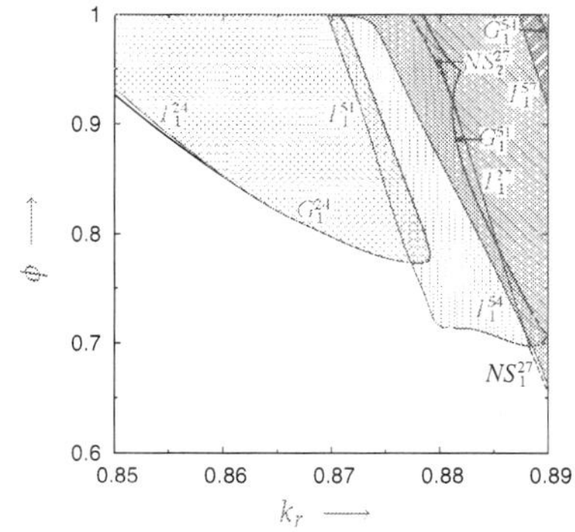

Fig. 13. Bifurcations of three-phase periodic points observed in symmetric three-coupled system

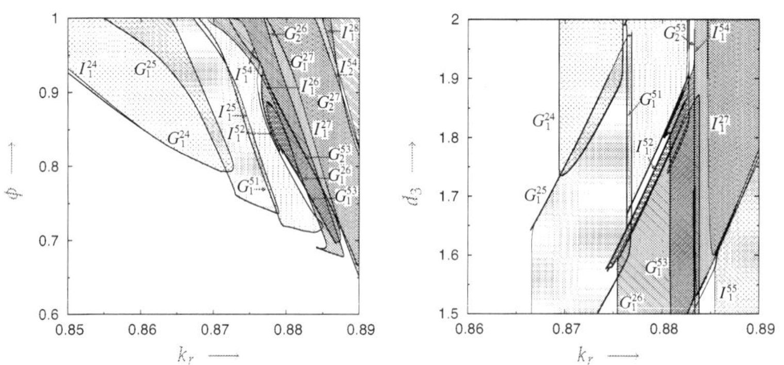

(a) $d_1 = 2, d_2 = 1.9$, and $d_3 = 1.8$

(b) $d_1 = 2, d_2 = 1.9$, and $\phi = 0.8$

Fig. 14. Bifurcations of three-phase periodic points observed in asymmetric three-coupled system

branching because of the asymmetric system. There is a stable three-phase periodic point in each parameter region shaded by a pattern. The shape and size of the whole shaded parameter region where there are three-phase periodic points are similar to those in Fig. 13.

As seen in Fig. 14(b), we also computed the bifurcations of three-phase periodic points observed at $d_1 = 2, d_2 = 1.9$, and $\phi = 0.8$ on the (k_r, d_3)-plane. As we can see from the figure, there are several stable three-phase periodic points even if the value of d_3 is set as small as 1.5. This suggests that our dynamic image-segmentation system can work for an image with three regions having different gray levels.

4. Application to Dynamic Image Segmentation

We demonstrated successful results for dynamic image segmentation carried out by our system with appropriate parameter values according to the results analyzed from the two- and three-coupled systems. Our basic concept was that we assigned system parameters to certain values such those in-phase oscillatory responses, which are unsuitable for dynamic image segmentation. They do not appear but a multiphase periodic point with as many phases as image regions does occur.

4.1 Image with two image regions

Let us consider a dynamic image segmentation problem for the 8-bit gray-level image with 256×256 pixels shown in Fig. 15(a). This is a slice from the X-ray CT images of the human head from the Visible Human Dataset (Ackerman, 1991). Using a thresholding method, we transformed the gray-level CT image into a binary image in preprocessing with $\forall i, p_i = \{0, 255\}$, where p_i denotes the ith pixel value. Here, the black and white correspond to 0 and 255. The process image contains the two white image regions shown in Fig. 15(b). The upper region corresponds to teeth and the mandible bone, and the lower regions indicate the cervical spine.

We need a neuronal network system to segment the binary image consisting of 256×256 neurons and a global inhibitor. The DC-input value to the ith neuron, d_i, was set to 2.0 for neurons corresponding to pixels in the two white image regions based on $d_i = 2p_i/255$. Therefore, we can design system-parameter values according to the analyzed results for the symmetric two-coupled system in Figs. 5 and 8.

Based on the information in the bifurcation diagrams, we set the two unfixed parameters to $k_r = 0.885$ and $\phi = 0.8$, which correspond to a parameter point in the left neighborhood of NS_1^1 in Fig. 5, so that no in-phase oscillatory responses appear from any initial values but a fixed point or an out-of-phase 36-periodic point does occur. Note that, any of the out-of-phase periodic points in Fig. 8(b) are available for dynamic image segmentation, and the period of the periodic point used in dynamic image segmentation corresponds to the period each segmented image appeared in output images that were exhibited in a time series.

The binarized image was input to our dynamic image segmentation system with 256×256 neurons and a global inhibitor. According to an out-of-phase 36-periodic point, our system output images in the time series shown in Fig. 15(c), i.e., images were dynamically segmented successfully. Note that the output images sequentially appeared from the top-left to the bottom-right, and they also began to appear in each line from the left; moreover, output images corresponding to state variables in the transient state were removed. We confirmed from the series of output images that the period where each image region appeared was 36.

4.2 Image with three image regions

We considered the 8-bit gray-level image with 128×128 pixels shown in Fig. 16(a). It has three image regions: a ring shape, a rectangle, and a triangle. To simplify the problem, the color in each image region was made into a monotone in which the pixel values were 255, 242, and 230 so that these values corresponded to $d_1 = 2$, $d_2 = 1.9$, and $d_3 = 1.8$ according to $d_i = 2p_i/255$. To dynamically segment the target image, we needed a neuronal network system consisting of 128×128 neurons and a global inhibitor. The DC-input value to the ith neuron, d_i, was set to 2.0 for neurons corresponding to pixels in the ring shape, 1.9 for those in the rectangle, and 1.8 for those in the triangle. The neuronal network system with 128×128 neurons could be regarded as an asymmetric three-coupled system. Therefore, according to the analyzed results in Fig. 14, e.g., we set the unfixed parameter values to $k_r = 0.875$ and $\phi = 0.8$ such that a three-phase 25-periodic point occurred in the asymmetric three-coupled system.

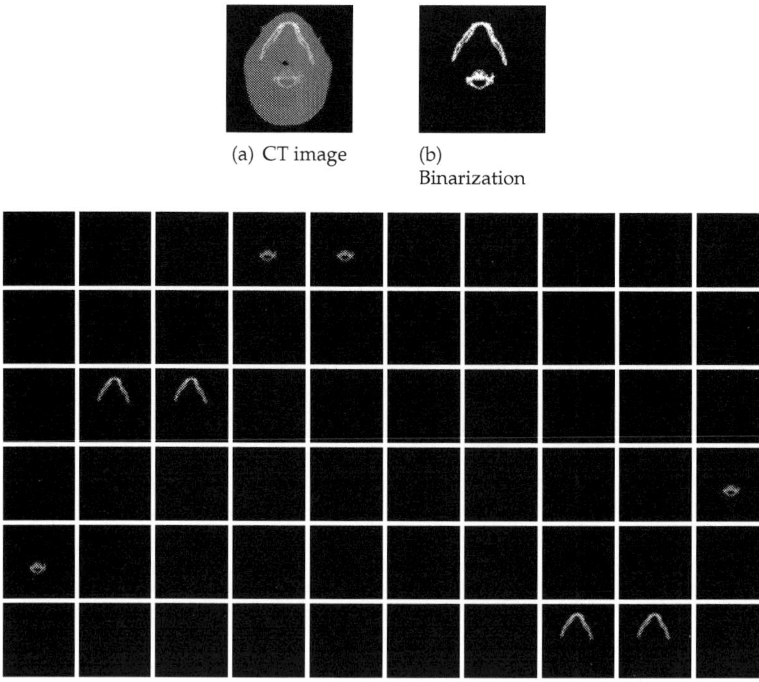

(a) CT image (b) Binarization

(c) Output images in time series

Fig. 15. Results of dynamic image segmentation based on out-of-phase oscillatory response

In trials for randomly given initial values, we achieved a successful result where three image regions appeared separately, as shown in Fig. 16(b). In addition, because the output images were generated according to a three-phase 25-periodic point observed in the asymmetric three-coupled system, we confirmed that the period where each image region appeared was 25. Note that we removed output images corresponding to state variables in the transient state. Our neuronal network system could work for a simple gray-level image with three image regions.

4.3 Image with many image regions

To segment an image with an arbitrary number of image regions using our dynamic image-segmentation system in one process, it is necessary for a multiphase periodic oscillatory response with as many phases as image regions to appear. As far as our investigations were concerned, however, it was difficult to generate a multiphase periodic point with many phases. Therefore, we proposed an algorithm that successively and partially segments an image.

Here, according to the previously mentioned results obtained from analysis, we considered a successive algorithm that partially segmented many image regions using two- and three-phase oscillatory responses. We let the gray-level image with five image regions in Fig. 17(a) be the target that should be segmented. To simplify the segmentation problem, we

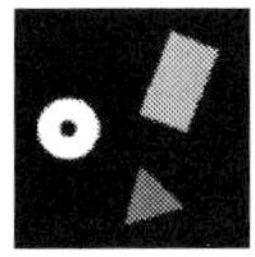

(a) Target image

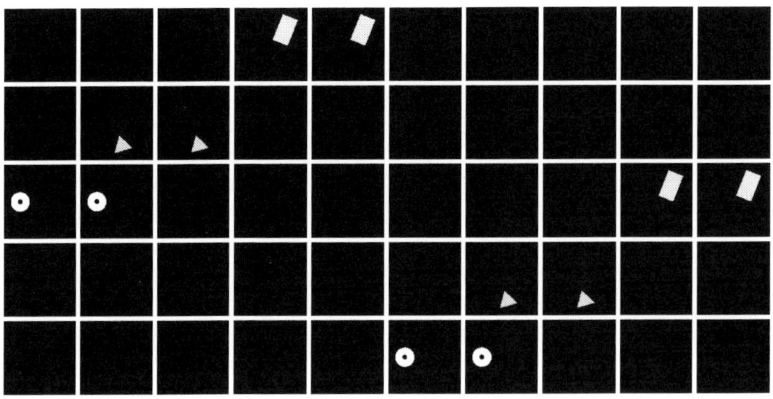

(b) Output images in time series

Fig. 16. Results of dynamic image segmentation based on three-phase oscillatory response

assumed that all pixels in an identical image region would have the same gray levels. Based on the analyzed results for two- and three-coupled systems, we set the system parameters to certain values such that no in-phase oscillatory responses occurred but a fixed point or a two- or three-phase oscillatory responses appeared.

We could obtain the three segmented images in Figs. 17(b)–(d) in the first step from the input image in Fig. 17(a) if a three-phase oscillatory response appeared. Note that the segmented images were extracted from output images in a time series by removing duplicate images and all black images.

Each segmented image in Figs. 17(b)–(d) became an input image for our system in the next step. We obtained the two images in Figs. 17(e) and 17(f) in this step from the input image in Fig. 17(b) using a two-phase oscillatory response; as well as this process, we also obtained the two images in Figs. 17(g) and 17(h) from the input image in Fig. 17(c) according to the two-phase response; whereas we obtained no output images from the input image in Fig. 17(d) because the system to segment the image corresponded to a single neuronal system, and a fixed point always appeared under the system-parameter values we assigned. Therefore, the segmentation of the image in Fig. 17(d) was terminated in this step.

The four images with only one image region in Figs. 17(e)–(h) are input images in the third step. As previously mentioned, we obtained no output images for an input image with only one image region. Therefore, our successive algorithm was terminated at this point in time. Thus, we could segment an image with an arbitrary number of image regions based on the successive algorithm.

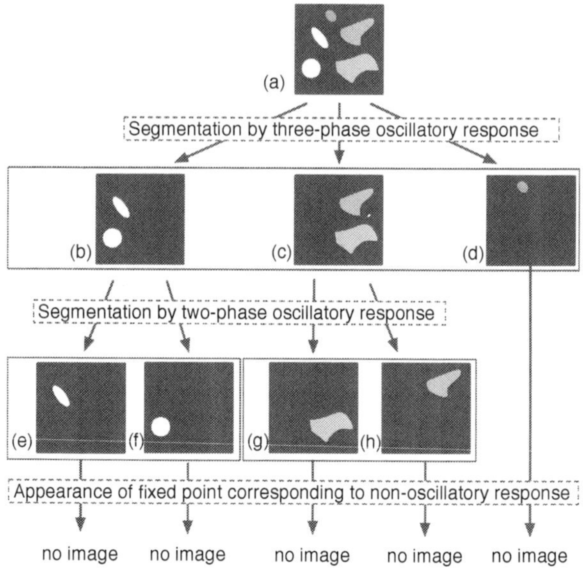

Fig. 17. Schematic diagram of successive algorithm using our dynamic image-segmentation system

5. Concluding remarks

We introduced a discrete-time neuron model that could generate similar oscillatory responses formed by periodic points to oscillations observed in a continuous-time relaxation oscillator model. The scheme of dynamic image segmentation was illustrated using our neuronal network system that consisted of our neurons arranged in a 2D grid and a global inhibitor. Note that we suggested that a neuronal network system where neurons are arranged in a 3D grid can be applied to segmenting a 3D image.

Images were dynamically segmented according to the responses of our system, and therefore, knowing about the bifurcations of the responses allowed us to directly set system-parameter values such that appropriate responses for dynamic image segmentation would appear. We derived reduced models that simplified our analysis of bifurcations observed in our neuronal network system and we found parameter regions where there was a non-oscillatory response or a periodic oscillatory response in the reduced models. According to the analyzed results, we set system parameters to appropriate values, and the designed system could work for two sample images with two or three image regions. Moreover, to segment an image with many image regions, we proposed a successive algorithm using our dynamic image-segmentation system.

We encountered three main problems that should be solved to enable the practical use of our dynamic image-segmentation system:

1. Development of a method that can form appropriate couplings between neurons for a textured image and a gray-level image containing gradation.

2. Development of a method that can give initial values to neurons and a global inhibitor so that an appropriate response will always appear.
3. Development of a method or system that can provide fast processing using our system to segment a large-scale image and a 3D image within practical time limits.

To solve the first problem, we proposed a dynamic image-segmentation system with a method of posterization (Zhao et al., 2003) used as preprocessing (Fujimoto et al., 2009a; 2010). However, their method of posterization involves high computational cost and a large memory, we are considering a neuronal network system with plastic couplings as weight adaptation (Chen et al., 2000). We proposed a solution to the second problem with a method that avoids the appearance of non-oscillatory responses (Fujimoto et al., 2011a). However, toward an ultimate solution, we are investigating parameter regions such that no inappropriate responses appear through bifurcation analysis. An implementation to execute our dynamic image-segmentation system on a graphics processing unit is in progress as a means of rapid processing.

6. Acknowledgments

This study was partially supported by the Ministry of Education, Culture, Sports, Science and Technology, Japan, Grant-in-Aid for Young Scientists (B), Nos. 20700209 and 22700234.

7. References

Ackerman, M. J. (1991). The visible human project, *J. Biocommun.* 18(2): 14.

Aihara, K. (1990). Chaotic neural networks, *in* H. Kawakami (ed.), *Bifurcation Phenomena in Nonlinear Systems and Theory of Dynamical System*, World Scientific, Singapore, pp. 143–161.

Aihara, K., Takabe, T. & Toyoda, M. (1990). Chaotic neural networks, *Phys. Lett. A* 144(6,7): 333–340.

Chen, K., Wang, D. L. & Liu, X. (2000). Weight adaptation and oscillatory correlation for image segmentation, *IEEE Trans. Neural Netw.* 11(5): 1106–1123.

Doi, K. (2007). Computer-aided diagnosis in medical imaging: Historical review, current status and future potential, *Comput. Med. Imaging Graph.* 31(4,5): 198–211.

FitzHugh, R. (1961). Impulses and physiological states in theoretical models of nerve membrane, *Biophys. J.* 1(6): 445–466.

Fujimoto, K., Musashi, M. & Yoshinaga, T. (2008). Discrete-time dynamic image segmentation system, *Electron. Lett.* 44(12): 727–729.

Fujimoto, K., Musashi, M. & Yoshinaga, T. (2009a). Dynamic image segmentation system for ultrasonic B-mode image based on its multi-scaled feature maps, *Proc. 2009 Int. Symposium on Nonlinear Theory and its Applications*, IEICE, Japan, Sapporo, pp. 495–498.

Fujimoto, K., Musashi, M. & Yoshinaga, T. (2009b). Reduced model of discrete-time dynamic image segmentation system and its bifurcation analysis, *Int. J. Imaging Syst. Technol.* 19(4): 283–289.

Fujimoto, K., Musashi, M. & Yoshinaga, T. (2010). Dynamic image segmentation system with multi-scaling system for gray scale image, *Proc. the Third Int. Conf. on Bio-inspired Systems and Signal Processing*, INSTICC Press, Valencia, pp. 159–162.

Fujimoto, K., Musashi, M. & Yoshinaga, T. (2011a). Discrete-time dynamic image segmentation based on oscillations by destabilizing a fixed point, *IEEJ Trans. Electr. Electron. Eng.* 6(5). (to appear).

Fujimoto, K., Musashi, M. & Yoshinaga, T. (2011b). FPGA implementation of discrete-time neuronal network for dynamic image segmentation, *IEEJ Trans. Electronics, Infomation and Systems* 131(3). (to appear).

Haschke, R. & Steil, J. J. (2005). Input space bifurcation manifolds of recurrent neural networks, *Neurocomputing* 64: 25–38.

Hodgkin, A. L. & Huxley, A. F. (1952). A quantitative description of membrane current and its application to conduction and excitation in nerve, *J. Physiol.* 117(4): 500–544.

Kapral, R. (1985). Pattern formation in two-dimensional arrays of coupled, discrete-time oscillators, *Phys. Rev. A* 31(6): 3868–3879.

Kawakami, H. (1984). Bifurcation of periodic responses in forced dynamic nonlinear circuits: computation of bifurcation values of the system parameters, *IEEE Trans. Circuits Syst.* 31(3): 248–260.

Musashi, M., Fujimoto, K. & Yoshinaga, T. (2009). Bifurcation phenomena of periodic points with high order of period observed in discrete-time two-coupled chaotic neurons, *J. Signal Processing* 13(4): 311–314.

Oppo, G.-L. & Kapral, R. (1986). Discrete models for the formation and evolution of spatial structure in dissipative systems, *Phys. Rev. A* 33(6): 4219–4231.

Pal, N. R. & Pal, S. K. (1993). A review on image segmentation techniques, *Pattern Recognit.* 26(9): 1277–1294.

Pikovsky, A., Rosenblum, M. & Kurths, J. (2003). *Synchronization: A universal concept in nonlinear sciences*, Cambridge University Press, Cambridge.

Rulkov, N. F. (2002). Modeling of spiking-bursting neural behavior using two-dimensional map, *Phys. Rev. E* 65(4): 041922.

Shareef, N., Wang, D. L. & Yagel, R. (1999). Segmentation of medical images using legion, *IEEE Trans. Med. Imaging* 18(1): 74–91.

Suri, J. S., Wilson, D. L. & Laxminarayan, S. (2005). *Handbook of Biomedical Image Analysis*, Kluwer Academic / Plenum Publishers, New York.

Terman, D. & Wang, D. L. (1995). Global competition and local cooperation in a network of neural oscillators, *Physica D* 81(1,2): 148–176.

Waller, I. & Kapral, R. (1984). Spatial and temporal structure in systems of coupled nonlinear oscillators, *Phys. Rev. A* 30(4): 2047–2055.

Wang, D. L. (2005). The time dimension for scene analysis, *IEEE Trans. Neural Netw.* 16(6): 1401–1426.

Wang, D. L. & Terman, D. (1995). Locally excitatory globally inhibitory oscillator networks, *IEEE Trans. Neural Netw.* 6(1): 283–286.

Wang, D. L. & Terman, D. (1997). Image segmentation based on oscillatory correlation, *Neural Comput.* 9(4): 805–836.

Zhao, L., Furukawa, R. A. & Carvalho, A. C. (2003). A network of coupled chaotic maps for adaptive multi-scale image segmentation, *Int. J. Neural Syst.* 13(2): 129–137.

24

Fuzzy Logic Based Interactive Multiple Model Fault Diagnosis for PEM Fuel Cell Systems

Yan Zhou[1,2], Dongli Wang[1], Jianxun Li[2],
Lingzhi Yi[1] and Huixian Huang[1]
[1]*College of Information Engineering, Xiangtan University, Xiangtan 411105,*
[2]*Department of Automation, Shanghai Jiao Tong University, Shanghai 200240,*
China

1. Introduction

The problem of fault detection and diagnosis (FDD) in dynamic systems has received considerable attention in last decades due to the growing complexity of modern engineering systems and ever increasing demand for fault tolerance, cost efficiency, and reliability (Willsky, 1976; Basseville, 1988). Existing FDD approaches can be roughly divided into two major categories including model-based and knowledge-based approaches (Venkatasubramanian et al., 2003a; Venkatasubramanian et al., 2003b). Model-based approaches make use of the quantitative analytical model of a physical system. Knowledge-based approaches do not need full analytical modeling and allow one to use qualitative models based on the available information and knowledge of a physical system. Whenever the mathematical models describing the system are available, analytical model-based methods are preferred because they are more amenable to performance analysis.

Generally, there are two steps in the procedure of model-based FDD. First, on the basis of the available observations and a mathematical model of the system, the state variable x and test statistics are required to be obtained. Then, based on the generated test statistics, it is required to decide on the potential occurrence of a fault. For linear and Gaussian systems, the Kalman filter (KF) is known to be optimal and employed for state estimation. The innovations from the KF are used as the test statistics, based on which hypothesis tests can be carried out for fault detection (Belcastro & Weinstein, 2002). In reality, however, the models representing the evolution of the system and the noise in observations typically exhibit complex nonlinearity and non-Gaussian distributions, thus precluding analytical solution. One popular strategy for estimating the state of such a system as a set of observations becomes available online is to use sequential Monte-Carlo (SMC) methods, also known as particle filters (PFs) (Doucet et al., 2001). These methods allow for a complete representation of the posterior probability distribution function (PDF) of the states by particles (Guo & Wang, 2004; Li & Kadirkamanathan, 2001).

The aforementioned FDD strategies are single-model-based. However, a single-model-based FDD approach is not adequate to handle complex failure scenarios. One way to treat this problem is the interacting multiple model (IMM) filter (Zhang & Li, 1998). For the IMM approach, the single-model-based filters running in parallel interact each other in a highly cost-effective fashion and thus lead to significantly improved performance. The initial estimate at the beginning of each cycle for each filter is a mixture of all most recent estimates from the single-model-based filters. It is this mixing that enables the IMM to effectively take into account the history of the modes (and, therefore, to yield a more fast and accurate estimate for the changed system states) without the exponentially growing requirements in computation and storage as required by the optimal estimator. The probability of each mode is calculated, which indicates clearly the mode in effect and the mode transition at each time. This is directly useful for the detection and diagnosis of system failures. In view of these, there is a strong hope that it will be an effective approach to FDD and thus has been extensively studied during the last decade, see (Zhang & Jiang, 2001; Yen &Ho, 2003; Tudoroiu & Khorasani, 2005; Rapoport & Oshman, 2007), and reference therein.

A shortcoming of the IMM approach lies in that the mode declaration of the IMM filter may not reflect a true faulty situation because the model probability of the nominal model tends to become dominant especially when 1) the states and control inputs converge to the steady state at a nominal trim flight, or 2) a fault tolerant controller works well after the first failure. Besides, the IMM filter with the constant transition probability matrix has a problem diagnosing the second failure. To cope with the abovementioned problems, a new FDD technique is proposed using IMM filter and fuzzy logic for sensor and actuator failures. In this study, fuzzy logic is used to determinate the transition probability among the models not only to enhance the FDD performance after the first failure but also to diagnose the second one as fast and accurately as possible.

On the other hand, fuel cell technology offers high efficiency and low emissions, and holds great promise for future power generation systems. Recent developments in polymer electrolyte membrane (PEM) technology have dramatically increased the power density of fuel cells, and made them viable for vehicular and portable power applications, as well as for stationary power plants. A typical fuel cell power system consists of numerous interconnected components, as presented comprehensively in the books (Blomen & Mugerwa, 1993), (Larminie & Dicks, 2000), (Pukrushpan et al. 2004b), and more concisely in the survey paper (Carette et al. 2001) and (Kakac et al. 2007). Faults in the fuel cell systems can occur in sensors, actuators, and the other components of the system and may lead to failure of the whole system (Hernandez et al. 2010). They can be modeled by the abrupt changes of components of the system. Typical faults of main concern in the fuel cell systems are sensor or actuator failures, which will degrade or even disable the control performance. In the last a few years, a variety of FDD approaches have been developed for various failures (Riascos et al., 2007; Escobet et al., 2009; Gebregergis et al. 2010). However, only simple failure scenarios, such as failure in sensor or actuator, are concerned therein. Moreover, upon FDD problem for the PEM fuel cell systems, there is little result so far by IMM approach.

In this chapter, a self-contained framework to utilize IMM approach for FDD of PEM fuel cell systems is presented. As mentioned above, the constant transition probability matrix based IMM approach has problem in diagnosing the second failure, even though a fault tolerant controller works well after the first failure. Therefore, in our study, fuzzy logic is introduced to update the transition probability among multiple models, which makes the proposed FDD approach smooth and the possibility of false fault detection reduced. In addition to the "total" (or "hard") actuator and/or sensor failures, "partial" (or "soft") faults are also considered. Compared with the existing results on FDD for fuel cell systems, more complex failure situations, including the total/partial senor and actuator failures, are considered. Simulation results considering both single and simultaneous sensor and/or actuator faults are given to illustrate the effectiveness of the proposed approach.

2. IMM for fault detection and diagnosis revisited

In this section, the details on generating the fault dynamics process using jump Markov linear hybrid dynamic models is first described. Then, the IMM estimation approach is developed for FDD.

2.1 Jump Markov hybrid systems

A stochastic hybrid system can be described as one with both continuous-valued base state and discrete-valued Structural/parametric uncertainty. A typical example of such a system is one subject to failures since fault modes are structurally different from each other and from the normal (healthy) mode. An effective and natural estimation approach for such a system is the one based on IMMs, in which a bank of filters running in parallel at every time with jumps in mode modeled as transition between the assumed models.

The IMM approach assumes that the state of the actual system at any time can be modeled accurately by the following jump Markov hybrid system:

$$x(k+1) = A(k,m(k+1))x(k) + B_u(k,m(k+1))u(k) + B_\omega(k,m(k+1))\omega(k,m(k+1)) \tag{1}$$

$$x(0) \in N(\hat{x}_0, P_0)$$

$$z(k) = C(k,m(k))x(k) + D_u(k,m(k))u(k) + D_\upsilon(k,m(k))\upsilon(k,m(k)) \tag{2}$$

with the system mode sequence assumed to be a first-order Markov chain with transition probabilities

$$P\{m_j(k+1) \mid m_i(k)\} = \pi_{ij}(k), \forall m_i, m_j \in S \tag{3}$$

and

$$\sum_j \pi_{ij}(k) = 1, 0 \le \pi_{ij}(k) \le 1, i = 1,...,s \tag{4}$$

where $x(k)$ is the state vector, $z(k)$ is the mode-dependent measurement vector, and $u(k)$ is the control input vector; $\omega(k)$ and $\upsilon(k)$ are mutually independent discrete-time process and measurement noises with mean $\bar{\omega}(k)$ and $\bar{\upsilon}(k)$, and covariances $Q(k)$ and $R(k)$; $P\{\cdot\}$ is the probability operator; $m(k)$ is the discrete-value modal state (i.e., the index of the normal or fault mode in our FDD scenario) at time k, which denotes the mode in effect during the sampling period ending at t_k; π_{ij} is the transition probability from mode m_i to mode m_j; the event that m_j is in effect at time k is denoted as $m_j(k) := \{m(k) = m_j\}$. The mode set $S = \{m_1, m_2, ..., m_s\}$ is the set of all possible system modes.

The nonlinear system (1)-(2), known as a "jump linear system", can be used to model situations where the system behavior pattern undergoes sudden changes, such as system failures in this chapter and target maneuvering in (Li & Bar-Shalom, 1993). The FDD

problem in terms of the hybrid system may be stated as that of determining the current model state. That is, determining whether the normal or a faulty mode is in effect based on analyzing the sequence of noisy measurements.
How to design the set of models to represent the possible system modes is a key issue in the application of the IMM approach, which is problem dependent. As pointed in (Li, 1996), this design should be done such that the models (approximately) represent or cover all possible system modes at any time. This is the model set design problem, which will be discussed in the next subsection.

2.2 Model set design for IMM based FDD

In the IMM method, assume that a set of **N** models has been set up to approximate the hybrid system (1)-(2) by the following **N** pairs of equations:

$$x(k+1) = A_j(k)x(k) + B_{uj}(k)u(k) + B_{\omega j}(k)\omega(k) \tag{5}$$

$$z(k) = C_j(k)x(k) + D_{uj}(k)u(k) + D_{\upsilon j}(k)\upsilon(k) \tag{6}$$

where $N \le s$ and subscript j denotes quantities pertaining to model $m_j \in \mathcal{M}$ ($\mathcal{M}$ is the set of all designed system models to represent the possible system modes in S. System matrices A_j, B_{uj}, $B_{\omega j}$, C_j, D_{uj}, and $D_{\upsilon j}$ may be of different structures for different j.
The model set design (i.e., the design of fault type, magnitude, and duration) is critical for IMM based FDD. Design of a good set of models requires a priori knowledge of the possible faults of the system. As pointed out in (Li & Bar-Shalom, 1996; Li, 2000), caution must be exercised in designing a model set. For example, there should be enough separation between models so that they are "identifiable" by the IMM estimator. This separation should exhibit itself well in the measurement residuals, especially between the filters based on the matched models and those on the mismatched ones. Otherwise, the IMM fault estimator will not be very selective in terms of correct FDD because it is the measurement residuals that have dominant effects on the model probability computation which in turn affect the correctness of FDD and the accuracy of overall state estimates. On the other hand, if the separation is too large, numerical problems may occur due to ill conditions in the set of model likelihood functions. A total actuator failures may be modeled by annihilating the appropriate column(s) of the control input matrix B_u and D_u:

$$x(k+1) = A(k)x(k) + [B_u(k) + M_{Bj}]u(k) + B_\omega(k)\omega(k) \tag{7}$$

$$z(k) = C(k)x(k) + [D_u(k) + M_{dj}]u(k) + D_\upsilon(k)\upsilon(k) \tag{8}$$

That is, choose the matrix M_{Bj} with all zero elements except that the jth column is taken to be the negative of the jth column of B_u.
Alternatively, the jth actuator failure may be modeled by an additional process noise term $\varepsilon_j(k)$:

$$x(k+1) = A(k)x(k) + B_u(k)u(k) + B_\omega(k)\omega(k) + \varepsilon_j(k) \tag{9}$$

$$z(k) = C(k)x(k) + D_u(k)u(k) + D_\upsilon(k)\upsilon(k) + \varepsilon_j(k) \tag{10}$$

For total sensor failures, a similar idea can be followed. The failures can be modeled by annihilating the appropriate row(s) of the measurement matrix C described as

$$z(k) = [C(k) + L_j]x(k) + D_u(k)u(k) + D_\upsilon(k)\upsilon(k) \tag{11}$$

or by an additional sensor noise term $e_j(k)$

$$z(k) = C(k)x(k) + D_u(k)u(k) + D_\upsilon(k)\upsilon(k) + e_j(k) \tag{12}$$

Partial actuator (or sensor) failures are modeled by multiplying the appropriate column (or row) of B_u (or C) by a (scaling) factor of effectiveness. They can also be modeled by increasing the process noise covariance matrix Q or measurement noise covariance matrix R. Here we consider more complex failure situations, including total actuator and/or sensor failures, partial actuator and/or sensor failures, and simultaneous partial actuator and sensor failures. These situations require that the FDD algorithm be more responsive and robust. It is difficult for single-model-based approach to handle such complex failure scenarios.

2.3 Procedures of IMM approach to FDD

The following procedures should be performed in the application of the IMM estimation technique for fault detection and diagnosis: (i) filter reinitialization; (ii) model-conditional filtering; (iii) model probability updating; (iv) fault detection and diagnosis; (v) estimate fusion.

The detailed steps for the IMM algorithm are described next (Zhang & Li, 1998; Mihaylova & Semerdjiev, 1999; Johnstone & Krishnamurthy, 2001).

Step 1. Interaction and mixing of the estimates: filter reinitialization (interacting the estimates) obtained by mixing the estimates of all the filters from the previous time (this is accomplished under the assumption that a particular mode is in effect at the present time).

1. Compute the predicted model probability from instant k to k+1:

$$\mu_j(k+1 \mid k) = \sum_{i=1}^{N} \pi_{ij}\mu_i(k) \tag{13}$$

2. Compute the mixing probability:

$$\mu_{i|j}(k) = \pi_{ij}\mu_i(k) / \mu_j(k+1 \mid k) \tag{14}$$

3. Compute the mixing estimates and covariance:

$$\hat{x}_j^0(k \mid k) = \sum_{i=1}^{N} \hat{x}_i(k \mid k)\mu_{i|j}(k) \tag{15}$$

$$P_j^0(k \mid k) = \sum_{i=1}^{N} \{P_i(k \mid k) + [\hat{x}_j^0(k \mid k) - \hat{x}_i(k \mid k)][\hat{x}_j^0(k \mid k) - \hat{x}_i(k \mid k)]^T\}\mu_{i|j}(k) \tag{16}$$

where the superscript 0 denotes the initial value for the next step.

Step 2. Model-conditional filtering

The filtering techniques such as (extended) Kalman filter, unscented Kalman filter, and particle filter can be applied for model-conditioning filtering. In this study, a linear Kalman filter is used as the individual filter of the IMM approach.

Step 2.1: Prediction step

1. Compute the predicted state and covariance from instant k to $k+1$:

$$\hat{x}_j(k+1 \mid k) = A_j(k)\hat{x}_j^0(k \mid k) + B_{uj}(k)u(k) + B_{\omega j}(k)\bar{\omega}(k) \tag{17}$$

$$P_j(k+1 \mid k) = A_j(k)P_j^0(k \mid k)A_j^T(k) + B_{\omega j}(k)Q_j(k)B_{\omega j}^T(k) \tag{18}$$

2. Compute the measurement residual and covariance:

$$r_j = z(k+1) - C_j(k+1)\hat{x}_j(k+1 \mid k) - D_{uj}(k)u(k) - D_{\upsilon j}(k)\bar{\upsilon}(k) \tag{19}$$

$$S_j = C_j(k+1)P_j(k+1 \mid k)C_j^T(k+1) + D_{\upsilon j}(k)R(k)D_{\upsilon j}^T(k) \tag{20}$$

3. Compute the filter gain:

$$K_j = P_j(k+1 \mid k)C_j^T(k+1)S_j^{-1} \tag{21}$$

Step 2.2: Correction step

Update the estimated state and covariance matrix:

$$\hat{x}_j(k+1 \mid k+1) = \hat{x}_j(k+1 \mid k) + K_j r_j \tag{22}$$

$$P_j(k+1 \mid k+1) = P_j(k+1 \mid k) - K_j S_j K_j^T \tag{23}$$

Step 3. Updating the model probability

The model probability is an important parameter for the system fault detection and diagnosis. For this, a likelihood function should be defined in advance, and then the model probability be updated based on the likelihood function.

1. Compute the likelihood function:

$$L_j(k+1) = \frac{1}{\sqrt{2\pi |S_j|}} \exp\left[-\frac{1}{2} r_j^T S_j^{-1} r_j\right] \tag{24}$$

2. Update the model probability:

$$\mu_j(k+1) = \frac{\mu_j(k+1 \mid k)L_j(k+1)}{\sum_{j=1}^{N} \mu_j(k+1 \mid k)L_j(k+1)} \tag{25}$$

Step 4. Fault detection and diagnosis

1. Define the model probability vector $\mu(k+1) = [\mu_1(k+1), \mu_2(k+1), \ldots, \mu_N(k+1)]$. The maximum value of the model probability vector for FDD can be obtained as

$$\mu_{\text{FDDmax}} = \max \vec{\mu}(k+1) \tag{26}$$

The index of the maximum value of the model probability vector component can be determined as

$$j = \text{find}(\mu_{\text{FDDmax}} == \vec{\mu}(k+1)) \tag{27}$$

2. Fault decision–FDD logic

The mode probabilities provide an indication of mode in effect at the current sampling period. Hence, it is natural to be used as an indicator of a failure. According to the information provided by the model probability, both fault detection and diagnosis can be achieved. The fault decision can be determined by

$$\mu_{\text{FDDmax}} \begin{cases} \geq \mu_T \Rightarrow H_j : \text{Delare fault corresponding to } j\text{th mode} \\ < \mu_T \Rightarrow H_1 : \text{No fault} \end{cases} \tag{28}$$

Or alternatively,

$$\frac{\mu_{\text{FDDmax}}}{\max\limits_{i \neq j} \vec{\mu}(k+1)} \begin{cases} \geq \mu_T' \Rightarrow H_j : \text{Delare fault corresponding to } j\text{th mode} \\ < \mu_T' \Rightarrow H_1 : \text{No fault} \end{cases} \tag{29}$$

Step 5. Estimate fusion and combination that yields the overall state estimate as the probabilistically weighted sum of the updated state estimates of all the filters. The probability of a mode in effect plays a key role in determining the weights associated with the fusion of state estimates and covariances. The estimates and covariance matrices can be obtained as:

$$\hat{x}(k+1 \mid k+1) = \sum_{j=1}^{N} \hat{x}_j(k+1 \mid k+1)\mu_j(k+1) \tag{30}$$

$$\begin{aligned} &P(k+1 \mid k+1) = \\ &= \sum_{j=1}^{N} [P_j(k \mid k) + (\hat{x}(k+1 \mid k+1) - \hat{x}_j(k+1 \mid k+1))(\hat{x}(k+1 \mid k+1) - \hat{x}_j(k+1 \mid k+1))^T]\mu_j(k+1) \end{aligned} \tag{31}$$

It will be seen from Section 4 that the transition probability plays an important role in the IMM approach to FDD. In this study, the transition probability is adapted online through the Takagi-Sugeno fuzzy logic (Takagi & Sugeno, 1985). The overall framework of the proposed fuzzy logic based IMM FDD algorithm is illustrated in Fig. 1.

It is worth noting that decision rule (28) or (29) provides not only fault detection but also the information of the type (sensor or actuator), location (which sensor or actuator), size (total failure or partial fault with the fault magnitude) and fault occurrence time, that is, simultaneous detection and diagnosis. For partial faults, the magnitude (size) can be determined by the probabilistically weighted sum of the fault magnitudes of the corresponding partial fault models. Another advantage of the IMM approach is that FDD is integrated with state estimation. The overall estimate provides the best state estimation of the system subject to failures. Furthermore, unlike other observer-based or Kalman filter based approaches, there is no extra computation for the fault decision because the mode probabilities are necessary in the IMM algorithm. Furthermore, the overall estimate is generated by the probabilistically weighted sum of estimates from the single-model-based filters. Therefore, it is better and more robust than any single-model-based estimate. This state estimate does not depend upon the correctness of fault detection and in fact, the accurate state estimation can facilitate the correct FDD. The detection threshold μ_T is universal in the sense that it does not depend much on the particular problem at hand and a robust threshold can be determined easily. In other words, the FDD performance of the IMM approach varies little in most cases with respect to the choice of this threshold (Zhang & Li, 1998). On the other hand, the residual-based fault detection logic relies heavily on the threshold used, which is problem-relevant. Quite different detection thresholds have to be used for FDD problems of different systems and design of such a threshold is not trivial. Moreover, without comparing with the threshold, the value of the measurement residual itself does not provide directly meaningful detection and indication of the fault situations.

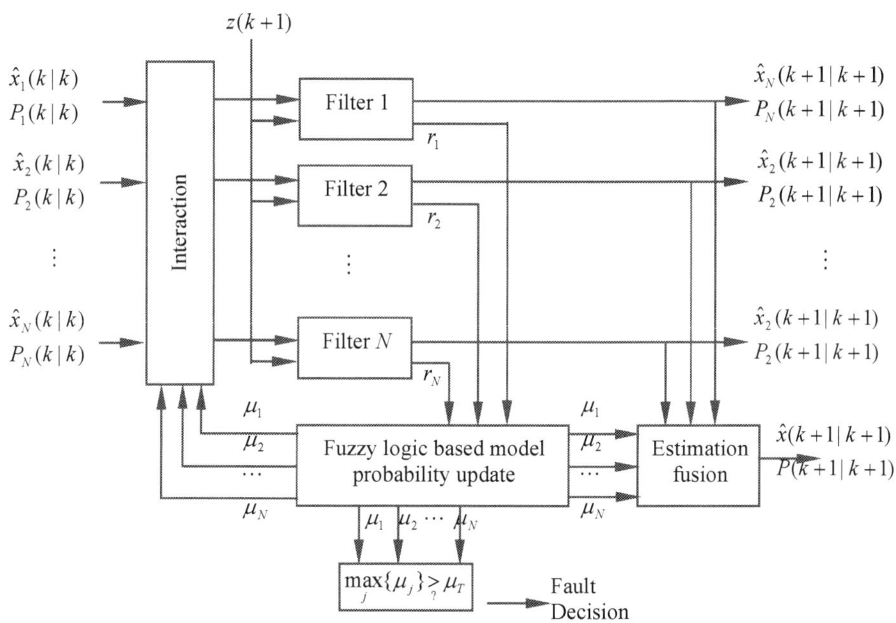

Fig. 1. Block diagram of the proposed fuzzy logic based IMM FDD approach

3. Update of transition probability by fuzzy logic

As aforementioned, the transition probability plays an important role in interacting and mixing the information of each individual filter. However, an assumption that the transition probability is constant over the total period of FDD can lead to some problems. Even if the fault tolerant control treats the first failure successfully, the unchanged transition probability can mislead the FDD to intermittently declare a false failure alarm. This is because the fact that the normal mode before the first failure occurrence is not the normal mode any longer. The declared fault mode should be changed to a new normal mode after the first failure. On that account, the fuzzy-tuning algorithm of the transition probability is proposed in this study.

The transition probability from any particular failure mode to the normal mode is generally set larger than others in order to prevent a false fault diagnosis. However, it may have a bad influence on performing correct fault diagnosis because the model probability of the healthy mode tends to increase again as the current failed system converges to the steady state by the fault tolerant control law even after a fault occurs. This problem can be overcome by adjusting the transition probability after the fault occurrence. For example, if the model probability of a certain failure mode remains larger than that of any other mode for an assigned time, the transition probability related to the corresponding failure mode should be increased. On the other hand, the transition probability related to the previous mode should be decreased to reflect the fact that the failed mode selected by the fault decision algorithm becomes currently dominant. In this work, the fuzzy-tuning algorithm is adopted to adjust the transition probabilities effectively.

Now introduce a determination variable C_i which decides whether or not the transition probabilities should be adjusted. First, the initial value of each mode's determination variable is set to zero. The increment of the determination variable can be obtained through the fuzzy logic with inputs composed of the model probabilities at every step. If the determination variable C_i of a certain mode exceeds a predefined threshold value C_T, then the transition probabilities are adjusted, and the determination value of each mode is initialized. The overall process is illustrated in Fig. 2.

3.1 Fuzzy input

A fuzzy input for adjusting transition probabilities includes the model probabilities from the IMM filter. At each sampling time, the model probabilities of every individual filter are transmitted to the fuzzy system. In this work, the membership function is designed as in Fig. 3 for the fuzzy input variables "small," "medium," and "big" representing the relative size of the model probability.

3.2 Fuzzy rule

The T-S fuzzy model is used as the inference logic in this work. The T-S fuzzy rule can be represented as

$$\text{If } \chi \text{ is } A \text{ and } \xi \text{ is } B \text{ then } Z = f(\chi, \xi) \tag{32}$$

where A and B are fuzzy sets, and $Z = f(\chi, \xi)$ is a non-fuzzy function. The fuzzy rule of adjusting transition probabilities is defined using the T-S model as follows

$$\begin{aligned} &\text{If } \mu_j \text{ is small, then } \Delta C_j^s = 0 \\ &\text{If } \mu_j \text{ is medium, then } \Delta C_j^m = 0.5 \\ &\text{If } \mu_j \text{ is big, then } \Delta C_j^b = 1 \end{aligned} \tag{33}$$

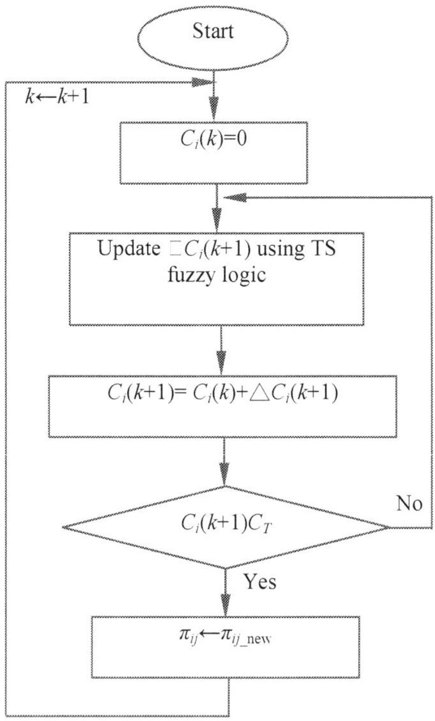

Fig. 2. Flowchart of T-S fuzzy logic for adaptive model probability update

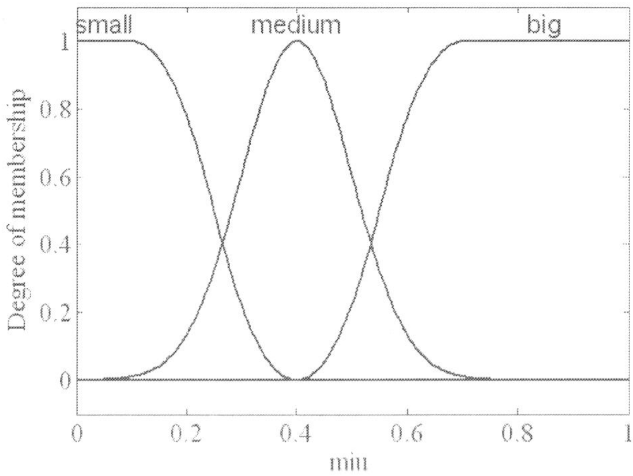

Fig. 3. Fuzzy membership function

3.3 Fuzzy output

The output of the fuzzy system using the T-S model can be obtained by the weighted average using a membership degree in a particular fuzzy set as follows:

$$\Delta C_j(k) = \frac{w_j^s \Delta C_j^s + w_j^m \Delta C_j^m + w_j^b \Delta C_j^b}{w_j^s + w_j^m + w_j^b} \tag{34}$$

where w_j^s, w_j^m, and w_j^b is the membership degree in the jth mode for group small, medium, and big, respectively. During the monitoring process, the determination variable of the jth mode is accumulated as

$$\Delta C_j(k+1) = C_j(k) + \Delta C_j(k+1) \tag{35}$$

The designed fuzzy output surface of the T-S fuzzy interference system is shown in Fig. 4.

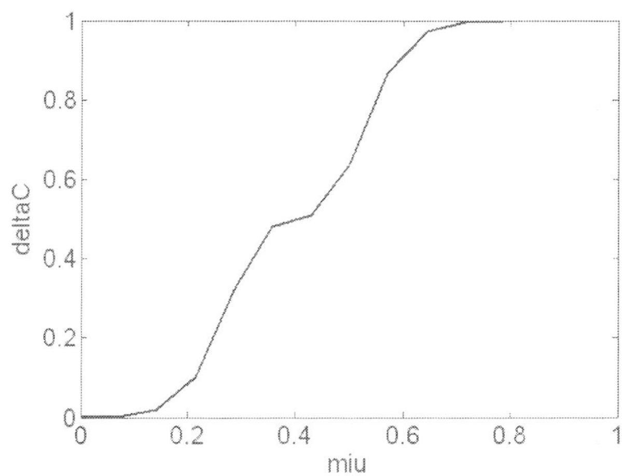

Fig. 4. Output surface of the fuzzy interference system

Once the determination variable of a certain fault mode exceeds the threshold value C_T, then all the elements of the transition probability matrix from the other modes to the corresponding fault mode are increased.

3.4 Transition probability design

The diagonal elements of the transition probability matrix can be designed as follows (Zhang & Li, 1998).

$$\pi_{jj} = \max\left\{ l_j, 1 - \frac{T}{\tau_j} \right\} \tag{36}$$

where T, τ_j, and l_j are the sampling time, the expected sojourn time, and the predefined threshold of the transition probability, respectively. For example, the "normal-to-normal" transition probability, π_{11}, can be obtained by $\pi_{11} = 1 - T / \tau_1$ (here τ_1 denotes the mean time between failures) since T is much smaller than τ_1 in practice. The transition probability from the normal mode to a fault mode sums up to $1 - \pi_{11}$. To which particular fault mode it jumps depends on the relative likelihood of the occurrence of the fault mode. While in reality mean sojourn time of total failures is the down time of the system, which is usually large and problem-dependent, to incorporate various fault modes into one sequence for a convenient comparison of different FDD approaches, the sojourn time of the total failures is assumed to be the same as that of the partial faults in this work.

"Fault-to-fault" transitions are normally disallowed except in the case where there is sufficient prior knowledge to believe that partial faults can occur one after another. Hence, by using (36), the elements of the transition probability related to the current model can be defined by

$$p_n = 1 - \frac{T}{\tau_n}, \quad \tilde{p}_n = \frac{1 - p_n}{N - 1} \tag{37}$$

$$p_f = 1 - \frac{T}{\tau_f}, \quad \tilde{p}_f = 1 - p_f \tag{38}$$

where p_n and p_f are the diagonal elements of the normal and failure mode, respectively, and $\tilde{p}_n$ and $\tilde{p}_f$ are off-diagonal elements to satisfy the constraint that all the row sum of the transition probability matrix should be equal to one. In addition, N is the total number of the assumed models, and τ_n and τ_f are the expected sojourn times of the normal and failure mode, respectively.

After a failure declaration by the fuzzy decision logic, the transition probability from the other modes to the corresponding failure model (say the mth mode) should be increased, whereas the transition probabilities related to the nonfailed model should be relatively decreased. For this purpose, the transition probability matrix of each mode is set as follows.

$$\pi_{ij} = \begin{cases} p_n, & i = j = m \\ p_f, & i = j \neq m \\ \tilde{p}_n, & i = j \text{ and } j \neq m \\ p_f, & i \neq m \text{ and } j = m \\ 0, & \text{otherwise} \end{cases} \tag{39}$$

4. PEM fuel cell description and modeling

The fuel cell system studied in this work is shown in Fig. 5. It is assumed that the stack temperature is constant. This assumption is justified because the stack temperature changes relatively slowly, compared with the ~100 ms transient dynamics included in the model to be developed. Additionally, it is also assumed that the temperature and humidity of the inlet reactant flows are perfectly controlled, e.g., by well designed humidity and cooling subsystems. It is further assume that the cathode and anode volumes of the multiple fuel cells are lumped as a single stack cathode and anode volumes. The anode supply and return manifold volumes are small, which allows us to lump these volumes to one "anode" volume. We denote all the variables associated with the lumped anode volume with a subscript (an). The cathode supply manifold (sm) lumps all the volumes associated with pipes and connection between the compressor and the stack cathode (ca) flow field.The cathode return manifold (rm) represents the lumped volume of pipes downstream of the stack cathode. In this study, an expander is not included; however, we will consider this part in future models for FDD. It is assumed that the properties of the flow exiting a volume are the same as those of the gas inside the volume. Subscripts (cp) and (cm) denote variables associated with the compressor and compressor motor, respectively.

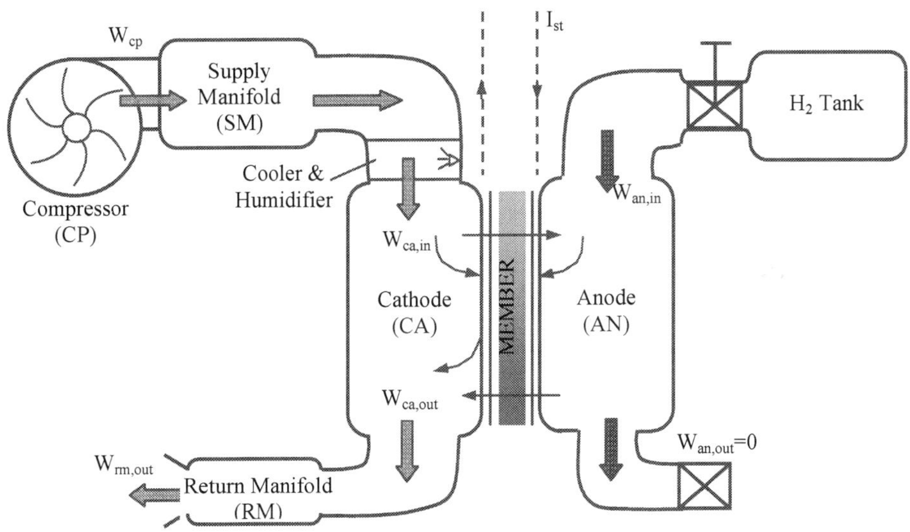

Fig. 5. Simplified fuel cell reactant supply system

The rotational dynamics and a flow map are used to model the compressor. The law of conservation of mass is used to track the gas species in each volume. The principle of mass conservation is applied to calculate the properties of the combined gas in the supply and return manifolds. The law of conservation of energy is applied to the air in the supply manifold to account for the effect of temperature variations. Under the assumptions of a perfect humidifier and air cooler, and the use of proportional control of the hydrogen valve, the only inputs to the model are the stack current, I_{st}, and the compressor motor voltage, v_{cm}. The parameters used in the model are given in Table 1 (Pukrushpan et al., 2004a). The model is developed primarily based on physics. However, several phenomena are described in empirical equations. The models for the fuel cell stack, compressor, manifolds, air cooler and humidifier are presented in state-space model as specified by (40)-(41) with the relating matrices given in Table 1.

$$\dot{x} = A_c x + B_{uc} u + b_{\omega c} \omega \tag{40}$$

$$z = C_c x + D_{uc} u + D_{\omega c} \omega \tag{41}$$

where $u=[v_{cm},I_{st}]^T$, and $z=[W_{cp},p_{sm},v_{st}]^T$, the stochastic noise or disturbance ω models the uncertainties caused by the linearization and measurement noises, etc. Note that the nominal operating point is chosen to be P_{net}=40 kW and λ_{O2} =2, which correspond to nominal inputs of I_{st}=191 Amp and v_{cm}=164 Volt. The state vector $x=[m_{O_2},m_{H_2},m_{N_2},\omega_{cp},p_{sm},m_{sm},m_{O_2},m_{w,an},p_{rm}]^T$. In more details, the fuel cell system model developed above contains eight states. The compressor has one state: rotor speed. The supply manifold has two states: air mass and air pressure. The return manifold has one state: air pressure. The stack has four states: O_2, and N_2 masses in the cathode, and H_2 and vapor masses in the anode. These states then determine the voltage output of the stack.

Symbol	Variable	Value
$r_{m,dry}$	Membrane dry density	0.002 kg/cm^3
$M_{m,dry}$	Membrane dry equivalent weight	1.1 kg/mol
t_m	Membrane thickness	0.01275 cm
n	Number of cells in stack	381
A_{fc}	Fuel cell active area	280 cm^2
d_c	Compressor diameter	0.2286 m
J_{cp}	Compressor and motor inertia	531025 kg.m^2
V_{an}	Anode volume	0.005 m^3
V_{ca}	Cathode volume	0.01 m^3
V_{sm}	Supply manifold volume	0.02 m^3
V_{rm}	Return manifold volume	0.005 m^3
$C_{D,rm}$	Return manifold throttle discharge coefficient	0.0124
$A_{T,rm}$	Return manifold throttle area	0.002 m^2
$k_{sm,out}$	Supply manifold outlet orifice constant	0.362931025 kg/(s.Pa)
$k_{ca,out}$	Cathode outlet orifice constant	0.217731025 kg(s.Pa)
k_v	Motor electric constant	0.0153 V/(rad/s)
k_t	Motor torque constant	0.0153 N-m/A
R_{cm}	Compressor Motor circuit resistance	0.816 V
h_{cm}	Compressor Motor efficiency	98%

Table 1. Model parameters for vehicle-size fuel cell system

Three measurements are investigated: compressor air flow rate, $z_1=W_{cp}$, supply manifold pressure, $z_2=p_{sm}$, and fuel cell stack voltage, $z_3=V_{st}$. These signals are usually available because they are easy to measure and are useful for other purposes. For example, the compressor flow rate is typically measured for the internal feedback of the compressor. The stack voltage is monitored for diagnostics and fault detection purposes. Besides, the units of states and outputs are selected so that all variables have comparable magnitudes, and are as follows: mass in grams, pressure in bar, rotational speed in kRPM, mass flow rate in g/sec, power in kW, voltage in V, and current in A.

In this study, the simultaneous actuator and sensor faults are considered. The fuel cell systems of interest considered here have two actuators and three sensors. Therefore, there are potentially only six modes, with the first mode being designated as the normal mode as (40)-(41) and the other five modes designated as the faulty modes associated with each of the faulty actuators or sensors.

$$A_c = \begin{bmatrix} -6.30908 & 0 & -10.9544 & 0 & 83.74458 & 0 & 0 & 24.05866 \\ 0 & -161.083 & 0 & 0 & 51.52923 & 0 & -18.0261 & 0 \\ -18.7858 & 0 & -46.3136 & 0 & 275.6592 & 0 & 0 & 158.3741 \\ 0 & 0 & 0 & -17.3506 & 193.9373 & 0 & 0 & 0 \\ 1.299576 & 0 & 2.969317 & 0.3977 & -38.7024 & 0.105748 & 0 & 0 \\ 16.64244 & 0 & 38.02522 & 5.066579 & -479.384 & 0 & 0 & 0 \\ 0 & -450.386 & 0 & 0 & 142.2084 & 0 & -80.9472 & 0 \\ 2.02257 & 0 & 4.621237 & 0 & 0 & 0 & 0 & -51.2108 \end{bmatrix}$$

$$C_c = \begin{bmatrix} 0 & 0 & 0 & 5.066579 & -116.446 & 0 & 0 & 0 \\ 0 & 0 & 0 & 0 & 1 & 0 & 0 & 0 \\ 12.96989 & 10.32532 & -0.56926 & 0 & 0 & 0 & 0 & 0 \end{bmatrix}$$

$$B_{uc} = \begin{bmatrix} 0 & 0 & 0 & 3.94668 & 0 & 0 & 0 & 0 \\ -0.03159 & -0.00398 & 0 & 0 & 0 & 0 & -0.05242 & 0 \end{bmatrix}^T, D_{uc} = \begin{bmatrix} 0 & 0 \\ 0 & 0 \\ 0 & -0.29656 \end{bmatrix}$$

Table 2. Parameters for the linear fuel cell model in (40)-(41)

$$A_1 = \begin{bmatrix} 0.1779 & 0 & -0.0333 & 0.0047 & -0.1284 & 0.0245 & 0 & -0.02 \\ 0.0012 & 0 & 0.0004 & 0.0002 & -0.0169 & 0.0019 & 0 & 0.002 \\ -0.0401 & 0 & 0.0263 & 0.0038 & -0.3963 & 0.0415 & 0 & 0.0663 \\ 0.0444 & 0 & 0.0177 & 0.0079 & -0.5741 & 0.0676 & 0 & 0.0806 \\ 0.0036 & 0 & 0.0012 & 0.0006 & -0.0517 & 0.0057 & 0 & 0.0059 \\ 0.0408 & 0 & 0.01 & 0.0053 & -3.9786 & 0.3265 & 0 & 0.0543 \\ -0.0004 & 0 & -0.0003 & -0.0001 & 0.0031 & -0.0005 & 0 & -0.0011 \\ 0.0035 & 0 & 0.0011 & 0.0006 & -0.0408 & 0.0048 & 0 & 0.0055 \end{bmatrix}$$

$$B_{u1} = \begin{bmatrix} 0.0451 & -0.0145 \\ 0.004 & 0 \\ 0.0878 & 0.0034 \\ 0.3634 & -0.0028 \\ 0.0123 & -0.0003 \\ 0.1474 & -0.0032 \\ -0.0007 & 0.0013 \\ 0.0097 & -0.0003 \end{bmatrix}$$

$$C_1 = \begin{bmatrix} 0 & 0 & 0 & 5.0666 & -116.446 & 0 & 0 & 0 \\ 0 & 0 & 0 & 0 & 1 & 0 & 0 & 0 \\ 12.9699 & 10.3253 & -0.5693 & 0 & 0 & 0 & 0 & 0 \end{bmatrix}$$

$$D_{u1} = \begin{bmatrix} 0 & 0 \\ 0 & 0 \\ 0 & -0.2966 \end{bmatrix}$$

Table 3. Parameters for the discretized model

Actuator (or control surface) failures were modeled by multiplying the respective column of B_{u1} and D_{u1}, by a factor between zero and one, where zero corresponds to a total (or complete) actuator failure or missing control surface and one to an unimpaired (normal) actuator/control surface. Likewise for sensor failures, where the role of B_{u1} and D_{u1} is

replaced with C_1. It was assumed that the damage does not affect the fuel cell system dynamic matrix A_1, implying that the dynamics of the system are not changed.
Let sampling period $T = 1$ s. Discretization of (40)-(41) yields the matrices for normal mode $A_1 = e^{A_c T}$, $B_{u1} = (\int_0^T e^{A_c \tau} d\tau) B_c$, $B_{\omega 1} = (\int_0^T e^{A_c \tau} d\tau) B_{\omega c}$, $C_1 = C_c$, $D_{u1'} = D_{u1}$, $D_{\upsilon 1'} = D_{\upsilon 1}$, which are specified in Table 3.
The fault modes in this work are more general and complex than those considered before, including total single sensor or actuator failures, partial single sensor or actuator failures, total and partial single sensor and/or actuator failures, and simultaneous sensor and actuator failures.

5. Results and discussion

Scenario 1: Single total/partial actuator faulty mode

First, in order to compare the performance between the conventional IMM and the proposed fuzzy logic based IMM approach, consider the simplest situation in which only a single total (or partial) sensor or actuator is running failure. Specifically, only partial failure for the actuator according to the second control input, i.e. stack current, I_{st}, is considered. The failure occurs after the 50th sampling period with failure amplitude of 50%. Two models consisting the normal mode and second actuator failure with amplitude of 50% are used for the IMM filter. The fault decision criterion in (29) is used with the threshold $\mu_T' = 2.5$. The transition matrix for the conventional IMM and the initial for the proposed approach are set as follows

$$\Pi = \begin{bmatrix} 0.99 & 0.01 \\ 0.1 & 0.9 \end{bmatrix}$$

The results of the FDD based on our proposed approach are compared with that of the conventional IMM filter. Fig. 6 (a) and (b) represent the model probabilities of the 2 models and the mode index according to (29) for the conventional IMM, respectively. From Fig. 6, it is obvious that the model probability related to the failure model does not keep a dominant value for the conventional IMM approach. On that account, momentary false failure mode is declared after the failure although the approach works well before the first failure occurs,

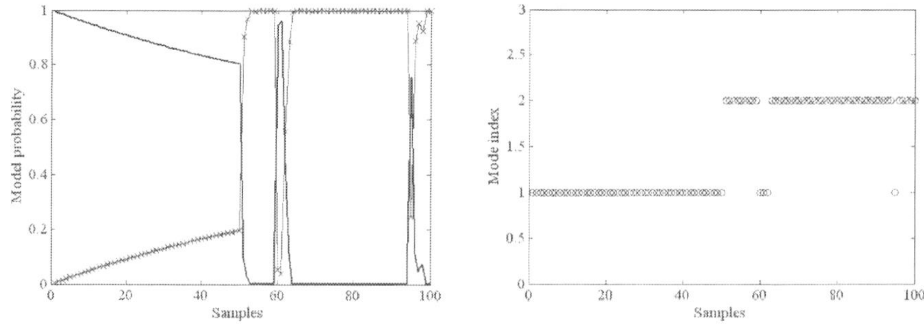

Fig. 6. The model probabilities and the mode index for the conventional IMM approach

just as shown in Fig. 6 (b). The performance of the proposed fuzzy logic based IMM approach is stable to hold a higher model probability than that of the conventional filter (cf. Fig. 7 (a)-(b)). This concludes that the improved IMM approach has better performance and, more importantly, reliability that the conventional IMM filter.

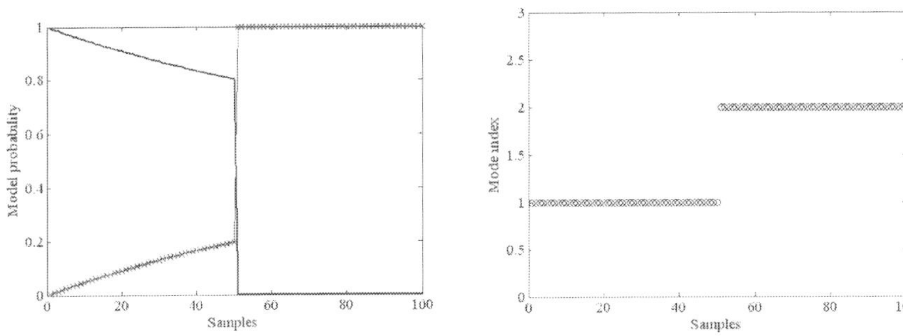

Fig. 7. The model probabilities and the mode index for the proposed fuzzy logic based IMM approach

Scenario 2: Single total/partial sensor/actuator faulty mode sequence

Consider the situation in which only a single total (or partial) sensor or actuator failure is possible. Then there are a total of 4 possible model (one normal plus 3 failure models) for sensor failure and 3 possible models (one normal plus 2 failure models) for actuator failures. Similarly, there are 4 partial sensor failure models and 3 partial actuator failures models. Due to the space limitation, only the simulation results for the sensor failure case are presented herein. Let the pairs (z_1, u_n), (z_2, u_{s1}), (z_3, u_{s2}), (z_4, u_{s3}) designate the measurements and corresponding causes associated with the normal/fault-free mode, and sensor fault for the first to the third sensor, respectively. Furthermore, let the pair (z_5, u_{s3p}) denote the measurement and corresponding causes associated with the partial fault for the third sensor. Consider the sequence of events designated by $z=[z_1, z_2, z_1, z_3, z_1, z_4, z_1, z_5, z_1]$ and $u=[u_n, u_{s1}, u_n, u_{s2}, u_n, u_{s3}, u_n, u_{s3p}, u_n]$, where the first, second, third total sensor failures, and the partial third sensor failure occur at the beginning of the time horizon windows [31, 50], [81, 110], [141, 180], and [211, 250], respectively. Note that z_1 corresponds to the normal mode. The faults persist for the duration of 20, 30, 40, and 40 samples, respectively.

Let the initial model probability for both the conventional IMM and the fuzzy logic based IMM approach $\mu(0)=[0.2, 0.2, 0.2, 0.2, 0.2]^T$. The transition matrix for the conventional IMM and the initial one for the proposed approach are set as

$$\Pi = \begin{bmatrix} 0.96 & 0.01 & 0.01 & 0.01 & 0.01 \\ 0.1 & 0.9 & 0 & 0 & 0 \\ 0.1 & 0 & 0.9 & 0 & 0 \\ 0.1 & 0 & 0 & 0.9 & 0 \\ 0.1 & 0 & 0 & 0 & 0.9 \end{bmatrix}$$

The mode indexes as a function of sampling period for the conventional IMM and the fuzzy logic based IMM approach are compared in Fig. 8.

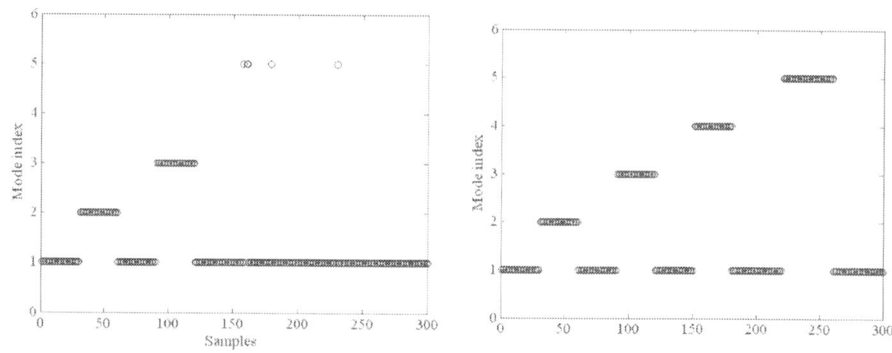

Fig. 8. The mode index in the 2nd scenario for (a) the conventional IMM; and (b) the fuzzy logic based IMM

Scenario 3: Simultaneous faulty modes sequence

Let the pairs (z_1, u_n), (z_2, u_{s1}), (z_3, u_{s2}), (z_4, u_{s3}), (z_5, u_{a1}), (z_6, u_{a2}) stand for the measurements and corresponding causes associated with the normal mode, sensor fault for the first to the third sensor, and the actuator fault for the first and second actuator, respectively. Furthermore, let (z_7, u_{a1s2}), (z_8, u_{a2s2}), (z_9, u_{a1a2}), (z_{10}, u_{a1s3}), (z_{11}, u_{a2s3}), (z_{12}, u_{s2s3}) designate the measurements and the inputs due to the presence of simultaneous double faulty modes caused by different combination of sensors and actuators, respectively. For simplicity and clarity, only sensor and actuator partial failures are considered herein.

The initial model probabilities are $\mu(0) = 1/N$, where N = 12 represents the number of modes; the threshold model probability $\mu_T' = 2.5$; and the initial one for the proposed approach are set as

$$\Pi = \begin{bmatrix} a & b & b & b & b & b & b & b & b & b & b & b \\ d & c & 0 & 0 & 0 & 0 & 0 & 0 & 0 & 0 & 0 & 0 \\ d & 0 & c & 0 & 0 & 0 & 0 & 0 & 0 & 0 & 0 & 0 \\ d & 0 & 0 & c & 0 & 0 & 0 & 0 & 0 & 0 & 0 & 0 \\ d & 0 & 0 & 0 & c & 0 & 0 & 0 & 0 & 0 & 0 & 0 \\ d & 0 & 0 & 0 & 0 & c & 0 & 0 & 0 & 0 & 0 & 0 \\ d & 0 & 0 & 0 & 0 & 0 & c & 0 & 0 & 0 & 0 & 0 \\ d & 0 & 0 & 0 & 0 & 0 & 0 & c & 0 & 0 & 0 & 0 \\ d & 0 & 0 & 0 & 0 & 0 & 0 & 0 & c & 0 & 0 & 0 \\ d & 0 & 0 & 0 & 0 & 0 & 0 & 0 & 0 & c & 0 & 0 \\ d & 0 & 0 & 0 & 0 & 0 & 0 & 0 & 0 & 0 & c & 0 \\ d & 0 & 0 & 0 & 0 & 0 & 0 & 0 & 0 & 0 & 0 & c \end{bmatrix}$$

where $a = 19/20$, $b = 1/220$, $c = 9/10$, and $d = 1/10$. Two faulty sequences of events are considered. The first sequence is 1-2-3-4-6-12, for which the events occur at the beginning of the 1st, 51st, 101st, 141st, 201st, 251st sampling point, respectively. The second sequence is 1-3-

5-7-8-9-10-11-12, for which the events occur at the beginning of the 1st, 41st, 71st, 111st, 141st, 181st, 221st, 251st, 281st sampling point, respectively. Note that z_1 corresponds to the normal mode. Then, for the first case the faults persist for the duration of 40, 40, 60, 50, and 50 samples within each window. For the second case the faults persist for 30, 40, 30, 40, 40, 30, 30, and 20 samples, respectively. For space reason, only the performance and capabilities of the proposed approach are shown. The results for the two cases are shown in Fig. 9 and Fig. 10, respectively. A quick view on the results, we may find that there is generally only one step of delay in detecting the presence of the faults. However, a more insight on both figures may reveal that at the beginning of the mode 4, it always turns out to be declared as mode 10, while taking mode 8 for mode 12, and vice versa. This may be attributed to the similarity between the mode 4 and 10, 8 and 12. However, the results settled down quickly, only 5-6 samples on average.

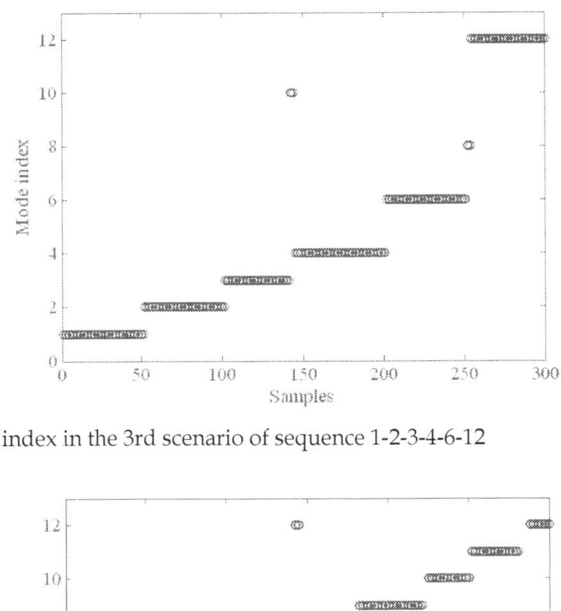

Fig. 9. The mode index in the 3rd scenario of sequence 1-2-3-4-6-12

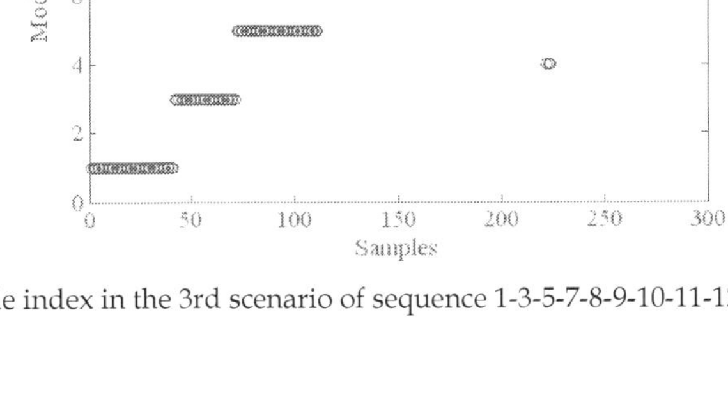

Fig. 10. The mode index in the 3rd scenario of sequence 1-3-5-7-8-9-10-11-12

6. Conclusion and future work

A self-contained framework to utilize IMM approach for fault detection and diagnosis for PEM fuel cell systems has been presented in this study. To overcome the shortcoming of the conventional IMM approach with constant transition matrix, a Takagi-Sugeno fuzzy model has been introduced to update the transition probability among multiple models, which makes the proposed FDD approach smooth and the possibility of false fault detection reduced. Comparing with the existing results on FDD for fuel cell systems , "partial" (or "soft") faults in addition to the "total" (or "hard") actuator and/or sensor failures have also been considered in this work. Simulation results for three different scenarios considering both single and simultaneous sensor and/or actuator faults have been given to illustrate the effectiveness of the proposed approach.

The scenarios considered correspond to representative symptoms in a PEM fuel cell system, and therefore the set of the considered models can't possibly cover all fault situations that may occur. Note that in case the fuel cell system undergoes a fault that it has not seen before, there is a possibility that the system might become unstable as a result of the IMM algorithm decision. It is indeed very difficult to formally and analytically characterize this, but based on our extensive simulation results presented, all the faulty can be detected precisely and timely.

It is worth mentioning that the main objective of this work was to develop and present simulation results for the applicability and the effectiveness of the fuzzy logic based IMM approach for fault diagnosis of a PEM fuel cell system. The proposed approach can be readily extended to IMM-based fault-tolerant control and provides extremely useful information for system compensation or fault-tolerant control subsequent to the detection of a failure. This work is under investigation and will be reported in the near future.

7. Acknowledgements

The work was supported by the National Natural Science Foundation of China (Under Grant 60874104, 60935001), and the Ph.D Scientific Research Foundation from Xiangtan University (Under Grant 10QDZ22).

8. References

Basseville, M. (1988). Detecting changes in signals and systems–A survey. *Automatica*, vol. 24, no. 3, pp. 309—326

Belcastro, C.M.; & Weinstein, B. (2002). Distributed detection with data fusion for malfunction detection and isolation in fault tolerant flight control computers. *Proceedings of the American Control Conference*, Anchorage, AK, May 2002

Blomen, L.; & Mugerwa, M. (1993). *Fuel Cell Systems*. New York: Plenum Press

Carette, L.; Friedrich, K.; & Stimming, U. (2001). Fuel cells - fundamentals and applications. *Fuel Cells Journal*, vol. 1, no. 1, pp. 5-39

Doucet, A.; de Freitas, N.; & Gordon, N. (2001) *Sequential Monte Carlo Methods in Practice*. New York: Springer-Verlag

Escobet, T.; Feroldi, D.; de Lira, S. et al. (2009). Model-based fault diagnosis in PEM fuel cell systems. *Journal of Power Sources*, vol. 192, no. 6, pp. 216-223

Gebregergis, A.; Pillay, P.; & Rengaswamy, R. (2010). PEMFC Fault Diagnosis, Modeling, and Mitigation, *IEEE Transactions on Industry Applications*, vol. 46, no. 1, pp. 295-303

Guo, D.; & Wang, X. (2004). Dynamic sensor collaboration via sequential Monte Carlo. *IEEE Journal on Selected Areas in Communications*, vol. 22, no. 6, pp. 1037—1047

Hernandez, A.; Hissel, D.; & Outbib, R. (2010). Modeling and Fault Diagnosis of a Polymer Electrolyte Fuel Cell Using Electrical Equivalent Analysis, *IEEE Transactions on Energy Conversion*, vol. 25, no. 1, pp. 148-160

Johnstone, A.L.; & Krishnamurthy, V. (2001). An improvement to the interacting multiple model algorithm. *IEEE Transactions on Signal Processing*, vol. 49, no. 12, pp. 2909—2923

Kakac, S.; Pramuanjaroenkijb, A.; & Zhou, X.Y. (2007). A review of numerical modeling of solid oxide fuel cells. *International Journal of Hydrogen Energy*, vol. 32, no. 7, pp. 761-786

Larminie, J.; & Dicks, A. (2000). *Fuel Cell Systems Explained*. Chicester: John Wiley & Sons, Inc.

Li, P.; & Kadirkamanathan, V. (2001). Particle filtering based likelihood ratio approach to fault diagnosis in nonlinear stochastic systems. *IEEE Transactions on Systems, Man, and Cybernetics, Part C*, vol. 31, no. 3, pp. 337—343

Li, X.R. (1996). Hybrid estimation techniques. In Leondes, C.T. (Ed.), *Control and Dynamic Systems*, vol. 76. New York: Academic Press, pp. 213-287

Li, X.R. (2000). Multiple-model estimation with variable structure-part II: model-set adaptation. *IEEE Transactions on Automatic Control*, vol. 45, no. 11, pp. 2047-2060

Li, X.R.; & Bar-Shalom, Y. (1993). Design of an interacting multiple model algorithm for air traffic control tracking. *IEEE Transactions on Control System Technology*, vol. 1, no. 3, pp. 186-194

Li, X.R., & Bar-Shalom, Y. (1996). Multiple model estimation with variable structure. *IEEE Transactions on Automatic Control*, vol. 41, no. 4, pp. 478-493

Mihaylova, L.; & Semerdjiev, E. (1999). Interacting multiple model algorithm for maneuvering ship tracking based on new ship models. *Information and Security*, vol. 12, no. 2, pp. 1124-1131

Pukrushpan, J.T., Peng, H.; & Stefanopoulou, A.G. (2004a). Control-oriented modeling and analysis for automotive fuel cell systems, *Transactions of the ASME*, vol. 126, no. 2, pp. 14-25

Pukrushpan, J.T.; Stefanopoulou, A.G. & Peng, H. (2004b). *Control of fuel cell power systems: principles, modeling, analysis, and feedback design*. New York: Springer- Verlag

Rapoport, I.; & Oshman, Y., (2007). Efficient fault tolerant estimation using the IMM methodology, IEEE Transactions on Aerospace and Electronic Systems, vol. 43, no. 2, pp. 492 - 508

Riascos, L.A.M.; Simoes, M.G.; & Miyagi, P.E. (2007). A Bayesian network fault diagnostic system for proton exchange membrane fuel cells. *Journal of Power Sources*, vol. 165, pp. 267-278

Takagi, T.; & Sugeno, M. (1985). Fuzzy identification of systems and its applications to modeling and control, *IEEE Transactions on System, Man, & Cyber*netics vol. 15, no. 1, pp. 116–132

Tudoroiu, N.; & Khorasani, K. (2005). Fault detection and diagnosis for satellite's attitude control system using an interactive multiple model approach, *Proceedings of 2005 IEEE Conf. Control Applications*, pp. 28-31, Toronto, Ont.

Venkatasubramanian, V.; Rengaswamy, R.; Kavuri, S.N.; & Yin, K. (2003a). A review of process fault detection and diagnosis part III: process history based methods. *Computers and Chemical Engineering*, vol. 27, no. 3, pp. 327-346

Venkatasubramanian, V.; Rengaswamy, R.; Yin, K.; & Kavuri, S.N. (2003b). A review of process fault detection and diagnosis part I: quantitative model-based methods. *Computers and Chemical Engineering*, vol. 27, no. 3, pp. 293-311

Willsky, A. (1976). A survey of design methods for failure detection in dynamic systems. *Automatica*, vol. 12, pp. 601 – 611

Yen, G.G.; & Ho, L.W. (2003). Online multiple-model-based fault diagnosis and accommodation, *IEEE Transactions on Industrial Electronics*, vol. 50, no. 2, pp. 296 - 312

Zhang, Y.; & Jiang, J. (2001). Integrated active fault-tolerant control using IMM approach, *IEEE Transactions on Aerospace and Electronic Systems*, vol. 37, no. 4, pp. 1221 - 1235

Zhang, Y.; & Li, X.R. (1998). Detection and diagnosis of sensor and actuator failures using IMM estimator. *IEEE Transactions on Aerospace and Electronic Systems*, vol. 34, no. 4, pp. 1293 – 1311

25

Discrete Time Systems with Event-Based Dynamics: Recent Developments in Analysis and Synthesis Methods

Edgar Delgado-Eckert[1], Johann Reger[2] and Klaus Schmidt[3]
[1]ETH Zürich
[2]Ilmenau University of Technology
[3]Cankaya University
[1]Switzerland
[2]Germany
[3]Turkey

1. Introduction

1.1 Definitions and basic properties

Discrete event systems (DES) constitute a specific subclass of discrete time systems whose dynamic behavior is governed by instantaneous changes of the system state that are triggered by the occurrence of asynchronous *events*. In particular, the characteristic feature of discrete event systems is that they are discrete in both their state space and in time. The modeling formalism of discrete event systems is suitable to represent man-made systems such as manufacturing systems, telecommunication systems, transportation systems and logistic systems (Caillaud et al. (2002); Delgado-Eckert (2009c); Dicesare & Zhou (1993); Kumar & Varaiya (1995)). Due to the steady increase in the complexity of such systems, analysis and control synthesis problems for discrete event systems received great attention in the last two decades leading to a broad variety of formal frameworks and solution methods (Baccelli et al. (1992); Cassandras & Lafortune (2006); Germundsson (1995); Iordache & Antsaklis (2006); Ramadge & Wonham (1989)).

The literature suggests different modeling techniques for DES such as *automata* (Hopcroft & Ullman (1979)), *petri-nets* (Murata (1989)) or *algebraic state space models* (Delgado-Eckert (2009b); Germundsson (1995); Plantin et al. (1995); Reger & Schmidt (2004)). Herein, we focus on the latter modeling paradigm. In a fairly general setting, within this paradigm, the state space model can be obtained from an unstructured automaton representation of a DES by encoding the trajectories in the state space in an n-dimensional state vector $x(k) \in X^n$ at each time instant k, whose entries can assume a finite number of different values out of a non-empty and finite set X. Then, the system dynamics follow

$$F(x(k+1), x(k)) = 0, \quad x(k) \in X^n$$

where F marks an implicit scalar transition function $F : X^n \times X^n \to X$, which relates $x(k)$ at instant k with the possibly multiple successor states $x(k+1)$ in the instant $k+1$. Clearly, in the case of multiple successor states the dynamics evolve in a non-deterministic manner.

In addition, it is possible to include control in the model by means of an m-dimensional control input $u(k) \in U^m$ at time instant k. This control input is contained in a so called control set (or space) U^m, where U is a finite set. The resulting system evolution is described by

$$F(x(k+1), x(k), u(k)) = 0, \quad x(k) \in X^n, u(k) \in U^m$$

In many cases, this implicit representation can be solved for the successor state $x(k+1)$, yielding the explicit form

$$x(k+1) = f(x(k), u(k)) \tag{1}$$

or

$$x(k+1) = f(x(k)) \tag{2}$$

when no controls are applied. As a consequence, the study of deterministic DES reduces to the study of a mapping $f : X^n \to X^n$, or $f : X^n \times U^m \to X^n$ if we consider control inputs, where X and U are finite sets, X is assumed non-empty, and $n, m \in \mathbb{N}$ are natural numbers. Such a mapping $f : X^n \to X^n$ is denoted as a *time invariant discrete time finite dynamical system.* Due to the finiteness of X it is readily observed that the trajectory $x, f(x), f(f(x)), ...$ of any point $x \in X^n$ contains at most $|X^n| = |X|^n$ different points and therefore becomes either cyclic or converges to a single point $y \in X^n$ with the property $f(y) = y$ (i.e., a fixed point of f). The *phase space of* f is the directed graph $(X^n, E, \pi : E \to X^n \times X^n)$ with node set X^n, arrow set E defined as $E := \{(x, y) \in X^n \times X^n \mid f(x) = y\}$ and vertex mapping

$$\begin{aligned} \pi \ &: \ E \to X^n \times X^n \\ (x, y) &\mapsto (x, y) \end{aligned}$$

The phase space consists of closed paths of different lengths that range from 1 (i.e. loops centered on fixed points) to $|X^n|$ (the closed path comprises all possible states), and directed trees that end each one at exactly one closed path. The nodes in the directed trees correspond to *transient states* of the system. In particular, if f is bijective[1], every point $x \in X^n$ is contained in a closed path and the phase space is the union of disjoint closed paths. Conversely, if every point in the phase space is contained in a closed path, then f must be bijective. A closed path of length s in the phase space of f is called a *cycle of length* s. We refer to the total number of cycles and their lengths in the phase space of f as the *cycle structure of* f.
Given a discrete time finite dynamical system $f : X^n \to X^n$, we can find in the phase space the longest open path ending in a closed path. Let $m \in \mathbb{N}_0$ be the length of this path. It is easy to see, that for any $s \geq m$ the (iterated) discrete time finite dynamical system $f^s : X^n \to X^n$ has the following properties

1. $\forall\, x \in X^n$, $f^s(x)$ is a node contained in one closed path of the phase space.
2. If T is the least common multiple of all the lengths of closed paths displayed in the phase space, then it holds

   $$f^{s+\lambda T} = f^s \ \forall\, \lambda \in \mathbb{N} \qquad \text{and} \qquad f^{s+i} \neq f^s \ \forall\, i \in \{1, ..., T-1\}$$

   We call T the *period number* of f. If $T = 1$, f is called a *fixed point system.*

In order to study the dynamics of such a dynamical system mathematically, it is beneficial to add some mathematical structure to the set X so that one can make use of well established mathematical techniques. One approach that opens up a large tool box of algebraic and graph theoretical methods is to endow the set X with the algebraic structure of a *finite field* (Lidl &

[1] Note that for any map from a finite set into itself, surjectivity is equivalent to injectivity.

Niederreiter (1997)). While this step implies some limitations on the cardinality[2] $|X|$ of the set X, at the same time, it enormously simplifies the study of systems $f : X^n \to X^n$ due to the fact that every component function $f_i : X^n \to X$ can be shown to be a polynomial function of bounded degree in n variables (Lidl & Niederreiter (1997), Delgado-Eckert (2008)). In many applications, the occurrence of events and the encoding of states and possible state transitions are modeled over the Boolean finite field $\mathbb{F}_2$ containing only the elements 0 and 1.

1.2 Control theoretic problems – analysis and controller synthesis

Discrete event systems exhibit specific control theoretic properties and bring about different control theoretic problems that aim at ensuring desired system properties. This section reviews the relevant properties and formalizes their analysis and synthesis in terms of the formal framework introduced in the previous section.

1.2.1 Discrete event systems analysis

A classical topic is the investigation of *reachability* properties of a DES. Basically, the analysis of reachability seeks to determine if the dynamics of a DES permit trajectories between given system states. Specifically, it is frequently required to verify if a DES is *nonblocking*, that is, if it is always possible to reach certain pre-defined desirable system states. For example, regarding manufacturing systems, such desirable states could represent the completion of a production task. Formally, it is desired to find out if a set of goal states $X_g \subseteq X^n$ can be reached from a start state $\bar{x} \in X^n$.

In the case of autonomous DES without a control input as in (2), a DES with the dynamic equations $x(k+1) = f(x(k))$ is denoted as *reachable* if it holds for all $\bar{x} \in X$ that the set X_g is reached after applying the mapping f for a finite number of times:

$$\forall \bar{x} \in X^n \exists k \in \mathbb{N} \text{ s.t. } f^k(\bar{x}) \in X_g. \tag{3}$$

Considering DES with a control input, reachability of a DES with respect to a goal set X_g holds if there exists a control input sequence that leads to a trajectory from each start state $\bar{x} \in X^n$ to a state $x(k) \in X_g$, whereby $x(k)$ is determined according to (1):

$$\forall \bar{x} \in X^n \exists k \in \mathbb{N} \text{ and controls } u(0), \ldots, u(k-1) \in U^m \text{ s.t. } x(k) \in X_g. \tag{4}$$

Moreover, if reachability of a controlled DES holds with respect to all possible goal sets $X_g \subseteq X^n$, then the DES is simply denoted as *reachable* and if the number of steps required to reach X_g is bounded by $l \in \mathbb{N}$, then the DES is called l-reachable.

An important related subject is the *stability* of DES that addresses the question if the dynamic system evolution will finally converge to a certain set of states ((Young & Garg, 1993)). Stability is particularly interesting in the context of failure-tolerant DES, where it is desired to finally ensure correct system behavior even after the occurrence of a failure. Formally, stability requires that trajectories from any start state $\bar{x} \in X^n$ finally lead to a goal set X_g without ever leaving X_g again.

Regarding autonomous DES without control, this condition is written as

$$\forall \bar{x} \in X^n \exists l \in \mathbb{N} \text{ s.t. } \forall k \geq l, f^k(\bar{x}) \in X_g. \tag{5}$$

In addition, DES with control input require that

$$\forall \bar{x} \in X^n \exists k \in \mathbb{N} \text{ and controls } u(0), \ldots, u(k-1) \in U^m \text{ s.t.} \forall l \geq k\ x(l) \in X_g, \tag{6}$$

---

[2] A well-known result states that X can be endowed with the structure of a finite field if and only if there is a prime number $p \in \mathbb{N}$ and a natural number $m \in \mathbb{N}$ such that $|X| = p^m$.

whereby $k = 1$ for all $\bar{x} \in X_g$.
It has to be noted that stability is a stronger condition than reachability both for autonomous DES and for DES with control inputs, that is, stability directly implies reachability in both cases.

In the previous section, it is discussed that the phase space of a DES consists of closed paths – so-called cycles – and directed trees that lead to exactly one closed path. In this context, the DES analysis is interested in inherent structural properties of autonomous DES. For instance, it is sought to determine *cyclic* or *fixed-point* behavior along with system states that belong to cycles or that lead to a fixed point ((Delgado-Eckert, 2009b; Plantin et al., 1995; Reger & Schmidt, 2004)). In addition, it is desired to determine the depth of directed trees and the states that belong to trees in the phase space of DES. A classical application, where cyclic behavior is required, is the design of feedback shift registers that serve as counter circuits in logical devices ((Gill, 1966; 1969)).

1.2.2 Controller synthesis for discrete event systems

Generally, the control synthesis for discrete event systems is concerned with the design of a controller that influences the DES behavior in order to allow certain trajectories or to achieve pre-specified structural properties under control. In the setting of DES, the control is applied by disabling or enforcing the occurrence of system events that are encoded by the control inputs of the DES description in (1). On the one hand, the control law can be realized as a feedforward controller that supplies an appropriate control input sequence $u(0), u(1), \ldots,$ in order to meet the specified DES behavior. Such feedforward control is for example required for reaching a goal set X_g as in (4) and (6). On the other hand, the control law can be stated in the form of a *feedback controller* that is realized as a function $g : X^n \to U^m$. This function maps the current state $x \in X^n$ to the current control input $g(x)$ and is computed such that the *closed-loop system*

$$\begin{aligned} h \ : \ & X^n \to X^n \\ & x \mapsto f(x, g(x)) \end{aligned}$$

satisfies desired structural properties. In this context, the assignment of a pre-determined cyclic behavior of a given DES are of particular interest for this chapter.

1.3 Applicability of existing methods

The control literature offers a great variety of approaches and tools for the system analysis and the controller synthesis for continuous and discrete time dynamical systems that are represented in the form

$$\dot{x}(t) = f(x(t), u(t)) \qquad \text{or} \qquad x(k+1) = f(x(k), u(k)),$$

whereby usually $x(t) \in \mathbb{R}^n$, $u(t) \in \mathbb{R}^m$, and $x(k) \in \mathbb{R}^n$, $u(k) \in \mathbb{R}^m$, respectively.
Unfortunately, traditional approaches to analyzing continuous and discrete time dynamical systems and to synthesizing controllers may fail when dealing with new modeling paradigms such as the use of the finite field $\mathbb{F}_2$ for DES as proposed in Section 1.1. From a mathematical point of view, one of the major difficulties is the fact that finite fields are not algebraically closed. Also non-linearity in the functions involved places a major burden for the system analysis and controller synthesis. In general, despite the simple polynomial shape of the transition function f (see above), calculations may be computationally intractable. For instance, determining the reachability set ((Le Borgne et al., 1991)) involves solving a certain set of algebraic equations, which is known to be an NP-hard problem ((Smale, 1998)).

Consequently, one of the main challenges in the field of discrete event systems is the development of appropriate mathematical techniques. To this end, researchers are confronted with the problem of finding new mathematical indicators that characterize the dynamic properties of a discrete system. Moreover, it is pertinent to establish to what extent such indicators can be used to solve the analysis and control problems described in Section 1.2. In addition, the development of efficient algorithms for the system analysis and controller synthesis are of great interest.

To illustrate recent achievements, this chapter presents the control theoretic study of *linear modular systems* in Section 2, on the one hand, and, on the other hand, of a class of *nonlinear* control systems over the Boolean finite field $\mathbb{F}_2$, namely, *Boolean monomial control systems* in Section 3, (first introduced by Delgado-Eckert (2009b)).

2. Analysis and control of linear modular systems[3]

2.1 State space decomposition

In this section, *linear modular systems* (LMS) over the finite field $\mathbb{F}_2$ shall be in the focus. Such systems are given by a linear recurrence

$$x(k+1) = A\,x(k), \quad k \in \mathbb{N}_0\,, \tag{7}$$

where $A \in \mathbb{F}_2^{n\times n}$ is the so-called system matrix. As usual in systems theory, it is our objective to track back dynamic properties of the system to the properties of the respective system matrix. To this end, we first recall some concepts from linear algebra that we need so as to relate the cycle structure of the system to properties of the system matrix.

2.1.1 Invariant polynomials and elementary divisor polynomials

A polynomial matrix $P(\lambda)$ is a matrix whose entries are polynomials in λ. Whenever the inverse of a polynomial matrix again is a polynomial matrix then this matrix is called *unimodular*. These matrices are just the matrices that show constant non-zero determinant. In the following, $\mathbb{F}$ denotes a field.

Lemma 1. *Let $A \in \mathbb{F}^{n\times n}$ be arbitrary. There exist unimodular polynomial matrices $U(\lambda), V(\lambda) \in \mathbb{F}[\lambda]^{n\times n}$ such that*

$$U(\lambda)(\lambda I - A)V(\lambda) = S(\lambda) \tag{8}$$

with

$$S(\lambda) = \begin{pmatrix} c_1(\lambda) & 0 & \cdots & 0 \\ 0 & c_2(\lambda) & & \vdots \\ \vdots & & \ddots & 0 \\ 0 & \cdots & 0 & c_n(\lambda) \end{pmatrix}, \tag{9}$$

in which $c_i(\lambda) \in \mathbb{F}[\lambda]$ are monic polynomials with the property $c_{i+1} \mid c_i$, $i = 1, \ldots, n-1$.

Remark 2. *The diagonal matrix $S(\lambda)$ is the Smith canonical form of $\lambda I - A$ which, of course, exists for any non-square polynomial matrix, not only in case of the characteristic matrix $\lambda I - A$. However, for λ not in the spectrum of A the rank of $\lambda I - A$ is always full and, thus, for any non-eigenvalue λ we have $c_i(\lambda) \neq 0$.*

Definition 3. *Let $A \in \mathbb{F}^{n\times n}$ be arbitrary and $S(\lambda) \in \mathbb{F}[\lambda]^{n\times n}$ the Smith canonical form associated to the characteristic matrix $\lambda I - A$. The monic polynomials $c_i(\lambda)$, $i = 1, \ldots, n$, generating $S(\lambda)$ are called invariant polynomials of A.*

[3] Some of the material presented in this section has been previously published in (Reger & Schmidt, 2004).

It is a well-known fact that two square matrices are similar if and only if they have the same Smith canonical form ((Wolovich, 1974)). That is, these invariant polynomials capture the coordinate independent properties of the system. Moreover, the product of all invariant polynomials results in the characteristic polynomial $\mathrm{cp}_A(\lambda) = \det(\lambda I - A) = c_1(\lambda) \cdots c_n(\lambda)$ and the largest degree polynomial $c_1(\lambda)$ in $S(\lambda)$ is the minimal polynomial $\mathrm{mp}_A(\lambda)$ of A, which is the polynomial of least degree such that $\mathrm{mp}_A(A) = 0$. The invariant polynomials can be factored into irreducible factors.

Definition 4. *A non-constant polynomial $p \in \mathbb{F}[\lambda]$ is called irreducible over the field $\mathbb{F}$ if whenever $p(\lambda) = g(\lambda)h(\lambda)$ in $\mathbb{F}[\lambda]$ then either $g(\lambda)$ or $h(\lambda)$ is a constant.*

In view of irreducibility, Gauß' fundamental theorem of algebra can be rephrased so as to obtain the unique factorization theorem.

Theorem 5. *Any polynomial $p \in \mathbb{F}[\lambda]$ can be written in the form*

$$p = a\, {p_1}^{e_1} \cdots {p_k}^{e_k} \tag{10}$$

with $a \in \mathbb{F}$, $e_1, \ldots, e_k \in \mathbb{N}$, and polynomials $p_1, \ldots, p_k \in \mathbb{F}[\lambda]$ irreducible over $\mathbb{F}$. The factorization is unique except for the ordering of the factors.

Definition 6. *Let $A \in \mathbb{F}^{n\times n}$ be arbitrary and $c_i = p_{i,1}^{e_{i,1}} \cdots p_{i,N_i}^{e_{i,N_i}} \in \mathbb{F}[\lambda]$, $i = 1, \ldots, \bar{n}$, the corresponding $\bar{n}$ non-unity invariant polynomials in unique factorization with N_i factors. The $N = \sum_{i=1}^{\bar{n}} N_i$ monic factor polynomials $p_{i,j}^{e_{i,j}}$, $i = 1, \ldots, \bar{n}$ and $j = 1, \ldots, N_i$, are called elementary divisor polynomials of A.*

In order to precise our statements the following definition is in order:

Definition 7. *Let $p_C = \lambda^d + \sum_{i=0}^{d-1} a_i \lambda^i \in \mathbb{F}[\lambda]$ be monic. Then the $(d \times d)$-matrix*

$$C = \begin{pmatrix} 0 & 1 & 0 & \cdots & 0 & 0 \\ 0 & 0 & 1 & \cdots & 0 & 0 \\ 0 & 0 & 0 & \cdots & 0 & 0 \\ \vdots & \vdots & \vdots & \ddots & \vdots & \vdots \\ 0 & 0 & 0 & \cdots & 0 & 1 \\ -a_0 & -a_1 & -a_2 & \cdots & -a_{d-2} & -a_{d-1} \end{pmatrix} \tag{11}$$

is called the companion matrix associated to p_C.

Based on Definition 7, it is now possible to define the *rational canonical form* of a given matrix.

Theorem 8. *Let $A \in \mathbb{F}^{n\times n}$ be arbitrary and $p_{i,j}^{e_{i,j}}$ its N elementary divisor polynomials, as introduced in Definition 6. There exists an invertible matrix T such that*

$$A_{\mathrm{rat}} = T^{-1}\, A\, T = \mathrm{diag}(C_1, \ldots, C_N) \tag{12}$$

where $C_1, \ldots, C_N$ are the companion matrices associated to the N elementary divisor polynomials of A.

Remark 9. *Except for the ordering of the companion matrices the matrix A_{rat} is unique. Furthermore, the number N is maximal in the sense that there is no other matrix similar to A that comprises more than N companion matrices.*

2.1.2 Cycle structure

As pointed out in the introductory section, the phase space of any discrete system may be decomposed into closed paths (cycles) and paths that terminate in some cycle. For ease of notation, let N_Σ denote the number of different-length cycles in a discrete system. Moreover, let the expression $\nu[\tau]$ denote ν cycles of length τ. For this notation it clearly holds $\nu_i[\tau] + \nu_j[\tau] = (\nu_i + \nu_j)[\tau]$. Then the formal sum (cycle sum)

$$\Sigma = \nu_1[\tau_1] + \nu_2[\tau_2] + \ldots + \nu_{N_\Sigma}[\tau_{N_\Sigma}] \tag{13}$$

is used to represent the entire cycle structure of a discrete system that has a total of ν_i cycles of length τ_i for $i = 1, \ldots, N_\Sigma$. The cycle structure is naturally linked to the notion of a periodic state, which shall be introduced for the particular case of linear modular systems.

Definition 10. *Let $x \in \mathbb{F}_2^n$ be a non-zero state of the LMS in* (7). *The period of x is the least natural number t such that $x = A^t x$. The period of the zero state $x = 0$ is $t = 1$.*

Without loss of generality, let the LMS in (7) be given in the elementary divisor version of the rational canonical form[4] (see Theorem 8). Hence,

$$x(k+1) = \mathrm{diag}(C_1, \ldots, C_N)\, x(k)\,. \tag{14}$$

The representation reveals the decomposition of (7) into N decoupled underlying subsystems, $x_i(k+1) = C_i\, x_i(k)$, associated to the companion matrices C_i with respect to each elementary divisor polynomial of A. By combinatorial superposition of the periodic states of the subsystems it is clear that the periods of the states in the composite system follow from the least common multiple of the state periods in the subsystems. Therefore, for the examination of the cycle structure, it is sufficient to consider the cycle structure of a system

$$x(k+1) = C\, x(k)\,. \tag{15}$$

In this representation, $C \in \mathbb{F}_2^{d\times d}$ is a companion matrix whose polynomial $p_C \in \mathbb{F}_2[\lambda]$ is a power of a monic polynomial that is irreducible over $\mathbb{F}_2$, whereby either $p_C(0) \neq 0$ or $p_C = \lambda^d$ ((Reger, 2004)). It is now possible to relate the cyclic properties of the matrix C to the cyclic properties of the polynomial p_C.

Theorem 11. *Let a linear modular system $x(k+1) = C\, x(k)$ be given by a companion matrix $C \in \mathbb{F}_2^{d\times d}$ and its corresponding d-th degree polynomial $p_C = (p_{\mathrm{irr},C})^e$, where $p_{\mathrm{irr},C} \in \mathbb{F}_2[\lambda]$ is an irreducible polynomial over $\mathbb{F}_2$ of degree δ such that $d = e\,\delta$. Then the following statements hold:*

1. *If $p_{\mathrm{irr},C}(0) \neq 0$, then the phase space of the system has the cycle sum*

$$\Sigma = 1[1] + \frac{2^\delta - 1}{\tau_1}[\tau_1] + \cdots + \frac{2^{2\delta} - 2^\delta}{\tau_j}[\tau_j] + \ldots + \frac{2^{e\delta} - 2^{(e-1)\delta}}{\tau_e}[\tau_e]\,. \tag{16}$$

   In the above equation, the periods τ_j, $j = 1, \ldots, e$ are computed as $\tau_j = 2^{l_j}\tau$, whereby τ represents the period of the irreducible polynomial $p_{\mathrm{irr},C}$ which is defined as the least positive natural number for which $p(\lambda)$ divides $\lambda^\tau - 1$. In addition, l_j, $j = 1, \ldots, e$, is the least integer such that $2^{l_j} \geq j$.

2. *If $p_{\mathrm{irr},C} = \lambda^d$, then the phase space forms a tree with d levels, whereby each level $l = 1, \ldots, d$ comprises 2^{l-1} states, each non-zero state in level $l-1$ is associated to 2 states in level l, and the zero state has one state in level 1.*

---

[4] Otherwise, we may always transform $\bar{x} = T\,x$ such that in new coordinates it will be.

Proof. Part 1. is proved in [Theorem 4.5 in (Reger, 2004)] and part 2. is proved in [Theorem 4.9 in (Reger, 2004)]. ■

Equipped with this basic result, it is now possible to describe the structure of the state space of an LMS in rational canonical form (14). Without loss of generality, it is assumed that the first c companion matrices are cyclic with the cycle sums $\Sigma_1, \ldots, \Sigma_c$, whereas the remaining companion matrices are *nilpotent*.[5] Using the multiplication of cycle terms as defined by

$$\nu_i[\tau_i]\nu_j[\tau_j] = \frac{\nu_i \nu_j \tau_i \tau_j}{\mathrm{lcm}(\tau_i, \tau_j)}[\mathrm{lcm}(\tau_i, \tau_j)] = \nu_i \nu_j \gcd(\tau_i, \tau_j)[\mathrm{lcm}(\tau_i, \tau_j)],$$

the cycle structure Σ of the overall LMS is given by the multiplication of the cycle sums of the cyclic companion matrices

$$\Sigma = \Sigma_1\, \Sigma_2\, \cdots\, \Sigma_c.$$

Finally, the nilpotent part of the overall LMS forms a tree with $\max\{d_{c+1}, \ldots, d_N\}$ levels, that is, the length of the longest open path of the LMS is $l_o = \max\{d_{c+1}, \ldots, d_N\}$. For the detailed structure of the resulting tree the reader is referred to Section 4.2.2.2 in (Reger, 2004).

The following example illustrates the cycle sum evaluation for an LMS with the system matrix $A \in \mathbb{F}_2^{5\times 5}$ and its corresponding Smith canonical form $S(\lambda) \in \mathbb{F}_2[\lambda]^{5\times 5}$ that is computed as in [p. 268 ff. in (Booth, 1967)], [p. 222 ff. in (Gill, 1969)].

$$A = \begin{pmatrix} 1\,0\,0\,1\,1 \\ 1\,1\,0\,0\,1 \\ 0\,0\,1\,0\,1 \\ 0\,0\,0\,0\,1 \\ 1\,0\,0\,0\,1 \end{pmatrix}, \quad S(\lambda) = \begin{pmatrix} (\lambda^2+\lambda+1)(\lambda+1)^2 & 0 & 0\,0\,0 \\ 0 & \lambda+1 & 0\,0\,0 \\ 0 & 0 & 1\,0\,0 \\ 0 & 0 & 0\,1\,0 \\ 0 & 0 & 0\,0\,1 \end{pmatrix}$$

Here the only non-constant invariant polynomials of A are

$$c_1(\lambda) = (\lambda^2+\lambda+1)(\lambda+1)^2, \quad c_2(\lambda) = \lambda+1$$

as indicated by the Smith canonical form. Thus, A has the elementary divisor polynomials

$$p_{C_1}(\lambda) = \lambda^2+\lambda+1, \quad p_{C_2}(\lambda) = (\lambda+1)^2, \quad p_{C_3}(\lambda) = \lambda+1.$$

Since none of the elementary divisor polynomials is of the form λ^h for some integer h, the system matrix A is cyclic. The corresponding base polynomial degrees are $\delta_1 = 2$, $\delta_2 = 1$ and $\delta_3 = 1$, respectively. Consequently, the corresponding rational canonical form $A_{\mathrm{rat}} = T\,A\,T^{-1}$ together with its transformation matrix T reads[6]

$$A_{\mathrm{rat}} = \mathrm{diag}(C_1, C_2, C_3) = \begin{pmatrix} 0\,1\,0\,0\,0 \\ 1\,1\,0\,0\,0 \\ 0\,0\,0\,1\,0 \\ 0\,0\,1\,0\,0 \\ 0\,0\,0\,0\,1 \end{pmatrix}, T = \begin{pmatrix} 1\,0\,0\,1\,1 \\ 0\,0\,0\,1\,1 \\ 1\,0\,1\,0\,1 \\ 0\,0\,1\,1\,1 \\ 0\,1\,1\,0\,1 \end{pmatrix}, T^{-1} = \begin{pmatrix} 1\,1\,0\,0\,0 \\ 1\,1\,1\,0\,1 \\ 0\,1\,0\,1\,0 \\ 1\,1\,1\,1\,0 \\ 1\,0\,1\,1\,0 \end{pmatrix}.$$

[5] A matrix A is called nilpotent when there is a natural number $n \in \mathbb{N}$ such that $A^n = 0$.

[6] A simple method for obtaining the transformation matrix T can be found in Appendix B of (Reger, 2004).

In view of Theorem 11, the corresponding periods are

$$\begin{aligned} p_{\mathrm{irr},C_1}(\lambda) &= \lambda^2+\lambda+1|\lambda^3+1 &\Longrightarrow&\quad \tau_1^{(1)}=3\\ p_{\mathrm{irr},C_2}(\lambda) &= \lambda+1 &\Longrightarrow&\quad \tau_1^{(2)}=1\\ \left(p_{\mathrm{irr},C_2}(\lambda)\right)^2 &= (\lambda+1)^2=\lambda^2+1 &\Longrightarrow&\quad \tau_2^{(2)}=2\\ p_{\mathrm{irr},C_3}(\lambda) &= \lambda+1 &\Longrightarrow&\quad \tau_1^{(3)}=1 \end{aligned}$$

Thus, the associated cycle sums are

$$\Sigma_1 = 1[1]+[3], \quad \Sigma_2 = 2[1]+[2], \quad \Sigma_3 = 2[1].$$

The superposition of these cycle sums yields the cycle sum of the overall LMS

$$\begin{aligned}\Sigma &= \Sigma_1\Sigma_2\Sigma_3 = \left(1[1]+1[3]\right)\left(2[1]+1[2]\right)\left(2[1]\right) = \left(2[1]+1[2]+2[3]+1[6]\right)\left(2[1]\right) = \\ &= 4[1]+2[2]+4[3]+2[6]\,.\end{aligned}$$

Therefore, the LMS represented by the system matrix A comprises 4 cycles of length 1, 2 cycles of length 2, 4 cycles of length 3 and 2 cycles of length 6.

2.2 Reachability and stability

In this section, the DES properties of reachability and stability as introduced in Section 1.2 are investigated. The DES analysis for both properties is first performed for systems with no controls in Subsection 2.2.1. In this case, we can prove necessary and sufficient conditions for reachability and stability for general (not necessarily linear) deterministic DES $f : X^n \to X^n$, without even requiring an algebraic structure imposed on the set X. However, to achieve equivalent results in the case of DES with controls, we need to endow the set X with the structure of a finite field and assume that the mapping $f : X^n \times U^m \to X^n$ is linear. This is presented in Subsection 2.2.2.

2.2.1 Reachability and stability for discrete event systems with no controls

The reachability analysis for DES with no controls requires the verification of (3). As mentioned in Section 1.1, any state $\bar{x} \in X$ either belongs to a unique cycle or to a tree that is rooted at a unique cycle. In the first case, it is necessary and sufficient for reachability from $\bar{x}$ that there is at least one state $\hat{x} \in X_{\mathrm{g}}$ that belongs to the same cycle. Denoting the cycle length as τ, it follows that $f^k(\bar{x}) = \hat{x} \in X_{\mathrm{g}}$ for some $0 \leq k < \tau$. In the latter case, it is sufficient that at least one state $\hat{x} \in X_{\mathrm{g}}$ is located on the cycle with length τ where the tree is rooted. With the length l_{o} of the longest open path and the root x_{r} of the tree, it holds that $x_{\mathrm{r}} = f^l(\bar{x})$ with $0 < l \leq l_{\mathrm{o}}$ and $\hat{x} = f^k(x_{\mathrm{r}})$ for some $0 < k < \tau$. Hence, $f^{l+k}\bar{x} = \hat{x} \in X_{\mathrm{g}}$. Together, it turns out that reachability for a DES without controls can be formulated as a necessary and sufficient property of the goal state set X_{g} with respect to the map f.

Theorem 12. *Let $f : X^n \to X^n$ be a mapping, let C_f denote the set of all cycles of the DES and let $X_{\mathrm{g}} \subseteq X^n$ be a goal state set. Then, reachability of X_{g} with respect to f is given if and only if for all cycles $c \in C_f$, there is a state $\hat{x} \in X_{\mathrm{g}}$ that belongs to c. Denoting l_{o} as the longest open path and τ as the length of the longest cycle of the DES, X_{g} is reachable from any $\bar{x} \in X^n$ in at most $l_{\mathrm{o}} + \tau - 1$ steps.*

Algorithmically, the verification of reachability for a given DES without controls with the mapping f and the goal state set X_{g} can be done based on the knowledge of the number ν of cycles of the DES[7]. First, it has to be noted that the requirement $|X_g| \geq \nu$ for the cardinality of X_g is a necessary requirement. If this condition is fulfilled, the following procedure performs the reachability verification.

Algorithm 13. **Input:** *Mapping f, goal state set X_g, cycle count ν*

1. *Remove all states on trees from X_g*
2. **if** $\nu = 1$ *and* $X_g \neq \emptyset$
   return *rechability verification successful*
3. *Pick $\hat{x} \in X_g$*
   Compute all states $\hat{X}_g \subseteq X_g$ on the same cycle as $\hat{x}$
   $X_g = X_g - \hat{X}_g$
4. $\nu = \nu - 1$
5. **if** $|X_g| \geq \nu$
   go to 2.
   else
   return *reachability verification fails*

That is, Algorithm 13 checks if the states in X_g cover each cycle of the DES. To this end, the algorithm successively picks states from X_g and removes all states in the same cycle from X_g. With the removal of each cycle, the variable ν that represents the number of cycles of the DES that were not covered by states in X_g, yet, is decremented. Thereby, reachability is violated as soon as there are more remaining cycles ν than remaining states in X_g.

Next, stability for DES with no controls as in (5) is considered. In view of the previous discussion, stability requires that all states in all cycles of the DES belong to the goal set X_g. In that case, it holds that whatever start state $\bar{x} \in X^n$ is chosen, at most l_o steps are required to lead $\bar{x}$ to a cycle that belongs to X_g. In contrast, it is clear that whenever there is a state $x \in X^n - X_g$ that belongs to a cycle of the DES, then the condition in (5) is violated for all states in the same cycle. Hence, the formal stability result for DES with no controls is as follows.

Theorem 14. *Let $f : X^n \times X^n$ be a mapping and let $X_g \subseteq X^n$ be a goal state set. Then, stability of X_g with respect to f is given if and only if X_g contains all cyclic states of the DES with the mapping f. Denoting l_o as the longest open path of the DES, X_g is reached from any $\bar{x} \in X^n$ in at most l_o steps.*

For the algorithmic verification of stability, a slight modification of Algorithm 13 can be used. It is only required to additionally check if the set $\hat{X}_g$ computed in step 3. contains all states of the respective cycle. In the positive case, the algorithm can be continued as specified, whereas the modified algorithm terminates with a violation of stability if $\hat{X}_g$ does not contain all states of a cycle.

In summary, both reachability and stability of DES with no controls with respect to a given goal state set X_g can be formulated and algorithmically verified in terms of the cycle structure of the DES. Moreover, it has to be noted that stability is more restrictive than reachability. While reachability requires that at least one state in each cycle of the DES belongs to X_g, stability necessitates that all cyclic states of the DES belong to X_g.

[7] Note that ν can be computed for LMS according to Subsection 2.1.2.

2.2.2 Reachability and stability under control

The results in this subsection are valid for arbitrary finite fields. However, we will state the results with respect to the (for applications most relevant) Boolean finite field $\mathbb{F}_2$. Moreover, the focus of this subsection is the specialization of (4) to the case of controlled LMS with the following form

$$x(k+1) = Ax(k) + Bu(k), \quad k \in \mathbb{N}_0 \tag{17}$$

with the matrices $A \in \mathbb{F}_2^{n\times n}$ and $B \in \mathbb{F}_2^{n\times m}$:

$$\forall \bar{x} \in \mathbb{F}_2^n \exists k \in \mathbb{N} \text{ and controls } u(0),\ldots,u(k-1) \in U^m \text{ s.t. } A^k\bar{x} + \sum_{j=0}^{k-1} A^{k-1-j}Bu(j) \in X_g. \tag{18}$$

In analogy to the classical reachability condition for linear discrete time systems that are formulated over the field $\mathbb{R}$ ((Sontag, 1998)), the following definition is sufficient for (18).

Definition 15. *The LMS in* (17) *is denoted as reachable if for any $\bar{x}, \hat{x} \in \mathbb{F}_2^n$, there exists a $k \in \mathbb{N}$ and controls $u(0), u(1),\ldots,u(k-1)$ such that $x(k) = \hat{x}$. If there is a smallest number $l \in \mathbb{N}$ such that the above condition is fulfilled for any $\bar{x}, \hat{x} \in \mathbb{F}_2^n$ and $k = l$, then the LMS is l-reachable.*

That is, if an LMS is reachable, then the condition in (18) is fulfilled for any given goal set X_g. To this end, the notion of *controllability* that is established for linear discrete time systems [Theorem 2 in (Sontag, 1998)] is formulated for LMS.

Theorem 16. *The LMS in* (17) *is controllable if and only if the pair (A, B) is controllable, that is, the matrix R with*

$$R = \begin{bmatrix} B & AB & A^2B & \cdots & A^{n-1}B \end{bmatrix} \tag{19}$$

has full rank n. Moreover, the LMS is l-controllable if and only if $R_l = \begin{bmatrix} B & AB & \cdots & A^{l-1}B \end{bmatrix}$ has full rank n for an $l \in \{1,\ldots,n\}$.

Noting the equivalence of controllability and reachability for linear discrete time systems as established in [Lemma 3.1.5 in (Sontag, 1998)], l-reachability for LMS can be verified by evaluating the rank of the matrix R_l. In case an LMS is l-reachable, an important task is to determine an appropriate control input that leads a given start state $\bar{x}$ to the goal state set X_g. That is, for some $\hat{x} \in X_g$ the controls $u(0),\ldots,u(l-1) \in U^m$ have to be computed such that $\hat{x} = A^l\bar{x} + \sum_{j=0}^{l-1} A^{l-1-j}Bu(j)$.

To this end, a particular matrix $L \in \mathbb{F}_2^{n\times n}$ is defined in analogy to [p. 81 in (Wolovich, 1974)]. Denoting the column vectors of the input matrix B as $b_1,\ldots,b_m$ (which, without loss of generality, are linearly independent), that is, $B = \begin{bmatrix} b_1 & \cdots & b_m \end{bmatrix}$, L is constructed by choosing n linearly independent columns from R_l with the following arrangement:

$$L = \begin{bmatrix} b_1 \; Ab_1 \; \cdots \; A^{\mu_1-1}b_1 \; b_2 \; Ab_2 \; \cdots \; A^{\mu_2-1}b_2 \; \cdots \; b_m \; Ab_m \; \cdots \; A^{\mu_m-1}b_m \end{bmatrix}. \tag{20}$$

In this expression, the parameters $\mu_1,\ldots,\mu_m$ that arise from the choice of the linearly independent columns of R_l are the *controllability indices* of the LMS (A, B). Without loss of generality it can be assumed that the controllability indices are ordered such that $\mu_1 \leq \cdots \leq \mu_m$, in which case they are unique for each LMS. The representation in (20) allows to directly compute an appropriate control sequence that leads $\bar{x}$ to a state $\hat{x} \in X_g$. It is desired that

$$\begin{aligned}\hat{x} &= A^l \bar{x} + \sum_{j=0}^{l-1} A^{l-1-j} \left[b_1 \cdots b_m\right] u(j) \\ &= A^l \bar{x} + \left[b_1 \cdots A^{l-1} b_1 \cdots b_m \cdots A^{l-1} b_m\right] \left[u_1(l-1) \cdots u_1(0) \cdots u_m(l-1) \cdots u_m(0)\right]^t\end{aligned}$$

In the above equation, $u_i(j)$ denotes the i-th component of the input vector $u(j) \in U^m$ at step j. Next, setting all $u_i(j) = 0$ for $i = 1, \ldots, m$ and $j \leq l - 1 - \mu_i$, the above equation simplifies to

$$\begin{aligned}\hat{x} &= A^l \bar{x} + \left[b_1 \cdots A^{\mu_1 - 1} b_1 \cdots b_m \cdots A^{\mu_m - 1} b_m\right] \left[u_1(l-1) \cdots u_1(l-\mu_1) \cdots u_m(l-1) \cdots u_m(l-\mu_m)\right]^t \\ &= A^l \bar{x} + L \left[u_1(l-1) \cdots u_1(l-\mu_1) \cdots u_m(l-1) \cdots u_m(l-\mu_m)\right]^t\end{aligned}$$

Since L is invertible, the remaining components of the control input evaluate as

$$\left[u_1(l-1) \cdots u_1(l-\mu_1) \cdots u_m(l-1) \cdots u_m(l-\mu_m)\right]^t = L^{-1}(\hat{x} - A^l \bar{x}).$$

Remark 17. *At this point, it has to be noted that the presented procedure determines one of the possible control input sequences that lead a given $\bar{x}$ to $\hat{x} \in X_g$. In general, there are multiple different control input sequences that solve this problem.*

Considering stability, it is required to find a control input sequence that finally leads a given start state to the goal state set X_g without leaving the goal state set again. For DES with no controls that are described in Subsection 2.2.1, stability can only be achieved if all cyclic states of an LMS are contained in X_g. In the case of LMS with control, this restrictive condition can be relaxed. It is only necessary that the goal set contains at least one full cycle of the corresponding system with no controls (for $B = 0$), that is, all states that form at least one cycle of an LMS. If l-reachability of the LMS is given, then it is always possible to reach this cycle after a bounded number of at most l steps.

Corollary 18. *The LMS in* (17) *is stable if it is l-reachable for an $l \in \{1, ..., n\}$ and X_g contains all states of at least one cycle of the autonomous LMS with the system matrix A.*

Next, it is considered that l-reachability is violated for any l in Corollary 18. In that case, the linear systems theory suggests that the state space is separated into a controllable state space and an uncontrollable state space, whereby there is a particular transformation to the state $y = \tilde{T}^{-1} x$ that structurally separates both subspaces as follows from [p. 86 in ((Wolovich, 1974))].

$$y(k) = \tilde{T} A \tilde{T}^{-1} y(k-1) + \tilde{T} B u(k-1) = \begin{bmatrix} y_c(k) \\ y_{\bar{c}}(k) \end{bmatrix} = \begin{bmatrix} \tilde{A}_c & \tilde{A}_{c\bar{c}} \\ 0 & \tilde{A}_{\bar{c}} \end{bmatrix} y(k-1) + \begin{bmatrix} \tilde{B}_c \\ 0 \end{bmatrix} u(k-1). \quad (21)$$

This representation is denoted as the *controller companion form* with the controllable subsystem $(\tilde{A}_c, \tilde{B}_c)$, the uncontrollable autonomous subsystem with the matrix $\tilde{A}_{\bar{c}}$ and the coupling matrix $\tilde{A}_{c\bar{c}}$.

Then, the following result is sufficient for the reachability of a goal state $\hat{y} = \begin{bmatrix} \hat{y}_c \\ \hat{y}_{\bar{c}} \end{bmatrix}$ from a start state $\bar{y} = \begin{bmatrix} \bar{y}_c \\ \bar{y}_{\bar{c}} \end{bmatrix}$, whereby $\hat{y}_c, \bar{y}_c$ and $\hat{y}_{\bar{c}}, \bar{y}_{\bar{c}}$ denote the controllable and reachable part of the respective state vectors in the transformed coordinates.

Theorem 19. *Assume that an uncontrollable LMS is given by its controller companion form in* (21) *and assume that the pair* $(\tilde{A}_c, \tilde{B}_c)$ *is l-controllable. Let* $\bar{y} = \begin{bmatrix} \bar{y}_c \\ \bar{y}_{\bar{c}} \end{bmatrix}$ *be a start state and* $\hat{y} = \begin{bmatrix} \hat{y}_c \\ \hat{y}_{\bar{x}} \end{bmatrix} \in Y_g$ *be a goal state. Then,* $\hat{y}$ *is reachable from* $\bar{y}$ *in k steps if*

- $k \geq l$
- $\hat{y}_{\bar{c}} = \tilde{A}_{\bar{c}}^k \bar{y}_{\bar{c}}$

Theorem 19 constitutes the most general result in this subsection. In particular, Theorem 16 is recovered if the uncontrollable subsystem of the LMS does not exist and $k \geq l$.
Finally, the combination of the results in Theorem 19 and Corollary 18 allows to address the issue of stability in the case of an uncontrollable LMS.

Corollary 20. *Consider an LMS in its Kalman decomposition (21). The LMS is stable if it holds for the uncontrollable subsystem that all states in cycles of* $\tilde{A}_{\bar{c}}$ *are present in the uncontrollable part* $\hat{y}_{\bar{c}}$ *of the goal states* $\hat{y} \in Y_g$*, whereby each cycle in the uncontrollable subsystem has to correspond to at least one cycle of the complete state* y *in* Y_g.

2.3 Cycle sum assignment

In regard of Section 2.1, imposing a desired cycle sum on an LMS requires to alter the system matrix in such a way that it obtains desired invariant polynomials that generate the desired cycle sum. Under certain conditions, this task can be achieved by means of linear state feedback of the form $u(k) = K\,x(k)$ with $K \in \mathbb{F}_2^{m \times n}$.
Since the specification of a cycle sum via periodic polynomials will usually entail the need to introduce more than one non-unity invariant polynomial, invariant polynomial assignment generalizes the idea of pole placement that is wide-spread in the control community. The question to be answered in this context is: what are necessary and sufficient conditions for an LMS such that a set of invariant polynomials can be assigned by state feedback? The answer to this question is given by the celebrated control structure theorem of Rosenbrock in [Theorem 7.2.-4. in (Kailath, 1980)]. Note that, in this case, the closed-loop LMS assumes the form $x(k+1) = (A + B\,K)x(k)$.

Theorem 21. *Given is an n-dimensional and n-controllable LMS with m inputs. Assume that the LMS has the controllability indices* $\mu_1 \geq \ldots \geq \mu_m$*. Let* $c_{i,K} \in \mathbb{F}_2[\lambda]$ *with* $c_{i+1,K} | c_{i,K}$, $i = 1, \ldots, m-1$*, and* $\sum_{i=1}^{m} \deg(c_{i,K}) = n$ *be the desired non-unity monic invariant polynomials. Then there exists a matrix* $K \in \mathbb{F}_2^{m \times n}$ *such that* $A + B\,K$ *has the desired invariant polynomials* $c_{i,K}$ *if and only if the inequalities*

$$\sum_{i=1}^{k} \deg(c_{i,K}) \geq \sum_{i=1}^{k} \mu_i, \quad k = 1, 2, \ldots, m \tag{22}$$

are satisfied.

Remark 22. *The sum of the invariant polynomial degrees and the n-controllability condition guarantee that equality holds for* $k = m$*. However, the choice of formulation also includes the case of systems with single input m. In this case, Rosenbrock's theorem requires n-controllablity when a desired closed-loop characteristic polynomial is to be assigned by state feedback. Furthermore, the theorem indicates that at most m different invariant polynomials may be assigned in an LMS with m inputs.*

Assigning invariant polynomials is equivalent to assigning the non-unity polynomials of the Smith canonical form of the closed-loop characteristic matrix $\lambda I - (A + B\,K)$. It has to be noted that although meeting the assumptions of the control structure theorem with the desired closed-loop Smith form, the extraction of the corresponding feedback matrix K is not a trivial task. The reason for this is that, in general, the structure of the Smith form of $\lambda I - (A + BK)$ does not necessarily agree with the controllability indices of the LMS, which are preserved under linear state feedback. However, there is a useful reduction of the LMS representation based on the closed loop characteristic matrix in the controller companion form as shown in [Theorem 5.8 in (Reger, 2004)].

Theorem 23. *Given is an n-dimensional n-controllable LMS in controller companion form* (21) *with m inputs and controllability indices* $\mu_1, \ldots, \mu_m$. *Let* $D_{\hat{K}} \in \mathbb{F}_2[\lambda]^{m \times m}$ *denote the polynomial matrix*

$$D_{\hat{K}}(\lambda) := \Lambda(\lambda) - \hat{A}_{\hat{K},\text{nonzero}}\, P(\lambda)\,,$$

where $\hat{A}_{\hat{K},\text{nonzero}} \in \mathbb{F}_2^{m \times n}$ *contains the m non-zero rows of the controllable part of the closed-loop system matrix* $\hat{A}_c + \hat{B}_c \hat{K}$ *in controller companion form, and* $P \in \mathbb{F}_2[\lambda]^{n \times m}$, $\Lambda \in \mathbb{F}_2[\lambda]^{m \times m}$ *are*

$$P(\lambda) = \begin{pmatrix} 1 & 0 & \cdots & 0 \\ \lambda & 0 & \cdots & 0 \\ \vdots & \vdots & \ddots & \vdots \\ \lambda^{\mu_1 - 1} & 0 & \cdots & 0 \\ 0 & 1 & \cdots & 0 \\ \vdots & \vdots & \ddots & \vdots \\ 0 & \lambda^{\mu_2 - 1} & \cdots & 0 \\ \vdots & \vdots & \ddots & \vdots \\ 0 & 0 & \cdots & 1 \\ \vdots & \vdots & \ddots & \vdots \\ 0 & 0 & \cdots & \lambda^{\mu_m - 1} \end{pmatrix}, \quad \Lambda(\lambda) = \begin{pmatrix} \lambda^{\mu_1} & 0 & \cdots & 0 \\ 0 & \lambda^{\mu_2} & \cdots & 0 \\ \vdots & \vdots & \ddots & \vdots \\ 0 & 0 & \cdots & \lambda^{\mu_m} \end{pmatrix}. \tag{23}$$

Then the non-unity invariant polynomials of $\lambda I - (\hat{A}_c + \hat{B}_c \hat{K})$, $\lambda I - (\hat{A}_{\text{nonzero}} + \hat{K})$ *and* $D_{\hat{K}}(\lambda)$ *coincide, whereby* $\hat{A}_{\text{nonzero}}$ *contains the nonzero rows of the controllable part* $\hat{A}_c$ *of the original system matrix.*

Theorem 23 points out a direct way of realizing the closed-loop LMS $y(k+1) = (\hat{A}_c + \hat{B}_c \hat{K}) y(k)$ with desired invariant polynomials by means of specifying $D_{\hat{K}}(\lambda)$. That is, if an appropriate $D_{\hat{K}}$ can be found, then a linear state feedback matrix $\hat{K}$ in the transformed coordinates can be directly constructed. Simple manipulations first lead to

$$\hat{A}_{\hat{K},\text{nonzero}} P(\lambda) = D_{\hat{K}}(\lambda) - \Lambda(\lambda) \tag{24}$$

from which $\hat{A}_{\hat{K},\text{nonzero}}$ can be determined by comparison of coefficients. Then, by Theorem 23, the feedback matrix

$$\hat{K} = A_{\text{nonzero}} - \hat{A}_{\hat{K},\text{nonzero}} \tag{25}$$

is obtained. Finally, the inverse coordinate transformation from the controller companion form to the original coordinates yields

$$K = \hat{K}\tilde{T}\,. \tag{26}$$

Hence, it remains to find an appropriate matrix $D_{\hat{K}}$. To this end, the following definitions are employed.

Definition 24. *Let $M \in \mathbb{F}_2[\lambda]^{n\times m}$ be arbitrary. The degree of the highest degree monomial in λ within the i-th column of $M(\lambda)$ is denoted as the i-th column degree of M and denoted by* $\text{col}_i(M)$.

Definition 25. *Let $M \in \mathbb{F}_2[\lambda]^{n\times m}$ be arbitrary. The highest column degree coefficient matrix $\Gamma(M) \in \mathbb{F}_2^{n\times m}$ is the matrix whose elements result from the coefficients of the highest monomial degree in the respective elements of $M(\lambda)$.*

Then, the following procedure leads to an appropriate $D_{\hat{K}}$. Starting with a desired cycle sum for the closed-loop LMS, an appropriate set of invariant polynomials – as discussed in Section 2.1 – has to be specified. Next, it has to be verified if the realizability condition of Rosenbrock's control structure theorem for the given choice of invariant polynomials is fulfilled. If the polynomials are realizable then $D_{\hat{K}}(\lambda)$ is chosen as the Smith canonical form that corresponds to the specified closed-loop invariant polynomials. In case the column degrees of $D_{\hat{K}}(\lambda)$ coincide with the respective controllability indices of the underlying LMS, that is, $\text{col}_i(D_{\hat{K}}) = \mu_i$ for $i = 1, \ldots, m$, it is possible to directly calculate the feedback matrix $\hat{K}$ according to (26). Otherwise, it is required to modify the column degrees of $D_{\hat{K}}(\lambda)$ by means of unimodular left and right transformations while leaving the invariant polynomials of $D_{\hat{K}}$ untouched. This procedure is summarized in the following algorithm.

Algorithm 26. Input: *Pair $(\hat{A}_c, \hat{B}_c)$ in controller companion form*[8] *controllability indices $\mu_1 \geq \cdots \geq \mu_m$, polynomials $c_{i,K} \in \mathbb{F}_2[\lambda]$, $i = 1, \ldots, m$ with $c_{j+1,K} | c_{j,K}$, $j = 1, \ldots, m-1$ and $\sum_{i=1}^{m} \deg(c_{i,K}) = n$.*

1. *Verify Rosenbrock's structure theorem*
   if *the inequalities in Theorem 21 are fulfilled*

   go to *step 2.*

   else

   return *"Rosenbrock's structure theorem is violated."*
2. *Define* $D^\star(\lambda) := \text{diag}(c_{1,K}, \ldots, c_{m,K})$
3. *Verify if the column degrees of $D^\star(\lambda)$ and the controllability indices coincide*
   if $\text{col}_i(D^\star) = \mu_i$, $i = 1, \ldots, m$

   go to *step 6.*

   else

   Detect the first column of $D^\star(\lambda)$ which differs from the ordered list of controllability indices, starting with column 1. Denote this column $\text{col}_u(D^\star)$ ($\deg(\text{col}_u(D^\star)) > \mu_u$)

   Detect the first column of $D^\star(\lambda)$ which differs from the controllability indices, starting with column m. Denote this column $\text{col}_d(D^\star)$ ($\deg(\text{col}_d(D^\star)) < \mu_d$)
4. *Adapt the column degrees of $D^\star(\lambda)$ by unimodular transformations*
   Multiply $\text{row}_d(D^\star)$ by λ and add the result to $\text{row}_u(D^\star) \rightarrow$ new matrix $D^+(\lambda)$
   if $\deg(\text{col}_u(D^+)) = \deg(\text{col}_u(D^\star)) - 1$

   $D^+(\lambda) \rightarrow$ new matrix $D^{++}(\lambda)$ and **go to** *step 5.*

   else

   Define $r := \deg(\text{col}_u(D^\star)) - \deg(\text{col}_d(D^\star)) - 1$

   Multiply $\text{col}_d(D^+)$ by λ^r and subtract result from $\text{col}_u(D^+) \rightarrow$ new matrix $D^{++}(\lambda)$.

[8] If the LMS is not given in controller companion form, this form can be computed as in [p. 86 in (Wolovich, 1974)].

5. *Set* $D^\star(\lambda) = (\Gamma(D^{++}))^{-1}D^{++}(\lambda)$ *and* **go to** *step 3.*
6. $D_{\hat{K}}(\lambda) := D^\star(\lambda)$ *and* **return** $D_{\hat{K}}(\lambda)$

It is important to note that the above algorithm is guaranteed to terminate with a suitable matrix $D_{\hat{K}}$ if Rosenbrock's structure theorem is fulfilled. For illustration, the feedback matrix computation is applied to the following example that also appears in (Reger, 2004; Reger & Schmidt, 2004). Given is an LMS over $\mathbb{F}_2$ of dimension $n = 5$ with $m = 2$ inputs in controller companion form (that is, $\tilde{T} = I$),

$$y(k+1) = \hat{A}_c\, y(k) + \hat{B}_c\, u(k), \quad \hat{A}_c = \begin{pmatrix} 0&1&0&0&0\\ 0&0&1&0&0\\ 0&0&0&0&0\\ 0&0&0&0&1\\ 1&0&0&1&0 \end{pmatrix}, \; \hat{B}_c = \begin{pmatrix} 0&0\\ 1&0\\ 0&0\\ 0&0\\ 0&1 \end{pmatrix}$$

from which the matrix $\hat{A}_{\text{nonzero}} = \begin{pmatrix} 0&0&0&0&0\\ 1&0&0&1&0 \end{pmatrix}$ can be extracted.

As a control objective, we want to assign the invariant polynomials[9] $c_{1,K}(a) = (a^2+a+1)(a+1)^2$ and $c_{2,K}(a) = a+1$, that is, according to the example in Subsection 2.1.2 this goal is equivalent to specifing that the closed-loop LMS shall have 4 cycles of length 1, 2 cycles of length 2, 4 cycles of length 3 and 2 cycles of length 6. An appropriate state feedback matrix K is now determined by using (26) and Algorithm 26.

$$\xrightarrow{1.} \quad \sum_{i=1}^{1} \deg(c_{i,K}(\lambda)) = 4 \geq \sum_{i=1}^{1} c_i = 3 \text{ and } \sum_{i=1}^{2} \deg(c_{i,K}(\lambda)) = 5 \geq \sum_{i=1}^{2} c_i = 5 \quad \surd$$

$$\xrightarrow{2.} \quad D^\star(\lambda) = \begin{pmatrix} (\lambda^2+\lambda+1)(\lambda+1)^2 & 0 \\ 0 & \lambda+1 \end{pmatrix} = \begin{pmatrix} \lambda^4+\lambda^3+\lambda+1 & 0 \\ 0 & \lambda+1 \end{pmatrix}$$

$$\xrightarrow{3.,4.} \quad D^+(\lambda) = \begin{pmatrix} \lambda^4+\lambda^3+\lambda+1 & \lambda^2+\lambda \\ 0 & \lambda+1 \end{pmatrix} \implies D^{++}(\lambda) = \begin{pmatrix} \lambda+1 & \lambda^2+\lambda \\ \lambda^3+\lambda^2 & \lambda+1 \end{pmatrix}$$

$$\xrightarrow{5.} \quad \Gamma(D^{++}) = \begin{pmatrix} 0&1\\1&0 \end{pmatrix} \implies D^\star(\lambda) = (\Gamma(D^{++}))^{-1}D^{++}(\lambda) = \begin{pmatrix} \lambda^3+\lambda^2 & \lambda+1 \\ \lambda+1 & \lambda^2+\lambda \end{pmatrix}$$

$$\xrightarrow{3.,4.,6.} \quad D_{\hat{K}}(\lambda) = \begin{pmatrix} \lambda^3+\lambda^2 & \lambda+1 \\ \lambda+1 & \lambda^2+\lambda \end{pmatrix}$$

With $D_{\hat{K}}(\lambda)$ the feedback matrix K can be computed. First, employing equation (24) yields

$$\hat{A}_{\hat{K},\text{nonzero}} \begin{pmatrix} 1&0\\ \lambda&0\\ \lambda^2&0\\ 0&1\\ 0&\lambda \end{pmatrix} = \underbrace{\begin{pmatrix} \lambda^3 & 0 \\ 0 & \lambda^2 \end{pmatrix}}_{\Lambda(\lambda)} + \underbrace{\begin{pmatrix} \lambda^3+\lambda^2 & \lambda+1 \\ \lambda+1 & \lambda^2+\lambda \end{pmatrix}}_{D_{\hat{K}}(\lambda)} = \begin{pmatrix} \lambda^2 & \lambda+1 \\ \lambda+1 & \lambda \end{pmatrix}$$

[9] Constructing the appropriate invariant polynomials based on the cycle structure desired is not always solvable and, if solvable, not necessarily a straightforward task (Reger & Schmidt (2004)).

and by comparison of coefficients results in $\hat{A}_{\hat{K},\text{nonzero}} = \begin{pmatrix} 0 & 0 & 1 & 1 & 1 \\ 1 & 1 & 0 & 0 & 1 \end{pmatrix}$. This implies that

$$K = \hat{K}\tilde{T} = (\hat{A}_{\hat{K},\text{nonzero}} + \hat{A}_{\text{nonzero}})\, I = \begin{pmatrix} 0 & 0 & 1 & 1 & 1 \\ 0 & 1 & 0 & 1 & 1 \end{pmatrix}.$$

3. Properties of Boolean monomial systems[10]

3.1 Dynamic properties, cycle structure and the loop number

The aim of this section is that the reader becomes acquainted with the main theorems that characterize the dynamical properties of Boolean monomial dynamical systems without deepening into the technicalities of their proofs. We briefly introduce terminology and notation and present the main results. Proofs can be found in Delgado-Eckert (2008), and partially in Delgado-Eckert (2009a) or Colón-Reyes et al. (2004).

Let $G = (V_G, E_G, \pi_G)$ be a directed graph (also known as digraph). Two vertices $a, b \in V_G$ are called *connected* if there is a $t \in \mathbb{N}_0$ and (not necessarily different) vertices $v_1, ..., v_t \in V_G$ such that

$$a \to v_1 \to v_2 \to ... \to v_t \to b,$$

where the arrows represent directed edges in the graph. In this situation we write $a \rightsquigarrow_s b$, where s is the number of directed edges involved in the *sequence* from a to b (in this case $s = t + 1$). Two sequences $a \rightsquigarrow_s b$ of the same length are considered different if the directed *edges* involved are different or the order at which they appear is different, even if the visited vertices are the same. As a convention, a single vertex $a \in V_G$ is always connected to itself $a \rightsquigarrow_0 a$ by an empty sequence of length 0. A sequence $a \rightsquigarrow_s b$ is called a *path*, if no vertex v_i is visited more than once. If $a = b$, but no other vertex is visited more than once, $a \rightsquigarrow_s b$ is called a *closed path*.

Let $q \in \mathbb{N}$ be a natural number. We denote with $\mathbb{F}_q$ a finite field with q elements, i.e. $|\mathbb{F}_q| = q$. As stated in the introduction, every function $h : \mathbb{F}_q^n \to \mathbb{F}_q$ can be written as a polynomial function in n variables where the degree of each variable is less or equal to $q - 1$. Therefore we introduce the *exponents set* (also referred to as *exponents semiring*, see below) $E_q := \{0, 1, ..., (q - 2), (q - 1)\}$ and define monomial dynamical systems over a finite field as:

Definition 27. *Let $\mathbb{F}_q$ be a finite field and $n \in \mathbb{N}$ a natural number. A map $f : \mathbb{F}_q^n \to \mathbb{F}_q^n$ is called an n-dimensional monic* monomial dynamical system *over $\mathbb{F}_q$ if for every $i \in \{1, ..., n\}$ there is a tuple $(F_{i1}, ..., F_{in}) \in E_q^n$ such that*

$$f_i(x) = x_1^{F_{i1}} ... x_n^{F_{in}} \;\forall\, x \in \mathbb{F}_q^n$$

We will call a monic monomial dynamical system just monomial dynamical system. The matrix[11] *$F_{ij} \in M(n \times n; E_q)$ is called the* corresponding matrix *of the system f.*

Remark 28. *As opposed to Colón-Reyes et al. (2004), we exclude in the definition of monomial dynamical system the possibility that one of the functions f_i is equal to the zero function. However, in contrast to Colón-Reyes et al. (2006), we do allow the case $f_i \equiv 1$ in our definition. This is not a loss of generality because of the following: If we were studying a dynamical system $f : \mathbb{F}_q^n \to \mathbb{F}_q^n$ where one of the functions, say f_j, was equal to zero, then, for every initial state $x \in \mathbb{F}_q^n$, after one iteration the system would be in a state $f(x)$ whose jth entry is zero. In all subsequent iterations the value of the jth*

[10] Some of the material presented in this section has been previously published in Delgado-Eckert (2009b).

[11] $M(n \times n; E_q)$ is the set of $n \times n$ matrices with entries in the set E_q.

entry would remain zero. As a consequence, the long term dynamics of the system are reflected in the projection $\pi_{\hat{j}} : \mathbb{F}_q^n \to \mathbb{F}_q^{n-1}$

$$\pi_{\hat{j}}(y) := (y_1, ..., y_{j-1}, y_{j+1}, ..., y_n)^t$$

and it is sufficient to study the system

$$\tilde{f} : \mathbb{F}_q^{n-1} \to \mathbb{F}_q^{n-1}$$

$$y \mapsto \begin{pmatrix} f_1(y_1, ..., y_{j-1}, 0, y_{j+1}, ..., y_n) \\ \vdots \\ f_{j-1}(y_1, ..., y_{j-1}, 0, y_{j+1}, ..., y_n) \\ f_{j+1}(y_1, ..., y_{j-1}, 0, y_{j+1}, ..., y_n) \\ \vdots \\ f_n(y_1, ..., y_{j-1}, 0, y_{j+1}, ..., y_n) \end{pmatrix}$$

In general, this system $\tilde{f}$ *could contain component functions equal to the zero function, since every component* f_i *that depends on the variable* x_j *would become zero. As a consequence, the procedure described above needs to be applied several times until the lower dimensional system obtained does not contain component functions equal to zero. It is also possible that this repeated procedure yields the one dimensional zero function. In this case, we can conclude that the original system* f *is a fixed point system with* $(0, ..., 0) \in \mathbb{F}_q^n$ *as its unique fixed point. The details about this procedure are described as the "preprocessing algorithm" in Appendix B of Delgado-Eckert (2008). This also explains why we exclude in the definition of monomial feedback controller (see Definition 62 in Section 3.2 below) the possibility that one of the functions* f_i *is equal to the zero function.*

When calculating the composition of two monomial dynamical systems $f, g : \mathbb{F}_q^n \to \mathbb{F}_q^n$ (i.e. the system $f \circ g : \mathbb{F}_q^n \to \mathbb{F}_q^n$, $x \mapsto f(g(x))$), one needs to add and multiply exponents. Similarly, when calculating the product $f * g$, where $*$ is the component-wise multiplication defined as

$$(f * g)_i(x) := f_i(x) g_i(x)$$

one needs to add exponents. However, after such operations, one may face the situation where some of the exponents exceed the value $q - 1$ and need to be reduced according to the well known rule $a^q = a \; \forall \, a \in \mathbb{F}_q$. This process can be accomplished systematically if we look at the power x_i^p (where $p > q$) as a polynomial in the ring $\mathbb{F}_q[\tau]$ and define the magnitude $red_q(p)$ as the degree of the (unique) remainder of the polynomial division $\tau^p \div (\tau^q - \tau)$ in the polynomial ring $\mathbb{F}_q[\tau]$. Then we can write $x_i^p = x_i^{red_q(p)} \; \forall \, x_i \in \mathbb{F}_q$, which is a direct consequence of certain properties of the operator red_q (see Lemma 39 in Delgado-Eckert (2008)). In conclusion, the "exponents arithmetic" needed when calculating the composition of dynamical systems $f, g : \mathbb{F}_q^n \to \mathbb{F}_q^n$ can be formalized based on the reduction operator $red_q(p)$. Indeed, the set $E_q = \{0, 1, ..., (q-1)\} \subset \mathbb{Z}$ together with the operations of addition $a \oplus b := red_q(a + b)$ and multiplication $a \bullet b := red_q(ab)$ is a commutative semiring with identity 1. We call this commutative semiring the *exponents semiring* of the field $\mathbb{F}_q$. Due to this property, the set of all n-dimensional monomial dynamical systems over $\mathbb{F}_q$, denoted with $MF_n^n(\mathbb{F}_q)$, is a monoid $(MF_n^n(\mathbb{F}_q), \circ)$, where $\circ$ is the composition of such systems. Furthermore, this set is also a monoid $(MF_n^n(\mathbb{F}_q), *)$ where $*$ is the component-wise multiplication defined above. In addition, as shown in Delgado-Eckert (2008), these two binary operations satisfy distributivity properties, i.e. $(MF_n^n(\mathbb{F}_q), *, \circ)$ is a semiring with identity element with respect to each binary operation. Moreover, Delgado-Eckert (2008) proved that this semiring is isomorphic to the semiring $M(n \times n; E_q)$ of matrices with entries in E_q. This result establishes on the one hand, that the composition $f \circ g$ of two monomial dynamical systems f, g is completely captured by the product $F \cdot G$ of their corresponding matrices. On the other hand, it also shows that the component-wise multiplication $f * g$ is completely captured by the sum $F + G$ of the corresponding matrices. Clearly, these matrix operations are defined entry-wise in terms of the operations $\oplus$ and $\bullet$. The aforementioned isomorphism makes it possible for us to operate with the corresponding matrices instead of the functions, which has computational advantages. Roughly speaking, this result can be summarized as follows: There is a bijective mapping

$$\Psi : (M(n \times n; E_q), +, \cdot) \to (MF_n^n(\mathbb{F}_q), *, \circ)$$

which defines a one-to-one correspondence between matrices and monomial dynamical systems. The corresponding matrix defined above can therefore be calculated as $\Psi^{-1}(f)$. This result is proved in Corollary 58 of Delgado-Eckert (2008), which states:

Theorem 29. *The semirings $(M(n \times n; E_q), +, \cdot)$ and $(MF_n^n(\mathbb{F}_q), *, \circ)$ are isomorphic.*

Another important aspect is summarized in the following remark

Remark 30. *Let $\mathbb{F}_q$ be a finite field and $n, m, r \in \mathbb{N}$ natural numbers. Furthermore, let $f \in MF_n^m(\mathbb{F}_q)$ and $g \in MF_m^r(\mathbb{F}_q)$ with*

$$f_i(x) = x_1^{F_{i1}} ... x_n^{F_{in}} \ \forall\, x \in \mathbb{F}_q^n,\ i = 1, ..., m$$
$$g_j(x) = x_1^{G_{j1}} ... x_m^{G_{jm}} \ \forall\, x \in \mathbb{F}_q^m,\ j = 1, ..., r$$

where $F \in M(m \times n; E_q)$ and $G \in M(r \times m; E_q)$ are the corresponding matrices of f and g, respectively. Then for their composition $g \circ f : \mathbb{F}_q^n \to \mathbb{F}_q^r$ it holds

$$(g \circ f)_k(x) = \prod_{j=1}^{n} x_j^{(G \cdot F)_{kj}} \ \forall\, x \in \mathbb{F}_q^n,\ k \in \{1, ..., r\}$$

Proof. See Remark and Lemma 51 of Delgado-Eckert (2008). ■

The dependency graph of a monomial dynamical system (to be defined below) is an important mathematical object that can reveal dynamic properties of the system. Therefore, we turn our attention to some graph theoretic considerations:

Definition 31. *Let M be a nonempty finite set. Furthermore, let $n := |M|$ be the cardinality of M. An* enumeration *of the elements of M is a bijective mapping $a : M \to \{1, ..., n\}$. Given an enumeration a of the set M we write $M = \{a_1, ..., a_n\}$, where the unique element $x \in M$ with the property $a(x) = i \in \{1, ..., n\}$ is denoted as a_i.*

Definition 32. *Let $f \in MF_n^n(\mathbb{F}_q)$ be a monomial dynamical system and $G = (V_G, E_G, \pi_G)$ a digraph with vertex set V_G of cardinality $|V_G| = n$. Furthermore, let $F := \Psi^{-1}(f)$ be the corresponding matrix of f. The digraph G is called* dependency graph *of f iff an enumeration $a : M \to \{1, ..., n\}$ of the elements of V_G exists such that $\forall\, i, j \in \{1, ..., n\}$ there are* ***exactly*** *F_{ij} directed edges $a_i \to a_j$ in the set E_G, i.e. $\left|\pi_G^{-1}((a_i, a_j))\right| = F_{ij}$.*

It is easy to show that if G and H are dependency graphs of f then G and H are isomorphic. In this sense we speak of *the* dependency graph of f and denote it by $G_f = (V_f, E_f, \pi_f)$.

Definition 33. *Let $G = (V_G, E_G, \pi_G)$ be a digraph. Two vertices $a, b \in V_G$ are called* strongly connected *if there are natural numbers $s, t \in \mathbb{N}$ such that $a \rightsquigarrow_s b$ and $b \rightsquigarrow_t a$. In this situation we write $a \rightleftharpoons b$.*

Theorem 34. *Let $G = (V_G, E_G, \pi_G)$ be a digraph. $\rightleftharpoons$ is an equivalence relation on V_G called* strong equivalence. *The equivalence class of any vertex $a \in V_G$ is called a* strongly connected component *and denoted by $\overleftrightarrow{a} \subseteq V_G$.*

Proof. This a well known result. A proof can be found, for instance, in Delgado-Eckert (2008), Theorem 68. ∎

Definition 35. *Let $G = (V_G, E_G, \pi_G)$ be a digraph and $a \in V_G$ one of its vertices. The* strongly connected component *$\overleftrightarrow{a} \subseteq V_G$ is called* trivial *iff $\overleftrightarrow{a} = \{a\}$ and there is no edge $a \to a$ in E_G.*

Definition 36. *Let $G = (V_G, E_G, \pi_G)$ be a digraph with vertex set V_G of cardinality $|V_G| = n$ and $V_G = \{a_1, ..., a_n\}$ an enumeration of the elements of V_G. The matrix $A \in M(n \times n; \mathbb{N}_0)$ whose entries are defined as*

$$A_{ij} := \textit{number of edges } a_i \to a_j \textit{ contained in } E_G$$

for $i, j = 1, ..., n$ is called adjacency matrix *of G with the enumeration a.*

Remark 37. *Let $f \in MF_n^n(\mathbb{F}_q)$ be a monomial dynamical system. Furthermore, let $G_f = (V_f, E_f, \pi_f)$ be the dependency graph of f and $V_f = \{a_1, ..., a_n\}$ the associated enumeration of the elements of V_f. Then, according to the definition of dependency graph, $F := \Psi^{-1}(f)$ (the corresponding matrix of f) is precisely the adjacency matrix of G_f with the enumeration a.*

The following parameter for digraphs was introduced into the study of Boolean monomial dynamical systems by Colón-Reyes et al. (2004):

Definition 38. *Let $G = (V_G, E_G, \pi_G)$ be a digraph and $a \in V_G$ one of its vertices. The number*

$$\mathcal{L}_G(a) := \min_{\substack{a \rightsquigarrow_u a \\ a \rightsquigarrow_v a \\ u \neq v}} |u - v|$$

is called the loop number of a. If there is no sequence of positive length from a to a, then $\mathcal{L}_G(a)$ is set to zero.

Note that the loop number $\mathcal{L}_{G'}(a)$ of the vertex a in a graph $G' = (V_G, E'_G, \pi'_G)$ may have a different value.

Lemma 39. *Let $G = (V_G, E_G, \pi_G)$ be a digraph and $a \in V_G$ one of its vertices. If $\overleftrightarrow{a}$ is nontrivial then for every $b \in \overleftrightarrow{a}$ it holds $\mathcal{L}_G(b) = \mathcal{L}_G(a)$. Therefore, we introduce the loop number of strongly connected components as*

$$\mathcal{L}_G(\overleftrightarrow{a}) := \mathcal{L}_G(a)$$

Proof. See Lemma 4.2 in Colón-Reyes et al. (2004). ∎

The loop number of a strongly connected graph is also known as the *index of imprimitivity* (see, for instance, Pták & Sedlaček (1958)) or *period* (Denardo (1977)) and has been used in the study of nonnegative matrices (see, for instance, Brualdi & Ryser (1991) and Lancaster & Tismenetsky (1985)). This number *quantizes the length* of any closed sequence in a strongly connected graph, as shown in the following theorem. It is also the biggest possible "quantum", as proved in the subsequent corollary.

Theorem 40. *Let $G = (V_G, E_G, \pi_G)$ be a strongly connected digraph. Furthermore, let $t := \mathcal{L}_G(V_G) \geq 0$ be its loop number and $a \in V_G$ an arbitrary vertex. Then for any closed sequence $a \leadsto_m a$ there is an $\alpha \in \mathbb{N}_0$ such that $m = \alpha t$.*

Proof. This result was proved in Corollary 4.4 of Colón-Reyes et al. (2004). A similar proof can be found in Delgado-Eckert (2009b), Theorem 2.19. ∎

Corollary 41. *Let $G = (V_G, E_G, \pi_G)$ be a strongly connected digraph such that V_G is nontrivial and $V_G = \{a_1, ..., a_n\}$ an enumeration of the vertices. Furthermore, let $l_1, ..., l_k \in \{1, ..., n\}$ be the different lengths of non-empty closed paths actually contained in the graph G. That is, for every $j \in \{1, ..., k\}$ there is an $a_{i_j} \in V_G$ such that a closed path $a_{i_j} \leadsto_{l_j} a_{i_j}$ exists in G, and the list $l_1, ..., l_k$ captures all different lengths of all occurring closed paths. Then the loop number $\mathcal{L}_G(V_G)$ satisfies*

$$\mathcal{L}_G(V_G) = \gcd(l_1, ..., l_k)$$

Proof. This result was proved in Theorem 4.13 of Colón-Reyes et al. (2004). A slightly simpler proof can be found in Delgado-Eckert (2009b), Corollary 2.20. ∎
The next results show how the connectivity properties of the dependency graph and, in particular, the loop number are related to the dynamical properties of a monomial dynamical system.

Theorem 42. *Let $\mathbb{F}_q$ be a finite field and $f \in MF_n^n(\mathbb{F}_q)$ a monomial dynamical system. Then f is a fixed point system with $(1, ..., 1)^t \in \mathbb{F}_q^n$ as its only fixed point if and only if its dependency graph only contains trivial strongly connected components.*

Proof. See Theorem 3 in Delgado-Eckert (2009a). ∎

Definition 43. *A monomial dynamical system $f \in MF_n^n(\mathbf{F}_q)$ whose dependency graph contains nontrivial strongly connected components is called* coupled monomial dynamical system.

Definition 44. *Let $m \in \mathbb{N}$ be a natural number. We denote with $D(m) := \{d \in \mathbb{N} : d \text{ divides } m\}$ the set of all positive divisors of m.*

Theorem 45. *Let $\mathbb{F}_2$ be the finite field with two elements, $f \in MF_n^n(\mathbb{F}_2)$ a* Boolean *coupled monomial dynamical system and $G_f = (V_f, E_f, \pi_f)$ its dependency graph. Furthermore, let G_f be strongly connected with loop number $t := \mathcal{L}_{G_f}(V_f) > 1$. Then the period number T (cf. Section 1.1) of f satisfies*

$$T = \mathcal{L}_{G_f}(V_f)$$

Moreover, the phase space of f contains cycles of all lengths $s \in D(T)$.

Proof. This result was proved by Colón-Reyes et al. (2004), see Corollary 4.12. An alternative proof is presented in Delgado-Eckert (2008), Theorem 131. ∎

Theorem 46. *Let $\mathbb{F}_2$ be the finite field with two elements, $f \in MF_n^n(\mathbb{F}_2)$ a* Boolean *coupled monomial dynamical system and $G_f = (V_f, E_f, \pi_f)$ its dependency graph. Furthermore, let G_f be strongly connected with loop number $t := \mathcal{L}_{G_f}(V_f) > 1$. In addition, let $s \in \mathbb{N}$ be a natural number and denote by Z_s the number of cycles of length s displayed by the phase space of f. Then it holds for any $d \in \mathbb{N}$*

$$Z_d = \begin{cases} \dfrac{2^d - \sum_{j \in D(d) \setminus d} Z_j}{d} & \text{if } d \in D(t) \\ 0 \text{ if } d \notin D(t) \end{cases}$$

Proof. See Theorem 132 in Delgado-Eckert (2008). ∎

Theorem 47. *Let $\mathbb{F}_2$ be the finite field with two elements, $f \in MF_n^n(\mathbb{F}_2)$ a* Boolean *coupled monomial dynamical system and $G_f = (V_f, E_f, \pi_f)$ its dependency graph. f is a fixed point system if and only if the loop number of each nontrivial strongly connected component of G_f is equal to* 1.

Proof. This result was proved in Colón-Reyes et al. (2004), see Theorem 6.1. An alternative proof is presented in Delgado-Eckert (2009a), Theorem 6. ∎

Remark 48. *As opposed to the previous two theorems, the latter theorem does not require that G_f is strongly connected. This feature allows us to solve the stabilization problem (see Section 3.3) for a broader class of monomial control systems (see Definition 54 in Section 3.2).*

Lemma 49. *Let $G = (V_G, E_G, \pi_G)$ be a strongly connected digraph such that V_G is nontrivial. Furthermore, let $t := \mathcal{L}_G(V_G) > 0$ be its loop number. For any $a, b \in V_G$ the relation $\approx$ defined by*

$$a \approx b :\Leftrightarrow \exists \text{ a sequence } a \rightsquigarrow_{\alpha t} b \text{ with } \alpha \in \mathbb{N}_0$$

is an equivalence relation called loop equivalence. *The loop equivalence class of an arbitrary vertex $a \in V_G$ is denoted by $\widetilde{a}$. Moreover, the partition of V_G defined by the loop equivalence $\approx$ contains exactly t loop equivalence classes.*

Proof. See the proofs of Lemma 4.6 and Lemma 4.7 in Colón-Reyes et al. (2004). ∎

Definition 50. *Let $G = (V_G, E_G, \pi_G)$ be a digraph, $a \in V_G$ an arbitrary vertex and $m \in \mathbb{N}$ a natural number. Then the set*

$$N_m(a) := \{b \in V_G : \exists\, a \rightsquigarrow_m b\}$$

is called the set of neighbors of order m.

Remark 51. *From the definitions it is clear that*

$$\widetilde{a} = \bigcup_{\alpha \in \mathbb{N}_0} N_{\alpha t}(a)$$

Theorem 52. *Let $G = (V_G, E_G, \pi_G)$ be a strongly connected digraph such that V_G is nontrivial. Furthermore, let $t := \mathcal{L}_G(V_G) > 0$ be its loop number and $\widetilde{a} \subseteq V_G$ an arbitrary loop equivalence class of V_G. Then for any $b, b' \in \widetilde{a}$ the following holds*

1. *$N_m(b) \cap N_{m'}(b') = \emptyset$ for $m, m' \in \mathbb{N}$ such that $1 \leq m, m' < t$ and $m \neq m'$.*
2. *$N_m(b) \cap \widetilde{a} = \emptyset$ for $m \in \mathbb{N}$ such that $1 \leq m < t$.*
3. *For every fixed $m \in \mathbb{N}$ such that $1 \leq m \leq t$ $\exists\, c \in V_G : \bigcup_{b \in \widetilde{a}} N_m(b) = \widetilde{c}$.*

Proof. See Theorem 111 in Delgado-Eckert (2008). ∎

Remark 53. *It is worth mentioning that since V_G is strongly connected and nontrivial, $N_m(b) \neq \emptyset$ $\forall\, m \in \mathbb{N}, b \in V_G$. Moreover, from (1) in the previous theorem it follows easily*

$$\left(\bigcup_{b \in \widetilde{a}} N_m(b)\right) \cap \left(\bigcup_{b \in \widetilde{a}} N_{m'}(b)\right) = \emptyset \text{ for } m, m' \in \mathbb{N} \text{ such that } 1 \leq m, m' < t \text{ and } m \neq m'$$

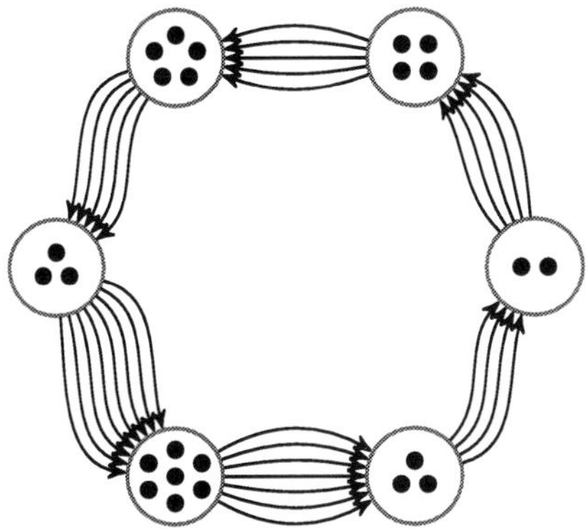

Fig. 1. Strongly connected dependency graph $G_f = (V_f, E_f, \pi_f)$ with loop number $\mathcal{L}_{G_f}(V_f) = 6$ of a 24-dimensional Boolean monomial dynamical system $f \in MF_{24}^{24}(\mathbb{F}_2)$. Circles (blue) demarcate each of the six loop equivalence classes. Essentially, the dependency graph is a closed path of length 6.

and because of (2) in the previous theorem clearly

$$\widetilde{a} = \bigcup_{b \in \widetilde{a}} N_t(b)$$

Given one loop equivalence class $\widetilde{a} \subseteq V_G$, the set of all the t loop equivalence classes can be ordered in the following manner

$$\widetilde{a}_i := \widetilde{a},\ \widetilde{a}_{i+1} = \bigcup_{b \in \widetilde{a}_i} N_1(b), ...\widetilde{a}_{i+j} = \bigcup_{b \in \widetilde{a}_i} N_j(b), ...\widetilde{a}_{i+t-1} = \bigcup_{b \in \widetilde{a}_i} N_{t-1}(b)$$

For any $c \in \bigcup_{b \in \widetilde{a}_i} N_{t-1}(b)$ it must hold $N_1(c) \subseteq \widetilde{a}_i$ (if $N_1(c) \cap \widetilde{a}_j \neq \emptyset$ with $j \neq i$, then $\widetilde{a}_i = \widetilde{a}_j$). Thus, the graph G can be visualized as (see Fig. 1)

$$\widetilde{a}_i \rightrightarrows \widetilde{a}_{i+1} \rightrightarrows \cdots \rightrightarrows \widetilde{a}_{i+j} \rightrightarrows \widetilde{a}_{(i+j+1)\ mod\ t} \rightrightarrows ... \rightrightarrows \widetilde{a}_{i+t-1} \rightrightarrows \widetilde{a}_{(i+t)\ mod\ t}$$

Due to the fact $\widetilde{a} = \bigcup_{b \in \widetilde{a}} N_t(b)\ \forall\ a \in V_G$, we can conclude that the claims of the previous lemma still hold if the sequence lengths m and m' are replaced by the more general lengths $\lambda t + m$ and $\lambda' t + m'$, where $\lambda, \lambda' \in \mathbb{N}$.

3.2 Boolean monomial control systems: Control theoretic questions studied

We start this section with the formal definition of a time invariant monomial control system over a finite field. Using the results stated in the previous section, we provide a very compact nomenclature for such systems. After further elucidations, and, in particular, after providing the formal definition of a monomial feedback controller, we clearly state the main control theoretic problem to be studied in Section 3.3 of this chapter.

Definition 54. *Let $\mathbb{F}_q$ be a finite field, $n \in \mathbb{N}$ a natural number and $m \in \mathbb{N}_0$ a nonnegative integer. A mapping $g : \mathbb{F}_q^n \times \mathbb{F}_q^m \to \mathbb{F}_q^n$ is called* time invariant monomial control system over $\mathbb{F}_q$ *if for* *every* $i \in \{1, ..., n\}$ *there are two tuples* $(A_{i1}, ..., A_{in}) \in E_q^n$ *and* $(B_{i1}, ..., B_{im}) \in E_q^m$ *such that*

$$g_i(x,u) = x_1^{A_{i1}} ... x_n^{A_{in}} u_1^{B_{i1}} ... u_m^{B_{im}} \ \forall \ (x,u) \in \mathbb{F}_q^n \times \mathbb{F}_q^m$$

Remark 55. *In the case* $m = 0$, *we have* $\mathbb{F}_q^m = \mathbb{F}_q^0 = \{()\}$ *(the set containing the empty tuple) and thus* $\mathbb{F}_q^n \times \mathbb{F}_q^m = \mathbb{F}_q^n \times \mathbb{F}_q^0 = \mathbb{F}_q^n \times \{()\} = \mathbb{F}_q^n$. *In other words,* g *is a monomial dynamical system over* $\mathbb{F}_q$. *From now on we will refer to a time invariant monomial control system over* $\mathbb{F}_q$ *as monomial control system over* $\mathbb{F}_q$.

Definition 56. *Let* X *be a nonempty finite set and* $n, l \in \mathbb{N}$ *natural numbers. The set of all functions* $f : X^l \to X^n$ *is denoted with* $F_l^n(X)$.

Definition 57. *Let* $\mathbb{F}_q$ *be a finite field and* $l, m, n \in \mathbb{N}$ *natural numbers. Furthermore, let* E_q *be the exponents semiring of* $\mathbb{F}_q$ *and* $M(n \times l; E_q)$ *the set of* $n \times l$ *matrices with entries in* E_q. *Consider the map*

$$\begin{aligned} \Gamma \ : \ & F_m^l(\mathbb{F}_q) \times M(n \times l; E_q) \to F_m^n(\mathbb{F}_q) \\ (f, A) & \mapsto \Gamma_A(f) \end{aligned}$$

where $\Gamma_A(f)$ *is defined for every* $x \in \mathbb{F}_q^m$ *and* $i \in \{1, ..., n\}$ *by*

$$\Gamma_A(f)(x)_i := f_1(x)^{A_{i1}} ... f_l(x)^{A_{il}}$$

We denote the mapping $\Gamma_A(f) \in F_m^n(\mathbb{F}_q)$ *simply* Af.

Remark 58. *Let* $l = m$, $id \in F_m^m(\mathbb{F}_q)$ *be the identity map (i.e.* $id_i(x) = x_i \ \forall \ i \in \{1, ..., m\}$*) and* $A \in M(n \times m; E_q)$ *Then the following relationship between the mapping* $Aid \in F_m^n(\mathbb{F}_q)$ *and any* $f \in F_m^m(\mathbb{F}_q)$ *holds*

$$Aid(f(x)) = Af(x) \ \forall \ x \in \mathbb{F}_q^m$$

Remark 59. *Consider the case* $l = m = n$. *For every monomial dynamical system* $f \in MF_n^n(\mathbb{F}_q) \subset F_n^n(\mathbb{F}_q)$ *with corresponding matrix* $F := \Psi^{-1}(f) \in M(n \times n; E_q)$ *it holds* $Fid = f$. *On the other hand, given a matrix* $F \in M(n \times n; E_q)$ *we have* $\Psi^{-1}(Fid) = F$. *Moreover, the map* $\Gamma : F_n^n(\mathbb{F}_q) \times M(n \times n; E_q) \to F_n^n(\mathbb{F}_q)$ *is an action of the multiplicative monoid* $M(n \times n; E_q)$ *on the set* $F_n^n(\mathbb{F}_q)$. *It holds namely, that*[12] $If = f \ \forall \ f \in F_n^n(\mathbb{F}_q)$ *(which is trivial) and* $(A \cdot B)f = A(Bf) \ \forall \ f \in F_n^n(\mathbb{F}_q)$, $A, B \in M(n \times n; E_q)$. *To see this, consider*

$$\begin{aligned} ((A \cdot B)f)_i(x) &= f_1(x)^{(A \cdot B)_{i1}} ... f_n(x)^{(A \cdot B)_{in}} = \prod_{j=1}^{n} f_j(x)^{(A_{i1} \bullet B_{1j} \oplus ... \oplus A_{in} \bullet B_{nj})} \\ &= (Aid \circ Bid)_i(f(x)) = (Aid)_i(Bid(f(x))) \\ &= (Aid)_i(fB(x)) = (A(Bf))_i(x) \end{aligned}$$

where $id \in F_n^n(\mathbb{F}_q)$ *is the identity map (i.e.* $id_i(x) = x_i \ \forall \ i \in \{1, ..., n\}$*). (cf. with the proof of Theorem 29). As a consequence,* $MF_n^n(\mathbb{F}_q)$ *is the orbit in* $F_n^n(\mathbb{F}_q)$ *of* id *under the monoid* $M(n \times n; E_q)$. *In particular (see Theorem 29), we have*

$$(\Gamma \cdot G)id = F(Gid) = f \circ g$$

[12] $I \in M(n \times n; E_q)$ denotes the identity matrix.

where $g \in MF_n^n(\mathbb{F}_q)$ *is another monomial dynamical system with corresponding matrix* $G := \Psi^{-1}(g) \in M(n \times n; E_q)$.

Lemma 60. *Let* $\mathbb{F}_q$ *be a finite field,* $n \in \mathbb{N}$ *a natural number and* $m \in \mathbb{N}_0$ *a nonnegative integer. Furthermore, let* $id \in F_{(n+m)}^{(n+m)}(\mathbb{F}_q)$ *be the identity map (i.e.* $id_i(x) = x_i \; \forall \; i \in \{1, ..., n+m\}$*) and* $g : \mathbb{F}_q^n \times \mathbb{F}_q^m \to \mathbb{F}_q^n$ *a monomial control system over* F_q*. Then there are matrices* $A \in M(n \times n; E_q)$ *and* $B \in M(n \times m; E_q)$ *such that*

$$((A|B)id)(x,u) = g(x,u) \; \forall \; (x,u) \in \mathbb{F}_q^n \times \mathbb{F}_q^m$$

where $(A|B) \in M(n \times (n+m); E_q)$ *is the matrix that results by writing A and B side by side. In this sense we denote g as the monomial control system* (A, B) *with n state variables and m control inputs.*

Proof. This follows immediately from the previous definitions. ∎

Remark 61. *If the matrix* $B \in M(n \times m; E_q)$ *is equal to the zero matrix, then g is called a* control system with no controls. *In contrast to linear control systems (see the previous sections and also Sontag (1998)), when the input vector* $u \in \mathbb{F}_q^m$ *satisfies*

$$u = \vec{1} := (1, ..., 1)^t \in \mathbb{F}_q^m$$

then no control input is being applied on the system, i.e. the monomial dynamical system over $\mathbb{F}_q$

$$\begin{aligned} \sigma \; &: \; \mathbb{F}_q^n \to \mathbb{F}_q^n \\ x &\mapsto g(x, \vec{1}) \end{aligned}$$

satisfies

$$\sigma(x) = ((A|0)id)(x,u) \; \forall \; (x,u) \in \mathbb{F}_q^n \times \mathbb{F}_q^m$$

where $0 \in M(n \times m; E_q)$ *stands for the zero matrix.*

Definition 62. *Let* $\mathbb{F}_q$ *be a finite field and* $n, m \in \mathbb{N}$ *natural numbers. A* monomial feedback controller *is a mapping*

$$f : \mathbb{F}_q^n \to \mathbb{F}_q^m$$

such that for every $i \in \{1, ..., m\}$ *there is a tuple* $(F_{i1}, ..., F_{in}) \in E_q^n$ *such that*

$$f_i(x) = x_1^{F_{i1}} ... x_n^{F_{in}} \; \forall \; x \in \mathbf{F}_q^n$$

Remark 63. *We exclude in the definition of monomial feedback controller the possibility that one of the functions* f_i *is equal to the zero function. The reason for this will become apparent in the next remark (see below).*

Now we are able to formulate the first control theoretic problem to be addressed in this section:

Problem 64. *Let* $\mathbb{F}_q$ *be a finite field and* $n, m \in \mathbb{N}$ *natural numbers. Given a monomial control system* $g : \mathbb{F}_q^n \times \mathbb{F}_q^m \to \mathbb{F}_q^n$ *with completely observable state, design a monomial state feedback controller* $f : \mathbb{F}_q^n \to \mathbb{F}_q^m$ *such that the closed-loop system*

$$\begin{aligned} h \; &: \; \mathbb{F}_q^n \to \mathbb{F}_q^n \\ x &\mapsto g(x, f(x)) \end{aligned}$$

has a desired period number and cycle structure of its phase space. What properties has g to fulfill for this task to be accomplished?

Remark 65. *Note that every component*

$$\begin{aligned} h_i \ : \ \mathbb{F}_q^n &\to \mathbb{F}_q, \ i = 1, ..., n \\ x &\mapsto g_i(x, f(x)) \end{aligned}$$

is a nonzero monic monomial function, i.e. the mapping $h : \mathbb{F}_q^n \to \mathbb{F}_q^n$ *is a monomial dynamical system over* $\mathbb{F}_q$. *Remember that we excluded in the definition of monomial feedback controller the possibility that one of the functions* f_i *is equal to the zero function. Indeed, the only effect of a component* $f_i \equiv 0$ *in the closed-loop system h would be to possibly generate a component* $h_j \equiv 0$. *As explained in Remark 28 of Section 3.1, this component would not play a crucial role determining the long term dynamics of h.*
Due to the monomial structure of h, the results presented in Section 3.1 of this chapter can be used to analyze the dynamical properties of h. Moreover, the following identity holds

$$h = (A + B \cdot F)id$$

where $F \in M(m \times n; E_q)$ *is the corresponding matrix of f (see Remark 30),* (A, B) *are the matrices in Lemma 60 and* $id \in F_n^n(\mathbb{F}_q)$. *To see this, consider the mapping*

$$\begin{aligned} \mu \ : \ \mathbb{F}_q^m &\to \mathbb{F}_q^n \\ u &\mapsto g(\vec{1}, u) \end{aligned}$$

where $\vec{1} \in \mathbb{F}_q^n$. *From the definition of g it follows that* $\mu \in MF_m^n(\mathbb{F}_q)$. *Now, since* $f \in MF_n^m(\mathbb{F}_q)$, *by Remark 30 we have for the composition* $\mu \circ f : \mathbb{F}_q^n \to \mathbb{F}_q^n$

$$\mu \circ f = (B \cdot F)id$$

Now its easy to see

$$h = (A + B \cdot F)id$$

The most significant results proved in Colón-Reyes et al. (2004), Delgado-Eckert (2008) concern Boolean monomial dynamical systems with a strongly connected dependency graph. Therefore, in the next section we will focus on the solution of Problem 64 for Boolean monomial control systems $g : \mathbb{F}_2^n \times \mathbb{F}_2^m \to \mathbb{F}_2^n$ with the property that the mapping

$$\begin{aligned} \sigma \ : \ \mathbb{F}_2^n &\to \mathbb{F}_2^n \\ x &\mapsto g(x, \vec{1}) \end{aligned}$$

has a strongly connected dependency graph. Such systems are called *strongly dependent monomial control systems*. If we drop this requirement, we would not be able to use Theorems 45 and 46 to analyze h regarding its cycle structure. However, if we are only interested in forcing the period number of h to be equal to 1, we can still use Theorem 47 (see Remark 48). This feature will be exploited in Section 3.3, when we study the *stabilization problem*.
Although the above representation

$$h = (A + B \cdot F)id$$

of the closed loop system displays a striking structural similarity with linear control systems and linear feedback laws, our approach will completely differ from the well known "Pole-Assignment" method.

3.3 State feedback controller design for Boolean monomial control systems

Our goal in this section is to illustrate how the loop number, a parameter that, as we saw, characterizes the dynamic properties of Boolean monomial dynamical systems, can be exploited for the synthesis of suitable feedback controllers. To this end, we will demonstrate the basic ideas using a very simple subclass of systems that allow for a graphical elucidation of the rationale behind our approach. The structural similarity demonstrated in Remark 53 then enables the extension of the results to more general cases. A rigorous implementation of the ideas developed here can be found in Delgado-Eckert (2009b).

As explained in Remark 53, a Boolean monomial dynamical system with a strongly connected non-trivial dependency graph can be visualized as a simple cycle of loop-equivalence classes (see Fig. 1). In the simplest case, each loop-equivalence class only contains one node and the dependency graph is a closed path. A first step towards solving Problem 64 for strongly dependent Boolean monomial control systems $g : \mathbb{F}_2^n \times \mathbb{F}_2^m \to \mathbb{F}_2^n$ would be to consider the simpler subclass of problems in which the mapping

$$\begin{aligned} \sigma \; &: \; \mathbb{F}_2^n \to \mathbb{F}_2^n \\ x &\mapsto g(x, \vec{1}) \end{aligned}$$

simply has a closed path of length n as its dependency graph (see Fig. 2 a for an example in the case $n = 6$). By the definition of dependency graph and after choosing any monomial feedback controller $f : \mathbb{F}_2^n \to \mathbb{F}_2^m$, it becomes apparent that the dependency graph of the closed-loop system

$$\begin{aligned} h_f \; &: \; \mathbb{F}_2^n \to \mathbb{F}_2^n \\ x &\mapsto g(x, f(x)) \end{aligned}$$

arises from adding new edges to the dependency graph of σ. Since we assumed that the dependency graph of σ is just a closed path, adding new edges to it can only generate new closed paths of length in the range $1, \ldots, n-1$. By Corollary 41, we immediately see that the loop number of the modified dependency graph (i.e., the dependency graph of h_f) must be a divisor of the original loop number. This result is telling us that no matter how complicated we choose a monomial feedback controller $f : \mathbb{F}_2^n \to \mathbb{F}_2^m$, the closed loop system h_f will have a dependency graph with a loop number $\mathcal{L}'$ which divides the loop number $\mathcal{L}$ of the dependency graph of σ. This is all we can achieve in terms of *loop number assignment*. When a system allows for assignment to all values out of the set $D(\mathcal{L})$, we call it *completely loop number controllable*. We just proved this limitation for systems in which σ has a simple closed path as its dependency graph. However, due to the structural similarity between such systems and strongly dependent systems (see Remark 53), this result remains valid in the general case where σ has a strongly connected dependency graph.

Let us simplify the scenario a bit more and assume that the system g has only one control variable u (i.e., $g : \mathbb{F}_2^n \times \mathbb{F}_2 \to \mathbb{F}_2^n$) and that this variable appears in only one component function, say g_k. As before, assume σ has a simple closed path as its dependency graph. Under these circumstances, we choose the following monomial feedback controllers: $f_i : \mathbb{F}_2^n \to \mathbb{F}_2$,

$f_i(x) := x_i, i = 1, ..., n$. When we look at the closed-loop systems

$$\begin{aligned} h_{f_i} &: \mathbb{F}_2^n \to \mathbb{F}_2^n \\ x &\mapsto g(x, f_i(x)) \end{aligned}$$

and their dependency graphs, we realize that the dependency graph of h_{f_i} corresponds to the one of σ with one single additional edge. Depending on the value of i under consideration, this additional edge adds a closed path of length l in the range $l = 1, .., n-1$ to the dependency graph of σ. In Figures 2 b-e, we see all the possibilities in the case of $n = \mathcal{L} = 6$, except for $l = 1$ (self-loop around the kth node).

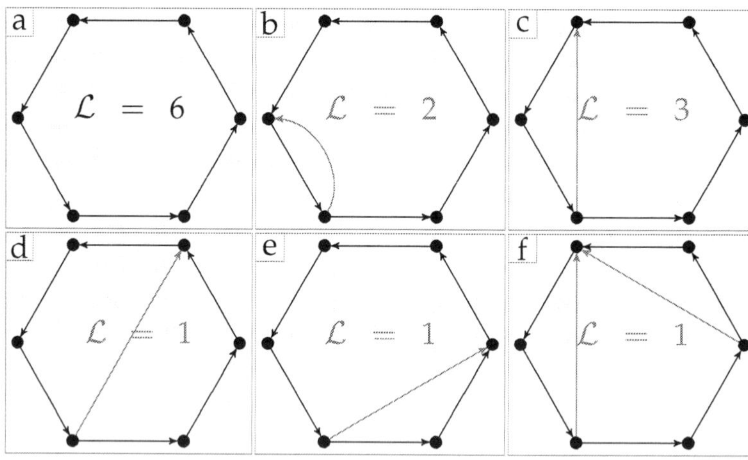

Fig. 2. Loop number assignment through the choice of different feeback controllers.

We realize that with only one control variable appearing in only one of the components of the system g, we can set the loop number of the closed-loop system h_{f_i} to be equal to any of the possible values (out of the set $D(\mathcal{L})$) by choosing among the feedback controllers f_i, $i = 1, ..., n$, defined above. This proves that the type of systems we are considering here are indeed completely loop number controllable. Moreover, as illustrated in Figure 2 f, if the control variable u would appear in another component function of g, we may loose the loop number controllability. Again, due to the structural similarity (see Remark 53), this complete loop number controllability statement is valid for strongly dependent systems.

In the light of Theorem 47 (see Remark 48), for the stabilization[13] problem we can consider *arbitrary* Boolean monomial control systems $g : \mathbb{F}_2^n \times \mathbb{F}_2^m \to \mathbb{F}_2^n$, maybe only requiring the obvious condition that the mapping σ is not already a fixed point system. Moreover, the statement of Theorem 47 is telling us that such a system will be *stabilizable* if and only if the component functions g_j depend in such a way on control variables u_i, that every strongly connected component of the dependency graph of σ can be forced into loop number one by incorporating suitable additional edges. This corresponds to the choice of a suitable feedback controller. The details and proof of this *stabilizability* statement as well as a brief description of a *stabilization procedure* can be found in Delgado-Eckert (2009b).

[13] Note that in contrast to the definition of stability introduced in Subsection 1.2.1, in this context we refer to stabilizability as the property of a control system to become a fixed point system through the choice of a suitable feedback controller.

4. Conclusions

In this chapter we considered discrete event systems within the paradigm of algebraic state space models. As we pointed out, traditional approaches to system analysis and controller synthesis that were developed for continuous and discrete time dynamical systems may not be suitable for the same or similar tasks in the case of discrete event systems. Thus, one of the main challenges in the field of discrete event systems is the development of appropriate mathematical techniques. Finding new mathematical indicators that characterize the dynamic properties of a discrete event system represents a promising approach to the development of new analysis and controller synthesis methods.

We have demonstrated how mathematical objects or magnitudes such as invariant polynomials, elementary divisor polynomials, and the loop number can play the role of the aforementioned indicators, characterizing the dynamic properties of certain classes of discrete event systems. Moreover, we have shown how these objects or magnitudes can be used to effectively address controller synthesis problems for linear modular systems over the finite field F_2 and for Boolean monomial systems.

We anticipate that the future development of the discrete event systems field will not only comprise the derivation of new mathematical methods, but also will be concerned with the development of efficient algorithms and their implementation.

5. References

Baccelli, F., Cohen, G., Olsder, G. & Quadrat, J.-P. (1992). *Synchronisation and linearity*, Wiley.

Booth, T. L. (1967). *Sequential Machines and Automata Theory*, Wiley, New York.

Brualdi, R. A. & Ryser, H. J. (1991). *Combinatorial matrix theory*, Vol. 39 of *Encyclopedia of Mathematics and its Applications*, Cambridge University Press, Cambridge.

Caillaud, B., Darondeau, P., Lavagno, L. & Xie, X. (2002). *Synthesis and Control of Discrete Event Systems*, Springer.

Cassandras, C. G. & Lafortune, S. (2006). *Introduction to Discrete Event Systems*, Springer-Verlag New York, Inc., Secaucus, NJ, USA.

Colón-Reyes, O., Jarrah, A. S., Laubenbacher, R. & Sturmfels, B. (2006). Monomial dynamical systems over finite fields, *Complex Systems* 16(4): 333–342.

Colón-Reyes, O., Laubenbacher, R. & Pareigis, B. (2004). Boolean monomial dynamical systems, *Ann. Comb.* 8(4): 425–439.

Delgado-Eckert, E. (2008). *Monomial Dynamical and Control Systems over a Finite Field and Applications to Agent-based Models in Immunology*, PhD thesis, Technische Universität München, Munich, Germany. Available online at http://mediatum2.ub.tum.de/doc/645326/document.pdf.

Delgado-Eckert, E. (2009a). An algebraic and graph theoretic framework to study monomial dynamical systems over a finite field, *Complex Systems* 18(3): 307–328.

Delgado-Eckert, E. (2009b). Boolean monomial control systems, *Mathematical and Computer Modelling of Dynamical Systems* 15(2): 107 – 137.
URL: *http://dx.doi.org/10.1080/13873950902808594*

Delgado-Eckert, E. (2009c). Reverse engineering time discrete finite dynamical systems: A feasible undertaking?, *PLoS ONE* 4(3): e4939.

Denardo, E. V. (1977). Periods of Connected Networks and Powers of Nonnegative Matrices, *Mathematics of Operations Research* 2(1): 20–24.

Dicesare, F. & Zhou, M. (1993). *Petri Net Synthesis for Discrete Event Control of Manufacturing Systems*, Kluwer.

Germundsson, R. (1995). *Symbolic Systems — Theory, Computation and Applications*, PhD thesis, Linköping.

Gill, A. (1966). *Linear Sequential Circuits: Analysis, Synthesis, and Applications*, McGraw-Hill, New York.

Gill, A. (1969). Linear modular systems, *in* L. A. Zadeh & E. Polak (eds), *System Theory*, McGraw-Hill, New York.

Hopcroft, J. & Ullman, J. (1979). Introduction to automata theory, languages and computation, *Addison-Wesley, Reading* .

Iordache, M. V. & Antsaklis, P. J. (2006). *Supervisory Control of Concurrent Systems: A Petri Net Structural Approach*, Birkhauser, Boston.

Kailath, T. (1980). *Linear Systems*, Prentice Hall, Englewood Cliffs.

Kumar, P. R. & Varaiya, P. P. (1995). *Discrete Event Systems, Manufacturing Systems, and Communication Networks*, Springer Verlag, NY.

Lancaster, P. & Tismenetsky, M. (1985). *The theory of matrices*, Computer Science and Applied Mathematics, second edn, Academic Press Inc., Orlando, FL.

Le Borgne, M., Benveniste, A. & Le Guernic, P. (1991). Polynomial dynamical systems over finite fields, *in* G. Jacob & F. Lamnabhi-Lagarrigue (eds), *Lecture Notes in Computer Science*, Vol. 165, Springer, Berlin, pp. 212–222.

Lidl, R. & Niederreiter, H. (1997). *Finite fields*, Vol. 20 of *Encyclopedia of Mathematics and its Applications*, second edn, Cambridge University Press, Cambridge. With a foreword by P. M. Cohn.

Murata, T. (1989). Petri nets: Properties, analysis and applications, *Proceedings of the IEEE* 77(4): 541 –580.

Plantin, J., Gunnarsson, J. & Germundsson, R. (1995). Symbolic algebraic discrete systems theory-applied to a fighter aircraft, *Decision and Control, IEEE Conference on*, Vol. 2, pp. 1863 –1864 vol.2.

Pták, V. & Sedlaček, I. (1958). On the index of imprimitivity of nonnegative matrices, *Czechoslovak Math. J* 8(83): 496–501.

Ramadge, P. & Wonham, W. (1989). The control of discrete event systems, *Proceedings of the IEEE* 77(1): 81 –98.

Reger, J. (2004). *Linear Systems over Finite Fields – Modeling, Analysis, and Synthesis*, PhD thesis, Lehrstuhl für Regelungstechnik, Friedrich-Alexander-Universität Erlangen-Nürnberg.

Reger, J. & Schmidt, K. (2004). A finite field framework for modelling, analysis and control of finite state automata, *Mathematical and Computer Modelling of Dynamical Systems* 10(3–4): 253–285.

Smale, S. (1998). Mathematical problems of the next century, *The Mathematical Intelligencer* 20(2): 7–15.

Sontag, E. D. (1998). *Mathematical control theory*, Vol. 6 of *Texts in Applied Mathematics*, second edn, Springer-Verlag, New York. Deterministic finite-dimensional systems.

Wolovich, W. A. (1974). *Linear Multivariable Systems*, Springer, New York.

Young, S. & Garg, V. (1993). On self-stabilizing systems: an approach to the specification and design of fault tolerant systems, *Decision and Control, IEEE Conference on*, pp. 1200 –1205 vol.2.

26

Discrete Deterministic and Stochastic Dynamical Systems with Delay - Applications

Mihaela Neamţu and Dumitru Opriş
West University of Timişoara
Romania

1. Introduction

The dynamical systems with discrete time and delay are obtained by the discretization of the systems of differential equations with delay, or by modeling some processes in which the time variable is $n \in \mathbb{N}$ and the state variables at the moment $n-m$, where $m \in \mathbb{N}, m \geq 1$, are taken into consideration.

The processes from this chapter have as mathematical model a system of equations given by:

$$x_{n+1} = f(x_n, x_{n-m}, \alpha), \tag{1}$$

where $x_n = x(n) \in \mathbb{R}^p$, $x_{n-m} = x(n-m) \in \mathbb{R}^p$, $\alpha \in \mathbb{R}$ and $f : \mathbb{R}^p \times \mathbb{R}^p \times \mathbb{R} \to \mathbb{R}^p$ is a seamless function, $n, m \in \mathbb{N}$ with $m \geq 1$. The properties of function f ensure that there is solution for system (1). The system of equations (1) is called *system with discrete-time and delay*. The analysis of the processes described by system (1) follows these steps.

Step 1. Modeling the process.

Step 2. Determining the fixed points for (1).

Step 3. Analyzing a fixed point of (1) by studying the sign of the characteristic equation of the linearized equation in the neighborhood of the fixed point.

Step 4. Determining the value $\alpha = \alpha_0$ for which the characteristic equation has the roots $\mu_1(\alpha_0) = \mu(\alpha_0)$, $\mu_2(\alpha_0) = \overline{\mu}(\alpha_0)$ with their absolute value equal to 1, and the other roots with their absolute value less than 1 and the following formulas:

$$\left.\frac{d|\mu(\alpha)|}{d\alpha}\right|_{\alpha=\alpha_0} \neq 0, \qquad \mu(\alpha_0)^k \neq 1,\ k = 1,2,3,4$$

hold.

Step 5. Determining the local center manifold $W^c_{loc}(0)$:

$$y = zq + \overline{z}\,\overline{q} + \frac{1}{2}w_{20}z^2 + w_{11}z\overline{z} + \frac{1}{2}w_{02}\overline{z}^2 + \dots$$

where $z = x_1 + ix_2$, with $(x_1, x_2) \in V_1 \subset \mathbb{R}^2$, $0 \in V_1$, q an eigenvector corresponding to the eigenvalue $\mu(0)$ and w_{20}, w_{11}, w_{02} are vectors that can be determined by the invariance condition of the manifold $W^c_{loc}(0)$ with respect to the transformation $x_{n-m} = x^1, ..., x_n = x^m$, $x_{n+1} = x^{m+1}$. The restriction of system (1) to the manifold $W^c_{loc}(0)$ is:

$$z_{n+1} = \mu(\alpha_0)z_n + \frac{1}{2}g_{20}z_n^2 + g_{11}z_n\bar{z}_n + \frac{1}{2}g_{02}\bar{z}_n^2 + g_{21}z_n^2\bar{z}_n/2, \tag{2}$$

where $g_{20}, g_{11}, g_{02}, g_{21}$ are the coefficients obtained using the expansion in Taylor series including third-order terms of function f.
System (2) is topologically equivalent with the prototype of the 2-dimensional discrete dynamic system that characterizes the systems with a Neimark–Sacker bifurcation.

Step 6. Representing the orbits for system (1). The orbits of system (1) in the neighborhood of the fixed point x^* are given by:

$$x_n = x^* + z_n q + \bar{z}_n\bar{q} + \frac{1}{2}r_{20}z_n^2 + r_{11}z_n\bar{z}_n + \frac{1}{2}r_{02}\bar{z}_n^2 \tag{3}$$

where z_n is a solution of (2) and r_{20}, r_{11}, r_{02} are determined with the help of w_{20}, w_{11}, w_{02}.
The properties of orbit (3) are established using the Lyapunov coefficient $l_1(0)$. If $l_1(0) < 0$ then orbit (3) is a stable invariant closed curve (supercritical) and if $l_1(0) > 0$ then orbit (3) is an unstable invariant closed curve (subcritical).
The perturbed stochastic system corresponding to (1) is given by:

$$x_{n+1} = f(x_n, x_{n-m}, \alpha) + g(x_n, x_{n-m})\xi_n, \tag{4}$$

where $x_n = x_{0n}$, $n \in I = \{-m, -m+1, ..., -1, 0\}$ is the initial segment to be $\mathcal{F}_0$-measurable, and ξ_n is a random variable with $E(\xi_n) = 0$, $E(\xi_n^2) = \sigma > 0$ and α is a real parameter.
System (4) is called discrete-time stochastic system with delay.
For the stochastic discrete-time system with delay, the stability in mean and the stability in square mean for the stationary state are done.
This chapter is organized as follows. In Section 2 the discrete-time deterministic and stochastic dynamical systems are defined. In Section 3 the Neimark-Sacker bifurcation for the deterministic and stochastic Internet control congestion with discrete-time and delay is studied. Section 4 presents the deterministic and stochastic economic games with discrete-time and delay. In Section 5, the deterministic and stochastic Kaldor model with discrete-time is analyzed. Finally some conclusions and future prospects are provided.
For the models from the above sections we establish the existence of the Neimark-Sacker bifurcation and the normal form. Then, the invariant curve is studied. We also associate the perturbed stochastic system and we analyze the stability in square mean of the solutions of the linearized system in the fixed point of the analyzed system.

2. Discrete-time dynamical systems

2.1 The definition of the discrete-time, deterministic and stochastic systems

We intuitively describe the dynamical system concept. We suppose that a physical or biologic or economic system etc., can have different states represented by the elements of a set S. These states depend on the parameter t called *time*. If the system is in the state $s_1 \in S$, at the moment t_1 and passes to the moment t_2 in the state $s_2 \in S$, then we denote this transformation by:

$$\Phi_{t_1,t_2}(s_1) = s_2$$

and $\Phi_{t_1,t_2} : S \to S$ is called *evolution operator*. In the deterministic evolutive processes the evolution operator Φ_{t_1,t_2}, satisfies the Chapman-Kolmogorov law:

$$\Phi_{t_3,t_2} \circ \Phi_{t_2,t_1} = \Phi_{t_3,t_1}, \quad \Phi_{t,t} = id_S.$$

For a fixed state $s_0 \in S$, application $\Phi : R \to S$, defined by $t \to s_t = \Phi_t(s_0)$, determines a curve in set S that represents the evolution of state s_0 when time varies from $-\infty$ to ∞.
An evolutive system in the general form is given by a subset of $S \times S$ that is the graphic of the system:

$$F_i(t_1, t_2, s_1, s_2) = 0, \quad i = 1..n$$

where $F_i : R^2 \times S \to R$.
In what follows, the arithmetic space R^m is considered to be the states'space of a system, and the function Φ is a C^r-class differentiable application.
An *explicit differential dynamical system of C^r class,* is the homomorphism of groups Φ : $(R, +) \to (Diff^r(R^m), \circ)$ so that the application $R \times R^m \to R^m$ defined by $(t, x) \to \Phi(t)(x)$ is a differentiable of C^r-class and for all $x \in R^m$ fixed, the corresponding application $\Phi(x) : R \to R^m$ is C^{r+1}-class.
A differentiable dynamical system on R^m describes the evolution in continuous time of a process. Due to the fact that it is difficult to analyze the continuous evolution of the state x_0, the analysis is done at the regular periods of time, for example at $t = -n, ..., -1, 0, 1, ..., n$.
If we denote by $\Phi_1 = f$, we have:

$$\Phi_1(x_0) = f(x_0), \Phi_2(x_0) = f^{(2)}(x_0), ..., \Phi_n(x_0) = f^{(n)}(x_0),$$
$$\Phi_{-1}(x_0) = f^{(-1)}(x_0), ..., \Phi_{-n}(x_0) = f^{(-n)}(x_0),$$

where $f^{(2)} = f \circ f, ... ,f^{(n)} = f \circ ... \circ f, f^{-(n)} = f^{(-1)} \circ ... \circ f^{(-1)}$.
Thus, Φ is determined by the diffeomorphism $f = \Phi_1$.
A C^r-class differential dynamical system with discrete time on R^m, is the homomorphism of groups $\Phi : (Z, +) \to (Diff^r(R^m), \circ)$.
The orbit through $x_0 \in R^m$ of a dynamical system with discrete-time is:

$$O_f(x_0) = \{..., f^{-(n)}(x_0), ..., f^{(-1)}(x_0), x_0, f(x_0), ..., f^{(n)}(x_0), ..\} = \{f^{(n)}(x_0)\}_{n \in Z}.$$

Thus $O_f(x_0)$ represents a sequences of images of the studied process at regular periods of time.
For the study of a dynamical system with discrete time, the structure of the orbits'set is analyzed. For a dynamical system with discrete time with the initial condition $x_0 \in R^m (m = 1, 2, 3)$ we can represent graphically the points of the form $x_n = f^n(x_0)$ for n iterations of the thousandth or millionth order. Thus, a visual geometrical image of the orbits'set structure is created, which suggests some properties regarding the particularities of the system. Then, these properties have to be approved or disproved by theoretical or practical arguments.
An *explicit dynamical system with discrete time* has the form:

$$x_{n+1} = f(x_{n-p}, x_n), \quad n \in N, \tag{5}$$

where $f : R^m \times R^m \to R^m$, $x_n \in R^m$, $p \in N$ is fixed, and the initial conditions are x_{-p}, x_{1-p}, ..., $x_0 \in R^m$.

For system (5), we use the change of variables $x^1 = x_{n-p}$, $x^2 = x_{n-(p-1)}, ..., x^p = x_{n-1}$, $x^{p+1} = x_n$, and we associate the application

$$F : (x^1, ..., x^{p+1}) \in \mathbb{R}^m \times ... \times \mathbb{R}^m \to \mathbb{R}^m \times ... \times \mathbb{R}^m$$

given by:

$$F : \begin{pmatrix} x^1 \\ \cdot \\ \cdot \\ x^p \\ x^{p+1} \end{pmatrix} \to \begin{pmatrix} x^2 \\ \cdot \\ \cdot \\ x^{p+1} \\ f(x^1, x^{p+1}) \end{pmatrix}.$$

Let $(\Omega, \mathcal{F})$ be a measurable space, where Ω is a set whose elements will be noted by ω and $\mathcal{F}$ is a $\sigma-$algebra of subsets of Ω. We denote by $\mathcal{B}(\mathbb{R})$ $\sigma-$algebra of Borelian subsets of $\mathbb{R}$. A *random variable* is a measurable function $X : \Omega \to \mathbb{R}$ with respect to the measurable spaces $(\Omega, \mathcal{F})$ and $(\mathbb{R}, \mathcal{B}(\mathbb{R}))$ (Kloeden et al., 1995).
A probability measure P on the measurable space $(\Omega, \mathcal{F})$ is a $\sigma-$additive function defined on $\mathcal{F}$ with values in $[0, 1]$ so that $P(\Omega) = 1$. The triplet $(\Omega, \mathcal{F}, P)$ is called a *probability space.*
An arbitrary family $\xi(n, \omega) = \xi(n)(\omega)$ of random variables, defined on Ω with values in $\mathbb{R}$, is called *stochastic process*. We denote $\xi(n, \omega) = \xi(n)$ for any $n \in \mathbb{N}$ and $\omega \in \Omega$. The functions $X(\cdot, \omega)$ are called the trajectories of $X(n)$. We use $E(\xi(n))$ for the mean value and $E(\xi(n)^2)$ the square mean value of $\xi(n)$ denoted by ξ_n.
The perturbed stochastic of system (5) is:

$$x_{n+1} = f(x_{n-p}, x_n) + g(x_n)\xi_n, \quad n \in \mathbb{N}$$

where $g : \mathbb{R}^n \to \mathbb{R}^n$ and ξ_n is a random variable which satisfies the conditions $E(\xi_n) = 0$ and $E(\xi_n^2) = \sigma > 0$.

2.2 Elements used for the study of the discrete-time dynamical systems

Consider the following discrete-time dynamical system defined on $\mathbb{R}^m$:

$$x_{n+1} = f(x_n), \quad n \in \mathbb{N} \tag{6}$$

where $f : \mathbb{R}^m \to \mathbb{R}^m$ is a C^r class function, called *vector field*.
Some information, regarding the behavior of (6) in the neighborhood of the fixed point, is obtained studying the associated linear discrete-time dynamical system.
Let $x_0 \in \mathbb{R}^m$ be a fixed point of (6). The system

$$u_{n+1} = Df(x_0)u_n, \quad n \in \mathbb{N}$$

where

$$Df(x_0) = \left(\frac{\partial f^i}{\partial x^j}\right)(x_0), \quad i, j = 1..m$$

is called *the linear discrete-time dynamical system* associated to (6) and the fixed point $x_0 = f(x_0)$. If the characteristic polynomial of $Df(x_0)$ does not have roots with their absolute values equal to 1, then x_0 is called a *hyperbolic fixed point*.
We have the following classification of the hyperbolic fixed points:

1. x_0 is a stable point if all characteristic exponents of $Df(x_0)$ have their absolute values less than 1.
2. x_0 is an unstable point if all characteristic exponents of $Df(x_0)$ have their absolute values greater than 1.
3. x_0 is a saddle point if a part of the characteristic exponents of $Df(x_0)$ have their absolute values less than 1 and the others have their absolute values greater than 1.
The orbit through $x_0 \in \mathbb{R}^m$ of a discrete-time dynamical system generated by $f : \mathbb{R}^m \to \mathbb{R}^m$ is *stable* if for any $\varepsilon > 0$ there exists $\delta(\varepsilon)$ so that for all $x \in B(x_0, \delta(\varepsilon))$, $d(f^n(x), f^n(x_0)) < \varepsilon$, for all $n \in \mathbb{N}$.
The orbit through $x_0 \in \mathbb{R}^m$ is *asymptotically stable* if there exists $\delta > 0$ so that for all $x \in B(x_0, \delta)$, $\lim_{n\to\infty} d(f^n(x), f^n(x_0)) = 0$.
If x_0 is a fixed point of f, the orbit is formed by x_0. In this case $O(x_0)$ is stable (asymptotically stable) if $d(f^n(x), x_0) < \varepsilon$, for all $n \in \mathbb{N}$ and $\lim_{n\to\infty} f^n(x) = x_0$.

Let $(\Omega, \mathcal{F}, P)$ be a probability space. The perturbed stochastic system of (6) is the following system:

$$x_{n+1} = f(x_n) + g(x_n)\xi_n$$

where ξ_n is a random variable that satisfies $E(\xi_n) = 0$, $E(\xi_n^2) = \sigma$ and $g(x_0) = 0$ with x_0 the fixed point of the system (6).
The linearized of the discrete stochastic dynamical system associated to (6) and the fixed point x_0 is:

$$u_{n+1} = Au_n + \xi_n Bu_n, \quad n \in \mathbb{N} \tag{7}$$

where

$$A = \left(\frac{\partial f^i}{\partial x^j}\right)(x_0), \qquad B = \left(\frac{\partial g^i}{\partial x^j}\right)(x_0), \quad i,j = 1..m.$$

We use $E(u_n) = E_n$, $E(u_n u_n^T) = V_n$, $u_n = (u_n^1, u_n^2, ..., u_n^m)^T$.
Proposition 2.1. (i) The mean values E_n satisfy the following system of equations:

$$E_{n+1} = AE_n, \quad n \in \mathbb{N} \tag{8}$$

(ii) The square mean values satisfy:

$$V_{n+1} = AV_nA^T + \sigma BV_nB^T, \quad n \in \mathbb{N} \tag{9}$$

Proof. (i) From (7) and $E(\xi_n) = 0$ we obtain (8).
(ii) Using (7) we have:

$$u_{n+1}u_{n+1}^T = Au_nu_n^TA^T + \xi_n(Au_nu_n^TB^T + Bu_nu_n^TA^T) + \xi_n^2 Bu_nu_n^TB^T. \tag{10}$$

By (10) and $E(\xi_n) = 0$, $E(\xi_n^2) = \sigma$ we get (9).
Let $\bar{A}$ be the matrix of system (8), respectively (9). The characteristic polynomial is given by:

$$P_2(\lambda) = det(\lambda I - \bar{A}).$$

For system (8), respectively (9), the analysis of the solutions can be done by studying the roots of the equation $P_2(\lambda) = 0$.

2.3 Discrete-time dynamical systems with one parameter

Consider a discrete-time dynamical system depending on a real parameter α, defined by the application:

$$x \to f(x, \alpha), \quad x \in \mathbf{R}^m, \; \alpha \in \mathbf{R} \tag{11}$$

where $f : \mathbf{R}^m \times \mathbf{R} \to \mathbf{R}^m$ is a seamless function with respect to x and α. Let $x_0 \in \mathbf{R}^m$ be a fixed point of (11), for all $\alpha \in \mathbf{R}$. The characteristic equation associated to the Jacobian matrix of the application (11), evaluated in x_0 is $P(\lambda, \alpha) = 0$, where:

$$P(\lambda, \alpha) = \lambda^m + c_1(\alpha)\lambda^{m-1} + \cdots + c_{m-1}(\alpha)\lambda + c_m(\alpha).$$

The roots of the characteristic equation depend on the parameter α.
The fixed point x_0 is called *stable* for (11), if there exists $\alpha = \alpha_0$ so that equation $P(\lambda, \alpha_0) = 0$ has all roots with their absolute values less than 1. The existence conditions of the value α_0, are obtained using Schur Theorem (Lorenz, 1993).
If $m = 2$, the necessary and sufficient conditions that all roots of the characteristic equation $\lambda^2 + c_1(\alpha)\lambda + c_2(\alpha) = 0$ have their absolute values less than 1 are:

$$|c_2(\alpha)| < 1, \quad |c_1(\alpha)| < |c_2(\alpha) + 1|.$$

If $m = 3$, the necessary and sufficient conditions that all roots of the characteristic equation

$$\lambda^3 + c_1(\alpha)\lambda^2 + c_2(\alpha)\lambda + c_3(\alpha) = 0$$

have their absolute values less than 1 are:

$$1 + c_1(\alpha) + c_2(\alpha) + c_3(\alpha) > 0, 1 - c_1(\alpha) + c_2(\alpha) - c_3(\alpha) > 0$$
$$1 + c_2(\alpha) - c_3(\alpha)(c_1(\alpha) + c_3(\alpha)) > 0, 1 - c_2(\alpha) + c_3(\alpha)(c_1(\alpha) - c_3(\alpha)) > 0, |c_3(\alpha)| < 1.$$

The *Neimark–Sacker (or Hopf) bifurcation* is the value $\alpha = \alpha_0$ for which the characteristic equation $P(\lambda, \alpha_0) = 0$ has the roots $\mu_1(\alpha_0) = \mu(\alpha_0)$, $\mu_2(\alpha_0) = \overline{\mu}(\alpha_0)$ in their absolute values equal to 1, and the other roots have their absolute values less than 1 and:

$$\text{a)} \quad \frac{d|\mu(\alpha)|}{d\alpha}\Big|_{\alpha=\alpha_0} \neq 0. \qquad \text{b)} \quad \mu^k(\alpha_0) \neq 1, \; k = 1, 2, 3, 4$$

hold.
For the discrete-time dynamical system

$$x(n+1) = f(x(n), \alpha)$$

with $f : \mathbf{R}^m \to \mathbf{R}^m$, the following statement is true:
Proposition 2.2. ((Kuznetsov, 1995), (Mircea et al., 2004)) *Let α_0 be a Neimark-Sacker bifurcation. The restriction of (11) to two dimensional center manifold in the point (x_0, α_0) has the normal form:*

$$\eta \to \eta e^{i\theta_0}(1 + \frac{1}{2}d|\eta|^2) + \mathcal{O}(\equiv^{\triangle})$$

where $\eta \in \mathbf{C}$, $d \in \mathbf{C}$. If $c = Re\, d \neq 0$ there is a unique limit cycle in the neighborhood of x_0. The expression of d is:

$$d = \frac{1}{2}e^{-i\theta_0} < v^*, C(v, v, \bar{v}) + 2B(v, (I_m - A)^{-1}B(v, \bar{v})) + B(v, (e^{2i\theta_0}I_m - A)^{(-1)}B(v, v)) > 0$$

where $Av = e^{i\theta_0}v$, $A^T v^* = e^{-i\theta_0}v^*$ *and* $< v^*, v >= 1$; $A = \left(\frac{\partial f}{\partial x}\right)_{(x_0,\alpha_0)}$, $B = \left(\frac{\partial^2 f}{\partial x^2}\right)_{(x_0,\alpha_0)}$ *and* $C = \left(\frac{\partial^3 f}{\partial x^3}\right)_{(x_0,\alpha_0)}$.

The center manifold in x_0 *is a two dimensional submanifold in* $\mathbb{R}^m$, *tangent in* x_0 *to the vectorial space of the eigenvectors* v *and* v^*.

The following statements are true:

Proposition 2.3. (i) *If* $m = 2$, *the necessary and sufficient conditions that a Neimark–Sacker bifurcation exists in* $\alpha = \alpha_0$ *are:*

$$|c_2(\alpha_0)| = 1, \ |c_1(\alpha_0)| < 2, \ c_1(\alpha_0) \neq 0, \ c_1(\alpha_0) \neq 1, \frac{dc_2(\alpha)}{d\alpha}\Big|_{\alpha=\alpha_0} > 0.$$

(ii) *If* $m = 3$, *the necessary and sufficient conditions that a Neimark–Sacker bifurcation exists in* $\alpha = \alpha_0$, *are:*

$$|c_3(\alpha_0) < 1, \ c_2(\alpha_0) = 1 + c_1(\alpha_0)c_3(\alpha_0) - c_3(\alpha_0)^2,$$
$$\frac{c_3(\alpha_0)(c_1(\alpha_0)c_3'(\alpha_0) + c_1'(\alpha_0)c_3(\alpha_0) - c_2'(\alpha_0) - 2c_3(\alpha_0)c_3'(\alpha_0))}{1 + 2c_3^2(\alpha_0) - c_1(\alpha_0)c_3(\alpha_0)} > 0,$$
$$|c_1(\alpha_0) - c_3(\alpha_0)| \neq 0, \ |c_1(\alpha_0) - c_3(\alpha_0)| \neq 1.$$

In what follows, we highlight *the normal form for the Neimark–Sacker bifurcation.*

Theorem 2.1. *(The Neimark–Sacker bifurcation). Consider the two dimensional discrete-time dynamical system given by:*

$$x \to f(x, \alpha), \quad x \in \mathbf{R}^2, \alpha \in \mathbb{R} \tag{12}$$

with $x = 0$, *fixed point for all* $|\alpha|$ *small enough and*

$$\mu_{12}(\alpha) = r(\alpha)e^{\pm i\varphi(\theta)}$$

where $r(0) = 1$, $\varphi(0) = \theta_0$. *If the following conditions hold:*

$$c_1: \quad r'(0) \neq 0, \qquad c_2: \quad e^{ik\theta_0} \neq 1, \ k = 1, 2, 3, 4$$

then there is a coordinates'transformation and a parameter change so that the application (12) is topologically equivalent in the neighborhood of the origin with the system:

$$\begin{pmatrix} y_1 \\ y_2 \end{pmatrix} \to \begin{pmatrix} \cos\theta(\beta) & -\sin\theta(\beta) \\ \sin\theta(\beta) & \cos\theta(\beta) \end{pmatrix} \left[(1+\beta) \begin{pmatrix} y_1 \\ y_2 \end{pmatrix} + \right.$$
$$\left. + (y_1^2 + y_2^2) \begin{pmatrix} a(\beta) & -b(\beta) \\ b(\beta) & a(\beta) \end{pmatrix} \begin{pmatrix} y_1 \\ y_2 \end{pmatrix} \right] + \mathcal{O}(\|+\|^{\triangle}),$$

where $\theta(0) = \theta_0$, $a(0) = Re(e^{-i\theta_0}C_1(0))$, *and*

$$C_1(0) = \frac{g_{20}(0)g_{11}(0)(1 - 2\mu_0)}{2(\mu_0^2 - \mu_0)} + \frac{|g_{11}(0)|^2}{1 - \overline{\mu}_0} + \frac{|g_{02}(0)|^2}{2(\mu_0^2 - \overline{\mu}_0)} + \frac{g_{21}(0)}{2}$$

$\mu_0 = e^{i\theta_0}$, $g_{20}, g_{11}, g_{02}, g_{21}$ *are the coefficients obtained using the expansion in Taylor series including third-order terms of function* f.

2.4 The Neimark-Sacker bifurcation for a class of discrete-time dynamical systems with delay

A two dimensional discrete-time dynamical system with delay is defined by the equations

$$\begin{aligned} x_{n+1} &= x_n + f_1(x_n, y_n, \alpha) \\ y_{n+1} &= y_n + f_2(x_{n-m}, y_n, \alpha) \end{aligned} \tag{13}$$

where $\alpha \in \mathbb{R}$, $f_1, f_2 : \mathbb{R}^3 \to \mathbb{R}$ are seamless functions, so that for any $|\alpha|$ small enough, the system $f_1(x, y, \alpha) = 0$, $f_2(x, y, \alpha) = 0$, admits a solution $(\overline{x}, \overline{y})^T \in \mathbb{R}^2$.
Using the translation $x_n \to x_n + \overline{x}$, $y_n \to y_n + \overline{y}$, and denoting the new variables with the same notations x_n, y_n, system (13) becomes:

$$\begin{aligned} x_{n+1} &= x_n + f(x_n, y_n, \alpha) \\ y_{n+1} &= y_n + g(x_{n-m}, y_n, \alpha) \end{aligned} \tag{14}$$

where:

$$f(x_n, y_n, \alpha) = f_1(x_n + \overline{x}, y_n + \overline{y}, \alpha); \; g(x_{n-m}, y_n, \alpha) = f_2(x_{n-m} + \overline{x}, y_n + \overline{y}, \alpha).$$

With the change of variables $x^1 = x_{n-m}$, $x^2 = x_{n-(m-1)}, \dots, x^m = x_{n-1}$, $x^{m+1} = x_n$, $x^{m+2} = y_n$, application (14) associated to the system is:

$$\begin{pmatrix} x^1 \\ x^2 \\ \vdots \\ x^{m+1} \\ x^{m+2} \end{pmatrix} \to \begin{pmatrix} x^2 \\ \vdots \\ x^{m+1} + f(x^{m+1}, x^{m+2}, \alpha) \\ x^{m+2} + g(x^1, x^{m+2}, \alpha) \end{pmatrix}. \tag{15}$$

We use the notations:

$$\begin{aligned} a_{10} &= \frac{\partial f}{\partial x^{m+1}}(0,0,\alpha), a_{01} = \frac{\partial f}{\partial x^{m+2}}(0,0,\alpha), \\ b_{10} &= \frac{\partial g}{\partial x^1}(0,0,\alpha), b_{01} = \frac{\partial g}{\partial x^{m+2}}(0,0,\alpha) \end{aligned}$$

$$\begin{aligned} a_{20} &= \frac{\partial^2 f}{\partial x^{m+1} \partial x^{m+1}}(0,0,\alpha), & a_{11} &= \frac{\partial^2 f}{\partial x^{m+1} \partial x^{m+2}}(0,0,\alpha), \\ a_{02} &= \frac{\partial^2 f}{\partial x^{m+2} \partial x^{m+2}}(0,0,\alpha), & a_{30} &= \frac{\partial^3 f}{\partial x^{m+1} \partial x^{m+1} \partial x^{m+1}}(0,0,\alpha), \\ a_{21} &= \frac{\partial^3 f}{\partial x^{m+1} \partial x^{m+1} \partial x^{m+2}}(0,0,\alpha), & a_{12} &= \frac{\partial^3 f}{\partial x^{m+1} \partial x^{m+2} \partial x^{m+2}}(0,0,\alpha), \\ a_{03} &= \frac{\partial^3 f}{\partial x^{m+2} \partial x^{m+2} \partial x^{m+2}}(0,0,\alpha) \end{aligned} \tag{16}$$

$$\begin{aligned}
b_{20} &= \frac{\partial^2 g}{\partial x^1 \partial x^1}(0,0,\alpha), & b_{11} &= \frac{\partial^2 g}{\partial x^1 \partial x^{m+2}}(0,0,\alpha), \\
b_{02} &= \frac{\partial^2 g}{\partial x^{m+2} \partial x^{m+2}}(0,0,\alpha), & b_{30} &= \frac{\partial^3 g}{\partial x^1 \partial x^1 \partial x^1}(0,0,\alpha), \\
b_{21} &= \frac{\partial^3 g}{\partial x^1 \partial x^1 \partial x^{m+2}}(0,0,\alpha), & b_{12} &= \frac{\partial^3 g}{\partial x^1 \partial x^{m+2} \partial x^{m+2}}(0,0,\alpha), \\
b_{03} &= \frac{\partial^3 g}{\partial x^{m+2} \partial x^{m+2} \partial x^{m+2}}(0,0,\alpha). & &
\end{aligned} \tag{17}$$

With (16) and (17) from (15) we have:

Proposition 2.4. ((Mircea et al., 2004)) (i) *The Jacobian matrix associated to (15) in* $(0,0)^T$ *is:*

$$A = \begin{pmatrix} 0 & 1 \dots & 0 & 0 \\ 0 & 0 \dots & 0 & 0 \\ \vdots & \vdots & \vdots & \vdots \\ 0 & 0 \dots & 1+a_{10} & a_{01} \\ b_{10} & 0 \dots & 0 & 1+b_{01} \end{pmatrix}. \tag{18}$$

(ii) *The characteristic equation of A is:*

$$\lambda^{m+2} - (2 + a_{10} + b_{01})\lambda^{m+1} + (1 + a_{10})(1 + b_{01})\lambda - a_{01}b_{10} = 0. \tag{19}$$

(iii) *If* $\mu = \mu(\alpha)$ *is an eigenvalue of (19), then the eigenvector* $q \in \mathbb{C}^{m+2}$*, solution of the system* $Aq = \mu q$*, has the components:*

$$q_1 = 1,\ q_i = \mu^{i-1},\ i = 2, \dots, m+1,\ q_{m+2} = \frac{b_{10}}{\mu - 1 - b_{01}}. \tag{20}$$

The eigenvector $p \in \mathbb{C}^{m+2}$ *defined by* $A^T p = \overline{\mu} p$ *has the components*

$$\begin{aligned}
p_1 &= \frac{(\overline{\mu} - 1 - a_{10})(\overline{\mu} - 1 - b_{01})}{m(\overline{\mu} - 1 - a_{10})(\overline{\mu} - 1 - b_{01}) + \overline{\mu}(2\overline{\mu} - 2 - a_{10} - b_{01})},\ p_i = \frac{1}{\overline{\mu}^{i-1}} p_1,\ i = 2, \dots, m, \\
p_{m+1} &= \frac{1}{\overline{\mu}^{m-1}(\overline{\mu} - 1 - a_{10})} p_1,\ p_{m+2} = \frac{\overline{\mu}}{b_{10}} p_1.
\end{aligned} \tag{21}$$

The vectors q, p *satisfy the condition:*

$$< q, p > = \sum_{i=1}^{m+2} q_i \overline{p}_i = 1.$$

The proof is obtained by straight calculation from (15) and (18).

The following hypotheses are taken into account:

H_1. The characteristic equation (19) has one pair of conjugate eigenvalues $\mu(\alpha)$, $\overline{\mu}(\alpha)$ with their absolute values equal to one, and the other eigenvalues have their absolute values less than one.

H_2. The eigenvalues $\mu(\alpha), \overline{\mu}(\alpha)$ intersect the unit circle for $\alpha = 0$, and satisfy the transversality condition

$$\frac{d}{d\alpha}|\mu(\alpha)|_{\alpha=0} \neq 0.$$

H_3. If $\arg(\mu(\alpha)) = \theta(\alpha)$, and $\theta_0 = \theta(0)$, then $e^{i\theta_0 k} \neq 1, k = 1, 2, 3, 4$.

From H_2 we notice that for all $|\alpha|$ small enough, $\mu(\alpha)$ is given by:

$$\mu(\alpha) = r(\alpha)e^{i\theta(\alpha)}$$

with $r(0) = 1$, $\theta(0) = \theta_0$, $r'(0) \neq 0$. Thus $r(\alpha) = 1 + \beta(\alpha)$ where $\beta(0) = 0$ and $\beta'(0) \neq 0$. Taking β as a new parameter, we have:

$$\mu(\beta) = (1 + \beta)e^{i\theta(\beta)} \tag{22}$$

with $\theta(0) = \theta_0$. From (22) for $\beta < 0$ small enough, the eigenvalues of the characteristic equation (19) have their absolute values less than one, and for $\beta > 0$ small enough, the characteristic equation has an eigenvalue with its absolute value greater than one. Using the center manifold Theorem (Kuznetsov, 1995), application (15) has a family of invariant manifolds of two dimension depending on the parameter β. The restriction of application (15) to this manifold contains the essential properties of the dynamics for (13). The restriction of application (15) is obtained using the expansion in Taylor series until the third order of the right side of application (15).

2.5 The center manifold, the normal form

Consider the matrices:

$$A_1 = \begin{pmatrix} a_{20} & a_{11} \\ a_{11} & a_{02} \end{pmatrix}, C_1 = \begin{pmatrix} a_{30} & a_{21} \\ a_{21} & a_{12} \end{pmatrix}, D_1 = \begin{pmatrix} a_{21} & a_{12} \\ a_{12} & a_{03} \end{pmatrix}$$

$$A_2 = \begin{pmatrix} b_{20} & b_{11} \\ b_{11} & b_{02} \end{pmatrix}, C_2 = \begin{pmatrix} b_{30} & b_{21} \\ b_{21} & b_{12} \end{pmatrix}, D_2 = \begin{pmatrix} b_{21} & b_{12} \\ b_{12} & b_{03} \end{pmatrix}$$

with the coefficients given by (16) and (17).

Denoting by $x = (x^1, \ldots, x^{m+2}) \in \boldsymbol{R}^{m+2}$, application (15), is written as $x \to F(x)$, where $F(x) = (x^2, \ldots, x^m, x^{m+1} + f(x^{m+1}, x^{m+2}, \alpha), x^{m+2} + g(x^1, x^{m+2}, \alpha))$.

The following statements hold:

Proposition 2.5. (i) *The expansion in Taylor series until the third order of function $F(x)$ is:*

$$F(x) = Ax + \frac{1}{2}B(x,x) + \frac{1}{6}C(x,x,x) + \mathcal{O}(|\S|^{\triangle}), \tag{23}$$

where A is the matrix (18), and

$$\begin{aligned} B(x,x) &= (0, \ldots, 0, B^1(x,x), B^2(x,x))^T, \\ C(x,x,x) &= (0, \ldots, 0, C^1(x,x,x), C^2(x,x,x))^T, \end{aligned}$$

where:

$$B^1(x,x) = (x^{m+1}, x^{m+2})A_1 \begin{pmatrix} x^{m+1} \\ x^{m+2} \end{pmatrix}, B^2(x,x) = (x^1, x^{m+2})A_2 \begin{pmatrix} x^1 \\ x^{m+2} \end{pmatrix},$$

$$C^1(x,x,x) = (x^{m+1}, x^{m+2})(x^{m+1}C_1 + x^{m+2}D_1) \begin{pmatrix} x^{m+1} \\ x^{m+2} \end{pmatrix}, \tag{24}$$

$$C^2(x,x,x) = (x^1, x^{m+2})(x^1 C_2 + x^{m+2}D_2) \begin{pmatrix} x^1 \\ x^{m+2} \end{pmatrix}.$$

(ii) *Any vector* $x \in R^{m+2}$ *admits the decomposition:*

$$x = zq + \overline{z}\,\overline{q} + y, \quad z \in C \tag{25}$$

where $zq + \overline{z}\,\overline{q} \in T_{\text{center}}$, $y \in T_{\text{stable}}$; T_{center} *is the vectorial space generated by the eigenvectors corresponding to the eigenvalues of the characteristic equation (19) with their absolute values equal to one and* T_{stable} *is the vectorial subspace generated by the eigenvectors corresponding to the eigenvalues of the characteristic equation (19) with their absolute values less than 1. Moreover:*

$$z = < p, x >, \quad y = x - < p, x > q - < \overline{p}, x > \overline{q}. \tag{26}$$

(iii) $F(x)$ *given by (23) has the decomposition:*

$$F(x) = F_1(z, \overline{z}) + F_2(y)$$

where

$$F_1(z,\overline{z}) = G_1(z)q + \overline{G_1(z_1)}\overline{q} + < p, N(zq + \overline{z}\,\overline{q} + y) > \overline{q} + < \overline{p}, N(zq + \overline{z}\,\overline{q} + y) > \overline{q}$$
$$G_1(z) = \mu z + < p, N(zq + \overline{z}\,\overline{q} + y) > \tag{27}$$
$$F_2(y) = Ay + N(zq + \overline{z}\,\overline{q} + y) - < p, N(zq + \overline{z}\,\overline{q} + y) > q - < \overline{p}, N(zq + \overline{z}\,\overline{q} + y) > \overline{q}$$

and

$$N(zq + \overline{z}\,\overline{q} + y) = \frac{1}{2}B(zq + \overline{z}\,\overline{q} + y, zq + \overline{z}\,\overline{q} + y) +$$
$$+ \frac{1}{6}C(zq + \overline{z}\,\overline{q} + y, zq + \overline{z}\,\overline{q} + y, zq + \overline{z}\,\overline{q} + y) + O(zq + \overline{z}q + y) \tag{28}$$

(iv) *The two-dimensional differential submanifold from* R^{m+2}, *given by* $x = zq + \overline{z}\,\overline{q} + V(z,\overline{z})$, $z \in \mathcal{V}_0 \subset C$, *where* $V(z,\overline{z}) = \overline{V}(z,\overline{z})$, $< p, V(z,\overline{z}) >= 0$, $\dfrac{\partial V(z,\overline{z})}{\partial z}(0,0) = 0$, *is tangent to the vectorial space* T_{center} *in* $0 \in C$.

Proof. (i) Taking into account the expression of $F(x)$ we obtain the expansion in Taylor series until the third order (23).
(ii) Because $R^{m+2} = T_{\text{center}} \oplus T_{\text{stable}}$ and $< p, y >= 0$, for any $y \in T_{stable}$, we obtain (25) and (26).
(iii) Because $F(x) \in R^{m+2}$, with decomposition (25) and $< p, q >= 1$, $< \overline{p}, q >= 0$, we have (27).
(iv) Using the definition of the submanifold, this submanifold is tangent to T_{center}.

The *center manifold* in $(0,0)^T \in \boldsymbol{R}^2$ is a two dimensional submanifold from $\boldsymbol{R}^{m+2}$ tangent to T_{center} at $0 \in \mathbb{C}$ and invariant with respect to the applications G_1 and F_2, given by (27). If $x = zq + \overline{z}\overline{q} + V(z,\overline{z})$, $z \in \mathcal{V}_0 \subset \mathbb{C}$ is the analytical expression of the tangent submanifold to T_{center}, the invariant condition is written as:

$$V(G_1(z), \overline{G_1(z)}) = F_2(V(z,\overline{z})). \tag{29}$$

From (27), (28) and (29) we find that $x = zq + \overline{z}\overline{q} + V(z,\overline{z})$, $z \in \mathcal{V}_0$ is the center manifold if and only if the relation:

$$\begin{aligned} &V(\mu z + < p, N(zq + \overline{z}\overline{q} + V(z,\overline{z}) >, \overline{\mu z} + < \overline{p}, N(zq + \overline{z}\overline{q} + V(z,\overline{z})) >) = AV(z,z) + \\ &+ N(zq + \overline{z}\overline{q} + V(\overline{z},\overline{z})) - < p, N(zq + \overline{z}\overline{q} + V(z,\overline{z})) > q - < \overline{p}, N(zq + \overline{z}\overline{q} + V(z,\overline{z})) > \overline{q} \end{aligned} \tag{30}$$

holds.
In what follows we consider the function $V(z,\overline{z})$ of the form:

$$V(z,\overline{z}) = \frac{1}{2}w_{20}z^2 + w_{11}z\overline{z} + w_{02}\overline{z}^2 + \mathcal{O}(|\ddagger|^{\ni}), \quad \ddagger \in \mathcal{V}, \in \mathbb{C}. \tag{31}$$

Proposition 2.6. (i) *If $V(z,\overline{z})$ is given by (31), and $N(zq + \overline{z}\overline{q} + y)$, with $y = V(z,\overline{z})$ is given by (28), then:*

$$G_1(z) = \mu z + \frac{1}{2}g_{20}z^2 + g_{11}z\overline{z} + g_{02}\overline{z}^2 + \frac{1}{2}g_{21}z^2\overline{z} + \dots \tag{32}$$

where:

$$\begin{aligned} &g_{20} = < p, B(q,q) >, \quad g_{11} = < p, B(q,\overline{q}) >, \quad g_{02} = < p, B(\overline{q},\overline{q}) > \\ &g_{21} = < p, B(\overline{q}, w_{20}) > + 2 < p, B(q, w_{11}) > + < p, C(q,q,\overline{q}) > . \end{aligned} \tag{33}$$

(ii) *If $V(z,\overline{z})$ is given by (31), relation (30) holds, if and only if w_{20}, w_{11}, w_{02} satisfy the relations:*

$$(\mu^2 I - A)w_{20} = h_{20}, \quad (I - A)w_{11} = h_{11}, \quad (\overline{\mu}^2 I - A)w_{02} = h_{02} \tag{34}$$

where:

$$\begin{aligned} h_{20} &= B(q,q) - < p, B(q,q) > q - < \overline{p}, B(q,q) > \overline{q} \\ h_{11} &= B(q,\overline{q}) - < p, B(q,\overline{q}) > q - < \overline{p}, B(q,\overline{q}) > \overline{q} \\ h_{02} &= B(\overline{q},\overline{q}) - < p, B(q,\overline{q}) > q - < \overline{p}, B(\overline{q},\overline{q}) > \overline{q}. \end{aligned}$$

Proof. (i) Because $B(x,x)$ is a bilinear form, $C(x,x,x)$ is a trilinear form, and $y = V(z,\overline{z})$, from (28) and the expression of $G_1(z)$ given by (27), we obtain (32) and (33).
(ii) In (30), replacing $V(z,\overline{z})$ with (32) and $N(zq + \overline{z}\overline{q} + V(z,\overline{z}))$ given by (28), we find that w_{20}, w_{11}, w_{02} satisfy the relations (31).
Let $q \in \boldsymbol{R}^{m+2}$, $p \in \boldsymbol{R}^{m+2}$ be the eigenvectors of the matrices A and A^T corresponding to the eigenvalues μ and $\overline{\mu}$ given by (20) and (21) and:

$$\begin{aligned} &a = B^1(q,q),\ b = B^2(q,q),\ a_1 = B^1(q,\overline{q}),\ b_1 = B^2(q,\overline{q}), C_1 = C^1(q,q,\overline{q}),\ C_2 = C^2(q,q,\overline{q}), \\ &r_{20}^1 = B^1(\overline{q}, w_{20}),\ r_{20}^2 = B^?(\overline{q}, w_{20}), r_{11}^1 = B^1(q, w_{11}),\ r_{11}^2 = B^2(q, w_{11}), \end{aligned} \tag{35}$$

where B^1, B^2, C^1, C^2, are applications given by (24).

Proposition 2.7. (i) *The coefficients g_{20}, g_{11}, g_{02} given by (33) have the expressions:*

$$g_{20} = p_{m+1}a + p_{m+2}b,\ g_{11} = p_{m+1}a_1 + p_{m+2}b_1,\ g_{02} = p_{m+1}\overline{a} + p_{m+2}\overline{b}. \tag{36}$$

(ii) *The vectors h_{20}, h_{11}, h_{02} given by (34) have the expressions:*

$$\begin{aligned} h_{20} &= (0,\ldots,0,a,b)^T - (p_{m+1}a + p_{m+2}b)q - (\overline{p}_{m+1}a + \overline{p}_{m+2}b)\overline{q} \\ h_{11} &= (0,\ldots,0,a,b)^T - (p_{m+1}a_1 + p_{m+2}b_1)q - (\overline{p}_{m+1}a_1 + \overline{p}_{m+2}b)\overline{q} \\ h_{02} &= \overline{h}_{20}. \end{aligned} \tag{37}$$

(iii) *The systems of linear equations (34) have the solutions:*

$$w_{20} = \left(v_{20}^1, \mu^2 v_{20}^1, \ldots, \mu^{2m} v_{20}^1, \frac{a + (\mu^2 - a_{10})\mu^{2m} v_{20}^1}{a_{01}}\right)^T - \frac{p_{m+1}a + p_{m+2}b}{\mu^2 - \mu} q - \frac{\overline{p}_{m+1}a + \overline{p}_{m+2}}{\mu^2 - \overline{\mu}} \overline{q}$$

$$w_{11} = \left(v_{11}^1, v_{11}^1, \ldots, v_{11}^1, \frac{a_1 + (1 - a_{10})v_{11}^1}{a_{01}}\right)^T - \frac{p_{m+1}a_1 + p_{m+2}b_1}{1 - \mu} q - \frac{\overline{p}_{m+1}a_1 + \overline{p}_{m+2}b_1}{1 - \overline{\mu}} \overline{q}$$

$$w_{02} = \overline{w}_{20}, v_{20}^1 = \frac{aa_{01} - b(\mu^2 - b_{01})}{(\mu^2 - a_{10})(\mu^2 - b_{01})\mu^{2m} - b_{10}a_{01}}, v_{11}^1 = \frac{b_1 a_{01} - a_1(1 - b_{01})}{(1 - a_{10})(1 - b_{01}) - b_{10}a_{01}}.$$

(iv) *The coefficient g_{21} given by (33) has the expression:*

$$g_{21} = p_{m+1}r_{20}^1 + p_{m+2}r_{20}^2 + 2(p_{m+1}r_{11}^1 + p_{m+2}r_{11}^2) + p_{m+1}C_1 + p_{m+2}C_2. \tag{38}$$

Proof. (i) The expressions from (36) are obtained from (33) using (35).
(ii) The expressions from (37) are obtained from (34) with the notations from (35).
(iii) Because $\mu^2, \overline{\mu}^2$, 1 are not roots of the characteristic equation (19) then the linear systems (34) are determined compatible systems. The relations (37) are obtained by simple calculation.
(iv) From (33) with (35) we obtain (38).

Consider the discrete-time dynamical system with delay given by (13), for which the roots of the characteristic equation satisfy the hypotheses H_1, H_2, H_3. The following statements hold:

Proposition 2.8. (i) *The solution of the system (13) in the neighborhood of the fixed point $(\overline{x}, \overline{y}) \in \mathbb{R}^2$, is:*

$$\begin{aligned} x_n &= \overline{x} + q_{m+1}z_n + \overline{q}_{m+1}\overline{z}_n + \frac{1}{2}w_{20}^{m+1}z_n^2 + w_{11}^{m+1}z_n\overline{z}_n + \frac{1}{2}w_{02}^{m+1}\overline{z}_n^2 \\ y_n &= \overline{y} + q_{m+2}z_n + \overline{q}_{m+2}\overline{z}_n + \frac{1}{2}w_{20}^{m+2}z_n^2 + w_{11}^{m+2}z_n\overline{z}_n + \frac{1}{2}w_{02}^{m+2}\overline{z}_n^2 \\ x_{n-m} &= u_n = \overline{x} + q_1 z_n + \overline{q}_1\overline{z}_n + \frac{1}{2}w_{20}^1 z_n^2 + w_{11}^1 z_n\overline{z}_n + \frac{1}{2}w_{02}^1\overline{z}_n^2 \end{aligned} \tag{39}$$

where z_n is a solution of the equation:

$$z_{n+1} = \mu z_n + \frac{1}{2}g_{20}z_n^2 + g_{11}z_n\overline{z}_n + \frac{1}{2}g_{02}\overline{z}_n^2 + \frac{1}{2}g_{21}z_n^2\overline{z}_n \tag{40}$$

and the coefficients from (40) are given by (36) and (38).
(ii) *There is a complex change variable, so that equation (40) becomes:*

$$w_{n+1} = \mu(\beta) w_n + C_1(\beta) w_n^2 \overline{w}_n + \mathcal{O}(|\Xi_\backslash|^\triangle) \tag{41}$$

where:

$$C_1(\beta) = \frac{g_{20}(\beta) g_{11}(\beta)(\overline{\mu}(\beta) - 3 - 2\mu(\beta))}{2(\mu(\beta)^2 - \mu(\beta))(\overline{\mu}(\beta) - 1)} + \frac{|g_{11}(\beta)|^2}{1 - \overline{\mu}(\beta)} + \frac{|g_{02}(\beta)|^2}{2(\mu^2(\beta) - \overline{\mu}(\beta))} + \frac{g_{21}(\beta)}{2}.$$

(iii) *Let $l_0 = Re(e^{-i\theta_0} C_1(0))$, where $\theta_0 = \arg(\mu(0))$. If $l_0 < 0$, in the neighborhood of the fixed point $(\overline{x}, \overline{y})$ there is an invariant stable limit cycle.*

Proof. (i) From Proposition 2.6, application (15) associated to (13) has the canonical form (40). A solution of system (40) leads to (39).
(ii) In equation (40), making the following complex variable change

$$z = w + \frac{g_{20}}{2(\mu^2 - \mu)} w^2 + \frac{g_{11}}{|\mu|^2 - \mu} w \overline{w} + \frac{g_{02}}{2(\overline{\mu}^2 - \mu)} \overline{w}^2 +$$
$$+ \frac{g_{30}}{6(\mu^3 - \mu)} w^3 + \frac{g_{12}}{2(\overline{\mu}|\mu|^2 - \mu)} w \overline{w}^2 + \frac{g_{03}}{6(\overline{\mu}^3 - \mu)} \overline{w}^3,$$

for β small enough, equation (41) is obtained. The coefficients g_{20}, g_{11}, g_{02} are given by (36) and

$$g_{30} = p_{m+1} C^1(q, q, q) + p_{m+2} C^2(q, q, q),$$
$$g_{12} = p_{m+1} C^1(q, \overline{q}, \overline{q}) + p_{m+2} C^2(q, \overline{q}, \overline{q})$$
$$g_{03} = p_{m+1} C^1(\overline{q}, \overline{q}, \overline{q}) + p_{m+2} C^2(\overline{q}, \overline{q}, \overline{q}).$$

(iii) The coefficient $C_1(\beta)$ is called *resonant cubic coefficient*, and the sign of the coefficient l_0, establishes the existence of a stable or unstable invariant limit cycle (attractive or repulsive) (Kuznetsov, 1995).

3. Neimark-Sacker bifurcation in a discrete time dynamic system for Internet congestion.

The model of an Internet network with one link and single source, which can be formulated as:

$$\dot{x}(t) = k(w - af(x(t - \tau))) \tag{42}$$

where: $k > 0$, $x(t)$ is the sending rate of the source at the time t, τ is the sum of forward and return delays, w is a target (set-point), and the congestion indication function $f : R_+ \to R_+$ is increasing, nonnegative, which characterizes the congestion. Also, we admit that f is nonlinear and its third derivative exists and it is continuous.
The model obtained by discretizing system (42) is given by:

$$x_{n+1} = x_n - akf(x_{n-m}) + kw \tag{43}$$

for $n, m \in N$, $m > 0$ and it represents the dynamical system with discrete-time for Internet congestion with one link and a single source.

Using the change of variables $x^1 = x_{n-m}, \ldots, x^m = x_{n-1}, x^{m+1} = x_n$, the application associated to (43) is:

$$\begin{pmatrix} x^1 \\ \vdots \\ x^m \\ x^{m+1} \end{pmatrix} \to \begin{pmatrix} x^2 \\ \vdots \\ x^{m+1} \\ kw - akf(x^1) + x^{m+1} \end{pmatrix}. \tag{44}$$

The fixed point of (44) is $(x^*, \ldots, x^*)^T \in \mathbf{R}^{m+1}$, where x^* satisfies relation $w = af(x^*)$. With the translation $x \to x + x^*$, application (44) can be written as:

$$\begin{pmatrix} x^1 \\ \vdots \\ x^m \\ x^{m+1} \end{pmatrix} \to \begin{pmatrix} x^2 \\ \vdots \\ x^{m+1} \\ kw - akg(x^1) + x^{m+1} \end{pmatrix} \tag{45}$$

where $g(x^1) = f(x^1 + x^*)$.
The following statements hold:

Proposition 3.1. ((Mircea et al., 2004)) (i) *The Jacobian matrix of (45) in $0 \in \mathbf{R}^{m+1}$ is*

$$A = \begin{pmatrix} 0 & 1 & 0 & \ldots & 0 \\ 0 & 0 & 1 & \ldots & 0 \\ \ldots & \ldots & \ldots & \ldots & \ldots \\ 0 & 0 & 0 & \ldots & 1 \\ -ak\rho_1 & 0 & 0 & \ldots & 1 \end{pmatrix} \tag{46}$$

where $\rho_1 = g'(0)$.
(ii) *The characteristic equation of A is:*

$$\lambda^{m+1} - \lambda^m + ak\rho_1 = 0. \tag{47}$$

(iii) *If $\mu \in \mathbf{C}$ is a root of (47), the eigenvector $q \in \mathbf{R}^{m+1}$ that corresponds to the eigenvalue μ, of the matrix A, has the components:*

$$q_i = \mu^{i-1}, \quad i = 1, \ldots, m+1$$

and the components of the eigenvector $p \in \mathbf{R}^{m+1}$ corresponding to $\overline{\mu}$ of the matrix A^T are:

$$p_1 = -\frac{ak\rho_1}{\overline{\mu}^{m+1} - mak\rho_1}, \; p_i = \frac{1}{\overline{\mu}^{i-1}} p_1, \; i = 2, \ldots, m-1, \; p_m = \frac{\overline{\mu}^2 - \overline{\mu}}{p\rho_1} p_1, \; p_{m+1} = -\frac{\overline{\mu}}{ak\rho_1} p_1.$$

The vectors $p \in \mathbf{R}^{m+1}$, $q \in \mathbf{R}^{m+1}$ satisfy the relation $\sum_{i=1}^{m+1} \overline{p}_i q_i = 1.$

The following statements hold:

Proposition 3.2. (i) *If $m = 2$, equation (47) becomes:*

$$\lambda^3 - \lambda^2 + ak\rho_1 = 0. \tag{48}$$

Equation (48) has two complex roots with their absolute values equal to 1 and one root with the absolute value less than 1, if and only if $k = \frac{\sqrt{5}-1}{2a\rho_1}$. For $k = k_0 = \frac{\sqrt{5}-1}{2a\rho_1}$, equation (48) has the roots:

$$\lambda_{1,2} = \exp(\pm i\theta(k_0)i),$$
$$\theta(a_0) = \arccos\frac{1+\sqrt{5}}{4}. \tag{49}$$

(ii) *With respect to the change of parameter*

$$k = k(\beta) = k_0 + g(\beta)$$

where:

$$g(\beta) = \frac{\sqrt{1+4(1+\beta)^6} - (1+\beta)^2 - \sqrt{5} + 1}{2k_0\rho_1}$$

equation (49) becomes:

$$\lambda^3 - \lambda^2 + ak(\beta)\rho_1 = 0. \tag{50}$$

The roots of equation (50) are:

$$\mu_{1,2}(\beta) = (1+\beta)\exp(\pm i\omega(\beta)), \quad \lambda(\beta) = -\frac{ak(\beta)\rho_1}{(1+\beta)^2}$$

where:

$$\omega(\beta) = \arccos\frac{(1+\beta)^2 + \sqrt{1+4(1+\beta)^6}}{4(1+\beta)^2}.$$

(iii) *The eigenvector $q \in \mathbb{R}^3$, associated to the $\mu = \mu(\beta)$, for the matrix A has the components:*

$$q_1 = 1, \quad q_2 = \mu, \quad q_3 = \mu^2$$

and the eigenvector $p \in \mathbb{R}^3$ associated to the eigenvalue $\overline{\mu} = \overline{\mu}(\beta)$ for the matrix A^T has the components:

$$p_1 = \frac{ak\rho_1}{2ak\rho_1 - \overline{\mu}^3}, \quad p_2 = \frac{\overline{\mu}^2}{\overline{\mu}^3 - 2ak\rho_1}, \quad p_3 = \frac{\overline{\mu}}{\overline{\mu}^3 - 2ak\rho_1}.$$

(iv) *a_0 is a Neimark-Sacker bifurcation point.*

Using Proposition 3.2, we obtain:

Proposition 3.3. *The solution of equation (43) in the neighborhood of the fixed point $x^* \in \mathbb{R}$ is:*

$$u_n = x^* + z_n + \overline{z}_n + \frac{1}{2}w^1_{20}z_n^2 + w^1_{11}z_n\overline{z}_n + \frac{1}{2}w^1_{02}\overline{z}_n^2$$
$$x_n = x^* + q_3 z_n + \overline{q}_3\overline{z}_n + \frac{1}{2}w^3_{20}z_n^2 + w^3_{11}z_n\overline{z}_n + \frac{1}{2}w^3_{02}\overline{z}_n^2$$

where:

$$w_{20}^1 = \frac{\mu^2(\mu^2-1)h_{20}^1 - (\mu^2-1)h_{20}^2 + h_{20}^3}{\mu^6 - \mu^4 + ak\rho_1}, w_{20}^2 = \mu^2 w_{20}^1 - h_{20}^1, \ w_{20}^3 = \mu^4 w_{20}^1 - \mu^2 h_{20}^1 - h_{20}^2$$

$$w_{11}^1 = \frac{h_{11}^3}{ak\rho_1}, \ w_{11}^2 = w_{11}^1 - h_{11}^1, \ w_{11}^3 = w_{11}^1 - h_{11}^1 - h_{11}^2$$

$$h_{20}^1 = 4ak\rho_2(p_3 + \overline{p}_3), \ h_{20}^2 = ak\rho_1(p_3q_2 + \overline{p}_3\overline{q}_2), h_{20}^3 = 4ak\rho_2(1 + p_3q_3 + \overline{p}_3\overline{q}_3)$$

$$h_{11}^1 = h_{20}^1, \ h_{11}^2 = h_{20}^2, \ h_{11}^3 = h_{20}^3$$

and $z_n \in \mathbb{C}$ is a solution of equation:

$$z_{n+1} = \mu z_n - \frac{1}{2}p_3 ak\rho_2(z_n^2 + 2z_n\overline{z}_n + \overline{z}_n^2) + \frac{1}{2}p_3(-ka\rho_1 w_{20}^1 - ka\rho_1 w_{11}^1 + \rho_3),$$

$rho_1 = f'(0), \quad \rho_2 = f''(0), \quad \rho_3 = f'''(0).$
Let

$$C_1(\beta) = -\frac{p_3a^2k^2\rho_2^2(\overline{\mu} - 3 - 2\mu)}{2(\mu^2-\mu)(\overline{\mu}-1)} + \frac{a^2k^2\rho_2^2|p_3|^2}{1-\overline{\mu}} + \frac{ak|\rho_2 p_3|}{2(\mu^2 - \overline{\mu})} + p_3(-ak\rho_1 w_{20}^1 - ak\rho_1 w_{11}^1 + \rho_3)$$

and

$$l(0) = Re(\exp(-i\theta(a_0))C_1(0)).$$

If $l(0) < 0$, the Neimark–Sacker bifurcation is supercritical (stable).

The model of an Internet network with r links and a single source, can be analyzed in a similar way.
The perturbed stochastic equation of (43) is:

$$x_{n+1} = x_n - \alpha k f(x_{n-m}) + kw + \xi_n b(x_n - x^*) \tag{51}$$

and x^* satisfies the relation $w = af(x^*)$, where $E(\xi_n) = 0$, $E(\xi_n^2) = \sigma > 0$.
We study the case $m = 2$. Using (46) the linearized equation of (51) has the matrices:

$$A_1 = \begin{pmatrix} 0 & 1\,0 \\ 0 & 0\,1 \\ -ak\rho_1 & 0\,1 \end{pmatrix}, B = \begin{pmatrix} 0\,0\,0 \\ 0\,0\,0 \\ 0\,0\,b \end{pmatrix}$$

Using Proposition 2.1, the characteristic polynomial of the linearized system of (51) is given by:

$$P_2(\lambda) = (\lambda^3 - (1+\sigma b^2)\lambda^2 - a^2k^2\rho_1^2)(\lambda^3 + ak\rho_1\lambda + a^2k^2\rho_1^2).$$

If the roots of $P_2(\lambda)$ have their absolute values less than 1, then the square mean values of the solutions for the linearized system of (51) are asymptotically stable. The analysis of the roots for the equation $P_2(\lambda) = 0$ can be done for fixed values of the parameters.
The numerical simulation can be done for: $w = 0.1$, $a = 8$ and $f(x) = x^2/(20 - 3x)$.

4. A discrete economic game with delay

The economic game is described by a number of firms that enter the market with a homogeneous consumption product at different moments n, where $n \in \mathbb{N}$. In what follows we consider two firms F_1, F_2 and x, y the state variables of the model that represent the firms'outputs. The price function of the product (the inverse demand function) is $p : \mathbb{R}_+ \to \mathbb{R}_+$, derivable function with $\lim_{x\to\infty} p(x) = 0$, $\lim_{x\to 0_+} p(x) = \infty$ and $p'(x) < 0$. The cost functions are $C_i : \mathbb{R}_+ \to \mathbb{R}_+$, $i = 1,2$, derivable functions with $C_i'(x) \neq 0$, $C_i''(x) \geq 0$. The profit functions of the firms, $\pi_i : \mathbb{R}^2_+ \to \mathbb{R}_+$, $i = 1,2$, are given by:

$$\pi_1(x,y) = p(x+y)x - C_1(x), \quad \pi_2(x,y) = p(x+y)y - C_2(y).$$

The non-cooperative game F_1, F_2, denoted by $\Gamma = (\mathbb{R}^2_+, \pi_1, \pi_2)$ is called *deterministic economic game*. The Nash solution of Γ is called *the solution of the deterministic economic game*.
From the definition of the Nash solution, we find that the solution of the deterministic economic game is given by the quantities $(\overline{x}, \overline{y})^T \in \mathbb{R}^2_+$ for which the profit of each firm is maximum. Thus, the Nash solution is the solution of the following system:

$$\begin{cases} \pi_{1x} = p'(x+y)x + p(x+y) - C_1'(x) = 0 \\ \pi_{2y} = p'(x+y)y + p(x+y) - C_2'(y) = 0. \end{cases} \tag{52}$$

A solution $(\overline{x}, \overline{y})^T \in \mathbb{R}^2_+$ of (52) is a (local) maximum for π_i, $i = 1,2$ if and only if:

$$p''(\overline{x}+\overline{y})\overline{x} + 2p'(\overline{x}+\overline{y}) < C_1''(\overline{x}), \quad p''(\overline{x}+\overline{y})\overline{y} + 2p'(\overline{x}+\overline{y}) < C_2''(\overline{y}).$$

At each moment n, $n \in \mathbb{N}$ the firms adjust their quantities x_n, y_n, proportionally to the marginal profits $\dfrac{\partial \pi_1}{\partial x}, \dfrac{\partial \pi_2}{\partial y}$. The quantities from the $n+1$ moment satisfy the relations:

$$\begin{aligned} x_{n+1} &= x_n + k(p'(x_n+y_n)x_n + p(x_n+y_n) - C_1'(x_n)) \\ y_{n+1} &= y_n + \alpha(p'(x_{n-m}+y_n)y_n + p(x_{n-m}+y_n) - C_2'(y_n)) \end{aligned} \tag{53}$$

where $m \in \mathbb{N}$, $m \geq 1$.
System (53) is a discrete dynamic economic game with delay.
With respect to the change of variables $x^1 = x_{n-m}, \ldots, x^m = x_{n-1}, x^{m+1} = x_n, x^{m+2} = y_n$ the application associated to (53) is:

$$\begin{pmatrix} x^1 \\ \vdots \\ x^m \\ x^{m+1} \\ x^{m+2} \end{pmatrix} \to \begin{pmatrix} x^2 \\ \vdots \\ x^{m+1} \\ x^{m+1} + k(p'(x^{m+1}+x^{m+2})x^{m+1} + p(x^{m+1}+x^{m+2}) - C_1'(x^{m+1})) \\ x^{m+2} + \alpha(p'(x^1+x^{m+2})x^{m+2} + p(x^1+x^{m+2}) - C_2'(x^{m+2})) \end{pmatrix}. \tag{54}$$

The fixed point of (54) is the point with the coordinates $(x_0, \ldots, x_0, y_0) \in \mathbb{R}^{m+2}$ where (x_0, y_0) is the solution of the following system:

$$p'(x+y)x + p(x+y) - C_1'(x) = 0, \quad p'(x+y)y + p(x+y) - C_2'(y) = 0 \tag{55}$$

In what follows we use the notations:

$$\rho_i = p^{(i)}(\overline{x}+\overline{y}),\ \mu_{i1} = C_1^{(i)}(\overline{x}),\ \mu_{i2} = C_2^{(i)}(\overline{y}),\quad i = 1,2,3,4 \tag{56}$$

the derivatives of $i = 1,2,3,4$ order of the functions p, C_1, C_2 in the point $(\overline{x}, \overline{y})$,

$$\begin{aligned} &a_{10} = \rho_2\overline{x} + 2\rho_1 - \mu_{21},\ a_{01} = \rho_2\overline{x} + \rho_1,\ a_{20} = \rho_3\overline{x} + 3\rho_2 - \mu_{31}, a_{11} = \rho_3\overline{x} + 2\rho_2,\\ &a_{02} = \rho_3\overline{x} + \rho_2, a_{30} = \rho_4\overline{x} + 4\rho_3 - \mu_{41}, a_{21} = \rho_4\overline{x} + 3\rho_3, a_{12} = \rho_4\overline{x} + 2\rho_3, a_{03} = \rho_4\overline{x} + 2\rho_3, \end{aligned} \tag{57}$$

$$\begin{aligned} &b_{10} = \rho_2\overline{y} + \rho_1, b_{01} = \rho_2\overline{y} + 2\rho_1 - \mu_{22}, b_{20} = \rho_3\overline{y} + \rho_2, b_{11} = \rho_3\overline{y} + 2\rho_2, b_{02} = \rho_3\overline{y} + 3\rho_2 - \mu_{32},\\ &b_{30} = \rho_4\overline{y} + 2\rho_3, b_{21} = \rho_4\overline{y} + 2\rho_3, b_{12} = \rho_4\overline{y} + 3\rho_3, b_{03} = \rho_4\overline{y} + 4\rho_3 - \mu_{42}, d_1 = b_{01} + k(a_{10}b_{01} - a_{01}b_{10}). \end{aligned} \tag{58}$$

Proposition 4.1. ((Neamţu, 2010)) (i) *The Jacobian matrix of the application (54) in $(x_0, \ldots, x_0, y_0)$ is:*

$$A = \begin{pmatrix} 0 & 1 \ \ldots & 0 & 0 \\ \ldots & \ldots\ldots & \ldots & \ldots \\ 0 & \ldots\ldots & 1 & 0 \\ 0 & \ldots\ldots & 1 + ka_{10} & ka_{01} \\ \alpha b_{10} & 0 \ \ldots & 0 & 1 + \alpha b_{01} \end{pmatrix}. \tag{59}$$

(ii) *The characteristic equation of A given by (59) is:*

$$\lambda^{m+2} - a\lambda^{m+1} + b\lambda^m - c = 0$$

where

$$a = 2 + ka_{10} + \alpha b_{01},\ \ b = (1 + ka_{10})(1 + \alpha b_{01}),\ \ c = k\alpha a_{01} b_{10}.$$

(iii) *The eigenvector $q \in \mathbb{R}^{m+2}$, which corresponds to the eigenvalue μ of the matrix A and satisfies the system $Aq = \mu q$, has the components:*

$$q_i = \mu^{i-1},\ i = 1, \ldots, m+1,\quad q_{m+2} = \frac{\alpha b_{10}}{\mu - 1 - \alpha b_{01}}. \tag{60}$$

The eigenvector $p \in \mathbb{R}^{m+2}$, which corresponds to the eigenvalue $\overline{\mu}$ of the matrix A and satisfies the system $A^T p = \overline{\mu} p$, has the components:

$$\begin{aligned} p_1 &= \frac{(\overline{\mu} - 1 - ka_{10})(\overline{\mu} - 1 - \alpha b_{10})}{m(\overline{\mu} - 1 - ka_{10})(\overline{\mu} - 1 - kb_{01}) + \overline{\mu}(2\overline{\mu} - 2 - ka_{10} - \alpha b_{01})}\\ p_i &= \frac{1}{\overline{\mu}^{i-1}},\ i = 2, \ldots, m-2,\ p_{m+1} = \frac{1}{\overline{\mu}^{m-1}(\overline{\mu} - 1 - ka_{10})} p_1,\ p_{m+2} = \frac{\overline{\mu}}{\alpha b_{10}} p_1. \end{aligned} \tag{61}$$

The vectors q, p given by (60) and (61) satisfy the condition

$$< q, p >= \sum_{i=1}^{m+2} q_i \overline{p}_i = 1.$$

The proof follows by direct calculation.

If $m = 1$, the following statements hold:

Proposition 4.2. (i) *If* $k \neq \frac{b_{01}}{a_{01}b_{10}}$ *and*

$$(k(a_{01}b_{10} - b_{01}a_{10}) - b_{01})^2 + 4ka_{10}a_{01}b_{10}(b_{01} - ka_{01}k_{10}) \geq 0$$

and α_0 *is a solution of the equation:*

$$ka_{01}b_{10}(b_{01} - ka_{01}b_{10})\alpha^2 + (k(a_{01}b_{10} - b_{01}a_{10}) - b_{01})\alpha - ka_{10} = 0$$

so that:

$$\alpha_0 k|a_{01}b_{10}| < 1, \quad |(b_{01} - ka_{01}b_{10})\alpha_0 + \lambda + ka_{10}| < 2,$$

then the equation:

$$\lambda^3 - a_0\lambda^2 + b_0\lambda - c_0 = 0 \tag{62}$$

has two roots with their absolute value equal to 1 and one root with its absolute value less than 1, where:

$$a_0 = 2 + ka_{10} + \alpha_0 b_{01}, \; b_0 = (1 + ka_{10})(1 + \alpha_0 b_{01}), \; c_0 = ka_{01}b_{10}\alpha_0. \tag{63}$$

(ii) *If for* $|\beta|$ *small enough,* $\Delta_1(\beta) \geq 0$, *where*

$$\Delta_1(\beta) = ((1+\beta)^2(b_{01}c_0 + ka_{01}b_{10}a_0) - 2c_0ka_{01}b_{10} - (1+\beta)^4 b_{01}(1 + ka_{10}))^2 -$$
$$-4ka_{01}b_{10}(b_{01}(1+\beta)^2 - ka_{01}b_{10})((1+\beta)^2 a_0c_0 - c_0^2 + (1+\beta)^4(1 + a_0c_0 - c_0^2) + (1+\beta)^6),$$

and a_0, b_0, c_0 *given by (63), then there is* $g : \mathbb{R} \to \mathbb{R}$, *with* $g(0) = 0$, $g'(0) \neq 0$ *so that the variable change:*

$$\alpha = \alpha(\beta) = \alpha_0 + g(\beta)$$

transforms equation (62) in equation:

$$\lambda^3 - a(\beta)\lambda^2 + b(\beta)\lambda - c(\beta) = 0 \tag{64}$$

Equation (64) admits the solutions:

$$\mu_{1,2}(\beta) = (1+\beta)e^{\pm i\theta(\beta)}, \quad \theta(\beta) = \arccos\frac{a(\beta)(1+\beta)^2 - c(\beta)}{2(1+\beta)^3}, \lambda(\beta) = \frac{c(\beta)}{(1+\beta)^2} \tag{65}$$

where:

$$g(\beta) = \frac{2c_0ka_{01}b_{10} + (1+\beta)^4 b_{01}(1+ka_{10}) - (1+\beta)^2(b_{01}c_0 + ka_{01}b_{01}a_0) + \sqrt{\Delta_1(\beta)}}{2ka_{01}b_{10}(b_{01}|1+\beta|^2 - ka_{01}b_{10})},$$
$$a(\beta) = a_0 + b_{01}g(\beta), \; b(\beta) = b_0 + b_{01}(1 + ka_{10})g(\beta), \; c(\beta) = c_0 + ka_{01}b_{10}g(\beta).$$

For $m = 1$, the model of a discrete economic game with delay (53) is written as:

$$\begin{aligned} x_{n+1} &= x_n + k(p'(x_n + y_n)x_n + p(x_n + y_n) - C_1'(x_n)) \\ y_{n+1} &= y_n + \alpha(p'(x_{n-1} + y_n)y_n + p(x_{n-1} + y_n) - C_2'(y_n)). \end{aligned} \tag{66}$$

We have:

Proposition 4.3. (i) *The solution of (66) in the neighborhood of* $(\overline{x}, \overline{x}, \overline{y}) \in \mathbb{R}^3$ *is:*

$$\begin{aligned} x_n &= \overline{x} + q_2 z_n + \overline{q}_2 \overline{z}_n + \frac{1}{2} w_{20}^2 z_n^2 + w_{11}^2 z_n \overline{z}_n + \frac{1}{2} w_{02}^2 \overline{z}_n^2, \\ y_n &= \overline{y} + q_3 z_n + \overline{q}_3 \overline{z}_n + \frac{1}{2} w_{20}^3 z_n^2 + w_{11}^3 z_n \overline{z}_n + w_{02}^3 \overline{z}_n^2, \\ u_n &= x_{n-1} = \overline{x} + q_1 z_n + \overline{q}_1 \overline{z}_n + \frac{1}{2} w_{20}^1 z_n^2 + w_{11}^1 z_n \overline{z}_n + w_{02}^1 \overline{z}_n^2, \end{aligned} \tag{67}$$

where z_n *is a solution of the equation:*

$$z_n = \mu(\beta) z_n + \frac{1}{2} g_{20} z_n^2 + g_{11} z_n \overline{z}_n + \frac{1}{2} g_{02} \overline{z}_n^2 + \frac{1}{2} g_{21} z_n^2 \overline{z}_n \tag{68}$$

and the coefficients from (67) and (68) are given by (36) and (38) for $m = 1$, *where* $a_{10}, a_{01}, a_{20}, a_{11}, a_{02}, a_{30}, a_{21}, a_{12}, a_{03}$ *are given by (57) and* $q \in \mathbb{R}^3$, $p \in \mathbb{R}^3$ *are given by (60), (61) for* $m = 1$.

(ii) *If* $l_0 = Re(e^{-i\theta(0)} C_1(0))$, *where* $\theta(\beta)$ *is given by (65) and then if* $l_0 < 0$ *in the neighborhood of the fixed point* $(\overline{x}, \overline{y})$ *there is a stable limit cycle.*

For $m = 2$, *the results are obtained in a similar way to Proposition 2.3.*

We will investigate an economic game where the price function is $p(x) = \frac{1}{x}$, $x \neq 0$, *and the cost functions are* $C_i(x) = c_i x + b_i$, *with* $c_i > 0$, $i = 1, 2$.

The following statements hold:

Proposition 4.4. *(i) The fixed point of the application (54) is* $(\overline{x}, \ldots, \overline{x}, \overline{y}) \in \mathbb{R}^{m+2}$ *where:*

$$\begin{aligned} \overline{x} &= \frac{c_2}{(c_1 + c_2)^2}, \\ \overline{y} &= \frac{c_1}{(c_1 + c_2)^2}. \end{aligned} \tag{69}$$

(ii) *The coefficients (56), (57) and (58) are:*

$$\begin{aligned} &\rho_1 = -(c_1 + c_2)^2,\ \rho_2 = 2(c_1 + c_2)^3,\ \rho_3 = -6(c_1 + c_2)^4, \rho_4 = 24(c_1 + c_2)^5, \\ &a_{10} = -2c_1(c_1 + c_2),\ a_{01} = c_2^2 - c_1^2, a_{11} = -2(c_1 + c_2)^3,\ a_{02} = 2(c_1 + c_2)^2(c_1 - 2c_2), \\ &a_{20} = 6c_1(c_1 + c_2)^2,\ a_{12} = 12(c_1 + c_2)^3(c_2 - c_1), a_{21} = 6(c_1 + c_2)^3(c_2 - 3c_1),\ a_{21} = a_{12}, \\ &a_{30} = -24c_1(c_1 + c_2)^3, b_{10} = c_1^2 - c_2^2,\ b_{01} = -2c_2(c_1 + c_2),\ b_{20} = 2(c_1 + c_2)^2(c_2 - 2c_1), \\ &b_{11} = 2(c_1 + c_2)^2(2c_2 - c_1), b_{02} = 6c_2(c_1 + c_2)^2,\ b_{30} = 12(c_1 + c_2)^3(c_1 - c_2),\ b_{21} = b_{30}, \\ &b_{12} = 6(c_1 + c_2)^3(c_1 - 3c_2),\ b_{03} = -24c_2(c_1 + c_2)^3. \end{aligned}$$

(iii) *The solutions of system (66) in the neighborhood of the fixed point* $(\overline{x}, \overline{x}, \overline{y}) \in \mathbb{R}^3$ *is given by (67). The coefficients from (67), (68) are:*

$$\begin{aligned} &g_{20} = p_2 a + p_3 b,\ g_{11} = p_2 a_1 + p_3 b_1,\ g_{02} = p_2 \overline{a} + p_3 \overline{b}, \\ &g_{21} = p_2 r_{20}^1 + p_3 r_{20}^2 + 2(p_2 r_{11}^1 + p_3 r_{11}^2) + p_2 C^1 + p_2 C^2, \end{aligned}$$

$$\begin{aligned} a &= (q_2, q_3)A_1(q_2, q_3)^T, \\ b &= (q_1, q_3)A_2(q_1, q_3)^T, \\ a_1 &= (q_2, q_3)A_1(\overline{q}_2, \overline{q}_3)^T, \\ b_1 &= (q_1, q_3)A_2(\overline{q}_1, \overline{q}_3)^T, \end{aligned}$$

$$\begin{aligned} &C^1 = (q_2, q_3)(q_2A_{11} + q_3A_{12})(\overline{q}_2, \overline{q}_3)^T, C^2 = (q_1, q_3)(q_1A_{21} + q_3A_{22})(\overline{q}_1, \overline{q}_3)^T, \\ &r_{20}^1 = (\overline{q}_2, \overline{q}_3)A_1(w_{20}^2, w_{20}^3)^T, \ r_{20}^2 = (\overline{q}_1, q_3)A_2(w_{20}^1, w_{20}^3)^T, \\ &r_{11}^1 = (\overline{q}_2, q_3)A_1(w_{11}^2, w_{11}^3)^T, \ r_{11}^2 = (q_1, q_3)A_2(w_{11}^1, w_{11}^3)^T, \end{aligned}$$

$$\begin{aligned} w_{20}^1 &= v_{20} - \frac{p_2a + p_3b}{\mu^2 - \mu} - \frac{\overline{p}_2a + \overline{p}_3b}{\mu^2 - \overline{\mu}}, \\ w_{20}^2 &= \mu^2v_{20} - \frac{p_2a + p_3b}{\mu^2 - \mu}q_2 - \frac{\overline{p}_2a + \overline{p}_3b}{\mu^2 - \overline{\mu}}\overline{q}_2, \\ w_{20}^3 &= \frac{a+(\mu^2-a_{10})\mu^2v_{20}}{a_{01}} - \frac{p_2a+p_3b}{\mu^2-\mu}q_3 - \frac{\overline{p}_2a+\overline{p}_3b}{\mu^2-\overline{\mu}}\overline{q}_3, \\ w_{02}^1 &= \overline{w}_{20}^1, \ w_{02}^2 = \overline{w}_{20}^2, \ w_{02}^3 = \overline{w}_{20}^3 \end{aligned}$$

$$\begin{aligned} w_{11}^1 &= v_{11} - \frac{p_2a_1 + p_3b_1}{1 - \mu} - \frac{\overline{p}_2a_1 + \overline{p}_3b_1}{1 - \overline{\mu}}, \\ w_{11}^2 &= v_{11} - \frac{p_2a_1 + p_3b_1}{1 - \mu}q_2 - \frac{\overline{p}_2a_1 + \overline{p}_3b_1}{1 - \overline{\mu}}\overline{q}_2, \\ w_{11}^3 &= \frac{a_1 + (1 - a_{10})v_{11}}{a_{01}} - \frac{p_2a_1 + p_3b_1}{1 - \mu}q_3 - \frac{\overline{p}_2a_1 + \overline{p}_3b_1}{1 - \overline{\mu}}\overline{q}_3, \end{aligned}$$

$$\begin{aligned} p_1 &= \frac{(\overline{\mu} - 1 - ka_{10})(\overline{\mu} - 1 - \alpha b_{10})}{(\overline{\mu} - 1 - ka_{10})(\overline{\mu} - 1 - kb_{01}) + \overline{\mu}(2\overline{\mu} - 2 - ka_{10} - \alpha b_{01})} \\ p_2 &= \frac{p_1}{\overline{\mu} - 1 - ka_{10}}, \ p_3 = \frac{\overline{\mu}}{\alpha b_{10}}p_1, \ q_1 = 1, \ q_2 = \mu, \ q_3 = \frac{\alpha b_{10}}{\mu - 1 - \alpha b_{01}}. \end{aligned}$$

(iv) *The variations of the profits in the neighborhood of the fixed point $(\overline{x}, \overline{y})^T \in \mathbb{R}^2$, are given by:*

$$\pi_{1n} = p(x_n + y_n)x_n - c_1x_n - b_1, \ \pi_{2n} = p(x_n + y_n)y_n - c_2y_n - b_2.$$

The above model has a similar behavior as the economic models that describe the business cycles (Kuznetsov, 1995), (Mircea et al., 2004).
The model can be analyzed in a similar way for the case $m > 2$.
For $m = 1$, the stochastic system associated to (53) is given by:

$$\begin{aligned} x_{n+1} &= x_n + k(p'(x_n + y_n)x_n + p(x_n + y_n) - c_1'(x_n)) + \xi_n b_{22}(x_n - \bar{x}) \\ y_{n+1} &= y_n + k(p'(x_{n-1} + y_n)y_n + p(x_{n-1} + y_n) - c_2'(y_n)) + \xi_n b_{33}(y_n - \bar{y}) \end{aligned} \tag{70}$$

where $(\bar{x}, \bar{y})$ is the solution of (55).

The linearized of (70) has the matrices:

$$A_1 = \begin{pmatrix} 0 & 1 & 0 \\ 0 & 1+ka_{10} & ka_{01} \\ \alpha b_{10} & 0 & 1+\alpha b_{01} \end{pmatrix}, B = \begin{pmatrix} 0 & 0 & 0 \\ 0 & b_{22} & 0 \\ 0 & 0 & b_{33} \end{pmatrix} \tag{71}$$

Using Proposition 2.1, the characteristic polynomial of (70) is given by:

$$P_2(\lambda) = \lambda(\lambda^2 - \lambda(a_{22}a_{33} + \sigma b_{22}b_{33}) - a_{23}a_{33}a_{31})(\lambda(\lambda - a_{22}^2)(\lambda - a_{33}^2 - \sigma b_{33}^2) - a_{23}^2 a_{31}^2), \tag{72}$$

where $a_{22} = 1 + ka_{10}$, $a_{23} = ka_{01}$, $a_{31} = \alpha b_{10}$, $a_{33} = 1 + \alpha b_{01}$.
The analysis of the roots for the equation $P_2(\lambda) = 0$ *is done for fixed values of the parameters.*
The numerical simulation can be done for $c_1 = 0.1$, $c_2 = 0.4$, $k = 0.04$, $\sigma = 0.4$.

5. The discrete deterministic and stochastic Kaldor model

The discrete Kaldor model describes the business cycle for the state variables characterized by the income (national income) Y_n and the capital stock K_n, where $n \in \mathbb{N}$. For the description of the model's equations we use the investment function $I : \mathbb{R}_+ \times \mathbb{R}_+ \to \mathbb{R}$ denoted by $I = I(Y, K)$ and the savings function $S : \mathbb{R}_+ \times \mathbb{R}_+ \to \mathbb{R}$, denoted by $S = S(Y, K)$ both considered as being differentiable functions (Dobrescu & Opriş, 2009), (Dobrescu & Opriş, 2009).
The discrete Kaldor model describes the income and capital stock variations using the functions I and S and it is described by:

$$\begin{aligned} Y_{n+1} &= Y_n + s(I(Y_n, K_n) - S(Y_n, K_n)) \\ K_{n+1} &= K_n + I(Y_n, K_n) - qK_n. \end{aligned} \tag{73}$$

In (73), $s > 0$ is an adjustment parameter, which measures the reaction of the system to the difference between investment and saving.
We admit Keynes's hypothesis which states that the saving function is proportional to income, meaning that

$$S(Y, K) = pY, \tag{74}$$

where $p \in (0, 1)$ is the propensity to save with the respect to the income.
The investment function I is defined by taking into account a certain normal level of income u and a normal level of capital stock $\frac{pu}{q}$, where $u \in \mathbb{R}$, $u > 0$. The coefficient $q \in (0, 1)$ represents the capital depreciation.
In what follows we admit Rodano's hypothesis and consider the form of the investment function as follows:

$$I(Y, K) = pu + r\left(\frac{pu}{q} - K\right) + f(Y - u) \tag{75}$$

where $r > 0$ and $f : \mathbb{R} \to \mathbb{R}$ is a differentiable function with $f(0) = 0$, $f'(0) \neq 0$ and $f'''(0) \neq 0$.
System (73) with conditions (74) and (75) is written as:

$$\begin{aligned} Y_{n+1} &= (1-sp)Y_n - rsK_n + sf(Y_n - u) + spu\left(1+\frac{r}{q}\right) \\ K_{n+1} &= (1-r-q)K_n + f(Y_n - u) + pu\left(1+\frac{r}{q}\right) \end{aligned} \tag{76}$$

with $s > 0$, $q \in (0,1)$, $p \in (0,1)$, $r > 0$, $u > 0$.
The application associated to system (76) is:

$$\begin{pmatrix} y \\ k \end{pmatrix} \to \begin{pmatrix} (1-sp)y - rsk + sf(y-u) + spu\left(1+\frac{r}{q}\right) \\ (1-r-q)k + f(y-u) + pu\left(1+\frac{r}{q}\right) \end{pmatrix}. \tag{77}$$

The fixed points of the application (77) with respect to the model's parameters s, q, p, r are the solutions of the following system:

$$\begin{aligned} py + rk - f(y-u) - pu\left(1+\frac{r}{q}\right) &= 0 \\ (r+q)k - f(y-u) - pu\left(1+\frac{r}{q}\right) &= 0 \end{aligned}$$

that is equivalent to:

$$qk - py = 0, \quad p\left(1+\frac{r}{q}\right)(y-u) = f(y-u). \tag{78}$$

Taking into account that f satisfies $f(0) = 0$, by analyzing (78) we have:

Proposition 5.1. (i) *The point of the coordinates* $P\left(u, \frac{pu}{q}\right)$ *is the fixed point of the application (77).*
(ii) If $f(x) = \arctan x$, and $p\left(1+\frac{r}{q}\right) \geq 1$ then application (77) has an unique fixed point given by $P\left(u, \frac{pu}{q}\right)$.
(iii) If $f(x) = \arctan x$ and $p\left(1+\frac{r}{q}\right) < 1$ then the application (77) has the fixed points $P\left(u, \frac{pu}{q}\right)$, $R\left(y_r, \frac{py_r}{q}\right)$, $Q\left(y_q, \frac{p}{q}y_q\right)$, where $y_q = 2u - y_r$ and y_r is the solution of the following equation:

$$\arctan(y-u) = p\left(1+\frac{r}{q}\right)(y-u)$$

Let (y_0, k_0) be a fixed point of the application (77). We use the following notations: $\rho_1 = f'(y_0 - u)$, $\rho_2 = f''(y_0 - u)$, $\rho_3 = f'''(y_0 - u)$ and

$$a_{10} = s(\rho_1 - p),\ a_{01} = -rs,\ b_{10} = \rho_1,\ b_{01} = -q - r.$$

Proposition 5.2. (i) *The Jacobian matrix of (77) in the fixed point* (y_0, k_0) *is:*

$$A = \begin{pmatrix} 1 + a_{10} & a_{01} \\ b_{10} & 1 + b_{01} \end{pmatrix}. \tag{79}$$

(ii) The characteristic equation of A given by (79) is:

$$\lambda^2 - a\lambda + b = 0 \tag{80}$$

where $a = 2 + a_{10} + b_{01}$, $b = 1 + a_{10} + b_{01} - a_{01}b_{10}$.
(iii) If $q + r < 1, \rho_1 < 1 + \dfrac{r(q+r-4)}{(q+r-2)^2}$ and $s = s_0$, where:

$$s_0 = \frac{q+r}{(1-q-r)(\rho_1 - p) + r}$$

then equation (80) has the roots with their absolute values equal to 1.
(iv) With respect to the change of variable:

$$s(\beta) = \frac{(1+\beta)^2 - 1 + q + r}{(1-q-r)(\rho_1 - p) + r}$$

equation (80) becomes:

$$\lambda^2 - a_1(\beta)\lambda + b_1(\beta) = 0 \tag{81}$$

where

$$a_1(\beta) = 2 + \frac{(\rho_1 - p)((1+\beta)^2 - 1 + \rho + r)}{(1-q-r)(\rho_1 - p) + r} - q - r, \quad b_1(\beta) = (1+\beta)^2.$$

Equation (81) has the roots:

$$\mu_{1,2}(\beta) = (1+\beta)e^{\pm i\theta(\beta)}$$

where

$$\theta(\beta) = \arccos \frac{a_1(\beta)}{2(1+\beta)}.$$

(v) The point $s(0) = s_0$ is a Neimark-Sacker bifurcation point.
(vi) The eigenvector $q \in \mathbb{R}^2$, which corresponds to the eigenvalue $\mu(\beta) = \mu$ and is a solution of $Aq = \mu q$, has the components

$$q_1 = 1, \quad q_2 = \frac{\mu - 1 - a_{10}}{a_{01}}. \tag{82}$$

The eigenvector $p \in \mathbb{R}^2$, which corresponds to the eigenvalue $\overline{\mu}$ and is a solution of $A^T p = \overline{\mu} p$, has the components:

$$p_1 = \frac{a_{01}b_{10}}{a_{01}b_{10} + (\overline{\mu} - 1 - a_{10})^2},$$
$$p_2 = \frac{a_{01}(\overline{\mu} - 1 - a_{01})}{a_{01}b_{10} + (\overline{\mu} - 1 - a_{10})^2}. \tag{83}$$

The vectors q, p given by (82) and (83) satisfy the condition $< q, p >= q_1\overline{p}_1 + q_2\overline{p}_2 = 1$.

The proof follows by direct calculation using (77).
With respect to the translation $y \to y + y_0$, $k \to k + k_0$, the application (77) becomes:

$$\begin{pmatrix} y \\ k \end{pmatrix} \to \begin{pmatrix} (1-sp)y - rsk + sf(y+y_0-u) - f(y_0-u) \\ -(r+q)k + f(y+y_0-u) - f(y_0-u) \end{pmatrix}. \tag{84}$$

Expanding F from (84) in Taylor series around $0 = (0,0)^T$ and neglecting the terms higher than the third order, we obtain:

$$F(y,k) = \begin{pmatrix} (1+a_{10})y + a_{01}k + \frac{1}{2}s\rho_2 y^2 + \frac{1}{6}s\rho_3 y^3 \\ b_{10}y + b_{01}k + \frac{1}{2}\rho_2 y^2 + \frac{1}{6}\rho_3 y^3 \end{pmatrix}.$$

Proposition 5.3. (i) *The canonical form of (84) is:*

$$\begin{aligned} z_{n+1} &= \mu(\beta)z_n + \frac{1}{2}(s(\beta)p_1 + p_2)\rho_2(z_n^2 + 2z_n\overline{z}_n + \overline{z}_n{}^2) + \\ &+ \frac{1}{6}(s(\beta)p_1 + p_2)\rho_3(z_n^3 + 3z_n^2\overline{z}_n + 3z_n\overline{z}_n^2 + \overline{z}_n^3). \end{aligned} \tag{85}$$

(ii) The coefficient $C_1(\beta)$ associated to the canonical form (85) is:

$$\begin{aligned} C_1(\beta) &= \left(\frac{(p(\beta)p_1 + p_2)^2(\overline{\mu} - 3 + 2\mu)}{2(\mu^2 - \mu)(\overline{\mu} - 1)} + \frac{|s(\beta)p_1 + p_2|^2}{1 - \overline{\mu}} + \right. \\ &+ \left. \frac{|s(\beta)p_1 + p_2|^2}{2(\mu^2 - \overline{\mu})}\right)\rho_2^2 + \frac{s(\beta)p_1 + p_2}{2}\rho_3 \end{aligned}$$

and $l_1(0) = Re(C_1(0)e^{i\theta(0)})$. If $l_1(0) < 0$ in the neighborhood of the fixed point (y_0, k_0) then there is a stable limit cycle. If $l_1(0) > 0$ there is an unstable limit cycle.
(iii) The solution of (76) in the neighborhood of the fixed point (y_0, k_0) is:

$$Y_n = y_0 + z_n + \overline{z}_n, \quad K_n = k_0 + q_2 z_n + \overline{q}_2\overline{z}_n$$

where z_n is a solution of (85).

The stochastic system of (76) is given by (Mircea et al., 2010):

$$\begin{aligned} Y_{n+1} &= (1-sp)Y_n - rsK_n + sf(Y_n - u) + spu\left(1 + \frac{r}{q}\right) + \xi_n b_{11}(Y_n - u) \\ K_{n+1} &= (1-r-q)K_n + f(Y_n - u) + pu\left(1 + \frac{r}{q}\right) + \xi_n b_{22}(K_n - \frac{pu}{q}) \end{aligned}$$

with $E(\xi_n) = 0$ and $E(\xi_n^2) = \sigma$.
Using (79) and Proposition 5.2, the characteristic polynomial of the linearized system of (5) is given by:

$$P_2(\lambda) = det \begin{pmatrix} \lambda - (1+a_{10})^2 - \sigma b_{11}^2 & -a_{01}^2 & -2a_{01}(1+a_{10}) \\ -b_{10}^2 & \lambda - (1+b_{01})^2 - \sigma b_{22} & -2b_{10}(1+b_{01}) \\ -b_{10}(1+a_{10}) & -a_{01}(1+b_{01}) & \lambda - (a_{01}b_{10}+ \\ & & +(1+a_{10})(1+b_{01})+ \\ & & +\sigma b_{11}b_{22}) \end{pmatrix} \quad (86)$$

The analysis of the roots for $P_2(\lambda) = 0$ can be done for fixed values of the parameters.

6. Conclusions

The aim of this chapter is to briefly present some methods used for analyzing the models described by deterministic and stochastic discrete-time equations with delay. These methods are applied to models that describe: the Internet congestion control, economic games and the Kaldor economic model, as well. The obtained results are presented in a form which admits the numerical simulation.
The present chapter contains a part of the authors' papers that have been published in journals or proceedings, to which we have added the stochastic aspects.
The methods used in this chapter allow us to study other models described by systems of equations with discrete time and delay and their associated stochastic models.

7. Acknowledgements

The research was done under the Grant with the title "The qualitative analysis and numerical simulation for some economic models which contain evasion and corruption", CNCSIS-UEFISCU (grant No. 1085/2008).

8. References

Dobrescu, L.; Opriş, D. (2009). Neimark–Sacker bifurcation for the discrete-delay Kaldor–Kalecki model, *Chaos, Soliton and Fractals*, Vol. 39, Issue 5, 15 June 2009, 519–530, ISSN-0960-0779.

Dobrescu, L.; Opriş, D. (2009). Neimark–Sacker bifurcation for the discrete-delay Kaldor model, *Chaos, Soliton and Fractals*, Vol. 40, Issue 5, 15 June 2009, 2462–2468 Vol. 39, 519–530, ISSN-0960-0779.

Kloeden, P.E.; Platen, E. (1995). *Numerical Solution of Stochastic Differential Equations*, Springer Verlag, ISBN, Berlin, ISBN 3-540-54062-8.

Kuznetsov, Y.A. (1995). *Elemets of Applied Bifurcations Theory*, Springer Verlag, ISBN, New-York, ISBN 0-387-21906-4.

Lorenz, H.W. (1993). *Nonlinear Dynamical Economics and Chaotic Motion*, Springer Verlag, ISBN, Berlin, ISBN 3540568816.

Mircea, G.; Neamţu, M.; Opriş, D. (2004). *Hopf bifurcation for dynamical systems with time delay and applications*, Mirton, ISBN, Timişoara, ISBN 973-661-379-8.

Mircea, G.; Neamţu, M., Cismaş, L., Opriş, D. (2010). Kaldor-Kalecki stochastic model of business cycles, *Proceedings of 11th WSEAS International Conference on Mathematics and Computers in Business and Economics*, pp. 86-91, 978-960-474-194-6, Iaşi, june 13-15, 2010, WSEAS Press

Mircea, G.; Opriş, D. (2009). Neimark-Sacker and flip bifurcations in a discrete-time dynamic system for Internet congestion, *Transaction on mathematics*, Volume 8, Issue 2, February 2009, 63–72, ISSN: 1109-2769

Neamţu, M. (2010). The deterministic and stochastic economic games, *Proceedings of 11th WSEAS International Conference on Mathematics and Computers in Business and Economics*, pp. 110-115, 978-960-474-194-6, Iaşi, june 13-15, 2010, WSEAS Press

27

Multidimensional Dynamics: From Simple to Complicated

Kang-Ling Liao, Chih-Wen Shih and Jui-Pin Tseng
Department of Applied Mathematics, National Chiao Tung University
Hsinchu, Taiwan 300, R.O.C

1. Introduction

The most apparent look of a discrete-time dynamical system is that an orbit is composed of a collection of points in phase space, in contrast to a trajectory curve for a continuous-time system. A basic and prominent theoretical difference between discrete-time and continuous-time dynamical systems is that chaos occurs in one-dimensional discrete-time dynamical systems, but not for one-dimensional deterministic continuous-time dynamical systems; the logistic map and logistic equation are the most well-known example illustrating this difference. On the one hand, fundamental theories for discrete-time systems have also been developed in a parallel manner as for continuous-time dynamical systems, such as stable manifold theorem, center manifold theorem and global attractor theory etc. On the other hand, analytical theory on chaotic dynamics has been developed more thoroughly for discrete-time systems (maps) than for continuous-time systems. Li-Yorke's period-three-implies-chaos and Sarkovskii's ordering on periodic orbits for one-dimensional maps are ones of the most celebrated theorems on chaotic dynamics.

Regarding chaos theory for multidimensional maps, there are renowned Smale-Birkhoff homoclinic theorem and Moser theorem for diffeomorphisms. In addition, Marotto extended Li-Yorke's theorem from one-dimension to multi-dimension through introducing the notion of snapback repeller in 1978. This theory applies to maps which are not one-to-one (not diffeomorphism). But the existence of a repeller is a basic prerequisite for the theory. There have been extensive applications of this theorem to various applied problems. However, due to a technical flaw, Marotto fixed the definition of snapback repeller in 2005. While Marotto's theorem is valid under the new definition, its condition becomes more difficult to examine for practical applications. Accessible and computable criteria for applying this theorem hence remain to be developed. In Section 4, we shall introduce our recent works and related developments in the application of Marotto's theorem, which also provide an effective numerical computation method for justifying the condition of this theorem.

Multidimensional systems may also exhibit simple dynamics; for example, every orbit converges to a fixed point, as time tends to infinity. Such a scenario is referred to as convergence of dynamics or complete stability. Typical mathematical tools for justifying such dynamics include Lyapunov method and LaSalle invariant principle, a discrete-time version.

However, it is not always possible to construct a Lyapunov function to apply this principle, especially for multidimensional nonlinear systems. We shall illustrate other technique that was recently formulated for certain systems in Section 3.
As neural network models are presented in both continuous-time and discrete-time forms, and can exhibit both simple dynamics and complicated dynamics, we shall introduce some representative neural network models in Section 2.

2. Neural network models

In the past few decades, neural networks have received considerable attention and were successfully applied to many areas such as combinatorial optimization, signal processing and pattern recognition (Arik, 2000, Chua 1998). Discrete-time neural networks have been considered more important than their continuous-time counterparts in the implementations (Liu, 2008). The research interests in discrete-time neural networks include chaotic behaviors (Chen & Aihara, 1997; Chen & Shih, 2002), stability of fixed points (Forti & Tesi, 1995; Liang & Cao, 2004; Mak et al., 2007), and their applications (Chen & Aihara, 1999; Chen & Shih, 2008). We shall introduce some typical discrete-time neural networks in this section.
Cellular neural network (CNN) is a large aggregation of analogue circuits. It was first proposed by Chua and Yang in 1988. The assembly consists of arrays of identical elementary processing units called cells. The cells are only connected to their nearest neighbors. This local connectivity makes CNNs very suitable for VLSI implementation. The equations for two-dimension layout of CNNs are given by

$$C\frac{dx_{ij}}{dt} = -\frac{1}{R}x_{ij}(t) + \sum_{(k,\ell)\in N_{ij}} [a_{ij,k\ell}h(x_{k\ell}(t)) + b_{ij,k\ell}u_{k\ell}] + I, \tag{1}$$

where $u_{k\ell}$, x_{ij}, $h(x_{ij})$ are the controlling input, state and output voltage of the specified CNN cell, respectively. CNNs are characterized by the bias I and the template set A and B which consist of $a_{ij,k\ell}$ and $b_{ij,k\ell}$, respectively. $a_{ij,k\ell}$ represents the linear feedback, and $b_{ij,k\ell}$ the linear control. The standard output h is a piecewise-linear function defined by $h(\xi) = \frac{1}{2}(|\xi+1| - |\xi-1|)$. C is the linear capacitor and R is the linear resistor. For completeness of the model, boundary conditions need to be imposed for the cells on the boundary of the assembly, cf. (Shih, 2000). The discrete-time cellular neural network (DT-CNN) counterpart can be described by the following difference equation.

$$x_{ij}(t+1) = \mu x_{ij}(t) + \sum_{(k,\ell)\in N_{ij}} [\tilde{a}_{ij,k\ell}h(x_{k\ell}(t)) + \tilde{b}_{ij,k\ell}u_{k\ell}] + z_i, \tag{2}$$

where t is an integer. System (2) can be derived from a delta operator based CNNs. If one collects from a continuous-time signal $x(t)$ a discrete-time sequence $x[k] = x(kT)$, the delta operator

$$\delta x[k] = \frac{x[k+1] - x[k]}{T}$$

is an approximation of the derivative of $x(t)$. Indeed, $\lim_{T\to 0} \delta x[k] = \dot{x}(t)|_{t=kT}$. In this case, $\mu = 1 - \frac{T}{\tau}$, where T is the sampling period, and $\tau = RC$. The parameters $\tilde{a}_{ij,k\ell}, \tilde{b}_{ij,k\ell}$ in (2) correspond to $a_{ij,k\ell}, b_{ij,k\ell}$ in (1) under sampling, cf. (Hänggi et al., 1999). If (2) is considered in conjunction with (1), then T is required to satisfy $\tau \geq T$ to avoid aliasing effects. Under this situation, $0 \leq \mu \leq 1$. Thus CT-CNN is the limiting case of delta operator based CNNs with $T \to 0$. If the delta operator based CNNs is considered by itself, then there is no restriction on T, and thus no restrictions on μ in (2). On the other hand, a sampled-data based CNN has been introduced in (Harrer & Nossek, 1992). Such a network corresponds to the limiting case of delta operator based CNNs as $T \to 1$. For an account of unifying results on the above-mentioned models, see (Hänggi et al., 1999) and the references therein. In addition, Euler's difference scheme for (1) takes the form

$$x_{ij}(t+1) = (1 - \frac{\Delta t}{RC})x_{ij}(t) + \frac{\Delta t}{C}\left(\sum_{k \in N_{ij}} a_{ij,k\ell}h(x_{k\ell}(t)) + b_{ij,k\ell}u_{k\ell} + I\right). \quad (3)$$

Note that CNN of any dimension can be reformulated into a one-dimensional setting, cf. (Shih & Weng, 2002). We rewrite (2) into a one-dimensional form as

$$x_i(t+1) = \mu x_i(t) + \sum_{k=1}^{n} \omega_{ik}h(x_k(t)) + z_i. \quad (4)$$

The complete stability using LaSalle invariant principle has been studied in (Chen & Shih, 2004a). We shall review this result in Section 3.1.

Transiently chaotic neural network (TCNN) has been shown powerful in solving combinatorial optimization problems (Peterson & Söderberg, 1993; Chen & Aihara, 1995, 1997, 1999). The system is represented by

$$x_i(t+1) = \mu x_i(t) + w_{ii}(t)[y_i(t) - a_{0i}] + \Sigma_{k \neq i}^{n} w_{ik}y_k(t) + a_i \quad (5)$$

$$y_i(t) = (1 + e^{\frac{-x_i(t)}{\varepsilon}})^{-1} \quad (6)$$

$$w_{ii}(t+1) = (1 - \gamma)w_{ii}(t), \quad (7)$$

where $i = 1, \cdots, n$, $t \in \mathbb{N}$ (positive integers), ε, γ are fixed numbers with $\varepsilon > 0$, $0 < \gamma < 1$. The main feature of TCNN contains chaotic dynamics temporarily generated for global searching and self-organizing. As certain variables (corresponding to temperature in the annealing process) decrease, the network gradually approaches a dynamical structure which is similar to classical neural networks. The system then settles at stationary states and provides a solution to the optimization problem. Equations (5)-(6) with constant self-feedback connection weights, that is, $w_{ii}(t) = w_{ii} =$ constant, has been studied in (Chen & Aihara, 1995, 1997); therein, it was shown that snapback repellers exist if $|w_{ii}|$ are large enough. The result hence implicates certain chaotic dynamics for the system. More complete analytical arguments by applying Marotto's theorem through the formulation of upper and lower dynamics to conclude the chaotic dynamics have been performed in (Chen & Shih, 2002, 2008, 2009). As the system evolves, w_{ii} decreases, and the chaotic behavior vanishes. In (Chen & Shih, 2004), they derived sufficient conditions under which evolutions for the system converge to fixed points of the system. Moreover, attracting sets and uniqueness of fixed point for the system were also addressed.

Time delays are unavoidable in a neural network because of the finite signals switching and transmission speeds. The implementation of artificial neural networks incorporating delays has been an important focus in neural systems studies (Buric & Todorovic, 2003; Campbell, 2006; Roska & Chua, 1992; Wu, 2001). Time delays can cause oscillations or alter the stability of a stationary solution of a system. For certain discrete-time neural networks with delays, the stability of stationary solution has been intensively studied in (Chen et al., 2006; Wu et al., 2009; Yua et al., 2010), and the convergence of dynamics has been analyzed in (Wang, 2008; Yuan, 2009). Among these studies, a typically investigated model is the one of Hopfield-type:

$$u_i(t+1) = a_i(t)u_i(t) + \sum_{j=1}^{m} b_{ij}(t)g_j(u_j(t - r_{ij}(t))) + J_i,\ i = 1, 2, \cdots, m. \tag{8}$$

Notably, system (8) represents an autonomous system if $a_i(t) \equiv a_i$, and $b_{ij}(t) \equiv b_{ij}$ (Chen et al., 2006), otherwise, a non-autonomous system (Yuan, 2009).
The class of Z-matrices consists of those matrices whose off-diagonal entries are less than or equal to zero. A M-matrix is a Z-matrix satisfying that all eigenvalues have positive real parts. For instance, one characterization of a nonsingular square matrix P to be a M-matrix is that P has non-positive off-diagonal entries, positive diagonal entries, and non-negative row sums. There exist several equivalent conditions for a Z-matrix P to be M-matrix, such as the one where there exists a positive diagonal matrix D such that PD is a diagonally dominant matrix, or all principal minors of P are positive (Plemmons, 1977). A common approach to conclude the stability of an equilibrium for a discrete-time neural network is through constructing Lyapunov-Krasovskii function/functional for the system. In (Chen, 2006), based on M-matrix theory, they constructed a Lyapunov function to derive the delay-independent and delay-dependent exponential stability results.
Synchronization is a common and elementary phenomenon in many biological and physical systems. Although the real network architecture can be extremely complicated, rich dynamics arising from the interaction of simple network motifs are believed to provide similar sources of activities as in real-life systems. Coupled map networks introduced by Kaneko (Kaneko, 1984) have become one of the standard models in synchronization studies. Synchronization in diffusively coupled map networks without delays is well understood, and the synchronizability of the network depends on the underlying network topology and the dynamical behaviour of the individual units (Jost & Joy, 2001; Lu & Chen, 2004). The synchronization in discrete-time networks with non-diffusively and delayed coupling is investigated in a series of works of Bauer and coworkers (Bauer et al., 2009; Bauer et al., 2010).

3. Simple dynamics

Orbits of discrete-time dynamical system can jump around wildly. However, there are situations that the dynamics are organized in a simple manner; for example, every solution converges to a fixed point as time tends to infinity. Such a notion is referred to as *convergence of dynamics* or *complete stability*. Moreover, the simplest situation is that all orbits converge to a unique fixed point. We shall review some theories and results addressing such simple dynamics. In Subsection 3.1, we introduce LaSalle invariant principle and illustrate its application in discrete-time neural networks. In Subsection 3.2, we review the component-competing technique and its application in concluding global consensus for a discrete-time competing system.

3.1 Lyapunov method and LaSalle invariant principle

Let us recall LaSalle invariant principle for difference equations. We consider the difference equation

$$\mathbf{x}(t+1) = F(\mathbf{x}(t)), \tag{9}$$

where $F : \mathbb{R}^n \longrightarrow \mathbb{R}^n$ is a continuous function. Let U be a subset of $\mathbb{R}^n$. For a function $V : U \longrightarrow \mathbb{R}$, define $\dot{V}(\mathbf{x}) = V(F(\mathbf{x})) - V(\mathbf{x})$. V is said to be a *Lyapunov function* of (9) on U if (i) V is continuous, and (ii) $\dot{V}(\mathbf{x}) \leq 0$ for all $\mathbf{x} \in U$. Set

$$S_0 := \{\mathbf{x} \in \overline{U} | \dot{V}(\mathbf{x}) = 0\}.$$

LaSalle Invariant Principle (LaSalle, 1976). Let F be a continuous mapping on $\mathbb{R}^n$, and let V be a Lyapunov function for F on a set $U \subseteq \mathbb{R}^n$. If orbit $\gamma := \{F^n(\mathbf{x}) | n \in \mathbb{N}\}$ is contained in a compact set in U, then its ω-limit set $\omega(\gamma) \subset S_0 \bigcap V^{-1}(c)$ for some $c = c(\mathbf{x})$.

This principle has been applied to the discrete-time cellular neural network (4) in (Chen & Shih, 2004a), where the Lyapunov function is constructed as

$$V(\mathbf{x}) = -\frac{1}{2}\sum_{i=1}^{n}\sum_{k=1}^{n} \omega_{ik} h(x_i) h(x_k) - \sum_{i=1}^{n} z_i h(x_i) + \frac{1}{2}(1-\mu)\sum_{i=1}^{n} h(x_i)^2,$$

and $h(\xi) = \frac{1}{2}(|\xi+1| - |\xi-1|)$ and $\mathbf{x} = (x_1, \cdots, x_n) \in \mathbb{R}^n$. Let us quote the main results therein.

Proposition (Chen & Shih, 2004a). Let W be a positive-definite symmetric matrix and $0 \leq \mu \leq 1$. Then V is a Lyapunov function for (4) on $\mathbb{R}^n$.

Consider the condition

$$\text{(H)} \quad \frac{1}{1-\mu}\left[\omega_{ii} - \sum_{k, j_k = \text{"m"}} |\omega_{ik}| + \sum_{j_k \neq \text{"m"},\, k \neq i} \delta(j_i, j_k)\omega_{ik} + z(i)\right] > -1.$$

Theorem (Chen & Shih, 2004a). Let W be a positive-definite symmetric matrix. If $0 < \mu < 1$ and condition (H) holds, then the DT-CNN with regular parameters is completely stabile.

Next, let us outline LaSalle invariant principle for non-autonomous difference equations. In addition to the classical result by LaSalle there is a modified version for the theorem reported in (Chen & Shih, 2004b). The alternative conditions derived therein is considered more applicable and has been applied to study the convergence of the TCNN.

Let $\mathbb{N}$ be the set of positive integers. For a given continuous function $\mathbf{F} : \mathbb{N} \times \mathbb{R}^n \longrightarrow \mathbb{R}^n$, we consider the non-autonomous difference equation

$$\mathbf{x}(t+1) = \mathbf{F}(t, \mathbf{x}(t)). \tag{10}$$

A sequence of points $\{\mathbf{x}(t)\}_1^\infty$ in $\mathbb{R}^n$ is a solution of (10) if $\mathbf{x}(t+1) = \mathbf{F}(t, \mathbf{x}(t))$, for all $t \in \mathbb{N}$. Let $\mathcal{O}_\mathbf{x} = \{\mathbf{x}(t) \mid t \in \mathbb{N}, \mathbf{x}(1) = \mathbf{x}\}$, be the orbit of $\mathbf{x}$. We say that $\mathbf{p}$ is a ω-limit point of $\mathcal{O}_\mathbf{x}$ if there exists a sequence of positive integers $\{t_k\}$ with $t_k \to \infty$ as $k \to \infty$, such that $\mathbf{p} = \lim_{k\to\infty} \mathbf{x}(t_k)$. Denote by $\omega(\mathbf{x})$ the set of all ω-limit points of $\mathcal{O}_\mathbf{x}$.

Let $\mathbb{N}_i$ represent the set of all positive integers larger than n_i, for some positive integer n_i. Let G be any set in $\mathbb{R}^n$ and $\overline{G}$ be its closure. For a function $V : \mathbb{N}_0 \times G \longrightarrow \mathbb{R}$, define $\dot{V}(t,\mathbf{x}) = V(t+1,\mathbf{F}(t,\mathbf{x})) - V(t,\mathbf{x})$. If $\{\mathbf{x}(t)\}$ is a solution of (10), then $\dot{V}(t,\mathbf{x}) = V(t+1,\mathbf{x}(t+1)) - V(t,\mathbf{x}(t))$. V is said to be a *Lyapunov function* for (10) if
(i) $\{V(t,\cdot) \mid t \in \mathbb{N}_0\}$ is equi-continuous, and
(ii) for each $p \in \overline{G}$, there exists a neighborhood U of p such that $V(t,\mathbf{x})$ is bounded below for $\mathbf{x} \in U \cap G$ and $t \in \mathbb{N}_1$, $n_1 \geq n_0$, and
(iii) there exists a continuous function $Q_0 : \overline{G} \to \mathbb{R}$ such that $\dot{V}(t,\mathbf{x}) \leq -Q_0(\mathbf{x}) \leq 0$ for all $\mathbf{x} \in G$ and for all $t \in \mathbb{N}_2$, $n_2 \geq n_1$,
or
(iii)′ there exist a continuous function $Q_0 : \overline{G} \to \mathbb{R}$ and an equi-continuous family of functions $Q : \mathbb{N}_2 \times \overline{G} \to \mathbb{R}$ such that $\lim_{t\to\infty} |Q(t,\mathbf{x}) - Q_0(\mathbf{x})| = 0$ for all $\mathbf{x} \in G$ and $\dot{V}(t,\mathbf{x}) \leq -Q(t,\mathbf{x}) \leq 0$ for all $(t,\mathbf{x}) \in \mathbb{N}_2 \times G$, $n_2 \geq n_1$.
Define

$$S_0 = \{\mathbf{x} \in \overline{G} : Q_0(\mathbf{x}) = 0\}.$$

Theorem (Chen & Shih, 2004a). Let $V : \mathbb{N}_0 \times G \to \mathbb{R}$ be a Lyapunov function for (10) and let $\mathcal{O}_\mathbf{x}$ be an orbit of (10) lying in G for all $t \in \mathbb{N}_0$. Then $\lim_{t\to\infty} Q(t,\mathbf{x}(t)) = 0$, and $\omega(\mathbf{x}) \subset S_0$.

This theorem with conditions (i), (ii), and (iii) has been given in (LaSalle, 1976). We quote the proof for the second case reported in (Chen & Shih, 2004b). Let $\mathbf{p} \in \omega(\mathbf{x})$. That is, there exists a sequence $\{t_k\}_1^\infty$, $t_k \to \infty$ as $k \to \infty$ and $\mathbf{x}(t_k) \to \mathbf{p}$ as $k \to \infty$. Since $V(t_k,\mathbf{x}(t_k))$ is non-increasing and bounded below, $V(t_k,\mathbf{x}(t_k))$ approaches a real number as $k \to \infty$. Moreover, $V(t_{k+1},\mathbf{x}(t_{k+1})) - V(t_1,\mathbf{x}(t_1)) \leq -\sum_{t=t_1}^{t_{k+1}-1} Q(t,\mathbf{x}(t))$, by (iii)′. Thus, $\sum_{t=t_1}^{\infty} Q(t,\mathbf{x}(t)) < \infty$. Hence, $Q(t,\mathbf{x}(t)) \to 0$ as $t \to \infty$, since $Q(t,\mathbf{x}(t)) \geq 0$. Notably, $Q(t_k,\mathbf{x}(t_k)) \to Q_0(\mathbf{x}(t_k))$ as $k \to \infty$. This can be justified by observing that

$$\begin{aligned}
&|Q(t_k,\mathbf{x}(t_k)) - Q_0(\mathbf{x}(t_k))| \\
&\leq |Q(t_k,\mathbf{x}(t_k)) + Q(t_k,\mathbf{p}) - Q(t_k,\mathbf{p}) + Q_0(\mathbf{p}) - Q_0(\mathbf{p}) - Q_0(\mathbf{x}(t_k))|.
\end{aligned}$$

In addition, $|Q_0(\mathbf{x}(t))| \leq |Q(t,\mathbf{x}(t))| + |Q(t,\mathbf{x}(t)) - Q_0(\mathbf{x}(t))|$. It follows from (iii)′ that $Q_0(\mathbf{x}(t_k)) \to 0$ as $k \to \infty$. Therefore, $Q_0(\mathbf{p}) = 0$, since Q_0 is continuous. Thus, $\mathbf{p} \in S_0$.
If we further assume that V is bounded, then it is obvious that the proof can be much simplified. In the investigations for the asymptotic behaviors of TCNN, condition (iii)′ is more achievable.
We are interested in knowing whether if an orbit of the system (10) approaches an equilibrium state or fixed point as time tends to infinity. The structure of ω-limit sets for the orbits provides an important information toward this investigation. In discrete-time dynamical systems, the ω-limit set of an orbit is not necessarily connected. However, the following proposition has been proved by Hale and Raugel in 1992.

Proposition (Hale & Raugel, 1992). Let T be a continuous map on a Banach space X. Suppose that the ω-limit set $\omega(\mathbf{x})$ is contained in the set of fixed points of T, and the closure of the orbit $\mathcal{O}_\mathbf{x}$ is compact. Then $\omega(\mathbf{x})$ is connected.

This proposition can be extended to non-autonomous systems for which there exist limiting maps. Namely,

($\mathbf{A}$) There exists a continuous map $\overline{\mathbf{F}} : \mathbb{R}^n \to \mathbb{R}^n$ such that $\lim_{t\to\infty} \|\mathbf{F}(t,\mathbf{x}) - \overline{\mathbf{F}}(\mathbf{x})\| = 0$, for all $\mathbf{x} \in \mathbb{R}^n$.

Theorem (Chen & Shih, 2004b). Assume that (10) satisfies ($\mathbf{A}$), the orbit $\mathcal{O}_{\mathbf{x}}$ is bounded, and $\omega(\mathbf{x})$, the ω-limit set of $\mathbf{x}$, is contained in the set of fixed points of $\overline{\mathbf{F}}$. Then $\omega(\mathbf{x})$ is connected. Under this circumstances, if $\overline{\mathbf{F}}$ has only finitely many fixed points, then the orbit $\mathcal{O}_{\mathbf{x}}$ approaches some single fixed point of $\overline{\mathbf{F}}$, as t tends to infinity.

Let us represent the TCNN system (5)-(7) by the following time-dependent map

$$\mathbf{F}(t,\mathbf{x}) = (F_1(t,\mathbf{x}), \cdots, F_n(t,\mathbf{x}))$$

where

$$F_i(t,\mathbf{x}) = \alpha x_i + (1-\gamma)^t \omega_{ii}(0)(y_i - a_{0i}) + \sum_{j\neq i}^{n} \omega_{ij} y_j + a_i,$$

where $y_i = h_i(x_i), i = 1, \cdots, n$ and h_i is defined in (6). The orbits of TCNN are then given by the iterations $\mathbf{x}(t+1) = \mathbf{F}(t,\mathbf{x}(t))$ with components $x_i(t+1) = F_i(t,\mathbf{x}(t))$. Note that $\mathbf{y} = H(\mathbf{x}) = (h_1(x_1), \cdots, h_n(x_n))$ is a diffeomorphism on $\mathbf{R}^n$. Let W_0 denote the $n \times n$ matrix obtained from the connection matrix W with its diagonal entries being replaced by zeros. Restated, $W_0 = W - \text{diag}[W]$. For given $0 < \gamma < 1$, choose $0 < b < 1$ such that $|\frac{1-\gamma}{b}| < 1$. We consider the following time-dependent energy-like function:

$$\begin{aligned} V(t,\mathbf{x}) = & -\frac{1}{2}\sum_{i=1}^{n}\sum_{j\neq i}^{n} w_{ij} h_i(x_i) h_j(x_j) - \sum_{i=1}^{n} a_i h_i(x_i) \\ & + (1-\alpha)\sum_{i=1}^{n}\int_0^{h_i(x_i)} h_i^{-1}(\eta)\,d\eta + b^t. \end{aligned} \tag{11}$$

Theorem (Chen & Shih, 2004b). Assume that W_0 is a cycle-symmetric matrix, and either one of the following condition holds,
(i) $0 \le \alpha \le \frac{1}{3}$ and $W_0 + 4(1-\alpha)\varepsilon I$ is positive definite;
(ii) $\frac{1}{3} \le \alpha \le 1$ and $W_0 + 8\alpha\varepsilon I$ is positive definite;
(iii) $\alpha \ge 1$ and $W_0 + 8\varepsilon I$ is positive definite.
Then there exists an $n_0 \in \mathbb{N}$ so that $V(t,\mathbf{x})$ defined by (11) is a Lyapunov function for the TCNN (5)-(7) on $\mathbb{N}_0 \times \mathbb{R}^n$.

3.2 Global consensus through a competing-component approach

Grossberg (1978) considered a class of competitive systems of the form

$$\dot{x}_i = a_i(\mathbf{x})[b_i(x_i) - C(x_1, x_2, \cdots, x_n)], \quad i = 1, 2, \cdots, n, \tag{12}$$

where $a_i \ge 0$, $\partial C/\partial x_i \ge 0$, $\mathbf{x} = (x_1, x_2, \cdots, x_n) \in \mathbb{R}^n$. In such a system, n is the number of competing populations, $a_i(\mathbf{x})$ refers to competitive balance, $b_i(x_i)$ represents interpopulation signal functions, and $C(x)$ stands for mean competition function, or adaptation level. System (12) was proposed as a mathematical model for the resolution to a dilemma in science for hundred of years: How do arbitrarily many individuals, populations, or states, each obey unique and personal laws, succeed in harmoniously interacting with each other to

form some sort of stable society, or collective mode of behavior. Systems of the form (12) include the generalized Volterra-Lotka systems and an inhibitory network (Hirsch, 1989). A suitable Lyapunov function for system (12) is not known, hence the Lyapunov method and LaSalle invariant principle are invalid. The work in (Grossberg, 1978) employed a skillful competing-component analysis to prove that for system (12), any initial value $\mathbf{x}(0) \geq 0$ (i.e. $x_i(0) \geq 0$, for any i) evolves to a limiting pattern $\mathbf{x}(\infty) = (x_1(\infty), x_2(\infty), \cdots, x_n(\infty))$ with $0 \leq x_i(\infty) := \lim_{t\to\infty} x_i(t) < \infty$, under some conditions on a_i, b_i, C.
System (12) can be approximated, via Euler's difference scheme or delta-operator circuit implementation (Harrer & Nossek,1992), by

$$x_i((k+1)\delta) = x_i(k\delta) + \delta a_i(\mathbf{x}(k\delta))[b_i(x_i(k\delta)) - C(\mathbf{x}(k\delta))],$$

where one takes $x_i(k\delta)$ as the k-th iteration of x_i. In this subsection, let us review the competing-component analysis for convergent dynamics reported in (Shih & Tseng, 2009). Consider the following discrete-time model,

$$x_i(k+1) = x_i(k) + \beta a_i(\mathbf{x}(k))[b_i(x_i(k)) - C(\mathbf{x}(k))], \tag{13}$$

where $i = 1, 2, \cdots, n$, $k \in \mathbb{N}_0 := \{0\} \bigcup \mathbb{N}$. We first consider the theory for (13) with $\beta = 1$, i.e.

$$x_i(k+1) = x_i(k) + a_i(\mathbf{x}(k))[b_i(x_i(k)) - C(\mathbf{x}(k))]. \tag{14}$$

The results can then be extended to (13). First, let us introduce the following definition for the convergent property of discrete-time systems.

Definition. A discrete-time competitive system $\mathbf{x}(k+1) = F(\mathbf{x}(k))$ is said to achieve *global consensus* (or *global pattern formation, global convergence*) if, given any initial value $\mathbf{x}(0) \in \mathbb{R}^n$, the limit $x_i(\infty) := \lim_{k\to\infty} x_i(k)$ exists, for all $i = 1, 2, \cdots, n$.

The following conditions are needed for the main results.
Condition (A1): Each $a_i(\mathbf{x})$ is continuous, and

$$0 < a_i(\mathbf{x}) \leq 1, \text{ for all } \mathbf{x} \in \mathbb{R}^n, i = 1, 2, \cdots, n.$$

Condition (A2): $C(\mathbf{x})$ is bounded and continuously differentiable with bounded derivatives; namely, there exist constants M_1, M_2, r_j such that for all $\mathbf{x} \in \mathbb{R}^n$,

$$M_1 \leq C(\mathbf{x}) \leq M_2,$$

$$0 \leq \frac{\partial C}{\partial x_j}(\mathbf{x}) \leq r_j,\ j = 1, 2, \cdots, n.$$

Condition (A3): $b_i(\xi)$ is continuously differentiable, strictly decreasing and there exist $d_i > 0$, $l_i, u_i \in \mathbb{R}$ such that for all $i = 1, 2, \cdots n$,

$$-d_i \leq b_i'(\xi) < 0, \text{ for all } \xi \in \mathbb{R},$$

$$b_i(\xi) > M_2, \text{ for } \xi \leq l_i, \text{ and } b_i(\xi) < M_1, \text{ for } \xi \geq u_i.$$

Condition (A4): For $i = 1, 2, \cdots, n$,

$$0 < d_i \leq 1 - \sum_{j=1}^{n} r_j < 1.$$

Theorem (Shih & Tseng, 2009). System (14) with a_i, b_i, and C satisfying conditions (A1)-(A4) achieves global consensus.

The proof of this theorem consists of three lemmas which depict the properties for the following terms:

$$\begin{aligned}
&g_i(k) = b_i(x_i(k)) - C(\mathbf{x}(k)),\ \Delta g_i(k) = g_i(k+1) - g_i(k),\\
&\hat{g}(k) = \max\{g_i(k) : i = 1, 2, \cdots, n\},\ \check{g}(k) = \min\{g_i(k) : i = 1, 2, \cdots, n\},\\
&I(k) = \min\{i : g_i(k) = \hat{g}(k)\},\ J(k) = \min\{i : g_i(k) = \check{g}(k)\},\\
&\hat{x}(k) = x_{I(k)}(k),\ \check{x}(k) = x_{J(k)}(k),\\
&\hat{b}(k) = b_{I(k)}(\hat{x}(k)),\ \check{b}(k) = b_{J(k)}(\check{x}(k)),\\
&\Delta\hat{b}(k) = \hat{b}(k+1) - \hat{b}(k),\ \Delta\check{b}(k) = \check{b}(k+1) - \check{b}(k),\\
&\Delta b_i(x_i(k)) = b_i(x_i(k+1)) - b_i(x_i(k)).
\end{aligned}$$

Let us recall some of the key lemmas to get a flavor of this approach.

Lemma. Consider system (14) with a_i, b_i, and C satisfying conditions (A1)-(A4). Then
(i) for function $\hat{g}$, either case ($\hat{g}$-(i)) or case ($\hat{g}$-(ii)) holds, where
($\hat{g}$-(i)): $\hat{g}(k) < 0$, for all $k \in \mathbb{N}_0$,
($\hat{g}$-(ii)): $\hat{g}(k) \geq 0$, for all $k \geq K_1$, for some $K_1 \in \mathbb{N}_0$;
(ii) for function $\check{g}$, either case ($\check{g}$-(i)) or case ($\check{g}$-(ii)) holds, where
($\check{g}$-(i)): $\check{g}(k) > 0$, for all $k \in \mathbb{N}_0$,
($\check{g}$-(ii)): $\check{g}(k) \leq 0$, for all $k \geq K_2$, for some $K_2 \in \mathbb{N}_0$.

Lemma. Consider system (14) with a_i, b_i, and C satisfying conditions (A1)-(A4). Then $\lim_{k\to\infty} \hat{b}(k) = \lim_{k\to\infty} C(\mathbf{x}(k)) = \lim_{k\to\infty} \check{b}(k)$.

4. Complicated dynamics

In this section, we summarize some analytic theories on chaotic dynamics for multi-dimensional maps. There are several definitions for chaos. Let us introduce the representative one by Devaney (1989):

Definition. Let (X, d) be a metric space. A map $F : \Omega \subset X \to \Omega$ is said to be *chaotic* on Ω if
(i) F is topologically transitive in Ω,
(ii) the periodic points of F in Ω are dense in Ω,
(iii) F has sensitive dependence on initial conditions in Ω.

It was shown in (Banks, et al., 1992) that condition (iii) holds under conditions (i) and (ii), if F is continuous in Ω. Let us recall Li-Yorke's theorem.

Theorem (Li & Yorke, 1975). Let J be an interval and let $f : J \to J$ be continuous. Assume there is a point $a \in J$ for which the points $b = f(a), c = f^2(a)$ and $d = f^3(a)$, satisfy

$$d \leq a < b < c \text{ (or } d \geq a > b > c).$$

Then for every $k = 1, 2, \cdots$, there is a periodic point in J having period k. Furthermore, there is an uncountable set $S \subset J$ (containing no periodic points), which satisfies:
(i) $\limsup_{n\to\infty} |f^n(p) - f^n(q)| > 0$, and $\liminf_{n\to\infty} |f^n(p) - f^n(q)| = 0$, for every $p, q \in S$ with $p \neq q$; (ii) $\limsup_{n\to\infty} |f^n(p) - f^n(q)| > 0$, for every $p \in S$ and periodic point $q \in J$.
Indeed, if there is a periodic point of period 3, then the hypothesis of the theorem will be satisfied. The notion of scrambled set can be generalized to metric space (X, d).

Definition. Let (X, d) be a metric space and $F : X \to X$ be a continuous map. A subset S of X is called a *scrambled set* of F, if for any two different points $\mathbf{x}, \mathbf{y} \in S$,

$$\liminf_{n\to\infty} d(F^n(\mathbf{x}), F^n(\mathbf{y})) = 0, \ \limsup_{n\to\infty} d(F^n(\mathbf{x}), F^n(\mathbf{y})) > 0.$$

A map F is said to be *chaotic in the sense of Li-Yorke* if it has an uncountable scrambled set. It was shown in (Huang & Ye, 2002) that for a compact matric space (X, d), if a map F is chaotic in the sense of Devaney then F is also chaotic in the sense of Li-Yorke.
Let us consider a differentiable map

$$F : \mathbb{R}^n \to \mathbb{R}^n; \tag{15}$$

we denote $\mathbf{x}_k = F^k(\mathbf{x}_0)$ for $k \in \mathbb{N}$ and $\mathbf{x}_0 \in \mathbb{R}^n$, and by $B_r(\mathbf{x})$ and $B_r^*(\mathbf{x})$ the closed balls in $\mathbb{R}^n$ with center at $\mathbf{x}$ and radius $r > 0$ under Euclidean norm $\|\cdot\|$ and certain norm $\|\cdot\|_*$, respectively.

Definition. Suppose $\mathbf{z}$ is a hyperbolic fixed point of a diffeomorphism map $F : \mathbb{R}^n \to \mathbb{R}^n$, and some eigenvalues of $DF(\mathbf{z})$ are greater than one in magnitude and the others smaller than one in magnitude. If the stable manifold and the unstable manifold of F at $\mathbf{z}$ intersect transversally at some point $\mathbf{x}_0$, the orbit $\{\mathbf{x}_k\}_{k=-\infty}^{\infty}$ of F is called a *transversal homoclinic orbit*.
For a diffeomorphism F, Smale discovered an elegant and significant result:

Theorem (Smale, 1967). If the diffeomorphism map F has a transversal homoclinic orbit, then there exists a Cantor set $\Lambda \subset \mathbb{R}^n$ on which F^m is topologically conjugate to a full shift of a symbolic dynamical system with N symbols, for some positive integer m.

Remark. The above theorem can be generalized to maps which are not diffeomorphisms under some extended definition of transversal homoclinic orbits, see Theorem 5.2 and Section 7 in (Hale & Lin, 1986) and Theorem 5.1 in (Steinlein & Walther, 1990).

4.1 On Marotto's theorem

Analytical theory on chaotic dynamics for multi-dimensional systems is quite limited; yet some important progresses have been made. In 1978, Marotto introduced the notion of snapback repeller and extended Li-Yorke's theorem to multi-dimensional maps. This result plays an important role in the study of chaos for higher but finite-dimensional noninvertible maps.

The point $\mathbf{z} \in R^n$ is called an *expanding fixed point* of F in $B_r(\mathbf{z})$, if F is differentiable in $B_r(\mathbf{z})$, $F(\mathbf{z}) = \mathbf{z}$ and

$$|\lambda(\mathbf{x})| > 1, \text{ for all eigenvalues } \lambda(\mathbf{x}) \text{ of } DF(\mathbf{x}), \text{ for all } \mathbf{x} \in B_r(\mathbf{z}). \quad (16)$$

If F is not a one-to-one function in $\mathbb{R}^n$ and $\mathbf{z}$ is an expanding fixed point of F in $B_r(\mathbf{z})$, then there may exist a point $\mathbf{x}_0 \in B_r(\mathbf{z})$ with $\mathbf{x}_0 \neq \mathbf{z}$ such that $F^{\ell}(\mathbf{x}_0) = \mathbf{z}$ for some positive integer ℓ. The original definition of snapback repeller is as follows.

Definition (Marotto, 1978). Assume that $\mathbf{z}$ is an expanding fixed point of F in $B_r(\mathbf{z})$ for some $r > 0$. Then $\mathbf{z}$ is said to be a *snapback repeller* of F if there exists a point $\mathbf{x}_0 \in B_r(\mathbf{z})$ with $\mathbf{x}_0 \neq \mathbf{z}$, $F^{\ell}(\mathbf{x}_0) = \mathbf{z}$ and $\det(DF^{\ell}(\mathbf{x}_0)) \neq 0$ for some positive integer ℓ; see Fig. 1.

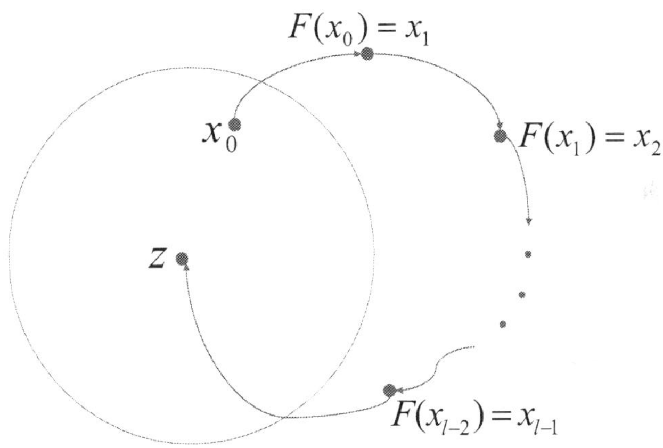

Fig. 1

It is straightforward to see that a snapback repeller gives rise to an orbit $\{\mathbf{x}_k\}_{k=-\infty}^{\infty}$ of F with $\mathbf{x}_k = \mathbf{z}$, for $k \geq \ell$, and $\mathbf{x}_k \to \mathbf{z}$ as $k \to -\infty$. Roughly speaking, the property of this orbit is analogous to the one for homoclinic orbit. In addition, the map F is locally one-to-one at each point $\mathbf{x}_k$, since $\mathbf{x}_0 \in B_r(\mathbf{z})$ and $\det(DF^{\ell}(\mathbf{x}_0)) \neq 0$. This leads to the trivial transversality, i.e., the unstable manifold $\mathbb{R}^n$ of full dimension intersects transversally the zero- dimensional stable manifold of $\mathbf{z}$. Therefore, snapback repeller may be regarded as a special case of a fixed point with a transversal homoclinic orbit if the latter is generalized to mappings which are not one-to-one.

Theorem (Marotto, 1978). If F possesses a snapback repeller, then F is chaotic in the following sense: There exist (i) a positive integer N, such that F has a point of period p, for each integer $p \geq N$, (ii) a scrambled set of F, i.e., an uncountable set S containing no periodic points of F, such that
(a) $F(S) \subset S$,
(b) $\limsup_{k\to\infty} \|F^k(\mathbf{x}) - F^k(\mathbf{y})\| > 0$, for all $\mathbf{x}, \mathbf{y} \in S$, with $\mathbf{x} \neq \mathbf{y}$,
(c) $\limsup_{k\to\infty} \|F^k(\mathbf{x}) - F^k(\mathbf{y})\| > 0$, for all $\mathbf{x} \in S$ and periodic point $\mathbf{y}$ of F,
(iii) an uncountable subset S_0 of S, such that $\liminf_{k\to\infty} \|F^k(\mathbf{x}) - F^k(\mathbf{y})\| = 0$, for every $\mathbf{x}, \mathbf{y} \in S_0$.

Remark. As the implication of this theorem yields the existence of uncountable scrambled set, we may say that existence of snapback repeller implies chaos in the sense of Li-Yorke. However, there is a technical flaw in the original derivation. Consider the following two statements:
(A): All eigenvalues of the Jacobian $DF(\mathbf{z})$ are greater than one in norm.
(B): There exist some $s > 1$ and $r > 0$ such that

$$\|F(\mathbf{x}) - F(\mathbf{y})\| > s\|\mathbf{x} - \mathbf{y}\|, \text{ for all } \mathbf{x}, \mathbf{y} \in B_r(\mathbf{z}). \tag{17}$$

That (A) implies (B) may not be true for the Euclidean norm in multi-dimension. In addition, if $\mathbf{z}$ is a fixed point and there exists a norm $\|\cdot\|_*$, such that

$$|\lambda(\mathbf{x})| > 1, \text{ for all eigenvalues } \lambda(\mathbf{x}) \text{ of } DF(\mathbf{x}), \text{ for all } \mathbf{x} \in B_r^*(\mathbf{z}),$$

then

$$\|F(\mathbf{x}) - F(\mathbf{y})\|_* > s \cdot \|\mathbf{x} - \mathbf{y}\|_*, \text{ for all } \mathbf{x}, \mathbf{y} \in B_r^*(\mathbf{z}), \tag{18}$$

still may not be satisfied. This is due to that the norm constructed for such a property depends on the matrix $DF(\mathbf{x})$ which varies at different points $\mathbf{x}$, as the mean-value inequality is applied. Several researchers have made efforts in modifying the definition of snapback repeller to validate the theorem. In 2005, Marotto gave a revised definition of snapback repeller. Note that a fixed point $\mathbf{z}$ of F is *repelling* if all eigenvalues of $DF(\mathbf{z})$ exceed one in norm. For a repelling fixed point $\mathbf{z}$, if there exist a norm $\|\cdot\|_*$ on $\mathbb{R}^n$ and $s > 1$ such that (18) holds, then $B_r^*(\mathbf{z})$ is called a *repelling neighborhood* of $\mathbf{z}$. Note that if $\mathbf{z}$ is a repelling fixed point of F, then one can find a norm $\|\cdot\|_*$ and $r > 0$ so that $B_r^*(\mathbf{z})$ is a repelling neighborhood of $\mathbf{z}$, see (Robinson, 1999).

Definition (Marotto, 2005). Let $\mathbf{z}$ be a repelling fixed point of F. Suppose that there exist a point $\mathbf{x}_0 \neq \mathbf{z}$ in a repelling neighborhood of $\mathbf{z}$ and an integer $\ell > 1$, such that $\mathbf{x}_\ell = \mathbf{z}$ and $\det(DF(\mathbf{x}_k)) \neq 0$ for $1 \leq k \leq \ell$. Then $\mathbf{z}$ is called a *snapback repeller* of F.
The point $\mathbf{x}_0$ in the definition is called a *snapback point* of F. While Marotto's theorem holds under the modified definition, its application becomes more inaccessible; indeed, it is a nontrivial task to confirm that some preimage of a repelling fixed point lies in the repelling neighborhood of this fixed point. From practical view point, condition (16) which was adopted in his original version, is obviously easier to examine than finding the repelling neighborhood for a fixed point. In (Liao & Shih, 2011), two directions have been proposed to confirm that a repelling fixed point is a snapback repeller for multi-dimensional maps. The first one is to find the repelling neighborhood $\mathcal{U}$ of the repeller $\mathbf{z}$ which is based on a computable norm. This is the key part in applying Marotto's theorem for practical application, as one can then attempt to find a snapback point $\mathbf{x}_0$ of $\mathbf{z}$ in $\mathcal{U}$, i.e., $F^\ell(\mathbf{x}_0) = \mathbf{z}$, $\mathbf{x}_0 \in \mathcal{U}$ and $\mathbf{x}_0 \neq \mathbf{z}$, for some $\ell > 1$. The second direction is applying a sequential graphic-iteration scheme to construct the preimages $\{\mathbf{z}_{-k}\}_{k=1}^\infty$ of $\mathbf{z}$, such that $F(\mathbf{z}_{-k}) = \mathbf{z}_{-k+1}$, $k \geq 2$, $F(\mathbf{z}_{-1}) = \mathbf{z}$, $\lim_{k\to\infty} F(\mathbf{z}_{-k}) = \mathbf{z}$. Such an orbit $\{\mathbf{z}_{-k}\}_{k=1}^\infty$ is a homoclinic orbit for the repeller $\mathbf{z}$, in the generalized sense, as mentioned above. The existence of such a homoclinic orbit leads to the existence of a snapback point in the repelling neighborhood of repeller $\mathbf{z}$. Therefore, without finding the repelling region of the fixed point, Marotto's theorem still holds by using

the second method. More precisely, two methodologies were derived to establish the existence of snapback repellers:
(i) estimate the radius of repelling neighborhood for a repelling fixed point, under Euclidean norm,
(ii) construct the homoclinic orbit for a repelling fixed point by using a sequential graphic-iteration scheme.
In some practical applications, one can combine (i) and (ii) to achieve the application of Marotto's theorem. These two methodologies can then be combined with numerical computations and the technique of interval computing which provides rigorous computation precision, to conclude chaotic dynamics for the systems, such as the transiently chaotic neural network (TCNN) and the predator-prey system (Liao & Shih, 2011). Let us recall the results therein.

Repelling neighborhood:
Proposition (Liao & Shih, 2011). Consider a continuously differentiable map $F : \mathbb{R}^n \to \mathbb{R}^n$ with fixed point $\mathbf{z}$. Let

$$\begin{aligned} s_1 &:= \sqrt{\text{minimal eigenvalue of } (DF(\mathbf{z}))^T DF(\mathbf{z})}\,, \\ \eta_r &:= \max_{\mathbf{w}\in B_r(\mathbf{z})} \|B(\mathbf{w},\mathbf{z})\|_2 \\ &= \max_{\mathbf{w}\in B_r(\mathbf{z})} \sqrt{\text{maximal eigenvalue of } (B(\mathbf{w},\mathbf{z}))^T B(\mathbf{w},\mathbf{z})}, \end{aligned}$$

where $B(\mathbf{w},\mathbf{z}) := DF(\mathbf{w}) - DF(\mathbf{z})$. If there exists a $r > 0$ such that

$$s_1 - \eta_r > 1, \tag{19}$$

then $B_r(\mathbf{z})$ is a repelling neighborhood for $\mathbf{z}$, under the Euclidean norm.

There is a second approach which is based on the estimate of the first and second derivatives of F. This estimate is advantageous for quadratic maps since their second derivatives are constants. Let $\sigma_i(\mathbf{x})$ and $\beta_{ij}(\mathbf{x})$ be defined as

$$\begin{aligned} \sigma_i(\mathbf{x}) &:= \sqrt{\text{eigenvalues of } (DF(\mathbf{x}))^T DF(\mathbf{x})}, \\ \beta_{ij}(\mathbf{x}) &:= \text{eigenvalues of Hessian matrix } H_{F_i}(\mathbf{x}) = [\partial_k \partial_l F_i(\mathbf{x})]_{k\times l}, \end{aligned}$$

where $i, j = 1, 2, \cdots, n$. Let α_r and β_r be defined as

$$\alpha_r := \min_{\mathbf{x}\in B_r(\mathbf{z})} \min_{1\le i\le n} \{\sigma_i(\mathbf{x})\} \tag{20}$$

$$\beta_r := \max_{1\le i\le n} \max_{\mathbf{x}\in B_r(\mathbf{z})} \max_{1\le j\le n} |\beta_{ij}(\mathbf{x})|. \tag{21}$$

Proposition (Liao & Shih, 2011). Consider a C^2 map $F = (F_1, \cdots, F_n) : \mathbb{R}^n \to \mathbb{R}^n$ with fixed point $\mathbf{z}$. Let α_r and β_r be defined in (20) and (21). If there exists $r > 0$, such that

$$\alpha_r - r\sqrt{n}\beta_r > 1, \tag{22}$$

then $B_r(\mathbf{z})$ is a repelling neighborhood of $\mathbf{z}$, under the Euclidean norm.
The conditions (19) and (22) are computable numerically and the value r can be found from numerical computation. Furthermore, if there exists a snapback point $\mathbf{x}_0$ in $B_r(\mathbf{z})$, i.e., $\mathbf{x}_0 \in B_r(\mathbf{z})$, and $F^{\ell}(\mathbf{x}_0) = \mathbf{z}$ for some integer $\ell > 1$, then $\mathbf{z}$ is a snapback repeller. Hence, the map F is chaotic in the sense of Marotto.

Sequential graphic-iteration scheme:
We recall an approach which is developed to exploit the existence of snapback repeller, without estimating the repelling neighborhood. In particular, it is a scheme to construct homoclinic orbits for repelling fixed point $\bar{\mathbf{x}}$ of F: $\{\bar{\mathbf{x}}_{-j} : j \in \mathbb{N}\}$ with $F(\bar{\mathbf{x}}_{-1}) = \bar{\mathbf{x}}$, $F(\bar{\mathbf{x}}_{-j}) = \bar{\mathbf{x}}_{-j+1}$, for $j \geq 2$, and $\lim_{j\to\infty} F(\bar{\mathbf{x}}_{-j}) = \bar{\mathbf{x}}$.

Theorem (Liao & Shih, 2011). Assume that there exists a compact, connected, convex region $\Omega = \Pi_{i=1}^{n}\Omega_i \subset \mathbb{R}^n$, so that the C^1 map $F = (F_1, F_2, \cdots, F_n) : \mathbb{R}^n \to \mathbb{R}^n$ satisfies

$$|\frac{\partial F_i}{\partial x_i}(\mathbf{x})| > 1 + \sum_{j=1, j\neq i}^{n} |\frac{\partial F_i}{\partial x_j}(\mathbf{x})|, \text{ for all } i = 1, \cdots, n, \ \mathbf{x} \in \Omega,$$

and has a repelling fixed point $\bar{\mathbf{x}}$ in $\Omega \subset \mathbb{R}^n$. For $i = 1, \cdots, n$, set

$$\hat{f}_{i,(1)}(\xi) := \sup\{F_i(x_1', \cdots, x_{i-1}', \xi, x_{i+1}', \cdots, x_n') : x_j' \in \Omega_j, j \in \{1, \cdots, n\}/\{i\}\},$$
$$\check{f}_{i,(1)}(\xi) := \inf\{F_i(x_1', \cdots, x_{i-1}', \xi, x_{i+1}', \cdots, x_n') : x_j' \in \Omega_j, j \in \{1, \cdots, n\}/\{i\}\},$$

for $\xi \in \mathbb{R}^1$. Also assume that $\hat{f}_{i,(1)}$ and $\check{f}_{i,(1)}$ both have fixed points in Ω_i, for all $i = 1, \cdots, n$, and

$$\bar{\mathbf{x}}_{-\ell+1} \in \mathbb{R}^n \setminus \Omega, \ \bar{\mathbf{x}}_{-\ell} \in \text{int}(\Omega)$$

hold, for some $\ell \geq 2$. Then there exist a sequence of nested regions $\{\Omega_{(k)}\}_{k=1}^{\infty}$ with $\Omega_{(k+1)} \subseteq \Omega_{(k)} \subset \Omega$, and preimages $\bar{\mathbf{x}}_{-k-1} \in \Omega_{(k)}$ of $\bar{\mathbf{x}}$ under F, $k \in \mathbb{N}$. If furthermore, $\|\Omega_{i,(k)}\| \to 0$, as $k \to \infty$, for all $i = 1, \cdots, n$, then $\{\bar{\mathbf{x}}_{-k}\}_{k=1}^{\infty}$ is a homoclinic orbit for $\bar{\mathbf{x}}$. Moreover, if

$$\det(DF(\bar{\mathbf{x}}_{-k})) \neq 0, \text{ for } 1 \leq k \leq \ell - 1$$

holds, then $\bar{\mathbf{x}}$ is a snapback repeller and F is chaotic in the sense of Marotto's theorem.

Remark. (i) The existence of this homoclinic orbit guarantees the existence of the snapback point without finding the repelling neighborhood. (ii) The conditions in the above theorem are formulated for DF and the one-dimensional maps $\hat{f}_{i,(1)}(\xi)$ and $\check{f}_{i,(1)}(\xi)$ (the upper and lower maps), hence they are easy to examine in applications. For example, for TCNN map, we can find explicit and computable conditions such that all conditions in the theorem are satisfied.

4.2 Applications and extensions

We review some applications of snapback repeller and chaotic dynamics in (Marotto, 1979a, 1979b). Consider a two-dimensional mapping $F : \mathbb{R}^2 \to \mathbb{R}^2$ of the form $F(x, y) = (f(x), x)$, with $f : \mathbb{R} \to \mathbb{R}$ being differentiable.

Lemma (Marotto, 1979a). (i) If f has a stable periodic point z of period p, then $F(x,y) = (f(x),x)$ has a stable periodic point (z,y_0) of period p where $y_0 = f^{p-1}(z)$. (ii) If f has a snapback repeller, then $F(x,y) = (f(x),x)$ has a transversal homoclinic orbit.
Using these results, one can investigate the dynamics of the following difference equation:

$$x_{k+1} = f(x_k, bx_{k-1}), \tag{23}$$

where $b, x_k \in \mathbb{R}$ and $f : \mathbb{R}^2 \to \mathbb{R}$ is differentiable. We rewrite (23) into the following two-dimensional system:

$$\begin{aligned} x_{k+1} &= f(x_k, by_k) \\ y_{k+1} &= x_k. \end{aligned} \tag{24}$$

Moreover, when $b = 0$, (23) is the following scalar problem

$$x_{k+1} = f(x_k, 0). \tag{25}$$

It was shown that the dynamics of (23) or (24) are determined by those of (25), if b is close to 0:

Theorem (Marotto, 1979a). (i) If (25) has a stable periodic point x_0 of period p, then there exists $\epsilon > 0$ such that (24) has a stable periodic point $(x(b), y(b))$ of period p for all $|b| < \epsilon$. In this case $(x(b), y(b))$ is a uniquely defined, continuous function of b with $x(0) = x_0$. (ii) If (25) has a snapback repeller, then (24) has a transversal homoclinic orbit for all $|b| < \epsilon$, for some $\epsilon > 0$.

Next, let us consider another class of two-dimensional map $G : \mathbb{R}^2 \to \mathbb{R}^2$ which is determined by two scalar equations $f(x)$ and $g(y)$ where $f, g : \mathbb{R} \to \mathbb{R}$ are differentiable and $G(x,y)$ is defined by $G(x,y) = (f(x), g(y))$.

Lemma (Marotto, 1979a). (i) If one of the mappings f and g has a snapback repeller and the other has an unstable fixed point, then $G(x,y) = (f(x), g(y))$ has a snapback repeller. (ii) If one of the mappings f and g has a snapback repeller and the other has a stable fixed point, then $G(x,y) = (f(x), g(y))$ has a transversal homoclinic orbit.

Now, we consider the dynamics for systems of the form:

$$\begin{aligned} x_{k+1} &= f(x_k, by_k) \\ y_{k+1} &= g(cx_k, y_k), \end{aligned} \tag{26}$$

where $f, g : \mathbb{R}^2 \to \mathbb{R}$ are differentiable, and $b, c \in \mathbb{R}$ are close to 0. If $b = c = 0$, then (26) can be simplified to the uncoupled system:

$$x_{k+1} = f(x_k, 0) \tag{27}$$

$$y_{k+1} = g(0, y_k). \tag{28}$$

Theorem (Marotto,1979a). (i) If one of the (27) and (28) has a snapback repeller and the other has an unstable fixed point, then (26) has a snapback repeller for all $|b|, |c| < \epsilon$, for some $\epsilon > 0$.

(ii) If one of the (27) and (28) has a snapback repeller and the other has a stable fixed point, then (26) has a transversal homoclinic orbit for all $|b|, |c| < \epsilon$, for some $\epsilon > 0$.

Remark. By examining the simplified systems, the above results exhibit the dynamics of system (24) or (26) under some small perturbations of certain parameters. However, these theorems do not provide any indication about the estimate of ϵ.

Next, let us recall the Hénon map

$$\begin{aligned} x_{k+1} &= y_k + 1 - a x_k^2 \\ y_{k+1} &= b x_k, \end{aligned}$$

which can be equivalently written as

$$\begin{aligned} u_{k+1} &= b v_k + 1 - a u_k^2 =: f(u_k, b v_k) \\ v_{k+1} &= u_k, \end{aligned} \tag{29}$$

where $f(u,v) = v + 1 - au^2$. It was shown in (Marotto, 1979b) that $u_{k+1} = f(u_k, 0)$ has a snapback repeller, when $a > 1.55$. Hence (29) has a transversal homolinic orbit for all $a > 1.55$ and $|b| < \epsilon$, for some $\epsilon > 0$.

In (Li, et al., 2008), they considered a one-parameter family of maps H_λ on $\mathbb{R}^n \times \mathbb{R}^m$ with $H_0(\mathbf{x}, \mathbf{y}) = (F(\mathbf{x}), G(\mathbf{x}))$ and continuous $F : \mathbb{R}^n \to \mathbb{R}^n$ and $G : \mathbb{R}^n \to \mathbb{R}^m$ or $H_0(\mathbf{x}, \mathbf{y}) = (F(\mathbf{x}), G(\mathbf{x}, \mathbf{y}))$ with continuous maps $F : \mathbb{R}^n \to \mathbb{R}^n$ and $G : \mathbb{R}^n \times \mathbb{R}^m \to \mathbb{R}^m$. They used the covering relations method proposed by Zgliczyński in (Zgliczyński, 1996, 1997) to prove that if $n = 1$ and F has a positive topological entropy, or if $n > 1$ and F has a snapback repeller, then any small perturbation H_λ of H_0 has a positive topological entropy. Without using hyperbolicity, the covering relations method still provides a way to verify the existence of periodic points, the symbolic dynamics and the positive topological entropy. Moreover, they also applied this method to obtain a new proof for García's result (García, 1986) that if a map has a snapback repeller then it has a positive topological entropy. One can obtain similar results by using this method with other structure, such as a hyperbolic horseshoe.
Since the definition of snapback repeller proposed by Marotto relies on the norm, the following definition independent of norm was proposed.

Definition (Li, et al., 2008). Let $F : \mathbb{R}^n \to \mathbb{R}^n$ be a C^1 function. A fixed point $\mathbf{z}$ for F is called a *snapback repeller* if (i) all eigenvalues of the derivative $DF(\mathbf{z})$ are greater than one in absolute value and (ii) there exists a sequence $\{\mathbf{x}_{-i}\}_{i \in \mathbb{N}}$ such that $\mathbf{x}_{-1} \neq \mathbf{z}$, $\lim_{i \to \infty} \mathbf{x}_{-i} = \mathbf{z}$, and for all $i \in \mathbb{N}$, $F(\mathbf{x}_{-i}) = \mathbf{x}_{-i+1}$, $F(\mathbf{x}_{-1}) = \mathbf{z}$ and $\det(DF(\mathbf{x}_{-i})) \neq 0$.

Remark. Although the above definition is independent of norm on the phase space, it requires the existence of the pre-images for the repeller. The sequential graphic-iteration scheme outlined above provides a methodology for such a construction.

Note that item (i) implies that there exist a norm $\|\cdot\|_*$ on $\mathbb{R}^n$, $r > 0$ and $s > 1$, such that $\|F(\mathbf{x}) - F(\mathbf{y})\|_* > s\|\mathbf{x} - \mathbf{y}\|_*$ for all $\mathbf{x}, \mathbf{y} \in B_r^*(\mathbf{z})$. Hence F is one-to-one on $B_r^*(\mathbf{z})$ and $F(B_r^*(\mathbf{z})) \supset B_r^*(\mathbf{z})$. Therefore, if there exists a point $\mathbf{x}_0 \in B_r^*(\mathbf{z})$ such that $F^\ell(\mathbf{x}_0) = \mathbf{z}$ and $\det(DF^\ell(\mathbf{x}_0)) \neq 0$ for some positive integer ℓ, then item (ii) of the above definition is satisfied. In addition, in (Li & Chen, 2003), they showed that this norm can be chosen to be the Euclidean norm on $\mathbb{R}^n$, under the condition that all eigenvalues of $(DF(\mathbf{z}))^T DF(\mathbf{z})$ are greater than one. However, this condition is more restrictive, due to that a repelling fixed point has the potential to be a snapback repeller, without satisfying this condition.

Theorem (Li, et al., 2008). Let H_λ be a one-parameter family of continuous maps on $\mathbb{R}^n \times \mathbb{R}^m$ such that $H_\lambda(\mathbf{x}, \mathbf{y})$ is continuous as a function of $\lambda \in \mathbb{R}^l$ and $(\mathbf{x}, \mathbf{y}) \in \mathbb{R}^n \times \mathbb{R}^m$. Assume that $H_0(\mathbf{x}, \mathbf{y}) = (F(\mathbf{x}), G(\mathbf{x}))$, where $F : \mathbb{R}^n \to \mathbb{R}^n$ is C^1 and has a snapback repeller and $G : \mathbb{R}^n \to \mathbb{R}^m$. Then H_λ has a positive topological entropy for all λ sufficiently close to 0.

Theorem (Li, et al.,2008). Let H_λ be a one-parameter family of continuous maps on $\mathbb{R}^n \times \mathbb{R}^m$ such that $H_\lambda(\mathbf{z})$ is continuous as a function of $\lambda \in \mathbb{R}^l$ and $(\mathbf{x}, \mathbf{y}) \in \mathbb{R}^n \times \mathbb{R}^m$. Assume that $H_0(\mathbf{x}, \mathbf{y}) = (F(\mathbf{x}), G(\mathbf{x}, \mathbf{y}))$, where $F : \mathbb{R}^n \to \mathbb{R}^n$ is C^1 and has a snapback repeller, $G : \mathbb{R}^n \times \mathbb{R}^m \to \mathbb{R}^m$, and $G(\mathbb{R}^n \times S) \subset \text{int}(S)$ for some compact set $S \subset \mathbb{R}^m$ homeomorphic to the closed unit ball in $\mathbb{R}^m$. Then H_λ has a positive topological entropy for all λ sufficiently close to 0.

Moreover, it was shown in (Li & Lyu,2009) that if F has a snapback repeller and G is a small C^1 perturbation of F, then G has a snapback repeller, positive topological entropy, as the implicit function theorem is applied. Moreover, G is chaotic in the sense of Li-Yorke. More precisely,

Theorem (Li & Lyu, 2009). Let F be a C^1 map on $\mathbb{R}^n$ with a snapback repeller. If G is a C^1 map on $\mathbb{R}^n$ such that $\|F - G\| + \|DF - DG\|_\star$ is small enough, where $\|\cdot\|_\star$ is the operator norm on the space of linear maps on $\mathbb{R}^n$ induced by the Euclidean norm $\|\cdot\|$, then G has a snapback repeller, exhibits Li-Yorke chaos, and has positive topological entropy.

Corollary (Li & Lyu, 2009). Let $F_\mu(\mathbf{x})$ be a one-parameter family of C^1 maps with $\mathbf{x} \in \mathbb{R}^n$ and $\mu \in \mathbb{R}^l$. Assume that $F_\mu(\mathbf{x})$ is C^1 as a function jointly of $\mathbf{x}$ and μ and that F_{μ_0} has a snapback repeller. Then map F_μ has a snapback repeller, exhibits Li-Yorke chaos, and has positive topological entropy, for all μ sufficiently close to μ_0.

In (Shi & Chen, 2004, 2008), they generalized the definitions of expanding fixed point, snapback repeller, homoclinic orbit, and heteroclinic orbit for a continuously differentiable map from $\mathbb{R}^n$ to general metric spaces as follows. Herein, $B_r^d(\mathbf{x})$ denotes the closed balls of radius r centered at $\mathbf{x} \in X$ under metric d, i.e.

$$B_r^d(\mathbf{z}) := \{\mathbf{x} \in \mathbb{R}^n : d(\mathbf{x}, \mathbf{z}) \le r\}.$$

In the following, we introduce the coupled-expanding map.

Definition (Shi & Chen, 2008). Let $F : D \subset X \to X$ be a map where (X, d) is a metric space. If there exists $\ell \ge 2$ subsets V_i, $1 \le i \le \ell$, of D with $V_i \cap V_j = \partial_D V_i \cap \partial_D V_j$ for each pair of (i, j), $1 \le i \ne j \le \ell$, such that

$$F(V_i) \supset \cup_{j=1}^{\ell} V_j, \; 1 \le i \le \ell,$$

where $\partial_D V_i$ is the relative boundary of V_i with respect to D, then F is said to be *coupled-expanding* in V_i, $1 \le i \le \ell$. Moreover, the map F is said to be *strictly coupled-expanding* in V_i, $1 \le i \le \ell$, if $d(V_i, V_j) > 0$, for all $1 \le i \ne j \le \ell$.

Definition (Shi & Chen, 2004). Let $F : X \to X$ be a map on metric space (X, d). (i) A point $\mathbf{z} \in X$ is called an *expanding fixed point* (or a *repeller*) of F in $B_{r_0}^d(\mathbf{z})$ for some constant $r_0 > 0$, if

$F(\mathbf{z}) = \mathbf{z}$ and

$$d(F(\mathbf{x}), F(\mathbf{y})) \geq \lambda d(\mathbf{x}, \mathbf{y}), \text{ for all } \mathbf{x}, \mathbf{y} \in B^d_{r_0}(\mathbf{z})$$

for some constant $\lambda > 1$. Moreover, $\mathbf{z}$ is called a *regular expanding fixed point* of F in $B^d_{r_0}(\mathbf{z})$ if $\mathbf{z}$ is an interior point of $F(\text{int}(B^d_{r_0}(\mathbf{z})))$.

(ii) Let $\mathbf{z}$ be an expanding fixed point of F in $B^d_{r_0}(\mathbf{z})$ for some $r_0 > 0$. Then $\mathbf{z}$ is said to be a *snapback repeller* of F if there exists a point $\mathbf{x}_0 \in \text{int}(B^d_{r_0}(\mathbf{z}))$ with $\mathbf{x}_0 \neq \mathbf{z}$ and $F^\ell(\mathbf{x}_0) = \mathbf{z}$ for some positive integer $\ell \geq 2$. Moreover, $\mathbf{z}$ is said to be a *nondegenerate snapback repeller* of F if there exist positive constants μ and δ_0 such that $\text{int}(B^d_{\delta_0}(\mathbf{x}_0)) \subset \text{int}(B^d_{r_0}(\mathbf{z}))$ and

$$d(F^\ell(\mathbf{x}), F^\ell(\mathbf{y})) \geq \mu d(\mathbf{x}, \mathbf{y}), \text{ for all } \mathbf{x}, \mathbf{y} \in B^d_{\delta_0}(\mathbf{x}_0);$$

$\mathbf{z}$ is called a *regular snapback repeller* of F if $F(\text{int}(B^d_{r_0}(\mathbf{z})))$ is open and there exists a positive constant δ_0^* such that $\text{int}(B^d_{\delta_0^*}(\mathbf{x}_0)) \subset \text{int}(B^d_{r_0}(\mathbf{z}))$ and $\mathbf{z}$ is an interior point of $F^\ell(\text{int}(B^d_\delta(\mathbf{x}_0)))$ for any positive constant $\delta \leq \delta_0^*$.

(iii) Assume that $\mathbf{z} \in X$ is a regular expanding fixed point of F. Let U be the maximal open neighborhood of $\mathbf{z}$ in the sense that for any $\mathbf{x} \in U$ with $\mathbf{x} \neq \mathbf{z}$, there exists $k_0 \geq 1$ with $F^{k_0}(\mathbf{x}) \notin U$, $F^{-k}(\mathbf{x})$ is uniquely defined in U for all $k \geq 1$, and $F^{-k}(\mathbf{x}) \to \mathbf{z}$ as $k \to \infty$. U is called *the local unstable set* of F at $\mathbf{z}$ and is denoted by $W^u_{loc}(\mathbf{z})$.

(iv) Let $\mathbf{z} \in X$ be a regular expanding fixed point of F. A point $\mathbf{x} \in X$ is called *homoclinic* to $\mathbf{z}$ if $\mathbf{x} \in W^u_{loc}(\mathbf{z})$, $\mathbf{x} \neq \mathbf{z}$, and there exists an integer $m \geq 1$ such that $F^m(\mathbf{x}) = \mathbf{z}$. A homoclinic orbit to $\mathbf{z}$, consisting of a homoclinic point $\mathbf{x}$ with $F^m(\mathbf{x}) = \mathbf{z}$, its backward orbit $\{F^{-j}(\mathbf{x})\}_{j=1}^{\infty}$, and its finite forward orbit $\{F^j(\mathbf{x})\}_{j=1}^{m-1}$, is called *nondegenerate* if for each point $\mathbf{x}_j$ on the homoclinic orbit there exist positive constants r_j and μ_j such that

$$d(F(\mathbf{x}), F(\mathbf{y})) \geq \mu_j d(\mathbf{x}, \mathbf{y}), \text{ for all } \mathbf{x}, \mathbf{y} \in B^d_{r_j}(\mathbf{x}_j).$$

A homoclinic orbit is called *regular* if for each point $\mathbf{x}_j$ on the orbit, there exists a positive constant $\tilde{r}_j$ such that for any positive constant $r \leq \tilde{r}_j$, $F(\mathbf{x}_j)$ is an interior point of $F(\text{int}(B^d_r(\mathbf{x}_j)))$. Otherwise, it is called *singular*. A point $\mathbf{x}$ is called *heteroclinic* to $\mathbf{z}$, if $\mathbf{x} \in W^u_{loc}(\mathbf{z})$ and there exists a $m \geq 1$ such that $F^m(\mathbf{x})$ lies on a different periodic orbit from $\mathbf{z}$.

Notice that if a map F on $\mathbb{R}^n$ has a snapback repeller, and is continuously differentiable in some neighborhood of $\mathbf{x}_j = F^j(\mathbf{x}_0)$, for $0 \leq j \leq \ell - 1$, then the snapback repeller is regular and nondegenerate. For continuously differentiable finite-dimensional maps, the definition of snapback repeller has been extended in (Shi & Chen, 2004, 2008) to the maps in the general metric space, through introducing the two classifications: regular and singular, nondegenerate and degenerate. It was proved that a map F is a strict coupled-expansion and chaotic in the sense of both Devaney and Li-Yorke if F has a nondegenerate and regular snapback repeller or a nondegenerate and regular homoclinic orbit to an expanding fixed point. Moreover, if F is C^1 in $\mathbb{R}^n$ and has a snapback repeller under Marotto's definition, then the snapback repeller is nondegenerate and regular. Therefore, F is chaotic in the sense of Marotto, Devaney, and Li-Yorke. In addition, more general scenario for degenerate and regular snapback repeller, was studied in (Shi & Yu, 2008).

4.3 Some remarks

We summarize some results concerning the above-mentioned notions.
(i) For a compact metric space (X,d), chaos in the sense of Devaney implies chaos in the sense of Li-Yorke.
(ii) If a map F has a snapback repeller $\mathbf{z}$, then F is chaotic in the sense of Marotto and Li-Yorke.
(iii) If a map $F : \Lambda \to \Lambda$ is topologically conjugate to the symbolic dynamical system $\sigma : \Sigma_2^+ \to \Sigma_2^+$, for some Cantor set Λ, then F is chaotic on Λ in the sense of Devaney and Li-Yorke.
(iv) For a complete metric space (X,d) and a map $F : X \to X$, if F has a regular nondegenerate snapback repeller $\mathbf{z} \in X$, then there exists a Cantor set Λ so that $F^m : \Lambda \to \Lambda$ is topologically conjugate to the symbolic dynamical system $\sigma : \Sigma_2^+ \to \Sigma_2^+$, for some integer m. Consequently, F^m is chaotic on Λ in the sense of Devaney and Li-Yorke.
(v) For a complete metric space (X,d) and a C^1 map $F : X \to X$, if F has a Marotto's snapback repeller $\mathbf{z}$, then $\mathbf{z}$ is also a regular nondegenerate snapback repeller. Hence, F^m is chaotic in the sense of Devaney and Li-Yorke, for some integer m.
(vi) If a map F has a transversal homoclinic orbit, then there exists a Cantor set Λ so that $F^m : \Lambda \to \Lambda$ is topologically conjugate to the symbolic dynamical system $\sigma : \Sigma_2^+ \to \Sigma_2^+$, for some integer m. Consequently, F^m is chaotic on Λ in the sense of Devaney and Li-Yorke.

5. Acknowledgements

The authors are supported, in part, by the National Science Council of Taiwan, under NSC-2115-M-009-012.

6. References

Arik, S. (2000) Global asymptotic stability of a class of dynamical neural networks, *IEEE Trans. Circuits Syst. I*, Vol. 47: 568–571.

Banks, J., Brooks, J., Cairns, G., Davis, G. & Stacey, P. (1992) On Devaney's definition of chaos, *Amer. Math. Monthly*, Vol. 99: 332–334.

Bauer, F., Atay, F. M. & Jost, J. (2009) Synchronization in discrete-time networks with general pairwise coupling, *Nonlinearity*, Vol. 22: 2333–2351.

Bauer, F., Atay, M.F. &, Jost J. (2010) Synchronized chaos in networks of simple units, *Europhys. Lett.*, Vol 89: 20002.

Buric, N. & Todorovic, D. (2003) Dynamics of Fitzhugh-Nagumo excitable systems with delayed coupling, *Phys. Rev. E*, Vol. 67: 066222.

Campbell, S. A. (2006) Time delays in neural systems, in McIntosh, A. R. and Jirsa, V. K.(ed.), *Handbook of Brain Connectivity*, Springer-Verlag, New York, pp. 65–90.

Chen, H. C., Hung, Y. C., Chen, C. K. & Liao, T. L. (2006) Image-processing algorithms realized by discrete-time cellular neural networks and their circuit implementations, *Chaos, Solitons and Fractals*, Vol. 29 (No. 5): 1100–1108.

Chen, L. & Aihara, K. (1995) Chaotic simulated annealing for combinatorial optimization, *Neural Networks*, Vol. 8: 915–930.

Chen, L. & Aihara, K. (1997) Chaos and asymptotical stability in discrete-time neural networks, *Physica D*, Vol. 104: 286–325.

Chen, L. & Aihara, K. (1999) Global searching ability of chaotic neural networks, *IEEE Trans. Circuits Syst. I: Fundamental Theory and Applications*, Vol. 46: 97–993.

Chen, S. S. & Shih, C. W. (2002) Transversal homoclinic orbits in a transiently chaotic neural network, *Chaos*, Vol. 12 (No.3): 654–671.

Chen, S. S. & Shih, C. W. (2004a) Dynamics for discrete-time cellular neural networks, *Intern. J. Biburc. Chaos*, Vol. 14 (No. 8): 2667–2687.

Chen, S. S. & Shih, C. W. (2004b) Asymptotic behaviors in a transiently chaotic neural networks, *Discrete and Continuous Dynamical systems*, Vol. 10: 805–826.

Chen, S. S. & Shih, C. W. (2008) Solving TSP via Neural Networks, in Federico Greco(ed), *Travelling Salesman Problem*, I-Tech Education and Publishing, pp. 117–134.

Chen, S. S. & Shih, C. W. (2009) Transiently chaotic neural networks with piecewise linear output functions, *Chaos, Solitons and Fractals*, Vol. 39: 717–730.

Chua, L. O. & Yang, L. (1988) Cellular neural networks, theory, *IEEE Trans. Circuits Syst.*, Vol. 35: 1257–72.

Chua, L. O. (1998) *CNN: A Paradigm for Complexity*, World Scientific.

Devaney, R.L. (1989) *An Introduction to Chaotic Dynamical Systems*, Addison-Wesley, New York.

Forti, M. & Tesi, A. (1995) New conditions for global stability of neural networks with application to linear and quadratic programming problems, *IEEE Transations on Circuit Systems-I: Fundament Theory and Application*, Vol. 42 (No. 7): 354–366.

García, B.C. (1986) Chaos and topological entropy in dimension $n > 1$, *Erg. Theory Dyn. Syst.*, Vol. 6: 163–165.

Grossberg, S. (1978), Competition, decision, consensus, *J. Math. Anal. Appl.*, Vol. 66: 470 –493.

Hale, J. K. & Lin, X. (1986) Symbolic dynamics and nonlinear semiflow, *Annali di Matematica Pura ed Applicata*, Vol. 144: 229–259.

Hale, J. & Raugel, G. (1992) Convergence in gradient-like systems with applications to PDE, *ZAMP*, Vol. 43: 63–124.

Hänggi, M., Reddy, H. C. & Moschytz, G. S. (1999) Unifying results in CNN theory using delta operator, *IEEE Int. Symp. Circuits Syst.*, Vol. 3: 547–550.

Harrer, H. & Nossek, J. A. (1992) An analog implementation of discrete-time cnns, *IEEE Transactions on Neural Networks*, Vol. 3: 466–476.

Hirsh, M. (1989) Convergent activation dynamics in continuous time networks, *Neural Networks*, Vol. 2: 331–349.

Huang, W. & Ye, X. (2002) Devaney's chaos or 2-scattering implies Li-Yorke's chaos, *Topology Appl.*, Vol. 117: 259–272.

Jost, J. & Joy, M. (2001), Spectral properties and synchronization in coupled map lattices, *Phys. Rev. E*, Vol. 65: 016201.

Kaneko, K. (1984) Period-doubling of kink-antikink patterns, quasi-periodicity in antiferro-like structures and spatial intermittency in coupled map lattice-toward a prelude to a field theory of chaos, *Prog. Theor. Phys.*, Vol. 72: 480–486.

LaSalle, J. P. (1976) The stability of dynamical systems, *Regional Conference Series in Applied Mathematics*, Vol. 25, SIAM, Philadelphia.

Li, C. & Chen, G. (2003). An improved version of the Marotto theorem, *Chaos, Solitons and Fractals*, Vol. 18: 69-77.

Li, M. C., Lyu, M. J. & Zgliczyński, P. (2008) Topological entropy for multidimensional perturbations of snap-back repellers and one-dimensional maps, *Nonlinearity*, Vol. 21: 2555– 2567.

Li, M.C. & Lyu, M.J. (2009) A simple proof for persistence of snap-back repellers, *J. Math. Anal. Appl.*, Vol. 52: 669-671.

Li, T.Y. & Yorke, J.A. (1975) Period three implies chaos, *Amer. Math. Monthly*, Vol. 82: 985–992.

Liang, J.L. & Cao, J. (2004) Exponential stability of continuous-time and discrete-time bidirectional associative memory networks with delays, *Chaos, Solitons and Fractals*, Vol. 22 (No. 4): 773–785.

Liao, K. L. & Shih, C. W. (2011) Snapback repellers and homoclinic orbits for multi-dimensional maps, Submitted.

Liu, Y.R., Wang, Z.D. & Liu, X.H. (2008) Robust stability of discrete-time stochastic neural networks with time-varying delays, *Neurocomputing*, Vol. 71: 823–833.

Lu, W. & Chen, T (2004) Synchronization analysis of linearly coupled networks of discrete time systems, *Physica D*, Vol. 198: 148–168.

Mak, K. L., Peng, J. G., Xu, Z. B. & Yiu, K. F. (2007) A new stability criterion for discrete-time neural networks: Nonlinear spectral radius, *Chaos, Solitons and Fractals*, Vol. 31 (No. 2): 424–436.

Marotto, F. R. (1978) Snap-back repellers imply chaos in $\mathbb{R}^n$, *J. Math. Anal. Appl.*, Vol. 63: 199–223.

Marotto, F. R. (1979a) Perturbations of stable and chaotic difference equations, *J. Math. Anal. Appl.*, Vol. 72: 716–729.

Marotto, F. R. (1979b) Chaotic behavior in the Hénon mapping, *Commun. Math. Phys.*, Vol. 68: 187–194.

Marotto, F. R. (2005) On redefining a snap-back repeller, *Chaos, Solitions and Fractals*, Vol. 25: 25–28.

Peterson, C. & Söderberg, B. (1993) Artificial neural networks, in C. Reeves(ed.), *Modern Heuristic Techniques for Combinatorial Optimization*, Blackwell Scientific Publishing, Oxford, England, pp. 197–242.

Robinson, C. (1999) *Dynamical Systems: Stability, Symbolic Dynamics, and Chaos 2nd edn*, Boca Raton, FL: CRC Press.

Roska, T. & Chua L. O. (1992) Cellular neural networks with nonlinear and delay-type template, *Int. J. Circuit Theory and Appl.*, Vol. 20: 469–481.

Shi, Y. & Chen, G. (2004) Chaos of discrete dynamical systems in complete metric spaces, *Chaos, Solitons and Fractals*, Vol. 22: 555–571.

Shi, T. & Yu, P. (2008) Chaos induced by regular snap-back repellers, *J. Math. Anal. Appl.*, Vol.337: 1480–1494.

Shih, C. W. (2000) Influence of boundary conditions on pattern formation and spatial chaos in lattice systems, *SIAM J. Applied Math.*, Vol. 61 (No. 1): 335–368.

Shih, C. W. & Weng, C. W. (2002) On the templates corresponding to cycle-symmetric connectivity in cellular neural networks, *Intern. Bifurc. Chaos*, Vol. 12: 2957–2966.

Shih, C. W. & Tseng, J. P. (2009) Global consensus for discrete-time competitive systems, *Chaos, Solitons and Fractals*, Vol 41: 302–310.

Smale, S. (1967) Differentiable dynamics systems, *Bull. Amer. Math. Soc.*, Vol. 73: 747–817.

Steinlein, H. & Walther, H. (1990) Hyperbolic sets, transversal homoclinic trajectories, and symbolic dynamics for C^1-maps in Banach spaces, *J. Dyna. Diff. Equa.*, Vol. 3: 325–365.

Wang, L. & Zou, X. (2008) Convergence of DiscreteąVTime Neural Networks with Delays, *International Journal of Qualitative Theory of Differential Equations and Applications*, Vol. 2 (No. 1): 24–37.

Wu, J. (2001) *Introduction to Neural Dynamics and Signal Transmission Delay*, Walter de Gruyter, Berlin.

Wu, Z., Su, H., Chu, J. & Zhou, W. (2009) New results on robust exponential stability for discrete recurrent neural networks with time-varying delays, *Neurocomputing*, Vol. 72: 3337–3342.

Yua, J., Zhang, K. & Fei, S. (2010) Exponential stability criteria for discrete-time recurrent neural networks with time-varying delay, *Nonlinear Analysis: Real World Applications*, Vol. 11: 207–216.

Yuan, L., Yuan, Z. & He, Y. (2009) Convergence of non-autonomous discrete-time Hopfield model with delays, *Neurocomputing* ,Vol. 72: 3802–3808.